# SOVIET FOREIGN POLICY
# IN A CHANGING WORLD

D0145284

# SOVIET FOREIGN POLICY IN A CHANGING WORLD

*Edited by*

## ROBBIN F. LAIRD
*Institute for Defense Analyses*

## ERIK P. HOFFMANN
*State University of New York at Albany*

Aldine de Gruyter
New York

# About the Editors

**Robbin F. Laird** is Senior Researcher, Strategy, Forces, and Resources Division, Institute for Defense Analyses, Alexandria, Virginia. He is author of *France, the Soviet Union, and the Nuclear Weapons Issue;* coauthor of *Technocratic Socialism: The Soviet Union in the Advanced Industrial Era, The Soviet Union and Strategic Arms, The Politics of Economic Modernization in the Soviet Union,* and *"The Scientific-Technological Revolution" and Soviet Foreign Policy;* and coeditor of *The Soviet Polity in the Modern Era.*

**Erik P. Hoffmann** is Professor of Political Science, The Nelson A. Rockefeller College of Public Affairs and Policy, State University of New York at Albany, and Senior Associate, Research Institute on International Change, Columbia University. He is coauthor of *Technocratic Socialism: The Soviet Union in the Advanced Industrial Era, The Politics of Economic Modernization in the Soviet Union,* and *"The Scientific-Technological Revolution" and Soviet Foreign Policy;* editor of *The Soviet Union in the 1980s;* and coeditor of *The Conduct of Soviet Foreign Policy* and *The Soviet Polity in the Modern Era.*

Aldine de Gruyter
A Division of Walter de Gruyter, Inc.
200 Saw Mill River Road
Hawthorne, New York 10532

Library of Congress Cataloging-in-Publication Data
Main entry under title:

Soviet foreign policy in a changing world.

  1. Soviet Union—Foreign relations—1975–
—Addresses, essays, lectures.   I. Laird, Robbin F.
(Robbin Frederick), 1946–      . II. Hoffmann,
Erik P., 1939–      .
DK289.S67  1986      327.47      85–18712
ISBN 0-202-24166-1 (lib. bdg.)
ISBN 0-202-24167-X (pbk.)

Printed in the United States of America
10 9 8 7 6 5 4 3 2

*To Vivian Louise Laird*
*and*
*Neil and Paul Hoffmann*

# CONTENTS

Introduction

## I. ISSUES

Contents

## VIII. THE THIRD WORLD

## IX. THE FUTURE

# INTRODUCTION

Erik P. Hoffmann
Robbin F. Laird

The purpose of this anthology is to deepen Western understanding of the sources, substance, and significance of contemporary Soviet foreign policy. Our book is designed for students of Soviet politics, comparative foreign policies, and international relations. Also, it is structured to meet the needs of government, business, and media officials and of citizens concerned about the USSR's international aims, activities, and accomplishments. The present work complements our anthology on Soviet domestic politics—*The Soviet Polity in the Modern Era* (Hawthorne, N.Y.: Aldine Publishing Co., 1984). Together, these volumes provide a comprehensive survey of notable Western writings about Soviet external and internal behavior and their interrelationships. Competing viewpoints are juxtaposed primarily in the first and last parts of both books, and authoritative analyses of key topics are presented primarily in the other parts.[1]

A distinctive feature of this collection is its numerous contributions from present and past officials of the United States Government and from full-time researchers in organizations that advise government officials. These contributions provide some of the most insightful and knowledgeable interpretations of Soviet foreign policy. Also, they reflect the concerns of Americans inside and outside of government who participate in public debate about international politics. We hope to raise the level of this debate by stimulating informed and independent-minded analysis of Soviet international activities and of their policy implications for the West. In a word, the present anthology is of policy relevance as well as of academic and general interest. It is written for Western policymakers and their advisors as well as for the university community and the inquisitive public. Almost all our authors are American, and the others are European or Canadian.

We intend to supplement, not supplant, the preeminent histories of Soviet international behavior—Adam B. Ulam's *Expansion and Coexis-*

*tence: The History of Soviet Foreign Policy, 1917–73*, 2nd ed. (New York: Praeger Publishers, 1974) and *Dangerous Relations: The Soviet Union in World Politics, 1970–1982* (New York: Oxford University Press, 1983); succinct texts such as Joseph L. Nogee and Robert H. Donaldson, *Soviet Foreign Policy since World War II*, 2nd ed. (Elmsford, N.Y.: Pergamon Press, 1984) and Alvin Z. Rubinstein, *Soviet Foreign Policy since World War II: Imperial and Global*, 2nd ed. (Boston: Little, Brown and Co., 1985); less policy-oriented anthologies such as Erik P. Hoffmann and Frederic J. Fleron, Jr., eds., *The Conduct of Soviet Foreign Policy*, 2nd ed. (Hawthorne, N.Y.: Aldine Publishing Co., 1980); and collections of Soviet writings such as Fred Schulze, ed., *Soviet Foreign Policy Today: Reports and Commentaries from the Soviet Press* (Columbus, Ohio: Current Digest of the Soviet Press, 1983).

Part I presents different Western views on key issues such as the tsarist and Stalinist legacies, the motivations and priorities of present-day Soviet leaders, the USSR's power vis-à-vis other nations, the relationships between Soviet domestic and international politics, and the appropriate ways of studying the USSR's foreign policy. For example, is Soviet international behavior primarily aggressive or defensive? How responsive have been the Soviet political system and its policies to Western diplomacy and to scientific-technological and socioeconomic developments at home and abroad? What kinds of available data can help to answer such questions? To be sure, the USSR has become more permeable to external influences and its policies have become more differentiated in various geographical and issue areas since Stalin's death in 1953. But it is much easier to describe the mounting complexities of public policies than to analyze the effects of different factors on a political system's goals, capabilities, and policy outputs and outcomes. Weighing the importance of political-administrative variables and their shifting relationships is both an art and a science. Such assessments are especially subjective when a nation's leadership (e.g., the USSR's) is highly secretive about its policymaking procedures and its military and economic activities abroad. Nonetheless, Western analysts must characterize and explain Soviet international behavior, and their conclusions will be greatly influenced by the questions they pose. Likewise, Western leaders must initiate policy toward the USSR and respond to Soviet policy, and their assessments of the Soviet polity and society will decisively shape their judgments about mutual and conflicting interests and appropriate actions.

Part II focuses on the formulation and implementation of Soviet foreign policy. Our selections elucidate the origins and effects of Soviet views of the international arena, identify key personnel and institutions, and present case studies of a covert and overt policy instrument ("active measures") and of a constructive policy (arms limitation). Westerners know very little about national policymaking and administration in the

USSR. But Soviet published sources are yielding more and better information about the *diverse* perspectives of leading Communist party officials and their advisors. One can distinguish between "rentier" and "speculator" tendencies in the Soviet leadership and between "conservative," "centrist," and "modernizer" orientations toward particular issues. Linking these tendencies and orientations to Soviet bureaucratic coalitions and to the competition over power and policy is highly problematical. Nonetheless, top party leaders recognize the increasing interconnections between foreign and domestic issues (e.g., economic reform, defense spending) and acknowledge the mounting difficulties in vital domestic and international spheres (e.g., technological innovation, Eastern Europe). Candid debates about such interconnections and difficulties have become more common in the Soviet media and have played a growing role in policy formulation and implementation. Also, since 1970 the USSR has considerably expanded its diplomatic, commercial, and scientific-technological ties with Western, Communist, and Third World countries and has participated in extensive arms control negotiations with the United States. Hence, foreign observers—on the basis of more extensive contact with Soviet officials and more open disagreements *within* the Soviet policy community—have been able to glimpse additional aspects of Soviet bureaucratic politics and to make better informed guesses about the Soviet policy process.

Part III reflects our judgment that military power is the crucial instrument of Soviet foreign policy. We do not present separate sections on Soviet diplomacy or international economic relations. Strategic and conventional arms make the USSR a superpower—not the diminishing appeal of its socioeconomic system to other nations. As our contributors note, Soviet views of national security have shifted under successive leaderships, and Soviet political and military goals have intertwined. The USSR's attainment of strategic parity with the United States about 1970 and the continuation of Brezhnev's unprecedented arms buildup were integral parts of the Soviet policy of détente. Likewise, Soviet conceptualizations of détente never precluded the use of conventional forces to advance the USSR's interests in the Third World. Indeed, Soviet leaders deployed their enhanced naval, air, and ground capabilities to support selected "wars of national liberation." Soviet strategic conservatives acknowledged that "the scientific-technological revolution in military affairs" was decisively altering the nature and conduct of war, but they were skeptical about the prospects of regulating nuclear or nonnuclear competition and deemed it necessary to win an all-out nuclear war if such a war became unavoidable. In contrast, Soviet strategic modernizers stressed the importance of avoiding even a "limited" nuclear exchange and of curbing the spiraling nuclear arms race, *while* projecting power throughout the world with conventional forces.[2] The different orientations of Soviet strategic conservatives and strategic modernizers reflect a broader conflict among party officials regarding the impact of scientific and technological advances on world politics, East-West relations, and the economic development of the USSR.[3]

Parts IV to VIII examine Soviet policy toward the major areas of the globe—the United States, Western Europe, Eastern Europe, the Far East, and the Third World. The structure of each section is similar. We begin with an essay (or essays) that provides historical context about the evolving relationship between the USSR and the area. We then focus on the military aspects of the relationship. We progress to the economic dimensions of the relationship. And we conclude with a comprehensive analysis of the present-day relationship. Space limitations preclude individual chapters on the USSR's interaction with important countries, except the other superpower—the United States—and the other major Communist power—China. However, historically grounded assessments of Soviet successes and failures in specific regions are warranted by the increasing differentiation of Soviet foreign policy and by the mounting complexity of the international environment. Broad generalizations about the short- and long-term objectives of Soviet policy are increasingly difficult to verify. Also, sweeping generalizations about the substance of Soviet policy are becoming more and more suspect as the USSR tailors its activities to diverse and changing political-administrative, socioeconomic, and scientific-technological conditions at home and abroad. Furthermore, the USSR's collective leaderships have not produced clearly delineated, consistently pursued, and carefully coordinated programs in certain geographical and issue areas. These circumstances stimulate competition within and among the Soviet diplomatic, economic, intelligence, and military bureaucracies, which have latitude to pursue their special interests in interpreting and implementing policy. Hence, our contributors analyze the intended and actual Soviet policies in key regions of the world, focusing on large and medium-sized countries of particular importance to the USSR and basing their conclusions on empirical evidence from a wide variety of sources, Soviet and non-Soviet.

Part IX offers competing assessments of the Soviet polity's capacity for change, the future aims of Soviet foreign policy, and the USSR's challenges to the industrialized democracies. Will the heightening pressures for political and economic reforms bring innovations in Soviet international activities under Mikhail Gorbachev? Will the new generation of party leaders adjust its "tactics" to external and internal changes in order to fulfill traditional goals or adjust its "strategies" to changing conditions in order to fulfill redefined goals? To be sure, Western commentators agree that portentous scientific-technological breakthroughs have taken place since World War II, and many stress that the bipolar world of the 1940s has become multipolar in the 1980s. But American, West European, and Japanese analysts have different views about the USSR's global ambitions, the ramifications of Soviet military power, the linkages between Soviet defense spending and socioeconomic problems, the malleability of Soviet policies and policymaking procedures, and the possibility and desirability of arms limitation accords and commercial ties. Hence, Western government officials and researchers dispute the characteristics and course of Soviet foreign policy and the most effective ways of changing, countering, or coping with it. Such disputes will continue to have an enormous impact on East-West and North-South relations throughout the 1980s and quite probably thereafter.

Before immersing oneself in this anthology and reassessing one's views about the USSR's international activities, the reader should recall that the Soviet Constitution of 1977 affirms: "The USSR's foreign policy is aimed at ensuring favorable international conditions for building communism in the USSR, protecting the Soviet Union's state interests, strengthening the positions of world socialism, supporting the peoples' struggle for national liberation and social progress, preventing wars of aggression, achieving general and complete disarmament, and consistently implementing the principle of the peaceful coexistence of states with different social systems."[4] Hence, "peaceful coexistence" is the core principle of Soviet foreign policy, includes major confrontational and cooperative elements, and presumes that "progressive" changes are emerging from continuous "struggle" in the international arena. Since the early 1970s party spokespersons have often referred to "peaceful coexistence" as "détente"—a "relaxation of tensions" for the purpose of furthering the USSR's interests in its global political, economic, and military competition with the West.

Soviet leaders since Lenin have stressed that the USSR's goals and policies must be adapted to the current period, which has distinctive characteristics shaped by the aspirations and accomplishments of competing socioeconomic systems and by the "correlation of forces" among nations. During the 1970s, for example, top party officials believed that the USSR could simultaneously support "national liberation movements," develop and stockpile strategic and conventional weapons, *and* participate more fully in the East–West and North–South division of labor. On the one hand, Angola was the first in a series of major Soviet and Soviet-supported adventures in the Third World. On the other hand, nuclear arms limitation agreements and expanded U.S./USSR economic and scientific-technological cooperation were actively pursued and still seemed within reach. Many Soviet leaders have emphasized the importance of commercial and diplomatic ties with Western Europe and Japan as well as the pitfalls of Soviet-American trade and arms control talks since the mid 1970s. Indeed, some Soviet commentators have concluded that vigorous pursuit of the two chief elements of détente— selected East-West *cooperation* in economic relations and strategic arms limitation and selected East-West *confrontation* in the Third World—has the added advantage of weakening the Atlantic alliance.

The Soviet invasion of Afghanistan in 1979 underscored the sizable gap between Soviet and American conceptions of détente and the differences between the American and West European conceptions. The USSR calls for collaboration and mutual restraint in East–West relations within Europe as a means of continuing—even accelerating—the rivalry with the West in the Third World. The United States advocates East–West cooperation and restraint within Europe as a means of reducing international tensions and of stabilizing the multifaceted Soviet–American competition. The Carter and Reagan administrations' responses to the war in Afghanistan made very clear the American rejection of the Soviet interpretation of détente. However, American political, military, and economic power have been unable to deter the Soviet leadership from acting on its own conception of détente, especially vis-à-vis selected African and Asian countries in the 1970s and major West European democracies in the 1970s and 1980s.

Western and Eastern Europe have been caught between the superpowers. From the outset, the West Europeans refused to define the Afghanistan crisis in East–West terms, perceiving it to be a regional crisis requiring regional responses. East–West détente within Europe was dealt a glancing blow but not a piercing—let alone a fatal—wound. West Europeans have consistently stressed the centrality of détente relationships within Europe. Acknowledging the ongoing East-West competition outside of Europe, West European leaders have assessed that competition largely in terms of its effects on European affairs. This position is congruent with the USSR's support for selected diplomatic, commercial, and scientific-technological cooperation between Western and Eastern Europe and between Western Europe and the USSR. However, the similar West European and Soviet perspectives about collaboration in Europe probably contributed to the Soviet leadership's misunderstanding of the significance of Atlantic ties for the *military* security of Western Europe. As the deployment of intermediate-range nuclear weapons in Western Europe in 1984 demonstrated, top Soviet leaders had developed unrealistic expectations about achieving military détente in Europe on Soviet terms.

No sooner had these tendencies in West-West and East-West relations begun to crystallize after the Soviet occupation of Afghanistan than the East and West were plunged into the Polish crisis. The gains the Politburo thought it had realized from the Afghanistan war—in particular, the greater independence of Western Europe from the United States—were immediately jeopardized by unprecedented confrontation between the state, workers, and Catholic church in Poland. Moreover, the Polish drama revived East European assertiveness, which had been stifled after the Soviet invasion of Czechoslovakia in 1968. Greater national consciousness was especially evident in the desire of the Polish party-government, labor unions, and church to resolve their differences without being dictated to from the Kremlin. By the mid-1980s, the Romanians, East Germans, Hungarians, and even the Bulgarians were manuevering for leeway from the USSR in order to develop distinctively national forms of socialism.

Elites and ordinary citizens in Eastern Europe have begun to perceive a *choice* between overt Soviet interference and the identification and resolution of domestic problems without such interference. These evolving perspectives are the products not only of de-Stalinization and desatellization but of détente itself. Détente has been a *gamble* in both the East and West. The East has risked unleashing major destabilizing changes in the Soviet bloc by encouraging greater interdependence and openness to the West. The West has risked political and military vulnerability and economic dependence on the USSR as well as fissures in the Atlantic alliance.

Soviet and West and East European leaders have taken relatively compatible views of détente. Unlike the United States, Western Europe has maintained a détente relationship with the USSR throughout the 1970s and 1980s. This relationship is based on political, economic, and scientific-technological ties that both sides perceive to be mutually advantageous. Had the Soviet–West European bonds created in the early 1970s failed to constrain the USSR from dispatching additional Red Army troops into Poland in the early 1980s, West European governments and citizens would have been much more inclined to accept President Reagan's sharp criticism of Soviet motivations and behavior. But, because the USSR did not directly intervene in Poland, the West Europeans' support for commercial and diplomatic collaboration increased.

In contrast, Soviet and American leaders have struggled to find a similar and workable interpretation of détente. Not surprisingly, relations between the two superpowers deteriorated precipitously after the Nixon–Kissinger period of promising beginnings and unwarranted expectations. Leading American executive and legislative branch officials began to comprehend and counter the USSR's simultaneous emphasis on long-term East–West economic and strategic arms cooperation as well as unfettered East–West economic and conventional arms competition in the Third World. But the Soviet policy of détente depends much less on international collaboration than does the American policy. Hence, American leaders have not been able to implement their conceptions of détente, and American and West European leaders have striven to alter their partner's views of their own interests and those of the Atlantic alliance.

Western observers often overlook or minimize the diverse *Soviet* interpretations of détente. Soviet leaders and analysts perceive East–West relations as a dynamic mix of conflict and cooperation and of centrifugal and centripetal tendencies. But conservatives emphasize

East–West conflict and West–West cooperation; modernizers emphasize
East–West cooperation and West–West conflict; and there are numerous
centrist positions.[5]

Soviet modernizers underscore the opportunities for improving the
USSR's economic growth and productivity through selective interdependencies with the formidable industrialized Western powers.
Soviet conservatives underscore the possibilities for exacerbating "the
general crisis of capitalism" and for promoting the independence of
socialist states from the "degenerating" capitalist systems. The first
orientation stresses the cooperative elements of détente and the vulnerabilities generated by East–West confrontation. The second orientation stresses the adversarial elements of détente and the vulnerabilities
generated by East–West collaboration. Some centrists favor closer East–
West ties to avoid domestic economic reforms, whereas others favor
closer East–West ties to spur domestic economic reforms. And some
centrists prefer ties with the United States, whereas others prefer ties
with Western Europe and/or Japan.

For Soviet conservatives, "the forces of Atlantic solidarity" are in the
ascendancy in the West, and "the class unity" and exploitativeness of
the Western powers continuously endanger the socialist bloc countries.
Disunity in the West does not dissuade conservatives from such conclusions, not even the disarray in the Atlantic alliance that followed the
Red Army's occupation of Afghanistan and the imposition of martial law
in Poland. Instead, conservatives stress the "regressive" nature of the
ferment in Poland and the long-term political, military, and commercial
advantages of an intrabloc or self-sufficient strategy of economic development. Conservatives acknowledge that this strategy increases the
cost of producing many goods and services, but they insist that the
maintenance of one-party rule throughout Eastern Europe and the
collective defense of the USSR and its allies are much more important
than economic efficiency.

For Soviet modernizers, "interimperialist contradictions" are so deep
that détente with Western Europe can be maintained even with strong
American opposition. There exist "realist" as well as "adventurist"
elements in the West, and the former are willing to engage in
"businesslike" relations with the USSR and its allies at a time when the
Soviet-type economies are experiencing considerable difficulties. Modernizers, much more than conservatives, are facing up to unpleasant
domestic and international realities. The USSR's economy is suffering
declining growth rates. Food shortages have become a major political as
well as an economic problem. The Soviet labor force is expanding at a
snail's pace. Diminishing productivity increases in industry and agriculture, inadequate production returns on research and development expenditures, and inefficient managerial practices and organizational technologies continue to retard the USSR's economic progress. Even the
reduced energy subsidies to Eastern Europe are enervating the Soviet

economy. And world capitalism, especially the technologically sophisticated American and Japanese economies, are making dramatic advances in the 1980s.

According to Soviet modernizers, more and better foreign economic ties with capitalist, socialist, and Third World countries are important means of coping with these realities. Especially beneficial to the Soviet economy are export-oriented industries that produce high-quality manufactured goods for Western markets. But the USSR has few such industries. Probably its most beneficial foreign trade is conducted through natural resource pay-back arrangements—for example, the mammoth natural gas deal between the USSR and numerous West European nations. Soviet modernizers are apprehensive that further heavy-handed use of the USSR's military power, especially in areas of primary concern to the Western allies, would curtail vital East–West commercial links and greatly reduce the USSR's participation in the international division of labor. They argue that insularity would seriously undermine the USSR's overall economic development, which in turn would limit military capabilities. Stressing the importance of science-based technology for civilian as well as military industries, modernizers conclude that confrontation with the West decreases the USSR's national security and should be mitigated if at all possible.

Thus, there exist different Soviet views of international politics and very different Western views. Although the sources of these differences are numerous, the Soviet-American rivalry is being shaped more and more by an increasingly interdependent world and by unprecedented scientific-technological and socioeconomic changes. Foremost among these changes is the capacity of nuclear weapons to destroy the human species.[6] Given the critical importance of East–West relations and the proliferation of regional, global, and outer-space problems and opportunities, American government officials and citizens must continuously reassess Soviet perspectives, pursuits, and performance. The USSR presents a formidable military challenge—but less formidable economic and ideological challenges—to the United States and other Western nations. It is imperative that we better understand these challenges if we are to compete and cooperate effectively and judiciously with the USSR in the future.

## Notes

[1] The coeditors have made equal contributions to the conceptualization and compilation of both volumes.

[2] See, e.g., Erik P. Hoffmann and Robbin F. Laird, *"The Scientific-Technological Revolution" and Soviet Foreign Policy* (Elmsford, N.Y.: Pergamon Press, 1982); Robbin F. Laird and Dale R. Herspring, *The Soviet Union and Strategic Arms* (Boulder, Colo.: Westview Press, 1984); and Robbin F. Laird, *France, the Soviet Union, and the Nuclear Weapons Issue* (Boulder, Colo.: Westview Press, 1985).

[3] See, e.g., Erik P. Hoffmann and Robbin F. Laird, *Technocratic Socialism: The*

*Soviet Union in the Advanced Industrial Era* (Durham, N.C.: Duke University Press, 1985); and Erik P. Hoffmann and Robbin F. Laird, *The Politics of Economic Modernization in the Soviet Union* (Ithaca, N.Y.: Cornell University Press, 1982).

[4]"Constitution (Fundamental Law) of the Union of Soviet Socialist Republics," in Robert Sharlet, *The New Soviet Constitution of 1977: Analysis and Text* (Brunswick, Ohio: King's Court Communications, 1978), p. 85. Translation by *The Current Digest of the Soviet Press*.

[5]For detailed elaboration, see our books cited in Notes 2 and 3.

[6]The following lines are adapted from a speech by Robbin F. Laird and Erik P. Hoffmann for delivery by a presidential candidate.

# CONTRIBUTORS TO THIS VOLUME

Hannes Adomeit
  *Stiftung Wissenschaft und Politik*
David E. Albright
  *Air War College*
Vernon V. Aspaturian
  *Pennsylvania State University*
Seweryn Bialer
  *Columbia University*
Lester R. Brown
  *Worldwatch Institute*
Zbigniew Brzezinski
  *Columbia University*
Center for Defense Information
  *Washington, D.C.*
Stephen F. Cohen
  *Princeton University*
Joseph J. Collins
  *U.S. Military Academy*
Timothy J. Colton
  *University of Toronto*
Alexander Dallin
  *Stanford University*
Karen Dawisha
  *Princeton University*
Charles Gati
  *Union College*
Harry Gelman
  *The Rand Corporation*
Roy Godson
  *Georgetown University*
Rose E. Gottemoeller
  *The Rand Corporation*
Franklyn Griffiths
  *University of Toronto*
Thane Gustafson
  *Georgetown University*
John P. Hardt
  *U.S. Library of Congress*
Dale R. Herspring
  *U.S. Department of State*

Erik P. Hoffmann
  *State University of New York
    at Albany*
David Holloway
  *University of Edinburgh*
Jerry F. Hough
  *Duke University*
William G. Hyland
  *Georgetown University*
Stephen S. Kaplan
  *The Brookings Institution*
George F. Kennan
  *Institute for Advanced Study*
Robert W. Kitrinos
  *U.S. Department of Defense*
Robbin F. Laird
  *Institute for Defense Analyses*
F. Stephen Larrabee
  *Institute for East-West Security
    Studies*
Robert Legvold
  *Columbia University*
Marian Leighton
  *U.S. Department of Defense*
William H. Luers
  *U.S. Department of State*
Edward N. Luttwak
  *Georgetown University*
Paul Marer
  *Indiana University*
Richard Pipes
  *Harvard University*
Alvin Z. Rubinstein
  *University of Pennsylvania*
Marshall D. Shulman
  *Columbia University*
George P. Shultz
  *U.S. Department of State*
Richard H. Shultz
  *Tufts University*

Dimitri K. Simes
  *Carnegie Endowment for*
    *International Peace*
Helmut Sonnenfeldt
  *The Brookings Institution*
Angela E. Stent
  *Georgetown University*
John J. Stephan
  *University of Hawaii at Manoa*
Kate S. Tomlinson
  *U.S. Library of Congress*

Adam B. Ulam
  *Harvard University*
Elizabeth Kridl Valkenier
  *Columbia University*
Allen S. Whiting
  *University of Arizona*
Donald S. Zagoria
  *Hunter College, City University*
    *of New York*
William Zimmerman
  *University of Michigan*

# I

*Issues*

# 1        ZBIGNIEW BRZEZINSKI

## *The Soviet Union: Her Aims, Problems, and Challenges to the West**

This essay will examine the distinctive nature of the Soviet Union as a world power and assess the special character of the Soviet challenge to the international system. The basic theses of this analysis can be stated briefly at the outset:

1. That the expansionism of the Soviet imperial system is a unique organic imperative produced by the sense of territorial insecurity on the part of the system's Great Russian national core;
2. That as a result of the Great Russian stake in the imperial system a genuine evolution of the Soviet system into more pluralistic forms is not likely in the foreseeable future;
3. That the political priorities and bureaucratic distortions of the Communist system confine the Soviet Union to the role of a one-dimensional military world power;
4. That the Soviet Union—which now has military global reach but which lacks political global grasp—feels herself both too strong internationally to accommodate to the status quo and too weak domestically not to fear it;
5. That as an organically expansionist, but one-dimensional military world power lacking the capacity to effect a genuine revolution in the world system, the Soviet Union is confined to the essentially negative role of disrupter of wider and more cooperative international arrangements;
6. That a major disruption of the international political system could occur as a consequence of Western failure to offset Soviet military power while not coping effectively with the mushrooming crises in the strategically and geopolitically central zones of the Middle East and Central America.

*Reprinted by permission of the author and publisher from Adelphi Papers, no. 189 (Spring, 1984), pp. 3–12. Copyright 1984 by The International Institute for Strategic Studies.

**A Uniquely Organic Imperialism**   The Soviet Union is the political expression of Russian nationalism. The Great Russians dominate the multinational Soviet Union, populated by some 270 million people, and through the power and resources of that Union, they dominate in turn a cluster of geographically contiguous states numbering approximately an additional 115 million people. In effect, about 135 million Great Russians exercise political control over a political framework that cumulatively encompasses some 385 million spread over much of the Eurasian Continent.

This is not to say that the system is one of simple national oppression. The Great Russians rule as much by cooptation as by suppression. The historical record of Russian imperial preponderance is replete with examples of successful cooptation, corruption, and integration of foreign elites, of the gradual absorption politically and even culturally of ethnically related peoples, of the creation of a sense of a larger community. Nonetheless, in the background of this process is the reality of Moscow's power, which is applied ruthlessly whenever a given nation chooses to resist domination and especially if it seeks to detach itself from the Russian-dominated larger whole.

The distinctive character of the Russian imperial drive is derived from the interconnection between the militaristic organization of Russian society and the territorial imperative which defines its instinct for survival. As often noted by both Russian and non-Russian historians, from time immemorial Russian society expressed itself politically through a state that was mobilized and regimented along military lines, with the security dimension serving as the central organizing impulse. The absence of any clearly definable national boundary made territorial expansion the obvious way of assuring security, with such territorial expansion then breeding new conflicts, new threats, and thus a further expansionary drive. A relentless historical cycle was thus set in motion: insecurity generated expansionism; expansionism bred insecurity; insecurity, in turn, would fuel further expansionism.

Russian history is consequently a history of sustained territorial expansionism. This sustained expansion from the northeast plains and forests of Muscovy has lasted—almost on a continuous basis—for more than 300 years. It has involved a push westward against major power rivals, resulting in the eventual expulsion of Sweden from east of the Baltic and in the partition of the Polish–Lithuanian Republic; it has involved the persistent drive southward, culminating—in the wake of defeats inflicted on the Ottoman Empire—in the subordination of the Ukrainian Cossacks and the Crimean Tatars and in the absorption of several Caucasian nations and of Muslim central Asia; it has involved a steady stream of settlers, penal colonists, and military explorers eastward, along the brim of the Chinese empire, all the way to Kamchatka. Such territorial expansion is doubtless—both in scale and in duration—one of the most ambitious examples of a relentless imperial drive in known history.

The Russians have come in this manner to control the world's largest real estate. They do so by the relatively dense inhabitation of its inner core—the large area known as European Russia—and by settling in smaller but still politically significant numbers in strategically significant colonial outposts in the Baltic region (including Kaliningrad), parts of Byelorussia, East Ukraine, the northeast shore of the Black Sea, large parts of Kazakhstan, and along a great security belt spanning the trans-Siberian Railroad all the way to the Soviet Far East. The empty vastness of Siberia has thus been effectively sealed off and remains available for gradual colonization.

In the process, the Russians have come to dominate the weaker peoples inhabiting some of these territories, by subordinating them politically, coopting them culturally, and even sometimes decimating them biologically. The non-Russian nations are controlled from the center and prevented from coalescing against the politically dominant Great Russians, who populate the strategically located central inner core of the multinational state.

The Russian imperial system—with its mixture of cooptation, subordination, and strategic settlement—thus emerged in a manner that differs profoundly from the experience of other recent empires. Naval expansion to remote lands, followed by limited settling, was not the method. The Russian method was much more organic—a process of steady seepage into contiguous territory, with the atavistic instinct for survival dictating the perceived need to acquire more land, with "insecurity" being translated into persistent expansion. As a result, and contrary to many journalist clichés, Russia historically was not so much a victim of frequent aggression but rather the persistent aggressor herself, pressing from the center in this or that direction, whenever opportunity beckoned. Any list of aggressions committed in the last two centuries against Russia would be dwarfed by a parallel list of Russian expansionist moves against her neighbors. The vaunted Russian sense of insecurity exists—but not because Russia was so frequently attacked but because her organic expansion has prompted, and was prompted by, territorial acquisitiveness, with its inevitably antagonist ripple-effects.

An additional, and enduring, consequence of such sustained territorial expansion has been the emergence of an imperial consciousness among the Great Russian people. Such a notion of "imperial consciousness" is difficult to define, but difficulty of definition is not a negation of the phenomenon. There is something strikingly imperial in the insistence of the Russians describing themselves as the "Big Brother" of other dominated peoples, in the spontaneous determination to build huge Russian orthodox cathedrals in the very centers of dominated capitals (as in Helsinki and Warsaw—and even to replace the Warsaw *Sobor*, which the newly emancipated Poles blew up in 1919, 30 years later with the monumental Stalin Palace of Culture), in the deeply rooted feeling that somehow the non-Russian nations of the Soviet Union and of Eastern Europe must be retained as part of Mother Russia's special domain. Anyone who has seen, or read reports of, how the Soviet ambassadors stationed abroad handle their periodic joint sessions with fellow ambassadors from the Warsaw Pact obtains a first-hand insight into imperial and hierarchical relations.

Great Russian imperial consciousness is a complex web of religious messianism, which has long associated Moscow with the Third Rome, of nationalistic instincts for survival and power, and of the more recent universalistic ideological zeal. In addition, territorially expansive insecurity has been reinforced by the Communist obsession with internal and external enemies, reinforcing an already existing paranoiac attitude toward the outside world. This complex web of motivations has helped to generate and sustain a world outlook in which the drive to global preeminence, for decades measured by competition with the U.S., has become the central energizing impulse. That impulse sustains the predatory character of Great Russian imperialism.

It is this drive toward global preeminence as well as the vested interest in the imperial system that inhibits the prospects of a qualitatively significant evolutionary change in the character of the Soviet system. Without Soviet intervention, Czechoslovakia under Dubcek or Poland under Walesa probably would have become social democratic republics, with Communist totalitarianism effectively dismantled.

But Soviet intervention occurred for the very same reason that internal evolution toward greater political pluralism within the Soviet Union will be intensely, and probably even more successfully, resisted for a very long time to come. The reaction against peaceful change in Eastern Europe stemmed from the same impulses, which make Great Russians fear any significant relaxation of central Moscow control. A genuinely far-reaching decentralization of the Soviet system, even if only economic, would pose a mortal danger to Great Russian imperial control, and thus, in the Russian psyche, eventually to the security of the Great Russian people. After all, what does "only economic" decentralization mean in political terms insofar as the Soviet Union is concerned? Inevitably, it would have to mean a greater degree of autonomy for the non-Russians who would be then in a position to translate greater economic self-determination into growing political self-determination.

To the majority of the Great Russians that is a highly threatening prospect. *Any* significant national self-assertion on the part of the non-Russians also constitutes a challenge to Russian territorial preeminence and could possibly even pose a biological threat to Great Russian national survival. Where would genuine decentralization, the acceptance of more democratic norms, the institutionalization of pluralism eventually lead? Where, indeed, could one even draw proper lines between the Great Russians and the others, given the demographic intermingling of the recent decades? There would be escalating tensions, eventually even head-on conflicts in a variety of areas: in some of the Baltic Republics which have been heavily settled by unwelcome Great Russians; in the culturally comingled areas of Byelorussia and the Ukraine; certainly on the fringes of the Caucasian and Central Asian Republics.

The dismantling of the overseas British and French Empires did not mean the end of either Britain or France. The dismantling of the territorially contiguous Russian Empire could even threaten Russia herself, given the absence of natural frontiers. The difficulties the French faced in Algeria would be dwarfed on the peripheries of the purely Great Russian lands. Any attempted disentangling along national lines would be messy and bloody, and awareness of that prospect makes almost every Great Russian instinctively wary of tolerating any significant devolution of Moscow's central control. The instinct for survival gives the autocratic, highly centralized, and imperial Soviet system unusual staying power, neutralizing the kind of inner self-doubt and imperial fatigue that induced the British and French to accede to the dismantling of their Empires.

## A One-Dimensional World Power of a New Type

Western observers of the Soviet system have been loath to concede that the political centralism of the Soviet system has staying power and that the Russian imperial impulse is vitally inherent to that system. It is certainly more reassuring to believe that both conditions are evanescent: that the system will mellow because of either containment or economic development (or a combination of both), and that its imperial drive will wane with the allegedly inevitable fading of Marxist zeal. The transformation of the system and the waning of its imperial ambitions will thus relieve the West of the obligation of having to face up to the much more difficult dilemma of determining how to historically coexist in the nuclear age with a powerful and closed political system motivated by vague but highly unsettling global goals.

But what if the Soviet system does not mellow, and what if her military power continues to grow? Rarely, if ever, do Western observers address themselves to the international implications of this issue, except occasionally from the extreme right perspective, cast usually in highly Manichaean and moralistic terms. Yet the issue demands attention and, above all, sober realization that for many decades to come an uneasy historical—but not entirely peaceful—coexistence with a militarily powerful Soviet Union may continue to teeter on the edge of the nuclear abyss.

The point of departure for a realistic appraisal of the relationship must be recognition of the special character of the Soviet system as a world power. The Soviet Union is a world power of a new type in that her might is one dimensional, with the result that she is essentially incapable of sustaining effective global dominance. The fact of the matter is that the Soviet Union is a global power only in the military dimension, but in no other. She is neither a genuine economic rival to the United States nor—as once was the case—even a source of a globally interesting ideological experiment. This condition imposes a decisive limitation on the Soviet capability to act in a manner traditional to world powers or claimants to the status of world power.

Traditionally, both the dominant world military power, as well as its

principal rival, possessed relatively matching political and socioeconomic systems, each with the capability for sustained and comprehensive
preeminence. From the late Middle Ages on, naval power has been the
central instrument for exercising global military reach, and the powers
exercising it (to the extent that such global reach can be said to have
existed in the age of slow communications and weapons of limited
lethality) and their principal rivals were—broadly speaking—Portugal
and Spain (during much of the sixteenth century); followed by the
Netherlands and France (during the seventeenth century); by Britain,
and then first France and later Germany (during the eighteenth,
nineteenth, and part of the twentieth centuries); and finally by the
United States and the Soviet Union (during the second half of the
twentieth century). In all cases until the most recent, the contest was
between powers at a comparable level of development, with the rival
quite capable of providing also wider commercial and political leadership as a supplement to its military preeminence. In effect, the rival, in
displacing the preeminent global power, could both provide and sustain
equally comprehensive leadership.

The unusual quality of the Soviet global challenge is that the Soviet
Union is manifestly unequipped to provide constructive and sustained
leadership in the event that she should succeed in unseating the United
States as the leading world power. The Soviet Union could not provide
global financial leadership. Her economy could not act as the locomotive
for global development and technological innovation. Her mass culture
has no wider appeal (and her leading intellectuals and artists have been
steadily fleeing the Soviet Union). In brief, American displacement
could not be followed by a Soviet replacement.

The main reason for this condition is to be found in the Russian
Communist system itself. Its bureaucratization, centralization, and
dogmatization of decision making have stifled socioeconomic initiative
to an unprecedented degree. As a result, the Soviet record in all the
nonmilitary dimensions of systemic performance ranges from the average to the mediocre. It still takes literally a *political* decision at the highest
level for the Soviet economic system to produce some item that is
generally competitive worldwide. Soviet economic performance over
the years has required social sacrifice altogether disproportionate to the
actual output. Perhaps never before in history have such a gifted people,
in control of such abundant resources, labored so hard for so long to
produce relatively so little.

Comparative studies of socioeconomic development, as for instance
by Professor Cyril Black of Princeton, show that today the Soviet Union
occupies in world rankings of social and economic indexes a place
roughly comparable to that which it held at the beginning of this
century. Black's conclusion was that "In the perspective of fifty years,
the comparative ranking of the USSR in composite economic and social
indices *per capita* has probably not changed significantly. So far as the
rather limited available evidence permits a judgment, the USSR has not
overtaken or surpassed any country on a *per capita* basis since 1917 with
the possible exception of Italy, and the nineteen or twenty countries that

rank higher than Russia today in this regard also ranked higher in 1900 and 1919. The *per capita* gross national product of Italy, which is just below that of the USSR today, was probably somewhat higher fifty years ago."[1]

In other words, the extraordinary sacrifices, the unprecedented loss of life, the sustained social deprivation that every Soviet citizen has felt have yielded results comparable to those achieved by other societies at much smaller social cost. Moreover, the pace of Soviet economic development after World War II has been only average, despite the fact that initially the Soviet Union had the statistical advantage of recovering from an artificially low plateau generated by wartime devastation. In 1950, the Soviet GNP accounted for about 11% of the global product; three decades later it is still 11%. No wonder that Soviet propagandists now prefer not to recall Khrushchev's challenge of 1960 to surpass the United States in absolute production by 1970 and in relative *per capita* production by 1980.

The picture is just as bleak in the social and cultural dimensions of Soviet life. Recent studies point to a decline in male longevity, to the poor state of Soviet health care, to increasing infant mortality, and to the spread of alcoholism. Intellectual and artistic life has become stifled; social innovation has been shackled by bureaucratic inertia. In brief, the Soviet Union is not a society capable of projecting world-wide an appealing image, a condition essential to the exercise of global leadership.

The main effect of this poor performance is twofold. First of all, it magnifies the traditional Russian and the doctrinaire Communist suspicions regarding the outside world. That world is perceived as bent on dismantling Moscow's empire and on promoting an anti-Communist counterrevolution. The outside thus continues to look threatening to the USSR, despite the Soviet attainment of the status of a global military superpower. Though the Soviet Union takes great pride in her new military prowess, and has used it to claim coequal status with the United States, in the Soviet perception of the world the U.S. looms as a giant, with her finances, communications, and mass media enveloping the world with many tentacles. American technology (for instance, currently microelectronics) keeps on providing the American military establishment with new capabilities which the Soviets take more than seriously. In the Far East, there looms the potential for a Chinese–Japanese constellation, while in the West there is always the magnetic pull on Eastern Europe of a Europe that has not fully resigned itself to an indefinite post-Yalta division.

All of that enhances Soviet paranoia and contributes directly to the second major effect of the one-dimensional character of Soviet global power. It generates an erratic pattern of accommodation and competition with the United States, in which, on the one hand, the Soviet Union seeks to attain a condominium with Washington and yet, on the other, fears becoming locked into the role of the junior partner in effect committed to the maintenance of the global status quo. That status quo Moscow rejects for it would not only perpetuate American preponderance but—in Soviet eyes—it would serve as the point of departure for policies designed to promote "peaceful evolution" of a contained Soviet Union (i.e., her political subversion).

As a result, the promotion of regional conflicts, the inhibition of wider and more genuinely international cooperation, and opposition to what is called "world order" are strategies that the Kremlin finds compatible with its own one-dimensional global military power. That military power permits the USSR to play a wider role in keeping with the Soviet imperial consciousness, it reduces the fear that regional conflicts could precipitate a head-on collision with the United States, and it enables the Soviet Union to use military leverage to undermine American preeminence in areas hitherto considered as safe U.S. havens. Particularly important and effective in this respect is the Soviet ability (in excess of the American) to deliver promptly from her large inventories huge amounts of military equipment to Soviet clients and would-be friends. In effect, a policy of gradual undermining of American global preeminence is a key aspect of the historical self-definition of the Soviet Union as a global power.

And that leads to a broader conclusion still: the real danger to the West is not that the Soviet Union will someday succeed in imposing a *Pax Sovietica* on the world. Rather, it is that the Soviet Union, as a one-dimensional world power committed to the disruption of the existing arrangements, because such disruption is essential to the displacement of the U.S., will contribute decisively not to a world revolution in existing international arrangements but to greater global anarchy from which all will suffer.

## A Partially Revised Perspective on the Soviet Challenge

Implicit in the foregoing conclusion are some revisions of the prevailing Western view regarding the nature of the Soviet threat. In the immediate post-World War II era, the West was preoccupied with the fear that vast Soviet armies would pour westward, literally swamping Western Europe. Internal high-level American discussions—as recent studies by Professor D. A. Rosenberg show[2]—focused heavily on the question of how the U.S. should respond, given her limited but monopolistic nuclear arsenal. Berlin became the symbolic lynchpin of Western resolve, with the blockade providing an American–Soviet test of wills.

Western, and notably U.S., anxiety mounted further after the Communist invasion of Korea, leading for the first time to comprehensive U.S. nuclear war planning and the creation of the SAC (Strategic Air Command) as the principal means of massive retaliation. In the late 1950s, Khrushchev's missile boasting precipitated more intensified U.S. efforts to offset the allegedly emerging Soviet advantage, resulting by the early 1960s in a considerable U.S. strategic superiority. However, by the late 1970s and early 1980s, with the U.S. homeland also fully vulnerable to a Soviet attack, the Soviet Union was again perceived as being on the verge of obtaining a politically significant military edge, with President Reagan even explicitly proclaiming that the Soviet Union is already strategically superior to the United States.

In fact, during much of the postwar era the Soviet challenge to the West—contrary to prevailing perceptions—was not primarily military, and even now the much more important military dimension of the Soviet threat needs to be seen in a broader political framework. During the immediate postwar years, Stalin did engage in some peripheral probes designed to establish the resilience of the new geopolitical realities, but his challenge was not primarily a military one. Indeed, the West greatly overestimated the existing Soviet military capabilities, in apparent ignorance of the large-scale demobilization of the Red Army. To be sure, the West, and especially the U.S., disarmed most hastily, but the West confronted an East that was socially exhausted and militarily also readjusting to a peacetime status.

The primary challenge in those years was in fact ideological–political. The Soviet Union emerged from World War II with unprecedented prestige. She was hailed and idealized in the West, and not only by fellow travellers. Many in the West so desperately wanted to believe that the USSR would remain also a postwar ally that they bent over backward to see the Soviet point of view on the contentious international issues. Moreover, to the populations of war-devastated countries, the Soviet Union projected the image not only of a victor but also of any apparently successful socioeconomic system. It was that image that generated the ideological support and invited political imitation. An enormous American effort, above all the Marshall Plan, was required to neutralize that appeal—and it was on this front, and not purely on the military level, that the initial historical confrontation occurred. This is not to deny the importance of NATO or of the Korean War in the containment of the Soviet Union, but it is to postulate that the political–ideological dimension was then critical in the rivalry.

The next crucial phase in the Soviet challenge occurred during the late 1950s and early 1960s. Khrushchev's policy of premature globalism, based on deliberately falsified claims of missile superiority, collapsed during the Cuban crisis of 1962. Khrushchev's challenge was predicated, however, also on a more generalized historical vision in which economic optimism was the decisive element. The Soviet leader's vulgar "We will bury you" was not—as it was widely perceived at the time—a physical threat but a historic gauntlet, derived from misplaced confidence that American economic stagnation and Soviet economic dynamism would result in the emergence by the 1970s of the Soviet Union as the world's preeminent economic power.

That did not happen. In 1980 the Soviet Union was as behind the United States as it had been a quarter of a century ago. It is also now behind Japan. The vaunted technological race ended with the American flag on the moon. Today the Soviet economy is widely perceived as being, if not in crisis, then at least noninnovative and confronting increasingly difficult trade-offs. Soviet agriculture is clearly an undisputed failure. The Soviet system more generally has lost its ideological appeal and that, too, detracts from Soviet global influence.

By the 1980s, however, Soviet military power had acquired, for the first time, genuine global reach, compensating thus for the lack of systemic appeal. This new condition was clearly gratifying to the Soviet leaders, and anyone who has dealt with them can testify to their pride in the Soviet Union's new status as a global superpower.

But global reach is not the same thing as global grasp. The Soviet challenge today, as already noted, is one-dimensional and therefore it cannot be the point of departure for either comprehensive global leadership, or even for an enduring global partnership with the United States. The ambivalent condition of one-dimensional power induces an outlook on the world which is a combination of possessive defensiveness and disruptive offensiveness.

To be sure, it is quite doubtful whether the Soviet leaders operate on the basis of some broad revolutionary blueprint or that they even have a systematic long-term strategy. In real life, most decision makers are so compelled to respond to circumstances and to cope with a myriad of specific issues that they simply lack the time and the intellectual inclination to engage in any systematic long-term definition of policy goals. Doubtless the Soviet leaders are no exception. But the Soviet leaders do operate in the context of an orientation in which the retention of what the USSR controls and the disruption of what the U.S. seeks to organize provide lodestars for more specific tactics and strategies.

It is important to recall here that there is a basic difference between a genuinely revolutionary world power and a disruptive world power. Napoleonic France threatened not only the status quo; France's socioeconomic development was such that France could serve as the center of a new international order that would have emerged if Napoleon had prevailed over Britain and Russia. In that sense, France was a genuinely revolutionary power. To an ominous degree, both Hitler's Germany and Tojo's Japan had also the revolutionary potential for creating a new international system, in the event that German and Japanese arms had won victory.

In contrast, the Soviet Union is limited to a disruptive, but not a truly revolutionary role. She is confined to that role by the nature of her one-dimensional power and also by the character of nuclear weapons. Nuclear weapons eliminate the possibility of a central war serving as the revolutionary cataclysm. Until the advent of the nuclear age, a world power could be displaced by its rival through a head-on military confrontation, with military victory then translated into premier status by the exercise of the other attributes of national power, such as the economy, finances, science, and national culture. The nuclear age has had the effect of making these other means of exercising world domination also become the more critical instruments for *achieving* such world domination.

Yet it is in these other attributes of power that the Soviet Union is most deficient. Moreover, there is no reason to believe, given the inherent limitations of the Soviet system, that this situation will soon alter to the Soviet Union's benefit. The Soviet Union is thus condemned to seeking global status neither by head-on nuclear collision nor by a peaceful socioeconomic competition. The only way open to it is that of attrition and gradual disruption of stable international arrangements so that the U.S. suffers directly and indirectly.

The most effective way of pursuing such a strategy of disruption is to achieve and maintain sufficient military power to deter U.S. reactions and to intimidate the friends of the U.S, while encouraging trends hostile to American interests in those particular strategically vital areas which possess the greater potential for a dynamic shift in the global political–economic balance. Today, these areas are, above all, the Middle East and Central America.

Accordingly, what happens in these two strategically and geopoliti- cally sensitive zones will determine the longer range pattern of the American–Soviet relationship and define the Soviet global role. A pro- gressive deterioration of the political stability of the Middle East, com- bined with the gradual political reentry of the Soviet Union into a region from which it has been excluded since 1973, could have far-reaching implications for American relations with both Europe and the Far East. The strategic salience of this region is such that any qualitatively important decline in American influence, especially if matched by a corresponding rise in Soviet political presence, is bound to have far- reaching and worldwide strategic consequences for the nature of the American–Soviet global equation.

Similarly, how the United States handles her new dilemmas in Central America, and in the longer run also the U.S.–Mexican relation- ship, is bound to affect the global balance, and therefore also the Soviet world role. As in the Middle East, it is again not so much a matter of what the Soviet Union may be doing as of how the United States conducts herself, either by commission or by omission. If American policy results in the Americanization of sociopolitical conflicts to such an extent that the western hemisphere is increasingly turned against the United States, and the American–Mexican problems become conse- quently so complicated that the United States loses the capacity for helping constructively in the resolution of Mexico's internal problems, the result will be a far-reaching decline in American global standing.

That, in turn, would reinforce the Soviet imperial consciousness and the expansionary impulse, while strengthening further the existing structure of Soviet power and the basic character of the system. Indeed, it is appropriate to recall in this connection that insofar as Russian historical experience is concerned, internal political change of truly significant character has tended to occur only in the wake of external defeats, whereas external successes have tended to reinforce centralism and ideological control. Moreover, as Arnold Horelick has shown in a recent RAND study, an improved Soviet domestic performance also tends to encourage a more assertive external behavior and the surfacing of greater external ambitions.[3]

In contrast, external setbacks have induced profound reassessments of Russian internal policies and have occasionally produced even signifi- cant systemic changes. Thus, despite the internal weakness of the Tsarist regime, its pervasive corruption, and its mindless bureaucracy, the basic structure of its power endured for a long time—and collapsed finally only because of the massive military defeat inflicted upon it during the three devastating years of World War I. Moreover, the occasional periods of internal reform that occurred during the 1860s and in the first decade of the twentieth century followed immediately upon external defeats suffered by Russia in the Crimean conflict and in the Russo/Japanese War, respectively. The great Russian historian, V. O. Kluchevsky (as cited in Horelick's paper) notes that "a Russian war carried to a successful issue has always helped to strengthen the previously compounded order," but "progress in Russia's political life at home has always been gained at the price of Russia's political misfortune abroad."

By having become a global military power, the Soviet Union has *de facto* broken through the U.S. policy of geographic containment. At the same time, by expanding her exposure at a time when her own capacities are still very one dimensional, the Soviet Union is exposing herself to the possibility of overextension and even eventually to some major external misfortune, because of some protracted military–political misadventure. And in that respect the Soviet strategy of deliberate exploitation of global turbulence could turn out historically to have been a case of playing with fire.

The policy implications that follow from the foregoing analysis can be posited briefly as the following:

• The military dimension of the East–West competition, notably of the U.S.–Soviet rivalry, is negatively of critical importance. Although the rivalry is not likely to be finally resolved by a clash of arms, the West must exercise every effort to make certain that the Soviet Union does not gain a military edge which would enable it to attempt political intimidation.

• Arms-control arrangements should be assessed primarily in terms of their contribution to the maintenance of a stable East–West military balance. That is their central role. Arms control, moreover, should be pursued without historical illusions regarding the impact of any agreement on the character of the Soviet system and its relationship with the West, for the long-term political rivalry will not be ended even by a comprehensive arms-control arrangement.

• A major Soviet external misfortune is likely to have the most immediate impact on Eastern Europe. This region is manifestly restless and resentful of Soviet control. Any sign of Soviet weakness, any prolonged and debilitating Soviet foreign entanglement will be exploited to break the weakest link in the Soviet imperial chain. Moreover, it is a region that is most susceptible to Western ideas and culturally attracted by Western Europe. It offers, therefore, a topical focus for Western policies designed to dilute the Soviet imperial impulse.

• Western, and especially American, efforts to maintain and promote regional stability, notably in such vital areas as Central America and the Middle East, are going to be decisive in determining whether Soviet global influence expands, to the detriment of international stability.

American passivity in the Middle East and U.S. overengagement in Central America are the most immediate geopolitical dangers.

• The positive task of shaping a wider international system that genuinely embraces the newly emancipated Third World, and thus replaces the narrower European world order that collapsed in the course of World War II, will have to be pursued for quite some time to come without constructive Soviet involvement. The Soviet Union—too strong not to be a rival, yet feeling herself too weak to be a partner—cannot be counted upon to become a true participant in the constructive global process since her systemic interests are diametrically opposed to the preservation of the status quo in a world which the Soviet Union can disrupt but not dominate.

• Historical coexistence with the Soviet Union will remain dominated by the largely negative task of avoiding a nuclear catastrophe. It will be Western acts, of commission or omission, that will ultimately determine whether that historical coexistence—a coexistence that at best for a long time to come will be precariously peaceful—will eventually produce a more harmonious relationship or deteriorate into wider global anarchy.

## Notes

[1]Cyril E. Black, "Soviet Society: A Comparative View," in *Prospects for Soviet Society*, ed. A. Kassof (New York: Praeger, 1968), pp. 42–43.

[2]David Alan Rosenberg, "The Origins of Overkill: Nuclear Weapons and American Strategy, 1945–1960," *International Security* (Spring, 1983), pp. 3–71.

[3]Arnold L. Horelick, "External Implications of Soviet Internal Developments," prepared for the RAND–SWP Conference, 24–27 June 1983 (Santa Monica, Calif.: RAND Corporation, 1983).

# 2

# CHARLES GATI

## The Stalinist Legacy in Soviet Foreign Policy*

The central arguments of this essay are that Stalin's foreign policy was less aggressive and revolutionary than is commonly assumed; that his successors' foreign policy has been more aggressive and revolutionary than is commonly assumed; and that there has therefore been more continuity in the conduct of Soviet foreign policy than is commonly assumed. All of these arguments run counter to widely held Western views.

Since Stalin's death in 1953, many Western students of Soviet foreign policy have emphasized "change" rather than "continuity" in the international orientation of the Soviet Union—change for the better, evolution toward moderation and restraint. They seem to have concluded that Soviet foreign policy—responding both to a new external environment and to different internal circumstances—has successfully shed its Stalinist past. They believe that the Soviet Union, having substantially reduced its revolutionary commitments, has become an essentially status quo power—steady and ambitious but not reckless, at times assertive but not adventurist, and invariably pragmatic. Rather than an aggressive revolutionary power, the Soviet Union is thus seen as primarily, if not exclusively, interested in protecting its own security and achievements in an atmosphere of relative international stability.

Is such a general appraisal of post-Stalin Soviet foreign policy—and the cautious optimism it has produced in the West— really warranted? Did de-Stalinization in foreign policy accompany Soviet domestic de-Stalinization?

I think not. The year 1953 was not a watershed in Soviet foreign policy. A comparison of post-Stalin Soviet foreign policy patterns with

*Reprinted by permission of the author from *The Soviet Union in the 1980s,* ed. Erik P. Hoffmann (New York: The Academy of Political Science, 1984), pp. 214–226. A longer, earlier version appeared in *The Soviet Union since Stalin,* eds. Stephen F. Cohen, Alexander Rabinowitch, and Robert Sharlet (Bloomington, Ind.: Indiana University Press, 1980). Copyright 1980 by Charles Gati.

Stalinist behavior from 1928 to 1953 reveals far more continuity than change. As a basic approach to the outside world, Stalin's conduct of foreign policy was calculating and circumspect, and his historic mix of expansion-and-accommodation, or revolutionary assertiveness-and-peaceful coexistence, which served the Soviet state so well for so long, has remained deeply ingrained in the Soviet political mind. On balance, Stalin cannot be said to have placed more emphasis on revolution making than his successors have on upholding or maintaining the status quo. Essentially cautious and opportunistic, the Soviet leaders since Lenin have displayed revolutionary assertiveness when and where it seemed safe to do so, while favoring the status quo and peaceful coexistence when and where it seemed necessary or useful to do so. All of them, and perhaps especially Stalin, consistently refused to risk the security of the Soviet Union for distant, revolutionary goals. After all, as early as the mid-1920s, Stalin had already advocated a largely inward-looking posture for the emerging Soviet state—"socialism in one country"—against Trotsky's more radical, outward-looking alternative of "permanent revolution."

It is true, of course, that the scope of Soviet foreign policy has changed. Stalin did not develop a coherent policy toward the colonial areas of Asia and Africa, for example, while his successors have certainly done so toward what is now called the Third World. It is also true that some of the issues on the Soviet agenda are new—such as the current preoccupation with and the management of nuclear weapons systems. And it is true that it remained for Stalin's successors to cope with such problems as the rise of new communist party-states and to define the meaning of "socialist internationalism" and "international relations of a new type." Yet, important as some of these changes in the scope, issues, and problems of Soviet foreign policy may seem, they are not so far-reaching as to assume that Stalin himself would not have made them. Indeed, if Stalin could now survey the achievements, strategies, and methods of Soviet foreign policy since 1953, he would likely endorse its general thrust and congratulate his successors on their skillful adaptation of his approach to new international circumstances.

Furthermore, even if one were inclined to dismiss as political rhetoric Khrushchev's remark that so far as foreign policy toward the West was concerned he and his colleagues did regard themselves as Stalinists, the fact remains that Stalin's foreign policy has never been subjected to extensive criticism in the Soviet Union—not even during the height of the domestic de-Stalinization campaign in the mid-1950s. In fact, Stalin was criticized for only two foreign policy faults: the country's military unpreparedness on the eve of World War II and his unduly harsh, and ultimately counterproductive, treatment of Yugoslavia in 1948 and 1949 (and, by implication, the rest of Eastern Europe). He was not accused of excessive aggressiveness or adventurism, nor did his successors ever promise to de-Stalinize Soviet foreign policy and indeed place it on new foundations.

The reason for the apparent gap between the promise and early pursuit of domestic de-Stalinization, on the one hand, and the lack of de-Stalinization in foreign policy, on the other, is self-evident. While his successors believed that Stalin's domestic policies—particularly the intimidation and terror aimed against the Soviet elite—began to threaten the cause of socialism within the Soviet Union, his foreign policy record spoke well of his skills in promoting Soviet security and the cause of socialism abroad. After all, when Stalin became *primer inter pares* in 1928, the Soviet Union was weak and vulnerable, an essentially second-rate power; yet by 1953, it was recognized as one of the two superpowers. His successors, having inherited a tested and successful approach to the outside world, had no reason either to criticize or to change the basic orientation of Stalin's foreign policy.

Stalin's Foreign Policy Revisited  The emphasis in Western studies on "change" rather than "continuity" in Soviet foreign policy since 1953 stems in part from an undue emphasis on Stalin's foreign policies from the end of World War II to the Korean War. Admittedly, this was an era of expansion and unprecedented aggressiveness in Soviet foreign relations, beginning with the Soviet domination of Eastern Europe, the Berlin crisis of 1948–1949, and the unnecessary and avoidable conflict with Yugoslavia—all coupled with intransigent statements and undiplomatic posturing. While some of these policies were indicated by the geopolitical opportunity that World War II had created, Stalin probably did push too hard during the early years of the cold war. His aggressiveness provided the glue for Western unity against the Soviet Union—as expressed by the Truman Doctrine, the establishment of NATO in 1949, and even the consideration of such radical countermeasures as the use of atomic weapons against Moscow during the Berlin confrontation (recommended by Churchill but quickly rejected by both the British and United States governments). To the extent that Stalin's postwar policies led to the mobilization of the West and the containment of further Soviet advances, therefore, these policies were not only unduly assertive but—from the perspective of long-term Soviet interests—probably counterproductive.

Aggressive Soviet behavior in the early years of the cold war, however, was only one aspect of the Stalinist pattern in foreign policy. During Stalin's reign, a pragmatic Soviet Union first sought to ally itself with Nazi Germany and then formed a grand coalition with such bastions of imperialism as England and the United States. Communists fought along with noncommunists in the Spanish Civil War. In the early 1930s, the Soviet Union concluded a number of treaties and cooperative agreements with such bourgeois states as France, Poland, and Czechoslovakia. In 1935, the Seventh Congress of the Communist International, reversing the Comintern's 1928 Sixth Congress, issued an analysis that justified the broad, flexible, coalition-seeking approach—the "Popular Front" strategy—adopted by Communist parties everywhere. And to accommodate the Soviet Union's immediate foreign policy needs, Stalin repeatedly modified certain features of Marxist–Leninist ideology pertaining to international relations.

Stalin's thinking in nonideological, power–political terms—meaning that he recognized both the uses and the limitations of Soviet power—was even demonstrated during the expansionary postwar era. A reluctant supporter of uncertain revolutionary causes abroad, Stalin denied extensive assistance not only to his comrades in the French Communist party but also to Mao's revolutionary forces in the Chinese civil war. He maintained relations with Mao's enemy, the Kuomintang's Chiang Kai-shek, as long as the outcome of the civil war was in doubt. Even in Eastern Europe, in the fall of 1945, when Stalin thought that he might need Western cooperation, he dramatically reversed previous decisions and as a gesture of goodwill ordered competitive elections in Bulgaria and then agreed to free elections in Hungary. Moreover, while purging Jews in the Soviet Union, he supported the Zionist cause for the establishment of a Jewish state in Palestine—no doubt calculating that such a state would weaken the British in the Middle East. And, finally, around 1950 Stalin gave new emphasis the old concept of "peaceful coexistence" and subsequently initiated the coalitionary "peace campaign" of the early 1950s.

Although this brief summary cannot do justice to the complexities of Stalin's foreign policy, it does suggest that Stalin was a rather cautious guardian of the Soviet Union's international interests. During his last years, as Adam Ulam noted, his policies "created an air of tension which, apart from being a source of danger to Russia, was largely unnecessary."[1] Moreover, the language he used to assess international developments and explain Soviet goals abroad contained more ideological referents than can be found in his successors' pronouncements. But Stalin's actual policies invariably reflected his sensitivity to the international balance of forces. As a result, he made all the necessary compromises in order to gain time and strength.

Has anything important really changed since Stalin's time? Surely both the internal and external environments of Soviet foreign policy have changed. Neither the Soviet domestic scene nor the world at large is the same as it was in the 1940s and 1950s. Very much at issue, however, is the influence these internal and external environments have had on the conduct of Soviet foreign policy.

## Internal Influences on Soviet Foreign Policy

The first and by far the most important change in the internal environment of Soviet foreign policy has been the substantially increased relative power of the Soviet Union since Stalin's reign. Although its economy remains uneven and technologically inferior to that of the West, the diverse and steadily growing military capability of the post-Stalin Soviet Union attests to its new status in world politics.

If Stalin's foreign policy had in part stemmed from a sense of weakness and insecurity, what policy change would follow enhanced

Soviet domestic strength? To answer this question, one should assume that the Soviet leaders believe some or most of their self-congratulatory messages about the successes of the Soviet state. But has the new Soviet leaders' confidence about internal strength helped them overcome their often-noted historic sense of insecurity vis-à-vis the outside world, especially the West? Has their self-confidence about domestic strength led them to pursue a more accommodating foreign policy?

Alternatively, one may suppose that, despite their remarkable achievements, the post-Stalin leaders still lack sufficient confidence in the viability of the Soviet domestic order. Perhaps they measure their accomplishments against more ambitious ultimate objectives or against the power of the United States and thus find these accomplishments lacking. Their self-congratulatory messages may be no more than the official optimism and wishful thinking characteristic of political discourse everywhere. In that case, the Soviet leaders' apparent lack of self-confidence about the internal health of the Soviet Union should reinforce their historic sense of inferiority vis-à-vis the outside world, especially the West. Such lack of self-confidence about domestic strength could prompt them to compensate for perceived weakness at home by pursuing an assertive or even aggressive foreign policy.

In his analysis of the interwar period—an era of considerable Soviet weakness—Alexander Dallin concluded that "perceived weakness need not always produce a conciliatory mood in Moscow; nor does the willingness to seek a détente or compromise need to stem from weakness alone."[2] Similarly, in his analysis of the post–Stalin years—an era of increasing Soviet strength—Morton Schwartz presented two contrary interpretations as equally plausible. In one passage, he said: "Convinced of their superiority—a conviction strengthened by their vast military power—the Kremlin leaders may be anxious to flex their new muscles. Thus, in the years ahead they may probe for ways to expand Soviet influence around the world." In another passage, however, Schwartz concluded: "A secure Soviet leadership has already become a somewhat more relaxed Soviet leadership."[3]

Unable to reach a firm conclusion about causality, no Western analyst has been able to offer conclusive evidence about the validity of any of the following hypotheses:

1. Domestic weakness leads to foreign policy accommodation.
2. Domestic weakness leads to foreign policy assertiveness.
3. Domestic strength leads to foreign policy accommodation.
4. Domestic strength leads to foreign policy assertiveness.

The validation of any of these hypotheses would have considerable implications for Western policy. It would indicate whether the West should try to encourage a strong and confident Soviet Union or whether it should try to keep Moscow weak and uncertain of its relative power position. But without such a validation, any advice about "keeping" the Soviet Union weak or strong must be prudent and qualified. No one knows how much the Soviet Union's newly acquired domestic strength will influence its foreign policy. But common sense argues against a Western policy that would seek an internally strong and confident

Soviet Union, because it would entail excessive risks for Western security in exchange for tempering, presumably, Moscow's "nervous aggressiveness."

The second frequently discussed change in the post-Stalin domestic order has been the apparent decline of ideological rigidity. The reason given for a more pragmatic and flexible Soviet approach to the outside world is that the new leaders did not experience the early, prerevolutionary days and that their mindset was thus formed during the years of socialist construction. As party bureaucrats, managers, soldiers, and engineers, they have devoted their lives to practical tasks, not to the making of revolution. While they have certainly participated in political intrigues, most did not take part in prerevolutionary conspiracies.

Moreover, the new Soviet leaders have repeatedly modified Stalin's ideology of international affairs. Wars were once said to be inevitable; now they are not. Revolutions were once said to be inevitable; now there can be a peaceful transition to socialism. The international class struggle used to be the major dogma of foreign policy; now it receives less public emphasis than peaceful coexistence. Autarky was to exclude devious foreign influences; now it is the international division of labor and even interdependence that pave the road to socialism and communism. Automation used to show capitalist inhumanity; now computers (often imported) are the new signposts of the scientific–technological revolution. At Lenin's grave, Stalin pledged to uphold the sacred and unshakable unity of the international communist movement; now his successors have yet to find an ideologically adequate explanation for Soviet military contingency plans against China.

Yet it remains doubtful whether Stalin's successors have been less influenced by ideological precepts than Stalin was supposed to have been. After all, ideological innovation and foreign policy flexibility, not doctrinal rigidity, were Stalin's traits, and his successors have only outperformed him in ideological gymnastics. But even if one were to assume otherwise, does the professed decline of ideological rigidity amount to flexibility? Does more flexibility necessarily translate into an accommodating or moderate foreign policy? It may well be, instead, that neither of these hypotheses is valid:

1. Rigid ideological environment leads to foreign policy assertiveness.

2. Decline of ideological zeal leads to foreign policy accommodation.

Without denying the steady erosion of faith since Lenin's days and the far-reaching, though only long-term, implications of this process for the future of Soviet political culture, what should be emphasized, therefore, is that the necessity of legitimizing every twist and turn in foreign policy by ideological incantation is hardly a novel phenomenon in Soviet history. Stalin offered an eloquent ideological rationale for the "hard" line adopted in 1928, as he did for the "soft" line in 1935. His successors presented an ideological explanation for their 1968 military intervention in Czechoslovakia (the "Brezhnev Doctrine") and for their more recent détente policies toward the West ("peaceful coexistence").

Stalin saw no way to avoid confrontations between the forces of socialism and imperialism. In 1953 and 1954, however, Malenkov revised Stalin's assessment, stating that because of the destructive quality of atomic weapons and the increasing might of the Soviet Union, an all-out war with imperialism was no longer inevitable. That was good news, of course, but one must note that (1) Stalin's belief in the inevitability of war did not propel him to begin such wars (as he always sought to enhance Soviet power and influence gradually, indeed incrementally); and that (2) his successors have not denounced "small" or "just" wars: the so-called wars of national liberation (e.g., Cuba, Vietnam, and Cambodia) and military intervention in their sphere (e.g., Hungary and Czechoslovakia). In the final analysis, Malenkov's revision of Stalin's dogma merely signifies the acceptance of, and the concurrent ideological rationalization for, what Stalin had practiced. The same can be said about other changes in the "ideological environment" of Soviet foreign policy since Stalin's time. For example, *Pravda* still holds that "there are essentially no neutrals in the struggle between the two world systems."[4] And according to the authoritative Soviet *Diplomatic Dictionary*, peaceful coexistence "is a specific form of class struggle between socialism and capitalism."

The third change in the domestic environment of Soviet foreign policy since Stalin has been identified as the broadening of the decision-making process, including the rise of elite factions and competing interests. Foreign policy alternatives are debated more openly among a wider circle of advisers and decision makers. Resource allocation between military and nonmilitary uses, for example, is a particularly lively issue. Concurrently, the Soviet view of international life has become more sophisticated, with specialists now covering all conceivable aspects of foreign policy analysis and international relations theory from the classical balance of power to simulation and beyond.

The controversial issue here is less the existence of "conflicting domestic pressures" and factional political struggle (which had been particularly evident during the three succession crises of 1953–1957, 1964–1968, and the early 1980s) than their consequence for foreign policy. Political deals and compromises in the Kremlin need not lead to an accommodating foreign policy, because the deal could also produce "relaxation" at home and "vigilance" abroad. In other words, the mere existence of divergent interests, needs, views, perceptions, and approaches cannot be said to ensure any consistent pattern in Soviet foreign policy—conciliatory, centrist, or belligerent. A compromise among competing interest groups does not require a foreign policy of restraint.

Nor can one necessarily expect moderation from a divided post-Stalin foreign policy elite, even if it is better informed and more sophisticated. After all, more expertise does not necessarily mean more caution.

Since we do not know how incoming foreign policy information is processed, the parameters of the policy debates, and, in particular, the political benefits or penalties derived from the transmittal of "bad news" and the offering of new ideas, it is difficult to judge the validity of any of the following hypotheses:

1. Narrow (Stalinist) decision making leads to foreign policy assertiveness.
2. Broadening of the decision-making process leads to foreign policy accommodation.
3. Limited knowledge of international life leads to foreign policy assertiveness.
4. Expanding knowledge of international life leads to foreign policy accommodation.

## External Influences on Soviet Foreign Policy

The apparent lack of causality between domestic inputs and foreign policy makes it particularly apposite to explore the external environment of Soviet conduct. Can that environment be the source of change in Soviet foreign policy?

To begin with, the members of the international community engage in activities that have a bearing on the Soviet Union. States engage in generally self-serving activities, though not necessarily contrary to the interests of the Soviet Union. Under all circumstances, however, given the military might, economic power, political influence, and the global reach of the Soviet Union—in short, its preeminent position in the international system—most states have reason to seek to alter some aspect of Soviet foreign policy. In turn, since the Soviet Union does not operate in a political, military, or economic vacuum, it has to respond to at least some of these attempts to influence its behavior.

The primary external demands on the Soviet Union are (1) for foreign policy "moderation" (i.e., demands on Moscow to help maintain the status quo by refraining from war and intervention) and (2) for "assistance" (i.e., demands to help change the status quo by extending political support and economic as well as military aid). Since these two broad categories of demands are mutually exclusive, the Soviet Union— taking into account domestic needs, pressures, and preferences as well—must evaluate and respond to such contradictory external demands, trying to satisfy as many of its more important or more powerful foreign audiences and constituencies as possible. Simply stated, the Soviet Union is linked to too many external causes, issues, and audiences whose demands on and expectations of the Soviet Union greatly differ. Moscow can satisfy some of these demands and expectations some of the time; it cannot satisfy all of them all of the time.

Since Stalin's reign, the international environment has dramatically changed. The world communist movement has disintegrated. The communist bloc that Stalin built after World War II has all but ceased to act as a united entity. Almost 100 new and, in many cases, radical states have emerged. Those rich in resources have come to present a major challenge to the Western industrialized world. Interdependence is a new economic fact of international life. The "leading role" of the United States in the Atlantic alliance has eroded. The "liberation" of Eastern Europe is no longer on the Western agenda. Finally, the extraordinarily rapid modernization of weapons systems, spearheaded by the United

States, has led to fundamental revisions in the concepts and strategies of warfare.

Some of the changes in the international system, such as the development of new weapons, require Moscow to exercise caution and accommodation; others, such as the rise of new states, may mean opportunities for the expansion of Soviet influence. It seems that the Soviet Union can respond to external influences calling for moderation in two ways. First, it can respond tactically—an essentially limited adjustment to external demands. This response is the well-known "one step backward," a temporary concession whose primary purpose is to gain time. This type of response originated with Lenin, and it has long been recognized as part of the repertoire of Soviet diplomacy.

The other kind of reaction, as William Zimmerman has suggested, is far more complex and seldom recognized. It can begin, perhaps, as a tactical adjustment to international reality; but over time—if properly stimulated and reinforced—it would transform itself into a learned response. Learning from the benefits of experience and subjected to carefully orchestrated external stimuli, the Soviet Union would thus become capable of genuine and lasting attitude-modification and "structural adaptation."[5] If the Soviet Union has the capability to produce such a response, as Zimmerman argued, the implications would be far-reaching indeed. It would signal a major opportunity—and responsibility—for the outside world to influence the Soviet foreign policy elite and to contribute to lasting change. The United States, for example, could act and speak in such a way as to reinforce the position of "moderates" in the Kremlin; it could attempt to show, by words and deeds, the benefits of détente and cooperation for both sides.

Unfortunately, there is reason to be skeptical about the possibility of achieving a "lasting adaptation" in Soviet foreign policy as a consequence of external influences. For one thing, there is the practical problem of policy coordination by the outside world. Neither now nor in the future can Western leaders know the parameters of internal debates on foreign policy in the Kremlin. But, assuming that they could make a good guess at the choices discussed, can the outside world then coordinate its policies in such a way as to bring about the desired result? Even though the United States is the most closely watched and surely the most important single external input, it is not the only one; and even if it could develop a set of finely tuned policies aimed at properly "educating" and influencing the Kremlin, the foreign policies of other nations would cancel out or at least mitigate the impact of the United States's efforts.

Even more fundamental is the problem of conceiving the appropriate mix of external inputs. It is not at all clear whether the outside world should be or should appear to be weak or strong, reassuring or threatening, in order to generate "moderation" in Soviet foreign policy. Soviet strategic superiority, for example, could help the Soviet leaders overcome their historic sense of inferiority vis-à-vis the West—a possibly valid but rather risky assumption—and thus produce a more accommodating Soviet foreign policy. Alternatively, the United States could aim at strategic superiority, following the long-held belief that it can influence the Soviet Union only from a position of strength. But if that approach only reinforces a sense of inferiority in the Soviet leadership, the concessions will likely be only tactical or short lived.

Accordingly, unless the West has some reasonably accurate assessment of the impact of external "strength" versus external "weakness" on the Soviet foreign policy debates—in other words, unless it knows what combination of external incentives and prohibitions may pave the way to a lasting tendency toward foreign policy moderation—it cannot be confident about the international environment producing such moderation in Moscow. This is not to deny the import of what the non-Soviet world does or is, or how it goes about conducting its relations with the Soviet Union; it is only to suggest that external environmental influences entering into the calculations of the Soviet leadership will generate no enduring change in Soviet conduct. Finally, it is not a set of often conflicting demands, conditions, or policy inputs that make for change; only the balance of perceived needs will do so: the Soviet leaders themselves must decide that external developments demand policy reassessment.

## The Balance of Perceived Needs: Key to "Change"?

So far, this essay has focused on the logic of assigning change to Soviet foreign policy on the basis of analyzing the internal and external environments of Soviet conduct. Yet, fascinating as it is to speculate about changing influences on Soviet behavior, the ultimate criterion for a judgment has to be the record—the output—of Soviet foreign policy itself.

Six "new departures" stand out in the history of Soviet foreign policy:

1. The Soviet Union discarded the early ideal of "revolutionary diplomacy" almost immediately after its establishment in 1917. Accepting the practice of what it had once regarded as "bourgeois" diplomatic intercourse with the outside world, the Soviet leaders promptly decided to enter into regular negotiations with other states and generally observe diplomatic protocol. Mainly because Lenin wanted to make peace with Germany and thus to cement his shaky regime at home, he did not hesitate to tell Trotsky that the very survival of the Soviet state required the adoption of "old" diplomatic practices.

2. The Communist International's "exclusionary" strategy of the 1920s—better known as the "United Front, from below"—was replaced in the early 1930s by the "inclusionary," or Popular Front, strategy. Sanctioned at the Soviet-dominated Seventh Comintern Congress in 1935, the new approach encouraged all Communist parties to cooperate with the noncommunist left in order to form a united front against the rise of fascism. Inherent in this fundamental shift was the danger of reducing the once-sacred "leading role" and ideological purity of Communist parties. Yet Stalin accepted the potential danger of ideological erosion by socialists, social democrats, and others because he assumed

that only a broader left coalition could ensure the security of the Soviet Union and defeat the greater danger—Nazi Germany and its allies.

3. Compared with the cautious, quasi-isolationist posture in the interwar period, Stalin initiated an expansionary phase in Soviet foreign policy after World War II. With the establishment of pro-Soviet regimes in Eastern Europe, "socialism in one country" gave way to "socialism in one region," because the prewar revolutionary rhetoric could now be translated into policy. As noted earlier, the change was due to the opportunity created by World War II and the lack of countervailing power in the international system.

4. Around 1950–1951, the confrontationist strategy of the postwar years was replaced by the peace campaign in Europe and the sudden opening to the Third World. Unable to break the European impasse and unwilling to risk a military showdown with the United States, Stalin— and subsequently his successors—shelved the rigid "two-camp" doctrine of 1946–1947, resuscitated the "peaceful coexistence" line, and shifted to a rather low-tension policy toward the outside world. Clearly, the Berlin crisis and the Korean War demonstrated that the confrontationist strategy had failed to advance Soviet interests and should therefore be modified. For years to come, the Soviet Union was to look beyond the old world for new gains, relying less on the military than on the economic instrument of foreign policy.

5. Since the mid-1950s, Stalin's successors have come to accept, however grudgingly, a degree of experimentation in Eastern Europe. Khrushchev's overture to Tito in 1955 marked the beginning of greater Soviet tolerance toward national traditions and characteristics in Eastern Europe. Despite subsequent interventions aimed at curtailing far-reaching liberalization in the region, Stalin's insistence on strict uniformity was altered—no doubt because it had created chronic and dangerous instability.

6. The Soviet Union, having learned during the Cuban missile crisis that its inferior military posture vis-à-vis the United States had been a major political handicap, initiated a massive program of military investments in the 1960s to catch up with, and possibly surpass, the United States in the arms race. An estimated 12–15% of the Soviet GNP has since been devoted to military procurements, presumably in order to avoid the kind of humiliation that Moscow suffered in 1962.

These are among the more important new departures—some accommodating, some assertive in character—in the history of Soviet foreign policy. They suggest three conclusions.

First, in each case the Soviet leaders embarked on a new course either when the previous policy had failed or when a new opportunity for expansion had presented itself. Irrespective of whether the new course was initiated under Stalin or his successors, it was usually the Soviet leaders' perception of policy failure that prompted the adoption of new approaches and solutions. In 1955, Khrushchev used the issue of Tito's rehabilitation as part of his political struggle against those who, like Molotov and Malenkov, had been implicated in the early anti-Tito campaign under Stalin. On the whole, however, the perceived needs of the Soviet state rather than political infighting can be said to have produced new departures in Soviet conduct.

Second, the record of Soviet foreign policy indicates tactical adjustments rather than lasting adaptations. While it may be premature to make a definitive judgment about the most recent period, it is quite clear that, as Zbigniew Brzezinski and others have noted, Soviet policy toward the outside world has been characterized by a cyclical pattern— "by alternating offensive and defensive phases."[6] On the same point, Henry Kissinger said: "Peace offensives, of course, are not new in Soviet history. Peaceful coexistence has been avowed since the advent of Communism in Russia. It was stressed particularly between 1934–1939; between 1941–1946; at the time of the Geneva Summit Conference of 1955; again on the occasion of Khrushchev's visit to the United States in 1959; and following the Cuban Missile Crisis in 1962. . . . On each occasion the period of relaxation ended when an opportunity for expanding Communism presented itself."[7] Given the cyclical pattern of the past, it would require excessive optimism, if not naïveté, to emphasize aspects of lasting change in Soviet foreign policy since Stalin.

Third, the records of both Stalin and his successors suggest neither a rigid "master plan" for global conquest nor a conservative policy aimed at the maintenance of the status quo. If there has been a basic pattern in Soviet foreign policy since Lenin, it is characterized by the persistent, though cautious, pursuit of opportunities abroad—"persistent" because the overall objective of advancing Soviet influence has not changed and "cautious" because the Soviet leaders have sought to promote Soviet influence so gradually as to make strong and concerted Western countermeasures unjustifiable.

Post-Stalin Soviet foreign policy reflects a curious paradox. While the internal and external environments in which it operates are different now, the Soviet leaders—under conflicting pressures, impulses, and demands for both change and continuity—have nonetheless continued to rely on the old, historic mix of assertiveness-and-accommodation. Stalin's heirs must assume that this mix has been successful, and hence they perceive no need even for the kind of change that de-Stalinization has signified in the domestic realm.

## Notes

[1]Adam B. Ulam, *Expansion and Coexistence* (New York; Praeger, 1968), p. 543.

[2]Alexander Dallin, "Soviet Foreign Policy and Domestic Politics: A Framework for Analysis," in *The Conduct of Soviet Foreign Policy*, 2d ed., eds. Erik P. Hoffmann and Frederic J. Fleron (Hawthorne, N.Y.: Aldine, 1980), pp. 41–42.

[3]Morton Schwartz, *The Foreign Policy of the USSR: Domestic Factors* (Encino & Belmont, Calif.: Dickenson, 1975), pp. 89–91.

[4]*Pravda*, April 30, 1969.

[5]William Zimmerman, "Choices in the Postwar World: Containment and the Soviet Union," in *Caging the Bear: Containment and the Cold War*, ed. Charles Gati (Indianapolis: Bobbs-Merrill, 1974), pp. 85–108.

[6]Zbigniew Brzezinski, "The Competitive Relationship," in *Caging the Bear: Containment and the Cold War*, ed. Charles Gati (Indianapolis: Bobbs-Merrill, 1974), pp. 157–199.

[7]Henry A. Kissinger, *The Troubled Partnership: A Reappraisal of the Atlantic Alliance* (Garden City, N.Y.: Doubleday, 1966), pp. 189–190.

# 3

# ROBERT LEGVOLD

## *The Nature of Soviet Power**

I For three decades, Soviet power has obsessed American foreign policy. By it we have judged our own; because of it we have committed ourselves far from home and justified our commitment in terms of the menace it represents; around it we have made a world order revolve. For us, Soviet power has been the ultimate measure and the central threat, a seminal idea and a source of orientation.

Should it still be, however, now that international politics are changing so? Or should it still be, because Soviet power is changing so? Is the evolution of the international setting altering the meaning of growing Soviet power? Or is the growth of Soviet power undermining the meaning of an evolving international setting? The ambiguous relationship between the two makes it much harder to know what role the Soviet Union ought to play in our concerns. Judging the significance of larger and more modern Soviet military forces becomes increasingly difficult when traditional frames of reference no longer hold, when the old rules and characteristics of international relations yield to new ones, when the uses to which military power can be put are depreciated, and when the concept of security as such loses its precision, swollen by strange anonymous sources of insecurity, many of them economic in nature. It is a world in which fewer and fewer of our problems are caused by the Soviet Union or can be solved by it, save for the ultimate matter of nuclear war.

Yet, amidst the loosening of the old order—the deteriorating hierarchies and orthodoxies, the growing number of political actors and political axes, the new imperatives of interdependence—there is also the distracting spectacle of ever-expanding Soviet military power. During these years of passage, the Soviet Union has busied itself with a vast buildup of its armed forces, introducing new technologies, enlarging numbers, and most significantly venturing into areas far from its historic

*Reprinted by permission of the author and publisher from *Foreign Affairs* 56, no. 1 (October, 1977), pp. 49–71. Copyright 1977 by Council on Foreign Relations, Inc.

spheres of concern. The Soviet Union has spent the decade turning itself into an authentic global superpower able to apply military force in the remotest regions of the world. With the capacity apparently has come the vocation.

"Soviet Russia," Henry Kissinger and his closest counselors used to say, "is only just beginning its truly 'imperial' phase." The prospect does not fit comfortably with our image of the other processes reforming world politics. Hard pressed to reconcile these two perceptions—of an increasingly interdependent (and decentralized) world and of an increasingly "imperial" Soviet Union—we have tended not to try. We have responded rhetorically ("The United States seeks to give the Soviet Union a stake in a more stable and humane international order") rather than conceptually. And having no clear concept of the relationship between the transformation of Soviet power and the transformation of the global political setting, we have concentrated on familiar apprehensions: Where there is instability, what is the Soviet ability to interfere? How do we keep the Soviet Union from intervening in Angola or in Yugoslavia? Or how do we frustrate Soviet intervention when it occurs? (Phrased by the Ford Administration, the question was: "How do we create a calculus of risks and benefits that will induce the Soviet Union to behave?") What is the political and psychological impact on our NATO allies of strategic parity or the growth of the Warsaw Pact's conventional forces? What does the Soviet Union hope to accomplish by adding to its military advantage in Central Europe? How well served are Soviet aims by the tensions between Greece and Turkey, the West's economic dislocations, or the possible entry of French or Italian Communists into their governments?

Like our apprehensions, our perception of the Soviet Union as such tends to be narrowly cast. There is a remarkable consensus in most of what is being said about the Soviet Union and the nature of its changing power. People may disagree over details and over what it all adds up to for us, but on the central characteristics nearly everyone agrees. The common portrait is of a late-arriving military leviathan, in the bloom of military expansion, self-satisfied at last to have matched the power of its great imperialist rival, and fascinated by the potential rewards in the continued accumulation of arms.

But most are also agreed that the Soviet Union is a seriously flawed power: economically disadvantaged, technologically deficient, bureaucratically sclerosed, and threatened by a society that is, in Zbigniew Brzezinski's words, "like a boiling subterranean volcano [straining] against the rigid surface crust of the political system." Something of a deformed giant, Enceladus with 50 withered arms, mighty in military resources and exhilarated by its strength, but backward in other respects and sobered by the need to enlist the West's help in overcoming these problems.

From these two perceptions it is only a short step to another widely shared impression: Unable to influence others by the force of its ideology, plagued by an economy that does not measure up, and discredited by its repressive habits at home and among allies, the Soviet Union has but one major trump, its military power. Some argue that this is a historic condition, that all of the regime's expectations have been deceived, save for the accomplishments of force. The failure of the European revolution, capitalism's resilience despite the Great Depression and the constant cycle of lesser economic crises, the collapse of communist unity almost as soon as unity became a practical dream, the unruliness of change in the theoretically revolutionary regions of the Third World, all these are the wreckage of earlier hopes. The Soviet Union's triumphs, they contend—from the conquest of power to the spread of empire, from the early victories in the civil war to the historic defeat of Nazi Germany—have proved to generations of Soviet leaders the trustworthiness of force alone.

Others are simply commenting on what appears to be the Soviet Union's comparative advantage. But either way, because of this perception, our concluding observation takes on greater moment. For, in one form or another, nearly everyone who makes the Soviet Union an interest notes the contrast in what we and they want for the world. Even those who believe the Soviet Union is losing its taste for revolutionary transformations and settling down to traditional power politics nonetheless stress the conflict in the two nation's underlying values. Whether the reasons reach back several centuries, as some insist, or merely back to different political systems, as others suggest, the Soviet Union remains an alienated competitor.

If there is truth in this assessment—and, to a degree, it is utterly true—it is a narrow-minded truth, which does not help us sort out the subtler aspects of the Soviet challenge. I say narrow-minded truth because it bears so little relationship to the Soviet Union's self-image; because it is so thoroughly *our* view of the world. Claiming greater honesty and accuracy on our side is only a partial way out and no service to ourselves, not if the Soviet Union is acting according to its own view. Thus, we have twice handicapped our analyses: first, by not grappling with the interconnection between the evolution of the international order and the evolution of Soviet power and, second, by giving short shrift to the way the Soviet Union views these issues.

We need a broader and richer framework within which to judge the changing nature of Soviet power, one that also incorporates the Soviet understanding of the changing nature of everyone's power. That is what I have tried to sketch here, starting with what seem to me the most conspicuous features of change in the international order, but measured against the lingering and complicating influence of the old order. There follows a brief description of both the new and the faded forms of power and a few comments on Soviet power judged accordingly. My primary concern, however, is the Soviet perspective on these issues. Therefore, I have devoted the second half of the essay to their perceptions of the evolving nature of power within an evolving international setting.

II    Five elements of change strike me as central. The first of these is the transformation of alliances, a specific manifestation of the general erosion of hierarchies. Not that partnerships are ended or that the power to compel loyalty has in all instances dissolved, but the premises of unity are in most cases no longer what they used to be. Among the industrialized countries of the West, the will to subordinate parochial national interests to traditional security concerns and common enterprises thrives less. In the other camp, the core alliance remains intact, but the original socialist alliance long ago disintegrated with Tito's challenge and the Sino–Soviet split. Moreover, the Soviet Union's extended alliance with West European communism is foundering at the moment on the same reluctance to subordinate national concerns.

The second element of change is the exponential growth of interdependence, confronting nations with the peculiar risk of suffering more the more others suffer, and fusing their prospects for prosperity—no longer merely their prospects for tranquility. Gradually and timidly the socialist countries are being drawn into the same process, a process with unfamiliar rules of restraint and mutual concern.

Third, in this increasingly interdependent world, the collapse of the old international economic order and the challenge raised to a new one of, by, and for the industrialized capitalist societies, have rewritten the political agenda, converted economics to a still higher form of politics, and introduced a critical revisionism, sponsored this time not by the East but by the South instead. Together the second and third elements of change have made the issue of national security far more complex than defending the integrity of one's territory and political values. Increasingly, the stake is also in the security of foreign markets and key resources, in the freedom from economically dislocating external price increases, and even in the success of other governments' domestic economic programs.

Fourth, there is growing regionalization of international politics, the particular form taken by the disintegration of a simplistically bipolar world. Ambitious states like Iran and Nigeria exert greater leadership within their own regions, and in the regions of Africa, Latin America, and Southeast Asia many of the local states make it increasingly plain that the stewardship of outside powers is no longer necessary. In Europe and Asia, new or restored power centers have emerged, creating a looser and more complicated geometry underpinning the structure of international politics. And cutting across this new structure, the proliferation of nuclear weapons adds to the complexity and hazards of change.

Finally, at the pinnacle where power was once concentrated, a fundamental shift has occurred in the military balance between the two superpowers. The Soviet Union is no longer the United States' relative inferior in strategic nuclear power. For nearly a decade, it has been our rough equal, and, in the minds of many, a self-confident military competitor eager to do still better.

This last development represents in fact a specter from the old order and is the chief reason we have been slow to think our way through the implications of the Soviet Union's altered power in an altered setting. For two things are at work and both stimulate ancient reflexes: one is the evolution of the whole of Soviet military power and the other is our enduring image of the role military power plays in Soviet conceptions.

Seeing the Soviet Union draw abreast in the strategic arms race has been hard enough. But to face in the same short period the realization that the Soviet Union is turning itself into a first-class naval power capable of challenging our mastery of the seas and meanwhile straining to improve its massive power in Europe has been vastly more disconcerting. All at once, the Soviet Union has as many, indeed more and larger, missiles than we; it has most of the same (though perhaps somewhat retarded) technologies, MIRV, mobile land-based missiles, and rudimentary high-energy lasers; and still it presses on with new generations of weapons systems. Just as suddenly its navy is out on the high seas, sailing oceans where it has never been before, assuming missions it has never had before, and building ships it has never needed before. But even more disturbing, in Europe, where it already had the advantage, the Soviet Union not only has improved the quality of its arms and the number of its forces on the Central European front, it has radically altered the balance in the Mediterranean and on the northern flank.

Add to this the place that we have long assumed war occupies in Soviet theory, and inevitably our perspective shrinks to a rather traditional set of apprehensions. For the assumption that the Soviet Union accepts the utility of war is deeply ingrained. Because the Soviet leaders have never repudiated Clausewitz's dictum of "war as the extension of policy," we have taken this to mean that they still regard the resort to arms as a legitimate instrument of policy. Hence, their apparent conviction that war, even nuclear war, is "winnable" and their unwillingness to accept Western notions of strategic nuclear deterrence. Dedicated to the idea of prevailing in a nuclear conflict, they are, we assume, less intimidated by the prospect of its outbreak and therefore less concerned with doctrines designed to avoid it or, in the event, to limit it. Even granted that they want war no more than we, the way they conceive war and the way they prepare for it prove to us that the Soviet leaders believe in the practical effect of both the threat and the arsenal of war.

For many, the next step in the analysis is obvious: If intellectually the Soviet leaders acknowledge the utility of force and if practically they are dependent on it, then not surprisingly they appear bent on achieving the largest possible margins of military advantage. This is the culminating premise. The Soviet Union is driven—to the limits of its resources and our complacency—to seek superiority over us: to amass still greater forces in Central Europe, that the West Europeans may be properly cowed; to fashion a navy more powerful than ours, that we and our friends may be held hostage to our economic dependencies; to build the capacity for projecting power to the far corners of the globe, that new and volatile nations may be opened to Soviet influence; and, ultimately, to overshadow the American strategic nuclear deterrent, that all these other enterprises may be safely pursued.

Viewed like this, it is no wonder that the Soviet–American relationship is soon largely reduced to its military dimension, our attention fixed on the contingencies and circumstances in which the Soviet Union could exploit its military power, and the solution found in our own military strength. Those who think we find the solution in too much military strength simply reinforce the narrowness of our analysis. Because their arguments usually turn on a more optimistic assessment of the military balance—rather than on any disbelief in our original assumptions about the place of force in Soviet theory, something they are more likely to regard as irrelevant than as wrong—they confine the issue still further to a great debate over comparative military capabilities. Thus, they reduce the Soviet threat but not our preoccupation with it.

III How ironic that we should be so easily seduced by our traditional apprehensions and so content to build our analysis around the military–political dimension. Interdependence, the other great theme these days, is supposed to depreciate the value of military power. Theoretically the rules are different in an interdependent world, requiring different means. (Theoretically—goes the response—the Soviet Union is not sufficiently a part of this world.)

Though old habits and a lack of imagination prevent us from adjusting, there is also a growing suspicion that conventional means of influence are not what we once thought. The notion that foreign aid, military assistance, cultural diplomacy, or any of the other elements of a nation's presence actually translate into leverage over another nation's decisions convinces us less and less, even when it is our adversary's aid, arms, and propaganda effort. Except in rare instances, power is not something usefully approached as a matter of devising, accumulating, and deftly applying mechanisms of influence. Not primarily at least.

For power, we sense, is increasingly unrefinable; increasingly indistinguishable from the setting in which it exists. Power is the capacity to reshape parts of the international order and for the powerful that is a capacity to compromise—to make concessions. Power is allowing monetary regimes or the law of the sea to take another form, allowing the International Monetary Fund, the General Agreement on Tariffs and Trade (GATT), or the Common Market to be changed or supplanted, and allowing other global economic goals, such as income redistribution, to have their day. In this case, there is nothing tangible or portable about it, and by its "application" little chance of imposing change.

Power, however, is also increasingly a matter of managing interdependence and, therefore, increasingly a matter of the structure and range of one's dependencies. To be positioned at the intersection of numerous and different forms of interdependence is power—unless too many of them are seriously unequal. So is opting out of interdependent relationships to the extent that minimizing vulnerabilities enhances power; but by sidelining itself, a nation also reduces its power to the extent that the rewards of participation are passed up. That is only the start, however, for power in an interdependent world also depends on how fungible others' dependencies are (that is, how easily their dependencies in one realm can be converted to offset yours in another) and how serviceable your vulnerabilities are (that is, when interdependence is asymmetrical, how much others hurt themselves by hurting you).

IV   If power is to be measured in terms of a country's ability to ferry material support great distances to friends fighting in settings like Angola in 1975, the Soviet Union is immeasurably stronger than it was 15 years earlier when Patrice Lumumba needed help. But if it is to be measured in terms of a country's ability to intervene over the same distances with its own military forces when it does not have friends or when we move to prevent it, the Soviet Union is not strong enough. If it is to be assessed in terms of a country's ability to obtain the material resources that it needs without fear of outside interference, the Soviet Union is less well-off than it was 10 years ago but a good deal better off than we. But if it is to be assessed in terms of a country's ability to influence the economic decisions of others impinging on its interests, the Soviet Union is better off now but not nearly so well off as we.

The trouble is we do not know how to evaluate the power of the Soviet Union. We do not have a sufficiently comprehensive and systematic set of criteria by which to judge. We do not even have sufficient criteria by which to disagree among ourselves. Of course, if we reduce the task to evaluating Soviet military power, we have the grounds for disagreeing but not for weighing its share of the many other resources by which nations try to shape world politics. To supplement the calculation of Soviet military power with other traditional indexes—such as the strength of its economy, the stability of its alliance(s), or the character of its adversaries—accomplishes little. What is more important, that Khrushchev's precise timetable for exceeding our per capita GNP has been long abandoned along with his accompanying fanfare? Or, that the Soviet economy continues to grow more rapidly than those of the vast majority of the world, including our own? Or is the sharp decline in the growth of Soviet total factor productivity more important than either? What is more striking about the large percentage of Soviet resources devoted to national defense, the dedication that it implies or the burden that it represents? And what is more significant about our discovery that this percentage has been even larger than we originally thought, the still greater dedication that it implies or the inefficiency that it betrays? Were we sure of the answers to these questions, we would still have to decide how they balance off against, say, the evolving character of the Chinese threat or the strengths and weaknesses of the Soviet Union's East European alliance.

Neither are we much helped by the tendency to substitute for an analysis of the resources serving Soviet foreign policy a summary of the trends favoring Soviet foreign policy, particularly when the summary is only that. In part, the problem is the same as with undifferentiated and unintegrated categories of power. Not only is it difficult to tell which trends matter most: the American failures in Indochina or the Soviet exclusion from the Middle East; the triumph of the MPLA in Angola or the destruction of Allende in Chile; the disruption on NATO's southern flank or the failed rapprochement after Mao's death. But it is still more treacherous discerning grand patterns among these trends, especially when many trends are quickly reversed. Moreover, the implications of any single trend often defy easy categorization. Take, for example, the case of Eurocommunism. Would the Soviet Union be strengthened by having the Italian Communist Party in government? Who knows? How does a leader in Moscow or one in Washington weigh the damage done to Soviet peace of mind in Eastern Europe by the PCI's heterodoxy, against the reinforcement of the USSR's foreign policy in Western Europe by the Party's lingering orthodoxy? How, when the Soviet leader wants a strong Left to constrain the Italian government but momentarily fears the effect on détente of a government that actually includes the Left?

In part, however, the problem with focusing on trends is in distinguishing their effects. After all, our concern with Soviet power is in what it can accomplish, and this cannot be automatically or easily inferred from what happens.

Given these pitfalls, it makes more sense to put a certain distance between ourselves and the problem of the Soviet Union's evolving (military) power. We need to stand back and contemplate the more basic question of the Soviet Union's ability to shape or alter different parts of its environment. Ultimately this is what determines the importance of the Soviet ability to affect events.

If one starts with interdependence, that complex network of involvements dominating so many of the stakes in international politics, including the structure of the international economic order, the Soviet Union's influence remains marginal. It will not do to dismiss this state of affairs as the Soviet Union's choice, as a game it prefers not to play, and may be the better off thereby. For clearly the Soviet Union *has* chosen to play and would like to play more, were the rules more within its control. Increasingly it has a stake in interdependence but little leverage over the governing institutions and rules. The Soviet Union, as the economist says, is a price-taker.

A third of the animal protein in Soviet diets comes from fish mostly caught off other nations' coasts. To fish there, the Soviet Union is increasingly obliged to enter into joint ventures aiding the development of the poorer countries' fishing industries. Since the early 1960s, the annual increase in Soviet food imports has exceeded that of Japan, the world's largest food importer, and the Soviet Union is now contractually bound to buy at least six million metric tons of American wheat and corn every year. The Soviet Union counts, and has counted for some years, on buying substantial quantities of foreign technology to reverse productivity lags in Soviet industry and agriculture; to pay for it, it exports a growing portion of its petroleum production—but if it is to maintain these levels of export, it must tap its more inaccessible reserves, and for that it needs more Western technology. Together with its friends in Eastern Europe, it now owes $46 billion to outsiders, including $28 billion to foreign commercial banks.[1]

For all that, however, the Soviet Union has precious little voice in shaping the larger system in which it buys, sells, and borrows. It is a member of none of the major international economic institutions, unless the United Nations Conference on Trade and Development (UNCTAD) be one, and there it is generally disregarded. It has not been much consulted by anyone, including the South, when monetary schemes, balance-of-payment adjustment arrangements, commodity agreements, and regulations of direct foreign investments are discussed. And its own particular pet concerns—such as most-favored-nation agreements, bilateral trade agreements, and a larger role for gold—wait on the goodwill of the capitalist powers and often on their diminished apathy.

Our standard explanation misses the point: The point is not that the organization of the Soviet economy makes the Soviet Union an unsuitable participant, but that the international economic order need not accommodate the national organization the USSR prefers. Our notion that this is no comment on Soviet power is plainly wrong; in an interdependent world, self-sufficiency is inefficiency, increasingly so in the Soviet Union, and the Soviet leadership knows it. How much of a world power is a nation without much power in the world economy?

On the other hand, not all crucial transactions take place in the economic sphere and not all crucial stakes are material. There is also, for want of a more revealing term, the political order. In theory, the maximum concern is with the Soviet capacity for making the world over in its own image, but few believe any longer in putting the issue so simplistically. Rather, we respond to an incoherent muddle of concerns, beginning with the pace at which the Soviet Union is acquiring footholds or facilities around the world, which jeopardize our power, and finishing with the pace at which change is occurring, which jeopardizes our values. In a place like southern Africa, the two become confused—but that is more a matter of our weakness than Soviet strength. Not that we fear for racism, but violent change may give rise to radical regimes, and many think there are too many of them already. More immediately, radical regimes may well accord the Soviet Union new facilities for its expanding global military power, which, according to the more pessimistic among us, could be used to shut off the flow of indispensable resources to Western economies. Worried about the fate of our own power and values, we tend to be sloppy about distinguishing between the aggrandizement of Soviet power and the advancement of Soviet values.

Our carelessness arises out of the mistaken apprehension that the growth of Soviet (military) power, and change, like that in Angola, necessarily aid Soviet foreign policy in dealing with its various tasks: that they interact to make it easier for the Soviet Union to sell its Asian collective security scheme or mobilize opposition to Diego Garcia. It also blinds us to the possibility that change may work against the Soviet Union, even in its own camp, quite apart from the growth of Soviet (military) power.

In the military realm, the Soviet Union is unquestionably stronger than it was, but the nature and sweep of its strength is worth exploring. Where arms are an uncontested entrée, the Soviet Union has a growing capacity to influence and, in some rare instances like Angola, to decide events. But sometimes, as in the Horn of Africa, even where order is breaking down and the Soviet access considerable, confusion and cross-cutting interests foil effective Soviet influence. In general, the Soviet Union has a conspicuously greater capacity than it did to constrain our use of military force and, to that extent, to influence events. But where it is the shadow of Soviet power that worries us, as in Europe, if Soviet influence grows, it will largely be influence that *we* have created; when the actual resort to force is so implausible, then dangers like that of "Finlandization" are far more a matter of our state of mind than of actual Soviet capabilities.

Moreover, the capacity to influence, even to control, events guarantees neither control after the event nor control over the larger patterns of change. By and large the Soviet Union is, as we are, the beneficiary or victim of the processes of change, not their source. Nothing in the evolution of Soviet power is altering that. Some have used the images of gardener and architect to identify the nature and limits of our power: The Soviet Union, like us, remains a gardener.

V     None of what has been said so far addresses the constraints a changing international order does or does not impose on Soviet behavior.[2] This, it seems to me, has a great deal to do with the way the Soviet Union judges these issues. For while in some respects it judges these issues as we do, in other important respects, it does not. Thus, Soviet writers and leaders are as sensitive as our own to the rapid transformation of world politics. Like our own, they recognize the fragmentation of power ("the multiplicity of forces each standing up for its own interests"), the transformation of capitalist and proletarian internationalism, the emergence of other axes, North–South and West–West, to compete with the East–West axis, and the growth of interdependence (in its praiseworthy form, the "international division of labor"). But they superimpose on these common perceptions a fundamentally different conception of the underlying forces at work.

For them, the key to the current transformation resides in the shifting "correlation of forces," the balance between history's progressive and retrograde forces—their sense of linear history, predicated on the eternal advance of the Soviet Union and those with whom it identifies and the equally certain retreat of those with whom it does not. At the moment, they contend, the correlation of forces has been radically altered by the dramatic increase in Soviet military power, the continued success of the socialist economies, the growth of the national liberation struggle, an unprecedented convergence of crises in the industrialized capitalist countries, and the strengthening of "democratic" and "peace-loving" forces within the other camp.

Whether they really believe the balance of trends has shifted so swiftly and so unambiguously is difficult to tell. But, in a sense, that is not crucial: first, because the Soviets do not underestimate the residual strength of capitalist societies, least of all the United States, nor over-estimate their own military strength. On the contrary, they have the deepest regard for the powers of recovery in Western societies, for their economic dynamism even when decelerated, and for the United States' preeminence among and continued dominance over them; they also seem to understand the limitations of their own military power—in fact, in contrast to many in the West, they still tend to see themselves as militarily inferior to the United States in most respects.

Second, the precise level of Soviet optimism is less important than the conceptual framework sustaining it. It is more important that the Soviet Union, however sensitive to specific trends, still ultimately reduces the evolution of international relations to a single contest. It still imposes (a Soviet speaker would say, understands) the juxtaposition between two historic forces, between two social systems and in these terms judges the ultimate significance of global change.

We make a mistake, therefore, to doubt the force of this idea, to consign it to that category of devices by which the Soviet regime finds self-justification, or to repress it in our haste to transform the Soviet Union into a historically recognizable problem. The mistake has three consequences: It obscures a basic asymmetry in our two conceptions of international change; it conceals the trouble a Soviet observer has with our conception of international change; and it makes it more difficult to understand the role that the Soviet Union assigns itself in promoting international change.

In the first instance, Americans have gradually learned to divide their preoccupations. One of the consequences of a changing environment, we think, is the increasingly diffuse quality of the challenges that it raises. Our problems and the solutions, to the extent that our problems have solutions, exist on different planes and in separate contexts. However much these are interwoven, they cannot any longer be forced into one dimension. On the other hand, the Soviet view of this increasingly intricate environment is still refracted through a single dimension.

Thus, for example, we take the contestation over the new international economic order (NIEO) to be a serious new focus of American foreign policy, and, because the challenge comes from the South, distinct from our competition with the Soviet Union. (Indeed, as an acknowledgment of interdependence and a moderated East–West contest, we now invite the Soviet Union to join us in aiding the developing nations.) But for the Soviet Union the North–South emphasis is misconceived, not merely because this tends to feature a "rich–poor" dichotomy, and the Soviet Union does not like its own ranking, but because a rich–poor dichotomy makes the issue income redistribution, and income redistribution has to do with buying off the oppressed, not revolutionizing the system. Properly conceived, the struggle over a new international economic order is between the two social systems, with the socialist countries in the forefront. As a symptom of imperialism's vulnerabilities, the Soviet Union supports the struggle for a more equitable international economic order; but, recognizing how powerful the industrialized capitalist states remain in this sphere, it prefers to emphasize other areas of change, ones better served by the "shifting correlation of forces," ones that have more to do with restructuring East–West relations, or, as Soviet writers put it, ones more directly concerned with reducing the risks of war, strengthening peaceful coexistence, and advancing "extensive and constructive cooperation."

In the second instance, our insensitivity to Soviet conceptions prevents us from seeing how much we remain the Soviet Union's preoccupation. (Too many people who do take Soviet formulas seriously are no exception, because they confound the "struggle between two social systems" with a struggle between two states or two sets of states.) If there is one great impediment to progressive change, one great benefactor of a reactionary order, in Soviet eyes, it is the United States. China may be a more immediate and noxious threat to the Soviet Union, but its larger meaning is as an objective ally of the antiprogressive forces led by us. Thus, when our theorists and leaders speak of adjusting to systemic change, creating new equilibriums, fashioning a sounder balance of power, and building on interdependence, these are not treated by the Soviets as concepts for a safer, more stable, and more humane international order, but as a design for saving as much as possible of the old one.

Because of Vietnam and the growing strength of the Soviet Union, Soviet writers say, the American leaders have a more realistic appreciation of the limits of their power and a more constructive approach to relations with the Soviet Union (until the human rights initiatives of the Carter Administration). No leader more symbolized that change than Henry Kissinger, but Kissinger the theorist, it has often been noted in Soviet analyses, believes in the "balance of power system" and, "however praised or embellished" that concept may be, it is designed to preserve the status quo not only in the international–political but, above all, in the social sphere—"to maintain and strengthen reactionary regimes," to stifle "revolutionary changes in the life of the people."

According to Soviet observers, it is not the imperatives of interdependence, particularly those of reciprocity and mutual restraint, that move American leaders, but rather the opportunities they see in the fragmentation of power. (The concept of interdependence, they say, becomes in our hands a rationalization for Western exploitation of the Third World and an artifice for salvaging imperialist collaboration under American leadership.) By capitalizing on the conflicts among various "power centers," Soviet analysts maintain, the United States hopes to make itself the arbiter of the system, the regulator of the "equilibrium," and the equilibrium that most bothers them is the so-called "pentagonal world" (the USSR, the United States, China, Western Europe, and Japan). It is not restraint that we are attempting to build into the system, according to them, but flexibility for ourselves, the kind that preserves others' dependencies and frees our hands to control adverse change, to "export counter-revolution."

In turn, Soviet commentators make no bones about their own country's large and active role in the evolution of the international order. As they say, the restructuring of international relations "can never be spontaneous or automatic." Marxist–Leninists cannot rely on "spontaneous development" in international affairs. "Any fundamental restructuring of international relations must be duly planned, controlled, and corrected." Since international politics, in contrast to the imperialists' view, are not a social system, subject to endless, directionless mutations—a "system" whose structure cannot be rectified, only manipulated and exploited—but a process, the progressive forces of the world can and must act to protect and foster this process. The process, of course, is the shifting "correlation of forces," and the Soviet Union, according to its spokesmen, has a growing responsibility for its advance.

Ambitious, militarily strengthened, buoyed by the course of events, persuaded that we are the key obstacle to a more preferable international order, this seemingly is not the kind of Soviet Union that we want to live with. Nor is it one much in step with an encumbered international environment dominated by mutual dependencies. How much worse that it also, according to many of us, invests military power with a high instrumental value.

This, however, misconceives the problem, and no part of it more than the military dimension. For the instrumentalism we see in the Soviet approach to military power is, in the first instance, the instrumentalism they attribute to *us*. The interplay is not easy to sort out, but it starts with our misrepresentation of their theory. Thus, the Soviet concepts that we consult to prove their instrumentalism are in fact those analyzing ours. Their loyalty to Clausewitz, for example, has nothing to do with rationalizing war as an instrument of Soviet foreign policy; it is a way of explaining the phenomenon of war and imperialism's proclivity to war as a means. In twisting their meaning, Soviet commentators complain, we "deliberately lump together the theoretical proposition characterizing the essence of war and the proposition concerning the expediency, or otherwise, of war as a means of achieving political objectives." (This disclaimer we may believe or not, but we have no business using Clausewitz to prove their commitment to war as an instrument of foreign policy.)

Seeing military power as an instrument of foreign policy, of course, is much different from proposing war as an instrument of foreign policy. We, they say, have made military power not only an instrument, but *the* instrument, of our postwar foreign policy. And we have not only made it the instrument of our foreign policy—that is, our frequent and ultimate recourse in controlling international change—but we have turned the threat of (nuclear) war into a prop for our frequent military interventions. That is why, according to them, we seek strategic superiority, why we reject parity, why we resort to the subterfuge of "strategic sufficiency" (the formula of the early Nixon years), why we concoct concepts like the "doctrine of limited nuclear options" (deterrence in the late Nixon and Ford years)—why, in short, we struggle to make nuclear war safe, and why we chase so frantically after technological advantage. Our particular approach to deterrence theory, they think, represents our never-ending struggle to salvage political utility for nuclear arms, to make them a shield for the exploitation of other forms of military power. (Our equivalent is the notion that the Soviet commitment to "winning" a nuclear war represents a commitment to an arms buildup that will permit winning without fighting—not, as Soviet theorists claim, a way of fighting a war that others start and hope to win.)

There is no way of knowing whether some or all within the Soviet leadership would be willing to try where we "have failed," whether they can imagine a plausible structure to the strategic balance that would profit Soviet foreign policy. But three lesser conclusions are within our reach: first, to the extent that the Soviet leaders are wrestling with the problem of integrating military power and foreign policy—and they are—it is at the lower end of the spectrum, where we have regularly applied military force to foreign policy ends. To judge from their building programs, they have not yet decided how far they want to go in developing an ability to project force, how far they want to go in preventing or duplicating our practices. Second, the areas where foreign policy and military power are the most likely to mingle are those geographically and naturally isolated from the central balances. Third, we pay an unnecessary price for our original invidious image of the Soviet Union: In truth, the Soviet Union feels better about itself and the course of events than we assume; trusting events, it is more likely to assign its military power the task—beyond defense—of preventing others from interfering with change than of imposing change.

For, in fact, the Soviet Union does not see itself as only militarily potent and otherwise as economically disadvantaged, technologically deficient, bureaucratically sclerosed, and so on. Its leaders admit to a broad range of problems and limitations but, where we constantly view these in terms of fundamental systemic weaknesses, they regard them as normal and corrigible defects. And where we focus on these defects, treating them as a basic disparagement of the Soviet experience, they tend to downplay them, instead emphasizing their accomplishments, and thus retain a genuine faith in the transcendent significance of that experience. (One could exchange "they" and "we" in these two sentences; that is, the same contrast exists in reverse.)

On the other hand, we tend to analyze the effect of Soviet ideology in narrow, utilitarian terms, that is, by the impact that it has on others by its power to attract, and by this standard we see the Soviet Union still more weakened. While a Soviet leader is also concerned with the force of ideology, as a practical matter he is more likely to focus on trends that correspond with his values than on the precise number of orthodox disciples that his country inspires (outside the critical sphere of Eastern Europe). Rather than judge the issue only by the number of socialist states in the world or genuine Marxist–Leninists, he will take heart from the number that merely reject the other way; even more will his optimism depend on the basic rhythm of change, say, in Indochina or southern Africa.

There is another side to the story. For the Soviet Union is not only, or even first, the servant of history; it is also a state with mundane interests, like adding Western computers to its economy, securing

recognition for the territorial status quo in Eastern Europe, and discouraging the United States from deploying cruise missiles. Its recourse
has been the process of détente, which the Soviet leaders say is not only
compatible with the process of an evolving correlation of forces, but an
essential part of it. Détente is the refinement and restraint that the Soviet
Union brings to the basic contest between two social systems. Theoretically, it is the framework within which the Soviet Union bridges the gap
between its private needs and the historic vision, but the recriminations
of the French Communist Party (against those who would sacrifice social
change to détente) and of "some representatives" of national liberation
movements indicate that it has not been fully successful.

Were the Soviet participation in détente but a tactical expedient, a
kind of winter quartering of the troops, a policy choice to be discarded at
the first sign of inconvenience, we might have a right to a more primitive
view of the Soviet approach to international change. But it is not. It is a
profound and long-term commitment dictated by the Soviet leaders'
inability to conceive a better way to pursue their three elemental
objectives: (1) nurturing both the processes that restrain the change the
Soviet Union fears and those that ease the way to the change it desires;
(2) sanctifying the Soviet Union's status as a global power coequal with
the United States (that there may be, in Andrei Gromyko's words, "no
question of any significance which can be decided without the Soviet
Union or in opposition to it"); and (3) securing the economic and
technological benefits of the "international division of labor." By the
last, the Soviet Union engages itself in the interdependent world. This
interdependent world, which includes collaboration between socialist
and capitalist states, now has the status of a phenomenon determined
by "objective realities and laws." And Soviet leaders admit that "no
single state is able for long to achieve full development if it cuts itself off
from the rest of the world."


VI  I remember those maps from early television programs on the
Soviet Union—or on the communist world as it was then. How the color
spread like spilled paint across the areas of Soviet control and ambition.
Whatever else it may be, 20 years later, the Soviet global thrust is not
that. Indeed it is not even a proper "global thrust," much less an
"imperial thrust," if by that we mean the extension of power *and*
control, or the attempt to control. The Soviet empire still ends at the Elbe
River. And, as far as power is concerned, while the Soviet Union's is
clearly enlarged, at least that part of it that is military, we should
remember that the portion of military power that is abroad is largely
redeployed, not additional, power and remains vastly inferior to our
own. That is, while the Soviet Navy is modernizing, it is less its
transfiguration that should catch our eye, for this has been slow and
ambiguous, than the simple decision to send the old navy out to sea.
Moreover, of all the naval-related areas, the one in which the Soviet
Union lags farthest behind us is in its ability to project force.

It is entirely possible that the Soviet Union intends to improve its capacity for projecting power, that it is ready to try to influence events more actively in various parts of the world, and that it believes the timely application of military power may be a primary means. But, if so, the effort will be made with relatively few illusions about the permanence of change or about the limits of influence or about the permanence of influence yielded by change. The closer to home (and to the central military balances), the less utility military power has for Soviet foreign policy, and the more the Soviet Union must rely primarily on processes like détente to influence the trends of concern to it. In the grey area in between, like Yugoslavia, there is no evidence that the Soviet Union regards its military power as an important part of policy, but neither is there any evidence that it disregards the fear that it may be.

In general, the notion of a Soviet global thrust has less to do with the application of power (toward control) than it does with status and access (derived from power). That is, the key proposition is Gromyko's: namely, the Soviet Union as a participant in decisions of concern to it. This indisputably depends, in the Soviet mind and, in part, in reality, on the growing mass of Soviet military power, strategic nuclear power in particular. But it also depends, in larger part, on the nature of local circumstances and, as events in the Middle East have proved since the 1973 war, these are often more powerful.

Phrasing the problem so basically, of course, does not help much in dealing with specific aspects or applications of Soviet power, but this kind of framework (not necessarily this particular one) is essential if we are to have a perspective in which to fit our specific judgments. Too often these days we focus on particular dimensions of Soviet power without the broader perspective—and end by inventing implications.

# VII
Looked at from a distance, what ultimately is the significance of a changing setting in assessing Soviet power? And where do these considerations intersect with the problem of competing Soviet and American perspectives? The answer to the first question, it seems to me, comes out of the fundamental evolution in our perception of the constraints on Soviet power. At the outset, that is 30 years ago when George Kennan wrote his famous essay on the subject, we viewed these constraints as too frail, and so we substituted ourselves. Faced with what we deemed to be a messianic expansionist state, which for whatever reasons—the one Kennan stressed was the regime's failure to consolidate its absolute power at home—was struggling to fill "every nook and cranny available to it in the basin of world power," our response was fateful and straightforward: We must, Kennan argued and we agreed, "confront the Russians with unalterable counterforce at every point where they show signs of encroaching upon the interests of a peaceful and stable world."

Since then, however, the international setting has grown constantly more complex, adding powerful new constraints and rendering our own role less obvious. The filled power vacuums in Europe and Asia, the fractured monolith of socialism, and most of all the shadow of nuclear war have transformed the context in which we contemplate Soviet ambition. To these commonplaces, we might add the Soviet Union's growing stake in what for it has long been a repugnant international order. The paradox stems not only from the Soviet Union's commitment to economic cooperation with the West and the utility it sees in, say, a stable law of the seas, but also from the disruptions it cannot afford to sponsor if it counts on Western forbearance in the face of its growing global role.[3]

Within this sturdier environment—sturdier because of the obstacles it raises to crude expansionism, not because we have been able to maintain our own mission of checking Soviet power at every point—the Soviet–American rivalry has now evolved into something less intensive and something more extensive. The elusiveness of opportunity and the distractions of multiple international challenges account for the loss of intensity. The broadening of the rivalry reflects the USSR's developing global vocation, or, to extend Kennan's original notion, it reflects the shift in Soviet preoccupation from the struggle to secure Soviet power against the external world to a quest for a larger place in it.

Détente has been the process by which we come to terms with both circumstances—with both the changing constraints on Soviet power and the changing nature of the threat it poses. It is also the nearest we have to a replacement for the policy (or process) of containment, now that the extension of Soviet dominion has been essentially contained. The new task is to temper the use of its extended power. (A Soviet speaker would say that détente is the process by which his country capitalizes on its growing power to curb American excesses, or the process by which the United States is led to embrace the principle of peaceful coexistence.)

The contest between us continues—that is the essence of peaceful coexistence—but for us, and presumably for the USSR, détente introduces the new prospect of managing, not merely maintaining, our rivalry. It is an historic opportunity but one with almost insuperable internal tensions. For, on the one hand, we in our rivalry are challenged to collaborate consciously and explicitly in order to moderate the contest; on the other hand, we in our collaboration must cope with the permanent reality of the contest, a reality constantly underscored by global instabilities and constantly heightened by the evolution of the Soviet Union's military power. The delicate task of designing and perhaps even codifying the "rules of the game," if that is what we set out to do in the Moscow agreements of 1972, is continually interrupted by moments of chaos when in Chile, Angola, Indochina, or perhaps Yugoslavia our conflicting interests are reemphasized.

The unhappy consequences of this problem are essentially three, each of which carries its own implicit resolution, though none is within easy reach. The first is the preeminence reserved for the military dimension. It is inevitable and, frankly, desirable that both sides maintain their defenses. Regrettable as it may be, the probable truth is that nuclear weapons, in some rough equilibrium, have kept the peace between us in the past and will be needed to keep it in the future. And the other parts of our military establishment are equally essential, not because the USSR is demonstrably eager to sweep across the North German plain at the first opportunity, but because, as the last war in the Middle East demonstrated, events in which the USSR has a heavy stake, but over which it has little control, may tempt it to invoke the threat of military intervention.

Still, we both have—or believe we have—an interest in holding these forces to a minimum. Because neither side trusts the other's conviction, however, because the "rules of the game" remain so rudimentary and suspect, and, in these circumstances, because those responsible for national security in both countries demand large margins for error, we move constantly the other way. And the motion becomes our pre-occupation: Those who see the Soviet side in the arms race in sinister terms judge détente accordingly; those who worry about the dangerous or destabilizing aspects of the arms race base the viability of détente primarily on success in controlling arms. In the process, neither group is coming to grips with the instrumentalism the United States and the Soviet Union each sees in the other's approach to military power.

The first group doubts that the Soviet Union could misunderstand the character and purpose of our military forces and is thus led to a heightened mistrust of Soviet motives; as a consequence, it places its faith instead in further arming—even as the soundest avenue to arms control. The second group, preoccupied with the enormous specific problems of negotiating SALT, MBFR, and now the proposed de-militarization of the Indian Ocean, tends to repress the dilemma of mutual United States and Soviet misperceptions about the role of force in each other's foreign policy. For ultimately the dilemma can only be dealt with by relating our defense preparations to our arms control efforts; it can only be addressed by weighing the secondary costs in the other side's distorted perceptions of the significance of the way we choose to defend ourselves, the arms we build, and the doctrines we formulate. Until both countries make that effort, arms control—whether SALT, MBFR, or other negotiations to follow—will remain a fragmented and unsystematic enterprise that may produce agreements but only marginal and ambiguous progress toward a moderated contest.

The second consequence flows from the first. Because of the central place accorded the military dimension, key aspects of the USSR–U.S. relationship are broken down and split from their context. I have just commented on how much the processes of arming and of negotiating arms control become divorced from the basic problem of military power in both sides' perceptions. Similarly, because of the prominence granted traditional security concerns, the natural effects of processes like in-terdependence are distorted, and in their place we substitute a pre-occupation with their manipulation—by us for gain, against us we fear to our disadvantage. Finally, and in the long run, the process of restructuring USSR–U.S. relations tends to lose its coherence, and we end, as in Kissinger's last days, by focusing on specific tension areas that threaten to accentuate East–West conflict or be accentuated by it or, as in the Carter instance, by concentrating on disembodied elements of the relationship such as human rights and arms control.

The third consequence—that is, the interruption in the search for more explicit "rules of the game"—follows from the other two. Though we tend to forget it now, relatively concrete patterns of restraint were discussed at the outset of détente. At the time, the two sides consciously set out to reduce the dangerous, extraneous, or unproductive burdens of competition, actually writing some of these restraints into the Basic Principles of United States–Soviet Relations (the document signed at the May 1972 summit). They included the crucial principle of parity—as stated in the Basic Principles neither side would "either directly or indirectly seek unilateral advantage over the other"—an idea most relevant to the strategic arms race, but in the Soviet mind one sanctioning equality in all forms of power. There were others such as the notion of substituting economic interdependence for (our) earlier economic warfare against the Soviet Union and (their) economic autarky, which was again, in implication, written into the Basic Principles. There was also the important concession, on each side's part, that the other's claimed dedication to peaceful coexistence, that is, to restraint in its foreign policy, might now have real meaning. Indeed, the idea of peaceful coexistence was written into the Basic Principles.

Others might be added, derived more from the observer's imagination, but the point is that the search in general was long ago disrupted: Parity as a principle fell victim to the widespread suspicion on both sides' part that it was for the other only a momentary indulgence for want of a choice. Interdependence as a principle has been eroded and partially discredited by the politics of linkages; and peaceful coexistence as a principle suffers from the effects of Angola and the 1973 Middle East war.

The dialectical quality of détente, with its competitive/cooperative essence, makes it hard to revive the search for "rules," for a more explicit *modus vivendi*, for a moderation of means in lieu of agreement over ends. But the search is ultimately the only hope we have of restoring coherence to the quest for a restructured Soviet–American relationship. It includes new and untried standards of behavior like those suggested by Marshall Shulman some years ago—one, the principle of "noninterference by force in processes of internal change," the other, the "right of free access," permitting nations to "compete, not for the control of territory, but for the establishment of mutually beneficial and nonexploitative relations, and thereby for political influence." These are the decisive "rules of the game," for it is they that will tell us how much either side really trusts a moderated contest and wants its advantages.

## Notes

[1] See Richard Portes, "East Europe's Debt to the West: Interdependence Is a Two-way Street," *Foreign Affairs*, July 1977, pp. 751–782.

[2]In urging that we cast our evaluation of Soviet power more broadly, I am aware that I have slighted considerations that many others feature. I have made no effort to appraise the impact of change within the socialist world on Soviet power; no effort to judge whether Soviet power is diminished by the continued erosion of "proletarian internationalism" beyond Eastern Europe but enhanced by its preservation within Eastern Europe; or whether it is enhanced by the rising influence of communists and their allies beyond the Soviet sphere but diminished by the cost of maintaining its own influence within this sphere. Or, whether the combinations are the opposite (because I do not know and because the judgment is history's). I have not attempted to explore the impact on Soviet power of the conflict with China or of our China diplomacy (because the impact is obvious). Nor have I commented on the power that the Soviet Union derives from our growing bilateral economic cooperation—from the so-called "hostage capital" it possesses or the ready-made lobbies that it inherits (because the leverage flows both ways and because this is a marginal consideration in the larger scheme of things).

[3]If after Angola and the 1973 Middle East War this sounds doubtful, we should not lose sight of the relatively narrow limits within which the Soviet Union acted in both instances, neither case ever being the reckless incursion that many in the West imagined.

# 4  EDWARD N. LUTTWAK

## The New Dynamics of the Soviet Empire: From Optimism to Pessimism*

From the day of its birth in Lenin's *coup d'état* of 6 November 1917 (October by the old calendar), and until very recently indeed, the Soviet regime has been fundamentally optimistic, albeit for reasons that have varied over time.

At first, the Bolsheviks were optimistic about the future even in the midst of famine and civil war, because they were quite certain that revolutions similar to their own would soon break out in Germany and the other industrialized countries. This expectation was reflected in the conduct of Lenin's new-made government toward the Central Powers, whose armies were pressing hard against a disintegrating Russian front at the time of the *coup d'état*. When a peace conference was convened in Brest-Litovsk on 3 December 1917, the Bolshevik delegation under Trotsky was ordered to employ delaying tactics with the Germans and Austro–Hungarians, in the belief that revolution would overtake those countries not just soon but actually in a matter of days or weeks. It was only at the end of February 1918, when the Germans resumed their advance to penetrate deeply into Russian territory, that Lenin decided to accept their terms. But this did not mean that the estimate of imminent revolution had been abandoned. On the contrary, Lenin's readiness to surrender huge territories including Poland, the Baltic provinces, much of the Ukraine, Finland, and even the Caucasus—very much more than the Germans had actually conquered—was due to his belief that the loss would soon be restored by the emergence of a fraternal Bolshevik Germany (and indeed his concessions were reversed, but only by the Allied victory in November).

*Reprinted by permission of the author from *The Grand Strategy of the Soviet Union* (New York: St. Martin's Press, 1983), pp. 21–41, 117. Copyright 1983 by Edward N. Luttwak.

During its first years, the Bolshevik regime could easily sustain belief in the imminence of world revolution. The mutinies and soldiers' "Soviets" in the French army and the German navy (which were imitated briefly in other armies also, albeit on a smaller scale), the sharp rise in political agitation by trade unionists and assorted socialists and revolutionaries throughout Europe and beyond, and the actual Bolshevik uprisings in Germany and Hungary that briefly brought to power Soviet-style regimes, inspired the worldwide "red scare" of 1919–1920, and they could also inspire red hopes.

By the time this first reason for optimism had waned, another had come to take its place. If the political millennium would have to wait, an economic revolution could still be accomplished. Central planning would allow the Soviet Union to achieve rapid economic growth toward an unprecedented prosperity, thus eventually offering an irresistibly attractive model which all other countries would eventually have to copy. Not itself part of the Marxist inheritance, but rather the offspring of the systems of economic control invented in both Germany and Britain during the great war just ended (which had made possible the huge and indeed utterly improbable increases in war production of the two countries), the direction of the economy by central planning seemed an innovation of epic proportions to the Soviet leaders.

From the inauguration of the first 5-year plan in 1928, the course seemed to be set for the achievement of high and sustained rates of growth that would eventually allow the Soviet Union to overtake every other economy and move far ahead. And this great result was to be achieved by a method remarkably simple: The state would appropriate all production, allowing a minimum for personal consumption; the surplus would be used not to build factories and equip farms to produce consumer goods and food, but rather to expand the economy's energy supply, railways, and other basic infrastructures, and above all to increase the output of "producer" goods. By continuing to provide only a minimum of resources for immediate consumption while investing the maximum in machine tools to make yet more machine tools, the stage would eventually be reached when a greatly enlarged Soviet industry could turn to produce equipment to make consumer goods and farm machinery in great quantities; then the Soviet consumer would finally enjoy an unprecedented abundance.

Only three things were needed to ensure the success of the scheme: the control of all capital by the state, so that the long-term growth priorities could be enforced; the enthusiasm of the public, or at least the willingness of all to work for very little while awaiting the great day; and peace.

The first requirement was so easily achieved in industry and commerce that its extension to agriculture seemed at least feasible if not easy. Factory owners and businessmen in general had either fled abroad or else they had been reduced to a frightened silence. The peasants, it is true, were very much in place and now the owners of the lands they tilled, but, just as the factories had been "collectivized," the peasants too would have to give up their petty rights of ownership to form collectives. To do this was not a matter of ideology but rather an essential part of the whole scheme: The surplus production to be used for investment would largely have to come from the land, and the state bureaucracy could scarcely squeeze all there was from millions of independent farms. Hence the peasants would have to be organized into large units under Party control so that their production could be more easily extracted by the state. What followed, of course, were all the miseries and massacres of forced collectivization, which opened a wound which has turned out to be incurable.

The second requirement, maximum work for minimum immediate reward, was to be met by a combination of inspiring propaganda and police terror. Films, posters, books, and songs explained the scheme and harnessed the enthusiasm of the young for the great projects that were the centerpieces of the plan; the competitive spirit was exploited in production "races" between work-teams and factories; high achievers were given personal recognition in medals and publicity—in sum, all the tricks of political propaganda and all the devices of commercial promotion were exploited in wave after wave of exhortation. As for the terror, that too was thoroughly done: Shirkers were imprisoned, "saboteurs" were shot, and tens of millions of peasants were collectivized by brutal compulsion. Propaganda and police were in themselves diversions from the production effort; but to the extent that production could be enhanced and consumption squeezed further, the resources given to the secret police and the Agitprop would handsomely pay for themselves.

The third requirement, peace, was a function of international politics, which were beyond the exclusive control of the Kremlin leader who otherwise controlled so much; but Stalin did what he could. A major war would inevitably interrupt the Soviet Union's steady ascent to the centrally planned millennium—the key to its eventual worldwide political victory—and thus the Soviet Union followed a genuine peace policy, at least until 1939.

The prospect of an impending economic supremacy served to maintain the fundamental optimism of the Soviet leadership for several decades, perhaps until as late as the end of the 1960s. But then finally it must have been recognized in the Kremlin that the perpetuation of the central planning system, in effect a special kind of war economy, could not after all serve as the reliable highway to prosperity. Until the end of the 1960s, the ravages of the war—and before that the original poverty of the Russian empire—could serve as plausible excuses, not only for their propaganda, but for the rulers themselves. But after 40-odd years of central planning, the great intellectual discovery was made, if only gradually and perhaps never completely: that central planning could indeed serve well in wartime to produce arms and ammunition in response to fixed specifications and quantity targets, but that it could not channel the right amounts of the right resources into the very many, very varied, and always changing paths of peacetime economic development. In sector after sector, the Soviet system strives to produce more obsolescent goods even as radically new ones have already appeared on the world scene; it is not that too little is produced, but rather that the wrong things are produced: adding machines, even in the greatest number, cannot compete with digital computers any more than great quantities of cast iron can substitute for the right amounts of the right kinds of plastic. The very visible symptom of the Soviet economic failure was the slow rate of innovation, but the cause was the very structure of the system itself.

The other discovery of the late 1960s was equally sinister: In the wake of huge investments in agriculture, a fundamental structural malady was revealed there also. Under Stalin's policy, Soviet farming had been starved of machinery and fertilizers; it was natural therefore to presume that given great quantities of both, all would be well. But when Soviet agriculture did finally receive vast resources, it turned out that there was a far more intractable obstacle to an adequate productivity: the state of the peasantry, which collectivization had long before deprived of the will to work carefully and well. Soviet agriculture absorbs more than seven times as much investment as its American counterpart, but the return on that investment is spectacularly low: Between 1950 and 1977, the capital stock of Soviet agriculture increased 11.9 times to yield an increase in output of 250%. At present, added investment yields almost nothing.

The world is full of dissatisfied consumers, and the prospect of an indefinite delay in delivering the long-promised abundance to the Soviet consumer was the least part of the regime's predicament. The decline in the rate of growth was far more serious, for in the Soviet case, uniquely, economic failure undermines the very legitimacy of the regime. The welfare of two entire generations had been ruthlessly sacrificed to the pursuit of economic supremacy, the declared goal of Soviet national strategy since 1928, and the consequences of disappointing long-stoked expectations were awesome. Palliatives such as the importation of Western technology, excuses old and new, and grim forecasts of an impending great depression in the capitalist world, could all serve to reduce the immediate political damage, but obviously the regime could no longer remain optimistic on economic grounds. Instead of overtaking the advanced economies, the Soviet economy was itself being overtaken.

## Imperialism: The Last Stage of Soviet Optimism

Once again the waning of one hope coincided with the birth of another, of a radically different sort. If the Soviet Union could no longer hope to conquer the world by the novel method of becoming its irresistibly successful economic and social model, it could instead pursue the lesser but still grandiose aim of becoming the world's leading military power. By sheer chance, the belated recognition of economic failure by the Soviet leaders at the end of the 1960s happened to coincide with the beginning of the abrupt and phenomenal decline of the United States as a military power. Already great in absolute terms, the decline was yet greater in comparison with the Soviet Union: While the armed strength of the United

States was consumed both morally and materially in unsuccessful warfare, and was then further diminished by budgetary reductions year after year until at least 1976, the Soviet Union was steadily enhancing its capital of military equipment (in quality above all) and also of sound expertise.

During the same period, the authority of the United States on the world scene was relentlessly eroded by violent social disarray, by the perceptible loss of nerve of its policy elite, and by the public attack upon all the institutions of power. All this engendered a fatal lack of tenacity in American conduct overseas, which culminated in the outright abandonment of Cambodia, Laos, and South Vietnam. The damage was then further compounded by a foreign policy of indecision, renunciation, and outright retreat, which continued for several years after the final defeat suffered in Indochina. During that same period, the Soviet Union in contrast reaffirmed its strength and determination by forceful action in Czechoslovakia (which, it was soon noted, evoked no lasting sanction) and then proceeded to broaden the range of its influence; always a great power, it became for the first time a global power also. While American prestige was sinking, the Soviet Union was gaining in authority from the reliable if grim continuity of its policies. Moreover, as an inevitable consequence of the Strategic Arms Limitation negotiations, the Soviet Union received a full and formal recognition of its coequal status as a superpower—also for the first time.

As a result of these sharply divergent trends, there could be no doubt in whose favor the global balance was shifting during the 1970s, and neither localized setbacks, such as the loss of Egypt as a client, nor all the varied consequences of Chinese hostility could alter the fundamental fact that the Soviet Union was emerging as the world's leading military power.

The Soviet Union thus found itself in the 1970s much more powerful and also distinctly poorer than its leaders could reasonably have predicted even a mere decade before. It was thus only natural that the goal of economic supremacy, which had become utterly unrealistic, should have given way to the pursuit of imperial power as the new dominant aim of Soviet national strategy.

This momentous change was of pervasive effect especially because it converged with the other great transformation, the restoration of Russian nationalism. One must exercise great care in trying to understand such complicated matters and their yet more complicated implications, but one thing is immediately obvious: While the pursuit of economic supremacy was fully consistent with the aspirations of all the nationalities of the empire, and those of the client-states too, the pursuit of imperial primacy on the world scene could only be a source of genuine satisfaction to the Russians themselves. Had the Soviet Union become a voluntary confederation as Lenin had once hoped, all its nationalities might have shared in the psychological rewards of imperial status; to some extent this might have been true even if only the highest leadership itself had remained transnational, as in Stalin's day. But in a Soviet Union so clearly ruled by Russians, the members of all other nationalities must regard themselves as subjects, and they can hardly gain much satisfaction from the prospect of further expanding the imperial domain of the Russian people.

Actually the novel pursuit of imperial power may be a new cause of resentment to the non-Russians. When the Soviet Union was still giving its highest priority to industrialization and growth, the sacrifices imposed on the population would be less painful in the degree that they offered the prospect of a happy future for coming generations. Many Russians, and perhaps most, might still willingly accept economic sacrifice for the sake of increasing yet further the power of a Soviet state that has become so clearly a Russian empire. But that cannot be so for the other nationalities. For the non-Russians, the pursuit of external power, with all the military expense that it entails, and all the aid given to the menagerie of radical Third World states, must merely seem a cause of their poverty; many, no doubt, believe it to be the leading cause. All Soviet citizens, Russians and non-Russians alike, are certainly well aware of how greatly their standard of living has improved during the last 30 years or so. On the other hand, they also know that the peoples of all other industrialized countries (including their own client-states) enjoy a much higher standard of living than themselves. It is a fair guess that the non-Russians are much more likely to blame military expenditures, and the cost of supporting overseas dependencies such as Cuba, South Yemen, and Vietnam, for the stringencies so vividly manifest in their daily lives.

There is one additional factor. While the restoration of Russian nationalism long preceded the advent of the new era of Soviet imperialism (and indeed it was virtually a precondition of the great change), the two phenomena reinforce one another. The success of the Soviet Union as a power on the world scene stimulates Russian national pride, and incidentally encourages all those manifestations of chauvinism that must unfailingly evoke the reactive nationalism of the non-Russians; on the other hand, Russian national pride further encourages the striving to globalize Soviet power. To the extent that the non-Russians do not in fact share in the psychological rewards of empire, the rise of Soviet power tends to antagonize the non-Russians, who pay their full share of the cost. Thus, for both economic and psychological reasons, the new primacy given to external aggrandizement intensifies ethnic tensions inside Soviet society. The failure to fulfill the original transnational promise is basic, but its consequences must be aggravated by the present direction of Soviet policy. This is the link between the last phase of optimism and the advent of pessimism.

The Advent of Pessimism   If the Soviet leaders estimated during the early 1970s that the United States was in sharp decline as a world power and perhaps that it was destined to revert to isolationism, theirs would have been a pardonable error. True, many social indicators—and the election of 1968 above all—proved conclusively that, for all the antiwar agitations and all the riots, the great majority of the American people remained firmly conservative and deeply patriotic. But such sentiments could only guarantee political stability at home. A foreign policy of substance and action requires much more: not just the vague approval of the general public, but rather the specific support of Congress and of the media and policy elites that influence Congressional dealings with foreign affairs. And such support can only be forthcoming if those elites are in turn confident of themselves and of the ability of the American government as a whole to act wisely overseas. And on both counts there was much evidence by the early 1970s to support the prediction that the United States would indeed retreat from the world scene, if only gradually.

While outright isolationism had never truly been the American stance and never would be by choice, in view of the retreat from globalism manifest by, say, 1972, it would have been reasonable to forecast that the perimeter of serious American concern would soon be restricted to Western Europe, Japan, and possibly the Middle East, in addition to the western hemisphere. Similarly, while the United States would not of course disarm, the trends pointed to a great reduction in American military strength, particularly in regard to forces for distant intervention.

Had the United States been confronted by evidence of a sharply diminished Soviet military effort, a responsive decline in American defense expenditures would have been inevitable, since the procedures of Congressional budget-making for defense mean that every American military "program" must be cast as a response to some Soviet "threat"; had the overall "threat" diminished, the defense budget would have declined also. But all procedures aside, such an outcome would have been consistent with the implicit national strategy of the United States, in which the foreign policy instruments of choice are economic, technological, and cultural, while military power is merely the instrument of necessity. The reaction of Soviet leaders to the great decline in American military power and foreign policy activism was naturally entirely different. For them, the accumulating evidence that America was in retreat could only be a powerful encouragement to yet more activism overseas, since now their efforts would no longer be countered, as in the past, by American reactions. Moreover, since military power must be the primary instrument of choice for the Soviet Union, lacking as it is in economic leverage, cultural influence, and social appeal, the appropriate response to the decline of American military power was to increase the Soviet as much as possible. With the goal of achieving a clear primacy in military power at least within reach—as it could never be when the United States was seriously competing—the incentive to enhance the strength of the Soviet armed forces was very greatly increased. In the past, some Kremlin leaders could argue that the inevitable American response would soon deprive the Soviet Union of whatever advantage could be gained by additional military spending, but once it became clear that the Americans would not seriously respond, all had to agree that it was indeed worthwhile to make the extra effort.

If the broad implication of the forecast of American decline was that

more Soviet military expenditure was warranted, the specific implication was that more effort should be devoted to the increase of long-range
intervention capabilities, especially the Soviet surface navy as well as
airlift capacity, both for direct Russian use and also to convey Cuban and
other client-forces usable overseas. The American retreat thus created a
powerful added incentive to globalize Soviet power. So long as the
United States still had almost 1000 warships, any Soviet flotilla sent far
from Soviet shores would be dwarfed by American naval forces on the
scene, but if a greatly diminished American navy was to be expected, an
increased Soviet naval effort would become profitable, since in the
future the Soviet navy would actually be able to outmatch its declining
counterpart. What was true for the Soviet navy was valid for the Soviet
military in general: Once a goal previously beyond reach becomes
attainable, it is bound to evoke an added effort.

By the beginning of the 1970s, it seemed that the Soviet Union could
indeed look forward to the day when it would become the world's
greatest military power and its only truly global power. A global reach
for the Soviet Union would not of course mean global domination. Nor
could the Soviet Union attain preclusive security, whereby its safety
would be fully assured by the physical ability to defeat any attack before
it could inflict any damage. Since the United States—and not only the
United States—would still retain control of long-range nuclear weapons
against which there is no fully reliable defense, the Soviet Union would
still have to rely on deterrence. For Russians especially, deterrence is a
most uncomfortable device, since its workings depend on others' calculations of risks and benefits. But certainly, even with such inevitable
limitations, the achievement of a global primacy could justify for the
Soviet leaders all the costs and all the risks of the pursuit of imperial
power.

Matters did not turn out as so many, almost certainly including the
Soviet leaders, had believed they would. By 1976, if not before, a net
majority of the American public had clearly rejected the counsels of the
media and foreign policy elites, which remained largely inimical to the
restoration of an activist foreign policy and to the rehabilitation of
American military strength. But in faithful reflection of public opinion,
Congress began to press with increasing success for higher defense
spending, and by 1977 a President of contradictory impulses found
himself compelled to spend more on defense than he might have
wished, quite unable to proceed with his declared intent to disengage
from Korea, and forced to maintain a greater American navy than he
desired.

Strategy is made of paradox, irony, and contradiction, and it was only
natural in that unnatural realm that it was the Soviet attempt to exploit
the favorable trend that caused its abrupt reversal. In more detached
fashion, it can be said that a Soviet national strategy necessarily based
on military power (in the absence of any other comparative advantage)
evoked a competitive reaction from the United States, whose own
national strategy would otherwise have given less weight to that particular instrument of policy, in which the United States has a comparative
disadvantage.

By 1980 matters had evolved to the point where it was clear that the United States would soon be competing in full force, both in the building of armaments and in the activism of its foreign policy. Finally, by the beginning of 1981, the Soviet Union was presented with solid evidence of American determination to regain a global primacy in military power in the budget plans that a new administration unveiled and which Congress would obviously support in large measure. To be sure, no conceivable increase in American defense expenditures could gain any sort of superiority in continental land warfare forces, but for the strategic-nuclear and naval forces that was a perfectly feasible goal. Soviet ballistic missiles could not be usefully outmatched in quantity or even in quality, but they could be outclassed by the development of weapons of radically new form; and if Soviet submarines would still deny a true naval supremacy to the United States, its surface fleet at least could regain a clear ascendancy over the Soviet. As for continental land warfare, in which the combination of powerful Soviet ground forces, large antiaircraft forces, and less impressive tactical air forces would certainly remain stronger than the American combination of strong tactical airpower and weak ground forces, the overall strategic context made any direct comparisons irrelevant, since the United States would not confront the Soviet Union alone, but rather in alliance with many other countries in both Europe and East Asia. The exception—and it is one of great significance—is the region of the Persian Gulf, where the United States has vital interests but lacks allies of any genuine military capacity.

It is true, of course, that an optimistic Soviet observer could find good reasons to discount the strength of the countries which would be associated with the United States in a continental conflict. In Western Europe, such allies as have well-equipped armies are the most vulnerable and therefore the least resolute; other allies deploy forces which are mostly made up of ill-equipped infantry, and much larger in form than substance, and others still, who do have forces of high quality, are weakened by shortages of modern equipment. As for East Asia, Japan for all its industrial capacity is still quite unable to protect its vital sea lanes or even the country itself, while the People's Republic of China (PRC) for all its millions of militiamen and soldiers, could not protect more than a part of its territory against Soviet invasion and has no significant offensive strength. That fact, and the parallel inability of the European alliance to stage any serious offensive against the Soviet Union, mean that China and Western Europe could not assist one another if either were attacked.

But as against all these undoubted weaknesses and deficiencies in the array of American alliances there is the simple fact that the Soviet Union is now encircled by enemies. Some are possessed of real military strength, even if of limited dimensions; others have at least the economic potential to acquire great military power in the future; and three of the antagonists of the Soviet Union have nuclear weapons, in addition to the United States itself. Americans may judge the British, French, and Chinese nuclear forces now aimed at the Soviet Union as technically weak in various ways and of insignificant size, but they would not treat them lightly if they were aimed at the United States. A classic paradox of strategy has been at work to the disadvantage of the Soviet Union: When a powerful country becomes yet more powerful, its strength may drive the very weakest of its neighbors into a frightened neutrality or outright client status, but neighbors marginally more secure will instead be stimulated to build up their own strength and to cooperate with one another against the great antagonist that threatens them all. The Soviet Union is thus the true author of its own encirclement.

An optimism based on the hope of achieving an imperial primacy need not give way to regime pessimism merely because of the global reaction to the Soviet pursuit of global power—a reaction natural and inevitable and by no means sufficient in itself to deny the Soviet Union what it so assiduously seeks. As for the great reversal in the substance of American military policy manifest by 1981, that indeed was rather more abrupt and entailed a more powerful rearmament than could have been expected even a year earlier; but, on the other hand, past experience and current economic forecasts both suggest that the upsurge in American military spending will not be sustained for more than a few years. That, to be sure, would suffice to deprive the Soviet Union of a great part of the gains it achieved in the military competition during the 1970s, but the relative position of the Soviet Union would still show a very great improvement as compared to, say, 1967.

Just as it did in the 1960s, when the United States was moving ahead in many areas of the military competition, the Soviet Union could now keep up its own armament effort and rely on the superior tenacity of the long-lived Kremlin leaders to overcome eventually the effects of the temporary American upsurge. Similarly, the Soviet Union could count on the continuing growth of its power to dissolve the fragile alliances that were engendered by its past military growth. For the upkeep of alliances against a rising threat will only persist if that threat falls within a middle range. If the threat is small, there will obviously be no sufficient reason to overcome all the natural diversities that pull allies apart, but if the threat is so great that any attempt at a joint defense seems futile, then too the alliance will collapse. In that circumstance, diplomatic conciliation—that is, appeasement—will seem the wiser choice, certainly less costly and perhaps less dangerous also.

Counting on the inconsistency of the great and ever-turbulent American democracy, and on its readiness to turn away from activism overseas to domestic concerns as soon as some foreign venture proves to be disappointing, the Kremlin leaders may persevere in their long-term military program and in their foreign policy, which seeks, as always, to separate the United States from its allies, clients, and friends.

By the classic paradox of strategy, the new American effort to restore a tolerable balance of military power which should eventually consolidate the alliance offers in the meantime great opportunities for Soviet diplomacy to divide the alliance. If the United States remains firm in its intent, and if it is successful in its major military program, and if the alliances are kept together in the interim, then a reconstructed balance of power will emerge by the end of the 1980s, in which the Soviet advantage in land power will once again be offset by the strength on land of cohesive allies and by American (and allied) advantages in strategic-nuclear and naval capabilities. It was on that asymmetry that the overall military balance of the entire postwar era was based, and it was the decline of American strength at sea and in strategic-nuclear forces that destabilized the balance of military power during the 1970s.

The opportunity for Soviet diplomacy to divide the United States from its allies arises because allies made insecure by the diminished strength of their protector must now be exposed to all the stresses of the new policy of rearmament even while being still in the state of weakness created by the American policies of the recent past. So long as the Western Alliance was drifting gently into an increasing weakness, with Soviet–American arms control talks underway to relieve anxiety and offer hopes of a costless stability, the Alliance could be as comfortable as a patient drifting into a coma under heavy sedation. Now the patient is being told to rise and work, and all the unfelt wounds inflicted in the past begin to hurt.

In so far as the American rearmament is strategic-nuclear, it raises the fear that the Soviet Union will be tempted to exploit its present advantage to make permanent gains, before the advent of newly powerful American strategic-nuclear forces once again imposes the full restraints of deterrence upon Soviet conduct. In so far as the American rearmament is "conventional" it must impose increased defense costs on the allies as well, since in some degree or other they each will have to make their gestures toward sharing the burden. As for rearmament in the middle category of forces—the battlefield nuclear weapons (mainly artillery shells and short-range missiles), tactical nuclear weapons (mainly bombs for fighter-bombers), and theater weapons (mainly missiles of trans-European range)—that places a special stress on the politics of the European allies, because in being forced to think of those weapons they are confronted by the strategic predicament that they strive so greatly to forget: An alliance which relies for its protection more on deterrence than on defense obtains security more cheaply, but at a correspondingly greater risk of catastrophe. In due course, the fruits of the new American policy should greatly reassure European opinion, but in the meantime costs, risks, and stresses all increase—while the benefits of added security are not yet forthcoming.

If the Soviet leaders were still optimistic about the long-term future of their system they could therefore see advantageous prospects in Europe, and elsewhere too for that matter. In east Asia, the fundamental poverty of China guarantees an equally fundamental military weakness, and this in turn keeps open the possibility of forcing by threats a reversal of Chinese policy, from hostility to conciliation. Certainly there is no solid base of security for Chinese foreign policy, which constantly affronts and provokes the Soviet Union even while having no adequate shield of deterrence or defense. Chinese nuclear weapons, the dense population of the eastern rim, and the *de facto* American alliance can all provide some degree of security; but they cannot suffice to protect the vast and scarcely populated Chinese hinterland, where no serious guerrilla resistance would be feasible, which American conventional strength could hardly reach, and whose (nonnuclear) invasion could never warrant nuclear retaliation upon Soviet cities. In the meantime, the basic conditions that make Chinese politics so unstable will continue in being. Optimistic Soviet observers may thus calculate that sooner or later a leadership less ill-disposed to the Soviet Union will emerge in Beijing, if only because the present opening to the West entails cultural intrusions that must in some degree erode the very foundations of China's totalitarianism.

Soviet leaders who were still optimistic could also see ample opportunities in the rest of east Asia, for each country of that region is poor or insecure or internally unstable or all of those things. Japan is the exception, but even in her case it is clear enough that the continued industrial evolution of that country on present lines is unlikely, for it would eventually lead to the elimination of the entire industry of the United States and Western Europe—a thing most unlikely to be tolerated. And it is only the Soviet Union that offers an alternative as a potential large-scale buyer of both consumer and producer goods, in exchange for raw materials, including perhaps oil and gas reexported from the Middle East.

And so the survey could go on, from country to country and region to region, to find everywhere causes of weakness and disarray which afford scope for a Soviet diplomacy which offers security and support to its clients and which presents a many-sided threat to those who resist its offer.

But to sustain optimism about the long-term competition with the United States and about the international scene more generally, the Soviet leadership must first remain optimistic about the future of its own system. Mankind has a great capacity to remain in a state of optimism even in circumstances most adverse, but it is difficult to see how Andropov or his proximate successor in the Kremlin (if there is one) can remain optimistic about the future of the regime. The Soviet economy is perceptibly falling behind, and the entire demographic base is changing in a way that is ultimately incompatible with the continued Russian domination.

The members of the gerontocracy who ruled the Soviet Union with Brezhnev at their head could be excused if they failed to see what lies ahead for the Soviet system. The old men of the Kremlin who could look back on the astonishing rise of Soviet fortunes must have found it very hard to see the future in a gloomy light. Their very long careers began during the grim terror of the purges; they survived the sinister tragedy of Hitler's war, in which the fortunate among the Soviet population survived in extreme misery and semi-starvation, while those less fortunate died by the million. Men who must have vividly remembered the phenomenal hardships of those years could hardly be greatly worried by the diminishing rate of increase in Soviet per capita consumption.[1] Men who lived through the days when German guns could be heard in the streets of Moscow would scarcely be alarmed by the danger of some fractional increase in Belgian defense budgets, nor even by the greater fact that the Soviet Union now confronts the possibility of a Sino–

American alliance in addition to the old Euro–American alliance. Nor would men who once solved nationality problems by deporting entire peoples see much to fear even in the relentless demographic change that is steadily increasing the proportion of the most intractable nationalities. Above all, old men who saw the Soviet economy recover from the devastation of a war unusually destructive to yield a modest prosperity, as well as a spectacular growth in armaments, were unlikely to be greatly alarmed by obscure phenomena such as the declining rate of growth of labor productivity. Although Andropov is scarcely much younger, he may have a different view—and may act upon it if he should survive in power.

In any case, harsh facts ignored do not disappear, and the ills of the Soviet economy and of Soviet society are becoming steadily more acute. As the products which the Soviet economy must produce become more varied and more complex, as innovation imposes change at an accelerating rate, central planning in the Soviet style accomplished by mandatory production quotas is less and less effective. That much was already publicly acknowledged by authorized Soviet economic experts as long as two decades ago; since then there have been many administrative reforms and all sorts of incentive schemes, but those efforts have failed, since the central planning mechanism ("Gosplan") remains the economy's controlling brain. Soviet economic experts certainly know full well by now that dynamic entrepreneurship and efficient management (the missing elements) cannot coexist with planning that specifies very exactly all output targets and all prices. It is obvious enough that the system cannot provide a sufficient reward for the dynamic entrepreneur or the efficient manager; it is the obedient administrator who lives best in the world that planning makes, and that is what the system gets.

We may therefore be sure that if the Gosplan's mandatory planning system has not been abolished it is for a very good reason, namely that the Party's power structure requires its preservation. So long as the official ideology remained a strong force in Soviet life, the Party's mass of middle-ranking officials could be well employed as the keepers and teachers of the ideology. But in the modern Soviet Union the official ideology is no longer a live body of guiding ideas, in constant need of reinterpretation and propagation. Now fossilized, Marxism–Leninism has become instead an official religion, since its propositions have become dogmas; Soviet Marxism–Leninism now has its ceremonies, rituals, and idols, chiefly the figure of Lenin himself—whose bust presides over all schoolrooms, offices, and places of public assembly. But if the ideology has become dogmatic religion, the Party could not likewise become a priesthood. The tens of thousands of officials who make up the base of the Party's power structure could only retain their importance by finding nonideological roles for themselves—and they have, as managers. It is they who are the directors of factories and farms, the managers of wholesale agencies and retail shops, the heads of service enterprises, design bureaus, and research centers; and then of course they fill the ranks of the gigantic economic bureaucracy, with its double structure of "all-Union" and republic ministries.

Some of those men and women are no doubt talented professionals, eager to emulate the best of Western standards, who would much prefer to be free to act on their own instead of being captive to the central planning process. But many more, inevitably, are essentially political hacks who have risen to managerial status because of their standing in the Party. For them, the plan is not an unwelcome straitjacket but rather the essential guarantee of their ability to cope. Since they lack the talents of the entrepreneur, since they could not possibly be efficient as managers, their professional survival depends on the preservation of the present system, which rewards the obedient administrator, gives only small incentives for efficiency, and offers no compensation for the risks that the true entrepreneur must face.

Since the entire power structure of the Soviet Union is based on the allegiance of the mass of middle-ranking officials, it is the imperative priority of regime survival that prohibits any drastic economic reform. And yet without a liberalization true and wide, there can be no escape from the circumstances that result in the declining effectiveness of the Soviet economy. Actually superior to any free enterprise system in a warlike environment in which the goal is the supply of a few essentials for civilians and the maximum output of a fully specified range of products for the armed forces, and still able to sustain military innovation in all circumstances (the aviation design bureaus, for example, operate in a competitive fashion), the Soviet economy becomes less and less effective as its setting is further and further removed from that of a war economy.

There is therefore every reason to believe that the decline in the *relative* effectiveness of the Soviet economy will simply continue. It is not that its total output will decline or even fail to keep up with, say, the American GNP, but rather that its output will consist more and more of the wrong products, that is, outdated products—a phenomenon long manifest in sectors of rapid innovation, such as computer technology or female fashions.

This being the case, the regime's increasing reliance on the appeal of Russian nationalism is politically the right course to follow—at least in the short term—because it is precisely the Russians who must feel the greatest sense of economic deprivation, since they compare themselves with West Europeans. The increasing proportion of Central Asians must by contrast feel the least sense of relative deprivation, since they compare themselves with their counterparts across the near borders in Turkey, Iran, Afghanistan, and China. But in the long run it is inevitable that the license given to Russian nationalism will stimulate the responsive self-assertion of the other nationalities, including the Central Asian nations, and that in turn must eventually erode the very basis of the Soviet order.

A more immediate link between the nationalities question and the economic problem is the increasing role of Central Asians in the labor force, which imposes a dilemma between bringing Central Asian workers into the established centers of industry—with the certainty of thereby increasing ethnic frictions—and the building of new industries in Central Asia, which would entail the greater long-run risk of increasing the economic power of the Asian republics. In fact, to channel new investments to Soviet Central Asia would assure the decline of the Russian-dominated centers of established industry, a course that must be politically unacceptable to a Russian-based regime.

The complex of internal problems facing the new Soviet leadership may seem deceptively similar to the economic and demographic problems now so vividly manifest in the West, namely slow growth, the "guest-worker" problem of Europe, illegal immigration for the United States, and the decline of the traditional industries of the northeast United States, Belgium, northeast France, Britain, and the Ruhr. The very great difference is that in the Soviet case the imperatives of regime survival deny "natural" solutions which, however painfully, lead to a gradual adjustment of economy and society.

If Andropov or any other new leaders of the Soviet Union are already possessed of a whole battery of novel ideas until now concealed from us, or alternatively if they are willing to carry out a whole new revolution by disestablishing the Party from the economy and restoring transnationalism in word and deed, they may remain optimistic. Otherwise, it is difficult to imagine how they can view the long-term future of the Soviet system with confidence.

## Military Optimism and Its Consequences

In what follows, the long-term pessimism of the Kremlin leadership is not assumed as fact but merely put forward as theory. Quite separately, it is argued that—also for the first time—Soviet leaders old and new have *operational confidence* in their armed forces, specifically that they now have good reason to believe that the Soviet armed forces can execute offensive operations with speed and precision, to win clean victories in short order against a variety of potential enemies in a variety of settings—so long as the risk of a nuclear reaction by the victim is low and the Soviet forces themselves do not need to employ nuclear weapons to accomplish their goals. This great change alone suffices to increase the risk of war by choice, which is inherent in a great military empire that rightly sees itself as encircled by enemies, some of which are very vulnerable.

To the extent that the notion of long-term Soviet pessimism is accepted, a correspondingly higher estimate must be made of the risks that the leaders of the Soviet Union might accept in their never-ending quest for total security. For it is notorious that the conjunction of a long-term regime pessimism with current military optimism is the classic condition that makes deliberate war more likely. Even in the presence of tempting opportunities, leaders optimistic about the long-term future of their regime will not willingly choose to go to war, because they expect that their strength will only become greater in the future. That of course was the condition of the Soviet Union until very recently. Again, leaders who lack confidence in the ability of their armed forces to carry out offensive operations reliably and well will not start wars either; rare indeed is the leader who in the end goes to war by deliberate choice fully expecting that the struggle will be costly, long, and of uncertain result. But when leaders are pessimistic about the long-term future of their regimes and at the same time have high confidence in the strength and ability of their armed forces, then all that they know and all that they fear will conspire to induce them to use their military power while it still retains its presumed superiority. Only thus can today's strength be exploited to improve the prospects for a future which seems unfavorable. To convert a transitory military advantage into a permanent gain of security for the regime, there must be some profitable war in prospect. Profitable wars were rare even before the nuclear age, but once the urgency to act before it is too late is strongly felt, men will easily persuade themselves of the high likelihood of victory, of its small cost, and of its great benefits. It was under such a pressure that Germany accepted the Hapsburg call to go to war in 1914, and an unfavorable future was Hitler's best justification for going to war in 1939—although characteristically it was his own mortality that Hitler invoked to explain the urgency of war. More seriously, it was the gloomy prospect of the loss of empire, in conjunction with high military confidence (and a fatal misreading of the American temper) that drove the Japanese to their Pearl Harbor decision in 1941.

Quite naturally, the opinions of most Western observers of Soviet conduct were based on the behavior of a Soviet Union that was perhaps expansionist, but essentially nonaggressive and, above all, always prudent. That indeed was the conduct that could be expected from a regime that was both optimistic of its long-run future and also sceptical of its current military strength. It is understandable that this opinion should persist: To confuse prudence imposed by circumstances with restraint inherent in the very nature of the regime is easy enough, since the conditions that made the Soviet leaders greatly reluctant to accept risks persisted for so long, year after year, decade after decade. But if the theory of regime pessimism and the further claim that the Soviet leaders now have operational confidence in their armed forces are both accepted, it follows directly that a radically different pattern of Soviet external conduct is now unfolding before us—a pattern to which the invasion of Afghanistan already belongs.

Many intellectual reputations and much political capital are invested in the notion of a Soviet Union fundamentally nonaggressive. We must therefore suspect the eagerness with which many specialists invented *ad hoc* explanations to reconcile the invasion of Afghanistan with their model of a defensive and prudent Soviet Union. In the perspective of eternity such opinions may of course turn out to have been right—and not merely in the trivial sense that all expansion can always be explained away as prudential and defensive—but it is here argued that they are wrong, and indeed that the new phase of Soviet imperial strategy had emerged several years before the invasion of Afghanistan. The debate must continue, but the possibility that Soviet conduct is being considered on a basis of outdated assumptions should at least be seriously examined.

# Note

[1]A 5% annual growth over 1966–1970, but only 2.9% in 1971–1975 and less than that in the years since. *Soviet Economy in a Time of Change*, vol. 1 (U.S. Government Printing Office, 1979), Table 4, p. 768.

# 5

# STEPHEN F. COHEN

## Soviet Domestic Politics and Foreign Policy*

Soviet Russia has been on our minds—a virtual obsession—for exactly 60 years. During these 60 years, far more has changed in the Soviet Union, and in the world, than in our perceptions and ideas. Even now, as a new American debate on Soviet domestic and foreign policy unfolds, it seems clear that much of our thinking still bears deep traces of that narrow consensus once admired as "bipartisanship," and that in many quarters cold-war attitudes and misconceptions are as firmly lodged as ever. This should alarm us, not only because of the sterile foreign policies this kind of thinking once produced, but because of the way these cold-war attitudes have distorted our own domestic values and priorities.

Any rethinking about Soviet intentions and behavior abroad must begin with an understanding of Soviet domestic politics and society. Indeed, American thinking about Soviet foreign policy over the years has almost always emphasized this connection; and, by the same token, most of our misconceptions of Soviet intentions abroad have derived from misconceptions of the character and direction of Soviet domestic factors. In particular, the tenacious view of a continuously revolutionary and militantly expansionist Soviet Union, a view that dominated American thinking for so long and has now, after a short decline, reappeared in opposition to détente, is based on a static, ahistorical image of a fundamentally unchanged and unchanging Soviet system. Just as observed alterations in Soviet foreign policy are dismissed, in this view, as merely tactical maneuvers in a relentless drive for world conquest, so too are internal changes said to be secondary to the basic continuities that determine the real nature of the Soviet Union and its intentions abroad.

*Reprinted by permission of the author from *Détente or Debacle: Common Sense in U.S.–Soviet Relations*, ed. Fred W. Neal (New York: Norton, 1979), pp. 11–28. This chapter is based on a statement made to a subcommittee of the U.S. House of Representatives' Committee on International Relations in October, 1977. Copyright 1977 by Stephen F. Cohen.

No informed person will deny that the Soviet political system continues to be a highly authoritarian and often repressive one, which systematically deprives its citizens of elementary political liberties, or that the USSR is a formidable international adversary with great power ambitions around the world. Nor will a careful student any longer argue either of two once-popular extremes—that there is an immutable irreconcilability between the Soviet Union and the United States; or, on the other hand, that modern history is somehow moving toward a "convergence" between the two systems. The rejection of these two excessive perspectives should be our starting point, the minimal consensus from which different perspectives proceed. Beyond this, however, there is an almost unlimited potential for disagreement among knowledgeable people.

We have learned a great deal about Soviet life in recent years, but this knowledge has demonstrated mainly that none of our conceptions or models of the Soviet Union are adequate—that all are far too simplistic. The main thing we have learned is that behind the crumbling facade of political and social conformity, there is a tremendous diversity and complexity of reality at every level of Soviet life. Students of Soviet economics, for example, have begun to speak less of an omnipotent centralized planned economy and more of a "multicolored" economy of official and unofficial components, state and private enterprises, controlled and free transactions, of red, white, grey, and black markets.[1] We need the same kind of "multicolored" approach to Soviet reality in general, which conforms as little to our models as it does to official Soviet ones, whether we are discussing the high politics of the Communist Party or the everyday life of ordinary citizens.

In this connection, I want to make four very general points about Soviet politics and society. They concern realities often obscured but which influence Soviet intentions and behavior abroad in important ways. First, the history of the Soviet Union provides many examples of internal change, and there is no reason to exclude the possibility of further change in the future. Second, the Soviet leadership today faces—as will its successor—an array of serious domestic and foreign problems; and while these problems should not be construed as crises that seriously enfeeble or endanger the system, neither should they be minimized. Third, there is within both Soviet society and the establishment itself a great diversity of opinion, political outlook, and proposed solutions to these problems. And fourth, this diversity of opinion must nonetheless be understood in the general context of a deep rooted political and social conservatism, which is widespread among Soviet officials and ordinary citizens alike.

## Change in the Soviet System

To understand that Soviet history has witnessed periodic and far-reaching internal changes is to reject the popular view of an immutable Soviet system. The fact that the main institutions of the political system—the Communist Party, the official Marxist–Leninist ideology, the planned state economy, the political police, and so forth—have continued to exist over the years says little. It is a commonplace of political history that deep changes in the working and nature of a political system often occur within a continuous institutional framework, and in this process the institutions themselves are inwardly changed. The American Presidency and the English Parliament continue to exist; but they are not the same institutions they were in the nineteenth century. Nor do the American and English political systems function just as they did 100 years ago. Even the names that historians customarily give to the main periods in Soviet political history bespeak the deep changes that have recurred since 1917: War Communism, the New Economic Policy, Stalinization, de-Stalinization.

The most recent of these great changes in the Soviet Union must be kept in mind when we talk about the present and the future. Our focus on the continuing authoritarianism and political abuses in the Soviet Union obscures the fact that during the Khrushchev years there occurred in that country an authentic political and social reformation. Virtually every area of Soviet life was affected by the changes, however contradictory and ultimately limited, of 1953–1964, from the end of mass terror and freeing of millions of prison camp victims, the measures introduced to limit at least some of the worst bureaucratic abuses and privileges, the civic awakening and growing political participation of educated society, and the array of economic and welfare reforms, to revisions in Soviet foreign policy that led to what we now call détente.

For our own thinking, the significance of this reformation (sometimes called de-Stalinization), which changed the Soviet Union for the better in many fundamental ways, is threefold. First, it reminds us that current Soviet abuses of power and violations of civil rights, however deplorable, are far more limited and less severe than in the Stalinist past. Second, it is evidence that a short time ago there existed inside the Soviet Union, within the Soviet political establishment, and apart from international pressures, significant forces for reform. There is no reason to assume that such forces do not still exist. And third, it helps us to understand the conservative reaction that followed the overthrow of Khrushchev in 1964 and continues today. In another society, this reaction would be considered normal. In American and English politics, for example, it is thought to be virtually axiomatic that periods of reform are followed by conservative backlashes.

Some of the major problems faced by the Soviet leadership today are common to industrial societies, but many are the direct legacy of Soviet historical development, the limitations of the reforms of 1953–1964, and the conservative reaction after 1964. Western specialists disagree as to which problems are the most serious, much depending on the specialist's own interests. Suffice it to itemize a few that Soviet citizens themselves emphasize.

At home, there is a chronic decline in industrial and technological development and persistently low labor productivity; a collective agricultural system which still cannot reliably feed the population; widespread consumer grumbling and housing shortages; a politically restive intellectual class; disenchantment with official values among young people; growing birth rates and nationalist sentiments among the major non-Slav groups, and a declining birth rate among Russians; a small but defiant dissident movement along with a large readership of uncensored (*samizdat*) literature; and, in the realm of political authority, the still unresolved, and pertinent, question of the terrible crimes of the Stalin era. More generally, I would stress the overarching administrative problem of a centralized bureaucratic system created in the very different conditions of the 1930s, which still prevails in all areas of Soviet life—political, economic, social, cultural, scientific—and which generates and institutionalizes a multitude of inefficiencies, Catch 22s, and popular resentments. On another level, I would stress the manifestations of rampant alcoholism and family disintegration, and, from the party's viewpoint, the revival of religious belief, because they reflect or impinge upon so many other problems.

At the same time, the Soviet leadership, for all its gains as a great power since 1945, can find little solace in foreign policy achievements. There is the perceived menace of China; the recalcitrant empire in Eastern Europe, which has been the scene of a major crisis every decade; the advent in Western Europe of so-called Eurocommunist parties, whose success threatens to complete the de-Russification of international communism; the familiar problem of Third-World "allies," who become fickle or difficult to control, as in Egypt and India; and the staggering costs of a global competition, however peaceful, with the United States.

The main thing to be said about these problems is not that they portend an imminent crisis, but that they represent long-term and hopelessly intertwined dilemmas and impose severe constraints on domestic and foreign policy, and that there is no real majority view as to their solution.[2] In part, this is because no majority consensus has been allowed to develop through an uncensored public discussion. But, equally, it is because of the deep divisions on every major issue and problem, even among Soviet officials and party members.

For many years, misled by the silence and conformity imposed by Stalin's terror, we imagined something that did not exist—a homogeneous Soviet officialdom and even society. The complex reality is now clear: The diversity of Soviet opinion is probably equal to that in any "open" society (though more private, of course), ranging from orthodox Marxism–Leninism to Russian Orthodox religion, from democratic to authoritarian, liberal to neofascist, from left to right. More important for our purposes, variations of this diversity exist within the political establishment and even inside the ruling Communist Party.

This will surprise those who take seriously official claims of a "monolithic" party, who continue to speak meaninglessly of "the Soviets," "the Communist mind," and "ideological blueprints," and who imagine an unbridgeable gulf between the party-state and society-at-large. In fact, it may be that a monopolistic political party inescapably acquires a more diverse membership than do parties in multiparty systems simply because there is no organized alternative.[3] Whatever the case, it makes no sense to think of the Communist Party, with its more than 15 million members, or the Soviet state, which employs virtually the entire population, as somehow remote or apart from society. At the very least, we must understand that while the party-state seeks to direct and control society, it is permeated by the diverse, conflicting attitudes of that society.

It is in this context that we can gain a better perspective on the dissident movement, which has come to figure so prominently in American thinking and, alas, is in danger of becoming the hostage of our foreign policy. Western specialists have trouble reconciling two seemingly contradictory truths. On the one hand, we know that the emergence and persistence of open dissent is an important development in Soviet history. On the other hand, we know that the active dissidents are very small in numbers and political impact.

How can we reconcile these truths? By realizing, I think, that most of the different trends of thought expressed openly by dissidents are to be found, in at least some subterranean form, within Soviet officialdom. This does not mean that dissident activists are spokesmen for real or potential oppositionists inside the establishment, but simply that dissident views reflect in significant measure, however obliquely, the array, and disarray of attitudes among officials as well.

Most important for our thinking about future Soviet and American policy are the competing political trends inside the Communist Party, and particularly at its middle and upper levels. Our knowledge here is imprecise, and this advises caution and against speculation. But it is safe to say that the three main trends, which have formed and struggled over the past 25 years, may be termed reformist, conservative, and reactionary or neo-Stalinist.[4] I use these terms loosely to designate amalgams of party opinion, not single-minded groupings.

Party reformers, who are certainly now the weakest in number and influence, include some advocates of authentic democratization, but many more administrators, managers, or technocrats who only want more initiative, and hence some liberalization, in their own areas of responsibility, be it the economy, science, culture, or international affairs. The conservatives, who have predominated almost everywhere in Soviet politics since the mid-1960s, also include various types, from sincere believers in the virtues of the status quo to cynical defenders of vested bureaucratic interests. Some lean toward the moderate reformers, some toward the neo-Stalinists. The party's neo-Stalinist wing can only be called reactionary. Its solutions to contemporary problems are couched in an extreme Russian chauvinism and nostalgia for the more despotic ways of the Stalin days, though short of the mass terror which, as they know, victimized Soviet officials capriciously, regardless of political outlook.

Although these party trends are part of the power struggles that range more or less continuously across all the important policy areas, it would be wrong to think that they have nothing in common. All are proud of the Soviet Union's achievements at home and abroad, nationalistic and patriotic in one way or another, loyal to the party system, and, to take a specific example, fearful about China. Nor are they incapable of collaboration in various areas of policymaking. Like politics elsewhere, much of Soviet politics involves compromises and coalitions. Most reformers and conservatives seem now to favor, for example, détente and expanding economic relations with the West, though for different reasons; reformers hope détente will promote economic reform at home, while conservatives hope it will enable them to avoid it. At the same time, there has been a growing conservative–neo–Stalinist coalition in cultural and intellectual policy in recent years.

Future change in the Soviet Union will depend in large measure on the struggle between these trends in the party. Change can be for the better or the worse, of course, toward liberalization or back toward a harsher authoritarianism. Since its inception in 1964, and especially since 1966–1968, the conservative or centrist Brezhnev government has turned increasingly toward the party's neo-Stalinist wing, particularly in domestic affairs. The bleak prospect of still greater neo-Stalinist influence, or even a leadership dominated by these party elements, cannot be excluded. I personally, however, have not yet succumbed to the chronic pessimism that seems eventually to come over many Western specialists on the Soviet Union. I do not rule out the possibility of another wave of reform, during or in the aftermath of a leadership succession.

## Soviet Reform and Conservatism

Any genuine reform requires, however, two conditions, both of which concern us. First, it must be reform with a Soviet face. Those among us who argue that Soviet reform must be patterned on Western examples or imposed from abroad understand little about Russia or the process of reform in general. No reform movement anywhere, but especially in a country as historically self-conscious as the Soviet Union, can be successful estranged from its own history and culture. It must find inspiration, roots, and ultimately legitimacy within its native—in this case, Russian and Soviet—political and historical traditions. A Soviet reformism couched in Westernism, or encumbered by foreign sponsors, would be tainted and doomed. For this reason alone, the best hope are those Soviet innovators who reason in terms of the existing system, whether they call themselves liberal socialists, communist reformers, democratic Marxist–Leninists, or simply doers of small deeds, and not those who repudiate the whole Soviet experience since 1917.

Second, much will depend upon the international environment, and thus American policy and behavior. Soviet reform has a chance only in conditions of a progressive relaxation of tensions between the USSR and its foreign adversaries. Worsening international relations will drive the Soviet Union back into her isolation and past, strengthening reactionaries and further diminishing reformers of all stripes. Or to take a different example, a complete break between the Soviet Communist Party and the Eurocommunist parties of Italy, France, and Spain would be an unfortunate development. These European parties have been a source of some restraint and liberal influence on the Soviet leadership, and a break would only further reduce this kind of Western influence and strengthen hard-line tendencies in the Soviet Union.

If this perspective on the future is one of guarded optimism, my last general point about the Soviet domestic scene is different. Despite the diversity of Soviet opinion, the predominant outlook, again both among officials and ordinary citizens, is a profound conservatism. This conservatism is strongest, of course, among the older generation, which still dominates middle and upper levels of officialdom, but it also appears to play a role in the attitudes of the younger generations.

By "Soviet conservatism" I mean the everyday gut sentiments that characterize social and political conservatism elsewhere, including in our own country. It is a deep sentimentality about one's own past, about the commonplace and familiar, an instinctive preference for existing routines and orthodoxies (however obsolete), and a fear of things new as somehow threatening and potentially chaotic. Politically, it is not always a flat rejection of any change; but it is an almost prohibitive insistence that change be very slow, tightly controlled, based on "law and order" (which is also a Soviet catchphrase) lest "things will be worse," and hence it is an instinctive, though often conditional, deference to political authorities that guard the present against the future, including the armed forces and the police.

That a system born in revolution and still professing revolutionary ideas should have become one of the most conservative in the world may seem preposterous. But history has witnessed other such transformations, as well as the frequent deradicalization of revolutionary ideologies.[5] Moreover, there are specific, and mutually reinforcing, sources of this Soviet conservatism. All of those factors variously said to be the most important in Soviet politics have contributed to it: the bureaucratic tradition of Russian government before the revolution; the subsequent bureaucratization of Soviet life, which proliferated conservative norms and created an entrenched class of zealous defenders of bureaucratic status and privilege; the geriatric nature of the present-day elite; and even the official ideology, whose thrust turned many years ago from the creation of a new social order to extolling the existing one.

Underlying all the factors making for Soviet conservatism is the Soviet historical experience, which is still for a great many citizens the story of their own lives. If few nations have achieved so much in so short a time, none has suffered such a traumatic history. In 60 years, man-made catastrophes have repeatedly victimized millions of Soviet citizens—the first European war, revolution, civil war, two great famines, forcible collectivization, Stalin's great terror, World War II. Every family has lost someone dear, often more than once. These memories live with an intensity that is hard for us to imagine. The victims have often been the essential elite of any nation's progress—the young, the strong, the enterprising, the gifted. No less remarkable than the Soviet Union's achievements is the fact that they were accomplished in the face of these colossal losses. Out of this experience in living memory have developed the underlying joint pillars of Soviet conservatism—a sense of great national pride and earned prestige from the achievements, together with an anxiety that the next disaster forever looms and must be guarded against.

Because we are slow to recognize this conservatism, we have yet to calculate fully its influence on Soviet domestic or foreign politics. At home, it is an important bond—a truly collective sentiment—between the government and the majority of the people. It affects all areas of policymaking, all segments of the population, high and low, and even political dissidents, who fear international turmoil as much as they object to the government.

Its influence on foreign policy cannot be easily exaggerated. Above all, this conservatism informs Soviet leaders' acute sense of national prestige, a crucial element in their outlook obscured by our rival notions that they are either aggressive ideologues or cynical realists. When offended, this prestige factor can cause them to postpone, or even jettison, international relations that they otherwise desire, be it economic, trade, or arms limitation agreements. On the other hand, when they perceive a ratification of Soviet prestige and status, it can lead them to join in international agreements that included provisions not to their liking, such as the Helsinki accords of 1975.

To put this differently, we usually discuss Soviet policy in military terms of "strategic parity." This is important, of course. But the larger Soviet striving in recent times has been for political parity, equal respect as the other superpower—full recognition of its achievements and rightful place in the world. As with the United States, this striving means both conserving and where possible enhancing the Soviet Union's status in a changing world. It is manifest in the Soviet infatuation with traditional diplomatic protocol, global meddling, and obsessive counting of everything from Olympic medals to strategic weapons. And nothing is more insulting than persistent suggestions in the West that the achievements and power status of the Soviet Union are somehow illegitimate.

Righteous indignation about foreign "interference in our internal affairs" is often a hypocritical dodge. But when a Soviet official complains, to take a recent example, that "James Carter has assumed the role of mentor to the USSR,"[6] we hear the voice of hurt pride and genuine resentment. The "surprising adverse reaction in the Soviet Union to our stand on human rights," which President Carter now acknowledges, should have surprised no one. It proved to be "a greater obstacle to other friendly pursuits, common goals, like in SALT, than [President Carter] had anticipated"[7] because, contrary to American spokesmen, there was for Soviet leaders a "linkage." Perceiving a direct affront to their self-esteem, they reacted—as they did when confronted by the Jackson–Vanik and Stevenson Amendments in 1974— accordingly, and predictably.

The ways that this conservatism can influence Soviet behavior are too numerous to explore here. A last example must suffice. American critics of détente and SALT see aggressive military intentions in the circumstance that "Americans think in terms of deterring war almost exclusively. The Soviet leaders think much more of what might happen in such a war."[8] Given the Soviet unpreparedness and loss of perhaps 20 million people in the last war, we should be surprised if it were otherwise. Indeed, a Soviet government that did not make some efforts in this direction, for example, the civilian defense programs in which our anti-détente lobby sees such ominous implications, would hardly be a Soviet government at all.

## No Alternative to Détente

What does all this tell us more concretely about Soviet foreign policy and prescribe for American policy? For me there is no sane or moral or otherwise desirable alternative to what is now called, somewhat loosely, détente. If we begin with the simplest literal meaning of the word—a relaxation of historical tensions between Washington and Moscow—and with its foremost objective—a reduction of the possibilities of war through strategic arms control—the alternative, an "Era II of the Cold War," is plainly unacceptable in the nuclear age. Those Americans, and their Soviet counterparts, who insist that détente is a "one-way street," that "we have nothing to gain from it," or that the two countries share no basic interests, should say openly that they prefer a world of escalating arms races, nuclear proliferation, and mounting risks of mutual destruction by design or mishap.

Reducing the risks of nuclear war is the first, indispensable, and irreproachable reason for détente. There is, however, even among its American (and Soviet) advocates, a spectrum of thinking about the desirable nature and scope of détente. Some advocate a narrow policy centered almost exclusively on military issues. While this position is preferable to the flatly anti-détente one, it is one-dimensional and unrealistic. Cooperation in the area of military safeguards is inseparable from broader forms of cooperation that promote stable relations between the two countries. I favor a policy of détente that can go beyond relaxation of tensions to full relations on all levels, but one consistent with intractable realities and free of extravagant expectations. For this we need an understanding of détente considerably broader than today's events.

Just as the history of the cold war did not begin in 1947–1948, but in 1917, what we now call détente did not begin in 1972. Leaving aside early milestones such as our belated recognition of the Soviet Union in 1933, the contemporary history of détente began in the Eisenhower–Khrushchev era, and not with the Nixon–Brezhnev phase. In short, détente is a historical process with previous stages of development that include both progress and setbacks. At different stages, quite different issues have been in the forefront and have defined the status of détente at the time—pullbacks from military confrontation, cultural exchanges, summitry, Berlin, Cuba, the Middle East, arms talks, trade, Jewish emigration, human rights.

It is therefore essential that détente as an ongoing and future process not be understood as something ultimately determined by one or more current events. This kind of political gimmickry, practiced sometimes by the opponents of détente as well as Nixon–Kissinger proponents of détente, can only produce unrealistic expectations and needless disillusionment, as we are now witnessing. A durable détente policy must be both historical and long-sighted.

Even in the best circumstances, there will be tough bargaining, resentment, serious misunderstandings, sharp disagreements, and open conflicts of national interests between the United States and the USSR. The goal is to reduce these elements progressively at each stage. We are, after all, talking about "détente" between long-standing rivals with very different social systems, political traditions, and orthodoxies, and not about Anglo–American relations. To imagine that these differences will disappear, or even diminish notably, in an appointed time because of proclamations is dangerous nonsense.[9] To promise détente without conflict, or to reject détente because of the conflict, is silly illogic. It is like saying that the job of diplomacy is only to formalize what already unites nations, and not to reconcile what divides them.

Two primary conditions for a progressively broadening détente are already present. First, there are substantial domestic forces for détente in both countries, despite parallel controversies about its dangers, strong opposition, and fluctuating internal conditions. Alarmist warnings about secret Soviet "intentions" and strategic "blueprints" fly in the face of the realities. Escalating military expenditures, the danger of mutual destruction, economic problems, and other domestic factors have brought a sizable part even of the conservative Soviet establishment away from old autarkic habits to acceptance of fuller relations with the West.

In other words, the main thrust of Soviet conservatism today is to preserve what it already has at home and abroad, not to jeopardize it. A conservative government is, of course, capable of dangerous militaristic actions, as we saw in Czechoslovakia and Vietnam; but these are acts of imperial protectionism, a kind of defensive militarism, not a revolutionary or aggrandizing one. It is certainly true that for most Soviet leaders, as presumably for most American leaders, détente is not an altruistic endeavor but the pursuit of national interests. In one sense, this is sad. But it is probably also true that mutual self-interest provides a more durable basis for détente than lofty, and finally empty, altruism.

The second existing condition is a shared philosophy of détente. Both sides now officially define détente as including both cooperation and competition, in peaceful conditions, between the two countries. If cooperation through SALT eliminates or significantly reduces military competition, we have no reason to fear the other kinds of competition, assuming we have confidence in our system. If American business firms cannot be allowed to trade freely with Soviet agencies, it speaks poorly for the capitalism the United States claims to profess. If the Soviet leadership's refusal to give up what it calls "ideological struggle," which so alarms our critics of détente, deters us, this speaks poorly for our own ideology, which emphasizes the virtue of conflicting ideas.

Without exaggerating or blinking away the competitive and conflictual aspects, we should pursue the cooperative component of détente vigorously and imaginatively. Global areas of cooperation, such as strategic arms control, ecology, and food shortages, may require protracted negotiations and the participation of other nations. But there is a wide range of immediate opportunities for fuller bilateral relations in the areas of trade, education, culture, science, sports, and tourism, to name a few.

Détente is too important to be left to governments alone. A variety of nongovernmental American organizations and citizens have been pursuing these kinds of relations, sometimes in the face of official American indifference and even obstructionism, for many years. They should be encouraged, and their ideas and expertise solicited, so that détente will become not merely fuller government-to-government relations, but institution-to-institution, profession-to-profession, citizen-to-citizen relations, both as a buffer against leadership changes in both countries and as a way of building popular support here and in the Soviet Union. Meanwhile, the American government should make its own direct contribution by, among other things, promoting trade by granting to the Soviet Union favorable tariff and credit provisions,[10] funding larger and more diverse exchanges of people, and pressing for liberalized entry-visa procedures and fewer travel restrictions in both countries.

American policy alone cannot, of course, guarantee the future of détente. This requires no less a pro-détente Soviet leadership with sufficient support in its own high establishment to withstand the inevitable setbacks in Soviet–American relations. And this returns us to the Soviet domestic scene.

Supporters of the Jackson–Vanik Amendment and other restrictions on détente have, so to speak, a half-idea. They argue, correctly, that the future of détente must be related to change inside the Soviet Union. Unfortunately, they seem not to understand that domestic change can also be for the worse, and that liberalizing change depends upon the respective political fortunes of trends and groups inside the Soviet establishment. These proponents of a kind of remote American interventionism in Soviet politics violate what should be our first axiom: We do not have the wisdom or the power, or the right, to try directly to shape change inside the Soviet Union.[11] Any foreign government that becomes deeply involved in Soviet international politics, or for that matter in Soviet emigré politics (whose many different "ambassadors" will continue to appeal to us), will do itself and others more harm than good.

What the United States can and should do is influence Soviet liberalization *indirectly* by developing a long-term American foreign policy, and thereby an international environment, that will strengthen reformist trends and undermine reactionary ones inside the Soviet Union. This means a further relaxation of tensions, increasing contacts on all levels, and drawing the Soviet Union into full, stable relations with the Western countries—in short, détente. This is not, in the lingering rhetoric of another generation, "appeasement." Such a policy allows for hard bargaining for our own national interests and private demands for certain kinds of Soviet behavior. But it is predicated on an American conduct that takes into account the nature of Soviet conservatism and is not calculated to offend needlessly the self-image and prestige of the Soviet establishment. Our new interventionists fail on all counts. Bombastic ultimatums, discriminatory congressional restrictions, and condescending preachments addressed publicly to the Soviet leadership offend the conservative majority, vivify the xenophobic prophecies of the reactionaries, and make meaningful reform suspect, if not impossible, as a concession to outside pressure.

## The "Human Rights" Campaign

This brings us, finally, to the issue of political rights[12] in the Soviet Union, which (for better or worse) has become a central focus in our current debate over détente. The question is terribly complex, even agonizing, especially for people with first-hand knowledge of the Soviet Union. And like other issues that are translated superficially into a Manichean choice between morality and immorality, it creates acrimonious divisions and false illusions.

Our own disagreements about American policy toward Soviet political rights should be among Americans equally committed to political liberties as a universal principle. The real question is not the validity of this principle, but whether specific American policies actually promote political liberties and safeguard dissent in the Soviet Union. There are, for example, knowledgeable Westerners who have had extensive contact with Soviet dissidents over the years, who admire them as courageous individuals and as representatives of a noble cause, but who have deep misgivings about recent American measures in this area. Furthermore, speaking for myself, it is fully consistent to want a larger moral aspect in American foreign policy, especially after our immoral and even criminal commissions in Vietnam and Chile, and still disapprove of certain American measures directed against Soviet violations of political rights. This does not reflect, as is sometimes charged, a bias in favor of left-wing dictatorships and against right-wing ones, but concern for the actual consequences of a specific policy.

American proponents of a hard-line policy exhort us to rally behind "our friends, the Soviet dissidents." But the Soviet dissident community is itself deeply divided into at least three groups on the question of American policy.[13] The larger group does insist that a tough American line on behalf of Soviet political rights has been, and will continue to be, only beneficial. They want more, and stronger, of the same. A second group acknowledges that recent American actions have caused the democratic movement setbacks and hardships, but insists that they will be beneficial in the long-run—how and when is left unclear. The third group argues that tougher American policies, from Senator Jackson's to President Carter's, have had, and can only have, a negative impact because, by going beyond diplomatic pressure to open confrontation, they galvanize Soviet conservative and reactionary opposition and jeopardize both active dissidents and reformers inside the Soviet system.

General references to "the Soviet dissidents" are therefore meaningless. Dissident opinion is far too diverse. Indeed, there are even Orthodox nationalist dissidents who dislike both détente and American interference in Soviet affairs. But even the numerical fact that most dissident activists want a hard-line American policy does not prove its wisdom. It reflects instead the fact that since 1972 many Soviet protesters have increasingly lost hope in internal sources of change and thus, for reasons of politics and morale, have looked increasingly to pressure from outside and specifically from the United States. We can understand this psychological development; but good sense tells us that it is bad for us and for them.

The proof is, as we say, in the pudding. President Carter's human rights campaign of early 1977 (insofar as it was directed at the Soviet Union), like earlier measures linking trade and détente to levels of Jewish emigration, has done more harm than good. It may be inexact to call President Carter's campaign a policy since, as Andrew Young has stated, it "was never really set down, thought out and planned."[14] It may even be that the campaign originated as much with domestic American political concerns.

Whatever the case, the "adverse reaction in the Soviet Union" was unanticipated. Though it is possible that a new Soviet crackdown on dissidents was planned even before President Carter took office, the nature and dimensions of the crackdown were made worse by American statements and actions. Each dramatic act of the Carter Administration's campaign—sharp warnings on behalf of Soviet dissidents in late January, the President's personal letter to Andrei Sakharov in early February, his White House meeting with exiled dissident Vladimir Bukovsky in early March—was followed by new acts of Soviet repression at home, from the arrests of Aleksandr Ginzburg and Yuri Orlov in February to the interrogation of American correspondent Robert Toth in June. We must see clearly what ensued—a dangerous game of political chicken, reminiscent of the cold war, played at the highest levels. ("We're not going to back down," declared President Carter.)[15] The victims were both our "common goals" and Soviet dissidents themselves.

Why did the Carter Administration's campaign become counterproductive? I do not think that the reason is to be found in the President's general statements on human rights and Helsinki. In signing these accords, the Soviet leadership must have reconciled itself to something along these lines, particularly from a new American administration, as part of the "ideological struggle." The reason was rather the way in which the campaign directly assaulted, even if only inadvertently, all those aspects of Soviet conservatism I discussed earlier. Two highly publicized episodes—the President's letter to Sakharov and the White House invitation to Bukovsky—are vivid examples.

The Carter campaign began in January 1977, and thus coincided with the sixtieth anniversary year of the Russian revolution, when Soviet conservatism and official self-esteem were in continuous celebration and at their most acute. The Administration's first statements and President Carter's letter then came on the heels of an extraordinary event and one of Sakharov's rare mistakes—his public suggestion that Soviet authorities themselves were responsible for the fatal bombing in a Moscow subway in early January. Scarcely any dissidents took this suggestion seriously, and Sakharov himself later seemed to regret it.[16] More important, the bombing was an exceptional event that greatly alarmed and embarrassed Soviet authorities. The decision to issue a Presidential statement on Soviet civil rights in the form of a letter to Sakharov on this unusual occasion was, to be kind, very bad judgment. Nothing could have been more offensive to official Soviet sensibilities or to have assured a stronger reaction. (It may also have confirmed doubts among some Soviet officials about the authenticity of American concern for Soviet political rights.)

The Bukovsky affair raises similar questions of judgment. In December 1976, the Soviet government exchanged Bukovsky, a defiant and brave dissident then in his eleventh year of prison camps and mental hospitals, for the jailed Chilean Communist leader Luis Corvalan. This, too, was an extraordinary development. The Soviet Union not only dealt equally with what it calls a "fascist dictatorship," it also acknowledged for the first time its own political prisoners. International publicity had made Bukovsky's personal fate an embarrassment. But it seems likely that the Soviet decision to risk its prestige in this dramatic way also had the larger purpose of weighing the feasibility, and political costs, of future agreements for the release of other Soviet prisoners.

Any such possibility was aborted, at least for the time, by President Carter's invitation to Bukovsky. Their meeting, which had the earmarks of a public relations coup against former President Ford's rebuff to Aleksandr Solzhenitsyn, allowed Bukovsky to denounce the Soviet government from the White House, implied that his release was a triumph of American policy, and thereby probably persuaded Soviet leaders that the political costs of such releases were too high. If our real concern is the plight of people, and not a propaganda victory, where is the morality in this outcome?

The same criticism applies to earlier American campaigns, culminating in the Jackson–Vanik Amendment of 1974, to make trade and détente dependent upon levels of Soviet Jewish emigration. The net effect was, as we know, to diminish that emigration considerably. But other questions were similarly ignored during the presidential primary season, when the issue of Jewish emigration came to the fore. Did the almost exclusive focus on Jews who wished to leave, with scant regard for other groups, reflect a moral commitment to the principle of open borders or the political power of Jewish lobbies in this country? How much thought was given to the frightful backlash that this campaign was certain to have on Soviet Jews who did not wish to emigrate? And how can monthly or annual quotas, and Soviet compliance, be determined when no one knows how many Jews actually want to leave?

The case against these kinds of short-sighted, highly publicized, and politically volatile campaigns that link American policy to specific events, issues, or prominent dissidents inside the Soviet Union is, I think, overwhelming. They involve us in complexities and ramifications beyond our control and in moral ambiguities beyond our resolution. Inside the United States, they encourage a revival of cold-war attitudes which could again distort our own domestic priorities, while undermining public support for détente. Internationally, they generate tensions and confrontations between Moscow and Washington detrimental to our mutual interests, endanger private concessions already granted by Soviet and East European authorities (in the area of family reunification, for example),[17] and, perhaps most important, they create an atmosphere unconducive to Soviet liberalization. Inside the Soviet Union, they arouse the conservative majority against American "interference," taint both dissidents and reformers as "Western agents," abet the party's neo-Stalinist wing, and further divide and misguide the dissident community.[18]

Indeed, the most ominous of recent Soviet reactions is neither the new arrests, which arguably would have come anyway, nor the setbacks in SALT negotiations, which after a decent interlude will move ahead, but the official Soviet campaign linking dissidents, and potentially any reformer, to the American government and specifically to the CIA. The emptiness of this charge is matched only by its grim revival of one of the worst themes of the Stalinist past. It seems to be, alas, a response to the Carter Administration's own campaign and plain evidence that the neo-Stalinists have gained new influence in Soviet affairs.[19]

## The Lessons To Be Learned

The lessons to be learned are not all negative. They teach us that whatever potential the American government has for influence on the Soviet leadership in the area of political rights must be exercised in private negotiations and not through public ultimatums, sermons, and other confrontations of national prestige. Since "quiet diplomacy" appears to have acquired a sinister connotation, let us call it simply "diplomacy."

The Soviet leadership wants détente and the various agreements that it encompasses. In the proper place and manner, American representatives, from the President to State Department officials, can and should make clear that American public support for these relations depends significantly upon the status of political rights in the Soviet Union. Modest concessions and achievements are possible, certainly at first in the areas of emigration and family reunification. Despite its abominations in other areas, the Nixon–Kissinger administration did in fact achieve a great deal in this way. If our purpose is to help people, why scorn it?

At the same time, the American government should push for fuller relations at all levels with the Soviet Union. Not only because this will promote a general international environment more conducive to Soviet liberalization, but because these diverse contacts create additional opportunities for direct influence. The Soviet Union has demonstrated its desire for expanded, regularized transactions with, for example,

American business, scientific, and other academic groups, which in turn gives these groups some influence on their Soviet counterparts and thus indirectly on Soviet policymakers.

Moreover, it is at this profession-to-profession level that outcries against specific violations of political rights can be most effective. A good example is the campaign on behalf of Academician Sakharov waged successfully by the American Academy of Sciences in 1973. An organized protest by a professional association and directed to its Soviet counterpart is more effective because it does not directly confront the Soviet government's prestige; it allows the Soviet leadership at least the fiction of referring the matter to a lesser Soviet body, and it thus draws a broader (and frequently more liberal) segment of Soviet officialdom into the deliberations. In brief, unlike official campaigns by the American President or Congress, it leaves room for concessions.

The final guideline simply reiterates the axiom I tried to formulate earlier. Any policies that involve the American government deeply in the quite different world of Soviet domestic (or emigré) politics will end badly. It is neither indifferent nor platitudinous to emphasize that the Soviet future must be decided by people in the Soviet Union and in their own way. I believe that even modest reform within the existing system would be good for them, for us, and for the world, and that this remains a real possibility. But the main contribution our government can make is more concern for our own problems at home, and a calm policy of restraint and détente abroad.

## Notes

[1]See, for example, A. Katsenelinboigen, "Coloured Markets in the Soviet Union," *Soviet Studies*, January 1977, pp. 62–85.

[2]As an example of how these problems are related and create interlocking constraints, consider the following. Beginning with the Khrushchev period, the Soviet leadership has made repeated promises and unfolded several unsuccessful campaigns to satisfy the consumer desires of the population. This is, I think, a genuine commitment, deriving partly from ideological tenets of communism, which sounds in official statements increasingly like the Welfare State plus consumerism, and partly from a need to counter political demands of the intelligentsia. But this commitment to a mass consumer-goods program is inseparable from other areas of domestic and foreign policy. It involves a restructuring of economic life and thus raises the question of reforms in the planning, industrial, and agricultural sectors. It involves new techniques of economic decision making and thus the problem of centralized power. It involves capital investments and allocations incompatible with escalating military budgets and grandiose commitments abroad. Meanwhile, Soviet consumerism is part of the leadership's concept of a peaceful competition abroad with the United States, as well as its anxiety that working-class discontent over prices and wages in Eastern Europe could be replicated in the Soviet Union.

[3]Ilya Erenburg, the late Soviet writer, once remarked, complaining about some of his fellow party members, that the problem with having only one party is that anybody can get in.

[4]There are several informed accounts of these trends, though categories and

labels sometimes vary. See, for example, Roy A. Medvedev, *On Socialist Democracy* (New York, Norton, 1975), chap. iii; and Alexander Yanov, *Détente after Brezhnev: The Domestic Roots of Soviet Foreign Policy* (Berkeley, California, University of California, Institute of International Studies, 1977). Much first-hand information on reformers and neo-Stalinists is available in the *samizdat* journal *Politicheskii dnevnik* (2 vols., Amsterdam, 1972 and 1975). Since the 1950s, these trends have been associated with, and articulated in, various official journals.

[5]See Robert C. Tucker, *The Marxian Revolutionary Idea* (New York, Norton, 1969), chap. vi.

[6]*The New York Times*, June 9, 1977.

[7]*Ibid*, June 26, 1977.

[8]Paul Nitze quoted in Charles Gati and Toby Trister Gati, *The Debate over Détente* (Headline Series, no. 234, New York, 1977) p. 27.

[9]Historians will find some whimsy, or at least understatement, in the following: "Two years is a relatively short time in which to alter the long-standing practices of sovereign nations, either in regard to one another or to their citizenries." The Commission of Security and Cooperation in Europe, *Report to the Congress of the United States on Implementation of the Final Act of the Conference on Security and Cooperation in Europe: Findings and Recommendations Two Years after Helsinki* (Washington, August 1, 1977), p. 5.

[10]This means, of course, reviving the Trade Act of 1972 by repealing the Jackson–Vanik Amendment and the Stevenson Amendment, which severely restricted Export–Import Bank credits to the USSR. For a persuasive argument in favor of expanding trade, see Daniel Yergin, "Politics and Soviet-American Trade: The Three Questions," *Foreign Affairs*, April 1977, pp. 517–538; and on the more general aspects of détente, Marshall D. Shulman, "On Learning to Live with Authoritarian Regimes," *ibid.*, January 1977, pp. 325–338.

[11]An unfortunate example of this lack of wisdom and potential for mischief was Senator Jackson's attack on the well-known dissident Roy Medvedev as "nothing but a front man, a sycophant for the leadership." Senator Jackson went on to liken Medvedev to "certain Jews [who] fronted for Goering, Goebbels, and Hitler" (*The New York Times*, January 28, 1975). Expelled from the party, subjected to periodic searches, and out-of-work, Medvedev is a democratic Marxist who tries to speak to and for reformers inside the party.

[12]The Carter Administration has defined this issue in terms of Soviet *human rights*, which is inexact. The issue is political rights or liberties. The term *human rights* includes a whole range of economic and other welfare problems, in which the Soviet Union, in the world context, can boast considerable achievement.

[13]For full examination of this subject, see Frederick C. Barghoorn, *Détente and the Democratic Movement in the USSR* (New York, Free Press, 1976).

[14]*The Washington Post*, June 6, 1977.

[15]*The New York Times*, January 31, 1977.

[16]Various explanations of the bombing circulated in Moscow. The most frequent theory linked it to food shortages, poor living conditions, rumors of price increases, and other discriminatory practices in provincial towns outside Moscow. This theory viewed it as a Polish-style protest.

[17]Prime Minister Trudeau and Chancellor Schmidt have expressed concern, for example, that increased movement of people from Eastern Europe to Canada and West Germany may be jeopardized (*The New York Times*, July 17, 1977). Austrian Chancellor Kreisky expressed similar concerns earlier (*The International Herald Tribune*, March 16, 1977).

[18]On February 7, 1977, the prominent dissident Yuri Orlov said publicly, "I think after the State Department statement on Ginzburg I will not be arrested."

He was arrested 3 days later. This is, of course, subject to different interpretations, one being that Orlov's own statement made certain his arrest.

[19]On March 21, 1977, in a speech little noted outside the Soviet Union, Brezhnev made an unusual distinction between internal critics. Constructive critics were to be thanked; mistaken but "honest" critics were to be forgiven; but "anti-Soviet" critics, who had Western support and were often "imperialist agents," were to be punished. In the Soviet context, these distinctions suggested some flexibility and even a little "liberalism." My guess is that Brezhnev was trying to guard against neo-Stalinist excesses in the anti-dissident campaign (See *Komsomol'skaia Pravda*, March 22, 1977).

# 6

# WILLIAM ZIMMERMAN

## *What Do Scholars Know about Soviet Foreign Policy?**

It has been almost a quarter-century since Daniel Bell observed that "the road to hell must be paved twice over with the thousands of books claiming to discover the truth about Russia."[1] In the interim, yet more publications have appeared and new methods have been introduced to the study of Soviet politics, domestic and foreign. During the 1960s and 1970s, in fact, there appeared to be emerging a reasonably coherent consensus among Western scholars about what it was that we, as specialists, knew about Soviet foreign policy.[2] But, the widespread realization that the Soviet Union had become, for the first time really, a power with global military force projection capabilities; the equally widespread sense that there had been a shift during the 1970s in the global distribution of power between the United States and the Soviet Union; the Soviet Union's manifest buildup of its strategic weaponry, its navy, and its conventional weapons, most notably in central Europe; the Soviet invasion of Afghanistan, an action in some ways both surprising and ominous against the backdrop of traditional Soviet behavior; the Soviet "noninvasion" of Poland, a "nonaction" in some respects as puzzling as the Soviet action in Afghanistan; all these have called into question the state of the West's knowledge about Soviet foreign policy.

It is to that this essay is addressed. What follows therefore is one research practitioner's view of what specialists know about Soviet foreign policy. In particular I shall address four questions. The first question is epistemological, indeed almost metaphysical: What does it mean to say we know something about Soviet foreign policy? The second, obviously, is what do scholars know of some theoretical and policy relevant significance about Soviet decision-making and foreign policy behavior? The third follows in part from the first and has a bearing on the policy relevance, or lack thereof, of scholarly knowledge about

*Reprinted by permission of the author and publisher from *International Journal* 27, no. 2 (Spring, 1982), pp. 198–219. Copyright 1982 by Canadian Institute of International Affairs.

Soviet foreign policy: To wit, what can't we know about Soviet foreign policy? (I assume that knowledge about discrete events and facts is not really at issue here.) Finally, by way of conclusion, I honor a long tradition in essays of this kind by identifying what we don't know *that we can know* if we will but do the research.

As a scholar with an incorrigible empiricist bent, I take "to know" to mean that there exists a falsifiable, replicable basis for a generalization, in this instance about present or past Soviet foreign policy, and that that explanation dominates by far all the alternative explanations of the same data. Such knowledge may take the form of the positivist's covering law: if $X$, then $Y$. It may also be expressed in probabilistic terms: in $a$, $b$ conditions, actor $x$ tends or tends overwhelmingly (read respectively: more often than not, much more often than not) to behave in certain specified ways.

The "truth"—what we know—about Soviet behavior in this sense is most definitely truth with a small "t." There does exist a rather voluminous literature that professes to know the Truth about the Soviet Union with a capital "T." That literature, by analogy to the more general history of science, I and others have called an essentialist perspective on the Soviet Union.[3] It dismisses *all* changes in Soviet policy as mere tactics—as many such changes have been—and claims to have fathomed the nature of communism. Such views make claims about Soviet foreign policy which are almost wholly nonfalsifiable; Secretary of State John Foster Dulles was engaging in such thinking when he dismissed a Soviet troop reduction announcement in 1955 as further evidence of Soviet mendacity, since such troop reductions would weaken the North Atlantic Treaty Organization (NATO). When increasing, maintaining, or decreasing Soviet troop deployments are all evidence of Soviet bad intentions, we are in the world of metaphysics and values, not knowledge in my sense. Likewise, when Aleksandr Solzhenitsyn[4] claims that "there exist no 'better' variants of communism, that it is incapable of growing 'kinder,' that it cannot survive as an ideology without using terror, and that, consequently, to coexist with communism is impossible," he is not making an empirical claim. Rather, he is asserting that communism is irredeemable, that whether, for instance, mass purges occur or not is for him immaterial and that coexistence is undesirable, not impossible.

Within the empirical realm—the realm of small "t" truth—the claim to know does not exclude the possibility that there may be alternative explanations for parts of a data set or other body of evidence. I am, for instance, quite comfortable in making the claim that we know that in the post-Stalin period, Soviet cultural penetration of Eastern Europe has diminished over time. I have developed a reasonable operational measure of cultural penetration (translations from Russian as a percentage of total translations undertaken in particular East European countries) which fits, lagged by a year, with virtually everything we know from other sources about Eastern Europe and Soviet behavior in Eastern Europe. (Those data, which I have used elsewhere, are reproduced in Table 6.1.) It does not trouble me that people can look at particular data

Table 6.1. *Russian-Language Books as a Percentage of the Total Number of Books Translated in East European Countries*[a]

| | Albania | Bulgaria | Czechoslovakia | GDR | Hungary | Poland | Rumania | Yugoslavia |
|---|---|---|---|---|---|---|---|---|
| 1954 | NA[b] | 66 | 64 | NA | 59 | 70 | NA | 7 |
| 1955 | NA | 69 | 52 | NA | 48 | 57 | 47 | 21 |
| 1956 | NA | 63 | 47 | NA | 40 | 47 | 53 | 23 |
| 1957 | NA | 63 | 31 | NA | 16 | 30 | 32 | 10 |
| 1958 | 57 | 50 | 24 | NA | 27 | 22 | 43 | 10 |
| 1959 | 44 | 49 | 26 | NA | 25 | 20 | 44 | 10 |
| 1960 | 61 | 54 | 26 | NA | 30 | 23 | 44 | 10 |
| 1961 | 48 | 57 | 24 | NA | 23 | 26 | 49 | 13 |
| 1962 | 39 | 51 | 24 | NA | 30 | 27 | 37 | 9 |
| 1963 | 34 | 53 | 23 | NA | 22 | 23 | 34 | 13 |
| 1964 | 58 | 46 | 16 | NA | 20 | 23 | 24 | 13 |
| 1965 | 26 | 43 | 16 | NA | 16 | 23 | 11 | NA |
| 1966 | 16 | 37 | 11 | NA | 13 | 25 | 9 | 11[c] |
| 1967 | 26 | 33 | 12 | NA | 15 | 23 | 8 | 11 |
| 1968 | 19 | 34 | 15 | NA | 13 | 20 | 8 | 12 |
| 1969 | 25 | 37 | 8 | NA | 10 | 19 | 5 | 8 |
| 1970 | 28 | 39 | 9 | NA | 11 | 21 | 10 | 13 |
| 1971 | 17 | 36 | 13 | 41 | 10 | 19 | 5 | 12 |
| 1972 | 7 | 44 | 18 | 73 | 11 | 17 | 10 | 8 |
| 1973 | 10 | 44 | 24 | 42 | 11 | 16 | 6 | 7 |

[a]While there are a number of possible explanations for the above figures, the trend over time seems unmistakably linked to changes in Soviet relations with particular European communist states, especially when one compares the impact of truly significant events (Hungary, Poland in 1956, Czechoslovakia in 1968) lagged a year. From United Nations, Statistical Office, *Statistical Yearbooks*.
[b]NA = Not available.
[c]1965–1966 combined.

points and argue that one or another of them can be explained by something other than my generalization. The basis for the claim to know something about Soviet relations with Eastern Europe from these data is that the data are all congruent with the generalization, and the generalization is parsimonious. With it one need not resort to *ad hoc* and *ad seriatim* explanations. We need not be troubled by the presentation of alternative explanations. They are always possible; I am told that there are people who are not institutionalized who believe man has not yet reached the moon and who believe instead the whole event was staged.

At the same time, it is important that scholars should exercise great care in making claims about the degree of confidence we have in the transferability of our knowledge. As with all science, what we know about Soviet foreign policy is largely about present and past behavior. To a greater extent than we sometimes care to acknowledge, we make estimates about the future. Scientists certainly know that if the sun rises tomorrow it will rise in the east, and we have great confidence based on past experience extending back some 4 billion years that it will rise, though a catastrophic astronomic event may occur destroying the earth, or the sun, or both. Even in this extreme instance, however, there is a difference in the confidence levels of the estimates that (1) the sun will rise tomorrow and that (2) if the sun rises at all, it will be in the east.

While a trivial example, it is not a trivial point about the state of our knowledge about Soviet foreign policy. We can extrapolate about future Soviet relations, but candor dictates that we specify the future context in which the prediction obtains. Recently, for instance, I estimated the degree of inequality that is likely to characterize relations between the states of the Soviet–East European hierarchical regional system during the 1980s.[5] I confidently predicted that, using a widely accepted measure of interstate inequality, Soviet–East European relations in the 1980s would remain distinctly hierarchical, and specifically within a range bounded by measures of inequality for United States relations with other NATO states, and current United States relations with Latin America. Such a statement involves a series of assumptions relating to the changes in gross national product for the East European states-members of the Warsaw Treaty Organization and the USSR, and assumptions that the Soviet Union will survive 1984 and that a united communist Germany will not occur. All these are nonheroic assumptions; even so, the claim to know an important proposition about future Soviet–East European relations remains context-dependent.

The context-dependent nature of knowledge about Soviet foreign policy warrants special emphasis in the early 1980s. In realms other than Eastern Europe (where structural change has been relatively minor in the entire post-World War II period), the context of Soviet behavior has changed substantially and arguably in ways that invalidate a substantial part of what has passed for received wisdom about Soviet foreign policy.

Consider the following example of something we "know." Any list of propositions about Soviet behavior would emphasize the paramount security concern which Soviet élites have universally ascribed to Eastern Europe since World War II. Institutionally, this priority has been recognized in the nonmembership in the Warsaw Treaty Organization of such clients of the Soviet Union as Mongolia, Vietnam, and Cuba—strongly suggesting that Moscow's commitment to defend "real socialism" (the current Moscow term) in Eastern Europe is far greater than for other Soviet allies. Militarily, similarly, Soviet force deployment policies have long emphasized the role of the army in a way consonant with giving priority to East European concerns. The centrality of Eastern Europe in the Soviet security calculus, however, may well presuppose a set of conditions and attitudes on the part of the Soviet élite that no longer exists. As a continental power ruled by élites socialized by the experience of two great wars with Germany in this century, any conceivable Soviet (indeed Russian) leadership circa 1955 would have calculated its security priorities in such a way that Eastern Europe took pride of place. Thirty-five years after World War II solved, as it were, the German problem, in an international system in which the USSR has become a genuinely global power, it is much less certain that all future Soviet élites will attach unquestioned precedence to Eastern Europe.

Indeed, even with respect to our knowledge of the past, we constantly find in the study of Soviet foreign policy, as in social science generally, that there is an embarrasingly brief half-life to our most well-established generalizations. To take another illustration from Soviet–East European relations: Until quite recently it had been well established that since the 1960s the Warsaw Treaty Organization has demonstrated the applicability of the Olson–Zeckhauser theorem that in an alliance, small states pay relatively less than their share to obtain a "public good," defense, than do the more powerful states.[6] Hence, small states get a relatively "free ride." Recent research by William Reisinger, however, has shown that the proposition did not continue to hold throughout the 1970s and that instead a more complicated bargaining model provides a better "postdictive" explanation.[7] Reisinger's analysis is a healthy reminder to us all that whatever modicum of knowledge there is extant about Soviet foreign policy is highly contextual and often subject to revision.

All these caveats notwithstanding, scholars nevertheless do know important things about Soviet foreign policy. First, we know that many widely held propositions, some of them of long duration, some of them more recent, are wrong. This in and of itself is significant and characteristic of the progress of knowledge in other realms as well where, typically, hypothesis falsification is central to the accumulation of knowledge.

Some notions which still warranted consideration 25 years ago, when Bell wrote his "Ten Theories" article, have long since been discredited. Serious people no longer give any credence to single-factor explanations that were then rather widely held. The Third Rome hypothesis has died a quiet death, unicausal Russian national character explanations are passé, and while the development of a Soviet blue-water navy has rekindled speculation about overarching Soviet interest in warm water ports, only a few in the 1980s seriously think that Russians, whether in their tsarist or their Soviet garb, have a unique and overpowering urge to the sea. (The realization that not even lemmings have an urge to the sea may have helped.)

More importantly, many early concrete generalizations have been shown to be of little relevance to the understanding of Soviet foreign policy over the last quarter-century. Perhaps the most important of these early generalizations was the notion that there existed a uniquely Bolshevik style, and that an understanding of Bolshevism had substantial implications for contemporary Soviet foreign policy behavior. Likewise, it has not been that many years since one of the leading students of Soviet foreign policy could assert that those who speculate about the possibility of a Sino–Soviet split do not understand the nature of communism.

Most recent notions that seemed to constitute an important element in our font of knowledge about the Soviet Union have also been discredited. I have already mentioned the temporal limitations of the relevance for Soviet–East European relations of the Olson–Zeckhauser theorem. One could mention some others, ranging from interpretations of specific events, such as Khrushchev's ouster in 1964 (still in public, quite mistakenly, attributed to his foreign policy vis-à-vis the West), to broader, more significant propositions. For instance, a widespread view held that ideology erosion would occur last in the area of foreign policy. A considerable body of literature has shown that this, while a quite attractive a priori generalization, simply does not withstand scrutiny.

It is what we know, surely, not what we know we do not know, that is more interesting. What follows is a brief inventory of some of the major propositions about Soviet foreign policy that will withstand serious scrutiny. It is necessarily selective and meant to illustrate broad points. I shall consider, first, Soviet relations with communist states; second, Soviet behavior in the international system generally; and third, links between Soviet foreign policy and Soviet domestic politics.

One of the big generalizations, surely, about relations among communist states pertains to the consequences of the nature of power seizure for the future evolution of relations between the Soviet Union and the communist state in question. Basically, it turns out that countries that achieve communist régimes in a manner akin to the Soviet pattern are those communist states with which the Soviet Union most frequently has contentious relations. Communism, long seen as likely to put an end to the national question, has, in many respects, exacerbated interstate relations such that Soviet relations with other states who came to power like the Soviet Union have often proved conflictual: One wonders how pleased, in retrospect, the Soviet leadership is that Albania, Yugoslavia, and China, for instance, have communist régimes. Certainly, one great consequence of the Sino–Soviet split has been to call into question an old Soviet belief that a communist takeover represented in all cases a genuinely "progressive" occurrence, that is, an occurrence congruent with Soviet foreign policy interests. It is difficult to imagine, for instance, that a pro-Chinese, communist takeover in India would be viewed by Moscow as anything other than an unmitigated disaster.

A second big point about communist international relations is that whereas a quarter of a century ago one could quite reasonably distinguish Soviet relations with other communist states and Soviet relations with all the rest of the world, in the aftermath of the Sino–Soviet split, this clear-cut dichotomy no longer obtains. Perhaps the most striking illustration of this proposition is that in recent years the Soviet Union has proposed to the Chinese that Soviet–Chinese relations be based on the principle of peaceful coexistence. Whatever else has characterized Soviet foreign policy in the past, it has always, until now, been that proletarian internationalism was the central theme of Soviet relations with communist states. To propose that Soviet–Chinese relations be constructed on the basis of relations between states of opposing social systems, to use Soviet jargon, is compelling evidence that the old dichotomy between Soviet relations with communist states and Soviet relations with the rest of the world has lost its predictive value.

Rather, it is only in Soviet–European relations that one can speak of a distinctive set of communist international relations. In that set of relations, too, we know that there have been a number of major developments. The time when it was appropriate to speak of a Soviet bloc as a unitary actor has long past. Domesticism, to use Brzezinski's phrase, has come to the fore. As we have watched the reemergence of genuine interstate relations, albeit between exceedingly asymmetrical units measured in power terms, we have witnessed also the gradual reassertion of the significance of state boundaries in Soviet relations with Eastern Europe. There was a time, we know, when East European states had become little more than front organizations like the Ukrainian Soviet Socialist Republic, or like other transmission-belt social organizations such as trade unions. It is a narrow example, but makes a point, when we recall that in the early postwar period, Bulgaria cast fewer votes against the Soviet Union in the United Nations General Assembly than did the Ukrainian SSR. In the last 25 years, by contrast, the attributes of the East European states as penetrated systems have been reduced. As well as the decreasing cultural penetrations of Eastern Europe by the Soviet Union, research has illustrated the transformation of Soviet economic relations with Eastern Europe. In the early postwar period the Soviet Union manifestly exploited Eastern Europe. Indeed the USSR took out of Eastern Europe roughly the same amount as the United States put into Western Europe via the Marshall Plan. Subsequently, by contrast, it has become arguable whether Eastern Europe was being exploited by the Soviet Union economically, or whether the Soviet Union was being "exploited" by Eastern Europe. The overwhelming consensus of Western scholarship, in fact, is that for a considerable period, until the Soviet Union increased its oil prices following the 1973 jump in oil prices, Eastern Europe was exploiting the Soviet Union economically. This, it was argued, was a condition the Soviet Union tolerated to ensure political quiescence and political cooperation in Eastern Europe.

An additional central point above Soviet behavior with communist states, and until recently a proposition which applied only to Eastern Europe, has been that the Soviet Union only intervenes in communist states. Since World War II, that proposition has obtained consistently if by intervene one is referring to large-scale Soviet use of its own military forces. The underlying theme, and the one that makes the Afghanistan invasion seem consistent with Soviet behavior in Eastern Europe, is that the Soviet Union attaches very great significance to perpetuating historical gains. The Soviet leadership simply does not like to lose and is willing to invoke substantial resources to prevent a historically retrograde action on its periphery or to prevent a state from adopting an anti-Soviet policy. This is not to say the Soviet Union will always interfere militarily to prevent a communist state from reorienting its foreign policy or to prevent fundamental internal transformations. It did not, for instance, in Yugoslavia; and as of this writing has not intervened militarily in Poland, although I, for one, have been repeatedly surprised such an action did not occur. Rather, it is to suggest that a Soviet decision to commit its own forces is taken quite rarely, but that one such instance is to prevent the loss of previous gains. Small wonder that Enrico Berlinguer, leader of the Italian Communist party, has made oblique but pointed reference to NATO as the shield which would protect Italian independence even under communist rule. One of the great dangers of a communist takeover anywhere is that it markedly increases the likelihood that the Soviet Union might decide to intervene in the event of some future transformation. What remains ambiguous, an ambiguity of which the Yugoslavs are perhaps most acutely aware,[8] is whether the Soviet Union's commitment to defend socialism, whether the citizens of a particular country wish to be defended or not, extends to Eastern Europe alone, or whether, given the Soviet Union's increased domain, the responsibility is likely to extend to the Balkans and elsewhere outside of Eastern Europe. This again calls into question whether what we have known about traditional attachment to Eastern Europe in the Soviet scale of priorities will persist in the 1980s.

When we turn to Soviet behavior in the international system, here too there are several propositions we can claim to know. The first in a list of truly substantial propositions about Soviet behavior in the international system relates to performance. That literature is now sufficiently substantial to allow us to declare with some confidence that, contrary to those who have argued that whatever other virtues and foibles the USSR may have, it is advantaged in its international competition with democratic pluralist systems, the international performance capabilities of the Soviet Union are not distinctive. Whether one examines Soviet and American ability to adjust to failed policies, the relative efficacy of Soviet and American aid to Third World states, or Soviet and American alliance behavior, the conclusion remains the same: The Soviet Union either performs no better or perhaps even worse internationally than the United States.[9] Indeed this extends generally to Soviet relations with the Third World. The staying power of the Soviet Union in particular Third World countries turns out to be very limited indeed. Whether one has in mind early Soviet relations with Ataturk's Turkey, Soviet relations with China in the 1920s, or the post-World War II experience of the Soviet Union in Guinea, Ghana, Indonesia, Sudan, Egypt, or Somalia, the story is, repeatedly, one of a Soviet presence achieved, followed by a Western write-off, followed ultimately by an untoward and unseemly Soviet departure.

The second proposition pertains to the basis for much of what we have observed about Soviet behavior in the international system. The observed Soviet propensity to prevent historically retrograde steps bespeaks a broader attribute of Soviet behavior: namely, the Soviet élites' strong attachment to ensuring an overall reputation for credibility. This is strikingly manifest in Soviet utterances. Moscow uses words very carefully, especially in depicting its own past, present, or future behavior. Whenever serious studies have been undertaken, they have shown, contrary to widespread belief, a strong mesh between deeds and words, or at least some tortured construction of the latter. One instance is Soviet treaty behavior. With respect to Soviet relations with equals, Soviet behavior has generally been rather congruent with Soviet treaty obligations, at least by narrow constructions of the terms of such arrangements. Similarly, analysis of Soviet statements about Soviet foreign policy per se in the central organs, *Pravda* and *Izvestia*, shows a manifest Soviet preoccupation with a reputation for careful expression. With few minor exceptions relating to the maintenance of diplomatic pretenses, the Soviet Union lies only in situations where the stakes are extremely high. There is an excellent reason for this. To retain credibility, it is entirely rational to time a surprise. Soviet behavior has been quite congruent with such an understanding of the rational timing of surprise. Credibility is a resource. Without it, a state would engage in strategic surprise with only minimal success. Hence there is an optimal moment to time surprises such as lies only to coincide with extraordinary, and extraordinarily important, events.[10]

Interestingly enough, however, here too, one wishes to be careful about specifying context. When my colleague, Robert Axelrod, and I examined Soviet strategic lying over the entire postwar period, we found that there were few instances indeed, the Cuban missile crisis being the most obvious and striking, when the Soviet Union was caught in an outright lie about its own foreign policy behavior. As the Soviet domestic policy arena expands, however, it may well be that the Soviet leadership will increasingly lie about Soviet foreign policy in order to play domestic political games. Should the Soviet Union lose its previous ability to compartmentalize its signals to external and domestic audiences, a generalization which has held for 35 years may become increasingly unreliable.

A third major proposition about Soviet behavior in the international system relates to the overall theme about the care with which the Soviet Union commits its military forces. Just as Soviet behavior in relation to the communist states reveals that the USSR has used major military force only when the continued existence of a pro-Soviet communist régime is threatened, so too the body of careful literature which examines Soviet use of force, whether directly or for political purposes, reveals an almost unbroken pattern of low risk-taking in the more general international arena.[11] Indeed, the Soviet use of force reveals a sharp distinction between situations where there is no risk of confronta-

tion with the United States and those with even low risk of confrontation with the United States. In that respect, Soviet use of force in Eastern
Europe (where the United States has made it abundantly clear time and
time again it will take no military action) and Soviet use of force
elsewhere, in instances such as Angola in the mid-1970s where the
United States committed itself not to intervene, are appropriately seen
as being of a piece, as is the pronounced Soviet preference for proxies
(most recently Cuba and Vietnam).

I would in turn relate this observation about the low risk-taking
proclivities of Soviet élites in part to a dilemma which inheres in the
Soviet Union's relation to the overall international system. Soviet élites
still profess to aspire to transform the international system, and very
likely some of them actually have such an aspiration. As the Soviet
Union has enhanced its capacity to influence events in the international
system, it has found increasingly that it has a stake in maintaining the
very order which it seeks to transform. Marx knew whereof he spoke
when he thought it would be those who had nothing to lose but their
chains who would lead the revolution. The Soviet leadership is quite
aware that it has more to lose than its chains. In the aftermath of the one
act in the post-World War II period least consonant with an overall
picture of low Soviet risk-taking, the Cuban missile crisis, Moscow
noted that "gone are the days" when the workers of the world have
"nothing to lose but their chains."[12]

A final characteristic attribute of Soviet behavior in international
systems which we may now safely claim "to know" concerns the
reactive nature of Soviet foreign policy. (How reactive, and reactive to
what, other than George Kennan's famous "logic of force," is a subject
of considerable dispute.) The realization that Soviet foreign policy is, to
some important extent, reactive, represents a significant change in
specialists' thinking over the last 20 years when the overwhelming
tendency was to see Soviet foreign policy as driven largely by internal
forces.

It is ironic, however, that given the long-standing tendency to view
Soviet foreign policy generally as largely deriving from domestic
sources, how little cumulative knowledge exists about the link between
domestic politics and domestic political processes and Soviet foreign
policy behavior. Remarkably, it has only been in the past year that the
first really comprehensive study of linkage between domestic policy and
Soviet foreign policy has been published.[13] Nevertheless, there are some
genuinely important propositions about domestic links to foreign policy
that we as Soviet specialists may be said to know. One is that a major
basis of support for the régime stems from foreign policy gains. While it
would be difficult to specify how much support for the régime is
bolstered by foreign policy achievements, it is certain that a substantial
fraction of the support a Soviet citizen may render the Soviet leadership
stems from the achievement of world power status and consonant
particular measures indicative of that status such as, on the one hand,
bilateral arms control agreements with the United States, and, on the
other, support for revolutionary causes globally.

A second well-substantiated proposition relates to the role of ideology in foreign policy. This is a hackneyed topic, no doubt, but in the atomic age and with the elongation of Soviet time horizons about the ultimate triumph of communism, there has been a demonstrable erosion of the relevance of ideology to foreign policy. Ideology continues to serve as the language of politics and, to a considerable extent, it remains the language of analysis, although there was a noticeable tendency in the 1960s and 1970s for Soviet specialists to adopt the vocabulary and tools of their Western counterparts. As, for instance, my *Soviet Perspectives on International Relations* showed, ideology has neither hindered nor enhanced the general Soviet appraisal of international relations.[14] Aside from Soviet assessments of relations among communist states, the maintenance of élan domestically through retaining doctrinal purity internationally has been consistently sacrificed to the aspiration to pursue foreign policy goals rationally and efficiently.

This, in turn, has profound implications for the erstwhile tendency to explain the moving forces of Soviet foreign policy as stemming from the nature of the political system. Instead, if we have learned anything about the linkage between internal Soviet developments and Soviet foreign policy, it is that a plurality of perspectives exists within the Soviet élite and Soviet attentive public on foreign policy. Those perspectives invariably point to quite different policy prescriptions, whether the issue is East–West relations broadly or Soviet relations with particular Third World states. Whenever, over the last 15 or 20 years, Western specialists on the Soviet Union have examined carefully Soviet utterances pertaining to foreign policy issues, significant differences have always been identified. A view of Soviet foreign policy that depicts an élite with undifferentiated goals, high purposiveness, an unquestioning belief in the utility of force, or an unchanging view of the nature of the enemy just will not withstand serious scrutiny. Even on such crucial matters, scholars concerned with cumulative knowledge about the Soviet Union have found repeatedly that to understand the structured patterns of debate in the press over a particular issue requires an examination of institutional position and individual differences. Moreover, we know that the dimensions of that debate are such that a substantial fraction of it can be described along a single left–right continuum. Some in that dialogue emphasize will, politics, and activism, and sharply differentiate between friend and foe—traditional left themes throughout the history of Soviet power. Others stress objective conditions and economics, caution against premature action, and muddle the distinctions between friend and foe, as rightist themes have typically done over the years.[15] Moreover, recent research by Peter Hauslohner indicates that the size and heterogeneity of the Soviet attentive public on foreign policy is increasing. For the first time we now witness regional party secretaries, the traditional prefects, acting like something akin to United States senators—and hence the title of Hauslohner's distinguished article.[16]

If these propositions may be said to represent fairly some of the more important propositions about what we know, the broad range of omissions and level of abstraction suggest how far we as specialists have yet to go. Just as there is no end to our worries, there is no end to our need for future research. Let me, by way of conclusion, indicate what are the most pressing needs.

I have already suggested what amounts to a central theme, namely, the fundamental change in the context in which the Soviet Union finds itself internationally and, to a lesser extent, domestically, and what bearing that has on future Soviet behavior. For instance, all our notions about Soviet risk-taking are based on the assumption the Soviet Union is not in a position of overwhelming preponderance. What would occur should the Soviet Union achieve strategic preponderance? We now know that the Soviet Union is a genuine global power. What implications does this have for its priorities vis-à-vis Eastern Europe? We know the Soviet Union faces a period of diminished growth; in Eastern Europe the situation, of course, is far more acute. Will the Soviet leadership be able to deal with its "participation crisis" as it strives to adjust to the changing ethnic composition of the Soviet Union qua multinational empire at a time when the pie is expanding much more slowly than heretofore? Will that adjustment entail acts that spill over into foreign policy behavior?

But there is much more to be learned as well, even if the change in context does *not* invalidate our previous knowledge concerning, for instance, relations among communist states. We have little sense about the range and possibilities that exist for future Soviet relations with China. Three years ago, just prior to the Soviet invasion of Afghanistan, there was an emerging Western consensus that Soviet relations with China would improve and that this would be, ironically, further evidence that ideology played a minimal role in the explanation of contemporary Soviet foreign policy. After the Chinese attack on Vietnam it appeared no future prospects for improvement were in sight. The Reagan administration's slight tilt away from the People's Republic to Taiwan has raised once again the issue of whether there can be a fundamental change in Sino–Soviet relations.

With respect to Eastern Europe, there is an almost incredible embarrassment in the state of our research. Zbigniew Brzezinski's *The Soviet Bloc* was first published in 1960. There have been special studies of particular aspects of Soviet–East European relations and efforts to conceptualize Soviet–East European relations, but no monograph comparable to *The Soviet Bloc* has been published in the last 20 years. Specifically, there is little by way of systematic research pertaining to the USSR's political penetration of Eastern Europe since the passing of the consular/embassy system when Moscow's ambassador basically dictated policy and when Soviet citizens sat on the Central Committee of the Polish Workers' party. We do not have, for instance, much of a sense of the role of Soviet advisers, military and nonmilitary, in Eastern Europe over the last quarter-century. Nor have we resolved whether the Warsaw Treaty Organization is to be seen fundamentally as an organization directed against the West or whether it is primarily an instrument for control in Eastern Europe, a vehicle through which East European military élites are socialized into ties with the Soviet Union.[17] Even an issue as exhaustively explored as Soviet–East European integration has produced little by way of systematic cumulative knowledge. Specialists are still at odds, whether integration across multiple sectors can be achieved or whether the impediments to integration of socialist states first identified theoretically by Jacob Viner 35 years ago will continue to operate.

As for Soviet behavior in the international system, it turns out to be as difficult to see a motive at 6000 miles as it was in the past. Scholars have provided little by way of explicit knowledge to guide the policymaker in assessing whether Soviet strategic policy is aimed toward achieving strategic preponderance or whether the Soviet Union is either content with equality or could be made to be resigned to being content with equality. This key question is one which scholars can address. David Finley has provided, if not an irrefutable case, at least a strong argument that the immense Soviet procurement of weapons in central Europe has been prompted primarily by an effort to achieve political gains through the display of military might.[18] Equally imaginative research might go a long way to increasing at least the confidence in our estimates of Soviet proclivities for strategic hegemony or parity. Much needs to be done also in the area of Soviet resolution of hard choices as, for instance, when it is faced with opportunities to improve East–West relations or to advance the cause of some radical anti-imperialist movement in the Third World. Time and again over the last 20 years such hard choices have confronted the Soviet Union, and the Soviet choice has not been consistent across those instances. Specifying the conditions in which one or the other option is more likely is a central part of our research agenda.

This, in turn, leads directly again to domestic links to foreign policy. Simply because of our knowledge of actuarial tables, we know that a whole new élite is likely to emerge in the Soviet Union in the next 5–7 years. It is not just Brezhnev who is a member of the current gerontocracy, not just the Politburo, but almost the entire Central Committee. We know from what cohort the new élite will emerge. Unless something radically different from the past transpires, they will emerge from the group who are now the regional party secretaries in the Soviet Union. We know that these people have expressed themselves in a wide variety of ways on foreign policy themes in recent years. Similarly, we know something about the general link between institution and policy stance and socialization and policy stance, but it is precious little. Likewise, we know that a left–right dimension still captures a great bit of the variation in foreign policy attitude and that one can often tie particular institutions or their media instruments to foreign policy stances. But we do not know whether within particular apparatuses the intragroup differences in orientation are greater than the intergroup differences. And we certainly have very little idea about what new élites are likely to think about foreign policy when they actually exercise power. (My own fairly strong instincts are to emphasize on-the-job socialization into role, rather than recruitment socialization, but that is really little more than a moderately well-founded prejudice.)

In short, there is much that we do not know. Some of it we cannot know. One of the problems that persists in relations between policymakers and academics is that policymakers want to know the answers to single-shot questions. Will the Soviet Union, for instance, intervene in Poland in the next several weeks? Academics do not know the answer to that and ought not to claim that they can know the answer. This is not the kind of scientific knowledge which can be achieved. One can predict the general pattern of behavior of molecules but one cannot predict the motion of particular molecules, and physicists would reject as absurd a request for such information. I can make some statements about countries in which the Soviet Union is most and least likely to intervene militarily, but when, or whether in a particular context, is simply not within the realm of scholarly capabilities. There is very little we can know about Soviet foreign policy in the future except to specify limits or ranges. We are not likely now or in the future to know much about the intimate workings of the Politburo, especially as its behavior relates to foreign policy.

Nevertheless we can still know a lot if we will but do the research. To make this point relatively vividly, let me illustrate by giving an example of something few specialists would ever have suspected could be predicted about Soviet foreign policy. Some research I and Glenn Palmer have recently done shows that over the past 25 years, there exists a strong correlation between the words used by the Soviet finance minister in the annual budget message to describe upcoming Soviet military spending and to characterize the nature of the American threat, and annual changes in Soviet defense spending as estimated in ruble terms by most Western sources, if we build into our assessment a knowledge of the five-year-plan cycle.[19] It is a remarkable finding. It is genuinely surprising to discover that there exists a striking relationship between the changes in the Soviet finance minister's words in the annual budget speech and subsequent Soviet military procurement patterns. I am convinced that this example is but one instance where surprising knowledge about issues or topics in Soviet foreign policy can be obtained from open sources through basic research.

My conclusion, then, is the traditional call for further research. The minor chord in that call is a pessimistic one: It distresses me that so little by way of basic knowledge has accumulated, and there is genuine reason to worry who will constitute the cadres to undertake future research. The dominant chord struck, though, is optimistic; over the years we have shown that we can generate with some confidence important propositions about Soviet foreign policy. Moreover, there is reason to believe new basic research will enrich that accumulation.

## Notes

[1]Daniel Bell, "Ten Theories in Search of Reality: The Prediction of Soviet Behavior," reprinted in *Process and Power in Soviet Foreign Policy*, ed. Vernon V. Aspaturian (Boston 1971), p. 289.

[2]William Zimmerman, "Rethinking Soviet Foreign Policy: Changing American Perspectives," *International Journal* 25 (Summer, 1980), pp. 548-562.

[3]Especially William Welch, *American Images of Soviet Foreign Policy* (New Haven, 1970).

[4]Aleksandr Solzhenitsyn, "Misconceptions about Russia Are a Threat to America," *Foreign Affairs* 58 (Spring, 1980), p. 797.

[5]Morris Bornstein, Zvi Gitelman, and William Zimmerman, eds., *East–West Relations and the Future of Eastern Europe* (London, 1981), p. 92.

[6]Harvey Starr, "A Collective Goods Analysis of the Warsaw Pact after Czechoslovakia," *International Organization* 28 (Summer, 1974), pp. 521–532.

[7]William Reisinger, "East European Military Expenditures: Collective Good or Bargaining Offer?" Unpublished manuscript, University of Michigan, May, 1981.

[8]The ambiguity is nicely captured in two statements. Brezhnev (*Pravda*, November 16, 1976) spoke of "The authors [who] in fairy tales try to depict Yugoslavia as some kind of poor, defenseless Little Red Riding Hood whom the terrible rapacious wolf—the Soviet Union—threatens to tear to pieces and devour." *Novoye Vremya* (no 3, 1980) by contrast asked: "What is the international solidarity of revolutionaries? . . . . Does it consist, under justified, extraordinary conditions, in sending material aid including military aid, all the more so when it is a case of blatant, massive outside intervention? . . . History . . . confirms the moral and political rightness of this form of aid and support."

[9]Robert S. Walters, *American and Soviet Aid: A Comparative Analysis* (Pittsburgh, 1970). Robert O. Freedman, *Economic Warfare in the Communist Bloc* (New York, 1970). Ole R. Holsti, P. Terrence Hopmann, and John D. Sullivan, *Unity and Disintegration in International Alliances: Comparative Studies* (New York, 1973).

[10]Robert Axelrod and William Zimmerman, "The Soviet Press on Soviet Foreign Policy: A Usually Reliable Source," *British Journal of Political Science* 11 (1981), pp. 193–200.

[11]Stephen S. Kaplan, *Diplomacy of Power* (Washington, 1981).

[12]"The Policy of Peaceful Coexistence Proves Its Worth," *World Marxist Review* 5 (December, 1962), p. 6.

[13]Seweryn Bialer, ed., *The Domestic Context of Soviet Foreign Policy* (Boulder, 1981).

[14](Princeton, 1969).

[15]Alexander Dallin, "Soviet Foreign Policy and Domestic Politics," in *The Conduct of Soviet Foreign Policy*, eds. Erik P. Hoffmann and Frederic J. Fleron (New York, 1980), pp. 36–49.

[16]Peter Hauslohner, "Prefects As Senators: Soviet Regional Politicians Look to Foreign Policy," *World Politics* 33 (January, 1981), pp. 197–233.

[17]Christopher D. Jones, *Soviet Influence in Eastern Europe* (New York, 1981).

[18]David D. Finley, "Conventional Arms in Soviet Foreign Policy," *World Politics* 33 (October, 1980), pp. 1–35.

[19]"Words and Deeds in Soviet Foreign Policy: The Case of Soviet Military Expenditures." Paper presented at the 1982 International Studies Association annual meeting, Cincinnati, Ohio, March 25–27, 1982.

# 7

# HANNES ADOMEIT

## Soviet Ideology, Risk-Taking, and Crisis Behavior*

If it is correct that there are operational principles and recurring patterns of behavior which are specifically Soviet, what accounts for them? "Soviet ideology" must be an important part of the answer—a conclusion that is likely to contradict conventional wisdoms in American scholarship.[1] It may be useful, therefore, to look more closely at the arguments put forward in support of the thesis that Soviet ideology need not be taken all too seriously in the analysis of post-World War II Soviet foreign policy and to state in more detail why, in the argument of this study, ideology continues to matter.

One reason for the reluctance in American scholarship to attribute a significant role to Soviet ideology in shaping Soviet behavior very likely has something to do with the image in the mind of the analyst associating "ideological" with "irrational," "reckless," "adventurist," and the like, but contrasting it with "pragmatic," "opportunist," or "realistic."[2] Ideology as a factor shaping Soviet behavior is as a consequence being eroded in the mind of the analyst when he is faced with instances where Soviet representatives display diplomatic skill, act as shrewd and calculating businessmen, or pay much attention to military power as an instrument of furthering state interests.

Another possible explanation for the Western diagnosis of the erosion of ideology in Soviet foreign policy is to be found in a very narrow—and hence inadequate and misleading—definition. "Ideology" is often conceived of as nothing but the equivalent of the degree of Soviet support for world revolution, and sometimes even this is measured by the degree to which the Soviet Union is willing to employ military force on behalf of local communists in various areas of the world. As a consequence, the importance of ideology in Soviet foreign policy is being reduced for the Western analyst when the Soviet leaders apparently close their eyes to the oppression of local communists while engaging in cooperation with the oppressors at the state level (as in many countries of the Arab world), stand by with folded arms as Marxist regimes are being crushed (as in Chile), or fail to exploit alleged or real advantages for deepening the "crisis of capitalism" (as in the wake of the oil crisis after 1973).

Other explanations have much to do with the philosophical pre-conditioning of the Western analyst. To scholars reared in the Anglo–Saxon tradition of empiricism and pragmatism, the very thought that leaders in the practical realm of politics in the twentieth century should be guided in their actions by a rigid belief system appears incredible or inconceivable.[3] They find the Hegelian form of Soviet ideology difficult to grasp, and "the pronouncements of Soviet ideologists appear to them similar to the chants and litanies of some esoteric religious cult."[4]

These basic tendencies of analysis have been much reinforced recently. On the one hand, there are many scholars now who have had some form of contact with their Soviet counterparts, and an increasing number of them are able to read the Soviet scholarly output of the various institutes of the Academy of Sciences of the USSR in the original. Many of their Russian counterparts appear to be (and often are) men of reason, and many of the scholarly analyses, give or take some of the obligatory references to Lenin, resemble Western modes of analysis. Hence the conclusion that Western and Soviet perspectives on the international system are essentially similar.[5] On the other hand, the basic tradition of empiricism and pragmatism has found specific expression recently in the behavioral revolution in the social sciences with the generation of pressures, often justified, for more stringent measurement and higher standards of verification. These pressures have been extended to Soviet studies. But there are tremendous problems of "operationalizing" a research problem such as the influence of ideology in Soviet foreign policy. As a result it often appears more appropriate to delete a factor such as ideology altogether than to lay open a research plan to the charge of being unscientific because an immeasurable factor has been introduced. Ideology, therefore, has often been eroded by default rather than design.

In order to arrive at a realistic assessment of ideology as a factor of Soviet behavior it is necessary to abandon some faulty distinctions altogether, to recognize that the term has a broad scope, and to acknowledge that what matters most are not so much the perceptions and products of the *institutchiki*, or the thin apologias and rationalizations of lower- and middle-level *apparatchiki* one is allowed to meet, but the probable belief system and actual, observable behavior of the political leadership.

The broad *scope* encompassed by Soviet ideology needs to be considered first. As summarized by Alfred Meyer, Soviet ideology can be said to include, among other parts, a philosophy called dialectical materialism; generalizations about man and society, past and present, called historical materialism; an economic doctrine called political economy, which seeks to explain the economics of capitalism and imperialism, on the one hand, and of socialist construction, on the other; and a body of political thought, or guidelines, now called scientific communism, which deals, first, with the strategy and tactics of communist revolutions and, second, with political problems of socialist states.[6]

The next stage in the examination of the problem of ideology is to assume that there may be a variety of *functions* played by each individual part of Soviet ideology, to make allowance for the possibility that the manifold activities in politics and society may be influenced by ideology to differing degrees, and to be aware of the problem that the relative importance of various aspects of ideology may change over time. The precise delimitation of functions of ideology may be a matter of preference (there will always be overlaps to a certain extent), but their existence itself has not been in dispute.[7] They could be called as follows: (1) analytical or cognitive function; (2) operational or tactical function; (3) utopian, revolutionary, or missionary function; (4) legitimizing function; (5) socializing function.

Briefly, the analytical function refers to a conscious process and asks questions such as "How do the Soviet leaders see the world?" and "What, in the view of the Soviet leadership, are the basic structural elements of the international system, the sources of conflict, the factors accounting for stability or change, and so on?" The second function is more difficult to define. It can be taken as meaning (a) that the Soviet leadership is acting on the basis of the results of analysis (the impact of perception on behavior); (b) that the Soviet leadership codifies and formalizes the main line of a particular era in world affairs, defines the scope of peaceful coexistence, sets forth its view on the correlation of forces and the like, and arrives from there at the main tasks to be pursued (that is, the impact of doctrine on behavior); or (c) that there exist deeply engrained operational principles formed by ideology (the impact of socialization and experience on behavior). It is within this function of ideology that the left/right dichotomy finds its proper place of discussion.

The third function of ideology—the utopian, revolutionary, or missionary function—is often (but incorrectly) taken to be the only one that matters. It is also the one that is at the basis of the dichotomy of ideology versus "the national interest." By referring to it the analyst asks questions such as "To what extent is world revolution still a goal of Soviet foreign policy?," "To what extent is the Soviet leadership committed to supporting local communists and their bids for power?," and "What is the role of the USSR within the international communist movement?"

The fourth function has two important dimensions—one domestic, the other international. Legitimacy of power in the USSR is based on Marxism–Leninism; although other forms of legitimacy may eventually emerge, at the present state of development it would appear that any Soviet leader, or leadership, attempting to deviate from that basis would be destroying the very ground on which he or it is operating. By extension this applies to the legitimacy of Soviet rule in Eastern Europe, where the Soviet system has been transplanted and where it is being protected by the various means of control available to the Soviet Union.

The last function rests in the dialectical interplay between ideology and the education, upbringing, experience, and career patterns of the top leadership. This must lead an open-minded analyst to ask: "What kind of psychological makeup of the leadership results from socialization processes in the Soviet Union?" Behind such a question would lie the assumption that the experiences in the control and organization of society, and the criteria of success or failure in the domestic *kto-kogo* struggle, are apt to be transplanted by the successful leaders to the international arena.

As regards Soviet behavior in the Berlin crises of 1948 and 1961, nothing could be further from the truth, therefore, than the statement, "ideology had nothing to do with it." Combined operational, legitimizing, and socializing aspects of Soviet ideology (functions 2, 4, and 5 of the above categorization) have much to do with the shaping of Soviet interests affected in the crises and with the existence (and persistence) of the following operational principles:

1. Do not embark on forward operations against an opponent which are not carefully calculated in advance and move forward only after careful preparation.
2. "Push to the limit," "engage in pursuit" of an opponent who begins to retreat or make concessions, but "know when to stop" (in conditions of challenging an adversary); "resist from the start" any encroachment by the opponent, no matter how slight it appears to be, but "don't yield to enemy provocations" and "retreat before superior force" (in conditions of responding to a challenge by an adversary).[8]
3. Before engaging in forward operations "carefully construct a fall-back position" so as to meet unexpectedly high resistance by the adversary.
4. Never lose sight of the political objectives to be achieved, and in pursuing them do not let yourself be diverted by false notions of bourgeois morality.

Concerning the operational aspect, some of the axioms summarized above could have been taken straight from Lenin's *"Left-Wing" Communism, an Infantile Disorder*, for instance, the admonition that "To tie one's hand beforehand, openly to tell the enemy, who is at present better armed than we are, whether we shall fight him, and when, is stupidity and not revolutionariness"[9] or the advice that

The more powerful enemy can be conquered only be exerting the utmost effort, and by necessarily, thoroughly, carefully, attentively and skillfully taking advantage of every, even the smallest "rift" among the enemies.[10]

When Lenin adds in characteristic polemical fashion that those who did not understand this "do not understand even a particle of Marxism" he makes a charge that to some degree also applies to adherents of the "erosion of ideology" view when they juxtapose as antitheses "ideology," on the one hand, and "opportunism" or "pragmatism," on the other, thereby overlooking the fact that rigidity in doctrine does not by any means imply rigidity in tactics.[11] Attention must be paid to the Leninist distinction between short-term considerations and long-range ideological goals. In a certain sense, as Leo Labedz has argued, all politics, ideological or not, tend to be concerned first of all with short-term considerations.

> But there is a difference between policies which appertain to nothing else, and those which take long-term considerations, ideological or other, as their frame of reference. To confuse the two as "pragmatic" in the same sense is to misunderstand the character of Soviet policies in the past, and . . . at present.[12]

The view that the education, upbringing, experience, and career patterns ("socialization") of the Soviet leaders account for specific behavioral patterns in domestic and international politics impinges on the argument that the Soviet leaders are cynical with regard to ideology, in particular to the aspect of a universal classless society. Well they might be. Revolutionary idealism and romanticism may very well be regarded as a thing of the past, and "ideological evolution during six decades of Soviet history can be summarized as a reluctant retreat from the utopian and universalistic claims of Marxist doctrine *without, however, their abandonment.*"[13] In addition to that, other aspects of ideology have become more pronounced (legitimacy, for instance, which will be dealt with presently), and still others have been retained. To be counted among them are the ideas that life, including "international life," is an unending struggle, that this struggle can only end with the victory of one socioeconomic system over the other, and that to stand still, and not to plan for advances and gains, means falling behind and to be thrown on the rubbish heap of history. In Western societies, by analogy, processes of secularization have progressed far, but the influence of Protestantism and Catholicism will tend to affect even the cynic's behavior (as does the influence of ideology in the USSR) because he will not be able to rid himself of unquestioned assumptions and ideas which he takes as given or erroneously holds to be self-evident.

Even if the credibility of Soviet ideology is wearing thin and, in international politics, is becoming more of a liability than an asset, it is still a fallacy to argue that ideology is "nothing but *ex post facto* rationalization" (*Rechtfertigung*) and has nothing to with motivation (*Antrieb*). Rationalization and motivation, for an individual, a political leadership, or a state (and particularly when it comes to a state conforming to the notion of "an ideology in power"), can be *mutually reinforcing* mechanisms.[14] This leads directly to the problem of legitimacy.

No matter whether it is the power of the Soviet leadership, the power of institutions (the party, the armed forces, the police, the courts, and so on), relations among the countries of the socialist community (that is, the exercise of Soviet control and influence in the ruling communist states), or Soviet claims—open or tacit—to preeminence in the international communist movement, all of this is justified in terms of ideology. Criteria of achievement and well-being, too, are used by the Soviet leadership to elicit cooperation and compliance. Such criteria, however, belong to the realms of practical politics and expediency. They are only subsidiary to and derivative of the basic ideological principles.

Marxism, as Robert Wesson has argued, would probably have been "effectively if not overtly left behind as the new state settled down after the revolution, to be replaced by a straightforward faith of patriotism, Russianism and loyalty to the new rulership," but it was "indispensable because the new Soviet state undertook to govern a multinational domain."[15] Marxist internationalism was practically dropped during the war, but it became important again as the Russian armies recovered the Ukraine and other minority areas. "As Soviet forces asserted hegemony over nations of Eastern Europe, the role of ideology became still more vital."[16] This much, at least, seems to be granted also by adherents to the "erosion of ideology" school. Although, in their view, ideology has come to play a much lesser role in Soviet foreign policy in general, Eastern Europe is nevertheless being regarded as an exception.[17]

The fallacy of this view can be shown quite simply, and quite legitimately, by substituting "Soviet sphere of influence" or "socialist community" for "Eastern Europe." As Cuba, Mongolia, and Vietnam belong to it, as Angola, Ethiopia, and South Yemen are allied with it, and as strenuous efforts are made to integrate Afghanistan in it the (as they perceive it) "limited" and "regional" importance of ideology is immediately transformed into a phenomenon of global significance. For all these reasons, to say that the USSR is only a "new name for old Russia" would be to convey the wrong idea; to assume that Soviet foreign policy is merely Russian imperialism in a new garb would be, as Vernon Aspaturian put it, "a catastrophic mistake."[18]

Certainly these considerations are valid with regard to East Germany and the Berlin crises. To assert that the GDR was but a new name for old East Germany would not only have been anathema to the SED leadership in 1961, but it would have been an idea extremely alien to *all* Germans, no matter what their political orientation, because in their conception old East Germany (*Ostdeutschland*) used to begin east of "East Germany"—odd as this may sound in English.[19] But the legitimizing function of Soviet ideology enters forcefully into both crises because the type of system in the making on German soil in 1948, and the system as it existed in 1961, derived their tenuous claim to legitimacy neither from German history nor from achievement but exclusively from ideology. The problems for the Soviet Union were complicated by the fact that ideology had not only to swim against *currents of nationalism* in Germany and cope with a singular *lack of socialist achievement* there but also to contend with strong rival variants of *German Marxism* as opposed to Russian Bolshevism.

This threefold challenge to ideological legitimacy of the Soviet zone of occupation, and later the GDR, took different forms in the two crises, but in both cases the challenge is inseparable from important or (if one prefers) vital Soviet interests as defined by the respective leaderships. In

1948 options other than confrontation were still open to the Soviet Union. In recognition of nationalism as a strong political force some form of neutralized Germany might have been preferable to an irredentist, hostile West Germany as a spearhead of "American imperialism"; in recognition of Marxism and independent socialism as a strong current in Germany some form of third road for that country could have prevented its inclusion in schemes of "capitalist encirclement" such as NATO. With such a Germany, neutralized and democratic–socialist, some form of friendship and cooperation was possible. But all this could have happened only *if* there had been dramatic change in Soviet ideology toward the genuine acceptance of "many roads to socialism " externally and the opening up of the Soviet system to a kind of "socialism with a human face" internally. It is in large measure because of the rigidity and the unacceptable face of Stalinist ideology that these theoretical alternatives had no chance of being tried out in practice.

In 1961 the threefold challenge to ideological legitimacy had by no means disappeared. The challenge was evident in the form of an economically successful West Germany and its claim of sole representation, in West Berlin as a center of attraction for East Germans and East Europeans, and in the rising attractiveness of social democracy as a political force. It was evident also in the fact that the Soviet-type system on German soil had been thoroughly discredited and was suffering a worsening political and economic crisis. But by then the GDR had become so much bound up with the USSR, and economically and politically had become so much part and parcel of the Soviet bloc, that alternatives other than physical action to remedy this state of affairs no longer seemed to exist.

In sum, Marxist–Leninist ideology furnished important portions of the analytical and perceptual framework, operational principles, and legitimation of Soviet behavior in both crises. These are the constant features. However, when comparing the role of ideology in the two Berlin crises there is also one feature of change. In 1948 a broad congruence of elements of the left still existed, both in doctrine and in actual policy. But in 1961 such congruence was absent, as demonstrated by the fact that the predominant elements of the right coexisted with confrontation.

Two explanations can be offered for this development. First, by 1961 the greater complexity of international relations and the increasing diversity in the international communist movement and of Soviet society and politics almost inevitably had led to inconsistencies and contradictions in the various elements of Soviet theory and practice. Congruence of left/right priorities and commitments had become a thing of the past. Second, in 1948 Soviet doctrine still clung to leftism not only in the form of the "two camps" theory but also the Leninist thesis on the "fatal inevitability of war." This thesis, as I have argued, was a dangerous thing for crisis diplomacy, and it is not surprising that it was first "clarified" and then modified by Stalin and finally abandoned by Khrushchev.[20] By 1961 it had become standard Soviet practice to try to combine a rightist ideological approach of the "carrot" toward the West with that of a military and political "big stick."

The discussion of ideology as a factor shaping Soviet behavior in the two Berlin crises underlines the fact that it is difficult to uphold the distinction between "Marxist–Leninist ideology" and "the Soviet national interest." Even authors who subscribe to the validity of such a dichotomy for analytical purposes hasten to add the reservation that this is a "crude antithesis."[21] This is true not only because Soviet ideology is a complex phenomenon but also because "the Soviet national interest" (like any national interest) is a highly subjective and ambiguous concept, capable of manipulation and almost limitless reinterpretation, so that in reality political leaders are faced with a complex tangle of interests (in the plural), always changing according to specific social, economic, military, political, *and* ideological conditions, both of an international and domestic dimension, and making it necessary every time to distinguish between costs, benefits, and risks of a long-term or short-term nature.

Despite these complexities one must be wary of worrying about a tautological trap that in reality does not exist. It could be argued that "national interests," vital or peripheral, can be defined only *ex post facto*: more specifically, that the relative importance of particular interests can be measured only in retrospect by the degree of commitment made by a particular state on their behalf. However, this argument resembles recent criticisms of Darwin's theory of natural selection. By defining fitness as "differential reproductive success" (that is, by considering evolution as a change in numbers, not as a change in quality), a vacuous tautology results because natural selection is no more than "the survival of those who survive." However, certain morphological, physiological, and behavioral traits can be considered *a priori* superior as designs for living in new environments. Certain traits "confer fitness by an engineer's criterion of good design, not by the empirical fact of their survival and spread."[22]

Similarly, in international relations political leaders and analysts are able to make their own *a priori* judgments as to the degree to which a particular state's interests are involved, whether they are of primary or secondary importance, and whether the design to safeguard the various interests is adequate, effective, legitimate, and the like. The mutually perceived balance of interests thus comes to be of crucial importance for the origin, course, and outcome of international crises. For an actor to succeed in conveying the idea that vital interests are at stake for himself, and only secondary interests for the adversary, confers to him tremendous advantages in the bargaining process.

## Notes

[1]See Hannes Adomeit, *Soviet Risk-Taking and Crisis Behavior: A Theoretical and Empirical Analysis* (London: Allen and Unwin, 1984), pp. 56–58.

[2]The image also often implies that the more "pragmatic" the Soviet Union becomes, the easier it will be to deal with it, and the greater the tendency for the Soviet Union to become a status quo-oriented power.

[3]This is a point made by Alfred G. Meyer, "The Functions of Ideology in the Soviet Political System," *Soviet Studies* 17, no. 3 (January 1966), p. 273

[4]*Loc. cit.*

[5]See Adomeit, *Soviet Risk-Taking and Crisis Behavior*, p. 57.

[6]Meyer, "The Functions of Ideology in the Soviet Political System," p. 273. Meyer also included the official history of the CPSU and pronouncements made by the party concerning the interpretation of current affairs and the setting of goals and priorities.

[7]The first four of the five functions named above conform roughly to distinctions made by Marshall Shulman. Similar distinctions have appeared in print, e.g., William Zimmerman, *Soviet Perspectives on International Relations* (Princeton: Princeton University Press, 1969), pp. 282–283.

[8]Alexander George, "The 'Operational Code': A Neglected Approach to the Study of Political Leaders and Decision-making," *The Conduct of Soviet Foreign Policy*, 2nd ed., eds. Erik Hoffmann and Frederic Fleron (Hawthorne, N. Y.: Aldine, 1980), pp. 165–190.

[9]V. I. Lenin, *"Left-Wing" Communism, an Infantile Disorder: A Popular Essay in Marxist Strategy and Tactics* [written in 1920] (New York: International Publishers, 1969), p. 59.

[10]*Ibid.*, p. 53.

[11]This is a point made long ago by Zbigniew Brzezinski and Samuel Huntington, *Political Power* (New York: Viking, 1964), p. 66, but it is still right.

[12]Leo Labedz, "Ideology and Soviet Policies in Europe," paper delivered at the Twentieth Annual Conference of the International Institute for Strategic Studies (IISS), September 7–10, 1978, p. 3. See also my paper, "Ideology in the Soviet View of International Affairs," delivered at the same conference, which very much agrees with Labedz's approach and conclusions. Both papers are published in *Prospects of Soviet Power in the 1980s*, ed. Christoph Bertram (London: Macmillan, 1980).

[13]Labedz, "Ideology and Soviet Policies in Europe," p. 6.

[14]*Ibid.*, p. 3.

[15]Robert G. Wesson, "Soviet Ideology: The Necessity of Marxism," *Soviet Studies* 21, no. 1 (July 1969), p. 69.

[16]*Loc. cit.*

[17]See Adomeit, *Soviet Risk-Taking and Crisis Behavior*, pp. 36 and 190.

[18]Vernon V. Aspaturian, "Ideology and National Interest in Soviet Foreign Policy," in *Process and Power in Soviet Foreign Policy* (Boston: Little Brown, 1971), p. 331.

[19]The West Germans, and politically indifferent "East Germans," have always referred to "East Germany" as *Mitteldeutschland* (Central Germany). If the SED rejected this label it was not because of its disagreement with the geographical distinction, but because what it wanted was to see the official political term of "German Democratic Republic" implanted in the consciousness of the Germans.

[20]See Adomeit, *Soviet Risk-Taking and Crisis Behavior*, pp. 113–114, 177–180, and 221–222.

[21]Robin Edmonds, *Soviet Foreign Policy* (London: Oxford University Press, 1975), pp. 153–154. The author also concedes that "Soviet historians and statesmen are guilty neither of dishonesty nor cynicism when they claim, in effect, that what is good for their country is good for world communism." To this can be added the view that "Soviet ideology itself defines 'national interest,' 'power,' and 'world revolution' in such a way as to make them virtually as indistinguishable as the three sides of an equilateral triangle" (Aspaturian, "Ideology and National Interest," p. 333). Finally, there should be little disagreement with the argument that "Depending on the perceptions of fact and value

among these people [Soviet leaders], Soviet national interest may be served by the aggressive pursuit of power by Communist Parties in all countries. Or, Soviet national interest may not be served by such a course at all. The national interest is a *conclusion*, derived logically from premises of fact and value, some of which may have been drawn from, or conditioned by, the precepts of Marxism–Leninism" [Jan Triska and David Finley, *Soviet Foreign Policy* (New York: Macmillan, 1968), p. 114].

[22]Stephen Jay Gould, "Darwin's Untimely Burial," *Natural History* 85, no. 8 (October 1976) p. 26. To demonstrate the point the author adds that "it got colder before the mammoth evolved his shaggy coat."

# II

*Policymaking and Implementation*

# 8

# ADAM B. ULAM

## *Anatomy of Policymaking**

Contemplating the vast volume of Kremlinology produced in this country since World War II, a layman might well paraphrase Karl Marx's famous thesis on Feuerbach and complain that various experts have only interpreted the Soviet Union in different ways, while the urgent need is to find out how its policies can be changed. There have been many prescriptions as to how the United States, through its own policies, might influence the USSR to alter a disquieting pattern of Soviet behavior on the world scene. But before trying to formulate such prescriptions, we must first of all try to understand the process of Soviet policymaking.

To repeat what this author wrote in another study, "The student of Soviet affairs has as his first task to be neither hopeful nor pessimistic, but simply to state the facts and tendencies of Russian politics. It is when he begins to see in certain political trends the inevitabilities of the future and when he superimposes upon them his own conclusions about the desirable policies of America towards the USSR that he is courting trouble."[1] American policymaking ought to profit by a dispassionate analysis of the Soviets' motivations and actions, but it cannot be a substitute for such analysis.

The fulcrum of the Soviet political system is the 20-odd full and alternate members of the Politburo and those Central Committee Secretaries who are outside it. Yet we still need to know more about how this group operates and its relationship to the wider Soviet political elite and to the Soviet people at large. For our purposes, it is especially important to establish some analytical guidelines about how the inner ruling group arrives at its decisions on foreign policy and to what extent it is susceptible to influences from the larger international environment.

Elitist and secretive as the process of Soviet decision making is in general, it is especially so when it comes to foreign policy. One may find

*Reprinted by permission of the author and publisher from *The Washington Quarterly* 6, no. 2 (Spring, 1983), pp. 71–82. Copyright 1983 by The Center for Strategic and International Studies, Georgetown University.

occasionally in the Soviet press and in the utterances of lower officials fairly far-reaching criticisms, particularly of the country's economic systems and performance. It is almost inconceivable for such public discussion to take place in connection with any major Soviet position on international affairs. This taboo is observed also when it comes to Moscow's past foreign policy.

Those who see the Soviet system moving toward pluralism or who hypothesize about the growing influence of the military in decision making disregard the exclusive prerogative of decision making to which the inner ruling group, especially in the Brezhnev era, has held with such tenacity. Even Nikita Khrushchev, who intermittently attempted to enlarge his political base by using the Central Committee to curb his fellow oligarchs, guarded jealously the party's monopoly of power. He could speak slightingly in the presence of foreigners about Andrei Gromyko, then "only" minister of foreign affairs, but not yet a member of the charmed circle; and he dismissed Zhukov largely because the marshal had helped him in his 1957 scrap with the Vyacheslav Molotov faction, and it was intolerable that a professional soldier should be allowed to interfere in settling future disputes on the Soviet Olympus.

In their turn, Leonid Brezhnev and his colleagues were especially insistent not only on preserving the party's role as the only source of political power, but also on recouping the narrower oligarchy's pre-rogative as final arbiter in policymaking. There is a Soviet equivalent of the U.S. National Security Council, but it is presided over ex officio by the general secretary, and nothing indicates that it is more than an advisory body to the Politburo. Since 1964 the Central Committee has been relegated again to being a forum where decisions of the top leadership are announced and perhaps explained in greater detail than they are to the public at large, but not debated. Emperor Paul I once told a foreign ambassador that the only important public figures in Russia were those to whom he talked, and even their influence disappeared once they were no longer in actual conversation with the sovereign. The only participants in the decision-making process in the USSR, outside the 20-odd members of the inner circle, are those whom it chooses to consult, and only while it does so. Unless he is simultaneously a member of the Politburo, the status of the head of an important branch of the government—the armed forces, security, foreign ministry, or economic planning—is similar to that of a high civil servant in the West rather than that of a minister and policymaker.

Because of its very rigidity, and in view of the average age of the ruling oligarchy, the pattern we just sketched is likely to become exposed in the future to increasing strains and might well break down, at least temporarily, during a succession struggle or a situation similar to that of 1956–1957 and the early 1960s. Then the inner group splits into hostile factions and, especially on the latter occasion, the leader found himself increasingly out of tune with his senior colleagues.

For the present and immediate future we must assume, however, that the USSR will continue to be governed under a system where policy options and moves are freely discussed by and fully known only to some

25 people, and the ultimate decisions are made by an even smaller group—the 13 or 15 full members of the Politburo.

This being so, we have little reason to expect basic changes in the Soviet philosophy of foreign relations. The present leaders and their prospective successors have seen the Soviet Union develop from the backward, militarily and industrially weak state of the early 1920s to one of the two superpowers of the post-1945 world. They have been brought up in the belief that the Soviet Union's connection with the worldwide communist movement has been a source of strength to their country, and it is only recently that they have had occasion for doubt on that score. Their formative years witnessed the Soviet system surviving the ravages of terror and the tremendous human and material losses of World War II. As rising bureaucrats in the immediate postwar period, the people of the Politburo generation could observe how Soviet diplomacy managed to offset the Soviet Union's industrial and military inferiority vis-à-vis the principal capitalist state, and even when the country's resources had to be devoted mainly to the task of recovery from the war, the USSR still managed to advance its power and influence in the world at large.

In brief, very little in their own experience or in the international picture, as it has evolved during the past 20 years or so, could have persuaded the Kremlin that its basic guidelines for dealing with the outside world needed revision. The external power and influence of the USSR has been used in propaganda at home to demonstrate the viability and dynamism of the Soviet system and its historical legitimacy. Granted the essentially conservative approach of the present leadership of the Soviet Union toward international affairs, one could hardly imagine it responding to a specific internal emergency by contriving a dangerous international crisis. But the Kremlin still persists in seeking to impress upon its people the paradoxical dichotomy of world politics: The imperialist threat remains as great as ever, and yet the USSR is steadily growing more powerful. Both beliefs are seen as essential to preserving the cohesion of Soviet society. The average Soviet citizen is never to be dissuaded from seeing the capitalist world as a source of potential danger to his country and its allies. By the same token, he must not lose faith in the ability of his government and its armed forces to repel this threat and to ensure even in this nuclear age the security and greatness of the USSR and of the entire socialist camp. It would take an extraordinary combination of domestic political, social, and economic pressures to form a critical mass capable of impelling the regime to change its outlook on world politics.

It is virtually impossible to conceive of the Soviet system surviving in its present form were its rulers to abandon explicitly, or even implicitly, the main premises behind their foreign policy. Practically every feature of Russian authoritarianism is ultimately rationalized in terms of the alleged foreign danger inherent in the existence of the "two struggling camps," one headed by the USSR and the other, the capitalist one, by the United States. Writing at the most hopeful period of détente, and painting a very rosy picture of the future of Soviet–American relations.

Georgi Arbatov still had to add the caveat, "There can be no question as to whether the struggle between the two systems would or would not continue. That struggle is historically unavoidable."[2] If the struggle continues, the Soviet citizen must be made to believe that his side is steadily forging ahead on the world stage. Otherwise, what can compensate him psychologically for his perception—increasingly unsuppressible—that life is freer and materially more abundant in the West?

To be sure, this official rationale of Soviet foreign policy becomes vulnerable in cases where its ideological premises cannot be readily reconciled with the nationalist ones, and it is mainly on that count that one can foresee the possibility of popular reactions at home affecting the course of foreign policy. Tito's apostasy could be dismissed by the Kremlin as being in itself not of great significance. The burdens inherent in standing armed guard over Eastern Europe or in suppressing the Afghan insurgency have been explained in the official media by the necessity of warding off the class enemy and, less explicitly, in terms of Russia's historical mission and interests antedating the Revolution. All these developments could be intepreted as still not in conflict with the thesis that communism is a natural ally and an obedient servant of the Soviet national interest.

However, the Sino–Soviet conflict has struck at the very heart of the ideology/national interest *Weltanschauung* of Soviet foreign policy. In his *Letter to the Soviet Leaders*, Aleksandr Solzhenitsyn formulated very cogently the essential dilemma that has confronted the Kremlin in public since the eruption of the dispute, in fact since Mao's forces conquered the mainland. It is another communist state, and precisely because it is communist, writes Solzhenitsyn, it has posed the greatest threat to Russia's future. Thus, even when it comes to the outside world, he charges, one can readily see how this false ideology has had disastrous consequences for the true interests and security of the Russian people and threatens it eventually with having to fight for survival. This is not the isolated opinion of a writer and dissident who abhors every aspect of communism. Fear of China because of its enormous size, vast industrial–military potential, and the nature of its regime and ruling philosophy is probably the most visceral reaction of the average Soviet, insofar as his outlook on world affairs is concerned. No other aspect of the regime's policy has had so wide approval among the Soviet population as its efforts to contain and isolate the other great communist state.

It is important to note that even this problem has not been allowed to affect the official rationale of Soviet foreign policy. This rationale is still couched in terms inherited from the era when the world communist movement was monolithic in its subservience to Moscow. When it first erupted in public, the Sino–Soviet dispute might well have prompted a foreign observer to prophesy that its implications were bound to change not only the Kremlin's actual policies, but its whole approach to international situations. The confrontation between ideology and reality inherent in the clash ought to have led to a thorough reevaluation of the former, not merely as a justification but also as an operating principle for foreign policies. The USSR should have abandoned even the pretense that what it was doing in Africa, the Near East, and other areas was in the furtherance of socialism.

Yet, in fact, such secularization of Soviet foreign policy has not taken place. One might object that the USSR has tried to cope with the Chinese problem without any ideological inhibitions. It has attempted to enlist the United States in a joint effort to stop or delay China's nuclear development. It has encouraged India to attack and fragment China's only major ally in Asia. The Kremlin viewed with equanimity the massacre of the pro-Beijing Indonesian Communist party, and it encouraged and helped Vietnam in its open defiance of its huge neighbor. Ideological kinship has not restrained the Soviet Union from hinting at times that it might have to resort to a preemptive strike against China.

Yet, for all such unsentimental measures and attitudes, the Soviet leadership has refused to draw what to an outsider would be the logical deductions of its predicament with China. The doctrine of the two camps is still being maintained as stoutly as when the two great communist powers were linked "by unshakeable friendship" and alliance against a potential capitalist aggressor. China's departure from the straight and narrow path of "proletarian internationalism" has been explained in the official Soviet rhetoric as a temporary lapse, while even at the most hopeful periods of peaceful coexistence, the conflict with the capitalist world has been presented as an unavoidable and permanent feature of world politics. There have been fairly serious armed clashes along the Sino–Soviet border, and a sizable proportion of the Soviet armed forces is deployed along the frontier. Those Russian military manuals, however, that are accessible to the public discuss at length the dangers and various scenarios of conventional and nuclear warfare between the USSR and the capitalist powers, while not even alluding to the possibility of a war with another communist power.

This bizarre pattern of behavior cannot be ascribed solely to the Soviet leaders' cynicism and ability to divorce their actions entirely from their words. Nor can it be attributed to some lingering ideological scruples. Given a truth serum, a Soviet statesman would readily confess that barring something very unexpected, the danger of unprovoked capitalist aggression against the USSR is virtually nil, while the possibility of China someday advancing territorial and other claims on his country is very real indeed. The immobilism of the Soviet foreign policy doctrine finds its roots in the nature of the political system as a whole. The 13 or so men at the apex of the Soviet power structure have to think of themselves not only as rulers of a national state, but also as high priests of a world cult, which in turn is the source of legitimacy for the system as a whole and for their own power in particular. Could that legitimacy (and with it, the present political structure of the Soviet Union) endure, were its rulers to renounce one of the most basic operating tenets of communist political philosophy?

To a Westerner it might appear that the regime could greatly strengthen itself by curtailing its expansionist policies abroad and by concentrating on raising the living standards of the Soviet people. It would gain in popularity, the argument would continue, by being more explicit about the real dimension of the problem the USSR faces in relation to China and by putting the alleged threat from the West into proper perspective. But it is most unlikely that the present generation of leaders would, or feels it could, afford to heed such arguments. They remember how even Nikita Khrushchev's modest and clumsy attempts at domestic liberalization and at relieving the siege mentality of his countrymen had, in their view, most unsettling effects on the party and society. Without a continuing sense of danger from abroad, economic improvement at home, far from being an effective remedy for political dissent, is in fact likely to make it more widespread. For the die-hards within the elite, even some of the side effects of détente, such as increased contacts with and knowledge of the West, must have appeared potentially harmful, because they brought in their wake ideological pollution and threatened the stability and cohesion of Soviet society.

History has played an unkind trick on the masters of the USSR. Probably no other ruling oligarchy in modern times has been so pragmatically minded and power-oriented as the current Soviet one. Compared to them, even Nikita Khrushchev, who joined the party in 1918 during the Civil War, showed some characteristics of a true believer. Ironically, it is precisely because of power considerations that the rulers cannot disregard ideological constraints on their policies.

A superficial view of Soviet politics would lead us to believe that a Soviet statesman enjoys much greater freedom of action, especially in foreign affairs, than his Western counterpart. He can order and direct rather than having to plead or campaign for his program. If he has to persuade others, it is a small group rather than an unruly electorate or a partisan legislature. The Politburo's decisions are not hammered out in the full glare of publicity or subjected to immediate public debate and criticisms. Whatever the fears, hesitations, and divisions among the rulers, they seldom become known outside the precincts of the Kremlin. Hence, how can a democracy avoid finding itself at a disadvantage when negotiating with the Kremlin? Neither budgetary constraints nor fear of public opinion can deflect Brezhnev and company from a weapons policy or an action abroad that they believe to be necessary for their purposes and for the prestige and power of the USSR.

This picture, while correct in several details, is greatly misleading overall. The structure of the decision-making process in the USSR enables the Kremlin to be free from many of the constraints under which nonauthoritarian governments must operate. Yet, the nature of the Soviet political system creates its own imperatives, which the leaders must heed and which may make the leaders' choice among foreign policy options more difficult and cumbersome than is the case in a democracy. Superbly equipped as it is for moving rapidly and effectively on several fronts, the Soviet political mechanism has not shown equal capacity during the last 20 years for effectively braking the momentum of its policies once launched. Whether the Soviet political mechanism can develop such braking devices must be of special interest to any student or practitioner of international affairs.

The immediate background of Soviet policies in the 1980s lies in the series of agreements and understandings reached between the USSR and the United States, as well as other states of the Western bloc, which set up the foundations of what has come to be known as détente. It would be a gross oversimplification on our part to view détente as simply an attempt by the Kremlin to deceive the West or, conversely, as a definitive change in Moscow's philosophy of international affairs. Soviet leaders sought a temporary accommodation with the West and a consequent lowering of international tension for reasons inherent in their interpretation of the world scene as of 1970.

Even if undertaken solely as a tactical maneuver, détente was not cost-free for the Soviets. Domestically it gave more resonance to the voices of dissent and placed the government under the obligation of relaxing restrictions on Jewish emigration, a concession that would have been unthinkable a few years earlier. Abroad, it was bound to raise doubts and suspicions in the minds of the Soviet Union's clients and friends. Only a few weeks after the Nixon–Brezhnev summit, Anwar Sadat ordered some 20,000 Soviet military personnel out of Egypt, a step very largely motivated by his conviction that his country's foreign policy now had to be more balanced between the two superpowers.

The Soviet policymakers' usual skill at having their cake and eating it too was thus put to a severe test. The 1972–1973 period offers a convincing example of the Soviet Union's sensitivity to its antagonists' actual policies and of the importance it places on its perception of the overall condition of the noncommunist world. In 1972 the economy of the West as a whole was still flourishing and expanding. Political stability appeared to be returning in the United States. With his successes in the international field, Nixon was virtually assured a second term. This political and economic strength of the West, as well as several other international developments, added up to compelling reasons for the Soviets to pull in their horns.

How long this restraint would have prevailed in the councils of the Kremlin and whether there was any possibility of more fundamental alteration in Soviet foreign policy remains unknown. Within a year and a half of the inauguration of détente, the premises on which the Soviets' restraints had been based began to crumble. By the end of 1974 Moscow was bound to conclude that the West was not nearly as stable and strong politically or economically as it had appeared to be in 1972.

Beginning in 1974, the USSR became much less concerned about U.S. reactions to its policies abroad, even the ones that were openly directed at undermining the influence and interests of the United States and its friends. Unlike the case of the 1973 Middle Eastern conflict, Soviet actions in Angola, Ethiopia, and South Yemen betrayed little hesitation or fear that they might bring effective U.S. countermeasures or even seriously damage overall Soviet–U.S. relations, thus diminishing the benefits the USSR was reaping from détente. To be sure, the Soviets have always been aware of how sensitive the United States is to what happens in the Middle East, and in comparison the average American knows little and cares less about Angola or South Yemen. However, what should have been cause for alarm to U.S. policymakers was not so much the targets but the character of Soviet activities in Africa. It was not merely another example of the Soviet skill at scavenging amidst the debris of Western colonialism and wresting yet another country from its nonaligned or pro-Western position through ideological appeal or an alliance with the local dictator or oligarchy. Angola was the testing ground for a new technique of Soviet imperial expansion.

The experiment was allowed to succeed and thus became a precedent for further employment of this technique. Nonnative, up to now Cuban, troops would be used to establish Soviet presence in the country and to maintain the pro-Soviet regime in power. Thus, wars of "national liberation" could be carried out and won by the pro-Soviet faction, because it was helped not only by Soviet arms and advisers, but also by massive infusion of communist bloc troops. Had the general international situation remained similar to that of 1972–1973, it is unlikely that the conservative-minded Brezhnev regime would have attempted such a daring innovation as projecting Soviet power into areas thousands of miles away from the USSR.

The reasons for the Kremlin's confidence that this innovative form of international mischief-making was not unduly risky were probably very similar to those that persuaded North Vietnam about the same time to launch a massive invasion and to occupy the south. A North Vietnamese general spelled out candidly the rationale of his government's actions and why it was certain the United States would not interfere. "The internal contradictions within the U.S. administration and among U.S. political parties had intensified. The Watergate scandal had seriously affected the entire United States. . . . It faced economic recession, mounting inflation, serious unemployment and an oil crisis."[3]

This revealing statement illustrates well the hard-boiled pragmatism of the Soviets and their disciples and how free they can be of the dogmas of their own ideology in their socioeconomic evaluations of a given situation. According to classical Marxist–Leninist doctrine, an internal crisis impels the capitalists to act more aggressively and to seek a remedy for economic troubles, as well as to distract the attention of the masses through imperialist adventures. Here we had quite a realistic analysis of the reasons for this country's acquiescence in North Vietnam's flagrant violation of the agreement it had signed only 2 years before, and of the debilitating effects of domestic crisis on a democratic country's foreign policies. The statement demonstrates once again how in their calculus of potential risks and gains in world politics, the Soviets tend to go beyond the arithmetic of nuclear missiles, tanks, and ships and pay even closer attention to the psychopolitical ingredients of the given situation. It did require a degree of sensitivity to U.S. politics to perceive how seriously American foreign policy was harmed by reopening the wounds of Vietnam and by pitting Congress against the executive branch. The Watergate affair had crippled America's capacity to act effectively abroad, especially when it came to meeting the Soviet and/or communist challenge in the Third World.

It was less remarkable for the Kremlin to draw the proper lesson from the energy crisis that now grips the West's economy. If the world's leading industrial nations were incapable of synchronizing their policies to counteract or soften the blow from the Organization of Petroleum Exporting Countries, a blow more serious in its implications to the West than anything done by the Soviet Union since World War II, how could they be expected to mount concerted action to deal with the Soviets' expansion in Africa or outright invasion of a neighboring country?

The effect of the Soviets' redefinition of détente in light of the economic crisis in the West weakened American leadership, and the fissiparous tendencies within the Atlantic alliance could be observed at the 1979 Vienna Brezhnev–Carter summit. Anxious as the Russians were to seal SALT II and to prevent relations between the two countries from deteriorating, there was little at Vienna of that studied courting of the Americans that had characterized the 1972 Moscow conference. This time there were no grandiloquent declarations about both countries scrupulously respecting each other's broad policy interests throughout the world. Instead, Brezhnev chose to lecture Carter and his entourage in public on the impermissibility and uselessness of trying to link the fate of SALT II and détente to Soviet restraint in foreign policy. "Attempts also continue to portray social processes taking place in one or another country or the struggles of the peoples for liberation as 'Moscow's plots or intrigues.' Naturally, the Soviet people are in sympathy with the liberation struggle of various nations. . . . We believe that every people has the right to determine its own destiny. Why then pin on the Soviet Union the responsibility for the objective course of history, or what is more, use this as a pretext for worsening our relations?"[4] With the worldwide configuration of forces now much more in their favor than it had been in 1972, it was probably genuinely incomprehensible to the Soviet leaders how anyone could expect them to abide by the same obligations and cautions they had pledged to observe on the earlier occasion.

## Choices and Projections

Their actions in the recent past and present offer a suggestive guide to Soviet leaders' choices and decisions in the future. While it is of little use to try to divide the Kremlin decision makers into hawks and doves or to try to divine who might represent the hard or soft factions, there is within the Politburo and its affiliates a considerable division of opinion when it comes to foreign policy. These differences, however, are not found in any permanent groupings or factions, but in the fluctuation between two main tendencies present in the mind of the leadership as a whole.

One such approach might be likened to that of the rentier. This view holds that the USSR can afford to be patient and circumspect in its foreign policies, eschew risky ventures abroad, and continue to collect the dividends of its past successes and the inherent and worsening afflictions of the capitalist world. The rentier's attitude is based not so much on the preachings and certitudes of Marxism as on the deductions from the historical experiences of the Soviet state, especially since World War II, when the United States has been its only real rival for worldwide power and influence. The Americans have been unable to oppose effectively the Soviets' advance, and they are unlikely to do so in the future. The cumbersome procedure of American foreign policymaking and the unruly democratic setting in which it operates will always place the United States at a disadvantage vis-à-vis the flexible and unconstrained apparatus of Soviet diplomacy. Hence, it is unwise to provoke the Americans and risk a confrontation, when the U.S. position is bound to grow weaker and that of the USSR stronger in the natural course of events.

The rentier puts the "imperialist danger" in a pragmatic perspective. It does exist as a general tendency within the capitalist world, but with proper caution on Moscow's part, it will not assume the form of a concrete menace. The United States was not able to threaten the USSR at the time of greatest American superiority. It is not likely to do so now, when there is general awareness in the West of what a nuclear war might mean. The Reagan administration's early rhetoric has already been blunted by the realization that the Soviet Union cannot be intimidated and that both the economic realities and the realities of European politics will not permit the United States to regain superiority in strategic weapons or to match quantitatively those of the USSR.

The rentier would urge the Soviets to moderate the pace of their nuclear arms buildup and to be prepared to offer timely concessions in the course of negotiations. The USSR has already gained great political advantages from having surpassed the United States in several categories of these weapons and would compound the gains by making what the world at large (if not the Pentagon) would hail as a magnanimous gesture—say, stopping the production of the Backfire bomber. Piling up arms eventually becomes politically counterproductive. The goal is to disarm the West psychologically and prevent it from recouping the momentum toward political integration; and Soviet military intimidation, if kept up for too long, is bound to have the opposite effect.

The same reasoning would apply to the general guidelines of Soviet policies throughout the world. Having established bridgeheads in Africa and the Caribbean, the Soviet Union would be making an error by trying to expand them too blatantly. The problems facing the United States in those areas are essentially intractable, and it is much better for Moscow to wait upon events in the Third World than to attempt to give history a push, for example in South Africa. The USSR must refrain from any action likely to touch on a raw nerve of American politics, such as identifying itself with the extreme Arab position on Israel or reaching too obviously for control of the oil routes. In most of these areas of contention, time is essentially working for the Soviet Union, and precipitate actions by the Soviets might tend to reverse the trend.

The rentier's case on this last point becomes most debatable when the Politburo discussions turn to Eastern Europe and China. But even there, the rentier instinct would plead for a conservative approach. Soviet bloc countries can always be handled, though preferably not by military means. In China, it is true, time does not seem to work in the Soviets' favor. But for the balance of the 1980s and probably considerably beyond that, China can be contained, provided that the West and Japan do not launch a massive effort to help Beijing modernize its economy and become a major industrial (and hence military) power. Therefore, the need to contain China makes it all the more important to exercise restraint and blend firmness with conciliatory gestures in their approach toward the West.

The other side of the Soviet leadership's split personality might be called that of the speculator. For him the imperialist danger is not merely a doctrinal or propaganda phrase. It is not that he believes any more than the rentier that the United States is about to attack the USSR or engineer a revolution in East Germany or Poland. But only the constant growth in power by the Soviet Union and its avowed readiness to contemplate nuclear war have kept the West off balance and have prevented it from more explicit attempts to undermine the socialist camp. The USSR, therefore, must not desist from active and aggressive exploitation of the weaknesses and vulnerabilities of the world capitalist system, even where it involves a possibility of a major clash with the United States. Such brinksmanship becomes especially important for the immediate future, because any lessening in the Soviets' militancy would be read by Washington as a vindication of tough U.S. rhetoric, would encourage the United States to play to the hilt the China card, and could embolden the West Europeans to follow Washington's pleas to join in applying economic pressures upon the Soviet Union.

The speculator would not desist from trying to enhance and exploit whatever military advantages the USSR has already secured over the United States. To give up any of those advantages would be a grave mistake politically, even more so than militarily. It is awe of Soviet military might that has kept the United States from interfering in the Czechoslovak and Polish crises, has made the Europeans fearful about offending Moscow by imposing effective economic sanctions, and in fact makes them ever more eager to propitiate the Soviet colossus with trade and credits. Any slackening in the arms buildup would be taken in the West as confirmation of the thesis that internal economic and other problems have made the USSR more malleable to defense and international issues and that consequently one can pressure the Soviets to alter not only their military and foreign policies but also their domestic ones. One has to negotiate with the United States and NATO on tactical and strategic nuclear arms, but to offer any one-sided concessions, even if not substantive, would be most damaging for the USSR's image and bargaining position.

The speculator would stress the necessity of militancy, and not only from the angle of relations with the West. In the years ahead some Third World leaders might well be tempted to imitate Sadat's gambit and exploit the USSR for their own purposes, only to switch to the other side once the Soviet connection had been fully exploited. In retrospect it may have been a mistake to make Egypt the fulcrum of Soviet policies in the Middle East and to pour so much money and effort into buttressing its regime without obtaining a firmer grasp on its internal politics. Future Soviet ventures in the Third World must not only lead to a temporary discomfiture for the West, but also result in firm Soviet ideological and military control over the new client.

Analysts in the West and even some figures within the Soviet establishment keep pointing to Afghanistan as an illustration of the dangers of overt and precipitate Russian aggression. In fact Afghanistan, for all its troublesome aspects, has served as a salutary lesson to those of Moscow's protégés who might contemplate following Egypt's example and try to get the benefits of Soviet political and economic support while maneuvering between the two camps. For all the initial indignation, the Afghanistan coup served to strengthen the Muslim world's respect or fear of the USSR. When a mob tried to attack the Soviet embassy in Teheran, it was protected (unlike the embassy of another power) by the forces of that very fundamentalist Muslim regime. Direct Soviet military intervention is not something to be used too often, but once in a long while it serves as a useful reminder that the USSR is not to be trifled with.

Similar considerations indicate that the Soviet Union cannot afford to be a passive observer or just assist occasionally and indirectly in the erosion of U.S. influence in Latin America or that of the West in general in Africa. In fact it is doubtful whether this process can continue to benefit the Soviet Union's interests, unless the latter promotes it energetically with more than just rhetoric and military supplies. All radical and liberation movements are inherently unstable and volatile in their political allegiance. If rebuffed in their pleas for more active Soviet help, they may turn to others or tend to disintegrate. It would thus be a mistake for Moscow to stand aside if and when armed struggle erupts in South Africa or in the case of a violent confrontation between the forces of Left and Right in a major Latin American country.

Our speculator tends to question, not explicitly of course, the thesis tht "the objective course of history" must favor the Soviet cause. Where would the USSR be today if it had allowed "objective factors" to determine the fate of Eastern Europe? In Latin American, Africa, and Asia one ought not to confuse the emotional residue of anticolonialism and local radicalism with a secular tendency toward communism or with automatic gravitation of the new and developing societies toward the Soviet model. Anticapitalism and perhaps anti-Western sentiments may be the common denominator of most radical and liberation movements in the non-Western world. But once in power, if they feel they can afford it, such movements tend to seek freedom from any foreign tutelage. Their leaders have grown sophisticated enough to understand the complexities of the international scene and, if left to themselves, they would prefer to be genuinely nonaligned and able to play one side against the other.

It is not by patiently waiting upon events but by bold coups that Soviet power and influence have been projected into all areas of the globe, and it is not the "inherent logic of economic and social development" but the greatly expanded naval and airlift capabilities that have maintained and enlarged those enclaves of influence. And so for the balance of the 1980s the objective course of history must continue to be carved out by strenuous Soviet efforts including, when necessary, the use of military force.

Political and economic stability is a natural ally of the capitalist world. The USSR, therefore, can have no interest except in special cases in a general U.S.–Soviet understanding that would lessen the intensity of political ferment in the troubled areas of the world or reduce appreciably the present level of international tension. The speculator rejects the practicality or desirability of any long-term accommodation between the USSR and the United States. Even if it pursues the most peaceful policies, the United States will always represent a standing danger to the Soviet system and the socialist camp, simply by virtue of what it is. Close relations with the democracies lead inevitably to ideological pollution at home and to the weakening of the political vigilance and social discipline that is *sine qua non* of a communist regime.

The rentier and the speculator would disagree most violently concerning the degree of urgency of the Chinese problem. The activist rejects emphatically the notion that the USSR can afford to sit and watch while China's economy is being modernized and its stockpile of nuclear weapons keeps growing. Some efficacious solution to the problem must be found during the next few years. Perhaps the intrafaction struggle that has been going on in China since the Cultural Revolution might assume the proportions of a civil war. Barring that rather slim hope, the USSR would have to take some measures beyond simply trying to contain China. Perhaps Beijing could still be enticed to paper over its dispute with the Soviets and be pushed again onto a collision course with the United States. Conversely, a moment might come when the Soviets will have sufficiently intimidated the West to compel it to leave them a free hand for even the most drastic resolution of their Chinese dilemma. Since the Sino–Soviet dispute heated up, and even when relations between Washington and Beijing were at their worst, it has in fact been America's nuclear power that has been a key factor in restraining the Soviets from trying to resolve the conflict by force.

Neither of the two impulses currently coexisting in the minds of the Politburo is likely to achieve complete mastery during the balance of the decade. Ascendancy of the rentier mentality would clearly make the Soviet Union much less of a destabilizing force in the world arena and in the long run could open up prospects of a major change in the Soviets' philosophy of international relations. The speculator motif, if dominant, would greatly increase the danger of an all-out war. For the immediate future the Soviet leaders can be expected to seek a middle course between the two approaches, the benefits and risks of either determined by their perceptions of the strengths and weaknesses of the noncommunist world.

## Notes

[1]Henry L. Stimson and McGeorge Bundy, *On Active Service in War and Peace* (New York: Octagon, 1947), p. 644.

[2]Georgi Arbatov, "Soviet-American Relations," in *The Communist* (Moscow: February, 1973), p. 110.

[3]Fox Butterfield, "Hanoi General Was Surprised at Speed of Saigon's Collapse," *New York Times*, April 26, 1976.

[4]Quoted in *State Department Bulletin*, no. 2028 (Washington, D.C.: U.S. Government Printing Office, July 1979), p. 51.

9

ERIK P. HOFFMANN
ROBBIN F. LAIRD

*Soviet Perspectives on "The Scientific–Technological Revolution" and International Politics**

Present-day Soviet policymakers and theorists are keenly sensitive to the reciprocal relationships between scientific and technological change and international politics. We have documented this contention extensively in our books *"The Scientific–Technological Revolution" and Soviet Foreign Policy* and *The Politics of Economic Modernization in the Soviet Union.* Here we will identify the chief parameters of consensus among Soviet leaders and commentators on these themes. We will then discuss the major differences between Soviet conservative and modernizing orientations. Finally, we will argue that the competition between conservative and modernizing tendencies has been and will continue to be a central component of Soviet politics.

**Consensus in Soviet Thinking**    Soviet analysts underscore at least eleven major changes that "the scientific–technological revolution" (STR) has introduced into contemporary international relations. Here, briefly stated, are these generally agreed upon and influential Soviet assessments of the STR as an "objective" force in world politics.

First, the STR has launched a "revolution in military affairs." Scientific discoveries and technological innovations have dramatically increased the destructiveness of warfare, endangering the very existence of the human species. Modern weaponry cannot be manufactured or deployed without advanced scientific research and technological virtuosity, especially in the fields of nuclear energy and guided missile systems.

*Reprinted in revised form by permission of the authors and publisher from *"The Scientific–Technological Revolution" and Soviet Foreign Policy* (Elmsford, N. Y.: Pergamon Press, 1982), pp. 174–190, 196–197, 233–235. Copyright 1982 by Pergamon Press.

Because both strategic and conventional weapons are becoming more automated, the capacity of a nation to win or deter wars increasingly rests upon its scientific and technical potential. N. A. Lomov asserts: "The ever growing role of science in strengthening the military might of a state is now a clearly expressed pattern. Without considering this pattern, it is impossible to examine with sufficient profundity and completeness the present military capability and prospects for strengthening the military might of a state."[1] Hence, the STR makes necessary the rapid modernization of armaments and of the strategies and tactics for waging and preventing war. International competition in this sphere is intense and ongoing.

Second, the STR generates a number of "global problems" whose resolution would benefit socialist, capitalist, and Third World countries. The reduction of environmental pollution and ecological imbalances, for example, increasingly necessitates international cooperation. R. A. Novikov declares: "In this epoch, the further progress of human civilization requires more than ever before the direction of social energy to deal with the preservation of nature, the utilization of natural resources, the rational and comprehensive management of the entire system of 'man–society–nature' from the standpoint not only of the present but of the long run, not only from a national but from a global ecological perspective."[2] Some Soviet analysts acknowledge the emergence of an environmental crisis in advanced capitalist *and* developed socialist societies, implicitly calling into question the advantages of socialist planning and management. But Soviet commentators maintain that, by encouraging "self-criticism" on environmental issues and by initiating international efforts to resolve environmental problems, the leaders of developed socialist states can help to reduce the abuse of nature and can demonstrate to their own citizens and to other peoples the superiority of socialist problem-solving capabilities.

Third, the STR creates opportunities to cope with dilemmas that result from powerful demographic forces, such as the more than doubling of the world's population in the second half of the twentieth century and the concomitant shortages of food, energy, and raw materials. Soviet spokesmen emphasize the importance of international collaboration, especially between the most industrialized socialist and capitalist states, to develop the resources of the world's oceans. N. I. Lebedev adds: "The current scientific–technical revolution makes it objectively necessary and possible to arrange for long-term economic, scientific, and technical ties in many other fields requiring collective effort: exploration and development of outer space, transport (especially airborne), peaceful uses of atomic energy, and the battle against the most widespread and dangerous diseases."[3]

Fourth, the STR promotes "the internationalization of economic life." Soviet theorists maintain that the specialization and concentration of production are "objective laws" governing industrial development throughout the world. The pursuit of economic self-sufficiency can lead to wasteful duplication of efforts by competing nations. Soviet conservatives stress the importance of integrating the Comecon economies and of selectively expanding links with advanced capitalist and Third World economies. Soviet modernizers call for greater emphasis on East–West commercial ties. But most conservatives and all modernizers would agree with M. M. Maksimova that, "In the conditions of the current STR, all countries are equally interested in making use of its achievements and in implementing the advantages of the international division of labor, which is providing ever new opportunities for the enhancement of social production, the acceleration of technological progress, and the establishment of higher living standards for the population."[4] Or, as V. L. Mal'kevich states: "Foreign economic ties in the age of the STR stimulate the development of the productive forces, the deepening of international specialization, the emergence of new types of productive activity, scientific research, and satisfaction of rising social requirements."[5]

Soviet officials and researchers recognize that present-day international economic relations are generating problems as well as opportunities. The USSR's economy has become increasingly open or permeable to economic disturbances from the external environment. The centralized planning and management systems of Soviet-type economies do not respond promptly or flexibly to fluctuations in world prices and to the supply of and demand for imports and exports. To be sure, the USSR benefited considerably from the inflated prices of oil and gold in the late 1970s. But the rising prices of grain, the stagnating prices of oil, and the declining prices of gold in the 1980s have made it much more difficult for the USSR to plan its foreign trade and to manage its hard-currency debt. These difficulties have been compounded by Eastern Europe's mounting dependency on subsidized energy imports from the Soviet Union and by the chaos in the Polish economy in the early 1980s, especially Poland's huge debt to Western banks and governments. With the creditworthiness of the entire Soviet bloc undermined, and with production and distribution bottlenecks disrupting the economies of numerous Comecon countries, some of the liabilities of socialist economic integration became more apparent and troublesome to the Brezhnev administration. In short, the Soviet optimism about international economic ties in the early 1970s was tempered by a more cautious assessment of the costs and risks of extensive participation in and exposure to the increasingly unstable and unpredictable global economy of the 1980s.

Fifth, the STR spurs the internationalization of scientific and technological activity.[6] Previously, the exchange of manufactured goods and natural resources had been the basic type of economic interaction among states. But, in the era of the STR, fundamental scientific research and technical know-how transcend national borders. A Soviet scientist or an engineer may well have more professional skills and interests in common with a Western specialist in the same field than with Soviet colleagues in his own institution. Collaboration among the scientists and technical experts of different countries and the dissemination of existing knowledge promote mutually advantageous economic growth and productivity and reduce the duplication of primary research and its practical applications. International team studies and the sale of licenses, for example, are particularly important in fields where the costs and risks of talent- and time-consuming research and development (R&D) are extremely high. Moreover, certain scientific and technological projects (e.g., space and energy R&D) are so costly and complex that long-term international financing is often required.

Soviet conservatives and modernizers think that the coordination of East–West scientific, technological, and economic policies is unfeasible, given the basic differences between socialist and capitalist systems and the multifaceted competition between them. But Soviet analysts emphasize the importance of integrating the economies of the USSR and its Comecon partners and of expanding *some* economic ties between socialist and capitalist nations. Hence, most conservatives and all modernizers would agree with Lebedev and Mal'kevich that

> Scientific–technical autarky is an impermissible luxury. In the final analysis it holds back scientific and technical progress, and consequently the growth of each country's productive forces. . . . No country, even the most highly developed, can secure maximum results in all areas of science, technology, and material production. For as the volume of knowledge grows in breadth and depth, the STR penetrates every sphere of economic activity. The multiformity and complexity of scientific and technological progress require much greater expenditure of manpower and finance for research and development and the material embodiment of their results. The scale of the integrated problems confronting science and technology at the present time makes it obligatory for individual countries to join their efforts for common goals.[7]

Sixth, the STR enhances the importance of a nation's ability to compete in an increasingly internationalized science–technology–production cycle or division of labor. In order to become more competitive in the world economy, the USSR must use scarce resources more effectively and efficiently, produce more and better industrial and agricultural goods, market its wares abroad (especially manufactured items) more successfully, generate more hard currency, and more skillfully select and thoroughly assimilate the products, services, and information that can be purchased or obtained from other nations. Both conservatives and modernizers perceive international scientific–technical and economic competition to be integrally connected with domestic economic challenges and pressures, and they recognize the importance of coordinating domestic and international objectives. Modernizers emphasize that in order to improve the quality and quantity of Soviet industrial and agricultural products and to meet the growing demands and needs of Soviet consumers, the closer linking of domestic production with foreign trade is becoming more and more significant. A major Soviet study concludes: "Foreign economic ties give us great additional opportunities for successfully fulfilling [our] economic plans, for saving time, for increasing the efficiency of production, for accelerating scientific and technological progress, and for attaining the primary objective—the further upgrading of the standard of living of the Soviet people."[8]

Seventh, the STR fosters scientific, technological, and economic cooperation between East and West, which, in turn, increases the likelihood and longevity of political accords. Georgii Skorov argues that "tension between countries always forces each of them to harden its position. At the same time, extension of commercial and economic relations on an equal and mutually profitable basis always provides the conditions for closer attention to the partner's opinion, induces pursuit of a more flexible policy, and justifies a tendency to compromise."[9] A. P. Aleksandrov, president of the USSR Academy of Sciences, affirms that the importation of foreign experience promotes *the strengthening of trust and the growth of economic incentive for the preservation of peace*. Long-term agreements would give these changes a stable instead of a chance character."[10] In a word, the selective expansion of international scientific, technological, and economic ties is an integral part of the Soviet concept of détente.

Eighth, the STR heightens the significance of nonmilitary forms of power in the international arena. As Oleg Bykov puts its: "Neither strategic nor technical innovations can help imperialism to regain the capability of resolving the question of war and peace at its own discretion. For with the present correlation of forces, including the strategic equilibrium, military might becomes less and less suitable a means of resolving the differences between the two social systems [socialism and capitalism]."[11] The mounting international influence of Japan derives almost entirely from its economic successes, and the rising assertiveness of Western Europe vis-à-vis the United States is similarly grounded on its commercial accomplishments and interests. Such factors must be given more and more weight when assessing a nation's overall capabilities and when predicting the future of "interimperialist contradictions."[12]

However, Soviet commentators stress that the *relative* scientific, technological, and economic capabilities of industrialized states are a major source of political influence. This argument has some important implications for East–West relations that Soviet spokesmen rarely address (e.g., the continuing "technology gap"). As for relations among the Western powers, a comprehensive Soviet–East German study affirms: "The growth of the role of Western Europe does not automatically entail the weakening of the positions of the USA. The USA continues to command a massive economic potential, and far [outpaces] its West European rivals in the areas of science and technology. In the military sphere Western Europe keeps [oriented toward] the USA as the power which commands the greatest stockpile of nuclear weapons in the capitalist world. In the political sphere the USA has kept hold of certain means of influencing the course followed by some West European states."[13].

Ninth, the STR establishes new forms of international dependency, especially in scientific and technological fields. G. A. Arbatov declares that "states which cannot create a sufficiently powerful scientific and technical potential of their own are faced with a difficult dilemma. They have to choose between falling seriously behind . . . or tying themselves firmly to a country which possesses such a potential."[14] At the same time, Soviet leaders and analysts emphasize that the STR introduces new forms of interdependence as well. Highly industrialized nations must secure diverse and stable natural resource bases. Hence, some Third World countries with technological dependencies possess commodities that establish reverse dependencies.[15] Oil is a particularly important example of the capitalist world's need to maintain businesslike relations with a cartel of developing nations (OPEC). Also, the STR creates a demand for certain previously unusable raw materials. For instance, the aluminum industry is the only consumer of bauxite.

Tenth, the STR has sparked a worldwide "information explosion." As Y. Kashlev observes, "The objective social, political, scientific, and technological processes of the modern world are enhancing the role of information and propaganda in society and international relations."[16] This is due in part to a "dramatic and unparalleled expansion of communication technology," and to an "expansion of international economic, commercial, financial, scientific, technical, cultural, and other links."[17] Indeed, many regions of industrialized nations are becoming increasingly permeable to ideas and information from other regions and from abroad. Also, the political leaders of industrialized nations are striving to improve the transmission and processing of information, because effective decisions in virtually all issue areas depend upon a continuous flow of accurate and timely data from domestic and international environments. Y. Zakharov affirms: "This is an objective process which stems from the general laws of development of the productive forces and the requirements of the international division of labor. The STR is speeding up this process."[18]

Eleventh, the STR produces increasingly complex and shifting international relationships, which, in turn, necessitate adjustments in the foreign and domestic policies and policymaking processes of modern industrialized states. Traditional diplomacy must be supplemented by the contributions of greater numbers of civilian and military politician–administrators, technical specialists, and production executives. These officials often work in ostensibly "domestic" functional areas, but they have a growing stake in defining the international interests of the state. Diplomatic, commercial, military, and intelligence activities are being transformed by experts who analyze segments of the international environment and, less frequently, internal/external linkages. For example, many Soviet analysts are publicly and privately acknowledging the need to modify some of the institutions and operations of the USSR's highly centralized economic system, in order to improve the growth and productivity of the economy and to compete more successfully in world markets. Top political officials retain the power to ignore this specialized knowledge. But most socialist and capitalist leaders are thought to be using such information and counsel to identify and assess the problems and opportunities spawned by the STR, and to formulate and implement differentiated national policies that seek to *preserve* their currently held values in a rapidly changing international system.[19]

Thus, leading Soviet officials and theorists understand that the STR is profoundly influencing international politics in the contemporary era.

As Lebedev succinctly concludes: "Scientific and technical progress has made our world smaller and more crowded. The masses react to problems of war and peace much more sensitively than before. Wars, particularly world wars, have always been a calamity for the masses. However, formerly wars had never jeopardized the physical existence of entire countries and peoples. In view of the huge stockpiles of thermonuclear weapons, the life of every person in the world now depends on the intelligent solution of problems of foreign policy."[20]

## Soviet Conservative and Modernizing Perspectives

Soviet leaders and international affairs specialists differ, however, in their assessments of "intelligent" foreign policy initiatives and responses. Soviet conservatives and modernizers disagree about foreign policy priorities, the most effective means of implementing them, and the risks and costs of alternative programs. Officials also debate the nature and significance of important processes of change, such as the STR and the "the general crisis of capitalism," and their political implications, such as the merits of pursuing relatively autarkic or interdependent strategies of development. The military and civilian sectors of the Soviet economy continuously compete for scarce resources, which is another fundamental source of bureaucratic conflict over power and policy.[21]

Conservatives stress that Soviet foreign policy should actively support the "objective" and "subjective" forces that will eventually make the polities and societies of capitalist and Third World nations similar to those of the USSR; modernizers stress that socialist, capitalist, and Third World countries have more and more mutual interests in contemporary international relations and should adjust their foreign policies (but not necessarily their sociopolitical systems) accordingly. Most conservatives and all modernizers share Mal'kevich's belief that the "STR has appreciably accelerated the [economic merging] of nations, has intertwined their economic contacts and *interests*, notably in scientific research and industry."[22] Modernizers view this process with confidence and as a potential benefit, whereas conservatives view it with caution and as a potential liability.

Assessing the effects of the STR on West–West relations and East–West détente, Soviet modernizers emphasize that major cleavages are developing between Western Europe and the United States. These cleavages are widening primarily because of the capitalist powers' different economic and security interests. West European countries, modernizers argue, are seeking to increase scientific, technological, and economic cooperation with the Soviet bloc, in order to enhance their economic competitiveness vis-à-vis the United States and Japan and to reduce their political dependence upon the United States. East–West diplomatic and commercial relations, as well as the limitation of strategic arms and the reduction of conventional military forces, can and must be "mutually advantageous" to socialist and capitalist states in the coming decades. Political and economic ties with Western countries will spur the development of the Soviet economy, modernizers contend, and will eventually induce all Western nations to accept the Soviet interpretation of détente or will increasingly split the Western alliance.

Soviet conservatives, in contrast, underscore that the West's approach to East–West relations "is dominated by a unity of class interests, displaying a tendency toward coordinating their political courses."[23] The military–industrial complexes of Western Europe and the United States have compelling mutual interests, conservatives maintain. Most West European countries and Japan, notwithstanding their growing economic power, lack the motivation and capabilities to transform that power into political leverage vis-à-vis the United States. The policies of America's allies are greatly influenced, conservatives argue, by the continued U.S. superiority in many key areas of scientific research and technological innovation in military and nonmilitary spheres.

Evaluating the impact of the STR on the global economy and the USSR's economy, Soviet modernizers emphasize that foreign economic ties have beneficial effects on domestic growth and productivity. The quality, mix, pricing, cost-efficiency, and profitability of Soviet products can be enhanced or "rationalized" by the challenge of competing in world markets. Two Western analysts contend that "subject to certain conditions—above all a satisfactory degree of openness to foreign technology and preparedness for its infusion—the transfer of technology from a developed country to a medium developed country becomes the dominant source of growth in the medium developed country."[24] This premise, and the feasibility and desirability of applying it in the USSR, are central to the thinking of Soviet modernizers.

Soviet conservatives, however, favor less extensive and more selective importation of advanced technology. Most conservatives believe that Western computers, telecommunications, and automated production systems can improve the performance of the Soviet economy, thereby preserving its highly centralized features and forestalling systemic reforms. Conservatives tend to view the importation of Western technology as a "one-shot" or "quick-fix"[25] approach to pressing problems. Whereas modernizers argue that Western imports are a means of continuously stimulating indigenous technological innovation, conservatives stress that overreliance on Western technology perpetuates "sluggishness" in the Soviet science–technology–production cycle. Brezhnev, having shifted from the modernizing position he shared with Kosygin in the early and mid-1970s, articulated a conservative position on East–West technology exchange at the Twenty-sixth Party Congress in 1981. "We must look into the reasons that we sometimes lose our [competitive advantage in certain fields of science, technology, and production] and spend large sums of money to purchase from foreign countries equipment and technologies that we are fully capable of producing ourselves, and often of a higher quality too."[26]

In short, Soviet conservatives and modernizers have different perspectives on the economic effects of importing sophisticated Western technology, whereas their perspectives on the appropriate nature and volume of high technology imports are much more similar. For instance, photocopying machines are anathema to conservatives and most modernizers, and both are eager to import sizable quantities of oil drilling equipment and of piping and turbines for the compressor stations needed to transport natural gas long distances.

Analyzing the consequences of "the STR in military affairs" on the Soviet–American strategic rivalry, Soviet modernizers emphasize the importance of balancing military and general political and economic capabilities. Modernizers argue that civilian sectors should derive more benefits ("spin-offs") from science-based technological advances in the military sphere. Strategic modernizers affirm that the STR dramatically alters the nature of contemporary warfare every decade or so, and that Soviet goals and methods should be reconceptualized and adjusted accordingly. For example, conventional military forces and economic competitiveness are viewed as increasingly significant modes of advancing Soviet global interests. Moreover, modernizers think that strategic arms limitation agreements are an important means of reducing the likelihood of nuclear war between the superpowers. Because of the emergence of "realistic" Western leaders and public opinion, effective arms control treaties can be negotiated. Lebedev, for one, affirms that national security cannot be guaranteed by the continuous modernization of strategic arms, and he concludes that "in international relations a nuclear war can no longer be a means of attaining political objectives."[27] Hence, modernizers underscore the benefits of maintaining strategic parity and the pitfalls of either the Soviet or American pursuit of strategic superiority.

Soviet conservatives stress the primacy of both the strategic and conventional military components of national security. Conservatives reiterate that survival in a hostile international environment takes precedence over all other claims on human and material resources. Strategic conservatives anticipate that new weapons technologies, together with much better military training of the traditional armed forces and of the general population (e.g., civil defense), will ensure victory in any kind of war that aggressive capitalist leaders might initiate. Conservatives are less sanguine than modernizers about reducing the chances of a military confrontation with the West through arms control, economic ties, or diplomatic negotiations, and about limiting a war, once started, to conventional combat or intermediate-range ("theater") nuclear exchanges. Conservatives view the overall military superiority of the Soviet bloc as the major means of furthering the global interests of the USSR and as the most effective deterrent to the expansion of Western, especially American, political, economic, and military influence throughout the world. Modernizers, in contrast, imply that the actual or perceived Soviet quest for strategic superiority might spur U.S. leaders to use their formidable military capabilities to advance American interests more aggressively, and might broaden the U.S. interpretation of these interests to include new substantive and geographical areas and new "linkages" between areas.

Briefly stated, Soviet conservatives and modernizers disagree about the merits of pursuing strategic superiority. Conservatives stress the risks and costs of failing to confront the global military and sociopolitical challenges posed by the common interests of bellicose capitalist states. Modernizers emphasize the economic challenges presented by contemporary capitalism and the diverging interests of Western nations, whose policies are shaped by both "belligerent" and "realistic" elements. Conservatives do not belittle the benefits of nuclear parity, but, unlike modernizers, they perceive strategic superiority to be a feasible and desirable means of enhancing national security. In order to achieve strategic superiority, conservatives affirm, the Soviet military and heavy industrial sectors must continue to receive a disproportionate share of scarce resources. Modernizers, however, advocate more equitable allocation of science-based high technology to military and civilian industries. Hence, conservatives have a strong vested interest in the argument that military power is the primary component of political influence in the generally hostile present-day international environment. But modernizers contend that both economic and military power are vitally important in the increasingly interconnected and differentiated world being shaped by the STR.

## Conservatives versus Modernizers

Whereas Stalin's conception of "socialism in one country" combined a domestic strategy of rapid industrialization with highly selective importation of Western technology, Khrushchev's view of "socialism" and "communist construction" and Brezhnev's view of "developed socialism" linked internal goals to a different international orientation. Stalin's successors have pursued a strategy of economic development that is predicated upon the broadening and deepening of interdependent relationships with a dynamic global economy and a more and more fragmented international political system. The USSR's policy of active peaceful coexistence and détente with the most industrialized powers of the West, particularly in the late 1950s and early 1970s, and the USSR's persistent efforts to expand long-term trade and industrial cooperation with diverse West European and Third World countries, demonstrate that many contemporary Soviet leaders have viewed economic interdependence as a key policy objective.

The increasingly multipolar world of the 1970s and 1980s (especially the relative decline of American influence) and the growing impact of science and technology on world politics (especially the balance of strategic power between the United States and the USSR, the proliferation of nuclear weapons among other nations, and the burgeoning of international economic ties) have significantly altered the external environment in which Soviet foreign policy must operate. Brezhnev's "collective leadership" viewed the world outside of the Soviet bloc as a veritable sea of change. Soviet spokesmen, particularly modernizers, acknowledge that international trends and events are having a mounting effect on conditions within the USSR, and that the USSR's exposure to foreign economic influences is increasing because of the "objective" characteristics of the STR (especially the expanding international division of labor).

At the same time, Brezhnev and his colleagues sought to preserve traditional goals and institutional relationships. The Brezhnev administration underscored the soundness of conservative Soviet values and of the basic features of the existing Soviet political system. But top party and state officials recognize that changes of some kind are needed to sustain minimal rates of socioeconomic progress and to adjust long-standing priorities and authority patterns in a new and uncertain historical context. For example, top Soviet leaders clearly understand the political, as well as the economic, importance of preventing further slippage in the rates of growth of industrial and agricultural output and productivity in the USSR, and of meeting the public's rising dissatisfaction with inadequate food, housing, consumer goods, health care, and social services.

Which changes in the Soviet polity and economy constitute "reform"? Which changes constitute "adaptation" of the traditional policies and political–administrative procedures to new domestic and international circumstances? These questions have been continuously debated in each one of the post-Stalin administrations. Indeed, even the technical criteria and standards for making such judgments have been disputed in most issue areas.

Soviet leaders and analysts have fueled this debate by repeatedly proclaiming that the STR is bringing portentous changes at home and abroad. Brezhnev asserted at the Twenty-fifth Party Congress in 1976: "The revolution in science and technology requires a cardinal change in the style and methods of economic activity, a determined struggle against stagnation and the rigidities of routine, genuine respect for science, and the ability and desire to seek advice and to take it into consideration."[28] Because of the global nature of the STR, and because of the closer integration of the Soviet economy in the world economy, Brezhnev's statement has major implications for domestic and foreign policy and for the strategies that link them. These implications are not at all self-evident, however, and Soviet bureaucratic coalitions have competing interests in different interpretations of official policy and strategy and of internal and external conditions.

Hence, the Brezhnev leadership, by legitimizing politicized but circumspect debate about the causes, content, and consequences of the STR, cautiously encouraged within-system reassessment of political and socioeconomic changes throughout the world and of their ramifications for Soviet domestic and foreign policy. Soviet analysts, in making such evaluations, often implicitly raise questions of fundamental importance about the institutional, as well as the policy, aspects of Soviet political and economic development. For example, if "cardinal" change is needed in the economy (see Brezhnev's statement just quoted), what corresponding changes are necessary in the role of the Communist Party, especially in its relations with state and production organizations?

Succinctly put, officials in the Khrushchev and Brezhnev administrations formulated and expressed many competing views about domestic and international politics. Also, Soviet leaders have become increasingly aware of the interconnections between—even the inseparability of—domestic and foreign policies in the era of the STR. Consequently, different Soviet perspectives on international relations often advocate or imply different internal policies and institutional relationships. Soviet conceptualizations of "developed socialism," for instance, have been considerably influenced by favorable judgments about economic progress in highly industrialized capitalist countries.[29] Jerry Hough notes that the Soviet authors of an exceptionally authoritative book emphasize the universal or "objective" features of the STR, and he observes that "many of the structural differences between the Western and Soviet economies are attributed to the process of industrialization; hence, the authors . . . are implicitly saying that [these structural innovations in capitalist countries] *not only should, but must be adopted in the Soviet Union.*"[30]

We have seen that contemporary Soviet leaders and theorists hold many similar views about the STR and international politics. We have also observed that, within these parameters of consensus, leading Soviet officials and analysts debate the nature of international change and particularly its implications for diplomatic, economic, and military policy. Both conservative and modernizing premises were incorporated into the important Twenty-fourth Party Congress program in 1971, and the two orientations were given about equal weight. The competition between conservative and modernizing tendencies continued throughout the 1970s and mid-1980s, in response to the successes, failures, and unanticipated consequences of Brezhnev's "grand design." Generally speaking, the conservative tendency gained ground until 1982—due in part to the mounting inertia and frustrations of the aging Soviet leadership (especially in coping with the increasingly serious economic problems of the Comecon countries) and to the Soviet leaders' perceptions of a more threatening international environment (e.g., U.S.–Chinese political, economic, and military collaboration).

Brezhnev and his successors have stressed that détente must be grounded upon the armed strength of the USSR. The significant buildup of the USSR's military power since the 1960s enables the Soviet bloc to interact with capitalist states from a position of strength, rather than vulnerability, and to establish mutual rather than unilateral dependencies.[31] Hence, "the shift in the correlation of forces in favor of socialism" stems largely from the growth of Soviet military power throughout the world.

However, Soviet efforts to cooperate with the West in certain fields are based on confidence in the USSR's economic and scientific potential as well as in its military capabilities.[32] Soviet commentators argue that the most efficient development and utilization of scientific, technical, and economic resources require an international division of labor. Autarky is wasteful and short-sighted, modernizers emphasize. Scientific and technological progress, together with economic growth and productivity, can be accelerated by closer integration of the Comecon economies and by carefully selected commercial ties with highly industrialized capitalist nations, conservatives agree. Conservatives and modernizers recognize deficiencies in the USSR's science–technology–production cycle, and both strongly support the policy of détente, which is striving to improve the performance of the Soviet economy under difficult and changing circumstances. Conservatives and modernizers acknowledge the mushrooming of international economic interdependencies and the increasing openness of the Soviet economy to external disturbances, and both policy groups are responding to these "objective" forces in their own ways.

Soviet modernizers affirm that it is commercially advantageous to socialist and capitalist countries for the latter to provide know-how and credits to help the USSR extract, transport, and market its energy, mineral, and other natural resources. If some Western nations choose not to do so, adequate assistance will almost certainly be forthcoming from other capitalist governments, corporations, and banks in the short or long run. And, as conservatives stress, Soviet scientists and engineers possess the skills and can be given greater resources and incentives to produce new technologies—more slowly and expensively, perhaps, but at less political risk and cost.

Most contemporary Soviet leaders do not prefer an autarkic strategy, but it is perceived to be a possible alternative, especially in light of the mixed political and economic results of the Soviet détente policy of the 1970s. Conservatives argue that the USSR's capacity to pursue interdependent *or* independent courses of development gives Soviet officials a broader range of choice in international diplomatic and commercial activities than that of their counterparts in the industrialized West. Conservatives stress that the USSR, primarily because of its vast untapped raw material resources in Siberia and the Far East, is much less dependent upon the Third World than is the industrialized West and hence has greater freedom to maneuver in the international arena. Western dependence on foreign sources of energy, conservatives imply, is a vulnerability that is undermining the entire capitalist way of life. Modernizers insist that greater Soviet participation in the world economy contributes significantly to the growth and productivity of the Comecon economies.

In fact, different strategies of economic development have competed or have been implemented simultaneously in the Soviet Union for a long time. Thane Gustafson observed in 1981:

> Throughout the Soviet period there has been an uneasy coexistence between foreign imports and home-grown enterprise (the latter usually entailing some degree of reform) as the two principal strategies for technological innovation, the former predominating in some periods (such as the First Five-Year Plan, 1928–1932) and the latter in others (such as the Second Five-Year Plan, 1933–1937). Logically, the two strategies should complement one another; but in practice they have tended to compete, and the balance between them swings with the state of mind of the Politburo. The last fifteen years have been somewhat exceptional, for both

strategies have been pursued simultaneously, and more vigorously than ever before.[33]

Two Westerners, V. Sobeslavsky and P. Beazley, elaborate:

The import of large quantities of foreign technology is accompanied by piecemeal reform of the existing organizational structure of Soviet industry. Both alternatives are thus by no means mutually exclusive, but, on the contrary, one complements the other. Nevertheless, it is the relative importance of one over the other that counts, and in this respect it must be concluded that at least in the USSR import of technology clearly receives an immeasurably higher priority than the promotion of indigenous technological innovation.[34]

Neither the conservative nor the modernizing tendency is likely to predominate in the near future. Some of the chief reasons behind the considerable support for conservative *and* modernizing orientations under the Brezhnev administration were: the legitimation of circumscribed debate about policy alternatives and administrative effectiveness; the perceived complexity and fluidity of the domestic and international environments and their interconnections; the perceived need for diverse inputs into policy making and implementation; and the perceived importance of making differentiated and flexible initiatives and responses to ongoing and interrelated problems and opportunities in a period characterized by increasing scarcities and difficult choices.

Moreover, the criteria and standards for evaluating conservative and modernizing perspectives and policies are not at all clear-cut. Philip Hanson, for one, concludes: "The commercial transfer of Western technology to the USSR has economic consequences for the recipient nation that are somewhere between 'massive assistance' and zero effect. To be slightly less imprecise, the consequences appear to fall well short of the former but are nonetheless sufficiently far above the latter to be of importance to Soviet policymakers."[35] The Soviet leadership, we submit, is similarly uncertain or divided about the actual effects of the international transfer of technology and about the past and future impact of specific scientific and technical developments on the economy and polity of the USSR. With "collective" or group decision making at many stages and levels, with continued disjunctions between administrative powers and responsibilities, with a general reluctance to alter the technological, informational, and incentive systems into which new equipment is implanted, and with questionable technical and statistical measures of effectiveness and efficiency, party and state leaders are likely to resort to highly politicized but often parochial (departmental and local) judgments when evaluating conservative and modernizing programs or combinations thereof.

Nonetheless, leading Soviet officials view the STR as a factor critical to the acceleration of domestic economic and sociopolitical progress and to the conduct and deterrence of modern wars. These powerful pressures for and constraints on interdependence have considerably influenced Soviet perspectives on the changing nature of East–West relations. Soviet analysts frequently observe that the STR is a compelling "objective" pressure for détente and that détente consists of the simultaneous development of collaboration and conflict between socialist and capitalist states. While Soviet modernizers emphasize the cooperative elements of East–West détente, conservatives emphasize the adversarial. While modernizers stress the importance of establishing ground rules for East–West political, economic, and military competition, conservatives stress the difficulties of creating and maintaining such ground rules. While modernizers underscore the benefits of advancing Soviet global interests by economic and conventional military means, conservatives underscore the primacy of military capabilities and of strategic arms in particular. Hence, the different policy implications of Soviet conservative and modernizing orientations are portentous indeed.

Although the unprecedented scientific, technical, and economic developments since World War II have created powerful incentives for international cooperation, we conclude by emphasizing the importance of *political* perspectives and pursuits. Other nations' intentions, capabilities, and priorities are not easily or objectively ascertainable in the increasingly fragmented international system of the 1980s. Perceptions and interests differ considerably within and among countries. Competing assessments of external and internal environments and competing strategies of political, economic, and social development are becoming more and more salient elements of contemporary intergovernmental and transnational relations. Politicized judgments and choices, not the inexorable "demands" of science and technology, will decisively shape East–West interaction and world politics for the foreseeable future.

## Notes

[1] N. A. Lomov, ed., *Scientific–Technical Progress and the Revolution in Military Affairs*, translated and published under the auspices of the U.S. Air Force (Washington, D. C.: U.S. Government Printing Office, 1974), p. 31.

[2] R. A. Novikov, "Obshchaia kharakteristika osnovnykh mezhdunarodnykh aspektov problemy okruzhaiushchei sredy i prirodnykh resursov na sovremennom etape," in *Problema okruzhaiushchei sredy v mirovoi ekonomike i mezhdunarodnykh otnosheniiakh* (Moscow: Mysl', 1976) p. 31.

[3] N. I. Lebedev, *A New Stage in International Relations* (Elmsford, N. Y.: Pergamon Press, 1978), p. 131.

[4] M. M. Maksimova, "The Soviet Union and the World Economy," *Social Sciences* 4 (1978), p. 130.

[5] V. L. Mal'kevich, *East–West Economic Cooperation and Technological Exchange* (Moscow: Social Sciences Today, 1981).

[6] See, for example, Y. Sheinin, *Science Policy: Problems and Trends* (Moscow: Progress, 1978), pp. 122 ff.

[7] Lebedev, *A New Stage*, p. 129; and Mal'kevich, *East–West Economic Cooperation*, p. 23.

[8] *Vneshniaia torgovlia SSSR: Itogi deviatoi piatiletki i perspektivy* (Moscow: Mezhdunarodnye otnosheniia, 1977), p. 30.

[9]Georgii Skorov, in Foreword to Mal'kevich, *East–West Economic Cooperation*, p. 15.

[10]A. P. Aleksandrov, interview in *Literaturnaia gazeta*, February 18, 1976, translated in *Daily Report: Soviet Union* (Washington, D.C.: FBIS, February 27, 1976), pp. A5–A6 (emphasis added).

[11]Oleg Bykov, "The Key Problem of Our Time," *Social Sciences* 4 (1980), p. 159.

[12]See, for example, L. Maier *et al.*, "Zapadnoevropeiskii tsentr imperialisticheskogo sopernichestva," *Mirovaia ekonomika i mezhdunarodnye otnosheniia* 12 (1978), pp. 22–32.

[13]V. N. Shenaiev *et al.*, eds., *Western Europe Today: Economics, Politics, the Class Struggle, and International Relations* (Moscow: Progress, 1980), p. 290.

[14]G. A. Arbatov, "Nauchno-tekhnicheskaia revoliutsiia i vneshniaia politika SShA," in *SShA: Nauchno-tekhnicheskaia revoliutsiia i tendentsii vneshnei politika* (Moscow: Mezdunarodnye otnosheniia, 1974), p. 26.

[15]See, for example, R. A. Avakov, *Ravivaiushchiesia strany: Nauchno-tekhnicheskaia revoliutsiia i problema nezavisimosti* (Moscow: Mysl', 1976).

[16]Y. Kashlev, "International Relations and Information, " *International Affairs* 8 (1978), pp. 82.

[17]Y. Kashlev, "International Relations," p. 82; Y. Zakharov, "International Cooperation and the Battle of Ideas," *International Affairs* 1 (1976), p. 86.

[18]Zakharov, "International Cooperation," p. 86.

[19]See, for example, N. M. Nikol'skii, *Nauchno-tekhnicheskaia revoliutsiia: Mirovaia ekonomika, politika, naselenie* (Moscow: Mezhdunarodnye otnosheniia, 1970). Nikol'skii analyzes the effects of the STR upon the institutions and processes of diplomacy on pp. 163–188.

[20]Lebedev, *A New Stage*, p. 58.

[21]For elaboration of the discussion about Soviet conservatives and modernizers in this and the following section, see Erik P. Hoffmann and Robbin F. Laird, *The Politics of Economic Modernization in the Soviet Union* (Ithaca, N. Y.: Cornell University Press, 1982).

[22]Mal'kevich, *East–West Economic Cooperation*, p. 23 (emphasis added).

[23]Shenaiev *et al.*, *Western Europe Today*, p. 310.

[24]V. Sobeslavsky and P. Beazley, *The Transfer of Technology to Socialist Countries* (Cambridge, Mass.: Oelgeschlager, Gunn & Hann, 1980), p. 110.

[25]Thane Gustafson, *Selling the Russians the Rope? Soviet Technology Policy and U.S. Export Controls* (Santa Monica, Calif.: Rand, 1981), p. 69.

[26]"Brezhnev's Report to the Congress," in *Current Digest of the Soviet Press* 33, no. 8 (March 25, 1981), p. 18.

[27]Lebedev, *A New Stage*, p. 94.

[28]"Brezhnev: Central Committee Report," in *Current Soviet Policies VII*, p. 18.

[29]See Erik P. Hoffmann and Robbin F. Laird, *Technocratic Socialism: The Soviet Union in the Advanced Industrial Era* (Durham, N. C.: Duke University Press, 1985).

[30]Jerry Hough, "The Evolution in the Soviet World View,"*World Politics* 32, no. 4 (July 1980), p. 521 (emphasis added).

[31]See, for example, A. A. Grechko, "Rukovodiashchaia rol' KPSS v stroitel'stve armii razvitogo sotsialisticheskogo obshchestva," in *Voprosy istorii KPSS* (May 1974), translated in *Strategic Review* (Winter 1975).

[32]See Zhores Medvedev's perceptive comments on the Soviet approach to détente in *Soviet Science* (New York: Norton, 1978), pp. 137–203.

[33]Gustafson, *Selling the Russians the Rope?*, p. 70.

[34]Sobeslavsky and Beazley, *The Transfer of Technology*, p. 112.

[35]Philip Hanson, *Trade and Technology in Soviet–Western Relations* (New York: Columbia University Press, 1981), p. 5.

# 10

## JERRY F. HOUGH

## *The Foreign Policy Establishment**

Western observers are quite aware of the advanced age of the top Politburo members and of the ensuing problems created for the coming leadership succession. Far fewer recognize that similar problems exist for the Soviet foreign policy elite and that a complete turnover of personnel must surely take place within its core over the next 5 years. The changes deserve careful consideration, for a gap of some 15 years exists beween the top foreign policymakers and those most likely to succeed them, at least in posts that deal with the West.

The locus of influence and power is not easy to determine. A relatively obscure adviser may have a decisive impact upon events, whereas a man in a high post may be frozen out of the process by which decisions are really made. Nevertheless, a person in a top position does have access to the inner circle, and if his views had been found unacceptable, he could have been—and normally would have been—replaced by someone whose perspective was more congenial.

If one defines the inner circle of the foreign policy establishment by the nature of their responsibilities and the Politburo or Central Committee status accorded them, the following seem to have been the inner fifteen in early 1980: Leonid I. Brezhnev, party general secretary and chairman of the Presidium of the Supreme Soviet; Aleksei N. Kosygin, chairman of the Council of Ministers; Mikhail A. Suslov, second secretary of the Central Committee and top foreign policy assistant to Brezhnev among the Central Committee secretaries;[1] Andrei A. Gromyko, minister of foreign affairs; Iurii V. Andropov, chairman of the KGB (an institution that has the functions of the CIA as well as those of internal security); Dmitrii F. Ustinov, minister of defense; Boris N. Ponomarev, secretary of the central committee and head of the international department; Konstantin V. Rusakov, secretary of the Central

*Reprinted by permission of the author and publisher from *Soviet Leadership in Transition* (Washington, D. C.: The Brookings Institution, 1980), pp. 109–130. Copyright 1980 by The Brookings Institution.

Committee and head of the socialist countries department; Vasilii V. Kuznetsov, first deputy chairman of the Presidium of the Supreme Soviet; Ivan V. Arkhipov, deputy chairman of the Council of Ministers and chairman of the Council of Ministers' Foreign Economic Commission; Nikolai S. Patolichev, minister of foreign trade; Semen A. Skachkov, chairman of the State Committee for Foreign Economic Relations (despite its title, really the foreign aid agency); Nikolai M. Pegov, head of the foreign personnel department of the Central Committee,[2] Andrei M. Aleksandrov-Agentov, personal assistant to the general secretary (with special responsibility for relations with the United States); and Anatolii I. Blatov, personal assistant to the general secretary (with special responsibility for relations with Western and Eastern Europe). Except for the two personal assistants, all these men are full members of the Central Committee, and eight of them are full or candidate members of the Politburo.

As one examines the biographies of these top foreign policymakers, several facts become obvious. The first is the similarity in their backgrounds. As Table 10.1 indicates, ten were born between 1904 and 1909, and nine were in college during the First Five-Year Plan period, 1928–1932. Typically for that period, nine graduated from engineering institutes, one from an industrial academy, one from an agricultural institute, and one from a secondary specialized educational institution (technicum) for transportation. At least nine came from a worker or peasant family, and nearly all took a big step up when they were sent to college in the 1920s and the early 1930s. (Eleven were between 25 and 33 years of age when they graduated from college.) Only three are not members of the Brezhnev generation; the others are classic members.

Table 10.1. *The Core of the Foreign Policy Establishment, 1980*[a]

| Name | Date of birth | Date of college graduation |
|---|---|---|
| Aleksandrov-Agentov, Andrei M. | 1918 | 1940 |
| Andropov, Iurii V. | 1914 | 1936[b] |
| Arkhipov, Ivan V. | 1907 | 1932 |
| Blatov, Anatolii I. | 1914 | 1940 |
| Brezhnev, Leonid I. | 1906 | 1935 |
| Gromyko, Andrei A. | 1909 | 1934 |
| Kosygin, Aleksei N. | 1904 | 1935 |
| Kuznetsov, Vasilii V. | 1901 | 1926 |
| Patolichev, Nikolai S. | 1908 | 1937 |
| Pegov, Nikolai M. | 1905 | 1938 |
| Ponomarev, Boris N. | 1905 | 1926 |
| Rusakov, Konstantin V. | 1909 | 1930 |
| Skachkov, Semen A. | 1907 | 1930 |
| Suslov, Mikhail A. | 1902 | 1928 |
| Ustinov, Dmitrii F. | 1908 | 1934 |

[a]Source: 1977 yearbook of the *Bol'shaia sovetskaia entsiklopediia.*
[b]Andropov actually graduated from a technicum in this year. He never graduated from a university.

A second striking fact about the top Soviet foreign policymakers is the length of time during which they have had an opportunity to work together—an extraordinarily long period when compared with American experience. Indeed, six of the most important officials have held their present jobs for at least 20 years. Suslov, for example, has been a Central Committee secretary since 1947 and a leading foreign policy official since at least 1954, when he was named chairman of the Foreign Policy Committee of one of the houses of the Supreme Soviet.[3] Gromyko was appointed minister of foreign affairs in 1957, but before that had been first deputy minister from 1949 to 1957 (with a short interruption as ambassador to Great Britain), and head of the American desk of the ministry (then called a people's commissariat) as early as 1939 and ambassador to the United States in 1943. Ponomarev worked in the executive committee of the Comintern in 1936 and was then moved into party work upon its abolition. Essentially he was the number-two man in the international department of the Central Committee from 1944 until he became its head in 1955. Kuznetsov's job was newly created in 1977, but from 1955 to 1977 he had been first deputy minister of foreign affairs. Since 1958 Patolichev and Skachkov have been minister of foreign trade and chairman of the State Committee for Foreign Economic Relations, respectively.

Another three in the inner circle of foreign policy officials have served in their posts for a decade or longer. Aleksandrov-Agentov has been Brezhnev's personal assistant since the early 1960s; Rusakov essentially head of the socialist countries department since 1968;[4] and Andropov (who was Rusakov's predecessor from 1957 to 1967), chairman of the KGB since 1967.

Ustinov has been minister of defense for a much shorter time (since Grechko's death in 1976), but from 1965 to 1976 he had been Central Committee secretary in charge of the defense industry and the military and intimately involved in decision making as a candidate member of the Politburo. (He had also been a USSR minister or higher in the defense industry from 1941 to 1965.) Arkhipov's tenure as deputy chairman of the Council of Ministers has likewise been limited to the period since 1974, but for the previous 15 years he had been first deputy chairman of the State Committee for Foreign Economic Relations. He was one of the dozen or so men who had been a party official under Brezhnev's direct supervision in Dnepropetrovsk or Moldavia in the late 1930s and the 1940s and who had become prominent in the Brezhnev era. It is therefore quite likely that his real access to the inner circle of foreign policymakers from 1959 to 1974 was greater than his governmental position would indicate. Only Pegov is a relative newcomer to the inner circle in Moscow, and even he became an ambassador in 1956, retaining his membership in the Central Committee.

It is incredible to think that in 1980 the head of the international department of the Central Committee (and a candidate member of the Politburo) had been appointed a key member of the Comintern executive committee to help implement the Popular Front in the 1930s, that the present minister of foreign affairs was serving as ambassador to the

United States when Franklin D. Roosevelt was president, and that the principal Central Committee secretary for foreign policy was speaking before the Cominform at roughly the time of the Stalin–Tito split in 1948. In no other major country have the same foreign policy officials been occupying such central posts for so long.

Yet precisely because of the age and tenure of these officials, it seems nearly certain that within 5 years—and probably much sooner—almost none of them will be having an impact on Soviet foreign policy. Even the three ""younger" men—the KGB chairman, Andropov, and Brezhnev's personal assistants Aleksandrov-Agentov and Blatov—hold positions whose occupants have fared poorly in other periods of leadership transition. With a change in top foreign policymakers imminent, the question that obviously interests everyone the most is what their successors will be like.

The Older Generation

Two-thirds of the top fifteen foreign policymakers had first been appointed to posts in this area after Stalin's death, perhaps in part because of the peculiar impact of the purge on the foreign policy establishment. Despite the frequent assumption in the West that contact with foreigners made an official especially vulnerable to the Great Purge of 1937–1938, a fairly high proportion of the leading foreign policymakers actually survived. Viacheslav Molotov, the top Politburo specialist on foreign policy was not touched, nor was the top Politburo specialist on foreign trade (Anastas Mikoyan), the Central Committee secretary who dealt with foreign affairs (Andrei Zhdanov), the commissar of foreign affairs (Maxim Litvinov), the chairman and secretary of the Comintern (Georgii Dimitrov and Dmitrii Manuilsky), the chairman of the Trade Union International (Solomon Lozovsky), or the director of the principal foreign policy research institute (Eugene Varga). The ambassadors to the United States, England, France, Italy, and Germany were also not arrested, although ambassadors to other countries often were.[5] On the eve of the war, the commissar of foreign affairs was Molotov (born in 1890); the first deputy commissar was Andrei Vyshinsky (born in 1883), a former Menshevik who had been the chief prosecutor in the show trials of 1936–1938; and the three deputy commissars were Litvinov (born in 1876), Lozovsky (born in 1878), and Vladimir Dekanozov (born in 1898). The situation was quite unlike that in commissariats dealing with internal policy, where the purge had eliminated most of the older men.

At levels below the top in the foreign policy establishment, the situation was also unlike that in other policy areas, but in the opposite way. In the party apparatus, in economic management, in the soviets, and in the military, the Great Purge brought incredibly quick promotion to the kinds of people who were in any case likely to receive it at a more leisurely pace over the next 10 to 15 years. The new officials tended to have received appropriate education in the late 1920s or the 1930s and to have worked in lower-level jobs in their specialty before being thrust upward.

Nothing of the sort happened in the foreign policy realm. Perhaps the problem was a lack of young men with the appropriate education to promote. Soviet social science education in the 1920s and the first half of the 1930s tended to be general in content, emphasizing broad class conflict rather than specific information. During the cultural revolution, the social science faculties were closed down altogether, and when they were reopened, the regime was emphasizing the importance of traditional history, with dates, leaders, concrete events, and so forth. Therefore, in the late 1930s, men with social science backgrounds who were in their late twenties and early thirties had received a type of training that the leadership had now repudiated. Perhaps younger men who had worked in the Commissariat of Foreign Affairs had also spent too much time abroad and, unlike older men, were thought to have been affected by foreign influences at an impressionable age.

Whatever the cause, almost no men in the foreign policy establishment who were in their thirties were promoted in the wake of the purge. Or at least if any such were promoted, almost none remained in their posts for long. (Diplomatic sources at the time reported that the really sweeping wave of removals of junior and middle-level officials of the Commissariat of Foreign Affairs occurred not in 1937–38, but in the spring of 1939, after Molotov replaced Litvinov as the commissar of foreign affairs.[6]) A Soviet biographical directory of scholars studying the Orient reveals a few commissariat officials of the 1930s who continued to work within it in the 1940s,[7] but almost none reached the rank of counselor, minister, or ambassador in the postpurge period. Except for the type of older, high-level officials already mentioned, only two of several hundred postpurge officials of this rank stationed either in Moscow or abroad had entered the diplomatic corps before 1936.[8]

The basic structure of the Commissariat of Foreign Affairs was (and is) geographical, and the basic officials below the level of deputy commissar were the heads of departments (otdels). Biographies have been found of thirteen men who held the post of departmental head in the period 1939–1941. They were born in 1905 on the average (in fact, eight were born between 1904 and 1906). Their previous backgrounds varied, but they often had engaged in some kind of research or educational activity, and a number had the Soviet equivalent of the Ph.D. degree. Their work invariably focused on the internal Soviet situation rather than on the outside world. Some of them graduated from the Institute of Diplomatic and Consular Officials, which had a short term of study, but most seem to have been appointed directly from the outside.

In short, the pattern of selection suggests that the regime was looking for officials who were relatively uncorrupted by foreign contact, but whose work had forced them to learn a foreign language and had demonstrated their ability to learn and communicate.[9] Although many had been sent abroad as part of some delegation or exchange, the biographical data indicate that many, if not most, of the department heads were administering a department that dealt with a part of the world they had never seen. Lower officials often had no foreign language.

A typical example of a new department head, though somewhat

younger than the average, was Andrei Gromyko, who was appointed head of the American department in 1939. Gromyko, who was born in 1909, had joined the party in 1931, and until 1936 had been first a student in agricultural economics in Belorussia. Upon receiving his degree, he had gone to work in the Institute of Economics of the Academy of Sciences in Moscow, and in 1939 he was the responsible secretary of the institute's journal, *Voprosy ekonomiki*. From this post he received a direct appointment as head of the American countries department of the commissariat. Soon he was sent to Washington as a counselor at the Soviet embassy, and in 1943—at the age of 34—he became ambassador to the United States.

The passage of time both eased and intensified the Soviet problem with diplomatic personnel. On the one hand, the outsiders like Gromyko gradually became more expert in the performance of their duties, and those who had been appointed to lower posts in embassies abroad brought their first-hand experience of foreign countries with them when they returned to Moscow. Officials were usually rotated between the field and the home office every 3 or 4 years, but the level of experience of the leading officials continuously rose throughout the Stalin period, for they were all chosen from the same generation. In 1946 the average department head of the Ministry of Foreign Affairs had been born in 1907 and had entered diplomatic work in 1939; in 1952 the average department head had been born in 1907 and had entered diplomatic work in 1940. The deputy ministers of 1952 had been born a year earlier and had had 2 more years of diplomatic experience.

On the other hand, the rise of the Soviet Union to Great Power status, coupled with the gradual increase in the number of independent countries in the third world, required a steady increase of personnel in the diplomatic corps. As a result, the regime continued to recruit men (and only men) from other lines of work into the Ministry of Foreign Affairs in the postwar period. For many years the average age of entry stayed at about 31.[10] But after the immediate postpurge period, most entered the Ministry of Foreign Affairs at fairly low levels, often received training at the Higher Diplomatic Academy, and spent years rising upward in orderly fashion.

In other parts of the foreign policy establishment the situation was even worse in the 1940s. Journalists covering the outside world seem to have been particularly affected by the purge. Although the biographies of a few Soviet Orientialists indicate that scholars were sometimes recruited to fill the gap,[11] many posts were simply not filled, so that "a kind of "vacuum'" was created.[12] In 1945 the leading governmental newspaper, *Izvestiia*, did not have a single foreign correspondent, and the Tass office in New York City was headed by an American until January 1944.[13]

By the early 1950s, as discussed further below, the conditions within journalism were gradually being corrected, but those within the scholarly community were falling into worse disarray. During the 1920s and early 1930s, a quite substantial community of those studying the outside world had been created, a large proportion of them in their thirties (those born between 1895 and 1905). These scholars were Marxists, unlike most of the traditional history and literature specialists and, no doubt, were of varying degrees of sophistication. The existence of the Comintern, however, at least gave them contact with the outside world and some sense of the international turmoil in left-wing politics.

Then a series of disasters befell Soviet social science. One can clearly see from Table 10.2 the deteriorating situation in Oriental studies, which must be similar to that in European studies: In the late 1930s, 1940s, and early 1950s the proportion of "younger" scholars (those born after 1906) in the field of economics and politics was much lower than that proportion of scholars in the previous generation. Some scholars of the contemporary scene were hit by the purge,[14] and at roughly the same time a number of party institutes that had served as the base for many such scholars were closed. Contact with foreigners soon dried up. Except for Eugene Varga's Institute of the World Economy and World Politics and a new Pacific Institute opened during the war (incorporated into the Institute of Oriental Studies in 1950), the major remaining institutes for training young scholars were the traditional centers for the study of history or literature, supplemented by the Institutes of Geography and Ethnography. These centers, together with the colleges and universities (which did not teach contemporary politics and economics of foreign countries), provided the only jobs and so further shaped career choices. The war sharply curtailed all higher and postgraduate education, and in 1949 Varga's institute was closed after a hail of criticism directed toward scholars who overestimated capitalism's ability to survive. All these developments sharply reduced the number of people who studied the outside world and led to a retreat from politically dangerous contemporary subjects to much safer—and less policy-relevant—ones.

Table 10.2. *Distribution of Soviet Scholars in Oriental Studies by Field of Study and Year of Birth, 1935–1953[a,b]*

| Year of birth | Politics, economics[c] | Ethnography, geography | History, languages, literature[c] |
|---|---|---|---|
| 1894 and earlier | 13 | 1 | 72 |
| 1895–1905 | 54 | 3 | 86 |
| 1906–1912 | 24 | 7 | 68 |
| 1913–1919 | 12 | 3 | 55 |

[a]Calculated from the biographies of S. D. Miliband, *Biobibliograficheskii slovar' sovetskikh vostokovedov* (Moscow: Nauka, 1975). This source seems quite complete, although scholars who did not publish are excluded.

[b]Scholars who studied the civilizations in Central Asia, Transcaucasia, and other areas now within the Soviet Union are excluded.

[c]A historian whose work, or a significant part of it, comes within a decade or two of the present is included under politics and economics.

The Creation of a New Corps of Specialists    Since the shortage of trained young personnel was partly the result of the disruption of education during the war, the end of the war brought some relief for the problem. By the late 1940s and early 1950s the universities were once more turning out undergraduates and graduate students trained in history, some of whom made their way into the international field. In addition, three institutes began training undergraduates directly for this field. The old Moscow Institute of Eastern Studies seems to have added a substantial social science component to its undergraduate curriculum, and the Ministry of Foreign Trade's Institute of Foreign Trade seems to have expanded its enrollment. More important, an entirely new undergraduate institute was created in 1944: the Moscow State Institute of International Relations (MGIMO). Its first class graduated in 1948, and its second class—the legendary class of 1949—produced an unusually high proportion of the top advisers of the Brezhnev period.

MGIMO was attached first to Moscow University and then to the Ministry of Foreign Affairs. Its leading professors were drawn from Moscow University and other relevant institutes in Moscow on a part-time basis, and Ministry of Foreign Affairs officials also served as part-time instructors. For example, Anatolii Dobrynin, the present ambassador to the United States, led a seminar in the late 1940s. Compared with Moscow University, MGIMO had excellent language instruction, oral as well as reading. Some 300 students were admitted each year and grouped by the language they were studying. Perhaps one-third to one-half were in the English group; smaller numbers were in German and French. Spanish was not added until much later.

The students of the late Stalin period were to be the new elite in the realm of international relations, but in contrast to the policy followed in creating the domestic and the military elites in the late 1920s and early 1930s, no effort was made to draw into international relations students of working class or peasant origin. Complete data are available on the social backgrounds of 198 scholars working on the economics, ethnography, geography, and politics of Asia and Africa who were born in the 1920s. (Incidentally, it may be recalled from Table 10.2 that in the late Stalin period there had been only forty-six such scholars born between 1906 and 1919.) Seventy-four percent of these scholars come from white-collar families, and all the evidence suggests a similar percentage in every part of the foreign policy establishment.

Although MGIMO was later to become a prestigious institute to which members of the elite strove to send their sons, the competition to enter it was not severe in the early years, perhaps because of the memories of 1937–1938. At least one man has admitted that after returning from the army, he chose to enroll in MGIMO rather than in an engineering institute because he had forgotten his mathematics during the war.[15] Some of the students were delivered to classes in their fathers' limousines and some (perhaps the same ones) "thought that they should be sent to different countries as ambassadors immediately after receiving their diplomas."[16] But such students, according to those who described them, were not the successful ones. For instance, the former student who mentioned his chauffeured classmates dismissed them with a self-satisfied "Where are they now?"

The members of the future foreign policy elite were also somewhat different in age from their future counterparts in civilian spheres. As has been mentioned, study of the outside world did not require mathematics and science. And the war may have helped to develop language skills among some in the military and a curiosity about the outside world in many others. Therefore, a substantial number of the wartime generation are found among the early foreign policy graduates. Being older and having a wealth of experience not possessed by the young secondary school graduates, they tended to dominate the student bodies of institutes such as MGIMO in the early years and to have the pick of the assignments.

After graduation, the students of the foreign relations institutes were recruited by all the agencies that were short of personnel. Many of the MGIMO graduates simply went into the Ministry of Foreign Affairs, and many of the graduates of the Institute of Foreign Trade entered the Ministry of Foreign Trade. A second important source of employment for the postwar international graduates was journalism. The leading foreign affairs journals, the newspapers, and Tass hired voraciously from the first three or four classes of MGIMO graduates[17] and then launched them on specialized, internationally oriented careers.

The journalists covering the other Communist countries were primarily drawn from those reporting the domestic Soviet scene, but those stationed in the non-Communist world in the last 30 years have almost never been shifted between international and domestic reporting. This is even reflected in the term that has regularly been applied to them as a matter of course: *zhurnalist-mezhdunarodnik* (journalist–internationalist). Many of these journalists have moved from one geographic area to another, but they almost always have been assigned to countries where they know the language.

The death of Stalin produced an enormous expansion in the third sphere of employment for the young international graduates—that of scholarly research. At the Twentieth Party Congress in 1956, Khrushchev revised a number of Lenin's central tenets about the capitalist system (e.g., the inevitability of war among capitalist states), and later at the congress one of his closest associates, Anastas Mikoyan, pointed out one of the necessary corollaries to this new skepticism about long-established dogmas:

The course of history shows that all the most fundamental propositions of Marxism–Leninism find unceasing confirmation during the present stage of the development of imperialism. But this general confirmation is not enough. We are obligated to study concretely when, where, and to what degree this occurs.

We seriously lag in the study of the contemporary stage of capitalism. We are not engaged in a deep study of facts and figures, but often limit ourselves to seizing upon individual facts as signs of a coming crisis and the impoverishment of the toilers for purposes of propaganda. We do not make a comprehensive and deep evaluation of phenomena which occur in the life of foreign countries.[18]

Shortly after the Twentieth Congress, the Varga Institute was reestablished as the Institute of the World Economy and International Relations (IMEMO) under the USSR Academy of Sciences.[19] Varga was 77 at the time, and the directorship of the institute was given to Anushavan A. Arzumanian, a man with extraordinary political connections. He had been one of the organizers of the Armenian Komsomol during the civil war and had then spent years in political work in Armenia. He has especially close ties with Mikoyan; the two men had in fact married sisters. During World War II Arzumanian entered political work in the army and, in retrospect, was fortunate to have been assigned to work in the political department of the Eighteenth Army. The head of the political department was Leonid Brezhnev.[20]

Whether because of its political connections or not, IMEMO prospered after 1956. At the end of that year, it had 170 research associates, including 95 doctors and candidates of science. By January 1974 not only had it increased in size to 572 research associates (including 286 doctors and candidates of science), but at least four of its sections had become independent institutes: the Institute of the USA and Canada, the Institute of the International Workers' Movement, the Institute of Africa, and the Institute of Latin America. These institutes, whose leading officials were often former IMEMO senior scholars, had by that time more than 725 research associates, including 375 doctors and candidates of science.[21]

Scholarship on international subjects was expanded in other parts of the Academy of Sciences as well. The Institute of Oriental Studies, which Mikoyan had severely criticized at the Twentieth Party Congress ("If the entire East has awakened during our time, then this institute still dozes until the present day") was substantially expanded, especially its work on contemporary matters. A new Institute of the Far East (which concentrates on China) was established, and in 1961 an Institute of the Economy of the World Socialist System was formed out of a section of the Institute of Economics.

The rapid expansion in the number and size of the foreign policy institutes created a big personnel problem. Even with the return of some of the older scholars who had (in the words of a later obituary) "worked in the coal industry of Vorkuta [a famous camp],"[22] there were simply not enough scholars to fill the newly created slots. Until the number of degree programs was greatly increased, people were recruited from any likely source. In particular, many journalist–internationalists were drawn into the institutes.

These men, it should be emphasized, were not simply engaging in academic research. The Ministry of Foreign Affairs has had little research staff, and this apparently is also true of the KGB. The scholarly community working on contemporary problems—and there are some 2000–3000 of them in Moscow—are supposed to fill the gap. Like scholars everywhere, they are expected to publish books and articles, but those doing policy-relevant work—and there is great pressure to do so—can spend 25% of their time or more on classified work usually called "the director's assignments." (The director in question is the director of the institute.) These assignments, which themselves reflect demands or requests from higher authorities, can range from the preparation of a short informational memorandum to a prediction of future developments in the area of their specialization or even to participation in a group working out different policy options for consideration by the Politburo.

The expansion of a scholarly community strongly oriented toward policy questions created another pool of cadres who could be used for other purposes. There was indeed a movement of scholars— though not a large one—into the posts directly involved in policymaking. Economists in particular were sometimes drawn into the Ministry of Foreign Affairs; politically oriented scholars were more often recruited for work in the Central Committee apparatus, especially in the groups of consultants of the Central Committee who work full-time on long-range questions.

## Generational Change

In areas like journalism and scholarship, the mass influx of new personnel had an impact upon these institutions almost immediately. Because of the "vacuum" between them and the older specialists, the new recruits moved into middle-level posts earlier than would otherwise have been the case.

The first breakthrough of the younger generation into important leadership posts occurred in the Central Committee apparatus. The secretary heading the international department, Boris Ponomarev (born 1905), retained a number of subordinates who were roughly of his generation. For example, as late as 1979, the deputy head of the international department for Africa was Rostislav Ul'ianovsky, who was born in 1903, and the head of the sector for North America was Nikolai Mostovets, who was born in 1912. But in the Khrushchev period a brain trust (the group of consultants) was created and attached both to the international department and the department for relations with socialist countries and then to the latter alone. The group reported first to the Central Committee secretary, Otto V. Kuusinen, and then in 1964 to his successor, Iurii Andropov. Its first head was Fedor Burlatsky (born 1927), its second, in 1964, Georgii Arbatov (born 1923), and its third, in 1967, Alexander Bovin (born 1930). The international department began to receive younger officials. In particular, Vadim Zagladin (born 1927) became deputy head of the department for Europe in 1967 and then in 1974 the first deputy head of the department, and Karen Brutents, who was born in 1924, became the deputy head for most of the third world.

The second locus of generational change in the foreign policy establishment was the scholarly community. Obviously the great influx of young scholars into the newly created institutes had an impact on them almost immediately, especially because of the near-absence of a middle generation. Already in the early 1960s the young scholars were beginning to become section heads in the institutes, and early in the Brezhnev era they began moving into the directorships. In January 1964 the directors of the institutes of the Academy of Sciences studying the outside world were born in 1907 on the average. By 1969 five of the eight institutes were directed by men born between 1921 and 1928, and a sixth director was born in 1918. The deputy directors of the institutes were almost all born in the 1920s.

The principal figure among the international specialists in the scholarly community was Nikolai Inozemtsev, the director of IMEMO after Arzumanian's death in 1966. When the Institute of the USA and Canada and the Institute of the International Workers' Movement were created out of IMEMO sections, former scholars from IMEMO headed them. Inozemtsev became a candidate member of the Central Committee as early as 1971 and was also named a member of the Presidium of the Academy of Sciences. He was in a key position to influence personnel decisions. In 1978, when the director of the Institute of Oriental Studies died, Inozemtsev was able to have a deputy director of IMEMO appointed as his replacement.[23]

A similar generational change occurred among the journalist–internationalists. Good biographical data on the journalists are not available prior to 1967, but since then the data are almost complete.[24] Throughout the 1970s nearly all the important figures covering the international scene—the leading correspondents as well as the foreign editors of the newspapers, Tass, and radio–television—were almost all born later than 1923, and a growing number of the correspondents stationed abroad were born in the 1930s and even in the 1940s. Only among the commentators can members of earlier generations still be found.

Of all the subgroups within the foreign policy establishment, the Ministry of Foreign Affairs was the slowest to undergo generational change. In 1952 the average age of the deputy ministers was 45, in 1964 it was 56, and by 1980 it had risen to 65. The heads of the departments of the ministry and the ambassadors to the large non-Communist countries were somewhat younger, but, as Table 10.3 indicates, became increasingly older between 1941 and 1980: They averaged 35 and 34, respectively, in 1941 and 57 and 58 in 1980. These middle-level officials tended to be older than their counterparts among international scholars and journalists.

By the late 1970s men born in the middle and late 1920s were beginning to rise toward the top and to be interspersed among men of Gromyko's (and Brezhnev's) generation. For example, at present the three deputy ministers of foreign affairs overseeing relations with Africa, the Afghanistan–Iranian area of the Middle East, and Latin America (L. F. Il'ichev, S. P. Kozyrev, and N. S. Ryzhov) average 73 years of age, whereas the deputy ministers for the United States and for foreign policy planning (G. M. Kornienko, A. G. Kovalev) are 54 and 56, respectively.

Because of the pattern of training in the late 1930s and the 1940s, many of the men of the wartime and postwar generations who began to

Table 10.3. *Average Year of Birth of Officials of the Ministry of Foreign Affairs, 1941–1980[a]*

| Year | Deputy ministers | Heads of departments | Ambassadors to large countries[b] |
|---|---|---|---|
| January 1941 | 1884 | 1905 | 1906 |
| January 1946 | 1880 | 1907 | 1902 |
| January 1952 | 1906 | 1907 | 1903 |
| January 1957 | 1908 | 1909 | 1907 |
| January 1964 | 1907 | 1912 | 1911 |
| January 1971 | 1908 | 1917 | 1914 |
| January 1977 | 1912 | 1919 | 1918 |
| January 1980 | 1914 | 1922 | 1921 |

[a]Individual biographies, most of them drawn from the three editions of *Diplomaticheskii slovar'* (Moscow: Izdatel'stvo politicheskoi literatury, 1948–1950, 1960–1964, and 1971–1973). For 1980 data, see National Foreign Assessment Center, *Directory of Soviet Officials*, vol. 2: *National Organizations* (Washington, D.C.: Central Intelligence Agency, 1979).

[b]Only non-Communist countries with over 15 million population in 1978—a total of thirty-one, although the Soviet Union at no one time had ambassadors in all of them.

assume important positions came from three or four graduating classes of only a few Moscow institutes. Indeed, a considerable number graduated from a single class, the class of 1949 of the Moscow Institute of International Relations: Vadim Zagladin, the first deputy head of the international department of the Central Committee; Nikolai Inozemtsev, the director of IMEMO; Georgii Arbatov, the director of the Institute of the USA and Canada; the two foreign policy editors of *Pravda* during the Brezhnev period; and a series of middle-level officials.

It is impossible to specify which men will replace the current group of septuagenarians who dominate Soviet foreign policy, but unless very improbable choices are made, the successors will amost surely be 10 to 15 years younger. The minister of foreign affairs was born in 1909, his first deputy ministers in 1917 and 1925 (and the latter is the man in charge of relations with the West and the Middle East); the head of the international department of the Central Committee was born in 1905 and his first deputy in 1928; the minister of foreign trade was born in 1908 and his new first deputy in 1933; the deputy chairman of the Council of Ministers in charge of foreign economic policy was born in 1907 and the deputy chairman representing the Soviet Union in the Council of Economic Mutual-Assistance (the agency coordinating economic plans with East Europe) was born in 1928; the minister of defense was born in 1908 and his first deputy ministers in 1914, 1918, and 1921 (and the younger two are more important than the older one). If the leadership wants important new officials with foreign policy experience who come from the 1910–1918 generation, it can find a few (e.g., Mikhail Zimianin, the Central Committee secretary in charge of ideological questions), but probably by the early 1980s the top Soviet foreign policy elite will have undergone a near-complete transformation. A strong majority of the new elite will have been selected from members of the wartime and postwar generations—men whose work experience will have taken place largely in the post-Stalin period.

Generational
Differences
in Attitude
In analyzing the attitudes of most of the Soviet spe- cialized elites, one is often driven to speculate on relatively weak data. For the foreign policy special- ists, however, much better evidence exists. The scholars and quite a few Central Committee officials write articles that often express differences of opinion or imply different assumptions about the outside world. Because this is also an elite with whom Westerners have a good deal of personal contact, it is possible to gain some feeling about differences within the group.

If one carefully analyzed the foreign policy debates over a long period, one obviously would not find total uniformity of views among those of any age. There are nonconventional thinkers among members of the Brezhnev generation and very traditional analysts among the postwar generation. Nevertheless, the generational difference in atti- tudes is striking, and relatively young Soviet scholars acknowledge and discuss it freely.

Basically, for all their growth in sophistication, the older specialists on the outside world have found it very difficult to free themselves from the set of ideas they developed when young. Those who had worked with Varga before the closing of his institute in 1949 and had shared his views had, of course, no difficulty in breaking away from the most primitive dogmas of the late-Stalin period. Indeed, they delighted in obtaining revenge in the late 1950s and early 1960s. Yet it is striking how many of the leading innovators of the 1950s and early 1960s became relatively conservative figures in the 1970s. They had not changed their earlier views, whereas younger scholars began moving beyond them and conceptualizing the outside world in different terms.

The differences between the generations are difficult to explain suc- cinctly to an audience that is unfamiliar with the Soviet terms of debate. In general, the traditional Leninist view had treated "capitalism" or "imperialism" (an exact synonym for advanced capitalism) almost as a living thing—as a monster reaching its tentacles into the colonial world. (The parallels with the American image of "totalitarianism" are strik- ing.)

Specialists of the postwar generation, on the other hand, are unlikely to even use the word *imperialism* as the subject of a sentence, especially if they are specialists on the United States or Western Europe. The younger scholars see the world in more differentiated terms and are likely to find local explanations for an event rather than blame it on the machinations of the imperialists. Specialists on Latin America, for ex- ample, study not only American policy toward Latin America, but also relations between Brazil and Argentina, and so forth. They do not simply explain the overthrow of Allende by the American intervention, but rather emphasize Chilean internal factors. In the process, political explanations for events tend to be much more prominent in analyses made by the postwar generation, especially those under 45.[25]

In fact, the attitude of the postwar generation toward the outside world tends to be different from that of its predecessors. The older generation often came to international studies through an interest in and dedication to the international Communist movement. Emotional commitment was as important as curiosity in guiding their work, and many worked in the Comintern or its institutes. Members of the younger generation, by contrast, often chose their careers because of their fascination with the West and their desire to travel abroad. The scholars among them who arose within the system of the Academy of Sciences are driven more by simple intellectual curiosity. Instead of being absorbed in thoughts about how to promote change in the West, they are more likely to wonder which aspects of Western development have or ought to have relevance for the Soviet future.

To the extent that the middle-aged and younger members of the foreign policy establishment tend to be modernizers—and even Westernizers—in Soviet politics, they tend to be strong supporters of détente. They have a sense that xenophobia and cold war relations with the West are associated with reaction at home—with a fundamentalist, ultranationalist mentality that bodes no good for them personally or for the values to which they adhere.

The attitudes of diplomats, KGB agents, and journalists are harder to document, for the first two groups do not publish and the third serves propagandistic purposes. No one who has met the younger men working in these occupations in the West has failed to be impressed by the degree of their fascination with Western culture and fashion and by their attraction to inside-dopester political explanations for events.

The postwar generation of foreign policy specialists is not, of course, composed largely of passivists or of people who believe that the Soviet Union should function as a small, uninvolved power. Those who are inclined to think that way are as unlikely to be chosen for top positions as their counterparts in the United States. The basic viewpoint of these specialists remains Marxist, and when the outside world seems threatening, they often appear to fall back on more traditional images. At these times they see policy determined by the "ruling circles" in the United States, and in a paranoid way they sometimes seem to betray an anxiety that "ruling circles" and "forces hostile to the Soviet Union" are synonymous. Even an extremely sophisticated scholar may state with pride that he has come to understand that power is not concentrated in many of the places that were emphasized by Marxists in the past, but then he may admit that he still does not know precisely where it is located—and do so in a manner that suggests he believes there is such a place.

Yet it is a Marxism that fully accepts Varga's judgments about the ability of capitalism to survive for a long time. (As Inozemtsev, the director of IMEMO, said in 1970, life "again and again" shows that Varga was correct.)[26] It is a Marxism that is trying to come to grips with the fact that big businessmen seem more favorable to détente than many other groups in the United States and that these businessmen lose on such issues as the Jackson–Vanik Amendment to the Trade Act of 1974, with the fact that statistical studies seem to show that high military expenditures are associated with higher unemployment than lower, and so forth.

No Soviet leadership—in fact, no leadership in Russia, regardless of the nature of the political system in that country—is going to usher in a period of bliss in Russian–American relations, for the world remains sufficiently bipolar to produce strains and suspicions, whoever the leaders are on each side. The next Soviet leader will almost surely not be drawn from the foreign policy specialists, and his basic values will be determined by forces within the party leadership and within society as a whole rather than by those within the foreign policy establishment. Nevertheless, his chief advisers and policymaking lieutenants in the foreign policy realm will almost surely be men who are considerably younger than their predecessors. Instead of having had little exposure to the West in their twenties and thirties (or even later) and of having worked for decades in the stultifying atmosphere of the rigid Stalin ideology, they will be men who have studied the West for decades, who have traveled extensively, and who seem more interested in the benefits of cooperation than in scoring points in a competition with the United States. It is difficult to believe that this will not create the possibility for some change in Soviet behavior, at least if the external environment permits it.

## Notes

[1]Westerners often treat Andrei **Kirilenko as the** second secretary, for he exercises the overall supervision of **the economy and the** party apparatus that have been associated with that *de facto* post **in the past. But at** recent party congresses, Suslov has been listed as the second man **in the Secretariat—and, of** course, alphabetical order can scarcely explain that position. See *XXV s"ezd Kommunisticheskoi partii Sovetskogo Soiuza [24 fevralia–5 marta 1976 goda]*, *Stenograficheskii otchet* (Moscow: Politizdat, 1976), vol. 2, p. 328.

[2]It is possible that Pegov is not a significant figure in policymaking and is concerned only with personnel selection. However, he is a Central Committee member and has been an ambassador since 1956.

[3]Suslov attended some Cominform meetings in the Stalin period and may well have had responsibility for relations with Eastern Europe. But his speech at the Nineteenth Party Congress in 1952 suggested his responsibility only for education, science, culture, internal propaganda, and the like—that is, the slot handled by P. N. Demichev and now M. V. Zimianin in the Brezhnev period.

[4]Rusakov actually holds two posts now—Central Committee secretary and department head—and the former post is a relatively new one. For a period he was Brezhnev's personal assistant for relations with socialist countries instead of Central Committee department head, but the latter position was left empty during that time.

[5]For a list of top officials purged, see Teddy J. Uldricks, "The Impact of the Great Purges on the People's Commissariat of Foreign Affairs," *Slavic Review* 36 (June 1977), pp. 188–89.

[6]*Foreign Relations of the United States: The Soviet Union, 1933–1939* (U.S. Government Printing Office, 1952), p. 772.

[7]S. D. Miliband, *Biobibliograficheskii slovar' sovetskikh vostokovedov* (Moscow: Nauka, 1975). See, for example, the biographies of I. V. Samylovsky and A. F. Sultanov on pp. 494 and 537.

[8]The biographies have been published in three editions of *Diplomaticheskii slovar'* (Moscow: Izdatel'stvo politicheskoi literatury, 1948–50, 1960–64, and 1971–73).

[9]For a different assessment of the language ability of the replacement generation as a whole, see Uldricks, "Impact of the Great Purges on the People's Commissariat of Foreign Affairs," pp. 195–196.

[10]The figure of 31 is based on the biographies of 269 men who first entered diplomatic work from 1936 through 1952. Since 233 of these men entered in the period from 1936 through 1948, the generalization may well not apply to the 1949–52 period when the number of biographies available is still rather small.

[11]For example, see the biography of M. A. Korostovtsev in Miliband, *Biobibliograficheskii slovar' sovetskikh vostokovedov*, p. 273.

[12]*Zhurnalist*, March 1967, pp. 16–17.

[13]*Ibid.*, June 1974, p. 71.

[14]Of the forty-seven specialists on the politics and economics of Asia and Africa who were born between 1895 and 1905 and who had entered scholarly work before the purge, 28% died in the period 1939–42 or apparently were sent to a concentration camp. Of the seventy-four specialists on history, languages, and literature of a like background, 20% died or disappeared in this period, but one-third of this group seem to have died of bombing or hunger in the Leningrad blockade. (Leningrad was the center for historical and literary work, whereas those working on politics or economics tended to be in Moscow.) These figures are calculated from the biographies in Miliband, *Biobibliograficheskii slovar' sovetskikh vostokovedov*. This source does not give the cause of death, and both figures are probably several percentage points high because a few of the deaths must have been natural.

[15]This man is Oleg K. Ignatev, the *Pravda* observer for Latin America, Asia, and Africa in 1977. He also reports the relatively minor competition for admission (*nebol'shoi konkurs*) in 1946, a point confirmed in interviews with others (*Altaiskaia pravda*, July 30, 1977, p. 4).

[16]*Zhurnalist*, November 1970, p. 61, and June 1976, p. 69.

[17]See the articles by the foreign editor of *Izvestiia* at the time, Vladimir Kudriavtsev, in *Zhurnalist*, March 1967, pp. 16–17, and December 1974, p. 29. Biographies of Soviet journalists can be found in *Zhurnalist* since 1967 and in *Molodoi kommunist* since 1973. By the summer of 1977, eighty-six biographies of journalist–internationalists had been found in which the college the person attended was specified. Fifty-six percent graduated from MGIMO, 14% from one of the Eastern studies institutes, 6% from graduate institutes of foreign relations (the Higher Diplomatic School or the Institute of the World Economy and International Relations of the Academy of Sciences), 3% from the Institute of Foreign Languages, 2% from the Institute of Foreign Trade, and 19% from all other institutions (half of them from Moscow University).

[18]XX s"ezd Kommunisticheskoi partii Sovetskogo Soiuza [14–25 fevralia 1956], *Stenograficheskii otchet* (Moscow: Gospolitizdat, 1956), vol. I, p. 323.

[19]William Zimmerman, *Soviet Perspectives on International Relations, 1956–1967* (Princeton University Press, 1969), pp. 37–39.

[20]*Mirovaia ekonomika i mezhdunarodnye otnosheniia*, May 1974, pp. 117 and 118, contains a description of Arzumanian's career; the information on his wartime experiences is on p. 118.

[21]The statistics of this paragraph come from *ibid.*, p. 120.

[22]*Ibid.*, April 1977, p. 156.

[23]E. M. Primakov. His biography is found in *Bol'shaia sovetskaia entsiklopediia* (Moscow: Izdatel'stvo "Sovetskaia entsiklopediia," 1975), vol. 20, p. 582.

[24]See note 17.

[25]See Jerry F. Hough, "The Evolution in the Soviet World View," *World Politics* 32 (July 1980), and Jerry F. Hough, "The Evolving Soviet Debates on Latin America," *Latin American Research Review*, forthcoming.

[26]*Mirovaia ekonomika i mezhdunarodnye otnosheniia*, January 1970, p. 124.

# 11

## ROSE E. GOTTEMOELLER

## Decision Making for Arms Limitation in the Soviet Union*

When the Soviet Union embarked on strategic arms limitation negotiations in 1969 it entered a new phase in its relations with the United States. The two countries had had prior dealings in the arms control arena, but never for intense, protracted discussions of an issue so vital to both—the size and shape of their respective strategic nuclear arsenals. The Strategic Arms Limitation Talks (SALT) ultimately produced agreements between the two sides, but they also engendered considerable discord and misunderstanding.

One source of misunderstanding for the U.S. side was the very nature of the negotiating partner. To American delegation members, the Soviet delegation seemed incapable of free give-and-take on the issues. Moreover, the Soviet procedure for staffing the delegation seemed ponderous, intricate, and insufferably slow. By the time the SALT II Agreement was completed in 1979, Americans were accustomed to a lengthy Soviet reaction time, and the Soviets had grown used to, however unwillingly, delays caused by U.S. presidential elections and transition processes that often meant lengthy delays in negotiations. Neither side offered optimistic target dates for initiating the next major U.S.–Soviet arms control negotiation, which, as it turned out, were talks on Intermediate Nuclear Forces (INF) that began in November 1981.

American negotiators, however, by that time had acquired a better understanding of how arms control decisions were reached in the Soviet Union. They had observed their Soviet counterparts for more than a decade in Geneva, Vienna, and Helsinki. They talked with them at informal gatherings and interacted on scores of issues. American SALT participants began to understand the major differences between the Soviet and American processes.

This chapter draws upon the observations that these American par-

*Reprinted in revised form by permission of the author and publisher from Hans G. Brauch and Duncan L. Clarke, eds., *Decisionmaking for Arms Limitation: Assessments and Prospects* (Cambridge, Mass.: Ballinger Publishing Co., 1983), pp. 53–80. Copyright 1983 by Ballinger Publishing Co.

ticipants have made throughout the 10-year SALT process.[1] Their conclusions are joined with other sources on Soviet policymaking to form a
picture of how arms control decisions are reached in the Soviet Union.
Although a process of great interest to Western observers of the Soviet
scene, Soviet arms control decision making can probably never be
completely understood by anyone outside the Kremlin establishment.
Given this limitation, the chapter reflects the fair degree of consensus
that Westerners have reached after observing and discussing Soviet
activities during the SALT negotiations. Where possible, it also reflects
the comments and observations of Soviet participants in the process.

## The Soviet Arms Control Bureaucracy

In the Soviet Union, arms control lacks a ready
institutional spokesman such as the U.S. Arms Control and Disarmament Agency, which was formed
for the express purpose of giving arms control a
quasi-independent voice in the U.S. government. Nevertheless, among
top Soviet leaders a commitment to arms control negotiations apparently does exist. Throughout the tensions and crises of the late 1970s,
Secretary Brezhnev and his colleagues on the Politburo consistently
supported arms control efforts. Their speeches during that period rarely
failed to reflect Soviet enthusiasm for the arms control process. The
Politburo, in other words, is evidently one source for the Soviet arms
control commitment.[2]

*The Politburo* The top decision-making body in the Soviet Union is
the Politburo. Brezhnev himself publicly stated that Soviet national
security decisions are the product of consensus in the Politburo.[3] Valentin Falin, a member of the Central Committee apparatus, has been
even more specific:

> Our decision-making system differs from the American in that it is more
> centralized. In international or national security affairs the American
> Secretaries of State and Defense can make a good many decisions on their
> own. In our case all foreign policy and national security questions must be
> discussed and decided in the Politburo.[4]

In the Soviet ruling hierarchy, the Politburo is at the peak of the
Soviet Communist Party (CPSU) bureaucracy. It sets general policy
directions but also deals with very specific national security and arms
control issues. Below it, as indicated in Figure 11.1, is the Party's Central
Committee, to which it is theoretically responsible; the Central Committee Secretariat, a second important policymaking body; the Secretariat's departments, which are staff organs; and the national, regional,
and local Party apparatus. The Soviet government bureaucracy, headed
by the Council of Ministers, is officially a separate entity with its own
important functions. These functions, however, seem to pertain more to
policy implementation than policy formulation.

Because the Politburo must address so many issues, it probably
divides responsibility for preparing initial policy positions among its

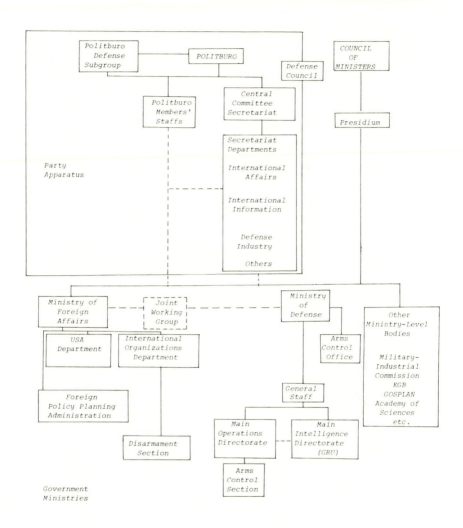

**Figure 11.1.** *Soviet Arms Control Bureaucracy. Note: The relationships indicated are approximate. They do not show all the levels of discourse that are possible among the various actors. For example, the relationship of the Defense Council to other agencies is unknown, but its role is evidently that of a high-level mediating body. Likewise, the position of the Defense Ministry's arms control office in its hierarchy is unknown. [Adapted from Thomas W. Wolfe,* The SALT Experience *(Cambridge, Mass.: Ballinger Publishing Company, 1979), p. 51.]*

members. It then collectively assents to the finished product. Brezhnev once indicated that disputed issues are dealt with through Politburo subgroups rather than an arduous process of consensus building among all Politburo members.[5] One such subgroup, it seems likely, is devoted to defense and arms control matters.

*The Central Committee Secretariat* The Secretariat also plays a role in the foreign policy process. Officially, the Secretariat is charged with ensuring implementation of Politburo decisions. Unofficially, it is a powerful policymaking body in its own right. "The Secretariat *frames* policy decisions," according to a senior Soviet official. "By the time an issue reaches the Politburo, the framework for decision is usually already there."[6] In the foreign policy sphere, this activity can involve coordinating and organizing information and analysis from various sources, a duty that guarantees the importance of the Secretariat's departments.[7] The Politburo, however, can also directly call upon experts in order to receive advice and information that is not filtered through the Secretariat. In this way, it is possible for Politburo members to hear the opinions of government and academic specialists without "interference" from the Central Committee apparatus.[8] The 1973 appointment of the foreign minister, defense minister, and KGB chief to the Politburo, in fact, may have heralded efforts by the top leadership to gain more direct access to, and control over, important government ministries.[9]

The Politburo and Secretariat actually appear to be an interlocking policy directorate where lines dividing responsibilities are unclear. Several of the top leaders are members of both bodies.[10] The Politburo, however, reportedly takes precedence in foreign policy. As a Soviet official explained it, "The Secretariat does not have competence in areas of state, as opposed to party, fundings and expenditure."[11] Arms control issues thus are probably handled most often in the Politburo.

*The Defense Council* The Defense Council is another device that has been used to draw specialists from outside the Party apparatus into arms control decision making. The Defense Council brings together Politburo members, senior military officers, and Party and government representatives to formulate policy on defense and arms control. Its permanent membership probably includes the CPSU general secretary, the chairman of the Council of Ministers, the minister of defense, the KGB chairman, the minister of foreign affairs, and perhaps the Central Committee secretary for ideology and the Central Committee secretary for cadres. Military leaders and lower echelon government officials and Party advisers would then be invited to participate as issues required.[12]

On arms control matters, the Defense Council seems to serve as a forum where the political leadership's policy commitment can be reconciled with the concerns of the professional military. Thomas Wolfe has suggested that Brezhnev and his colleagues may use the council to line up support on arms control among military leaders. The military, in turn, would have an opportunity to present a unified arms control position to the political leadership.[13]

Henry Kissinger's perception of Brezhnev's Defense Council role contradicts this emphasis on consensus building. In his recollections of the 1972 Moscow Summit, Kissinger wrote that Brezhnev apparently needed the support of Kosygin and Podgornyy to convince the full Politburo to accept a policy decision. However, Kissinger noted, Brezhnev's position as chairman of the Defense Council seemed to give him exclusive authority on military matters, including SALT.[14] If this interpretation is correct, Brezhnev's personal power may have been a major factor governing the interaction of the political leadership with the military in the Defense Council setting. Nevertheless, Kissinger's account also reaffirms that Brezhnev's authority in what was then the ruling triumvirate did not ultimately excuse him from seeking agreement with the other top leaders. Kissinger described how SALT concessions that Brezhnev made personally had to be withdrawn, evidently after consultations within the Politburo.[15]

Decisions reached in the Defense Council are likely to be accepted by the Politburo arms control subgroup and, in turn, by the full Politburo.[16] The Politburo members of the Defense Council are probably, in fact, the same individuals who serve in the arms control subgroup. These entities are thus the most important seats of arms control decision making in the Soviet system. The top Soviet leadership retains as much control over the process as possible. This control even may extend to formulating the details of negotiating positions for individual rounds of negotiations. Little responsibility for decisions, it seems, is left to those below the very highest level.

This highly centralized system means that much information flows up to the Politburo from sources throughout the government and Party. Brezhnev and his colleagues are, no doubt, constantly deluged with demands for decisions, and not only on defense and arms control. Centralized decision making extends to important issues throughout the Soviet economy and society.

To prevent the flood of information from overburdening individual leaders and clogging the system, good staff work would be required. Expert staffers would be needed to process information, select the most important details, and draft reports for presentation to the Politburo. Their duties would give them considerable influence because they would be straddling the information channels to the highest levels of government.

From available evidence, staff work is, indeed, crucial to Soviet leaders. High-level staffers are actually influential decision makers in their own right because they select the issues and background information that appear on the desks of the Politburo members. However, for the purpose of this discussion, I will maintain the distinction, as do the Soviets, between decision makers in the leadership and the staffers who work for them.

It must also be stressed that an all-embracing commitment to secrecy is an important reason why Soviet decision making is so top-heavy. Information is a commodity that is not shared lightly among the echelons of the Soviet government system nor handed out to the general public. Staffs are privy to different types and volumes of information. Those nearest the Politburo have the best access and, hence, the broadest understanding of policy issues. But information is tightly compartmented throughout the government.

*Leadership Secretariats* Each Central Committee secretary and, doubtless, each Politburo member has his own personal staff whose members possess impeccable political credentials and long-standing ties with their superior. Brezhnev's staff attracted the greatest attention in the West because its members were more in evidence thanks to Brezhnev's many trips abroad and visits with foreign leaders during the détente era. Brezhnev's personal secretariat, as the staff is often called, included long-time Brezhnev aides, Party veterans with experience in international affairs, and some junior experts.[17] This makeup is probably typical of the staffs of the other top leaders.

The leadership secretariats are doubtless active in considering arms control issues, although probably not in a strict bureaucratic structure. It is more likely that a small number of individuals handle a large number of issues in a fluid environment without the traditional organizational hierarchy of other Soviet bureaucracies.[18] Perhaps a number of staffers are familiar with arms control issues and shift responsibility for a specific problem according to various priorities.

But the leadership secretariats do have an important liaison function, for they are the medium through which staff work performed at lower levels reaches the top leadership.[19] The departments of the Central Committee Secretariat are one step below the personal staffs but have traditionally performed a great volume of staff work for the Politburo. The approximately 23 departments have a permanent staff of about 1000. Thus, unlike the personal staffs of the leaders, the Central Committee apparatus is a large bureaucracy. Its duties include gathering and processing information, proposing policy, advising the Politburo on the domestic and international situation, and monitoring policy implementation.[20]

Of the 23 departments, probably only a few are directly concerned with arms control. The likeliest candidates are the International Affairs Department, headed by Boris Ponomarev; the International Information Department, headed by Leonid M. Zamyatin; and the Defense Industry Department, headed by I. D. Serbin.

*Central Committee Departments* The International Affairs Department, which handles foreign policy related to capitalist countries and the Third World, employs experts capable of advising the Politburo on political matters related to arms control.[21] The staff is said to be made up of "well-educated, widely traveled technocats"[22] who evidently acquire responsibility for particular issue areas. For example, Ponomarev's first deputy, Vadim V. Zagladin, has been entrusted with significant tasks in the arms control arena. Zagladin has been the first senior Kremlin official to comment on major U.S. arms control initiatives. He has also been instrumental in launching important Soviet initiatives.[23]

The International Information Department was established in February 1978, apparently to remedy weaknesses in the presentation of Soviet foreign policy to the world outside the Soviet Union.[24] In the early 1980s, as preparations unfolded for U.S.–Soviet negotiations on European-based intermediate-range nuclear forces (INF), the International Information Department evidently also acquired a specific role in the Soviet arms control bureaucracy. The department's chief, Leonid Zamyatin, and his first deputy, Valentin Falin, became extremely active in "selling" Soviet INF positions to audiences in Western Europe and the United States. Zamyatin, who was said to enjoy Brezhnev's confidence,[25] accompanied the general secretary on several foreign trips to serve as his spokesman.[26] Falin likewise has traveled widely outside the Soviet Union, although his previous experience as ambassador to West Germany has apparently led him to concentrate on Soviet–German relations.[27] In general, extensive media experience and many years of service abroad seem to characterize International Information Department staffers.

The International Information Department has begun to produce background briefings in a format familiar to Western journalists, perhaps in an effort to provide them with information that they would feel they could use. In the context of the INF negotiations, such briefings have included discussions of Soviet military doctrine, weapons programs, and arms control proposals.[28] The department thus has been playing an important role in laying the groundwork in the West for Soviet arms control initiatives. To do this, it doubtless must remain in close contact with the upper layers of the arms control bureaucracy in Moscow. In fact, its duties may well include advising that bureaucracy on how to make initiatives acceptable to Western public opinion.

The Defense Industry Department, with responsibility for implementing weapons research and development and production policies,[29] almost certainly has an arms control role. The department reportedly has authority to request information from the General Staff of the Armed Forces, Central Committee Departments responsible for individual military industries, the Military Directorate of the State Planning Commission (GOSPLAN), and deputy defense ministers.[30] It is therefore in an excellent position to know development and deployment stages for individual weapon systems and where those systems fit into overall Soviet military plans.

In addition, the Defense Industry Department apparently keeps track of production potential in individual military industries.[31] Because of this knowledge, it would be aware of some of the constraints that may prevent full production of a weapon system. The information available to the Defense Industry Department, therefore, would be indispensable for formulating arms control negotiating strategies.

*General Staff and Defense Ministry* The International Affairs Department, the International Information Department, and the Defense Industry Department have independent authority to request information from government agencies at lower levels. Such agencies are part of the Soviet government hierarchy, not the Communist Party apparatus, and are generally considered to be less influential than the Central Committee Secretariat. Individual agencies, however, *are* centers of expertise that have not been duplicated elsewhere in the Soviet system.

The General Staff of the Soviet Armed Forces is one example of such a center. Officially subordinate to the Ministry of Defense, the General Staff nevertheless maintains a special position as the source of Soviet military doctrine and strategy. A stronghold of military professionalism, the General Staff is the seat of knowledge on defense matters in the Soviet Union. Traditionally, it has protected this knowledge from wide dissemination and certainly from independent scrutiny and comment.[32]

The Soviet leadership thus far has not attempted to intrude on the General Staff bailiwick by setting up competing centers of expertise on military affairs. Civilian analysts in the Soviet Union concentrate on Western strategic doctrine. They do not comment on Soviet doctrine or posture. The General Staff, in other words, enjoys a monopoly on information that forms the basis for training and equipping the Soviet armed forces, including strategic forces.[33]

In a staffing role for arms control negotiations, the General Staff reportedly interacts with the Central Committee Secretariat, as mentioned above. Probably its most important inputs, however, go through the Defense Council. As Michael Checinski points out, "The most effective kind of pressure on the Defense Council takes the form of military strategy and doctrine prepared by the Soviet General Staff."[34] The General Staff thus would provide the background for any unified military position on a negotiation. Nonmilitary members of the Defense Council would lack alternative sources of information to assess the military's position.

The Main Operations Directorate is probably the locus of the General Staff's arms control support work. Its arms control section would be best situated to serve as the military's monitor of a negotiation's progress. Its responsibilities are also likely to include providing arms control decision makers with information on the deployment status of Soviet strategic forces and on the status of new weapon systems under development.[35]

Although the Ministry of Defense has formed a separate office to handle arms control issues, little is known about its personnel, position in the hierarchy, or responsibilities.[36] American negotiators noted that during the SALT talks, Soviet Defense Ministry representatives reported to Moscow via channels separate from those used by the General Staff representatives. The Americans were unable to discern whether the two groups performed different functions, however.[37] The General Staff, because it has provided the chief military delegates to SALT,[38] seems to be the military organization most actively involved in arms control.

On the other hand, the Ministry of Defense contains organizational entities that may be very important to Soviet arms control decision making. The armaments directorate, created in 1970, is a likely example. Arthur Alexander suggests that the armaments directorate is responsible for major new weapons programs, those "characterized by high levels of priority, uncertainty and costs."[39] The directorate may also, according to Alexander, provide a link between force planning and weapons procurement. These roles could place the directorate in a position to represent Defense Ministry interests during negotiations, bureaucratic or otherwise, on arms control. The fact that General Nikolay Alekseyev heads the directorate bears out this supposition. An early delegate to the SALT negotiations, Alekseyev returned to Moscow and the directorate position as a deputy minister of defense. In his new job, Alekseyev reportedly continued to be involved with SALT problems.[40]

*Ministry of Foreign Affairs*  The Ministry of Foreign Affairs (MFA) is a natural participant in the arms control arena, although in the past it has suffered from excessive compartmentalization. U.S. SALT negotiators, for example, have recounted how MFA representatives on the Soviet delegation were denied access to information under the purview of Soviet military representatives.[41] The ministry's main contribution has evidently been to provide the diplomatic perspective divorced from military policy requirements.

Thus, the MFA has traditionally participated as an actor familiar with the negotiating partners and the international negotiations process. The chief Soviet SALT negotiators have been senior Foreign Ministry officials.[42] Other SALT delegation members have come from the ministry's International Organizations Department, Policy Planning Administration, and American desk.[43] Compared to the high-level staffing bodies in the Central Committee Secretariat, however, the MFA has been constrained in acquiring military information that would allow it to expand its role into the overall national security sphere.

The Ministry's diplomatic expertise does give it a unique utility, however. The activities of Anatoliy Dobrynin, the Soviet Union's ambassador to the United States, illustrate its importance. Although Dobrynin has no full-time place in the Soviet arms control bureaucracy, he has frequently used his position to contribute to the negotiating process. He can thus be considered an important part of Soviet arms control decision making involving the United States. During SALT I, for example, Dobrynin and Henry Kissinger opened secret backchannel discussions to resolve deadlocks that had developed during the negotiations in Vienna and Helsinki. Kissinger has recounted that Dobrynin, acting on behalf of the Politburo, could informally explore options that would be impossible to raise formally through the delegations. He also, according to Kissinger, performed the function of providing the Politburo with "a sophisticated assessment of conditions" in the United States.[44]

However important Dobrynin was to the SALT process, his role is difficult to generalize to other men and other negotiations. It is unclear, for example, that a replacement would be able to enjoy Dobrynin's wide access to Washington policymakers, at least in the early stages of an appointment. Indeed, after the Nixon and Ford presidencies, questions arose about the ease of Dobrynin's entrée to the White House and State Department, especially in light of the U.S. ambassador's perennial access problems in Moscow.[45] Furthermore, Soviet ambassadors are often moved to new assignments every few years. They do not always remain in one place for lengthy periods, as Dobrynin has. Thus, in many cases they would not have the contacts and information necessary to conduct backchannel discussions.

In general, the MFA's role may gradually be expanding as the Soviet arms control bureaucracy absorbs the experience of negotiating SALT I and II. In particular, the volume of cooperation between the ministries of Defense and Foreign Affairs may have expanded considerably in the 1970s. Some Western observers have posited, as shown in Figure 11.1, the post-SALT I addition of a Defense–Foreign Affairs group to coordinate work and provide support for negotiations.[46] Such a group would symbolize some breakdown in the lateral rigidity of the system and, presumably, an improved position for the Foreign Ministry.

As mentioned earlier, a second indicator that the MFA's role may be expanding is the fact that its head, Andrei Gromyko, acquired full Politburo rank in 1973, along with the heads of the Defense Ministry and KGB. Western observers have felt that this improved status has strengthened the Foreign Ministry's links to the top leadership while loosening the Central Committee Secretariat's control over it.

*Defense Research and Production* Judging from the contributions that Soviet scientists, engineers, and managers have made to achieving the SALT agreements, the Soviet scientific and industrial establishments are evidently active in arms control processes. Their exact roles are difficult to define, however, because of the separation that the Soviets maintain between the defense and civilian sectors. Weapons research and procurement remain largely apart from the civilian economy, partly because of secrecy requirements, but also because of the need to overcome the inefficiencies endemic to centralized planning and the Soviet civilian industries.[47] Arms control in the Soviet system thus naturally falls under the purview of defense sector specialists. Lacking access to information about weapon programs, a specialist from civilian research or manufacturing would be of little help to the arms control policy process.

The secrecy that cloisters the defense sector also prevents Western observers from developing a clear idea of how scientists and production managers contribute to arms control decision making. Certain organizations have been clearly identified with the process, but the exact nature of their roles is uncertain. For example, the Military–Industrial Commission caught the attention of U.S. SALT participants when its chairman, L. V. Smirnov, emerged from the background to negotiate some unresolved SALT I issues during the final hours of the Moscow Summit in May 1972.[48] The commission is evidently a high-level body with authority to coordinate defense research and production for projects where multiple ministries are involved. Some analysts conclude that the commission may, in addition, be involved in economic planning and setting priorities for the defense industry sector.[49] If so, Smirnov would not only have an intimate knowledge of weapons programs, he would also be in a position to advance SALT trade-offs involving them.

Other analysts, however, assert that the Military–Industrial Commission's responsibility does not extend beyond directing and coordinating the huge military–industrial bureaucracy.[50] Its focus, they say, is policy implementation, not formulation.[51] If this is the case, Smirnov may not have owed his starring role in the SALT I finale to the policymaking functions of his commission, but rather to his close association with the top leadership.

The Military–Industrial Commission is an important force in Soviet defense procurement. It is less clear that it has a formal, constant place in arms control matters. Smirnov's role in SALT I may well have been related to a personal tie to Dmitry Ustinov, who was then Party secretary (in the Central Committee Secretariat) in charge of defense research and production.[52] Such relationships are common in the Soviet system and are often an important source of an individual's power and influence.

The State Planning Commission, or GOSPLAN, indisputably fulfills a planning function, for it is within this organization that plans are set for the pace and direction of the Soviet economy. Westerners have long felt that GOSPLAN must have a role in arms control decision making because GOSPLAN would know what procurement plans would be upset by arms control measures and what sectors of the defense industry would be relieved of pressure by those same measures. It has never been clear, however, how GOSPLAN contributes its inputs to the decision-making process. One view is that the Military Department of GOSPLAN, with responsibility for providing an interface between the civilian and military sectors of the economy, is the likeliest candidate. According to this view, the department's chief, V. N. Novikov, would be the only individual "competent to estimate the real capabilities of the factories and R&D enterprises."[53] He would, therefore, be best able to advise those charged with formulating arms control negotiating positions.

The State Committee for Science and Technology performs both planning and implementation functions. It plans directions for Soviet civilian research and development and also sees that those plans are carried out. Its responsibilities include furthering Soviet participation in international scientific exchanges and coordinating the acquisition of foreign technologies. Those duties require its personnel to be acquainted with foreign products, probably including weapons, and accustomed to dealing with foreigners on science and technology issues. Committee staff may therefore be useful advisers on arms control questions.[54]

The bulk of defense research and production is handled by nine "full-time" defense ministries that are supplemented by others that produce goods, such as automobiles, for both the civilian and defense sectors.[55]

Unlike the Defense or Foreign Affairs ministries, the defense production ministries do not appear to make routine inputs to arms control policy. Petr Pleshakov became minister of the Radio Industry while serving as a principal with the Soviet SALT delegation,[56] but the other ministries were not regularly represented by delegation members.

Nevertheless, the ministries doubtless provide information on the status of research and production programs when called upon by entities such as the Central Committee's Defense Industry Department. When this information is used to formulate Soviet negotiating positions, the ministries could be said to have a place in arms control decision making. Their location in the bureaucratic hierarchy suggests, however, that their access to top leaders is somewhat limited.

Institutes in the USSR Academy of Sciences and the Soviet university system also carry out defense-oriented research, much of it apparently devoted to very advanced technologies. However, these programs, like their counterparts in the defense industries, are "closed"; that is, limited to defense sector personnel and facilities.[57] The Academy's representative at the SALT negotiations, Aleksandr Shchukin, had worked on missile guidance systems and continued to direct a staff researching guidance problems in Moscow.[58] Prior to the SALT I negotiations, Shchukin also apparently chaired an academy study group devoted to preparing recommendations on arms control proposals.[59] His delegation and study-group roles probably gave him considerable influence on Soviet SALT policymaking.

Like Shchukin, other prominent Soviet scientists seem to have played important roles. Their influence is apparently felt most often through the consulting relationships that they develop with top Soviet leaders who are seeking information outside the regular Kremlin staff channels.[60] In addition, since the academy's head, Anatoly Aleksandrov, reportedly attends Politburo meetings frequently,[61] he can presumably present the academy's views to the top leadership. Whatever the access enjoyed by individual scientists, however, the academy as a whole—especially its civilian sector—does not seem to contribute technical information for arms control decisions through a well-established institutional staff structure.

*Intelligence Agencies* The Committee for State Security (KGB) and the Main Intelligence Directorate (GRU or Military Intelligence) are organizations whose place in the arms control bureaucracy is not clearly understood. Both undoubtedly serve as sources of raw intelligence data on NATO weapon systems, but they also probably produce analysis on the directions of U.S. military research and development.[62] Thus, they almost certainly have a major role in arms control processes. How their inputs reach top policymakers, however, is largely unknown. One Soviet official has noted that on urgent foreign policy problems, the KGB and GRU may or may not be called upon to report to the Politburo, but that Politburo-level figures, such as former KGB chief Yuri Andropov, would be "virtually automatic participants" in the process.[63]

The GRU, likewise, seems to have easy access to the Soviet leadership. Officially subordinate to the General Staff,[64] it apparently can be called on to provide information and analysis to the Central Committee departments, perhaps in conjunction with the Main Operations Directorate, site of the staff's major arms control support group. In addition, the Chief of the General Staff would presumably be able to present GRU findings directly to fellow members of the Defense Council, thus bypassing the Central Committee apparatus.

*Social Science Institutes* In addition to research facilities address-ing technical issues, the USSR Academy of Sciences oversees social science institutes that pursue political questions germane to arms con-trol. Some Western observers argue vigorously that these institutes have a vital role in Soviet foreign policymaking; others argue with equal vigor that they are ignored by the top leadership and are used only to coopt foreign visitors. Still others assert that the true role of the institutes lies somewhere between these two extremes. The issue remains unresolved.

Where arms control decision making is concerned, two of the in-stitutes bear consideration: the Institute of World Economy and In-ternational Relations (IMEMO) and the Institute of the USA and Canada (IUSAC). Both have arms control sections and both have been extremely active in hosting Western academic and government visitors to the Soviet Union. Researchers associated with the institutes have also traveled extensively abroad, meeting with foreign colleagues, speaking before audiences on arms control issues, and writing in Western jour-nals and newspapers.

The most direct influence on Soviet leaders seems to come from individuals at the top of the institute hierarchies, including Georgiy Arbatov, director of the IUSAC. As important foreign policy specialists, they apparently participate in formulating foreign policy decisions on a fairly regular basis. Either they are asked to serve as consultants to the Central Committee departments, or they are invited to advise the Secretariat or Politburo directly.[65] In the first case, they may be asked to prepare a written assessment of a particular situation. If called into a Politburo session, they could of course express their opinions in person.

Specialists like Arbatov, as one source states, "retain frequent enough contact with men of at least [Central Committee] Secretariat level to make an important contribution to the policy machine."[66] Mikhail Voslenskiy reports that Arbatov could telephone Konstantin Chernenko directly when the latter was serving as head of the Central Committee's General Department, the powerful entity that manages the final flow of policy papers to the top leadership. According to Voslenskiy, Cher-nenko readily agreed on one occasion to distribute an Arbatov paper to the full Politburo.[67]

The high-level institute contributions reportedly tend to be of a longer range nature than those intended to answer a specific diplomatic initia-tive from the other side.[68] On arms control matters, this long-range orientation may mean that institute specialists have less to do with day-to-day negotiating tactics than with helping to advise Soviet leaders throughout the course of a negotiation by providing important insights into the other side's style and possible motives. In any case, since the specialists lack regular access to information on Soviet weapon systems and military policy, their ability to contribute to specific Soviet negotiat-ing positions would be limited.

Institute personnel at lower levels probably only participate in arms control policymaking through the demands for staff support that their superiors place upon them. In general, the arms control sections of the institutes do not appear to participate routinely in formulating arms control policy, although they undoubtedly would supply information on

Western positions and constraints if called upon directly by the Central Committee apparatus or Minsitry of Foreign Affairs. Thus, as with the more technically oriented institutes, the academy's social science institutes seem to play a role through knowledgeable, high-level individuals who are admitted to the policy process.[69]

Conclusions      Western observers generally agree that Soviet arms control decision making is characterized by a compact group of decision makers—the Communist Party's Politburo—supported by staff groups that extend from the Party apparatus through the governmental ministries. In the Brezhnev era, the Politburo decided issues on the basis of consensus among all of its members. Subgroups of the Politburo, however, apparently took responsibility for resolving difficult problems. When subgroup members presented their solutions to the full Politburo, their colleagues usually accepted the solutions without further study.

Below the senior policymaking level, high-level staffers control the flow of information to their superiors. Because responsibility for decisions is retained by such a compact group, staff work is particularly important. The leadership's personal secretariats do seem to wield considerable influence. They are joined by another entity in the Party apparatus—the Central Committee Secretariat. Secretariat departments, which number some twenty-three, evidently perform staff functions ranging from processing information and preparing policy options to evaluating policy and monitoring its implementation.

The Central Committee departments evidently have a strong hold on the ministerial bureaucracies, because they provide the avenues through which ministry positions normally reach the Politburo. However, certain organizations, such as the General Staff of the Soviet Armed Forces and the Ministry of Foreign Affairs, retain an independent position because they are the sole center of expertise on particular subjects. Nevertheless, the Central Committee departments remain in a very strong position.

The exceptional importance of staff work means that the Politburo must apparently circumvent routine bureaucratic procedures to acquire alternative sources of advice and expertise. As the SALT talks progressed in the late 1970s, evidence accumulated that Soviet leaders attempted to do just that. Top Kremlin decision makers apparently sought, and found, means to circumvent normal staff channels in order to broaden their information base. These means included granting direct access to certain ministerial bureaucracies and inviting technical and foreign-area specialists to report directly to the Politburo. Rather than having to communicate through the Academy of Sciences structure to the Central Committee apparatus, for example, high-level scientists and Americanists increasingly were able to voice their views firsthand in Politburo meetings.

In the early 1970s, Soviet leaders seemed concerned, above all, that the military establishment—professional soldiers as well as representatives of defense research and production—should contribute to developments in the arms control arena. By the early 1980s, this heavy military emphasis had changed somewhat, as best symbolized by the 1978 formation of the International Information Department in the Central Committee apparatus. The department was apparently formed to improve the reception abroad for Soviet foreign policy, including arms control initiatives. Soviet leaders evidently concluded that Western publics could affect the progress of arms control negotiations and so decided that they should be taken into account.

This greater concern with political impact apparently led the Politburo to admit more nonmilitary actors into the policy process. However, there are still important factors limiting their participation in arms control decision making. For example, General Staff/Defense Ministry expertise is still, it seems, accepted as sufficient to generate advice on military matters. The product no doubt of custom and concern for secrecy, such acceptance means that the military's requirements tend to escape question. The Soviet leadership hence must enter its political concerns into the decision-making process in the face of military requirements at least somewhat immune to alteration. As a result, although military advisers may escape question, political and foreign policy advisers probably do not.

Since the early 1980s, the Soviet leadership transition has also had an influence on Soviet arms control decision making. Brezhnev died after nearly 20 years of rule, leaving behind bureaucratic routines that had long been subject to his preferences and those of his colleagues in the Politburo. The process as we know it, therefore, was established when the regime was remarkably constant. Even actions that originally were innovations became routine as individuals maintained their positions in organizations and staff structures for many years. However, with the Brezhnev generation's passing, those whose access to the leadership was unimpeded may be losing it. Arms control decision making, therefore, may be undergoing change.

Brezhnev at the height of his power was clearly able to dominate Kremlin decision making on SALT. However, his authority at that time did not excuse him from seeking agreement with other top leaders—they could, in fact, override him if he went too far. Brezhnev's "exclusive authority" seemed in fact to be limited by his incomplete grasp of technical issues. This gap is entirely proper, since heads of state are not supposed to be caught up in the details of silo dimensions. On the other hand, technical expertise was represented by other Politburo and Defense Council members, whose organizations were indeed responsible for military policy and weapon development programs. Brezhnev was a strong enough leader to impose his will in general issue areas important to him (e.g., arms control), but the details of how "his" policy was accomplished were still subject to tight scrutiny by his fellows and their expert staffs.

What differences emerge when the strong leader disappears, along with his powerful peers? First, the absence of a strong leader means that there is no one to exercise a strong influence over the direction of policy.

Instead, probably a number of Politburo members are jostling to have an influence over the policies that they consider most important—policies that may or may not include arms control for a given individual. Second, the disappearance of the leader's peers means that powerful individuals long in command of government and Party organizations have been replaced by powerful individuals often new to the bureaucracies and issues in their charge. Until they learn the ins and outs of their organizations, they cannot be said to represent expertise to the same extent that Brezhnev's peers did.

The practical results of these changes seem to be several. Although the Soviet leadership's devotion to continuity guarantees some degree of arms control commitment, arms control is probably somewhat lost in the flood of issues that the new Politburo group is grappling with. Unless forced to confront arms control by outraged public opinion or another strong influence (the Reagan administration's Strategic Defense Initiative may be an example), the current leaders would perhaps be glad to leave it alone. In that way, they would gain time to learn the ins and outs of the Soviet arms control bureaucracy, especially as it involves the expert staffs over which they must gain control in order to be effective actors in that arena.

This requirement to develop staff relationships is another important practical result of the leadership changes. The departments of the Central Committee (CC) Secretariat are working with CC secretaries newly charged with national security responsibilities. These include Grigory Romanov, whom Andropov brought to Moscow to become the CC secretary in charge of monitoring the defense industry; and Mikhail Gorbachev, who became the CC secretary charged with economic strategy and foreign policy during Andropov's tenure.[70] Although secretariat staffing procedures are probably routine, the demands that these two men make on the staff must differ from those of their predecessors. Dmitry Ustinov, who held the defense industry portfolio for years before becoming Defense Minister, participated in the major Soviet defense buildup of the 1960s and 1970s. He therefore probably had an across-the-board grasp of defense issues when he participated in SALT policymaking in the 1970s. Romanov, by contrast, although long active in naval development issues, did not have such a wide access, so his secretariat staff is probably focused on understanding his needs for information.

Staffing relationships are probably even more in a state of flux in the area of personal secretariats. It is well known that Brezhnev had a personal staff of a few individuals with well-developed expertise on foreign policy issues. Such individuals apparently staff the issues that their boss considers most important, ensuring that he has the information needed to make a decisive presentation of his point of view. They probably also keep him abreast of his rivals' pet positions. These activities require a network of contacts within the Kremlin and government establishments. If an assistant is newly arrived with his boss in the Kremlin's inner sanctum, these contacts take time to develop. If a leader acquires an assistant in his ascent to power, the relationship between them takes time to develop. Both of these possibilities would hamper the effectiveness of a personal secretariat in the short run.[71]

A final area where staffing personalities and procedures may be changing involves the system of consulting relationships built up during the Brezhnev years. During that period, the Politburo began increasingly to call upon top experts to present their views directly to the Politburo, not through the agency hierarchies and the Central Committee staff. The Central Committee staff itself called upon individual scientists and academic specialists in the same way. These consulting relationships are perhaps the closest the Soviet leaders have come to seeking alternative advice on touchy matters such as weapon development programs.

The roster of consultants to the Politburo and Central Committee is probably undergoing some changes as relationships disappear and new individuals are brought in to serve the needs of the current Politburo. This process almost certainly involves the eclipse of individuals, at least temporarily. Indeed, the "consulting" concept may somewhat lose favor as too ad hoc a method at a time when the leadership is struggling to establish new routines. It is unlikely that such disfavor would continue for long, however, given the potential advantages for the leadership that the concept entails.

In summary, certain aspects of Soviet arms control decision making are likely to remain constant no matter what the status of those in power. The actual decision makers will remain a compact group at the Politburo/Defense Council level. They will obtain information on which to base decisions from a number of organizations and individuals. At the ministerial level, these will maintain rather strict secrets from each other. At the level of the Central Committee departments, information will become less compartmented and more useful in formulating policy options. Certain organizations, for example, the General Staff, will continue to monopolize information in their areas of expertise. They will be called upon to report their advice and opinions directly to the top leadership, probably in the Defense Council.

The innovations of the Brezhnev years, for example, the use of consultants to bypass normal information channels, will probably continue. These mechanisms, however, along with the individuals involved, will change in importance over time. During a transition period when leaders are concerned with establishing their positions, such ad hoc arrangements may be less in use than during periods when staffs and leaders are firmly ensconced and ready to do business.

## Notes

[1]The recollections of delegation members and other U.S. officials involved in SALT have appeared in John Newhouse, *Cold Dawn: The Story of SALT* (New York: Holt, Rinehart and Winston, 1973); Mason Willrich and John B. Rhinelander, eds., *SALT: The Moscow Agreements and Beyond* (New York: The Free Press, 1974); Gerard Smith, *Doubletalk: The Story of the First Strategic Arms Limitation Talks* (Garden City, N.Y.: Doubleday, 1980); Henry Kissinger, *White*

*House Years* (New York: Little, Brown, 1979); Raymond L. Garthoff, "Negotiating with the Russians: Some Lessons from SALT," *International Security* 2 (Spring 1977), pp. 3–24; Raymond L. Garthoff, "SALT I: An Evaluation," *World Politics* 32 (October 1978), pp. 1–25; Raymond L. Garthoff, "Negotiating SALT," *The Wilson Quarterly* 1 (Autumn 1977), pp. 76–85; Thomas W. Wolfe, *The SALT Experience* (Cambridge, Mass.: Ballinger Publishing Company, 1979); Strobe Talbott, *Endgame: The Inside Story of SALT II* (New York: Harper and Row, 1979); U.S. Congress, House of Representatives Committee on Foreign Affairs, *Soviet Diplomacy and Negotiating Behavior: Emerging New Context for U.S. Diplomacy,* Special Studies Series on Foreign Affairs Issues, Vol. 1 (Washington, D.C.: U.S. Government Printing Office, 1979).

[2]Western observers are divided about the sincerity of this commitment. Some feel that the Soviet leadership genuinely desires limitations on strategic arms. Others conclude that the Soviets enter negotiations primarily to constrain the United States and thereby improve their own strategic position. See Gerard Smith, *Doubletalk*, pp. 461–62; Harry Gelman, *The Politburo's Management of Its America Problem* (Santa Monica, Calif.: The Rand Corporation, April 1981), R-2707-NA, pp. 42–44.

[3]Theodore Shabad, "Brezhnev, Who Ought to Know, Explains Politburo," *New York Times*, June 15, 1973.

[4]Henry Brandon, "How Decisions Are Made in the Highest Soviet Circles," *The Washington Star*, July 15, 1979.

[5]Shabad, "Brezhnev, Who Ought to Know, Explains Politburo."

[6]Ned Temko, "Who Pulls the Levers of Power in the Soviet Machine?" *The Christian Science Monitor*, February 23, 1982.

[7]*Ibid.*

[8]Elizabeth Teague, *The Foreign Departments of the Central Committee of the CPSU*, A Supplement to the Radio Liberty Research Bulletin, Radio Free Europe-Radio Liberty, Washington, D.C., October 27, 1980, p. 4.

[9]*Ibid.*, pp. 2, 4; Arthur J. Alexander, *Decision-Making in Soviet Weapons Procurement* (London: International Institute for Strategic Studies, 1978/79), Adelphi Papers Nos. 147–148, pp. 11, 13; William E. Odom, "The Soviet Military and Foreign Policy," *Survival* (November–December 1978), p. 280.

[10]Temko, "Who Pulls the Levers of Power in the Soviet Machine?"

[11]*Ibid.*

[12]Wolfe, *The SALT Experience*, pp. 52, 57–58. See also Alexander, *Decision-Making in Soviet Weapons Procurement*, pp. 14–16; Marshall D. Shulman, "SALT and the Soviet Union," in Willrich and Rhinelander, eds., *SALT: The Moscow Agreements and Beyond*, p. 112; Edward L. Warner, III, *The Military in Contemporary Soviet Politics: An Institutional Analysis* (New York: Praeger, 1977), p. 46. In the 1970s, participation in the Defense Council by Central Committee secretaries may have been determined by the personal power of those who occupied those positions. For example, ideology secretary Mikhail Suslov, until his death in January 1982, was evidently an extremely powerful figure in Kremlin politics.

[13]Wolfe, *The SALT Experience*, p. 58.

[14]Henry Kissinger, *White House Years*, p. 1214.

[15]*Ibid.*, pp. 1220–1222.

[16]Karl F. Spielmann, *Analyzing Soviet Strategic Arms Decisions* (Boulder, Colo.: Westview Press, 1978), p. 53.

[17]Alexander, *Decision-Making in Soviet Weapons Procurement*, p. 13; Wolfe, *The SALT Experience*, p. 53; Kenneth A. Myers and Dimitri Simes, *Soviet Decision Making, Strategic Policy, and SALT* (Washington, D.C.: Georgetown University Center for Strategic and International Studies, December 1974), pp. 14–17.

[18]Alexander, *Decision-Making in Soviet Weapons Procurement*, p. 13.

[19]Myers and Simes, *Soviet Decision Making, Strategic Policy, and SALT*, p. 16.

[20]Elizabeth Teague, *The Foreign Departments of the Central Committee of the CPSU*, p. 3.

[21]Wolfe, *The SALT Experience*, p. 54; and Gelman, *The Politburo's Management of Its America Problem*, p. 25. For an émigré account of the International Department's importance, see Vladimir Sakharov, *High Treason* (New York: G. P. Putnam's Sons, 1980), pp. 248–250. Another account is Leonard Schapiro, "The International Department of the CPSU: Key to Soviet Policy," *International Journal* (Winter 1976–1977), pp. 41–55.

[22]Teague, *The Foreign Departments of the Central Committee of the CPSU*, p. 24.

[23]See, for example, John F. Burns, "Senior Soviet Aide Calls Reagan Plan a Welcome Change," *New York Times*, November 21, 1981. Burns stated that Zagladin is "believed to be an influential Soviet foreign policy adviser to Brezhnev."

[24]Herwig Kraus, *The International Information Department of the Central Committee of the CPSU*, Radio Liberty Research Bulletin No. RL 95/80, Radio Free Europe-Radio Liberty, Washington, D.C., March 4, 1980, p. 4; and Teague, *The Foreign Departments of the Central Committee of the CPSU*, p. 5.

[25]Teague, *The Foreign Departments of the Central Committee of the CPSU*, p. 26.

[26]Kraus, *The International Information Department of the Central Committee of the CPSU*, p. 2; "A Tribute to a Spry Brezhnev Brings an Edgy Soviet Reply," *New York Times*, November 25, 1981.

[27]Teague, *The Foreign Departments of the Central Committee of the CPSU*, pp. 25–26.

[28]See, for example, Hamburg DPA in German, October 29, 1981, translated in the *Daily Report: Soviet Union* of the Foreign Broadcast Information Service, FBIS-SOV-81-210, October 30, 1981; and Josef Riedmueller dispatch, *Suddeutsche Zeitung* in German, October 30, 1981, translated in the *Daily Report: Soviet Union* of the Foreign Broadcast Information Service, FBIS-SOV-81-211, November 2, 1981.

[29]Alexander, *Decision-Making in Soviet Weapons Procurement*, p. 11.

[30]Michael Checinski, *A Comparison of the Polish and Soviet Armaments Decisionmaking Systems* (Santa Monica, Calif.: The Rand Corporation, January 1981), R-2662-AF, pp. 67–68.

[31]*Ibid.*, p. 68.

[32]Alexander, *Decision-Making in Soviet Weapons Procurement*, pp. 13–14, 16.

[33]For more on the General Staff, see Alexander, *Decision-Making in Soviet Weapons Procurement*, pp. 17–18; Wolfe, *The SALT Experience*, pp. 62–64; Warner, *The Military in Contemporary Soviet Politics*, pp. 24–26, 240–41, 243. John Erickson, *Soviet Military Power* (London: Royal United Services Institute, 1971), pp. 16, 21. For the Soviet description of the General Staff (*general'nyy shtab*) see the *Sovetskaia voennaia entsiklopediia*, Voenizdat, Moscow, Vol. 2, pp. 511–13.

[34]Checinski, *A Comparison of the Polish and Soviet Armaments Decision-making Systems*, p. 69.

[35]Warner, *The Military in Contemporary Soviet Politics*, p. 243.

[36]*Ibid.*

[37]Myers and Simes, *Soviet Decision Making, Strategic Policy, and SALT*, pp. 27–28, 31.

[38]Warner, *The Military in Contemporary Soviet Politics*, p. 240.

[39]Alexander, *Decision-Making in Soviet Weapons Procurement*, p. 17.

[40]Smith, *Doubletalk*, p. 48. For more on Alekseyev, see Erickson, *Soviet Military Power*, pp. 16, 24.

[41]U.S. Congress, House of Representatives, Committee on Foreign Affairs, *Soviet Diplomacy and Negotiating Behavior*, p. 455.

[42]Igor S. Glagolev, "The Soviet Decision-making Process in Arms-Control Negotiations," *Orbis* 21 (Winter 1978), p. 77. Raymond Garthoff reports that the Soviets intended to appoint a senior military man to head their SALT I delegation, but they ultimately followed the U.S. lead and appointed a diplomat. See his "The Soviet Military and SALT," in *Soviet Decisionmaking for National Security*, eds. Jiri Valenta and William C. Potter (Boston: George Allen & Unwin, 1984), p. 142.

[43]Myers and Simes, *Soviet Decision Making, Strategic Policy, and SALT*, p. 24; Glagolev, "The Soviet Decision-making Process in Arms-Control Negotiations," p. 771; Shulman, in *SALT: The Moscow Agreements and Beyond*, p. 111.

[44]Kissinger, *White House Years*, pp. 139–40.

[45]For discussion of this issue, see Gelman, *The Politburo's Management of Its America Problem*, pp. 69–70.

[46]Wolfe, *The SALT Experience*, p. 61. Raymond Garthoff claims that as early as 1968, steps were taken to coordinate the arms control work of the Defense and Foreign Affairs Ministries. See Raymond L. Garthoff, "SALT and the Soviet Military," *Problems of Communism* 24 (January/February 1975), p. 29; Arkady Shevchenko describes such interagency cooperation taking place as early as 1957. See his *Breaking with Moscow* (New York: Alfred A. Knopf, 1985), p. 83.

[47]For a discussion of this issue, see David Holloway, "Soviet Military R&D: Managing the 'Research-Production Cycle,'" in *Soviet Science and Technology: Domestic and Foreign Perspectives*, eds. John R. Thomas and Ursula M. Kruse-Vaucienne (Washington, D.C.: The George Washington University, 1977).

[48]John Newhouse, *Cold Dawn*, pp. 250–60; Kissinger, *White House Years*, pp. 1233–38, 1241.

[49]Wolfe, *The SALT Experience*, p. 59.

[50]Checinski, *A Comparison of the Polish and Soviet Armaments Decision-making Systems*, p. 71.

[51]Alexander, *Decision-Making in Soviet Weapons Procurement*, p. 21.

[52]Ustinov died while serving as Minister of Defense in December 1984. The role of personal contacts has been, in some ways, institutionalized through the Party's *nomenklatura* system. According to Leonard Schapiro, "The right to participate in the appointment of personnel depends on a series of documents to which the term *nomenklatura* applies. These set out the appointments to be filled and the particular officials at different levels, both party and state, who are entitled to be consulted and to decide on the appointments listed. These lists cover virtually all responsible appointments in the country. Nothing is known of the method in use for solving any cases of conflict in the selection of personnel. It is fairly certain that the weight of the party decision will tend to predominate in most cases." Leonard Schapiro, *The Government and Politics of the Soviet Union* (New York: Vintage, 1967), p. 127. Recent émigré accounts have clarified the importance of the *nomenklatura* system. See, for example, Michael Voslensky, *Nomenklatura* (Garden City, N.Y.: Doubleday, 1984).

[53]Checinski, *A Comparison of the Polish and Soviet Armaments Decision-making Systems*, pp. 57–58, 71.

[54]For more on the State Committee for Science and Technology, see Louvan E. Nolting, *The Structure and Functions of the U.S.S.R. State Committee for Science and Technology* (Washington, D.C.: U.S. Department of Commerce, Bureau of the Census, November 1979), Foreign Economic Report No. 16.

[55]For a full listing, see Alexander, *Decision-Making in Soviet Weapons Procurement*, p. 22.

[56]Smith, *Doubletalk*, p. 48.

[57]Holloway, in *Soviet Science and Technology*, fn 93, p. 223.

[58]Smith, *Doubletalk*, p. 47

[59]Shulman, in *SALT: The Moscow Agreements and Beyond*, pp. 111–12. According to Wolfe, there was some question as to the study group's continued existence after SALT I. See *The SALT Experience*, p. 66.

[60]Wolfe, *The SALT Experience*, p. 66.

[61]Temko, "Who Pulls the Levers of Power in the Soviet Machine?"

[62]John Barron, *KGB: The Secret Work of Soviet Secret Agents* (New York: Reader's Digest Press, 1974), pp. 76, 102.

[63]Ned Temko, "It's Not 'Democracy' But Many Soviets Have a Say," *The Christian Science Monitor*, February 24, 1982.

[64]Warner, *The Military in Contemporary Soviet Politics*, p. 243.

[65]Temko, "It's Not 'Democracy' But Many Soviets Have a Say."

[66]*Ibid.*

[67]Voslensky, *Nomenklatura*, p. 384.

[68]Temko, "It's Not 'Democracy' But Many Soviets Have a Say."

[69]For more on the academy's social institutes, see Blair A. Ruble, *Soviet Research Institutes Project, Volume II: The Social Sciences* (Washington, D.C.: The United States International Communication Agency, January 1981); Rose E. Gottemoeller and Paul F. Langer, *Foreign Area Specialists in the USSR: Training and Employment of Specialists* (Santa Monica, Calif.: The Rand Corporation, January 1983), R-2697-RC.

[70]Ellen Jones, "The Defense Council in Soviet Leadership Decisionmaking." Paper presented at colloquium on Soviet National Security Decisionmaking, Kennan Institute for Advanced Russian Studies, May 3, 1984, p. 42; "Potential Successors to Andropov and Some Who Will Help Decide," *New York Times*, February 11, 1984.

[71]Chernenko has inherited several of Brezhnev's *and* Andropov's personal staff. Perhaps the most influential of these in the arms control area is Andrei Aleksandrov-Agentov, who became an aide to Brezhnev in 1963 and has since served as a foreign policy adviser to each Soviet leader. See Alexander Rahr, "Chernenko's Aides," *Radio Liberty Research Brief*, RL 426/84, November 9, 1984.

# 12  ROBERT W. KITRINOS

## The CPSU Central Committee's International Department*

As the first communist party to seize and retain power, the Communist Party of the Soviet Union occupies a privileged position in the international communist movement. Indeed, despite periodic challenges to its leadership and a mixed record in protecting and supporting foreign communists, the CPSU remains the dominant actor in this movement. This is largely due to the USSR's ascendancy to superpower status and the advantages this status confers on the CPSU. Thus, the Soviet Union is able to extend political, economic, and organizational assistance to leaders of sympathetic Marxist–Leninist movements in their quest for national power. It also demonstrates the Soviet leadership's willingness to employ assertive and indirect means to support revolutionary movements abroad.

Initiating and coordinating the dissemination of effective propaganda and manipulating sensitive or unstable political situations are critical elements of this aspect of Soviet foreign policy. Such an undertaking requires the establishment of formal and informal channels by which CPSU representatives can regularly meet with sympathetic political leaders, recruit local government officials, conduct propaganda and "disinformation" campaigns, and instruct local surrogates on Soviet policies. Orchestrating this effort, however, is no easy task. Most of these activities cut across traditional institutional and functional lines and potentially involve jurisdictional disputes between the party and the state bureaucracy. To be effective, the institution responsible for overseeing these activities must occupy a privileged position within the Central Committee apparatus, be invested with considerable authority, and be headed by a relatively high-ranking and powerful party member.

The Central Committee's International Department (ID) is apparently

*Reprinted in revised form by permission of the author and publisher from *Problems of Communism* 33, no. 5 (September–October, 1984), pp. 47–65.

such an organization. Until recently, however, the ID was mostly ignored in Western studies of Soviet foreign policy. What little was known was either scattered throughout the literature or buried in the numerous articles on traditional Soviet diplomacy. During the past decade, though, considerable material has surfaced that indicates that the ID plays a far more significant role in Soviet politics than had been previously thought.[1] Indeed, the ID has been increasingly recognized in the West not only as the major actor in the CPSU's dealings with nonruling foreign communist movements, but also as an organization that exercises considerable influence in the formulation of Soviet foreign policy.[2] This essay pieces together this material in order to present a more complete picture of the ID, noting in particular its origins, organizational structure, relationship with other Soviet institutions, mission, dealings with international and bilateral fronts, and overall effectiveness. It must be pointed out that there are few means of verifying some of this new information, since the inner workings of the department and much of its international activities are regarded as sensitive information and thus shielded by the CPSU. Nonetheless, the ID deserves far more comprehensive coverage than it has received to date. It is in this vein that the present study was undertaken.

Origin    The ID today is the product of several reorganizations within the CPSU Central Committee which began in the mid-1940s and were designed to define its role and status. Created in 1943, the year the Communist International (Comintern) was disbanded, the ID was tasked to handle relations with foreign communists.[3] During its first decade and a half, however, the department underwent numerous changes. In 1948, the CPSU Central Committee was reorganized and the ID was renamed the International Relations Department (*Otdel Vneshnikh Snosheniy*).[4] Two years later, for reasons not known in the West, the International Relations Department was replaced by a Foreign Policy Commission (*Vneshnepoliticheskaya Kommissiya*) and a Department for Cadres of Diplomatic and Foreign Trade Organs (*Otdel Kadrov Diplomaticheskikh i Vneshnetorgovykh Organov*).[5] Six years after that, in 1955, the Foreign Policy Commission was again renamed, this time reverting to its original designation, the ID.

These changes were usually accompanied by changes in the department's leadership or a refinement of its mission. While presumably headed at the outset by Andrey Zhdanov (who signed the announcement dissolving the Comintern),[6] the new department was reportedly first run by Dmitriy Manuil'skiy, then by Georgiy Dimitrov.[7] The ID's first deputy chief appears to have been Boris N. Ponomarëv who, having served as a Soviet representative on the Comintern's Executive Committee (1936–1943), brought to the position a wealth of experience in managing the international communist movement. The department's primary function during this formative stage was presumably to maintain the CPSU's links with the outside world through its contacts with foreign communists and to commission/supervise various studies on the world situation, the results of which were to be used for policy purposes.[8]

Three events in the late 1940s seem to have enhanced significantly Ponomarëv's career and, by extension, the political fortunes of the ID, of which he became chief in 1955: his appointment as first deputy chief of the newly established Communist Information Bureau (Cominform) in 1947;[9] the election of Mikhail Suslov to the Central Committee Secretariat the same year; and the sudden death of Zhdanov the following year, on August 31, 1948. Under the tutelage of his new mentor, Suslov, Ponomarëv rose to prominence in the CPSU Central Committee and continued to benefit from Suslov's 35-year reign as a dominant figure in the formulation of Soviet foreign and domestic policy. Ponomarëv became a candidate member of the CC in 1952, a full member in 1956, and a secretary in 1961. Little is known about the department's status within the Soviet system or about its activities between 1949 and 1955, though Ponomarëv's writings during this period suggest that he was primarily concerned with the rise of West European socialists and with Tito's pursuit of an independent policy.[10] According to a former member of the Soviet Information Bureau, Ponomarëv was appointed by Malenkov as his personal assistant in 1953. Later that year, when Khrushchev asserted his authority, Ponomarëv moved back to the ID.[11]

Following the decisions of the 1957 Conference of World Communist Parties, the Cominform was disbanded, the journal *Problems of Peace and Socialism* founded, and the International Department's section that dealt with ruling communist parties split off to become a separate Central Committee Department—the Department for Liaison with the Workers' and Communist Parties.[12] The ID retained responsibility for relations with nonruling communist parties. As a result, the ID expanded its activities into what CPSU General Secretary Nikita Khrushchev saw as a new horizon in Soviet foreign relations, namely, the Third World.

Indeed, by the mid-1950s, the Soviet Union had reformulated its policy toward the Third World, revealing a willingness to send arms and economic aid to a large part of the world hitherto ignored by Stalin. But the Soviet bureaucracy was ill-equipped to deal with areas such as the Middle East, since it lacked even well-trained Arabic language specialists.[13] Furthermore, not all members of that bureaucracy were receptive to Khrushchev's courting of noncommunist leaders in Third World nations; thus, in some cases, Politburo decisions were not being implemented.[14] Following several changes in the leadership of the Ministry of Foreign Affairs (MFA)—long-time head Vyacheslav Molotov was replaced by Dmitriy Shepilov, who was in turn replaced by Andrey Gromyko[15]—the ID and the Department for Liaison with the Workers' and Communist Parties assumed greater responsibility for ensuring that party foreign policy directives were carried out by government organs.[16] This new role enabled these departments to become more active in the process of formulating and executing Soviet foreign policy.[17]

Organizational    During the late 1950s, the U.S. government es-
Structure         timated the staff of the ID at between 100 and 150,
                  a figure that is often still quoted today.[18] Owing to
the considerable increase in the department's responsibilities since then,
the ID may now have as many as 200 employees, but this is only
conjecture. The organization of the department is never discussed in the
Soviet press.[19] Furthermore, to augment its staff, the department essentially functions as an "umbrella" organization, relying on the services of numerous other organizations, such as the research institutes of
the USSR Academy of Sciences, the various branches of the Soviet
intelligence services, the Ministry of Foreign Affairs, international front
organizations, and numerous bilateral friendship or cultural societies.
Indeed, one specialist familiar with the department's inner workings
notes that the ID "can request information on any subject from any
government agency, invite for consultation any individual, and communicate directly with any revolutionary organization in the world."[20]
    In terms of scope of responsibilities, the ID has no counterpart in the
United States. It incorporates some of the functions that come under the
jurisdiction of the National Security Council, the Congressional intelligence and foreign relations committees, the CIA, and even the
Departments of State and Labor. The ID is concerned only with political
considerations, however; it does not decide military policy, as this is the
preserve of the Ministry of Defense and the Defense Council.[21]
    As the head of the department, Ponomarëv is no doubt more in-
volved in high-level administration than he is in day-to-day supervision
of operations. He spends a considerable portion of his time preparing
for the weekly meetings of the Politburo and CC Secretariat (including
helping to set the agenda),[22] conferring with his deputies on routine as
well as pressing issues, and dealing with the heads of the KGB, the
Ministry of Foreign Affairs, the Ministry of Defense, and various research institutes of the Academy of Sciences. He also must attend a
variety of official and social functions, give speeches, and greet and see
off CPSU as well as foreign dignitaries at the airport. Moreover, he
seems to be endlessly consulting with foreign political leaders either
abroad or in Moscow.
    Responsibility for day-to-day affairs appears to have fallen to Vadim
V. Zagladin, a full CC member and the department's first deputy chief,
who functions as "acting chief" during Ponomarëv's frequent
absences.[23] He is generally responsible for West European affairs and is
himself a specialist on West Germany. Next in line are six deputy chiefs
who are responsible for geographic regions and, in some cases, functional areas: Vitaliy Shaposhnikov (Scandinavian countries and international social organizations); Rostislav Ul'yanovskiy (South Asia;
national liberation movements in Asia and Africa); Pëtr Manchkha
(Africa); Ivan Kovalenko (Far East); Karen Brutents (Middle East and
Latin America); and Anatoliy Chernyayev (North America and the
United Kingdom). These men supervise the work of their respective
sectors, coordinate this work with their counterparts in the Soviet

government, task research institutes to conduct supportive work, receive foreign delegations, brief the Politburo and Secretariat, and oversee Soviet activity in their geographic and functional areas.

Without exception, these men are experienced and highly qualified. Three (Ul'yanovskiy, Brutents, and Kovalenko) are former academics; the others are journalists.[24] Most are active in organizations that do work in areas of interest to the department. Zagladin, for example, serves on the Board of the State Committee for Science and Technology (GNTK), which assists the Ministry of Foreign Trade and the State Committee for Foreign Economic Relations, as well as the KGB and the Main Intelligence Directorate (GRU) of the Ministry of Defense, in determining what technology to procure from the West.[25] Though the acquisition of technology constitutes an important part of Soviet trade with Western Europe, Zagladin is not known to have scientific expertise. (His background is in journalism/propaganda.) Thus, his role is more likely that of a political dignitary familiar with the West and possibly a guide in directing the Soviet intelligence services to potentially cooperative sources where scientific and technical information may be procured most expeditiously from the West.

Ul'yanovskiy is another example. In addition to his responsibilities as department deputy chief, he is a deputy chairman of the Soviet Committee for Solidarity with Asian and African Countries (SKSSAA), the Soviet affiliate of the parent international front group, the Afro–Asian Peoples' Solidarity Organization (AAPSO). The ID uses the Soviet contingent at SKSSAA central headquarters as a conduit to funnel money to AAPSO. The SKSSAA serves several other useful purposes as well: It acts as a buffer between dissident groups and the Soviet Union when these groups need arms or funds; functions as an "unofficial" welcoming committee for those groups to whom the Soviet government does not grant diplomatic recognition and which the CPSU wants to keep at a distance; and serves as a propaganda outlet for the Soviet Union in the Third World. The activities of the SKSSAA are in part overseen by Ul'yanovskiy and the section of the ID that deals with international front groups.

Below the deputy chiefs are numerous sectors organized along geographic–linguistic lines—for example, "Germanic Europe" or "Francophone West Africa"—or along functional lines, such as "International Social Organizations" or "Liaison and Protocol." Heading up these units are sector chiefs who supervise the work of "responsible workers" (*referenty*) and "instructors" (*instruktory*).[26] Responsible workers may in fact be senior analysts who head the country or functional desks and oversee the work of more junior colleagues. Instructors are apparently responsible for verifying that party decisions are implemented by government agencies (e.g., the KGB and Ministry of Foreign Affairs), though they may also be responsible for issuing instructions or directives to pro-Soviet, nonruling communist parties.[27] The task of issuing instructions to Soviet government agencies may be done quite informally (perhaps by making a phone call) or through formal channels, such as sending a department directive to the agency in question.[28] It is through the work of the various sectors that the department maintains contact with nonruling communist parties and revolutionary groups; provides arms and funds to certain groups; oversees the Soviet government agencies charged with implementing policy decisions; and analyzes intelligence reports and puts them in a framework whereby policy recommendations can be made to the CC Secretariat and Politburo.

There are several sectors within the department, such as "Liaison and Protocol," formerly headed by Deputy Sector Chief Grant Akopov, about which even less is known. For example, there may be a special sector responsible for receiving and storing classified materials from the intelligence services as well as for keeping archives on nonruling communist parties.[29] There may also be a separate sector tasked to handle codes and communications.[30]

Complementing the ID's regular staff is a full-time consultants group, headed by Yuriy Zhilin, which is made up of academics from the research institutes of the USSR Academy of Sciences. Unlike the basic staff of the department, who have enough to do keeping up with the day-to-day developments in their areas, these consultants conduct in-depth research, carry out long-range studies, and help draft major doctrinal statements. They may also assist in writing major speeches.[31] Unlike their colleagues in the research institutes, these individuals probably have access to classified material. In addition, there are numerous part-time consultants working on specific research projects. The precise number of full- and part-time consultants employed by the ID is not known.[32]

Liaison with Foreign Communists

High-ranking ID officials meet with representatives of the nonruling communist parties on a regular basis in an effort to coordinate policy, strategy, and tactics. These consultations may take place in Moscow, Eastern Europe, or locally. For example, in the summer of 1979, according to a CIA study of Soviet covert action and propaganda, the leaders of selected West European communist parties visited Moscow, where they were instructed by CPSU representatives (presumably of the ID) to use their influence on the French and Italian communist parties in order to convince the leaders of those two parties to come into line with Soviet policy toward Western Europe.[33] Prior to this meeting, the CPSU Central Committee had sent a delegation to visit one West European communist party ostensibly to discuss vacations and schooling in the USSR for members of that party. The actual motive for the delegation's visit, according to the CIA study, was to provide the local party's senior officials with advance information and instructions regarding the Soviet position on SALT II and on the projected Carter–Brezhnev summit.[34]

Foreign communists also contribute generally to the Soviet intelligence-gathering effort, sending reports on a regular basis to Moscow on situations or events taking place in their countries. In a broad sense, this amounts to a sharing of intelligence and views. CPSU

General Secretary Leonid Brezhnev admitted as much during his speech at the Twenty-sixth Party Congress in February 1981:

> We have regularly briefed fraternal Parties on our internal developments and our actions in the field of foreign policy. . . . Contacts with foreign communists enable our Party, too, to get a better idea of the situation in individual countries.[35]

There is no pretense, however, that all parties are equals in these exchanges. Indeed, in Moscow's view, the interests of a foreign communist party must be subsumed when necessary to the interests of the CPSU and the Soviet Union. In recent years, some communist parties have balked at the CPSU's application of this principle. For the most part, these have been legal communist parties, such as those in Italy, France, and Japan, whose status permits them to pursue a more independent stance vis-à-vis the CPSU. Illegal communist parties, however, are more reliant on the CPSU for financial and logistical support; hence, they are generally careful not to jeopardize their ties with their patron.[36]

The ID controls the activities of foreign communists in several ways. One primary source of control, notes Elizabeth Teague, is financing, even if it is sometimes applied indirectly:

> What may be a substantial source of revenues for non-ruling CPs is income derived from the large numbers of CP newspapers and journals that are imported by the USSR to be sold throughout the country. These are the only foreign-language Western sources of information freely and regularly available to the Soviet population, so they are assured a steady sale. Soviet displeasure can sometimes be expressed by withdrawing these newspapers from sale; this happened, for example, after the invasion of Czechoslovakia in August, 1968. . . .[37]

Another means by which the department can subsidize foreign communist parties is through the use of trading organizations. According to the testimony of Soviet defector Stanislav Levchenko before the U.S. Congress Permanent Select Committee on Intelligence on July 14, 1982, a foreign trading company will be permitted to import Soviet goods or export foreign goods to the USSR with the provision that 15–20% of the net profit be delivered to a certain political party.[38] In other cases, the trading company may be wholly owned by the local communist party, as was the case with the Tudeh party in Iran.[39] Finally, and particularly in the case of illegal communist parties, the ID may use KGB officers stationed in Soviet embassies to transfer funds to local communist parties.[40]

Another service provided by the ID is training. A local communist party selects for review by the ID certain candidates to receive training at the CPSU party schools.[41] If accepted, the names of the nominees are forwarded to the Organizational Party Work Department, which then places students in appropriate programs.[42]

Today, one of the chief means by which the International Department seeks to direct the international communist movement is the conference mechanism. These conferences may be bilateral, regional, or international in attendance and may focus on either general or specific issues. They are invariably sponsored by one or more of the international communist front groups and are designed to bring together foreign communist parties and radical groups in order to achieve support for Soviet policies.[43]

## The ID and Other Political Parties

By 1964, the ID had assumed responsibility for handling the CPSU's relations with other political parties, revolutionary groups, and so-called national liberation movements.[44] This was done primarily in order to capitalize on the hostility toward the West prevalent in the Third World and to enable the Soviets to bring about the eventual acceptance by these countries of Marxism–Leninism. As Khrushchev told an Egyptian delegation visiting the USSR in 1959:

> We are not going to push you to Communism, since we do not believe that people can be pushed into Paradise with a stick. You have liberated yourselves and are happy with what you call nationalism. But let me tell you, Arab nationalism is not the zenith of happiness. I don't want to force you into Communism, but I believe that some members of the delegation are going to become future Communists. Because life itself will impose Communism.[45]

Another reason why the ID was assigned this task concerns protocol. As a section of the CPSU, the ID represents the party, not the Soviet government. Thus, the ID can receive delegations from such opposition or revolutionary groups without giving the impression that the Soviet Union is altering its policy toward the government in power. This also enables the Ministry of Foreign Affairs to continue to pursue "official" state-to-state relations with the nations in question.

The ID is most active in receiving delegations from the Third World. These groups are not always communist, though they often employ similar political slogans. The utility of these meetings is twofold. On the one hand, they provide the ID with a forum to make a pitch for the virtues of a united front strategy; on the other hand, they enable department personnel to gauge the diversity within the international movement and direct their policies accordingly. Since the mid-1960s, when Soviet leaders first realized that Third World communist parties tended to be weak and controversial, the CPSU has encouraged "progressive" sections of the national bourgeoisie to cooperate with local communist parties in forming antiimperialist (read anti-West and anti-capitalist) fronts in order to achieve a firm power base.[46] In 1971, this issue was addressed by Rostislav Ul'yanovskiy:

> Petty bourgeois ideology, which usually has a nationalistic and anti-imperialist spearhead with religious overtones, dominates the masses in one form or another and will evidently do so for a long time to come. . . . A realistic revolutionary approach to the matter reveals that socialism must often be built not out of the ideal matter that an advanced working class alone can be, but of the poor material that objective reality puts at the

revolutionary's disposal. The masses can gradually be led to an understanding of scientific socialism.[47]

Ul'yanovskiy terms those noncommunists who support the anti-
imperialist front as either "national" or "revolutionary" democrats
depending upon the degree of cooperation between the party in question and the CPSU. Likewise, the ID deputy chief currently responsible
for the Middle East and Latin America, Karen Brutents, notes that the
Twenty-fourth Congress of the CPSU (1971) called for the Central
Committee (presumably through the ID) to expand and strengthen its
ties with the revolutionary democratic parties of the developing
countries.[48] Establishment of a network of ID representatives stationed
in Soviet embassies for this and numerous other purposes had already
begun at least by the late 1960s.[49] This, according to Brutents, will help
the CPSU attain one of its major goals with regard to revolutionary
democratic parties, namely that of facilitating their transition to communism:

> The existence and even widening of political schoolings and differences
> within revolutionary democracy should be connected with . . . the con-
> tinuing evolution of revolutionary democracy. This evolution is a peculiar-
> ity of peasant and petty-bourgeois democracy; a peculiarity manifesting
> the transitional character of revolutionary democracy itself as a political
> force. . . . The amplitude of revolutionary democracy's political dynamic
> can be illustrated in, . . . on the one hand, the names of men who have
> become renowned Communists [and], on the other hand, the names of
> those who have degenerated. . . .[50]

Owing to their general responsibility for supervising Soviet policy
toward the Third World, Ul'yanovskiy and Brutents are concerned with
the current and future directions of revolutionary groups. One can
assume, however, that ensuring the formation of anti-imperialist fronts
in the Third World is the CPSU's immediate goal; facilitating their
transition to communism is a longer term ambition.

The ID also maintains links with the socialist parties of Western
Europe and Japan. This is due primarily to the Soviet leadership's
recognition that social democrats in these countries wield considerable
political power and, therefore, cannot be ignored.[51] Accordingly, ID
officials have encouraged socialist–communist cooperation with a view
to strengthening Soviet–West European relations and lessening the
likelihood of an East–West confrontation.

The ID's primary goal with regard to West European socialists since
the 1970s has been to enlist their support in the Soviet campaign to block
or delay the deployment of NATO's intermediate-range nuclear forces
(INF).[52] To accomplish this task, the ID has relied to a considerable
degree on bilateral consultations. In October 1979, for example, ID First
Deputy Chief Zagladin participated in a major front group rally in
Belgium, then met with members of the Dutch Parliament in The
Hague.[53] Department Chief Ponomarëv summed up the value of such
contacts in March 1981:

A number of personalities of social democratic parties observed that the peace initiatives put forward by the 26th CPSU Congress are contributing to the struggle against the conservative militarist forces inspired by the new U.S. administration. Members of the British Labour Party adopted a special resolution in support of the new peace initiatives of the Soviet Union. Many FRG [West German] Social Democrats and certain SPD [Social Democratic Party of Germany] personalities expressed a positive view of the Soviet proposals. SPD Chairman W. Brandt observed that the reaction to L. I. Brezhnev's report refutes the viewpoint of those who in past months have constantly claimed that a new stage in the arms race between East and West is absolutely inevitable.[54]

Bilateral consultations, however, provide only one means of influencing West Europeans. The Soviet Union has also made considerable use of both positive and negative propaganda ploys—granting interviews with high-ranking ID officials to West European newspapers,[55] on the one hand; disseminating forgeries of "official" documents and of Western periodicals, on the other—to garner support for its campaign against the INF deployment. Another ploy is the worldwide dissemination of the writings of Soviet foreign affairs specialists, which have been translated and published by the state publishing house, Progress Publishers. These articles are often written or commissioned by ID officials and are highly propagandistic. The ID also supervises Soviet radio broadcasts to Western Europe, a responsibility it shares with the International Information Department of the CPSU Central Committee.[56] Finally, and perhaps most important, the ID supervises the operations of 13 international front groups, which are used by the CPSU to co-opt communists and noncommunists alike into supporting programs and policies that serve Soviet interests.

## International and Bilateral Fronts

One of the major functions of the ID is acquiring international support for Soviet policy. To this end, the department has made extensive use of various front groups, especially those specifically tasked to promote "world peace."[57] These organizations typically have Soviet affiliates, which are directed and funded by the ID. In addition to directing such parent international front groups as the World Peace Council (WPC), the World Federation of Trade Unions (WFTU), and the Afro–Asian Peoples' Solidarity Organization,[58] the ID operates a large number of bilateral front groups. Both types of front groups serve Soviet interests quite well. On the one hand, they invariably adopt policy stands that mirror Soviet perceptions. On the other hand, by being formally independent of the USSR and by minimizing the role that communists play in their activities, these organizations are able to attract far more adherents than if their leanings were explicitly articulated.

Historically, the Soviet Union has used front groups to mobilize those elements in foreign societies who are unwilling to join a communist party but are sympathetic to some of the principles such a party espouses. Typically, this group included individuals who are unwilling to commit themselves to party discipline or who support the USSR only on certain issues.[59] Today, international front groups attract essentially the same type of participants and serve the same functions. Originally under the direction of the Comintern,[60] these organizations are now administered through the Mass Movements Sector of the ID,[61] which is overseen by Deputy Chief Vitaliy Shaposhnikov and headed by Grigoriy Shumeyko.[62]

Funding for international front groups is apparently handled in several ways. While these organizations do take in donations and earnings from publications, evidence strongly suggests that they receive the bulk of their operating expenses from the USSR.[63] According to Ruth Tosek, a former senior interpreter for several Moscow-controlled front groups:

> All funds of these organizations, in local and hard currency, are provided above all by the Soviet Union, and also by other East European satellite countries on the basis of set contribution rates, paid by the governments of these countries, through various channels.[64]

In the case of the WPC, funding goes from the ID to Oleg Kharkhardin of the Soviet Committee for the Defense of Peace, then to a Soviet representative at WPC headquarters in Helsinki. Until 1979, according to a U.S. interagency intelligence study, Soviet control of WPC finances in Helsinki was handled by Aleksandr Lebedev.[65] Presumably his replacement, Tair Tairov, handles this function today.[66]

The Afro–Asian Peoples' Solidarity Organization was set up in Cairo in 1957 as a jointly run Soviet–Egyptian front group. Today, it is nominally based in Egypt, though most of its activities take place in Cyprus, Vietnam, or Geneva. Funding in this case, as noted earlier, is extended by the ID through AAPSO's Soviet affiliate, the Soviet Committee for Solidarity with Asian and African Countries, to a Soviet representative at the parent organization, either S. I. Kalandrov or Anatoliy Sofronov.[67] The Soviet affiliate, in each case, functions as a subsector of the ID, thereby insulating financial transactions and policy directives from the CPSU as a whole.

Another way in which the CPSU funds international front groups is by holding congresses in the USSR. All expenses are paid for by the front's Soviet affiliate, including air fare.[68] These subsidies are usually provided through a so-called public foundation—the Soviet Peace Fund—which receives "donations" from Soviet workers (some of whom contribute as much as a day's wages), from Soviet recipients of international awards (such as the Nobel prizes), and from a portion of the gate receipts from Soviet sports competitions.[69] In this way, the Soviet Peace Fund functions as a branch of the ID.

As noted, the CPSU uses its affiliates as unofficial welcoming committees for foreign delegations that the party or government has chosen not to receive. This tactic has been used to receive such individuals as Nayif Hawatimah of the Democratic Front for the Liberation of Palestine (DFLP) when officials of other groups that have higher status, such as the Palestine Liberation Organization (PLO), are also visiting at the invitation of the party or government.[70]

Soviet affiliates may also be used as buffers between the CPSU/Soviet government and revolutionary groups or national liberation movements. For instance, a visiting delegation may make a request for arms or training. The Soviet affiliate sends this request, which presumably has first been screened and cleared by the ID, to the CC Secretariat or Politburo for review. Once the deal is approved, the ID makes arrangements with the Soviet General Staff to provide whatever is required.[71]

In addition to the international front groups, there are roughly 80 bilateral "friendship" or "cultural" organizations throughout the world.[72] Like the larger, international fronts, the governing bodies of these organizations include Soviet operatives, who report to the ID's International Governmental Organizations section,[73] and foreigners sympathetic to the CPSU. Membership rolls usually include not only staff of the local Soviet embassy, who frequently serve as honorary or ex officio members, but also members and fellow travelers of the local communist party.[74] In some cases, these friendship societies provide a convenient cover for CPSU representatives, who can use their positions to maintain close ties with local communists and dissidents, conduct Soviet intelligence operations,[75] and distribute propaganda material.

## The Ministry of Foreign Affairs

The ID's relationship with the Ministry of Foreign Affairs is presumably close and sometimes cooperative. Analysts from both organizations could be expected, in the interest of efficiency, to communicate with one another on a regular basis and work together coordinating and drafting policy recommendations for the Central Committee and Politburo.[76] Indeed, in many regards the two are natural allies. For example, both might have an institutional interest in seeing that Soviet policy in one area does not jeopardize Soviet relations in other areas. Thus, writes a Soviet émigré with knowledge of this subject, "on many policy issues, representatives of the International Department . . . may find their positions more closely attuned to those of the Foreign Ministry . . . than to those of the Department for Liaison with Ruling Workers' and Communist Parties, . . . [which] in turn, might look for support outside the party apparatus. . . ."[77]

Nonetheless, in theory at least, the ID appears to have a more important role in the process of foreign policy formulation than does the MFA, especially as regards policy toward the Third World. For one thing, senior ID personnel such as Zagladin, Brutents, and Ul'yanovskiy have established reputations as experts in their fields. For another, the ID acts as a filter through which information on the developing world and capitalist countries is funneled to Soviet leaders: Recommendations on policy issues, based upon inputs from the Ministry of Foreign Affairs, the Soviet intelligence services, and the Ministry of Defense, are made by the ID and sent to the general secretary's aides who assist in preparing the agenda for Secretariat (and Politburo) meetings.[78]

During these weekly Secretariat meetings, if necessary, selected specialists from a variety of quarters may be invited to provide further information.[79] Proposals are then approved, rejected, or returned to the ID for further study. The Secretariat may approve a recommendation either outright or provisionally, stipulating in the second instance that it be presented to the Politburo for final approval. In essence, however, matters are usually decided at the Secretariat level or even within the International Department before they reach the Politburo.[80] According to one source, "the Secretariat *frames* policy decisions, and by the time the issue is presented to the Politburo, the framework for the decision is usually [pre]determined."[81] Thus, the MFA's views on foreign policy represent only a portion of the information upon which party leaders base their decisions.

In practice, of course, the Ministry of Foreign Affairs may have considerably more influence in this process, especially given Andrey Gromyko's rise to prominence after the recent succession from Yuriy Andropov to Konstantin Chernenko. Previously, Gromyko's input was through the initial proposals and information sent by the MFA to the ID or, in the final stage, after the Secretariat had submitted its findings to the Politburo, where Suslov's commanding presence presumably prevailed in foreign policy matters. Thus, had Gromyko disagreed with the Secretariat's proposals, his only means of countering them was to persuade the other Politburo members that the Secretariat's analysis and recommendations were faulty—which might have been quite difficult since half of the Politburo members concurrently belong to the Secretariat.[82] Now, however, in the absence of Suslov it seems highly unlikely that Gromyko's input or preferences on any foreign policy issue would go unheeded, particularly in such areas as Soviet–American relations or arms control.

## Relations with the KGB

In addition to the Ministry of Foreign Affairs, the ID deals extensively with the Soviet intelligence services, particularly the KGB. This relationship essentially exists on two levels—the analytical and the operational. On the one hand, the ID receives KGB reports and recommendations based upon both raw and evaluated intelligence, which in turn form the backdrop for policy proposals submitted by the department to the CC Secretariat and Politburo. On the other hand, the ID enlists KGB operatives to carry out special projects on the party's behalf.

One of the major ways in which the two agencies interact is through the sharing and evaluation of intelligence. Prior to the 1970s, political/economic intelligence gathered in or about foreign countries was funneled through the information department of the KGB's First Chief Directorate. There, intelligence was evaluated, collected, and distributed to policymakers, including those in the ID.[83] While attempts were made to verify the authenticity and accuracy of the information gathered, only minimal analysis was done by the KGB's information department.[84] The task of analyzing and producing finished intelligence reports appears to have been left to the ID.[85] This was an enormous undertaking, as the ID simply lacked the staff to handle the work.

In an effort to cope with the ever-increasing glut of information, the ID drew more and more upon the research institutes of the USSR Academy of Sciences.[86] Selected academics were given access to varying amounts of foreign literature and possibly diplomatic reports.[87] ID analysts, however, still bore the burden of having to integrate classified material into the work of academics. As the Soviet Union became more active in the Third World during the late 1960s, greater demands were placed upon the information-channeling system, and it is unlikely that the Soviet leadership was able to make effective use of all the information at its disposal.

To help alleviate this problem, during the early 1970s, the CPSU upgraded the status of the KGB's information department to that of Service I[88] and expanded its role to include more intelligence analysis.[89] It now publishes a classified summary of daily events and regularly produces forecasts of world developments for use by the Soviet leadership.[90] According to a recent source, Service I makes "a conscientious, scholarly effort" to give the Politburo and other clients objective and accurate analysis.[91] Even though Service I has been able to alleviate part of the ID's analysis burden, leaving the latter greater freedom to explore policy issues, it still is unable to digest, analyze, and disseminate all the information made available from Soviet resources.[92] Thus, the KGB continues to work closely with the ID in order to produce intelligence products that provide the Soviet leadership with the necessary understanding of developments in the noncommunist world.

In addition to coordinating intelligence analysis with Service I, the ID also interacts with other branches of the KGB. It frequently enlists the KGB's Active Measures Service (known as Service A), which is responsible for conducting disinformation and propaganda operations abroad. Service A, in close collaboration with the relevant CC departments, including the ID, has been very active during recent years in disseminating forgeries of Western documents, planting bogus or misleading articles in the foreign press, spreading rumors and false reports, and using clandestine radio stations to spread disinformation.[93]

The idea for a propaganda campaign, according to John Barron, may originate within the Politburo, the ID, Service A, or the KGB *Residentura* (Residency) abroad.[94] Operations that are of a particularly sensitive nature must be approved by either the Politburo or the CC Secretariat.[95] Important campaigns are then monitored by the various agencies and departments involved through a "top secret" bulletin published by Service A.[96]

Making up Service A are about 200 staff officers, most of whom operate out of KGB headquarters ("the Center"), which is located just outside Moscow.[97] Service A does not station personnel abroad, and it must rely on KGB staff officers assigned to the *Residenturas* to implement a propaganda or disinformation campaign abroad. In those operations involving the use of foreign communists, the ID plays a supportive, perhaps even supervisory, role, since the KGB usually must obtain the department's approval before embarking upon such operations.[98]

The ID also appears to be involved in directing the KGB in covert operations of economic destabilization. According to one account, these include:

> Setting up dummy companies to take out loans from local banks and defaulting on them, buying into local banks and companies themselves, recruiting local businessmen and contractors by throwing business their way or through bribery, buying interest in technology-oriented Western companies through a third country, and buying real estate the same way.[99]

Research     Since the mid-1960s, the ID has increasingly drawn upon
Institutes   the research institutes of the USSR Academy of Sciences
             in order to support its work. These institutes proliferated
during the Khrushchev years, and under the Brezhnev leadership conducted studies more relevant to policymaking. Consequently, as noted above, the ID now employs numerous full- and part-time scholars to conduct research projects. Selected experts may also take part in ad hoc committees, made up of department, Ministry of Foreign Affairs, and KGB personnel, that study particular problems or monitor important events.[100] However, this is the exception rather than the rule, since it is the institute directors, deputy directors, or section chiefs who are usually involved in these activities. Individual academics conducting special research for the ID are brought on as full-time consultants. These researchers probably have access to classified materials.

The extent to which the ID controls these organizations is uncertain; what is clear, however, is that research institutes are playing an increasingly important support role in the ID's efforts to keep Soviet policymakers informed of world events. Secretary Ponomarëv stressed the value and role of the research institute in his keynote address before the Oriental Institute of the USSR Academy of Sciences (IVAN) when it was presented with the Order of the Labor Red Banner in 1980.

> Emphasis is rightly being placed here on the combination of fundamental research with an analysis of current events on the practical day-to-day plane. . . . IVAN's scientific collective should analyze the ongoing changes in depth, comprehensively and in good time, in order that it might always be on top of matters and completely ready to provide a scientific answer to the questions posed by life and not only correctly spot what is new, but also skillfully forecast the development of events.

> Serious demands are being made of Soviet oriental science by the prospects of the Soviet Union's political, economic and cultural cooperation with the oriental countries. . . . The tasks confronting you, comrades, are big and difficult, as you can see. . . . The party and Soviet people expect of orientalists fundamental works collating the new phenomena and trends in the struggle of the oriental peoples and also a prompt analysis of current events.[101]

Other research institutes also regularly conduct studies for the ID, including the Institute of the International Workers' Movement (IMRD), the Institute of World Economics and International Relations (IMEMO), the Far East Institute (IDV), the Africa Institute (IA), the Latin American Institute (ILA), and the Institute of the United States of America and Canada (ISShAK).[102] Each of these think tanks publishes its own journal, except for the Oriental Institute and the Africa Institute which copublish *Narody Azii i Afriki* (Peoples of Asia and Africa) and *Aziya i Afrika Segodnya* (Asia and Africa Today). The ID helps monitor the political tone of the articles published in these journals by having ID personnel sit on the various editorial boards. For example, Karen Brutents, the department's deputy chief for the Near East, serves on the editorial board of *Aziya i Afrika Segodnya*, as does the Near East sector chief, Yuriy Gryadunov; moreover, Zagladin, Brutents, and Nikolay Mostovets, the sector chief responsible for North America, are members of the editorial staff for ISShAK's publication, *SShA: Ekonomika, Politika, Ideologiya*.

When a scholar acquires a position at one of these research institutes and develops a reputation for his products, he may begin doing policy-relevant work for the ID. These scholars are tasked through the institute's director and accordingly, projects are referred to as "the director's assignments."[103] A scholar may be asked to participate in studies which take up at least 20% of his time, or he may take part in an ad hoc committee, or if he is particularly well-known, may present his views at CC Secretariat or Politburo meetings.[104] This work is always classified and does not appear in the open press, though it may be circulated among select scholars.[105]

While Soviet researchers generally play little role in the policy-formulation process, they have a number of informal ways by which they attempt to influence policymakers. One of the most frequent ways that they give their unsolicited views is through "floating" an article in the Institute's journal.[106] This may be done openly or by writing under a pseudonym. Another way that scholars attempt to influence policymakers is through contacting friends, classmates, or former students who occupy positions in the ID.[107] For example, Nikolay Inozemtsev (the late director of IMEMO) and Georgiy Arbatov (the director of ISShAK) were classmates of Vadim Zagladin, the first deputy chief of the ID, at the Moscow State Institute of International Relations.[108]

More formal means by which scholars are able to influence policymakers are through the publication of their views in "classified" publications—"Spravki, Spetzbulletany," initiative notes or memoranda, and Information Bulletins. A *Spravka* is a report based upon a study done by academics for the ID after the study's completion. The conclusions of a *Spravka* may form the basis of a change in policy or serve as a justification for the continuation of a policy.[109] *Spetzbulletany* (Special Bulletins) are regular publications containing summaries of various classified reports which are submitted to the ID.[110] According to one source, the *Spetzbulletin* inside IVAN has a circulation of 250 registered copies, and special permission was required to read it.[111] Little is known about the memoranda notes, but it is likely that these are short and concise personal views of current events sent by a scholar, on his own initiative, to the institute's director. If the director finds them particularly insightful, he may forward them to the ID. According to a former member of IMEMO, views stated in memoranda can result in the adoption of a new policy.[112] Sometimes an *Information Bulletin* is mentioned, but it is unclear whether this is the same as the *Spetzbulletin* previously mentioned. One source maintains that an *Information Bulletin* is published by IMEMO and ISShAK four to six times a year and is restricted to the Central Committee staff, the MFA, the General Secretary's assistants, the editors of the major newspapers and international relations journals, and probably the appropriate KGB foreign sections.[113]

In order to conduct policy-relevant work, specialists are given access to the *"White" TASS* and the *"Red" TASS Bulletin*. The *White TASS* gives a limited review of foreign newspapers and the wire services for each day and is supplemented by brief analysis. The *Red TASS Bulletin* reprints lengthy passages from articles and commentaries in the foreign press.[114] It is not known to what degree, if any, that scholars are given access to other classified information, but it is likely that only a very select group of academics is accorded this privilege, probably only institute directors and their deputies.[115]

Although employed essentially as support research staff of the ID, foreign ministry, and the Soviet intelligence services, the institutes' scholars are also used to disseminate Soviet propaganda to the general Soviet populace as well as to foreigners. They may be called upon to soften the impact of unpopular or potentially unfavorable policies, such as the Soviet invasion of Afghanistan, by providing "scholarly," pro-Soviet versions of the events in question. Moreover, quite frequently, the ID will use institute specialists to prepare articles for *Pravda, Novoye Vremya* (New Times), or *Aziya i Afrika Segodnya* on specific issues, such as the political motivations behind NATO's deployment of a new generation of nuclear missiles in Western Europe. These articles may be written independently, or under the direction of the department representative on the journal's staff. Research institute specialists also contribute to the intelligence-gathering effort aimed at foreigners and their countries. As the Soviet citizens most likely to come in contact with foreigners, both in the USSR and abroad, they are in the best position to garner information on the backgrounds of their foreign counterparts, to compile biographic sketches that may be of some intelligence value, and to assess prevailing moods in foreign countries. Their position as "academics" enhances this capability, as foreigners are more apt to speak freely with professional colleagues than they would with officials of either the party or the state.[116]

It must be emphasized that only a select few of the research institute staffers do work for the ID. Despite the attention that these institutes are given in the West, they may actually have very little impact on Soviet foreign policy formulation. Indeed, according to one informed source, most of the work done by ISShAK for Central Committee departments winds up in the wastepaper basket.[117] Nevertheless, although their precise role in Soviet foreign policy remains uncertain, the institutes do appear to provide, upon request, background material for department studies and serve as training facilities for party cadres.

**The Soviet Press**    An important domestic function of the ID is its general supervision of the Soviet media's coverage of party policy toward communist and radical movements in nonbloc countries. Even here, however, lines of institutional authority are somewhat complex. According to a former Soviet editor, whose views were cited in a recent Rand Corporation study:

> The International Department keeps an eye on all . . . journals [in its policy area], but the general direction is determined by the Propaganda Department. It's a complicated system. The Propaganda Department can make no decision about a given journal or its specific subject matter: it checks up on basic facts, clears up specific problems. The other is done by Ponomarëv's office. He has constant charge of the kitchen. He determines the political line, the content, and everything else. But the article could not be published without the Propaganda Department because the Propaganda Department leads in all matters of ideology. The Propaganda Department can influence an article from the point of view of general directions.[118]

There also exists a CPSU Central Committee International Information Department (IID) whose responsibilities have never been openly defined. Its staff appears to be much smaller than that of the ID, and it is apparently overshadowed by the ID as well. According to a former KGB officer, the IID is responsible for improving the timing, responsiveness, and coordination of the major overt propaganda outlets (T.V., radio, newspapers) of the USSR for internal consumption first and foreign audiences second.[119] Its targeting of Soviet audiences is particularly important in light of modern information technology's ability to deliver news into the USSR without Soviet regulation. Therefore, the IID appears to focus primarily on propaganda vis-à-vis the Soviet mass media, while the ID is more concerned with implementing Soviet covert propaganda plans abroad.

The handling of information on foreign affairs is not the domain just of the Central Committee apparat, however. The Ministry of Foreign Affairs also exercises a degree of control over the Soviet press, as does the KGB. But the foreign ministry's influence in this area is not so great as was once thought by Western Soviet specialists. For example, Barron claims that only 30% of the articles appearing in the foreign affairs weekly *Novoye Vremya* are written or arranged by the journal's own staff; the bulk of the materials is written by staffers of the ID (30%), the KGB Service A (20%), and the Ministry of Foreign Affairs (20%).[120]

The ID also supervises the work of the international communist journal, *Problems of Peace and Socialism (PPS)*, which is published in Prague. The journal, published in 37 languages and distributed in 145 countries, was founded in 1958, a year after the Cominform was dissolved, in an effort to reinvigorate the international appeal of communism. Originally intended to serve as an open forum for discussion, *PPS* has increasingly become a means of putting forth the CPSU line.[121] Nonetheless, those communist parties that produce their own national editions, such as the Communist Party of Canada which publishes the North American English edition of *PPS* under the title of *World Marxist Review*, exercise editorial control over the material that appears in their journals, often editing or omitting articles as they see fit.

The ID has relied on both direct and indirect means to control the publication of *PPS*. On the one hand, high-ranking ID figures such as Ponomarëv, Zagladin, Shaposhnikov, and Ul'yanovskiy openly exert their considerable influence when necessary;[122] on the other hand, ID personnel routinely serve on the editorial board and journal staff. Moreover, the journal's chief editor is a Soviet citizen, Yuriy A. Sklyarov, who succeeded another Soviet citizen, Konstantin Zarodov, who died in early 1982. Sklyarov was formerly *Pravda*'s deputy chief editor and is an alternate member of the CPSU Central Committee. ID officials maintain an active role in *PPS*, writing articles and heading CPSU delegations to its conferences.[123]

It is quite difficult to determine how political lines of control run in the USSR. While the ID appears to have primacy in editorial control over publications concerning Soviet policy toward the Third World, the foreign ministry probably exercises control of articles dealing with the United States, SALT, and Soviet diplomatic relations.[124]

Conclusion    The ID of the CPSU Central Committee is a subject worthy of scholarly attention. For one thing, as shown throughout this chapter, the ID seems to play an important role in the formulation and implementation of Soviet foreign policy; for another, its leaders are both interesting and accomplished. Yet, very little is known about the actual operations of the ID. This study has bridged this gap by showing the ID in its institutional role, that of bringing together, for the purposes of policymaking and policy implementation, the activities of various Soviet government and party organizations responsible for covering foreign affairs.

The ID is an institution without parallel in the United States and appears to lend itself uniquely to communist bureaucracy. Like most organizations, its strength is dependent upon both the personalities of its leaders and the scope of its operations. Consequently, its influence with the Politburo has no doubt varied over the years. Some analysts might argue that the ID's influence has waned since its heyday during the 1960s when Ponomarëv and Ul'yanovskiy were younger and more dynamic. Yet today, with Zagladin and Brutents as its key figures, the ID probably does its best work on Western Europe, the Middle East, and Latin America, despite the inherent constraints the Soviet Union faces in these regions. The ID has been in existence in one form or another for over 40 years, and regardless of the fluctuations in its influence on policymakers in the CC Secretariat or in the Politburo, it will continue to play a major role in Soviet policy.

## Notes

[1]See, for example, Leonard Schapiro, "The International Department of the CPSU: Key to Soviet Policy," *International Journal* (Toronto), Winter 1976–1977, pp. 41–55; Jerry F. Hough, "Soviet Policymaking toward Foreign Communists," *Studies in Comparative Communism* (Los Angeles, Calif. (Autumn 1982), pp. 167–183; and Vladimir Petrov, "Formation of Soviet Foreign Policy," *Orbis* (Philadelphia, Penn.) (Fall 1973), pp. 819–850.

[2]Schapiro, *loc. cit.*, p. 44.

[3]Two sources indicate that an "international" section existed within the CPSU Central Committee prior to 1943. In his memoirs, Alexandre Barmine, a former Soviet diplomat stationed in Athens during the late 1930s, notes that he telephoned someone in the foreign bureau of the Central Committee in January 1937 (*One Who Survived* [New York: G. P. Putnam's Sons, 1945], p. 309). Louis Fischer also mentions the existence of a CC bureau, run by Karl Radek, that supplied Stalin with information on the international situation. See his *Men and Politics: An Autobiography* (New York: Duell, Sloan and Pearce, 1941), p. 434.

[4]S. A. Abramov, "Organizational-Party Work of the Soviet Communist Party in the Years of the Fourth 5-Year Plan," *Voprosy istorii KPSS* (Moscow) (March 1979), p. 64.

[5]*Ibid.*

[6]Gunther Nollau, *International Communism and World Revolution: History and Methods* (London: Hollis and Carter, 1961), p. 212. Barton Whaley, in perhaps the earliest study discussing the International Department in detail, suggests that the department's original chief was Aleksandr Shcherbakov (1943–1945), followed by Georgiy Malenkov, Zhdanov, perhaps Aleksey Kirichenko, and then Ponomarëv. See his *Soviet Clandestine Communication Nets* (Cambridge, Mass.: Center for International Studies, MIT, September 1969), p. 60. Recent studies by Werner Hahn and by Gavriel Ra'anan, however, indicate that Zhdanov was the original head of the ID. See Hahn's *Post-War Soviet Politics: The Fall of Zhdanov and the Defeat of Moderation, 1946–1953* (Ithaca, N.Y.: Cornell University Press, 1982), pp. 219–220; and Ra'anan's *International Policy Formation in the USSR: Factional "Debates" during the Zhdanovshchina* (Hamden, Conn.: Archon Books, 1983), pp. 13, 25, 28.

[7]Milovan Djilas, *Conversations with Stalin* (New York: Harcourt, Brace and World, 1962), p. 24. See also Hough, *loc. cit.*, p. 169.

[8]A Soviet novel by Aleksandr Chakovskiy mentioned that leaders of an International Department participated in a 1943 study of expected international problems in the aftermath of World War II. See FBIS, *Trends in the Communist Media*, April 11, 1979, p. 28.

[9]Elizabeth Teague, "The Foreign Departments of the Central Committee of the CPSU," *Radio Liberty Research Bulletin*, October 27, 1980, Supplement, p. 8.

[10]Teague, *loc. cit.*, p. 10.

[11]I. Glagolev. *Post-Andropov Kremlin Strategy* (N.P., 1984), p. 12. Dr. Glagolev provides some interesting observations about the activities of the ID between World War II and the 1960s. Had the author chosen to maintain this focus, he would have contributed to the existing information about the ID. Instead, most of the book is a diatribe against communism and replete with rather absurd accusations that American statesmen such as Kissinger, Brzezinski, McNamara,

and Mondale operated under the influence of Soviet manipulation and disinformation.

¹²For more information on the division of labor between the two departments, see Hough, *loc. cit.*, pp. 171–172; Petrov, *loc. cit.*, pp. 824–827; and Wallace H. Spaulding, "The World Communist Movement and its Allies," in *Transnational Parties*, ed. Ralph M. Goldman (Lanham, Md.: University Press of America, 1983), pp. 47–50.

¹³Mohamed Heikal, *The Cairo Documents* (New York: Doubleday, 1973), pp. 124-125.

¹⁴Karen Dawisha, "The Limits of the Bureaucratic Politics Model: Observations on the Soviet Case," *Studies in Comparative Communism* (Winter 1980), p. 304.

¹⁵*Ibid*; see also Jerry F. Hough and Merle Fainsod, *How the Soviet Union Is Governed* (Cambridge, Mass.: Harvard University Press, 1979), p. 215.

¹⁶Dawisha, *loc. cit.*, p. 304. A former CC apparatchik, Abdurakhman Avtorkhanov, disputes this view. He maintains that "the departments of the Central Committee do not have the right to issue instructions or directives either to the minister of foreign affairs or his colleagues on matters of foreign policy." See his *The Communist Party Apparatus* (Cleveland, Ohio: World Publishing Co., 1966), p. 347.

¹⁷The ID shared this responsibility with the Department for Liaison with Workers' and Communist Parties of Socialist Countries. See Dawisha, *loc. cit.*, p. 304.

¹⁸Hough, *loc. cit.*, p. 174.

¹⁹*Ibid.* For a list of the ID staff, see Wallace Spaulding, "Addenda on the International Department," in *Problems of Communism*, September–October 1984, pp. 68–74.

²⁰Petrov, *loc. cit.*, p. 826; and Steven A. Grant, "Soviet Americanists," *US International Communications Agency Research Report* (Washington, D.C.), R-1-80, February 15, 1980.

²¹For Soviet policymaking on national security issues, see Michael Sadykiewicz, "Soviet Military Politics," *Survey* (London) (Winter 1982), pp. 179–210; and Arthur J. Alexander, "Decision-Making on Soviet Weapons Procurement," in *The Defense Policies of Nations: A Comparative Study*, eds. Douglas J. Murray and Paul R. Viotti (Baltimore, Md.: Johns Hopkins University Press, 1982), pp. 153–194.

²²This was certainly likely during Brezhnev's tenure, since secretaries and department heads were required "as a matter of routine to send such information and recommendations to Brezhnev's personal secretariat." See Kenneth A. Meyers and Dimitri Simes, *Soviet Decision Making, Strategic Policy, and SALT* (Washington, D.C., Center for Strategic and International Studies, Georgetown University, December 1974), p. 16; and Petrov, *loc. cit.*, pp. 823–824.

²³See, for example, Teague, *loc. cit.*, p. 39.

²⁴It is probably easier for journalists to join the ID given the rigorous screening process they must go through during their careers. Moreover, within the party hierarchy, international affairs journalists are considered more prestigious than academics. See Dimitri K. Simes, "National Security under Andropov," *Problems of Communism* (Washington, D.C.) (January–February 1983), p. 37.

²⁵Oleg Penkovsky, *The Penkovsky Papers*, trans. by Peter Deriabin (London: Collins, 1965), pp. 69, 101–103; John Barron, *KGB: The Secret Work of Soviet Secret Agents* (New York, Readers Digest Press, 1974), p. 76; Miles Costik, "The Targets of Soviet Technological Espionage," *Current Analysis* (Washington, D.C.) (December 31, 1982), pp. 15–17; and Henri Regnard, "The Theft of Western

Technology," *Journal of Defense and Diplomacy* (McLean, Va.) (April 1984), pp. 44–48, 64.

[26]Hough and Fainsod, *op. cit.*, p. 422. Hough maintains that the ID avoids using the term *instruktory* because of its connotation. Instead, it classifies its staff *referenty*. Thus, this is unclear.

[27]*Ibid.*

[28]Lilita Dzirkals, Thane Gustafson, and A. Ross Johnson, *The Media and Intra-Elite Communication in the USSR*, R-2869 (Santa Monica, Calif.: Rand Corporation, 1982), p. 20.

[29]See, for example, Veljko Micunovic, *Moscow Diary* (Garden City, N.Y.: Doubleday, 1980), pp. 101–102.

[30]See Stefan Possony, *Defense and Foreign Affairs* (London) (November 1975), p. 9. According to Possony, ID officials on foreign duty have their own system of codes and communications. David Kahn also suggests this as he notes that "the several branches of a Soviet mission—diplomatic, secret police, military, commercial, and political (Communist Party)— all have their own keys and, in larger embassies, cipher clerks. See *The Codebreakers* (New York: McMillan, 1967), p. 662.

[31]Hough, *loc. cit.*, p. 175.

[32]Within the department is a "Secretariat" about which little is known. According to one source, personnel assigned to this group make up the department's office staff or clerical help (Hough and Fainsod, *op. cit.*, p. 422). It is not known whether they are attached to each sector or are part of an administrative affairs section. The "Secretariat" is headed by M. I. Kovalev.

[33]U.S. House of Representatives, Permanent Select Committee on Intelligence, *Soviet Covert Action (The Forgery Offensive)*, Hearings before the Subcommittee on Oversight, February 6, 19, 1980 (Washington, D.C., U.S. Government Printing Office), p. 82. (Hereafter *Soviet Covert Action.*)

[34]*Ibid.* In another case, a delegation from a West European communist party met with ID officials in Moscow to discuss a new Soviet propaganda and political action campaign designed to woo the political Left in Western Europe away from NATO and the United States. Delegates were encouraged to open up a dialogue with local social democratic parties, the main target of the offensive, on the subject of disarmament.

[35]*Information Bulletin* (Toronto) (April 1981), p. 9.

[36]An example of an illegal communist party that was heavily dependent on the USSR for financial and logistical support was the People's (Tudeh) Party of Iran, which was forced by circumstances to bear the burden of the shifting trends in Soviet–Iranian relations. In 1959, the Soviet Union created in Baku the clandestine National Voice of Iran (NVOI) in order to lend support to the Tudeh party and to put forth the Soviet position in Iran. During the 1970s, however, another pro-Soviet clandestine radio station, Radio Peyk-i Iran, was closed down when Soviet–Iranian relations improved. And in December 1979, when the Soviet leadership recognized that religious leaders were going to succeed in overthrowing the Shah, Tudeh Secretary General Iraj Iskandari was suddenly removed for having previously gone on record that he would not cooperate with religious leaders "if the matter concerned the creation of a theocratic state." See *Al-Nida* (Beirut), December 17, 1978. For a recent account of Soviet–Iranian relations, see Zalmay Khalilzad, "Islamic Iran: Soviet Dilemma," *Problems of Communism* (January–February 1984), pp. 1–20.

[37]Teague, *loc. cit.*, p. 15. According to former KGB Major Stanislav Levchenko, the ID provided foreign communist journalists in Moscow with a personal aide and a monthly stipend of 300 rubles. See John Barron, *KGB Today: The Hidden Hand* (New York, Readers Digest Press, 1983), p. 60–61.

[38]U.S. House of Representatives, Permanent Select Committee on Intelligence, *Soviet Active Measures*, Hearings before the Subcommittee on Oversight, July 13, 14, 1982 (Washington, D.C., U.S. Government Printing Office, 1982), p. 165. (Hereafter *Soviet Active Measures.)*

[39]U.S. Central Intelligence Agency, *The Tudeh Party: Vehicle of Communism in Iran*, ORE 23–49 (July 18, 1949) (declassified April 7, 1975), pp. 12–13; and CIA, "Information Report: Historical Sketch of the Tudeh Party" (June 30, 1952) (declassified April 7, 1975), p. 5. According to Gholam Husayn Qa'empanah, a member of the Tudeh party's Central Committee, following the revolution in 1978–1979, the Tudeh party used a commercial company as a cover to send information to the Soviets and, in turn, to receive financial, material, and other forms of aid from Moscow. See Tehran Domestic Television Service (in Persian), October 10, 1983, trans. in Foreign Broadcast Information Service, *Daily Report: South Asia*, October 13, 1983, pp. I/3–19.

[40]According to KGB defector Stanislav Levchenko, during his years as a KGB operative in Japan (1975–1979), the ID provided funds to Philippine Communists (presumably to members of the pro-Soviet Philippine Communist Party—PKP) on a regular basis, using KGB officers to deliver the money to that party's courier in Tokyo. See *Soviet Active Measures*, p. 166.

[41]Teague, *loc. cit.*, p. 15.

[42]For an example of such cooperation, see *Pravda* (Moscow), August 2, 1983, p. 4.

[43]Spaulding, "The World Communist Movement," pp. 39–52.

[44]Oded Eran, "Soviet Perceptions of Arab Communism and its Political Role," in *The U.S.S.R. and the Middle East*, eds. Michael Confino and Shimon Shamir (New York, Halsted Press, 1973), p. 117; and Bertil Haeggman, *Det Internationella Terroristnaetet* [Terrorism: Warfare in Our Time] (Malmoe, Sweden: Berghs Foerlag, 1978), pp. 159–163.

[45]Heikal, *op. cit.*, p. 152.

[46]Bhabani Sen Gupta, "An Approach to the Study of Soviet Policies for the Third World," in *Soviet Economic and Political Relations with the Developing World*, eds. Roger E. Kanet and Donna Bahry (New York, Praeger, 1975), p. 122.

[47]Rostislav Ul'yanovskiy, "Marxist and Non-Marxist Socialism," *World Marxist Review* (Toronto), no. 9, 1971, pp. 118–127.

[48]See Wallace Spaulding, "Addendum 2: ID Representatives Abroad," *Problems of Communism* (September–October 1984), pp. 74–75.

[49]Karen N. Brutents, *National Liberation Revolutions Today*, Vol. 2 (Moscow, Progress Publishers, 1977), p. 215.

[50]*Ibid.*, p. 216.

[51]Soviet strategy with respect to West European social democrats, of course, has fluctuated throughout the years. During the 1930s, for example, German social democrats were denounced by Soviet leaders as "social fascists." See Ruth Fischer, *Stalin and German Communism: A Study in the Origins of the State Party* (Cambridge, Mass.: Harvard University Press, 1948), pp. 655–656.

[52]Wynfred Joshua, "Soviet Manipulation of the European Peace Movement," *Strategic Review* (Washington, D.C.) (Winter 1983), p. 10.

[53]*Soviet Covert Action*, p. 72.

[54]*Kommunist* (Moscow), no. 5, March 1981.

[55]These interviews are often conducted by the pro-Soviet communist media. For example, see the interview with Vadim Zagladin in *L'Humanité* (Paris), July 15, 1983, p. 5.

[56]*Kommunist*, no. 5, March 1981, pp. 6–7.

[57]For a comprehensive review of Soviet representation on the "presidential boards" and secretariats of the major front groups, see Wallace Spaulding,

"Communist International Fronts in 1983," *Problems of Communism* (March–April 1984), pp. 52–61.

[58]The Soviets technically share control of AAPSO with Egypt; however, since Egypt altered its policies vis-à-vis the West and the Soviet Union, AAPSO activities have taken place outside of Egypt, in such countries as South Yemen, India, Cyprus, and Vietnam. This has effectively shut the Egyptian government out of the organization.

[59]U.S. Department of State, "World Peace Council: Instrument of Soviet Foreign Policy," *Foreign Affairs Note* (Washington, D.C.), April 1982, p. 2.

[60]The use of front groups by the CPSU dates back to the 1920s when Otto Kuusinen, a veteran Finnish communist who subsequently became a member of the CPSU, told a meeting of the Comintern Executive Committee that a "whole solar system of organizations and small committees around the Communist Party, working under the influence of the Party, although not under its mechanical leadership," should be created. (See Ian Greig, *The Assault on the West* [Petersham, England, Foreign Affairs Publishing Co., 1968], p. 39.) Two years later, Willi Munzenberg, a German citizen doing organizational work for the Comintern, elaborated upon this idea, stressing, among other things, that front groups could be a means "to arouse the interest of apathetic and indifferent workers, who were not interested in Communist propaganda and have to be attracted in new ways [and] to act as bridges for those who sympathise with Communism but have not taken the final step and joined the Party" (*ibid.*, p. 40).

[61]U.S. State Department, "World Peace Council," p. 3.

[62]U.S. Central Intelligence Agency, Directorate of Intelligence, *Directory of Soviet Officials: National Organizations* (August 1982), p. 13.

[63]U.S. State Department, "World Peace Council," pp. 2–3.

[64]From a letter in the *New Statesman* (London, October 17, 1980), quoted in *ibid.*, p. 2, n. 1.

[65]*Soviet Active Measures*, p. 39.

[66]CIA, *Directory* (August 1982), p. 280.

[67]*Soviet Active Measures*, p. 160.

[68]*Ibid.*

[69]*Ibid.*

[70]Nayif Hawatimah of the Democratic Front for the Liberation of Palestine (DFLP) was recently in Moscow as a guest of SKSSAA, while concurrently Faruq Al-Qaddumi, chief of the PLO's Political and International Department, arrived as a guest of the Soviet government. This fits well with Soviet diplomatic policy, since the USSR accords quasi-diplomatic status to the PLO, but considers the DFLP only a political/paramilitary organization, albeit pro-Soviet. For Hawatimah's visit, see TASS International Service (in Russian), July 12, 1983, trans. in Foreign Broadcast Information Service, *Daily Report: Soviet Union*, July 12, 1983, p. H/1.

[71]*Soviet Active Measures*, p. 160.

[72]*Soviet Covert Action*, p. 82.

[73]The International Governmental Organizations Sector is headed by Aleksey Legasov. Beneath him are Mikhail Andreyev and V. G. Savel'yeva, who is the only woman known to work in the department. See CIA, *Directory* (September 1978), pp. 22–24; and Teague, *loc. cit.*, p. 37.

[74]*Soviet Covert Action*, p. 83.

[75]*Ibid.*

[76]Dev Murarka, "Soviet Foreign Policy—An Unknown, Efficient Mechanism," *Suomen Kuvalehti* (Helsinki), no. 39, September 25, 1981, p. 2; and Meyers and Simes, *op. cit.*, p. 19.

[77]Meyers and Simes, *op. cit.*, p. 23.

[78]See, for example, Petrov, *loc. cit.*, pp. 823–824.

[79]Ned Temko, "Who Pulls the Levers of Power in the Soviet Machine?" *The Christian Science Monitor* (Boston, Mass.), February 23, 1982, p. 12.

[80]Dawisha, *loc. cit.*, p. 322, no. 42.

[81]Temko, *loc. cit.*, p. 13.

[82]By at least one account, rendered *before* Gromyko's recent ascendance, the MFA's position vis-à-vis the International Department was not "affected substantially by Gromyko's promotion to the Politburo" in April 1973. See Dawisha, *loc. cit.*, p. 322, no. 42, where she recounts a statement to this effect of an MFA sector chief.

[83]Cord Meyer, *Facing Reality: From World Federalism to the CIA* (New York: Random House, 1980), p. 314; and Barron, *KGB Today*, pp. 446–447.

[84]Barron, *KGB: Secret Work*, pp. 76–77; and *idem. KGB Today*, p. 446. Several writers have mentioned the past existence of an "Information" department or center which conducts analysis of intelligence information. Barton Whaley notes that in 1947, a Committee on Information (KI or Komitet Informatsiy) was created to centralize all Soviet foreign intelligence operations. The KI was directed by a group of senior foreign service chiefs subordinate to the Party. The KI was never quite successful, as it proved difficult to manage and was responsible for numerous bureaucratic battles. Accordingly, it was abolished in 1951. Former KGB officer Anatoliy Golitsyn states that the KI's function was to prepare long-range studies and analyses for the Soviet leadership. He adds that after 1951 it was placed under the operational control of the Ministry of Foreign Affairs until 1958, whereupon it was subordinated to the Central Committee directly. Golitsyn believes that it exists today under the cover of the State Committee for Foreign Cultural Relations. Angello Codevilla also alludes to the continued existence of an "Information Center" staffed by personnel from several agencies which collect intelligence. The purpose of the organization is to provide assessments based on intelligence information for policymakers. The personnel of this section remain tied to their parent organizations but work through a chief analyst who drafts and signs the final document. If the Information Center exists, it probably is either subordinate to or part of the ID, rather than as Golitsyn asserts, the State Committee for Foreign Cultural Relations (Whaley, Soviet Clandestine Communication Networks, pp. 119–120; Anatoliy Golitsyn, *New Lies for Old*; and Angello Codevilla, "Comparative Historical Experience of Doctrine," in *Analysis and Estimates*, ed. Roy Godson [Washington, D.C., National Strategy Information Center, 1980], p. 19).

[85]Meyer, *op. cit.*, p. 324.

[86]Jerry F. Hough, *The Soviet Leadership in Transition* (Washington, D.C.: The Brookings Institution, 1980), p. 123; Ronald Russell Pope, "Soviet Foreign Affairs Specialists: An Evaluation of Their Direct and Indirect Impact on Soviet Foreign Policy Decision-Making Based on Their Analysis of Cuba, 1958–1961, and Chile, 1969–1973." Ph.D. diss., Philadelphia, Penn., University of Pennsylvania, 1975, pp. 12–14; and Meyers and Simes, *op. cit.*

[87]Petrov, *loc. cit.*, p. 843.

[88]*Soviet Covert Action*, p. 61.

[89]Barron, *KGB Today*, p. 446. As a result of this expanded role, Service I is now the third-largest section within the KGB's First Chief Directorate.

[90]*Ibid.*

[91]*Ibid.*

[92]*Ibid.*

[93]*Soviet Active Measures*, p. 10.

[94]Barron, *KGB Today*, p. 447.

[95]*Ibid.*; Meyer, *op. cit.*, p. 312; and *Soviet Covert Action*, p. 65.

[96]Barron, *KGB Today*, p. 447.

[97]*Soviet Active Measures*, p. 10.

[98]Meyer, *op. cit.*, p. 312.

[99]Vladimir Sakharov and Umberto Tosi, *High Treason* (New York, G. P. Putnam's Sons, 1980), p. 249.

[100]Jiri Valenta, "From Prague to Kabul: The Soviet Style of Invasion," *International Security* (Cambridge, Mass.) (Fall 1980), p. 122, n. 13.

[101]*Narody Azii i Afriki* (Moscow), no. 1, 1981, pp. 4–13.

[102]The function performed by TASS in translating and providing limited analysis of the foreign news media is apparently very similar to the job done by the Foreign Broadcast Information Service (FBIS) and the Joint Publications Research Service (JPRS) of the U.S. government with the exception that anyone may subscribe to FBIS and JPRS publications.

[103]Hough, *Soviet Leadership in Transition*, p. 123.

[104]Petrov, *loc. cit.*, p. 844.

[105]Oded Eran, *The Mezhdunarodniki* (Ramat Gan, Israel: Turtledove Publishing, 1979), p. 306.

[106]Karen Dawisha, *Soviet Foreign Policy toward Egypt* (London: Macmillan, 1979), p. 146; and Pope, *loc. cit.*, p. 13.

[107]Dawisha, *Soviet Foreign Policy toward Egypt*, p. 146.

[108]Hough, *Soviet Leadership in Transition*, p. 124.

[109]Eran, *Mezhdunarodniki*, p. 148.

[110]*Ibid.*, p. 306. The author states that copies could not be brought home and that all stencils had to be destroyed.

[111]*Ibid.* Former ISShAK researcher, Galina Orionova, who defected to the West, noted that in addition to the regular library of Soviet publications, two classified libraries existed at her institute. One held Western publications, and the other held Western publications dealing with the USSR (Nora Beloff, "Escape from Boredom: A Defector's Story," *Atlantic Monthly*, November 1980, p. 44).

[112]*Ibid.* The author's sources indicated that Georgiy Arbatov and the late Nikolay Inozemtsev were particularly influential with Secretary Ponomarëv. The same may be true of Yevgeniy Primakov, the head of IVAN, who was a protégé of Inozemtsev. See Hough, *Soviet Leadership in Transition*, p. 124.

[113]I. Glagolev "The House on Old Square," *Posev* (Frankfurt), no. 9 (September 1978), p. 29.

[114]Leonid Vladimirov, "Problems of a Soviet Journalist," *Conflict Studies*, no. 56 (April 1975), p. 6.

[115]According to Orionova, the main sources for researchers at ISShAK are Western publications, the TASS reports, and interviews with foreigners (Beloff, *loc. cit.*, p. 44).

[116]U.S. Central Intelligence Agency, "The Institute of the U.S.A. and Canada—U.S.S.R. Point of Contact for Americans," in *Soviet Active Measures*, p. 70. According to Orionova, when foreigners visited the institute, the staffers had to fill out two forms: one on where the visitors went; the other on their personal lives and background. This information was sent to Dr. Rodimir Bogdanov, a KGB officer assigned to the institute. See Nora Beloff, "Escape from Boredom: A Defector's Story," *The Atlantic Monthly* (Boston, Mass.) (November 1980), pp. 46–47.

[117]Beloff, *loc. cit.*, pp. 46–47. For a different view, which sees the institute's influence as growing, see Tyrus Cobb, "National Security Perspectives of Soviet 'Think Tanks,'" *Problems of Communism* (November–December 1981), pp. 51–59.

[118]Cited in Dzirkals, Gustafson, and Johnson, *op. cit.*, p. 21.

[119]See the interview of S. Lenchenko in Richard Shultz and Roy Godson, *Dezinformatsia: Active Measures in Soviet Strategy* (N.Y.: Pergamon, 1984), p. 180. Also see Radio Liberty, "The International Information Department of the Central Committee of the CPSU," March 4, 1980.

[120]Barron, *KGB Today*, p. 82.

[121]Wallace Spaulding "New Head, Old Problems of Peace and Socialism," *Problems of Communism* (November–December 1982), p. 57–58.

[122]For example, Arab Communists responded to the crackdown on Sudanese Communists in May 1971 by airing their differences with Moscow. The secretary general of the Lebanese Communist Party, Nicholas Shaoui, wrote in *World Marxist Review* (September 1971) that the working class should form the nucleus of the "united front." Ul'yanovskiy responded by writing a critique of this view in the same journal. See Ul'yanovskiy, "Marxist and Non-Marxist Socialism." For more background on this exchange, see Robert O. Freedman, *Soviet Policy toward the Middle East since 1970*, 3rd ed. (New York, Praeger, 1982), pp. 65–67.

[123]See Spaulding, "New Head, Old Problems." For more information on *PPS*, Sklyarov, and the death of Konstantin Zarodov, see *Radio Liberty Research Bulletin*, RL 171/82, April 22, 1982; and RL 225/82, June 2, 1982.

[124]Dzirkals, Gustafson, and Johnson, *op. cit.*, p. 22.

# 13

## ROY GODSON
## RICHARD H. SHULTZ

## "Active Measures" in Soviet Strategy*

Disagreement clearly exists in the West over the importance Moscow places on the utility of overt and covert propaganda and political influence techniques as instruments of its foreign policy. There are those who believe that these techniques continue to play a central role in Kremlin strategy. Others disagree, maintaining that the Kremlin no longer regards them as important.

Based on several years of research in the U.S. and Western Europe, it seems clear, however, that propaganda and covert political influence techniques do in fact constitute significant instruments of Soviet foreign policy and strategy. Even prior to the Bolshevik seizure of power, Soviet leaders rejected the Western distinction between periods of war and peace. From their perspective politics is a continual state of war carried out by a wide variety of means, only sometimes requiring military operations. Indeed, included in this approach are *all* means deemed effective.

Soviet leaders now use the term "active measures" (*activnyye meropriatia*) to describe an array of overt and covert techniques for influencing events and behavior in, and the actions of, foreign countries. (Prior to the 1960s, the term *dezinformatsia* was used in some Soviet circles to describe these activities.) The term "active measures," as used here, includes attempts to influence the policies of another government, undermine confidence in its leaders and institutions, disrupt relations with other nations, and discredit and weaken governmental and nongovernmental opponents. This frequently involves attempts to deceive the target (foreign governmental and nongovernmental elite or mass audiences) and/or to distort the target's perception of reality.

Active measures are conducted overtly through officially sponsored

*This chapter summarizes the findings in Richard H. Shultz and Roy Godson, *Dezinformatsia: Active Measures in Soviet Strategy* (London and New York: Pergamon-Brassey's, 1984). Copyright 1984 by National Strategy Information Center, Inc.

foreign propaganda channels, diplomatic relations, and cultural diplomacy. Covert political techniques include the use of covert propaganda, oral and written disinformation, agents-of influence, clandestine radios, and international front organizations. In practice, these
techniques often are interrelated and coordinated.

While other nations from time to time may employ some of these
techniques, the Soviet Politburo uses them in a very different way—
qualitatively and quantitatively. Soviet overt and covert techniques are
much more centrally coordinated and intensive. They are also systematically and routinely conducted on a worldwide scale. Soviet leaders use
covert means in most noncommunist states to enhance dramatically
their themes of overt propaganda, employing intentional misrepresentation, exaggeration, and outright falsehoods on a very large scale. These
overt and covert political campaigns are frequently sustained over long
periods of time. Few, if any, Western governments emulate these
activities in peacetime.

Since the early days of the post-World War II period, the U.S. and the
NATO Alliance have been the main targets of Soviet active measures.
Kremlin leaders have consistently sought to discredit, isolate, and
separate the U.S. from its allies. The ongoing Soviet campaign against
the modernization of NATO's intermediate range nuclear forces (INF)
demonstrates these propositions. For some years, the Soviets have
mounted a large-scale campaign of coordinated diplomatic moves, overt
propaganda, and covert political action aimed at preventing such modernization; so far this has not been successful.

Because Soviet leaders, both in their doctrine and actions, emphasize
the importance of these tactics and devote extensive organizational and
financial resources to them, it is surprising that Western scholars have
devoted little attention to this subject to date.

The Soviet leadership has global ambitions and approaches world
politics as a continual state of conflict and war. While specific policies
reflect the situation and issues unique to a given period, the following
broad objectives of Soviet foreign policy have been identified by many
Western scholars: (1) To preserve, enhance, and expand security in
those areas under the influence of the USSR; (2) to divide Western
opponents of the Soviet Union by driving wedges between them and
disrupting alliance systems; (3) to retain the primacy of the USSR in the
communist world; (4) to promote "proletarian internationalism" and
"national liberation movements" which serve Soviet interests; and (5) to
minimize risk and avoid serious involvement on more than one front at
a time. The specific instruments deployed to achieve these objectives at
any given time are based on Moscow's assessment of what it calls the
"correlation of forces." This is an assessment of military, economic, and
political forces as well as international movements, particularly those
affecting the internal affairs of noncommunist countries. According to
Soviet commentary:

> The foreign policy potential of a state is dependent not upon its own forces
> and internal resources but to a considerable extent on such factors as the

existence of reliable socio-political allies among other states, a national contingent of congenial classes, mass international movements, and other factors active on the world scene.[1]

Influencing national and international political and social forces appears to constitute an important objective in Soviet strategy.

An examination of the years 1960–1980 demonstrates that the leadership of the CPSU regarded active measures as an indispensable instrument to influence these forces. Active measures were used in the 1960s when the Soviet Union was militarily inferior to the West; in the 1970s during the period of détente; and in the late 1970s when the Soviets came to believe the "correlation of forces" had begun to move in their favor but when they were seeking to shift it even more.

Most Western specialists assume (although there is little concrete evidence to support their propositions) that Soviet foreign policy decisions are made by the Politburo, the apex of the CPSU. The Politburo also appears to approve general active measures programs. Since the late 1950s at least three major organizations under Politburo control apparently have planned and conducted active measures. They are the International Department of the CPSU, the International Information Department, and a section of the KGB's First Chief Directorate. Since its creation in the late 1950s, the International Department (ID) has been headed by Boris Ponomarëv, who is now a candidate member of the Politburo. The ID almost certainly coordinates and reviews inputs concerning Soviet foreign policy and active measures from the Ministry of Foreign Affairs and various "think tanks" under the Academy of Sciences. It also plans and coordinates active measures with similar departments in the Communist parties of other Soviet bloc countries as well as with nonruling Communist parties, revolutionary movements, major international fronts, and national liberation movements throughout the world. Moreover, the ID has responsibility for operating a number of clandestine radios that broadcast to the noncommunist world.

The International Information Department (IID) of the CPSU was created in 1978 to coordinate overt propaganda aimed at foreign audiences. Prior to that time this task was incorporated into the work of the CPSU's Department for Agitation and Propaganda and later the Information Department.

The IID now appears to control the foreign operations of TASS, Novosti, international radio broadcasting, periodicals and books sent abroad, and embassy information departments. It is headed by Leonid Zamyatin, a member of the Central Committee, former head of the press department of the Ministry of Foreign Affairs, and a former director of TASS.

Although the primary purpose of the KGB is internal security, its First Chief Directorate carries out espionage and active measures abroad. In the late 1950s the KGB began to increase its active measures activities. First a Department D (for *dezinformatsia*) was created, and then in the 1960s this was upgraded to a Service A (for *activnyye meropriatia*) of the

First Chief Directorate. This group assists KGB "residences" ("stations" in Western parlance) in each country to engage in covert active measures, as well as to coordinate covert active measures with the intelligence services of other Soviet bloc countries.

While it is difficult to estimate the numbers of personnel involved in overt and covert Soviet active measures, recently available information suggests that 10,000–15,000 people are involved, with a budget, in the late 1970s, of $3 to 4 billion per year.

A systematic examination of several major Soviet propaganda outlets from 1960 to 1980 reveals a pattern of "messages" which Moscow wanted Western Europeans and Americans to "hear" over the 20-year period. The "International Review" column of the authoritative Soviet daily *Pravda* was analyzed using a computerized form of content analysis to ensure that the authors did not focus selectively on themes as a result of bias. Then this basically quantitative approach was supplemented by a more qualitative assessment of selected articles from *New Times*, a world affairs weekly published by the ID of the CPSU and distributed worldwide in several languages.

Using these methods, we found that Soviet propaganda from 1960 to 1980 underscored that the U.S. and NATO were (1) aggressive, adventurous, and provocative; (2) militaristic, promoting arms races and cold war; (3) opposed to a negotiated settlement of international issues; (4) in the throes of political, economic, and social crises; (5) threatening communist bloc unity and conducting anti-Soviet bloc propaganda and political action. While the U.S. consistently was characterized as *the* major threat to world peace, careful analysis of Soviet propaganda indicates that in reality the Kremlin did not perceive any direct threat or challenge to its security interests emanating from alleged U.S. aggressiveness and militarism. Moscow asserted a threat without describing how the U.S. military or the U.S. government were threatening the Soviet leadership. The incongruity between Soviet propaganda and Moscow's actual threat perception may be explained partially by considering the tactical foreign policy objectives of the Kremlin rather than its immediate security concerns.

By the late 1960s and the 1970s Moscow's foreign propaganda became increasingly sophisticated. Instead of only one or two themes, the Soviets concentrated on half a dozen. The number of elements within Western governments and societies that were targeted increased. Soviet propaganda also became increasingly flexible, enabling Moscow to respond rapidly to critical issues and events of the day.

The Soviets operate secretly to promote and enhance the effectiveness of their overt propaganda. The Kremlin goes to enormous lengths to hide covert techniques, and it is not easy to detect or document them. Nevertheless it *is* possible to demonstrate persuasively that the Soviets integrate overt propaganda with covert political techniques to multiply the effectiveness of their overall effort. For example, the Kremlin manipulates at least thirteen major international front organizations.

The origins of the post-World War II international fronts can be traced to the Comintern (Communist International) in the 1920s. This was described by Willi Munzenberg, the Communist expert on organizing fronts: "We must penetrate every conceivable milieu, get hold of artists and professors, make use of theaters and cinemas, and spread abroad the doctrine that Russia is prepared to sacrifice everything to keep the world at peace."[2] In 1935 Comintern official Otto Kuusinen was more explicit: "We want to attack our close enemies in the rear. . . . But how can we do so if the majority of working class youth follow not us, but for instance the Catholic priests or the liberal chameleons?" The answer, according to Kuusinen, was "to create a united youth front."[3]

These commentaries illuminate the tasks of front organizations. They are to employ propaganda and active measures to promote Soviet foreign policy objectives within other nations by creating coalitions of communists and noncommunists (from many segments of society) who do not appear to be under Soviet control.

After World War II, responsibility for directing and coordinating the various international fronts was assigned to the Communist Information Bureau (Cominform) and then in the late 1950s to the ID of the CPSU.

One of the most important international fronts is the World Peace Council (WPC) which Moscow created in 1949. Indeed, the other important fronts, the World Federation of Trade Unions, the World Federation of Democratic Youth, and the International Union of Students clearly follow the lead of the WPC.

Moscow, of course, tries to mask its control of the fronts. In the years immediately following World War II, these organizations were based in Western capitals (until they were expelled), and Soviet officials were not appointed to top posts of these ostensibly nongovernmental organizations. But Moscow maintains its influence by controlling the leaders and staff of the WPC and its national affiliates in almost every Western and Third World country. Also, Moscow provides most of the WPC funds. In the late 1970s the U.S. government estimated Soviet annual expenditure on the fronts at $63 million; approximately one-half of this is spent on the WPC.

Since its creation the WPC and most of its national affiliates have supported Soviet foreign policy almost unswervingly. They play the role of independent and nongovernmental organizations, however, in international forums such as those sponsored by the United Nations. Through their national affiliates they also influence national peace movements in directions favored by Moscow.

Another covert active measure used by Moscow is the agent-of-influence, one of the most complex and difficult measures to document. Agents-of-influence include the unwitting but manipulated individual, the trusted contact, and the controlled covert agent. *An unwitting but manipulated person* is one who is unaware that he/she is being directed and/or financed by the Soviet Union, because he/she is hired or directed by a trusted contact or controlled covert agent. *A trusted contact* is a Soviet term used to describe a person who may not be a formally recruited, paid, or controlled agent but who wittingly uses his/her influence to advance Soviet interests. *An agent-of-influence* is a person who is not an intelligence officer but who, when recruited, uses his/her influence to promote Soviet objectives in ways unattributable to Moscow. The agent-of-influence may be a journalist, a prominent private citizen, a government official, a labor leader, or an academic. The main objective of the influence operation is the use of the agent's position—be it in government, politics, labor, or journalism—to support and promote political conditions desired by the Kremlin.

Moscow uses agents-of-influence as one element of a carefully orchestrated effort. Insiders label this orchestration *Kombinatsia*. This refers to the skill of relating, linking, and combining various agents-of-influence (at various times and places) with overt propaganda to enhance effectiveness. These actions comprise one more component of the overt/covert approach employed by the Kremlin.

Generally, the KGB is responsible for conducting agent-of-influence activities. The first phase entails the development of strong covert personal relationships with important figures in foreign societies. Once such a relationship has been established, the next step is to secure the active collaboration of the individual on matters of mutual interest. In return the KGB will provide remuneration tailored to meet the specific needs or vulnerabilities of the person involved.

One of a number of recent cases is that of Pierre Charles Pathe in France. Because Pathe was a prominent citizen, operated as an agent-of-influence over a long period of time, wrote a great deal, and was convicted, it is possible to trace many of his activities with a great deal of assurance.

Pathe apparently came to Soviet attention in 1959 when he wrote favorably about the Soviet Union. After accepting an invitation from the Soviet Ambassador to France, a relationship with the KGB was established. In 1961 he began to publish—with Soviet encouragement and financial support—a confidential journal/newsletter. At the same time he wrote for other journals and newspapers under the assumed name of Charles Morand.

In 1976 he launched a biweekly newsletter entitled *Synthesis*, for which he received partial funding from Moscow. At the height of its popularity the subscribers included 139 Senators and 299 deputies of the French Parliament, 41 journalists, and 14 ambassadors, that is, 70% of the Chamber of Deputies and 47% of the Senate, and a substantial number of important journalists and diplomats. In 1978 his clandestine relationship with the KGB came to the attention of French counterintelligence. He was tried, convicted, and jailed.

An analysis of the seventy issues of *Synthesis* from 1976–1979 indicates that there were two general themes: (1) denigration of and attacks upon Western interests and policies; (2) defense of the USSR and its allies. Pathe omitted from the publication any material which might render the USSR and its friends vulnerable to criticism, muted that criticism which could not be avoided, and included material which actively supported or defended the views of the Soviet Union and its allies.

Forgeries are another significant weapon in the Soviet arsenal of active measures. From the earliest days of the Bolshevik regime, Moscow has used forged documents to discredit and deceive opponents. One major example was the use of forgeries in the "Trust" operations of the 1920s to lure important counterrevolutionaries and their friends, such as Sidney Reilly, back to Russia—and to capture and death.

During the years from 1960 to 1980 forged documents continued to play an important role. These forgeries appear to have been coordinated with other overt and covert operations and were closely related to specific Soviet objectives. During the early 1960s and the latter half of the 1970s, many forged documents were targeted to discredit the U.S. and NATO. Some took the form of authentic-looking but nonetheless false U.S. government documents and communiqués. Some were altered or distorted versions of real U.S. documents. Others were entirely fabricated. Apparently manufactured by the KGB's First Chief Directorate and other Soviet bloc intelligence services, they sought to portray the U.S. as the major threat to world peace and to create suspicion and discord in relations between the U.S. and its West European allies.

In the early 1960s, for example, the Soviets circulated forged U.S. State Department documents designed to show that the U.S. was doing everything possible to sabotage all negotiations with the USSR, especially on disarmament matters. False Defense Department documents surfaced purporting to provide medical evidence that Strategic Air Command personnel were psychotic and in danger of initiating nuclear war! In the late 1970s, Moscow also began to recycle false documents initially circulated in the late 1960s and early 1970s.

Among other notable forgeries is a letter to NATO Secretary General Luns by the Supreme Allied Commander Alexander Haig stating that NATO needed to consider further use of limited nuclear weapons in wartime. Another forged letter from Luns informed the U.S. Ambassador that the Belgian government was compiling files on journalists who opposed deployment of the neutron warhead, implying that the journalists would be suppressed.

We have interviewed former Soviet bloc intelligence officers who specialized in covert political techniques in the early 1960s through the late 1970s. A former Senior Czech intelligence officer (Ladislav Bittman) and a former Soviet intelligence officer (Stanislav Levchenko) describe specific methods of planning, implementing, and evaluating Soviet active measures. They reveal the high degree of control exercised by the Kremlin over active measures conducted by the KGB and Eastern bloc services. Both are convinced that Soviet leaders view these techniques as very important. They report that during the period they served as intelligence officers, the already extensive organizational and financial resources devoted to these activities were increased because Moscow was convinced of their efficacy. As a result, Soviet leaders enhanced their ability to conduct active measures on a massive worldwide scale against the U.S. and NATO.

Bittman reports that when he was operating under the cover of a press attaché in Vienna from 1966–1968, he ran four or five secret agents in Austria and West Germany at any one time. Some were politicians, others journalists. The journalists were not asked to support particular Soviet policy positions but rather to undermine NATO and help create rifts among the NATO allies. During this tour, Bittman said, the Czech Disinformation Department (in which he served as Deputy Chief) focused on forgeries, rumor, and intrigue in order to deceive and mislead the West. The KGB not only provided the Czech intelligence service with general guidance but actually placed KGB advisers within the Czech service in Prague.

Levchenko worked first for one of the International Department fronts in Moscow and later under the cover of a *New Times* correspondent in Tokyo. In Tokyo he recruited a number of politicians and journalists as agents-of-influence. In the late 1970s he was handling 10 agents from all parts of the political spectrum (the democratic left to the more conservative governing party). According to Levchenko, the KGB had about 200 agents in Japan at the time. Their top priorities were to collect intelligence, to prevent further Japanese–U.S. cooperation, and to provoke distrust between Japan and the U.S. Levchenko also described the financial and political means the ID uses to control the international fronts and how the fronts were coordinated with other covert and overt active measures programs.

To recapitulate:

- Examination of the years between 1960 and 1980 demonstrates that the Soviet leaders devoted extensive resources to discrediting, isolating, and splitting the Western alliance through the use of propaganda and political influence activities as part of their broader political–military strategy. For these purposes, the Politburo developed a highly centralized and tightly coordinated organizational structure for planning and implementing active measures.

- Moscow's overall propaganda message basically has remained unchanged during recent decades. Whether the Western allies have perceived East–West relations to be in a period of cold war or a period of détente, Soviet overt propaganda has continued to portray the U.S. and NATO in negative and defamatory terms. However, Moscow's propaganda campaign against the West has become more sophisticated, complex, and flexible.

- Analysis of Soviet propaganda strongly suggests that the Kremlin does not perceive any imminent threat or danger from the U.S. They rarely use foreign propaganda to warn the U.S. and NATO of *genuine* anxiety. Rather, Soviet leaders to a great extent use propaganda as part of a political–military strategy that seeks to weaken the Western alliance.

- It is clear that Moscow actively combines overt and covert political techniques to manipulate, mislead, and deceive Western targets. When Soviet overt propaganda takes up a theme, Moscow usually plays the same message through its international fronts and agents-of-influence, simultaneously using techniques such as forgeries to further its objectives.

Will the Soviets in the 1980s continue to use overt and covert propaganda and political influence techniques against the U.S. and other members of the Western alliance? Will these activities escalate? The answer appears to be "yes." Moscow apparently has been impressed with its own programs, as can be seen by the growth in the size and scope of its active measures. Moreover, the KGB and CPSU officials who were part of this growth are still in place in the hierarchy.

These developments carry important policy implications for the U.S. and its allies. Until recently, however, the NATO countries have paid little attention to active measures in Soviet strategy and have just begun to explain them to their citizens. For example, educational activities have been undertaken to show journalists and politicians how the Soviets target them. In addition to defensive or protective activities, the Reagan Administration has initiated positive action to assist democratic forces around the world. National Security Decision Directive (NSDD) 77 and the establishment of the National Endowment for Democracy are tangible indications of Washington's general direction in the early 1980s. But one cannot be sure that the U.S. and the NATO governments will effectively sustain such initiatives. Nor can we know the extent to which nongovernmental organizations in these states and the Western media will support or impede this policy direction. It is far from clear that the West is prepared to meet the challenge posed by Soviet active measures.

## Notes

[1]A. Serjiyen, "Leninism on the Correlation of Forces as a Factor of International Relations," *International Affairs* (May 1975), p. 103.

[2]Based on confidential Comintern documents first published in 1924 in German by the German Trade Union Federation (ADGB) under the title "The Third Column of Communist Policy—IAH (International Worker's Aid)." Quoted in English in *Labour Magazine* (December 1924). The quotations were authenticated by Willi Munzenberg's widow, Babette Gross, in her book entitled *Willi Munzenberg—A Political Biography* (Lansing, Mich.: Michigan State University Press, 1974), pp. 121 and 133.

[3]*Seventh Congress of the Communist International*, abridged stenographic report of proceedings, July–August 1935 (Moscow: Foreign Languages Publishing House, 1939), p. 489.

# III
## *Military Power*

# 14

## HELMUT SONNENFELDT
## WILLIAM G. HYLAND

*Soviet Perspectives on Security**

**Introduction** The purpose of this essay is to explore Soviet conceptions of security. More particularly, we are concerned with determining how successive Soviet leaderships have sought to define the security requirements of the Soviet Union, how they have gone about satisfying these requirements, and how successful they have been.

To examine the security conceptions of any nation, or those of its leaders, is at best fraught with difficulties. Security is not a fixed or quantifiable condition, although some of its elements are concrete enough. But it is in many respects a state of mind, which is affected by many stimuli, some going far back into historic experience.

The Soviet case is beset by particular problems because so much of the USSR's own discussion of security issues is either shrouded in secrecy or obscured by ritualistic and convoluted terminology. Soviet conduct is, of course, visible and constitutes a major and important body of evidence. But the motivations behind the conduct, and the debates and judgments associated with it, are rarely elucidated in the documentary material that is only sporadically available. It hardly needs to be noted that there is no investigative reporting in Moscow, nor a Freedom of Information Act, nor any wholesale opening of archives. Thus, even at this late date, we must still rely on speculation about the Soviet role in the invasion of Korea in 1950 or, to take a more recent example, about the calculations, expectations, and objectives that led Khrushchev to deploy missiles to Cuba in 1962. For written material, we have to rely almost entirely on the public record such as official releases, speeches, articles, and diplomatic communications.

Publicly available pronouncements, of course, cannot be discounted.

*Reprinted by permission of the authors and publisher from Adelphi Papers, no. 150 (Spring, 1979), pp. 1–19, 24. Copyright 1979 by The International Institute for Strategic Studies.

They serve, among other things, as one form of communication between the Soviet leadership, the subordinate elites, and the population at large. They are also used in some measure to communicate with foreign Communist parties and with the outside world generally. Careful scrutiny of these materials over time can and does provide some insight into Soviet concerns and goals.

Analysis of official or officially inspired Soviet materials has been intensively conducted in the West for more than 30 years now. It has produced a methodology which involves in the main a search for shifts in emphasis or phrasing, frequently minute, which are interpreted to reflect policy changes or differences among the leadership elite. At the same time, most Western analysts believe that the Soviet Union usually means what she says on policy matters and should be taken at her word; that is to say, the reiteration of statements should be accorded substantial weight. We tend to agree with these approaches to the analysis of the contents of public Soviet materials.

But it needs to be remembered constantly that in sifting these materials one is still dealing only with very partial evidence, and that what is withheld almost certainly greatly outweighs in importance what is accessible. Among other things, we are denied the kind of "feel" that we might gain from an occasional sampling of the papers used by top leaders in their deliberations. It is a lack of which one is particularly conscious when dealing with an issue like security, which involves intangibles.

The absence of what would normally be considered historical evidence has been somewhat offset in recent years by the intensification of contact between Soviet and foreign representatives at summit level and below. Most of these occur in a bargaining context. They lack the candor and, generally speaking, the informality and the broad range of topics which characterize meetings among Western leaders, for example. They do offer a hint, but only a hint, about the preoccupations of Soviet leaders. In addition, Soviet representatives (below decision-making levels on the whole, but members of the governing elite) participate in increasing numbers in exchanges with foreign counterparts. Over the past few years they have adapted their discourse to a terminology and a style more compatible with those of Western debates about the issues that concern us here.

But even the greater intensity and variety of contacts and the decline of jargon leave considerable room for doubt about whether the USSR thinks about security issues in the terms to which we are accustomed in our own deliberations over these issues. In any event, anyone who has participated in discussions with Soviet representatives will be aware that, even if the terms of discussion have become more compatible, differences in substance and perception remain wide and deep.

Thus, the problem of inadequate and defective evidence is compounded by the problem of perspective. Any attempt by foreigners to comprehend and represent the conceptions of other nations and their leaders is always beset by pitfalls; these dangers are almost certainly more pronounced when dealing with the USSR.

Relations with the USSR have been a matter of enormous concern for Americans and many others for more than a generation. Issues are involved which have the gravest and most far-reaching implications. Almost inevitably in such circumstances, the line between analysis and policy preferences becomes quite fine. Indeed, experience has demonstrated that certain analytical conclusions are not merely a contribution to scholarship or theory; they may well become the basis for action. To call on an example from the past, one needs only to read some of the official American documents now available for the 1949–1950 period to see the close connection between conclusions reached about the nature of the Soviet Union and her objectives, on the one hand, and the policy options considered and advocated, on the other.

We recognize, therefore, that we cannot be fully objective in the pages that follow. Inevitably, we will be presenting something of our own view of Soviet perspectives, based on evidence with the imperfections we have noted.

Our discussion focuses on Soviet security perspectives. But security is, in part, a function of power, although the correlation is far from a simple one. Many a nation lacking some of the principal prerequisites of power nevertheless feels relatively secure against external attack or pressure. Other more powerful nations may be troubled, and often are, by anxieties concerning their survival or freedom of action. Some states seek to curb their fears by accumulating military power; others rely on alliances as well, on skillful diplomacy, on the manipulation of their putative adversaries, and on many other devices and courses. For the USSR, power—especially its military component— has long been considered the principal means of assuring survival and the creation of conditions in which the regime can pursue its domestic and other aims. Consequently, in undertaking this examination of the Soviet view and pursuit of security, we will constantly encounter the question of Soviet power and its role and purposes. But we will also encounter the complexities of the interaction between security and power, particularly as, for the USSR, concepts like alliances, interdependence, and international institution-building until now have played a far less significant role in the search for security than has been true for most Western nations.

The approach we have used in our discussion is basically chronological. That is, viewing Soviet conduct as a whole, we will trace the evolution of Soviet security conceptions through various stages from the Revolution to the present. The essay is organized roughly around the leadership periods of Lenin, Stalin, Khrushchev, and Brezhnev. We recognize, of course, that changes in Soviet leadership are not necessarily coterminous with historical periods, especially when the problem under study is partly affected by developments and events that are either not at all, or only very indirectly, under Soviet control. Still, we have found this rough division of the period under consideration useful for our purposes, acknowledging that the stages in the evolution we are seeking to trace are not wholly congruent with the tenures of the four men who have ruled the USSR since 1917.

The
Revolutionary
Perspective

There has been a tendency in Western analysis to regard Soviet "goals" as immutable and to interpret changes in policy and fluctuations in the tone and climate of East–West relations as essentially "tactical" shifts. This is far from a unanimous Western view, but it is widely and tenaciously held. It is encouraged by the USSR herself because of her constant insistence that she is operating on the basis of "scientific" doctrines or even laws (which the USSR herself "discovers" and inteprets); that she is the agent of history, which is said to be on her side; and that, while policies are adapted to new and changing conditions, the commitment of Soviet policy to "Leninist" prescriptions remains unwavering. There is a large body of Soviet pronouncements that holds strategy to be broadly unchanging while allowing for—indeed, urging—shifts in tactics as required by prevailing circumstances.

One consequence is that analysts speculate endlessly about where tactics end and strategy begins. Similarly, the somewhat contrary point is often made that when "tactics" are infinitely flexible, they are bound sooner or later to affect even the most devoutly held goals; resolution of these conflicting views is unlikely to be accomplished by abstract argument.

Turning to the problem of security, then, it can readily be seen that the quest for it has been among the most basic and persistent Soviet concerns since the Revolution. Survival is the most fundamental task of any state, and hence of the governments of all states. It is also the most basic element in any concept of security. Very soon after the Revolution the Bolshevik state began to manifest a degree of concern about its survival not dissimilar to that of other states or of its Tsarist predecessor.

Indeed, at the outset the new Soviet government could not ignore this most elementary aspect of security: A large part of the Soviet Union was occupied by the German army. Bolshevik authority was tenuous, and war or peace was an urgent political question in 1917. What constituted the most effective means of securing Soviet power was an urgent, practical problem and no longer a theoretical proposition to be debated by exiles in the coffee houses of Zurich. Soviet pronouncements insist that Lenin set the fundamental course even then, and that Soviet policy has simply been elaborated in the light of modern conditions.

Yet it seems obvious that the question of what constitutes security has been answered differently at various times in the history of the Soviet Union. And, despite the generally high degree of uniformity of Soviet pronouncements on matters of high policy, it has been answered differently by different Soviet leaders.

In the early days of the Revolution, and for many years before it occurred, most Bolsheviks appeared to be genuinely convinced that after the Revolution had taken place in Russia, similar upheavals in adjacent countries would quickly follow. Communist theory, in fact, had assumed that more advanced "capitalist" countries would have their revolutions well before backward Russia. In the event, it was believed that Russia and her ruling proletariat would soon find themselves surrounded by class allies who had wrested power from the bourgeoisie; frontiers and state sovereignty would lose their meaning, and class solidarity would override national differences as old political entities became caught up in revolutionary change. The security problem would thus no longer present itself in its traditional form.

These early notions constituted perhaps the most radical departure from the conventional conception of security which had evolved historically in the system of states and nations that had developed since the Middle Ages. The Bolsheviks did not see themselves at first as governing a state but as leading a revolutionary detachment, part of a movement which, if not world-wide, would be widespread, at least in Europe. Security to them meant the physical survival and the further development of the regime that had been established in a part of Russia; it was an important but nevertheless temporary problem. It also meant safeguarding the regime's ability to institute the societal and other changes it planned—but still in the context of a broader, revolutionary environment. The content of these notions of survival and development did not in themselves differ significantly from those entertained by rulers of traditional states. What was new was the conception that survival and the fulfillment of revolutionary goals depended on similar events occurring in adjacent and other countries, and the conviction that these events would then merge into a single universal movement.

Since the survival of the Russian Revolution and the implementation of its goals were seen as depending on revolutions elsewhere, it was only natural that the Russian revolutionary vanguard should seek to trigger such revolutions and help to sustain them. Thus, security clearly was not confined within the old frontiers of Russia, nor within the areas where the Russian revolutionaries held sway (which were far smaller than the territory of Russia, however defined at that fluid moment); it became consciously and deliberately contingent on events well beyond those territorial confines. Yet the capacity of the Russian revolutionaries to affect events beyond the borders of the Soviet Union, and even within their own area of more or less tenuous control, was highly circumscribed. They did have certain ties with revolutionaries elsewhere, but their principal instruments were the presumed force of their ideas and doctrines, and the illusion that history had ordained a revolutionary tide in the capitalist world at that particular moment. These notions, however, proved to be false, and the more clearly their falsity was demonstrated, the more the Bolsheviks, lacking at that time other, traditional manifestations of power, resorted to conspiratorial, clandestine, and other means of encouraging revolutionary movements.

Events unfolded quite differently from expectations. Soviet-style revolutions were confined to a very few countries and proved to be short-lived. Circumstances in the Soviet Union, and the manner in which Lenin's Bolsheviks staged the take-over of the country's government and other institutions, proved to be virtually unique. The USSR soon found herself confronting problems typical of those encountered by states functioning within a system of states. Having challenged the outside world with revolutionary upheaval, she now had to cope with

numerous threats to her own territorial integrity and to the survival of
the new regime. While in many countries, adjacent as well as more
distant, there sprang up Communist parties and other groups sympathetic to the Soviet state, these turned out to have only a limited
capacity to support the Soviet rulers' quest to secure themselves against
external threats. Their capacity to buttress the new regime in its struggles against internal enemies was even more limited. The novel notions
of security and how to promote it entertained by the Russian Bolsheviks
thus had only a very brief life, although they continued to color the
security conceptions that subsequently evolved.

The Communist rulers of the USSR had to adjust to the fact that their
earlier definitions of the conditions for survival and of how to ensure it
were no longer pertinent and may indeed have been no more than
hopes in the first place. But they were convinced that if the country and
the hope of eventual widespread revolution were to survive, the regime
itself had to be preserved. To Soviet leaders, and to the evolving elite
with which they surrounded themselves, national security (to use a
Western term) became synonymous with regime security.

These redefinitions of security, which began in Lenin's lifetime, did
not come easily. Many of the early disputes and schisms in the regime
revolved precisely around the ability of the new revolutionary state to
survive. Even before Lenin's death important sections of the revolutionary leadership remained persuaded that the Soviet Union and her
regime could not long survive as an island in a capitalist sea. They were
dubious about, and opposed to, Lenin's domestic concessions, as in the
case of the New Economic Plan, by which he sought to safeguard the
economic viability of the Soviet Union. Some also doubted the wisdom
and propriety of Lenin's willingness to deal with capitalist powers in the
early 1920s in an effort to prevent the formation of hostile coalitions
against the Soviet state. Hence the alternative policy associated broadly
with Trotsky, that of permanent revolution and active support for
revolutionary movements and enterprises in other countries, continued
to enjoy support.

Stalin's victory established an enduring conception of security that in
its fundamental elements was essentially traditional. The Soviet Union
was a state which had to stand guard over her frontiers and territorial
integrity. To do so, she needed military forces to deter or ward off
potential invaders; she could utilize—and even to an extent rely upon—
the admittedly fragile but still not insignificant protection of the
"bourgeois" international order and its legal norms; she could seek
alliances or other forms of association, including economic ones, with
other members of the traditional state system; and she could and would
try to manipulate the external balance of power. Before turning to this
new period and the evolution of more traditional security policy, it is
worth noting some of the effects of this early period on both the Soviet
Union and her adversaries.

First, the Communist International absorbed much of the energy of
the Soviet regime and in a sense supplanted more normal forms of
diplomacy. Since the Soviet Union was excluded from the European

councils, her reliance on foreign Communists was in part a natural reaction, but it may be that the alliance gave the Soviet regime a false impression of the ability of foreign Communists to influence events. In any case, the maintenance of party links with Moscow were a constant source of suspicion abroad and continued to play a role in the exclusion of the Soviet regime from European affairs.

Second, the question of the "legitimacy" of the Soviet regime lingered on for a considerable period. The Soviet Union herself contributed to the notion that what was happening in the USSR was transitory and bound to be replaced by some new revolutionary order in Europe. The regime's opponents abroad also continued to hope and believe (though for different reasons) that it would not last. There was widespread expectation that some upheaval would take place or, if not, that the regime's character would evolve in a more benign and traditional direction.

Thus, in the post-Lenin period the regime found itself having to define its own interests, and being forced to do so in a climate still essentially hostile, if not overtly threatening.

## Consolidation and New Danger

Traditional conceptions of security—and far from revolutionary methods of safeguarding it—continued to be accompanied by other elements that gave Soviet views of security a special character. Even as Stalin established the most rigid and repressive internal order and created the first modern totalitarian state, he believed in and practiced a form of forward defense deriving from the Bolshevik notion that class solidarity extended beyond national frontiers. Particularly when the external dangers to her security mounted in the mid-1930s, through the consolidation of the Nazi regime in Germany, the Soviet Union sought to build "reserves" among Communist parties and sympathizers abroad to consolidate her own strength. She gradually ended the sectarian phase of the external Communist parties, ordering and pressing them to seek allies among non-Communist parties and other groups so as to form united fronts against the Fascist threat.

It is quite possible that Stalin saw these alliances as temporary arrangements dictated by the Nazi threat and that, in some instances at least, he envisaged subsequent stages when Communist takeovers could be staged (for example, in Spain). In other words, the Soviet conception of security, while heavily conditioned by anxieties about external dangers (as well as internal threats from residual "capitalist" elements), retained offensive aspects harking back to earlier notions of spreading Communist revolutions and class alliances transcending national borders. Pretensions to the leadership of the international working class were muted but not renounced. This was the united-front tactic, in fact, built on the mechanisms of the Comintern which had its origins in the early revolutionary optimism that had prevailed immediately after the Revolution. And, under Soviet orders, Communists sought to retain their separate identity to avoid contamination by other groups and theories.

Still, for the time being at least, such offensive aspects were sub-ordinated to more immediate concerns: the search for allies wherever they could be found, including alliances formed through a "collective security" system; and the effort to deter and delay external aggression and prevent the isolation of the USSR in the event of such aggression.

In the end, these concerns led to an alliance with the enemy himself, when it appeared that neither united fronts nor alliance arrangements could be worked out with the Western democracies and with Germany's potential victims in Eastern and Southeastern Europe. (The Western democracies and their Polish and Romanian associates may have been short-sighted in their failure to enter into defense arrangements with the USSR—most historians believe this to be the case. But it is worth reflecting that it was not the first time, and certainly not the last, that the Soviet Union's own conduct and the legacy of her revolutionary pretensions served to heighten the dangers to her own security and prevent cooperative measures that might have reduced them.)

The Nazi–Soviet alliance quintessentially represented the use of a traditional means of seeking safety or of delaying danger—the manipulation of external forces. But, cynicism (or realism) apart, it was another instance, and perhaps the most dramatic up to that time, of a recognition that the imperatives of security required certain entanglements with the external world of class enemies. Moreover, as the period between 1939 and 1941 was to show, in Soviet eyes the interests of security even required the propitiation of the potential enemy with economic and military support while class allies were left to their own devices—and in consequence deserted the socialist motherland in droves. In addition, as had been evident on earlier occasions after the Revolution, security considerations were seen as ample justification for the acquisition of territory and demands for spheres of influence and control (as advanced in Soviet–Nazi diplomatic haggling in 1940), with no regard for "revolutionary" conditions or the interests and concerns of indigenous Communist parties.

Thus, in the 20 years after the consolidation of Soviet power, the regime's security conception had evolved from considerations determined largely by the expectations of Communist revolutionary doctrines to ones quite similar to those that had traditionally assured the physical survival of nation-states in times of peril. Since they had not envisaged a single Communist state, Communist doctrines appeared to have little to offer to meet these concerns in practical terms, although they were used to consolidate further Stalin's domestic power. Externally, the Soviet Union was concerned with her essential territorial integrity and physical security; she sought to extend her frontiers as far as possible against the incursions of the potential enemy; she sought allies, regardless of political orientation; she tried to buy time with economic and other concessions; and she set aside revolutionary goals abroad both because they obstructed the palliation of more fundamental anxieties about survival and because, if pursued, they might even have heightened the threat.

It may be said that at this moment of grave danger and considerable weakness the Soviet definition of security involved the most elementary imperative of survival and little else. When the dangers confronting the regime became even graver after the Nazi invasion, it did not, in seeking to assure its survival, shrink from moderating certain of the internal essentials of Communist rule by invoking, *inter alia*, nationalism, patriotism, military discipline and prestige, faith and religion to motivate and mobilize the population against the external threat. The survival of the country and the survival of the leadership were still essentially synonymous, but a certain dilution of the character of the regime occurred which, in conjunction with but quite separately from the external threat, might in fact have placed its survival in question, had the Soviet Union not succeeded in reversing her military fortunes.

The point here is not just that Stalin proved extremely flexible and cynical in pursuing his goals; it is somewhat simpler but no less important: Soviet conceptions of fundamental interests and of how to protect and advance them have not been immutable. The means chosen by, or forced upon, the regime in the pursuit of its interests have involved not only choices normally described as tactical or expedient, but also some that could not have been readily derived from the basic Marxist–Leninist texts or even from the statements of the very practitioners of the policies outlined above. The Soviet conception of security, and the actions designed to safeguard it, must then be seen in the light as much of Soviet operational conduct as of Soviet pronouncements and the Marxist–Leninist classics. Predispositions stemming from the Bolshevik heritage of the leadership can be and have been significantly affected by other factors.

*World War II and After*  World War II—still referred to, characteristically, as the Great Patriotic War—was plainly a deeply traumatic experience for the Soviet Union. Not only did it cause enormous destruction and human suffering, but it shook the regime to its foundations. Had German occupation policy been less brutal and stupid, large portions of the population (especially, but not exclusively, non-Russians) might well have defected from the Soviet state. As it was, hundreds of thousands—if not millions—of soldiers and civilians surrendered or were captured. A large number agreed to serve against the Soviet Union, and many others refused to return there. In the end capitalist allies were needed to help sustain the USSR's military efforts and defeat the enemy.

It is hardly surprising that, even in the exhilaration of victory, Stalin should have had uppermost in his mind not abstract questions about a just and lasting peace settlement, but the fundamental issue of how to prevent such catastrophes from recurring. The territorial buffers he had hurriedly erected in the short period before disaster struck had been of little use. The military preparations he had undertaken had been flawed and inadequate. The "socialist transformations" implemented in the years between the Revolution and the war had done little, if anything, to inspire in the population loyalty to the regime; the opposite was closer to the truth, and traditional Russian values and symbols had had to be reintroduced to inspire the populace to sacrifice and heroism.

Throughout the wartime conferences Stalin was determined to assure for the USSR territorial gains that would provide a more effective buffer against attack. Where he did not or could not subsume territory, he operated on the premise that mere hegemony over adjacent land was insufficient and that the political order of such territories itself had to be transformed to fit the Soviet pattern. Either Soviet military occupation or the proximity of Soviet military power facilitated the process—and certainly justified it in Stalin's eyes, whatever the preferences, traditions, and other circumstances of the populations involved.

It is not clear whether the establishment of a satellite empire in the form in which it emerged in the late 1940s in Eastern and Southeastern Europe was already clearly part of Stalin's wartime design. The wartime and immediate postwar arguments about Poland indicate that the essentials were clear to Stalin, and he then adapted the pace, intensity, and particular methods of the satellization process to the circumstances obtaining in the individual countries concerned. To some degree, he also considered potential foreign reaction. The security concerns of the USSR were thus transformed and expanded to include the security of the new empire and the maintenance of the regimes imposed on the populations with the aid of Moscow-trained Communists. (Czechoslovakia was only marginally exceptional, in the sense that her Communist party, though still a minority, was larger than those of other East European countries. Yugoslavia was a separate case, since the Tito regime had established itself essentially by its own efforts, although Tito and many of his associates also had extensive connections with Moscow.)

Stalin's conception of security in the postwar world, of course, was not confined to the physical protection of the Soviet Union against renewed miltary threats. Since the safety of the regime, and the political order over which it presided, were of equally crucial concern, especially in the light of wartime events and the dilution of party orthodoxy, Stalin saw the East European satellite empire as more than a military buffer. He regarded it also as constituting the outer lines of defense against various forms of ideological and psychological challenge that emanated from the "capitalist" world, a wall from behind which conformity could be reimposed only with great difficulty on the peoples of the USSR. This concern with external subversion was almost certainly reinforced by the recognition that the Soviet population would be called upon to make extraordinary sacrifices in terms of their living standards and well-being as the regime pressed forward with reconstructing the industrial base of the country and the maintenance of large military forces. If the East European buffer states were to play this role, it became as essential to identify the survival of their regimes with the physical security of the countries themselves as was the case with the Soviet Union herself. It was, moreover, not sufficient that these regimes should carry the Communist label. (Actually, of course, according to the Soviet ritual, they were not yet Communist regimes but regimes run by Communists, engaged in building socialism as a preliminary to the eventual construction of Communist societies. The Soviet Union herself was said to be still only building socialism.) It was vital that the regimes should be intensely loyal and subservient to the Stalinist regime in Moscow. The designation "People's Democracy" was attached to each of them, and they were instructed to follow the model "pioneered" by the USSR in the era of socialism in one country. This course carried the seeds of later difficulties.

There had thus emerged an extended concept of security which involved the territorial integrity of both the Soviet Union and the newly acquired empire as well as the ideological and structural conformity of all the parts of the empire and its subordination in all major respects to the needs and concerns of the USSR.

Although the establishment of this empire was portrayed as resulting from a renewal of the revolutionary tide which had subsided after the 1917 Revolution, it had in fact occurred as a result of the use and refinement of largely traditional means of power. Stalin had wielded force, directly and indirectly, to create the empire. But he had not done so indiscriminately; that is, he acted where he judged the risks of doing so to be acceptable in terms of possible Western responses. Later, in 1948–1949, when Yugoslavia failed in several respects to conform to Soviet prescriptions, he was prepared (in his view, perhaps, only temporarily) to overlook one defection because the risks and costs of preventing it seemed to him excessive. This decision probably did not stem so much from fear of Western intervention as from the realization that Tito commanded sufficient support to enable him to put up vigorous resistance to the application of Soviet force.

The question of why Stalin chose to establish buffers in the form of satellites only in Eastern Europe is still open. He had, of course, made demands upon Turkey and Iran, which were designed to provide the USSR with territorial and other advantages associated with security. He had also laid claim to former Italian colonies in the Mediterranean area. But when they were rejected, he refrained from pressing these ambitions, presumably because he considered that resistance might embroil the USSR in complications which he was not then prepared to countenance. In the case of Finland he preferred a form of neutrality and indirect hegemony to satellization, perhaps because he recognized that the establishment of a subservient and conformist pro-Soviet Communist regime would be far more difficult than in Eastern and Southeastern Europe and because he was less certain of Western passivity. He did, of course, impose territorial concessions and other constraints on Finland. In the case of the Far East he held on to territories seized from Japan or Japanese control at the end of the war, but he was not ready to challenge the United States' dominant postwar position on Japan's main islands.

In general, Stalin displayed considerable caution in pressing or undertaking actions which he judged would halt or reverse American withdrawal from the Soviet periphery. The wartime meetings had evidently persuaded him that this was the American intention. Indeed, it was one of the ironies of the split with Yugoslavia that Stalin viewed the latter's intervention in the Greek civil war as potentially detrimental to Soviet security because of possible British and American reactions. Stalin's instinct was right: It was the fragility of the Greek situation, along with fears about the integrity of Turkey, which triggered the first major American decisions leading to the permanent involvement of the United States in Europe.

Stalin displayed similar caution with regard to Communist prospects in France and Italy. He was concerned more with consolidating what he had than with expansion, and he was probably doubtful about whether he could maintain over Communist activities in these more distant areas the kind of control he considered essential in countries adjacent to the USSR. In general, although it was not fully apparent at the time, Stalin had serious doubts about the contribution that would be made to Soviet security by Communist regimes that came to power largely on their own strength. Although Communist theory held that Communist revolutions would be essentially compatible with the Soviet regime, Stalin seems to have been unconvinced. Yugoslavia was already an object lesson; China and Albania were also to defect soon after Stalin died.

Stalin had increased substantially the sphere of dominant Soviet power and had thereby seemingly strengthened the physical security of the USSR. Yet he never lost the siege mentality that had marked Soviet evolution in the 1920s and 1930s. "Capitalist encirclement" remained for him a reality, both in terms of the military threat to the Soviet Union that he envisaged and in terms of potential connections between internal opposition to the regime and external enemies. Internal repression was therefore as necessary an expedient for him as defense against external aggression.

These very attitudes and the policies they produced resulted in developments which left the position of the USSR considerably less secure than Stalin had hoped. For among the consequences of his policies were the creation of a new Western alliance system, including, after 1950, the permanent stationing of large numbers of American combat forces on the European continent, the gradual incorporation of West Germany in the alliance system, and the development of a potent American nuclear arsenal, together with systems capable of delivering these new weapons on to Soviet soil.

From the late 1940s onward Stalin, facing these developments, had to raise his sights above the consolidation of his homeland and empire to ways of impeding the formation of a potent, new, hostile coalition. This gave rise to the peace movement and its campaigns against the nuclear weaponry that was being acquired by the United States and the alliance system in process of construction in the West. Some of the united-front tactics employed in the 1930s against Hitler were revived, and a certain diplomatic flexibility began to manifest itself (e.g., in the resolution of the Berlin blockade).

Meanwhile, Stalin laid the economic and technological foundation for expanded Soviet military power which looked beyond the defense of the Soviet perimeter and incorporated nuclear weapons in the USSR's military forces. Stalin died as these developments were under way; his successors were left to cope with and build upon them.

Observers of the Stalinist era have pointed out that Stalin's vision was a limited one, coinciding with Soviet artillery range. Within these limits he was, in fact, relatively successful; a dominant position in Eastern Europe, diminished German strength, a weak China, and some voice in Japan's future made the USSR relatively more secure than before the war.

Stalin had assumed that the postwar settlement was to be a "spheres of influence" arrangement. What actually happened, however, was that the USSR's inferior nuclear position inevitably limited her power. At the time, of course, few understood that Stalin was a rather conservative statesman. Western opinion attributed to him and to the USSR the most grandiose aspirations and ambitions. In 1950, in the famous American policy paper, NCS-68, the Soviet Union emerged as a towering giant, casting her shadow over almost all of the world and bent on total conquest. This view was corroborated, shortly after the document was promulgated, by the invasion of Korea. But if Khrushchev is to be believed, this was initially a rather casual affair, with Stalin approving an adventure by Kim Il Sung, which Western statements could have led Stalin to believe was a relatively safe probe. On January 12, 1950 Secretary Acheson had, after all, said the defensive perimeter excluded South Korea.

In short, the immediate postwar period saw the extension of the USSR's security perimeter, but by 1953 the process had about run its course. The limits had been determined first in Iran, then in Greece and Turkey, then in Germany, and finally in the Far East.

Few observers would claim that the position of the Soviet Union was "secure" in 1953. Indeed, Stalin's heirs apparently regarded it as unsatisfactory. In his memoirs Khrushchev gives a summary of this moment: "We had doubts of our own about Stalin's foreign policy. He overemphasized the importance of military might for one thing, and consequently put too much faith in our armed forces." Khrushchev goes on to describe Soviet nervousness over dealing with the Western powers and the Soviet delegation's sense of inferiority in meeting the Western leaders at the Geneva summit in 1955. Yet, freed from Stalin's restraint, his successors began to broaden their horizons and to grope for definitions of security more suited to the emerging situation. For this was no longer simply the post-World War II era, but a time of dramatic changes in military technology and the world political map.

## The Uncertain Superpower: Khrushchev

It is a commonplace but nevertheless valid contention that the transition from Stalin to Khrushchev reflected the shift from a regional conception of security to a global one, from a basically defensive orientation to an offensive one, and from the era of World War II to the nuclear-rocket age.

In the simplest terms, what happened was that Stalin's successors found that it was not only feasible to project Soviet influence beyond the more traditional range of her neighboring areas, but that this might well pay dividends in terms of the security of the Soviet state. The Soviet Union, however, was quite slow to discover the political consequences of the colonial era's end, having originally regarded newly independent nations like India as likely to remain in the capitalist camp. The process of "liberation" was already well advanced when Khrushchev and his colleagues began to make their first tentative forays into the Third World.

What did they expect to achieve? The advantages were obvious. If some of the Soviet Union's principal adversaries were caught up in the agonies of relinquishing their colonial holdings, this process might not only be encouraged but could also reinvigorate the broader revolution the older generation had expected, albeit in advanced capitalist countries, 30 years earlier.

Involvement in this process of "liberation" also had the attraction that in the various struggles the USSR, not the West, was the "legitimate" power; indeed, it was the USSR that provided a model for transforming relatively weak and backward countries into modern industrial powers, for organizing an economy and forcing its development, and even for reconstructing the social and political order.

Although she was still facing capitalist encirclement in Eurasia, it was thought, the Soviet Union might in turn be able to leapfrog the containment barriers and to encircle the capitalists. A simple calculation revealed that Soviet security—that is, the security of the heartland—would be reinforced if the positions held by the enemy were weakened over a broad front in areas where the Western world still saw its essential reserves.

The story of the USSR's involvement with Nasser, Nehru, Sukarno, etc., need not be rehearsed. But it is worth noting that doctrinal rationalization was elaborated *ex post facto* and piecemeal; the policy was well launched before the Twentieth Party Congress and the international Communist meetings of the late 1950s.

The very process of elaborating theories concerning "national democracies" and the like probably reinforced the belief that the policy was, in fact, advantageous. Nevertheless, the fact remains that the Soviet Union's reading of historical development was erroneous. The Soviet model was not widely adopted; local Communists were only marginally effective and sometimes a burden; the West accommodated itself slowly to neutrality; its losses in Asia and Africa were to some extent compensated for by the reawakening of Western Europe: NATO expanded; Germany began to rearm; and the treaty of Rome envisaged European unity.

There was also the problem that, as time passed, newly won Soviet advantages and positions had to be reinforced. Stalin had made the complete control of the Eastern European parties synonymous with Soviet security, permitting no deviations and underwriting his position with the physical presence of the Red Army. This approach was both impracticable and inappropriate to the new era and the regions to which Soviet attention turned. Most of the political forces in these regions were unsuited to the imposition of old-style Comintern discipline and were far from the Soviet homeland. Thus, the Soviet Union was forced to commit herself increasingly to the defense—at least in political and economic terms—of a highly disparate aggregation of states, political parties, and movements. And in so doing, she was obliged to accept new obligations and risks in areas where her control was far from complete.

In short, the arena of Soviet security concern expanded and the policy instruments multiplied, but the gains were tenuous and had to be consolidated periodically. In the course of adopting a global policy, the USSR was gradually transforming her techniques in ways that drew on the expertise of her only true global competitor, the United States.

Indeed, the process of expansion was accompanied inexorably by a growing confrontation with the one power capable of countering the USSR. Where Stalin might have envisaged various political combinations with the capitalists in 1938–1939, the range of options available to Khrushchev was more constricted. Soviet security was, above all, defined in terms of competition with the United States. Moreover, that competition was at the highest level a military one. The United States had the longest strategic reach. For the first time the USSR could be threatened directly and devastated by a power that was not bordering on or near her own territory. The nuclear competition could not be affected by "national liberation" as such; nor was there any firm ideological basis for examining the relationship between the destructiveness of nuclear war and the USSR's political aims.

The problem of adjusting to the nuclear age was obviously a cardinal security issue in the 1950s. It was debated in the military literature and, presumably, in other forums. It had to be confronted during a period of internal tensions and power struggles. What evidence there is suggests that it was one of the issues debated among the various political contenders. Malenkov's deviation, emphasizing the dangers and even the inutility of nuclear war, is well known. It is doubtful that it was an accidental misstatement. Probably it represented a cautious viewpoint that took account of the possibility, even the necessity, of accommodations with the West. The position that prevailed must have argued for political maneuvering but involved doctrinal adjustments that avoided the fundamental conflict with Marxist–Leninist prescriptions on war.

The major decisions proclaimed at the Twentieth Party Congress in 1956 reflected a rather clever compromise. The inevitability of war was qualified: it was no longer "fatal"; war could be prevented. The means by which it would be circumvented were associated with the new "social and political forces" that would combine to deter the capitalists. It is worth pausing to note the confusion surrounding the doctrine of the inevitability of war. It stemmed from prerevolutionary notions concerning relations among capitalist states. The wars that were said to be inevitable were those generated by the inherent antagonisms and conflicts between capitalist states fighting for markets, resources, etc. It was in the era of socialism in one country that the notion was transformed into one applying to relations between socialist and capitalist states. Capitalism, that is, would delay its own demise by resisting forcibly the onward march of socialism. In its original version, the inevitability-of-war doctrine served to benefit the advance of revolution, since the "peoples" would rebel against the recurrent bloodshed engendered by capitalism and would find their salvation in socialism. As the prospect of intracapitalist wars seemed to dim after World War II, the emphasis shifted to the inevitability of capitalist–socialist war. Even then, well into the Khrushchev period, the greatest gains of socialism were said to have been the results of the two intracapitalist world wars (World War II having become a modified socialist–capitalist one only after 1941). The advent of nuclear weapons complicated adherence to the doctrine of inevitable socialist–capitalist war, since it seemed to make the USSR an implicit advocate of such a war. Moreover, if a catastrophic war were inevitable, there was a danger that the Soviet populace would become apathetic and resigned; the "preventability" of war both allowed for active policies and gave the population hope for prolonged peace.

Meanwhile, Soviet diplomacy would attempt to neutralize the nuclear issue. In effect, what emerged was a more vigorous and diversified version of Stalin's tentative return, in the late 1940s and early 1950s, to some of the popular front approaches of the 1930s. To some extent, Soviet security again became dependent on the manipulation of political forces—Communists, nationalists, neutralists—outside the immediate areas of Soviet control. It was in this context that the principle of "peaceful coexistence" was revived. It was no doubt viewed as a soporific; it permitted the Soviet leaders to avoid more fundamental choices, and it was useful in rationalizing of policies that had already been adopted out of necessity.

But was it wholly tactical? One can only speculate, but it seems plausible that, having resurrected a doctrinal expression to suit their purposes, the Soviet leaders, in continually defining and defending the "preventability" and coexistence doctrines, found them increasingly comfortable and convenient. Almost certainly, Mao's insistence on the likelihood, and even the desirability, of a cataclysmic showdown found no support in Moscow. In short, tactics blended with strategy. Despite changing external conditions and the growth of Soviet power, the general line of peaceful coexistence has been maintained, and at no point since 1956 has any Soviet leader challenged the contention that a world war was no longer inevitable—nor has there been any real effort to define the limits of the period of coexistence.

To be sure, the Soviet Union recognized that there were fatalistic, passive, and defeatist connotations to peaceful coexistence (as well as to the "inevitability of war"). Enormous energy has been expended on defining what peaceful coexistence is *not* (it does not, for example, exclude "struggle" or the support of national liberation). Some basic ambiguities have been permitted, and it is this grey area between devastating war and placid peace that has provided Western analysts with endless scope for speculation about real Soviet "intentions."

But it is also reasonable to conclude that Khrushchev introduced a period of considerable confusion in Soviet security policy. For one thing, he was entranced by nuclear rockets. The political potential he saw in them emerges clearly from his memoirs, in which he belittles "rifles and bayonets" and claims that the USSR's defense depends on the "quality and quantity of our nuclear missile arsenal." The Soviet warning to Britain and France in the Suez crisis of 1956 foreshadowed the more aggressive conduct of the USSR after 1957. Not only could the Soviet Union compensate for intercontinental inferiority by holding Europe hostage, but the threat of a "missile gap" offered a chance to achieve some of the recurrent Soviet aims in a period of offensive pressures. Thus Khrushchev's demands in 1958–1960 were strikingly reminiscent of earlier Soviet demands: the exclusion of the West from Berlin and final settlement of the German problem.

The events of the period cannot be recounted here. Khrushchev ran a gigantic bluff that became increasingly complicated and dangerous. In some desperation, he sought a breakthrough by means of a bold stroke in Cuba. He failed and thereby brought the optimistic and most assertive phase of his policy to a close.

Any assessment of Soviet security in the Khrushchev period must note some major internal developments and the state of international Communism. First, the initial "thaw," the subsequent de-Stalinization, and the disappearance of mass terror had a bearing on security problems. Stalin's successors were less paranoid, though still concerned about internal enemies. Having lived through the various plots and counterplots concocted by Stalin, they must have concluded that the internal threat was exaggerated. In the light of what happened in Poland and Hungary, however, one must ask why Khrushchev launched his internal repudiation of Stalin. Moreover, why did he promote the reconciliation with Tito, going so far as to revise the doctrine of a single road to socialism?

It is important to remember that de-Stalinization and internal liberalization were by no means unanimously supported policies; they were resisted at very high levels and were thus instruments in Politburo struggles. Most important, de-Stalinization was not a process which the Soviet Union had foreseen in all its consequences once it had spread outside her borders. Far from operating on a master plan, it seems probable that the Soviet Union became engaged in a series of *ad hoc* decisions and struggles. De-Stalinization was a weapon against Malenkov and Molotov. The reconciliations with Tito accorded with the same strategy.

In retrospect, the various cross-currents of domestic and foreign policy were much stronger throughout Khrushchev's period than was generally recognized. Much as Stalin feared that his "enemies" had never accepted the legitimacy of his own rule, Khrushchev continued to see "Stalinists," or at least professed to see them, as his principal opponents. Thus his policies, which might otherwise have seemed reasonable, were often justified and defended in strident and dogmatic terms. His obsession with Stalin, which comes through in his memoirs, had the effect of driving him to extremes; his own apprehensions compounded his tendency to overreact and overachieve.

Indeed, it may be that Khrushchev felt driven to prove that his anti-Stalinism would be crowned with success: Where Stalin ignored the Third World, Khrushchev courted it; where Stalin insisted on iron rule,

Khrushchev proclaimed relaxations; where Stalin ruled Eastern Europe through the army and the KGB, Khrushchev hoped for loyalty to principles; where Stalin sought security in the Red Army, Khrushchev sought it in the strategic rocket forces (though he bluffed about their strength). The result was that Khrushchev defined Soviet interests so broadly that he became overcommitted, and some breakdown or retrenchment was probably inevitable.

One can only speculate about the extent to which Khrushchev was also driven by his resentment or fear of China. Khrushchev claims in his memoirs that he told his comrades as early as 1954 that conflict with China was "inevitable." Whether or not this is true, his policies hastened the conflict. It is likely that by 1959, when China claims Khrushchev halted Soviet assistance for her nuclear weapons program, China had acquired the status of an adversary, if not an outright enemy. This was not fully appreciated at the time; until 1964 it was believed in the West that there was a continuing prospect of a Soviet–Chinese reconciliation. Since the split was fully confirmed after Khrushchev's fall, it is probable that his antipathy toward or apprehensions about China were not personal predilections but reflected a new dimension of Soviet security concerns.

A review of the Khrushchev period proffers certain conclusions. First, the Soviet Union began to view her security in much broader geographical and functional terms, and in doing so she accepted commitments and risks that made the management of national security policy more complex. Second, the nuclear issue assumed more urgency and the competition with the United States came to be judged more and more in terms of the strategic nuclear balance. Third, the relaxation of tension inside the USSR accelerated centrifugal tendencies in the Communist orbit, leading to a partial reconciliation with, but also concessions to, Yugoslavia and a deepening split with China—in effect stimulating pluralism. Fourth, the shift from regionalism to globalism cost the Soviet Union a good deal: It imposed new military–economic burdens but yielded only a marginal weakening of the regime's main adversaries abroad. By 1964 national security for the USSR was a complex equation. It involved calculations concerning the internal repercussion of foreign policies, the cost of sustaining large economic and political commitments in Eastern Europe as well as in much more remote areas, the burden of armaments to offset Western build-ups, and the ideological and doctrinal consequences of the era of disintegrating Communist ranks. In this light, it is not surprising that more elements of the Soviet bureaucracy, particularly the military, were drawn into policy deliberations.

## The Accumulation of Power: Brezhnev

We do not have access to any systematic, internal Soviet definition of the security status of the USSR in the mid-1960s. Nor can we say precisely how the Soviet Union defined the notion of security at that point in her history.

If security is to be regarded chiefly as a function of military power, the Soviet sense of security must have been substantially greater then than at any other time in the country's history. Security (defined as safety from imminent attack) was certainly greater than in the past. It should be observed, however, that even in the mid- and late 1920s, as well as in the 1940s, when the USSR's military power was much less formidable, her security concerns revolved chiefly around a generally hostile environment which might, over a longer or shorter period of time, evolve toward active aggression—or, more accurately, toward active resistance to Soviet incursion. Soviet fears of imminent, active aggression were justifiably greatest in the late 1930s, as intensive German rearmament proceeded amidst violent hostility against Bolshevism, thinly disguised claims to "living space" adjacent to or even within the USSR, and in the context of the anti-Comintern pact. In the postwar world there may have been intermittent fears of imminent strategic attack, but they were associated with crises often caused by the USSR's own actions.

By any measure Soviet power had vastly increased between 1945 and 1965. Ground and air forces had been modernized and were deployed in substantial numbers in all areas where attacks might conceivably occur (with some exceptions in the Far East). Large reserves were maintained. The navy was in the process of evolving from a coastal defense force designed to support a land battle to one that could be used, at least for purposes of showing the flag, in more remote places. A squadron was permanently deployed in the Mediterranean, and some facilities were available in Cuba. Plans were under way to increase and diversify the navy and to enlarge the merchant marine. Long-range intervention forces, in the form of air transports, airborne divisions, and amphibious forces, were making their appearance. Strategic forces, though numerically and technically inferior to those of the United States, were growing with sustained momentum and were losing their initial vulnerability to preemptive or preventive strikes by the United States. Industry and technology were harnessed to a permanent effort to maintain and improve these forces.

These developments in their totality had begun to place a serious question mark over Western strategy for the defense of Europe. The West could no longer place unqualified reliance on the first use of nuclear weapons to compensate for disadvantages in conventional theater forces and for extended overwater lines of communication. In addition, at this stage the United States was increasingly preoccupied with the war in Vietnam, which deflected forces and energies from the power competition with the USSR. The Soviet Union almost certainly considered it in her interest to see the United States thus diverted, although that judgment came gradually to be qualified. Along with this preoccupation in Asia, the United States found her presence and influence in the Middle East seriously impaired after the 1967 war, largely—but not wholly—to the benefit of the USSR.

But if these trends in the power equation were a necessary condition, they still did not turn out to be a sufficient condition for security. For one thing, despite her enormous gains in power, the Soviet Union remained obsessed by the notion of inequality. She still saw the United States as an established world power and herself merely as an aspiring one. American influence, although less imposing than before and despite declining relative military power, remained widespread and deep-seated. Soviet influence, meanwhile, was increasing generally but continued to fluctuate, and it seemed much less secure than that of the United States and, indeed, of other physically much weaker Western powers. Economic and cultural ties between the West and the Third World, although often challenged by the latter, still seemed more durable than similar ties between the USSR and the Third World. The appeals of Soviet ideology were more superficial than real; political ties were vulnerable to changes in Third World regimes and nationalist resistance. Soviet efforts at transforming positions of influence into outposts of power (and hence security) frequently met only temporary success and at times outright failure.

Closer to home, Soviet power and a quarter of a century of Communist rule had failed to eradicate strivings for national identity in Eastern Europe. Beneath the crust of Stalinism—and probably encouraged by it—popular hostility toward the Soviet Union and resistance to imposed uniformity grew. The regional economic, military, and political structures which Khrushchev had sought to substitute for crude and direct domination had not produced the commonwealth of which he had dreamt. If anything, centrifugal forces revived with renewed force. If, as the Soviet Union argued, her power was forcing the West to accept a form of peaceful coexistence, this very evolution also increased the pressures in Eastern Europe to renew earlier ties with the Western world and to reduce dependence on the USSR. The Prague Spring in 1968 demonstrated that popular resistance to incorporation in the Soviet order remained a strong, latent force, ready to erupt in defiance of virtually certain Soviet military action calculated to crush it.

These trends, and the diverse expression they found in the several East European countries, showed that continued Soviet dominance did not necessarily spell control of events. Interestingly enough, it was in the face of these realities that Khrushchev's successors set out in the late 1960s to seek Western confirmation of Soviet hegemony in Eastern Europe. (The renewed pressures for a European security conference and for confirmation of the "results of World War II" clearly had this intent.) Ironically, the Soviet Union thus sought legitimacy for her position from her putative enemies. The Soviet Union no doubt believed that her power entitled her to this. Ironically, her allies in the West, the Communist parties, found it difficult to offer help unreservedly to the Soviet Union. By this time, these parties were seeking increasing voter acceptance by demonstrating, in form if not in substance, that the era of total subservience to the USSR had ended in the international Communist movement.

In many ways, the persistent and mounting challenge from Peking was an even more serious threat to the sense of security which great and growing power might have conferred upon the Soviet Union. Here was not only a separate and competing pole of attraction and orthodoxy in the Communist world; Peking also challenged the Soviet quest for influence and recognition in the Third World. More than that: Although she was backward in terms of modern military capacity, China voiced claims to Soviet territory and did not shrink from frontier altercations. If the Soviet

Union approached the rest of the world with a sense of grievance over real and imagined wrongs perpetrated on her and her Tsarist predecessors, China managed to place the Soviet Union on the defensive by identifying her with "unequal" treaties of the past. Whatever the turmoil of the "Great Leap Forward" and the "Cultural Revolution," the Soviet Union could not shake off the nightmare of nearly a thousand million determined people eventually gaining the power to seek to redress the wrongs of the distant and recent past. The dream of nonantagonistic contradictions had long since evaporated, and there was scant comfort in the claim that the Chinese leaders had left the path of Marxism–Leninism. The USSR could retain intact the illusion that there can be no basic conflict between genuine revolutionaries, but she could not ignore the fact that here was a hostile power abutting on millions of square kilometers of rich but sparsely populated Soviet land, which was linked with European Russia by fragile communications and peopled at the rim by non-Russians whose affinity with Muscovite rule had its own historic uncertainties.

The accumulation of military force and the extension of its reach beyond the Eurasian landmass thus had not overcome some of the inherent flaws in the polity that the Soviet rulers had constructed over half a century. At the same time, the sense of power conferred on the Soviet Union by the steady shift in the military balance increased the Soviet appetite for tangible and intangible pay-offs. As in the past, this appetite had its defensive as well as offensive elements. But, for the first time since the Revolution, aspiration was being buttressed by great and growing power. In this respect, the late 1960s (and the period since then) differed from the optimistic phase of Khrushchev's term of office. While he was fascinated by modern weaponry, he had, like others before him, seen as the most potent sources of growing Soviet influence the nature of the Soviet system and the supposed confluence of revolutionary currents. His successors seemed less sanguine on these counts and relied more on the (by then) cumulative impact of raw power. It was not so much that they intended to use this power directly, although they plainly did not exclude that possibility; they believed, rather, that power would pay political dividends. Indeed, they believed that the USSR was entitled to these dividends; that she was entitled to be treated and respected as a superpower; and that this role should be given formal recognition through treaties and understandings, above all with the United States.

The Soviet concept of security thus became closely associated with the concept of equality and with the determination that the USSR should have her rights of access, presence, and influence acknowledged on a world-wide basis in form as well as substance. As power grew, so did the definition of security. The safety of the homeland was the principal consideration; the inviolability of Soviet predominance in Eastern Europe was a close second; "friendly" powers elsewhere on the Soviet periphery were next; and entitlement to a role at least equal to that of the United States elsewhere came last.

Yet the implementation of such plans was problematic. The homeland was safe from land attack, but it could not be protected either from vast

destruction if nuclear war should break out or from infection by alien
ideas. Eastern Europe was in the Soviet camp but full of cross-currents
which diluted Soviet control. While Soviet power based in the area
aimed an arrow at the West, the region was also an avenue for Western
influence. Other countries on the periphery, while not actively hostile
toward the Soviet Union, were far from friendly and were not deterred
from maintaining and building military forces and alliances that enabled
them to resist Soviet pressures. China was hostile, an active rival, and,
in Soviet eyes, potentially a long-term physical threat. Japan was moderately friendly but hardly supine. Further afield the Soviet presence
was growing but remained contested and uneven.

Security had thus become a goal whose attainment would require
ever-increasing measures of military power and unceasing effort. As
Soviet security was being defined in terms of the security situation of the
United States—the Soviet Union was now demanding "equal
security"—commitment to it was increasingly open-ended. Even if
Soviet missile forces reached rough numerical parity with those of the
United States, as they did in the late 1960s, that still did not spell a
condition of equality. For American missile technology was more advanced than that of the Soviet Union; the USSR faced not only the
United States but Britain and France as well, who represented the
"forward-based" systems of the United States; and the USSR needed
strategic forces to act as a threat (or deterrent) to China. If Soviet ground
forces were substantially more extensive than those of the United States,
the USSR was still not in a position of parity *vis-à-vis* the United States,
because the latter had no land enemy comparable with China. Indeed,
wherever the Soviet Union looked she seemed to feel herself in need of
"compensation," either for discriminations and disadvantages suffered
in the past or for contemporary or future ones. A natural consequence of
this outlook was that as "compensation" was piled on "compensation,"
the United States and others against whom the Soviet Union measured
her security considered their own interests to be in jeopardy and
undertook a variety of counteractions which in turn established new
military requirements for the USSR. [It should be noted that during the
Vietnam war particularly, but at other times too, the United States and
her allies did not, in fact, respond to all accretions in Soviet power.
Indeed, real defense outlays, apart from Vietnam-related expenses,
declined steadily during the 1960s and 1970s. Moreover, with increasing
personnel costs, outlays on military hardware declined even more
sharply. Individual programs, such as the introduction of multiple
independently targetable reentry vehicles (MIRV) in American land- and
sea-based missile forces, did proceed, however.]

Brezhnev and his colleagues had thus inherited from Khrushchev the
conviction that the Soviet Union could not and should not be satisfied
with securing the borders of the homeland and its Western outposts but
should strive for a status resembling that of the United States. Khrushchev had had the notion that the Soviet Union could match and
overtake the economic strength of the United States and that this would
render the Soviet example irresistible elsewhere in the world. Military
power, which Khrushchev did not neglect but which he had tried to

channel into particular areas, would be the concomitant of economic power and the power of example. Brezhnev was realistic enough to see the failings of this conception. Once he had consolidated his political position at home, he muted the themes of economic and ideological competition and generally sought to avoid head-on collisions with the USSR's principal antagonists, the United States and China. He proceeded methodically to build Soviet military power in all its dimensions and, having failed in his overtures to China and then in efforts to contain and surround her with Soviet allies, shifted to an "opening to the West." It was this strategy that was shaped in the period leading up the Twenty-fourth Communist Party Congress in 1971 and proclaimed in programmatic terms on that occasion.

*Defense and Security* The unveiling of the "peace program" of the Twenty-fourth Party Congress marked the start of the present period. It has been characterized by a continuation of older political–security concerns, especially in Europe, by some new elements, especially in relations with the United States, and by some enduring uncertainties over China and Asia and over the question of leadership succession. Above all, it has been a period in which commitment to the growth of the Soviet Union's military power has become an increasingly predominant characteristic of the regime. This has raised persistent questions abroad about Soviet intentions—about how the USSR will conduct her policies in an era of military parity, if not superiority.

By the time of the Twenty-fourth Party Congress, the "détente" with the Federal Republic of Germany was well advanced. The Eastern treaties were a culmination of postwar aims to ratify the *status quo*, although they were by no means entirely the product of skillful Soviet policy; changes in West Germany played a considerable role in the conclusion of the treaties and the Soviet Union prudently worked with the new forces. But the consolidation of a European détente, as defined by the USSR, proved elusive. The West introduced new demands involving respect for human rights and increased contacts at the very time when the older issues of territorial integrity, recognition of borders, etc., were being settled. And at the same time, the willingness of the Soviet Union to temper or resist these new trends was inhibited by her growing economic interest in securing trade and credits from Western Europe. Reversion to harsher Soviet alternatives in Europe would thus entail economic losses that might not seem justified by any political advantages to be gained from taking a harder line. On the other hand, the Soviet Union faced the dilemma of whether or not she should risk the further military relaxation in Europe which the West was demanding ever more insistently.

Soviet superiority in conventional military forces, of course, has been an essential support for Soviet policy since 1945. But this advantage clearly raises for the Western partners the question of the terms for continuing the European détente, especially as each cycle of force modernization seems to create new advances. A persistent Western search for some means to eliminate some, if not all, of the USSR's conventional military advantages could pose problems which Soviet regimes in the past have managed to evade. The basic security issue is whether the Soviet Union could afford to compete and coexist in Europe under conditions of near parity of conventional forces in Central Europe. Could she, in fact, withdraw large numbers of her forces as a result of a negotiated settlement or agree to stabilize a regional balance of nuclear forces? How would this affect her security interests in Eastern Europe?

How these questions are eventually answered will depend in part on the Soviet perception of the China problem. A prominent analytical line is that the Soviet Union has sought a period of relaxation in the West in order to consolidate her buildup in the East. This is plausible and consistent with the evidence provided by the share of Soviet military resources devoted to China. But it is an explanation more of tactics than of a well-defined strategy. What does the Soviet Union do in the post-Mao period?

It seems likely that at one time the USSR harbored hopes that after Mao a *modus vivendi* could be agreed with China; while this is still possible, especially given the propensity for internal turmoil in the Chinese leadership, the entire relationship seems to be shifting to a new level of geopolitical competition ushered in by the Chinese economic modernization program, the Sino–Japanese treaty, the conflict in Indochina, and normalization with the U.S.

We can only note that the Soviet treaty with North Vietnam is a new element in Soviet security policy; it has antecedents in friendship treaties with several Third World countries, but the Soviet Union could not have been oblivious to the risk that this particular treaty might become a blank check. At present all that can be hazarded is that the odds on a confrontation with China are now shorter. The prospect of Western willingness to underwrite Chinese economic and military modernization must raise the old specter of encirclement. It also raises the question of whether and which Soviet policies will be adopted to break up a hostile coalition. "Encirclement" clearly does not accord with the regime's appreciation of Soviet power and its consequent demand for "equal security." Soviet leaders must be asking themselves whether they can accept a policy of détente with the West which could lead to an underwriting of Chinese armament efforts by the USSR's European détente partners.

The question of how to manage a European détente and a Chinese confrontation inevitably involves a consideration of Soviet policy toward the United States. The decision taken in the early 1970s to enter into a period of relaxation with Washington was not a sudden one. The factors which appear to have prompted the decision are: (1) the conclusion of the Eastern treaties, which required a further payment in the Berlin negotiations that involved the United States; (2) the American opening to China in 1971, which helped to produce the American–Soviet summit of 1972; (3) the prospect of an antiballistic missile (ABM) race; (4) economic needs; and (5) the ascendency of Brezhnev. All (except perhaps the last factor) necessitated an active policy of maneuver.

Of course, the Soviet Union expected dividends, primarily in the form of economic assistance, which she needed in a period of intensive economic development requiring major inputs of capital and technology, but also in the form of the curtailment of certain areas of strategic competition. Having embarked on the détente policy, the Soviet Union found that, as it evolved, she could not disengage herself from it, even though it yielded smaller dividends than expected and elicited new challenges.

The point is that the Soviet Union became to some extent the prisoner of her own commitments. Having proclaimed the irreversibility of détente, she could not easily dismiss it as a temporary aberration without calling into question the judgment of her own leadership. Having entered into the Strategic Arms Limitation Talks (SALT) negotiations and signed one treaty of indefinite duration, she could not easily jettison the process, even though it had become more complex. Having committed herself to multibillion dollar programs, she could not run political risks that could jeopardize them.

This is not to say that the Soviet Union has been straining to abandon the line of the Twenty-fourth Party Congress. Brezhnev's personal identification with it is a powerful impediment to such a course. Moreover, new gains have been achieved, and others may be looming. In Africa, in particular, the Soviet Union has found a novel approach to the projection of her power—through proxy military forces. This was foreshadowed to some extent in the Middle East, when Soviet forces were in combat along the Suez line during the tensions of 1970–1971. But the stationing abroad of sizable forces of a Soviet ally is new; it provides new leverage in an area of major Western concerns. The impressive fact is that the Soviet Union has accepted the concomitant risks with apparent equanimity. The two incursions—in Angola and in Ethiopia—thus suggest that the Soviet Union has already reappraised the opportunities and inhibitions of a more forward policy. The most intriguing question is whether this reappraisal reflects only an assessment of local conditions or a broader evaluation of a change in the overall balance of power.

In any case, the more traditional notion of security relating to the periphery of the USSR has probably received a new impetus by events along her southern periphery, particularly in Afghanistan, but also in Turkey and Iran. At present, the situation in Iran is uncertain. The Soviet Union has played a cautious hand—in part because of her interest in a continuous flow of natural gas, in part because the religiously motivated opponents of the Shah could have undesired effects on the USSR's own Muslim population, and in part because the Soviet Union has probably not yet seen an effective indigenous Iranian force with which to ally herself. Nevertheless, she has issued solemn warnings against foreign intervention, asserting her own state security interests because of the proximity of her borders. Moscow is probably as uncertain about the future course of events as anyone, but it must at least be harboring hopes of, and possibly taking some action to encourage, a more congenial regime in an area which Russians have historically viewed with a mixture of fear and ambition.

At the same time, the peace program of the Twenty-fourth Party Congress has suffered the effects of a number of events, some well beyond Soviet control: the resignations of Brandt and Nixon; Soviet expulsion from the Middle East and the revival of American presence and influence there; the modest economic benefits of relations with the United States; and the reappearance of human rights as an international political issue.

The Soviet Union has thus encountered some serious contradictions. On the one hand, her military power has grown both absolutely and relatively. Her reach has made itself felt in distant places, and favorable tides may be running on the USSR's southern rim. On the other hand, there is a budding relationship among the Soviet Union's principal adversaries—Western Europe, Japan, China, and the United States. The Soviet Union seems to recognize this, but how she will handle it is far from clear. At present she appears to be still at the stage of issuing "serious" warnings.

Yet it must be clear to the Soviet regime that the USSR neither has been able to translate her military preponderance into lasting favorable political alignments nor to neutralize alignments she considers inimical. Thus the curious paradox of strategic nuclear power seems to have affected the Soviet Union perhaps even more than it has affected the United States.

Finally, it is obvious that for more than a decade Soviet security has been defined and presided over by a group of leaders who will not survive more than a few more years. One can only speculate about the turmoil that the change of leaders will provoke. The most fascinating aspect is that a new leadership will inherit a position of far greater power than any of its predecessors; but it will also inherit a new set of problems, particularly in the management of economic resources, which in part is the price to be paid for the massive increases in Soviet power.

Conclusion        The emerging situation for Soviet security policy in the next decade could resemble that of 1958–1962, when Khrushchev attempted to turn a military advantage into lasting geopolitical gains. But there would be a significant difference: Soviet military power would meanwhile have gone through some 20 years of modernization and enlargement. Strategic forces would be massive and diverse rather than rudimentary. Close to a generation of momentum in military growth would be behind the Soviet leadership of the day, and by all indications this momentum would not be arrested, even if anticipated economic slowdown increased its relative cost.

Yet when all of this is added up, would Soviet leaders in the end dismiss the forces that would be arrayed against them in any open and direct challenge to the international geopolitical balance? Would political leaders, including those principally charged with the development and modernization of the Soviet economy and with managing far-flung ties with the outside world, accept without serious reservation estimates that the gains to be derived from pressure, threats, and, ultimately, the use of force, are inevitably destined to outweigh the costs? Would Soviet leaders, even assuming they believed themselves to have gained substantial military advantages, be certain of their ability to control the course of crises or war? How certain would Soviet leaders be that the gains they made through pressure or force would, in fact, enhance the security of the Soviet state and the progress of its political system?

None of these questions can be answered conclusively by drawing on the experience of the past. Nothing in that portion of Soviet discourse available to us sheds clear light on the answers. The Soviet attacks on Finland, Poland, and Bessarabia in 1939–1940 took place in the anticipation of fairly imminent attack, but with a green or amber light from the enemy-to-be who was then still an ally. The moves into Angola and Ethiopia seem to have been based on the calculation that the risks were modest, and therefore they do not give us much guidance for gauging Soviet reaction in situations in which risks may be judged to be more serious. On the other hand, Soviet actions in successive crises over Berlin, the Middle East, and Cuba, in which assertiveness was followed by caution when risks became higher than apparently anticipated, do not provide clear answers either. All these crises occurred before the military balance had reached the state prevailing now or that which is expected to prevail in the next 5 to 10 years.

We thus reach a point where speculation about Soviet behavior must inevitably merge with expectations of American behavior and that of other powers in the world. We do not see a Soviet leadership brimming with optimism about the prospects of the USSR in relation to the United States, the Western world generally, China, and others. But nor do we see that leadership overcome with pessimism. Its economic and other plans project effort and sacrifice for years to come. Its external economic and other commitments are also essentially long-term. Its military plans seem to envisage further cycles of modernization and improvement.

How a new leadership will handle this inheritance we cannot say. But whatever departures from Lenin it adds to those sanctioned already by its predecessors, we tend to believe that it will continue to adhere to Lenin's adaptation of Clausewitz: "War is the continuation of the policies of peace; and peace, the continuation of the policies of war." If we are right in that judgment, then the West has it in its power to help the Soviet Union remain true to the scripture in this one fateful instance, by making certain that no meaningful political gain and no security advantage can be obtained from resort to the threat or use of force.

# Note

[1]V. I. Lenin, *Bourgeois Pacifism and Socialist Pacifism* (March 1919).

# 15

# DAVID HOLLOWAY

# Military Power and Political Purpose in Soviet Policy*

The growth of Soviet military power in the 1960s and 1970s has caused anxiety, alarm, and disillusionment in the West. Widely different interpretations of this military buildup have been advanced. Some have seen it as evidence of the Soviet Union's determination to achieve decisive military superiority over its adversaries and to extend its power and influence by means of military force. Others, more in sorrow than in anger, have viewed it as springing from a deep-seated sense of insecurity and a desire to defend Soviet interests against real or imagined dangers. The entry of Soviet combat troops into Afghanistan and the overthrow of the government in Kabul have not resolved Western disagreements about the sources of Soviet policy. Those who see that policy as inherently expansionist have taken the invasion of Afghanistan as confirmation of their views, while for those who see Soviet policy as rooted in anxiety, the intervention merely points to the depth of Soviet insecurity.

Soviet leaders have argued that increased Soviet military power contributes to better, more cooperative East–West relations by forcing Western governments to adopt a more "realistic" and less hostile approach to the Soviet Union. In Western eyes, however, the very growth of Soviet military power has cast doubt on the professed Soviet desire for better relations and on the Soviet interest in East–West cooperation. The Soviet action in Afghanistan has highlighted Western fears, while the Western response seems to contradict the Soviet view that greater Soviet power means better relations with the West.

The Afghan crisis has closed one chapter in East–West relations. The détente of the late 1960s and the 1970s appears to have run its course. Since the mid-1970s the prospects for further progress had diminished. But now the supporters of détente have to devote their energies to

*Reprinted by permission of the author and publisher from *Daedalus* 109, no. 4 (Fall, 1980), pp. 13–30. Copyright 1980 by The American Academy of Arts and Sciences.

salvaging what was achieved rather than to pressing for a further easing of tensions. Whatever course East–West relations now take, Soviet military power will continue to pose difficult problems for Western governments. But the Soviet leaders too will face difficult decisions, inasmuch as the growth and exploitation of military power may make impossible those relations with the West they say they want. It remains important, therefore, to try to understand Soviet perspectives on military power and its contribution to political purposes.

The prospect of a major turnover in the Soviet leadership makes the issue of Soviet military power more urgent. The Brezhnev years have seen a steady decline in economic performance, alongside the steady growth of military power. The new leadership may therefore find it extremely difficult to maintain a large defense effort, revive economic growth, and satisfy the consumer. A redefinition of priorities or a major reform of the system of economic planning and management could have repercussions on foreign policy. Indeed, the succession raises wide-ranging questions about the distribution of power in the Soviet Union, about the prospects for changes in policy, and about the effects of domestic problems on foreign and defense policy. All of these need to be considered in deciding what, if anything, Western governments can do to influence the choices the Soviet leaders make.

It is not surprising that Western disagreements about Soviet military policy have spilled over into controversy about the nature of the Soviet state. The one area of agreement is that Soviet military power has increased over the last 20 years, though even here major differences can be found in interpreting the significance of this increase. The divergencies of view both reflect and contribute to the lack of consensus that exists in the West, and in particular in the United States, on questions of defense policy. (Indeed, they may tell us more about American thinking than they do about Soviet policy.) The object of this essay is to throw light on Soviet military policy by exploring Soviet conceptions of security and military power, by analyzing the role and content of Soviet military doctrine, and by examining the effect of domestic factors on Soviet defense policy. The focus is not Soviet military power as such, for this has received constant examination, but the articulation of military power and political purpose, which is less often studied. The problems of analysis are immense and need no rehearsal here. But an understanding of Soviet policy requires that the military and political elements be taken together, for it is the relationship between the two that raises the most important questions.

## Military Power and the Soviet State

There is a tendency in the West to see Soviet conceptions of security as fixed and monolithic. Soviet statements encourage this impression by stressing the continuity of policy, while the principles of democratic centralism lay down that once a policy is formulated no disagreement may be voiced. Western governments, on the other hand, like to portray each policy decision as marking a new departure, and this naturally helps to stimulate open disagreement. In fact, however, Soviet leaders have defined their security interests in different ways at different times, as military and political conditions have changed. Similarly, Soviet views of security are not monolithic, for differences in perspective can be identified in Soviet thinking.

Soviet conceptions of security are nonetheless rooted in a distinctive historical and cultural experience that continues to exert a strong influence on Soviet thinking about military power. Even the legacy of the prerevolutionary state, with its powerful military–bureaucratic apparatus, can still be discerned. War and the preparation for war provided a major stimulus for domestic reforms and gave the state a dominant role in economic development. Rivalry with more advanced powers imposed a heavy military burden on Russian society. The Russian state expanded by assimilating weak or unstable areas and subjugating them by military force. At the same time the great invasions of Russian territory helped to engender a deep sense of insecurity about threats from outside the state. Insecurity and expansion were not mutually exclusive, but mutually reinforcing.

When the Bolsheviks seized power, they did not anticipate this inheritance, for they expected revolution to sweep through Europe. While the initial seizure of power was accomplished quickly, its consolidation was opposed in a bitter civil war and by the intervention of the leading capitalist powers. The Bolsheviks were victorious, but with the failure of revolution in Europe, they faced the task of socialist construction without aid from more advanced socialist partners. The young, economically backward proletarian state stood alone in a world that it regarded with hostility and suspicion, sentiments that were reciprocated in full measure.

In these difficult conditions, the course the Soviet Union took under Stalin's leadership had far-reaching consequences for Soviet security. Socialism was to be constructed in one country; a rapid industrialization drive would enable the Soviet Union to "catch up and overtake" the advanced capitalist powers. The "defense of socialist achievements" would be secured by Soviet military power, supported by a strong industrial base.[1] Alongside economic autarky a kind of autarkic security was pursued. Soviet security was now to depend more on Soviet efforts than on political events elsewhere in the world. Non-Soviet Communist parties were transformed into instruments of Soviet foreign policy, helping to oppose anti-Soviet forces and trying to prevent them from uniting.

On June 22, 1941, the war for which the Soviet Union had long prepared began with an attack that took Stalin by surprise. The opening months proved disastrous as the German armies advanced to the outskirts of Moscow. The newly created Soviet industry provided the material basis for a triumphant, though very costly, victory. The moral basis of victory was provided by an intense patriotism that the party did its utmost to encourage. After the bitter social conflicts and repression of the 1930s, the war against Germany (the "Great Fatherland War") drew regime and people together in a common struggle.

Victory brought territorial gains that must have been inconceivable in the dark months after the German invasion. The Red Army's liberation of Eastern Europe from Nazism laid the foundation on which a socialist camp could be built. The Soviet Union no longer stood alone against the capitalist world. But in spite of the victorious outcome, the initial German attack left a profound mark on Soviet thinking about the prevention of war and the preparation for war. The attempt to prevent war through a combination of diplomacy and military power had failed; the Red Army had been caught unready for the German attack; the Soviet Union had suffered enormous losses of men, materiel, and territory in the first months of the war; victory had been achieved at a huge cost.

The very success of the Red Army in pushing the German armies back to Berlin created disputes with the Western allies, and these soon degenerated into the intense hostility of the Cold War. The Soviet Union had suffered a severe economic setback during the war, while its chief postwar adversary had emerged, if anything, stronger. The Soviet Union lagged in those new military technologies, notably nuclear weapons, that had undergone rapid development during the war. The gains of victory were thus partially offset by Soviet economic and technological backwardness. The Soviet Union's ground forces in Europe provided it with a major advantage, but once again the imperative of "catch up and overtake" had to be obeyed if inferiority was to be avoided.[2]

At the end of the war Stalin launched major research and development programs (nuclear weapons, rockets, radar, and jet-engine technology) to make good the lags in military technology. By the mid-1950s the growing stockpile of nuclear weapons raised fundamental questions about the relationship of war to policy and about the appropriate structure for the armed forces in the nuclear age, questions that have preoccupied Soviet military thought ever since. The discussions of the 1950s led to the establishment of the Strategic Rocket Forces as a separate service in December 1959, and to a major reformulation of Soviet military doctrine, which now emphasized preparation for nuclear war.[3]

In an important sense, the Soviet "military buildup" (to use the common term) began in the years of the First Five Year Plan (1928–1932). The Politbureau decreed in 1929 that the Red Army should have no fewer troops than its probable enemies in the main theater of war, and should be stronger than the enemy in the decisive forms of armament—aircraft, artillery, and tanks.[4] But the current buildup has its origins in the transformation of the Soviet armed forces for nuclear warfare between 1954 and 1964. Khrushchev tried to substitute firepower for manpower and to cut the size of the armed forces, apparently with the aim of reducing, or at least limiting, the military burden. This policy met with considerable military opposition, which was strengthened by the international crises of the early 1960s and by the defense policy of the Kennedy Administration.

Khrushchev was finally unsuccessful, and it is from the defeat of his policy that the present buildup can be traced. His successors have eschewed his exclusive emphasis on nuclear war and have pursued a "balanced" force structure that would be ready for various contingencies. A determined effort brought strategic parity with the United States by the late 1960s (and parity remains the public Soviet description of the strategic balance). The ground forces have been expanded, in particular along the frontier with China, and have been steadily modernized. The air forces, too, have continued to receive more modern equipment. Soviet naval presence has extended throughout the world. The supply of arms and advisers to Third World countries has grown substantially. All this has amounted to a formidable accumulation of military power, not according to a blueprint, but through a series of interlocking decisions.

## Military Power and Security

It is in the light of this experience that present policies should be viewed. Leading members of the Brezhnev Politbureau came to positions of some power during the 1930s, and this has had a marked influence on their approach to problems of military power. The creation of a strong industrial state, victory in the war with Germany, the attainment of strategic parity with the United States, and 35 years of peace since 1945—these are regarded by this generation as among its greatest achievements. It is in the creation of military power that the Soviet Union has come closest to "catching up and overtaking" the advanced capitalist powers.

It is not surprising, therefore, that the present generation of leaders has come to see military power as one of the main guarantees of Soviet security and of the Soviet position in the world. Official Soviet thinking sees the world in terms of an irreconcilable conflict between socialism and capitalism; it is from this that the Soviet state derives its *raison d'être*. It is true that the Soviet concept of the "correlation of forces," which is used to analyze this conflict, does not place primary emphasis on military power. It is also true that Soviet history indicates that political, military, and economic elements are interwoven in Soviet conceptions of security. But the very success of the Soviet Union in creating military power means that the law of comparative advantage gives the military instrument a major role in Soviet external policies.

The Soviet Union conducts its relationship with the West from a position of military strength but economic weakness. It has used arms transfers and military advisers as major instruments of policy in Africa and Asia. In its relations with other socialist states, military power has also been an important factor. In Hungary and Czechoslovakia, the Soviet leaders used military force to prevent political setbacks, while the Soviet relationship with China has now acquired a crucial military dimension. From the point of view of Soviet security, the creation of a socialist camp has not been an unambiguous gain, and its cohesion has been maintained only by military force.

The Soviet use of military force must, however, be seen in perspective. Compared with American, British, and French forces, the Soviet armed forces have engaged in little combat since 1945 and have been used less actively as an instrument of policy. By and large, Soviet leaders have used military force circumspectly and have sought to avoid precipitating a major conflict with the West. The Soviet style of active military intervention has been to use overwhelming force as an earnest of political and military commitment in the hope of crushing resistance at once and establishing firm control quickly. This has been rather different from the American practice of intervening at a low level and raising the commitment as resistance is encountered. Yet it would be wrong to try to discover permanent rules of Soviet behavior, because the context in which the Soviet Union exercises its military power is changing. Since World War II the Soviet Union has moved from being a continental military power to being a global one, with a growing ability to project military power around the world. This extension of military power has been driven primarily by the desire to counter those threats that can be posed to the Soviet homeland from afar, but it has provided the basis for more active use of military force for limited political purposes.

The current Soviet military buildup began at a time when world politics had a clear bipolar structure, with the Soviet Union and the United States as the dominant powers. The growth of Soviet military power has certainly altered the relationship with the United States to the Soviet advantage. But since the 1950s new forces have emerged to transform the international system. Fissiparous tendencies, both East and West, have complicated international relations. By the late 1960s, when the Soviet Union attained strategic parity with the United States, Japan and the European Economic Community had become major centers of economic power, while the Sino–Soviet conflict had degenerated into military confrontation. And the emergence of the new states of Asia and Africa has provided a new arena for East–West rivalry.

From the Soviet point of view (as from the American), the international environment has become more complex, presenting opportunities but also dangers. Soviet opportunities for the exploitation of military power have grown most notably in Africa and Asia, while the increased ability of the Soviet Union to project military power gives governments on those continents a choice of superpower patronage and protection in their internal and external relations. But it should not be supposed that the Soviet Union is always the initiator, or always the beneficiary, of anti-Western developments. To suppose this would be to impose a political perspective that is not always appropriate to a world that has moved away from a clear bipolar structure.[5]

The greatest danger for the Soviet Union is that the various centers of power in the world will combine against it. Elements of such a combination have been evident, motivated in large part by the desire to offset growing Soviet military power; in turn, this countervailing power has provided the Soviet leaders with further reasons for military forces. It is not clear, therefore, that the growth of military power has resulted in a commensurate increase in Soviet security. Of course it is not inevitable that other states will react by increasing their own forces: They may feel intimidated, or find that accommodation to Soviet interests is the appropriate response. But Soviet leaders are faced with some delicate judgments in assessing the political effects of their military policy.

In the nuclear age, military power cannot provide a sure guarantee of security. Because of the destructiveness of nuclear weapons, and because of the present impossibility of effective defense against ballistic missiles, each state's security is contingent, to a greater or lesser degree, on the actions of other states. For Soviet leaders, schooled in the Stalinist approach to security, this has proved particularly unsettling. Ballistic missile defense has been attractive to the Soviet leadership because it would mean that Soviet security did not depend, in the words of one Soviet general, on the "good will of the other side."[6] But in the absence of effective defense, such dependence does exist. Thus nuclear weapons have posed military and political problems for Soviet policy. These problems have been the central concern of Soviet military doctrine.

## Military Doctrine

It was widely expected 10 years ago that the strategic arms limitation talks would lead to a better mutual understanding of military doctrine by the United States and the Soviet Union, but it is not clear that this has happened. The earlier American view of Soviet military doctrine as backward and primitive has been replaced by a greater awareness of the distinctiveness of Soviet ideas. It is no longer widely believed that Soviet strategic conceptions must converge on the American. Indeed, a reverse influence can now be discerned in which Soviet writings have influenced American thinking about the prevention and conduct of nuclear war. It is undoubtedly healthy that Soviet thinking is no longer dismissed as unworthy of serious attention. But there are disagreements in the West about precisely what Soviet thinking is.

The most contentious issue in Western debates about the nature of Soviet military thinking is whether the Soviet Union believes that it can fight and win a nuclear war. It is argued by some commentators that Soviet doctrine—in particular, the commitment to the Clausewitzian view of war as a continuation of politics by violent means—shows that the Soviet leaders do hold to this belief and that they accept the practical consequences that follow from it. Others object, saying this is a misreading of Soviet doctrine, that the Soviet leaders accept that a relationship of mutual deterrence—in the sense of mutual vulnerability to devastating retaliatory strikes—exists between the superpowers and, further, that they accept this as the only practicable relationship with the United States at the present time.[7] The issue is not a simple one, for the evidence available to us is far from complete; nor, indeed, should we suppose that there is a monolithic Soviet view on this question.

The most convenient way to approach this issue is through an examination of the structure of Soviet military doctrine. Military doctrine is defined in the Soviet Union as the system of views that a state holds at a given time on "the purposes and character of a possible war, on the preparation of the country and the armed forces for it, and also on the methods of waging it."[8] Military doctrine, in the Soviet view, has two closely connected sides: the political (which is dominant) and the military–technical. The former sets out the political purposes and character of war and their implications for defense policy; the latter deals with the methods of waging war and the organization, equipment, and combat readiness of the armed forces. In practice, these two sides are not only connected, but overlap as well; yet the analytical distinction is important. Soviet use of the term "doctrine" is more restricted than the American; one does not find, for example, references to "naval doctrine." At the same time, however, it is also more general, because it merges with the principles that underlie Soviet foreign policy.

Stalin's death opened the way for discussion of the implications of nuclear weapons for military doctrine. In 1954 Malenkov declared that in the nuclear age world war would mean the end of world civilization. In saying this he was not being un-Marxist, for both Engels and Lenin had pointed to the possibility that weapons might be developed that would make war senseless.[9] But Malenkov was being less than astute in terms of the leadership politics of his day, and he was criticized for his outspokenness. At the Twentieth Party Congress in 1956, however, Khrushchev announced that war between socialism and capitalism should no longer be considered "fatally inevitable." This was because there now existed a world socialist camp, and because the Soviet Union possessed the means to deal a "crushing rebuff" to any aggressor.[10] This was an important innovation, and one that has remained central to Soviet thinking. Growing Soviet power would make a world war less likely because it would give the Soviet Union an increasing ability to deter an attack on itself or its allies.

The political side of Soviet doctrine stresses the importance, and the possibility, of preventing a war between the socialist and capitalist powers. The military side attends to the question of waging such a war "if the imperialists should unleash it" (to use the standard Soviet qualification). Deterrence is a political rather than a military concept and receives almost no attention in the military press. The Soviet leaders have seen the prevention of war as something to be achieved by means of a "peace policy"—a foreign policy that seeks to reduce the risks of war—backed by military might. In the words of Marshal Ustinov, the present minister of defense, the basis of Soviet military doctrine lies in "the unity of the peaceful foreign policy of the Soviet state and its readiness to give the necessary rebuff to an aggressor."[11] No contradiction is seen between the prevention of war and the preparation for war: War can be prevented only by being prepared to wage it.

The Soviet conception of deterrence is thus different from the American, and is embedded in the notion of war prevention. Soviet doctrine has never accepted the principle of assured destruction as a guide to force planning. (It does not follow from this, however, that the Soviet leaders reject the existence of a relationship of mutual deterrence between the two superpowers.) One way to explore Soviet thinking about mutual deterrence is to examine the discussion of deterrence by an

influential Soviet social scientist, Fyodor Burlatskii.[12] In his view, the
strongest argument the advocates of nuclear deterrence have is that, in
spite of international tension and crises, a third world war has been
avoided. Burlatskii claims, however, that three different hypotheses can
be advanced to explain this. First, war has been made senseless by the
threat of mutual destruction or irreparable damage. Second, the creation
of a bipolar international system after World War II led to a balance of
power that made victory by one side over the other doubtful (or
impossible). Third, the forces of peace have been stronger than the
forces interested in unleashing thermonuclear war.

Each of these factors, writes Burlatskii, has played its part in preventing world war, but the third has been most important. While war may
have become senseless in a technical sense, he argues, the important
question is whether the "imperialist conquerors" take this into account;
nuclear war may be senseless, but someone might start it nonetheless.
War must be prevented not merely through the threat of mutual
destruction, but by tackling the political conflict that might give rise to it.
This is why the third factor is decisive for Burlatskii. By the relationship
between the forces of war and the forces of peace, he means not only the
balance of power within the bipolar system (with the Warsaw Pact
naturally identified with the forces of peace); he has in mind also those
political elements in the West that oppose a strengthening of NATO, as
well as the nonaligned and anti-Western policies of the new states of the
Third World.

Burlatskii's identification of the forces of peace is crude, but his
overall argument is interesting. It reflects a widely held Soviet view that
the relationship of mutual deterrence is not a foolproof mechanism for
preventing war; in spite of the Soviet Union's best efforts, the catastrophe of nuclear war might occur. The true significance of the Clausewitzian view that war is the continuation of policy by other means is that
the possibility of war has to be assessed in terms of the political conflict
that might cause it, and not merely in terms of the balance of armaments
between the two sides. Two consequences follow from this view. The
first, which Burlatskii advocates, is the pursuit of radical moves to
change the character of international relations. But the second is the
course that Soviet policy has pursued more vigorously: preparation for
the wars that might take place.

It should not be surprising that the Soviet approach to deterrence is
different from the American, for deterrence, although founded on hard
material facts, is essentially a psychological relationship and is therefore
strongly influenced by cultural and historical factors. It is here that the
Soviet experience—in particular, perhaps, the memory of June 22,
1941—bears on Soviet thinking about the prevention of nuclear war. At
the end of his detailed study of the German attack, the Soviet historian
Anfilov concludes, in the light of historical experience, that to prevent
the West from unleashing a new world war it is essential not only to be
vigilant and to maintain constant combat readiness, but also to mobilize
political forces for peace.[13] In Soviet eyes, the prevention of war is not
only a matter of the balance of military strength, but the object of a wider
policy that embraces political elements as well.

The
Development
of Military
Doctrine

It may be useful to explore the relationship between the military and political sides of doctrine by tracing briefly the development of that doctrine in the nuclear age. After Stalin's death the military press began to discuss the implication of nuclear weapons for the conduct of warfare. In 1957 the Ministry of Defense organized the first of a series of conferences on nuclear war. These were followed closely by the Party leadership and formed the basis of the new military doctrine that Khrushchev unveiled in January 1960.[14] The focus of the new doctrine was the possibility of war between the Warsaw Pact and NATO; in such a war the chief weapon would be nuclear-armed rockets. The Strategic Rocket Forces were now to form the main strike force of Soviet military power. Khrushchev's outline of the new doctrine was very general, and in the following years intensive debates took place on a number of unresolved issues—for example, would such a war be long or short? Were the ground forces essentially occupation forces that would move into enemy territory after a nuclear strike, or would they take a major part in actual combat? These discussions centered on the question of what a nuclear war would be like and how it should be waged.[15]

At the same time, the acquisition by the Soviet armed forces of growing numbers of nuclear weapons and long-range rockets raised the question of the relationship between military power and foreign policy. The thesis that war was not inevitable opened the way for much greater stress on peaceful coexistence between socialism and capitalism. It seemed also to offer the possibility of political gains for the Soviet Union. Soviet nuclear forces would help to deter the West from attacking the Soviet Union or its allies. They would also, Khrushchev hoped, make possible a more active foreign policy. Soviet priority in testing an ICBM and launching an artificial earth satellite seemed to confirm Khrushchev's belief that the correlation of forces was moving rapidly in the Soviet favor. His prognostications about attaining full communism by 1980 were matched by his optimistic expectation of making major foreign policy advances. In a series of crises in the late 1950s and early 1960s he tested the political possibilities of the new military relationship with the United States by attempting to use a presumed Soviet military advantage to win concessions from the West. These attempts proved unsuccessful and culminated in the debacle of the Cuban missile crisis.[16]

Khrushchev's successors introduced some important changes of emphasis in force structure and in the political exploitation of military power. In the debates about military strategy Khrushchev had sided with those who relegated conventional forces to a secondary role. This position was criticized for depriving Soviet military power of flexibility. Stress was now laid on the need to prepare to fight different kinds of war; in particular, since 1967 the possibility of a conventional campaign in Europe has been taken seriously. After Khrushchev's fall, the military buildup was greatly influenced by the effort to eradicate imbalances in the structure of the armed forces. Khrushchev's defense policy was also criticized for depriving Soviet foreign policy of flexibility, forcing it to choose between passivity and risky challenges to the West. In effect, his successors agreed with the taunt the Chinese had flung at him after the Cuban missile crisis, that his policy was a mixture of adventurism and "capitulationism."

The Brezhnev leadership inherited from Khrushchev a considerable inferiority in strategic forces. They rejected this as unacceptable on both military and political grounds and made strenuous efforts to catch up with the United States. By the late 1960s the attainment of parity with the United States and the prospect of intense competition in antiballistic missile systems—in which the Soviet Union might well fare worse—raised new questions of military policy; in particular, was mutual vulnerability the only possible relationship with the United States, or should the Soviet Union strive for a significant strategic superiority? At this time it seems to have been accepted by the Soviet military and political leaders alike that mutual deterrence—in the sense of mutual vulnerability to devastating retaliatory strikes—was an objective phenomenon.[17] While not altogether happy with this relationship, they saw it as preferable to American superiority and as satisfactory insofar as an American attack was thereby deterred. It was accepted further that strategic arms competition did contain an action–reaction element, and that any attempt to achieve a decisive superiority would provoke a countervailing action from the other side. In other words, the choice the Soviet leaders faced was not one between parity and superiority (for superiority is clearly desirable), but between parity and a dangerous competition for superiority, the outcome of which was by no means certain. It made sense, therefore, to enter negotiations with the United States to stabilize the strategic relationship. The SALT agreements have not, of course, halted strategic arms competition, but they appear to have confirmed, in Soviet eyes, the correctness of the Soviet position. In the mid-1970s Soviet doctrine came to state more explicitly that superiority was not the goal of Soviet policy.[18]

This conception of the strategic relationship was one of the underpinnings of the peace program adopted at the Twenty-fourth Party Congress in 1971. Soviet thinking has not conceived of mutual deterrence as a sure mechanism for preventing world war. If mutual deterrence was to be accepted as an objective fact, then further measures had to be taken to reduce the risk of war, and this was one of the aims of the Soviet peace program. At the same time, the Soviet leaders believed that growing Soviet military power would help to make Western governments adopt a more accommodating attitude to Soviet interests. Détente, while helping to reduce the risk of war, would also provide a framework in which Soviet interests could be pursued and Soviet influence extended. Perhaps the most important gain for the Soviet Union in this period has been the international recognition of the postwar status quo in Europe.

One consequence of the acceptance of strategic parity has been that more attention has been given to the use of military power as an instrument of policy below the strategic level. Parity had helped to neutralize American strategic power; more strenuous efforts could now be made to restrict Western and Chinese power and influence outside the central military balances. The Soviet Union's move to a global military role was in the first instance motivated by the desire to counter American strategic power. But through the supply of arms and military advisers, and with the help of proxy forces such as the Cuban troops, the Soviet Union has increasingly tried to use its military power to support political change to its own advantage around the world. It is as if the Soviet Union, having achieved recognition of its superpower status at the strategic level, now wished to play a superpower's military role in shaping the destiny of the countries of the Third World.[19]

Doctrine and Policy   Soviet writings about the conduct of nuclear war should be approached with the political as well as the military side of doctrine in mind. Those who draw from such writings the conclusion that the Soviet leaders think they can fight and win a nuclear war fail to relate them to the political side of Soviet military doctrine. The widespread Soviet acceptance of the position that war is a continuation of policy by other means does not suggest that nuclear war is regarded as an effective instrument of policy. Soviet writers are careful to distinguish between the nature of war and the expediency of initiating a particular conflict. Nor do Soviet statements about the possibility of victory in nuclear war necessarily indicate that such a war is regarded as an instrument of practical policy. If deterrence is not seen as foolproof, it makes sense to pay attention to how a nuclear war would be fought and how the survival of the state could best be assured in the event of such a war. In this context, victory retains significance as a concept: It is certainly to be striven for if war does break out; it is important for maintaining the morale of the armed forces; it seems to be entailed by the ideological notion that socialism must triumph over capitalism—for war cannot be thought of as reversing the movement of history. But Soviet writers stress the unprecedented destruction that would follow from a general nuclear war. There is little evidence to suggest that the Soviet leaders think victory in the present circumstances would be anything other than catastrophic.[20]

The relationship between the political and military sides of Soviet doctrine has not always been easy or unambiguous. Some members of the Party leadership have wondered whether, if war with the West could be avoided, the costly preparation for such a war was necessary; they have also doubted whether it made sense to speak of victory in such a war. Malenkov in the early 1950s and Khrushchev in the early 1960s appear to have had doubts of this kind and to have advocated something akin to a policy of minimum deterrence. Members of the High Command, on the other hand, have taken seriously their responsibility to prepare to wage war and have pressed for the means with which to do so. Whatever disagreements they may have had about the forces required for waging a nuclear war, they seem to have been agreed that such a war should be prepared for.[21]

The present position appears to be something of a compromise. It seems to be accepted that, in present circumstances, parity is the best possible relationship with the United States; the pursuit of a significant superiority would be risky and dangerous. But Soviet doctrine has not abandoned the principle that war should be prepared for: The military–technical side of doctrine attends to the question of how war is to be waged. Within the relationship of parity, efforts have been made to enhance Soviet strategic capabilities and to limit, through such measures as civil defense, the damage that a nuclear strike would inflict on Soviet society. At the same time, research and development work on new ABM technologies suggests that vulnerability is not seen as something immutable, and a technological breakthrough in this area might lead to a revision of doctrine. The Soviet view that war should be prepared for has a bearing on Soviet negotiating behavior at SALT, for the details of the agreements may have considerable significance for Soviet fighting capabilities. It also has a bearing on the strategic relationship with the United States, for Soviet measures to enhance their own capabilities appear to the West to be eroding the balance of mutual deterrence.

The closest Soviet doctrine comes to providing a criterion of sufficiency is in its statement that superiority in armaments is not the goal of Soviet policy.[22] Part of the reason for the adoption of this criterion is the fear that a drive for superiority will provoke countervailing action by other powers. But what does it mean to eschew superiority? What precise meaning is to be given to terms such as "parity" and "equality"—equality with all potential enemies or just with the United States? In the absence of an agreed strategic calculus, how is a judgment to be made about what will provoke a justified—as opposed to an "artificial"—reaction from the other side?

These questions are not posed to suggest that doctrine is of no importance either in making Soviet policy or in understanding it. But doctrine is not regarded in the Soviet Union as the key to specific decisions, nor should it be seen by outside observers as the key to understanding Soviet policy. Doctrine does provide a framework for the formulation of policy, but it does not determine the outcome of the policymaking process. Moreover, the framework of doctrine has evolved in response to changes in the military-political environment. It was reformulated for the rocket-nuclear age and has been adapted since then to meet the realities and exploit the opportunities of changing military relationships in the world. More important, Soviet doctrine is not monolithic. Within its framework, substantial ambiguities, cross-currents, and differences of emphasis may be found. Stress can be put on the preparation for war or on the pursuit of political measures to prevent it; on the possibility of victory or on the destructiveness of nuclear war; on the offensive political uses of military power or on the need for accommodation with the West. Variation can be found in Soviet writings, and this presumably reflects divergencies of opinion inside the Soviet Union. Thus one should beware of imputing to Soviet leaders a single undifferentiated view on these profoundly important matters. And, although doctrine is an important guide to Soviet thinking and Soviet intentions, one cannot move directly from a reading of Soviet doctrine to conclusions about policy.

The Making
of Policy    The possibility of major shifts in Soviet policy has been
one of the most contentious issues in Western debates
about the Soviet Union. Some have argued that under
the post-Brezhnev leadership policy will continue much as before, either
because major changes are systemically impossible, or because policy
has been based on a consensus rooted in the Party-State apparatus.
Others have argued that the pressures for major changes in policy are
very powerful, and that the Soviet system possesses the capacity to meet
new challenges of the kind, for example, posed by declining economic
performance. These issues are far too large to examine in detail here, but
they are obviously relevant to Soviet defense policy in the 1980s.

In order to assess the possibility of a shift of resources away from
defense, it is important to understand the position of the defense sector
in the Soviet system. Since the years of the First Five Year Plan, Soviet
leaders have given high priority to the creation of military power, and
this priority has become institutionalized in the structure of the Soviet
state. The defense sector has enjoyed a privileged position in the
economy, not merely in the allocation of resources, but also in its
institutional arrangements, which are designed to shield it from shortcomings elsewhere in the economy. The organization of the defense
sector has a marked influence on the patterns of Soviet weapons
development and production: Institutional stability in military research
and development appears to generate pressure for follow-on systems;
defense production is less prone than American to the "feast or famine"
syndrome. The defense sector shows signs of a strong bureaucratic
momentum.

The high priority given to defense is embedded not only in Soviet
institutions, but also in Soviet political culture. The military burden is
heavy, but the legitimacy of the defense effort appears to be high. The
armed forces stand as a symbol of national power and integrity. This
symbolic appeal is strengthened by the very extensive "military–
patriotic education" that the Party conducts. This does not glorify war in
the fascist manner, but it does cultivate patriotic sentiments and military
virtues and helps to foster the respect and esteem that the armed forces
appear to enjoy. This provides a favorable context in which to continue a
high level of military effort.[23]

Just as the military–political nexus is central to Soviet doctrine, so is
the relationship between the Party leadership and the High Command a
key factor in defense policymaking. There have been strains and tensions in this relationship, but it should not be seen as fundamentally one
of conflict. Although some of the mechanisms of Party control have been
criticized, the principle of Party supremacy has never seriously been
challenged. There have been disagreements about defense policy, but in
no case do these appear to have taken the form of a clash between the
High Command on the one side and the Party leadership on the other.[24]
The Soviet state has been so much influenced by war and the preparation for war that it is wrong to see the military as the driving force of
defense policy.

While the principle of Party supremacy is assured—and is reflected in the structure of the central decision-making bodies—the Party leaders do not appear to exercise the kind of detailed control over military decisions that Stalin, for example, enjoyed. There are two main reasons for this. One is the sheer complexity of the decisions, which makes it extremely difficult for political leaders to control all aspects of policy. The other is the diffusion of power that has taken place at the center since Stalin's death. In the Soviet Union this has been described as a move toward a more scientific form of policymaking, in which the claims of professional expertise and special competence are recognized.

The armed forces have been well placed to take advantage of this shift of power. In the various leadership struggles since Stalin's death, members of the High Command have proved useful allies whom no cautious Party leader would antagonize unnecessarily. The Ministry of Defense and the General Staff are institutions of undoubted competence and have a monopoly of expertise in the military field; there is, for example, no Central Committee department to monitor the military activities of the Ministry or the General Staff. Moreover, the details of military policy are shrouded in secrecy, so that discussion of specific decisions will be restricted to a very narrow circle. Even the size of military expenditure is kept secret, and this helps to fend off claims from civilian ministries for scarce resources.

For all of these reasons there is a very strong military influence on the formulation of defense policy, and this is likely to have an effect on the practical meaning given to such concepts as parity and equality. When the Party leaders make decisions about Soviet weapons programs, they presumably receive briefings from the General Staff about the military balance and the need for the new systems. The scanty evidence available suggests that the presentation of the threat will be made—naturally enough—in a way that supports the requirements for the new weapons.[25] The secrecy that surrounds the Soviet defense effort will make it extremely difficult for anyone to challenge the General Staff case. Thus the details of the policymaking process can affect the way in which doctrine is translated into practice. One result of this is that fears expressed by foreign governments about Soviet armaments policies will be seen by the Soviet leadership as artificially concocted for political reasons. As a consequence, the military balance becomes an object of manipulation both in domestic policymaking and in relations with other states; the arguments about the significance of the SS-20 for the military balance in Europe show how the definition of the balance can be a major source of disagreement in international politics.

One military writer has argued that only the armed forces' own research institutes can make political and diplomatic evaluations of new systems.[26] It is, of course, always open to the Politbureau to call on the advice of outside experts, but there is no evidence that this is done in making judgments about the political or arms control impacts of new weapons. It seems unlikely that the Ministry of Foreign Affairs or the policy-oriented institutes of the Academy of Sciences have a say in major decisions, even though they might be particularly interested in the political effects of the deployment of a system such as the SS-20 IRBM.

Secrecy also makes it difficult for foreign governments to influence the acquisition of specific weapons. It is usually only when testing begins that it becomes clear what the characteristics of the new systems are, and by that time the development may have acquired considerable momentum. This secrecy has the advantage, from the Soviet point of view, of reducing political pressures on defense policy, but it also carries the disadvantage that the political repercussions on other governments may be difficult to foresee and control.

Although the priority given to the military effort is embedded in the political and economic system, it would be a mistake to see the militarization of Soviet society as absolute. The legacy of Russian and Soviet history is not uniform; even today there exist many different political currents inside the Soviet Union, and the diversity is very wide if the views of contemporary dissidents are taken into account. Moreover, in looking at Russian and Soviet history one can see its contingent character and the openness of choices at critical junctures—between 1905 and 1914, in 1917, in the 1920s, and even in the 1950s, for example. Further, the militarization of Soviet society is a relative, not an absolute, phenomenon—a matter of more or less, not of either/or.[27]

The Soviet Union does face problems other than those of military policy. There has been a slow, but steady, decline in economic performance, and this has provoked intense debates about economic reform in the post-Stalin period. With the abandonment of terror as an instrument of rule, the Party leaders have had to search for new sources of legitimacy for the state. Greater effort has been made to secure popular support—for example, through the provision of better goods and services to the population. As a result, the priorities of resource allocation have become more complex than they were under Stalin. For these reasons, it is argued by some observers, economic pressures will eventually force a diversion of resources away from the military effort.

It is indeed true that the military burden is heavy and that there are many pressing needs toward which resources might be directed. Besides, leadership succession offers the opportunity for various political forces to come into play, and for the formulation of new political strategies. Some commentators have suggested that we might witness a new industrialization debate, comparable in significance to that which took place in the 1920s.[28] This might lead to a shift of resources away from defense to a more eager search for accommodation with the West. Such a possibility should certainly not be ruled out, although Party leaders who wished to reorder priorities in a significant way would encounter opposition from the High Command and from the defense sector, as well as from inside the Party itself.

But there is another possibility that should be noted: that the armed forces and the defense sector will be used to help solve the problems outlined above. This, in fact, is already happening. The armed forces perform important social and political functions: Military service is seen to have a major socializing effect on young men and to help in bringing the different national groups closer together; through extensive "military–patriotic education" the Party seeks to tap the deep patriotism of the Soviet people as a source of legitimacy. In the economy, the defense sector has served as the model for recent reforms, now that the prospect of a shift toward some form of market socialism has effectively been abandoned. This is an ambiguous development, for while it indicates the leading role of the defense sector in the economy, it also points to an awareness of the need for reform. It is not clear whether this line of reform will be successful. Nor is it clear what its political implications are. It might accompany marginal shifts of resources away from defense; or it might help to strengthen the political weight of the defense sector and enhance the priority of defense expenditure.

I have examined in this chapter the relationship between military power and political purpose in Soviet policy. The subject is a complex one, and it has been possible to touch on only some aspects of it here. I looked at the role given to military power in Soviet foreign policy and suggested that the emphasis placed on it is a consequence not only of the Russian and Soviet experience, but also of the international context of Soviet development. Moreover, I argued that the relationship between military power and foreign policy was a complex one in which the contribution of military power to foreign policy changed over time.

These complexities and changes are registered by the development of Soviet military doctrine. The military–technical side of Soviet doctrine, which has received considerable attention in the West in recent years, reveals how seriously the Soviet Union takes the possibility of nuclear war. But Soviet military doctrine can be properly understood only if its political and military side are examined in relation to each other. Only in this light can Soviet thinking on deterrence and the possibility of nuclear war be understood. Moreover (although I have not been able to argue the point here), if Soviet doctrine is viewed in this way, the differences between Soviet and American thinking are seen to be smaller than many writers have portrayed them.[29]

The fact that Soviet doctrine has changed is important, for it indicates that one should not take an "essentialist" view of Soviet policy, seeing it as springing from some innate characteristic of Russian culture or the Soviet system, impervious to phenomena in the real world. The development of Soviet doctrine suggests that Soviet policy involves a learning process, while the apparent existence of divergent thinking in the Soviet Union suggests that the process of learning has not stopped. Of course, what the Soviet Union is learning may very well be contrary to Western interests. But the point to note here is that an essentialist view of Soviet policy has, at its worst, two profound practical consequences: First, it means that one does not have to listen to what the Soviet Union says, because one knows essentially what it is trying to do; second, one does not have to heed the effect of one's own actions on the Soviet Union, because Soviet policy remains essentially the same.[30]

This is not to deny that Soviet conceptions of security and attitudes to military power are strongly influenced by Russian and Soviet history and by the internal structure of the Soviet state. But this influence is neither so strong nor so uniform as to inhibit all change. At the same time, however, these elements do make it difficult for Western governments to exert remote and precise pressure on Soviet military decisions: The policymaking process is largely closed to outside influence. Soviet policy has indeed reacted to Western policies, but not always in the way Western governments have wished. Foreign actions are refracted through the Soviet policymaking process, in which Soviet perceptions, military doctrine, foreign policy objectives, and domestic influences and constraints come into play. Moreover, the Soviet policymaking process appears to be rather inflexible; consequently, its ability to respond rapidly to external initiatives may not be very great. Western policy, to be effective, will have to be consistent and long-term. All this helps to make dealing with the Soviet Union very difficult. But it does not make it impossible.

All the indications are that the Soviet Union's security environment will become more complex as the 1980s progress. What course a new leadership will take is impossible to predict. It might adopt a more flexible policy to prevent that combination of its adversaries that appears to be one of the chief Soviet anxieties or to devote its energies to internal problems. It might adopt a more belligerent policy, seeking to use the military power it has accumulated, relying on that miltary power to ward off danger. Domestic problems, coupled with tighter control and more fervent nationalism at home, might even push the Soviet leaders in this direction. One thing seems certain, however; no Soviet leadership would willingly give up the gains in military power that the Soviet Union has made, at considerable cost, in the 1960s and 1970s. At best, it might be more accommodating in the effort to stabilize existing relationships. Western governments, if they seek such accommodation, should not foreclose its possibility through their own actions or through a breakdown in political communication with the Soviet Union.

## Notes

[1]On this period, see Julian Cooper, *Defence Production and the Soviet Economy, 1929–41*, CREES Discussion Paper, University of Birmingham, 1976.

[2]See, for example, Molotov's speech of February 6, 1946, in V. M. Molotov, *Problems of Foreign Policy* (Moscow: Foreign Languages Publishing House, 1949), pp. 31–32.

[3]For Khrushchev's speech, see *Zasedaniya Verkhovnogo Sovyeta SSSR pyatogo sozyva (chetvyortaya sessiya). Stenograficheskii otchet.* (Moscow: Izdanie Verkhovnogo Sovyeta SSSR, 1960), pp. 10–59.

[4]*Istoriya vtoroi mirovoi voiny 1939–1945*, vol. 1 (Moscow: Voenizdat, 1973), p. 258.

[5]Robert Legvold, "The Super Rivals: Conflict in the Third World," *Foreign Affairs* (Spring 1979).

[6]Major General N. Talenskii, "Anti-Missile Systems and Disarmament," *International Affairs*, no. 10 (1964), p. 18.

[7]The most notable proponent of the first view has been Richard Pipes, in "Why the Soviet Union Thinks It Could Fight and Win a Nuclear War," *Commentary* (July 1977); for the second view, see Raymond L. Garthoff, "Mutual

Deterrence and Strategic Arms Limitation in Soviet Policy," *International Security* (Summer 1978); and Robert L. Arnett, "Soviet Attitudes towards Nuclear War: Do They Really Think They Can Win?" *Journal of Strategic Studies* (September 1979).

[8]*Sovyetskaya Voennaya Entsiklopedia*, vol. 3 (Moscow: Voenizdat, 1977), p. 225.

[9]F. Burlatskii and A. Galkin, *Sotsiologiya. Politika. Mezhdunarodnye otnosheniya* (Moscow: Izd. "Mezhdunarodnye Otnosheniya," 1974), p. 287.

[10]*XX s"yezd KPSS: stenograficheskii otchet,* vol. 1, Gospolitizdat, 1956, pp. 36–38.

[11]D. F. Ustinov, *Izbrannye rechi i stat'i* (Moscow: Izd. politicheskoi literatury, 1979), p. 329; this is taken from an article originally published in *Kommunist*, no. 3 (1977).

[12]Burlatskii and Galkin, *Sotsiologiya. Politika.*, pp. 286–288. This part of the study was written by Burlatskii and has been published in English, in Fyodor Burlatskii, *The Modern State and Politics* (Moscow: Progress Publishers, 1978). Burlatskii has been a consultant to the Central Committee. But I am examining his discussion here not because he may be, or have been, influential, but because it seems to me to throw light on Soviet thinking about deterrence.

[13]V. A. Anfilov, *Bessmertnyi Podvig* (Moscow: Izd. "Nauka," 1971), p. 532. This, of course, is relevant to the current Soviet anxiety about encirclement. On this point, see also Raymond L. Garhoff, "Soviet Views on the Interrelation of Diplomacy and Military Strategy," *Political Science Quarterly* (Fall 1979), especially p. 400.

[14]For the speech, see Note 3; on the background, see *50 let Vooruzhennykh Sil SSSR* (Moscow: Voenizdat, 1968), p. 521; and Harriet Fast Scott and William F. Scott, *The Armed Forces of the USSR* (Boulder, Colo.: Westview Press, 1979), p. 41.

[15]On these debates, see especially Thomas W. Wolfe, *Soviet Strategy at the Crossroads* (Cambridge, Mass.: Harvard University Press, 1964).

[16]Herbert S. Dinerstein, *The Making of a Missile Crisis. October 1962* (Baltimore: Johns Hopkins University Press, 1976). From his study of the years leading up to the crisis, Dinerstein concludes that in Soviet–U.S. relations "the most grievous wounds have been self-inflicted. Exaggerated fears or misplaced confidence have produced a veritable catalogue of disasters" (p. 238).

[17]On this, see especially the article by Garthoff cited in Note 7.

[18]The most important statement was that by Brezhnev in his speech at Tula in January 1977, when he said that Soviet policy was "not a course aimed at superiority in armaments, but a course aimed at their reduction" (*Pravda*, January 19, 1977). In an article in *Pravda* (August 2, 1979), the Chief of the General Staff, Marshal Ogarkov, quoted this passage and wrote: "We have no other doctrine." See also *Sovyetskie Vooruzhennye Sily. Istoriya stroitel'stva* (Moscow: Voenizdat, 1978), p. 453: "Every violation of this [strategic] equality, the supply of new systems of armament to armies, is fraught with serious consequences: it will provoke retaliatory pressures and lead to a new spiral in the arms race, to a destabilization of the international situation, to new political difficulties."

[19]For Soviet discussions of the use of military power in this way, see *Voennaya Sila i Mezhdunarodnye Otnosheniya*, V. M. Kulish (ed.) (Moscow: Izd. "Mezhdunarodnye Otnosheniya," 1972), and Admiral S. G. Gorshkov, *Morskaya Moshch Gosudarstv* (Moscow: Voenizdat, 1976).

[20]These issues are discussed with reference to a considerable body of Soviet material in the article by Arnett cited in Note 7.

[21]Raymond L. Garthoff, *Soviet Military Policy* (London: Faber and Faber, 1966), p. 59.

[22]In his Tula speech, Brezhnev declared that "the defensive potential of the

Soviet Union ought to be sufficient so that nobody will risk disturbing our peaceful life. Not a course aimed at superiority in armaments . . . " (see Note 18). In the joint communique issued after Brezhnev's visit to West Germany in May 1978 it was stated that "the two sides consider it important that no one should seek military superiority. They proceed from the assumption that approximate equality and parity are sufficient to ensure defense" (*Soviet News*, May 9, 1978). These statements mark a change in Soviet doctrine, for the second volume of the Soviet Military Encyclopedia, published in 1976, contains an entry on "military–technical superiority" that declares that "Soviet military doctrine . . . gives a program of actions for ensuring military–technical superiority over the armed forces of probable enemies" (*Sovyetskaya Voennaya Entsiklopedia*, vol. 2 [Moscow: Voenizdat, 1976], p. 253). This may indicate a certain ambivalence in Soviet thinking as to whether equality really is enough.

[23] I have tried to provide a more extensive discussion of these questions in "War, Militarism and the Soviet State," *Alternatives* (Spring 1980).

[24] For an analysis of military–political relations, see Timothy J. Colton, *Commanders, Commissars and Civilian Authority* (Cambridge, Mass.: Harvard University Press, 1979).

[25] See, for example, the interesting account of a briefing given by General Staff officers to the American side at the Brezhnev–Nixon summit meeting of July 1974 by Joseph Kraft in *The New Yorker*, July 29, 1974, p. 70: "The Americans were disheartened. One of those present said he thought that Brezhnev had been 'sold a bill of goods' by the Soviet military. Subsequently, the Americans checked the Soviet assessment and discovered it was technically justifiable, provided all the optimistic statements made by American admirals and generals about the new weapons were taken at face value and interpreted at what would be from the Russian point of view the worst possible fashion."

[26] V. M. Bondarenko, *Sovremennaya Nauka i Voennoe Delo* (Moscow: Voenizdat, 1976), p. 41.

[27] For further discussion, see the article cited in Note 23.

[28] See John Hardt, "Military Economic Implications of Soviet Regional Policy," NATO Economic Secretariat, 1979.

[29] This is an important issue, precisely because of the influence that a certain reading of Soviet doctrine has had on American thinking. For a Soviet analysis that stresses that alongside acceptance of the principle of assured destruction there has been in American strategic thought a constant search for ways of using strategic power in a more active and offensive manner, see M. A. Mil'shtein, "Nekotorye kharakternye cherty sovremennoi voennoi doktriny SShA," in *SShA*, no. 5 (1980), pp. 9–18.

[30] I owe the idea of the "essentialist" approach to understanding Soviet policy to Alex Dallin.

# 16

## STEPHEN S. KAPLAN

## The Satisfaction of Operational Objectives*

Now that the USSR has achieved strategic parity with the United States and its conventional military units are more capable than they were in the past, the use of Soviet armed forces as a foreign policy instrument is increasingly determined by decision making in the Kremlin rather than by the USSR's ability to intervene militarily. Soviet leaders no doubt will be influenced by prior experiences bearing similarity to current issues. Foreign observers seeking clues to future Soviet behavior might also look to the historical record.

Soviet armed forces, when used as a political instrument, are an uncertain means for achieving specific objectives abroad. In the incidents explored here in depth, positive outcomes and their retention for at least a few years vary greatly with circumstances and with how Soviet military power is used. The realization of broader outcomes important to Soviet interests also is problematic.

China and Eastern Europe — The two most serious challenges to the USSR, which precipitated large Soviet political–military operations, were China's heightened hostility toward the Soviet Union in the late 1960s and periodic rebellions in Eastern Europe. The political character of Eastern Europe and relationships in Asia would probably be different if Soviet armed forces had been absent from these regions during the past several decades. Soviet military formations exercised almost continuous deterrence against major change opposed by the USSR. However, when general deterrence failed in Eastern Europe, Soviet military units were a virtual flop as a discrete political instrument aimed at compelling the reversal of unwanted developments or deterring other undesirable behavior. Moscow

*Reprinted by permission of the author and publisher from *Diplomacy of Power: Soviet Armed Forces as a Political Instrument* (Washington, D.C.: The Brookings Institution, 1981), pp. 641, 646–668.

achieved its operational objectives against Peking, but only after many months of Soviet military activity and a threat to wage nuclear war against China—and at an enormous long-term cost.

The Soviet military buildup east of the Urals and in Mongolia during the several years before the clash on March 15, 1969 did not result in conciliatory Chinese behavior but rather in more blatant hostility toward Moscow. Although the border actions and further Soviet buildup after the violence on March 2, 1969 did not provoke new Chinese border provocations and may indeed have been an effective deterrent, it was only after the Kremlin threatened a nuclear strike against China that Peking felt compelled to enter negotiations with the USSR. Even then Peking did not accept Soviet positions in the negotiations but used the talks as a hedge against preemptive Soviet military action and to buy time to build a favorable political environment in which to confront the USSR and increase its own military capabilities. Thus the USSR obtained relatively little after exerting maximum force short of war. By going so far to obtain a secure border in the short term, a dynamic dangerous to long-term Soviet security and global interests was set in motion.

As Thomas Robinson argues, the fear generated by this coercive diplomacy, which compelled an isolated China to enter into negotiations, also led Peking to mortgage its economic, foreign, and defense policy to create a greater military and global political base—an anti-Soviet global entente—that would make the USSR more wary of threatening China and increase Peking's ability to resist coercion. A decade after the Ussuri River clashes China was in political and economic alliance with the United States, Europe, and Japan against the USSR. Soviet attempts to intimidate China and the USSR's expanded air and naval presence in the Far East and Sea of Japan, which were related in part to the Sino–Soviet conflict, kindled serious Japanese anxiety about Soviet intentions and reinforced Tokyo's interest in closer relations with Peking and the acquisition of more capable defense forces. The United States and Europe became even more suspicious of the USSR when Moscow dramatically increased the capabilities of its conventional forces in the Far East at a time when Soviet forces in Europe were being reinforced. Improved Chinese relations with the United States and the European members of the North Atlantic Treaty Organization (NATO) and Japan caused considerable friction between the West and the USSR—the West welcoming a stronger China as a counterbalance to increased Soviet power and the USSR perceiving in this a global anti-Soviet entente.

In Eastern Europe military power was orchestrated to ensure subservience to the USSR and socialist orthodoxy. But the Poles stood up to Nikita Khrushchev and his cohorts in October 1956 and did not reform their leadership or hand power over to the Soviet-allied Natolinist faction. Movements by the Soviet army in and around Poland and of warships in the Baltic may have assured the loyalty and cohesiveness of the Natolinists, but this faction could not command the armed forces and remained an unpopular party minority. Nor is there a case for arguing that Moscow's show of force deterred a radical assertion of independence by Warsaw. Wladyslaw Gomulka himself was a stern Communist, opposed to liberalization and disposed strongly toward a firm alliance with the USSR. Having prevented Soviet military intervention with a unified following and a credible threat of violent and determined resistance, Gomulka assured further Soviet restraint by following *his* preferred course, which was acceptable to the USSR. What paid off was Khrushchev's gamble to back away militarily and give the Poles time to pursue their promised course. Moscow's political use of force was a failure, although the Poles could not ignore their environment and Soviet demands. But what Warsaw feared was military suppression—it was not impressed by mere demonstrations of force. Moreover, as Michel Tatu points out, Gomulka feared West Germany and the prospect of a united Germany at least as much as he did the USSR.

Nor did the deployment of Soviet units to Budapest during the first phase of the Hungarian crisis (October 23–31) or the buildup of forces and actions early in the second phase (beginning November 1) compel dissident workers and students to end their rebellious behavior and be content with promises of reform. Hence the new team led by Imre Nagy and János Kádár, who initially replaced Ernö Gerö, was unable to channel the rebellion. Had the dissidence been quelled early on, Nagy, like Kádár, probably would have been satisfied with mild reforms within a continued satellite framework. But Nagy turned away from Moscow completely after the insurrection and the USSR's new military moves. Kádár, who was more loyal to the USSR and more impressed by the Soviet army than Nagy, also was not emboldened by Moscow's behavior to try to rally Hungarians against the rebels and Nagy. Kádár merely took a back seat while Soviet authority and socialist orthodoxy were reimposed by force.

Soviet military demonstrations also did not induce effective bold behavior by Czechoslovak leaders loyal to the USSR in 1968, either before or after the August intervention by Warsaw Treaty Organization forces. Before the definitive action in August, Prague perceived the various movements and activities of Soviet and other Eastern European armed forces as theater. Alexander Dubček and his associates might have allowed the liberalization to proceed more rapidly in the absence of surrounding Soviet military power, but Moscow's political use of armed forces in the spring and early summer did not compel the reversal of developments distasteful to the Kremlin. The USSR's invasion and physical seizure of control, which the Czechoslovaks did not attempt to deter or resist violently, bought the Kremlin time, but more than 7 months passed before Prague was compelled to accept Moscow's political diktat. This was brought about not by a show of force but by a verbal ultimatum delivered by Marshal Grechko.

The lessons of the political–military operations orchestrated against Poland, Hungary, and Czechoslovakia apply to the actions directed at East Germany, Rumania, and Yugoslavia. The East German riots in 1953 were not ended by shows of force or by bolstering the will of the East German authorities but by violent suppression, like that in Hungary.

Nor was Tito coerced by Stalin's exertion of military pressure against Yugoslavia, or Nicolae Ceausescu by demonstrative actions ordered by Leonid Brezhnev's team. The danger of full-scale Soviet intervention caused both Tito and Ceausescu, like Gomulka and Dubček, to exercise self-restraint in their assertions of independent behavior; but this restraint appears to have been unrelated to the Kremlin's discrete uses of the military. Possibly, Soviet demonstrations of force caused other Eastern European leaders to fear suppression by and continue to respect Soviet military power; they might otherwise have inferred that the USSR was unwilling to resort to military means.

The restoration of loyalty and communist order in Poland, Hungary, and Czechoslovakia was not followed by the unraveling of the new regimes in those countries. In Poland, Gomulka remained a stalwart, conservative Marxist–Leninist. Decollectivization of agriculture, a less hostile relationship between church and state, and acceptance of economic assistance from the United States accompanied by a slow but sure tightening and then reversal of liberalization placed communism on a firmer footing, thereby giving the USSR a more stable and reliable ally. Still, Moscow had to consider that its failure in using the Soviet army to coerce the Poles and its willingness to gamble on Gomulka was taken as a sign of weakness in Eastern Europe and opened the way to the insurrection in Budapest.

Just as Gomulka had done with Poland, Kádár restored Hungary as a loyal Soviet ally and placed communism there on a stronger, national foundation. An important difference between the two leaders, however, was that Gomulka followed an increasingly conservative course and Kádár gradually introduced into Hungary the most liberal regime in Eastern Europe. The brutal suppression of insurgency in Hungary was probably a powerful deterrent to further eruptions of independence elsewhere in Eastern Europe in the short term. Such eruptions would have been plausible if both Poland and Hungary had successfully stood up to Moscow. Definitive Soviet action in Budapest gave credibility to the concurrent strengthening of the Soviet army elsewhere in Eastern Europe in November 1956.

The suppression in Hungary undermined the prospect of détente that had developed after Stalin's death. Yet if Moscow had been prepared in any event to enter into vigorous competition with the West over the then emerging Third World and to provoke confrontation over Berlin and the future of West Germany, the cold war would probably have gained renewed vigor even if the events in Hungary had not occurred. The restoration of control in Hungary and of Soviet authority elsewhere in Eastern Europe was important to Khrushchev's diplomacy directed at the West and to the USSR's strategy for dealing with Peking's demands in the late 1950s and early 1960s. But Hungary was a dark stain on the image of the USSR in most of the world and undermined propaganda about principled Soviet behavior and the Kremlin's pretensions of moral leadership. The blow to the image of the USSR and its allies was greater still as a result of the 1968 intervention in Czechoslovakia. Earlier, many outside of the USSR believed the Kremlin had become more benevolent;

and in the Third World and even in the West, Moscow had capitalized on U.S. interventions in Southeast Asia and the Dominican Republic to build itself up and put the United States down. But the August intervention encouraged Eurocommunism and the further fragmentation of the Communist world. Once again Moscow reinforced the perspective that west of the Bug River the presence of the Soviet army was an imperial one, intended to control countries next to the USSR at least as much as to defend them and the USSR against Western aggression. Although dissidence in Eastern Europe was probably not responsible for the further buildup of Soviet military power there, Moscow nevertheless had greater reason to doubt the steadfastness of its allies in a European crisis. It was clear that despite the web of economic and social ties that the USSR had created in the preceding quarter of a century, its position in Eastern Europe remained exceedingly fragile.

The invasion of Czechoslovakia and the announcement of the Brezhnev doctrine also led to Albania's formal withdrawal from the Warsaw Treaty Organization and frightened China into reassessing its relations with the United States and adopting a firm antagonistic posture on the Sino–Soviet border. To the extent that the March 2, 1969, incident on Damansky Island was related to this stiffer attitude in Peking—aimed at showing Moscow that China was not a pushover—the intervention in Czechoslovakia may have caused a major rearrangement in global relations unfavorable to the USSR.

Still, not to intervene forcefully in Czechoslovakia would have meant accepting the possible disintegration of Soviet authority in Eastern Europe. Had Czechoslovakia been allowed to establish a new socialist democracy and distance its foreign policy from Soviet aegis, the repercussions might have included an even more serious situation in Poland in 1970, an emboldened Rumania, an even more liberal Hungary, and growing dissidence in East Germany. With no Soviet armed forces in Czechoslovakia, both the USSR and NATO would have perceived the Soviet security system in the west and Moscow's ability to intimidate Western nations as significantly weaker. The intervention into Czechoslovakia precluded these possibilities and led to the establishment in Prague of one of the tightest regimes in Eastern Europe. The establishment of Group Soviet Forces Czechoslovakia reinforced the USSR's military posture toward NATO, which was not commensurately reinforced. Nor was détente very much delayed.

**The Korean Peninsula and the Vietnam War**    Moscow's cautious and subtle coercive diplomacy in response to conflict on the Korean peninsula and in the Vietnam War did not fail. Although largely the result of coincidence, U.S. behavior did conform to the objectives of Moscow's political–military diplomacy in these affairs. U.S. forces did not attack Manchuria after Chinese forces entered the Korean War or invade North Korea again in 1951; nor did U.S. forces direct violence at North Korea after the *Pueblo* was seized in 1968. Moreover, after the United States decided not to retaliate in 1968, the arrival of several Soviet warships around the U.S. *Enterprise* and its escorts in the Sea of Japan may even have played a role in compelling the task force's withdrawal. Finally, the 1972 presence of Soviet warships in the South China Sea was not followed by further U.S. bombing of Soviet merchantmen in the Haiphong harbor.

However, Stalin did not attempt to deter U.S. entry into the Korean War on the U.S.-led drive across the Thirty-eighth parallel to the Yalu.[1] Nor did Moscow attempt to militarily deter the United States from beginning the air war against North Vietnam in 1965 or to compel U.S. withdrawal thereafter. The 1972 Soviet naval presence in Vietnam was not meant to compel the United States to stop its bombing against North Vietnam in response to Hanoi's Easter offensive; no Soviet military response accompanied the U.S. bombing attacks in December 1972. The limit to which the Kremlin went in using Soviet military men on behalf of Hanoi was to dispatch personnel whose technical skills quietly raised the cost of the war to the United States, as Soviet fighter pilots did during the Korean War. Soviet military men in North Vietnam, in the role of willing hostages, also constrained U.S. bombing decisions. The Johnson administration's decision not to invade North Vietnam or initiate strategic bombing of Hanoi and Haiphong resulted from U.S. concern about prospective Soviet and Chinese reactions.

The stance taken toward the United States by Moscow after North Korean airmen shot down a U.S. Navy EC-121 in 1969 also was not followed by retaliation against North Korea, and after a brief interval the large U.S. task force that had been deployed into the Sea of Japan was withdrawn. In this instance the Soviet stance was conciliatory and Soviet warships acted cooperatively to support the search and rescue effort. Rather than being used to deter a U.S. attack on North Korea or even to compel U.S. withdrawal from the Sea of Japan, Soviet military units were used instead to induce the Nixon administration to recall its armada. This the administration did, although Moscow's diplomacy, at most, probably only affirmed Washington's decision.

The Kremlin's restriction of its objectives and use of force to coerce the United States in these conflicts in Northeast and Southeast Asia, though accompanied by success in meeting narrow goals, seems to have been poorly received by the Communist nations threatened by the United States and whose allegiance Moscow wished to retain. However, Moscow wanted to avoid confrontation with the United States and, in the late 1960s and 1970s, to foster détente. The Kremlin's prudence, born out of concern to ensure paramount security and foreign policy interests, created dissatisfaction among Moscow's allies. Had it not been for their continuing dependence on the USSR for assistance, the Soviet Union's allies might have openly denounced Moscow.

It is unlikely that Peking was satisfied by the deployment of Soviet ground and air units in northern China in late 1950 after Pyongyang's aggression failed and U.S. troops approached the Manchurian border. If, as appears to be the case, Moscow pressed Peking to realize the utility of North Korea's invasion of the South and assured Mao Tse-tung and his colleagues that a quick victory could be obtained at little cost, it is likely that the Chinese expected the Soviet army and air units to accept the burden or at least fight alongside Chinese forces when things did not go according to plan and disaster loomed. At best, Peking may have viewed Soviet behavior with resignation, believing that Soviet–American fighting in Korea would escalate to include U.S. nuclear strikes against China. Kim Il-Sung wanted far greater support from the USSR, however. It was apparent to him that Stalin was not willing to wage war against U.S. forces on behalf of North Korea. After Moscow's military withdrawal from the North before June 1950 and then failure to avert the occupation of North Korea in the fall, Kim and his associates could not have been impressed by the Soviet deployment to North Korea of easily withdrawn aircraft or even of Soviet army units after the front had been stabilized and U.S. objectives sharply limited.

The Kremlin's delayed military response to the U.S. buildup after the *Pueblo* was seized also was not reassuring to Pyongyang, and Moscow's behavior in the EC-121 affair and after the murder of two U.S. officers in the demilitarized zone in 1976 seemed to leave Kim disgusted. Only North Vietnam may have expected little political–military support from the USSR and been relatively content with the military support it received. North Vietnamese doubts that the Kremlin would be ready to act coercively to derail the escalating air war against the North in 1965 may have owed much to their witness of Soviet support given to China during the 1958 offshore islands crisis and to Cuba during the missile crisis, when Peking and Havana were greatly disappointed.

The displeasure of the USSR's allies probably did not surprise Moscow. At best, Moscow could have hoped only to persuade its allies that Soviet military power was limited and that stronger action was futile, although Stalin also might have tried to rationalize Soviet caution with the argument that the USSR needed to be protected as the source of international communism.

Although Soviet deployments in China during the Korean War reinforced the credibility of the 1950 Sino–Soviet mutual defense treaty, the absence of strong coercive diplomacy on behalf of North Korea gave the West more than a hint of Soviet prudence and a greater sense of optimism and confidence in Western military capabilities. This more positive outlook than the one held in the beginning of the Korean War was also based on the absence of Soviet aggression toward Western Europe, despite Soviet hostility to both NATO rearmament and the movement toward the rearmament of West Germany. Soviet deployments in Manchuria during the Korean War possibly made the United States more circumspect in its thinking about China in the 1958 Quemoy crisis. Moscow's minimal support of North Korea in 1950 may have encouraged the Eisenhower administration to act more boldly in the Middle East in the late 1950s and the Johnson administration to attack North Vietnam in 1964. The limited Soviet support given to Hanoi may similarly have made U.S. policymakers more confident about Soviet restraint during the 1967 Middle East war.

Soviet caution in Southeast Asia was essential, though, to the improvement of U.S.–Soviet relations that was finally made possible when the air war against North Vietnam was ended in early 1968. Soviet military intervention on behalf of Hanoi might have unified American public opinion, galvanized NATO, and allowed the United States to escape the international stigma brought on by its unilateral military intervention in Southeast Asia. Moscow's restraint in reacting to the U.S. military buildup following the *Pueblo* seizure and Soviet cooperation after the EC-121 was shot down also allowed détente to go forward, as did Soviet reticence after the United States renewed air attacks on North Vietnam in 1972. The nuclear nonproliferation and SALT I treaties, agreements on Berlin and West Germany, the development of East–West trade, and Soviet economic relations with Japan all might have been delayed or precluded by a serious U.S.–Soviet confrontation. The complications of U.S.–Soviet and Soviet–Japanese relations, brought on by Soviet military activity and accompanying statements during the *Pueblo* affair—delayed and restricted as they were—reveal what might have happened if the Soviet show of force in these incidents had been larger and more pointed. A superpower confrontation in 1976, had the USSR reacted strongly to the U.S. deployments following the murders in Korea's demilitarized zone in July, might have severely threatened U.S.–Soviet relations.

Although North Korea and North Vietnam remained dependent on the USSR for military and economic aid, their recognition that Soviet support in the face of U.S. military power was fragile and that Moscow's global interests were preeminent weakened their trust in the USSR and belief in international communism as it was interpreted in Moscow. Soviet behavior seemed to endorse self-interested behavior and self-reliance. Whether a show of force in support of North Vietnam would have induced Hanoi to openly side with the USSR in the Sino–Soviet conflict during the period of U.S. military engagement in Southeast Asia is arguable. However, Soviet conciliation of the United States in the instance of the EC-121 clearly helped undermine relations between Moscow and Pyongyang and pressed the latter toward improved relations with Peking. What Moscow did appreciate was the absence of new provocation by North Korea against the United States, which might have threatened superpower accord. The attack on the EC-121 immediately followed the release of the *Pueblo* crew, despite Moscow's limited support—intended as a restraint—to Pyongyang in the *Pueblo* case. Moscow's distance from Pyongyang in the EC-121 affair made clear that allies who might get into trouble with the United States on their own account could not rely on the USSR for help.

The Third
World

In the Third World the USSR did not obtain very stable positions as a result of its coercive diplomacy on behalf of allies. Also, the ramifications of incidents to which the United States, China, and European NATO nations were attentive included serious debits to Soviet interests. Nevertheless, most of the outcomes related to Soviet operational objectives in the Third World were positive in the short term, and the gains were retained for several years. Soviet military units were most useful in coercing antagonists of Moscow's Third World allies.

Moscow did not attempt to use its warships in the Mediterranean to deter an Israeli attack on Egypt and Syria in June 1967, although the squadron was probably meant to caution Washington against using the Sixth Fleet against the Arabs after hostilities ensued. In fact, the Sixth Fleet was not used militarily, and when paratroops in the USSR were alerted on the last day of the war, after Israeli units moved toward Damascus, the United States was motivated to pressure Israel against further movement in this direction. Although the United States had no intention of acting against the Arabs (at least when they were on the defensive) and Israel did not intend to assault the Syrian capital, coercive Soviet behavior did precede these favorable outcomes.

After the 1967 war, the deployment of Soviet warships to Egyptian harbors to deter new Israeli attacks seemed to be successful, and Moscow's deployment of missile crews and fighter aircraft to the Middle East in 1970 compelled Israel to end deep penetration raids on central and upper Egypt and, finally, attacks in the Suez Canal area. Israel was forced to face Soviet military resistance directly, and the United States again felt it necessary to pressure Israel by delaying new warplane sales and refusing to issue a declaration of caution to Moscow.

In the 1973 conflict, neither the United States nor Israel—after it had launched several attacks on Soviet merchant vessels and aircraft in Syria—interfered with Soviet airlifts and sealifts to Egypt and Syria; Israel did not move to seize Damascus; U.S. military forces played no role in the fighting; and, after Brezhnev coupled a threat of unilateral military intervention with demonstrative actions by Soviet airborne and aircraft units to threaten unilateral military intervention, the Nixon administration pressured Israel to recognize the cease-fire on the west bank of the Suez Canal, which Israel did.[2]

Coercion also did not fail in two essentially interstate Third World conflicts (Guinea and Ethiopia) and in direct confrontation between the USSR and a Third World nation (Ghana). Portugal did not attack Guinea again after Soviet naval vessels were deployed to West African waters. Although by themselves the global condemnation suffered by Portugal as a result of its attack on Conakry and Lisbon's fear of further isolation from the West might have deterred new violence against Guinea, it is also possible that Soviet gunboat diplomacy was a necessary condition for Portuguese restraint, particularly in the long term. Somalia was clearly disheartened by Moscow's political–military support of Ethiopia in the struggle over the Ogaden region, and Somali troops were forced to withdraw from Ethiopian territory. However, Mogadishu was not coerced by a threat of Soviet military action but was driven from the battlefield by Cuban and Ethiopian military men armed with Soviet equipment. And Ghana, after Soviet naval vessels had been deployed to the Gulf of Guinea in 1969, released the two Soviet trawlers and their crews that had been held in custody for 5 months. Although Accra probably would have released the vessels and crews in any case,

Moscow's naval diplomacy probably influenced the timing of the release. Moreover, if Moscow had meant to deter the Ghanaians from harming the crew members to extract information, its effort did not end in failure.

Soviet leaders could take less satisfaction from the behavior of insurgent groups threatening Soviet friends, although no ally that Moscow supported was placed in more danger by domestic opponents after Soviet help was received; indeed, each ally found its position substantially improved. Also, in each incident involving an insurgency against a Soviet ally, antagonists suffered significantly and had to limit their objectives to avoid total defeat. Only the Kurds in Iraq were beaten decisively. The Soviet air support given to Gaafar Mohammed al-Nimeiry's government in Sudan did not compel the Anyanya rebels to end their struggle or compel Ethiopia, Uganda, or Zaire to stop helping the insurgents. Those outcomes were obtained 2 years later, after Moscow's relations with Nimeiry had weakened considerably and as a result of a political settlement that conceded many of the Anyanya demands. However, the decision to appease the rebels, made as it was in a climate of poor relations with the USSR, might indicate that continued Soviet military support had been essential to the containment of the secessionists.

More effective was the air support given to Iraq to help suppress the Kurdish rebellion. Iran did not increase its military support of the Kurds and finally withdrew it completely. The Kurds, who had already been forced to retreat, were thus forced to end their rebellion. That Iran reversed its position as it did seemed related not only to Baghdad's agreement to a favorable border adjustment and cessation of anti-Iranian activities in Iraq but also to Moscow's expanded—that is, military—presence in Iraq and Tehran's fear of additional Soviet deployments and clashes between Iranian and Soviet military men.

Angola was still a different story. With the aid of Soviet and Cuban military support, forces of the National Front for the Liberation of Angola (FNLA) and the National Union for the Total Independence of Angola (UNITA) were largely driven from the battlefield; moreover, neither Zaire, South Africa, nor the United States attempted to interfere with the Soviet airlift or sealift of Cubans and military matériel to southern Africa. It is important, however, that like the Anyanya insurgents and the Eritrean and Ogaden rebels, the FNLA and UNITA were not crushed completely or compelled to reach a political accommodation with the MPLA. Moscow's use of military means frustrated their objectives, but neither these groups nor their allies were intimidated enough to give up their cause. They remained a continuing threat requiring substantial governmental concessions in Sudan and the continued presence of a large Cuban garrison and commensurate Soviet military assistance in Angola and Ethiopia.

With the partial exception of the Arab side in the 1973 Middle East war, no Soviet ally involved in the Third World cases examined occurring after the 1967 Middle East war was defeated by a Chinese or Western ally or an actor supported by a Western proxy. Nor was any regime receiving Soviet political–military support overturned. In the October war, although Syria lost some territory, Egypt at least achieved a political victory by crossing the Suez Canal and holding a position in Sinai.

But if antagonists of Soviet allies in the Third World generally did what Moscow wanted them to do, the beneficiaries of Soviet military diplomacy did not often react so favorably. President Nasser, for example, was greatly disappointed by Moscow's support during the June war even if, having experienced Soviet behavior in the Suez and Lebanon crises, he was not terribly surprised. From Moscow's point of view, massive Soviet arms transfers and the show of force aimed at Israel after the 1967 war were critical to the USSR's retention of strong relations with Egypt and use of Egyptian bases; by providing air defense to Egypt in 1970 Moscow was able to reaffirm its relationship with Cairo, obtain further access to Egyptian military facilities in Egypt, and, in 1971, negotiate with Cairo a Treaty of Friendship and Cooperation. But these gains were not lasting. The creation of a powerful air defense, increasingly manned by Egyptians, and Israel's respect for the August 1970 cease-fire reduced Egypt's dependence on the USSR. At the same time, Cairo was angered by Moscow's refusal to deliver the armaments that the Egyptians believed were necessary to end the "no war–no peace" status quo with Israel. Exposure of the Ali Sabry plot and Soviet approval of the failed coup in Sudan made President Anwar Sadat positively suspicious of Moscow's intentions. Consequently, in 1972, Sadat terminated the large Soviet military presence in Egypt, took over the military equipment manned by Russian units and the facilities being developed for the Soviet navy, and denied Soviet naval aircraft the use of Egyptian airfields.

Soviet military diplomacy during the 1973 war did not prevent Syria from losing more territory and Egyptian forces from suffering a military disaster on the west bank. Sadat and President Hafiz al-Assad of Syria were not at all pleased by Soviet military diplomacy or the level of military matériel they received during the 1973 conflict. Moscow wanted to associate the USSR with the limited Arab gains made early in the conflict and to avoid blame for the success of Israel's counterattacks and further thrusts. But the USSR did not manage to secure an image of being a dependable patron supportive of the Arab cause. Rather, Soviet behavior was perceived in Egypt and in other Arab countries as calculated to limit Egyptian and Syrian military capabilities as a way to keep the Arabs dependent on the USSR; hence, Moscow was held responsible by the Arabs for their losses. Arms deliveries and Soviet threats on behalf of first Syria and then Egypt were not publicly acknowledged by Assad or Sadat during or after the war. In fact, Soviet relations with Egypt deteriorated after 1973 until finally, in early 1976, Sadat not only denied Soviet naval vessels the use of Egyptian facilities but also abrogated the 1971 Treaty of Friendship and Cooperation with the USSR. Cairo's disdain toward Moscow's help in clearing the Suez Canal, offered to supplement the work of U.S. and British teams, symbolized Egypt's declining interest in ties with the USSR.

India did not reject the USSR after its 1971 conflict with Pakistan, as Egypt did after 1973. Why did the Indians, on the one hand, and the Egyptians and the Syrians to a degree, on the other, react differently to Soviet military diplomacy on their behalf? Most important, perhaps, the Indians, unlike the Arabs, won a decisive military victory, leaving no need for a scapegoat. Second, the USSR appears either to have done everything New Delhi asked it to do to deter hostile behavior by China and the United States or else offered this assistance preemptively. Finally, India apparently did not consider itself or its victory dependent on the Soviet Union; its self-respect remained intact and it did not feel a strong need to assert itself in its relations with the USSR.

Syria suffered a major military failure between the June and October wars when it was forced to withdraw from Jordan in 1970. Moscow gave Damascus questionable military backing on that occasion—unlike its response to Egypt 6 months earlier and to India a year later—and conveyed to Damascus a prognosis of doom. This Soviet behavior, Syria's 1967 war experience, and the loss of further territory in 1973 convinced Damascus of the limited utility of a strong alliance with the USSR. Hence, despite Soviet replenishment of Syrian arsenals and diplomatic support given after the October war, Moscow ultimately found its relationship with President Assad rocky. Syria did not offer the USSR increased use of military facilities to compensate for the loss of those in Egypt; Assad refused to sign a treaty of friendship and cooperation with the USSR; and Damascus took positions far from the Soviet line on several important issues. Also, after the 1973 war, relations improved between Washington and Damascus.

In Sudan President Nimeiry was gratified by the USSR's counterinsurgency support in the early 1970s. But even before the USSR backed an ultimately unsuccessful coup in 1971, Nimeiry had followed a policy of socialism without communism and had grown increasingly wary in his relations with the USSR. When Moscow then overreached itself in Sudanese affairs in 1971, as was to occur soon in Egypt, Soviet relations with Sudan deteriorated precipitately.

The access to Guinean facilities that Soviet naval vessels and reconnaissance aircraft gained did appear directly related to Moscow's political–military support of Guinea. But in accepting Moscow's protection, President Touré, like Sadat and Nimeiry, became concerned about increased dependence on the USSR. Similarly, Prime Minister Sirimavo Bandaranaike of Sri Lanka, after gaining Soviet military support in 1971, reacted to the demonstration of Soviet and Indian military power in the Indo–Pakistani war by ending criticism of a U.S. naval presence in the Indian Ocean and welcoming port visits by the U.S. Navy and American military and economic assistance. In other words, the prime minister sought balance in Sir Lanka's relationships when its regime was fairly secure, since the country's fundamental interest lay in its freedom of action. In the case of Guinea, the Kremlin was not allowed to construct a naval facility on Tamara Island, and naval assistance was accepted from Peking.

Moscow appeared to obtain firmer relations with the MPLA in

Angola and with President Mengistu's regime in Ethiopia. Moscow supported the MPLA and Ethiopian forces in their times of crisis, and both Angola and Ethiopia—formerly influenced by NATO members— maintained especially close relations with the USSR and Cuba. Both African regimes continued to be dependent, however, and may find this dependency less palatable if they become more secure. Before his death in 1979, President Agostinho Neto was already receptive to substantial economic exchange with the West and improved relations with Zaire and took a pragmatic view of the insurgency in Namibia. The Kremlin therefore had some reason to doubt the durability of cozy relations with at least Angola. But the USSR did obtain in these countries friendly, socialist-oriented regimes distrustful of the West, offering the USSR special entrée. Their identity with Soviet values is important. President Neto declared the MPLA a Marxist–Leninist organization, Addis Ababa accepted considerable tutelage from Soviet and Cuban advisers, and both regimes signed treaties of friendship and cooperation with the USSR. Moscow considers their sympathy to the cause of liberation in southern Africa another advantage. If, in the future, relations with Luanda and Addis Ababa sour over differences in policy, and military access previously obtained is lost—as has happened in other countries that have received substantial Soviet political–military and other support—these regimes might still be an asset to the Kremlin insofar as the West finds it difficult to deal with them.

A broad conclusion about the utility of Soviet political–military diplomacy as a way to reinforce relations with allies is that such support is appreciated and can help obtain access to military facilities and close political relations; but these gains are conditional. They depend on a continued identity of interests and harmony of strategies for the achievement of mutual objectives. When a Third World leader perceives the USSR as being overbearing or unsupportive, the question "What have you done for me recently?" is more relevant to him than "What did you do for me in the past?" In this context a decline in dependence on the USSR for national or regime security has often led to a serious reversal in relations. Moscow thus has been able to preserve good relations most effectively (1) with governments especially insecure and isolated from other sources of support; (2) when it confined itself to helping a regime retain power rather than undermining it or redirecting its policies; and (3) when the demands made on the USSR were palatable. The status of the Soviet Union typically has not been that of imperial overlord but of guest worker. Still, nations, or at least regimes, sometimes find the support they receive to be necessary and can see no option other than dependency for long periods of time. "Put all your energy into remaining independent," Charles de Gaulle advised a young monarch a long time ago; but, at least for a while, national leaders often are willing to compromise their independence to retain the fruits of alliance.[3]

Increased dependence of Soviet allies creates difficulties between them and the USSR that are well illustrated by longer term developments in their relations. In the late 1970s President Sadat allied himself with the United States and the West and sought from the NATO bloc armaments, economic assistance, and foreign investments as well as support for his bold strategy for obtaining peace with Israel and, with it, the Arabs' lost territories. Unwilling to provide Egypt with the armaments Sadat considered necessary for bringing about a military victory and opposed to Sadat's independent stance in the Arab–Israeli conflict and conciliation of the United States, the USSR became thoroughly estranged from Egypt. President Nimeiry also drew closer to the West and China after obtaining a peaceful settlement of the Anyanya insurgency in 1972, which lessened his dependence on Soviet military support. As a part of this realignment Soviet advisers were expelled from Sudan in 1977. In close entente, Egypt and Sudan vigorously opposed the Kremlin's political–military support of Ethiopia in the conflict on the Horn of Africa.

Although President Assad of Syria did not reject the USSR and did allow Soviet warships increased access to Syrian facilities, Moscow remained unable to consolidate relations with Damascus.[4] Relations with the USSR suffered as a result of Syrian conflict with the Palestine Liberation Organization in Lebanon, and differences with Moscow also arose over Syrian openness to U.S. efforts to achieve an Arab–Israeli settlement. Evidence of President Assad's independence and flexibility included increased U.S. economic assistance to Syria, Syrian arms purchases in Western Europe, and decreasing numbers of Soviet arms transfers and military advisers in Syria. Closer accord between Moscow and Damascus after the 1978 Camp David summit conference pointed up President Assad's continued pursuit of a strategy different from the one followed by President Sadat, not a newfound identity with Soviet interests or objectives in the Middle East.

After the Kurdish insurgency was dealt with successfully, Soviet relations with the Baath party in Iraq also became unsteady. Baghdad adopted a stance independent from Moscow in the Arab–Israeli dispute, forced the Soviet embassy to move as a result of suspicions about eavesdropping, opposed Soviet support of Ethiopia directed against Eritrea, exchanged oil for Western technology, and circumscribed and executed local Communists. Such positions eventually led to the termination of Soviet aircraft refueling in Iraq and to expressions of anger about unauthorized overflights. Iraq also opposed the Soviet Union's activities in Afghanistan and South Yemen.

It is too soon to talk about long-term outcomes with reference to Angola and Ethiopia. President Touré did allow the USSR use of Guinean facilities for naval reconnaissance and for refueling transport aircraft en route from Cuba and the Soviet Union during the Angolan civil war; but relations weakened and the use by Soviet reconnaissance aircraft of facilities in Conakry was restricted when Touré sought economic assistance from the West and the USSR did not provide the desired volume of military assistance. President Touré may also have been irritated by Soviet intrusion into Guinean domestic affairs, as occurred in Egypt, Sudan, and perhaps Iraq. The regime in Guinea-Bissau, which gained independence in 1974, shared with the USSR a similar perspective on national liberation in Africa and appreciated the USSR's support. But the new government in Bissau did not allow the USSR to direct its decision making; nor was Moscow given military bases or even routine access to local air or naval facilities. China, in fact, was a larger donor of aid than was the USSR. Bissau's ties with Moscow slipped considerably when, in the late 1970s, Soviet advisers became unpopular, dispute arose over Soviet fishing practices, and more Western aid was obtained.

On the other hand, Soviet relations with Ghana did not suffer long-term damage as a result of Moscow's coercive diplomacy in the 1968–1969 trawlers incident. Neither Ghana nor the USSR ever publicized the Soviet naval presence in Ghanaian waters, and the coming to office of the Busia government less than a year later and the 1972 coup led by Colonel Ignatius K. Acheampong may well have erased Accra's official memory of Moscow's gunboat diplomacy. Moreover, although relations with the USSR remained cool in the early 1970s, the new military government supported the cause of liberation movements in Africa and had difficult economic relations with the West. In 1975–1976 Accra gave support to the MPLA in Angola, Soviet–Ghanaian economic relations were improved, and military attachés were exchanged for the first time in a decade.

Neither did Soviet relations with Iran suffer as a result of increased overflights of Iran in 1973 following large arms purchases by the shah from the United States or because of Moscow's coercion of Tehran to withdraw its support of the Kurds in 1974. After Iran and Iraq came to terms in early 1975 the shah was prepared to buy arms from the USSR as a partial counterbalance to his weapons purchases from the United States, which were endangered by anger in the United States about policies of the Organization of Petroleum Exporting Countries (OPEC).

What were the wider ramifications of Soviet efforts in the Third World? Although U.S. policymakers awarded some legitimacy to Soviet actions intended to defend allies that supported international norms valued by the West, the larger the Soviet military effort the more damage was done to Soviet–American relations and the harder U.S. policymakers tried to follow policies harmful to Soviet interests.[5] The minimal Soviet military support given to Syria and Egypt during the June war and its immediate aftermath provoked no serious U.S. countermeasures and did not hinder improved superpower relations. Soviet efforts on behalf of Guinea, Sudan, and Iraq as well as the bullying of Ghana attracted only the barest attention and no noticeable U.S. counteractions. Apparently the United States was willing to accept small doses of Soviet political–military diplomacy aimed at ensuring the territorial integrity of nations, preserving recognized regimes, and securing Soviet assets (Ghana). In addition, U.S. sympathy was evoked by Egypt's suffering of deep penetration raids by Israel in 1969–1970, the encirclement of the Egyptian Third Army during the October war, and Ethiopia's disintegration in 1977.

Nevertheless, the large Soviet deployment to Egypt and Cairo's greater dependence on the USSR in 1970 caused the United States to take a more balanced position between the Arabs and Israel—one that both Nasser and then Sadat sought as a way not only to satisfy Arab objectives in the confrontation with Israel but also to reduce long-term Egyptian dependence on the USSR. Soviet military support of the Arabs in the 1973 war reinforced this dynamic by leading the United States to further induce the Arabs with support while strengthening Sadat's view that reliance and dependence on the USSR was a mistaken strategy for regaining lost Egyptian territory, Gaza, and the West Bank. President Assad, too, was drawn closer to the United States. Moreover, the Soviet airlifts to Egypt and Syria, the Brezhnev ultimatum and related military activities in the USSR, and the consequent superpower confrontation in the Mediterranean during the 1973 war raised a serious question about détente in the United States for the first time, although U.S. support of Israel also led to serious discord within NATO and contributed to the Arab oil embargo, which was disastrous to Western economies.

Doubts of many in the United States and elsewhere in the West about Soviet intentions were reinforced by Soviet military support of the MPLA in Angola and of Ethiopia. Because of these interventions the United States spent more on defense, strengthened its relations with China, and became more cautious in negotiations with the USSR on strategic arms limitation and several other matters. European NATO nations slowly began to react similarly, and in Africa a number of nations entered into an overt, though informal, alliance against the Soviet presence on the continent. In addition, U.S. unwillingness to counter Soviet and Cuban activities in Angola contributed to French military intervention in conflicts in Chad, the western Sahara, Zaire, and elsewhere. These interventions may have led Soviet allies in Africa to think more critically about the utility of Soviet military intervention to their interests.

The other side to this Western and regional alarm in Africa, however, was the credibility and respect accorded Soviet military capabilities. Just as the image of the USSR had suffered when Moscow had offered the Arabs less than full support in 1967, doubts arose in the mid-1970s about American will and military capabilities because of U.S. restraint during the Angolan civil war and the conflict on the Horn of Africa. China appeared to be a completely unworthy patron. Hence, the climate was ripe for improved relations with the USSR, although not necessarily for Soviet influence. Leaders like Joshua Nkomo of the Zimbabwe African Peoples Union (ZAPU) and Sam Nujoma of the South West African People's Organization were given reason to rely more heavily on the USSR for support in their insurgencies in Rhodesia and Namibia. The apparent ability of the USSR to enable its allies to emerge triumphant may have led these revolutionary groups and perhaps others to discount the value of maintaining closer relations with the West. Also, although the USSR lost its military facilities in Somalia in 1977, President Siad Barre suggested in 1979 the possibility of a reconciliation with the Soviet Union.[6] Appearances of Soviet as well as U.S. naval vessels in response to the *Pueblo* seizure, the Indo–Pakistani war, the October war, and the civil war in Lebanon gave many the impression that the Soviet Union could render U.S. military power politically impotent. Uncontested Soviet military diplomacy in support of the MPLA, leading to the defeat of U.S. and Chinese clients (FNLA and UNITA), and of Ethiopia reinforced the impression of burgeoning Soviet military power and decreasing U.S. ability to affect the course of Third World crises.

Moreover, although some African nations with close relations to the West disapproved of the Soviet interventions in Angola and Ethiopia, at least as many African capitals were not upset. Earlier the USSR had not been rebuffed when it had intimidated Ghana in 1969; the placid reaction was evidently made possible by the lack of publicity linking the deployment of Soviet warships to the release of the trawlers and their crews. Nor had the USSR offended African sensibilities by its naval support of Guinea and the PAIGC against Portugal, which had not been played up either. In the case of Angola, the considerable Soviet and Cuban effort mounted in 1975–1976 was offset by the assistance, though limited, given to the UNITA and FNLA by South Africa, the United States, China, and even Zaire (perceived by many as a U.S. client and even stooge). Still others found Agostinho Neto's social values and attitudes toward economic development and national liberation in southern Africa congenial and were therefore willing to ignore foreign intervention on behalf of the MPLA. A large number of African and other Third World nations were highly sympathetic to Soviet–Cuban support ensuring Ethiopian sovereignty and territorial integrity. In this, Moscow's claim of principled behavior was reinforced by its abandonment of Somalia, a long-time friend, and the USSR's consequent loss of access to Somali air and naval facilities.

Conclusion   Did the Kremlin use military power prudently or provocatively? Was Moscow sensitive to the ramifications of its use of force as a political instrument? Was the use of Soviet armed forces appropriate and well tailored to the USSR's operational objectives and larger interests? What difference did it make that some and not other types and sizes of armed forces units were chosen? And how significant to outcomes were particular military movements and activities? Standards used to obtain answers to these questions are the timing of Soviet military moves and consequent perceptions of target actors; the attention paid by Moscow to making coercive diplomacy appear legitimate as well as Moscow's subtlety when blatant coercion was likely to be counterproductive; and the extent to which forces of different size and character as well as varying activities were efficient and associated with favorable outcomes.

Invariably Moscow used military power with great deliberation. In Eastern Europe shots were fired by Soviet troops only in East Germany in 1953 and in Hungary in November 1956, after an earlier intervention and withdrawal. Coercive (as opposed to suppressive) military behavior in Eastern Europe was not accompanied by any violent action; instead, warnings and threats were coupled with attempts at discussion and negotiation. Violence occurred periodically along the Sino–Soviet border, but Chinese territory was not seized and held, deep penetration raids were not made, and engagements were carefully limited. The threat to use nuclear weapons against China was preceded by 6 months of lesser coercion and attempts at more traditional diplomacy.

Particular circumspection was shown when the United States was an actor. Before hostilities broke out on the Korean peninsula in 1950 virtually all Soviet military men were withdrawn from North Korea; the later deployments of combat forces into Manchuria and North Korea were unannounced; and air operations were begun surreptitiously and only over Communist territory. U.S. naval operations were never interfered with. During the Vietnam War the supportive role played by Soviet military men was also minimal and deniable. Yet Soviet personnel were well placed in northern China and Vietnam during these two conflicts to provide practical support to Peking and Hanoi and to help deter U.S. air attacks.

Despite the presence of both U.S. and Soviet naval forces in the Sea of Japan after the *Pueblo* was seized, the timing of the major Soviet reinforcement precluded even the appearance of a superpower crisis; and while the harrassment of U.S. ships was unexpected, Washington recognized it as an expression of displeasure about the proximity to the USSR of a U.S. task force, not as a threat related to the issue at hand. Moscow's use of only intelligence-gathering vessels and several destroyers and its cooperative behavior following the shooting down of the EC-121 a year later clearly portrayed a desire to avoid superpower confrontation.

In the Third World, where, in contrast to Europe and northern Asia, Soviet security was not directly at stake, Moscow used military power effectively and subtly, showing an ability to minimize damage to its interests abroad while applying its capabilities incisively. In general, Soviet leaders were adept at legitimating their use of force, timed their introduction of military means well, showed good sense in the types of forces called on, and did not gloat over successes. The Kremlin preferred a naval presence, covert tactical air assistance, logistical support, and the use of Cuban combat formations over the open deployment of Soviet military units in Third World nations. Moscow knew that it was better to create new political facts rather than risk issuing ultimatums. In the Middle East, Africa, and southern Asia, Soviet armed forces were used neither recklessly nor clumsily, but with prudence and sensitivity.

# Notes

[1] Had Chinese forces failed to rout U.S. ground units in North Korea in the fall of 1950, Stalin might even have accepted a Western reunified peninsula. After all, the United States had already obtained strong positions in Iran and Turkey, which also border the USSR.

[2] It would be a mistake to view Israel's crossing of the Suez Canal and encirclement of the Egyptian Third Army as a failure in Soviet deterrence. The

opportunity to carry out this brilliantly executed operation was not recognized until after Israeli troops were on the west bank.

[3]The quotation is cited by André Malraux, *Felled Oaks: Conversation with de Gaulle* (Holt, Rinehart and Winston, 1972), p. 29.

[4]Richard B. Remnek, "The Politics of Soviet Access to Naval Support Facilities in the Mediterranean," in *Soviet Naval Diplomacy*, ed. Bradford Dismukes and James M. McConnell (Pergamon, 1979), pp. 378, 381.

[5]I am indebted to the theoretical work on asymmetries of motivation and the protection of the status quo done by Alexander George *et al.* in *The Limits of Coercive Diplomacy* (Little, Brown, 1971) and by James M. McConnell, "The 'Rules of the Game': A Theory on the Practice of Superpower Naval Diplomacy," in *Soviet Naval Diplomacy*, ed. Dismukes and McConnell, pp. 240–280.

[6]U.S. Foreign Broadcast Information Service, *Sub-Sahara Africa* (January 23, 1979), p. B4.

# 17

## MARIAN LEIGHTON

## Soviet Strategy toward Northern Europe and Japan*

Moscow's targeting of SS-20 missiles on Japan and its warnings to Tokyo against rearming or engaging in defense cooperation with the United States constitute an Asian equivalent to the Soviet campaign of harassment and intimidation on NATO's northern flank. Not only do the patterns of Soviet coercion against northern Europe and Japan display striking and disquieting similarities, but the geopolitical and strategic characteristics of the two regions are also remarkably similar.

Norway, the key to the defense of NATO's northern flank, is one of the most strategic pieces of land in the world. Just 200 miles off the tip of northeastern Norway lies the Kola Peninsula, site of the Soviet Union's most extensive complex of military bases and headquarters for its powerful Northern Fleet. In order to gain access to the Atlantic Ocean, this fleet must cross the narrow, ice-free stretches of water along Norway's northern coast. There it is subject to constant surveillance by Norwegian and other NATO monitoring facilities. Norway not only must provide its allies with warning of a Soviet naval breakout before the fleet reaches the Greenland–Iceland–United Kingdom (G–I–UK) Gap, but it must guard the sea lines of communication (SLOCs) in the Atlantic by which U.S. reinforcements could reach Europe in wartime.

Norway's defense tasks have increased greatly with the steady growth of Soviet land-based air power on the Kola Peninsula and naval (particularly submarine) strength off the Norwegian coast. The Barents Sea, directly north of Norway, is a virtual Soviet lake, and control of the Norwegian Sea, to the west, would be strongly—and probably successfully—contested by the USSR in the initial stages of any East–West conflict in Europe. In recent years, the Northern Fleet's exercise area has been extended from the Barents into the Norwegian and even the North Sea. Moreover, the Barents Sea serves as a sanctuary for the

*Reprinted in revised form by permission of the author and publisher from *Survey* 27, no. 118/119 (Autumn–Winter, 1983), pp. 112–130, 133–134, 150–151. Copyright 1983 by *Survey*.

Soviet Union's ballistic missile submarines (SSBNs). Although the Yankee-class submarines must move into the Atlantic in order to be in firing range of their U.S. targets, the Delta-class boats, equipped with 4200-nautical-mile-range missiles, can strike at the United States from "home waters" in the Barents.

Japan, like Norway, lies in an area where, until recently, Western seapower enjoyed supremacy. The country is also vitally dependent, as is Norway, upon transoceanic links with its U.S. ally for reinforcements in case of war. Today, the Soviet Union is extending its defense perimeter in the Pacific as well as the Atlantic. The Soviet Pacific Fleet, like its Northern counterpart, monitors, patrols, and exercises in an ever-widening zone.

Vladivostok, an ice-free port off the Sea of Japan, is the headquarters for the Soviet Pacific Fleet. Just as Northern Fleet warships moving from the Kola Peninsula to the open Atlantic must cross chokepoints under NATO surveillance, so Pacific Fleet vessels going from Vladivostok to the open Pacific must pass through straits controlling entry to and egress from the Sea of Japan.

The Sea of Okhotsk, directly north of Japan, is analogous to the Barents Sea in its status as a virtual Soviet lake and as a sanctuary, test firing-range, and staging area for Delta-class submarines which, like those off Norway, can strike targets in the United States from Soviet "home waters." The Kurile Islands constitute a natural barrier guarding the Soviet Far Eastern coast from penetration by hostile naval forces. The Kola Peninsula performs a similar function along NATO's northern flank.

Further analogies between the regions north of Norway and around Japan relate to serious territorial disputes in both areas. The islands of Etorofu and Kunashiri (part of the Southern Kurile chain) and Shikotan and the Habomai group (the Lesser Kuriles), off the coast of Japan's northernmost home island of Hokkaido, were seized by Soviet troops at the end of World War II. Although on some past occasions Moscow offered to return at least some of these "Northern Territories" in the context of signing a peace treaty with Tokyo, it now calls the island question nonnegotiable. As a sign of its determination to retain the territories permanently, the Soviet Union conducted a military build-up there, beginning in 1978.

Japanese forces assigned to defend Hokkaido would be greatly out-numbered in a contest with Soviet forces. The situation is similar to that of northern Norway, where two Soviet motorized rifle divisions, total-ling some 27,000 men and outfitted with a sizable complement of snow vehicles, face a mere 500 Norwegian border guards across the 150-mile-long frontier.

The status of the Svalbard (Spitsbergen) archipelago constitutes a bone of contention in Soviet–Norwegian relations in some respects not unlike that of Japan's "Northern Territories." An international treaty signed by some 40 countries, including the USSR, grants Norway sovereignty over Svalbard and mandates it permanent demilitarization.

The Soviet Union, however, has sought relentlessly to undermine Norwegian sovereignty by engaging in illegal military activities on the archipelago.

Just as the Kola Peninsula looms across the Norwegian frontier, so Sakhalin Island lies beyond northern Hokkaido and Kunashiri. A heavily fortified region, Sakhalin contains, *inter alia*, at least two motorized rifle divisions, radar installations, and large airfields capable of handling Soviet Backfire bombers. (Hokkaido's vulnerability became manifest when a defecting Soviet pilot in a MiG-25 easily penetrated the island's airspace and reportedly circled undetected in search of a landing place.)

Disputes over economic resources in the waters off Norway and Japan constitute still another parallel in the context of Soviet policy toward these regions. Soviet–Norwegian relations have been inflamed by quarrels over demarcation of the continental shelf in the Barents Sea and over fishing rights. The shelf is also believed to contain sizeable oil deposits. In 1978 Moscow and Oslo signed a temporary accord drawing the Barents Sea boundary line west of the median that Norway seeks ultimately to establish. The accord also grants the USSR a fishing monopoly in certain disputed waters. The Kremlin is attempting to use this temporary agreement to prejudice negotiations leading to a final resolution of the disputed issues.

The Sea of Okhotsk has long been the scene of Soviet–Japanese fishing disputes and may contain the potential for a struggle over oil resources. Thousands of Japanese fishing trawlers have been seized and fined for operating in waters off Sakhalin and the disputed "Northern Territories."

Last, but certainly not least in terms of analogies, important restraints govern the conduct of both Norwegian and Japanese foreign policy. Far from acknowledging these restraints as signs of moderation, the Soviet attitude toward these countries combines contempt for their relative military weakness with threats of dire consequences should they abandon their restraints.

Norway joined NATO only on condition that no foreign troops or military bases would be allowed on Norwegian soil in peacetime, that no allied air or naval activity east of 24°E longitude would be permitted, and that no allied maneuvers would be staged in the northernmost county of Finnmark. The Norwegian government later forbade the deployment of nuclear weapons in the country in peacetime. In addition, Oslo has given prior notice of major military exercises on Norwegian soil and has conducted them along relatively predictable lines, with an accent on defensive rather than offensive operations. More recently, in compliance with the Final Act of the Helsinki Conference on Security and Cooperation in Europe, Norway has invited Warsaw Pact observers to these exercises. Oslo has announced forthcoming military maneuvers even if they do not reach the 25,000-man threshold dictated by the Helsinki accords. With regard to the strategically sensitive Barents Sea, Norway has restricted offshore oil drilling operations north of latitude 62°N to its own state-controlled oil companies.

In an interview with the conservative daily *Aftenposten*, January 2, 1978, then Norwegian Foreign Minister, Knut Frydenlund, reiterated that:

> We belong to NATO, but during the formulation of our defense policy we have taken as much account of the Soviet Union as can be reasonably expected of a country's government. Our base policy, nuclear policy, and severe restrictions on military maneuvers all constitute what in Helsinki terminology we call confidence-inspiring measures. And they are unilateral Norwegian measures.

Denmark, like Norway, forbids nuclear weapons or allied troops to be stationed on its territory in peacetime. There have been rumblings of dissatisfaction with this policy of restraint, however, because of growing Soviet military activity off the Danish coasts and on the edges of Danish airspace. If modifications in these policies of restraint are contemplated, they will result not, as Moscow contends, from "imperialist" warmongering or "outside (i.e., NATO) pressure" on Oslo or Copenhagen, but rather from the alarming Soviet military activity along NATO's northern flank.

The restraints on Japanese military policy were not self-imposed like those of Norway and Denmark, but were incorporated into the postwar Japanese Constitution that was drafted under American supervision during the Occupation period. Article 9 of the Constitution stipulates that "the Japanese people forever renounce war as a sovereign right" and that "land, sea and air forces, as well as other war potential, will never be maintained." In 1954 the Japanese government created the Self-Defense Forces (now roughly 260,000 strong) but forbade them from acquiring "offensive" weapons or operating abroad. The government also decreed that defense spending should not exceed 1% of the gross national product. The U.S.–Japan Security Treaty, signed in 1960, obligates the United States to come to Japan's defense in case of attack but does not impose a mutual obligation on Japan. In 1968 Tokyo adopted a self-restraining policy in the form of the "three non-nuclear principles—no manufacture, possession, or 'introduction' of atomic weapons" into Japan.

The Soviet Union's top priority vis-à-vis Europe and Japan is to preclude their coalescence into an alliance (in fact if not in name) that would work hand in glove with the United States (and perhaps with China) to thwart the Kremlin's global ambitions. While the USSR appears obsessed with fears of a war on two fronts, however, its own military preparations reflect a strategy to fight on two fronts. Having engaged during the past two decades in a massive military build-up aimed largely at Europe, the Soviets have embarked on an unprecedented build-up of their forces in Northeast Asia. Unlike the half-million or so Soviet troops stationed along the Sino–Soviet frontier—troops equipped to wage a land war with China—the new deployments in the Soviet Far East suggest acquisition of a capability to take on U.S. forces in the Pacific, neutralizing Japan in the process.

Although the likelihood of a Soviet invasion of either northern Norway or northern Japan in the absence of a generalized war appears remote, the towering presence of Soviet military power so close to these countries creates psychological pressures and doubts as to whether U.S. support would be forthcoming in the event of such attacks. Moreover, Moscow, which believes firmly in the utility of military power as an instrument of political leverage, has sought to manipulate its regional military prowess to dictate to the northern flank countries and, increasingly, to Japan on political issues. The Soviets want to bring about a reflexive accommodation by countries in both regions to Moscow's foreign policies and thus to establish predominant Soviet influence without having to resort to war. As William F. Buckley, Jr. wrote of this Soviet objective in another context, "Some dare call it Finlandization."

NATO's Northern European Command (AFNORTH) has its headquarters at Kolsaas, near Oslo, and covers Norway as well as the Baltic area—including Denmark, the West German state of Schleswig-Holstein, and the Baltic approaches. Under AFNORTH is the Joint Baltic Command (COMBALTAP), which consists of Danish and West German forces. This chapter will concentrate on Norway as the key to the defense of the northern flank.

Norway may be viewed as an umbilical cord linking West Germany—the European heart of NATO—with the United States. As the *Frankfurter Allgemeine Zeitung* has pointed out, "The 'front in Central Europe,' where four American divisions stand, can be held only if the northern flank can be covered. The [U.S.] Seventh Army can pose a creditable deterrence outside the Iron Curtain only if a security cordon stretches from the Baltic Sea outlets to Spitsbergen." Loss of the northern flank would prevent the reinforcement of West German forces either via Scandinavia or through the Baltic and would render virtually impossible the U.S. ability to resupply its European allies by sea. A substantial proportion of U.S. airborne reinforcements also would be unable to reach the Central Front.

Norway, as mentioned above, lies in the shadow of the Kola Peninsula. The 400-mile stretch of the Barents Sea from the North Cape (situated on an island off the northernmost Norwegian province of Finnmark) to the Svalbard Archipelago constitutes a major chokepoint for Soviet naval forces leaving the Kola area for the open ocean.

Norway lies along both the Soviet Northern Fleet's access route to the Atlantic and along the Warsaw Pact's maritime route to the Baltic via the North Sea. The Arctic Ocean between northern Norway and Svalbard is warmed by the Gulf Stream and offers the Soviet fleet year-round access to European waters. As the experience of World War II indicates, however, hostile forces in northern Norway can harass Soviet naval operations out of Kola, while enemy concentrations in southern Norway can hinder Warsaw Pact movements through the Baltic exits.

Denmark's strategic importance to the northern flank lies both in its role as a bridge between Norway and the NATO countries on the Central Front (especially Germany) and as the guardian of the Belts and Sounds (notably the Oresund Strait between Denmark and Sweden, the

Kattegat and the Skaggerak) leading from the Baltic to the North Sea and the Atlantic. The latter role also bolsters the defense of southern Norway, thus allowing Norwegian defense forces to concentrate on northern Norway.

As I have written elsewhere,[1] it is useful to speak of two military theatres impinging on Norway: the "northern theatre," where Soviet naval forces based on the Kola Peninsula would try in wartime to disrupt the reinforcement of Norway by its NATO allies and to neutralize air and naval bases and electronic surveillance systems, and the "southern theatre," where the Soviet Union's Baltic Fleet and armies based in the Leningrad Military District could attempt to block the Baltic approaches and hamper the movements of West German troops assigned to aid Norway.

Norway is the only NATO country besides Turkey that has a common border with the USSR. The 150-mile border results from a Soviet–Finnish treaty of 1947, by which Finland ceded territory lost in wartime as well as additional land along what is now the Norwegian–Soviet frontier.[2] At the time the common frontier was created, Norway's security was not seriously at stake because U.S. and British maritime supremacy in the waters around northern Europe was unchallenged. The enormous growth of the Soviet Northern Fleet and its transformation from a coastal defense force into a blue-water fleet (along with the rest of Moscow's navy) has irrevocably altered the security environment along NATO's entire northern flank. In the view of many observers, the preponderance of Soviet military power on the Kola Peninsula and the surrounding seas has placed Norway and her Scandinavian neighbors effectively behind the Soviet front lines.

An emerging factor of great significance for the strategic environment in northern Europe is Moscow's interest in exploring the feasibility of military operations against North America under the polar ice-cap. In order to carry out submarine probes in this area, the Soviet Union will guard jealously its strategic prerogatives in the north European seas. These seas lie along the shortest direct route between the USSR and the United States.

Japan, like Norway, lies in an area where, until recently, Western seapower enjoyed supremacy. The country also is vitally dependent, as is Norway, upon transoceanic links with its U.S. ally for reinforcements in case of war (as well as for peacetime supplies of food from the West and oil from the Middle East).

The Sea of Japan was a virtual preserve of the U.S. navy for more than 25 years, and General Douglas MacArthur's famous landing at Inchon—a turning point in the Korean war—probably would have been impossible were it not for control of this sea and of various islands off the North Korean coast. Today, Soviet naval combatants use the Sea of Japan for sea trials. By contrast, the United States has denuded its naval forces in the Pacific by transferring ships to the Indian Ocean in the aftermath of the crisis in Iran and Afghanistan.

Soviet naval vessels crossing from the Pacific Fleet headquarters at Vladivostok to the open ocean, face geographical obstacles similar to those confronting warships en route from the Kola Peninsula to the open Atlantic. In both instances, these consist of chokepoints subject to surveillance by unfriendly powers. En route from Vladivostok to the open Pacific are three sets of straits around the edges of the Sea of Japan. The Soya (or La Perouse) Strait runs between Sakhalin (part of the USSR) and the northernmost Japanese island of Hokkaido and separates the Sea of Japan from the Sea of Okhotsk. The Tsugaru Strait lies between Hokkaido and the main Japanese island of Honshu. The Tsushima Strait (together with the Korea Strait) runs between Japan and South Korea and separates the Sea of Japan from the East China Sea. The strategic importance of all these waterways for the USSR is so great that Japan's recent announcement that it would mine or otherwise blockade them in a crisis situation set off an international war of words between Moscow and Tokyo.

General Edward C. Meyer, the U.S. Army Chief of Staff, has likened Japan to a cork in a bottle that holds back a massive surge of Soviet warships from Vladivostok to the Pacific (and Indian) Ocean. Iceland plays an analogous role on NATO's northern flank by "corking" a potential flood of Soviet submarines from their Kola bases into the open Atlantic. When Japanese Prime Minister Yasuhiro Nakasone declared his intention of turning his country into an "unsinkable aircraft carrier," he was using another phrase long applied to Iceland.

The extensive presence of Soviet submarines, particularly of the nuclear variety, in the waters off northern Europe and Japan raises serious questions about the feasibility of sending U.S. aircraft carriers to do battle along the periphery of the USSR. The carriers and their escorts would be subject to withering fire from the Soviet submarines as well as from Soviet land-based airpower.

While much attention in recent strategic discussions has focused on Vladivostok, the importance of Petropavlovsk, a key submarine base for the Soviet Pacific Fleet, has received less notice. Petropavlovsk lies on the Kamchatka Peninsula, just north of the Kurile Islands. Like the Northern Fleet bases on the Kola Peninsula, Petropavlovsk offers access to the open ocean through waters that are navigable all year round with the help of icebreakers. Submarines from Petropavlovsk and from adjacent Talinskaya Bay can deploy into the open Pacific without crossing the straits around the Sea of Japan, but they would be under surveillance by U.S. installations on the Aleutian Islands and Alaska.

The Soviet Union is pressing for the permanent stationing of submarines and surface warships at Cam Ranh Bay in Vietnam, from where they could also reach the Pacific without passing through narrow chokepoints.[3] As the USSR increases its access to naval and air bases in Indochina and steps up its reconnaissance flights along the Chinese coast, it will be able to forge a ring around Japan as solid as that around Norway.

Petropavlovsk is also a major port and naval base on the northern sea route. The military as well as economic potential of this route has been greatly enhanced in recent years with the USSR's use of atomic-powered icebreakers to keep the passage open. The Kremlin is anchoring both ends of the northern sea route with military strongholds. This process is virtually complete at the European end and is based on the Kola Peninsula.

Even when one allows for Russia's alleged paranoia where defense is concerned, the build-up on the Kola Peninusla far exceeds the requirements for a strictly defensive role ("unless one accepts 'defense in depth' in terms of a secured and enlarged geographic zone and the domination of contiguous waters").[4] The naval and air components of the build-up in particular reflect the Soviet posture of forward deployment. Also of great significance are the accelerating emplacement of infrastructure that is applicable for both military and economic purposes and the drive to promote colonization, industrialization, transportation, and communications links and the overall economic modernization of the Kola region. This activity, in turn, should be viewed in combination with the ambitious new "virgin lands" program, an attempt to raise agricultural yields by 50% as well as to consolidate small towns into larger cities and to speed industrialization in the vast "non-black-earth zone" stretching from the Arctic frontier southward beyond Moscow and from the Baltic states westward to the Urals. The total picture is one of building a secure rear base for defense in depth as well as for possible thrusts beyond the northern and Baltic boundaries.

The Soviets have enlisted Finland's assistance (as a partner in joint industrial projects and a source of manpower and financial largesse for the building of militarily-applicable infrastructure) in developing the northwestern corner of the USSR, including the Soviet–Finnish border region.

Since the beginning of World War II, the population of the Kola Peninsula and Murmansk Oblast has more than tripled—from about 300,000 to one million—and the growth continues. Murmansk, the world's largest city north of the Arctic Circle, is the terminus of a railway line from Leningrad and of the North-East Passage across the Arctic. In addition to the warships that use Murmansk as a point of egress, the numerous fishing trawlers, merchant vessels, and other civilian ships operating out of Murmansk and nearby Arkhangelsk, could be used as troop carriers to help launch a surprise attack on NATO's northern flank.

Murmansk Oblast was enlarged at the end of World War II with incorporation of the city of Pechenga (the former Finnish Petsamo). An ice-free port on the Barents Sea, it serves as a principal home port for Northern Fleet warships, a base for a Soviet naval infantry brigade, and an exercise area for Soviet amphibious units. It is also the northern terminus of an Arctic highway.

Shipbuilding and repair—largely military-related—is a major economic activity in and around the Kola Peninsula. It has been said, for example, that the submarine yards at Severodvinsk alone have an annual output equal to that of all U.S. submarine-building facilities combined.

The military build-up on the Kola Peninsula apparently results from the discovery during World War II of serious vulnerabilities in that sector. The "Great Patriotic War" also indicated the great need for coordination between the Soviet Union's northern and Baltic-based military forces. Weakness in this sphere nearly cost Russia the war and has now been corrected. For instance, recent enlargement of the Baltic–White Sea Canal has dramatically improved Soviet ability to coordinate the activities of the Northern and Baltic fleets, as well as to facilitate transit between the Kola bases and the naval maintenance and repair facilities in the Leningrad area, without sailing either around Norway or through the Baltic straits under the eye of Danish coastal surveillance.

These and other improvements in coordination among Soviet forces have resulted in the emergence of a northwestern theatre of operations (TVD)[5] as a strategic entity in its own right. Having incorporated the means of linking its Baltic, North and Norwegian Sea, and Atlantic Ocean components, this operational theatre presages an unprecedented danger for NATO's northern flank.

The Soviet Union's Far Eastern complement to the strategic bastion around the Kola Peninsula and the White Sea is developing north of Japan on the Sea of Okhotsk and the Kamchatka Peninsula. The Sea of Okhotsk, which is virtually encircled by Soviet territory, makes a natural strategic sanctuary and protective barrier for the USSR's Asian land-mass. Blanketed with an air defense network consisting of radars, missiles, guns, and interceptor aircraft, the areas surrounding the sea would be all but impossible for hostile planes to breach. Enemy sub-marines would be deterred by the fact that the Sea of Okhotsk is covered by ice for about 5 months of the year. Submarines would have to surface in order to fire their missiles. The Soviets, for their part, presumably use the frozen sea to practice the under-ice operations that they seem to view as increasingly important.

The Soviet ring around the Sea of Okhotsk has been closed with the fortification of the Southern Kurile Islands, which control passage from the Pacific to the Sea of Okhotsk (across which supplies from Siberia to Kamchatka are transported) and which are claimed by Japan. As noted, the quarrel between Moscow and Tokyo over these islands is somewhat similar to the dispute between the USSR and Norway over the Svalbard Archipelago.

The Kurile Island chain, extending from the southern tip of the Kamchatka Peninsula to a point directly northeast of Hokkaido, serves the Soviet Union both as a defensive barrier against hostile intrusions into the Sea of Okhotsk and as an offensive arm pointed at Japan. Hugging the eastern littoral of the Sea of Okhotsk is Kamchatka, which the USSR is ringing with naval bases (notably the submarine base at Petropavlovsk) and naval air installations. The eastern shores of Kam-chatka are washed by the Bering Sea, site of the recent sinking of a Soviet nuclear submarine—one of many evidently engaged in training operations in the world's northern seas.

There are two naval bases on Sakhalin, at Korsakov and Aleksan-drovsk, and a third may be established at the port of Kholmsk. An important submarine base is located in the central Kuriles on Simushir Island. Submarines are built in the shipyards at Komsomolsk, on the

Amur River in southeastern Siberia. From there they sail to Nikolaevsk and into the Tatar Strait, which affords entry into the Sea of Okhotsk. Other shipbuilding and repair facilities dot the Siberian and Far Eastern regions, notably in the vicinity of Vladivostok.

Soviet emplacement of a military–industrial complex in the north-western USSR has its parallel in the Far East, notably around Sakhalin and Kamchatka, but also in the area around Vladivostok, where the new port of Vostochny at Nakhodka, on the Sea of Japan, is potentially important for military as well as commercial activity. With some two-thirds of its national territory in Asia, the USSR is determined to make its mark as a Pacific power, both in an economic and a strategic sense. Moscow is trying to enlist the help of Japan in tapping energy and mineral resources and setting up joint industrial ventures in Siberia and the Far East, just as it has sought the assistance of Finland in the northwest. A pipeline running from Sakhalin (where joint Soviet–Japanese exploration for oil and natural gas has been underway) through the 40-mile-wide Soya Strait to Hokkaido is one of the most promising projects from Moscow's standpoint.

Construction of the Baikal–Amur Mainline (BAM) railway, Russian colonization of the Eastern regions, and the overall industrialization and modernization of the area along the Sea of Okhotsk, spanning Siberia, Sakhalin, Kamchatka, and the Kurile Islands, are designed to create a vast secure rear base like that in the northwestern USSR and a defense in depth against China and the West in Asia.

In 1978, in the wake of an important journey to the Soviet Far East by Communist Party leader Leonid Brezhnev and the Soviet Defense Minister Dmitri Ustinov, a theatre high command was established to coordinate the activities of the Far Eastern, Trans-Baikal, and Siberian Military Districts, as well as Soviet units stationed in Mongolia. By all indications, the missions of these districts in wartime would be aimed not only against China but against Japan and the Pacific theatre as well. Coordination of wartime missions by a regional authority in this vast area is reminiscent of Soviet planning for joint Northern Fleet–Baltic operations in northern Europe under the aegis of the northwestern theatre of operations.

In line with the role of Europe as Moscow's prime foreign policy target, the forces designed for deployment in the European theatre traditionally received the greatest attention from Soviet military planners. The strategic importance of the complex of bases on the Kola Peninsula for the defense of the USSR necessitated the transformation of this area into a redoubt that inevitably overshadowed the small and relatively weak countries of northern Europe.

Just as the occupation of Norway and Denmark by Nazi Germany in World War II was the prerequisite for the subsequent attack on the USSR—notably Leningrad—so now the "Finlandization" or control of Norway by the Soviet Union would be a prelude to applying decisive pressure on West Germany, NATO's heartland.

The northwestern TVD, based on the Leningrad Military District and covering the bulk of Scandinavia, has an increasingly coherent structure adapted for offensive land, sea, and air operations against NATO's northern flank. Roads and railways have been constructed to enable troops to move northward rapidly from the Leningrad region to Murmansk Oblast. Domestic waterways similarly facilitate the movement of warships from the Leningrad and Baltic areas to the Kola Peninsula.

Soviet airpower based on Kola has been greatly augmented with the deployment of the MiG-23 Flogger, the SU-19 Fencer, and, most recently, the Backfire supersonic bomber which is capable of deep penetration strikes with nuclear weapons. The 40-odd airfields on the Kola Peninsula hold more than 300 fighters and long-range bombers in all, as well as some 20 medium-range transport planes and more than 50 maritime reconnaissance aircraft. Several hundred naval aircraft, including Backfires, operate with the Northern Fleet. Units of the Soviet Naval Air Force designed for antiship and antisubmarine missions operate continuously over the Barents and Norwegian Seas and the North Atlantic. Soviet MI-24 "Hind" helicopter gunships, which have proved their worth against the insurgents in the mountains of Afghanistan, now are deployed on the Kola Peninsula and may well be earmarked for missions in the mountainous terrain near the Soviet–Norwegian frontier.

With regard to the Northern Fleet, Soviet military expenditures during the past decade have focused heavily on the strategic submarine force, of which some two-thirds are with that fleet. The Northern Fleet is now believed to include about 70 nuclear-powered submarines. The Delta-class subs (each armed with 16 SS-N-8 missiles) have a 4200-nautical-mile range, while the Yankee-class subs (outfitted with SS-N-6 missiles) have a range of 1500 nm. Both classes of submarine use the Barents Sea as their principal area of peacetime deployment, exercise, and patrol. In wartime, the Yankees would have to move into the western half of the Atlantic in order to reach targets in the United States, but the Deltas could remain in the Barents as a reserve force for second-strike operations. Thus, the Soviets will insist on maintaining this sea as a strategic redoubt and will not tolerate intrusions there by NATO naval forces.

"The growth in Soviet submarine deployments [along NATO's northern flank] is awesome," declared Rear Admiral Ronald F. Marryott, commander of the U.S. airbase at Keflavik, Iceland. He cited a 300% increase in the number of Soviet nuclear-powered submarines alone that sailed past the Icelandic coasts during the past decade.[6]

Aside from its submarine components (which include more than 130 nonnuclear attack subs), the Northern Fleet has been strengthened in recent years with such major additions as the USSR's first aircraft carrier, the *Kiev* (equipped with up to 20 KA-25 "Hormone" antisubmarine helicopters and 12 Yak-36 vertical take-off planes) and the first Rogov-class amphibious landing ships—the largest of their kind in the Soviet navy. The Rogovs can accommodate both helicopters and hovercraft. Moreover, many of the Northern Fleet's surface combatants have undergone such modernization measures as the replacement of their gun units with missile batteries. The fleet has about 70 major surface warships.

Increased Soviet military activity in the northern theatre has its counterpart in the Baltic arena, where the USSR, assisted by its Warsaw Pact allies, has all but transformed this maritime gateway to Russia into a communist lake. The Baltic Fleet in times past was the USSR's chief naval arm, but it suffers even more than its Northern counterpart from geographical constraints. While the Northern Fleet must break out of the Murmansk area through a series of "gaps" to reach the open ocean, the Baltic Fleet is subject to a bottling up by Western naval forces that could mine or otherwise block the Baltic exits in the event of an East–West crisis. Preventing the entry of NATO naval forces into the Baltic and keeping open the Baltic entrances for Warsaw Pact reinforcements are important wartime missions of the Northern Fleet in the Baltic theatre.

As a result of the recent build-up (involving especially the growing quantity and quality of amphibious and assault landing ships),[7] the Baltic Fleet's strength far exceeds what local requirements would warrant, even if the Swedish navy were added to NATO forces in the Baltic. Evidence from Soviet naval exercises indicates, however, that the Baltic Fleet's operational commitments may now extend to the North Sea and parts of the Atlantic. The North Sea links the two vital areas of Allied naval operations on the northern flank and serves as the conduit for bringing British reinforcements to the Continent. North Sea ports are also major terminals for U.S. troops and supplies destined for the northern flank.

A joint Soviet, East German, and Polish amphibious force permanently stationed in the Baltic could attack Denmark with an extremely high likelihood of success. "This is not to say that the Warsaw Pact powers necessarily intend to do so," a British observer noted several years ago, "but it is a capability which they have chosen to acquire and which they did not possess before."[8] A 2000-man naval infantry regiment is attached to the Soviet Baltic Fleet.

Addressing himself to the Soviet naval build-up, Norwegian Prime Minister Kaare Willoch has pointed out that:

> It is of particular importance for the northern areas that the Soviet Fleet is a major factor in the Soviet Union's strategy. . . . We do not think that this build-up is aimed at the Nordic area, but . . . it would be naïve to ignore the fact that these military forces are there and that, objectively speaking, it would be advantageous for Soviet strategy to have control over Norwegian territory.[9]

The Soviet ground force build-up on the Kola Peninsula has been less spectacular than that of the naval and air strike forces; but that is cold comfort for Norway, which has a mere 500 border guards at Kirkenes facing two Soviet motorized rifle divisions (totalling some 27,000 men) deployed between the Norwegian frontier and the Murmansk railway. These units reportedly are equipped with an abnormally large complement of snow vehicles and are maintained in an extremely high state of readiness. They are supported by Scud surface-to-surface missiles, by SAM-4 antiaircraft missiles, and by an army artillery regiment. There are at least five Soviet divisions deployed on the Kola Peninsula, in addition to the two divisions along the border. The total number of troops in place would thus be at least 70,000. Other contingents that can be brought to bear on Kola include at least three airborne divisions, a naval infantry brigade (based at Pechenga) of 3000–4000 men, and so-called naval pioneers, consisting largely of demolition experts and frogmen. Moreover, the ground and air forces in the region can be speedily reinforced with the addition of six more motorized rifle divisions and an airborne division from the Leningrad Military District. Still other sizable reinforcements could reach the Kola Peninsula within 2 weeks from the Moscow Military District.

The Soviets clearly are capable of launching a *blitzkrieg* against Norway not only from the Kola Peninsula but also across Finland and northern Sweden. The Norwegians almost certainly would have to yield Finnmark and fall back upon the province of Troms, immediately to the south, while awaiting NATO reinforcements to regain the lost territory. However, if the Soviets succeeded in seizing Norwegian coastal bases before the reinforcements arrived, Backfires could be flown from there to attack incoming NATO convoys.

A new challenge to the northern flank arose in 1976 with the stationing in the Baltic Sea of six Soviet Golf-class submarines, each carrying three SS-N-5 missiles with a 750-mile range. Since Soviet submarines in the Barents Sea can deliver nuclear strikes against northern European targets, the Baltic-based subs probably are intended chiefly for purposes of intimidation—although they also bolster the Warsaw Pact's theatre nuclear strike force. When the submarines (which are diesel-powered) first appeared in the Baltic, littoral countries assumed that they were on temporary maneuvers or were en route to nearby repair facilities. When it became clear that they were permanent launching platforms for atomic warheads, both NATO and Swedish officials protested to the Kremlin. The Swedish cited Soviet hypocrisy in deploying such weapons in an area that Moscow advocates as a "sea of peace and cooperation."

The deployment of Soviet mobile, land-based SS-20 nuclear missiles, beginning in 1977, represents perhaps the greatest threat to date to NATO's northern flank (and to all of Western Europe and Japan). The Kremlin has given short shrift to NATO's concerns. When U.S. arms control negotiator Paul Nitze complained to his Soviet counterpart, Yulii Kvitsinsky, that the 3000-mile-range SS-20s could strike as far north as northern Norway, Kvitsinsky first denied the charge and then declared contemptuously, "So why should you worry if we kill a few reindeer?"[10]

A development worth watching with respect to NATO's northern flank is the construction in Rostock, East Germany, of a site for Soviet SA-5 "Gammon" antiaircraft missiles. According to a recent article in the *Wall Street Journal*, the SA-5 can be armed with a nuclear warhead. If these missiles, which already form part of the USSR's air defense network, are placed in Eastern Europe, the consequences for NATO's northern flank would be grim. Western military strategists believe that SA-5s in East Germany could be used to "fight Western reconnaissance planes of the AWACS E 3-A type, to achieve air superiority in the western Baltic in case the straits to the North Sea should be opened in a war, and to threaten ground targets in north Germany with nuclear weapons."[11]

Moscow's military build-up vis-à-vis northern Europe has its counterpart in Northeast Asia, where Japan is both literally and figuratively as much under the gun as are Norway and her Scandinavian neighbors. Forward deployment is the chief characteristic of Soviet military configurations in both regions. As former U.S. Defense Secretary Harold Brown noted during a 1979 visit to Tokyo, the Russians are "pushing at the edge in northeast Asia . . . as elsewhere."[12]

In line with its strategy of achieving readiness not only for a land war with China, but also for a Pacific conflict, the USSR has dramatically expanded and upgraded its Pacific Fleet. Moscow's policy of according preferential treatment to the Northern Fleet in terms of delivery schedules and provisions of top-class equipment has been modified. Partly because the Northern Fleet already possesses the newest Soviet naval systems, and partly because Moscow is concerned about the possible emergence of a U.S.–Japanese–Chinese coalition in Asia, modernization of the Pacific Fleet has assumed a high priority. The fleet contains roughly 600 combat ships. These include about 135 submarines (a sixfold increase in one decade), of which some 65 are nuclear-powered. According to Western military sources in Japan, the fleet is receiving one or two new SSBNs every year.[13]

More than 70 major surface combatants, well over 350 planes and helicopters, 150 amphibious units, and a 6000-man naval infantry (Marine) force, belong to the Pacific Fleet. In the past few years the aircraft carrier *Minsk* (designed for antisubmarine warfare), Rogov-class amphibious assault ships, two missile-carrying cruisers, and three modern destroyers have been added to the Pacific Fleet.[14] The *Minsk* (together with a sister ship expected to join the fleet on a permanent basis) presumably will be assigned to protect the SSBNs in the seas around Japan during a war and has carried out flag-showing missions in southeast Asia.

The number of ship-days at sea for the Pacific Fleet rose from 7000 in 1975 to 11,500 in 1980, and apparently continues to increase. A permanent naval command to coordinate ship movements has been set up in the central Kurile Islands, with direct communication links to Petropavlovsk. Access to naval and air bases in Vietnam has extended the fleet's range into southeast Asia and the Indian Ocean and has poised the Soviet navy to interdict the sea lanes running from the oil-rich Persian Gulf to Japan in an international crisis.

Dwelling at length on the Pacific Fleet's capabilities, the 1981 volume of the *Far Eastern Economic Review's Asia Yearbook* noted that:

> Even if the *Minsk* group and its accompanying submarines may have problems in detecting and destroying US nuclear-powered submarines because of their quietness and high performance, it can demonstrate Soviet military power to the countries around the Western Pacific, the South China Seas and the Indian Ocean in peacetime. Ivan Rogov is an

amphibious assault ship capable of carrying at a minimum either some 800 troops or 40 tanks and landing them through its bow ramp or stern dock as well as by hovercraft or helicopter—new capabilities not found in the conventional Soviet amphibious vessels like the Ropucha and Alligator classes. Ivan Rogov, given air cover and anti-submarine protection, would be a useful means of intervening in local conflicts around the Western Pacific and the Indian Ocean, carrying out commando operations or simply backing up friendly countries.

Tokyo has watched the increase in Pacific Fleet strength with considerable anxiety. "The [Japanese defense] strategists . . . once thought only in terms of an attack from the Soviet Union on . . . Hokkaido. Now the growing weight of Soviet seapower exposes other home islands to danger."[15] Counterpoised to the massive Soviet Pacific Fleet is the small Japanese navy (limited in size by Japan's Constitution, which forbids the establishment of "offensive" forces and by the country's reliance on U.S. naval power for protection). The Japanese navy's largest ship is a 4000-ton helicopter carrier. There are no known plans to build U.S.-style aircraft carriers.

Moscow's build-up of naval strength in the Far East has been matched by an impressive growth of airpower. The total number of warplanes in the Soviet Far East exceeds 2200. Nuclear-capable MiG-23s, with a range enabling them to hit targets anywhere in Japan, have replaced older models of the MiG in the Soviet Far East and on Etorofu Island north of Japan. Fincers (fighter–interceptors), Bears (in both reconnaissance and antisubmarine warfare models), and other modern aircraft have also entered the Pacific-oriented inventory.

By far the most significant addition to Soviet airpower in the Pacific region, however, has been the supersonic Backfire bomber. From its bases on Kamchatka and Sakhalin, the Backfire can hit Japan with nuclear-tipped cruise missiles and return to base without refueling. Backfires have also been assigned to Soviet naval aviation, with a mission to interdict vital sea lanes in the event of war. It would be impossible for ships carrying reinforcements from the United States either to Japan or NATO's northern flank to avoid entering the path of Backfires based on Kamchatka or Kola, respectively. In addition, the great-circle aerial routes around the North Pole are within range of the Backfires.

Since 1978, the USSR has deployed SS-20 missiles east of the Urals. There are about 110 of these missiles there now, and all are within reach of Japan. The Soviets contend that if Moscow and Washington sign an accord limiting SS-30s in Europe, missiles above the agreed limit could be transferred to Soviet Asia. A Japanese Foreign Ministry spokesman called such a prospective transfer "totally unacceptable, out of the question."[16] But Soviet Deputy Foreign Minister Mikhail Kapitsa told his hosts during a visit to Japan that Moscow would deploy intermediate-range missiles wherever it saw fit, without taking Japanese opinion into consideration.[17]

Moscow's military build-up in northeast Asia has not neglected the ground forces. In mid-1981 the Japanese Defense Agency told the Diet (parliament) that 51 Soviet army divisions were stationed in the Soviet Far East—an increase of five from the previous year. According to the JDA official, 20 of these divisions were deployed in areas other than the Sino–Soviet frontier (15 divisions in the Maritime Provinces and the rest on Sakhalin and Kamchatka), and thus seemed earmarked for use in the Pacific theatre.[18] These forces have been upgraded both quantitatively and qualitatively. They no longer lag behind their comrades deployed against the European theatre in terms of receiving the latest generation of weaponry.

Soviet commentaries contend that Japan's defeat in World War II did not result from the atomic bombings of Hiroshima and Nagasaki but rather from the decimation of the Japanese Kwantung Army in Manchuria at the hands of the Soviet troops. Soviet military writers also glorify the victory against Japanese forces in the Battle of Khalkin Gol along the Manchurian border in 1938. Moscow's recounting of these battles evidently is intended to remind Japanese "neo-imperialists" of the "lessons of history." Applied to the present period, the "lessons" are that Soviet military prowess should be respected, and that Japan should avoid antagonizing the USSR.

The USSR has resorted increasingly to shows of force aimed at intimidating its adversaries and at gaining political leverage over them by demonstrating the hopelessness of trying to resist Soviet military power.

Most disturbing of all the provocative incidents staged by the USSR in Norwegian waters have been the intrusions of Soviet submarines into Norwegian fjords, evidently with the aim of spying on submarine-detection devices and testing Norway's antisubmarine capabilities. In view of their so-called "ninth of April complex," created by the surprise German U-boat landings on that date in 1940, the Norwegians are peculiarly wary of this kind of Soviet naval activity.

Submarine sightings have become virtually routine occurrences—as have Moscow's denials of the penetrations. On June 30, 1983, after Norway's navy detected a submarine (evidently Soviet) in Andsfjord, in the vicinity of the NATO base off Andoey Island, *Agence France-Presse* reported that this was the latest of some 230 alleged violations of Norwegian territorial waters by unidentified submarines since 1970. Some Norwegian military officers speculate that the submarines are on training missions. Other officers believe that the USSR wants to use the Norwegian fjords, which are exceptionally deep, for wartime operations by Soviet submarines, including SSBNs.[19] The depth of the fjords has frustrated Norwegian efforts to force the intruding submarines to the surface by means of depth charges and even missiles. A number of the submarines were prowling in a region not far from Norway's principal naval defense center.

The most dramatic incident of Soviet submarine probes in northern European waters occurred in October 1981 when a Whiskey-class submarine ran aground on a rocky outcropping near Sweden's top-security naval base at Karlskrona, on the Baltic. "Whiskey on the Rocks" was a symbol of Soviet contempt for Swedish neutrality at a time when Social Democrat Olaf Palme, a leading proponent of détente and disarmament, had just regained the prime ministership. Far from expressing regrets for the incident, however, the Soviets continued to send their submarines into Swedish waters—all the while professing their desire to turn the Baltic into a "sea of peace."

Japan, like the countries along NATO's northern flank, has experienced Soviet military provocations that are evidently intended both for gaining political leverage and conducting dry runs for wartime operations.

During the Soviet Union's worldwide *Okean II* exercises in 1975, four naval task forces took up positions around Japan. Then, in July 1976:

> Soviet warships sailed through the Sea of Japan and, via the Tsushima Straits, continued southwards past Okinawa. Simultaneously, Soviet reconnaissance aircraft from . . . bases in the Vladivostok area flew southwards on both sides of the Japanese islands to back up the Soviet naval units. It was noted in the Japanese press that this was the first time that the USSR had sent its aircraft to fly down both sides of the home islands.[20]

Maneuvers by Soviet naval task forces and flights by reconnaissance and antisubmarine aircraft around Japan have become increasingly frequent. The regular flights of "Bear" reconnaissance planes over Japan en route from the Soviet Union to Vietnam have come to be dubbed the "Tokyo Express." More than 150 Soviet warships cross the Tsushima Straits each year; the number passing through other chokepoints in the area has increased steadily. Moreover, Soviet intelligence-collecting ships called AGIs operate extensively off the Japanese shores. The large number of fishing trawlers, merchant ships, and oceanographic research vessels that ply these waters must also be regarded—as Admiral Sergei Gorshkov, Commander-in-Chief of the Soviet Navy so regards them— as integral components of Soviet naval might that can perform military-related missions when needed.

During a large-scale U.S. naval exercise in the northern Pacific in the autumn of 1982, Backfire bombers staged simulated missile strikes against two American aircraft carriers for the first time. The Soviet intention evidently was to demonstrate to Japan the vulnerability of the U.S. forces on which it depends for protection. In the meantime, according to the Japanese Defense Agency, Soviet warplanes have been making an average of 240 flights yearly just beyond Japan's airspace, thus causing the Air Self-Defense Force, as well as U.S. aircraft based in the country, to "scramble" repeatedly. The pattern is analogous to that along NATO's northern flank, where warning and reaction time in the event of a Soviet attack have been reduced drastically.

Moscow's provocative behavior toward the countries of NATO's northern flank and Japan might be expected to be counterproductive by drawing Norway (along with Denmark and even neutral Sweden) closer to NATO and causing Japan to step up even further its military collaboration with the Western allies. There are powerful hurdles to such developments, however—hurdles that the Soviet Union recognizes and exploits to the hilt.

First, there are strong neutralist and pacifist constituencies in Scandinavia and Japan. Although public opinion polls indicate that a healthy majority of Norwegians favor continued participation in NATO, there is widespread concern about maintaining the delicate "Nordic balance."[21] Thus, for example, abandonment by Norway and Denmark of their "base and ban" policies could upset the strategic equilibrium throughout the Nordic region. It is noteworthy in this regard that Norwegian defense planners tend to view prestocking, or prepositioning, of equipment for NATO's use as supporting rather than contradicting the "no-base" policy. Japan, with its "nuclear trauma," will probably be just as vocal about maintaining its "three non-nuclear principles" as Norway is about adhering to "base and ban."

The inherent difficulty that parliamentary democracies face in rallying their populations around a vital national defense issue which falls short of all-out enemy attack militates against the probability of major changes in Norwegian and Japanese military policies. One can imagine, for example, the tremendous political turmoil that would accompany a fully-fledged effort to delete the "no-war" clause from the Japanese Constitution. In Norway, the Labor Party and other groups on the Left tried repeatedly to prevent the Storting from voting funds for NATO's theatre nuclear force modernization. They came within a hair's breadth of success.

Financial pressures also inhibit greater participation by the northern flank countries and Japan in military activities with their allies. Norway, one of the few countries that adhered to the 1977 NATO decision to devote 3% of the GNP to defense, now feels forced to reduce its defense expenditures—at least temporarily—by decreasing the number of military conscripts and keeping at least one of its frigates in port.

A desire on the part of Scandinavian and Japanese businessmen to maintain lucrative economic and trade relations with the USSR constitutes still another barrier to major changes in the countries' defense policies in a direction likely to alienate the Soviets. For example, when Tokyo imposed economic sanctions on Moscow after the invasion of Afghanistan, Japanese companies, engaged in providing technologically advanced products for the Soviet market, protested vocally. Soviet propaganda exploited their resentment toward their government by emphasizing that the sanctions (imposed in conjunction with the United States) caused Japan to fall from second to fifth place among the USSR's trading partners in the capitalist world. The businessmen's fears that European firms had seized their share of Soviet commerce were thus confirmed. Fishermen in both Japan and Norway also have a vested interest in preventing a serious deterioration in their countries' relations with the Soviet Union.

Finally, there is a sizable element of wishful thinking among various groups in Scandinavia and Japan (including groups well versed in foreign affairs) to the effect that the USSR's dramatic military build-up is not really directed at their countries but relates only to the superpowers' rivalry. A corollary to this type of thinking is that bluff and bluster have long characterized Soviet behavior toward the outside world and that the Kremlin's offensive will not spill over from the propaganda to the military realm.

While the Norwegians, Japanese, West European NATO members, and Americans persistently attempt to divine Moscow's military intentions, Soviet capabilities continue to grow. The USSR can be expected to continue blending threats and cajolery to vitiate efforts by NATO Europe, Japan, and the United States to pool their defense efforts. To the extent that it succeeds, the Kremlin will pursue with impunity its strategy of isolating, neutralizing, and encircling the major political and economic power centers of the non-communist world.

## Notes

[1] Marian K. Leighton, *The Soviet Threat to NATO's Northern Flank* (National Strategy Information Center, New York, 1978), pp. 2–3.

[2] A recent article in the Soviet military newspaper *Krasnaya zvezda* (Red Star) took note of Soviet offensive operations in 1944 against the Nazis in the Norwegian–Finnish border area. As a result of these operations, "the enemy was driven out of the Soviet polar regions. Fulfilling their international duty, Soviet servicemen liberated northern Norway from the German fascist invaders." *Krasnaya zvezda*, 11 March 1983.

[3] The Soviet navy's access to the U.S.-built base at Cam Ranh Bay in Vietnam is particularly unsettling from Japan's standpoint. Cam Ranh Bay was the staging area for the Japanese fleet that decimated the Russian Baltic fleet in the Tsushima Strait in 1905, in the major naval battle of the Russo–Japanese War. Are Soviet naval strategists contemplating a Tsushima-in-reverse during a future conflict? Cam Ranh Bay has still another historical connotation. It was the Japanese move into Cam Ranh that led the United States to impose oil sanctions against Japan—a catalyst for World War II in the Pacific.

[4] See John Erickson, "The Northern Theater: Soviet Capabilities and Concepts," in *Strategic Review* (Summer 1976), p. 6.

[5] In Soviet parlance, a TVD (*teatr voennykh deistvii*) is a subsection of a theatre of war (*teatr voiny*). Thus, for example, the northwestern TVD is a component of the European theatre.

[6] The *Washington Post*, 11 July 1983.

[7] For details, see Leighton, *op. cit.*, pp. 20–21.

[8] The *Manchester Guardian Weekly*, 27 March 1977.

[9] Quoted in *Hufvudstadsbladet* (Helsinki), 1 March 1983.

[10] John Barry, "Geneva behind Closed Doors," *The Times* (London), 31 May 1983.

[11] *Die Welt* (Bonn), 19–20 February 1983.

[12] The *New York Times*, 21 October 1979.

[13] Drew Middleton, the *New York Times*, 4 July 1980.

[14] See *Asia Yearbook (Far Eastern Economic Review)*, 1983, p. 23; *US News & World Report*, 8 December 1980, p. 35; and the *Baltimore Sun*, 26 November 1981, p. 13. Also, Osamu Kaihara, "Japan's 'Sea-Lanes' Mission Is Wishful Thinking," in the *Wall Street Journal*, 29 August 1983, p. 13.

[15] *Business Week*, 23 June 1980, p. 58.

[16] The *New York Times*, 8 May 1983.

Marian Leighton

[17]*Asiaweek*, 29 April 1983, p. 17.

[18]See *News-World* (New York), 26 August 1981. U.S. troops in Japan were pared from 65,000 to 45,000 in the period 1972–1981.

[19]The *Washington Post*, 4 June 1983.

[20]David Rees, "The Gorshkov Strategy in the Far East," in *Pacific Community* (January 1978), p. 144.

[21]For details of this concept, see Leighton, *op. cit.*, especially pp. 76–77.

# 18

## JOSEPH J. COLLINS

## The Soviet–Afghan War: The First Four Years*

The Soviet–Afghan war has now lasted longer than World War II did for the Soviet Union. At its initiation in December 1979, the invasion appeared to be yet another dramatic extension of Soviet influence, with the same promise of success already achieved by proxy in Angola and Ethiopia.

Now, 4 years later, the invasion appears more a blunder than a daring extension of influence. The Soviets, despite the presence of 4% of their ground forces, are no closer to securing Afghanistan than they were in 1980. Moreover, although they are learning valuable military lessons, the war has become a persistent, though not a life-threatening, problem for the Soviet military. Having built an army for World War III on the plains of Europe, the Soviets are finding that it is not performing well in a counterinsurgency role in the mountains of South Asia.

The purpose of this chapter is to address: (1) the political situation in Afghanistan; (2) current Soviet military strategy and operations; (3) the prospects for a negotiated settlement; and (4) conclusions that Western military thinkers might draw from the 4 years of war to date.[1]

On the domestic scene, the Soviets apparently believed that a decisive show of armed might, coupled with a change in rulers, would reunite the ruling party, restore order to Afghanistan, and prevent a potential "encirclement" of the Soviet Union. All of this would, at the same time, preserve the neosocialist "revolution" on their southern border. Delivered in the combat trains of the Soviet invasion force, Babrak Karmal, the Soviet-picked replacement for Hafizullah Amin, was to restore domestic political order, while the Soviet forces were to frighten the guerrillas back to their villages. To put it mildly, the Soviets have not accomplished their objectives. Babrak Karmal has failed in his efforts to reunite the Khalq ("Masses") and Parcham ("Banner") factions of the People's Democratic Party of Afghanistan. Khalq–Parcham in-

*Reprinted by permission of the author from *Parameters* 14, no. 2 (1984), pp. 49–62. Copyright 1984 by Joseph J. Collins.

fighting continues and is still a major problem for the Afghan army, traditionally a Khalqi stronghold. In September 1982, the Khalqi general commanding the Central Army Corps was found shot dead in his office under circumstances apparently not connected to the fighting. In May 1983, the Khalqi Deputy Defense Minister physically assaulted the Defense Minister after having been passed over for promotion. Military defections are frequent and even Afghan communists have been reported fighting alongside the *Mujahiddin*. In all, the rate of military accessions barely equals the rate of desertions. The army is still less than one-third the size it was in 1978, and it is close to useless as a military force.[2]

Between 20 and 25% of the prewar population have become refugees. As a result of Soviet military operations, the population of the cities has swelled, with the population of Kabul now three times its prewar size. In the spring of 1983, Babrak Karmal still claimed that without Soviet support, "It is unknown what the destiny of the Afghan Revolution would be. . . . We are realists and clearly realize that in store for us yet lie trials and deprivations, losses and difficulties."[3] Just 2 weeks before, Prime Minister Keshtmand had admitted that one-half of the country's schools and three-quarters of its communication lines had been destroyed since 1979.[4]

# Current Military Operations

The current situation in Afghanistan pits roughly 105,000 to 120,000 Soviet and 30,000 Afghan troops against 85,000 to 100,000 freedom fighters. Soviet forces (the Fortieth Army), according to unclassified sources, are composed of seven motorized rifle divisions and five air assault brigades (about 2000 men each), backed up by an undisclosed number of "airborne/ranger" units, around 240 gunships, 400 other helicopters, several squadrons of MiG-21s and -23s, and at least one squadron of Su-25 attack aircraft. The deployment of this latter aircraft is significant in that the Soviets have chosen Afghanistan as the location for its first operational deployment.[5] Recent reports indicate that MiG-25s configured for reconnaissance may also be in the country. Persistent reports also have an unknown number of Cuban, Vietnamese, and East European advisors and troops in Afghanistan.[6]

Soviet forces include more than 80,000 ground forces, 30,000 general support troops, and 10,000 air force personnel. These forces are supported by about 30,000 support and air force personnel in the southern part of the USSR. Divisional deployments are geographically balanced, with about one-third of the ground force total in the Kabul area and other major deployments at Mazar-i-Sharif and Quandoz in the north, Herat and Farah in the west, Kandahar in the south, and Jalalabad in the east. Major airbases are located in Herat, Shindand, Farah, Kandahar, Kabul, Bagram, and Jalalabad.

The freedom fighters come from at least six loosely organized and disunited resistance groups and fight in anywhere from platoon to regimental strength. Armaments vary, with some units having one

Kalashnikov (AK) automatic rifle per platoon, while other units have nearly all of their fighters equipped with AKs.[7] Fire support is limited, in the main, to rocket-propelled grenades, machine guns, and mortars. Although some analysts put foreign aid to the freedom fighters at the $100 million level, relatively little materiel has found its way to fighting units.[8] Some recent observers have noted that the open-market price of an AK in Pakistan—about $2800—had not declined appreciably from 1979 to 1982. The best source of arms is still the Soviet and Afghan forces. One active local commander estimated that 80% of his weapons came from the Soviets or Afghan forces.[9]

Overall, since mid-1980 the Soviet position in Afghanistan has deteriorated, though not yet to the point where it might jeopardize the entire operation. While territorially based estimates are necessarily suspect, experts have increased their estimate of rebel-controlled territory from 75% of the country (December 1980) to as much as 90% (December 1981).[10] It would be more accurate to say that perhaps as much as 90% of Afghan territory is controlled by neither the Soviets nor the freedom fighters on a permanent basis. Soviet forces are free to move in strength into almost any area, but neither they nor their Afghan allies possess the numerical strength to occupy and pacify major areas of the country. In most cases, the freedom fighters, of course, depend too much on mobility and concealment for their survival to establish effective control. In any case, the major cities and base areas are only safe for the Soviets during daylight hours. In the countryside, only the narrow strip joining the PRC to Afghanistan, the Wakhan Corridor (which has been occupied by the Soviets), and the thinly populated areas in the extreme northwest and southwest of the country are relatively free of rebel activity.

To date, Soviet strategy appears to have been to hold the major centers of communications, limit infiltration, and destroy local strongholds at minimum cost to their own forces. In essence, the Soviet strategy is one wherein high technology and superior tactical mobility are used as force multipliers and as means to hold Soviet casualties to a minimum. In effect, Soviet policy has been a combination of "scorched earth" and, in anthropologist Louis Dupree's words, "migratory genocide."[11] Numerous reports have suggested that Soviet forces, in particular their helicopter gunships, have been deliberately used to burn crops and destroy villages to force the population—the main source of resistance logistical support—to flee to Pakistan or Iran. Other reports imply that the Soviets have used a "free fire zone" approach in areas with strong resistance forces.[12]

Soviet terror tactics have increased in their ferocity since mid-1980. Though few would accuse the Afghans of restrained behavior toward their enemies, the Soviet monopoly on high technology has magnified the destructive aspects of their behavior. One expert testified:

The International Red Cross and other humanitarian organizations are denied access to Afghanistan. Between last October 26 and November 2 [1981], three hospitals, operated by a French humanitarian medical organization, in three separate provinces, were demolished by helicopters that singled them out for bombing and rocketing. Helicopters set the crops aflame just before the harvest; village granaries are emptied and destroyed—all in an effort to starve the people into submission. The planes often bear Afghan markings, but the pilots are Soviet, as they have been since mid-1979—although they reportedly sometimes wear Afghan uniforms.[13]

The use of plastic, caseless mines, usually dropped from helicopters, has greatly affected the resistance's morale and ability to maneuver. One resistance leader noted in 1982:

> The Soviets also drop small antipersonnel mines by helicopter. These mines are in the form of watches, ballpoint pens or even books. They have caused enormous damage among the civilian population and livestock, and many women and children have lost feet or hands. The children have now learned not to touch such objects, but to explode them by throwing stones at them.[14]

Total Soviet casualties (killed or wounded) have been estimated at 20,000, and the Soviets may have suffered again as many casualties from sickness and disease. Exact figures on the number of Soviets killed in action are impossible to obtain, but responsible analysts have cited estimates from 5000 to 10,000.[15] To the end of 1982, the freedom fighters may have suffered ten times the number of Soviet casualties, with undoubtedly a higher percentage of deaths as well. In all, despite the costs, the Soviets are preparing for a prolonged stay. Permanent logistical facilities and barracks are being constructed. Airfields are being upgraded, and the construction of a permanent bridge across the Amu Darya has been completed. The tour of duty for Soviet soldiers has been set at 2 years, with a quarter of the force being rotated semiannually.[16]

Operationally, new or untried Soviet equipment (e.g., the improved BMP, the AK-74 rifle, the Hind helicopter, scatterable mines, the AGS-17 automatic grenade launcher) has been tested, and some technical innovations have been made. For example, the Soviets have experimented with a new main armament on their standard BMP infantry fighting vehicle. Based on their Afghan experience, they have moved to replace the slow-firing 73mm cannon with an automatic 30mm cannon.[17] This change will enable Soviet ground forces to achieve an even larger volume of suppressive fire. The use of helicopters is also an important facet of operations in Afghanistan. Helicopters are used for resupply, reconnaissance, troop transport, fire support, and command and control. Pilot training in Afghanistan is superb. As one Soviet officer described it,

> Flying in the mountains and above the desert, plus the real possibility of coming under fire by anti-aircraft weapons which are making their way from Pakistan to the bandits operating on [Afghan] territory—this is a real training school. . . . No wonder they say that after a month in Afghanistan helicopter pilots can be awarded the top proficiency rating without testing their piloting ability.[18]

This pilot training is also costly, however. The rebels have shot down as many as 300 Soviet helicopters, mostly of the troop-carrying variety, with small arms and antitank weapons.

According to two highly detailed U.S. State Department reports, Soviet forces have used chemical weapons in at least 15 provinces of Afghanistan. Witnesses have made a total of 59 separate incident reports, and the State Department noted that at least 36 of the reports were corroborated by additional evidence. Amazingly, the Soviet use of chemical weapons—incapacitants, lethal chemicals, and perhaps even mycotoxin biological weapons—has continued apace even after the first detailed U.S. report appeared in March 1982. The reports conservatively estimate that the attacks have resulted in 3000 deaths. One other ominous detail did not go unnoticed: Detailed survey and monitoring operations following some of the strikes showed that the Soviets were obviously "interested in studying after-effects, lethality, or some other quasi-experimental aspect of a new chemical weapon."[19]

While the question of mycotoxins, artificially manufactured biological weapons, is still the subject of some controversy, the use of other lethal chemicals—blood and nerve agents—in Afghanistan has been proven beyond question. In addition to the statements of hundreds of eyewitnesses, the more significant proofs of lethal agent usage include:

- The film of Dutch journalist Bernd de Bruin, who himself was wounded in an attack in which numerous Afghans perished.

- The fact that chemical battalions were left in place after extraneous military equipment was withdrawn in June 1980.

- The testimony of a Soviet POW who was engaged in postattack survey and monitoring operations.

- The testimony of another Soviet POW who detailed chemical storage sites in Afghanistan and who had seen Soviet soldiers who were contaminated by agents directed at the guerrillas.

- Positive test results on two Soviet protective masks taken from dead Soviet soldiers in September and December 1981 and on another obtained in Febuary 1982.[20]

Why the Soviet Union would use chemical agents is not difficult to understand. These weapons generate panic. They can also be used to guard exposed flanks and to clear built-up areas or caves of deadly snipers or ambushers. In other words, while inflicting damage and inducing panic among the enemy, they enable the user to conserve troop strength and to minimize his own casualties.

There is very little reliable information on the performance of Soviet troops in Afghanistan. A distillation of the scant information that is available reveals the following:

- The initial invading divisions—except the airborne units—were Category 3 units, manned primarily by Central Asian reservists. These units were poorly trained and unreliable. Collusion with the freedom fighters was commonplace. Ghafoor Yussofzai, a former lawyer and now a resistance leader, gave this eyewitness testimony of collusion between Central Asian soldiers and their co-religionists:

> When the Soviets first entered our country in 1979 . . . most of the soldiers were Soviet–Central Asians. This is because they speak a language akin to our own. And the Russians certainly thought that through the use of Soviet–Central Asian troops they could more easily control us. And these Soviet–Central Asian soldiers were told that they [were] coming to defend us in Afghanistan from American, Chinese, and Pakistan military attacks. When these people (Soviet–Central Asians) realized that the only people they were fighting in Afghanistan were Afghans . . . then these Soviet–Central Asians began helping us. They began leaving us packages with ammunition and weapons and caches. They left it in the ground and covered it with earth and just left a little of it emerging. In the beginning we were very suspicious and cautious and poked at this with sticks afraid that they would prove to be mines. And when we finally uncovered these things, we found out that they were parcels of weapons and ammunition that these Soviet–Central Asians were leaving for us. The Soviets (Russians) finally became aware that this was going on and [have] since withdrawn Soviet–Central Asian troops from Afghanistan and now they have just brought their own red-faced troops.[21]

• The initial complement of regular forces was not trained in counterinsurgency or mountain warfare techniques. In December 1981, one Soviet source even reported that "it took a while for [an Afghan] soldier to believe that the majority of Soviet servicemen had first seen mountains here—in Afghanistan." Not finding the Chinese or American "agents" whom they had been told were causing the trouble has also been bad for morale. Recent interviews with Soviet POWs indicate widespread discontent among Soviet forces.[22]

• The pace of operations ranges from frantic "offensives" or "damage limiting" operations to long periods of boredom. Soviet soldiers are apparently not coping very well with this and reports of the use of hashish have surfaced. Indeed, numerous separate sources have confirmed the widespread use of hashish and the fact that Soviet soldiers have traded truck parts, uniforms, ammunition, and even rifles for hashish or other local drugs.[23]

• Soviet tactics still tend toward an overreliance on motorized rifle and tank troops employed in sweep or "hammer and anvil" operations. Air assault operations—usually of company or battalion strength—are becoming more important, although they are usually conducted in conjunction with movements by motorized rifle units. Tanks are apparently being used mostly in a fire support role. Much of the Soviets' operational experience apparently has been in road-clearing operations, designed to keep open the ground lines of communication. On the whole, airborne and air assault troops seem to be held in higher esteem by the freedom fighters than troops from the motorized divisions.

An Afghan army colonel who later defected to the resistance observed the Soviet forces as both ally and adversary. He characterized them as "oversupervised," "lacking initiative," and addicted to "cookbook warfare," wherein proven "battle recipes" are mechanically applied to new situations. S. B. Majrooh, another close observer, said that Soviet soldiers were "generally undisciplined, isolated, and not motivated."[24]

Ambushes of various sizes have proved to be very effective. An Afghan army major described guerrilla tactics in a conversation with a Soviet reporter:

> Usually they operate in groups of 30–40 men. They used to assemble in larger gangs. They prefer to use ambushes by bridges, or in defiles. They destroy the bridge or block the road and then open fire from the commanding heights. If a strong army subunit is moving, they allow the reconnaissance and the combat security detachment to go by. All of a sudden, they open up with volleys of well-aimed fire and then rapidly withdraw. They mine the roads, then cover the mined areas with small arms fire. The hand of professional foreign instructors can be felt at work.[25]

A Soviet defector evaluated the freedom fighters as follows:

> The *mujahidin* were brave when they began their resistance and they still are. Resistance is still strong. Pilots as well as all soldiers in the Soviet Army respect the courage and tactics of the *mujahidin* and recognize their successes.[26]

The Soviet populace is eager to learn about what is happening in Afghanistan, but censorship within the military and the media is strictly enforced. Accounts of Soviet soldiers in combat are rare, usually anecdotal, and very heavy on propaganda content. Despite this fact, some truth has emerged in Soviet sources, perhaps because the leadership wants to squelch rumors that may even be worse than the reality. Early in 1983, *Krasnaya zvezda* reported:

> Service on Afghanistan's soil makes special demands on all servicemen. It is not easy being far from our motherland. . . . The difficult climate conditions take their toll. The lack of roads presents quite a few difficulties. And how exhausting exercises in the mountains are, when each meter takes a tremendous and intensive effort and it is hard to breathe. . . . There are considerable other ordeals. The dushmans are continuing their piratical onslaughts.[27]

Soviet efforts to date have not produced the desired results. Contrary to Soviet propaganda, the bulk of the fighting has been done by Soviet troops, sometimes opposed by mutinous Afghan army forces. A Western summary of recent major combat actions included the following:

> Between April 13 and July 15, 1981, at least 107 high-level Afghan Communist officials and Soviet officers were assassinated in Kabul, on two occasions at the very gate of the Soviet Embassy at midday. In Herat, a no-man's land for two years, Soviet soldiers are killed in their barracks. Unable to wrest Kandahar from the resistance, the Russians bombed much

of it into rubble in June; two weeks later, the resistance again controlled Kandahar. On June 19, the main Soviet airbase at Bagram was set ablaze, and fuel, ammunition dumps, and aircraft were destroyed. In July, the resistance won Gulbahar on the north–south supply road. The landscape is littered with ruined Soviet tanks and armor.[28]

A captured Soviet tank officer, a Captain Sidelniko, added that in a series of three raids on Bagram in 1981 and 1982, the rebels had destroyed 38 aircraft. A French doctor, based on an actual count of burned vehicles in seven provinces, estimated Soviet vehicle losses throughout Afghanistan at 3000 to 4000.[29]

The number of major battles involving multiple, battalion-sized units apparently increased from 1981 to 1983. Although there were periodic reports of intraresistance fighting, three major groups formed the "Islamic Unity of Afghan Mujahidin" coalition early in 1981 and a year later fought a coordinated battle in Paktia Province in which they defeated two Soviet regiments, destroying 25 vehicles and killing 60 Soviet soldiers in the process. Other reports of coordinated operations appeared early in 1983, but they are far more the exception than the rule.[30]

There are few accurate accounts of entire battles by which we can judge the state of Soviet military art in Afghanistan. One month-long operation in 1982 was witnessed by *Christian Science Monitor* correspondent Edward Giradet.[31] The battle was apparently designed to eliminate the 3000 fighters of Ahmed Shah Massoud who had been implicated in numerous raids, including at least one successful penetration of Bagram air base. Four previous Soviet forays into the Panjshir Valley had failed to eliminate this unit of freedom fighters. While the operation was significant because of its size, it was also important because it appeared to represent an archetypical Soviet "battle recipe" that has been used time and again in Afghanistan.

After an entire week of aerial bombardment, Soviet and Afghan forces were inserted by helicopter into the narrow east–west Panjshir Corridor on May 17, 1982. The freedom fighters, having been previously warned of the Soviet battle plan, had escaped down the side valleys or onto the top of the ridge lines. As a *Pravda* military correspondent noted, the first waves of attackers encountered "a multilevel system of fire prepared in advance."[32] Three days later a tank/motorized rifle force entered the valley, bringing the total of Soviet and Afghan forces to between 12,000 and 15,000. A series of sharp engagements followed, and within the first 10 days, 50 Soviet and Afghan vehicles and 35 helicopters (at least by resistance reports) were destroyed in the fighting. The freedom fighters may have netted 100 Soviet rifles. The Soviets destroyed up to 80% of the dwellings in some areas and killed nearly 200 freedom fighters and close to 1200 civilians, more than 1% of the Panjshir's population, but they were forced to begin withdrawing on June 13. In early September, Soviet fighter planes again began bombing the Panjshir Valley. The sixth Soviet offensive against Massoud's forces had begun.

As a result of the increased fighting, and following a December 1981 visit by Marshal Sokolov, a First Deputy Defense Minister, the Soviets added 20,000 additional troops to their "limited contingent" in Afghanistan.

Peace Process    Throughout the war, the Soviet assessment of the immediate situation in and concerning Afghanistan has been primarily negative. Numerous officials have expressed concern over the problem. In March 1981, in response to prodding by American members of a panel in Cincinnati, Ohio, Vitaly Kobysh, deputy head of the Central Committee International Information Department, characterized the invasion as "a mistake."[33] A month later, Yuri Velikanov, a Soviet diplomat stationed in the strategically important Seychelles Islands, stated, "For us, Afghanistan is an embarrassment. There were mistakes when we went in, and we are looking for ways to get out."[34]

Indeed, the Soviets have incentives to negotiate. Not only is the war a drain of up to $3 billion per year,[35] but it also distracts the leadership from more important issues and is a stumbling block to improving relations with China and Iran, the latter country being especially significant now that Soviet–Iranian relations are at a very low point. Having perceived a pro-Iraqi tilt on the part of the Soviets, the Ayatollah has severely curtailed the activities of Soviet diplomats in Iran and has arrested more than 1500 members of the Iranian communist Tudeh Party.[36] Soviet patience is also wearing thin. As one Soviet analyst told Karen Dawisha, "There must come a point at which we can no longer support a regime which hurls the people back into the sixteenth century."[37] Although that point has not yet arrived, it seems fast approaching.

Because of the battlefield situation, international pressure, and the desire to improve its image, since February 1980 the Soviets have been seeking a diplomatic way to extricate themselves from the Afghan quagmire. To comprehend these efforts, two cautionary notes must be made. First, Soviet peacemaking attempts have been conducted in the context of continuing to fight in Afghanistan. Moreover, as described above, though the Soviets are not yet committed to a battlefield victory in Afghanistan, they have reinforced their limited contingent by more than one-fourth its original size and they have consistently improved their logistical and basing infrastructure in Afghanistan. In short, they have not evidenced any desire for "peace at any price."

Although there have been changes in nuance and some rather interesting unofficial statements, the formal Soviet position has changed little since February 1980. However, there have been two significant changes in the Soviet position concerning the role of third parties and the pace of the withdrawal.

Up to the summer of 1981, the Soviets rejected peace plans put forward by, *inter alia*, the United States, France, and the European Community. This last initiative, the "Carrington Plan," was rejected in

July 1981 because it did not include the Karmal government in early discussions; it did include rebel representation; and it spoke of neutralization, which the Soviets saw as a much more heinous state than nonalignment and which implied that the Karmal government would cease to exist.[38] This last item violated the Soviet pledge that it would not go behind Karmal's back and their assertion that the gains of the "revolution" were permanent. Brezhnev himself said at the Twenty-sixth Party Congress:

> We do not object to the questions connected with Afghanistan being discussed in conjunction with the questions of security in the Persian Gulf. Naturally here only the international aspects of the Afghan problem can be discussed, not internal Afghan affairs. The sovereignty of Afghanistan must be fully protected, as must its nonaligned status.[39]

The United Nations, in conjunction with Pakistan and Afghanistan and in accordance with a General Assembly resolution in November 1980, began negotiations on the conduct of trilateral indirect talks among Afghanistan, Pakistan, and Iran to be held under U.N. auspices. Pakistan and Afghanistan agreed in principle to the format in January 1981, and the Soviets and Afghans agreed formally to pursue this avenue in August 1981. Iran has refused to participate but is being kept informed of the talks.[40]

The format of the talks is innovative. U.N. representatives have talked to one side and then the other, obviating the need for the Pakistanis to recognize the Karmal government. Absent that recognition, the Pakistanis can negotiate without admitting to the Soviet charge that Pakistani support for the resistance is equivalent to "outside interference." The Pakistani position is clear. They want total Soviet withdrawal, restoration of the nonaligned and independent status of Afghanistan, freedom from outside intervention, and the safe return home of the Afghan refugees.

Meetings took place in June 1982 and intermittently thereafter. Although there have been numerous reports of a "light at the end of the tunnel," by the end of 1983 little apparent progress had been made. In October 1982, Karmal characterized the responses of Iran and Pakistan to Afghan peace initiatives in the following manner: "Iran and Pakistan have so far not adopted concrete and constructive positions."[41] In February 1983, after a subsequent round of talks, Karmal stated that these discussions could bear fruit "whenever the other side shows readiness to conduct talks with the necessary realism and goodwill."[42] At about the same time, the usually optimistic U.N. Secretary General Javier Perez de Cuellar characterized as naive the idea "that Mr. Andropov will withdraw Soviet troops tomorrow."[43] In April 1983, after two more rounds of talks, Andropov himself characterized the talks as useful and "having some prospects," but, he added, the Pakistanis were "still being held by their sleeve by their overseas friends."[44]

There has been some slow movement by the Soviets on the question of the pace of troop withdrawals. Although their initial position stated that they would begin to withdraw only after all "interference" had stopped, since 1981 there have been preliminary indications that a Soviet troop withdrawal could be phased into a peace agreement. Brezhnev himself had said:

> An agreement on a political settlement would make it possible to establish, with the concurrence of [the] Afghan side, a time schedule and procedures for the withdrawal of Soviet troops from Afghanistan. . . . Troops could be withdrawn as accords that have been reached are implemented.[45]

Aside from this glimmer, there have been only rare flashes of hope on a peaceful solution to this problem. When Brezhnev died in November 1982, many thought that Andropov, long rumored to have been against the invasion, would quickly move to end the war. These rumors were supported by some observers, like President Zia ul-Haq, who noted on meeting Andropov that there was a "hint of flexibility" in the Soviet attitude toward Afghanistan.[46] Even the chief editor of *Pravda*, Viktor Afanasyev, who is also a full Central Committee member, went beyond the official line when he told a Japanese newspaper:

> I do not think military power can settle everything. That is why the Soviet Union intends to withdraw its troops sooner or later. There is no knowing when the conditions for withdrawal will be met, but it is essential that a government which is nonaligned and has good-neighborly relations with the Soviet Union can exist in Afghanistan. It need not be a Soviet-type socialist government.[47]

The Soviet media soon contradicted Afanasyev and retorted that the Soviet position remained unchanged. Six months after Brezhnev died, Andropov indicated how little movement there had been in the Soviet position:

> Our plans for a political settlement of the Afghan problem are no secret. We have repeatedly stated them publicly. Leonid Ilyich Brezhnev spoke about that. We consider that as soon as outside interference in the affairs of Afghanistan has been terminated and non-resumption of such interference guaranteed, we shall withdraw our troops. Our troops are staying in that country at the request of the lawful Afghan Government— that government which was then in power—and they continue staying there at the request of the lawful government headed by Babrak Karmal. We are not after anything for ourselves there. We responded to the request for assistance from a friendly neighboring country. It is, however, far from being a matter of indifference to us what is happening directly on our southern border.[48]

Even the rumors—ably assisted by the comments of many Soviet academics—that the USSR would be willing to sacrifice Karmal and his government for a settlement appear to be without basis in fact. The future of the Karmal government is still a major sticking point in the talks. The Soviets insist on its legitimacy, and Pakistan has continued to reiterate Zia's stand of December 1982: "We have always stated that Pakistan will not talk to this man who came to be the head of the Afghan regime by riding on Soviet tanks. We will not talk to him."[49]

Overall, Soviet efforts to gain a peace in Afghanistan have not progressed very far, and at the end of 1983 both sides were still far apart on a number of issues, including the fate of the Karmal regime, the scope and speed of the Soviet withdrawal, and the nature of international guarantees of the solution. The Soviets have not put all their effort into making peace. The rigidity of their proposals, when coupled with their military measures inside Afghanistan, suggests that even though they are pessimistic about the present situation in Afghanistan, they apparently do not perceive the costs of continued operations in Afghanistan as unacceptable. It is quite possible, as an American diplomat in Moscow has said, that they believe that they have absorbed the worst of the costs (the grain embargo, the Olympic boycott, etc.) and that now it is simply a matter of endurance and fortitude, virtues which their historical experience and highly authoritarian government have given them in great quantities.[50] The Soviets are prepared for peace on their terms or the continuation of warfare at the present level for the foreseeable future.

It is not difficult to understand why there has been such little change in Soviet peace proposals. The potential for disintegration of the People's Democratic Party of Afghanistan is still present and, in Soviet eyes, the threat to Soviet security is there as well. Indeed, there is even less likelihood that a new, non-PDPA regime could ever—given cultural constraints— behave in a "good neighbor" fashion toward the Soviet Union. The specter of encirclement is still present, and so is the threat of lost prestige. It is one thing to desert an ally, but it is even more damaging to your prestige if you try very hard to save him and then fail. The Soviets are caught in a trap of their own construction. As a Pakistani diplomat said,

> The Soviets can continue to occupy the country, but they cannot win over the people. The longer they stay, the more they alienate the people. The more they alienate the people, the longer they must stay. This Russian dilemma is also the Afghan dilemma, and both seem condemned to suffer its consequences.[51]

Conclusions    The Soviet experience in Afghanistan supports a number of conclusions of interest to anyone concerned with Soviet military issues. First, with regard to organizational framework, the Afghanistan experience suggests that armies will do well only those things for which they habitually prepare and practice. Soviet forces performed well in the movement into Afghanistan, but they have done poorly in dealing with the insurgency itself. To date, the Soviets are only beginning to adjust to the conditions present in Afghanistan. Short of genocide, the methods in use at present will continue to be ineffective.

Second, in the area of doctrine, Afghanistan appears as a unique case.

The Soviets entered Afghanistan not expecting to fight, but very soon found themselves embroiled in a full-blown counterinsurgency. While the Soviets have in the past shown a strategic appreciation for limited war, they were put in the awkward position of having a force structure and operational and tactical doctrines that did not match the military situation. Moreover, it was a situation that required an independent, decentralized style of command somewhat alien to the Soviet experience.

In analyzing the Soviet–Afghan war, one finds much data to support the image of the dogged, inflexible Russian who time and again attempts to make circumstance adapt to practiced technique. The observations of German generals at the close of World War II appear to have retained a measure of their validity:

> The commanders of Russian combined arms units were often well trained along tactical lines, but to some extent they had not grasped the essence of tactical doctrines and therefore often acted according to set patterns, not according to circumstances. Also, there was the pronounced spirit of blind obedience which had perhaps carried over from their regimented civilian life into the military field. . . .
>
> The inflexibility of Russian methods of warfare was evidenced repeatedly. Only the top Russian command during the last years of the war was an exception. This inflexibility manifested itself as high as army level; in divisions, regiments, and companies it was unquestionably the retarding factor in the way the Russians fought.[52]

Tactical adaptations, as noted above, have taken place and are in evidence even in Soviet accounts of battles in Afghanistan. The Soviet military press is replete with articles discussing mountain training and exhorting leaders to pay more attention to developing the elusive "initiative" and physical fitness among their subordinates. For example, *Voennyi vestnik* (*Military Herald*) showed a steady increase in articles on mountain warfare from none in 1978, to three in 1979, to 15 in 1981.[53] Time and experience may enable the Soviets to turn this evolving body of information into a working doctrine, but they will probably be inhibited in the near future from getting directly involved in another counterinsurgency.

Third, one ought not to believe that the Afghan experience has been totally negative for the Soviet armed forces. The Soviet experience in Afghanistan has given them valuable experience in mobilization. Unfortunately, from their point of view, many of the lessons learned were painful. The performance of Central Asian troops in the initial invasion was poor, and this could lead to greater emphasis on reserve training and changes in active-duty manning policies. Marshal Ogarkov, the Soviet chief of staff, highlighted the role of the reserves in a 1981 article in *Kommunist*:

> If an aggressor unleashes a war, the prepared reserves of personnel and equipment assigned to formations and units must reach them in extremely short periods of time. Hence, the task of constant readiness for immediate

mobilization deployment of troops and naval forces is of great state significance.

Later he added that "supplying the troops with prepared reserves of personnel and equipment predetermines the need for efficiently planned measures even in peacetime."[54] All in all, the Soviet reserve forces and mobilization procedures bear further watching. Changes based on their experience in Afghanistan may already be taking place.

In the areas of weapons and personnel, Afghanistan has been a prize (though a very expensive one) for the Soviet military. Training deficiencies will have been detected and combat experience, though it tends to be fleeting, will ensure a more seasoned Soviet army. Particularly significant here has been the performance of Soviet pilots. We can be assured that the Soviets will hone their fire support skills to a fine edge in Afghanistan. If nothing else, Soviet command cadres in future conflicts will be better able to control their air and ground firepower.

As noted above, nearly all analysts give high marks for proficiency to Soviet airborne and air assault troops. NATO planners should take note of this fact. In any NATO–Warsaw Pact conflict, NATO rear areas may be subject to intense pressure from elite, combat-experienced units that do not suffer from the general malaise of their motorized rifle and tank brethren in Afghanistan.[55]

One Soviet "adaptation" which should alarm the West is the use of chemical weapons. The use of these weapons in Afghanistan and Southeast Asia again confirms, not surprisingly, that the Soviets find them put to their best use against unprotected subjects incapable of retaliation. Afghanistan is proof positive that the Soviets do not consider these devices as "special weapons." Considerations of utility and not morality will govern Soviet use of them in future conflicts.

The Soviet use of chemical and biological weapons in Afghanistan also suggests that the validity of future arms control agreements rests heavily on whether the West can retaliate in kind if those agreements are violated. It is clear from the experience in both Southeast Asia and Afghanistan that the various treaties that the Soviets have signed on chemical and biological weapons are of questionable value in curbing either the manufacture or use of such weapons by the Soviet Union.

Finally, one should reflect on the efficacy of learning lessons from recent history. The contest in Afghanistan is far from over. Years from now, the record of events may be far different than what it appears today. The Soviets believe that time is on their side and that they do not need a quick victory. The Soviet ability to "hang tough" and "muddle through" far surpasses our own. A French doctor, himself a veteran of the Soviet–Afghan war, sadly noted:

> The Russians do not need smashing victories to announce to their citizenry, as Soviet public opinion does not influence Soviet policy. Catastrophes, such as that in the Salang tunnel where several hundred Soviet and communist-regime troops (and civilians) were killed, do not incite an outcry in Moscow for Soviet "boys" to come home. The Soviet army can wait it out as long as it did for the Basmachi revolt to end—and it waited for that for 20 years. It can wait even longer if necessary.[56]

## Notes

[1]See also Joseph J. Collins, "Afghanistan: The Empire Strikes Out," *Parameters* 12 (March 1982), pp. 32–41.

[2]On factional feuding, see U.S. Department of State, "Soviet Dilemmas in Afghanistan," Special Report no. 72, June 1980, pp. 1–3; U.S. Department of State, "Afghanistan: Three Years of Occupation," Special Report no. 106, December 1982, pp. 1, 6–7; K. Wafadar, "Afghanistan in 1981: The Struggle Intensifies," *Asian Survey* 22 (February 1982), pp. 148–150; and U.S. Department of State, "Afghanistan: Four Years of Occupation," Special Report no. 112, December 1983, pp. 4–6.

[3]Tass in English, 28 April 1983, in FBIS-Soviet Union-III-89-4/6/83, p. 2.

[4]"U.N. Official Confers on Afghan Fighting," *The New York Times*, 12 April 1983, p. 6.

[5]The deployment of the Su-25 was confirmed in an unofficial 1982 State Department document entitled "Glossary of Soviet Military Terms," and in Drew Middleton, "Soviet Said to Be Raising Quality of Air Force," *The New York Times*, 26 September 1982, p. 7. For order of battle information, see David Isby, "Afghanistan 1982: The War Continues," *International Defense Review* 15 (no. 11, 1982), pp. 1523–1526; and Special Report no. 112, pp. 1, 3. Isby uses 152,000 as the number of Soviet troops in Afghanistan, while the State Department uses 105,000. The range 105,000–120,000 will be used throughout this chapter.

[6]"Troops of 5 Soviet Allies Reported Fighting Guerrillas in Afghanistan," *The New York Times*, 20 December 1982, p. 10; and Drew Middleton, "Afghanistan: A Year Later," *The New York Times*, 26 December 1980, p. 3. See also, Agence France Presse dispatch (Spanish), 28 November 1980, in FBIS-South Asia-VII-232-2/1/80, p. C8. See also, *Washington Times*, 16 June 1983, p. 2.

[7]Compare Jere Van Dyk, "Afghan Arms: From Missiles to Ramshackle Rifles," *The New York Times*, 12 January 1982, p. 2; and articles in *The Christian Science Monitor* cited in note 31, below.

[8]On foreign assistance to the freedom fighters, see Michael Kaufman, "Afghans Said to Get New Guns After Trip to Egypt," *The New York Times*, 22 January 1981, p. 3; and "Afghan Rebels Bristle with New Arms," *The New York Times*, 14 April 1981, p. 3. See also Carl Bernstein, "Arms for Afghanistan," *The New Republic*, 18 July 1981, pp. 8–10; and Anwar Sadat's oblique confirmation of the U.S. role in "Sadat Says U.S. Buys Soviet Arms in Egypt for Afghan Rebels," *The New York Times*, 23 September 1981, p. A15. More recent reports place foreign assistance (U.S. and Saudi) between $30 and $50 million per year, 1980–1982. See Leslie Gelb, "U.S. Said to Increase Arms Aid for Afghan Rebels," *The New York Times*, 4 May 1983, p. 1; and "The Afghan Connection," *Time*, 16 May 1983, p. 12.

[9]Jere Van Dyk, "Afghan Arms: From Missiles to Ramshackle Rifles," and Francis Fukyama, *The Future of the Soviet Role in Afghanistan*, Rand Research Note N 1579-RC (Santa Monica, Calif.: Rand, September 1980), p. 12. For the local commander's estimate, see William Branigin, "Mujaheddin Say U.S. Should Provide Training, Weapons," *The Washington Post*, 18 October 1983, pp. A12ff. A French doctor, Lauren Lemonnier, an eyewitness to the fighting in the Panjshir, confirmed the 80% figure in her remarks at the Center for the Study of Human Rights Conference on Afghanistan, Columbia University, 2 February 1984.

[10]Drew Middleton, "Afghanistan: A Year Later," and U.S. Department of State, "Afghanistan: Two Years of Occupation," Special Report no. 91, December 1981.

[11]Nicholas Wade, "Afghanistan: The Politics of Tragicomedy," *Science*, 1 May 1981, pp. 521–523.

[12]See Rosanne Klass' statement in U.S. Congress, Senate Committee on

Foreign Relations, *Hearings on the Situation in Afghanistan*, 97th Cong., 2d sess., 8 March 1982, pp. 71–75.

[13]*Ibid.*, pp. 72–73.

[14]*Les Nouvelles Afghanistan*, 10 (July–December 1982), pp. 4–16, in JPRS 81812, 21 September 1982, p. 21.

[15]U.S. Government sources now use 10,000 as the high-range estimate of Soviet KIAs. This fact was announced by Ambassador Charles Dunbar, former U.S. chargé d'affaires in Kabul, at the Harvard–State Department Conference on Afghanistan, Cambridge, Mass., October 1983.

[16]Special Report no. 72, p. 3.

[17]Mining operations are described in George Wilson, "Soviets Lay Mines to Slow Afghan Guerrillas, Arms," *The Washington Post*, 8 July 1980, p. 1. Photographs of the new scatterable mines can be found in *Soldier of Fortune* (April 1981), pp. 23–24. Also see DIA, *Review of Soviet Ground Forces* (May 1980, February 1981, June 1981), for details on AK-74 and AGS-17. On the improved BMP (M1981), see DIA, *Review of Soviet Ground Forces* (April 1982 and December 1983), and the photograph in *The New York Times*, 8 November 1982, p. 1.

[18]Col. V. Stulovskiy, "Stationed in Afghanistan," *Voyennoye znaniye* (March 1981), as cited in Douglas Hart, "Low Intensity Conflict in Afghanistan: The Soviet View," *Survival* 24 (March 1982), pp. 66–67. For a description of helicopters in resupply and medevac roles, see *Komsomolskaya Pravda*, 4 February 1983, p. 4.

[19]U.S. Department of State, "Chemical Warfare in South Asia and Afghanistan," Special Report no. 98, March 1982, and Special Report no. 104, November 1982. The quote is from the former publication, p. 23.

[20]*Ibid.* See also, Special Report no. 106, p. 5, and the unpublished U.S. State Department collection of media reports, "Reports of the Use of Chemical Weapons in Afghanistan, Laos, and Kampuchea, Summer 1980," pp. 4–30.

[21]"Soviet Human Rights Violations in Afghanistan," the unedited transcript of a presentation by five Afghans on the massacre at Padkahwab-e-Shana, Georgetown Center for Strategic and International Studies, Washington, D.C., 1 February 1983, pp. 21–22.

[22]The quote can be found in *Krasnaya zvezda*, 31 December 1981, p. 2, in FBIS, *Daily Report-Soviet Union*, 6 January 1982, p. D4. An interview with a Soviet officer POW can be found in an Agence France Presse dispatch of 29 April 1982, from Hong Kong. An interview with Soviet enlisted defectors can be found in *Die Welt*, 29 October 1982, p. 8, translated in FBIS, *Daily Report-Soviet Union*, 2 November 1982, pp. D1–D3; and in "Soviets' 'Dirty War' in Afghanistan," *U.S. News and World Report*, 19 December 1983, p. 13. Also see "Soviet Soldier Tells of Deserting to Afghans," *Washington Times*, 23 January 1984, p. 2.

[23]*Ibid.*; *Die Welt*, 29 October 1982, p. 8; Alain Fadeux, "Soviet Captives Describe Afghan War Roles," *The Washington Post*, 28 September 1981, p. 15; Jere Van Dyk, "Afghan Arms: From Missiles to Ramshackle Rifles," Stuart Auerbach, "Standoff in Afghanistan Tarnishes Red Army's Image," *The Washington Post*, 27 December 1981, p. 1; and Agence France Presse dispatch of 3 December 1980, in FBIS, *Daily Report-South Asia 8*, no. 235, 4 December 1980, pp. C2–C3.

[24]On road clearing, see, for example, *Komsomolskaya Pravda*, 7 August 1981, p. 2, in FBIS, *Daily Report-Soviet Union*, 13 August 1981, pp. D5–D9; and *Krasnaya Zvezda*, 7 January 1984, p. 3. The quote on performance is from an interview with Colonel A. A. Jalali, Washington, D.C., 6 April 1983. S. B. Majrooh, now director of the Afghan Information Service in Pakistan, made these remarks at the Harvard–State Department Conference, October 1983.

[25]*Pravda*, 5 June 1980, in U.S. Air Force, *Soviet Press: Selected Translations* (September 1981), p. 273.

[26]*Die Welt*, 29 October 1982, p. 8.

[27]*Krasnaya zvezda*, 26 February 1983, p. 1.

[28]Rosanne Klass, "Afghans Battle On," *The New York Times*, 30 July 1981, p. 19.

[29]On the Soviet captain, see Agence France Presse dispatch of 29 April 1982 from Hong Kong. The figure on destroyed vehicles comes from Dr. Claude Malhuret at the Harvard–State Department Conference on Afghanistan, October 1983.

[30]Interview with Colonel A. A. Jalali, former assistant chief of the Military Committee of the Islamic Unity of Afghan *Mujahiddin*, in Washington, D.C., 6 April 1983. See also, "Major Soviet-led Drive is Reported in Afghan War," *The New York Times*, 21 April 1983, p. 11; and William Claiborne, "Afghan Rebels Said to Team Up, Ambush Convoy," *The Washington Post*, 13 April 1983, p. 22.

[31]See the series of articles in *The Christian Science Monitor* by Edward Giradet, entitled "With the Resistance in Afghanistan," 22 and 28 June and 2, 7, and 9 July 1982. Also see the description in Special Report no. 106, pp. 2–4.

[32]*Pravda*, 3 August 1982, p. 6. Both the *Pravda* military correspondent, a rear admiral, and Giradet reported that the *Mujahiddin* had at least portions of the Soviet battle plan prior to the start of the battle.

[33]This remark was made during the question and answer session following Kobysh's address before the Section on Soviet-American Relations, at the 23d Annual International Studies Association Convention in Cincinnati, Ohio, 26 March 1982.

[34]Michael T. Kaufman, "Ports and Oil Spur Naval Buildup by U.S. and Soviet," *The New York Times*, 20 April 1981, pp. 1, 12.

[35]Remarks by State Department official at the "National Forum on Afghanistan" sponsored by the University of Nebraska and the U.S. Department of State, Washington, D.C., 13 December 1983.

[36]See *Radio Liberty Research Bulletin*, RL202/83 (May 1983), p. 3.

[37]Karen Dawisha, "The USSR in the Middle East," *Foreign Affairs* 61 (Winter 1982–1983), p. 448. On Iranian aid to the Afghan resistance, see "Khomeini Helps the Afghans," *Foreign Report*, 22 September 1983, pp. 1–2; and "Khomeini and the Afghans," *Foreign Report*, 20 October 1983, pp. 5–6.

[38]*Pravda*, 5 August 1981, p. 4, in *Current Digest of the Soviet Press* (CDSP)-33-31, pp. 5–6.

[39]The quote is reprinted in FBIS-Soviet Union-2/24/81, p. 20.

[40]The best sources on these negotiations are Selig Harrison, "Dateline Afghanistan: Exit through Finland?" *Foreign Policy* (Winter 1980–1981), pp. 163–187; and "A Breakthrough in Afghanistan?" *Foreign Policy* (Summer 1983), pp. 3–26.

[41]Press release, cited in FBIS-East Europe-II-196-9/8/82, p. F4.

[42]*Patriot* (New Delhi), 10 February 1983, pp. 1, 7, in FBIS-South Asia-VIII-41-3/1/83, p. C3.

[43]"U.N. to Press Afghan Efforts," *The New York Times*, 30 March 1983, p. 4.

[44]*Pravda*, 25 April 1983, p. 2.

[45]*Pravda*, 23 May 1981, pp. 1–2, in CDSP-33-21, pp. 6–8.

[46]Richard Bernstein, "Zia Says Soviet May be Flexible on Afghan War," *The New York Times*, 10 December 1982, pp. 1, 8.

[47]Cited in *Yomiuri Shimbun* (Tokyo), 17 November 1982, p. 5. For a Soviet "rebuttal" of this "soft" line, see the unsigned editorial in *Pravda*, 16 December 1982, p. 4.

[48]*Pravda*, 25 April 1983, pp. 1–2.

[49]Richard Bernstein, "Zia Says Soviet May be Flexible on Afghan War."

[50]Interview with U.S. Foreign Service Officer Robert Clark in Moscow, 3 January 1983.

[51]Quoted in Lord Saint Brides, "Afghanistan: The Empire Plays to Win," *Orbis* 24 (Fall 1980), p. 536.

[52]On the general subject of military style, see Chris Donnelly, "The Soviet

Soldier: Behavior, Performance, Effectiveness," in *Soviet Military Power and Performance*, ed. John Erickson and Eric Feuchtwanger (London: Macmillan, 1979), pp. 114–120. The quotes are from Department of the Army Pamphlet no. 20-230, *Historical Study: Russian Combat Methods in World War II*, November 1950 (rpt. 1983), pp. 12, 25.

[53]Defense Intelligence Agency, *Review of Soviet Ground Forces* (July 1982), pp. 13–16.

[54]Nikolai Ogarkov, "For Our Soviet Motherland: Guarding Peaceful Labor," *Kommunist* (no. 10, 1981), in JPRS 79074, 25 September 1981, p. 95. Ogarkov repeated the point in a recent pamphlet and added his concern over Russian language proficiency in the armed forces, a fact which could very well be related to the poor performance of Central Asian reservists in the initial invading force. See *Always in Readiness to Defend the Homeland* (January 1982), in U.S. Air Force, *Soviet Press: Selected Translations*, nos. 9 and 10, 11 and 12, 1982; and no. 1, 1983. The appropriate passages are in pp. 19–22 in no. 1, 1983.

[55]On air assault units, see Roger E. Bort, "Air Assault Brigades: New Element in the Soviet *Desant* Force Structure," *Military Review* 63 (October 1983), pp. 21–39. Although their Soviet designation is in question, a former Afghan army colonel related to this author that, at least informally, they are referred to as "storm brigades" by the Soviets.

[56]Claude Malhuret, "Report from Afghanistan," *Foreign Affairs* 62 (Winter 1983–1984), p. 435.

# IV

*The United States*

# 19

# GEORGE F. KENNAN

## The United States and the Soviet Union, 1917–1976*

I  When, in the year 1917, Russian society was overtaken by the most tremendous and far-reaching upheaval it had ever known, American opinion-makers were poorly prepared to understand either the meaning or the implications of this event.

This was partly because there was little understanding in the United States of that day for Russian history or for the nature of the political society in which these events were taking place. Russian studies had been developed in North America only on the tiniest and most rudimentary of scales. Knowledge of Russia rested on the tales of the occasional traveler or on the reports of press correspondents, very few of whom were qualified to see deeply into the great political and social stirrings that tormented the life of Russia in those final decades of Tsardom. The traditional antipathy of Americans for the Tsarist autocracy was understandable enough; but it was seldom balanced by any realistic examinination of the nature of the possible alternatives. And in the final years before World War I, governmental and journalistic opinion in the United States had tended to be preempted by the problem of the treatment of Jews within the Russian Empire, to the detriment of the attention given to other and even deeper aspects of the slow crisis in which Russian society was then embraced.

This was the situation as of 1914. But as World War I ran its course, and particularly in the year 1917, there came to be imposed upon this general shallowness of understanding a far more serious source of confusion: America's own involvement in the war. If it be conceded that one of the most stubbornly ingrained characteristics of American democracy has been its inability to accept and experience military involvement without becoming seriously disoriented by it and without permitting it to distort judgment on other questions of policy, then it must be said

*Reprinted by permission of the author and publisher from *Foreign Affairs* 54, no. 4 (July, 1976), pp. 670–690. Copyright 1976 by Council on Foreign Relations, Inc.

that never did this weakness reveal itself more sharply and fatefully than in American outlooks on Russia during World War I. Entering the war only a few weeks after the first of the two Russian revolutions of 1917, Americans resolutely declined, from that time on, to view Russian developments from any standpoint other than that of the war against Germany, and not of a thoughtful and objective image of that war, at that, but rather as it was perceived through the grotesquely distorting lenses of wartime propaganda and hysteria.

Thus both Russian revolutions of that fateful year were seriously misperceived. The first—the fall, that is, of Tsardom and its replacement by a regime which was liberal–democratic at least in intent—was welcomed less in its possible significance for the future of Russia than because it was seen—wholly incorrectly—as releasing forces of enthusiasm for the war effort previously suppressed by a supposedly pro-German imperial court. The second revolution, in November, which brought the Bolsheviks to power, was misunderstood by reason of the widespread belief that the Bolshevik leaders were German agents; as a result of which the new regime, not generally expected to last very long in any case, was opposed less for what it really was than out of resentment for its action in taking Russia out of the war.

It was only after the termination of hostilities against Germany that the way was cleared, in theory at least, for a view of Russian communism as a political phenomenon in its own right. But by this time a new welter of bewildering and misleading factors had entered in: such things as the passions and uncertainties of the Russian civil war; the exaggerations of propaganda on both sides; our own semi-involvement in the Allied intervention; the measures of the new Communist regime with relation to Tsarist debts and foreign property, etc. It was not, really, until the early 1920s, after the termination of the Russian civil war and the overcoming of the famine of 1921–1922, that the meaning of what had occurred in Russia since 1917 began to emerge from the turmoil of events with sufficient clarity to permit the beginnings of thoughtful and reasonably informed debate in the United States over the nature of the problem which the installment of Lenin and his associates in the traditional seats of Russian power presented for American statesmanship.

II   Before considering the nature of this problem and of the responses with which it met, it would be well to have a glance at one particular involvement of the United States which occurred in the confusion of those immediate postrevolutionary years and the main effect of which was to muddy the waters of mutual understanding for decades to come. This was America's part in the Allied intervention of 1918–1920. Precisely because this action has so often been depicted by Soviet propagandists as an unsuccessful effort by the American government to unseat the Soviet regime, it is important to recognize its essential origins and dimensions.

The United States only sent troops to two areas of Russia: the European north, in the neighborhood of Arkhangelsk on the White Sea, and eastern Siberia. Both of these areas were far from the main theaters of the Russian civil war then in progress. In neither case was the decision to dispatch these troops taken gladly or—one may say—independently, in Washington. In neither case was it motivated by an intention that these forces should be employed with a view to unseating the Soviet government. In neither case would the decision have been taken except in conjunction with the World War then in progress, and for purposes related primarily to the prosecution of that war.

First—as to northern Russia. President Wilson consented to the dispatch of American forces to that region only in the face of a massive misunderstanding on his part of the situation prevailing there, only with great misgivings and skepticism as to the usefulness of the undertaking, and only when it had been insistently urged upon him by the British and French, with the support of Marshal Foch, then Supreme Allied Commander in Europe, all of whom portrayed it as a measure required by the war effort against Germany. What brought him to the decision was well described by his Secretary of War, Newton Baker, in a letter written some years later. He had convinced the President, Baker wrote, that the decision was unwise:

> [B]ut he told me that he felt obliged to do it anyhow because the British and French were pressing it upon his attention so hard and he had refused so many of their requests that they were beginning to feel that he was not a good associate, much less a good ally.

The three battalions of American troops (for that is all it amounted to) were sent to Arkhangelsk, and served there, under British command. The decisions as to how and for what purposes they would be employed were British decisions, not American ones. The uses to which they were put were ones of which Wilson was ignorant at the time, ones he had never envisaged, ones of which, had he known of them, he would unquestionably have disapproved. That the units remained there after the end of the war with Germany was due to the fact that they were held there, over the winter of 1918–1919, by the frozen condition of the White Sea. When the ice broke up they were removed as soon as this could be accomplished.

As for the troops that were sent to Siberia: The consent to the dispatch of these units was given only when Wilson's unwillingness to send them had been worn down by 6 months of pleading from the Western Allies. Their missions were restricted to the guarding of the Suchan coal mines, in the Maritime Province, and of certain sections of the Trans-Siberian railroad north of Manchuria—services, that is, that were of high importance to the lives and comfort of the inhabitants of the region, regardless of politics. The areas in question were, at the time of the dispatch of the units, thousands of miles removed from the main theaters of the Russian civil war; and the units took no part in that war. Their presence probably gave some satisfaction and comfort to the non-Bolshevik Russian forces in Siberia (although little love was lost between those forces and the Americans), and it may have had some effect in delaying the eventual extension and consolidation of Bolshevik power in the area. But this, so far as Wilson's intentions were concerned, was incidental. That they remained as long as they did, and were not withdrawn in 1919, was due rather to suspicion of the Japanese (who also had troops in the area) on the part of the Americans rather than to hostility toward the Bolsheviks.

The task of attempting to understand the permanent elements of the Soviet-American relationship will be best served if these regrettable episodes of the final weeks and immediate aftermath of World War I be left aside, as the pathetic by-products of wartime confusion, weariness, and myopia that they really were, and the focus of attention be shifted to the more enduring sources of conflict that were destined to complicate the relationship over ensuing decades.

# III

The first and most fundamental of these sources of conflict was of course the ideological commitment of the Bolshevik-Communist leadership. This was something wholly new in the experience of American statesmanship. It was the manifestation of a form of hostility Americans had never previously encountered. Americans had known, of course, the phenomenon of war, as a situation defined and recognized by international law. But war was (normally) the expression of a hostility limited both in time and in intent. It was limited in time because it was coincidental with the existence of a formal state of war. It was limited in intent because the aims it was designed to serve were normally ones of a limited nature: the transfer of a province from one sovereignty to another, a change in the arrangements governing maritime commerce, the replacement of one ruler by another for dynastic reasons, etc.

But what American statesmen now saw themselves faced with, in the person of the new Russian-Communist regime, was something quite different: a governing faction, installed in the seats of power in another great country, which had not even dreamed of declaring war formally on the United States but which was nevertheless committed, by its deepest beliefs and by its very view of its place in history, to a program aimed at the overthrow of the entire political and social system traditional to American society—committed, that is, to a program calculated to inflict upon the society of the United States a damage more monstrous in the eyes of most Americans than any they might expect to suffer from even the worst of purely military defeats at the hands of the traditional sort of adversary.

This situation was destined to undergo many changes and modifications in the course of the ensuing decades. There would be times when the ideological hostility on which it was based would be soft-pedaled for reasons of tactical expediency. In general, the cutting edge of the hostility would be progressively blunted over the course of the decades by the erosion of frustration and the buffeting of contrary events; so that it would come, with the years, to assert itself more as a rhetorical exercise than as a guide to policy. Particularly with respect to the United States, where its chances for political success were singularly slender, this messianic dedication would gradually lose its bite with the passage of the years, so that Americans would ultimately come to fear it less for its possible effect upon themselves than for its effect on other peoples: its effect, that is, in alienating those peoples from that portion of the international community with which America could have a comfortable and friendly relationship and adding them to that other sector (to be greatly increased in the Third World after World War II) in which America, and all that she stood for, would be regarded only with prejudice, misunderstanding, and rejection.

But these would be gradual changes. They lay, as of the early 1920s, well in the future. They were not yet generally visible or predictable. The American statesmen of that day had to take the ideological challenge at its own words, and deal with it accordingly.

It would be wrong, of course, to suppose that this sort of hostility remained one-sided, or even that it was wholly one-sided from the start. It naturally bred its own reaction on the part of many Americans; and it would be idle to pretend that this reaction was always thoughtful, reasonable, devoid of prejudice, sensitively responsive to the nature of the challenge itself. It was a reaction that would manifest itself, down through the years, in many ways, most of them unpleasant: in the anti-Red hysterias of 1919–1920 and 1950–1953; in the vulnerability of large sections of the American public to the sanguine urgings of the Chinese–Nationalist and "captive nations" lobbies; in the exaggerated military apprehensions and phantasmagoria of the post-World War II period. Hampering at every turn the development of a sound and effective response to the challenge which had provoked it (or provided the rationalization for it), this exaggerated reaction would constitute at all times a complication of the Soviet-American relationship in its own right. And it was not slow in making itself felt in the immediate aftermath of the Revolution. It was one with which American policymakers were obliged to contend from the start, in their efforts to design an effective response to the challenge in question.

Before proceeding to examine this response, it would be well to note that there were two features of this unprecedented relationship that were fated to constitute basic and unalterable elements of the problem it presented for American statesmanship. One was the fact that, fiery as were the assertions of intent upon the part of this ideological opponent to destroy *our* system, and heartily as this challenge was accepted by sections of our own public opinion, neither side was in a position, or ever would be in a position, to achieve the total destruction of the other. Each might hope for it; each might do what little it could to abet processes that seemed to run in that direction. But neither could, by its own action, achieve it; nor did ulterior forces produce this result. The result was that each had to accept, for better or for worse, the other's existence and to start from there in the designing of policy.

This—"peaceful coexistence" if you will—was a reality of the relationship from the beginning. It did not need a Khrushchev or a Brezhnev to discover it or create it.

The other inalterable element of this problem, destined to become wholly visible and compelling only in later years but also present, in reality, from the start, was the fact that in this complicated world of ours there could be no international relationship which was one of total antagonism or total identity of interests—none which did not contain both sorts of ingredients, however uneven the mix. Just as there could be no relationship of friendship undiluted by elements of rivalry and conflict, so there could be no relationship of antagonism not complicated by elements of occasional common purpose or desiderata.

The fact that these *were*, precisely, the basic elements of the problem was not always clearly visible to all the American statesmen who had to deal with it, any more than it was to all sections of American private opinion. But the fact was always there, on the visible surface or below it; and those who attempted to ignore it risked the prospect of being yanked back sooner or later, and sometimes in painful ways, to the plane of reality.

IV It would be unfair to search in actions of the American statesmen in the 1917–1920 period for the elements of a serious and considered response to this problem. The situation was too chaotic, their oversight over events too imperfect, to expect this of them. But with the end of Allied intervention, and with the gradual grinding to a halt of civil conflict in Russia, the situation became clearer; and it is instructive to observe the emergence of a more systematic and principled response.

The first to make the attempt to design such a response were those who were responsible for the conduct of American diplomacy at the end of the Wilson Administration.

These did not really include Wilson himself, except as the influence of his thinking from earlier days still made itself felt. He lay, at that time, ill and helpless in the White House. But it was impossible for his assistants not to take some attitude toward the problem, and this they proceeded to do. It was a purely ideological attitude, as uncompromising in its acceptance of the Bolshevik challenge as were the authors of that challenge in their creation of it. It was succinctly expressed in the note that Secretary of State Bainbridge Colby addressed to the Italian government on August 10, 1920:

> It is not possible for the Government of the United States to recognize the present rulers of Russia as a government with which the relations common to friendly governments can be maintained. This conviction has nothing to do with any particular political or social structure which the Russian people themselves may see fit to embrace. It rests upon a wholly different set of facts.
>     . . . Upon numerous occasions the responsible spokesmen of this Power . . . have declared that it is their understanding that the very

existence of Bolshevism in Russia, the maintenance of their own rule, depends, and must continue to depend, upon the occurrence of revolutions in all other great civilized nations, including the United States, which will overthrow and destroy their governments and set up Bolshevist rule in their stead. . . . We cannot recognize, hold official relations with, or give friendly reception to the agents of a government which is determined and bound to conspire against our institutions.

The essential features of this response are easily observed. It accepted the first of the elements of the problem noted above: the existence of the Soviet state and the impossibility, for the United States, of doing anything to change that situation, beyond the refusal to accord formal diplomatic recognition. It revealed no awareness of the second element: namely the existence of a limited area of common interest; indeed, its authors would have been skeptical of the thesis that such an area existed, or could exist. Nothing of this nature was visible to them.

This declaration was, of course, one of the swan songs of the Democratic Administration of that day. That Administration shortly was to be replaced by the first of the successive Republican Administrations of Harding, Coolidge, and Hoover.

The Republicans accepted the reasoning of the Colby note, as far as it went; but to the motivation of the policy of nonrecognition they added one more feature not present in Mr. Colby's pronouncement. This was a reference to the failure of the Soviet government to recognize any obligation in principle to assume the foreign debts of previous Russian regimes or to reimburse foreigners for property previously owned by them in Russia and now nationalized by the Soviet authorities. In the view of these Republican statesmen, the Soviet government, in order to regularize its relations with the United States, would not only have to cease its advocacy of revolution in the United States and its ill-concealed support for elements working to that end, but would have to assume the financial obligations incurred by previous Russian regimes to the U.S. government and to American nationals.

On this, the relationship rested for 13 years. Individual American businessmen were not prevented from traveling in Russia and trading with the Soviet foreign trade monopoly, at their own risk. Herbert Hoover, emerging with halos of glory from his leadership of the American relief effort in Europe at the end of the war, was not prevented from organizing and conducting in Russia, in 1921–1922, as a private undertaking, the magnificent work of the American Relief Administration, which saved several million people from starvation and may well, for all anyone can tell, have saved the Soviet regime itself from utter failure and collapse. But the American government itself was officially blind to a regime whose attitude and behavior it found unacceptable as a basis for formal relations.

The Soviet government, for its part, was quite aware, over the years in question, of the complexity of its relations with the Western countries, and of its need for certain forms of collaboration with them even in the face of ideological hostility. It did not, however, find itself too adversely affected by the American stance. What it wanted from the Western powers was trade, recognition, and credits. Trade it got, without difficulty, from all of them, including even the United States. Recognition it received, mostly in the years 1924–1925, from all the leading European powers. Commercial credit, too, it succeeded in obtaining from some of them, notably the Germans, within the relatively narrow limits prescribed by circumstances. All these benefits were achieved without paying the price the U.S. government was demanding: which was the suppression of the Comintern and the sort of activity its existence implied, as well as major concessions in the field of debts and claims. Thus the incentive on the part of the Soviet leaders to meet these American demands became weaker with the passage of the years. They wanted American recognition and financial help; but they were not prepared to pay, and did not need to pay, the price the Republican Administrations of 1921–1933 were demanding.

V Franklin Roosevelt's assumption of the presidency, in 1933, marked, of course, a fundamental turning point in the relationship. To him, the old question of debts and claims seemed, in itself, unimportant, likewise the issue of propaganda. He recognized that these issues engaged the feelings and interests of important segments of American opinion, and thus presented domestic-political problems he would have to meet; but he could not have cared less about them from his own concept of America's external interests.

On the other hand, he was, in contrast to his Republican predecessors, very conscious indeed of the existence of at least one area of common interest with the Soviet Union: with relation, namely, to the threat of Japanese penetration onto the mainland of Asia. This was shortly to be supplemented by similar feelings on his part with relation to Hitler's obvious intention to win for Germany a dominant position on the European continent.

Franklin Roosevelt was contemptuous from the start of the reasoning of the State Department and of the upper-class Eastern establishment which had for so long inspired Republican policy toward Russia. He was much influenced by Mr. William C. Bullitt, the brilliant and charming dilettante who, as a very young man, had been sent to Russia in 1919, during the Peace Conference, by Lloyd George and Colonel House, had returned convinced that it *was* possible to deal with Lenin and his associates and disgusted with the Allied leaders for declining to do so. FDR, persuaded as he was of his own great powers of ingratiation and persuasiveness, readily lent his ear to Mr. Bullitt's suggestions that the Soviet leaders, being human, would now be responsive to a more friendly and conciliatory approach, and that, having even more to fear than did the Americans from a Japanese penetration into Manchuria (not to mention an expansion of Nazi power into Eastern Europe) they could easily be made into an asset from the standpoint of possible resistance to these developments. And the result, of course, was the reestablishment of diplomatic relations between the two countries in the autumn of 1933.

It was characteristic of FDR that the preliminary Soviet–American agreements (the so-called Roosevelt–Litvinov letters), on the basis of which the establishment of diplomatic relations was arranged, were ones designed, in his own eyes, not at all to assure to the United States any real advantage in the forthcoming official relationship, but rather to meet the prejudices and disarm the criticisms of groups within the American political community whose opposition to recognition was to be expected. Such of the wording of the Litvinov letters as appeared to assure a cessation of subversive propaganda and activity with relation to the United States, and a settlement of the questions of debts and claims, was thus far too vague and full of loopholes to satisfy anyone really wishing to see these issues resolved; and in this sense it could be charged, and was, that Roosevelt's acceptance of it constituted a direct misleading of the American public. But there is no reason to suppose that FDR doubted that desirable results could be obtained in the end, by one means or another, regardless of the precision of the language of the understandings. For real gains in the Soviet–American relationship the President was inclined to rely not on written documents but on the power of his own charismatic personality.

The result, for anyone who knew anything about Russia, was predictable. The issues of debts and claims were never resolved; it remained for the passage of time to drain them of most of their meaning. The propaganda and the support for subversion did not cease. Trade, instead of increasing, declined. The Soviet authorities, recognition having now been obtained, the Japanese threat having for the moment slightly abated, and it having become clear that in any case the Americans were not going to fight the Japanese for their benefit, now lost interest either in making good on the concessions they had semi-promised or in making new ones. The new American Embassy in Moscow, founded initially with exuberant optimism under the auspices of Mr. Bullitt as the first Ambassador, soon fell victim to the age-old Russian aversion to dealing with the resident-diplomat (regarded as too avisé, too guarded and skeptical, too patient, and too little susceptible to being rushed into hasty agreements) and its preference for dealing directly with the foreign statesman, innocent of any close personal knowledge of Russian realities.

So Mr. Bullitt, not surprisingly, left in disgust after a year or so of frustration, to join at a later date the ranks of the Soviet Union's most bitter critics and opponents on the Washington scene. His successor, Mr. Joseph E. Davies, a man to whom for various reasons the appearances of good relations were more important than their reality, made a valiant attempt, if not a very plausible one, to maintain those appearances. But he, too, soon gave up the struggle, and retired from the Russian scene in 1938. The American Embassy was felt, thereafter, to share for years to come the dim semi-existence customarily led by the Moscow diplomatic corps, isolated, guarded, seen but not heard, useful—in this case—primarily as a school for young Russian-speaking diplomats, obliged to contemplate and to study the Russian scene while they pondered the reasons for their own isolation.

The years immediately following the resumption of Soviet–American relations were, of course, the years of the purges. With the millions that perished in those fearful agonies, there perished also—there could not help but perish—the magical afterglow of the hope and idealism of the Lenin period. By the end of the 1930s not even the greatest enthusiast could ignore the dread hand of terror, denunciation, and moral corruption that had gripped Russian society. Only the most wishful and uninstructed of foreign sympathizers, outraged by the phenomenon of European fascism and inclined to give the benefit of the doubt to anything that even appeared to oppose it, could retain the illusion that here was a superior and more humane civilization.

But such sympathizers did, of course, exist in the United States. They were encouraged by what seemed to them to be the implications of the economic crisis that had now overtaken their own "capitalist" country. They encouraged, and helped to preserve, in Franklin Roosevelt and certain of those around him a somewhat battered but undefeated partiality for the Soviet regime: a readiness to dismiss the tales of the horror and injustice of the purges as just some more of the anti-Soviet propaganda that had been pouring out from reactionary circles ever since the Revolution, and a readiness to continue to believe in the essential progressiveness of the Soviet "experiment," all the more acceptable, seemingly, by way of contrast to the European fascism and Japanese militarism just then advancing upon the world scene.

The Nazi–Soviet Non-Aggression Pact of 1939 was, of course, a great blow to people who held these views. Together with the ensuing Russian attack on Finland and taking over of the Baltic states, this unexpected development was enough to suppress down to the year 1941 the latent pro-Sovietism just described. But it was not a mortal blow. The inclinations in question survived, below the surface, into the eventful year of 1941. And when in June of that year Russia herself was invaded by Hitler, it was as if the unhappy events of 1939–1940 had never occurred: Robert Sherwood's moving play on the suffering of the Finns under the Russian attack was soon revised with the replacement of the Finns by the Greeks, and the Russians by the Germans. A new era, once again dominated by the fact of America's being at war, was beginning to dawn in the history of Soviet–American relations.


VI  Never, surely, has the congenital subjectivity of the American perception of the outside world been more strikingly illustrated than in the change of attitude toward Russia that followed Pearl Harbor and the ensuing German declaration of war on the United States, in December 1941. Gone, as if by magic, were most of the memories and impressions of the past. Forgotten, now, were the Russian purges, along with the reflection that the men now running Russia's war effort and diplomacy were the same who had once conducted those bloody persecutions.

Forgotten, too, were the cruelties only recently perpetrated by Beriya's police establishment upon the innocent populations of Eastern Poland and the Baltic states. Forgotten was the fact that Russia's involvement in the war was neither the doing nor the preference of her own rulers: that, on the contrary, they had made desperate efforts to remain aloof from it, and would, had this been possible, have witnessed without a quiver of regret further Western reverses in the war, provided only that the contest was sufficiently bloody and prolonged to exhaust Germany's war-making potential along with that of its Western opponents. Ignored, in large measure, was the fact that the demands which Stalin was making on his Western allies, even as early as the end of 1941, were substantially the same as those he had placed before Hitler as the price for Russia's initial neutrality. In place of all this there emerged, and was systematically cultivated in Washington, the image of a great Soviet people, animated by the same noble impulses of humane indignation and yearning for a future free of all tyranny by which Americans conceived themselves and their allies to be animated, fighting with inspiring heroism and grandeur against an opponent in whose repulsive political personality all the evil of an imperfect world seemed to be concentrated.

The image was, of course, not wholly wrong. The heroism was there. So was the grandeur of the effort. That the Western powers owed their military victory to that effort, in the sense that without it their victory could never have been achieved, was undeniable. It was also true that a great proportion of the Soviet people conceived themselves to be fighting for the defense of their homeland—an aim with which Americans could at least sympathize even if the homeland was not theirs.

But what was important, of course, in the given circumstances, was not what the mass of the Soviet people conceived themselves to be fighting for but what their rulers perceived as the uses they wished to make of victory; and this, as the past had shown, was a different thing.

Weighty reasons were offered for the idealization of the Soviet ally, and the encouragement of belief in the possibilities of postwar collaboration with it, that inspired so much of Franklin Roosevelt's wartime policy. Without a belief on the part of the public that Russians and Americans were fighting for the same thing it would have been impossible, it was said, to maintain American enthusiasm for the war effort and the readiness to give aid to Russia in the pursuit of that effort. Without American aid, without American moral support, without expressions of American confidence in Russia, Stalin might have been tempted, it was argued, to make a compromise peace with the Nazis, permitting Hitler to concentrate his entire great force against the West.

There was much in these arguments. The weakest part of them was perhaps that which most appealed to the American military establishment, now the center of American policymaking: the fear of a complete Russian collapse or (as the tide turned) of a separate Russian–German peace. Stalin, of course, would have loved the latter, though not until the Germans had been expelled from at least the pre-1938 territory of the Soviet Union; and once things had gone that far, and the Germans had begun to crumble, then his own appetite was stimulated to a point where he saw no need to stop. But that fear of such a development, coupled with a sense of humiliation over their own inability (until 1944) to pick up a larger share of the military load, haunted the American military leadership throughout the war and inclined them to give moral and material support to their Soviet opposite numbers in every possible way, is clear.

Behind this whole argument, however, there lay a deeper question: and that is whether it ever pays to mislead American opinion, to be less than honest with it, even in the interests of what is perceived by the political leadership as a worthy cause. It is characteristic of wartime psychology that the end tends to be seen as justifying the means. But when the means include the manipulation of opinion by the creation and propagation of unreal images, there is always a price to be paid at a later date; for the distortions thus engendered have some day to be straightened out again.

And so it was in the years after 1945. It must be said in defense of FDR and his associates that they probably never fully realized (although they came closest to it in the days just preceding the President's death) the extent to which they *were* actually misleading American opinion on this point. Amid the stresses of a great war effort it is particularly easy for the wish to play father to the thought. Stalin, too, encouraged, in his own delicate and cautious way, the propagation of this myth: soft-pedaling, while the war was in progress, certain forms of criticism of the Western Allies, and making adroit use of those idealistic semantic generalities which can mean all things to all people.

But the fact remains, however extenuating the circumstances, not only was the unreal dream of an intimate and happy postwar collaboration with Russia extensively peddled to large portions of the American public during the war, but they were encouraged to believe that without its successful realization there could be no peaceful and happy future at all.

The events of the final weeks of the war and of the immediate post-hostilities period rapidly demolished this dream. Event after event: the behavior of the Soviet forces in the half of Europe they overran; the growing evidence that the Soviet authorities had no intention of permitting the free play of democratic forces in the countries of that great region; their cynical reluctance to collaborate in the restoration of economic life and stability in areas they did not control; the continued secretiveness and inscrutability of Soviet policymaking and political action; the failure to enter upon any extensive demobilization of the Soviet armed forces; the narrow, suspicious and yet greedy behavior of Soviet representatives in the new international organizations—all these things fell heavily upon a public in no way prepared for them; nor was there any Franklin Roosevelt, now, with his talent for the leadership of opinion, to make the transition in company with those whom he had, wittingly or otherwise, misled—to ease them out of the wartime euphoria he had once eased them into.

The results were not unnatural. Unrequited love now turned only too easily into unreasonable hatred. To people taught to assume that in Russian–American postwar collaboration lay the only assurance of future peace, the absence of that collaboration, in the light of a conflict of aims becoming daily more visible, inevitably conduced to visions of war. To people unsettled by the recent experience of being at war, the real personality of Russia, in all its vast complexity, was often lost to view; and in its place, assuming in many respects the aspect of the late-departed Hitler, there emerged one of those great and forbidding apparitions to the credence in which mass opinion is so easily swayed: a monster devoid of all humanity and of all rationality of motive, at once the embodiment and the caricature of evil, devoid of internal conflicts and problems of its own, intent only on bringing senseless destruction to the lives and hopes of others.

Neither of these reactions—neither the exorbitant wartime hopes nor the angry postwar disillusionment—were shared by all sections of American opinion; and where they were shared, not all experienced them in like degree. There were those who labored, with moderate success, to correct them. Alone the effect of these aberrations might not have been deep or enduring. But they happened to fall in, most fatefully, with the emergence of a new pattern of fears and misunderstandings—this time of a military nature.

The failure of the Soviet government to carry out any extensive demobilization in the posthostilities period has already been mentioned. Here again, taken outside the context of ulterior circumstances, this might not have been unduly alarming. For centuries it had been the custom of Russian rulers to maintain in being, even in time of peace, ground forces larger than anyone else could see the necessity for. The reasons for this must be assumed to have been primarily of a domestic political and social nature. But this time the circumstances—and along with the circumstances, the reactions—were different in a number of respects.

In the first place, in contrast to the situation of earlier decades and centuries, the Russian armed forces now had an area of deployment in the very heart of Europe, with secure lines of support and communication behind them. In the past, it had been possible to employ their great numerical strength in Western Europe only after first overcoming both the geographic and the military impediments of the territory that lay between Russia's traditional western borders and the industrial heartland of the European continent. Now, a Soviet offensive, if one wished to launch one, could be started from within 60 miles of Hamburg or 100 miles of the Rhine. To military planners, trained to give greater weight to capabilities than to intentions, this could not fail to be disturbing. And not to military planners alone. The peoples of Western Europe, all of whose memories, with one or two exceptions, included the overrunning of their homelands by foreign troops at one time or another, and usually within the past century, suffered from *la manie d'invasion* and found it difficult to believe that the Russians, having already overrun so many countries since 1944, should not wish to overrun more.

Second, Western strategists, inclined anyway, for reasons of professional prudence and others, to a chronic overrating of the adversary's capabilities, now found themselves confronting no longer the traditional primitive and slow-moving Russian ground forces, defensively strong on their own ground but not well fitted for offensive purposes against a strong Western opponent, but rather, modern, mechanized units with equipment little inferior, sometimes not inferior at all, to that of the Western armies themselves. The result, of course, was increased anxiety.

But overshadowing both of these factors, as a source for the militarization of American thinking about the problem of relations with Russia, was of course the development by the Russians of a nuclear capability, visible from 1949 onward.

The writer of these lines knows no reason to suppose that the Soviet leadership of Stalin's day ever allotted to the nuclear weapon anything resembling a primary role in its political–strategic concepts. There is no reason to doubt that Stalin saw this weapon as he himself described it: as something with which one frightened people with weak nerves. Not only was he aware from the start of its potentially suicidal quality, but he will be sure to have recognized, as one in whose eyes wars were no good unless they served some political purpose, that for such purposes the nuclear weapon was ill suited: it was too primitive, too blindly destructive, too indiscriminate, too prone to destroy the useful with the useless.

Merciless as he could be, and little as his purposes may have coincided with ours, Stalin was entirely rational in his external policies; war, for him, was not just a glorified sporting event, with no aim other than military victory; he had no interest in slaughtering people indiscriminately, just for the sake of slaughtering them; he pursued well-conceived, finite purposes related to his own security and ambitions. The nuclear weapon could destroy people; it could not occupy territory, police it, or organize it politically. He sanctioned its development, yes— because others were doing so, because he did not want to be without it, because he was well aware of the importance of the shadows it could cast over international events by the mere fact of its inclusion in a country's overt national arsenal.

But it was not to this weapon that he looked for the satisfaction of his aspirations on the international plane. Indeed, in view of the physical dangers the weapon presented, and the confusion which its existence threw over certain cherished Marxist concepts as to the way the world was supposed to work, he probably would have been quite happy to see it removed entirely from national arsenals, including his own, if this could be done without the acceptance of awkward forms of international inspection. And if his successors were eventually forced into a somewhat different view of the uses of the weapon, as they probably were, it was surely the Western powers, committed from the start to the first use of the weapon in any major encounter, whether or not it was used against them, that did the forcing.

Little of this was perceived, however, on the Western side—and on the American side in particular. Once again, the interest in capabilities triumphed over any evidence concerning intentions. The recognition that the Russians had the weapon, and the necessary carriers, served as sufficient basis for the assumption that they had a desire to use it and would, if not deterred, do so.

In part, this was the product of the actual discipline of peacetime military planning. The planner has to assume an adversary. In the case at hand, the Russians, being the strongest and the most rhetorically hostile, were the obvious candidates. The adversary must then be credited with the evilest of intentions. No need to ask *why* he should be moved to take certain hostile actions, or whether he would be likely to take them. That he has the capability of taking them suffices. The mere fact that they would be damaging to one's own side is regarded as adequate motive for their execution. In this way not only is there created, for planning purposes, the image of the totally inhuman and totally malevolent adversary, but this image is reconjured daily, week after week, month after month, year after year, until it takes on every feature of flesh and blood and becomes the daily companion of those who cultivate it, so that any attempt on anyone's part to deny its reality appears as an act of treason or frivolity. Thus the planner's dummy of the Soviet political personality took the place of the real thing as the image on which a great deal of American policy, and of American military effort, came to be based.

Nor does this exhaust the list of those forces which, in the aftermath of World War II, impelled large portions of influential American opinion about Russia into a new, highly militaristic, and only partially realistic mold. The fall of China to its own Communists, a development that was by no means wholly agreeable to the Soviet leadership, came soon to be regarded as the work of Moscow, implemented (was there ever an odder flight of the imagination?) not directly but through the agency of naïve or disloyal Americans. Out of this, and out of the related discovery that there was political mileage to be made by whipping up suspicions of fellow citizens, there emerged the phenomenon known as McCarthyism, the unquestioned premise of which was the existence of a diabolically clever Russian–Communist enemy, consumed with deadly hostility and concerned only with our undoing. And not long thereafter came the misreading by the official Washington establishment of the nature and significance of the Korean War—a misreading by virtue of which an operation inspired overwhelmingly by local considerations related to the situation in the Manchurian–Korean area, and one from which the Soviet government studiously kept its own forces aloof, came to be regarded and discussed in Washington as, in effect, an attack by the Soviet Red Army across international borders, and as only the first move in a sort of Hitlerian "grand design" for military world conquest.

It was out of such ingredients that there emerged, in the late 1940s and early 1950s, those attitudes in American opinion that came to be associated with the term "cold war." These were never to dominate all of American opinion. Many people, while generally prepared to give a polite show of outward credence to the image of the Soviet adversary just described, remained aware of the scantiness of their own information and were prepared, by and large, to reserve judgment. In their extreme form the fixations in question remained the property of a small but strongly committed right-wing minority, the electoral weakness of which was repeatedly demonstrated, and of the military budgeteers and nuclear strategists, who had little electoral significance at all.

Nevertheless, the image of the Soviet Union as primarily a military challenge was now widely accepted. And for reasons that warrant more scholarly investigation than they have received, the resulting fixations acquired a curiously hypnotic power over the professional political community. A certain show of bristling vigilance in the face of a supposed external danger seems to have an indispensable place in the American political personality; and for this, in the early 1950s, with Hitler now out of the way, the exaggerated image of the menacing Kremlin, thirsting and plotting for world domination, came in handy. There was, in any case, not a single Administration in Washington, from that of Harry Truman on down, which, when confronted with the charge of being "soft on communism," however meaningless the phrase or weak the evidence, would not run for cover and take protective action.

These observations should not be misunderstood. The reality that deserved recognition in place of this exaggerated image was never its opposite. There were indeed, throughout this period, as there always had been before, threatening elements in both Soviet rhetoric and Soviet behavior. That behavior remained marked at all times, in one degree or another, by features—disrespect for the truth; claims to infallibility; excessive secrecy; excessive armaments; ruthless domination of satellite peoples; and repressive policies at home—that were bound to arouse distaste and resentment in American opinion, and thus to feed and sustain the distorted image of Soviet Russia we have just had occasion to note. It is not too much to say, in fact, that if the Soviet leaders did not want to live with this image, they could have done a great deal more than they actually did to disarm it; a few obviously specious peace congresses and the ritualistic repetition of professions of devotion to the cause of "peace" (as though peace were some sort of abstraction) were never enough.

Most serious of all, as distortions of understanding from the Soviet side—particularly serious because massively and deliberately cultivated—were the dense clouds of anti-American propaganda put out, day after day, month after month, and year after year, in the postwar period by a Soviet propaganda machine that had never been inhibited by any very serious concern for objective and observable truth, and was now more reckless than ever in its disregard for it. The extremes to which this effort was carried, particularly in those final months of Stalin's life that coincided with the high point of the Korean War, were such as to be scarcely conceivable except to those who experienced them at first hand. Here, the United States was portrayed, of course, as the most imperialist, militaristic, and generally vicious of all aggressors. And this affected the climate of relations at both ends; for, on the one hand, the very extremism of these attacks confirmed Americans in their view of the sinister duplicity of Soviet policy (why, it was asked, should a government that was really of peaceful intent have such need for the lie in the statement of its case?); while, on the other hand, those Soviet leaders and officials who had a part in the making of policy, despite the cynicism with which they launched this propaganda, could not help being affected by it themselves, and were influenced according-ly in their interpretation of American behavior.

Against this background of mutual misunderstanding, the course of Soviet-American relations in the immediate postwar years, and to some extent down into the Khrushchev era, was determined by a series of spontaneous misinterpretations and misread signals which would have been comical had it not been so dangerous. The Marshall Plan, the preparations for the setting up of a West German government, and the first moves toward the establishment of NATO, were taken in Moscow as the beginnings of a campaign to deprive the Soviet Union of the fruits of its victory over Germany. The Soviet crackdown on Czechoslovakia and the mounting of the Berlin blockade, both essentially defensive (and partially predictable) reactions to these Western moves, were then similarly misread on the Western side. Shortly thereafter there came the crisis of the Korean War, where the Soviet attempt to employ a satellite military force in civil combat to its own advantage, by way of reaction to the American decision to establish a permanent military presence in Japan, was read in Washington as the beginning of the final Soviet push for world conquest; whereas the active American military response, provoked by this Soviet move, appeared in Moscow (and not entirely without reason) as a threat to the Soviet position in both Manchuria and in eastern Siberia.

And so it went, less intensively, to be sure, after Stalin's death, but nonetheless tragically and unnecessarily, into the respective mininter-pretations of such later events as the bringing of the Germans into NATO, the launching of the first Sputnik, the decision to introduce nuclear weapons into the continental components of NATO, the second and prolonged Berlin crisis provoked by Khrushchev in the late 1950s and early 1960s, and finally the Cuban missile crisis. Each misreading set the stage for the next one. And with each of them, the grip of military rivalry on the minds of policymakers on both sides was tightened and made more final.

VII    One of the most fateful effects of this preoccupation with the military aspects of the relationship was to dull in a great many Amer-icans, including many legislators, opinion-makers, and policymakers, the sensitivity to real and significant changes occurring in Soviet society and leadership. Most fateful of all was their effect in obscuring the significance of Stalin's death. The changes that followed on that event were of course gradual ones, and ones of degree. In part, they were the objects of deliberate efforts at concealment on the part of the new leadership. All this, admittedly, made them not always easy of recogni-

tion. But they were important. They greatly deserved American attention. And they were not undiscernible to trained and attentive eyes, of
which the American government had a number, if it had cared to use
them.

The Khrushchev era, and particularly the years from 1955 to 1960,
presented what was unquestionably the most favorable situation that
had existed since the 1920s for an improvement of relations with Russia
and for a tempering of what was by this time rapidly becoming a
dangerous, expensive, and generally undesirable competition in the
development of armed forces and weapons systems. Khrushchev certainly had his failings—among them, his boasting, his crudeness, his
occasional brutalities, his preoccupation with Soviet prestige, and his
ebullient efforts to ensure it—most of these were the failings of a man
who was outstandingly a peasant *parvenu*, not born to the habit or
expectation of great power and with a tendency to overdo in the exercise
of it. But he was intensely human, even in relations with the ideological
opponent. One could talk with him—talk, so far as he was concerned, to
the very limits of one's physical stamina (his own appeared to be
unlimited).

The primitive and naïve nature of Khrushchev's faith in Marxist–
Leninist principles as he understood them was, strange as this may
seem, an advantage; for it caused him to wish, even in confrontation
with the capitalist visitor, to convince, to convert, and—to this end—to
communicate. This, from the standpoint of efforts to reach a better
understanding, was far better than the crafty cynicism of a Stalin. To
which must be added the recollection that Khrushchev's secret speech,
at the Twentieth Congress of the Party in 1956, dealt to the extreme
Stalinist tendencies in the Party and in the world communist movement
a blow from which they were never fully to recover.

The Khrushchev period, too, was of course not lacking in serious
crises. In addition to the Berlin crisis mentioned above, there was, above
all, the Hungarian rebellion of 1956. It should not be taken as an apology
for the Soviet action at that time if one points out that this action was
neither correctly understood nor usefully reacted to on the American
side. The misunderstanding arose (as it was again to do in the face of the
Czechoslovak crisis of 1968) from the apparent inability of a great many
Americans to understand that the Soviet hegemony over Eastern Europe, established by force of arms in the final phases of the war and
tacitly accepted by this country, was a seriously intended arrangement
that the Soviet leadership proposed to maintain, if necessary, by the
same means with which they had acquired it.

As for the American reaction: The resort to armed force by the
Western powers was never a feasible alternative; the conflict could not
have been limited; and even Hungary was not worth a nuclear war.
Where the United States might usefully have acted was by an offer to
make certain modifications in its military posture in Western Europe if
the Soviet government would let things in Hungary take their course.
But the preoccupations of the American Secretary of State at that
moment with the deplorable happenings of the Suez crisis, together

with the already firm commitment of the United States and the other NATO members against anything resembling a disengagement in Europe, made such an offer impossible.

The situation remained, therefore, essentially unchanged. In certain relatively powerless sectors of the American government establishment people continued to explore, patiently and with insight, the possible channels of approach to a less dangerous and more hopeful state of affairs. But in other and more powerful echelons other people continued to carry on with the concepts born of the Korean War, as though Stalin had never died, as though no changes had occurred, as though the problem were still, and solely, the achievement of superiority in preparation for a future military encounter accepted as inevitable, rather than the avoidance of a disastrous encounter for which there was no logical reason at all and which no one could expect to win. The interests of the gathering of military intelligence continued to be given precedence over the possibilities for diplomatic communication. And who does not remember the result? The almost predictable accident occurred. The U-2 plane was brought crashing to the ground in the center of Russia, carrying with it the prestige of Khrushchev; discrediting him in the eyes of his own colleagues, shattering his ascendancy over the Soviet military establishment, hastening the end of a career already seriously jeopardized by other factors.

VIII    Four years were still to elapse before Khrushchev's final fall—years marked by President Kennedy's rather unsuccessful effort to establish a personal relationship with Khrushchev, and by the further complication of the Cuban missile crisis. Whether the unwise effort to put missiles in Cuba was something forced upon Khrushchev by his own colleagues, or whether it was a last desperate gamble on his part with a view to restoring his waning authority, seems still to be uncertain; but that it completed the destruction of his career is not. And from 1965 on, with LBJ now in the White House by his own right and with Khrushchev removed from the scene, a new period opened in Soviet–American relations.

The omens, at the outset of Mr. Johnson's incumbency, were not, by and large, wholly unfavorable. The shock of the recent unpleasantnesses still weighed, to be sure, upon the atmosphere of relations. But even the fall of Khrushchev had not canceled out many of the favorable changes in Soviet conditions against which Soviet–American relations had to proceed; modest improvements, and gradual ones, to be sure, but not without their significance. The terror had been mitigated. The independence of the secret police had been greatly curtailed. There had been some relaxation of the restrictions on association of Russians with foreigners. There was a greater willingness on the part of the authorities to permit many forms of participation by Soviet citizens in international life, culturally and in the sports. Theses changes were, to be sure, only partially recognized in Washington. Many people, as the future would show, remained quite blind to them. But LBJ and his Secretary of State, Dean Rusk, were not wholly oblivious to them, nor did they fail to try to take some advantage of them. The result was that certain gains were made, in the 1966–1968 period which, if one had been able to build further on them, might well have developed into the sort of thing that later, in the early 1970s, came to be known as "détente." (The word was in fact even then in use.) Agreements were reached on the opening up of direct airline communications, on the establishment of consular representation in cities other than the respective capitals, and (in very modest measure) on certain fishing problems. New arrangements for cultural exchange were agreed upon, and the first soundings were taken for what were later to be the SALT talks and the collaboration in space exploration and research.

These beginnings soon fell victim, however, to two developments: first, the Soviet action in Czechoslovakia in 1968; second, and of much greater importance, the American involvement in Vietnam. It was not until the first could be forgotten, and the second brought into process of liquidation in the early 1970s, that prospects again opened up for further progress along the lines pioneered by Messrs. Johnson and Rusk some 4 to 6 years earlier.


IX    The positive results of the phase of Soviet–American relations that came to be known (somewhat misleadingly) as the Nixon–Kissinger détente are too recent to require extensive recapitulation. These results were compressed, for the most part, into an extraordinarily short period, but one full of activity: from the time of the Kissinger visit to China in the summer of 1971 to the Brezhnev visit to the United States in June 1973. The individual bilateral agreements arrived at in the course of the various negotiations and high-level visits were too numerous to be listed here. They covered some 15 to 20 subjects, sometimes overlapping, and sometimes representing successive stages in the treatment of a single subject. Not all of them were of great political importance; a number of them represented beginnings, rather than the full-fledged achievement of wholly open, fruitful and secure arrangements; but they represented steps forward. The most important of them was, without question, the SALT agreement signed by Messrs. Nixon and Brezhnev on the occasion of the former's visit to Moscow in May 1972.

These were all bilateral Soviet–American agreements. They were flanked, of course, in their early stages, by the achievements of what came to be called Chancellor Willy Brandt's "Ostpolitik." (Again, this was a poor term—as though this were the first German government, or the last, ever to have a policy toward the East.) There were also the highly confusing and largely meaningless negotiations that were to lead, eventually, to the Helsinki agreements—multilateral negotiations in which the Americans took only an unenthusiastic and secondary part. But by and large, the Nixon–Kissinger détente was a movement of a positive nature in bilateral Soviet–American relations, observed even with some uncertainty and misgiving by America's European allies.

From the Soviet standpoint this effort of policy was stimulated and made possible by two changes in the international situation that marked the early 1970s: the liquidation of America's Vietnam involvement and the Nixon visit to Peking, followed by the establishment of a de facto American–Chinese official relationship. At the American end it was of course simultaneously the presence in positions of authority in Washington of two men: Richard Nixon, then at the height of his power and prestige, bringing to the White House a reputation as a cold war hardliner which gave him a certain margin of immunity from right-wing attack as he moved to improve relations with Russia; and Henry Kissinger, who brought to the operation a measure of imagination, boldness of approach, and sophistication of understanding without which it would have been difficult of achievement.

Both sides saw in this effort toward the improvement and enrichment of the relationship a chance for reducing the dangers of unlimited rivalry and proliferation in the field of nuclear weaponry; and both, be it said to their credit, were aware of the immense, almost mandatory, importance of progress in this direction. In addition to this, the Soviet side saw reinforcement for itself in its relations with Communist China, and a measure of assurance against too intimate or exclusive an association between that power and the United States. The American side was astute enough to realize that the various rigidities that marked the cold war, both as a state of mind in America and as a condition of American–Soviet relations, were not conducive to American interests in other areas of the world. In addition to this it is evident that Mr. Nixon was not wholly indifferent to the domestic-political fruits to be derived from the drama of successive summit meetings.

These recognitions, however, also roughly defined and delimited the aims and the scope of détente. Beyond them, it was not possible to go. The Soviet leaders were determined that the development should not affect the intactness of the dictatorship at home; nor was it to hinder them from continuing to adopt, with relation to the problems of third countries, a rhetorical and political stance of principled revolutionary Marxism, designed to protect them from charges by the Chinese Communists that they were betraying the cause of Leninism–Marxism. There is no evidence that they ever attempted to conceal from their Western opposite numbers the nature or the seriousness of these reservations.

Whether, in their actions affecting the 1973 Middle Eastern war and—somewhat later—Angola, the Soviet authorities did not violate at least the spirit of the earlier understandings with Messrs. Nixon and Kissinger is a question that surpasses the limits of this examination. But some people on the American side certainly thought that this was the case; and the impression was used to justify the very clear changes that did occur in American policy.

The pressures against détente had never been absent in Washington, even at the height of its development; they had only been repressed by the momentary prestige and authority of the White House. As the power of the Nixon presidency disintegrated in 1973 and 1974, the anti-détente forces moved again to the battle lines, and with great effectiveness. This was, to some extent, only to be expected; for the overdramatization of the earlier contacts and negotiations had bred false hopes and concepts of what could be achieved; and a certain disillusionment was inevitable. The signs of this reaction were already apparent in late 1973. Efforts to save the situation by another (and very misconceived) Nixon visit to Moscow, in June 1974, were unavailing. Some limited further progress was made, to be sure, in the field of cultural exchanges. But by this time, resistance in the Pentagon and elsewhere to any further concessions of consequence in the SALT talks, as well as to any acts of self-restraint in the development of American weapons programs, was too strong to be overcome, particularly by a desperate and harassed Nixon, or even by a bewildered Gerald Ford, by no means personally unresponsive to hard-line pressures.

The Jackson–Vanik Amendment, and the subsequent demise of the trade pact, dealt a bitter blow to any hopes for retaining the very considerable momentum that had been obtained in the development of Soviet–American relations. The very modest and tentative results of the Vladivostok meeting led only to new protests and attacks from anti-détente forces that now had the bit in their teeth and were not to be gainsaid. By the beginning of 1975, although the various cultural agreements reached under the heading of détente were still in effect and were being, so far as can be judged from the public reports, punctiliously observed by both sides, the prospects for further success in the SALT talks had been heavily damaged, and along with them the political atmosphere in which, alone, further progress could be made in the improvement of the Soviet–American relationship generally.

What followed—the wrangling over the language of the Helsinki agreements, the conflict over Angola, even the most recent spate of expressions of alarm in Washington over the pace of development of the Soviet armed forces—these were in the main the products rather than the causes of the limited deterioration of the Soviet–American relationship which the period since mid-1973 has witnessed.

X    It would be idle to pretend, as the year 1976 runs its course, that the prospects for the future of Soviet–American relations are anything less than problematical. Formidable impediments continue to lie across the path of any efforts at improvement. The Soviet authorities will no doubt continue to adhere to internal practices of a repressive nature that will continue to offend large sections of American opinion. They will continue to guard what they regard as their right or their duty to subject the United States to periodic rhetorical denunciation and to give to anti-American political factions in third countries forms of support that Americans will find unreconcilable with a desire for good relations with this country. They will, rather because they are Russians than because they are Communists, continue to cultivate and maintain armed forces on a scale far greater than any visible threat to their security would seem to warrant. They will continue what they will describe as efforts to achieve parity with the United States in naval and long-range nuclear capabilities; and others will continue to be in doubt as to whether these are not really efforts to achieve a decisive, and irrevocable, superiority. They will continue to hide all their undertakings behind a wholly unnecessary degree of secrecy—a secrecy which invites exaggerated fears on the other side and enhances the very dangers to which it is supposed to be responsive. None of this will be helpful to the development of the relationship.

On the other hand, the Soviet leadership has, and will continue to have, a high degree of awareness of the dangers of a continued nuclear competition. Along with all its exaggerated military efforts, it does not want, and will not want, a world war. It has a keen realization of the suicidal nature of any nuclear war; and it has too many internal problems to allow it to wish to assume inordinate risks. It is now governed, furthermore, by a relatively old, habit-worn, and weary bureaucracy, which is going to have to give over in the relatively near future. Waiting in the wings is a new generation of officials who, insofar as one is able to judge them at all, would appear to be no less rough than their elders, no less capable, and certainly no less nationalistic, but more pragmatic, less confined by ideological rigidities, less inhibited in association and converse with foreigners. To which must be added that curious streak of friendly and sometimes even admiring interest in the United States—a mixture of curiosity, eagerness for peaceful rivalry, and sometimes even real liking—that runs through the Soviet population and has never failed to be noted by observant American students of Russian life.

All these factors lend assurance that, given an American policy reasonably adjusted to these contradictions of the official Russian personality and conscious of the immensity of what is at stake in the future of the relationship, there need be no greater danger of apocalyptic disaster arising out of that relationship than there has been in the past—and the United States, after all, has contrived to live in the same world with this regime for over half a century without finding it necessary to resort to arms against it in order to protect American interests. Possibly there could even be a further successful effort to improve things.

But if this is to occur, American statesmanship will have to overcome some of the traits that have handicapped it in the past in dealing with this most unusual, most dangerous, and most serious of all the problems of foreign policy it has ever had to face. It will have to overcome that subjectivity that caused Americans to be strongly pro-Soviet at the height of the Stalin era and equally anti-Soviet in the days of Khrushchev, and to acquire a greater steadiness and realism of vision before the phenomenon of Soviet power. It will have to make greater progress than it has made to date in controlling the compulsions of the military-industrial complex and in addressing itself seriously to the diminution, whether by agreement or by unilateral restraint or both, of the scope and intensity of the weapons race.

American politicians will have to learn to resist the urge to exploit, as a target for rhetorical demonstrations of belligerent vigilance, the image of a formidable external rival in world affairs. And American diplomacy will have to overcome, in greater measure than it has done to date, those problems of privacy of decision and long-term consistency of behavior which, as Tocqueville once pointed out, were bound to burden American democracy when the country rose to the stature of a great power. In all of this, American statesmanship will need the support of a press and communications media more serious, and less inclined to oversimplify and dramatize in their coverage of American foreign policy, than what we have known in the recent past.

It is not impossible for American government and society to make these advances. To do so, they have only to match the best examples of American statesmanship in the past, but then to give to their achievements, this time, a more enduring commitment and a deeper general understanding than was the case at other high moments of American performance.

There is not, however, infinite time for the achievement of these results. Certain of the trends of international life at this moment for which the United States bears a very special responsibility, notably the steady expansion and proliferation of nuclear weaponry and the preposterous development of the export of arms from major industrial countries, are ones which it is impossible to project much farther into the future without inviting catastrophes too apocalyptic to contemplate. The greatest mistake American policymakers could make, as the country moves into the years of a new Administration, would be to assume that time is not running out on all of us, themselves included.

# 20

# FRANKLYN GRIFFITHS

## *The Sources of American Conduct:*
## *Soviet Perspectives and*
## *Their Policy Implications**

A new way of thinking and talking about Soviet foreign policy is needed, one that allows ready recognition of diversity in the outward behavior of a society whose leaders are bent on the containment of diversity within. The experience of the liberal democracies demonstrates that a dual policy of concurrent resistance and cooperation in dealing with the USSR suffers in the absence of public recognition of dualism in Soviet conduct. But how to contest the widespread assumption that the Soviet leaders are single-minded expansionists without falling into the other error of implying that the regime is divided into coalitions of moderates and diehards whose presence cannot be demonstrated with assurance? The answer is to be had in the identification of contrasting tendencies in the behavior of the Soviet Union that persist irrespective of momentary internal configurations of the regime.

Western analysts have debated the sources of Soviet foreign conduct for many years now. The effort to define and explain the opponent's behavior, sometimes referred to simply as "the threat," has seen the emergence of three main schools of thought which continue to vie for acceptance.[1] This chapter seeks to promote a new synthesis suited to the needs of Western policy in the latter half of the 1980s and beyond.

Some would explain Soviet conduct primarily by reference to what the USSR is or is supposed to be—a totalitarian political order that is irrevocably committed to world domination, that stays its hand only when confronted with superior force, and that invariably exploits Western good will in the furtherance of its aggressive aims. President

*Reprinted by permission of the author and publisher from *International Security* 9, no. 2 (Fall, 1984), pp. 3-5, 11, 24-46. Copyright 1984 by the President and Fellows of Harvard College and of the Massachusetts Institute of Technology.

Reagan's vision of the Soviet Union as an empire of evil is not far removed from this eccentric evaluation. It is however far removed from the data of Soviet behavior, as will be seen.

A more empirical assessment is associated with mainstream Western thinking about the containment of Soviet power. For this school of thought, the explanation of Soviet actions centers more on what the Kremlin does and less on what the Soviet system "is." A wider range of Soviet responses to Western moves is in principle allowed, mainly because the Soviet leaders are viewed not only as ideological thinkers but as realists who accommodate when forced to do so. Indeed, the elements of a tendency analysis lie buried in the foundations of Western thinking about containment: As George F. Kennan put it in 1947, the "expansive tendencies" in Soviet policy were accompanied by "tendencies which must eventually find their outlet in either the break-up or the gradual mellowing of Soviet power." [2] An overriding preoccupation with Soviet expansionism and with the mechanics of countervailing force has, however, served to inhibit the emergence of a comprehensive understanding of Soviet tendencies and how they might figure in a more balanced Western approach to the USSR.

Both schools of thought—they have been called "essentialist" and "mechanist," respectively—have relied heavily on strategic conceptions in accounting for Soviet behavior. In common with more conservative Soviet assessments of the politics of American policymaking, to be considered below, it is felt that the opponent is best understood in terms of its ability to implement a stragegy, or even "plan," devised by a small group of individuals at the pinnacle of the political system. This readiness to attribute a high level of centralization, intentionality, and self-control in the making of Soviet policies has been challenged by a growing body of research since the early 1960s.

A third, process-oriented school succeeded in drawing attention to what may be regarded as the quasi-pluralist character of Soviet politics and policymaking, to the presence of foreign policy debates and the use of ideology in advancing contrasting evaluations of the external setting, and to the complex linkages between Soviet domestic and foreign policy.[3] Not only was participation in the Soviet policy process shown to be more extensive, but the degree of Soviet responsiveness to Western actions seemed to be greater than previously recognized. At the same time, the dark side of Soviet domestic and foreign operations received less emphasis as hope rose for cooperation with the USSR and ultimately for internal reform of the Soviet regime.

Hope for change in relations with the Soviet Union seemed to be vindicated in the early 1970s as American policymakers led the way in derogating the significance of ideology in Soviet policy, in seeking the creation within the Soviet Union of vested interests in good behavior, and in acting broadly as though the Soviets were capable of offering an alternative to relentless expansionism in their dealings with the West. Just what this alternative was never received a proper explanation. Nor was there a public understanding of what might be required of the West to sustain it. The result was an excessive swing toward optimism about the future of East-West relations, and then the inevitable disillusion. With disillusion came a return to prominence of one-sided strategic explanations of Soviet conduct, and then an immoderate commitment to containment and confrontation with the USSR.

Experience shows that each of the available schools of thought on the sources of Soviet policy is inadequate when relied upon exclusively. Each captures and overstates selected aspects of a complex reality that must somehow be understood in its totality. The task of providing a new synthesis should be accomplished in a way that reduces the risk of oversimplification and excess in Western conduct. It should also produce a central concept that is simple enough to be readily understood and used by individuals who do not have professional knowledge of Soviet affairs. The analysis that follows seeks to meet this need mainly by establishing the proposition that there is an array of conflicting tendencies in the behavior of the Soviet system toward the United States. It does so primarily by examining stated Soviet perceptions of American foreign and military policymaking as reported in the published work of Soviet specialists during the Brezhnev era.

Perceptions of the American policy process as presented in the open by specialists may well diverge substantially from the operational evaluations of Soviet decision makers. Where Soviet decision making itself is concerned, the assessment of what is going on within the United States is likely to be only one of a great many considerations that shape Soviet conduct toward the principal adversary. Persistent variations in the writing of specialists as they consider the workings of the American system do nevertheless reveal a good deal about the predispositions of the regime in its approach to relations with the United States. This is because the things specialists say in public about the U.S. policy process reflect the proclivities of the leadership, and are advanced in part to justify preexisting preferences for Soviet policy toward America. By backtracking from stated specialist conceptions of American politics as put forward over an extended period of time, we stand to gain an initial understanding of Soviet tendencies, of what they tend to do in dealing with the United States.

Representing predispositions to act in given ways, tendencies are by definition future-oriented. To the degree that the tendencies in Soviet policy toward the United States can reliably be specified, it should be possible to reduce uncertainty both in anticipating what next in the Soviet Union's American policy, and in understanding it when it happens. As well, knowledge of contrasting tendencies in Soviet conduct that is derived from Soviet perceptions, as distinct from an external view of things, should add to the efficiency of policy toward the USSR. Knowing more about the structure of Soviet thinking about their relations with the United States, governments and attentive publics in the liberal democracies might be more discriminating in the use of resources to underwrite tendencies that deserve encouragement, while simultaneously acting to resist unwanted variants of Soviet conduct.

Greater economy in the commitment of resources and greater steadfastness in public support for a dual policy are essential prerequisites for a reduction in the severity of East-West conflict. To the degree that a tendency analysis of Soviet policy meets not only the foreign policy but the domestic political needs of dualism in Western and especially United States conduct, it should further the cause of East-West cooperation while encouraging measured responses to the continuing requirements of competition.

Images
of the
American
Policy
Process

Soviet thinking on the politics of American foreign and military policies may strike the Western reader as strange and forbidding, if not irrelevant. The Soviet reader would doubtless find an elaborate American discussion of nuclear deterrence equally difficult to assimilate. The comparison is intentional. Soviet national security thinking would seem ultimately to be expressed in the language of political economy, and not in military-strategic terms. The observations that follow provide an opportunity to begin to look at the requirements of national security from a Soviet point of view. As well, it should be emphasized that the literature we are about to consider is written by Soviets for Soviets. It is impenetrable to all but the most determined external observer. As such, it minimizes the risk of disinformation that sometimes comes with Western reliance on published Soviet sources. It allows us to listen to Soviets talking amongst themselves about the political economy of national security.

The specialist literature since 1945 yields four images of the U.S. political process. Each of these images has evolved in the course of protracted and sometimes polemical discussion of the opposing social system. Each has also responded to change in the political economy of American capitalism. Each however retains certain core attributes that remain unchanged. To simplify what might otherwise become an excessively complicated discussion, the account that follows is confined to the literature of the Brezhnev era as it concerns the American policy process and the role of the Presidency as represented in each of these images, designated I–IV.[4] In each case our concern is not so much with details as with the overall Soviet conception of how the United States makes policy and where the Presidency fits into the scheme of American political life.

Each of the four images was organized around certain persistent conceptions or stated beliefs, whereas the specifics and the authority of each were subject to significant change in the course of the Brezhnev era. The core attributes may be summarized as follows: subordination of the state and political life to an essentially unitary monopoly bourgeoisie (Image I); domination of the state and political life by an internally divided monopoly bourgeoisie (Image II); domination of a relatively self-sufficient state by the whole bourgeoisie and a divided monopoly stratum in the first instance (Image III); and the increasing self-sufficiency of the state and the state-monopoly or political elite as actors in their own right (Image IV). Despite the persistence of these core attributes, the work of specialists was subject to a process of modification that left the discussion in November 1982 quite different from that of October 1964. These modifications occurred in two phases which first saw support drain away from Image I, and then from Image IV as well.

During the period to 1973, the elaboration of innovating assessments that had begun under Khrushchev continued but with diminishing momentum. By 1970, Image I and its leading exponents in the Communist Party of the Soviet Union (C.P.S.U.) Central Committee's Academy of Social Sciences had effectively been discredited. As a result, Image II also became a repository for tempered Image I assessments, M.S. Dragilev of Moscow State University being a principal spokesman for what may be called the conservative coalition until his death in 1975. On the other hand, the Institute of the World Economy and International Relations of the USSR Academy of Sciences (IMEMO), which had spearheaded the process of analytical innovation in the Khrushchev years, withdrew to a position that favored Images II and III at the expense of IV. The volumes edited and written by its director, N. N. Inozemtsev, tended to straddle the midpoint in the debate, now veering to Image II, now to Image III. Deprived of its previous institutional support, Image IV was pressed forward principally by S. I. Tyulpanov of Leningrad State University after 1969. Tyulpanov endeavored to move the discussion into areas not previously addressed by E. S. Varga, the leading Image IV analyst of the Khrushchev and indeed the Stalin eras. In so doing, he indicated that his principal opponent was M. S. Dragilev.[5] Meanwhile, the Institute of U.S. Studies, founded in 1967 and later renamed U.S. and Canadian Studies, joined IMEMO in putting out Image II and III presentations. Its director, G. A. Arbatov, indicated a preference for Image III presentations.

As of the onset of détente with the United States in 1972–1973, the specialist discussion had experienced a consolidation that benefitted innovating perceptions. Though continuing criticism of the subordination thesis in the 1970s suggested that it retained influence behind the scenes or outside the confines of specialist discourse, Image I had been taken out of play.[6] Image II consequently gained in support. As well, Image III presentations indicated a readiness to absorb concepts and detail from Image IV assessments that would have been contentious some years earlier. And Image IV analysis was promising to break new ground.

In the remainder of the Brezhnev era, the discussion swung back toward positions of greater orthodoxy. Image IV was put on ice by 1974. This would seem to have been a consequence of the Western economic crisis, which reinforced Image II skepticism as to the economic and political capabilities of the capitalist system for self-regulation and effective competition with "socialism." In addition, the crystallization of Eurocommunism, and the unwillingness of the C.P.S.U. to concede in dealing with it, may well have obliged Soviet Eurocommunist specialists to fall silent. Tyulpanov nevertheless retained a position on the editorial board of the IMEMO journal through the end of the Brezhnev period. More importantly, IMEMO itself tilted increasingly toward an Image II view of things after 1975, this at the expense of Image III analyses. This left the Institute of U.S. and Canadian Studies somewhat exposed as a producer of Image II and III studies by mid-decade. As U.S.–Soviet relations deteriorated in years that followed, innovation in the specialist analysis of the American political process, and of the political economy of capitalism more generally, was arrested. Though there were exceptions, increasingly conservative assessments of American conduct and prospects came to prevail. As of November 1982, Images I and IV had both been reduced to the status of offstage presences in a specialist discussion that increasingly favored Image II at the expense of Image III commentary.

## Four Tendencies

To the extent we are able to surface the policy subtexts that accompanied the various images propagated by analysts working outside the decision-making arena, we should be in a position to begin to specify a set of conflicting predispositions or tendencies that figured in the regime's approach to the United States during the Brezhnev era,[7] and that may be expected to persist under the present leadership. In view of the relative scarcity of Image I and IV evaluations in the literature under review here, the corresponding tendencies are necessarily obtained more by inference than by reference to specific texts, which are more plentiful for Images II and III.

*Coercive Isolationism* In the absence of powerful countervailing considerations, Image I would orient the Soviet viewer toward a policy of confrontation with the United States. It would do so actively by depicting the American system in terms that left the USSR no other choice, and passively by screening out information that might be employed to justify an alternative course for Soviet policy. Active and passive effects are obtained by the use of a simple concept: the subordination of the state to the monopolies.

Frontal opposition to the United States is the appropriate response for the Image I observer who could expect little but the worst from the American government. Owing to the omnipotence of the most reactionary stratum of the ruling class and its unity of purpose on issues of importance, the policies implemented by the President would be inevitably and exclusively hostile to the Soviet Union. High levels of defense preparedness and political vigilance would be mandatory for the USSR, as would the readiness to repress counterrevolutionary activity promoted within the socialist camp by the United States. Furthermore, since not only the American but all capitalist governments are subordinated by the monopolies, the Image I observer would be inclined to favor not merely a posture of confrontation in relation to the United States, but a two-camp foreign policy.[8] Selective détente with America's allies could accordingly be seen as inappropriate or of dubious value in view of the reactionary nature of capitalist states. As well, the fact of subordination would make illusory many of the ideological and political compromises accepted by the communist parties of the capitalist countries, and by the C.P.S.U., in an effort to utilize the electoral or parliamentary path to power.[9] Since the dictatorship of the proletariat is thought to be virtually impossible to achieve prior to the anticipated economic and political collapse of modern monopoly capitalism, opportunities would be taken to exploit the greater revolutionary potential of the developing areas, and to deprive imperialism of the markets and raw materials on which it depends.[10]

The symbols, slogans, and policy preferences accompanying Image I texts tend to stress coercion and unilateral action, whether it be in the domestic and international conduct of the American government, or in Soviet and international communist behavior. They also point to a perceived need for high levels of mass mobilization and enforced unity within the USSR. Were Soviet policies to be constructed exclusively on the basis of an Image I assessment of the United States, the Soviet Union would quickly isolate itself from all but those it was able to subordinate, thereby reproducing an acute Cold War setting conducive to the reimposition of Stalinist totalitarianism within the USSR and Eastern Europe. We may therefore infer from Image I presentations a tendency to what may be called "coercive isolationism" in specialist thinking about policy toward the United States.

*Expansionist Internationalism* Image II is more complex and allows for greater flexibility in Soviet conduct. If its policy corollaries alone were to guide Soviet behavior toward the United States, the USSR would strive for global expansion in conditions of East–West détente and limited cooperation with Washington. This line of policy flows from an assessment of the American system that (*a*) gives the Soviet Union a choice other than confrontation, and (*b*) directs attention to the importance of external factors, principally the growth of Soviet power, in weakening an adversary that can alter its methods but not its essence as a hostile force. The proposition that authorizes Image II preferences for simultaneous expansion and tension-reduction is that of the domination of the American state by an internally divided monopoly bourgeoisie.

Owing to the presence of competition within the dominant stratum and the capacity of the monopolists to employ the state, not ineffectively at times, in a "goal-directed strategy of adaptation" aimed at meeting the needs of struggle with "socialism,"[11] the United States is neither likely to collapse internally nor to pursue a policy of unmitigated hostility toward the USSR. Conflicting tendencies in the orientation of the American monopoly bourgeoisie toward the Soviet Union are, moreover, seen to present opportunities to advance Soviet interests in ways that are denied when the adversary is viewed as monolithic in its rapacity and belligerence.[12] Rather than waiting for the millennial transformation of American capitalism, Image II analysis suggests an active interest in encouraging the erosion of American aggressiveness and global power. Since monopoly capital remains in firm control of the American political process, there would be clear limits on the capacity of the United States to deviate from a policy of strength as a consequence of internal political developments. A premium would therefore be placed on the furtherance of an external setting or correlation of forces that gradually disabled or "paralyzed" American imperialism.

Perceived Soviet successes in altering the global correlation and in demonstrating the unreality of American efforts to create situations of strength accordingly yield the assertion that it is not imperialism but the "conditions of its existence" that have changed.[13] Or, "The aggressive nature of imperialism has not changed and cannot change, it refrains from the use of arms only under pressure of the objective international situation. . . ."[14] As well, support for national liberation movements not wholly subordinated to the Soviet interest would be viewed with approval. The Angolan events of 1975, for example, are depicted as part of a larger process that serves to deliver "the strongest blow at the positions of capitalism as a whole, as a world social system."[15] Image II assessments may thus be taken to favor a Soviet policy of military might and global power projection that aims to outdo the United States and its allies in creating situations of strength.

Image II is associated with the view that the Atlantic Alliance is prone to greater disarray in conditions of diminished international tension.[16] By seeking to reduce tension through propaganda restraint, support for broad-front tactics of the communist movement, and a commitment to East–West negotiations, the Soviet Union could be expected not only to weaken allied support for U.S. policy positions, but to add to its own economic and political strength. On the last point, Image II analyses indicate an interest in utilizing Western economic capabilities and experience, American included, to bolster the capacity of the Soviet system to finance simultaneous increases in defense production and personal consumption.[17] Soviet efforts to promote détente and economic cooperation would however be centered on Western Europe insofar as the use of interimperialist contradictions were a primary aim. Image II evaluations thus point not only to a policy of strength and forwardness aimed at containing and ultimately isolating the United States, but to an interest in tension-reduction as a means of depriving America of reliable allies and increasing the capacity of the USSR to compete militarily and economically.

The tendency in Soviet thinking about policy toward the United States that is connoted by Image II presentations may be referred to as "expansionist internationalism." In common with the coercive isolationism of Image I, expansionist internationalism points to a heavy requirement for military capabilities, and to an interest in the acceleration of revolutionary change in the Third World. But in contrast to the self-isolation and passivity that flow from Image I assessments of the opposing social system, the expansionist tendency in specialist comment entails a vigorous global effort to contain and isolate the United States. Two-camp confrontation gives way to a détente posture and the exploitation of divisions between and within Western countries. Though a radical transformation of U.S. foreign and military policies is the ultimate goal of Soviet expansionist thinking, the opponent is perceived in a manner that inhibits the thought of acting to modify its conduct through direct bilateral action aimed at a *modus vivendi*. The expansionist orientation thus suggests a preoccupation not with the development of U.S.–Soviet bilateral relations as such, but with the furtherance of an international context in which America has less and less choice but to come to Soviet terms. Limited agreements with the United States may be feasible and desirable, but not at the cost of compromising the capacity of the USSR to promote continued change in the correlation of forces. Hence a preference for improved relations with America's allies and the maintenance of a less tense but still remote relationship with America itself.

*Reformative Internationalism* In contrast to the clear sense of policy direction that accompanies Image II assessments of the American system, the foreign policy and military corollaries of Image III appear to be somewhat indeterminate. Where Image II draws attention to inherent limits on the capacity of the United States to cooperate with the USSR. Image III filters the information in a way that allows for greater variety in American conduct as the result of interaction among nonmonopoly as well as monopoly actors who make diverse demands on a relatively autonomous apparatus of state. Internal political conflict, conditioned *inter alia* by changes in the correlation of forces and in the consequences of modern warfare,[18] is seen to incline American behavior in either a militaristic and "aggressive" or a relatively moderate and "realistic" direction. Should American policies take on an "aggressive" cast, the Image III viewer might well lend support to an expansionist Soviet effort to contest and otherwise demonstrate the unworkability of U.S. globalism.

But to the extent that American politics and policies are seen to entail a readiness to cooperate with Moscow, Image III analyses suggest an interest not only in encouraging American moderation, but in working out a long-term stabilization of political and military relations with the main opponent. Indeed, as distinct from the fixed expectation of political–military rivalry connoted by Image II presentations, Image III signals a preference for a reformation of East–West and Soviet–American relations in which military-strategic forms of conflict are replaced, as circumstance allows, by forms that stress economic and ideological competition. The construct that both allows for a greater measure of cooperation in Soviet policy and accounts for the relatively wide range of behavior that may in principle be expected from the United States is that of the domination of a relatively self-sufficient apparatus of state by the whole bourgeoisie and the heterogeneous stratum of monopolists in the first instance. The tendency in specialist thinking about Soviet policy that is associated with this image of the American system will be called "reformative internationalism."

Arbatov chose to provide Soviet readers with an exposition of the reformative case in the early 1970s. Stressing the existence of conflicting tendencies in the orientation of the American ruling class and its dominant stratum toward foreign and military affairs, Arbatov indirectly agreed with the Image II assessment that such differences were inherently tactical in nature.[19] But in the evaluation of "realistic" (also

called "moderate," "liberal," or "reformist") tactics and their significance, he diverged substantially from Image II argumentation. For a
variety of reasons, the American ruling class had been obliged to evolve
a "dialectical" or dual policy that envisaged concessions and compromises, as well as pressure and divisive cooperation in relations with
the Soviet Union and its allies.[20] In this more "subtle and differentiated
anti-communism," military power was employed increasingly as a
"shield" for other foreign policy tactics that included economic, scientific, technological, and cultural relations, and "even certain forms of
cooperation" with the Soviet bloc.[21] In developing these ties, the United
States aimed not only at the erosion of socialism, but at the avoidance of
nuclear war.[22] Moreover, where previously it had been thought that
imperialist aggressiveness would increase as the correlation of forces
shifted to its disadvantage, now it could be said that, "Among the more
sober-minded and far-sighted representatives of the bourgeoisie the
trend toward [acceptance of peaceful coexistence] will become more and
more pronounced as socialism grows stronger and the hollowness of
any other political line is laid bare."[23] Evidently the United States was
moving into an era in which frontal opposition to the USSR would
gradually be replaced by more subtle forms of struggle.

In sum, Soviet diplomacy was to implement a set of procedures
aimed not only at structuring the external context in which decisions on
U.S. foreign and military policy were made, but also at modifying
American public opinion.[24] As well, Moscow was to utilize the relative
self-sufficiency of the Presidency to alter the balance of forces within the
American ruling class.[25] To the extent that these efforts were successful,
the Soviet Union and the United States would both find themselves
pursuing dual policies that allowed for a growing measure of bilateral
cooperation in the midst of continuing conflict.

Contrary to the thrust of reformative thinking about policy toward
the United States, the years that followed Arbatov's presentation of the
argument for a dual policy oriented toward greater collaboration saw the
Presidency become less and less useful for the promotion of an American "realism" whose social base steadily narrowed. Faced with weaker
Presidents, fundamental American questioning of the role of the state in
economic and social life, the growth of congressional–executive rivalry,
the rightward shift of American public opinion, the increasing disability
of the Democratic Party, and finally the capacity of the Reagan Administration to mobilize public support for a return to policies of strength,
those favoring a reformative emphasis in Soviet policy could only have
been dismayed. Add to these considerations a growing awareness of
impediments to cooperation arising from the need to deal simultaneously with the Senate and the President,[26] and from the greater
responsiveness of the Congress itself to local interests and political
action committees,[27] and the American scene as viewed from Moscow
by the end of the Brezhnev era became one that all but denied the
immediate utility of a reformative perspective. For those who nevertheless clung to a preference for reformative internationalism as of November 1982, the choice would seem to have been one of keeping the option

of cooperation open and otherwise limiting damage in American–Soviet relations, or of lending support to an expansionist effort to constrain American choices by making clear the futility of a renewed globalism.

*Democratic Isolationism* Finally, some brief remarks may be ventured on the policy corollaries of the very few Image IV texts that have been considered here. When compared with reformative internationalist preferences for a gradual liberalization of American foreign and military policies, Image IV evaluations suggest an interest in more rapid and far-reaching transformations in American–Soviet relations, in the nature of American capitalism, and ultimately in the nature of the Soviet system as well. Indeed, the principal goal implied by Image IV writings appears to be the internal reform and democratization of Soviet "socialism" in a stabilized international setting. The tendency connoted by Image IV texts will therefore be referred to provisionally as "democratic isolationism."

Having discussed in detail the consequences of a war fought with nuclear weapons, F. Burlatskii and A. Galkin stated that self-regulating global mechanisms based on the spontaneous interaction of competing forces were no longer an acceptable means of assuring international stability.[28] Instead, they suggested, the prevention of nuclear war required the adoption of a strategy of "planned general peace" that consisted of "conscious, goal-directed and effective actions" in which the Soviet Union and the United States were in effect to lead the way.[29] Just how general peace was to be planned and brought about was not made clear. Evidently an evolving American capitalism whose differences with the USSR were essentially political, and in which the state played an increasingly autonomous role, was capable of taking part in such an exercise. Evidently the Soviet Union was in a position to reduce the severity of the political conflict that stood in the way of broadening cooperation to avert nuclear war.

Given that the sources of qualitative change in the capitalist system were primarily endogenous, a vigorous Soviet effort to advance the cause of socialism by acting to alter the world correlation of forces would have been seen as inherently misguided in the view of Tyulpanov and those for whom he spoke. Rather, Soviet policy should have been seeking to create conditions conducive to the realization of inner "democratic transformations" of the American system that had become possible with the advent of the state-monopoly phase of imperialism. Indirect Soviet military interventions in the developing countries would accordingly have met with disapproval, as would other military moves that served to brace the forces of order and constrain the forces of movement in America. Furthermore, to the degree that the C.P.S.U. began to speak the language not merely of Eurocommunism but of the Italian Communist Party,[30] the overt Soviet political threat to American capitalism could also be reduced. While this line of policy could have been expected initially to produce an American–Soviet accommodation similar to that implied by Image III assessments, the underlying aim would have been to further the socialist transformation of American society, as distinct from encouraging a moderation of American foreign policy.

The shortage of direct evidence for the isolationist tendencies at either end of the spectrum of specialist policy preferences suggests that both lacked regime support in the course of the Brezhnev years. This is in contrast to the status of the two internationalist tendencies that coexisted at the center: Both are relatively easily documented; both would seem to have been endowed with legitimacy. Yet it remains true that expansionist preferences were articulated more frequently and with greater assurance than was the case for the reformative orientation toward the United States. Indeed, had Arbatov not been explicit in making the case for a line of policy that emphasized collaboration with the principal adversary in the early 1970s, the Western analyst would be obliged to rely heavily on subtext or inference in specifying reformative internationalist preferences. Accordingly, if we are to select one tendency that predominated in the specialist literature of the Brezhnev era on the political economy of contemporary capitalism and the American policy process in particular, it must be expansionist internationalism.

## Structure in Soviet Policy

Taken together, the four tendencies identified here constitute a repertoire of specialist predispositions for Soviet policy toward the United States as they existed in the period 1964–1982, and as they may be expected to persist in the years ahead. These tendencies were articulated by individuals and, it would appear, in the interaction of informal groups and coalitions. They do not allow us to speak with assurance about the subjective perceptions and policy preferences of individuals or groupings of specialists. But they do tell us something about the orientations of the specialist community as a whole. The distinction is an important one.

Depending on the issue, the application of intraparty controls, the state of American–Soviet relations, and a host of other variables, a set of specialists or an individual such as Arbatov who might personally have favored an Image IV assessment and a reformative emphasis in Soviet policy toward the United States could have found themselves publicly presenting an Image III evaluation and privately endorsing an expansionist policy prescription on a given issue. We are not in a position to establish reliable correlations between the public pronouncements and the behind-the-scenes activities of specialists, or between their stated perceptions and their personal policy preferences as individuals. What we have before us is evidence not so much of subjective as of what may be called transactional perceptions and preferences—stated beliefs and predispositions that may or may not correspond accurately to subjective thinking, and that are the product more of influence and power relationships than of an unfettered search for the true and proper.

Though the Soviet data allow only very little to be said about the subjective orientations of individuals and informal groups, they do permit us to speak with confidence about enduring patterns in the overall body of communication among specialists during the Brezhnev era. Persistent regularities can readily be discerned in the published arguments of the community of professionals engaged in perennial discussion and debate about American capitalism and Soviet policy toward the United States. In short, we have before us a set of tendencies that tells us a good deal about the long-standing policy predispositions of the corps of Soviet specialists taken as a whole. Might these also be the tendencies of the Soviet political system, or more precisely of the regime insofar as it is not commensurate with the system as a whole?

To demonstrate conclusively that we have isolated the repertoire of established response patterns of the Soviet regime as it deals with its principal adversary, we would have to widen the analysis very considerably. We should consider variations in official action toward the United States during the Brezhnev years, in official statements including the speeches of leaders, in the print and electronic media as they concerned American affairs and American–Soviet relations, and in the *samizdat* literature as well. An inquiry of this kind would yield not only a more finely textured and less ideological presentation of uniformities in the Soviet approach to the United States, but an indication of the effects of persistent preferences originating from outside the regime on the relative influence of tendencies within the regime itself. Additional patterns of policy preference could, for example, be identified on the middle ground between expansionist and reformative internationalism. More copious evidence of support for the two isolationist tendencies might also be uncovered, thereby offsetting a possible bias toward expansionist internationalism in the literature under review here.[31] Antiwar and indeed pacifist attitudes among the Soviet intelligentsia and in the population at large could as well be found to provide a social base outside the regime for the democratic isolationist orientation toward the United States, as might Great Russian nationalist and chauvinist sentiment in the case of coercive isolationist responses. In addition, contrasting orientations toward China, which do not figure in the literature under consideration here, could be factored into the analysis. Most important for practical purposes, an enlarged inquiry stands to provide indicators for assessing the relative strength of the various tendencies, and for marking changes in the correlation among them. This much granted, there are reasons to believe that the four tendencies outlined here do begin to describe the main predispositions of the regime in its dealings with the United States.

For one thing, it is a task of senior specialists and lesser commentators to lend meaning to incoming information on American affairs and American–Soviet relations, to assist in defining centrally important features of the context in which foreign and domestic policies are made, and to do so in a manner consistent with the requirements of the Party. Though an examination of a more extensive body of data would undoubtedly produce a better understanding of Soviet tendencies, it would not likely offer a major improvement on the capacity of the specialist literature to inform us as to how Soviets themselves put the pieces together for purposes of policy discussion. Second, to the extent that the comments of specialist producers of integrated assessments are structured year in and year out to conform to the varied needs of consumers in senior positions in the Party, tendencies that are observable in specialist discourse should reflect, however indirectly, the propensities of the leadership in its dealings with America. Though the corps of specialists is by no means wholly conformist or wholly politicized in its assessments, the outer perimeters of debate and the character of discussion within these confines are clearly regulated by a leadership that remains willing to admit some diversity of expert analysis and policy prescription. As well, the Central Committee status of key spokesmen such as Inozemtsev and Arbatov supports the view that senior participants were voicing preferences distributed more widely within the Party. But aside from these considerations, which relate to the inner workings of the regime, a correspondence is to be observed between the set of tendencies under discussion here and variations in the outward behavior of the Soviet Union between 1964 and 1982.

As of the Twenty-third C.P.S.U. Congress early in 1966, for example, the correlation of tendencies in the Soviet Union's American policy had altered substantially in comparison with the situation at the time of Khrushchev's removal late in 1964. The tactics, slogans, and symbols of reformative internationalism—negotiation, arms agreements, détente, and positive internal Soviet references to "concessions"—had been withdrawn as the Vietnam War intensified and the new leadership revealed an aversion to reformism in foreign and domestic affairs. Democratic isolationist commentary—on themes such as "what disarmament will bring," or democratization of the Soviet system as conveyed by the notion of the "state of the whole people"—had been suppressed and offset by a resurgence of coercive isolationist preferences evinced in an attempted rehabilitation of Stalin and the reappearance of a two-camp propaganda on American–Soviet relations. Expansionist internationalism was clearly the order of the day as Moscow vigorously supported the intention of the North Vietnamese to defeat the United States in Indochina, maintained an arm's length bilateral relationship with Washington while greatly increasing Soviet armed strength, and endeavored to cultivate America's European allies in a renewed emphasis on the effort to extrude the United States from Western Europe.

Six years later, the correlation of tendencies in Soviet policy had assumed different proportions. Notwithstanding a second unsuccessful effort to rehabilitate Stalin at about the time strategic arms limitation talks began with the United States late in 1969, the force of coercive isolationist preferences had diminished by the time of the Moscow summit of 1972. The fortunes of democratic isolationism had correspondingly improved, as seen in the authorization of arguments favoring a basic revision of Soviet thinking and practice in regard to the United States and other advanced capitalist countries. This change in the relative influence of the two flanking tendencies would seem to have occurred in two phases. First, in 1969–1970, there appears to have been a polarization of preferences within the regime, as reflected in the strengthening of coercive and democratic isolationist impulses simultaneously. And then, in 1970–1971, as Brezhnev assumed the role of preeminent spokesman on foreign affairs and the way was cleared both for the Twenty-fourth Congress and for détente in Europe, coercive isolationist preferences evidently lost ground and the reformative inclination to negotiate directly with the main opponent began to gain at the expense of expansionism. This shift at the center was presumably a response to the attainment of approximate equivalence in strategic nuclear weapons, to the ensuing improvement in the Soviet arms bargaining position, and to evidence that a debilitated America was prepared to do business. As well, the opening for reformative internationalism would seem to have been widened by the onset of Sino–American cooperation, by a marked deterioration in Soviet economic performance, and by a perceived opportunity to apply American as well as Western European economic capabilities in stimulating Soviet economic growth and military strength in a manner that diminished the need for reform of the Soviet system.

As of the summit of 1972, reformative internationalism would seem to have approached a position of parity with expansionism in Soviet policy toward the United States. Cooperation with American allies was being pursued very actively and in an expansionist mode, as was the growth of strategic and conventional military capabilities in a setting of limited agreements on strategic arms control and leadership assertions of Soviet support for revolutionary transformations in the developing areas. Simultaneously, an attempt was being made, in SALT and in the development of American–Soviet economic relations, to alter the terms of competition with a seemingly more accommodating principal adversary. Any further accession of strength to reformative internationalism in Soviet policy would depend not only on the results of bilateral cooperation, but on the capacity of both sides to accept the risks of political and military demobilization in the midst of continuing rivalry.

A decade later, in November 1982, the relative strength of the tendencies in Soviet conduct had altered substantially once again. On the flanks, democratic isolationist argumentation had effectively been closed off since the mid-1970s, whereas coercive isolationist responses had acquired greater prominence in the effective repression of dissent, in the military intervention in Afghanistan, in the effort to intimidate the population of Poland, and in the reassertion of two-camp rhetoric in Soviet comment on American policy and American–Soviet relations. At the center of the policy spectrum, reformative internationalism had been reduced to overt reaffirmations of readiness to negotiate unaccompanied by any great flexibility in practice, but possibly accompanied by covert efforts to avoid Soviet action liable to underwrite the Reagan Administration's campaign to remobilize America. As to expansionist internationalism, after having recovered much of the ground lost in the experiment with reformative internationalism in the early 1970s, it too was increasingly muted as a consequence of the Reagan Administration's ability to deny Moscow the reduced tension that was essential to the pursuit of unilateral gain at acceptable levels of risk and cost. Soviet operations in the developing areas were consequently marked by notable restraint. On the other hand, cleavages in the Atlantic alliance and the appearance of mass antinuclear movements in the major NATO countries, the United States included, promised to hamper President Reagan's remobilization effort, if not to force the United States into a posture of restraint and cooperation with Moscow. Evidently preferring to face the NATO countries with the consequences of their decision to deploy new American intermediate-range nuclear weapons in Europe, the Brezhnev leadership sought to influence the impending West German election by pressing the cause of détente in Europe and continuing with its deployment of intermediate-range missiles. The net result, as compared with the situation in 1966 or 1972, was remarkable passivity in the American policy of a regime whose preferences added up to residual expansionism shaded by a very largely immobilized reformative internationalism and a propensity to strike out in coercive isolationist fashion.

Three brief cuts into Soviet policy over a period of 18 years do not provide a test of the fit between the tendencies articulated in specialist discussion and the behavior of the regime toward the United States. Nor do they offer a detailed explanation of shifts in the correlation of these tendencies. But they do indicate that variations in the regime's American policy can readily be described in terms of change in the relative influence of tendencies derived from the specialist literature. If to this we add the circumstantial evidence that specialists echo foreign policy preferences distributed more widely within the regime, we may conclude that the conflicting tendencies exhibited in specialist discourse did broadly reflect the repertoire of established response patterns in Soviet behavior toward the principal adversary between 1964 and 1982.

Soviet actions are not likely to be well understood when they are viewed in terms of a unilinear, internally consistent policy whose direction is deliberately changed by the leadership as circumstance requires. The evidence assembled here suggests that Soviet conduct is better regarded as internally contradictory, consisting of a series of persistent tendencies whose relative strength alters in response to international and domestic situational variables. As is the case with the specialist community, these tendencies are best read as uniformities in the behavior of the regime taken as a whole. Democratic isolationism aside, they represent tried and tested ways of dealing with situations that face the USSR. As is shown by the meager results of the effort since 1945 to promote democratic isolationism as a legitimate orientation to domestic and foreign affairs, the basic predispositions of the regime cannot readily be altered by lesser participants in the policy process. Nor is the leadership itself in a position to change these predispositions in short order. On the contrary, the established tendencies of the regime serve to structure the performance of leaders and lesser actors alike. Barring the appearance of a leader with dictatorial powers, or a crisis that forced the consideration of radically new responses, those engaged in the making of policy toward the United States must conform to the acquired response patterns of the regime, or fail.

But if structure in the form of dominant tendencies constrains and channels the conduct of actors within, these actors nevertheless remain free to alter the inflection of policy on specific issues, and thereby to modify the correlation of tendencies in the overall approach of the regime toward America. Though individual decision makers and those on the perimeter of the decision-making arena could well hew to particular orientations for policy toward the United States, we have no real way of knowing whether this is so. Under the circumstances, Soviet policymakers are best seen as "uncommitted thinkers" who produce a mobile consensus as together they vary the correlation of regime tendencies in processing a continuous sequence of issues that relate to America.[32] The result is a policy that at once displays remarkable continuity and a propensity to oscillate as tendencies are combined and recombined to produce an array of responses to the United States.

## Notes

[1] See the penetrating accounts in William Welch, *American Images of Soviet Foreign Policy* (New Haven: Yale University Press, 1970) and William Zimmerman, "Rethinking Soviet Foreign Policy: Changing American Perspectives," *International Journal* 35, no. 3 (Summer 1980), pp. 548–562. Zimmerman especially is relied upon here.

[2] "The Sources of Soviet Conduct," *Foreign Affairs* 25, no. 4 (July 1947), pp. 575, 582.

[3] See, for example, Marshall D. Shulman, *Stalin's Foreign Policy Reappraised* (Cambridge, Mass.: Harvard University Press, 1963); H. Gordon Skilling and Franklyn Griffiths, eds., *Interest Groups in Soviet Politics* (Princeton: Princeton University Press, 1971); Jerry F. Hough, *How the Soviet Union Is Governed* (Cambridge, Mass.: Harvard University Press, 1979); Alexander Dallin, "The Domestic Sources of Soviet Foreign Policy," in *The Domestic Context of Soviet Foreign Policy*, ed. Seweryn Bialer (Boulder, Colo.: Westview Press, 1981), pp. 335–408; and Jerry F. Hough, *Soviet Policy Debates about the Third World* (Washington, D.C.: Brookings, forthcoming).

[4] An earlier study by the author examined the literature from 1945 to 1970: Franklyn Griffiths, "Images, Politics and Learning in Soviet Behavior toward the United States," Ph.D. dissertation, Columbia University, 1972. This chapter updates the analysis to 1982. For several reasons there is no Soviet theory of American capitalism as such, nor is there a theory of the American political process. The Western observer is instead presented with semi-theoretical discussions of capitalism "in general," and with descriptive accounts of American internal politics that tend to avoid theoretical generalization. Soviet images of the American political process must therefore be derived from the literature on contemporary capitalism as well as those publications that deal explicitly with the United States. For detail on the derivation of images which centers on Soviet debate over the nature of state-monopoly capitalism, see Griffiths, "Images, Politics and Learning," pp. 117–123.

[5] S.I. Tyulpanov and V.L. Sheinis, *Aktualnye problemy politicheskoi ekonomii*

*sovremennogo kapitalizma* [Current Problems in the Political Economy of Contemporary Capitalism] (Leningrad: Izd-vo LGU, 1973), p. 10.

[6]In November 1970, the Academy of Social Sciences had been the recipient of a Central Committee resolution calling for measures to improve the quality of its work. See A.L., "Leninskie traditsii v podgotovke teoreticheskikh kadrov" [Leninist Traditions in the Preparation of Theoretical Cadres], *Voprosy ekonomiki*, no. 1 (1972), p. 156.

[7]A discussion of tendencies in Soviet politics is available in Franklyn Griffiths, "A Tendency Analysis of Soviet Policy-making," in Skilling and Griffiths, eds., *Interest Groups in Soviet Politics*, pp. 335–377.

[8]Arbatov hinted at the existence of a positive view of confrontation in the C.P.S.U., in referring to the presence in the communist movement of "sectarian groups and individuals who contend that imperialism's old, traditional policy . . . is more preferable from the standpoint of the revolution" (Arbatov, fn. 18, p. 238).

[9]See, for example, the criticism of the "parliamentary path" in K.I. Zarodov, *Leninizm i sovremennye problemy perekhoda ot kapitalizma k sotsializmu* [Leninism and Contemporary Problems of the Transition from Capitalism to Socialism], 2nd ed., rev. (Moscow: "Mysl," 1981), pp. 53, 252–253. Zarodov argued that Stalin favored the "peaceful" path; he also noted, evidently with approval, that the Communist Party of the United States left open the question of whether socialist revolution would be "non-peaceful" or peaceful (*Ibid.*, pp. 249, 56).

[10]Zarodov cited Lenin on the difficulty of revolution in the advanced capitalist countries (*Ibid.*, pp. 37–38). It is necessary however to reach back to the Khrushchev years for a clear Image I statement of the comparative revolutionary advantage in the developing areas: V.F. Khlepikov *et al.*, eds., *O gosudarstvenno-monopolisticheskom kapitalizme* [On State-monopoly Capitalism] (Moscow: Izd-vo AON i VPSh pri TsK KPSS, 1963), p. 58. For evidence of the extraordinary continuity of Image I thinking, compare M.F. Kovaleva, *K voprosu metodologii politicheskoi ekonomii kapitalizma* [On the Question of the Methodology of the Political Economy of Capitalism] (Moscow: "Mysl," 1969), with I.I. Kuzminov, *O gosudarstvenno-monopolisticheskom kapitalizme* [On State-monopoly Capitalism] (Moscow: Gospolitizdat, 1949). A criticism of the view that "the most important if not the sole path" to the destruction of capitalism was to deny it the markets and raw materials of the developing countries is to be found in I.A. Sokolov, "Leninskaya teoriya i sovremennyi imperializm" [Leninist Theory and Modern Imperialism], *SShA*, no. 1 (1970), p. 38.

[11]M.S. Dragilev *et al.*, eds., *Gosudarstvenno-monopolisticheskii kapitalizm: Obshchie cherty i osobennosti* [State-monopoly Capitalism: General and Specific Features] (Moscow: Politizdat, 1975), p. 23.

[12]N.N. Inozemtsev *et al.*, eds., *Uchenie V.I. Lenina ob imperializme i sovremennost* [Lenin's Teaching on Imperialism and the Contemporary World] (Moscow: "Nauka," 1967), p. 33.

[13]N.N. Inozemtsev *et al.*, eds., *Leninskaya teoriya imperializma i sovremennost* [The Leninist Theory of Imperialism and the Contemporary World] (Moscow: "Mysl," 1977), pp. 24–25, 194; N. N. Inozemtsev, *Sovremennyi kapitalizm: novye yavleniya i protivorechiya* [Contemporary Capitalism: New Phenomena and Contradictions] (Moscow: "Mysl," 1972), pp. 23, 106–110; and N. N. Inozemtsev *et al.*, eds., *Uglublenie obshchego krizisa kapitalizma* [The Deepening of the General Crisis of Capitalism] (Moscow: "Mysl," 1976), pp. 76–77.

[14]N.N. Inozemtsev *et al.*, eds., *Mirovoi revolyutsionnyi protsess i sovremennost* [The World Revolutionary Process Today] (Moscow: "Nauka," 1980), p. 114.

[15]Inozemtsev, fn. 13, *Uglublenie*, pp. 74–75. See also Inozemtsev, fn. 14, p. 114, for an endorsement of Soviet support for the Afghan "revolution." On the

matter of differentiation between the parties, see N.N. Yakovlev, ed., *SShA: Politicheskaya mysl i istoriya* [American Political Thought and History] (Moscow: "Nauka," 1976), pp. 173, 174, 194. Yakovlev looked forward to the day when "socialism is the absolutely decisive force" and opposed any attempt to "compromise" the policy of peaceful coexistence by subordinating Soviet dealings with third states to considerations of American–Soviet coexistence.

[16]N. N. Yakovlev, fn. 15, p. 196. This assessment may have been changing as the Brezhnev years drew to a close. As one observer noted, "In the past, it used to be assumed that interimperialist contradictions tend to exacerbate in periods of relative international calm and to abate during periods of crisis as a result of the self-preservation instinct of the Western ruling circles" (L. Vidyasova, "Inter-imperialist Contradictions and Imperialist Foreign Policy," *International Affairs* (Moscow), no. 3 [1982], p. 82).

[17]Inozemtsev's observations that modern capitalist practice allowed both objectives to be met simultaneously [fn. 13, *Sovremennyi kapitalizm*, pp. 49, 116), and that the Soviet Union could learn from capitalist experience (*ibid.*, p. 54), are suggestive. So also is his recognition that while U.S. defense expenditures rose significantly between 1954 and 1970, they declined as a proportion of G.N.P. (pp. 116–117).

[18] For comments on changes in the correlation of forces and the nature of war as causative factors, see, e.g., G.A. Arbatov, *The War of Ideas in Contemporary International Relations* (Moscow: Progress Publishers, 1973), pp. 230–232, 246, 264–265.

[19]*Ibid*, pp. 225, 229.

[20]*Ibid*, pp. 227, 225, 235–236, 238.

[21]*Ibid.*, pp. 236, 241, 59.

[22]*Ibid.*, pp. 236, 241, 246, 232, 264–265.

[23]*Ibid.*, 226, 245–246.

[24]Cf. Arbatov, fn 18, p. 41: "In the ideological struggle the basic aim of any class is to bring the largest number of people under the influence of its ideas and to tear them away from the spiritual influence of the class adversary." And: "ideological propaganda is used by a class as a means of undermining the spiritual unity of the class adversary and ensuring to itself the broadest possible influence in his ranks," (*ibid*).

[25]A direct interest in employing the state to influence the ruling class is suggested by Arbatov's observations that the strategic arms agreements of 1972 undermined the "aggressive" elements, and that détente and a normalization of relations would strengthen the hand of the moderates (*ibid.*, pp. 235, 253).

[26]R.G. Bogdanov and A.A. Kokoshin (*SShA: informatsiya i vneshnyaya politika* [Information and American Foreign Policy] [Moscow: "Nauka," 1970], pp. 47–48) report as justified West European opinions to the effect that negotiation with American administrations is impossible without considering the position of the Congress from the very outset. Another Image III observer, S. B. Chetverikov ("Vneshnepoliticheskaya rol kongressa SShA" [The Foreign Policy Role of the U.S. Congress], *Sovetskoe gosudarstvo i pravo*, no. 12 (1981), pp. 117–118) while commenting that the President remained the predominant force despite the growth of congressional power, makes note of a Presidential practice of referring to congressional constraints in an attempt to extract "additional concessions" from the Soviet Union.

[27]Chetverikov, fn. 26, pp. 113–114.

[28]F. Burlatskii and A. Galkin, *Sotsiologiya. Politika. Mezhdunarodnye otnosheniya* [Sociology. Politics. International Relations] (Moscow: "Mezhdunarodnye otnosheniya," 1974), p. 282.

[29]*Ibid.*, pp. 282, 291–302.

[30]Circumstantial evidence suggests that Tyulpanov favored a view of the capitalist system more in keeping with that of the Italian (P.C.I.) than the French Communist Party (P.C.F.). See *Le capitalisme monopoliste d'état*, 2 vols. (Paris: Editions sociales, 1971).

[31]Bias may arise, for example, from the responsibilities of IMEMO in articulating the formal ideology of the regime on developments in the capitalist world at large. The effect of IMEMO presentations could thus be to skew the distribution of opinion on the United States in particular. As well, we should be aware of possible bias in our own minds as we assess the significance of Soviet tendencies. Experience of political life in the liberal democracies suggests that power flows from the center of the policy spectrum, that positions to the right and left of center are deprived of influence the further they go. Russian and Soviet experience suggests however that the center is inherently weak. Hence the extraordinary variety of Soviet political controls to ensure that the center not only holds but dominates. Hence also the Soviet propensity to overrate the strength of the far right and far left in American politics—this evidently in an uncritical transposition from domestic Soviet experience to the evaluation of policy processes abroad. The appropriate framework in considering the correlation of forces in Soviet policymaking on relations with America may therefore be one that has the flanks exerting significant effects on the center. If this is so, the two "isolationist" tendencies could prove to be more potent than the Western observer might initially think.

[32]Cf. John D. Steinbruner, *The Cybernetic Theory of Decision* (Princeton: Princeton University Press, 1974), esp. pp. 129–131.

# 21

## ROBBIN F. LAIRD
## DALE R. HERSPRING

# The Soviet Union and Strategic Arms*

Characterizing the Soviet strategic challenge calls for answers to four central questions. First, do Soviet leaders believe in the reality of mutual deterrence? For the United States, the reality of mutual assured destruction (MAD) has historically formed the basis of strategic doctrine. MAD, as a doctrine, aims at persuading the enemy that the costs of a nuclear war (in terms of losses) far outweigh any possible gains.[1] MAD places primary emphasis on the need for both the United States and the Soviet Union to maintain mutual vulnerability. By this, the United States has meant the ability of each side to deliver a vigorous second strike that would inflict "unacceptable damage" on the side that initiated a first strike. As a consequence of this view, the United States believes that both sides are thereby dissuaded from beginning a nuclear war. Do Soviet leaders also believe in such dissuasion?

Second, do the Soviets believe they could survive and win a strategic nuclear war? This question can be posed in two other ways. Do the Soviets believe nuclear war is a rational instrument for achieving political ends? Has the Kremlin adopted a warfighting doctrine that it believes can enable it to win a nuclear conflict?

Third, do the Soviets accept strategic parity with the United States as a desirable, even inevitable, state of affairs or merely as a transient one? Specifically, do the Soviets believe that strategic parity exists? If so, are they prepared to accept such a condition over the long run? Most importantly, do they believe strategic superiority is possible in the light of U.S. capabilities and are they working toward achieving it?

*Reprinted by permission of the authors and publisher from *The Soviet Union and Strategic Arms* (Boulder, Colorado: Westview Press, 1984), pp. 1–8, 139–152. The views expressed in this chapter are the authors' and do not necessarily reflect those of the Institute for Defense Analyses or the U.S. Department of State. Copyright 1984 by Westview Press.

Fourth, does the Soviet approach to arms control embody a concept of strategic parity? Are the Soviet leaders seriously interested in limiting strategic arms or are they using arms control negotiations only as a vehicle for controlling—or defusing— Western efforts to meet the Soviet strategic challenge?

The characterization of the Soviet strategic arms effort has been a highly controversial process in the West. Some argue that the USSR primarily sees its strategic weapons as a deterrent to protect the Soviet Union from U.S. attack. The Soviets are in the strategic arms race to ensure that the United States does not gain a usable strategic superiority. From this point of view, the Soviets are interested primarily in strategic stability and parity, not in engaging in an unbridled arms race.

Others argue that the Soviet Union intends to achieve usable strategic superiority to advance its policy interests. Indeed, the strategic arms race is seen as caused primarily by the Soviet desire to establish global dominance by means of strategic superiority. The Soviets seek military superiority by winning the strategic arms race.

These two polar positions have entailed quite different responses to the four key questions identified in this introduction. To further elaborate these conflicting positions as well as to further analyze the nature of the four key questions, the views of Raymond Garthoff, a former member of the U.S. delegation to the Strategic Arms Limitation Talks (SALT), are compared with those of Richard Pipes, a former member of the National Security Council in the Reagan administration.

For Raymond Garthoff, mutual assured destruction is the basis not only of U.S. policy but of Soviet strategic policy as well.[2] As he sees it, the Soviet political and military leadership recognizes that "under contemporary conditions there is a strategic balance between the two superpowers which provides mutual deterrence; that the nuclear strategic balance is basically stable, but requires continuing military efforts to assure it stability and continuation."[3] As a consequence, Garthoff sees Soviet efforts in the strategic area as aimed primarily at maintaining a mutual deterrent capability, not at gaining strategic superiority. Furthermore, he maintains, the Soviet leadership recognizes that the strategic balance is unlikely to shift significantly in the forseeable future away from the reality of mutual assured destruction.

Garthoff then goes on to argue that "it is not accurate, as some Western commentators have done, to counterpose Soviet military interest in a warfighting and warwinning capability to a deterrent capability."[4] To the degree such capabilities are present, they are aimed at providing Moscow with "the most credible deterrent,"[5] in addition to serving as "a contingent resort if war should nonetheless come."[6] In practice, Garthoff would maintain, this means assuring that Moscow possesses the ability to deliver a credible and devastating retaliatory strike if that becomes necessary. Soviet nuclear weapons deployments do not imply a belief in the viability of nuclear war as a rational instrument of policy. Soviet leaders recognize that a nuclear war would be mutual suicide in terms of casualties and the amount of damage both sides would suffer. If, however, nuclear war should occur, Moscow's goal would be "to emerge from it victorious, that is, less totally destroyed than 'capitalism'."[7]

For Garthoff, the Soviets have accepted the existence of strategic parity since the early 1970s. This includes the Soviet military, which he maintains has acknowledged "throughout the 1970s . . . that while each side has certain areas of superiority, these balance out to yield an overall parity."[8] It is this parity that serves as the basis for Moscow's acceptance of the doctrine of mutual deterrence in Garthoff's view.

Despite their acceptance of parity, Soviet leaders continue to "display considerable suspicion of American intentions and concern over growing American capabilities."[9] The Soviets believe that the United States is engaging in an effort to obtain military "superiority." Moscow believes it must keep pace with the technological competition with the United States if it hopes to ensure that the Soviet nuclear deterrent remains credible. From this standpoint, Moscow's continuing strategic arms modernization program is explained by the technological competition with the United States.

Moscow's interest in strategic arms control negotiations is closely tied to its desire to maintain overall strategic parity. As Garthoff puts it: "The Soviet political and military leadership has recognized . . . that agreed strategic arms limitation can make a contribution, possibly a significant one, to reducing . . . otherwise necessary reciprocal military efforts."[10] As an example, he cites Moscow's willingness to sign the Anti-Ballistic Missile (ABM) Treaty. Had the United States continued with its ABM program, there was concern in Moscow that it could have restored the United States "to a position of superiority that could imperil the still unstable state of mutual assured destruction and mutual deterrence."[11] Thus, for Moscow, strategic arms treaties are not a vehicle for obtaining strategic superiority but an instrument for maintaining the nuclear balance.

In contrast to Garthoff, Pipes maintains that the Soviets reject the very basis upon which the Western concept of mutual deterrence is based. They believe in the possibility of winning a nuclear war and totally reject the concept of mutual vulnerability. Insofar as the concept of stability is concerned, "Soviet strategists regard 'mutual deterrence' to be a reality of the balance of nuclear forces as presently constituted, but they mean to alter this balance in their favor and in this manner secure a monopoly on deterrence."[12]

Furthermore, Pipes does not believe the Soviets are about to intentionally leave their country vulnerable to a second strike by the United States. Such a way of thinking is totally foreign to the Russian psyche. In fact, rather than retaliation, it is offensive actions combined with appropriate defensive measures against a retaliatory strike that are the focal point of Moscow's strategic policy. Finally, instead of avoiding any actions that might be viewed as threatening by the other side, the Soviets will do whatever they can get away with to assure their own defense. If the United States wants to follow a strategy of mutual deterrence, so be it; the Soviet Union is not interested.

Moreover, Pipes argues that although Moscow would prefer to avoid a nuclear war if at all possible, "Soviet doctrine . . . emphatically asserts . . . that its outcome would not be mutual suicide: the country better prepared for it and in possession of superior strategy could win and emerge a viable society."[13] Although Pipes does not directly deal with the question of whether or not the Soviet Union believes it can effectively employ the threat of using nuclear weapons for political purposes (e.g., to force the United States to back down in a crisis situation somewhere in the Third World), his heavy reliance on the Clausewitzian dictum that war is nothing more than a continuation of politics in another form at least opens the door for such an interpretation.

Pipes characterizes the Soviet strategic force posture as one which is counterforce in character. This means that Soviet strategic forces are primarily targeted at the enemy's military forces and especially the command and control facilities. The only purpose for such a doctrine, Pipes implies, is a desire to fight and win a nuclear war. In addition, unlike the United States, Moscow has devoted considerable effort to developing a defensive capability, most notably, air defense and civil defense programs. Such undertakings are clearly aimed, in Pipes's view, at developing a nuclear warfighting, warwinning capability. Although the Soviets would prefer to avoid fighting a strategic nuclear war, they recognize that it may someday occur and if that happens, Moscow intends to be in a position to win.

Strategic parity may in some instances be a fact of life. If this is the case, Pipes would maintain, the Soviets do not accept it as a desirable condition. They do not want to give the United States the capability of deterring them. Given the heavy military input into the making of Soviet strategic arms policy, the Soviets probably believe that the only viable long-term option is the attainment of strategic superiority. Moscow's continuing strategic arms buildup is explained primarily by the drive for strategic superiority. In a word, Moscow is not interested in a "sufficiency in weapons, but superiority."[14]

Because Pipes characterizes the strategic balance between the United States and the USSR as inherently unstable due to Moscow's push for superiority, he seriously questions the value of strategic arms control agreements. Such agreements have in the past, he notes, focused mainly on "numbers of strategic weapons."[15] Qualitative improvements are equally important in his opinion. Most significant in Pipes's view, however, are Soviet intentions. After all, he maintains, "The Soviets persist in adhering to the Clausewitzian maxim on the function of war."[16] As a result, mutual deterrence on which both SALT I and SALT II were based is absent in Moscow's eyes. For Moscow, arms control negotiations are primarily aimed at limiting U.S. capabilities, especially constraining U.S. technology. Nevertheless, Pipes leaves open the possibility that arms control negotiations could be in the U.S. interest, but only if more account is taken of the serious differences between U.S. and Soviet doctrine and policy than has been done in the past.

## The Argument

The argument in this chapter will incorporate elements from both positions. We will argue that the "objective reality" of the U.S.–Soviet strategic balance is one in which both sides are currently capable of inflicting high levels of damage to each other with the delivery either of first or second strategic strikes.

We maintain that Soviet leaders, both civilian and military, recognize the objective reality of assured destruction in an all-out nuclear war. The acceptance of assured destruction has led to important modifications in Soviet military and diplomatic strategy. For example, given Soviet perception that the costs of a nuclear war outweigh any possible gains, we argue that the significance of conventional and theater nuclear forces for Soviet strategy has increased markedly. Furthermore, not only have conventional and theater systems become more important in the military dimension, they are also playing an ever more important role in Moscow's diplomatic strategy. The Soviet leaders believe that the more stable the deterrent to escalation provided by the strategic nuclear balance, the more effective conventional military advantage becomes as a diplomatic currency. Conventional military power is an especially critical tool in expanding Soviet influence in the Third World. Without a secure strategic balance, the use of conventional forces in the Third World would create greater risks of unacceptable escalation.

The extensive and massive destruction that would result from an all-out strategic nuclear exchange has led the Soviets to reshape their military thinking. Soviet military writers have shifted the focus of their attention away from preparing to fight an all-out nuclear war against the West as the key military option. Rather, they have emphasized the creation of more flexible military options. Soviet military theorists and officials seek to create escalation dominance whereby the Soviets might prevail in a war with the United States without the fearful necessity of using strategic weapons. If the Soviets are developing a warwinning strategy, it is one founded on terminating a war in Europe without the need to risk significant strategic exchanges with the United States, because the United States would be deterred from using nuclear weapons by Soviet strategic nuclear power.

The Soviet approach to developing a military doctrine and force structure designed to win a war against the West is rooted in strategic deterrence that increases the military efficacy of military forces below the strategic nuclear threshold. It does not require the attainment of decisive Soviet strategic nuclear superiority. Strategic parity is thus a tolerable condition from a Soviet standpoint.

From a diplomatic standpoint, strategic parity with the United States, rather than superiority, is all that is required for the expansion of Soviet global influence. The loss of U.S. strategic superiority has been an integral part of the dispersion of global power, a process the Soviets hope to turn to their advantage. For Soviet analysts, the loss of U.S. strategic superiority is a critical component in gaining U.S. recognition of the Soviet Union as a power equal to itself. Soviet leaders also believe that strategic parity increases U.S.–West European tensions which they hope to exploit and thereby weaken the Western alliance.

Strategic parity has an inherent instability in the Soviet view due to the technological competition with the United States. The Soviet Union, of course, holds the United States responsible for "causing" the technological arms race. Nonetheless, in spite of technological uncertainties, the Soviets believe strategic parity will continue to prevail given the will of the Soviets not to lose in the strategic arms race.

The Soviets participated in the SALT talks in the 1970s and the Intermediate Nuclear Force (INF) and Strategic Arms Reduction Talks (START) in the 1980s to ensure that strategic parity remained within reach. The Soviets used these talks primarily to try to restrain U.S. technological virtuosity. The Soviets also participated in the talks in order to generate domestic pressure on Western governments from their publics to support parity, rather than superiority. In addition, Soviets participated in order to enhance the stability of the environment for their defense planning.

The Soviet strategic challenge in the 1970s and early 1980s has encompassed four major dimensions. First, the Soviet leaders have deployed strategic forces capable of inflicting assured destruction against U.S. territory and have recognized the "objective reality" of the U.S. ability to reciprocate. Second, Soviet leaders, while not anticipating a meaningful "victory" in conditions of all-out nuclear war, have developed a flexible military force structure in order to be able to prevail in a conventional war at the European theater level. They have also developed the military capability for the exercise of limited nuclear warfighting options as well. Third, the Soviet leaders have perceived strategic parity to be difficult to attain in light of U.S. military and technological capabilities. Fourth, the Soviets have acted on a concept of strategic parity in the arms control process that has contradictory political and technological faces. Politically, the Soviets have insisted on an equality with the United States that seriously complicates U.S. relations with and obligations to NATO. Technologically, the Soviets have tried to use the arms control process to limit U.S. modernization programs while protecting their most significant modernization programs, especially their ICBM forces.

In spite of such contradictions, arms control agreements were forged in the 1970s. But will the political and technological contradictions of the strategic parity problem become so exacerbated in the 1980s and 1990s that the arms control process of the 1970s becomes an historical relic, something akin to the Washington Naval Treaty of 1922?

The answer to this question has three parts. First, how will the Soviet Union view the strategic environment of the 1980s and 1990s? Second, what are the likely Soviet strategic responses to this environment and how will the United States view the subsequent strategic environment? Third, given the conflicting assessments of the evolving strategic environment, what are the prospects for arms control agreements?

## The Soviet View

Table 21-1 indicates the Soviet view of the strategic environment in terms of the interaction between political and technological factors. A significant political dimension is the desire to maintain "equivalence" with U.S. central or intercontinental systems. The major technological challenges to equivalence are the proposed U.S. modernizations, namely, the MX ICBM, the Trident submarine-launched ballistic missiles, and the bomber/cruise missile combinations. Another political dimension is the desire to main-

Table 21.1. *The Strategic Environment in the 1980s and 1990s (from the Soviet Perspective)*

| The political dimension of strategic parity | Western strategic programs (the "technological threat" to strategic parity) |
|---|---|
| 1. Maintain equivalence with the United States | 1. Qualitative transformation of U.S. forces (MX, Trident I and II, cruise missiles, and new manned bombers) |
| 2. Maintain assured destruction capability | 2. U.S. R&D programs (Midgetman, stealth bomber and cruise missiles, strategic defense, and ASW systems) |
| 3. Equal security<br>  a. Geographical asymmetries<br>  b. Third Country systems | 3.<br>  a. U.S. GLCMs and Pershing IIs<br>  b. French and British nuclear modernization |
| 4. Deny U.S. strategic superiority | 4. Qualitative transformation of U.S. forces together with French and British modernization programs |

tain assured destruction capabilities vis-à-vis the United States. The major U.S. technological threats to assured destruction are new ballistic-missile defense systems and the development of new technologies, such as the new stealth technologies, which will make it more difficult for the Soviet Union to destroy U.S. systems. Still another political dimension is the desire to ensure "equal security" with the United States. From the Soviet standpoint, two technological problems are critical challenges to equal security: (1) the United States capitalizing on geographical asymmetries by deploying ground-launched cruise missiles and Pershing IIs in Europe to gain strategic advantage; and (2) the West gaining strategic superiority through French and British nuclear modernizations developing outside the U.S.–Soviet strategic balance. A final political dimension is the desire to deny the United States the possibility of attaining usable strategic superiority. The Soviet Union might well be wary of the qualitative transformation of U.S. intercontinental and intermediate missile systems together with the French and British modernizations that could enable the United States to conduct a limited nuclear war from Europe that would wreak unacceptable damage on the Soviet homeland.

The qualitative transformation of U.S. strategic forces will especially threaten the mainstay of Soviet strategic power, namely, the ICBM. By 1988, the United States plans to deploy 100 MX missiles in fixed silos. Each MX will carry 10 warheads of a new type—the W87—with an explosive power of more than 300 kilotons. The W87 warhead will be carried by a new reentry vehicle, the Mk-21, which has a much more accurate guidance system than the Mk-12a, which is currently deployed on more than 300 Minuteman IIIs.[17] The 1000 MX warheads could hypothetically destroy almost the entire core of the Soviet ICBM force, the 308 SS-18s and 310 SS-19s. By 1998, the United States plans to deploy 20 Trident Class submarines, each with 24 missile tubes. The first 8 will carry the Trident I missiles, but by 1998 all will carry the Trident II or D-5 missiles. The D-5, which will be capable of carrying from 10 to 15 warheads, will have "the capability to attack all potential targets effectively from submarines."[18] The Trident force carrying a minimum of 4800 warheads when conjoined with the MX force could be theoretically capable of destroying the entire Soviet ICBM force in a first strike.

The United States also plans to deploy at least 4348 air-launched cruise missiles by 1990. "The extremely accurate ALCMs will be able to destroy the hardest Soviet targets."[19] The ALCMs will be supplemented by a force of 400 sea-launched cruise missiles by 1988. Not all SLCMs will carry nuclear warheads. In addition, the United States plans to deploy a force of 100 B1-B penetrating bombers by the late 1980s. From the Soviet perspective, the cruise missiles together with the bombers will significantly enhance U.S. second strike capabilities.

In addition to already programmed force modernizations, the United States has generated a number of programs that could further reduce the efficacy of the Soviet Union's strategic forces. For example, the United States appears to be moving in the direction of supplementing its fixed-silo ICBMs with a smaller, more survivable Midgetman.[20] In addition, the development of a stealth bomber would significantly increase U.S. ability to penetrate Soviet airspace.[21] The United States plans significant improvements in strategic defense. The navy plans to build a new class of attack submarines in the 1990s that will be larger, faster, quieter, and more lethal than the world's best nuclear attack submarine, namely, the Los Angeles Class SSN.[22] In addition, the United States has an active program in ballistic missile defense.[23] The United States reportedly believes that "an active defense could protect some high-value strategic assets from ballistic missile attack."[24]

President Reagan in a major speech in March 1983 underscored the U.S. desire to develop an effective defense against ballistic missiles while reducing the threat of mutual assured destruction.[25] The speech has been followed up by Pentagon studies on the feasibility of "high confidence" ballistic missile defense systems. By the late fall of 1983, key defense officials were reportedly encouraging the president to adopt an ambitious ballistic missile defense research-and-development program that would provide deployment options, possibly by the end of the decade or, at least, by the end of the century.[26]

In addition to the challenges posed by improvements in U.S. central systems, the Soviet Union faces nuclear challenges in the European theater that seriously complicate its quest for equal security. The United States will deploy nearly 600 missiles with hard-target capability in the European theatre. From the Soviet standpoint, these programs will enhance U.S. first strike capabilities as well as provide for a much more diversified second strike capability. France and Britain are also carrying out significant modernization programs. The two countries plan to have more than 1000 strategic warheads by the mid-1990s. For Moscow, such programs challenge the credibility of the Soviet conventional war-fighting option or, at a minimum, clearly complicate Soviet plans to exercise escalation dominance in a European war.[27]

The Soviet Union might be confident that in the absence of wide-spread and effective U.S. anti-ballistic missile deployments, the United States will not be able to reestablish strategic superiority on the central systems level. Moscow must be concerned, however, with the tech-nological challenge posed by Washington's strategic force moderniza-tion program. As Steinbrunner noted:

> Tacitly, the material pressure on the Soviet Union emerging from the Reagan Administration is qualitative in character. The apparent intention is to develop a more sophisticated, more diverse United States strategic arsenal rather than a larger one and thereby to force major adjustments in the large Soviet deployments. The implied purpose is to force the Soviets to waste the heavy investment they so recently completed by making it technically obsolete. (The most compelling threat from the Soviet perspec-tive is the Trident II ballistic missile, expected to give the United States submarine force the capability to attack hardened Soviet ICBM silos.)[28]

For the Soviet Union, the United States could most likely reestablish a semblance of strategic superiority by enhancing NATO strategic nuclear capability in the European theater. The U.S. long-range theater nuclear forces when conjoined with British and French strategic systems, *even if numerically inferior* to Soviet systems targeted against Western Europe, would still potentially lead to U.S. strategic superiority, from the Soviet standpoint. If Moscow hopes to fight a conventional war in Europe, the British and French independent nuclear forces represent serious threats. If either a conventional or nuclear war is limited to the European theater, the discharge of U.S. LRTNF, British, and French nuclear systems could wreak substantial damage on the USSR itself. In fact, the damage could be so substantial that Moscow would have to terminate the war in order to preserve what remained of its state and society. Such termination would occur in this scenario without the use of U.S. or Soviet central systems. U.S. territory would remain intact. As a result, the Soviet Union might conclude that the greatest threat to the strategic balance involves changes in Western strategic capabilities in the European theater. Moscow might feel that derailing such changes by military deployments, arms control measures, and various political actions is a central priority in the 1980s and 1990s.

**Soviet Strategic Programs**   The Soviets have a panoply of central strategic systems under development with which to define their response to U.S. strategic modernization efforts. To begin with, the Soviets are developing two new ICBMs. The SS-X-24 is a large, solid-fuel missile, first successfully tested in December 1982. It is a medium-sized ICBM carrying 10 warheads and is the replacement for the single warhead SS-11.[29] According to *Soviet Military Power*. "The

SS-X-24 will probably be silo-deployed at first. Mobile deployment could follow several years after initial operational capability is achieved in 1985. This ICBM is likely to be even more accurate than the SS-18 Mod 4 and SS-19 Mod 3."[30]

The Soviets are also testing a follow-on to the SS-13, known as the SS-X-25. A relatively small, single-warhead missile, it was probably designed to be deployed on a mobile launcher. Some Western sources claim that the SS-X-25 is actually a variant of the SS-16.[31] *Soviet Military Power* described the characteristics of the SS-X-25: "[It] is approximately the same size as the U.S. Minuteman ICBM. It will carry a single reentry vehicle. The SS-X-25 has apparently been designed for mobile deployment, with a home base with launcher garages equipped with sliding roofs; massive, off-road, wheeled transporter–erector launchers; and necessary mobile support equipment for refires from the launcher."[32]

The Soviets also have an important SLBM modernization program in the form of the Typhoon Class submarine. The Typhoon carries up to 20 SS-N-20 missiles and has "design features that would permit [the missiles] to poke up through the polar sea ice to fire. Flight time to United States missile silos would be 15 minutes, or half the time it would take other Soviet warheads to reach United States targets."[33] Two will be operational by the end of 1984, with three to four additional ones under construction. By the early 1990s, the Soviets could have eight Typhoon Class SSBNs operational.[34]

Moscow is also working to develop a new long-range strategic bomber, the Blackjack A. This bomber will be used in multiple roles in delivering both gravity bombs and ALCMs to intercontinental range and is expected to be operational in the late 1980s. The Soviet ALCM program is closely associated with the Blackjack. As an official U.S. government source noted: "The Soviets are developing at least one long-range ALCM with a range of some 3,000 kilometers. Carried by the Backfire, the Blackjack, and possibly the Bear, it would provide the Soviets with greatly improved capabilities for low-level and standoff attack in both theater and intercontinental operations. ALCMs could be in the operational force by the mid-1980s."[35] The 1984 version of this report indicated that the new ALCM could become operational on the Bear bomber as early as the end of 1984.[36]

The Soviet Union also has several programs aimed at strengthening its strategic defenses. Its air defense is being enhanced by the deployment of a new SAM systems (the SA-10 and SA-12) as well as the development of a new generation of look-down, shoot-down aircraft (Su-27, MiG-29, and MiG-31). Soviet anti-submarine warfare capabilities are being improved by the development of a new generation of SSNs. The Soviet Union is also pursuing ballistic missile defense systems. According to *Soviet Military Power*:

> The Soviets have developed a rapidly deployable ABM system for which sites could be built in months instead of years. A typical site would consist of engagement radars, guidance radars, above-ground launchers and the high-acceleration interceptor. The new, large phased-array radars under

construction in the USSR along with [existing radars] . . . appear to be designed to provide support for such a widespread ABM defense system. The Soviets seem to have placed themselves in a position to field relatively quickly a nationwide ABM system should they decide to do so.[37]

The Soviet Union could combine these programs in a number of alternative patterns to deal with its growing ICBM vulnerability and to protect its strategic assets for second strikes. One response could be to maintain fixed-site ICBMs but to protect them with ABM systems. A deployed ABM system has the advantage of undercutting the effectiveness of the French and British systems. It has the disadvantage, however, of stimulating an "analogous" U.S. response that might actually erode the effectiveness of Soviet strategic systems.

A second response could be to maintain the ICBM as the premier strike force but to use mobility to enhance survivability. The fixed-base ICBMs could be used as the first strike force, with a mobile ICBM force as the reserve or second strike force. The development of a common intermediate range/intercontinental missile (as in the SS-20/SS-16 pairing) would provide the Soviet Union with a much more flexible weapons mix.

A third response could be to develop a more balanced force or "triad" of ICBMs, SLBMs, and bombers. The SLBM could emerge as the first strike force as the Soviets develop hard-target kill capability in their SLBMs. The SLBMs could then be targeted on U.S. ICBMs with Soviet SLCMs targeted against U.S. bomber bases. Soviet mobile ICBMs could then be used in a second strike role, with long-range bombers providing further countervalue coverage of U.S. territory.

It is more difficult for the Soviet Union to formulate an adequate response to its conception of the Euro-strategic threat posed by U.S. nuclear weapons. The Soviet Union already has a full spectrum of nuclear weapons deployed in Europe. There is no readily apparent "analogous" response to U.S. LRTNF that has not already been made. Of course, greater numbers of SS-20s, SS-21s, SS-22s, or SS-23s could be deployed in response to American deployments.[38]

However, the Soviet Union has an even greater difficulty in defining an analogous response from the standpoint of a similar capability to use tactical or theater weapons to strike U.S. territory. One possibility might be the forward deployment of Soviet bombers carrying ALCMs to Cuba in order to threaten the United States. Another possibility might be the deployment of a new class of attack submarines armed with cruise missiles that could pose a serious undersea threat to the United States. If the Soviets intend to use their SLCMs in a land-attack role, they could pose an especially significant threat to U.S. $C^3$ systems and bomber bases. The closer a submarine can get to a land target, the less warning there would be of a cruise missile attack.[39] Soviet leaders will apparently focus on the forward deployment of SLCMs as their analogous response to U.S. deployments in Europe.[40]

Even more difficult to formulate would be a response to the modernization of French and British strategic forces. The Soviets already have a broad array of conventional and nuclear options to deal with British and French systems. New systems, as opposed to augmenting the capabilities of existing systems, seem unnecessary. From the strategic standpoint, Moscow could implement a policy that would treat the use of British and/or French strategic weapons against Soviet territory as if they were U.S. From a political standpoint, however, the Soviet leaders will continue to follow a policy of trying to exacerbate diplomatic relations among the Western allies in peacetime in the hope that serious disunity would be evident in wartime. In a wartime setting such disunity would allow the Soviet Union the possibility of reaching separate war termination agreements with each major Western power at the expense of the others.

## The U.S. View

The significant array of strategic programs that the Soviet Union has under development and its concomitant possibilities for alternative deployment mixes create a challenging strategic environment for the United States (see Table 21.2). The first political dimension, to maintain equivalence with the Soviet Union, is threatened by the qualitative transformation of Soviet forces. U.S. $C^3$ systems and bomber forces are especially threatened by Soviet SLBM and SLCM modernizations. In addition, the deployment of mobile ICBMs, if the United States is unable to respond for domestic reasons, might be especially challenging to U.S. targeting requirements. The second political dimension, to maintain assured destruction capability, is threatened by continued improvements in Soviet ABM and strategic air defense systems, especially if the Soviets decide to deploy a significant number of advanced ABM systems. The recent discovery by the United States of a probable ABM radar system in violation of the 1972 agreement raises such a prospect.[41] The third political dimension requires that the United States maintain a credible extended deterrence capability, that is, have sufficient nuclear forces to protect Western European as well as U.S. territory. The SS-20, SS-21, SS-22, and SS-23 deployments are especially threatening to the credibility of extended deterrence.[42] The fourth political dimension requires that the United States deny the Soviet Union the ability to attain military superiority. Especially threatening in this regard has been the Soviet effort to maintain conventional superiority in the Eurasian land mass while continuing to transform qualitatively their nuclear forces, both intercontinental and intermediate.

In light of the projected U.S. and Soviet assessments of the evolving strategic environment, will there continue to be significant opportunities for superpower arms control agreements? From the structure of the two assessments, the greatest probability for agreements seems to lie in the first two dimensions, namely, trying to maintain equivalence and assured destruction capabilities. Purely from a military-planning perspective, it would seem useful to have agreements to provide parameters to guide the modernization or qualitative transformation process.

Table 21.2. *The Strategic Environment in the 1980s and 1990s (from the U.S. Perspective)*

| The political dimension of strategic parity | Soviet strategic programs (the "technological threat" to strategic parity) |
| --- | --- |
| 1. Maintain equivalence with the Soviet Union | 1. Qualitative transformation of Soviet forces (SS-X-24, PL-5, Typhoon, Backfire–Blackjack/cruise missile combination) |
| 2. Maintain assured destruction capability | 2. R&D in ABM and strategic air-defense systems |
| 3. Maintain extended deterrence capability | 3. SS-20, SS-21, SS-22, and SS-23 deployments and their follow-on systems |
| 4. Deny Soviet military superiority | 4. Soviet conventional "superiority" in the Eurasian land mass combined with the qualitative transformation of Soviet nuclear forces |

For example, one Reagan administration official in describing the threat to the United States inherent in the shift of the Soviets to a mobile ICBM in the years ahead stated that: "Whether mobile weapons ever represent less of a threat than today's weapons depends upon the total number of warheads allowed on each side."[43] In other words, without controlling the number of deployed warheads, mobile ICBMs might well increase, rather than decrease, the Soviet threat to the United States.

It will remain useful to bargain about what constitutes equivalence, especially with regard to intercontinental strategic systems. The assured destruction dimension will be threatened by changing strategic defensive capabilities—ABM, anti-air, and ASW. ABM systems remain the area of greatest possibility for limitation, even if the 1972 agreements are modified to permit more possibility for ICBM protection, thereby obviating the need to go to mobile ICBMs. But if there are no controls on the numbers of warheads, ABM systems might well be rendered inefficacious.[44]

The least likely area for agreement involves resolving the intermediate nuclear forces problem in Europe. The United States wishes the Soviet Union to recognize, in effect, the Soviet threat to "extended deterrence" posed by Soviet INF systems. The Soviet Union, in turn, wishes the United States to recognize the U.S. and Western European threat to "equal security."

Thus, the Soviet approach to arms control in the 1980s will probably embody several objectives. Although the contours of the U.S. strategic modernization program are increasingly clear, the Soviet Union will hope to control the number of deployed U.S. systems.[45] Moscow is also interested in protecting its strategic modernization program from technological obsolescence by controlling as much as possible the introduction of new technologically advanced systems in the U.S. inventory, but the experience of the 1970s should make the Soviet Union less than sanguine in this regard. Finally, the Soviet Union will try to gain Western acceptance of the equal security concept whereby Soviet nuclear capability would be weighed against U.S., French, and British systems as a totality.

The arms control approach of the Reagan administration has separated the problem of limiting intercontinental from intermediate systems. Although there have been solid political reasons to separate the two forums, strategic and intermediate, there will be significant technological pressure to merge them when the Soviet Union begins to deploy mobile ICBMs. It would be politically and militarily questionable for any U.S. administration to leave uncounted mobile two-stage IRBMs while counting mobile three-stage ICBMs, for there would be obvious potential interchangeability between the two. In addition, as a general rule, incorporating intermediate forces into the Strategic Arms Reduction Talks would expand the scope of possible trade-offs.[46]

At U.S.–Soviet START which began in 1982, the United States has made a number of proposals aimed at controlling the process of modernizing intermediate strategic systems. On May 9, 1982, President Reagan indicated that the United States sought a two-phase reduction in strategic arms. In the first phase, land- and sea-based ballistic missiles would be reduced to 850 on each side. Warheads for these missiles would be limited to 5000, of which no more than 2500 could be deployed on ICBMs. In the second phase, the United States would consider limits on other systems, including long-range bombers and cruise missiles.[47]

The key rationale for the U.S. proposal was to halt and reverse the destabilizing growth in ballistic missile warhead numbers. The United States has been especially concerned with the heavy missiles, the SS-18s, and prefers a "deep cuts" approach to achieving equivalence in intercontinental systems. The U.S. position was modified, however, in June 1983. The new proposal allowed each side more land- and submarine-based missiles (somewhere between 850 and 1450 launchers) but would continue to limit the number of warheads these launchers could carry to 5000 on each side. The United States also continued to insist on a sublimit of 2500 ICBM warheads as well.

In August 1983, the chief U.S. START negotiator, Edward Rowny, indicated that progress in the START negotiations had reached the point where a preliminary agreement with the Soviet Union on guidelines for reducing intercontinental strategic weapons was possible. Such guidelines would include counting warheads rather than missile launchers, setting an overall ceiling on a number of warheads on each side, and agreeing on equality in total missile throw-weight or lifting power.[48]

But major difficulties remained. The Soviet Union proposed that all missile warheads and bomber-carried weapons be "aggregated" into a single total for nuclear weapons allowable for both sides. The United States, in contrast, proposed one limit for ballistic missile warheads, ICBMs, and SLBMs and another for bomber weapons. According to a

Reagan administration official, "The talks so far have revealed a major Soviet concern about the approximately 3,000 air launched cruise missiles with which the Reagan Administration plans to equip United States bomber forces."[49]

In October 1983, the administration introduced a version of the "build-down" approach to arms control at the START talks. Three proposals were at the heart of this approach. First, two old ICBM warheads would be destroyed for every new fixed land-based missile warhead, such as those on the MX. Second, three old SLBM warheads would be replaced by two new SLBM warheads, such as the D-5. Third, mobile ICBMs, such as the Midgetman, would be on a one-for-one basis. According to Leslie Gelb of the *New York Times*, "this would penalize modernization of potential first-strike weapons and reward modernization in the direction of submarine-launched and mobile missiles."[50]

The Soviets have been less than enthusiastic about Washington's basic START proposals. Initially, they proposed that the SALT II parameters be accepted with one major change, namely, the banning of ALCMs. After the new U.S. proposals in June 1983, the Soviets showed some movement from this position. They no longer sought a complete ban on new U.S. systems such as ALCMs. But the Soviets continued to reject any U.S. proposal that limited their ICBM force without limiting U.S. cruise-missile and bomber programs.[51] In addition, the Soviets have proposed that long-range nuclear weapons be limited to about 1100 multiple warhead missiles and bombers for each side but with no special limits on the SS-18 or SS-19 forces.[52]

Garthoff commented on the reason for Moscow's rejection to date of the U.S. START proposals:

From the Soviet perspective, the revised proposals are fatally flawed. . . . The advertised flexibility does not extend to the key provisions that made the Administration's original negotiating proposal fundamentally unacceptable to Moscow. These crucial flaws are not affected by the flexibility on total ballistic-missile numbers and are in fact made worse by the American plan to deploy the MX.

The 2,500 warheads ceiling would mean a cut of more than half in the Soviet warheads on intercontinental missiles, while permitting an increase in comparable American warheads. The President did not go so far as to impose explicit limitations on missile throw-weight . . . but he kept severe indirect constraints on throw-weight that would require Moscow to reduce by two-thirds its biggest and best strategic missiles, the SS-18 and SS-19, while Washington could go ahead with plans to build-up its MX and Trident II missiles.

Worse still, from the Soviet standpoint, while the proposed agreement would alleviate the vulnerability of American land-based intercontinental missiles . . . it would greatly increase the vulnerability of comparable Soviet missiles—which are the most important component of Moscow's strategic force. There would be no equality of sacrifice and no "equal security."[53]

It should be noted, however, that Soviet unwillingness to recognize the legitimacy of U.S. concerns over the vulnerability of U.S. ICBMs to

Soviet attack is at the heart of the current U.S. arms modernization program. Although the United States is now seeking additional counter-silo capabilities, it is doing so in reaction to Soviet force deployments. Because the Soviet Union has been unwilling to talk about the Minuteman vulnerability problem, the United States has concluded that its only recourse is likewise to threaten Soviet forces.

From a U.S. standpoint, Soviet insistence throughout the arms control negotiations of the 1970s and 1980s on protecting their strategic assets (especially the ICBM force) and on reducing the U.S. technological advantage has been, at the very least, troubling to the United States. Wolfe has noted that one of the core issues of the strategic arms talks has been "where to draw the line at which Soviet insistence upon safe margins of force levels would cease to represent legitimate compensation for technological and other asymmetries favoring the United States and would become a demand for unilateral advantage threatening to tip the strategic balance perceptibly in Soviet favor."[54] The United States is not about to let that happen.

In short, the strategic arms race during the next decade promises to make a determination of what constitutes parity very difficult. The Soviet Union is apparently unable to derail (despite their best diplomatic efforts to do so) U.S., French, and British modernization programs. These Western programs coupled with what the Soviets deem to be their appropriate responses will threaten to undermine parity as it was established in the strategic arms agreements of the 1970s. But parity will continue to exist in the form of mutual assured destruction, especially if the United States and the USSR do not engage in widespread deployments of ballistic missile defense systems.

It is not clear how, or if, superpower arms control talks will effectively curb technological competition or channel the Soviet and U.S. modernization processes into some form of bargained equivalence. There is a real danger that technological competition will become so intense that the effort to define parity through arms control agreements will collapse. This is particularly true if Moscow is confused by U.S. rhetoric, uncertain of U.S. policy goals toward the USSR, and convinced that Washington is out to regain the strategic superiority it lost in the 1960s through increased reliance on advanced technology. An open-ended and dangerously unregulated arms race could well be unleashed.

## Notes

[1]See, for example, Fritz Ermarth, "Contrasts in American and Soviet Strategic Thought," and Stanley Sienkiewitz, "Soviet Nuclear Doctrine and the Prospects for Strategic Arms Control," both in *Soviet Military Thinking*, ed., Derek Leebaert (London: George Allen and Unwin, 1981), pp. 50–69 and 73–91, respectively. See also Robert P. Berman and John C. Baker, *Soviet Strategic Forces* (Washington, D.C.: Brookings Institution, 1982), p. 33; and Keith B. Payne, *Nuclear Deterrence in U.S.–Soviet Relations* (Boulder, Colo.: Westview Press, 1982), pp. 11–27.

[2]Garthoff's views are taken from Raymond L. Garthoff, "Mutual Deterrence

and Strategic Arms Limitation in Soviet Policy," *Strategic Review* (Fall 1982), pp. 36–51 and pp. 58–63. Pipes's views are taken from Richard Pipes, *U.S.–Soviet Relations in the Era of Détente* (Boulder, Colo.: Westview Press, 1981), pp. 135–170, and Richard Pipes, "Soviet Strategic Doctrine: Another View," *Strategic Review* (Fall 1982), pp. 52–57.

[3]Garthoff, "Mutual Deterrence," p. 37.

[4]*Ibid*, p. 42.

[5]*Ibid*.

[6]*Ibid*.

[7]*Ibid.*, p. 44.

[8]*Ibid.*, p. 45.

[9]*Ibid*.

[10]*Ibid.*, p. 37.

[11]*Ibid.*, p. 44.

[12]*Pipes*, "Soviet Strategic Doctrine," p. 56.

[13]*Pipes, U.S.–Soviet Relations in the Era of Détente*, p. 136.

[14]*Ibid.*, p. 159.

[15]*Ibid.*, p. 168.

[16]*Ibid*.

[17]*Washington Post*, June 28, 1983, p. 7. Information in this section on U.S. systems has also been taken from Thomas B. Cochran *et al.*, *U.S. Nuclear Forces and Capabilities* (Cambridge, Mass.: Ballinger Publishing Co., 1984).

[18]U.S. Secretary of Defense, *Annual Report to Congress, Fiscal Year 1984* (Washington, D.C.: U.S. Government Printing Office, 1983), p. 222.

[19]U.S. Department of Defense, Chairman of the Joint Chiefs of Staff, *United States Military Posture, Fiscal Year 1984* (Washington, D.C.: U.S. Government Printing Office, 1983), p. 39.

[20]*New York Times*, May 16, 1983, p. 15; *Air Force Magazine* (August 1983), pp. 22–24.

[21]*Defense Electronics* (May 1983), p. 15; *Armed Forces Journal* (October 1983), pp. 24–25.

[22]*New York Times*, May 19, 1983, p. 17.

[23]See *Science*, July 1, 1983, pp. 30–32, and July 8, 1983, pp. 133–135, 138.

[24]*Annual Report to Congress*, p. 227.

[25]*New York Times*, March 24, 1983, p. 20.

[26]*Science*, November 25, 1983, pp. 901–902; *Washington Post*, November 27, 1983, p. 24; *Harper's* (January 1984), pp. 50–52, 54–57.

[27]See Robbin F. Laird, *France, the Soviet Union, and the Nuclear Weapons Issue* (Boulder, Colo.: Westview Press, 1985).

[28]John Steinbrunner, "Arms and the Art of Compromise," *The Brookings Review* (Summer 1983), p. 8.

[29]*Washington Times*, December 23, 1983, p. 4.

[30]*Soviet Military Power* (Washington, D.C.: U.S. Government Printing Office, 1984), p. 24.

[31]*Washington Times*, May 25, 1983, p. 5; *Washington Post*, May 12, 1983, p. l; *New York Times*, May 12, 1983, p. B-9; *Washington Post*, August 19, 1983, p. l; *New York Times*, August 20, 1983, p. 3.

[32]*Soviet Military Power*, 1984, p. 24.

[33]*Los Angeles Times*, June 26, 1983, p. 1.

[34]*Soviet Military Power*, 1984, p. 25.

[35]U.S. Department of Defense, *Soviet Military Power* (Washington, D.C.: U.S. Government Printing Office, 1983), p. 26.

[36]*Soviet Military Power*, 1984, p. 311.

[37]*Ibid.*, p. 34.

[38]*Washington Post*, October 11, 1983, p. 9; *Baltimore Sun*, October 26, 1983, p. 1.

[39]Joel Wit, "Soviet Cruise Missiles," *Survival* (November/December 1983), pp. 249–260.

[40]*Washington Post*, November 25, 1983, p. 1; *Baltimore Sun*, November 28, 1983, p. 1.

[41]*New York Times*, October 5, 1983, p. 8.

[42]Pierre Gallois, "L'Option Zero est Inacceptable pour l'Europe," *Geopolitique* (April 1983), pp. 104–112.

[43]*Washington Post*, August 19, 1983, p. 1.

[44]Paul Stares, "Reagan's BMD Plan: The Ultimate Defence?" *Armament and Disarmament Information Unit Report* (May–June 1983).

[45]*Washington Post*, July 2, 1983, p. 8.

[46]*National Journal*, October 1983, p. 2179.

[47]*Washington Post*, June 9, 1983, p. 7.

[48]*Washington Post*, September 21, 1983, p. 1.

[49]*Baltimore Sun*, September 9, 1983, p. 2.

[50]*New York Times*, October 5, 1983, p. 1.

[51]*New York Times*, June 10, 1983, p. 1.

[52]*Washington Post*, July 13, 1983, p. 1.

[53]*New York Times*, June 12, 1983, p. E-19; *Washington Post*, June 27, 1983, p.2; *Christian Science Monitor*, June 23, 1983, p. 1.

[54]Thomas Wolfe, *The SALT Experience* (Cambridge, Mass.: Ballinger Publishing Co., 1979), p. 156.

# 22 THANE GUSTAFSON

## Selling the Russians the Rope? Soviet Technology Policy and U.S. Export Controls*

**Introduction: A Critical Look at High-Technology Export Controls**

Is the United States putting itself in danger by failing to control more carefully the export of scientific knowledge, technology, and management know-how to the Soviet Union? Alarmed by the rapidly growing military strength of the Soviets, we wonder uncomfortably whether we have inadvertently contributed to it, through scientific exchanges, turnkey and training agreements, sales of licenses, or exports of high-technology products and processes. About 15 years ago, confident of our military strength and of the superiority of our civilian technology, and hopeful about the possibilities of cooperation with the Soviet Union, we began dismantling the virtual trade embargo we had maintained against Eastern Europe for nearly 20 years, and set about expanding trade and contracts. We are far from that optimism now.[1]

In the last few years the United States has moved, albeit for logical reasons that will be explained below, toward an export-control system that could be more complex, costly, and controversial than any we have had before. At the same time Americans remain ambivalent about the objectives of export controls and unclear about what such controls can achieve and what they cannot. Our thinking will be considerably clarified, however, if we bear in mind that the most important question about technology transfer in the long run is whether the receiving side is able to absorb the technology it imports, to diffuse it beyond one or two

*Reprinted in revised form by permission of the author and publisher from *Selling the Russians the Rope? Soviet Technology Policy and U.S. Export Controls* (Santa Monica, Calif.: Rand, 1981), pp. 1–10, 66–77. Prepared for the Defense Advanced Research Projects Agency. Copyright 1981 by The Rand Corporation.

showcase locations, and to build upon it to generate further technological advances of its own. Only then does technology transfer have its most lasting consequences.

If we rethink the export-control question on that basis, then our focus shifts from the characteristics of the proposed export or its potential end-uses (the issues that the American debate tends to dwell on most) to the Soviets' ability to learn from it. Here we must distinguish between two classes of cases: In certain high-priority sectors (notably military), where Soviet technological skills are already high, the Soviets' ability to learn from foreign technology is also high. Here, then, there is a clear case for export controls. In contrast, in the lagging areas in which most Soviet imports of foreign technology are concentrated, the Soviets' record in absorbing and learning from it is poor. The reasons are much the same as the ones that cause those areas to lag in the first place: They lie deep in the political and economic structure of the country, and (as we shall see) numerous reform measures in Soviet technology policy over the last 12 years or so have not altered them. Neither have high-technology imports visibly improved the Soviets' ability to innovate on their own, in some instances the opposite. It is this second class of cases, and the difficult matter of distinguishing it from the first, that most of the American uncertainty is about.

Within the second class of cases the most effective barriers to technology transfer are those erected by the Soviets against themselves. The effects of internal Soviet obstacles, in fact, dwarf those of the most stringent embargo the Western powers might devise. Consequently, so long as Soviet policies for technological innovation remain as ineffective as they are now, the claimed benefits of any expansion of U.S. export controls should be examined very carefully. Export controls have important if marginal political benefits, but they also have serious costs, and the task before us is to arrive at a sound balance between the two.

## Evolution of American Export-Control Policy

The basis for the present system of controls is the Export Administration Act of 1979 (Public Law 96–72), which mandates prior review and approval by the federal government of any proposed export that "would make a significant contribution to the military potential of any other nation or group of nations which would prove detrimental to the national security of the United States."[2] The agency with primary responsibility for this system is the Commerce Department's Office of Export Administration, but several other government offices must also review and concur, notably the Defense Department, which judges the possible military significance of proposed exports. In practice, decisions on controversial cases are made by consensus, which sometimes requires long negotiation to reach.

For more than 10 years, the successive versions of the Export Administration Act (the present Act is the fourth since 1969) have been uneasy compromises between two objectives, that of protecting the national security and that of promoting exports. During that period, on the whole, encouragement of foreign trade has been Congress's primary concern; and framers have attempted to limit and define precisely the situations in which export controls will be invoked. In the recent past, however, anxiety about national security has risen in Congress as in the rest of the nation, and the issue of reconciling the competing objectives in export-control legislation is coming once again to the fore. The matter is complicated by the fact that the distinctions involved are inherently slippery. Just about any export, including feed grain or drilling technology, can be considered a "significant contribution" to Soviet military potential, provided one adopts sufficiently broad definitions. Hence, every time the Act comes before Congress for review (as in 1974, 1977, 1979, and 1984), it gives rise to anxious debate.

To try to cope with the distinctions between military and civilian applications of exports, the Departments of Commerce and Defense maintain a Commodity Control List of items with possible military applications. The decision to grant or deny an export license for any item on that list requires judging, case by case, how likely it is that it will actually be diverted to a military end-use and, if the likelihood is considered high, whether suitable checks or alterations can be devised to remove the danger. It goes without saying that this process takes time, and one of the chief complaints of American companies and members of Congress over the years has been that the system is so cumbersome that it costs the United States valuable export business. On that count alone the present export-control system would be controversial. However, the real problems go deeper.

New generations of weapons rest on a multitude of advanced supporting technologies that cannot be said to be inherently either military or civilian. It follows that diversion to military uses constitutes less and less often a clear act that one can identify and control. Even the most plausible diversion scenarios have their ambiguities. Can a Sperry Univac 1100/10C computer, sold to a Soviet design agency in the synthetic-rubber industry, be diverted to perform three-dimensional differential equations for aircraft-wing stress analysis at the nearby Tupolev plant?[3] Amid the flurry of concern over whether it has been or might be, one should point out that synthetic rubber is of military importance too, and that a good eight-year-old computer technology is likely to have a greater marginal impact in that industry than in the top priority Tupolev facility, which presumably is already well provided for.

A further difficulty with the end-use principle, in the eyes of its critics at least, is that it tends to emphasize transfer of "hard" products and processes, physical quantities that can be identifiably diverted, whereas an equally crucial question is the transfer of know-how and supporting skills. In the computer example mentioned above, we worry about the quality of the software that the Soviets may be importing along with the Univac; and diversion of software is, of course, more difficult to spot and deter than that of hardware. Defenders of the present export-control system insist that such know-how and "soft" technology are recognized as problems and are adequately controlled; critics say they are not.

Washington's growing awareness of these issues in the mid-1970s led to the development of a new concept and a proposed new strategy based on so-called "critical technologies," which has now been incorporated into official policy in the 1979 Export Administration Act. The term arose out of a panel convened by the Department of Defense in 1975, chaired by the President of Texas Instruments, J. Fred Bucy. The panel's recommendations, issued the following year,[4] contained three important concepts that have since gained wide currency: (1) The proper object of control is the export of manufacturing and design know-how rather than end-products alone; (2) "active" mechanisms of transfer (such as turnkey or training arrangements) are more apt to be consequential than "passive" ones (such as trade fairs or export of finished products); and (3) rather than attempt to construct impermeable barriers to the transfer of militarily significant technology, the aim of the control system should be to retard the flow so as to protect lead-times in the military areas in which the United States has a significant edge.

Each of these three points has important implications. First, by stressing the *mechanism* of transfer, the Bucy criteria stress that the transfer of an object or a process may be less important than the transfer of a skill, and that one of the most important questions about such transfers is the *way* they are made. Second, by focusing on classes of technologies rather than specific items, the Bucy criteria appear to offer relief from the increasingly futile and time-consuming task of tracking down possible military end-uses and diversions. Finally, by emphasizing that the goal of American policy should be to preserve critical lead-times (thus conceding that it is hopeless to prevent military end-uses indefinitely), the Bucy criteria require us to think clearly about the nature and sources of the American lead, in other words, about what technological superiority really consists of in the first place and how it should be defended.

Despite these real virtues, there is serious question whether the critical-technologies approach will improve the export-control system. On the contrary, if we are not careful it could make the system more complex, cumbersome, and controversial than any we have previously had. The "Initial List of Militarily Critical Technologies," issued in October 1980 by the Department of Defense,[5] illustrates the danger. It contains a virtual roll-call of leading contemporary techniques, including videodisk recording, polymeric materials, and many dozens of others equally broad. If this collection had automatically become the basis for the official Commodities Control List (as some had urged during the debate over the 1979 Export Administration Act), the entire Department of Commerce would not have been large enough to administer the export-control program. Fortunately the Initial List has advisory status only, and one may be confident that it will undergo refinement before it becomes the actual basis for policy.

The underlying problem, which the legislative history of the successive versions of the Export Administration Act in the 1970s shows clearly, is that American policymakers have been uncertain about the effects and dangers of high-technology exports to the Soviet bloc.[6] What exactly are we trying to prevent the Soviets from doing? In what ways does imported Western technology enable the Soviets to do the things we fear? Can export controls stop them or slow them down? These three questions are central to any export-control policy, but there has been considerable confusion about all three of them. In particular, if our goal is to preserve lead-times it is soon apparent that we have two different sorts of lead-times to worry about: the lead embodied in individual weapons systems and that embodied in the underlying technologies that generate them. Each has its own dangers, and consequently each requires its own sorts of information and its own strategies. What is needed, in other words, is cooler and more systematic thinking about the effects and dangers of technology transfers. The next section offers some suggestions.

Effects and Dangers of Technology Transfer   In the broadest terms, transfers of technology have three classes of possible consequences: The Soviets may gain (1) direct, near-term military advantage; (2) indirect, longer-term military advantage; (3) a boost to their overall economic growth. Which of these should the United States try to limit through export controls?

*Direct, Near-Term Military Advantage* Imported Western technology could yield the Soviet Union a direct, short-term military advantage in two possible ways. The first is a transfer leading directly to a revolutionary Soviet breakthrough. The second is a transfer that suddenly fills a gap, overcomes a bottleneck, or completes a puzzle in an otherwise mature Soviet technology, enabling the Soviets to proceed to a rapid expansion of numbers or a sudden generational improvement in a major weapons system. As a hypothetical example, the revelation of the Ulam–Teller principle, during the crucial period when the Soviets were groping for an efficient fusion–fission coupling of their own, would have been an example of the first kind. A case of the second kind may have been the sale to the Soviet Union of high-precision micro-ballbearing grinders, used in the manufacture of highly accurate guidance systems for intercontinental missiles.

A subcategory in the second group is the inadvertent giveaway, in which the technology in question is a readily available item whose military significance the Russians may realize ahead of the Americans. A plausible hypothetical example is Kevlar, the casing material that contains the propellant in the Trident I, initially developed by DuPont for use in radial tires. Kevlar's potential military applications were realized by accident, when defense contractors happened to come across it at an aerospace fair on the West Coast.[7] In this case, the serendipitous discoverers happened to be Americans, but there is no reason why they could not have been Russians. Plastics and synthetic rubber, indeed, have been high on the list of chemicals and chemical equipment purchased by the Soviet Union in recent years. The job of anticipating such cases will become steadily more difficult in years to come, as new weapons systems incorporate a progressively wider range of supporting technologies, such as new synthetic materials and fuels, micro-electronics, and so forth.

As nightmarish as these possibilities sound, it is important to recognize that the chances of a sudden doomsday giveaway through trade are next to nil. First, the military balance between the two countries is stable and well buffered. In strategic weaponry, for example, the redundancy built into the U.S. Triad is so great that no single new weapon will confer meaningful advantage in the short term. The day when the simple invention of the stirrup swung the balance of power on the Asian continent is long over. (Of course, maintaining the Triad requires periodic deployment of new weapons systems. But such deployments— however heated the debate surrounding them—take decades to plan and execute, which shows how stable the basic system is.)

Second, major weapons systems rest on a multitude of different technologies, so that no single breakthrough will produce a sudden advantage; whether in undersea acoustics, look-down shoot-down air defense, missile guidance, "stealth" avionics or high-energy lasers, major developments come from an accumulation of advances over long years, most of them involving basic sciences that are being actively studied on both sides. Threats from such a quarter can be seen from a long way off, and therefore no single transfer can possibly produce a total surprise. (The enormous publicity given by the Western media to Soviet efforts in charged-particle-beam technology illustrates this point strikingly.)

Third, in the research sectors of immediate military relevance the Soviet Union maintains a level that may be better funded and in some cases more advanced than that of the United States.[8] Most of their weaknesses, as we shall see below, lie in traditionally "civilian," lower-priority, supporting technologies. Experience suggests that in high-priority sectors, in which the opponent is already well equipped and heavily engaged, the most important transfer is simply the sure knowledge that something is possible and is being achieved elsewhere. This appears to have been Fuchs' most important contribution to the Russians, for example, in the case of the hydrogen bomb.[9] Needless to say, the prevention of such transfers, though desirable, lies outside the export-control issue. The same is true of the fact that, where the West possesses a clearly superior technology of direct military importance, the Soviets have demonstrated the ability to spirit away what they need by means other than trade, as in the case of the design for the Side-winder missile.

In sum, the fear that the United States is unwittingly selling the rope that the Russians will shortly use to hang us is hardly credible. In the areas of technology that might yield direct military advances, the Soviets depend less (and are less willing to depend) on foreign trade than they do in other, traditionally lower-priority areas. No single export item will produce a lightning-bolt surprise, for any such transfer would be so obvious that it could not be overlooked; and even if it were it could not be converted into sudden strategic advantage. It goes without saying that the commercial export of technologies with clear and immediate military applications must be controlled where possible; but despite occasional headlines to the contrary there is no serious evidence that our present control systems (particularly the Munitions List) fail to do this. As we shall see in the next two subsections, the knotty parts of the technology transfer issue lie elsewhere.

*Indirect, Long-Term Military Advantage* The more difficult issue in export-control policy is not whether the West is selling the Russians the rope but whether we are selling them the capacity to make it themselves, by helping them to overcome technological lags in the broad industrial infrastructure needed for tomorrow's advanced weapons systems (not to mention tomorrow's economic growth, which we shall address next).

We are currently witnessing throughout the world a blurring of the boundaries between military and civilian technologies, and the Soviet Union is no exception. Tomorrow's weapons systems will depend on new materials and alloys, advances in communications and data processing, manufacturing and fabricating techniques, automation of assembly and auxiliary operations, new skills, and techniques of management. The traditional Soviet strategy of maintaining an isolated high-priority zone for military deployment and production, while simultaneously skimming the cream from the civilian economy for military use, becomes self-defeating when military technology requires the entire range of skills and techniques of an advanced industrial economy.[10] No small part of the current Soviet anxiety over the weaknesses of their R&D policy and their management of technological innovation stems from their increasing awareness of the backwardness of several crucial areas of what had hitherto been neglected as "civilian" technology. Therefore, the greatest benefit of foreign technology to the Soviets may be to bring up to a fully modern standard the "infrastructural" civilian technologies that are emerging as the crucial ones for tomorrow's military strength.

The question is, Can this problem be dealt with through any remotely feasible export-control policy? As soon as one shifts one's focus from weapons systems to the technologies embodied in them, virtually any high-technology product, process, or skill becomes militarily relevant. From there it is but a short step to declare that all advanced technologies should be subject to export controls. The Initial List of Militarily Critical Technologies, mentioned earlier, illustrates the problem: Its critical weakness is that it is simply a listing of techniques that, if exported to a military competitor, *could* be harmful to us; it does not contain any clear conception of how or why technology transfer actually takes place. It implicitly assumes that advanced technology is like virulent disease: It is enough for the recipient to be exposed for him to catch it.

However, studies of actual cases show that that is not how technology transfer works at all. Imported technology will not be of more than passing benefit to the Soviet Union unless that country is able to use it to develop its own innovative capacities, to generate further technology, and to diffuse it broadly and quickly. If the Soviets fail to gain that capacity, then imported technology will in many ways only perpetuate their backwardness and dependence (and we will see instances of that phenomenon in the next section), since by the time it is installed and functioning it is already out of date. *Therefore the crucial point to examine is the extent to which foreign technology helps overcome the root problems that have been holding back Soviet technological innovation in the first place.*

*Long-Term Economic Effects: Reinforcement or Displacement?* Foreign technology, whatever else it may do, contributes to the overall growth of the Soviet economy. In the near term, the higher productivity of Western products and processes gives a boost to quality or efficiency of Soviet output; in some specialties, such as the manufacture of mineral fertilizers, this effect is striking. Over the longer term, Western technology has served as a model and a standard, providing a stimulus to progress that is often lacking within the Soviet system itself.

The contribution of Western technology to Soviet growth may not be large in global terms.[11] But Soviet leaders have frequently used foreign technology to make a fast start in a branch of industry that has suddenly risen in importance and priority; this occurred notably in chemicals in the 1950s and 1960s, in the automotive industry in the 1960s and 1970s, and in the energy sector beginning in the 1970s. Thus foreign technology helps Soviet leaders respond rapidly to new policy needs.

These broad economic effects of foreign technology, rather than the narrower military ones, appear to be uppermost in the minds of the Soviet leaders themselves, for signs of economic trouble confront them wherever they look. Declining output and productivity, shortages of labor and key resources, low quality and poor performance—these are the symptoms of a disease whose existence the Soviet leaders themselves no longer try to deny. And one of the principal remedies to which the leaders have resorted, after lengthy debate and much swallowed pride, has been to import unprecedented quantities of foreign technology.

This development raises the most difficult questions of all for Western export-control policy. Is it in the interest of the United States to try to prevent the Soviet Union from turning to foreign technology to boost economic growth? And if so, are export controls the appropriate instrument for the job? The 1979 Export Administration Act, as we have seen, authorized the use of export controls to protect the national security, and particularly to prevent transfers that would contribute to the military potential of unfriendly powers. Should fertilizer plants, mills for specialty steels, or oil-drilling technology be banned on the grounds that, because they contribute to Soviet economic growth, they contribute significantly to Soviet military potential? This question has a variant that has proved especially thorny: What if imported technologies free resources that the Soviets can then displace toward the military sector?

Let us take up the latter question first: Its plausibility turns on several difficult questions of fact. First, do we really know that imported technology releases resources? Some Western experts argue, on the contrary, that foreign technology *ties up* scarce resources, because every ruble of imported equipment requires something like five rubles of investment support (in the form of supporting infrastructure and training of personnel), in order to absorb it and make it work.[12] If the priority of the receiving sector is high enough, it may have such a strong claim on scarce resources that it competes with the military.

A more fundamental objection to the displacement argument is that it assumes that the Soviet allocation system treats resources as fungible between the military and civilian sectors. That assumption cannot be demonstrated to be true. What little evidence we have concerning Soviet military spending (and, for that matter, military R&D) suggests a steady, incremental increase through the Brezhnev period, unaffected by the substantial ups and downs of trade in high-technology goods. In other words, there is no evidence that the Soviets would spend less on the military and more on the civilian economy in the absence of high-technology trade. The pattern corresponds instead to what we would expect to observe if the Soviets followed a lexical decision rule, with the military treated as first claimant until its "needs" (however defined) are met, and other claimants treated as residual.[13]

The displacement argument, furthermore, assumes that the civilian and military sectors are separate and competitive rather than complementary and mutually reinforcing. But is not an increase in oil drilling in Western Siberia as much a contribution to the military, in the long run, as it is to the "civilian" economy? Imported technology in recent years has been concentrated primarily in industries that the Soviets have been systematically building up rather than deliberately neglecting, industries to which the Soviets are simultaneously directing considerable native R&D. There is no denying that the military sector enjoys the highest priority in the land. What cannot be shown, however, is that the Soviets use foreign technology to wring every last kopeck from the civilian economy to benefit the military.

Still, there is no doubt that the extreme priority enjoyed by the military in the allocation of Soviet resources puts the rest of the economy under severe strain. If that strain became great enough, might not the Soviet leaders be forced to review their priorities and reroute some scarce resources to "civilian" purposes, the energy sector for example? Why then should the West help relieve the strain? An answer one sometimes hears is that, regardless of what happens to the military sector, a technologically backward or energy-starved Soviet Union is a special danger to the rest of the world. Consequently, in this view, it is not in the interest of the West to attempt to impede Soviet economic growth. But is it really true that the Soviets are depraved because they are deprived? There is no particular evidence either way. What stands out, instead, is the essential continuity of Soviet foreign policy over the years, through good economic times and bad. In sum, as one picks one's way through the thicket of arguments about Soviet economic growth, one reaches no clear answers.

Therefore let us reason instead from the standpoint of feasibility. Even if we should *like* to slow down Soviet economic growth (not necessarily a foregone proposition), it is quite another matter to ask whether we *can*, and whether export controls (or even embargoes) are the right instrument for the job. Here it is important to remember that the effects of export controls are inherently marginal. That is, they will not halt Soviet economic or military development; at most, they may slow it down slightly at the margin. (American defense planners mean nothing different when they speak of preserving this country's military lead-time; that is the same as a moving margin.) And as in any public policy, the sound aim is equilibrium at the margin, that is, to confine export controls to the classes of cases in which the marginal political benefits are readily identifiable and outweigh (or at least balance) the marginal political costs of obtaining them.

What happens if we apply this criterion to the three classes of effects of technology transfer that we have been discussing? The benefits of attempting to control near-term military effects are *immediate* and *specific*; those of controlling long-term economic effects are *remote* and *diffuse*. At the same time, the costs of the former are likely to be lower than those of the latter, since they are more likely to command the agreement of our allies and more likely to involve technologies in which the United States is genuinely dominant. It follows that, *from the standpoint of feasibility*, a system of controls narrowly defined around the prevention of near-term military effects is the one most likely to have results, while one broadly aimed at impeding Soviet economic growth is likely to be self-defeating.

But what about the middle category, that of long-term and indirect military effects? Here we need to ask one question: How *consequential* are the effects of technology transfer in each category? Near-term military effects, as alarming as they are, are nevertheless passing, because the military technologies of both countries are moving rapidly. What *really* maintains lead-times is the comparative ability of both countries to generate new advances, and here it is the long-term effects of technology transfer that may be the most consequential ones, if they affect that comparative ability to innovate. Consequently, the case for export controls in this middle category must turn on evidence that a proposed export package would help the Soviets remove fundamental obstacles standing in the way of their own innovative ability, in some way that the Americans are in a unique position to deny.

Conclusions    First, what exactly is at issue? No one in the United States questions the need to control exports of direct military importance. To the extent that American security continues to rest on a lead in critical military technologies, then safeguarding technological lead-times is in the nation's vital interest. Something like the present system of case-by-case evaluation, aimed at preventing clear and immediate military use of American technology by the Soviets, must and undoubtedly will continue.

Rather, the issue today is what to do about the possibility that the United States is giving away indirect military advantages through subtle channels that may call for more subtle defenses. The main danger is not so much the possibility of sudden and disastrous give-aways, but rather that high-technology trade may help the Soviets to upgrade over the longer term the traditionally neglected "civilian" industries that will provide broad, infrastructural support for new weapons systems tomorrow. Some of the most significant obstacles to Soviet military progress come from deficiencies in the civilian sector (e.g., computers, communications, energy, and new materials), and this drag can only increase in the future, as military development comes to depend more and more intimately on the combined technological skills of a nation's entire industry. But does foreign technology really enable the Soviets to overcome those obstacles, and could an expanded system of export controls prevent them from doing so?

The major weakness of the present system of controls, in the view of some of its critics, is that it allows important technology to slip through to our military competitors by paying too much attention to the export of products, and not enough to the control of skills, techniques, and know-how. Consequently the most recent U.S. legislation mandates the development of a review procedure that will control classes of critical technologies rather than individual products. Recent American thinking focuses particularly on "active" mechanisms of transfer, such as training agreements, long-term technical exchanges, extended workshops, and other apprenticeship-like arrangements that teach skills and know-how.[14]

It is important to explore carefully the implications of such a broadening, because it can lead to excesses. A recent example that gives food for thought is the decision made at the beginning of 1980 to bar Soviet representatives from attending two technical conferences in the United States—one on bubble memories and the other on laser fusion—in order to prevent transfer of the knowledge discussed there. The two meetings involved technical data directly related to development and manufacture; therefore the Department of Commerce held that the participation of the Soviets required a license, which the Department chose to deny. Other foreign delegates were asked to sign pledges that they would not reveal what they had learned at the meetings to colleagues from communist-controlled countries.[15]

This episode suggests what a broadened export-control doctrine could lead to: First, it tempts us to put pressure on allied governments and their citizens, to induce them to cooperate with our expanded export-control program, despite the fact that support for export controls has been declining abroad.[16] The Carter Administration experimented with economic reprisals against the French firm Creusot-Loire for concluding a contract with the Soviet Union that Washington disapproved of; and the logic of the critical-technologies approach, if we mean to apply it seriously, will lead us toward more measures of the same kind.

Second, the attempt to control "active" mechanisms of technology transfer may inhibit unimpeded and rapid international communication of technical skills and information, at a time when the United States is moving from the position of a dominant supplier of leading technology to that of a beneficiary of foreign advances, and is therefore increasingly dependent upon free exchange. Unless we are judicious about them, expanded export controls could cost us considerable good will among important commercial partners in the West.

To put these points in perspective, it is worth bearing in mind that in the total volume of Western high-technology exports to the Soviet Union the United States is a small player. American high-technology exports to the Soviet Union in 1979 amounted to $183 million ($270 million to Eastern Europe as a whole), about one-tenth the level of Soviet imports of advanced machinery and equipment from West Germany, France, and Japan combined (see Table 22.1). Direct scientific contact is also quite small. The 13 U.S.–Soviet bilateral agreements, at their height, involved little more than 1000 people from each side each year, most of them on carefully orchestrated and necessarily superficial two-week visits. The scientific exchange program conducted by the two countries' Academies of Sciences supports fewer than 250 man-months of visits from each side, few of them involving actual research.[17] Moreover, it is unlikely that extension of most-favored nation treatment and credits by the United States would change this situation much, because the Soviets have taken some care throughout the 1970s to diversify their sources of supply and to limit their indebtedness (see Table 22.2).

In view of these modest dimensions, it is clear that the effect of whatever policy the United States pursues will be slight compared to the actions of our principal allies, and slight also in its overall effect on Soviet science and technology, given how little actual contact there is between the two countries. The chances of gaining much support from other countries are small and growing smaller, for among the nations conducting high-technology trade with the Soviet Union one finds not only NATO allies (whose reluctance to apply stiffer export controls is of long standing), but also countries like Austria and Switzerland, which are unlikely to cooperate at all.

Consequently we should not imagine that an expansion of export controls would be free of serious political costs; indeed, it might be unenforceable at any cost. Before we make the attempt, therefore, we should be clear on whether technology transfer actually has the effects we fear and whether expanded export controls would make a substantial difference. Hence the emphasis of this chapter on the environment in which exported technology is received. We turn now to a summary of our essential findings.

Broadly speaking, in the last decade the Soviets have pursued two strategies simultaneously to improve the technological level of their economy. The first is a "quick-fix" approach, aimed at modernizing backward branches of industry quickly through large-scale imports of foreign equipment and plant. In certain industries, notably those which manufacture chemical equipment, agricultural technology, automobiles, machine tools, precision instruments, and pipeline and drilling equipment, the Soviets have relied on Western suppliers for a large part—in some cases the virtual entirety—of new productive capacity. The industries involved here have been a varied lot, and in no two cases has Western technology played exactly the same role. However, two general traits appear to hold for most of them.

Table 22.1. *Soviet Imports of Western Technology*[a]

| Index No. | Class of import | U.S.A 1977/1978 | West Germany 1977/1978 | Japan 1977/1978 | France 1977/1978 |
|---|---|---|---|---|---|
| 10 | Machinery, equipment, and transportation | 351/273.5 | 1041.5/1004 | 685/830 | 566.5/688 |
| 100–103 | Metal-cutting and shaping, and fabrication | 17/11 | 154/157 | 21/46 | 9/14 |
| 10515 | Electrical and power engineering | | | | |
| 100–111 | Equipment and manufacturing | | 14/12 | 11/18 | 30/23.5 |
| 113 | Facilities for same | 0.5 | 68.5/101 | 3.5/43 | 20.5/11.5 |
| 12303 | Metal rolling equipment | | | 25.5/157 | 3.5/29.5 |
| 127 | Petroleum—refining equipment | | | | 12/0.5 |
| 128 | Drilling, extraction, and exploration | 21/38 | 15/10 | | |
| 150 | Chemical-industry equipment | 113/42.5 | 274/238 | 286/233 | 350.5/406 |
| 154 | Road-building | 30.5/53 | | 17.5/34 | |
| 15501 | Pumps | 17/7 | 11.5/9 | 7.5/2 | 1/1.5 |
| 15931 | Computers | 8.5/25 | | 2/1 | 2.5/4 |
| 15932 | | | | | |
| 15941 | | | | | |
| 170–171 | Instruments and lab equipment | 8/8 | 17/12 | 12/10.5 | 8/10.5 |
| 178–179 | | | | | |

[a] In $10^6$ rubles, rounded to the nearest half million. SOURCE: *Vneshniaia torgovlia SSSR v 1978g.: statisticheskii sbornik* (Moscow: "Statistika," 1978).

Table 22.2. Soviet Imports of Metalworking Machinery and Equipment[a]

| Exports | 1970 | 1971 | 1972 | 1973 | 1974 | 1975 | 1976 | 1977 | 1978 |
|---|---|---|---|---|---|---|---|---|---|
| | | | | | Value (in thousands of rubles) | | | | |
| Total | 425,311 | 294,434 | 430,264 | 589,561 | 747,986 | 941,358 | 976,316 | 1,059,025 | 1,055,618 |
| From Developed West (DW) | 315,967 | 155,303 | 231,389 | 360,083 | 489,855 | 593,797 | 582,337 | 557,164 | 474,475 |
| F.R.G. | 65,733 | 39,290 | 90,355 | 126,491 | 185,522 | 203,968 | 240,288 | 230,228 | 182,916 |
| U.K. | 25,498 | 17,282 | 23,394 | 32,929 | 10,567 | 23,199 | 22,805 | 8,790 | 29,400 |
| U.S.A. | 11,534 | 10,039 | 20,480 | 51,495 | 55,439 | 91,318 | 71,064 | 34,205 | 17,491 |
| | | | | | Shares (in percentage) | | | | |
| DW of Total | 74.3 | 52.7 | 53.8 | 61.1 | 65.5 | 63.1 | 59.6 | 52.6 | 44.9 |
| F.R.G. of DW | 20.8 | 25.3 | 39.0 | 35.4 | 37.9 | 34.3 | 41.3 | 41.3 | 38.6 |
| U.K. of DW | 8.1 | 11.1 | 10.1 | 9.1 | 2.2 | 3.9 | 3.9 | 1.6 | 6.2 |
| U.S. of DW | 3.7 | 6.5 | 8.9 | 14.3 | 11.3 | 15.4 | 12.2 | 6.1 | 3.7 |

[a]SOURCE: Soviet trade handbook—*Vneshniaia torgovlia SSSR*, 1970–1978.

• The resort to massive imports has come suddenly each time, as a result of ad hoc political decisions to upgrade the priority of the industry concerned (e.g., the "chemicalization" campaign under Khrushchev). Therefore the turn to Western technology in such cases is only partly the result of the inability of the industry to respond to sudden demands placed upon it (e.g., to increase the output capacity of fertilizer from 10 to 100 million tons in one 5-year period, or more recently, to expand the output of light automobiles beyond one million new cars a year). The possibility of turning to foreign suppliers has given Soviet leaders a freedom for rapid maneuver that the Soviet economy's rigidity denies them.

• The quick-fix import programs rely on import of finished products above all, such as complete plants and heavy equipment. And while considerable training and demonstration are involved, they are centered primarily on the management of well-established technology, that is, that embodied in the finished product, rather than the transfer of skills that confer the ability to generate further innovation or diffuse the acquired technology rapidly.

These two features have implications that we shall return to below.

The second principal strategy is internal reform of the management of technological innovation. Though less spectacular than the first strategy, it is potentially further-reaching, since it is aimed at the root causes of Soviet backwardness. Soviet literature on technological innovation goes back more than 50 years, pointing to many of the same problems and complaints as today, but the 1970s and 1980s have witnessed an unprecedented degree of soul-searching and experimentation on the part of Soviet officials and experts at all levels. Such efforts testify to a growing Soviet recognition that their traditional approach to promoting economic growth and higher productivity is no longer adequate.

The crucial instrument in the traditional approach is the selective allocation of priority. For military purposes, for example, two principal techniques have long been used to secure scarce resources and manpower: a Manhattan-Project style of organization for large, high-priority ventures, combined with a systematic skimming of the highest-quality output from ordinary producers throughout the economy, by means of ubiquitous "military representatives" (voenpredy) stationed in factories in every industry, armed with the authority to select and commandeer output that meets the military's requirements. By means of such devices, the Soviets are able to concentrate effort, materials, and skills on the most important projects related to national security and other top priorities.

However, priority is by definition a scarce resource. There is evidence that some dilution of its effects has already occurred in the last two decades, as a result of the need to bring an ever-broader array of industries and technologies into play with each new generation of weaponry.[18] But priority that is no longer priority becomes meaningless, and attempting to spread it thinner is no substitute for thorough-going reform in the incentives and organization for innovation. Indeed, military related industries themselves have pioneered many such devices and they are now being extended to important civilian industries. One way of looking at recent Soviet experiments in technology policy is to consider them a wager on the Soviets' part that management devices perfected under high priority will yield good effects when applied where priority is lower.

Throughout the Soviet period there has been an uneasy coexistence between foreign imports and home-grown enterprise (the latter usually entailing some degree of reform) as the two principal strategies for technological innovation, the former predominating in some periods (such as the First Five-Year Plan, 1928–1932) and the latter in others (such as the Second Five-Year Plan, 1933–1937). Logically, the two strategies should complement one another; but in practice they have tended to compete, and the balance between them swings with the state of mind of the Politburo, from emphasis on independence to emphasis on fast catch-up, and back again.[19] The last 15 or so years have been somewhat exceptional, for both strategies have been pursued simultaneously, and more vigorously than ever before.

The simultaneous existence of these two strategies raises a number of questions. First, to what extent are they connected, that is, does a crash program of Western imports involve at the same time a reform of the management of innovation in the industry involved? Do recent Soviet experiments in the management of innovation make the Soviets better able to profit from transferred technology? Are the Soviet experiments in the management of innovation themselves a species of "higher-level" technology transfer, which might be prevented or regulated? What do Soviet problems with both strategies reveal about the root causes of Soviet lag in technological innovation, and what further guidance do they give us about appropriate policies for technology transfer? The findings of this report suggest some preliminary answers:

1. *Recent Soviet reforms in the management of technology are only distantly inspired by or related to Western technology as such.*

In Soviet writings one can see evidence of a limited "transfer" of Western thinking about the management of R&D and innovation, and in particular, some effort to learn from American methods. Soviet specialists on the United States have devoted considerable attention to the American system of R&D policy and administration, focusing notably on issues that are known to be of special concern in the Soviet Union (such as contracts, research parks, or the structure of research corporations).[20] We can tell that some of this knowledge actually finds its way to policymakers because American management methods have been copied in the Soviet space and military programs.[21]

On a broader plane, there has been a fashion in Moscow for Western management theory and Western-style computerization of management processes. Not only has Western management literature influenced a whole generation of Soviet management specialists, but through exchange programs and bilateral cooperation (as well as joint creations like the International Institute for Applied Systems Analysis), the Soviets are being exposed directly to Western techniques. They have based their own systems of management education on American models, notably the case method of the Harvard Business School. It is uncertain as yet how much actual change has been wrought by this movement, but it is undoubtedly a leaven in Soviet thinking about industrial productivity.[22]

These Western examples, however, have had only marginal effects on the reform effort as a whole. The Soviet experiments we have discussed in this report are primarily Soviet in inspiration, modeled on Soviet antecedents, and addressed to characteristically Soviet problems. The defects they are aimed at arise out of the Soviet system of planning and organization, and consequently address specifically Soviet worries about incentives, information flow, financing, priority-setting, coordination,[23] and failure of effective demand for innovation. That these problems are systemic, that is, generated by the Soviet economic and political system, can be seen from the fact that much the same issues and problems have been stock concerns in Soviet science-policy literature ever since the first Five-Year Plans.[24]

2. *Soviet crash imports and internal management reform do not appear to be directly related or mutually reinforcing.*

There is only a very partial overlap between the "long-term" reforms discussed in this report and the "quick-fix" import programs. The massive import of Western equipment is not usually accompanied in the same industry by a massive program to change management of innovation, and there is little apparent effort to exploit the synergistic effects that presumably exist when massive technology imports and internal management reform occur together. It is as though the two types of moves were decided upon independently, by different kinds of people. Most of the recent imports of Western technology, as already mentioned, have been concentrated in chemical equipment, machine tools, automotive manufacture, agricultural equipment, and, increasingly, in extraction and transmission of oil and gas. These are not, by and large, the ministries that have made the most highly publicized efforts to reform the management of technological innovation.[25] The main exceptions to this observation are the computer and instruments industries, to which we shall return below.

Why has there not been a better "fit" between the two strategies? For the moment we can only speculate. First, they address different problems in different time-frames. The attraction of massive imports is that they promise to be fast and simple, conferring quickly the capability to get an important job done. The Academy of Sciences, for example, has recently imported a lot of advanced Western instrumentation to improve Soviet performance in biochemistry and molecular biology, once-neglected subjects that have been promoted to top priority recently because of the possible industrial applications of genetic engineering. At the same time, the Academy has created special instrumentation associations to produce advanced equipment at home. The latter effort will take years, but in the meantime, thanks to imported instruments, the Soviets are making rapid strides in the life sciences. In this case (one of the few in which foreign imports and domestic management reform are clearly occurring simultaneously), the difference between the two approaches is manifest: Foreign imports provide for the present and management changes provide for the future (so their originators hope).

The difference in time-frames between the Western-import and management-reform strategies may, in turn, spell further differences, notably in the kinds of people and organizations associated with each. The State Committee on Science and Technology, for example, is heavily involved in both imports and reform, but each strategy is presumably handled by different divisions, imports by the "branch" divisions that correspond to each of the major branches of industry and agriculture, and management reforms by the "functional" divisions that focus on matters such as the economics and organization of research and inno- vation.[26]

To be sure, there is one mechanism, not yet discussed in this report, that gives the State Committee, at least on paper, the potential for uniting the import and management-reform strategies. This is the sys- tem of "integrated programs" (*kompleksnye programmy*), a list of 200-odd high-priority "problems" established and overseen by the State Com- mittee on Science and Technology. Each one encompasses the entire R&D cycle from basic research to final application in production. Together they cover one-quarter of the total budget for research and development of the country.[27] The "problems" are clearly of great potential importance as a management mechanism, for in addition to providing continuity from one stage to another in the R&D cycle, they afford the possibility, in principle at least, of systematically combining imported technology with internal changes. But it is not certain how effective the integrated programs have been in practice, because the influence of the State Committee over the ministries and their institutes appears weak, its control over funding and other resources is slight,[28] and its own internal organization may discourage a truly integrated approach.[29] Its influence over the trading organizations of the Ministry of Foreign Trade is equally uncertain.

The apparent failure to coordinate foreign imports and internal re- form may involve a question of risk: Foreign technology, at least, has proved itself and is known to produce predictable results. Management reforms, if they produce results at all, are hard to measure, unpredic- table in their effects, and probably slow to pay off. Soviet decision makers, in the short term, may place more confidence in the import strategy than in the management reform strategy. In essence, massive imports may be viewed as an extension of the "priority" method, that is, concentrating scarce resources on a need rather than implementing reforms to eliminate or alleviate the underlying problems.

The tenuousness of the connection between foreign technology trans- fer and internal reform must not be overstated. One can find examples of apparent ties between the two, such as the collaboration of NPO Plastpolimer with East German chemical engineers in launching the "Polymer 50" complex in Novopolotsk, or the interaction of "lead institutes" like the Paton Institute (electrowelding) or "production asso- ciations" like Elektrosila (heavy electrical equipment) with Western technologists (although we should bear in mind that all three of the organizations just named are long-standing and prestigious establishments despite their "new" labels, and as such more properly belong to Conclusion 4 below). Nevertheless, even in such cases one can trace no obvious synergistic effects coming directly from the simultaneous presence of foreign transfers and changes in the management of innovation.

The above is not meant to imply that Soviet leaders do not take reform of technological innovation seriously; on the contrary, it is clearly one of their dominant concerns. Rather, what lies behind all the possible explanations we have just enumerated is the plain fact that internal reform, since it involves changing basic incentives and patterns of communication throughout the industrial system, is a daunting proposition. Imported technology, on the other hand, does not require overhauling the economic system in order to put it to work. But as a consequence, the contribution of Western technology to Soviet innovative abilities is considerably diminished. The history of technological innovation and diffusion in the last two centuries teaches the importance of foreign example and instruction—but only if, at the same time, the political and economic institutions of the receiving country adjust accordingly.[30]

3. *Imports by themselves do not enable the Soviets to overcome dependence, but may actually increase it.*

The examples of the Soviet chemical and machine-tool industries, discussed in passing earlier, suggest that massive Western imports by themselves do not give the Soviets a capability for generating their own advances. Western imports have not compensated for these weaknesses; if anything, imports may have contributed to perpetuating them, by removing pressure for reform that the machine-tool industry might otherwise have been moved to respond to.

The Soviets have not passively accepted their weaknesses in these fields; they have attempted on several occasions to duplicate what they have been importing, but without conspicuous success (at least as far as one can judge from the anecdotal evidence available). It is not clear from the pattern of failures whether they are due primarily to weak science and engineering (the "supply" side of innovation), or weaknesses in management, incentives, and organization (the "demand" and "transmission" sides), or some combination of both (for one can presume that each affects the other two). Whatever the exact mix of reasons (and there is no reason to assume it is the same in every industry or branch), Western technology alone is apparently not enough to overcome them. Indeed, the very availability of Western technology may delay Soviet efforts to grapple with the root problems of innovation by making it less urgent in the short run to do so. The price, of course, is a continuing lag behind the Western state of the art, and though influential Soviets may feel humiliated by such lags,[31] they may be thought of as the logical outcome of quite rational middle-term strategies on the part of the leadership, particularly in the handful of areas, such as agricultural chemicals, in which the productivity of imported Western technology is spectacularly higher than what Soviet enterprise would be able to achieve on its own.

4. *The more highly developed the Soviets' indigenous capabilities in a given*

*branch of technology, the better able they are to profit from technology transfer (especially higher orders of transfer), and the less dependent they are likely to be.*

In some striking cases—such as heavy electrical equipment, welding, slag remelting, and heavy automotive equipment—the Soviets have demonstrated the ability to produce technology that, if not necessarily world-leading, is competent and capable of progress. It is internally generated, well adapted to Soviet needs and conditions, and increasingly competitive on world markets. In such areas the Soviets have demonstrated the ability to profit quickly and efficiently from Western technology, and the result is not dependence, but synergism, leading to an increase in Soviet technological strength in the fields concerned.

What accounts for this technological equivalent of the rich getting richer? This question actually contains two separate puzzles: First, what internal features of these industries account for their relative success? Second, what are the crucial skills or knowledge being transferred?

The traditional answer to the first question is high priority. But as we have seen earlier, there is considerable argument among Western specialists (and presumably among their Soviet colleagues, too) about what high priority actually does. Clearly, one thing that high priority does is to assemble the best available elements that go into new technology: the best equipment, skilled manpower, and facilities. However, high priority on the supply side alone engenders ineffective protected industries, like the royal manufactures that mercantilist monarchies nurtured at great expense in the eighteenth century. The Soviet Union has done better than that by coupling higher priority with high pressure: deliberate stimulation of competition (e.g., among rival aircraft designers),[32] strong user demand (as in the case of military customers), or clear yardsticks of performance with rewards attached (such as cost per kilowatt-hour of generated electricity).

The example of the automotive, machine-tool, and electrical equipment industries suggests a further principle: that political priority, in order to stimulate native innovative performance, must (in addition to the factors mentioned above) be sustained. Sudden increases in priority, on the contrary, appear to be counterproductive as far as indigenous technological innovation is concerned, especially if they are accompanied by a sudden flood of foreign technology. Thus, in plastics, synthetic fibers, agricultural chemicals, energy exploration (e.g., offshore technology), and gas transmission the impact of high priority has been too sudden for successful innovative performance in the context of a supply and training system that reacts slowly.

We turn now to the second question raised above: Where direct contact with foreign technology has had an obviously stimulative effect, what exactly are the useful elements being transferred? The case of the KamAZ foundry is instructive. By maintaining on permanent location at the Pullman Corporation a large rotating delegation of top engineers, the Soviet Union was gaining something that in the scale of possible transfers falls somewhere in the middle between the most concrete (such as finished products) and the most abstract (such as broad management philosophy): skills in the organization of design, assembly, maintenance, costing, and quality control. Such knowledge, half science and half art (the difference is crucial, because for science alone the Soviets are reasonably well-equipped), is best transferred through practical example and informal contact, in other words by a process that amounts to apprenticeship. These are subtle skills, whose transfer apparently requires close working contact over an extended period. What is striking, however, is that they also require a certain minimum level of skill, experience, and receptiveness on the part of the receiver. Technology, like contagious disease, requires a receptive host.

The conclusions we have outlined so far suggest that the interaction of various types of technology transfer with the Soviet environment produces three distinct zones, each featuring hypotheses with different implications for American policy:

A. *Transfer of finished products and processes as part of a Soviet crash program to improve an industry in which the Soviets start from a low level of capability.*

*Hypothesis*: In such cases the Soviet program of imports is poorly coordinated with internal improvements in the management of innovation, and yields no significant improvement in the Soviets' ability to generate and diffuse new technology on the basis of what they import.

*Implication for policy*: The consequence of such transfers is that they produce short-term gains in output capacity (such as synthetic fibers or plastics) rather than major improvements in innovative capabilities. From the standpoint of Western export-control policy, therefore, such transfers are of lesser concern, except insofar as they can be shown to overcome a major bottleneck in military-related production. Therefore the decision whether or not to grant an export license should depend primarily on whether the United States considers it expedient to contribute to the short-term production gains (such as increased oil production) for which the proposed export is intended.

B. *Transfer of skills and know-how in industries in which the Soviets have already shown considerable innovative proficiency.*

*Hypothesis*: The higher the native capacity of a given industry for innovation, the greater its ability to absorb and diffuse foreign technology as well.

*Implication for policy*: American policy in such cases should be to control transfers that involve "apprenticeship" relations (training, extensive joint work, etc.). However, any such policy must be tempered by a realization that the most that may be possible in such cases is a limited holding action, since the learning ability of the Soviets will be greater in such cases than in the backward industries, and in most instances they will have alternatives available from other countries.

C. *Transfer of general concepts about the management of incentive systems, information flow, division and coordination of tasks, etc.*

Transfer of "high-order" skills of this kind may be important as a source of general examples. However, Soviet problems in the overall management of innovation arise not so much from the lack of foreign models—for there is every evidence that Soviet specialists are well acquainted with the models—but rather from long-standing, deeply rooted systemic obstacles to their implementation in the Soviet context. In addition, the Western literature on management and organization of innovation is so abundant and ubiquitous that it is hard to imagine any control mechanism by which its transfer could be prevented.

**A Concrete Illustration: The Case of Computer Hardware and Software**   The Soviet computer industry in the late 1960s was a classic example of the effects of long neglect, compounded by faulty organization and management, limited user demand, and slow development of professional training. Since 1968, however, the Soviet computer field has enjoyed sustained political priority, which has taken the form not of a crash import program but rather an effort to build native skills while following Western example, largely as filtered through Eastern Europe. Whether this strategy is more the result of Western export restrictions or Soviet determination to build independent capabilities is difficult to say, but at any rate the Soviet computer industry is now reaching the same fateful stage in its development that its Western counterparts reached at the beginning of the 1970s: The chief limitation on further progress is not hardware but software. But in software the Soviet dependence on Western technology has been even greater than in hardware,[33] and their own innovative success has been smaller. Finally, the field of computers and computer applications is one of the few very clear cases in which Western management concepts have had a major impact on Soviet actions, resulting in efforts (however limited as yet) to change management structure in Western directions. What implications follow?

Export of much general-purpose computer hardware falls into Category A as described above, provided it can be modified (as in so-called "C" modifications to lessen the speed of Univac computers) to prevent military end-uses. This position is justified by the very rapid pace of technological advance in the West, which makes transferred hardware obsolete long before the Soviets have succeeded in copying it (the Ryad series, is a case in point), and paradoxically also by the high priority of computer development in the Soviets' eyes, which guarantees that any wide-spread type of computer hardware not transferred to the Soviet Union by way of commerce will cross the border by some other means.

Export of software falls into Category B, particularly that portion of it transferred by "live" apprenticeship.[34]

Finally, export of more general knowledge such as organization of service or computer applications in business falls into Category C. In some ultimate sense, this is the most important category of all. As Seymour Goodman ably argues, the concept of a technology as a package, including service, training, peripheral technologies and applications, is more vital in the computer field than perhaps any other.

However, such "conceptual" matter relating to the management of technology and innovation is easily transferred (indeed, its transfer is impossible to stop) but not easily applied. It falls therefore in Category C.

## Balancing the Benefits and Costs of Export Controls

The issue of technology transfer to the Soviet bloc is a new instance of a very old problem: how to prevent the diffusion of valuable skills across national boundaries. History teaches that the control of technology transfer is at best a rear-guard action, achievable (and then only briefly) at the cost of regulations and secrecy that carry harmful side-effects of their own. This fact has not prevented every advanced nation from trying to impose controls at one time or another; in fact, since the beginnings of the industrial revolution, periods of relatively free exchange and transfer have been briefer than eras of control. But in the end the transfer of technology depends less on the fact that knowledge and skills have been divulged than on the fact that the receiver knew how to make creative use of them. From the loss of the secrets of porcelain manufacture by the Chinese to the loss of the secrets of the Sidewinder by the Americans, the ultimate consequences depend on the ability of the receiver to profit from them—and on the ability of the donor to generate more.

It follows that balancing the political costs and benefits of export controls requires weighing their claimed effects in delaying the Russians against their costs in delaying us. An export-control policy based on the assumption that the enemy needs only to be exposed to superior American knowledge and skills in order to seize upon them, master them, and turn them into major gains prejudges the most important questions and may lead us into mistakes. The aim of this report has been to take a fresh look at the effects of technology transfers by calling attention to some of the important features of the Soviet context.

Naturally, this exercise is surrounded by uncertainties. To confirm or disprove the hypotheses advanced in this report, we would need to know a great deal more than we are ever likely to know, industry by industry, about Soviet strengths and weaknesses in generating and diffusing new technology. Neither do we know enough about how technological innovation works in general. We cannot predict in detail what kinds of transfers give Soviet technologists and managers the greatest help in improving their innovative performance—or for that matter our own. The translation of new ideas into new products and processes is still a mysterious business everywhere in the world, and no one explanation accounts for more than a fraction of the cases observed. This means, let us say it frankly, that it would be unwise to attempt to base any actual export-control policy on case-by-case evaluations of the Soviets' ability to absorb. The aim of this report is not to replace the critical-technologies approach with some sort of "critical-receivers" approach, for we simply do not have enough information or enough understanding to make it work.

Rather, the aim is to raise larger, cautionary questions about the broad course of export-control policy: Given the uncertainties surrounding any broadening of export controls, *in what direction is it safest to err?* The difficulties of technological innovation in the Soviet Union, and the largely negative results of recent reforms there, underscore some important points about innovation that are equally valid anywhere: First, however mysterious the details may be, it is clear that successful innovation depends on the presence of appropriate incentives and information. Potential inventors must know what opportunities exist and must stand to gain from good ideas, but also to lose from bad ones or from inaction. Potential users must know what has been invented and have both the motivation and the knowledge to choose correctly. If the Soviet system does not supply these incentives and information outside a narrow zone of closed high-priority projects, foreign imports will not fill the void.

Moreover, favorable climates for innovation, where they exist, are fragile. Regulation, however well-intentioned, introduces screens and filters between the perception of an opportunity for innovation and the inspiration and incentive to take advantage of it. Consequently, if the national purpose is to maintain the United States' technological lead, our first concern should be to remain good innovators ourselves. We should beware lest we hobble ourselves, as the Soviet system has so clearly succeeded in doing in the greater part of its industry.

What does this imply for export-control policy? The case for export controls is strongest in areas of immediate military relevance in which the United States has a clear lead over other Western countries. As one moves outside this zone, toward technologies that afford the Soviets longer term industrial gains and that are not areas of clear American superiority over the rest of the West, the political benefits of export controls become more diffuse and uncertain, while the costs become progressively greater. Any widening of export controls outside the first range into the second should be undertaken only with the greatest care.

## Notes

[1]Previous Rand work on the subject of technology transfer includes: Charles Wolf, Jr., *U.S. Technology Exchange with the Soviet Union: A Summary Report*, (The Rand Corporation, R-1520/1-ARPA, August 1974); Robert E. Klitgaard, *National Security and Export Controls* (The Rand Corporation, R-1432-1-ARPA/CIEP, April 1974).

[2]50 USC2401 et seq. A summary of the provisions and legislative history of the 1979 Act can be found in the *Congressional Quarterly Almanac* for 1979, pp. 300–305.

[3]Peter J. Schuypen, "Soviets' Univac Arouses Concern," *New York Times*, January 3, 1980, p. D1.

[4]Department of Defense, Office of the Director of Defense Research and Engineering, *An Analysis of Export Controls of U.S. Technology—A DoD Perspective*,

a report of the Defense Science Board Task Force on Export of U.S. Technology, Washington, D.C., February 1976.

[5]*Federal Register*, vol. 45, no. 192, October 1, 1980, pp. 65014–65019. A recent statement of Dr. Bucy's views will be found in "Technology Transfer and East–West Trade," *International Security*, vol. 5, no.3, (Winter 1981), pp. 132–151.

[6]Useful background will be found in Organization for Economic Cooperation and Development, Committee for Scientific and Technological Policy, *Technology Transfer Between East and West*, Paris, 1980. See also Marie Lavigne, *Les Relations Economiques Est–Ouest*, Presses Universitaires de France, Paris, 1979.

[7]Deborah Shapley, "Technological Creep and the Arms Race: ICBM Problem a Sleeper," *Science*, vol. 201 (September 22, 1978), p. 1104.

[8]For example, in an address in May 1979 to the Center on Science and International Affairs of Harvard University, Undersecretary of Defense William Perry stated that the Soviet Union may well be investing five times more effort in high-energy laser research than the United States.

[9]See the discussion by Herbert York in *The Advisors: Oppenheimer, Teller, and the Superbomb* (San Francisco: W.H. Freeman, 1976).

[10]In reality, there has always been considerable overlap between the Soviet civilian and military sectors, so what we are really talking about is differences of degree. Nevertheless, in recent years the degree of overlap has greatly increased. See for example Simon Kassel's study of sources of Soviet basic research for laser technology: *The Relationship Between Science and the Military in the Soviet Union* (The Rand Corporation, R-1457-DDRE/ARPA, July 1974). See also a suggestive work by John E. Kiser, III, "Civilian and Military Technology in the USSR: Is There a Difference?" (unpublished).

[11]See, for example, the discussion in Philip Hanson, "Western Technology in the Soviet Economy," *Problems of Communism* 27, no. 6 (November–December 1978), pp. 20–30. During the Ninth Five-Year Plan (1971–1975) 15% of the capital equipment installed was obtained from abroad, although not all, by any means, from the West. See *Izvestiia*, February 18, 1976, cited in A.I. Bel'chuk, ed., *Novyi etap ekonomicheskogo sotrudnichestva SSSR s razvitymi kapitalisticheskimi stranami* (Moscow: "Nauka)," 1978, p. 7.

[12]Some Soviet sources make the same point. See Bel'chuk, *op. cit.*, p. 14.

[13]We have benefited from the careful discussion of displacement and fungibility in Klitgaard, *op. cit.*, pp. 27–35.

[14]U.S. Congress, Public Law 96–72, Export Administration Act of 1972, September 29, 1979.

[15]Nicholas Wade, "Science Meetings Catch the U.S.–Soviet Chill," *Science*, vol. 207 (March 7, 1980), pp. 1056–1058.

[16]For a recent report, see Angela Stent Yergin, *East–West Technology Transfer: European Perspectives*, The Washington Papers, no. 75 (Beverly Hills, Calif., Sage Publications, 1980).

[17]The basis for the expanded exchanges of the 1970s was a series of eleven agreements signed by the American and Soviet governments between May 1972 and June 1974, which increased tenfold the volume of technical visits between the United States and the Soviet Union. For descriptions and evaluations, see Lawrence H. Theriot, "Governmental and Private Industry Cooperation with the Soviet Union in the Fields of Science and Technology," in U.S. Congress, Joint Economic Committee, *Soviet Economy in a New Perspective* (Washington, D.C.: U.S. Government Printing Office, 1976), pp. 753–755; National Academy of Sciences, National Research Council, *Review of the US/USSR Agreement on Cooperation in the Fields of Science and Technology* (Washington, D.C., 1977); and Loren R. Graham, "How Valuable Are Scientific Exchanges with the Soviet Union?," *Science*, vol. 202 (October 27, 1978), pp. 383–390; see also Francis W.

Rushing and Catherine P. Ailes, "An Assessment of the USSR–US Scientific and Technical Exchange Programs," in U.S. Congress, Joint Economic Committee, *Soviet Economy in a Time of Change*, vol. II (Washington, D.C.: U.S. Government Printing Office, 1979), pp. 605–624.

[18]For an interesting account of this phenomenon in military-sponsored Soviet work in radiolocation, see A. Fedoseev, *Zapadnia: Chelovek i sotsialism* (Possev, 1977).

[19]See Bruce Parrott's excellent description of this ambivalence in official Soviet policy in *Politics and Technology in the Soviet Union* (Cambridge, Mass.: MIT Press, 1983).

[20]See Thane Gustafson, "American Science Policy Through Soviet Eyes: A Reflection of Soviet Concerns and Priorities," in *Soviet Science and Technology: Domestic and Foreign Perspectives*, ed. John R. Thomas and Ursula M. Kruse-Vaucienne (Washington, D.C.: The George Washington University, 1977), pp. 83–100.

[21]Robert Campbell, "Management Spillovers from Soviet Space and Military Programmes," *Soviet Studies* 23, (1972), pp. 586–607.

[22]One of the most important vehicles for this kind of "transfer" is the monthly journal of the Institute for Economics of Industrial Production of the Siberian Division of the USSR Academy of Sciences, *Ekonomika i Organizatsiia Ekonomicheskogo Proizvodstva* (often referred to as "EKO").

[23]See Joseph Berliner, *The Innovation Decision in Soviet Industry* (Cambridge Mass.: MIT Press, 1976).

[24]For a discussion that illustrates this point strikingly, see Robert Lewis, *Science and Industrialization in the USSR: Industrial Research and Development 1917–1940* (New York: Holmes and Meier Publishers, 1979). It is remarkable how many of the complaints, as well as the proposed solutions, are the same from the 1930s down to the present day. For comparison, see Organization for Economic Cooperation and Development, *Science Policy in the USSR* (Paris, 1969).

[25]That is not to say that some overlap does not exist. The Ministry for Petrochemical Machine-Building (*Minneftekhimmash*), which imports large quantities of shipment from the West, has pioneered a general-contractor approach to supplying equipment to new plants. The Ministry of Agricultural Machine-Building (*Minsel'khozmash*) has experimented with a new approach to demand and has learned much from its export activities. (We are indebted to Nancy Nimitz for these observations.)

[26]The State Committee on Science and Technology has an unusual administrative structure that may be designed to prevent a separation between the "branch" and "functional" activities of the committee: Each deputy chairman is in charge of some of both kinds. For example, Deputy Chairman M.G. Kruglov oversees both the Instrument Making and Radio Electronics Directorate (Chief: A.P. Yurkevich) and the Organizations and Economics of Scientific and Technical Research Department (Chief: V.A. Pokrovskii).

[27]S. Tikhomirov, "Ot poiska do vnedreniia," *Pravda*, June 6, 1978. For a lengthier description of the functions and powers of the State Committee on Science and Technology (unfortunately somewhat out of date), see *Organizatsionno-pravovye voprosy rukovodstva nauki v SSSR* (Moscow, "Nauka," pp. 158–169). This section, by G.A. Dorokhova, tends to be somewhat skeptical about GKNT's actual powers and effectiveness.

[28]Academician Paton, for example, gives the impression that the funding role of the State Committee is to supplement that of regular sources of support, by commissioning "supplementary" research themes, presumably ones that fit the overall programs. But such supplementary funding appears modest, in comparison with "mainline" sources of support. For example, according to Paton, the

State committee funded 37 million rubles' worth of R&D in the Ukrainian Academy of Sciences during the period 1971–1975, spread out over 354 projects. That makes an average of about 20,000 rubles per project per year, certainly not a crucial increment. B.E. Paton, "Effektivnost' nauchnykh issledovanii i uskorenie protsessa vnedreniia," *Vestnik AN SSSR*, no. 3, 1977, p. 50. As for GKNT's power to reassign funding among participating ministries, it requires the ministries' consent, and is therefore presumably requested only with diplomacy and circumspection. (*Organizatsionno-pravovye voprosy rukovodstva naukoi v SSSR, op. cit.*, p. 124).

[29]According to an article by the Minister of Nonferrous Industry, P.F. Lomako, the State Committee on Science and Technology is hindered in overseeing any project that involves more than one branch of industry, because it is excessively narrowly structured by branch (P.F. Lomako, "Faktor vremeni," *Trud*, February 1, 1975).

[30]The earliest and still the most striking illustration in the modern era is the transfer of modern industrial skills from Great Britain to the Continent in the late eighteenth and early nineteenth centuries. See David S. Landes, *The Unbound Prometheus: Technological Change and Industrial Development in Western Europe from 1750 to the Present* (Cambridge, England: Cambridge University Press, 1969).

[31]See Parrott, *op. cit.*.

[32]See the memoirs of the noted military aircraft builder A. Iakovlev, *Tsel' zhizni: zapiski aviakonstruktora* (Moscow: Politizdat, 1970).

[33]S.E. Goodman, "Software in the Soviet Union: Progress and Problems," *Advances in Computers*, Vol. 18 (New York: Academic Press, 1979), pp. 231–287.

[34]See Charles L. Gold, Seymour E. Goodman, and Benjamin G. Walker, "Software: Recommendations for an Export Control Policy," *Communications of the ACM* 23, no. 4 (April 1980), pp. 199–207. Professor Goodman has been an active participant in the software subgroup of the Computers Technical Working Group (TWG.7), called to advise the Undersecretary of Defense on the composition of the Militarily Critical Technologies List mandated by the Export Administration Act. The group has prepared an unofficial summary of its views, which the author is grateful to have had the opportunity to draw upon.

# 23  LESTER R. BROWN

## U.S. and Soviet Agriculture: The Shifting Balance of Power*

Analysts of the U.S.–Soviet balance of power usually focus on relative military strength—the number of tanks, planes, nuclear warheads, and other items in the so-called strategic balance. But many other factors determine a country's overall power and influence. Among the most basic is a country's capacity to feed its people. By this measure the Soviet Union appears to be in deep trouble.

Massive spending has increased Soviet military strength in recent years, but the country has become weaker agriculturally. While the two superpowers now appear roughly equal in military strength, the advantage in agriculture has shifted dramatically toward the United States. The U.S. exportable food surplus is climbing, while Soviet dependence on food imports is growing.

This year the Soviet Union will try to import 46 million tons of grain, more than any country in history. Nearly one-fourth of all Soviet grain, feeding both people and livestock, will come from outside sources. Over one-half of this imported grain will come from the North American breadbasket, most of it from the United States.[1]

The Soviet economy is a planned economy, but these grain imports were not planned. They will fill part of the 68 million ton gap between the 1982 target of 238 million tons of grain and an actual harvest of some 170 million tons.[2] In the past the Soviets blamed bad weather for their shortfalls, but this explanation is beginning to wear thin. Recently the Soviet leadership has acknowledged failures within the agricultural system itself.

Evidence now indicates that the Soviet Union has moved beyond the good year/bad year oscillations of the late 1960s and early 1970s, when it

*Reprinted by permission of the author and publisher from *U.S. and Soviet Agriculture: The Shifting Balance of Power* (Washington, D.C.: Worldwatch Institute, 1982), pp. 5–7, 36–44, 48. The author is indebted to his colleague Edward Wolf for assistance with the research and analysis underlying this chapter. Copyright 1982 by Worldwatch Institute.

imported grain only after poor harvests, and must now import massive quantities of grain continuously. The fourth consecutive massive crop shortfall in 1982 signals a broad-based deterioration of Soviet agriculture that will create food shortages well into the future.

In contrast to poor harvests in Third World countries, which can lead to starvation, poor Soviet harvests largely threaten the supply of livestock products. The Soviet food problem is a shortage of meat, not bread. The issue, therefore, is not starvation but worker morale, a question of whether the system can provide the quality of diet that Soviet leaders and planners since Khrushchev have promised, and that Soviet citizens have come to expect.

The dramatic shift in the agricultural balance of power between the United States and Soviet Union has been decades in the making. But contrasting food surpluses and deficits have been highly visible only in the last decade or so. As recently as 1970 both countries were exporting grain—the United States 38 million tons and the Soviet Union 8 million tons. By 1981, however, U.S. grain exports had jumped to a staggering 115 million tons and the Soviets were importing 43 million tons.[3]

Not surprisingly, these huge food deficits trouble the Soviet leadership. In the Eleventh Five-Year Plan (1981–1985), released a year late at the November 1981 meeting of the Central Committee of the Soviet Communist Party, General Secretary Leonid Brezhnev said food was "the central problem of the whole Five-Year Plan."[4] His discussion of Soviet agricultural goals and prospects was extraordinarily dispirited, a far cry from Khrushchev's taunting "we will bury you" economic rhetoric of a quarter-century ago.

As the deterioration of Soviet agriculture continues, the need to import food will become even greater. Already the flow of grain from the United States to the Soviet Union is on the verge of being the largest ever between two countries, about to eclipse the current U.S. flow to Japan. The long line of ships that now connects American farms with the dining tables of the Soviet Union constitutes a new economic tie between the two countries, one that could eventually transform their political relations as well.

## The Effect on U.S.–Soviet Relationships

The new food connection between the United States and the Soviet Union may represent the most important change in relations between the two countries since the Cold War began a generation ago. It demonstrates in clear economic terms that the United States and the Soviet Union need each other. This is particularly true at a time when the productive capacity of U.S. farms continues to climb while growth in grain markets outside the Soviet Union has slowed because of a sluggish economy worldwide. The record grain deficits of the early 1980s in the Soviet Union show more than ever its dependence on U.S. agriculture.

Whether or not the Soviets import their grain directly from the United States is not the relevant issue. The vast U.S. grain exports, over 110 million tons per year in recent years and 55% of the world total, are what enable the Soviets to import record quantitites of grain. If U.S. export capacity had not doubled over the past decade, there would not be nearly enough grain to meet all world import demands at current prices, and certainly not enough to support the growth in Soviet imports.

Although American farmers are the most outspoken advocates of trade with the Soviet Union, the higher level of farm exports that Soviet imports make possible benefits the entire U.S. economy. As the U.S. oil import bill soared after the 1973 price increases, the enormous growth in farm exports paid much of the bill. Traditional export industries, such as automobiles, have sagged in international competition. Even high technology exports, such as commercial jet aircraft, are suffering.[5] In a stagnant economy the productivity and ingenuity of American farmers have helped the United States balance its international payments.

Great as the benefits of this expanded farm trade are for the United States, the Soviet Union has even more to gain. One can only imagine how long the lines would be at Soviet meat counters had it not been for U.S. grain. The Soviet Union is in deep trouble economically because it must import so much food, but it would be in even deeper trouble politically if the food were not available.

Both superpowers at times feel uneasy with their new trade dependency because it complicates a traditional adversarial relationship. The food connection does not ensure peaceful relations between the two countries, but it will make massive arms spending more difficult to justify. The American people and Congress may increasingly doubt that a country depending on the United States for so much of its food could be as dangerous as commonly portrayed. Hard-liners in the Soviet Union may be unable to convince Kremlin colleagues that the country which is feeding them is indeed a mortal enemy.

The evolution of U.S.–Soviet agricultural trade is a reminder that in the long run economic forces tend to override political considerations. With another bumper grain harvest likely in 1982, the United States will need Soviet markets more than ever. Indeed, U.S. Secretary of Agriculture John Block, eager to bolster farm income, has implored the Soviets to buy more U.S. grain.[6]

Internal stability within the Soviet Union, as well as in the Soviet Bloc, may depend more on grain imports than any other external factor. If the Reagan administration is serious about putting pressure on the Soviet Union, as it argues in opposing the pipeline, it should urge a joint embargo with U.S. allies Canada and Australia of all grain shipments to the Soviet Union. This would provide real and immediate economic pressure, but no such effort has been made. Instead, President Reagan has promised American farmers that the Soviets in 1982 will receive the biggest shipment ever of U.S. grain.[7]

In the absence of such an effort to press the Soviets, the Reagan administration arguments against the Yamal gas pipeline from northern Siberia to Western Europe sound insincere and unconvincing. In the short run, foregoing the pipeline would deny the Europeans industrial exports and employment, much as a grain embargo would deny American farmers a market. In the long run, failure to build a pipeline would deny West Europeans needed energy and a more diverse supply.

Arguing against the 3500 mile gas pipeline, Reagan notes that U.S. grain sales drain the Soviet Union of hard currency, while the pipeline will boost Soviet money supplies. But if the United States is unwilling to wield grain as an economic weapon against the Soviets (and face the consequences at home), its pipeline stand is unfair to Western Europe. Pipeline opposition also ignores eventual advantages to the United States. For U.S. farmers, earnings from the pipeline will eventually allow the Soviets to buy more U.S. wheat, feedgrain, and soybeans than they otherwise could. If U.S. agriculture seeks foreign markets in the late 1980s as eagerly as it currently does, the pipeline is a welcome development, something the United States should support rather than oppose.

The key decisions affecting the long-term fate of this new economic relationship between the superpowers are more likely to be made in Moscow than in Washington, as the Soviets endeavor to improve their agriculture. Soviet officials may not yet realize that the agricultural modernization they want is incompatible with centralized planning and management. If not, they will keep tinkering with the system, trying to make it work. One inevitable consequence of following this path will be declining morale among farm workers as frustrations with the inherent defects of the system mount. Without corrective action the Soviets face continued food shortages, rationing, and longer waits at the market. More broadly, shortages of high-quality foodstuffs, especially meat, will lower worker morale throughout Soviet society.

A second Soviet option is to launch economic reforms similar to those in Hungary, where managers in both industry and agriculture are relatively free of central control and have wide latitude to make independent decisions. No modest adjustments the Soviets can make, however, such as giving private farm plots more support, will arrest the broad-based deterioration. Only fundamental reforms, perhaps as great as any since the Communist Party came to power in 1917, will be adequate.

There are signs that the Soviet leadership is looking carefully at the Hungarian experience. Hungarian poultry producers are now aiding their Soviet counterparts, using techniques the Hungarians acquired from the West. Soviet Prime Minister Nikolai Tikhonov visited Hungary to examine firsthand the Hungarian successes and, in so doing, gave an implicit stamp of approval. Whether this interest will translate into Soviet decentralization along Hungarian lines remains to be seen.[8]

Given the complex interaction between modern agriculture and the rest of the economy, the farm economy cannot be reformed in isolation. It can succeed only as part of a restructuring of the entire economy. In assessing the prospects, *Washington Post* correspondent Dan Morgan notes that, "extensive economic reforms on the Hungarian model pose political risks for entrenched communist power structures. They imply a willingness to tolerate a more decentralized, disorderly system in which economic decisions are made by thousands of factory managers, small-scale entrepreneurs and farmers, not just a few party officials and bureaucrats."[9]

In effect the Soviet leadership faces two hurdles enroute to a productive agriculture: the decision to reform and the implementation of the reform. Launching reforms like those in Hungary will be far more difficult in the Soviet Union, with its longer bureaucratic tradition. Those now in power cannot remember working within a market economy, and farm workers accustomed only to taking orders cannot develop overnight the decision-making skills essential to successful decentralized agriculture. Robbin Laird of Columbia University notes that previous Soviet reform efforts "just fizzled out in the soggy mass of bureaucracy."[10]

For the United States, policy options are less clear-cut. The shift in the agricultural power balance in favor of the United States provides an opportunity to reshape relations with the Soviet Union. When two powers are evenly balanced it is difficult for either side to take major initiatives. Now that the balance has been decisively altered in the strategically important food sector, the United States can proceed from a position of strength.

While unfortunate for the Soviets, the deterioration of their agriculture does present a timely opportunity to lessen tensions between Washington and Moscow. An obvious beginning for the Reagan administration would be to slow down the arms race. Identified in the U.S. public mind as a Soviet hard-liner, President Reagan is well-positioned to engage the Soviets in serious discussions of reductions in both nuclear and conventional weapons. Just as hard-liner Richard Nixon was able to reopen the door to China and in so doing ensure a place in history, Ronald Reagan can lead U.S.–Soviet relations into a new era. In the absence of a successful major foreign policy initiative, the Reagan administration's principle claim to a chapter in the history books may be its generation of the largest U.S. budget deficits ever recorded.

Conditions within the Soviet Union suggest that the Soviets will respond to U.S. initiatives that would lessen international tensions and permit the Soviets to focus on internal reforms. In his missile-freeze speech in early 1982, President Brezhnev said, "We have not spent, nor will we spend, a single ruble more for these purposes than is absolutely necessary." As Soviet analyst Marshall Goldman notes, this departs from past statements, since Soviet leaders normally omit cost considerations when discussing military matters, and it may well reflect a Soviet interest in reordering priorities.[11]

For the United States the question is how to use this new advantage most effectively to reduce tensions between the two countries. Using food as a lever in U.S.–Soviet relationships requires an understanding of its limitations. While a joint grain embargo by the United States, Canada, and Australia could check more radical Soviet military actions, access to the U.S. exportable grain surplus cannot easily be put on the arms reduction negotiating table along with tanks in Europe and nuclear warheads. For the Soviets, it is embarrassing enough to import four times as much grain as India imported after its worst monsoon failure. To spotlight this shortcoming by directly linking it to arms reductions would be an unacceptable affront to Soviet national pride.

The Soviets have already indicated that they will resist the U.S. use of food for political purposes. In his May 24, 1982 address outlining the new "food program," President Brezhnev noted that "The leadership of certain states is striving to turn ordinary commercial operations such, for example, as grain sales, into a means of putting pressure on our country, into an instrument of political pressure."[12] This pre-emptive rhetoric, not needing to mention the United States by name, shows that the Soviets are fully aware of their dilemma, but will not easily bend to pressure.

The advantages of massive U.S. food shipments to the Soviet Union are not limited to economic benefits alone. These shipments are an important commercial transaction for the United States, but they also provide a form of insurance against a Soviet nuclear attack. Although the prospect of destroying its principal source of imported food will not necessarily prevent a Soviet nuclear attack, it is certainly a deterrent. Unlike a U.S. grain export embargo that would simply rearrange trade patterns, a nuclear attack that destroyed U.S. export capacity would decimate the world's exportable grain supplies, particularly since Canada's export capacity might also be destroyed. This would leave over a hundred grain-importing countries, including the Soviet Union, scrambling for the exports of Australia and Argentina, plus a few other small exporters.

While reducing tensions is obviously attractive to Moscow, there are significant advantages for Washington as well. Rising military spending is pushing budget deficits to record levels. In 1982, for the first time in U.S. history, the soaring public debt has pushed public borrowing above private borrowing, including that by both businesses and consumers.[13] This competition for capital from the U.S. Treasury has driven up interest rates and restricted corporate investment and consumer spending. The result has been economic stagnation, the highest unemployment in 40 years, and more farm and business failures than at any time since the Great Depression. In these circumstances, any budget relief would be welcome. But balancing the budget and reducing public borrowing depend on cuts in defense spending, pegged at a record $263 billion in fiscal year 1983.[14] Defense budget cuts in turn depend on substantial progress in arms reduction negotiations with the Soviet Union.

Countries worldwide also have an interest in reduced tensions between the superpowers. The Third World has a stake in Soviet reforms that would reduce its claims on the world's exportable food supplies. Recent Soviet grain purchases, though heavy, have not driven prices skyward as they did in the mid-1970s. But shortages could easily reemerge with the next poor world havest, as they did in 1972, when food shortages raised death rates in India, Bangladesh, and the Sahelian zone of Africa.

The Third World also has an economic interest in nuclear disarmament by the superpowers. Anything that reduces the threat of nuclear war benefits the more than 100 countries depending on U.S. grain exports. In the event of a U.S.–Soviet nuclear exchange, more people may die of starvation in the South than of radiation in the North.

The food connection between the two superpowers will not automatically usher in a new period of East–West cooperation and peace. But if wisely used, it could become the cornerstone on which to build a better relationship. The food connection between the two superpowers promises other changes in the long run. Frequent consultations under the grain agreement could lead to consultations in other areas as well. Just as the two countries now find it in their mutual interest to engage in massive food trade, they may also find it advantageous to cooperate in nonagricultural trade, scientific research, and even space exploration.

The importance of the dramatic shift in the agricultural balance of power lies less in the potential it provides for using food as a political lever than in the psychological effect the new commercial ties will have on political relations between the two countries. The long line of grain-laden ships linking U.S. farmers to Soviet consumers represents a major new economic tie between the two countries, one that could transform long-term political relationships as well.

## Notes

[1]U.S. Department of Agriculture (USDA), *Foreign Agriculture Circular* FG-21-82, July 1982.

[2]USDA Economic Research Service, *USSR Review of Agriculture in 1981 and Outlook for 1982* (Washington, D.C.: May 1982); USDA, *Foreign Agriculture Circular* FG-26-82, August 1982.

[3]USDA, *Foreign Agriculture Circulars* FG-13-82, April 1982 and FG-7-77, July 1977.

[4]USDA Economic Research Service, *USSR Review of Agriculture in 1981 and Outlook for 1982.*

[5]Hunter Lewis and Donald Allison, *The Real World War* (New York: Coward, McCann and Geoghegan, 1982).

[6]David Hoffman, "Soviets accept Reagan Offer to Extend Grain Sales a Year," *Washington Post*, August 21, 1982.

[7]James Kelly, "Very Down On the Farm," *Time*, August 16, 1982.

[8]John F. Burns, "Soviet Grain Crop: One More Failure," *New York Times*, June 21, 1982.

[9]Dan Morgan, "East Europe Tries Modified Capitalism," *Washington Post*, May 24, 1982.

[10]Quoted in Harry Anderson *et al.*, "A System that Doesn't Work," *Newsweek*, April 12, 1982.

[11]Marshall Goldman, "Let's Exploit Moscow's Weakness," *New York Times*, April 4, 1982.

[12]Serge Schmemann, "Brezhnev Offers Plan to Boost Soviet Food Supply," *New York Times*, May 25, 1982.

[13]Larry Kudlow, Chief Economist, Office of Management and Budget, in testimony before the Subcommittee on Housing and Community Development,

Committee on Banking, Finance and Urban Affairs, U.S. House of Representatives, Washington, D.C., June 3, 1982.

[14]Executive Office of the President, Office of Management and Budget, *The United States Budget in Brief* (Washington, D.C.: U.S. Government Printing Office, 1982).

# 24

## DIMITRI K. SIMES

## *The New Soviet Challenge and America's New Edge*[*]

What are the Soviets after? Their ambitions fall short of world domination but go far beyond narrowly defined security. The Kremlin not only
lacks a master plan, it does not even seem to have a clear-cut international agenda, except for dealing with the most immediate contingencies. Soviet literature on foreign policy issues and conversations
with Russian officials suggest that little mid- and long-term foreign
policy planning is under way.

At the same time this body of evidence confirms lasting themes
shared by Soviet policymakers. They include the deep-rooted feeling
that communist Russia is engaged in a history-shaping rivalry with the
industrial democracies, a rivalry that can be regulated but, as long as
capitalism exists, cannot be eliminated. The Kremlin also holds the
conviction that security on the periphery of the empire should be as
absolute as possible. Those who happen to live in the shadow of the
USSR are expected to accept geopolitical realities and behave accordingly. Finally, the Soviet elite and people alike are proud of having achieved
superpower status and are committed to maintaining it. The periodic
establishment of even short-lived footholds in the Third World perpetuates Soviet self-esteem and is perceived as proof of the growing
historical relevance of the Soviet Union.

Thus Soviet motives in the world arena are rooted in Russian imperial
aspirations and compounded by a sectarian Marxist–Leninist hostility to
anything noncommunist. This hostility alone rarely dictates Soviet actions, but it gives the competition with the West an additional element
of self-righteous intensity.

Still, the magnitude of Soviet power and the ruthless ways in which it
is being applied should not obscure the important transformation that

[*]Reprinted by permission of the author and publisher from "The New Soviet
Challenge," *Foreign Policy* 55 (Summer, 1984), pp. 125–131, and "America's New
Edge," *Foreign Policy* 56 (Fall, 1984), pp. 24–43. Copyright 1984 by the Carnegie
Endowment for International Peace.

America's Soviet rival has undergone. New and different ways are required to deal with it.

## The Roots of Rivalry

The U.S.–Soviet rivalry can only be managed. It cannot be eliminated so long as communist Russia remains simultaneously so powerful and so hostile to Western values and interests. Both countries have geopolitical interests on a global scale and are bound to compete. Moreover, while Washington and Moscow alike often attempt to avoid direct involvement in international trouble spots and to rely on allies and surrogates, where vital interests are concerned there is no substitute for a direct superpower role. Only the United States and the Soviet Union can balance each other.

Maintaining a situation of mutual nuclear vulnerability is hardly a prescription for good will and mutual trust. Yet there is no realistic alternative. It is to a considerable degree not even what the Soviets do, but rather what they are—armed to the teeth and able to destroy life on earth—that assures a continuing element of tension in the U.S.–Soviet relationship.

America and the Soviet Union are not on the same wavelength economically, either. Some opportunities for mutually beneficial trade exist: for example, American grain and Pepsi Cola for Soviet raw materials and vodka. But the basic economic interests of the two countries are incompatible. In terms of its export structure, the Soviet Union is very much a Third World country. In one sense, this backwardness creates a basis for cooperation with more technologically advanced countries such as the United States. But such cooperation, designed to spur Soviet development, would require massive Western investment for which there is no popular support, given the current political climate and Western economic problems.

Meanwhile, Moscow acts to protect its own interests. Moscow, for example, supported the oil price hikes of the 1970s not only out of a feeling of solidarity with the Third World at the expense of the West, but also because the Kremlin realized that higher world oil prices meant greater oil export revenues for the troubled Soviet economy. It is this money that permits Moscow to make massive purchases of American grain year after year.

But there are also other political and psychological factors at work that make the competition so antagonistic and on occasion plain nasty. Probably the most important element is that for different reasons the United States and the USSR tend to insist on nothing short of absolute security. One reason for the temptation is self-evident. The Soviet Union and the United States are the only two countries in the world so powerful that credible deterrence against all threats to their existence seems within reach. For centuries, the Europeans have had to operate in a political environment that had to be kept carefully balanced, where no dominant power was allowed to emerge. They had to maneuver, to enter coalitions, and to accept an element of uncertainty in their foreign policy conduct.

The Russians, and to an even greater degree the Americans, have preferred essentially to emphasize unilateral efforts. Of course, both the United States and the Russian empire have had to practice diplomacy. But unlike most European states, what these two continental powers bargained for had little to do with survival or the protection of their territory. The negotiations usually dealt with less vital matters— acquiring additional international real estate or gaining economic and political influence outside their borders.

But here the similarity stops. Being by far the strongest power in the Western Hemisphere, the United States could afford to feel basically secure. Russian history has been filled with invasions, blood, and tragedy. And Russians have viewed diplomacy as an unreliable instrument of the weak. The threats from Napoleon Bonaparte and Adolf Hitler forced the Russians temporarily to seek collective security. But in the long run despite numerous traumas the Russians have traditionally had the self-confidence of a people powerful enough to control their destiny. Vladimir N. Lamsdorf, a Russian diplomat during the late nineteenth century rule of Czar Aleksandr III, complained that "badmouthing of diplomacy had a great appeal to his majesty." According to Lamsdorf, who became foreign minister under Czar Nicholas II and one of whose descendants is now a minister in the West German government, diplomacy for Aleksandr presented the threat of a Westernized state within a state; he hoped to gain popularity by displaying "wild inclinations."[1] Throughout the centuries, a strong sentiment has developed in Russia that there can be no such thing as too much security and that self-reliance is the only certain means of survival.

To the Americans, Soviet insistence that an independent, and therefore less than friendly, Afghanistan represents an intolerable threat to Soviet security, is preposterous. Yet most Americans agreed with Reagan that a Grenada politically close to Cuba was a threat to the United States and endorsed the invasion of the island. Khrushchev's introduction of missiles to Cuba was widely viewed in the United States as a brutal provocation. However, the Soviet argument that Pershing II missiles should not be deployed in Western Europe close to Soviet borders is contemptuously dismissed. Conversely, the Politburo becomes extremely nervous at the slightest sign of U.S. involvement in Poland, yet fails to see what is wrong with supporting guerrillas in El Salvador and, for that matter, with an alliance with Cuba and a semi-alliance with Grenada, right in America's backyard.

The difficulty in understanding each other's concerns also reflects the strong American and Soviet belief in the righteousness of their respective causes. These convictions do not prevent American and Soviet leaders from acting pragmatically. Nevertheless, both assume that they have something terribly important and inherently good to share with the rest of the world. In the U.S. case it is the ideal of a democratic system of government marked by pluralism and tolerance. The Soviets rhetorically are committed to social equality but in fact are essentially offering the privilege of association with a military power already second to none. Their goods may be flawed, but the Soviets provide them with considerable pride.

Moralistic recriminations are even stronger because of the perceived shortcomings each sees in the other. The United States rightly complains that the Soviet Union increasingly turns to force and coercion in the absence of other efficient tools to protect and to expand its sphere of influence. Americans also strongly suspect that expansionism is inherent in the Soviet political culture. With ideology no longer a driving factor, legitimating the needs of the regime acquires a greater significance.

Deterioration of the domestic situation in particular may pique the leadership's interest in opportunities abroad. The argument should not be oversimplified. It is impossible to imagine a Politburo meeting where members support intervention in Angola because the harvest was bad. Yet some Soviet scholars privately suggest that economic difficulties put additional pressure on the Brezhnev leadership to come up with some spectacular accomplishments on the eve of the Twenty-fifth Communist Party Congress in February 1976. Since emerging troubles in the U.S.– Soviet relationship and the recent defeat of Communists and their allies in Chile and Portugal left little ground for boasting about foreign policy matters, Angola became a tempting target.

Still, Soviet officials, and especially ordinary people, almost never describe adventures in distant countries as something in which they take pride. Rather, such interventions are usually explained as unpleasant necessities in a competitive world. The Kremlin applauds when new regimes proclaim their Marxist–Leninist allegiance and a desire to be allied with the USSR. The Politburo becomes considerably less enthusiastic when support of these regimes requires a major investment in prestige and resources and especially a commitment of Soviet military personnel beyond a handful of advisors. At a time of economic scarcity the Soviet leadership can hardly improve its domestic credentials by engaging in costly and risky exploits in the Third World.

Unfortunately, the costs associated with involvement in Third World disputes can rarely be forecast with precision. When things go sour domestically, leaders feel a temptation to look for compensating successes and may seriously underestimate the costs. The temptation does not amount to a Pavlovian reflex. Still, such temptation may alter the prism through which the Kremlin views international developments.

In addition, dealing with the Soviets is no fun. They are secretive and polemical. When they feel provoked—and little is needed to provoke them—they may become exceptionally nasty and petty. Soviet officials take unusual liberties with the truth and act offended when their lies are exposed. Sometimes it appears that the Soviet elite, together with the majority of its subjects, has lost the ability to make a mental distinction between truth and falsehood and simply tries to figure out what is appropriate to think and say under the circumstances.

In turn, the Soviets complain about the inconsistency and unpredictability of U.S. foreign policy, of America's propensity to make sharp turns disregarding previous agreements and understandings. The role of domestic politics in U.S. policy formulation is another sore point with the Kremlin. The Soviet leadership is annoyed when popular pressures inside the United States work against Soviet interests. Since the leaders come from a totally different political tradition, they also feel bewildered, uncertain of exactly what motivates those "crazy" Americans. And their extreme suspicion prompts them to look for some sinister explanation.

An assessment of problems dividing the United States and the Soviet Union leaves little reason to believe that a foundation for a beautiful relationship is in sight. Soviet Russia today represents a tough rival and a difficult partner. But doing the United States in, promoting world revolution, and achieving global dominance are definitely not on the top of the Politburo's agenda. Contrary to what Soviet and American alarmists claim, the international situation today does not resemble the prewar late 1930s. The Soviet challenge is formidable, but it is also fairly traditional in terms of world politics. It is carefully calculated and accordingly, with some luck and skill, manageable.

Managing the competition with a declining but still powerful and ambitious Soviet empire with its growing global power and a finger on the nuclear trigger is, by definition, an extremely difficult and frustrating business. The temptation to develop simple formulas that promise lasting solutions can lead only to illusions, trouble, and policy reversals. What Americans need most in dealing with the Soviet Union is realism—about communist Russia, its power and intentions; about U.S. interests in relations with it; about the tools available to Washington, both coercive and inducive, for achieving desired ends; and about the way U.S. actions are likely to be perceived by Soviet policymakers.

A further condition for any effective policy toward Moscow is a greater willingness to take into account the inner workings of the American political process as it bears on U.S. policy toward the Soviet Union. Wonderful conceptual schemes, so logical, calibrated, and nuanced that no ordinary person can understand them, appeal to political scientists. But as long as the American foreign policy formulation process remains populist and media-oriented, such schemes are no more than irrelevant abstractions.

The United States is now addressing the Soviet challenge at a time when—to use the Kremlin's phrase—the correlation of forces is shifting against the adversary. The Soviets themselves now admit that "on the boundary of the seventies and the eighties [their] country has encountered difficulties."[2] What they fail to acknowledge—and may fail to understand themselves—is how profound these difficulties are and how inadequate are the stopgap solutions they have so far approved.

The new situation is uniquely advantageous in many respects. Having the Soviets on the defensive for a change feels good and opens new options for U.S. diplomacy. A modified American policy can exploit the unprecedented opportunities located on the nuclear minefield of the superpower rivalry. But a few words of caution are in order.

First, as the last decades of Austria–Hungary demonstrate, decadent empires are prone to the temptation to prove that history is still on their side or that at least the clock can be stopped. Flexing military muscles, striking back, and on occasion even engaging in risky adventures is not uncommon for such insecure but still-powerful regimes.

Second, the current troubled era could represent for the Soviets either a temporary phenomenon or an irreversible trend. Most students of Soviet affairs agree that major structural reforms will be very difficult to undertake. Thinking about radical departures in Soviet policies is particularly unfashionable during the current transition in the Kremlin. Yet this is not Russia's first period of stagnation and degradation. And in the past a combination of domestic failures and military defeats more often than not resulted not in the system's collapse but in the emergence of a strong and ruthless leader, willing and able to attack the problem head on. The fact that no Peter I (the Great) or at least Pëtr Stolypin, prime minister under Nicholas II, seems to be on the horizon does not necessarily mean that the Soviet Union can no longer produce one. Contributing to a Soviet crisis would not serve U.S. interests since no one can predict the outcome. Nor does it make sense to push the Soviet Union so hard in its hour of weakness that most of the people—to say nothing of the ruling elite—would feel deeply offended and eager for revenge.

## Operating within Established Margins

Since the late 1940s, the West's answer to the Soviet challenge has been containment. This highly mutable concept was nonetheless always based on three analytical assumptions—all of them currently inoperative to some degree. First was the supposition that the Soviet Union was committed to aggression and subversion beyond its post-World War II sphere of influence. Western Europe was considered an immediate target. Second was the sense that Soviet control over occupied territories was inevitable. Third was a belief that successful containment would eventually lead to "either the breakup or the gradual mellowing of the Soviet power," as George Kennan put it in 1947 in his Mr. X article in *Foreign Affairs*.

The advent of nuclear weapons coupled with political stabilization in Western Europe and the Far East have profoundly reduced chances of a calculated Soviet attack against the industrial democracies. The Persian Gulf, with its constant potential for turmoil, offers the Kremlin more attractive opportunities short of direct aggression. But even there, Moscow acts with considerable care. Cutting an adversary's access to oil supplies is not appealing enough to risk a suicidal nuclear confrontation. Soviet spokesmen admit that the United States has important interests in the Persian Gulf that Moscow is forced to take into account. Inside the Soviet orbit, instability, tension, and a struggle for independence are on the rise. The Soviet leadership is preoccupied with the increasingly difficult task of holding together its own. And while the Soviet regime has mellowed somewhat domestically—at least in comparison with Joseph Stalin's era—a similar moderation in Soviet foreign policy has not resulted. On the contrary, the period of greatest Soviet international assertiveness, and occasionally outright adventurism, coincided with former Premier Nikita Khrushchev's internal thaw.

Thus the Soviet challenge appears to be simultaneously less pressing and more indefinite than anticipated by the founding fathers of containment. In dealing with Moscow, Washington has to operate within fairly well established margins: The Soviet regime cannot be eliminated, and a genuine modus vivendi is not within reach. The view that the Soviet challenge can only be indefinitely managed clashes with the characteristic American belief that all problems have solutions. But any sensible long-term policy toward Moscow requires accepting this reality.

Certainly, in the age of nuclear parity there is no military solution to the Soviet challenge. Nor can the United States hope to develop a normal relationship with the Soviet Union similar to relations with other great states such as China that may differ considerably from America in both interests and values. After all, China is not a superpower, and it is the shadow of Soviet power that inspires Sino–American cooperation despite myriad serious disagreements.

Further, declaring the intent to free the Soviet Union from communism would be dangerous and counterproductive for the United States. It may be dangerous because the United States lacks the kind of leverage, knowledge about the Soviet elite and society, and self-discipline necessary to push the internal processes of another great power in a desirable direction. In the past, American efforts to influence Soviet domestic policies in most instances did more harm than good. The Jackson–Vanik amendment to the 1974 trade act, which linked trade benefits to the USSR with the Kremlin's emigration policies, is a perfect illustration. President Jimmy Carter's well-intentioned but ill-fated attempts to help Soviet dissidents is another.

Moreover, a thoroughly reformed Soviet Union may be anything but a blessing for the West. Some in the West fully believe the next generation of Soviet leadership—presumably better educated, more worldly, and more flexible than the current old guard—will seriously pursue reforms. Once these leaders learn the Hungarian lesson—that meaningful economic change is impossible without relaxing, but not lifting, political controls over society—the Soviet system will become simultaneously more humane and more inwardly oriented. The West will be able to welcome a new Soviet Union into the community of nations and offer economic cooperation to give Moscow an additional stake in the existing international order.

But as a rule, major economic and social reforms were undertaken in Russia after defeats in war and aimed primarily at assuring better military performance. Russian Westernizers such as Ivan IV (the Terrible) and Peter the Great used the most barbaric methods to modernize their nation. Even liberal reformers such as Aleksandr II used domestic change to prepare the Russian empire for new military exploits.

In the twentieth century the greatest Soviet Westernizer was V. I. Lenin, who transformed Russia and wanted to transform the rest of the world. In recent years, the closest thing to a hero for those among the elite committed to modernizing Soviet society was the late leader Yuri Andropov. Had he lived longer, the Soviet Union possibly could have become more efficient, but would it have become more free and open?

Moreover, many of the supposedly reform-minded younger members of the Soviet hierarchy are reported to be fierce patriots. Less inhibited than their predecessors by the trauma of World War II, these officials seem to take for granted that the USSR is and should remain a global military power second to none. Neither pressures nor promises of benefits from the West are likely to lead them to give up these ambitions. Some imply willingness to adopt elements of the market economy. But there is as yet no evidence that any influential segment of the Soviet ruling strata is interested in transforming the political organization of the country.

Even among dissidents, Russian imperial sentiment, contempt for the "excesses" of Western democracy, and a preference for autocracy are growing. Aleksandr Solzhenitsyn is a perfect example of a Russian who detests the communist regime but favors maintaining authoritarian controls under a different banner. The fear of chaos, of a breakup of the Russian empire, is stronger than the yearning for freedom and tolerance. Since Kievan Russia was defeated by the Mongols in the thirteenth century, Russia has always existed as a multinational entity built and maintained by force, not as a nation-state. Unlike the British, the French, and others who could surrender colonial possessions without irreparable damage to the core of their national identity, the Russians still have no clear self-image separate from their empire. Even true supporters of pluralistic democracy in the Soviet Union recognize the dangers of experimenting with political liberalization in a country where numerous ethnic and religious groups have been traditionally kept together by tight police controls.

Naturally, no country is forever imprisoned by its history, and Russia is no exception. Today, as before the revolution, there are supporters of democracy—most but not all forced outside the system. Their time may yet come. Still, the history of the Soviet Union should caution those who are eager to build Western policies on the anticipation of constructive change in the Soviet Union.

## Contributing to International Chaos

What is precisely the nature of the Soviet threat at this juncture? The most unlikely danger—even if its horrifying consequences demand grave concern—is a pre-emptive nuclear attack against the United States. Deterrence is sufficiently strong to preclude the possibility of a strike from the blue. The invasion of Western Europe is also not among probable contingencies. While critics on both sides of the Atlantic question the reliability of the American-nuclear unbrella, the element of uncertainty is too great and the risks too tremendous for Moscow to consider a blitzkrieg seriously.

An escalation of Third World conflict, with the Middle East being the prime contender, is a more realistic prospect. But outside of this periphery the Soviets act with caution. The postwar record suggests that when the United States demonstrates resolve—while avoiding provocation—Moscow knows when to stop and even to retreat.

Similarly, the Kremlin lacks both the political appeal and economic competitiveness to ride the tide of history in the Third World. The Soviet military reach is formidable and growing. But the Soviets are reluctant to commit ground troops in faraway regions. The number of surrogates is not unlimited, and these clients frequently encounter stiff resistance from indigenous forces and their patrons: the Vietnamese in Kampuchea, the Cubans in Angola, the Libyans in Chad, and the Sandinistas in their own country. Conversations with Soviet officials and experts suggest that the USSR already feels overextended. Easy victories are hard to come by, and long-lasting, costly engagements in remote regions seem to be unpopular not only among the Soviet people but also among important sectors of the elite concerned with the allocation of increasingly scarce resources. In addition, geopolitical adventures carry a considerable foreign policy price tag. Afghanistan and Kampuchea, for example, complicate the search for rapprochement with China and the Islamic countries.

Reagan administration officials claim that a new U.S. willingness to counteract Soviet expansionism is largely responsible for the USSR's relative moderation and shortage of successes in the Third World. Other factors are clearly also at work here, such as the need to consolidate gains and the lack of truly appealing targets. Also, as with Lebanon, the Kremlin may prefer to avoid a costly involvement in an environment where the Americans are likely to fall flat on their faces anyway. But U.S. readiness to move against Soviet-supported advances is bound to enter the Politburo's calculations. Finding itself face-to-face with America is hardly the Politburo's idea of an attractive Third World opportunity.

Neither Moscow's caution nor its failure to develop multidimensional links with postcolonial societies guarantees an automatic Soviet failure in the Third World. But particularly during the 1970s, the Kremlin has been forced to lower its earlier expectation regarding associating with and eventually providing leadership to the diverse community of developing countries. Still, some concern has been voiced that the Soviet Union is in a position to contribute to international chaos.

Even without the destructive influence of the USSR, the process of international change is neither orderly nor uniformly responsive to American interests. The Soviet Union was not responsible for the sudden rise in oil prices, which caused two of the greatest international convulsions in the last decade. If the first jump in oil prices can be partially attributed to the Kremlin's actions—arming Egypt and Syria, which enabled those countries to attack Israel—the second price jump cannot. Nor can the Soviet Union be blamed for the growing gap between developed and developing countries; for the inevitable contradictions between raw-material producers and consumers; for starvation and the lack of population controls in the Third World; or for the

Third World debt crisis, which threatens the international financial system. Nor are imprudent Western loans to Eastern Europe, particularly to Poland, attributable to Soviet actions or pressures.

The Soviets support so-called national liberation movements, but they do not create them. The collapse of colonial empires, widespread poverty in the Third World, the insensitivity of former colonial masters and the United States, and the well-established phenomenon of postcolonial ingratitude on the part of the newly independent countries, not Soviet intrigues, have created divisions between industrialized Western and developing states.

It is also an oversimplification to assume that the USSR is always tempted to contribute to international chaos, as it is a mistake to believe that the United States and the Soviet Union always find themselves on opposite sides in Third World disputes. Regarding the Iran–Iraq war, both superpowers, albeit for different reasons, prefer to put an end to the conflict. Both cautiously lean toward Iraq, and both complain about Iranian intransigence and fanaticism. Similarly, despite Islamabad's provision of sanctuary to Afghan revels, Moscow has avoided much-feared efforts to help aid separatist movements in Pakistan. The Soviet Union supports Colonel Muammar el-Qaddafi of Libya but only because he vehemently opposes the United States, Israel, and Arab moderates. Discussions with both Arab specialists and Soviets give an impression that Libya's terrorism is tolerated but hardly encouraged.

The Soviet Union is an ambitious, unscrupulous, but conservative global empire. Its ambitions and self-image of being an underdog, as well as its forced reliance on military might, frequently permit Moscow to benefit from international instability. But its conservatism, limited resources, and power disincline Moscow from actively seeking additional commitments and risking the possibility that events will tumble out of control. And who can be confident of being able to direct and control Third World conflicts?

Revolutions may be inevitable; their success is usually not. Soviet arms and Soviet support influence the outcome of numerous internal and international conflicts in the Third World. Syria, for example, was bound to oppose the U.S.-sponsored May 17, 1983 agreement between Lebanon and Israel. But Damascus may not have tried so boldly to torpedo the pact were no Soviet missiles and Soviet soldiers on Syrian soil. The USS New Jersey's big guns and the U.S. Marines might have made more of an impression on President Hafez al-Assad had Moscow abandoned his regime and had fighting spread inside the Syrian perimeter. And Cuban Premier Fidel Castro's willingness to anger the United States by becoming involved in Central America is surely increased by the presence of a Russian big brother behind his back.

There can be little doubt that the Soviet global presence is a major factor in shaping a new international environment where the United States has less room to maneuver. The Politburo apparently wishes to use Soviet might as a straitjacket on American power. Moscow is careful not to push its luck by challenging vital U.S. interests, such as Western

Europe, Japan, South Korea, and the Persian Gulf. But the United States cannot afford to lose room to maneuver outside these crucial but still rather narrow regions. Specific individual American interests in Africa, Latin America, and South Asia may not amount to vital concerns. Yet if the United States cannot take measured steps to protect these interests, truly vital concerns may be jeopardized. And one crucial objective of U.S. policy should be to prevent the Soviet-orchestrated paralysis of America's ability and willingness to play an assertive role on the global scale, including, when appropriate and necessary, the use of military force.

The Soviets cannot be contained everywhere. But Washington must deny them geopolitical momentum and maintain the credibility of U.S. forces at all rungs of the escalation ladder. Yet deterring Soviet power and retaining the ability to contain the Soviet empire carefully are conditions for an effective and imaginative policy, not policies in themselves. The Soviets do respect and understand force. Yet they cannot be contained by U.S. force alone. Force is even less useful for probing opportunities inside the Soviet orbit. The costs of Soviet expansionism, however, can be increased. Successful containment requires a wise definition of U.S. geopolitical priorities. The United States would also benefit from acting as decisively but as quietly as possible. If Washington's purpose is to stop the Soviets, not just embarrass them, it must leave the Kremlin room for retreat. The U.S. proclamation of a Soviet defeat after the Israeli military victory in Lebanon in 1982 was not only premature, it also put pressure on Moscow to prove its regional relevance. Yet in Afghanistan the Reagan administration skillfully manages to provide assistance to the rebels without needlessly creating the impression of a superpower confrontation at the gates of a nervous Pakistan.

Of equal importance is making local environments less hospitable to Soviet involvement. The Carter administration stressed developing ties with Third World countries, regardless of their official ideology and rhetoric, in order to provide an alternative to affiliation with the USSR. Unfortunately, eager to embrace Third World causes, the United States at that time did not sufficiently stress the other side of the coin: imposing penalties on those hostile to America and providing military and security assistance to governments and factions seeking U.S. cooperation. The Reagan administration has corrected this dangerous imbalance but in some instances has gone too far in the other direction. Excessive generosity to petty left-wing authoritarians in the face of verbal attacks on the United States and disregard of U.S. interests can only generate contempt for America. But failing to explore the limits of the flexibility of left-leaning states, which for various reasons may want to reduce dependence on the Soviet Union, is not a smart policy either.[3] The Carter administration, for example, was initially far too generous to the Sandinistas despite their well-known Cuban connection. The Reagan administration, by trying to bully them, may be helping to push Nicaragua further inside the Soviet orbit. Similarly, treating Syria as the Soviet surrogate in the Middle East was a mistake.

A Changed NATO Strategy

Nowhere can the United States benefit more from a sympathetic understanding of the dilemmas of Soviet clients than in Eastern Europe. Here, America has a historic opportunity to go beyond containment. The artificial division of Europe imposed by Soviet armies at the end of the World War II is becoming obsolete. The Iron Curtain cannot be destroyed by NATO's force but it is increasingly permeable, and the West can help accelerate the process.

Chances are that Eastern Europe will have to stay under Soviet domination for a long time, maybe for decades. But the West must realize that one Warsaw Pact government after another feels entitled and able to exercise a degree of autonomy. Moscow can no longer even assume that East Berlin will serve as a blind instrument of Soviet power. The need to differentiate among East European governments has been accepted by every U.S. administration since President Richard Nixon's. But building independent relationships with Soviet satellites has never become a true priority for American diplomacy. Further, the Reagan administration has given contacts with Eastern Europe a distinctive anti-Soviet twist. Yet provoking additional Soviet opposition to the erosion of Europe's political and economic barriers seems contrary to U.S. interests. The United States has a choice between attempting delicately to expedite a process of change already under way and adopting a more ambitious and outspoken approach that disregards geopolitical realities and that is bound to stiffen Soviet opposition.

Nothing America can do will change the Soviets' basically hostile approach to an increase in links across the great European divide. But pushing Warsaw Pact allies back into absolute obedience may cost Moscow dearly. Deprived of Western credits, East European regimes would insist on greater Soviet subsidies. And as the June 1984 Council for Mutual Economic Assistance summit meeting demonstrated, the Politburo is in no mood to provide for its allies during times of economic scarcity in the USSR. A Soviet-enforced tightening of internal screws may cause popular uprisings—something the Politburo can suppress but surely prefers to avoid.

Nor would uprisings, as long as NATO is neither willing nor able to come to their aid, be in the American interest. Soviet interventions interrupt and retard domestic evolution of East European societies and polarize the international climate in which these societies have to operate. The brutal suppression of revolts reminds the West of the evil nature of the Soviet empire. But such reminders are too costly in human and political terms.

Consolidation of Western ties with Eastern Europe may be retarded or even temporarily reversed by a heightened tension in the U.S.–Soviet relationship. After the Soviet walkout from the intermediate nuclear force negotiations in Geneva, Hungary and East Germany did try to protect their Western connections. In the long run, however, as their reluctant joining of the 1984 summer Olympic games boycott shows, Warsaw Pact states, except Romania in this instance, cannot help but side with the Soviet empire during periods of extreme tension. Just as a climate of hostility complicates Soviet relations with Western Europe, it threatens American relations with Eastern Europe. Still, America's allies are far more independent from Washington than Soviet allies are from Moscow. On balance, superpower polemics are more damaging to the Western alliance than the Eastern.

Ties with the East Europeans should be cultivated from a position of strength. Sensitivity to their situation inside the Soviet orbit requires more than de-escalating anti-Soviet rhetoric. Also needed are changes in NATO's military planning that would allow extending a modicum of encouragement to Warsaw Pact governments attempting to pursue an autonomous line, at least to those who share borders with NATO. The West cannot acquire the capability for a major offensive against Eastern Europe. The cost would be prohibitive, and anything smacking of building an offensive potential is bound to spark another bitter and possibly explosive NATO debate. Finally, scaring the Soviets with invasion preparations would only harden the divisions of Europe.

East Europeans striving for greater political flexibility do not need the threat of military assault by NATO. But they would profit from the West's ability to shake Moscow's confidence that all its satellites could get from the United States in their hour of trial would be sympathetic noises.

Addressing the dilemma of how to extend a modicum of deterrence to Eastern Europe without unduly alarming a state obsessed enough with security to destroy an unarmed South Korean airliner will be extremely difficult. The most NATO can realistically seek is to develop an arsenal and a strategy for military maneuver in central Europe that would enable the West to conduct operations inside Warsaw Pact territory. Such changes are already powerfully advocated by those who believe, like Harvard University political scientist Samuel Huntington, that "the threat of a conventional retaliatory offensive into Eastern Europe" is required for credible deterrence of aggression against NATO itself.[4] The difference, however, between a force posture designed for counterattack and posture for limited offensive operations in Eastern Europe in support of a local revolt is politically enormous but militarily next to nonexistent. Consequently, simply by building the capability for a retaliatory offensive, the West inevitably will affect Soviet calculations regarding the costs of crushing East European uprisings in countries bordering NATO.

Such a capability would involve nothing more than a moderate change of NATO's military penetration capabilities. It certainly would not involve the transformation of NATO into an offensive rather than purely defensive alliance. Acquiring the ability to help a Warsaw Pact government to stand up to the Kremlin would simply be a happy byproduct of legitimate Western defensive improvements. NATO would have to exercise caution and certainly should not brag about these options. In contrast to the "liberation" and "rollback" slogans of the 1950s, what is needed today is a military capability without rhetoric, rather than rhetoric without military capability. But the West should not be so sensitive to the Soviet preoccupation with protecting its East European domain that its legitimate defensive needs are sacrificed.

In fact, NATO strategy is heading exactly in this direction. The introduction of precision-guided munitions, the adoption of the air–land battle doctrine, the new emphasis on maneuver at the expense of war-of-attrition strategies are the beginning of a welcome and essential change. Evidence of the appearance of so-called operational maneuver groups—highly mobile division-sized formations—among Soviet forces makes the old concept of essentially static front-line defense increasingly outdated. Rejecting the option of extending deterrence eastward would not only deprive NATO of the ability to aid Soviet satellites militarily but also endanger its power to conduct a defense of Western Europe.

Eastern Europe is not the only area where it is essential to be firm without making the Soviets panic. In all its dealings with Moscow the United States needs not only courage and strength but also tact and clarity. The image of tactical unpredictability probably helped Nixon moderate Soviet behavior in the Middle East. But the Politburo still had a reasonably clear, if not always accurate, view of basic American objectives regarding Moscow and the rest of the world. Such clarity about fundamental U.S. interests, commitments, and determination is as crucial for a stable superpower relationship as maintaining the military balance.

The encounter with Carter made the Soviets confused and annoyed. Here was a president who promised to liberate the United States from "an inordinate fear of communism" and unilaterally canceled the B-1 bomber and yet openly embraced Soviet dissidents and broke with previous patterns of arms control negotiations. The experience with President Ronald Reagan has left the Kremlin downright angry and paranoid. The absence of clarity will lead Soviet subjects and the elites angrily to close ranks against America and make meaningful dialogue extremely difficult.

It is rarely possible to prove that some particularly disturbing Soviet step was caused by a misreading of U.S. policies. But states act on the basis of their perceptions. The Soviet leadership's apparent belief that the United States is seeking meaningful strategic superiority over the USSR surely influences Soviet military planning and the Kremlin's willingness to compromise at the bargaining table. The Reagan administration, including the president himself, seems to have come to the belated realization that it would be much wiser to explain new U.S. strategic programs in terms of deterrence rather than by a determination to "prevail with pride" in a protracted nuclear conflict with "the evil empire." The development of weapons systems in many respects speaks louder than words, but rhetoric often influences the context in which adversaries view these systems and the intent behind them.

In relations with the Soviet adversary, cooperation should rarely be an end in itself. Its primary function must be to contribute to managing the rivalry. This principle may help to develop some general guidelines for frequently distasteful but unavoidable cooperation with the Kremlin.

A New          First, the United States should not repeat the mistake
Diplomacy      made in 1972 and 1973 of signing agreements for their
               own sake. The criterion for agreements with an adver-
sary should not be, "Why not?" but rather, "Why yes?" If an arrangement is unlikely to bring considerable substantive benefits, America is
better off without creating misleading symbols of superpower harmony.

U.S.–Soviet cultural agreements, for example, contribute little to
geopolitical stability. Their contribution to mutual understanding is
doubtful as long as Soviet authorities determine who to send and what
to show. And Soviet artistic groups become subjected to hostile demonstrators in the United States, who rightly sense that the very presence
of Soviet performers projects the image of an artificial normalcy in the
relationship between the totalitarian empire and the American
democracy.

Further, cultural, scientific, and other exchange agreements often do
more harm than good to the climate of the relationship. Whenever
pressure builds in the United States to find a cheap way to protest
abhorrent Soviet actions, exchanges are suspended, visits canceled, and
passions on both sides needlessly raised to the boiling point. The only
alternative is to applaud the Bolshoi Ballet while Andrei Sakharov is
being tortured.

Not all exchanges with the USSR are objectionable. Let the Americans
enjoy Soviet ballet. And let American ballet companies benefit from its
defectors. But if there is a genuine interest in the exchanges beyond
politics' sake, they can be sponsored by private U.S. institutions without
official blessing.

Second, every possible effort should be made to avoid ambiguous,
excessively ambitious, and nonbinding declarations of intentions that
are bound to be interpreted differently by each side and lead to future
misunderstandings and mutual bitterness. Two such documents easily
come to mind: the 1973 U.S.–Soviet agreement on the prevention of
nuclear war and the 1975 Helsinki Final Act. The former agreement
required parties to enter consultations in case of conflicts with great
potential to turn nuclear. The wording was so vague that influential
voices in the United states raised a political storm when the USSR did
not specifically advise Washington about the forthcoming Arab attack
against Israel. The latter gave legitimacy to expectations in America that
the Kremlin was ready to relax domestic controls.

Certainly, no agreements between the United States and the USSR
can persuade either country to betray allies or to modify its system of
government. The Helsinki accords were useful in terms of putting
human rights on the East–West diplomatic agenda. They became a
treasured, if illusory, symbol of peace in the midst of a shattered
structure of East–West cooperation, especially to many West Europeans.
But they hardly contributed to the greater freedom of Soviet subjects
and to a better relationship between the blocs. Ultimately the accords
did more to embarrass the Soviets than to serve the original objective:
advancing détente and human rights.

Diplomacy sometimes requires intentional ambiguity. And political pressure both at home and in Western Europe may on occasion force the United States to accept an element of imprecision in agreements with the Soviets. But at a minimum it is important to examine carefully the purpose of confusing pieces of paper and to realize that by signing them Americans are not just promoting a more peaceful world but may also be laying political land mines over which both Washington and Moscow will eventually have to walk.

Third, the U.S.–Soviet relationship would benefit from playing down arms control. The record of U.S.–Soviet arms control negotiations suggests that while some useful agreements can be reached, their absence rarely seriously escalates the military competition. Signing superficially comprehensive, but in fact fairly meaningless, agreements at tastelessly pompous summit meetings hardly adds to arms control momentum. Instead, this practice leads to political polarization in the United States and eventually to trouble between the superpowers.

Was SALT II worth the trouble? Five years after the document was signed, both superpowers, in the absence of ratification, have not found the need to go beyond its sky-high limits. Yet the effort to ratify SALT II led to a divisive and frequently vicious political debate in the United States. And the eventual failure of this effort poisoned the U.S.–Soviet relationship and gave grounds for perceiving America as an unreliable partner.

Paradoxically, the development of some of the most controversial systems on both sides was fueled by arms control. U.S. cruise missiles were initially portrayed as bargaining chips. Their development was apparently among the reasons Moscow opted to fill Eastern Europe with SS-20 missiles. And one of the early arguments in favor of topping American missiles with multiple warheads was that it could offset the Soviet superiority in launchers codified by SALT I. Whether these arguments were rational or just rationalizations is not clear. More important, they worked.

Now that 15 years have passed since Soviet and American SALT delegations first met in Helsinki, it is time to admit that the process was fundamentally flawed. By attempting to do too much, the superpowers have accomplished too little; by pretending that the nuclear arms competition could be neatly separated from the basic rivalry, Washington and Moscow first created unrealistic expectations and, later, excessive recrimination.

Arms control will and should remain an important element of U.S.–Soviet diplomacy. But playing down its political significance will probably help the cause of actual arms limitations. Both Washington and Moscow seem to realize that the central strategic balance—fears of windows of vulnerability notwithstanding—is remarkably stable and that it makes little sense to invest too many precious resources into militarily and politically unusable systems.

But there is also the genuine danger that weapons in space and elsewhere may increase uncertainty, reduce warning time, and contribute to the emergence of a hair-trigger strategic situation. These dangers may be most effectively addressed piecemeal through incremental agreements. Such agreements will separate areas of overlapping interest from those where U.S. and Soviet interests diverge. By disregarding the trivial, incremental arms control will deal more effectively with the crucial.

Fourth, before concluding agreements with the Soviet Union, American leaders must ask whether the American political process can sustain them. If, as in the case of the 1972 trade agreement, they are bound to lead to political infighting in the United States, everybody may be better off without them. The structural problems of American democracy do make it hard to carry out a sophisticated and calibrated international strategy. But the system exists, and if it changes it will not be because of requirements for relations with the Soviet Union. There is nothing to apologize about. The USSR with its insensitivity, self-righteousness, and passion for secrecy is also a very difficult partner. Both governments have to recognize that their political processes preclude closeness and impose severe restrictions on possible cooperation. Keeping some distance from each other would actually be a mutual favor helping to avoid unnecessary friction between the two incompatibles.

The United States should explore specific limited agreements with the Soviets not so much as an investment in a better tomorrow but in terms of their own merit. If an arms control agreement blocks a destabilizing and expensive system or if an unsubsidized nonstrategic trade agreement helps U.S. farmers or creates industrial jobs, each should be pursued without other strings attached.

Fifth, concerning human rights issues, the difference between morality and moralism must be remembered. Highly publicized pressure on the Kremlin to halt repressive practices reminds Americans of the adversary's nature and pays off domestically, but it rarely helps the victims of persecution. They benefit more from quiet but forceful diplomacy that, without asking the Politburo to subscribe to American judgments about Soviet behavior, has a better chance to affect Soviet policy—at least at the margins.

Finally, if the Soviet challenge represents a paramount strategic problem for the United States, the American policymaking mechanism must become far better organized to cope with it. The State Department boasts special bureaus headed by officials at the assistant secretary level—for refugees, for international organizations, and even for international narcotics matters. Yet the Soviet Union and Eastern Europe are lost in the Bureau of European and Canadian Affairs. Surely the Soviet bloc is both important and unique enough to deserve a separate bureau directed by an assistant secretary. Similarly, Congress has no special subcommittee to monitor relations with the Soviet camp.

Such restructuring of the State Department and the congressional committee system will help separate concerns of Soviet policy from other pressing issues, give policymakers of both branches better access to top-ranking specialists, and, one hopes, attract more talented and ambitious individuals to careers in the Soviet and East European area.

No changes—substantive or organizational—will make managing the relationship with the Soviet Union anything but a most demanding and often disappointing long-term exercise. Yet while the dangers are great, the rivalry does not seem to be about to explode; it is the adversary, not the United States, that is slowly but steadily losing ground. The task of U.S. policy is to stay on top of this trend without blowing up the world. The strong can afford kid gloves.

# Notes

[1]F.A. Rotshteyna, *Dnevnik V.N. Lamzdorfa* (Moscow: Gosudarstvennoye Izdatelstvo, 1926), p. 215.

[2]*Izvestiya*, June 15, 1984, p. 3.

[3]See Dimitri K. Simes, "Disciplining Soviet Power," *Foreign Policy* 43 (Summer 1981).

[4]Samuel P. Huntington, "Conventional Deterrence and Conventional Retaliation in Europe," *International Security* 8, no. 4 (Winter 1983–1984), p. 41.

# V

*Western Europe*

# 25 ANGELA E. STENT

## The USSR and Western Europe*

**Soviet Goals toward Western Europe** Western Europe is a central concern of Soviet foreign policy because of both its intrinsic importance and its significance for Soviet relations with the United States. This constant interplay between the European and U.S. aspects of Soviet Westpolitik gives Soviet ties with Western Europe their peculiarly complex character. Nevertheless, the United States remains the key determinant of Soviet foreign policy toward Western Europe, and this framework provides the USSR with many opportunities to flirt with, manipulate, cajole, and threaten Western Europe.

There has been remarkable continuity in Soviet policy toward Western Europe since World War II, involving five basic objectives. These goals all add up to one basic desideratum: to divide and influence, if not conquer, Europe.

The focus of Soviet policy toward Western Europe was and remains Germany. The main preoccupation since 1945 has been to contain West Germany and control East Germany, to solve the German problem, and to prevent Germany ever again from threatening the USSR militarily or politically. Moscow has tried to manipulate the German Democratic Republic (GDR) and entice the Federal Republic of Germany (FRG) into developing a special relationship with the USSR by hinting at various possibilities for German reunification, although in reality it is highly unlikely that the Soviet Union would ever permit this. The USSR has dealt with the German problem by maximizing the ambiguities inherent in the situation and by exploiting the frustrated German wishes that are

*Reprinted in revised form by permission of the author and publisher from *The Washington Quarterly* 5, no. 4 (Autumn, 1982), pp. 93–104. A longer version of this chapter appears in Gerrit W. Gong, Angela E. Stent, and Rebecca V. Strode, *Areas of Challenge for Soviet Foreign Policy in the 1980s* (Bloomington, Ind.: Indiana University Press, 1984), pp. 1–51, 131–133. Copyright 1982 by The Center for Strategic and International Studies, Georgetown University.

an inevitable product of a divided Germany. Moscow holds the key to German reunification and has sought to benefit from this lever to the greatest extent possible.

Prior to the advent of the Social Democrat-Free Democrat coalition in Bonn, the chief Soviet goal toward West Germany was to secure recognition of the postwar geographical and political status quo. Since the Ostpolitik treaties, the USSR has sought to translate the legal resolution of the German problem into a long-term political solution, which has thus far proved elusive. Yet despite these problems, the success of Soviet-German détente has presented certain advantages for the USSR in its attempt to wean the FRG away from the United States.[1]

The second and interconnected Soviet goal toward Western Europe has been to encourage fissures within the Atlantic alliance. Here the USSR has been considerably aided by the United States' own difficulties in dealing with its allies and by the greater self-assertiveness of the European members of the North Atlantic Treaty Organization (NATO) in the 1970s. The USSR has not caused the problems within the alliance, but it has taken advantage of them. As long as the NATO alliance bickers over a wide range of issues, from nuclear strategy to economic policy to relations with the USSR, the nightmare of a cohesive Western alliance confronting the Soviet Union can be prevented. The Europeans believe that détente involves stabilizing East–West relations in Europe, but not necessarily limiting Soviet expansion in the rest of the world. This has ensured friction with Washington over how to interpret Soviet behavior and how to respond to Soviet actions.

The third set of Soviet goals has been to prevent a more coherent political, economic, and military West European integration. Although the Kremlin has less control in this area than it does in the previous two, it has sought to play different European countries off against one another. A united Europe might prove more impervious to Soviet attempts to divide and influence and might also act as a dangerous magnet to Eastern Europe, a reminder that it is indeed possible for smaller states within a hegemonic bloc to weaken the grip of their superpower ally.

Another possible danger for Eastern Europe that reinforces the interconnection between Soviet policy toward Eastern and Western Europe is the attraction of a more independent West European communism. A fourth Soviet goal has been to assist the growth of communism within Western Europe—but only up to a certain point. Communist parties in Western Europe can serve as a conduit of Soviet influence and act as an irritant to the stability of Western bourgeois governments. But they have become increasingly critical of Moscow since the 1968 invasion of Czechoslovakia; they question the legitimacy of the Soviet system and they diminish even further the attraction of a moribund Soviet ideology in Western Europe. While one can question whether the USSR would favor an improvement in the electoral fortunes of the Communist party of Italy at the present time, the Soviet Union continues to derive some concrete benefits from the strength of communist parties in Latin Europe, particularly through their criticisms of the United States.

A final and increasingly important Soviet interest in Western Europe has been economic. Since the failure of the 1965 Kosygin reforms, the USSR has apparently decided that it is politically too dangerous to introduce far-reaching, decentralizing economic reforms that might threaten the vested interest of those committed to the Stalinist economic system of centralization and unbalanced growth. Nevertheless, as growth rates decline and as the Soviet system faces chronic problems caused by the unwillingness to modify the ossified economic infrastructure, new ways must constantly be found to keep the economy functioning.

The Soviet Union decided in the late 1960s to import large amounts of West European technology and equipment, and West European countries have become more attractive trade partners since the prospects for U.S.–Soviet nonagricultural trade have shrunk. In addition to the economic benefits derived from this trade, the USSR has also gained politically. The greater the dependence of Western Europe on Soviet energy supplies, the greater the potential Soviet leverage over Europe. Moreover, the interest in East–West trade has created export lobbies in Western Europe that argue consistently and effectively against embargoes.

The USSR has varying degrees of leverage in these five areas; perhaps it has the greatest influence over the German situation because of its control over the GDR. Yet in all these areas the realization of Soviet goals is largely dependent on events within Western Europe.

This chapter will survey the most significant aspects of West European domestic and foreign policy from the Kremlin's point of view and discuss the extent to which new opportunities may arise in the next few years.

## Germany

*Foreign Policy* Ostpolitik determines West German relations with the USSR and also plays a major role in the Federal Republic's relations with the United States. The minimal Soviet goal is to maintain West Germany's interest in continuing bilateral détente with the USSR, and there is little doubt that the FRG will maintain its commitment to Ostpolitik.

The basic reason for the West German interest in détente stems from its unique position. To paraphrase Freud, geography is destiny. Germany is a divided nation, and the USSR controls the other Germany. West Germany has Soviet troops on its borders and is the West European nation most exposed to Soviet power. Any government in Bonn must have a continuing interest in maintaining a dialogue with the USSR and in attempting to ameliorate conditions within the GDR.

The first and most important pillar of German Ostpolitik is Bonn's *Deutschlandpolitik*. Intra-German relations were the prism through which much of the negotiations with the USSR and Eastern Europe were viewed, and they continue to determine Germany's Ostpolitik.

Chancellor Helmut Schmidt and his government do not believe that reunification is imminent, nor do West Germans believe that the USSR (not to mention Poland or France) would look on such a prospect with equanimity. But the point is that the constant search for maintaining and improving intra-German relations will be a focal concern of any German government in the 1980s.

There are costs to the USSR associated with this intra-German rapprochement. In some ways it has destabilized East German society by making it more open to West German influence. However, the advantage of this continuing West German interest in East Germany is that it enables the USSR to exercise leverage over the FRG because Moscow can control the pace of intra-German relations.

The second pillar of West German Ostpolitik, which is connected to the first, is the desire to maintain and strengthen ties between West Berlin and Bonn. Most Western officials agree that Berlin has been an "oasis of détente" since the invasion of Afghanistan, showing that the Soviets can use Berlin as a convenient point of pressure or reward.

The third pillar of German Ostpolitik is the bilateral relationship with the USSR. Germany has not gained much directly from this relationship. The Soviet Union is far more important for the FRG indirectly because of its control over the GDR and over Berlin. However, one direct benefit of bilateral détente has been the increased emigration of ethnic Germans from the USSR.

The fourth and final pillar of Ostpolitik is economic relations. West German–Soviet trade has increased eightfold since 1969. Trade with the USSR forms only 2.2% of total German trade, but for certain industries— particularly the Ruhr steel industry—it is disproportionately important. Mannessmann, for instance, exports 60% of its large-diameter pipe output to the USSR. About 100,000 West Germans are employed in trade with the Soviet Union. The Germans have been unwilling for both economic and political reasons to participate in trade sanctions against the USSR following the invasion of Afghanistan and the imposition of martial law in Poland, as their support of the Urengoi pipeline project shows. They reject the use of negative economic levers—particularly sanctions—against the USSR. This is partly a result of German historical experience, which suggests that the USSR is unlikely to alter its political behavior on significant issues in response to economic pressure.[2] The Germans are more amenable to the idea of trade carrots—using eco- nomic inducements to modify Soviet behavior on more marginal hu- manitarian issues, such as emigration—but they remain skeptical about the value of linking politics and economics, and this view is likely to persist in the 1980s.

Is there any possibility that Germany will reorient its Ostpolitik? It seems unlikely, unless there is a drastic change in the international system. The optimistic hope of *Wandel Durch Annaeherung* (change through rapprochement) has clearly not materialized. There has been East–West rapprochement, but no real change in the nature of Soviet control over its empire. German unity is no nearer now than it was 10 years ago. There is a consensus within West Germany that détente must continue because Germany is divided. The muted reaction to the imposition of martial law in Poland indicates that popular support for détente remains, even though there has been some disillusionment in recent months. As long as the Soviet Union occupies part of Germany, the FRG's room for maneuver is limited, and it will continue to seek accommodation with the USSR. There will be no significant new avenues for Soviet influence over German Ostpolitik in the next few years; but there is unlikely to be any significant diminution of the German commitment to détente.

"The Federal Republic," as Chancellor Schmidt reminded the nation in an address last year, "belongs to the West. Without the United States of America there is no security in Europe. Next to the Atlantic alliance the European Community remains a pillar of our policy."[3] The USSR realizes this fact of international life and admits that "the FRG's orientation on the United States as its 'main ally,' just as participation in NATO's military organization remains unchanged, of course."[4] The Federal Republic's Westpolitik is important to the USSR on several counts.

Through its role in NATO and its close ties to the United States, West Germany has become a significant target for the USSR. Yet Soviet policy toward Germany's Westpolitik has always been two-faced. On the one hand, the Soviet Union seeks to aid and abet conflicts between Bonn and Washington, and constantly reminds West Germany that the aggressive designs of the United States are not in its ultimate interest. On the other hand, the USSR seeks to use West Germany to influence U.S. policy positively, particularly on arms-control issues. Moscow, therefore, has some interest in closer U.S.–West German ties.

U.S.–German relations will continue to experience problems in the next few years over a range of political, economic, and military issues; however, it is unlikely that these chronic strains will offer the USSR any major opportunities for increased influence. Indeed, it is possible that a future Christian Democratic government might seek improved ties with the United States, and that relations between the two countries might well become somewhat less discordant.

*Domestic Politics—The Peace Movement* The domestic situation in Germany may well become more volatile in the next few years, affording new opportunities to the Soviet Union. The Federal Republic is in a transition period. The postwar economic giant has, for the first time, experienced a serious economic challenge to its stability, with rising unemployment rates. If these economic difficulties persist, then there is the question of whether the young German democracy can survive this challenge.

In the past few years, a heterogeneous coalition of antiestablishment groups has found one issue on which to unite: the question of intermediate-range nuclear force modernization. The peace movement has recently mushroomed in West Germany and is unlikely to be ephemeral. Moreover, the peace movement encompasses a number of issues and ideas that go beyond the narrow question of stationing a few hundred Pershing II and cruise missiles in Germany. This makes it a particularly interesting target for Soviet short-term and longer-term goals.

The German peace movement is an amorphous amalgam of left-wing political groups, environmentalists, Protestant church members, and Communist party members. It can mobilize hundreds of thousands of demonstrators. The "Krefeld Appeal," sponsored by former Bundeswehr General Kurt Bastian and others, calling for a reversal of the 1979 NATO decision to modernize forces and negotiate with the USSR at the same time, has collected over two million signatures.

The peace movement argues that a major new weapons escalation is underway; that this makes nuclear war more likely; that the United States is trying to recover nuclear superiority; that the United States and the Soviet Union want to fight a limited nuclear war in Europe while maintaining themselves as nuclear sanctuaries; and that the United States is a greater danger to world peace than is the USSR. This tendency seems to have been unaffected by the imposition of martial law in Poland.[5]

The peace movement does not represent a majority of the German population, but it contains an active, vocal minority. Regardless of whether the missiles are eventually deployed, in the longer run the USSR may reap considerable gains from its current support of the peace movement. Many of the movement's members are young, and some may become politically influential. It is impossible to estimate the impact of the current peace movement on the future German leadership, but the USSR definitely views the movement as a form of investment capital for the future.

Although the immediate focus of the movement is the missile issue, the deeper problem fueling it is the question of national identity. What does it mean to be a German? Why should Germany be allied with the United States? Why should it continue to pursue the "materialistic, bourgeois policies" of the economic miracle? These are issues being debated and they invoke a fundamental questioning of West Germany's postwar orientation.

The USSR may have ample reason for welcoming this questioning of the West German identity and the potential instability it implies. If one traditional Russian fear is of a strong Germany, then a Federal Republic plagued by a fundamental challenge to its Western orientation may well be desirable. If the USSR fears a cohesive Western Europe, then the more instability, the better. However, the questioning of national identity in West Germany inevitably has repercussions in East Germany. One of the prices that Moscow has paid for détente is greater penetration of East German society by West Germany. There are indications that a peace movement is growing in the GDR. This movement is not part of the Soviet-sponsored anti-U.S. campaign; rather it criticizes Soviet, as well as U.S., nuclear policies. The challenge for the USSR will be to manipulate instability in West Germany to its maximum advantage while minimizing the effects of this instability on the GDR.

As long as the division of Germany remains a focus of West German domestic politics, the opportunities and challenges for Soviet policy will remain.

France    *Foreign Policy* The USSR has always had fewer means of influencing France than it has in its relations with Germany. France is not a divided country, and its historical traditions and postwar goals have made it relatively impervious to Soviet influence; although it has certainly used relations with the USSR for its own ends. It is not dependent on Soviet goodwill as is the Federal Republic and therefore the quality of Franco–Soviet relations and the importance of French domestic and foreign policies are of a different order of magnitude compared to West Germany's.

Both the USSR and France in the past valued their relationship for its effects on their relations with other countries. DeGaulle used his détente policy as part of his dealings with Germany and the United States. The Soviets saw France under de Gaulle as their best means for eroding the Atlantic partnership, isolating the Germans, and impeding Western European integration.

Since de Gaulle's retirement, Franco–Soviet détente has fluctuated. Georges Pompidou and Valéry Giscard d'Estaing both began to distance themselves from the more blatantly anti-American aspects of Gaullism, and Giscard brought France into closer military cooperation with NATO by permitting French participation in NATO naval exercises and other cooperative ventures sponsored by NATO's Eurogroup. Nevertheless, Giscard retained an ongoing interest in détente, and it was clear in the 1981 elections that the USSR favored him. He made a point of continuing the dialogue with Moscow after the Soviet invasion of Afghanistan by meeting with Brezhnev in Warsaw in 1980.

Since his election, President Mitterrand has been far more critical of the USSR than his predecessors. This may partly be to counterbalance the presence of Communists in his cabinet. He has downgraded Franco–Soviet ties, endorsed the NATO two-track decision (although France, of course, will not have to take any of the missiles), and has announced increases in defense spending. Moreover, France has held the USSR responsible for the imposition of martial law in Poland.

Nevertheless, the Franco–Soviet relationship has not been entirely ruptured. In the economic sphere, ties have continued to expand. France has refused to cease subsidizing credits to the USSR and has defied the American sanctions aimed at halting the construction of the West Siberian pipeline.

It is too early to predict whether Mitterrand's harsher political stance toward the USSR represents a significant departure from the Gaullist détente of his predecessors, or whether it is a tactic that may alter with time.

Prior to the French rejection of U.S. pipeline sanctions, Franco–American relations had improved, largely because of Mitterrand's tough stance toward the USSR. Yet, except for their common assessment of the Soviet military threat, the two sides are divided on most other issues, particularly the Third World. It is a *mariage de raison* rather than a *mariage d'amour*, and one that may come apart.[6]

*Domestic Politics* French society is currently more stable and less receptive to Soviet propaganda than is West German society. Perhaps the most vivid illustration is that, in France, the mass demonstrations have recently been against martial law in Poland and not against the NATO modernization decision. France, unlike Germany, does not have a sizable peace movement.

The major domestic challenge facing France is economic, and here the USSR has some influence through the Communists. After a period of mutual recrimination in the 1970s, the French Communist party (PCF) moderated its criticisms and appeared to have returned to the Soviet fold. Recent Soviet articles praise the PCF's support for "internationalism" (i.e., Soviet foreign policy).[7] The PCF endorsed both the invasion of Afghanistan and the imposition of martial law in Poland.

Mitterrand's inclusion of Communists in his government reflects the Socialists' strength and the Communists' weakness. He took the PCF into the cabinet in order to assure trade union compliance with his economic policies, but he gave it minor positions—transport, health, the civil service, and vocational training. So far, his strategy has paid off. The PCF may, however, cease to be docile if Mitterrand's economic policies run into trouble and there is a clash with the unions. In an economic crisis the PCF might possibly leave the government to give its full support to the Communist-dominated CGT trade union. Ironically the PCF and USSR might have more influence over French society if the Communists were outside the government and they could disrupt the system more freely.

The prospects for significant Soviet influence in France over the next few years are relatively small. The best that the USSR can expect will be continued French interest in the practical aspects of détente, such as trade, despite harsher anti-Soviet rhetoric and increased clashes with Washington.

Britain    The United Kingdom has played a less important part in Soviet policy toward Western Europe than has either Germany or France, because its own foreign policy role has been less distinctive from Moscow's point of view than either of these two continental powers and because its international power is on the wane. Britain does not have the same significance for Moscow as does the FRG, for obvious geographical and political reasons. Moreover, unlike France, it has not sought to play a more autonomous role between the two superpowers. On the contrary, it is far more firmly identified with the United States than is either of its major continental neighbors, and it has emphasized transatlantic relations as the cornerstone of its policy. In theory, the USSR should be interested in Britain's close links to the U.S. because of London's potential influence on Washington's East–West policy. In practice, however, under the government of Conservative Prime Minister Margaret Thatcher—and even before—the United Kingdom has followed and supported U.S. policy toward the USSR (although it has disagreed with Washington over East–West trade) rather than seeking to determine it. Britain has conceived its function as that of alliance management and multilateral cooperation in East–West relations rather than formulation of a separate policy toward the USSR.

However, Britain has traditionally separated the political and economic aspects of its relations with the USSR, and it remains interested in expanding East–West trade, despite its harsher political stance toward the USSR under the conservatives. Indeed, the Soviets have manipulated this British interest in trade relations to punish the British for their political actions, particularly the expulsion of diplomats. For instance, after Prime Minister Wilson established a £950 million credit line with the USSR in an effort to improve the U.K.'s trade balance with the Soviet Union, Moscow showed little interest in drawing on the credits, and Britain continues to run a sizable deficit with the USSR.

The Soviet Union has, moreover, benefited from the United Kingdom's interest in selling equipment for the West Siberian natural gas pipeline and its adamant refusal to comply with U.S. extraterritorial sanctions. Indeed, after these American sanctions were imposed, the secretary of state for trade described them as "unacceptable" and issued an order to certain companies forbidding them to comply with the U.S. embargo. Thus, the USSR will be able to count on Britain's interest in expanded East–West economic relations for the foreseeable future, irrespective of which party is in power. Britain, like France, Germany, or Italy, favors this trade for economic reasons, particularly in a time of record unemployment and recession.

Although the British government will offer few opportunities for Soviet influence for some time to come, domestic developments in Britain are potentially of great interest to the Kremlin for two reasons: the shift to the left in the Labour party and the growing antinuclear movement in the United Kingdom. In the short run, therefore, the prospects for Soviet influence on British government policies are at best highly limited. In the long run, the possibility of Britain's pursuing policies that are more congenial to the USSR are somewhat brighter. However, as long as the United Kingdom remains firmly in the NATO alliance, the potential for Soviet gains will be restricted.

Italy   Italy is far less important to the USSR than is either the FRG or France, in foreign policy terms. However, the domestic situation in Italy may ultimately be of greater interest to the USSR in the coming years, particularly if the Communists continue to receive a sizable share of the vote.

In the late 1970s there was concern in the West that the Italian Communist party (PCI) might be taken into government. Since then, its fortunes have declined and in the last election it received 30.4% of the vote, as opposed to 34.4% in 1976. Nevertheless, it is not impossible that the PCI might one day come into a government coalition. The key question is what kind of influence the USSR might have over the PCI in the future.

As the largest Western Communist party with 1.7 million members, the PCI has always been of interest to the Soviet Union. Despite the party's condemnation of the Soviet invasion of Czechoslovakia, and its periodic criticism of Soviet policies in the 1970s, Soviet attacks on the PCI were comparatively mild. However, polemics have been escalating since the invasion of Afghanistan. After the imposition of martial law in Poland, the PCI threw off all restraints, explicitly accused the USSR of having a repressive foreign policy, and called for a European alternative to Soviet-style socialism. The USSR responded with a fierce attack in *Pravda*, accusing the PCI leadership of "direct aid to imperialism."[8] The significant question is whether the USSR would seriously consider splitting the PCI, as it is estimated that about 10% of its membership is pro-Soviet and another 30% would prefer a more "communist" leadership. At the moment, it appears that the USSR wants to avoid a formal break with the PCI because of the repercussions in its relations with other parties. It is more likely that the PCI leadership may contemplate some form of a de facto break with the USSR as this would undoubtedly enhance its electoral chances.

For the foreseeable future, relations between the PCI and USSR will remain extremely strained, but will probably not be formally broken. Meanwhile the PCI's role in promoting East–West trade will continue, as will Soviet attempts to win over Communist sympathizers. However, the USSR's ability to influence Italian politics will be limited by an unfavorable image in large segments of the Communist and non-Communist population.

## The European Community

The USSR has always had ambivalent, mainly negative, attitudes toward the European Community (EC). For many years, Soviet writers insisted that the attempt at European integration would fail, and they attacked the EC consistently. When it became apparent that the EC would not wither away, the USSR reluctantly toned down its rhetoric, and in 1972 Brezhnev publicly acknowledged its existence. Since then, the USSR has recognized the EC *de facto* by negotiating with it over fishing rights, but it still does not recognize it *de jure*.

The Soviet Union continues to pursue a contradictory policy toward the EC. On the one hand, it welcomes the "contradictions" between the United States and its European allies brought about by closer economic and political cooperation within Europe. On the other hand, the USSR fears the implications of any viable European integration, because this would diminish the Kremlin's ability to play one European country off against another. Moreover, by condemning the idea of West European integration, the Soviet Union detracts from the credibility of its argument in favor of greater East European integration. Yet a viable West European integration independent of U.S. control might also act as an unwelcome precedent for Eastern Europe. Given all of these contradictions, the ideal Soviet goal in Western Europe would be for the EC to continue to limp along and remain a source of problems for the United States as well of difficulties between individual member countries. In this way, true West European political integration would never be achieved.

For the foreseeable future, it does not appear that the Soviet Union will have to be seriously concerned about a more successful European integration. The EC's problems can only be summarized here, but they include financial disagreements, especially over individual members' contributions to the community budget; problems caused by the enlargement of the EC when Spain and Portugal join in 1984; the question of continuing British membership; and finally the difficulties of greater coordination in the political and security fields through the mechanism of European political cooperation.

The European Community remains in disarray. It will probably continue to survive *faute de mieux*, because a breakup of the EC could have several negative consequences. First, living standards would fall with the restoration of trade barriers; second, a breakup of the EC could undermine further the cohesion of the Atlantic alliance and could drive nations, such as Holland or Denmark, into nonalignment. Third, the desire to join the EC has had a stabilizing influence on the infant democracies in Spain and Portugal, and the demise of the EC might facilitate further military coups. In order to prevent disintegration of the EC, a more viable system for budget sharing may have to be introduced. Greater political cooperation may have to be encouraged, as well as more viable economic integration.[9]

Unless there is a major change in the international situation, all of these attempts at greater integration will prove problematic although not impossible. There is an asymmetry in the degree of commitment to the community, both financial and political, among its members, and this lack of balance will inevitably complicate further prospects for integration. From the Kremlin's point of view, there may be relatively little to worry about vis-à-vis the European Community in the 1980s.

East–West Trade    In the past decade, Western Europe's economic importance for the USSR has increased considerably. After a brief political honeymoon with the United States in the early 1970s, U.S.–Soviet relations soured, and Kissinger's grand design of entwining the Soviet Union in a web of economic and political interdependencies never materialized. Since the mid-1970s, the USSR has focused its attention on West European trade and has not been disappointed with the results.

There are three reasons for Soviet interest in trade with Western Europe, and these will continue to be important in the 1980s. The USSR is interested in importing equipment and technology from Western Europe to build up its economic infrastructure. It does not necessarily desire "state of the art" technology, because its economic system is unable to absorb and diffuse much of this technology efficiently. However, it is interested in standard equipment—such as pipe, pipelayers, and compressors for natural gas pipelines. There is considerable debate in the West over how important the contribution of Western technology is to Soviet economic development and how much Western technology imports strengthen the Soviet military-industrial complex. The Soviets provide little conclusive statistical evidence to resolve this discussion. Whatever the precise numbers, it is indisputable that imports of Western equipment ease the problems caused by the unwieldy innovation-averse, Stalinist economic system and lighten the trade-offs between guns and butter.

The USSR has also become increasingly interested in the export side of East–West trade, because of its growing hard-currency shortage. In the 1970s, energy exports became the most promising hard-currency earner for the Kremlin. At present, energy exports account for 73% of Soviet hard-currency earnings in the developed West, and oil for 55% of those earnings. The USSR will earn about $17 billion from energy exports to the West in 1982. As Soviet oil resources decline, natural gas export earnings will largely replace oil income. However, as energy and gold prices continue to fall, the USSR will find it increasingly difficult to finance its purchases of West European goods. Hence its continued interest in credits, to assist its ability to import.

Third, the Soviet Union clearly has a political interest in trade with Western Europe. Innumerable Soviet articles stress the dialectical interconnection between East–West trade and political détente. Whether or not the Soviet leaders really believe that trade promotes better political relations, the Soviet Union has correctly calculated that it can foster an influential East–West trade export lobby in various European countries that will pressure governments to maintain trade with the USSR. Western Europe is trade dependent with exports contributing as much as 30% of some countries' gross national product. The Kremlin may also have calculated that, by maintaining and possibly increasing West European dependence on Soviet energy imports, the USSR may eventually gain a useful lever in dealings with the West.

The construction of one or two natural gas export pipelines will not solve the problems of the Soviet economy. Trade with Western Europe may prevent negative economic growth rates, but it cannot save the Soviet economy from further difficulties. Growth rates have steadily been declining for the last decade, and will continue to do so in the 1980s. It will be hard enough for the USSR to maintain its military spending targets, and it is doubtful that it will be able to expand its purchases of Western goods. Nevertheless, even if the economic prospects themselves are dim, the West European commitment to East–West trade will remain, and will give the USSR some room for maneuver in its dealing with the NATO alliance.

Conclusions   The Kremlin's ability to realize its five major goals in Western Europe will remain limited. The German problem will continue to be the focus of Soviet concern in Europe. Both the West Germans and the Soviets will remain committed to the status quo, although both will strive for advances. For the Soviets, this would mean greater FRG distancing from the United States. For the West Germans, it would mean closer ties to the GDR while remaining firmly within the Atlantic alliance.

As long as West Germany can meet its current domestic challenges and preserve its commitment to Western democracy, the possibilities for greater Soviet influence will be circumscribed. The USSR will not be able to "Finlandize" or neutralize the FRG in the foreseeable future. However, it will be able to fuel opposition movements inside West German society by presenting itself as a peace-loving state and by reminding the West Germans of the negative consequences for their national unity of following the U.S. line too closely. The USSR will be limited in the degree to which it can woo the population of the Federal Republic by its awareness of the interconnection between protest movements in West Germany and greater unrest in East Germany.

The prospects for greater Atlantic alliance cohesion in the 1980s are not great, and friction between the United States and its partners will continue. The crises in Poland and Afghanistan have not brought the allies close together; they have indeed sharpened the differences between them. Nevertheless, despite the chronic difficulties of managing an alliance of democratic states, both the United States and Western Europe realize that their common interests outweigh their differences. There will be no major break in the alliance, although conflict over nuclear strategy, over how to deal with the USSR, and over East–West trade and technology transfer will persist.

The USSR will indirectly benefit from these strains, particularly in the economic field, but there is a limit to how far it can turn these Western quarrels to its own advantage. Disagreements with the United States do not automatically translate in most West European capitals into closer ties with the Soviet Union.

Problems with the United States are likely to intensify discussion of the need for greater West European unity, but it is doubtful that any significant progress will be made in that direction in the next few years. The European Community will not disintegrate but will be plagued by problems over budgetary allocations, enlargement, and general political questions of making concessions on sovereignty. The great hopes for European unity have obviously faded; but most EC members recognize the necessity for some form of coordination, even one that falls short of true integration. If relations with the United States deteriorate, this may revive some of the momentum toward unity.

The prospects for Communists holding significant government positions in future European cabinets are also not great. The French Communists are in the government precisely because the Socialists could govern without them, but want their assistance for France's economic programs. However, the PCF's electoral fortunes are declining. The polemics between the PCI and Moscow will continue and will at a minimum damage the USSR's image in Western Europe. They may even encourage East European dissidents striving to legitimize a non-Soviet socialist society. Moreover, as the older generation of Communists disappears from the scene, and younger members with little memory of the war gain positions of influence within the West European parties, it is less likely that the USSR will be able to create pro-Soviet Communist factions. Some parts of the PCI are not very different from left-wing members of the German Social Democratic party, and this process of convergence may continue. Whatever happens, communism is not the wave of the future in Western Europe.

On the economic front, energy is the most promising area for East–West trade in the 1980s. The Soviet Union at present appears a better credit risk than most of its allies, but to the extent that it is ultimately responsible for their debts, its attractiveness as a business partner may well diminish. Even if East–West trade does decline in the 1980s, the Europeans will remain unwilling to use this trade as a political lever.

The scenario for the Kremlin is, therefore, mixed. Opportunities to divide and influence Western Europe will remain, but the Soviet Union will come no nearer to controlling Western Europe than it does now.

## Notes

[1]See Angela Stent, "The U.S.S.R. and Germany," *Problems of Communism*, September–October 1981, pp. 1–24.

[2]Angela Stent, *From Embargo to Ostpolitik: The Political Economy of West German–Soviet Relations, 1955–1980* (New York: Cambridge University Press, 1982).

[3]"Erklaerung der Bundesregierung zur Lage der Nation," *Deutschland Archiv*, no. 5, 1981. p. 535.

[4]V. Mikhailov, "The FRG and Peace in Europe," *International Affairs* (Moscow) January 1982, p. 11.

[5]William E. Griffith, "Bonn and Washington: From Deterioration to Crisis?" *Orbis*, vol. 26, no. 1, Spring 1982, pp. 117–133.

[6]Pierre Lellouche, "The Odd Couple," *AEI Foreign Policy and Defense Review*, vol. 4, no. 1, 1982, p. 9.

[7]E.A. Arsenev, "B Avangarde Borby Frantsuskikh Trudiashchikhsia" ["In the vanguard of the French workers' struggle"] *Rabochii Klass i Sovremenny Mir*, no. 1, 1981, pp. 135–149.

[8]*Pravda*, April 24, 1982.

[9]*The Economist*, November 28, 1981.

# 26

## ROBBIN F. LAIRD

## *Soviet Nuclear Weapons in Europe**

There has rarely been a crisis in East–West relations more analyzed or debated than the NATO decision to deploy new medium-range American nuclear missiles in Europe. In December 1979 NATO agreed to the U.S. deployment of 108 Pershing II missiles and 464 ground-launched cruise missiles (GLCMs) in Europe. Scheduled deployment began in November 1983 to be completed by 1988. The systems are under American control, although located on NATO European territory.

At the time of the public announcement of the decision, Britain, West Germany, and Italy committed themselves to the deployment of the new missiles. Britain agreed to the basing of 160 GLCMs, West Germany to 108 Pershing IIs and 96 GLCMs, and Italy to 112 GLCMs. In principle, the Netherlands and Belgium agreed with the deployment but did not publicly commit themselves to basing these missiles on their territory.

NATO's December 1979 decision also entailed a commitment to try to negotiate with the Soviets in order to stabilize the theater nuclear balance. From NATO's standpoint, the main negotiating objective would be to lower the level of deployment of SS-20s and to ensure complete elimination of the SS-4s and SS-5s. The West would use the Pershing IIs and GLCMs, in part, as bargaining chips to induce the Soviets to negotiate.

The Western analytical literature has dealt with virtually all dimensions of the so-called Euromissile crisis. Some analysts have focused

*Reprinted by permission of the author and publisher from Robbin F. Laird, *France, the Soviet Union, and the Nuclear Weapons Issue* (Boulder, Colo: Westview Press, 1985), pp. 1–6, 29–43. The views expressed in this chapter are the author's and do not necessarily reflect those of the Institute for Defense Analyses or the U.S. Department of Defense. Copyright 1985 by Westview Press.

primarily on the West–West dimension of the Euromissile issue.[1] Others have focused on the U.S.–Soviet competition in intermediate nuclear weapons.[2] Still others have analyzed Soviet motivations and concerns evident in the crisis.[3]

The underlying argument of this essay is that Soviet behavior in the Euromissile crisis, in particular, and on the question of the enhancement of Western nuclear capability in Western Europe, in general, is motivated by concern that a stronger Western Europe, more independent and more capable of defending itself, might well be emerging. The Soviets hope to promote or, at least, to contribute to a crisis of statecraft in the West and thereby to impede the development among the Western powers of a more "mature" partnership between Western Europe and the U.S. The Soviets hope to contribute to the decline of Atlanticism without encouraging the further development of West European cooperation in economic, political, and military areas. The Soviets are especially concerned to impede the emergence of a better division of labor between Western Europe and the U.S. in the security area, which would allow the Americans to confront the Soviet Union more effectively within Europe and outside of Europe.

The Soviets are having to come to terms with an increasingly assertive Western Europe. Especially significant to the Soviets is the need to influence the shape and direction of West European foreign policy as the West struggles to define its policy in East–West relations. The increased assertiveness of Western Europe provides the Soviets with opportunities to undercut American influence in Western Europe and to try to hinder the development of various kinds of Western relationships which the Soviets find damaging to their interests. The Soviet objective is to reduce the room for maneuver or the margins of permissible error in Western security policies.

This chapter describes and analyzes the military and political roles of Soviet nuclear weapons in Europe. Paradoxically, the deployment of new-generation Soviet nuclear weapons strengthens the ability of the Soviets to conduct conventional military operations in Europe. By deploying new nuclear systems more capable of surviving an extended period of conventional warfare, the Soviets can more confidently prepare to wage an all-conventional campaign. The new Western Eurostrategic systems are an important threat to the viability of the Soviets' all-conventional option and complicate their attempt to exercise escalation dominance. The Soviets had hoped to reduce the Western threat by political bluster and arms diplomacy.

Politically, the superiority of Soviet theater nuclear systems (in the context of U.S.–Soviet parity in intercontinental nuclear systems) has been useful in increasing political tensions in the Western alliance. The Soviets have sought simultaneously to decouple Western Europe from the U.S. and to discourage West European military integration, especially the development of West European nuclear capabilities. The deployment of the new Western Eurostrategic systems tends to undercut these twin Soviet goals. Coupling will be increased and French and British nuclear capability enhanced as modernization proceeds.

The Military
Role of
Soviet
Nuclear
Weapons
in Europe

The basis for the exercise of political influence by the Soviet Union in Western Europe has been its military power. As R. A. Mason has noted, "since 1945 the Soviet Union has been in no position to exert economic pressure and any spread of Marxist–Leninist ideology has taken place despite its example rather than in its emulation. Apart from perennial encouragement of internal divisive and disruptive elements it is self-evident that military strength has been a primary instrument of Soviet diplomacy toward Western Europe."[4]

The political role of nuclear weapons in the Soviet exercise of influence is conditioned by perceptions of their military role. Hence, before analyzing the political role of Soviet nuclear weapons, it is necessary to identify how they might be used in a military confrontation in Europe.

As a European power, the Soviet Union would hope to fight a war against the West in such a way as to limit damage to the European landmass. The Soviets would like to be able to destroy Western forces in Europe to the extent necessary to ensure the capture of Europe, but without excessive damage to the Soviet Union, primarily, and Europe, secondarily.

The Soviets expect a war in Europe to involve substantial conventional operations.[5] Their key goal during conventional operations would be to degrade Western military forces in Europe, especially nuclear forces. The Soviets have become increasingly sensitive to the possibility and even the desirability of withholding nuclear strikes as long as possible or, in other words, of prolonging conventional operations in a war with the West as long as it is feasible to do so. As *Strategic Survey* has commented, "the presumed role of Soviet theater nuclear forces (TNF) would be to deter NATO from nuclear use while its nuclear capabilities were being degraded by Soviet conventional forces. Soviet TNF would thus be used for the preemption mission only when positive warning had been received that a strike by NATO's residual nuclear forces was imminent."[6] Thus, a key military objective of Soviet nuclear weapons in Europe is to make a conventional warfighting option more viable.

The Soviets deploy three basic types of nuclear weapon systems for potential use in a European nuclear war: short-, medium-, and long-range theater nuclear weapons. Soviet short-range, or battlefield, nuclear weapons are designed for use in relative proximity to Warsaw Pact forces. Soviet battlefield nuclear weapons consist of artillery pieces (especially 152-mm guns, both the self-propelled and towed versions) and short-range missile systems (the truck-mounted Frog and its replacement, the SS-21). Although NATO has a numerical advantage in battlefield nuclear weapons, the Warsaw Pact has significantly more short-range missile launchers. And as one authoritative Western source notes, "the greater range, and consequently the improved target coverage and survivability, of the Warsaw Pact's land-based missiles more than compensates for NATO's numerical advantage."[7]

Soviet medium-range theater nuclear systems consist of tactical aircraft that can carry conventional or nuclear armament and medium-range missile systems, the Scud B and the SS-12 Scaleboard (and their successors, the SS-23 and SS-22, respectively). The SS-22 and SS-23 have greater survivability, improved maneuver capabilities, and better reliability. These improved systems enhance the Soviets' conventional warfighting capabilities. As Stephen Meyer has noted, "These missiles might be called upon to survive an extended period of conventional warfare, throughout which enemy reconnaissance would try to locate them in preparation for attacks against them."[8]

The Soviets have steadily improved their capabilities to deliver nuclear strikes with their medium-range forces. This trend has been especially evident with regard to the enhancement over the past decade of the nuclear ground-attack capabilities of Soviet tactical aircraft. The most capable Soviet tactical aircraft, the Fencer and Flogger, were introduced in the mid-1970s and began to be deployed in significant numbers only in the late 1970s and early 1980s.

The Su-24 Fencer is the first modern Soviet aircraft specifically designed for ground attack. The Fencers have decisively strengthened the striking power of the Soviet air forces aimed at Western Europe. The Fencer can carry a large and diverse payload, including nuclear ordnance. It has the range to strike most significant military targets in Western Europe.

Although deployment of the Flogger did not begin until 1971, it is now the most widely deployed aircraft in Soviet Frontal Aviation. The Flogger D/J, or MiG-27, is a nuclear-capable, ground-attack aircraft that can attain high subsonic speed at low altitude.

Soviet long-range theater nuclear systems consist of a medium-range bomber force and an intermediate-range ballistic missile (IRBM) force. The medium-range bomber force consists of the Badger, Blinder, and Backfire aircraft. The Badger (2800-kilometer range) and the Blinder (3100-kilometer range) are older systems, but they are being upgraded to extend their service life. These older aircraft will eventually be replaced by the new Backfire bomber, first deployed in 1974. The range of the Backfire, at 4200 kilometers, is significantly greater than that of the Badger or Blinder. According to Strategic Survey: "This range allows it [the Backfire] to cover all of NATO Europe, as well as large areas of adjacent oceans, from bases in the USSR; perhaps equally important, it gives the aircraft increased loiter time at shorter range, and thus an enhanced capability to seek out mobile targets."[9]

The Soviet IRBM force consists of the older SS-4 and the new SS-20 medium-range missiles. The SS-4 missile uses liquid fuel and carries a single warhead. It is based in fixed silos and is potentially vulnerable to a preemptive NATO strike. The new SS-20 represents a significant improvement in every dimension. The SS-20 uses solid fuel, which allows it to be launched more quickly. The SS-20 is mobile, which makes it more capable of surviving preemptive strikes, and it carries three warheads, which significantly expands the target coverage of Soviet IRBMs. It is also much more accurate than the SS-4, giving it greater military utility.

The greater survivability of the SS-20 and the Soviets' ability to withhold Fencers and Backfires on their own territory allows the Soviets to more effectively ride out lengthy conventional operations. It has also provided them with improved nuclear warfighting capabilities. As Gregory Treverton has argued:

> The record of the last two decades clearly suggests that the USSR accords high priority to targeting Western Europe, probably a higher priority than most in the West have believed. The SS-20 underscores that priority. It demonstrates a traditional objective of Soviet efforts: to deter NATO's resort to nuclear weapons in war, to deter escalation if NATO goes nuclear and to have some chance of avoiding destruction on Soviet territory.[10]

If the Soviets thought in terms of conducting nuclear operations against NATO Europe, they would hope to draw a clear line between nuclear weapons used against European targets (East and West) and nuclear weapons used against Soviet or American territory. Several components in the Soviet theater nuclear arsenal would aid them in achieving this objective; others would not.

The short-range, or battlefield, nuclear weapons would provide the Soviets with a limited nuclear war option that would be compatible with limiting nuclear war to the European theater. Nuclear weapons would be limited in range, yield, and level of damage commensurate with the task of destroying NATO's military assets within Europe. From the standpoint of both warfighting and post-war recovery, limiting theater nuclear warfare to the level of battlefield weapons is desirable to the Soviets.

Use of either the medium- or long-range theater nuclear systems would involve serious possibilities of provoking at least selected nuclear strikes against Soviet territory. Nonetheless, the Soviets might try to generate a Eurostrategic option from their medium- and long-range theater nuclear systems. Such an option would involve a massive strike against NATO's theater nuclear assets, airfields, port facilities, and other military targets.

A Soviet Eurostrategic option might employ nuclear weapons located in Eastern Europe, perhaps supplemented by some long-range theater systems. The Scud-B and SS-23 missiles are already integrated into Soviet forces in Eastern Europe. The SS-12 Scaleboard and SS-22 are deployed on Soviet territory in peacetime but would move to Eastern Europe in wartime. The Warsaw Pact's nuclear-capable tactical aircraft could all operate from East European air bases. These medium-range systems would probably be supported by air strikes by Backfire, Badger, and Blinder bombers, which are normally based in the Soviet Union. If the Soviets were concerned to preserve fully the distinction between European and superpower territory, these systems could be deployed forward to Eastern Europe to provide more firepower for a Eurostrategic effort. One authoritative source notes that "SS-20 missiles are readily transportable and could be relocated westward at short notice."[11]

Such a Soviet Eurostrategic strike would be massive and designed to reduce significantly NATO's ability to continue the European war effort.

The Warsaw Pact ground forces would then attempt to move quickly to exploit the results of the theater nuclear strikes and to occupy Western Europe.

Above all, Soviet TNF systems are deployed to deter the West's use of nuclear weapons. The Soviets would hope to combine nuclear deterrence with the erosion of Western nuclear capability during the conventional campaign. As Stephen Meyer has articulated the role of TNFs in contemporary Soviet military strategy:

> Soviet nuclear forces are assigned the mission of deterring enemy TNF employment, while Soviet conventional forces go about the task of locating and destroying them. The main mission of reconnaissance and intelligence operations, then, is to locate enemy nuclear forces in the theatre. Soviet TNF will be husbanded in rear areas, safe from enemy conventional strikes, while Soviet *conventional* forces whittle down enemy TNF. Soviet expectations are that, as the war evolves, the theatre nuclear balance (i.e., the correlation of nuclear forces in the theatre) will move steadily in the direction of greater Soviet preponderance.[12]

Nonetheless, if widespread nuclear use in the theater became necessary, Soviet conventional forces are designed to operate under nuclear battlefield conditions (to the extent to which one can prepare for such an operation). As Jeffrey Record has noted:

> A significant feature of the Soviet tanks and armored fighting vehicles introduced into service during the past decade and a half is their incorporation of extensive CBR (chemical, biological and radiological) defensive systems that afford Soviet ground forces a far higher degree of survivability on a contaminated battlefield than even the latest vehicles fielded by NATO, most of which lack collective overpressure systems and adequate filtration devices. . . . That the Soviet aim has been to develop truly dual-purpose "conventional" forces—capable of operating in either a nuclear or non-nuclear environment—is also evident in an unparalleled regime of CBR warfare training and in a refusal to sacrifice investment in numbers to achieve qualitative improvements.[13]

In short, the Soviets would hope to deter NATO from using nuclear weapons by having a credible threat of retaliation. The Soviets would clearly wish to avoid exchanging intercontinental strategic nuclear strikes with the United States. They would hope that the strategic nuclear balance, which deters politically in peacetime, would deter the United States militarily in wartime from engaging in massive intercontinental strikes against Soviet territory. Eurostrategic weapons, especially the SS-20s, are useful militarily for deterring escalation to any nuclear level. They are, therefore, a significant component in the Soviets' effort to make a conventional warfighting option more viable.

In other words, the Soviets are hoping to raise the nuclear threshold to enhance their conventional military options in Europe. By enhanced conventional military power, the Soviets hope to increase their leverage over Western Europe. As R. A. Mason has argued:

Any reduction of dependence on nuclear weapons by NATO would replace one set of military problems by another and would pose complicated questions of defense appropriations to member nations. It might reduce the chances of the early use of nuclear weapons in a European conflict but would certainly facilitate the implementation of the Soviet Union's own military doctrine. It is probable, therefore, that the raising of the nuclear threshold, unless it were to be accompanied by Warsaw Pact conventional arms reduction, would strengthen the military element in Soviet policy toward Western Europe.[14]

The Political Role of Soviet Nuclear Weapons in Europe

Soviet European nuclear forces serve the political objective of exacerbating strains in U.S.–West European relations, besides contributing to any actual military effort. For the Soviets, achieving parity with the United States in intercontinental nuclear systems has helped undermine the American nuclear guarantee for Western Europe. A. F. Gorelova and Iu. P. Davydov have noted with favor the recognition by West Europeans that "after the loss by the U.S. of its 'nuclear superiority' in the context of 'nuclear parity' with the USSR, the reliability of the American security guarantee for Western Europe has declined."[15] The deployment of Soviet theater nuclear systems is designed in part to erode further the American security guarantee for Western Europe and thereby to weaken the political ties between Western Europe and the United States.

"Atlanticism," in the Soviet view, has allowed the United States to exercise considerable influence over political and economic developments within Western Europe. From the Soviet perspective, an Atlanticized Europe is one in which American definitions of Western security needs dominate Western Europe's security interests and political and economic relationships with the Soviet Union. Such an Atlanticized Europe was able to exist only under the specific conditions of absolute American predominance over Western Europe that existed in the late 1940s and early 1950s. As G. A. Vorontsov has noted, an Atlanticized Europe has rested upon "the military, economic and financial power of the United States, which guaranteed a commanding position in its relations with Western Europe."[16]

This type of Atlanticism has been seriously undercut by the changing balance of power (or, in Soviet terminology, the "shift in the correlation of forces") between the United States and Western Europe. The growth of West European economic power has led to the emergence of the West European "power center" in the capitalist world, a power center that has exercised growing assertiveness and even independence from the United States.[17]

In the Soviet view, "three centers of imperialism" have emerged, rather than a cohesive Western camp whose unity is enforced by American dominance.[18] The "correlation of forces" in the imperialist camp has shifted away from the United States in favor of Western

Europe and Japan. This redistribution of power has increased "interimperialist contradictions." As O. Bogdanov argued:

> With the change in the balance of strength between the chief centers of imperialism, the capitalist powers tended gradually to substitute "polycentrism" for "U.S.–centrism" in their economic and political lines. This involved abandoning the scheme of international economic relations resting on U.S. supremacy. U.S. economic and political overlordship clashed with the weakening of the U.S. position in the world capitalist economy. As a result, foreign economic relations tend increasingly to become an important area of interimperialist rivalry within the triangle of the U.S., the EEC, and Japan.[19]

The growing assertiveness of Western Europe limits the American ability to take unilateral actions to define Western interests. This limitation has, in turn, substantially undercut U.S. global flexibility. As Vorontsov added:

> Western Europe has now consolidated its economic weight and political influence to the extent that the United States cannot engage in any major actions in the international arena without its assistance and support. It is sufficient to recall Washington's persistent and extremely active endeavor to involve the West Europeans in "sanctions" against the USSR, the policy of confrontation with Iran, the plan for the creation of rapid deployment forces, and so forth.[20]

With the growing diversification of power in the Western world, American policymakers are trying to exercise leadership on the military front as a means of preserving U.S. political and economic dominance in the West. As the late N. N. Inozemtsev noted, an important aspect of the contemporary situation is that "the changes running against the United States in the economic and political positions in the leading West European countries and Japan have been taking place in the context of tremendous U.S. military superiority."[21] In other words, the United States is reduced to drawing upon its military dominance to protect its deteriorating position of leadership in the West. From a Soviet standpoint, NATO as an organization plays a major role in protecting American power in Western Europe and in limiting West European independence from U.S. security interests. As V. S. Shein underscored:

> Although U.S. economic, political, and even ideological positions in relations to Western Europe have become much weaker, particularly as a result of the development of West European integration, and now with the decline of American hegemony in the Atlantic world, NATO . . . has turned out to be the only instrument for imposing Washington's will on the states of Western Europe.[22]

The key lever through which the United States can exercise influence over NATO Europe is its nuclear weapons. As one group of Soviet analysts noted, "At the contemporary stage of the scientific–technological revolution in military affairs, the actual military potential of a given state depends primarily upon its possession or non-possession of nuclear weapons and the level of development of its nuclear-missile systems."[23] Given the overwhelming predominance of American nuclear arms within NATO, the United States is able to exercise a preponderant influence over NATO.

Nonetheless, the centrality of American nuclear weapons to NATO defense underscores a central contradiction between Western Europe and the United States. As the same group of Soviet analysts emphasized:

> The strategical calculations of the two centers of power make a strikingly different assessment of the character of a potential military conflict. In its endeavor to avoid destruction of its own territory the U.S. is oriented toward a limitation of operations to the European theater of action in the event of an armed conflict in this region, at least in its early stages. The West European military conceptions proceed from the necessity to ensure the broad participation of the U.S. in the conflict from the very moment of its inception. This diametrical opposition of their interests is breeding a chain reaction of fears in Western Europe and disagreements with the U.S. on such questions as the stationing of American troops in Western Europe, the reliability of the U.S.'s nuclear guarantees, the role of NATO outside of its geographical bounds, the possible involvement of Western Europe in the military undertakings of American global politics. . . .[24]

Soviet Eurostrategic capability contributes to precisely this contradiction of interests between Western Europe and the United States. Parity in intercontinental systems tends to deter the United States from using these systems to defend Western Europe and hence raises questions within Western Europe about the reliability of U.S. nuclear guarantees.

The modernization of Soviet Eurostrategic arms contributes to the Soviets' capability to conduct a nuclear war limited to Europe. But when the United States has tried to strengthen its European theater nuclear forces, the Soviets have stressed the dangerous quality of American "limited nuclear war" doctrines. They do this in part to exacerbate West–West tensions and to impede Western military development.

To the United States, the Soviets underscore the impossibility of a Eurostrategic war's being contained without escalation to intercontinental systems.[25] With such a claim the Soviets hope to convince the United States to cease developing theater nuclear forces with which to implement NATO's flexible response strategy.

To the West Europeans, the Soviets emphasize that U.S. preparation for, or emphasis upon, a limited nuclear war shows a lack of genuine American concern for West European security.[26] The Soviets thereby wish to convey the message that the United States is an offshore power not sharing the same security problems of the Soviet and West European "continental" powers.[27]

By pressuring both the American and European components of the alliance, the Soviets hope to obstruct the development of Western strategic power. The Soviets wish to slow the further development of a

Eurostrategic rung of the U.S. escalation ladder. Also, the Soviets wish to undercut the process of modernization of French and British nuclear forces.

Thus, the Eurostrategic problem is a deeply political one. The Soviets hope to increase their deterrent capability, to increase their leverage against Western Europe, and to obstruct Western strategic development by maintaining their Eurostrategic superiority in the context of intercontinental strategic parity. Colin Gray's characterization of the strategic arms race as being "about politics" could not be more aptly applied than to the political objectives served by Soviet Eurostrategic deployments.[28]

## The Impact of the Western Alliance's Eurostrategic Modernization

The opposition of the Soviet Union to the Western Alliance's Eurostrategic modernization is rooted in the negative effects of that modernization on the military and political roles of Soviet INF systems.[29] Militarily, the Soviets are concerned that the American, French, and British modernizations may so complicate Soviet military strategy that Western superiority can appear to be reestablished. Politically, the Soviets are concerned with the strengthening of U.S. ties to a Western Europe that will possess an enhanced independent nuclear capability as British and French forces are modernized.

The deployment of the new U.S. INF systems provides the Americans with a much more survivable nuclear force. The survivability of the new systems casts doubt on the Soviets' ability to preempt conventionally against them. The range and accuracy of the Pershing IIs and GLCMs provide the Americans with limited nuclear options, delivered from European territory, against Soviet command, control, and communications facilities.[30] Certainly, the Soviets acknowledge that the Americans believe they will have new options. As V. Nekrasov has argued:

> There is no doubt that the USA intends its missiles to be permanently stationed on this side of the Atlantic, for it sees the European continent as a theatre of possible hostilities lying close to the vital centres of the Soviet Union. The Pentagon believes it is a bridgehead that may witness the first exchange of nuclear strikes that would make the USSR capitulate, thus saving the USA from a crushing retaliatory blow by Soviet strategic forces.[31]

The French and British are also planning a significant modernization of their strategic nuclear forces, and the quantity and quality of these modernizations are significant. G. Seignious and J. Yates affirm: "New British and French nuclear forces will present the Soviet bloc with an entirely new situation . . . [for] Western Europe will soon possess a nuclear triad capable of escalating with the Soviets up to a devastating exchange level."[32] In particular, the growth of the arsenals of the independent nuclear powers in Western Europe presents the Soviets with alternative Western decision-making centers capable of inflicting severe damage on the Soviet Union. As Seignious and Yates have underscored:

> The real danger to the Soviet Union, however, is the vulnerability of its industries and population centers, the so-called soft targets. The destruction of just 34 refineries would halt all gas production in the Soviet Union. Eight well-placed warheads would curtail Soviet copper production. Almost all of the chemical industry would be destroyed in an attack on 25 cities, and the destruction of the city of Pavlodar would deny Moscow 65 percent of its aluminum output. In the eyes of the Kremlin leaders, each British and French SLBM-firing submarine will have, at the very minimum, the ability to destroy the Soviet copper, chemical, and gas-refining industries, as well as almost 70 percent of Soviet aluminum and oil production, while having several warheads each left over to attack Moscow, Murmansk, Leningrad, Volgograd, and the missile-testing center at Tyuratam.
>
> If Great Britain and France combined and coordinated their forces that are available at any given time, . . . they could . . . unquestionably destroy the Soviet Union as a superpower and probably as a viable country.[33]

The combined U.S., French, and British modernizations are significant militarily. From the Soviet point of view, the United States might be able to reestablish a semblance of strategic superiority by enhancing NATO's strategic nuclear capability in the European theater. The American INFs when joined with British and French strategic systems, even if numerically inferior to Soviet systems targeted against Western Europe, could still potentially lead to American strategic superiority, from the Soviet standpoint. If Moscow hopes to fight a conventional war in Europe, the British and French independent nuclear forces represent serious threats. If either a conventional or nuclear war is limited to the European theater, the discharge of American INFs and British and French nuclear weapons could inflict substantial damage on the USSR itself. In fact, the damage could be so great that Moscow would have to terminate the war to preserve what remained of its state and society. Such termination might occur without the use of American or Soviet intercontinental systems. American territory would remain intact. As a result, the Soviet Union might conclude that the greatest threat to the strategic balance involves changes in Western strategic capabilities in the European theater. Moscow might feel that derailing such changes by military deployments, arms control measures, and various political actions is a central priority in the 1980s and 1990s.

The Soviets will also have to contend with what they perceive to be the twin negative political effects of the Alliance's Eurostrategic modernization. On the one hand, the Americans are perceived to be using Euromissile deployments to bind Western Europe more closely to the United States. On the other hand, the potential for an independent West European strategic nuclear force is enhanced by the French and British modernizations.

The Soviets believe the Americans are trying to bind the West Europeans to U.S. interests by deploying Euromissiles. V. Baranovsky has articulated this Soviet perception as follows:

> Western Europe is generally aware of the fact that the course of strengthening the role of nuclear weapons in U.S. and NATO global and European strategy is viewed by Washington primarily as one of the most reliable methods of blocking the further development of centrifugal tendencies in U.S.–West European relations and in the North Atlantic Alliance. From time to time reports even get into the press that indisputably attest to the fact that all the clamor about the allies' confidence in the "nuclear guarantees" of their partner across the ocean are deliberately exaggerated first and foremost by the U.S. itself. The initial deployment of new American medium-range nuclear missile weapons in Western Europe is also aimed at cementing the NATO bloc and at binding its West European members even more to Washington's policy.[34]

There are forces in Western Europe that also consider the American Euromissiles to be instruments of coupling. According to V. Mikhnovich:

> Both France and England assume that the appearance of American first-strike weapons on European land will allow them to "bind" the U.S. strategic forces to the "defense" of their own interests. In this matter, "the preservation of the American nuclear deterrent potential and its steady modernization is, in our opinion, of critical importance," declared France's Minister of Foreign Affairs Claude Cheysson.[35]

There is little question that the Soviets oppose any coupling effect from the new U.S. missile deployments. What also concerns them is the possibility of the creation of a joint independent nuclear force in Western Europe under the aegis of Britain and France. The buildup of these two countries' nuclear potential is seen as a critical prerequisite for Western Europe's growing assertiveness within the Western Alliance.[36] The parallel British and French modernizations significantly enhance West European nuclear capability. Hence, the potential for a genuine European nuclear force is increasing.

What the Soviets would like to see is U.S.–West European nuclear decoupling, without the further development of Western Europe's own independent nuclear capability. As V. F. Davydov, in the most comprehensive Soviet analysis of the European nuclear force idea to date, articulated the Soviets' desired outcome:

> It appears that supplementing political detente with military detente would allow the United States the possibility of reducing the expenses of its involvement in the so-called "defense" of Western Europe; in turn, for the West European countries the processes of gradually abolishing the NATO structures formed during the "cold war" years would open up the way for decreased dependence on the U.S. without needing a sharp increase in military expenditures, including on nuclear forces, which

presupposes the redistribution of the "burden of responsibility" within NATO.[37]

Nonetheless, as William Garner has commented, the West European reaction to decoupling might be quite different. There might be "the acquisition by a confederation of West European powers of an independent nuclear force credible at all levels of combat. Thus, not only might a decoupled U.S. be less responsive to the Soviets, but a decoupled Europe might raise new threats fully equal to those they now perceive from the U.S. missiles."[38]

# Notes

[1]See, for example, William Hyland, "The Struggle for Europe: An American View," in *Nuclear Weapons in Europe*, ed. Andrew J. Pierre (New York: Council on Foreign Relations, 1984), pp. 15–44.

[2]See, for example, Jed C. Snyder, "European Security, East–West Policy, and the INF Debate," *Orbis* (Winter 1984), pp. 913–970.

[3]See, for example, William V. Garner, *Soviet Threat Perceptions of NATO's Eurostrategic Missiles* (Paris: The Atlantic Institute for International Affairs, 1983).

[4]R.A. Mason, "Military Strategy," in *Soviet Strategy toward Western Europe*, ed. Edwina Moreton and Gerald Segal (London: George Allen and Unwin, 1984), p. 166.

[5]The argument in this section is shaped by Phillip A. Petersen and Maj. John G. Hines, *The Soviet Conventional Offensive in Europe* (Washington, D.C.: Defense Intelligence Agency, 1983); and James McConnell, "Shifts in Soviet Views on the Proper Focus of Military Development," *World Politics*, April 1985, pp. 317–343.

[6]*Strategic Survey*, 1981–1982 (London: International Institute for Strategic Studies, 1982), p. 53.

[7]U.S. Department of Defense, *NATO and the Warsaw Pact* (Washington, D.C.: U.S. Government Printing Office, 1981), p. 46.

[8]Stephen Meyer, *Soviet Theatre Nuclear Forces*, part two, Adelphi Paper no. 188 (London: International Institute for Strategic Studies, 1984), p. 20.

[9]*Strategic Survey*, p. 51.

[10]Gregory Treverton, *Nuclear Weapons in Europe*, Adelphi Paper no. 168 (London: International Institute for Strategic Studies, 1981), p. 9.

[11]*NATO and the Warsaw Pact*, p. 45.

[12]Stephen Meyer, *Soviet Theatre Nuclear Forces*, part one, Adelphi Paper no. 187 (London: International Institute for Strategic Studies, 1984), p. 26, emphasis in original.

[13]Jeffrey Record, *NATO's Theater Nuclear Modernization Program* (Washington, D.C.: Institute for Foreign Policy Analysis, 1981), p. 52.

[14]Mason, "Military Strategy," pp. 194–195.

[15]Iu. P. Davydov, ed., *SShA-Zapadnaia Evropa: Partnerstvo i sopernichestvo* (Moscow: Nauka, 1978), p. 226.

[16]G.A. Vorontsov, *SShA i Zapadnaia Evropa: Novyi etap otnoshenii* (Moscow: Mezhdunarodnye otnosheniia, 1979), p. 11.

[17]See, for example, V. F. Davydov, T.V. Oberemko, and A. I. Utkin, *SShA i zapadnoevropeiskie "tsentry sily"* (Moscow: Nauka, 1978).

[18]V. M. Kudrov, "Tri tsentra imperializma: Tendentsii sootnosheniia sil," *SShA*, 1981, no. 10, pp. 15–25.

[19]O. Bogdanov, "Competition in the Capitalist World," *International Affairs* (1977), no. 4, p. 43.

[20]G. Vorontsov, "SShA i Zapadnaia Evropa v usloviiakh obostreniia mezhdunarodnoi obstanovki," *Mirovaia ekonomika i mezhdunarodnye otnosheniia* [hereinafter *Memo*] (1981), no. 11, p. 41.

[21]N. N. Inozemtsev, *Contemporary Capitalism: New Developments and Contradictions* (Moscow: Progress, 1974), p. 134.

[22]V. S. Shein, "SShA i NATO v kontse semidesiatykh," *SShA*, 1979, no. 6, p. 4.

[23]*Western Europe Today* (Moscow: Progress, 1980), pp. 160–161.

[24]*Ibid.*, p. 306.

[25]See, for example, the following: Maj. Gen. A. Slobodenko, "The Strategy of Nuclear Adventurism," *International Affairs* (1981), no. 1, pp. 26–33; A. Nikonov and R. Faramazian, "Opasnyi kurs nagnetaniia voennoi napriazhennosti," *Memo* (1981), no. 2, pp. 44–69.

[26]See, for example, the following: Iu. P. Davydov, "Razriadka, SShA i Zapadnaia Evropa," *SShA* (1979), no. 3, pp. 20–31; Iu. P. Davydov, "Kurs Vashingtona na napriazhennost' i Zapadnaia Evropa," *SShA* (1980), no. 10, pp. 31–42; Ia. Rakhmaninov, "For Peaceful and Fruitful Cooperation in Europe," *International Affairs* (1980), no. 7, pp. 3–9; V. Mikhailov, "The FRG and Peace in Europe," *International Affairs* (1982), no. 1, pp. 3–9.

[27]For the concept of the U.S. as an offshore power and a key component of Soviet strategy, see Uwe Nerlich, "Change in Europe: A Secular Trend?" *Daedalus* 110 (Winter 1981), pp. 71–103.

[28]Colin Gray, "The Arms Race Is about Politics," *Foreign Policy*, no. 9 (Winter 1972–1973), pp. 117–131.

[29]For an overview of Soviet views on the Eurostrategic problem, see Garner, *Soviet Threat Perceptions*.

[30]See Lt. Gen. D. Volkogonov, "Strategiia avantiurizma," *Zarubezhnoe voennoe obozrenie* (1984), no. 5, pp. 5–7.

[31]V. Nekrasov, "Realities of Modern Europe and 'Atlanticism'," *International Affairs* (1984), no. 5, p. 35.

[32]George M. Seignious II and Jonathan Paul Yates, "Europe's Nuclear Superpowers," *Foreign Policy*, no. 55 (Summer 1984), pp. 46–47.

[33]*Ibid.*, pp. 47–48.

[34]V. Baranovsky, "NATO: EES v politike imperializma," *Memo* (1984), no. 6, pp. 37–38.

[35]V. Mikhnovich, "Raschety i proschety," *Krasnaia zvezda*, June 14, 1984, p. 3.

[36]A. I. Utkin, "Vashington i problemy NATO," *SShA* (1983), no. 8, pp. 8–9.

[37]V. F. Davydov, "Diskussiia o evropeiskikh iadernykh silakh," *SShA* (1976), no. 3, pp. 71–72.

[38]Garner, *Soviet Threat Perceptions*, p. 91.

# 27

## JOHN P. HARDT
## KATE S. TOMLINSON

## Soviet Economic Policies in Western Europe*

**Overview** Two often conflicting tendencies have dominated Soviet policy toward Western Europe: the desire to wield political and ideological influence over a divided capitalist world and a need to draw upon the technological resources of the economically advanced Western countries. The interplay of these tendencies has formed Soviet policy toward Western Europe since the earliest days of the Soviet state. Divisions within the capitalist world present Soviet leaders with the opportunity to exert political and ideological influence over Western Europe. Thus, Soviet leaders have eagerly seized upon evidence of division within the West—either among the European countries or, particularly during the post-World War II era, between Western Europe and the United States. Efforts to enlarge or foster division within the West have been a prominent feature of Soviet foreign policy. Yet, at the same time, the Soviet Union has frequently sought expanded commercial relations with the West, particularly Western Europe, in order to advance its economic goals of modernization and growth. Soviet economic relations with Western Europe have not shown a steady progression, but have been marked by interruption and occasional equivocation. Discussions among the Soviet leadership on the risks and opportunities of expanded commercial relations with the West have tended to coincide with periods of division within the West. The continuation of

*Reprinted in revised form by permission of the author and publisher from *Soviet Policy toward Western Europe: Implications for the Atlantic Alliance*, ed. Herbert J. Ellison (Seattle: University of Washington Press, 1983), pp. 159–177, 190–201. The views are those of the authors, not necessarily those of the Congressional Research Service, the U.S. Congress, the U.S. International Trade Commission, or any other U.S. Government agencies. Copyright 1983 by the University of Washington Press.

détente and economic Ostpolitik in Soviet–West European relations during the 1980s sharply contrasts with the return to confrontation, tension, and trade restrictions in Soviet–American relations. Concurrently, the Soviet leadership's enthusiasm for technology transfer as a means of attaining growth and modernization may have cooled since its peak in the early 1970s.

Political factors dominate Soviet policy in the 1980s as in the past. During the post-Brezhnev years, however, issues of political economy such as commercial relations with Western Europe and alliance relations in Eastern Europe have also been high on the policy agenda. To be sure, when the Soviet leadership perceives threats to political or military security, national sovereignty, or systemic continuity, issues of political economy do not take precedence. During the 1970s, major threats to these values were not perceived, and the Soviet leaders felt able to concentrate on the needs of the economy and the agenda of political economy generally. The turn to the West for technology, grain, and credit was central to Moscow's policy of economic modernization.

In alliance relations, the Soviets sought to retain their hold over Eastern Europe by economic as well as military levers. In an era of détente, the Soviets gave the East European countries leeway to build their own economic bridges to West Europe and the United States. The Soviets hoped that the East Europeans could thereby foster economic modernization, consumer welfare, and political stability. An equally important reason for the leeway granted the East Europeans in their relations with the West was to reduce the drain on scarce Soviet energy and other raw materials.

With the continued division in the West on relations with the Soviet Union, the Soviet leaders have been tempted to exploit political divisions and move closer to an autarkic system. Reducing the level of interdependence with the West and increasing CMEA integration have always had an appeal for the Soviets. They could thereby reduce CMEA's dependency and vulnerable exposure to economic leverage by the West. But it is economically costly to reverse the trend toward overall East–West interdependence, and the Soviets may have been presented in the 1980s with the even more attractive option of pursuing a divided political and economic policy toward the West—continued détente and economic intercourse with Europe and a return to conflict and autarky in relations with the United States.

Changing Currents in Soviet–West European Economic Policy
In the early days of the Soviet state, the leadership saw the West as subject to escalating economic division and economic crises verging on collapse. In this apocalyptic vision it seemed that wartime division, fatigue, and economic weakness in the capitalist world had opened the path to the spread of the Bolshevik revolution to Western Europe—especially to Germany. Again, in the 1980s economic competition, economic crises, and differences in Western policies toward the East have

driven wedges in Western unity, especially between Western Europe and the United States.[1]

The themes of long-term Soviet policy have been to divide and weaken the West politically and to draw on the technological advances of the West: In 1917 conflicts dividing the West were seen as the way to the World Socialist Revolution, but by 1920 the goal of overcoming economic backwardness bound Moscow to the West. In the 1980s the opportunity to divide the NATO Alliance through the Peace Program and selective economic Westpolitik and to encourage a much-needed scientific–technological revolution with Western technology and credit was equally attractive to the Soviet Union.

There centrifugal political and centripedal economic forces have played across the history of Soviet policy in Europe for more than the six decades. The policies of the developed Western economies have alternatively fostered and impeded the success of these Soviet tendencies. Occasionally Western policies have been unified, but more often divided.

Europe has been a primary focus of Soviet foreign policy since the October Revolution. The United States has also played a critical role due to its technological prowess and acquisition of a leadership role in the Atlantic Alliance after World War II. From the Soviet point of view, the United States frequently acts as a European power in its role in NATO, CoCom, and other international organizations. Since the 1970s, however, the European countries have been playing more independent roles in East–West relations.

*The Stalinist System* In the pre-Five-Year-Plan period Western Europe, especially Germany, was to be the solution to both Soviet economic backwardness and political isolation—by revolution if the Communist "machine shop" of Germany could be added to the Soviet granary, or by trade as the two outcast nations joined in informal industrial and military cooperation. The aim of the modified autarky of the first Five-Year Plan (1928–1932) was to obtain critical technical imports to further industrialization. Trade missions preceded formal recognition as depression in the West made Soviet industrial import orders more desirable. With diplomatic recognition came further normalization of trade: tariff and credit privileges. Stalin, however, was chary about accepting normal Western commercial relations as he feared that interdependence in economic relations would lead to political dependence and vulnerability. His fears proved to have some basis as the German Reich used economic penetration to pave the way for later political and military control in Eastern Europe.

On the eve of World War II in 1938, Soviet bilateral ties with the Western countries were sharply reduced, although the special ties with Nazi Germany were temporarily deepened during the Nazi–Soviet Pact period.

With the wartime alliance Western, especially American military and industrial, aid became critical to Soviet survival. The wartime volume of Lend Lease was high but short lived.

Before the war's end the Soviet Union and the Western countries initiated a two-track policy leading toward the creation of global institutional interrelations. The political track continued to San Francisco and the establishment of the United Nations in 1945. The economic track, which was undertaken in a cooperative mode at Bretton Woods, was later derailed as the USSR chose not to join the IMF or World Bank or accept Marshall Plan aid.

Why Stalin renounced an active role in the postwar international economic system is not clear. Perhaps, as some Western analysts suggest, the war had left the Soviet economy so devastated that the Soviet Union could not hope to participate on an equal footing. Or, perhaps, as others suggest, Stalin did not see any advantage in participating in organizations that were likely to be dominated by and oriented toward the capitalist countries.[2]

Whatever the reason, Stalin rapidly returned the Soviet Union to the economic autarky of the 1930s. In the "two camps" speech of 1952 he justified the change of policy by describing the world as divided into two opposing systems—capitalist and socialist—between which only a minimum of economic interrelations were to be desired.[3] Concurrently, Stalin revived the totalitarian system of the 1930s, which had been relaxed during the war years, and sought to isolate Soviet citizens from all foreign influences. Many individuals who had come into contact with foreigners during the war were purged.

In the early 1950s less than 20% of Soviet trade was with noncommunist countries. Imports were limited to commodities needed to relieve short-term supply bottlenecks and were carefully balanced with exports to avoid indebtedness. Throughout the decade the East European and Chinese economies were tied to the Soviet economy through interlocking plans.

In turn, Western Europe adopted a policy of economic isolation from the Soviet Union in the wake of the 1948 U.S.–Soviet confrontation in Berlin. Its policy toward trade with the East paralleled that of the United States: a virtually complete embargo and economic warfare. Through CoCom, the informal export control system that began in 1950, the United States and the West European countries restricted all exports that could contribute to the East's military or economic performance. Slightly looser controls were applied to Yugoslavia, Romania, and Poland to encourage political independence from the Soviet Union. Tariffs on imports from the East were set high; and trade and credit facilities for bloc countries were restricted.

By the mid-1950s, the policy of "peaceful coexistence" with the capitalist countries began to take a more global, less isolationist, form under the post-Stalinist leadership. In addition, due to a sharp slowing down of growth rates in the CMEA countries, problems in developing new technology, and the desire for higher quality Western machinery and equipment, Soviet interest in expanding East–West trade greatly increased. But the renewed Soviet interest in Western imports was not matched by an increased ability to finance these imports. During the 1960s, therefore, trade was restricted by the small size of Soviet export earnings, the limited availability of Western government and private credits, and the small number of industrial cooperation agreements that could be concluded.

*Toward Ostpolitik/Westpolitik* When Khrushchev was ousted in October 1964, a collective leadership led by Leonid Brezhnev and Alexei Kosygin took power. Although the general objectives of Khrushchev's foreign policies in most cases continued under the new leadership—upholding Soviet political, ideological, and economic domination in Eastern Europe; avoiding direct military conflict with the West; containing the Chinese threat; maintaining Soviet influence over the world communist movement; increasing Soviet influence in the Third World; restraining Western military power; and improving access to Western products and technology—the manner in which these objectives were pursued did undergo significant changes. Whereas Khrushchev's foreign policy actively utilized military power for political gains (as in Cuba), the Brezhnev–Kosygin leadership, although it aimed to strengthen Soviet power in relation to the West, did not pursue a militarily aggressive foreign policy.

Just as the general foreign policy objectives remained unchanged from the Khrushchev to the Brezhnev–Kosygin leadership, the more narrow Soviet objective regarding Western Europe remained essentially unaltered: to prevent the development of a powerful West European military bloc; gain de jure recognition of the geographic status quo; gain access to West European technology; retain control of West European Communist parties; and maintain a policy of relaxation of tensions with the West European nations. To achieve these ends the Brezhnev–Kosygin leadership encouraged the development of a framework for orderly negotiations and the establishment of significant multilateral agreements in the fields of arms control, trade, science, and technology.

Concurrent with renewed Soviet interest in East–West trade was a Western movement toward lowering economic and ideological barriers to trade during the 1960s. The Western industrial countries diverged from U.S. policy and began to develop more independent Eastern policies. Chancellor Adenauer's embargo of pipe shipments from the Federal Republic of Germany to the Soviet Union in 1962, which was seconded by U.S. insistence and a NATO embargo order, was probably the end of an era of American dominance in East–West commercial policy. For the Germans it was the end of an era of isolating the USSR and of insisting on political concessions on such issues as the permanence of German borders and reunification as prior conditions for normal trade. Thus, the Soviets in 1962 were penalized by denial of critically needed oil pipe until or unless they took favorable political action on borders. The Soviets eventually built their own pipe but with delay of a year or two over the time that might have been required were German pipe available.

By 1966, the Soviet leadership had begun to develop closer ties with Italy and France, signing a variety of agreements on mutual consultation and scientific/economic cooperation, including an agreement for producing the Soviet version of the Italian Fiat in the Volga Valley. In addition to developing closer Italian and French ties, the Soviet leadership by 1966 exchanged a growing number of visits with their other European neighbors (with the notable exception of the Federal Republic of Germany)—including two trips to Moscow by British Prime Minister Harold Wilson, a visit to the Vatican and the Italian government by Andrei Gromyko, and visits to Finland and Austria by Kosygin and Nikolai Podgorny—in some cases signing trade agreements and joint cooperation agreements.

Soviet policy toward Europe not only emphasized closer political, economic, and technical ties between the West and the Soviet Union, but also encouraged the idea of new collective security arrangements as an alternative to NATO, in order to loosen European ties with the United States.

From 1966 to 1968 Soviet initiatives in Europe were moving in a positive direction until the August invasion of Czechoslovakia. The invasion created new problems for Soviet–West European relations and set back a number of previously attained Soviet policy objectives by (1) bringing a return of Cold War feelings about the Soviet military threat to Europe; (2) discouraging any weakening of NATO forces in favor of an all-European security system; (3) doing away with the image of a restrained, responsible, collective Soviet leadership encouraging détente or a relaxation of tensions; (4) causing a deterioration in Soviet–West German relations; (5) illustrating to the United States the need for greater attention to U.S.–West European relations; (6) threatening gains made by Western Communist parties; and (7) discouraging movement toward East–West cooperation.

By 1969, following the invasion, Soviet efforts once again centered on creating an atmosphere of détente in Europe: The Soviet Union proposed a European security conference to be held in Helsinki in 1970, signed the Renunciation of Force treaty with the FRG in 1971, which gave de jure recognition to the postwar borders and de facto recognition to the GDR; began bilateral talks with the FRG for further normalization of relations; and agreed to reopen Four-Power talks on Berlin. Critical additional steps forward were the 1972 and 1973 Brezhnev–Nixon summits in Moscow and Washington, which put the U.S. stamp of approval on Soviet détente with Europe. By 1973, when the Conference on Security and Cooperation in Europe (CSCE) and negotiations on mutual force reductions (MFR) opened in Europe, economic and technological ties between East and West began to grow closer, and trade turnover increased dramatically.

Although there was no basic shift in Soviet European policy after the invasion of Czechoslovakia, there was clearly a shift in emphasis. Gone was the insistence that NATO and the Warsaw Pact be replaced by an all-European security system and that the United States initiate a withdrawal from Europe. The new emphases were: (1) a desire to raise the level of consumption without cutting defense expenditures, and (2) a stronger desire to acquire Western capital and technology.

Soviet
Perspectives
on East–West
Interdependence
and Détente

*Break with Stalinist Autarky* The decision after the removal of Khrushchev to contract with Fiat to build a passenger car plant in Togliatti was a critical one in the setting of the Brezhnev–Kosygin strategy on technology imports from the West.[4] The Fiat contract, signed in 1966, followed by 1 year the conclusion of an agreement for scientific and technical cooperation between Italian firms and the Soviet government. The impact of the Fiat contract and related agreements on Soviet foreign trade was felt later as Soviet imports of Western machinery increased sharply. Donald Green and Herbert Levine quite reasonably place the beginning of a new strategy on technology in imports from the West in 1968.[5] One aspect of the new Soviet strategy was the conclusion of science and technology exchange agreements with Western governments. As noted above, agreements were signed with France and Italy in 1966. They were followed by agreements with the United Kingdom in 1968, Sweden in 1970, Canada in 1971, the United States in 1972, and Japan and West Germany in 1973. A common goal of the intergovernmental agreements was to complement and encourage commercial contracts on the model of the Fiat transaction.[6]

The decision to import automotive technology was broadened during the Ninth Five-Year Plan to include truck technology. As the Fiat arrangement had been the centerpiece of the Eighth Five-Year Plan, the Kama River truck plant became the major focus of Western machinery importation in the Ninth Five-Year Plan. The areas selected for special attention were widened from automotive technology to include technology and equipment for (1) natural gas, oil, timber, metal extraction, processing, and distribution, (2) metallurgical facilities, (3) chemical processes ranging from fertilizers to petrochemicals, (4) computer-assisted systems, (5) agrobusiness, and (6) regional development in the Baikal-Amur region of Siberia.

By Western standards many of the technologies sought by the Soviets (e.g., designs for automotive and tourist facilities) represented only "evolutionary" advances, or small incremental improvements in technology, rather than "revolutionary" advances. Although evolutionary in terms of the level of technology in the West, some technologies may bring about a significantly greater improvement in Soviet technological capabilities and result in substantial benefits to the Soviet economy.[7]

In seeking to expand the importation of foreign technology, whether revolutionary or evolutionary, Soviet decision makers appeared to be moving belatedly toward a foreign economic policy that conformed with the postwar policies of other industrialized countries. Soviet leaders appeared to have approved the growing technological interdependence of the world economy and therefore apparently decided to end the autarkic tendencies of Stalinist economic policy, ending a policy of denying themselves access to the world market. This interpretation does not conflict with the reality that the Soviet leaders selected particular Western streams of technology for top priority.[8] The pattern of cooperative agreements emphasizing computer applications and chemical and metallurgical processes followed the same strategy.

Soviet leadership statements and actions during the Ninth and Tenth Five-Year Plans increasingly advanced the official view that significant growth effects were likely to be achieved from selective Western technology transfer. West European exports of machinery and transport equipment to the USSR increased from $294 million in 1965 to almost $3 billion in 1976, appearing to illustrate Soviet intentions to increase growth through selective technology transfer from the West.[9]

A significant Western confirmation of the Soviet official view was the econometric assessment of Donald Green and Herbert Levine, which attributed up to 15% of the industrial growth in the period 1968 to 1973 to importation of Western machinery.[10] Sector analysis by Philip Hanson in the chemical fertilizer industry reached similar conclusions.[11] These views on the importance of Western imports to the Soviet economy suggest a certain degree of influence or leverage in the West with political potential. Just as the Soviet Union may use its energy exports for political reasons, the West European countries may counter with their technology exports.

Recomputations of Soviet trade statistics by Vladimir Treml, Jan Vanous, and others, while based on different methodologies, all show that the imports from the West and CMEA have been undervalued in Soviet statistics and represent increasingly critical inputs for individual sectors of the Soviet economy.[12] Whether the attendant interdependence and higher foreign trade participation ratios represent dependency or vulnerability is subject to some dispute among Western analysts.

Potential Western political leverage from exports of machinery and technological processes may not be the only Soviet problem. If the Soviets are to obtain the benefits in economic performance suggested in the Green–Levine approach, they may have to allocate high-quality domestic inputs for projects involving imported technology. Thus, imports may place heavy demands on their limited domestic supply of high-quality equipment and skilled manpower.[13] Imports, to be sure, may have dual consequences: releasing domestic resources for military use as well as consuming more resources to complete sophisticated civilian projects and, hence, diverting resources from military programs.

Several factors support the general conclusion that Soviet technology imports have a net resource-demanding or diverting effect in the domestic economy. First, the technology transfer process itself consumes domestic as well as foreign resources. The adaptation and absorption of technology that has been developed for another country requires considerable inputs from the Soviet economy. For example, Soviet engineers are needed to adapt foreign production techniques and product designs to local conditions. The Zhiguli passenger car, produced with the assistance of Fiat and modeled after the Fiat-124, required modifications of 65% of its parts in order to perform adequately under Soviet conditions.[14]

A second factor contributing to a large resource-demanding function is the high-quality requirements for domestic inputs for projects using Western technology. Frequently, the highest-quality domestic labor and material resources are needed to ensure that imports of advanced technology are effectively exploited. One example is the apparent diversion of experienced construction crews from high-priority Moscow projects to work on construction of the Western-assisted Volga and Kama River automotive plants. Likewise, skilled production workers have been recruited from other regions for the Soviet automotive industry.[15]

The third factor contributing to a large resource-demanding function is the increasingly complex and interrelated structure of the Soviet economy. Often, Western-assisted projects cannot function effectively without massive domestic investment in complementary industries and infrastructure. Foreign technology imports may be likened to a down payment on economic change; subsequent payments must be made by a selective revision in domestic resource-allocation priorities.

The long-term effect of Western technology transfers to the Soviet Union will probably be to strengthen the Soviet economy. At the same time, the net effect of such transfers may be to direct Soviet resource allocations toward those sectors of the economy that are the primary recipients of Western technology. Furthermore, the sophisticated nature of domestic investment requirements for projects using Western technology competes with the defense industries and other high-priority sectors.

If the resource-demanding function of Soviet imports of Western technology exceeds the resource-releasing function, as suggested above, the traditional Soviet high-priority investment sectors may be affected. For example, resources needed to complement technology imports may have to be diverted from military programs. If so, the traditional advocates of a high priority for military spending would undoubtedly exercise their considerable political power to impede change. They might readily accept the long-run utility of a more modern industrial base, but not at the expense of short-run cuts in key military programs. They might, however, be partially assuaged by the gains in administrative power over high-technology civilian projects offsetting their loss in resource priority. This would be more attractive if leadership policy seemed to give them no better alternative.[16] For these reasons, the domestic demands on Soviet resources are likely to be for high-quality products several-fold the value of imported products. Moreover, Soviet planners required that much high-quality domestic machinery would be used as possible to minimize the import requirements. In building a new project in the Urals, the Soviets rapidly constructed an entire urban industrial complex using a combination of Western imports and high-quality intermediate products. The intermediate products and the required infrastructure development were several-fold the value, in ruble equivalents, of the imported equipment. Several Soviet economists in informal discussions have suggested that imports were held down in 1976–1977 not just because of the hard-currency debt, but also because imported machinery would place demands on Gosplan for additional scarce resources several times the value of the imported equipment. These proportions may be higher or lower depending on the type of project, but a ratio substantially above 2:1 seems reasonable. A careful and detailed analysis of several large projects and their effects on supply plans is necessary to determine the resource-demanding ratio more precisely; but it is not possible with the available information.

If high-quality intermediate goods and infrastructure construction are required, will there be a choice between military and civilian economic growth?[17] In the estimation of U.S. intelligence agencies, the slowdown in Soviet defense spending from about 4% per annum in 1970–1976 to 2% per annum in 1976–1981 is largely due to the leveling off of military procurement. This may represent an unwillingness on the part of Soviet leaders to let investment take the entire brunt of the slowdown in industrial growth. Some suggest that the removal of Marshal Ogarkov as Chief of Staff was related to a "defense debate." A reference in a *Pravda* editorial on September 4, 1984 to a Chernenko statement favoring maintaining consumption outlays rather than upgrading defense supports this theory.

It seems likely that any major high-priority project in the civilian sector must draw on the pool of Western-type industrial products usually reserved for the military. Accelerating a major Siberian complex would seem to involve decisions that would change civilian–military priorities. This is likely simply because any large-scale, high-quality, timely construction in the Soviet Union appears to be done by the military builders and the only adequate supply of high-quality industrial goods appears to be found within the Ministry of Defense Industries. This hypothesis might, in turn, be supported by a detailed piecing together of available evidence in the defense economics field. However, as such information is largely covered by the Soviet Secrecy Acts, this conjecture will have to be left as an assumption.

*Industrial Cooperation: Toward Joint Ventures* A narrowly constrained transfer of technology, such as a one-time purchase of equipment or even turnkey plants followed by a reduction of Western ties, has not proved particularly successful for purposes other than relieving excess domestic demand at a given time. In a number of cases, the Soviets have established modern industrial plants based on Western technology imports, only to fall behind the rapid pace of technological progress in the West within a few years. The Soviets' inability to keep abreast technologically is a result of shortcomings in both their foreign commercial and domestic economic institutions.

The Soviet leaders' awareness of these and other problems has led them to consider more flexible arrangements for importing Western technology. The traditional Soviet approach has been giving way to a modified systems approach to technology transfer. The new approach is characterized by (1) a long-term or continuous connection, (2) complex or project-oriented management and distribution, (3) systems-related construction, production, management, and distribution, and (4) Western involvement both in the USSR and at home in the training and decision-making process.[18]

*Financing Western Technology Transfers*  A major constraint on Soviet technology imports from the West is the USSR's ability to finance such imports. During the 1970s, it had serious and chronic balance-of-payments deficits in its trade with the West and a rising level of hard currency indebtedness due to short-, medium-, and long-term borrowing from private and official Western banks. This situation was temporarily improved upon in 1974, when the large increase in oil prices enabled the Soviets to expand their hard-currency earnings. However, in 1975 and 1976, Soviet trade deficits again worsened. Concurrently, net Soviet debt to the West (gross debt minus deposits in Western banks) declined in 1972 to $555 million from a level of $582 million in 1971. Thereafter, net debt rose each year almost reaching the $10 billion mark by the end of 1976. Unwilling to allow continued increases in trade deficits and debt, the Soviets began to cut imports, especially of machinery and equipment, from the West. In addition, the Soviets increasingly sought product-payback arrangements with Western firms to avoid having to expend hard currency. According to estimates by the CIA, the Soviets managed to reduce the annual trade deficit from an average of $6 billion in the 1975–1976 period to an average of $2.9 billion in 1977–1980. Net debt rose to $11.1 billion in 1977, but then began to decline, sinking to $9.55 billion in 1980.[19]

In 1981, however, Soviet efforts to reduce trade deficits and debt came undone, due to the necessity of importing large amounts of grain from the West and of giving Poland a substantial amount of hard currency aid, and due to soft oil prices on the world market. The hard currency deficit increased from $2.5 billion in 1980 to $4 billion in 1981. Net debt ballooned from $9.5 billion in 1980 to $12.5 billion in 1981. These unfavorable developments occurred despite a reduction in nonagricultural imports to their 1978 level, large sales of gold in a soft market, increased borrowing, and a temporary draw-down in deposits in Western banks. The Soviet Union subsequently managed to improve its financial position vis-à-vis the West, earning current account surpluses on hard currency trade after 1981 and reducing net debt to $10.0 billion in 1982 and $10.9 billion in 1983.[20]

*Equivocation in Brezhnev's Modernization Policy*  In the Tenth Five-Year Plan (1976–1980), the first plan in the 15-year plan, there appeared to have been a major equivocation in the application of the new Brezhnev modernization strategy, especially as it involved Western technology transfer.[21] Serious delays in the plans for modernization in areas such as the following were costly to future Soviet economic performance: (1) projected production of Western auto and truck models; (2) development of the power-consuming industries and resource-development industries in East Siberia and the region around the Baikal–Amur railroad; (3) the development of the agrobusiness complexes required for modernizing the feed-grain livestock industry; (4) the development of long-distance alternating and direct current (AC and DC) transmission facilities for bringing cheap hydro- and coal-generated power from Siberia to markets in European Russia, and of importing transmission, exploration, extraction, and other facilities for petroleum and natural gas complexes to meet projections for increases in output both onshore and offshore; (5) the Kursk metallurgical project for pelletizing and direct metal reduction; and (6) the introduction of an effective, computer-assisted national economic reporting system.

The delays suggested debate within Soviet leadership on the priority of modernization, especially as it involved increased imports from the primary trading area, Western Europe. These differences of views may have represented equivocation on the part of Brezhnev.

Noting that the Soviet leadership decided to reduce the rate of growth of investment during the Tenth and Eleventh Five-Year Plans, Myron Rush concluded that the Brezhnev leadership was set on a course of sacrificing investment for a continuing defense build up,[22] although as noted above the U.S. intelligence estimates found defense spending growth slowing as well. Given the secular decline in the Soviet rate of growth in the 1970s and its continuation into the 1980s, the decline in both the growth rate of investment and in its share of national income imposed serious constraints on Soviet efforts to modernize key sectors of the economy. Efforts to increase the effectiveness of capital utilization and, thus, to foster the goal of modernization without significantly increasing investment were unlikely to succeed.

Others, especially Philip Hanson, argued that the earlier enthusiasm of Soviet leaders for imports of Western technology as a means of achieving a scientific and technological revolution in their economy had cooled.[23] The limited effectiveness of some major projects in auto-motives and computers may have fueled this skepticism. The expanded use of restrictions on key Western exports to the USSR for political purposes by the Carter and Reagan administrations raised the political cost of exploiting the Western technology connection. Thus far, the natural gas pipelines and the BAM are the only major high priority projects tied to Western trade in the 1980s.

On the other hand, there are those in Gosplan, the Ministry of Foreign Trade, the State Committee on Science and Technology, the academic institutes, and a number of ministries who still argue for an expansion of modernization based on Western technology. Their argu-ments are deflected for the time being by a shortage of hard currency, a low level of domestic investment, and a deferment of domestic reform.

*Energy: The Solution or the Problem?* The Soviet Union has been a net exporter of oil since 1955 and a net exporter of natural gas since 1970. During the 1970s, oil and oil product exports became the largest single earner of hard currency, bringing in over $4.5 billion in 1976. By 1980, natural gas exports had begun to become a major source of hard currency as well.

Because of the enormous demand and significant price increases for energy in 1973 and 1974, the USSR was able to finance a large share of high-priority imports with its oil-income windfall. Even without further energy price increases, the Soviet Union will likely continue to be a net energy exporter to the West throughout the 1980s in order to earn hard currency and finance imports. Out of a total of 135 million metric tons of oil available for export in 1980, the Soviets exported 75 million metric tons to Eastern Europe and 35 million metric tons to hard-currency countries; and out of the 59 billion cubic meters of gas available for export in 1980, 33 billion cubic meters were exported to Eastern Europe and 26 billion cubic meters to Western Europe.[24] In the 1980s, the share of oil in energy exports to Western countries is intended to decrease, while the share of natural gas is to increase.

In order to maintain energy exports as a major hard-currency earner, the Soviets had to produce or import significantly more drilling equipment, large-diameter pipe, submersible pumps, and other equipment. Without this equipment and technology, exploration and extraction would have been unlikely to keep up with energy demand. Therefore, the energy sector laid claim to a priority share of hard-currency income.

Attainment of the 1985 and 1990 oil production goals depends primarily on the rapid development of West Siberian deposits, on major improvement in the technology and equipment for oil exploration, development, and transport, and on the continued stability of present levels of output in the existing oil fields in West Siberia.

The volume of oil exports to the West is to some extent a function of production goals in the 1980s.[25] Should, for example, the goals for the 1980s be significantly underfulfilled, the Soviets could cut back on oil exports in order to maintain domestic supply and supplies to Eastern Europe. The more important variable that determines the size of oil exports, however, is the ability of these exports to finance large quantities of Western equipment, technology, and grain. As long as oil maintains its potential to earn large amounts of hard currency, it is likely oil exports will be kept high—even at the cost of cutting back on domestic and East European supplies.

During the 1980s, a high level of oil exports may become difficult if not impossible to maintain in the following cases: (1) if no new large field like Samotlar is discovered and proven out; (2) if adequate geophysical equipment and skilled labor to manage the equipment are not readily available; (3) if investment resources are not sufficient to support necessary infrastructure development, exploration, and extraction plans; and (4) if Western credits are not available to finance crucial equipment imports. Oil exports may represent the critical margin for Soviet hard currency income in the 1980s. (According to one estimate, in 1985 they may range up to $19.3 billion in current prices.[26])

Exports of natural gas are expected to rise sharply in the 1980s, as the output of gas increases and the pipeline network expands. The natural gas production goal of 635 billion cubic meters for 1985 is well within the Soviets' reach, largely due to substantial production increases from West Siberia, particularly in the Urengoi area. Fulfillment turns on the ability of the Soviets to make major improvements in pipeline construction, technology, and high-performance pipeline equipment. More and better pipelines resulted from expanded Western supply and financing arrangements.

The ability of the Soviets to import the large quantity of Western technology necessary for the rapid development of energy resources has been and will continue to be dependent upon their ability to earn hard currency; borrow at acceptable and affordable interest rates; arrange compensation agreements; participate in long-term cooperation agreements with the West; and maintain a high level of debt with Western nations.

To encourage long-term energy cooperation between East and West, among other goals, the Soviet Union, along with 34 other nations, signed the Helsinki Final Act, which supported the following long-term projects: (1) exchanges of electrical energy within Europe with a view to utilizing the capacity of electric power stations as rationally as possible; (2) cooperation in research for new sources of energy and, in particular, in the field of nuclear energy; and (3) cooperation in the perfecting of equipment for multimodal transport operations and for the handling of containers.[27]

Compensation agreements with the West are perhaps one of the best ways for the Soviets to import Western technology and develop resources as they often do not involve complex financing arrangements, but rely on barter with repayment through exports of the product resulting from the agreed project. Yakutia, Sakhalin, and Orenburg are successful examples of these compensation agreements. In all three cases the Soviets were able to commit future energy production for current purchases of energy services, equipment, and technology. For future East–West trade, the Soviets have indicated a strong preference for this type of agreement. A coal slurry pipeline from West Siberia may be among the innovative East–West energy projects of the late 1980s.

The Soviets also emphasize exports using substantial energy inputs. Those products that utilize energy in their production processes are said to "embody energy." The Soviets, therefore, have options when developing their energy intensive export industries, to export the raw materials—oil, gas, and coal—or to export products that "embody energy," such as large volumes of energy in processing mineral fertilizers, copper, and aluminum. Because the products can utilize cheap and available energy resources, such as thermal power, hydropower, and natural gas, they serve three useful purposes to the Soviets. First, developing these industries contributes to the modernization process as it encourages further development of the energy centers of East Siberia, where much of the natural gas and cheap hydropower is located. Second, utilizing a relatively small labor force, the production process for these embodied products does not add to the high-cost infrastructure development required for the development of raw materials. And third, by developing an exportable product, the Soviets are able both to reduce their dependence on oil and gas exports and to help finance their growing debt to the Western nations. Completion of the Baikal–Amur railroad and added hydro capacity in East Siberia increase the prospect of "energy embodied" exports, especially to the Pacific rim.

The Soviet Union has been economically supportive of East European energy needs at a high cost to its own welfare, increasing deliveries throughout the 1970s of oil, gas, and coal at less than world market prices. The Soviets exported 75 million metric tons of oil and 33 billion cubic meters of gas to Eastern Europe in 1980—the year they announced the leveling off of energy deliveries to Eastern Europe.[28] When the Soviets export energy to the Eastern countries they forego the hard currency they might have earned had they exported the energy to Western Europe. In 1975 alone the Soviets might have earned approximately $5.25 billion by selling to hard-currency countries instead of to Eastern Europe.[29] However, the Soviet shift in terms of CMEA energy trade is not clearly advantageous to either party:

> Soviet energy policy is a part of the overall dilemma in dealing with Eastern Europe. Energy policy has always loomed large in Soviet–East European economic relations. Under the impact of recent global energy trends, however, it has become a key lever of Soviet political control in the region. . . .
>
> Besides its vital goal of maintaining control over Eastern Europe, the Soviet Union is also interested in fostering the overall economic health and political stability of the region. Although supplies of Soviet energy are critical to attaining both these goals, the economic and political criteria for energy policy may conflict. On the one hand, flexible energy rationing by the Soviet Union in a tight supply market greatly increases its leverage and expands its policy options for dealing with a variety of problems in Eastern Europe. On the other hand, a reduction of energy deliveries, necessitated both by the declining growth of Soviet energy supplies and by expanding demand at home and abroad, may lead to slower growth in national and personal incomes in Eastern Europe and perhaps to political instability.[30]

These dilemmas are inherent in the CMEA rhetoric and practice during and following the CMEA Summit of June 1984. The official Soviet position was to move toward more CMEA integration and toward world market pricing (WMP). However, these policies have political and economic costs for Eastern Europe that may be too severe to sustain. The East European nations were placed during the 1970s on a multiyear moving average related to world market prices, which will draw them closer to Organization of Petroleum Exporting Countries (OPEC) pricing levels. Still, as soft or nonmarketable goods by Western standards are accepted in payment, the returns to the USSR are less than the price equivalents would suggest. Oil and gas prices will continue to rise, but due to the Soviet policy of maintaining economic order and control over Eastern Europe, they could end up being higher than WMPs, at least temporarily. That is, if the WMP falls to $27/bbl. in 1985, Eastern Europe could pay the equivalent of $28–29/bbl. in 1985 under a moving average pricing scheme. There are also dilemmas in West European energy policy and trade with the Soviet Union in assessing the benefits and costs of European energy imports of Soviet gas and oil and exports of Western energy equipment to the USSR. A central issue for the OECD has been: Are European gas imports a source of unacceptable vulnerability or energy security? Some Soviet energy imports are necessary as agreement has been reached on the need for diversity in energy supplies. "Secure" Norwegian gas supplies and the ability to shift from Soviet gas to indigenous fuel supplies in case of an interruption in supply and domestic "safety nets" are commonly considered the keys to Western European energy security. Throughout the 1980s, supply and demand equations for gas and total energy supplies will favor buyers rather than sellers. That is, in a soft energy market, Ruhrgas—the monopsonist—will have the short-term economic leverage rather than the putative gas-exporting monopolist—the Soviet Union. But agreement is still lacking on the future availability of "secure" (e.g., Norwegian) sources that are needed to offset dependence on Soviet gas until the mid or late 1990s, as the Troll field of Norway cannot be developed and producing until then at the earliest. As a result, the buyers' market of the 1980s is liable to be transformed into a sellers' market in the 1990s with the Soviet Union, the gas monopolist, having the key leverage over market price and supply in the 1990s.

*Raw Materials* Traditionally, raw materials have been a large export item for the Soviet Union. Metals—nickel, palladium, platinum, and chromium—in particular, have been exported in large quantities to the developed West, as have wood, wood products, diamonds, and gold. Future prospects for increased export earnings will depend on (1) raw material price trends in the West; (2) ability to increase the volume of raw material exports; and (3) ability to increase the volume of manufactured exports. Because of problems such as quality, marketing, servicing, and strong Western competition, it is unlikely that export of manufactured goods will contribute significantly to future export earnings.[31]

During the 1960s, the value of Soviet exports to the developed West rose because of an increase in the volume of exports rather than an increase in the price received. Oil, coal, wood, and wood products were the fastest growing exports. During the 1970s, by contrast, the value of exports to the developed West grew because of an increase in the prices received for major Soviet exports—oil, wood products, metals—rather than an increase in the volume exported. The volume of Soviet exports did not increase during the 1970s because of bottlenecks in the expansion of raw material production. An increase in domestic and CMEA demand for raw materials combined with sharply rising investment costs for Siberian exploitation were the primary deterrents to expanded exports. In an effort to relieve these problems, the Soviets encouraged increased CMEA and Western investment participation in raw materials projects.

The volume of Soviet nonenergy material exports during the 1970s was limited not only by bottlenecks in the raw materials industries, but also by Western recession. As early as 1974, economic activity in the West began to contract and inventories increased due to the recession. Hence, the demand for Soviet exports fell. This situation, combined with rising industrial equipment prices—resulting from Western inflation—and poor harvests, caused balance-of-payments problems for the Soviet Union. Imports of Western grain and technology, while helping somewhat to relieve short-term shortages and bottlenecks were particularly expensive for the Soviets because they coincided with reduced demand for Soviet exports.

Future increases in the volume of raw materials exports will depend upon the ability to commit more resources to development and exploitation, the availability of Western credits, and the ability to make compensation agreements and other payback arrangements with the West, especially in Siberian projects.

*Multilateral and Bilateral Agreements* Although both the European Community (EC) and the CMEA have submitted drafts for a treaty, the two organizations have not reached an agreement. Although the Soviet Union would encourage such an agreement—because it would bring a stronger commitment by the individual East European countries to the CMEA—many of the East European and Western countries prefer bilateral arrangements. The East European countries generally prefer bilateral contacts because they can minimize Soviet economic dominance and in some cases obtain more concessions from the West. Similar considerations seem to motivate West European countries to prefer bilateral over multilateral arrangements. Yet, it is conceivable that an agreement could be reached because the EC and the CMEA draft treaties mention some areas of agreement—such as economic prognoses, statistics, environmental protection, and standardization.[32]

Most commercial agreements between East and West have been bilateral rather than multilateral. Dating as far back as the 1960s, starting with the Federal Republic of Germany, and then expanding to other West European countries, the number of bilateral agreements in scientific, technical, and economic areas grew rapidly. Over time, these agreements evolved from simple licensing arrangements to highly complex joint-production and coproduction ventures and turnkey projects involving product compensation arrangements.

For Soviet purposes, turnkey projects have been most useful as they are the most efficient method of importing needed Western technology equipment, management skills, and marketing capabilities. These projects are used primarily in oil and gas development, exploration, and exploitation; major technological improvements in the production of computers, cars, trucks, and steel; developing, processing, and storing agricultural products; and livestock raising. Long-term agreements such as the U.S.–USSR Long-Term Grain Agreements and the 20-year FRG–Soviet economic agreement are models of preferred bilateral vehicles.

There is some question as to whether Western equipment and technology transfers in the form of turnkey projects or Western credits will have a major impact on the export capabilities of the Soviet Union. It seems likely that, instead, such imports will have a marginal impact on Soviet productivity and will relieve critical short-term bottlenecks.

*Nontrade Income* Tourism has been a modest earner of hard currency for the Soviet Union. According to the CIA, net receipts from tourism were between $300 and $400 million in recent years.[33] In the past, the uneven quality of Intourist, Aeroflot, and other Soviet facilities restricted the growth of tourism, but the construction of new facilities for the Moscow Olympic Games in 1980 significantly expanded and improved exisiting facilities.

Soviet merchant shipping has expanded at an impressive rate in the 1970s, allowing it to earn substantial hard currency. Its earning capacity will undoubtedly continue to grow again after the recession in the West ends and if East–West agreements on merchant marine activities are renewed.

## Issues in Soviet Relations with Europe

*Energy Policy and Interdependence* Conservative Europeans and some Americans fear that the construction of the pipeline from the Soviet Union to the border of Western Europe during the 1980s may make an economically unified Gaullist-type Europe "from Brest to Brest" a reality, but with Moscow playing the dominant role rather than Paris or another Western European capital. In their view, the Soviet Union might at some point use its economic leverage to encourage the removal of all Western export controls and to influence the extension of Western preferential credits and other trade concessions. Coupled with the perceived shift in the military balance to the Warsaw Pact, this trend, they warn, might lead to Soviet dominance of Europe.

On the other hand, there is another more widely held view that stresses the leverage that the pipeline will confer on the West European countries, the increasing independence of the East European countries, and the tendency among the West European Communist parties to diverge from the Soviet position on important political issues.[34]

In the 1980s, Soviet plans called for increases in all energy sources—oil, coal, hydro, nuclear, and gas.[35] Since proven Soviet gas reserves are equivalent to Saudi Arabia's oil reserves and since the Soviets are encountering difficulty in continuing to increase oil output, natural gas is projected to account for the predominant share of incremental energy production and hard currency earnings for the Soviet Union.

The key to the Soviets' ambitious plans for natural gas and for the maintenance of hard currency earnings is the construction of the export pipeline and domestic pipelines to bring the gas from Siberian fields to the center and border. The rate of pipeline construction in the USSR exceeds the rate in any other country by several times. According to Soviet estimates, the pipeline construction program will cost over 25 billion rubles. There may have been some opposition in the Politburo to the military-like priority for natural gas production, but when Leonid Brezhnev announced in November 1981 that the pipelines would have to be completed "without fail" by the end of the current Five-Year-Plan (i.e., by 1985), the issue was settled. The export line was largely completed and European deliveries were begun in late 1984 as contracted.

The gas supply agreements signed by the Soviet Union and the West European countries have long-term implications. Gas deliveries through the new export pipeline will continue for 25 years. The FRG, the largest purchaser, will import as much as 10.5 billion cubic meters (BCM) annually and France, the next largest customer, may purchase 8 BCM annually. Other European countries have agreed to import smaller quantities. While deliveries via the new pipeline began in 1984, they need not reach maximum contracted levels until 1987. These commitments are over and above the amount of Soviet gas that has been flowing into the West European gas network through the Orenburg and Northern Lights pipelines since the 1970s. With the deliveries of gas from the new pipeline, the share of Soviet gas in French, German, and Italian imports of gas from all sources will rise to about one-third. Soviet gas may thus account for 5–6% of all primary energy in these countries.

West European interest in the pipeline stems primarily from the policy of reducing dependence on oil imported from OPEC countries and of diversifying sources of natural gas. These policies are also designed to hold down the cost of energy. Unlike some on the other side of the Atlantic who believe that energy independence is an option for the United States, West Europeans do not perceive energy independence as a viable policy for Europe. In the European view, the way to achieve energy security and hold down prices is to diversify sources of supply. Thus, West European governments viewed the Soviet proposal as a means of offsetting the risks entailed in importing oil from OPEC and natural gas from other suppliers such as Algeria. The Italian energy agency, for example, used the Soviet price concessions to hold down the Algerian price for gas from a new pipeline via Sicily. Moreover, Europeans viewed the large Soviet equipment orders placed with firms in importing countries as providing substantial job and production prospects for many years. The orders would benefit the metallurgy and equipment sectors, which are highly competitive and have been stagnant in the past few years. A third motivation was the West European view that economic interdependence with the East might stabilize political relations and provide useful tools for Western diplomacy.

The Reagan administration disagreed with the European assessment and made concerted efforts to dissuade the West European countries, especially the FRG, the key participant, from accepting the Soviet offer. The administration's chief argument was that the additional gas deliveries would make major NATO allies dependent on Soviet gas, and, hence, vulnerable to Soviet threats to cut off the gas during a political crisis. The administration also argued against the pipeline on the grounds that it would provide the Soviets with large amounts of hard currency—perhaps as much as $11.1 billion annually by the mid-1980s, according to an estimate by the Defense Intelligence Agency—which could be used to pay for major purchases of high technology from the West. The administration proposed U.S. coal and revival of plans for development of nuclear electric power as European substitutes for Soviet gas. As a minimum precaution if they decided to go ahead with the pipeline, the U.S. urged the West Europeans to arrange stand-by facilities (e.g., Dutch or Norwegian gas).

The Federal Republic has claimed to have a virtually complete "safety net" (i.e., alternative supplies of non-Soviet gas and other fuels) through Dutch "surge capacity" contracts, new gas from Norway, domestic gas, and standby energy sources. An Algerian–Italian gas line would provide extra gas to Western Europe in the 1980s. Liquefied Nigerian gas and more Norwegian gas may be available in the 1990s as well as increased U.S. coal supplies. Public opposition to nuclear plants may limit expansion of nuclear electric power generation in all major West European countries except France. Premier Mitterand may rely on the ambitious French nuclear program as an offset to important gas dependency. While the indigenous safety nets may be a source of energy independence, "secure" alternatives to Soviet gas before the turn of the century seem problematic, as noted above.

In response to the presumed Soviet role in the Polish declaration of martial law on December 13, 1981, President Reagan banned U.S. sales to the Soviet Union of equipment and technical data for the refinement and transmission of gas and oil. This measure, which went into effect on December 30, 1981, effectively precluded U.S. companies from completing sales related to the pipeline. In particular, it blocked the General Electric Company (GE) from exporting patented rotors for the compressors the West European companies were to supply. After the declaration of martial law in Poland, France and West Germany reaffirmed their commitment to a policy of equipment supply to the pipeline, although that policy was more controversial in Italy.

Much to the consternation of the West European countries, President Reagan decided to expand the ban on U.S. sales of oil and gas equipment to overseas subsidiaries of U.S. firms and foreign companies that produce oil and gas equipment under U.S. licenses. The primary aim of the decision, which was announced on June 18, 1982, was to prevent U.S. subsidiaries in Europe and European-owned firms from shipping turbines with patented GE rotors to the Soviet Union for the pipeline, but oil and gas equipment for other uses was also affected.[36] Statements by the administration stressed the lack of improvement in the Polish situation as the main reason for the President's decision, but there remained some uncertainty in both Europe and the United States about the reasons for and, hence, the necessity of the broadened control.[37] The rationale of influencing Polish policy through action against the Soviet Union was at the center of the difference of opinion.

The European response was angry and unified. The British, French, Italian, and German governments and the European Community protested that the extraterritorial application of U.S. law was counter to international law and was an affront to European sovereignty. They also objected to the retroactive application of the controls to preexisting contracts and to the U.S. decision to extend its grain agreement with the Soviet Union for another year. They did not accept the Reagan administration's argument that grain sales and pipeline equipment exports should be viewed differently because the former reduced the Soviet Union's hard currency supply, while the latter would increase it. Given the recession and high rates of unemployment, European governments were also concerned about the potential loss of employment connected with the contracts. For these reasons, the governments of Britain, France, Italy, and the Federal Republic ordered or, lacking legal authority to do so, encouraged their companies to defy the ban. Since enough components for part of the Soviet order were already on European soil or could be manufactured by a French company, Alstom-Atlantique, the European response could partially frustrate the U.S. goal. The Reagan administration responded by blacklisting European firms as the banned equipment was shipped.

Even with the end of the U.S. sanctions in November 1983, the pipeline controversy, which coincided with a serious dispute over steel imports, remained an irritant in U.S.–West European relations. The European Community's protest note, which may be taken as an authoritative statement of its members' views, prophetically predicted that the expanded controls would not "delay materially" the pipeline.[38] The Reagan administration, however, argued that the dispute had raised the consciousness of other CoCom members to the dangers of strategic trade and hazards of dependency.

*Strategic Trade and CoCom*  Throughout the postwar period dual-use exports to the East (i.e., products and technologies with military as well as civilian applications) have been a contentious issue within the Atlantic Alliance. Since the establishment of CoCom in 1950 as a mechanism for coordinating the export policies of the Western countries, both the criteria for deciding which exports to restrict and the lists of embargoed goods have undergone substantial changes. At the U.S. lead, in the 1950s and through most of the 1960s CoCom sought to deny the Eastern countries all exports that would contribute to their economic as well as military capabilities. The late 1960s saw the adoption in U.S. legislation and, concurrently, in the CoCom guidelines of a criterion of controlling only those goods that would contribute to the military capabilities of the East. Along with the demise of the policy of economic warfare against the East and the change in the criteria for deciding which goods could be exported came a reduction in the length and scope of the lists of controlled goods.

Over the years there have been broad areas of agreement and disagreement between the West European countries, on the one hand, and the United States, on the other. All agree that "strategic" goods and technologies should be controlled in order to preserve Western security. There is general agreement, even in countries such as France and Italy, which are officially discreet about their participation in CoCom, that a mechanism for coordinating Western export policies is necessary. Beyond that, however, there are disagreements about what constitutes a "stragtegic" good and which ones with which capacities should be restricted. From the beginning the United States has tended toward a broader definition of strategic and has generally sought to control a broader array of goods than most of the West European countries. In addition, the process of compiling the lists of restricted goods and authorizing exceptions almost inevitably leads to charges that some members are seeking commercial advantages for their firms.

Another factor underlying the differences between Europe and the United States is that in Europe the consensus on the nature of East–West trade and the respective roles of Western countries in CoCom has shifted, whereas in the United States this shift is more ambiguous. The U.S. legislation, the Export Administration Act of 1979, reflected changes in perceptions of the nature of the Soviet threat and in views on the appropriate balance between preserving U.S. and Western security and maximizing economic benefits from trade.

While the legislation was basically in tune with European views, beginning in 1980 the philosophy of the American leadership and the implementation of policy harked back to the Export Control Act of 1949, the Battle Act of the 1950s, and even to the Trading With the Enemy Act of World War I. The new consensus in Europe, Canada, and Japan was in sharp contrast with the return to older perceptions in Washington. The contrast did not begin with, but was brought into focus by, the divergent European and American responses to the Soviet action in Afghanistan and martial law in Poland.

A similar phenomenon may be said to exist in the East. The CMEA-Six and Yugoslavia had accepted as desirable and preferable their broader Western connections and greater maneuvering room to spur system flexibility and external relations. Changes in Hungary and Poland represented the range of Soviet toleration in practice. Paralleling the change in U.S. policy, the Soviet Union in the 1980s had a marked inclination toward a return to great power dominance, adversarial relations, and Eastern system integration and independence from the West.

The Carter and Reagan administrations made two proposals for significant changes in CoCom's operations: (1) the incorporation of the "critical technologies" approach in CoCom's licensing guidelines, and (2) a tightening of controls on exports to the Soviet Union.

The critical technologies approach evolved from a study by the Defense Science Board, which was completed in 1976. Its chief conclusion was that the direct mechanisms of technology transfer such as technical documentation and training of Eastern personnel that may accompany East–West commercial relations are a more important means of technology transfer than exports of specific products.[39] Instead of focusing on the product being considered for export, the traditional approach to export licensing, the Board recommended focusing on the technology being transferred through a given transaction. Or, as it is often described, a "case" approach should be substituted for the "list" approach. As a follow-on to the study, the Export Administration Act of 1979 mandated the compilation of a list of militarily critical technologies (MCTL), which was completed in fall 1980 and made available in unclassified form to the general public in late 1984.

The Reagan administration continued and intensified its predecessor's initiatives to strengthen CoCom controls and to incorporate the critical technologies approach. These initiatives were pursued both in CoCom and in other fora. At the annual economic summits and at the high-level (ministerial) CoCom meetings held in 1982 and 1983 (the first since the late-1950s), the Reagan administration sought a commitment by the leaders of the Western alliance to strengthen the strategic embargo. Another element of the Reagan administration's approach was a series of studies by CoCom and NATO intended to provide agreed upon analyses of strategic trade and its implications for Western security.

Some of the major American proposals to CoCom during the early 1980s and their outcomes can be pieced together from published sources. Following the Soviet invasion of Afghanistan, the Carter administration proposed that CoCom refrain from granting exceptions to CoCom controls for exports to the Soviet Union (the "no-exceptions" policy) and from engaging in "major projects" in the Soviet Union. As noted above, CoCom adopted the "no-exceptions" policy, which remained in effect 4 years after the invasion.[40] The "major projects" proposal, however, was not adopted and, as noted above, firms from CoCom-member countries took over two major projects in the Soviet Union.[41] CoCom members also reacted unfavorably to a follow-on proposal calling for informal CoCom consultations on projects that involved more than $100 million in Western inputs and "process know-how" in "defense priority industries."

U.S. proposals on the critical technologies seem to have left West European officials with doubts about whether the approach is workable and with concern about the contents of the MCTL prepared by the Defense Department. Nonetheless, the other CoCom members seemed willing to adopt at least some elements of this approach. For example, during the 1978/1979 review of the CoCom lists, they agreed to the U.S. proposal to add specific references to technology as well as products to the CoCom strategic criteria and to include controls on technology in the CoCom lists themselves instead of in an "administrative principle" appended to the lists.[42] At the High Level CoCom Meeting in January 1982, the other CoCom members reportedly agreed to "redefine" CoCom's guidelines and procedures and to include modern technologies on the lists.[43] CoCom subsequently agreed to an American proposal to inventory emerging technologies and monitor their potential strategic significance.[44]

Primarily in the context of the 1982–1983 List Review, CoCom made significant changes in the list of controlled dual-use products and technologies, particularly in the area of electronics. Among the most important changes were the new guidelines on exports of computers and large, sophisticated telecommunication switches announced in May 1984.[45] New guidelines for computers had been under negotiation off and on since the 1978–1979 List Review, but agreement proved elusive until 1984. In essence, CoCom agreed to tighten controls on computers with the greatest potential military uses and to loosen controls on other machines. Thus, CoCom decontrolled personal computers except for portable, "ruggedized" models that could withstand battlefield conditions; raised the technical level of exportable general purpose mainframe computers; and tightened controls on "supermini" computers. Agreeing to the first controls on software not associated with hardware, CoCom also placed certain programs with military applications on the control list.

Despite the competition among firms in several West European countries to sell telephone exchanges to East European countries, CoCom agreed to ban the export of sophisticated telecomminications switches until 1988. CoCom also imposed controls on some components and technologies for manufacturing computers: silicon, printed circuit boards and manufacturing technology, and ceramics used in the production of semiconductors.[46] Other additions to the list included some robotics technology, certain metallurgical equipment and technologies, composite materials, space vehicles, and floating dry docks.

Officials of the Reagan administration have praised the work of its CoCom partners in strengthening strategic controls. They have also claimed considerable success in obtaining West European agreement to increased use of the critical technologies approach in CoCom and a commitment to more rigorous enforcement of CoCom controls by member governments. While agreeing with the Reagan administration's formulation that their economic relations with the East should be compatible with their political and security objectives, the Europeans undoubtedly made their own perspectives known at the summits and in CoCom. Sharp disagreements on some specific proposals were reported in the press, but by 1984 some officials were referring to a significant "convergence" in American and European polices.[47] Since CoCom's deliberations are confidential and public knowledge of its activities is fragmentary at best, definitive conclusions about the results of the U.S. initiatives in CoCom during the early 1980s cannot be reached. An assessment is also premature because CoCom's consideration of such important proposals as the critical technologies approach appears to be on-going and several of its new agreements, particularly on computer's and switches, are just being interpreted. Even in the context of heightened awareness of the strategic implications of trade with the East and of Soviet efforts to obtain Western technology, differences within CoCom are likely to persist on the specifics: Should a particular piece of equipment or technology be controlled? Should an exception be granted in a particular case?

Summarizing the European position on export controls in *Le Monde Diplomatique* in January, 1985, Dr. Marie Lavigne concluded that it is "most improbable" that an agreement can be reached in this area "beyond a very vague consensus on the principle of controlling strategic exports."[48]

*Credit as a Carrot or a Stick* Active use of credit and debt in East–West relations is a divisive policy in the West. Responses to the Polish debt crisis and to U.S. proposals to limit subsidies on credits to the Soviet Union illustrate the spectrum of Western views on appropriate use of credit policies. Few in Europe were in favor of precipitating a formal or de jure Polish default. Part of the reason was that West European governments and banks, which extended larger credits than their U.S. counterparts, stood to lose more in the event of a Polish default. But they also feared that if a formal declaration of default were made, Poland would no longer have any incentive to repay its debts and would have no other option than a closer Soviet orientation in economic and political policy. At the other extreme were those in the United States who favored precipitating a formal default on Polish debts guaranteed by the Commodity Credit Corporation.

U.S. commercial banks and some private citizens have proposed conditionality as a means of avoiding defaults, assuring repayment, and maximizing benefits to the West. Economic conditionality is familiar from its use by the International Monetary Fund. As applied to Poland and, in the future, possibly to other East European countries on the verge of formal default, economic conditionality might include the following elements: (a) provision of adequate and verifiable information, (b) the establishment of a consistent long-range stabilization program by the indigenous government; and (c) progress with the two preceding elements as a condition for rescheduling old loans. U.S. commercial banks have taken the lead in arguing for applying economic conditionality to the rescheduling of the Polish debt despite the initial lack of enthusiasm on the part of the West European banks.

Political conditionality is a more delicate issue with less clear precedent. But it is certainly not unknown for a country in debt to another or dependent on another for a key import to be responsive on a variety of political and economic issues. Political conditionality is the key to new loans to many Eastern countries. Political conditionality is, therefore, an issue primarily for Western political leaders—not bankers. The West European governments appear even more reluctant to apply political than economic conditionality. The Reagan administration has not raised the issue per se, but political conditionality would appear to be compatible with its use of economic leverage in diplomacy. The possibility of applying political conditionality may come up in the future; it was not included in the 10 Western governments' agreement to reschedule official Polish debts for 1981. The United States did, however, indicate that it intended to apply leverage by refusing to reschedule official Polish debts falling due in 1982 until martial law was lifted. European governments seconded this use of leverage.

Proposals to reduce the subsidization of credits to the Soviet Union divided the West along different lines.[49] The Reagan administration's proposals on credit stemmed from a philosophic aversion to interest rate subsidies in general and the belief that the Soviet Union should not continue to benefit from low-interest loans subsidized by Western governments. The French and, to a lesser degree, the British viewed subsidized credits as a necessary element of their commercial relations with all countries, including members of CMEA. German views and policies on credit were closer to those of the United States, although many would argue that the credit insurance offered by the government through the Hermes Corp. on loans to the USSR and East European countries is a subsidy.

Nonetheless, in late 1982 the Allies agreed to changes in the OECD Arrangement on Export Credits that raised the minimum interest rate participants would charge on loans to the Soviet Union, Czechoslovakia, and the GDR. The three nations were "graduated" from Category II (intermediate-income countries) to Category I (relatively rich countries charged the highest minimum interest rates), and the minimum interest rates for countries in Category I were raised. As a result, the minimum interest rate for most loans to the Soviet Union was raised from 8.75 to 12.4%. This rate was not applicable to credits denominated in the currencies of countries where interest rates were relatively low such as the Federal Republic and Japan. Instead, the participants set lower interest rates based on market rates in these countries for loans denominated in yen or Deutsche Marks. In October 1983, an automatic adjustment mechanism to keep the Arrangement's matrix of interest rates in line with market rates was added. Arrangement interest rates are not applicable to credits for agricultural commodities or to short-term credits (less than 2 years).

Whether the closer alignment of Arrangement and market interest rates virtually eliminated the subsidization of credits to the Soviet Union as the Reagan administration asserted is subject to controversy. Some observers argue that countries can circumvent the Arrangement by offering the Soviet Union credits in yen or D-Marks. In rebuttal, the Reagan administration argued that such credits should not be considered subsidized unless the interest rate is lower than the prevailing rate in Japan or the Federal Republic. It also argued that a loan at a lower interest rate in a weaker currency is not necessarily easier to repay than a loan at a higher interest rate in stronger currency.[50]

Prospects for the 1980s and 1990s
Constraints on Soviet Economic Interdependence Through the mid-1970s, the trend of Soviet trade with the West and, by extension, the level of Soviet interdependence with the West was upward. During the late 1970s through 1981, however, the trend was reversed. In 1977 the Soviet Union began to reduce nonagricultural exports, especially machinery and equipment, to improve its trade balance and debt position and, probably, to reduce demands on high quality domestic resources. According to calculations by Joan Zoeter, real imports increased by a modest 2% per annum during the 1977–1981 period, in comparison with an annual average of 20% during the 1971–1976 period.[51] Similarly, Philip Hanson notes the post-1977 decline in Soviet imports of technology, which in his view was temporarily broken by an increase in equipment imports for the pipeline in 1981. He concludes that "in some respects the Soviet Union could even be said to have reduced its economic involvement with the Western world."[52]

The outlook for Soviet–Western interdependence during the 1980s and 1990s will depend on financial and political factors such as the Soviets' ability to pay, Western willingness to engage in trade with the Soviet Union and to extend credit, Soviet attitudes toward interdependence and perceptions of the ability of the West to exert leverage through trade, and the transition to a new generation of leaders.

The Soviet liquidity crisis of 1981–1982, during which the Soviet Union requested deferral of payments to suppliers, complete as opposed to 85% financing of equipment imports for the pipeline, and gold sold on declining markets, raised new questions about the Soviet Union's ability to pay. The consensus of Western analysis is that the Soviet hard currency position will probably be more difficult for the remainder of the 1980s than it was during the early 1970s, but that it will not be a binding constraint on the Soviets' ability to continue critical imports of machinery and equipment.[53]

Likewise, Western willingness to export to the Soviet Union is unlikely to be a binding constraint. The West Europeans have shown no indication of plans to change their policies of promoting exports to the Soviet Union. Under the Carter and Reagan administrations, the United States has restricted technology exports. But, even if U.S. policy remains more restrictive in the 1980s and 1990s, the Soviet Union will probably be able to turn to West European and Japanese suppliers for most of its import orders.

As for the willingness of the West to finance trade, it should be noted that the Soviet Union is considered to be the most creditworthy borrower in Eastern Europe. Although repayment problems in Poland and Romania may have had temporary effect on the Soviet Union's ability to borrow on international markets, the loan syndications of 1984 are evidence of Western bankers' confidence in the USSR's creditworthiness. Wharton Econometric Associates predicted that Soviet net hard currency debt will increase by over 85% in current dollar terms from 1980 to 1988.[54]

As Hanson suggests, political considerations may be more important constraints on Soviet trade and interdependence with the West than financial exigencies. Soviet decisions about the amount of interdependence and about the amount of leverage available to the West that they are willing to accept will be made during the transition to a new generation of leadership. In all probability this period will also be a period of slow growth.

While a policy of muddling through—that is, keeping economic policy as it is—is an option for the Soviet leadership, it is not likely to result in a significant improvement in growth and relief of shortfalls in key sectors. Nor would such a policy be likely to advance Soviet international security goals. Likely alternatives for change in economic policy that are available to the Soviet leaders tend toward two divergent groupings: policies that foster economic modernization and interdependence with the global economy, and neo-Stalinist policies of extreme centralization, tight control, and isolation form the non-Communist world.[55] The modernization/interdependence and the control/security scenarios or tendencies can be described in terms of the differing policies they would entail for national economic development: the allocation of resources among "guns," "butter," and "modernization"; reform of planning and management; economic relations with the industrialized West; and relations with the smaller members of the Council for the Mutual Economic Assistance (CMEA). Of the two tendencies, the modernization/interdependence scenario is liable to yield the better economic results and is more likely to be chosen if

498    John P. Hardt and Kate S. Tomlinson

improving the economy is the first priority. If considerations of internal
and external security are paramount, the control/security option is more
likely to be adopted. While it would appear to advance the internal and
external security goals of the Soviet leadership, it would probably not be
so beneficial economically as the modernization/interdependence option.

These two scenarios have sharply divergent implications for Soviet
policy toward Western Europe. If the modernization/interdependence
option is chosen, Soviet policy will be likely to emphasize international
cooperation over competition. If the neo-Stalinist control/security option
is selected, competition and confrontation with the capitalist countries
are liable to be the focus of Soviet policy. A major factor in determining
the tendencies in Soviet policies will be the nature of the domestic power
struggle for succession. Western policies will have some influence on
succession outcomes. The influence is likely to be enhanced if the West
has a unified position on relations with the East.

# Notes

[1]For an analysis of the current situation in the West by an authoritative
Soviet commentator, see N. Inozemtsev, "XXVI s"ezd KPSS i nashi zadachi,"
*Mirovaya ekonomika i mezhdunarodnye otnosheniya*, no. 3 (March 1981), especially
pp. 18–23. For a review of Soviet–West European trade policy under Stalin, see
John P. Hardt and Ronda Bresnick, "Brezhnev's European Economic Policy," in
*Soviet Foreign Policy toward Western Europe*, ed. George Ginsburgs and Alvin Z.
Rubinstein (New York: Praeger Publishers, 1978), pp. 205–206.

[2]Thomas G. Paterson, *Soviet–American Confrontation* (Baltimore: Johns Hop-
kins University Press, 1973), pp. 154–156. For another view, see Daniel Yergin,
*Shattered Peace: The Origins of the Cold War and the National Security State* (Boston:
Houghton Mifflin Co., 1977), especially Part 3.

[3]In Leo Gruliow, ed., *Current Soviet Policies*, vol. I (New York: Columbia
University Press, 1953).

[4]John P. Hardt and George D. Holliday, *Technology Transfer and Scientific
Cooperation between the United States and the Soviet Union: A Review*, U.S. Congress,
House Committee on International Relations (Washington, D.C.: U.S. Govern-
ment Printing Office, May 1977), Part 2, Chapter 2. Sources of general interest
include J. N. Savelova, "Development of Technical Exchange between Socialist
and Capitalist Countries," *Voprosy Izobratelstva*, no. 7 (1975); E. S. Shershnev,
*USSR–USA Economic Relations* (Moscow: "Science" Publishers 1976); N. P.
Shmelev, "Socialism and the World Economy," *Mirovaya ekonomika i mezhduna-
rodniye otnosheniya*, no. 10 (1976); and *Economic Ties East–West: Problems and
Possibilities* (Moscow: "Thought" Publishers, 1976).

[5]Donald W. Green and Herbert S. Levine, "Macroeconomic Evidence on the
Value of Machinery Imports to the Soviet Union," in *Soviet Science and Technolo-
gy: Domestic and Foreign Perspectives*, ed. John R. Thomas and V. M. Kruse-
Vaucienne (Washington, D.C.: George Washington University Press, 1977).

[6]Lawrence H. Theriot, "U.S. Governmental and Private Industry Cooperation with the Soviet Union in the Fields of Science and Technology," *Soviet
Economy in a New Perspective*, U.S. Congress, Joint Economic Committee (Washington, D.C.: U.S. Government Printing Office, 1976).

[7]U.S. Department of Defense, Office of the Director of Defense Research

and Engineering, "An Analysis of Export Control of U.S. Technology: A DOD Perspective," a report of the Defense Science Board Task Force on Export of U.S. Technology (Washington, D.C., 1976), pp. 9–14.

[8]John P. Hardt and George D. Holliday, "Technology Transfer and Change in the Soviet Economic System," in *Technology and Communist Culture: The Socio-Cultural Impact of Technology under Socialism*, ed. Frederic J. Fleron, Jr. (New York: Praeger Publishers, 1977), pp. 189–192.

[9]U.S. Department of Commerce, Bureau of East–West Trade. This includes Austria, Belgium–Luxembourg, Denmark, France, the Federal Republic of Germany, Italy, the Netherlands, Norway, Sweden, Switzerland, and the United Kingdom. Machinery and transport equipment are classified as SITC 7.

[10]Green and Levine, *op. cit.*, pp. 394–424.

[11]Philip Hanson, "Soviet Mineral Fertilizer Industry," in *East European Integration and East–West Trade*, ed. Paul Marer and John M. Montias (Bloomington: Indiana University Press, 1980), pp. 252–280. See also Robert Campbell, "Technological Levels in the Soviet Energy Sector," in NATO Economics Directorate, ed., *CMEA: Energy, 1980–1990* (Newtonville, Mass.: Oriental Research Partners, 1981), pp. 265–276, and Stanislaw Gomulka, *Inventive Activity, Diffusion and the Stages of Economic Growth* (Denmark: Aarhus, 1976).

[12]See Vladimir G. Treml, "Foreign Trade and the Soviet Economy: Changing Parameters and Interrelations," in *The Impact of International Economic Disturbances on the Soviet Union and Eastern Europe*, ed. Egon Neuberger and Laura D'Andrea Tyson (New York: Pergamon Press, 1980), pp. 184–211. For a critique of Treml's analysis by Jan Vanous, see Wharton Econometric Forecasting Associates, Centrally Planned Economies, *Current Analysis*, July 14, 1982. Treml's response may be found in the August 6 issue. Another source of the arguments by Drs. Treml and Vanous is U.S. Congress, Senate Committee on Foreign Relations, *The Premises of East–West Commercial Relations: A Workshop Sponsored by the Committee on Foreign Relations*, United States Senate and Congressional Research Service, Library of Congress, Committee Print, 97th Congress, 2d session, December 1982 (Washington, D.C.: U.S. Government Printing Office, 1983), pp. 83–111.

[13]On this subject, see also George Holliday, "Western Technology Transfer to the Soviet Union: Problems of Assimilation and Impact on Soviet Imports," in U.S. Congress, Joint Economic Committee, *Soviet Economy in the 1980s: Problems and Prospects*, vol. 1. (Washington, D.C.: U.S. Government Printing Office, 1982), pp. 514–580.

[14]Hardt and Holliday, "Technology Transfer and Change," p. 204.

[15]George D. Holliday, *Technology Transfer to the USSR, 1928–1937 and 1966–1975: The Role of Western Technology in Soviet Economic Development* (Boulder, Colo.: Westview Press, 1979), p. 180.

[16]See John P. Hardt, "Soviet Commercial Relations and Political Change," in *The Interaction of Economics and Foreign Policy*, ed. R. Bauer (Charlottesville: University of Virginia Press, 1975), pp. 48–83.

[17]For other answers to this question, see Daniel L. Bond and Herbert Levine, "The Soviet Machinery Balance and Military Durables in SOVMOD"; Myron Rush, "The Soviet Policy Favoring Arms over Investment since 1975"; Gregory Hildebrandt, "Trade-offs between Growth and Defense," in *Soviet Economy in the 1980s*; and Richard F. Kaufman, "Causes of the Slowdown in Soviet Defense," *Soviet Economy* 1, no. 1 (1985), pp. 9–38.

[18]Hardt and Holliday, "Technology Transfer and Change," pp. 184–189.

[19]Joan Zoeter, "U.S.S.R.: Hard Currency Trade and Payments," in *Soviet Economy in the 1980s, Part 2*, pp. 479–488.

[20]*Ibid.*, pp. 482–488. The estimates of net Soviet debt at year-end 1982 and 1983 are from the CIA's *Handbook of Economic Statistics*.

[21]John P. Hardt, "Soviet Economic Capabilities and Defense Resources" in *The Soviet Threat: Myth or Reality?* (New York: Academy of Political Science, 1978), pp. 122–124.

[22]Rush, *op. cit.*

[23]Philip Hanson, "The Role of Trade and Technology Transfer in the Soviet Economy," in *Economic Relations with the U.S.S.R.*, ed. A. Becker (Lexington, Mass.: Lexington Books, 1983). See also U.S. Congress, Joint Economic Committee, *East–West Technology Transfer: A Congressional Dialogue with the Reagan Administration*, Joint Committee Print, 98th Congress, 2d session, December 19, 1984 (Washington, D.C.: U.S. Government Printing Office, 1984).

[24]ECE, *Economic Bulletin for Europe*, June 1981, p. 233.

[25]For a more detailed analysis, see U.S. Congress, Joint Economic Committee, *Energy in Soviet Policy* (Washington, D.C.: U.S. Government Printing Office, 1981), especially Chapters 2 and 4; Hedija H. Kravalis, "U.S.S.R.: An Assessment of U.S. and Western Trade Potential with the Soviet Union through 1985," in U.S. Congress, Joint Economic Committee, *East–West Trade: The Prospects to 1985* (Washington, D.C.: Government Printing Office, 1982), *passim.*: John P. Hardt, "Soviet Energy and Allied Security", in *World Energy Supply and International Security, Special Report*, October, 1983, Institute for Foreign Policy Analysis, Inc., Cambridge, Mass., and Washington, D.C., pp. 23–63; and Ed. A. Hewett, *Energy, Economics, and Foreign Policy in the Soviet Union*, Washington, D.C.: The Brookings Institution, 1984.

[26]Kravalis, *op. cit.*, p. 296.

[27]See Conference on Security and Cooperation in Europe, *Final Act* (Helsinki, 1975), Bulletin Reprint, U.S. Department of State, Washington, D.C.

[28]*Economic Bulletin for Europe*, p. 170.

[29]In 1982, when the price of oil had began to decline, the CIA estimated that the Soviets could have earned as much as $1 billion annually by switching the destination of oil from East to West.

[30]John P. Hardt, "Soviet Energy Policy in Eastern Europe," in Council on Foreign Relations, *Soviet Policy in Eastern Europe*, ed. Sarah Terry (New Haven: Yale University Press, 1984), p. 189. Cf. Jochen Bethkenhagen, "Soviet Energy Supplies as a Factor in East–West Relations," forthcoming in *Economic Relations with the Soviet Union, American and West German Perspectives*, ed. Angela Stent (Boulder, Colo.: Westview Press).

[31]See N. Smeliakov, "Soviet Deputy Foreign Trade Minister Discusses East–West Trade," *Novyy Mir* (December 1973) for a discussion on Soviet problems in exporting manufactured goods to the West and Kravalis, *op. cit.*, pp. 291–294.

[32]For a detailed analysis, see Max Baumer and Hanns-Dieter Jacobsen, "CMEA's 'Westpolitik' between Global Limitations and All-European Potentials," in U.S. Congress, Joint Economic Committee, *East European Economic Assessment, Part 2—Regional Assessments* (Washington, D.C.: U.S. Government Printing Office, 1981), pp. 872–886.

[33]Zoeter, "U.S.S.R.," p. 486.

[34]On the last point, see Joan Barth Urban, "The West European Communist Challenge to Soviet Foreign Policy," in *Soviet Foreign Policy in the 1980s*, ed. Roger E. Kanet (New York: Praeger, 1982), pp. 171–193.

[35]For background on Soviet energy policy, see Edward A. Hewett, "Near-Term Prospects for Soviet Natural Gas Industry and the Implications for East–West Trade; Jonathan P. Stern, "CMEA Oil Acquisition Policy in the Middle East and the Gulf: The Search for Economic and Political Strategies"; and Thane Gustafson, "Soviet Energy Policy," in *Soviet Economy in the 1980s, Part 1*, pp. 431–456.

[36]47 FR 27250.

[37]See, for example, Dan Quayle," A Worthy Objective—But You Wouldn't Know It," *Washington Post*, August 29, 1982, p. C8. Additional sources on the pipeline dispute include: U.S. Congress, Joint Economic Committee, *Soviet Pipeline Sanctions: The European Perspective*, Hearings, 97th Congress, 2nd session, September 22, 1982 (Washington, D.C.: U.S. Government Printing Office, 1982) and Steve Mufson, "Anatomy of Continuing Pipeline Controversy: U.S. Is in Sharp Fight with European Allies," *Wall Street Journal*, August 31, 1982, p. 1.

[38]Bradley Graham, "European Community Protests U.S. Sanctions against Pipeline," *Washington Post*, August 13, 1982, p. A12.

[39]"An Analysis of Export Control of U.S. Technology," see note 7.

[40]Testimony by William A. Root, Former Director, Office of East–West Trade, Department of State, to the Subcommittee on International Economic Policy of the Committee on Foreign Relations of the United States Senate on October 26, 1983," mimeo, p. 4 and Paul Lewis, "Allies Curb Computers for Soviet," *New York Times*, July 17, 1984, p. D7.

[41]Root, *op. cit.*, p. 3.

[42]John P. Hardt and Kate S. Tomlinson, "Economic Interchange with the U.S.S.R. in the 1980s: Potential Role of Western Policy toward Eastern Europe in East–West Trade," in *Economic Relations with the USSR*, ed. Abraham S. Becker (Lexington, Mass.: Lexington Books, 1983), p. A-9.

[43]"U.S. Allies Agree to Redefine Rules on Sales to Soviets," *Wall Street Journal*, January 21, 1982, p. 31.

[44]"Prepared Statement of Hon. Allen W. Wallis, Under Secretary for Economic Affairs, Department of State," in U.S. Congress, House Committee on Foreign Relations, Subcommittees on Europe and the Middle East and on International Economic Policy and Trade, *East–West Economic Issues, Sanctions Policy, and the Formulation of International Economic Policy*, Hearings, 98th Congress, 2d session, March 29, 1984 (Washington, D.C.: U.S. Government Printing Office, 1984). p. 23.

[45]For an authoritative summary and the technical details of the new guidelines for computers and telecommunications equipment, see the changes in the U.S. export control list published in the *Federal Register* on December 31, 1984. Other sources on computer and telecommunications controls include Paul Mann, "CoCom Agrees on Export of Computers," *Aviation Week & Space Technology*, July 23, 1984, pp. 21–22; "Technology Exports to Soviet Bloc," *Wall Street Journal*, July 23, 1984, p. 21; and David Buchan, "Waiting for the New Lists," *Financial Times*, January 28, 1985, p. 9.

[46]Root, *op. cit.*, p. 4 and Frederick Kempe and Eduardo Lachica, "CoCom Feuds over Trade to East Bloc," *Wall Street Journal*, July 17, 1984, p. 35.

[47]See, for example, Under Secretary Wallis' oral statement in *East–West Economic Issues*, p. 3.

[48]Marie Lavigne, "Les relations Est–Ouest sous hegemonie?" *Le Monde Diplomatique*, Janvier 1985, pp. 8–9.

[49]For German views on credit, see Axel Lebann, "Financing German Trade with the East," *Aussen Politik* (English ed.) 33, no. 2 (1982), pp. 123–137 and Joachim Jahnke, "Westliche Kreditpolitik gegenuber osteuropaischem Staaten. Die Problematik angesichts wachsender politischer Spannungen" (Western Credit Policies towards the East European States. The Problem of Growing Political Détente), *Europa Archiv*, no. 15 (August 10), 1982, pp. 459–466.

[50]See the letter from Allen Wallis, Under Secretary of State for Economic Affairs, to Representative Lee H. Hamilton, Chairman of the Subcommittee on Europe and the Middle East of the House Foreign Affairs Committee, reprinted in *East–West Economic Issues*, p. 57.

[51]Joan Zoeter, *op. cit.*, p. 484. For the Soviet perspective on the credit issue,

see N. Shmelev, "Kredity i politiki k otnosheniam Vostok-Zapad (Credit and Politics in East–West Trade Relations)," *Mezhdunarodnaya Zhizn'* (*International Life*), no. 3, 1984.

[52]Hanson, *op cit.*, p. 1. For a discussion of Soviet export performance in the 1970s, see Philip Hanson, "The End of Import–Led Growth? Some Observations on Soviet, Polish, and Hungarian Experience in the 1970s," *Journal of Comparative Economics* 6 (1982), pp. 130–147.

[53]See Zoeter, Kravalis, and Hanson, *op. cit.*

[54]Wharton Econometric Forecasting Associates, Centrally Planned Economies *Balance of Payments and Debt Report: Soviet Union*, March 19, 1984, p. 3.

[55]An earlier version of these scenarios appeared in John P. Hardt and Kate S. Tomlinson, "Economic Factors in Soviet Foreign Policy," in *Soviet Foreign Policy in the 1980s*, ed. Roger E. Kanet (New York: Praeger, 1982), pp. 37–57. For another view, see Morris Bornstein, "Soviet Economic Growth and Foreign Policy," in *The Domestic Context of Soviet Foreign Policy*, ed. Seweryn Bialer (Boulder, Colo.: Westview Press, 1981), pp. 227–255.

# 28

# HANNES ADOMEIT

## Capitalist Contradictions and Soviet Policy*

Politics, in the Marxist–Leninist view and in Soviet practice, is the craft of conflict; it consists of the skillful management of contradictions. Even a "more powerful enemy," according to one of Lenin's most basic statements on strategy and tactics,

> can be conquered by exerting the utmost effort, and by *necessarily*, thoroughly, carefully, attentively, and skillfully taking advantage of every, even the smallest, "rift" among the enemies, of every antagonism of interest among the bourgeoisie of the various countries, among the various groups or types of bourgeoisie within the various countries, by taking advantage of every, even the smallest, opportunity of gaining a mass ally, even though this ally be temporary, vacillating, unstable, unreliable, and conditional. Those who do not understand this do not understand even a particle of Marxism, or of scientific, modern Socialism *in general*.[1]

The principle of *divide et impera* is, of course, not new. For centuries it was used to great advantage by the Roman and other empires. As for the Soviet Union, it too has applied this principle. But today the utilization of conflict *between* capitalist countries ("interimperialist" contradictions) and conflict *in* capitalist countries ("intraimperialist" contradictions) seems to hold greater promise for Soviet foreign policy than ever before. The capitalist economies are experiencing lower growth and higher unemployment than at any time since World War II. New and old remedies for restoring sound economic dynamism—Keynesian, monetarist, or "supply side"—appear to have, in essence, failed. Economic projections point to high or even rising unemployment in the coming years.[2] Large government deficits and the perceived need to cut government spending collide with the same governments' major com-

*Reprinted by permission of the author and publisher from *Problems of Communism* 33, no. 3 (May–June, 1984), pp. 1–18. No copyright claimed.

mitments (some of which are legally binding) to maintain a costly social security net. All this could lead to sharper domestic conflicts over distribution of income and allocation of resources. Defense, in this context, might very well be regarded by the electorate as the prime sector for extensive cuts in expenditures.

Such a development may appear all the more probable because pacifist—mainly antinuclear—and neutralist currents ("peace movements") have increased in strength in the late 1970s, particularly in Western Europe. These currents, moveover, are by no means limited to environmentalist, communist, Marxist, or other groups at the fringes of Western society, but extend to the major churches, noncommunist labor unions, and social democratic parties. Finally, since the United States is the strongest military power of the Western alliance, with global commitments that could involve Western Europe in a military conflict with the Soviet Union, these currents more often than not are also anti-American or at least quite critical of American policies.

Internal conflicts within "capitalist countries," as can be seen, are closely connected with "contradictions" between them. Indeed, disagreement between the United States and Western Europe as a whole on matters of substance has become more severe, and the tone of the exchanges more acrimonious. Many issues are at stake, including the scope of defense efforts and equitable burden sharing, protectionism in trade, and the level of interest rates on domestic and international money markets. But they are all overshadowed by and intertwined with one problem of major importance—relations with the Soviet Union.

Whereas in the past, too, attitudes and policies toward the Soviet Union were often characterized by disagreements both within and among the Western European countries and the United States, the late 1970s and early 1980s present a different situation. In the perception of both West Europeans and Americans, the dividing lines today run much more sharply between Western Europe as a whole and the United States. Additionally, the differences in attitude and policy toward the Soviet Union are regarded on both sides of the Atlantic as encompassing a much broader range of issues than before.

Irritations began to accumulate during the Carter Administration, whose management of policy—from the European perspective, whether correct or incorrect—was damaging the alliance because of its vacillation, unpredictability, and lack of firmness. These irritations escalated to resentment and mutual recrimination over how to react to the Soviet intervention in Afghanistan: how to evaluate this Soviet move and Soviet intentions; how to deter the Soviet Union from future expansionism; whether or not to use sanctions and, if so, whether to apply them in selected areas or across the board of political, economic, financial, scientific, and cultural contacts.

Resentment has deepened under President Reagan, whose electoral victory and subsequent policies seem to many European policymakers and analysts to be just one of many shifts from one extreme to the other in U.S. policy. At issue are policies which seem to aim at "managing the decline of the Soviet empire" and making sure that this empire goes under with a "whimper" rather than a "bang"; the utility or disutility of arms control negotiations with the Soviet Union; the scope of modernization for NATO's theater nuclear forces; the validity of charges that West European foreign policies reflect dependence upon and deference to Soviet power; the degree to which Soviet policies are responsible for instability in the Third World; and, finally (back to square one after Afghanistan), how to react to the "internal intervention" and "normalization" in Poland.

At the root of almost all the controversies in alliance policy toward the Soviet Union lie differing interpretations of détente. As summarized by an American analyst, the countries of Western Europe—by and large, and with some differences among and within them—have concluded that

> détente, and its underlying premises about the "web of economic relationships," were valid and useful in the 1970s and remain applicable in the 1980s. By contrast, we in the United States—by and large, and also with differences among us—have concluded that détente and its premises "have been weighed in the balance and found seriously wanting." We have concluded that we should envisage drastic changes in our relations with the Soviet Union in general, and in our economic relations in particular.[3]

## Imperialist Contradictions over Time

Even under socialism, serious contradictions are admitted by Soviet spokesmen and scribes to exist, but are regarded as being "nonantagonistic" and hence solvable by definition.[4] This is not the case with three other types of contradictions: (1) the fundamental antagonism between the two opposed socioeconomic systems, socialism and imperialism; (2) conflicts *between* capitalist countries; and (3) conflicts in capitalist countries. These types of contradictions are seen as "irreconcilable." They will disappear only with the disappearance of the capitalist system itself.

As this disappearance may take a while yet, it is of considerable interest for any examination of Soviet objectives and policy toward the United States and Western Europe to note that formalized Soviet ideological perceptions about the three types of antagonistic contradictions have changed significantly over time. "How else," Lenin asked during World War I, "can the solution of [interimperialist] contradictions be found, except by resorting to *violence?*"[5] Capitalist wars for the redistribution of power and influence, colonies, markets, access to raw materials, cheap labor, and so on, he reiterated after the war, "are absolutely inevitable."[6] Furthermore, given the nature of the capitalist system, Lenin was also convinced that "a series of frightful collisions between the Soviet Republic and the bourgeois states will be inevitable."[7]

It was not until the last stages of Stalin's rule that a Soviet leader clearly stated which of the existing antagonistic contradictions were more likely to lead to war, those between capitalist states or those between capitalism and socialism. Stalin provided this clarification shortly before the Nineteenth CPSU Congress in 1952. "War with the USSR," in Stalin's view, would "certainly put into question the existence of capitalism itself."[8] To that extent, such a war was not as probable as were wars among capitalist states merely for realignment of power. According to Stalin:

> Outwardly everything would seem to be "going well": the USA has put Western Europe, Japan, and other capitalist countries on rations; [West] Germany, Britain, France, Italy, and Japan have fallen into the clutches of the USA and are merely obeying its commands. But it would be mistaken to think that things can continue to "go well" for "all eternity," that these countries will tolerate the domination and oppression of the United States endlessly, that they will not endeavor to tear loose from American bondage and take the path of independent development.[9]

Khrushchev was less impressed with the sharpness of conflict between the United States and the countries of Western Europe and Japan. To be sure, when he stated—at the Twentieth party congress in 1956— that "war is not fatalistically inevitable," he was referring to war between the two opposed world systems. Yet, war between capitalist states was no longer a topic for him. This is not surprising, as cooperation in the Atlantic Alliance increased steadily in the 1950s and as a new factor difficult to reconcile with traditional Marxist–Leninist precepts arose: capitalist integration.

The European Economic Community (EEC) was initially interpreted very much in the light of Lenin's criticism in August 1915 of the slogan of the United States of Europe (USE), which held that alliances under imperialism could only have a "temporary" and "reactionary" character. Internationally, USE could only be designed to reapportion colonies and markets in the competition with the United States and Japan; domestically (i.e., in Europe), it would be used to check the advances of socialism. But in any case, the whole experiment could not last. The contemporary equivalent of USE, however, *has* lasted and has been regarded by Soviet analysts as, by and large, quite successful.[10]

While the view about the relative success of the Common Market has stayed constant until recently, Soviet analysis of the economic and political *implications* of West European integration has evolved through several stages. At first, when the EEC was founded, it was thought that this venture in capitalist integration was directed primarily against the Soviet Union. In the second stage, the 1960s, integration was seen primarily as a device by the West European countries to assert themselves against the *défi américain*. In the third stage, the 1970s, Soviet experts came to the realization that the West European "power center" (*tsentr sily*)[11] was not developing as much in the direction of autonomy and independence from the United States as they had previously thought.

Most recently, the "current economic and political situation in the capitalist world system," according to one of the foremost Soviet analysts on Western integration, is characterized by "an unprecedented—for the postwar period—sharpening of imperialist contradictions among the USA, the Western European countries of the EEC, and Japan." It is a stage, to summarize the argument, that consists of a counteroffensive launched by the United States against the loss of its economic power to the other two main competitors and the further weakening of its "political hegemony."[12]

As these shifts in interpretation show, formalized ideological perceptions and international relations analysis have fairly accurately reflected actual trends. These interpretations almost invariably are couched in combative language and—in line with communist "group-speak"—tend to dramatize aspects of threat to the Soviet Union and of conflict among the capitalist "power centers." It takes some courage and standing in the Soviet political system, therefore, to deviate from this pattern and, moreover, to stand Leninism completely on its head by arguing the following:

> The strengthening of the international positions of the world socialist system, the successes of the national-liberation movement in the "Third World," and the sharpening of social antagonism and the growth of the democratic and working-class movement in the capitalist countries put clearly recognizable limits to the development of the competitive struggle and rivalry, the implementation of an autarkic policy by imperialism, grim protectionism, and trade and currency wars, not to speak of such extreme measures as interimperialist wars.[13]

The differences in this interpretation are quite significant. Growth in the power of socialist and developing countries, from the Leninist perspective, can have but one consequence: the creation of severe *constraints* on the export of capital and the possibilities of making "superprofits," and hence the *sharpening* of interimperialist contradictions up to the increased likelihood of violent conflict, rather than the "setting of limits to the competitive struggle and rivalry." Nevertheless, the author sticks to her point. Even though in her view, too, " American–West European contradictions have never been sharper in the postwar period than today," she also clarifies that "these two regions of the capitalist world [the United States and Western Europe] are linked by a close network of capital, growing interdependence of economic development, and alliance obligations."[14] Yet another warning against exaggerated perceptions of rivalry among the "power centers" of imperialism (rather than dramatization for maximum political effect) is contained in her observation that "Western Europe, *like the world as a whole*, is to a certain extent living through a critical period."[15]

The implications of this interpretation are quite obvious. If Western Europe and the United States are objectively closely linked, and if, furthermore, important problems exist that affect not only the capitalist countries but also the socialist countries and the Third World (i.e., problems of common concern to all socioeconomic systems), then there

might be definite limits beyond which it would not be useful, from the
Soviet point of view, to fuel divisions in the West.

Utility of              In view of the above, it might not be safe to assume
Contradictions    that the differences in perception and policy be-
                            tween the United States and Western Europe are
invariably the result of deliberate and successful Soviet diplomacy,
propaganda, and clandestine operations rather than of self-inflicted
pain. Second, it is by no means correct to proceed from the assumption
that the Soviet leadership is inexorably and singlemindedly trying to
maximize conflict between the United States and Western Europe rather
than attempting to unite Western policymakers behind certain policies
favorable to the Soviet Union.[16]

Time and again, when a "power center" or country "A" proves
unresponsive to overtures by Moscow, the Soviet leaders resort to
indirect approaches to change its course. By demonstratively engaging
in atmospheric improvements, offering political concessions, and placing economic orders in countries "B" or "C" which are more responsive
to Soviet overtures, the Soviets hope to produce a "spillover" or "band-
wagon" effect on "A." This technique could be seen at work during
1965–1969, when Soviet–French relations were designed to accelerate
the pace and broaden the scope of the incipient West German Ostpolitik. Similarly, Moscow's practice of selective détente (with strong dos-
ages nevertheless of warning and pressure) vis-à-vis Western Europe
since the end of 1979 can be interpreted as an attempt to blunt the edge
of American "hard-line" policies toward the Soviet Union and to induce
the United States to align its policies more closely with those of Western
Europe. This purpose of Soviet policy becomes quite apparent in Moscow's dialectical view concerning the divisibility of détente. The "concept of the divisibility of détente," according to N. Portugalov, "does in
our view correspond to a certain extent to political reality." It does apply
in the sense that "the events of Afghanistan must not, under any
circumstances, put in danger détente in Europe." And it remains
applicable while the United States is attempting "to shelve détente
policy, resume the cold war, put pressure on the USSR, and work
towards its isolation, etc." Détente, on the other hand, is "indivisible on
our continent, as well as in other regions, in quite a different sense. One
cannot, as some politicians in NATO countries do, support the continuation of détente in Europe and at the same time, and not only
verbally, act in solidarity with American policy which is directed at
undermining it."[17]

Soviet attitudes toward the issues dividing the United States and
Western Europe, therefore, can be subsumed by standard Soviet operating assumptions and procedures that posit a perennial "struggle of two
tendencies" in capitalist countries. On the one hand, there are said to be
the "sober" and "realist" forces acting in recognition of objective
tendencies and in line with the Zeitgeist (*dukh vremeny*). They are pitted
against, on the other hand, the "reactionary" and "ultra-rightist" forces,

the "madmen" who want to turn back the course of history. Such divisions pose the task for Soviet policy, to paraphrase Soviet arguments, of encouraging the progressive against the reactionary tendencies and of making sure that the former "triumph" over the latter.

Divisions of a similar kind—into more accommodating or more uncompromising leaders—may exist in the Soviet Union as well; and it may very well be true, as reported by a prominent West German journalist after a trip to Moscow, that among Soviet middle-level party officials and higher ranking international relations experts there are those who advocate the exploitation of American–West European differences as a matter of principle and as a goal per se, and those who caution against such course of action.[18] As for the latter, "we are realists," Vadim Zagladin is reported to have said, "and it would not be a realistic goal to drive a wedge between Western Europe and America."[19]

Similarly, as two Soviet international relations experts write, people in the West who claim that the Soviet Union is trying to drive a wedge between the United States and Western Europe "do not see or do not want to see the difference between a dialectical–materialist approach to foreign policy and petty politicking (*melkoe politikanstvo*)." The main criterion on which the USSR bases its foreign policy, they argue, is not the degree of unity or absence thereof among the Western powers but "the extent to which [they] cooperate in or, conversely, oppose the solution of important international problems."[20]

## Objectives of Soviet Policy

The emphasis on the "objective" nature of inter-imperialist contradictions, and the view that exacerbation of such differences by the USSR might be short-sighted, raise the question whether such arguments reflect genuine perceptions or are subtle attempts at deceiving the West. Before rushing to answer this question, it might be helpful to consider first the importance of Western Europe to Soviet policy and the objectives that the Soviet leaders may be pursuing.

Whatever the degree to which particular functions of ideology may have been eroded, Soviet concepts of international relations still proceed from the "fundamental contradiction between the two opposed socio-economic systems" as a basic fact of life.[21] On the opposing side, it is the United States that is regarded as by far the most powerful country—despite relative gains in economic power and political influence by Japan and Western Europe since World War II. Whereas Western Europe and Japan (and China, too) are looked upon as regional powers, the United States is seen as a global power whose strength or weakness will ultimately decide the outcome of the historic struggle between the two systems.

Western Europe has correctly been regarded by the Soviet leadership as the single most important region in this global competition. It is, from the Soviet point of view, both a lever and a potential prize. This is due to a number of reasons. Western Europe has a much more developed infrastructure and a much more developed technological and industrial base than the USSR. It is culturally more advanced, and its societies are more dynamic and more adaptable to change. Despite all the frictions, the European Economic Community is still functioning, attracting new members, and extending into political cooperation. All this has repercussions in the various countries of Eastern Europe. It reinforces the traditional affinities between the two halves of Europe. It makes the Western half a center of attraction and emulation for a significant portion of the population in the Eastern half, and hence it poses problems for Soviet control. Western Europe, beyond that, is an important political, economic, cultural and, last but not least, military bridgehead of the United States on the Eurasian landmass. Quite obviously, if this bridgehead were to be denied to the United States, the global power position of that country would be decisively weakened.

Taking these facts into consideration and looking at published Soviet analyses and the twists and turns in Soviet political approaches since World War II, it is possible to postulate the following six objectives of Soviet policy toward the Atlantic Alliance.[22]

1. To win recognition of the territorial and systemic status quo in Eastern Europe.
2. To make sure that the West European countries adhere to the Soviet definition of "peaceful coexistence," that is, that they observe a certain code of conduct in their relations with the Soviet Union, maintain "friendly" relations with it, abandon "policies from positions of strength," refrain from "interference in the internal affairs" of the USSR and the East European countries, and so on.
3. To retain and, if possible, to broaden access to Western technology, know-how, and credits so as to overcome the Soviet Union's perennial economic and technological inferiority vis-à-vis the West.
4. To limit as much as possible Western political cooperation in the frameworks of the European Community and NATO.
5. To deny to Western Europe any viable defensive option and to make sure that the West Europeans are acutely aware of their military vulnerability in relation to the Soviet Union.
6. To transform the pluralistic systems of Western Europe from within by encouraging and supporting communist parties and other "progressive" and "peace-loving" forces.

When looking at these probable Soviet objectives in more detail, care needs to be taken not to fall into the analytical trap of invariably and unquestioningly fitting every Soviet move, including moves of embarrassment, probing, or blunder, into a coherent strategic design. Care also needs to be taken not to neglect the possibility that Soviet objectives may be mutually contradictory. After all, international politics is made up of a complex web of actions and reactions, and, quite naturally, anything the Soviet Union does in one direction may contain the seeds of failure in another.

In fact, the dilemmas that lie at the heart of Soviet policy shifts are numerous. Pressure on Western Europe may make public opinion more responsive to Soviet demands but tends to strengthen hard-line, anti-Soviet currents in the United States. (It may lead to what one observer has called the "toothpaste syndrome": if you close the cap of the tube and squeeze hard, the net effect may be quite unpleasant.) Benevolent attitudes and far-reaching détente may bring trade and security gains but also raise the specters of "liberalization," waning of ideology, and erosion of the power and authority of the CPSU. Reduction in the military presence of the United States in Western Europe may open the way for increased Soviet influence but undermine the rationale for the Soviet military presence in Eastern Europe and encourage closer West European cooperation, including defense cooperation. Finally, support of tendencies in West Germany toward neutralism (i.e., toward the reestablishment of a unified German state) could help separate that country from NATO but it could also give rise to dangerous illusions and potentially explosive developments in East Germany.

Because of these and similar dilemmas, it is not surprising that in pursuing its objectives the Soviet leadership has vacillated between several approaches. The three most important ones can be typified as follows:

- "Europeanism," that is, encouragement of tendencies toward neutralism, foreign-policy autonomy, and the independence of Western Europe with an anti-American bias

- "Atlanticism," that is, Soviet–American cooperation, collusion, or condominium directed at jointly "solving" European and other world problems

- "Pan-Europeanism," a combination of the two, consisting in the abandonment of crude endeavors at either forcing the United States out of Europe or trying to settle matters bilaterally with Washington at the expense of Europe. It is, thus, an attempt at *persuading* the United States to consent to a reduction in its European role and encouraging an "all-European" consciousness among the Europeans.

Pursuit of Objectives    Although these different approaches toward Western Europe testify to a certain skill and inventiveness in Soviet diplomacy, none of them has turned out to be entirely successful. Frequent shifts of approach are the result. But even when one approach is dominant and played *forte* by the Soviet orchestra, one can always discern in the background (as if waiting, in turn, to become dominant) the countertheme played *piano* or *pianissimo*. The shifts are clearly shown by the record of Soviet policy toward the West since 1945.

*The Stalin Era: "U.S.—Go Home!"* In the immediate postwar years, as the grand alliance quickly disintegrated over questions such as quadripartite control and administration of Germany and Japan, reparations, the Ruhr, free elections in Eastern Europe, and Soviet designs in Greece, Turkey, and Iran, Stalin shifted to an anti-American stance. Several years of strident "U.S.—Go Home!" campaigns were to follow.[23] Burdened with the legacy of Lenin's "inevitability-of-war" thesis, verbal aggressiveness, and anti-American rhetoric, the Soviet Union blundered into the blockade of Berlin in 1948, only to find that if it wanted to avoid war under conditions of U.S. nuclear monopoly, and if it desired to find a solution to the German problem, it had to appeal to the theme of "after all, we are still allies."[24]

Given the circumstances, such appeals were, of course, in vain. The blockade enhanced the impetus for closer Atlantic defense cooperation, checked to some extent, at the popular level, by a Soviet-supported peace movement. Yet Soviet foreign policy soon recovered from the setback of the Berlin crisis. The explosion of the first Soviet nuclear device in August 1949, the victory of communism in China, and nationalist, anticolonialist uprisings in the French and British territories in North Africa and Asia apparently induced a new sense of Soviet strength and helped precipitate the Korean war. But that policy also defeated the purpose of the peace movement, undercut neutralist currents in Western Europe, led to the rearmament of West Germany, and provided the impetus for the reintroduction of sizable U.S. forces in Europe. Thus, there was no confirmation of Stalin's idea, quoted above, concerning the alleged West European (and Japanese) desire "to tear loose from American bondage."

*The Khrushchev Era: Contours of Condominium* Under Khrushchev, another approach was dominant. Claiming (prematurely) that the possession of nuclear weapons with intercontinental means of delivery, and other attributes of power, established rough military parity with the United States, he asserted political equality as well: "Where there are equal forces, there must also be equal rights and responsibilities."[25] On various occasions, moreover, Khrushchev stressed that "history has imposed upon our two peoples great responsibility for the destiny of the world," and that as regards the two countries, "our interests do not clash directly anywhere, either territorially or economically."[26] Apparently unaffected by Khrushchev's fall in October 1964, Soviet writings on U.S. foreign policy and U.S.–Soviet relations continued to see a "community of national interests" between the United States and the Soviet Union and to state that "the two countries' national interests do not collide either globally or anywhere regionally."[27]

Soviet strategy thus assumed the contours of a Soviet–American condominium, or dyarchy, in international relations. The superpowers, according to this approach, would demarcate their respective areas of vital interest, define the areas of common interest, agree on the status quo to be preserved, and establish rules of conduct to govern their competition.[28] Furthermore, the primary focus of competition was to be not military power but ideology and economic performance. Bilateral summitry (see, for instance, Khrushchev's meetings with Eisenhower at

Camp David in September 1959 and with Kennedy in Vienna in June 1961) and personal contacts at lower levels were to be the primary means of reaching agreement.

Yet the difficulties are quite obvious in a relationship of one power ideologically committed to *changing* the status quo with another power dedicated to *defending* world order. The state called upon by "history" to change the status quo will be tempted to use the special relationship as a protective umbrella under which to expand its power and influence. It will tend to interpret the agreed-upon code of conduct not as a mutual obligation but as a constraint on the freedom of action of the adversary. It will inevitably tend to regard its own sphere of influence as inviolable and that of its adversary as open to revision. The allies of the status quo-oriented power in such a condominium or dyarchy are likely to feel suspicious and insecure, since they can no longer be sure that their own vital interests will not be sacrificed. The danger of such a bilateral relationship, finally, is recurrent misperception and misunderstanding about the "rules of the game." For these reasons, "big two-ism" under Khrushchev did not prevent (and perhaps even substantially contributed to) the outbreak of serious international crises, including the Berlin and Cuban-missile crises, in 1961 and 1962.

*The Brezhnev Era: Defects of Détente* Khrushchev's successors tried several changes in approach, the first of which was facilitated by a confluence of several developments. The United States was militarily and politically preoccupied with the Vietnam war. West European government reaction to that U.S. engagement ranged from lukewarm support, at best, to thinly veiled opposition. Left-wing student unrest used the war as a rallying point for anti-American demonstrations. de Gaulle was calling for his *Europe des patries* and for a reduction in the role of the "peripheral" powers (the U.S. and the USSR) and of the two military alliances in Europe. His withdrawal from NATO's military organization seemed to herald the beginning of the eventual dissolution of the Atlantic Alliance.

The stage was thus set for the Soviet leadership under Brezhnev in 1965–1969 to try to mobilize West European sentiment against NATO, against participation of the United States and Canada in the "all-European" conference on security and cooperation, in favor of "independent" foreign policies and the dissolution of the military blocs. it was set, in short, for an attempt to fragment Europe and separate it from the United States. To support this attempt propagandistically, the "main document" adopted by the latest (and perhaps last) World Conference of Communist and Workers' Parties in Moscow in June 1969 proclaimed that peace and security in Europe meant "guaranteeing the European peoples their sovereign right to be masters of their continent without interference from the USA."[29]

But in the same year another set of factors converged to induce a change of approach in Soviet "Westpolitik." First, as de Gaulle left office and Willy Brandt formed a left-liberal coalition government, France's role as Moscow's *interlocuteur privilégié* diminished. The evolving Ostpolitik of the new West German government, not least because of the problems over Berlin, intra-German relations, and the borders issue, required quadripartite participation (i.e., inclusion of the United States in the negotiating process). Second, with the removal of Alexander Dubček from all positions of power, "normalization" in Czechoslovakia provided Moscow with new freedom of maneuver to launch a Peace Programme. Third, the Ussuri River clashes had transformed Sino–Soviet relations from latent to overt conflict; some initiative was needed to forestall U.S.–Chinese security cooperation. Fourth, the conviction had grown in the United States that it would be impossible to find a military solution to the Vietnam war and that Soviet "restraint" and good offices were needed to achieve "peace with honor" (in essence, a decent interval before the collapse of South Vietnam). Finally, the Soviet leadership had been unable to reverse the trend of declining growth rates in the Soviet economy and cope successfully with the necessary transition from extensive to intensive growth. Large-scale imports of Western—including American—technology, and access to know-how and credits, began to look like an attractive alternative to far-reaching economic reform.

Thus, on all levels of East–West interaction—political, legal, military, and economic—U.S. participation became a *conditio sine qua non*. This precondition was made even more stringent by the West as the bargaining process evolved, when two sets of linkages were made more explicit: (1) no ratification by West Germany of the Moscow treaty and the treaties normalizing relations with East Germany, Poland, and Czechoslovakia without a quadripartite agreement on Berlin; (2) no agreement by the West to the Conference on Security and Cooperation in Europe (CSCE) without Soviet consent to talks on mutual and balanced force reduction (MBFR). These linkages presupposed Washington's continued involvement in Europe.

It is not surprising, therefore, that the Soviet leadership in 1970 gave up its opposition to U.S. participation in the European security conference. It is, similarly, less surprising in retrospect that Brezhnev, in his speech in Tbilisi in May 1971, consented to talks on MBFR—even though NATO could not conceal its desire for the Soviet Union to help the West alleviate the pressures exerted by U.S. supporters of the "Mansfield amendment" for unilateral withdrawal of American troops.[30] The Soviet leadership had decided upon a *comprehensive* management of East–West relations and a *negotiated* withdrawal of U.S. forces. Their "all-European" security system was apparently designed to transcend the constraints of both "Europeanist" and "Atlanticist" approaches. Rather than—as in the first phase of Brezhnev's policy toward the West from 1965 to 1969—trying to achieve a fragmentation of the West and a separation of Europe from the United States through pressure and head-on propaganda campaigns to isolate West Germany and exclude the United States from European affairs, the Soviet leadership in this phase of policy allocated to the United States the noble task of presiding over a *voluntary* curtailment of its influence in Europe.

Brezhnev's détente strategy, therefore—in contrast to all previous phases of Soviet policy—did contain new elements. These included (1) the unprecedentedly broad scope of East–West agreements, ranging from general rules of conduct to cooperation in space, from the prevention of nuclear war to environmental protection, and from strategic arms limitation talks to cultural and scientific exchanges; (2) the unprecedentedly large scale of Western commitment envisaged for the expansion of East–West trade and the development of the Soviet and East European economies; and (3) the inclusion of the West European countries as well as the United States in the overall approach, limiting the traditional attempts at playing off the "power centers" of imperialism and individual "capitalist" countries against one another. These represented improvements in strategy to which Andropov's successors may eventually revert.

For the time being, however, Brezhnev's détente strategy has been shattered, for both internal and external reasons. First, Soviet ideology, with its formalized perceptions of global systemic antagonism and the "tactical" nature of compromise, persisted, casting serious doubt on Soviet intentions. Second, Soviet leaders continued to apply a double standard to the "rules of the game" and the commitment to maintain the status quo in Europe. While they were determined not to allow any relaxation of tension to undermine the ideological, political, and socioeconomic system in Eastern Europe, they continued to actively support "progressive" forces in order to induce political change in Western Europe. Third, Soviet leaders adopted a similar double standard as regards the Third World. Claiming that the Soviet Union was consistently pursuing a "policy of peace and friendship among nations" (i.e., détente), they also stated unambiguously that the USSR would continue to "give undeviating support to the people's struggle for democracy, national liberation, and socialism."[31] In practice, this meant expansionism at limited risk (through arms deliveries and Cuban and Vietnamese intervention) in areas ranging from Angola to Cambodia, and (through Soviet forces) in Afghanistan. Fourth, the Soviet leadership embarked on a large military buildup. After ratification of SALT I, it did not seem to be content with parity in the strategic competition with the United States but was striving for "parity plus." Beyond that, it was increasing Soviet preponderance in conventional and tactical nuclear power in Central Europe.

But Western attitudes and policies, too, contributed to the demise of détente. Foremost among the factors to be mentioned in this connection was the Western—notably American—impatience with the slow pace of change in the Soviet Union. There was an almost complete lack of awareness of the need felt by Soviet leaders to make sure that an opening to the West would not lead to a rapid crumbling of their control, at home and in Eastern Europe. Vociferous Western demands regarding human rights are but one important example of this lack of awareness.

Related to this was the failure of East–West economic interaction to increase in line with the possibilities for expansion—and with probable Soviet expectations. This development was triggered by the Jackson–Vanik and Stevenson amendments, and the concomitant refusal by the

United States to grant most-favored-nation status to the USSR or to
make available government-guaranteed credit exceeding U.S. $75 mil-
lion per year.

The collapse of détente in Soviet–American relations and the survival
of only limited détente in Soviet–West European relations raise questions about the effectiveness of Soviet policy in utilizing "imperialist
contradictions." Put differently, assuming that the earlier enumeration
of Soviet objectives is by and large correct, what are the policy areas in
which the Soviet leaders have made gains, and where have they
suffered losses?

Balance          Contrary to some assessments made in Western Europe
Sheet of         and (more so) in the United States, Soviet policy toward
Soviet           the West has not been an overall success story. The
                 record suggests that success and failure have been
Westpolitik      mixed, the failures lying primarily in the socioeconomic
                 realm (i.e., in the attempts to achieve objectives 1, 2, 3,
and 6, noted and analyzed earlier) and the successes in complicating
Western political and security cooperation and eroding the credibility of
NATO's doctrine of "flexible response" (i.e., objectives 4 and 5).

*Failures in the Ideological and Political Competition* The European security conference (CSCE), according to the Soviet agenda, was
to lead to the recognition not only of the territorial but also of the
systemic status quo in Europe. Some gains have been made, in the
Soviet view, on the territorial issues. The CSCE did indeed declare the
postwar borders in Europe to be "inviolable." But contrary to Moscow's
original designs, the Helsinki conference and the follow-up meetings in
Belgrade and Madrid never did codify legally or legitimize politically the
existing socioeconomic order in Europe. Nor did they endorse the kind
of political and military control the Soviet Union is exerting in Eastern
Europe.

If, from the Soviet perspective, further proof of this were needed, it
was amply provided by the Western responses to the developments in
Poland after July 1980. These responses included the open support for
Solidarity from the entire political spectrum in Western Europe and the
United States; the ill-concealed hope for the undoing of the "shameful
surrender" to Stalin at Yalta; the earnest belief in the "Finlandization" of
Poland as a realistic prospect. Finally, after the imposition of martial law
in December 1981, demands were put forward by Western governments
individually, as well as by the European Community and the NATO
Council of Ministers collectively, for the lifting of martial law, the release
of all internees, and the resumption of dialogue between the authorities
and Solidarity. These demands, moreover, were backed up by
sanctions—more substantive and severe on the part of the United States
and less stringent, more symbolic on the part of the West European
countries. Thus, neither the West European countries nor the United
States adhered to the code of conduct applicable, according to Soviet

interpretations of the CSCE Final Act, to the events in Poland—"non-interference in the internal affairs of sovereign states." Rather than cooperating with the Soviet Union in codifying the status quo in Europe, they had, in the Soviet view, tried their hardest to change it.

This points to the failure of Soviet diplomacy to achieve another of the objectives enumerated above, namely, transforming the pluralist systems of Western Europe, winning a greater degree of control over West European domestic policies, and channeling these policies in a pro-Soviet direction. In fact, all empirical evidence runs counter to the view expressed by an American correspondent that "bonds of sympathy and a community of interests are developing as rapidly between Western Europe and the Soviet Union as they are dissolving between Western Europe and the United States."[32] Obviously, it is necessary to make a distinction between some calculated adaptation to Soviet power and favorable images of the Soviet Union. Growth of Soviet power, it stands to reason, does not necessarily lead to improvements in the Soviet image. Indeed, the former may well damage the latter.

For example, recent public opinion polls show that a significant majority of West Germans believe that the aim of Soviet policy is not to achieve peaceful cooperation with the West but to dominate Western Europe. And because citizens feel *more* threatened by the Soviet Union now than a few years ago, according to the polls, the West Germans' opinion of Russia has become *less* rather than more favorable.[33] Similarly, even without detailed poll data, it is evident to any casual observer that there has been a spectacular deterioration of the Soviet image and influence in France. This was already true before the imposition of martial law in Poland and, in all likelihood, has increased since then. Concurrently, there has been broad support in France for Mitterrand's hard-line policies toward the communists at home, in relations with the Soviet Union, and on defense. Britain, in the last decade, has also been immune to an increase in Soviet influence. At the same time, it exemplifies a pattern common to other West European countries. Despite high unemployment figures, the country remains eminently "governable" and even retains an electorate that is prone to vote center-right rather than center-left or left.

The communist parties in Western Europe have been a prime instrument in Soviet attempts to transform the domestic systems and the foreign policy orientation of the countries concerned. However, in line with the declining attraction of Soviet ideology among Western intellectuals, the effectiveness of the communnist parties in promoting Soviet influence has decreased. More often than not, the impact that can be made by various "peace" campaigns on domestic politics in Western Europe crucially depends on the ability of the organizers to refute the charge that they are acting on behalf of the Soviet Union.

Furthermore, electoral support for communist parties has correlated nearly inversely with their pro-Moscow orientation. But more independent or even outright anti-Soviet positions do not help much either. Thus, "Eurocommunism," which thrived on the idea of a model of communism different from that of Soviet and East European

Marxism–Leninism, and which to many observers seemed to become a major political force in the late 1970s, is today a dead issue.

*Failures in the Economic Competition* Concerning economic issues (objective 3), the Soviet Union has abysmally failed in its attempt—still part of the official CPSU Programme adopted in 1961—to "catch up with and overtake" the United States in production by 1980. Soviet GNP stablilized at around 55% of U.S. GNP in the 1970s. Economic growth rates have shown a long-term declining trend. (According to Soviet figures, they fell from around 10% in the 1940s to approximately 8% in the 1950s, 6% in the 1960s, and 4% in the 1970s. Growth rates of 2% are probable for the 1980s.)[34] The USSR did not achieve its aim of overcoming the perennial technological inferiority vis-à-vis the West. The structure of Soviet foreign trade is still very much that of a developing country—importing finished products in exchange for raw materials and energy supplies. Furthermore, the Soviet leadership is faced with a whole set of economic problems: declining rates of investment, underdevelopment of economic infrastructure, adverse demographic trends, exhaustion of oil reserves in the European parts of the Soviet Union, labor shortages, lagging productivity, and low competitiveness on the world market—in short, difficulties in shifting from coercion to cooperation, and from mobilization to modernization, in economic affairs.

All this casts doubt on the existence of a Soviet economic strategy designed, as Richard Pipes has argued, "to make the West Europeans maximally dependent on the Eastern bloc" by deliberately "promoting heavy indebtedness of the Comecon countries" and achieving "maximum control of West European energy supplies."[35] To put it more cautiously, even if there were such a strategy, it has not worked very well. The primary reason for the interest of the Soviet leadership in East–West economic exchanges, in the foreseeable future, will be due not to Soviet external political objectives but to domestic economic requirements.

For a time, in the first half of the 1970s, the USSR was quite successful in achieving its goal of broadening access to Western technology, know-how, and credit. This soon began to change, however. A number of economic and political factors converged to limit East–West trade significantly. Such factors included (1) the burdening of Soviet–American trade with political preconditions, as noted above, in the early 1970s, and the deterioration of Soviet–American relations in the late 1970s; (2) the slowdown in the rates of growth of the Western economies in the wake of several "oil shocks," resulting in cutbacks of orders from Council for Mutual Economic Assistance (CMEA) countries; and (3) the change in the role of commercial credit from important driving force behind East–West trade to brake on its expansion.

In part because of the deterioration of Soviet–American relations, the Soviet Union has attempted to shift much of its trade to Western Europe and Japan. This has led to widely shared impressions in the West—notably in the United States—that this "punishment" of the United

States has been successful; that there has been a significant increase in Soviet–West European trade; and that the USSR, consequently, can easily do without trade exchanges with the United States.

These impressions do not correspond to the facts. There is no reason to suspect that, in principle, the Soviet leadership is no longer interested in engaging the huge U.S. economic and technological potential for the development of its Siberian resources. Many products and types of equipment are available only from the United States. And although there has been an increase in the absolute value of Soviet–West European trade (caused mainly by the significantly higher prices charged for Soviet oil), the share of the CMEA countries in overall West European trade has been falling steadily since the mid-1970s. In the early 1980s, there has been a slight increase again in the USSR's share, but a further decline in the share of the other European CMEA countries.[36] Credit relations conform to the same pattern. It is understandable that, for financial and economic reasons, the East European countries have increasingly come to be regarded by Western banks as credit risks. This should not apply to the Soviet Union, which possesses huge gold reserves and natural resources, and whose foreign indebtedness is quite low. Yet its creditworthiness, too, has significantly suffered. Net financing flows from Western banks to the Soviet Union have decreased to a trickle. This decrease cannot be explained solely on economic grounds. It is undoubtedly due to political reasons (i.e., to the general atmosphere of tension and uncertainty prevailing in East–West relations).[37]

In sum, despite the well-publicized gas-pipes-and-credit deal (the Urengoy pipeline project), it is difficult to maintain that there has been "business as usual" in Soviet–West European economic relations. "Economic relations between Eastern and Western Europe," as even some Soviet economists acknowledge, "are closely connected with American policy."[38] Furthermore, neither the scale of the economic exchanges nor the perceptions of the West European public concerning this issue make it safe to assume that Soviet leaders think they have managed to achieve—or are able to achieve—West European economic dependence on the Soviet Union. Quite the contrary. The Soviet leaders must be aware that on matters of East–West trade they are more of a *demandeur* than are the Western countries.

*Relative Success in the Military Competition* In contrast to the East–West competition in the ideological and socioeconomic spheres, the Soviet Union has been more successful in the East–West military competition (objectives 4 and 5). This is indicated by Soviet achievement of strategic parity or "parity plus"; modernization of Soviet intermediate-range and theater nuclear forces; further improvement in Soviet conventional military preponderance in Europe and the buildup of forces capable of power projection and intervention at and far beyond the periphery of the USSR.

In the Khrushchev era, as was mentioned above, the primary focus of competition between the two opposed world systems was declared to be ideological and economic. But starting with the Berlin and Cuban crises, the focus began to shift. Increasingly, the central sphere of competition between the two systems came to be military. This was perhaps not a conscious decision taken by the leadership under Brezhnev. But as the adversary superpower seemed to place such a great emphasis on military power in international relations, and as other Soviet means of influencing world events turned out to be relatively ineffective, this reorientation became ever more pronounced.

There are other reasons for this reorientation. Military competition is best suited to a centralized command economy in which military industry has been allocated a privileged position and national security receives top priority. Conversely, military competition is the sphere that is most controversial in Western pluralist systems. It is also the sphere where such systems are most vulnerable. Consequently, claims for a constant, let alone higher, budgetary share for defense expenditures against the background of a trend in almost all Western countries to cut government spending are likely to lead to domestic polarization. But the emphasis on military competition is bound for several reasons to lead as well to intra-Alliance polarization. In Western Europe the size of the military sector in the national economy is smaller than in the United States (i.e., the "military–industrial complex" is economically and politically less influential). Western Europe has a more extensive and costly social welfare net and strong social democratic parties committed to its protection.

The emphasis on military competition, moreover, is likely to be also a reflection of the belief held by the Soviet leadership that military power can successfully be transformed into political influence. Such transformation is probably regarded as working through perceptions or, more precisely, through a process of interaction between changes in the power relationship and the recognition of such changes. If, the Soviet leadership may reason, it can convincingly demonstrate that NATO has no viable defensive option in Western Europe, a process of political accommodation is likely to set in. This process could be furthered, to continue this reasoning, if the threat or use of force by the Soviet Union on the flanks, or in areas not directly covered by the NATO treaty, were to add to NATO's political, economic, and military constraints.

In order to accelerate such a political process of adaptation, the Soviet arms buildup, the Soviet stance in arms control negotiations, and the Soviet support for the "antiwar movement" have been integrated closely in one single approach. This much is undisputed by most political analysts. What is hotly debated, however, is the question whether West European political accommodation to or appeasement of Soviet military power is an accomplished fact; a discernible, on-going process; a conceivable, future possibility; or a distinct impossibility. It is undoubtedly a question that looms very large in the collective mind of the Soviet leadership as well.

From the Soviet perspective, looking at Western Europe and its role in the Western alliance, there are indeed some trends and issues that indicate an increase in Soviet influence over Western security relations. These trends are most likely, in the Soviet view, reflected in the following:

- The adoption of programs declared necessary by NATO but never implemented (e.g., the Long-Term Defense Program and the decision to increase defense expenditures by 3% in real terms)

- The announcement of production and deployment of the "neutron bomb" as necessary to counter Soviet superiority in tanks but the shelving (in part because of West European hesitation and domestic opposition) of these plans by President Carter

- The growth—in conjunction with the domestic opposition to the "neutron bomb"—of a "peace movement" in Western Europe, rallying pacifist, environmentalist, religious, and leftist political forces against nuclear weapons in general, and against NATO's plans for the modernization of intermediate range nuclear forces (INF) in particular

- Major divisions in important West European political parties, notably social democratic parties, and conflicts in coalition governments *in* Western Europe and *between* Western Europe and the United States concerning NATO strategy, Western security policy, and relations with the Soviet Union.

If trends and events such as these were interpreted by the Soviet leadership as proof that the transformation of Soviet military preponderance in Europe into political leverage is well under way, the outcome of the INF controversy must give the Soviet leadership cause for reappraisal. There can hardly be any doubt that, for the Soviet Union and the "peace movement" in Western Europe, blocking the deployment of Pershing II and cruise missiles had been an important test case of their ability to decide significant Western security issues in their favor. This test case they lost.

This loss must appear to the Soviet leaders as particularly painful since they had characterized NATO's dual-track decision as the most serious and most hostile measure taken against the Soviet Union since World War II. Thus they portrayed the dangers of deployment as equal to those of the Cuban missile crisis, warned that détente in Europe could not survive deployment, and threatened that the USSR would reply "both militarily and politically" and that the consequences would be "very grave indeed."[39] Soviet policy toward the United States and Western Europe, therefore, has arrived at a crucial juncture.

Prospects     On the one hand, the Soviet leaders may consider the West European "peace movement" to have suffered only a temporary setback, so that it still can be an effective political instrument for Soviet foreign policy. They may still regard the erosion of consensus over NATO strategy among West European political parties (e.g., the about-face of the West German Social Democratic Party on the dual-track decision) as significant enough to be strengthened by a tough Soviet stance. Such a stance would allow a leader or a collective leadership not to be perceived as weak during a succession period. It would not antagonize an important domestic political force—the military. And given the tremendous Soviet efforts in arms production and deployment over the past two decades, it would meet an inclination of the leadership—under the circumstances perhaps understandable—to "cash in" on its investment.

In practice, such a tough line could mean ever more threats of new deployments; closer military integration in the Warsaw Pact; pressure on the East European countries to increase their share of the defense burden; intransigence in arms control negotiations; further fueling of divergencies between the United States and Western Europe; and continued reliance on domestic pressures in NATO countries. Part of such a line could be interpreted as having begun with the Soviet walkout from the intermediate-range (INF), strategic (START) and conventional (MBFR) negotiations, and the adoption of certain countermeasures as announced in November 1983: (1) cancellation of the (self-proclaimed and arguably self-violated) moratorium on the construction of new missile sites in the European part of the Soviet Union; (2) stationing of short-range nuclear missiles in East Germany and Czechoslovakia; and (3) deployment of additional missiles in "ocean areas" around the United States.[40]

On the other hand, unceasing emphasis on military power does nothing to alleviate the Soviet Union's social and economic problems. It strengthens the role of the military, and of the orthodox political and ideological forces in the Soviet system, making decentralization and other economic reforms even more difficult to achieve. The continued priority for military production and for the military instrument in foreign policy does nothing to improve Soviet control in Eastern Europe. Indeed, it serves to undermine even further the legitimacy of this control among East Europeans. It further enhances the image in Western Europe of the USSR as a repressive garrison state founded on a rigid and antiquated ideology. A tough line could, more dangerously from the Soviet point of view, harden American attitudes even further and transform the U.S.–Soviet arms competition into a real arms race, which the USSR could still lose by a significant margin. The prospect of engaging the United States in large-scale economic ventures for the development of Soviet natural resources or of gaining access to U.S. technology and credit would practically vanish. In short, continued reliance on military pressure entails the risk for the Soviet leaders that they may overplay their hand.

In fact, they may already have realized that there is such a risk. For instance, the "countermeasures," which Andropov announced in November 1983, can be regarded as the very minimum that the Soviet Union had to adopt so as to save face. Militarily, some of the measures are fairly mild and inconsequential; others were planned in advance and merely received a more convenient packaging. But, significantly, Poland, Hungary, Bulgaria, and Romania have been exempted from the military countermeasures on the nuclear level. And there are good reasons for not forcing those countries, as well as East Germany and Czechoslovakia, to put further strain on their vulnerable societies and economies, either by making them increase their defense burden or by requiring them to cut off their trade with the West.

The "countermeasures" at the political level are by and large limited to posturing—and, for the Soviet Union, not very promising posturing at that. This is the case because both the Soviet Union and the East European countries have an interest in maintaining a reasonable working relationship with the West European countries, politically and economically. For this reason, too, nothing has come of the "new ice age" in intra-German relations of which East German leader Erich Honecker warned, should Pershing II and cruise missiles be deployed in West Germany.[41] Similarly, under current conditions of Soviet military advantage in Central Europe, prolonged abstention from arms control negotiations would damage Soviet interests more than those of the West. Abstention would take away one of the most effective Soviet means for influencing domestic political processes in West European countries and, for a change, would cast the Soviet Union in the role of the *enfant terrible* holding up arms control agreements. It is most likely for these reasons that the Soviet leadership decided to take part in the European Disarmament conference in Stockholm; that it very quickly agreed to a new date for the continuation of the MBFR talks in Vienna; and that it has hinted—even though cautiously—at the possibility of merging INF and START negotiations.[42]

If, as it appears, the scope for a "tough" line is limited, so too is the scope for a "soft" line. Any immediate, far-reaching shift away from the emphasis on military power (e.g., by agreeing to substantial cuts in conventional and nuclear forces in Europe, by lowering the rate of growth in arms production, and by consenting to genuine "equal security" for both the Soviet Union *and* Western Europe) may entail quite unpalatable consequences in the collective consciousness of the Soviet leadership. Given the relative weakness of political, ideological, economic, and cultural means for exerting influence, such consequences could include a significant decrease in political leverage in Europe. This, in turn, would have negative implications for the *global* role and status of the USSR. A reduced threat profile and lessening of tensions could also bring with it—as the 1970s have proven—difficult management problems in the Soviet Union and Eastern Europe. Undoubtedly, verbal aggressiveness and vivid portrayal of external threats are not only in conformity with Marxist–Leninist ideology but also useful for maintaining discipline at home and in the bloc, and hence will not easily be abandoned.

Finally, given the uncertainties of the succession process and the need for any leader or group of leaders to retain the support of the military as the single most powerful institution except for the CPSU, and given the palpable aversion to aiding, or being seen as aiding, President Reagan's reelection prospects, no major conciliatory initiative in Soviet–American relations is likely. This does not exclude tactical approaches to find out whether a relatively conciliatory American posture is merely a function of the election campaign or contains some substantive elements advantageous to Soviet interests. It also does not exclude a measure of selective détente in Soviet–West European relations.

By the same token, all this does not amount to a promising blueprint of "divide and rule," not least because the differences in the Western alliance at present are showing clear signs of abating. It may not even amount to a policy of muddling *through* but simply one of muddling *on*.

This would be due to the fact that the "socialist community" (*sotsialisticheskoye sodruzhestvo*), too, is riddled with contradictions. These contradictions, moreover, are probably even more severe than those in the Western alliance. They encompass the above-mentioned gap between military strength and the relative weakness of socioeconomic instruments for exerting influence internationally. But they also extend to the conflicts between ideological rigidity and an ever more complex reality, between internal stagnation and external ambitions, and between centralized command economies and widespread corruption, as well as between integrative tendencies at the center of the Soviet empire and autonomous aspirations at the periphery. Undoubtedly, these contradictions—whether "nonantagonistic" or not—greatly reduce the effectiveness of Soviet attempts at exploiting divisions in the opposite camp.

## Notes

[1] V. I. Lenin, *Left-Wing Communism, an Infantile Disorder: A Popular Essay in Marxian Strategy and Tactics* (New York: International Publishers, 1969), p. 59 (emphasis in the original). The essay was written in 1920.

[2] Projections of the OECD are that unemployment in North America will decline slightly until the first half of 1985 (to 8% of the labor force in the United States and 11% in Canada) while unemployment in Europe is likely to continue its upward drift, and could approach 12% of the labor force [see *OECD Economic Outlook* (Paris), no. 34, (December 1983), p. 48].

[3] Charles Wolf, Jr., Statement before the Senate Foreign Relations Committee, August 12, 1982 (unpublished mimeograph). The author is head of the International Security Program and Dean of the Graduate Institute at the Rand Corporation, Santa Monica, Calif.

[4] Andropov, for instance, warned that contradictions in socialist countries should be taken seriously lest they lead to "grave collisions"; see his "The Teaching of Karl Marx and Some Questions on the Building of Socialism in the USSR," *Kommunist* (Moscow), no. 3 (1983), pp. 9–23, esp. p. 21. For more detailed discussion of the problem of socialist contradictions, see A.P. Butenko, "Contradictions in Developed Socialism as a Social System," *Voprosy filosofii* (Moscow), no. 10 (1982), pp. 16–29.

[5] Quoted from Lenin's essay, *Imperialism: The Highest Stage of Capitalism* (New York: International Publishers, 1969), pp. 96–97 (emphasis in the original). The essay was written in Zurich in the spring of 1916.

[6] *Ibid.*, p. 10, Preface to the French and German editions, July 20, 1920.

[7] V.I. Lenin, Report to the Eighth Congress of the Communist Party, March 18, 1919, *Selected Works*, Vol. VIII (New York: International Publishers, 1943), p. 33.

[8] I.V. Stalin, *Economic Problems of Socialism in the USSR* (a collection of comments on a draft for a new textbook on political economy written between February and September 1952, that is, shortly before the nineteenth CPSU Congress in October 1952) (Moscow: Foreign Languages Publishing House, 1952), p. 39.

[9]*Ibid.*, pp. 38–39.

[10]One of the foremost Soviet experts on socialist integration, for instance, frankly acknowledges that "the level of the division of labor in CMEA does not satisfy the requirements of the countries participating in it. . . . CMEA lags behind the Common Market in that respect." See M. Senin (Director of the International Institute for the Study of Economic Problems of the Socialist World System at CMEA), *Socialist Integration* (Moscow: Progress Publishers, 1973), p. 178. Although published in 1973, Senin's appreciation of the differences in the depth of economic integration achieved by the two economic organizations remains valid more than 10 years later. One of the most recent indications of this is the postponement yet again of the much-delayed summit conference of the CMEA countries.

[11]The term "power center" became official Soviet usage when Brezhnev stated at the Twenty-fourth CPSU Congress: "By the early 1970's, the main centers of imperialist rivalry have become clearly visible: these are the USA— Western Europe (above all, the six Common Market countries)—Japan. The economic and political competitive struggle between them has been growing ever more acute." *The Twenty-fourth Congress of the Communist Party of the Soviet Union, March 30–April 9, 1971: Documents* (Moscow: Novosti, 1971), p. 20.

[12]Juri Schischkow, "Rivalry among the Three Imperialist Centers and the US Confrontationalist Course, "*Aussenpolitik* (East Berlin), no. 2 (1983), pp. 49–56, esp. pp. 49 and 53. For a more detailed examination of Soviet perceptions of West European economic integration, see Hannes Adomeit, "Soviet Perceptions of Western European Integration: Ideological Distortion or Realistic Assessment?" *Millenium: Journal of International Studies* (London) (Spring, 1979), pp. 1–24.

[13]M. Maksimova, "Capitalist Integration and World Development," *Mirovaya ekonomika i mezhdunarodnyye otnosheniya* (Moscow—hereafter *MEMO*), no. 4 (1978), pp. 14–24, esp. p. 19.

[14]M. Maksimova, Introduction to a Round-Table Discussion, "Problems of West European Integration," in *ibid.*, no. 11 (1982), pp. 107–111, esp. p. 111.

[15]*Ibid.*, p. 110.

[16]This is a point well made by Kenneth Pridham, "The Soviet View of Current Disagreements between the United States and Western Europe," *International Affairs* (London) (Winter 1982–1983), pp. 17–31.

[17]TASS commentary as published in *Neues Deutschland* (East Berlin), February 9–10, 1980. N. Portugalov is a senior Soviet journalist who writes on West Germany and European security issues and apparently is on the staff of, or otherwise attached to, the CPSU Central Committee Department on International Information (see *Le Monde* [Paris], March 2–3, 1980).

[18]Theo Sommer, "Do the Russians Want War?" *Die Zeit* (Hamburg), March 11, 1983, pp. 9–10.

[19]*Ibid.* Zagladin is First Deputy Head of the International Department of the CPSU Central Committee.

[20]S. Madzoyevskiy and D. Tomashevskiy, "Increase in International Tension and Western Europe," *MEMO*, no. 11 (1982), pp. 42–51, esp, pp. 50–51.

[21]See Hannes Adomeit, "Ideology in the Soviet View of International Affairs," in Christoph Bertram, ed., *Prospects of Soviet Power in the 1980's* (London: Macmillan, 1980), pp. 103–110.

[22]This summary of Soviet objectives draws on Christoph Royen, *Die sowjetische Koexistenzpolitik gegenüber Westeuropa: Voraussetzungen, Ziele, Dilemmata* (Soviet Coexistence Policy toward Western Europe: Preconditions, Goals, and Dilemmas), Series Internationale Politik und Sicherheit, ed. by Stiftung Wissenschaft und Politik (Baden-Baden: Nomos, 1978). Although this summary was

written in 1977–1978, changes that have occurred in the meantime have not rendered it outdated.

[23]More detail on this is provided by Pridham, *Loc. cit.*, p. 19.

[24]Such appeals are documented in Hannes Adomeit, *Soviet Risk-Taking and Crisis Behavior: A Theoretical and Empirical Analysis* (London: George Allen & Unwin, 1982), pp. 67–182.

[25]Khrushchev in a speech to graduates of Soviet military academies, *Pravda* (Moscow), July 9, 1961.

[26]*Ibid.*, December 31, 1961.

[27]Institute of the World Economy and International Relations, ed., *Dvizhu-shchiye sily vneshney politiki SShA* (Motive Forces in U.S. Foreign Policy (Moscow: Nauka, 1965), p. 507.

[28]This summary of Khrushchev's détente strategy follows Vernon Aspaturian, *Process and Power in Soviet Foreign Policy* (Boston: Little, Brown, 1971), p. 780. On Khrushchev's détente policies vis-à-vis the U.S. and their effect on Western Europe, see John Van Oudenaren, *The Leninist "Peace Policy" and Western Europe*, Research Monograph, Center for International Studies, Massachusetts Institute of Technology, Cambridge, Mass., January 1980, pp. 8–9.

[29]Text of the document as published in *Problemy mira i sotsializma* (Prague), June 1969.

[30]The NATO ministerial meeting in Reykjavik in June 1968 called for discussions on mutual and balanced force reductions. This call was formally reiterated at the NATO minsterial meeting in Rome in May 1970. For the context of the offer and the Soviet responses see Lothar Ruehl, *MBFR: Lessons and Problems*, Adelphi Paper no. 176 (London: International Institute for Strategic Studies, 1982), pp. 6–8.

[31]Quoted from Brezhnev's report to the Twenty-fourth CPSU Congress, March 30, 1971, *Pravda*, March 31, 1971.

[32]David A. Andelman, "Struggle over Western Europe," *Foreign Policy* [Washington, D.C. (Winter, 1982–1983), pp. 37–51, esp. p. 37].

[33]See, for instance, Elisabeth Noelle-Neumann, *The Germans: Public Opinion Polls, 1967–1980* (Westport, Conn.: Greenwood Press, 1981), pp. 428–430. The deterioration of the Soviet image in West Germany was measured in February 1977 and January 1980, the latter date reflecting the impact of the Soviet intervention in Afghanistan. It is doubtful that the events in Poland have in any way improved the Soviet image. It is interesting to note in the context of Soviet attempts to transform military power into political influence that a Louis Harris poll conducted in the spring of 1983 showed that a significant minority of West Germans (30%) thought that there is a nuclear imbalance in favor of the Soviet Union. However, a majority (58%) held that the Soviets would be unable to exploit their advantage (see *The Economist*, London, June 4, 1983). Similar results obtained in a Louis Harris survey made later in the year, as reported in *International Herald Tribune* (Paris), November, 29, 1983.

[34]According to a Central Intelligence Agency briefing on the Soviet economy by Henry Rowen, chairman of the National Intelligence Council, before the Joint Economic Committee, Subcommittee on International Trade, Finance, and Security Economics, December 1, 1982 (unpublished mimeo, p. 2), the Soviet economy—in terms of Western GNP—is expected to grow at an annual rate of 1 to 2%. Wharton Econometric Forecasting Associates say that "the Soviet economy will continue muddling through . . . with GNP growing at 2.0–2.5 percent annually" [WEFA, *Centrally Planned Economies: Current Analysis* (Washington, D.C.,) (February, 14, 1984), p. 13].

[35]Richard Pipes, ed., *Soviet Strategy in Europe* (New York: Crane, Russak, 1976), pp. 37–38.

[36]Concerning these economic trends, see Friedemann Müller *et al.*, *Wirtschaftssanktionen im Ost–West Verhältnis: Rahmenbedingungen und Modalitäten* (Economic Sanctions in the East–West Relationship: Conditions and Modalities), ed. under the auspices of the Stiftung Wissenschaft und Politik, Series Aktuelle Materialien, vol. 1 (Baden-Baden: Nomos, 1983), pp. 130–144.

[37]Credit drawings by the Soviet Union on the Eurodollar market declined from U.S. $750 million in 1975 to U.S. $400 million in 1979 and U.S. $153 million in 1982 (OECD, *Financial Market Trends* [Paris], no. 24, March 1983). Concerning interrelationships between East–West politics and finance, see Klaus Schröder, "East–West Financial Relations," in *Wirtschaftskrieg oder Entspannung?* (Economic Warfare or Détente?) (ed. Hans-Dieter Jacobsen and Reinhard Rode) (Bonn; Neue Gesellschaft, 1984).

[38]Yu. Andreyev, "East–West Economic Relations," *MEMO*, no. 12 (1982), p. 94.

[39]See, for instance, General and Deputy Minister of Defense, K. Mikhaylov, in an interview with the West German newspaper *Frankfurter Rundschau* (Frankfurt-am-Main), November 3, 1982.

[40]*Pravda*, November 25, 1983.

[41]"Letter by Erich Honecker to Chancellor Kohl," *Neues Deutschland*, October 10, 1983.

[42]Lt. Gen. Viktor P. Starodubov, a member of the General Staff of the Soviet Armed Forces and for the past 10 years a member of the Soviet team negotiating with the United States on strategic arms, for instance, stated in an interview that from the Soviet point of view Pershing II and cruise missiles "are considered to be strategic weapons." This is the standard Soviet position. But, more signifi- cant, he added that the "emplacement of missiles with a strategic purpose is in essence an attempt to bypass SALT II, particularly Article 12." (In this article, the parties committed themselves "not to circumvent the provisions of this treaty, through any other state or states, or in any other manner.") Starodubov did not explicitly say that he expected the subject of the European missiles to be merged into future discussions about strategic arms. But the linking of the new U.S. deployments in Europe and SALT suggests that this is the case—as does his comment that a resumption of strategic arms negotiations is likely because the limitation of such arms conformed to the "general political line" of the Soviet government (see *The Washington Post*, January 25, 1984).

That there is a close link between INF and START is acknowledged by other Soviet negotiators. Yuliy Kvitsinskiy, the chief of the Soviet team at the INF talks in Geneva, for instance, suggested on November 12, 1983—during the by now famous "walk in the park"—that the U.S. propose a limit of approximately 120 SS-20s (in exchange for zero U.S. missile deployment in Europe) in return for which the Soviet government would reserve the right to raise "in another forum" (i.e., in START) its demand for compensation for the British and French missiles and that it would "credit" the U.S. with 120 missiles in compensation for the SS-20s [see the detailed report in *The Times* (London), November 30, 1983].

# VI

*Eastern Europe*

# 29      F. STEPHEN LARRABEE

## Soviet Policy toward Eastern Europe: Interests, Instruments and Trends*

**Soviet Interests in Eastern Europe**    Since the end of World War II, the Soviet Union has maintained a strong interest in Eastern Europe. Moscow's readiness to use military force in East Germany in 1953, Hungary in 1956, and Czechoslovakia in 1968, as well as its "indirect intervention" in Poland in 1981, is indicative of the importance the USSR attaches to preserving these interests.

*Military/Security* For the Soviet Union, Eastern Europe represents an important buffer zone. The military-strategic importance of maintaining this buffer zone was underscored by the famous exchange between Churchill and Stalin over Poland at Yalta in February 1945 in which Stalin bluntly told the British Prime Minister that while Poland was a question of "honor" for Britain, it was a question of "security" for the USSR.[1] In Stalin's view Soviet security required control of Poland and other areas on the Soviet periphery; if this risked damaging relations with the allies, he was willing to pay that price.

Soviet interest in retaining Eastern Europe as a buffer zone has remained strong despite changes in military technology and expansion of Soviet power. From a military point of view, Eastern Europe offers Moscow a number of important advantages. First, it provides the Soviet Union with space for deployment and maneuvers well forward from the Soviet frontier.[2] Second, control of Eastern Europe allows Moscow to concentrate its forces for an attack on Western Europe well to the West of the Soviet Union and enhances the USSR's ability to launch a lightning offensive against NATO. It enables not only the stationing of troops, but also the preparation of lines of communication and reinforcements, as well as the prepositioning and storage of ammunition and

*Reprinted by permission of the author and publisher from *The Challenge to Soviet Interests in Eastern Europe: Romania, Hungary, and East Germany* (Santa Monica, Calif.: Rand, 1985), pp. 3–22. Copyright 1985 by The Rand Corporation.

materiel. Third, Soviet control of Eastern Europe increases the number of troops available to the Soviet Union in any conflict. By one calculation, the East European countries provide 37 divisions to the Warsaw Pact.[3] While the reliability of these forces in actual combat is open to question,[4] some of the troops could be expected to perform well, depending on how the war was initiated and against which forces they were deployed.

Finally, Eastern Europe also provides a staging area for political intimidation of Western Europe. The large-scale conventional forces stationed in Eastern Europe, along with their offensive posture, are a stark reminder of Western Europe's vulnerability. This is reinforced by the presence of Soviet short-range nuclear systems such as FROG and SCUD, which Moscow has recently begun to replace with newer, more accurate, mobile systems, the SS-21, SS-22, and SS-23. The fact that the Soviets took the unusual step of announcing their deployment reinforces the impression that their prime motivation was political rather than military: to show "resolve" and exploit antinuclear fears in Western Europe, especially West Germany.

*Ideological/Political* The Soviets also have a strong ideological/political interest in Eastern Europe. The preservation of the Leninist system, in which the communist party holds a monopoly of power, helps to ensure Soviet hegemony and control over the region. It allows Moscow to maintain links with a relatively small number of people, who exercise tight control over the societies they rule. It also facilitates the coordination of policy and makes it easier for Moscow to obtain political support for its foreign policy and security goals.

For these reasons, the Soviets have generally reacted strongly to any erosion of the leading role of the party in Eastern Europe, such as occurred in Czechoslovakia in 1968 and Poland in 1980–1981. Moscow's anxiety stems from a fear not only that such erosion could infect other countries in Eastern Europe, but also that over the long run it could have an effect upon the Soviet Union itself. It is no accident that one of Moscow's first actions after the outbreak of unrest in Poland in August 1980 was to reimpose jamming of Western radio broadcasts to the USSR and to stop the flow of tourists and Polish newspapers into the Baltic Republics, particularly Lithuania. A similar fear of ideological contamination was evident during the Prague Spring, particularly in the Ukraine.[5]

While ideology plays a less important role as a guiding force in Soviet foreign policy today than it has in the past, the *ideological* factor has remained important because of the challenge from the Chinese. Beijing represents an alternative model of development and has openly challenged Moscow's leadership within the communist movement. In the face of this challenge, the existence of a bloc of communist states that adhere closely to the Soviet model and support Soviet policy goals is a valuable asset, one that Moscow would be reluctant to relinquish.

Moscow's ideological/political and military/security interests are, of course, closely linked. Indeed, Moscow has at times been willing to accept a considerable degree of ideological deviance in order to preserve its security interests. Poland provides a good example. Traditionally, Moscow has been extremely sensitive to the dangers of "Bonapartism" and has insisted on strict party control over the military.[6] In the case of Poland, however, it both countenanced and encouraged the intervention of the military and the maintenance of military rule—in large part because the military was the only institution capable of preserving political stability in Poland, which Moscow considers important for its own security.

Hungary is another case in point. The Hungarian model, with its emphasis on economic decentralization, differs significantly from the Soviet model. Moreover, Hungary has recently introduced measures to encourage and promote the growth of the private sector in both agriculture and industry. These measures have been combined with a degree of political liberalization unparalleled elsewhere in Eastern Europe, not to mention the Soviet Union itself. Moscow has been willing to tolerate the Hungarian deviation for a variety of reasons, the most important of which has been Kadar's ability to provide loyalty *and political stability* within the framework of a communist one-party state.

*Economic* The Soviet Union has also derived certain economic benefits from its relationship, though these have varied over time. During the Stalinist period, the Soviet–East European economic relationship was exploitative and clearly favorable to the Soviet Union. It has been estimated, for instance, that the uncompensated flow of resources from Eastern Europe to the Soviet Union until Stalin's death amounted to about $14 billion—roughly the equivalent of the flow of resources from the United States to Western Europe under the Marshall Plan.[7]

However, this situation changed after Stalin's death. During the 1960s and 1970s (at least until CMEA prices were restructured in 1975), the Soviet Union paid an increasingly steep price to maintain its domination over Eastern Europe. While the exact balance of costs and benefits is difficult to calculate, the evidence strongly suggests that over the last two decades, the economic benefits to Eastern Europe have outweighed those to the USSR.[8]

*Political/Diplomatic* Moscow also has a strong political/diplomatic interest in Eastern Europe. East European support for Soviet foreign policy goals is an important asset in international forums such as the United Nations. Poland, for instance, played a particularly useful role in furthering Soviet interests as a member of the Middle East Peace-Keeping Force and the International Control Committee in Vietnam. There are also indications that a division of labor is emerging in regard to the Third World, where the GDR in particular has significantly expanded its political and military presence.[9] East European countries, especially Czechoslovakia, also serve as important sources of arms for many countries in the Third World and often act as conduits for weapons in situations in which the Soviet Union prefers for diplomatic reasons to restrict its own visibility.

While all the four interests discussed above have influenced Soviet policy in the postwar period, the relative weight Moscow has attached to each has varied over time. For every Soviet leader from Stalin to Chernenko, the military/security interest has been strong—indeed paramount. The idea of Eastern Europe as a buffer area was obviously more important militarily before the advent of intercontinental ballistic missiles, but Eastern Europe still remains important as a forward staging area for any Soviet attack on Western Europe. Today, however, the gains that Moscow acquires by maintaining large concentrations of troops in that area are primarily *political*: This overwhelming conventional superiority, backed by nuclear power, remains a useful instrument of political pressure.[10] The political utility of this superiority has been enhanced by Moscow's achievement of parity at the strategic level, as well as the across-the-board modernization or improvement of its theater nuclear and conventional forces which has taken place over the last decade. Indeed, this large-scale modernization, which has included the East European forces as well, may prove to be one of the most important legacies of the Brezhnev era.[11]

At the same time, Moscow's economic interests in Eastern Europe are clearly changing. The impact of the energy crisis has necessitated a restructuring of economic relations. While Moscow continues to subsidize Eastern Europe's economic development, this is becoming increasingly difficult—and costly—as the constraints on Moscow's own resources increase. The Soviet Union's continued willingness to provide subsidies to its East European allies and to bear the heavy costs of economic integration, however, underscores the high priority it continues to attach to maintaining political dominance in the area.

## Continuity and Change

Yet if Moscow's interest in Eastern Europe has remained relatively constant, its management of its relations with its East European allies has undergone visible change and modification over the past 35 years. In essence, the USSR has pursued two goals in Eastern Europe in the postwar period: stability and control. There has often been a tension between the two goals, however; maintenance of stability has required concessions to popular pressures and national differences, which at times have undermined Soviet control. The problem for Moscow has been—and remains—that of finding the right balance between the two goals.

Under Stalin, control was given almost exclusive priority over stability. After 1948, Stalin ruthlessly sought to impose the Soviet model on Eastern Europe through a policy of *Gleichschaltung*.[12] "National" communists, that is, those who had spent the war years in their home countries, were purged and often executed; in their place Stalin put loyal "Muscovites" who had spent long years in the Soviet Union and who could be counted on to faithfully carry out Soviet directives. A policy of forced industrialization and collectivization was introduced, and Eastern Europe became little more than an appendage of the Soviet Union.

*The Khrushchev Era* In the aftermath of Stalin's death in March 1953, his successors sought to find a new balance between control and stability. To defuse popular tensions in Eastern Europe and prevent them from erupting into open revolt, the new Soviet leadership introduced a number of reforms and partially dismantled the most onerous aspects of the Stalinist system. The pace of industrialization was reduced; terror was relaxed; and the New Course, with its emphasis on consumer goods, was introduced. Most of the changes instituted in the initial period after Stalin's death, though, were ad hoc measures; they did not constitute a systematic effort at restructuring Moscow's relations with the bloc. Moreover, in many instances, they served to exacerbate tensions in Eastern Europe rather than ameliorate them.

The upheavals in Hungary and Poland in 1956 underscored the need for Moscow to work out a more stable relationship with Eastern Europe—one that took into greater consideration East European traditions and culture but still preserved Soviet economic and political hegemony. In the aftermath of the unrest in both countries, Khrushchev consciously set out to restructure the USSR's relations with Eastern Europe in an attempt to forge a more cohesive, but at the same time more viable system of Soviet rule.

Khrushchev's relaxation of Soviet/East European relations, however, set in motion forces that undermined the very stability he had hoped to promote. One of the strongest and most corrosive of these was nationalism. The extent of "renationalization" differed from country to country. It went farthest in Romania and Poland—two countries with strong anti-Russian traditions—but by the time of Khrushchev's removal in October 1964, it had affected every country (with the possible exception of Bulgaria) to some degree. The result was a new, more vigorous Eastern Europe, one both more assertive vis-à-vis the Soviet Union and more differentiated internally.

As part of Khrushchev's de-Stalinization campaign, economic reforms were introduced throughout Eastern Europe. Again the degree and pattern of reform varied from country to country, but in general, the degree of party control over economic life—and in some cases over political life as well—was reduced.[13] This process went farthest in Czechoslovakia, where efforts to dismantle the Stalinist economic system spilled over into the political arena and led to widespread calls for broad political change, presenting Moscow with a major challenge to its hegemony.

The growing domestic differentiation coincided with, and to some extent was reinforced by, increased polycentrism within the bloc and the "socialist community" in general. Growing differences with China resulted in an open split after 1960; Albania defected into the Chinese camp a year later; and Romania embarked upon a more independent path after 1964.

The causes of the emergence of polycentrism were varied, but one in particular deserves mention: the process of limited détente fostered by Khrushchev in the aftermath of the Cuban missile crisis. The partial relaxation of tensions at this time helped to erode the barriers of the

Cold War and encouraged East European countries to take advantage of the new more fluid atmosphere in East–West relations to expand their autonomy in foreign policy and experiment domestically.

This process was given greater impetus by two other developments in the aftermath of Khrushchev's fall: (1) the preoccupation of Khrushchev's successors with internal consolidation, which tended to deflect their attention away from Eastern Europe and give the East European leaderships greater room for maneuvering; (2) the Soviet leadership's efforts after 1966 to pursue a more vigorous *Westpolitik*. The latter was reflected most visibly in Moscow's campaign for a European security conference that was officially launched at the Bucharest Conference in July 1966 and, to a lesser extent, in its initiation of bilateral discussions with Bonn over a renunciation-of-force agreement.

The major catalyst for change, however, came from Bonn's new *Ostpolitik*. As long as the Federal Republic of Germany (FRG) remained wedded to precepts of the Adenauer era, the Soviet Union could afford to play the role of the champion of détente with impunity. Once Bonn left the trenches of the Cold War, however, and embarked upon a policy of East–West reconciliation of its own, Moscow found its interests in Eastern Europe under serious threat. The shift in Bonn's policy tended to erode the credibility of the German threat, which was one of Moscow's main instruments for maintaining cohesion within the bloc, and led to a new interest in rapprochement with Bonn on the part of several East European countries.

This process seriously threatened Soviet rule in Eastern Europe and confronted Moscow with a new threat to its hegemony in the region. The threat was most serious in Czechoslovakia, where in January 1968 the Stalinist leader, Anton Novotny, was overthrown and replaced by a new Czechoslovak leadership under Alexander Dubček, which embarked upon a policy of far-reaching economic and political reform. But it also manifested itself in Poland, where Wladyslaw Gomulka faced mounting student unrest, on one hand, and a serious political challenge form Mieczyslaw Moczar, the head of the secret police, who played on Polish nationalism, on the other.

As in 1956, the Soviet leadership was too preoccupied with internal problems, particularly the consolidation of its power, to pay adequate attention to developments in Eastern Europe. And as in 1956, its policy during this period was marked by vacillation and hesitation. Both of these factors contributed to the ferment and unrest that manifested itself after 1964 in Eastern Europe. But the origins of this ferment lay in changes and experiments initiated by Khrushchev; to a large extent, Brezhnev and Kosygin reaped the harvest that Nikita Sergeevich had sown.

*The Brezhnev Counterreformation: 1969–1975*  The Soviet invasion of Czechoslovakia ushered in a new period in Soviet–East European relations, one marked by a reassertion of cohesion and control. In essence, the Soviet Union sought to carry out what J. F. Brown has aptly termed a "counterreformation": the reassertion of orthodoxy and restoration of Soviet control in Eastern Europe.[14] This policy had both a domestic and an international rationale. The domestic motivation was the long-standing Soviet desire for stability and control in Eastern Europe, the desire in particular to create the internal conditions which would make future Czechoslovakias both impossible and unnecessary. This was reinforced by foreign policy considerations, in particular Moscow's desire to pick up the threads of its détente diplomacy left dangling prior to the invasion. But as the Czechoslovak experience had shown, détente tended to have a destabilizing impact on the bloc; thus to withstand the disintegrative impulses that any return to détente was bound to unleash, Moscow first had to bolster cohesion within the bloc.

Paradoxically, while the invasion of Czechoslovakia was a reflection of the fragility of Soviet control in Eastern Europe, it actually served to strengthen the cohesion and stability that were a necessary precondition for any return to détente. The invasion underscored the limits of Soviet tolerance and the lengths to which Moscow was willing to go to preserve its hegemony in Eastern Europe. This had two important effects. In the West, it made clear that "the road to Prague lay through Moscow"—that is, that there could be no attempt to "build bridges" to Eastern Europe that by-passed Moscow. This implied a reordering of Western, especially West German, priorities in which top priority was given to improving relations with Moscow first and Eastern Europe second. In the East, the invasion had an important "demonstration effect," which facilitated Mocow's efforts to reestablish stability and control. Not only was the clock turned back in Czechoslovakia, but in the aftermath of the invasion, other Eastern European countries, including Romania, were reluctant to undertake new initiatives in either domestic or foreign policy.

The exception was Hungary, which proceeded with the introduction of its New Economic Mechanism (NEM) despite the invasion. The Soviet Union was willing to tolerate this deviation for several reasons: (1) Kadar was a proven ally; (2) the reform was introduced gradually and did not directly threaten the leading role of the party; (3) Hungary's deviation in domestic policy was not matched in foreign policy, where Budapest faithfully toed the Soviet line.

Yet Moscow did not give Hungary completely free rein. The demotion of Rezsó Nyers, the "Godfather of the NEM," and several other reformers at the March Central Committee Plenum in 1974 underscored the limits of the reform and marked a return to a more orthodox line. In part, the slowdown of the pace of the reform in the aftermath of the March Plenum was a reaction to domestic concerns—above all, the growth of discontent among the working class, which felt that the reform tended to benefit the middle classes at its expense—but Soviet pressure also appears to have played a role.

Moscow's effort to increase cohesion in the aftermath of Czechoslovakia manifested itself in two areas in particular: First, it moved to strengthen integration within Comecon, beginning at the Twenty-third Comecon Council session in April 1969. Two years later, at the Twenty-fifth Council session in July 1971, a "Comprehensive Program" was adopted which envisioned a long-range, multifaceted program of economic cooperation and integration. The Comprehensive Program put particular emphasis on greater coordination of national plans and joint investment projects. In 1975, at the Twenty-ninth Comecon Council session in Budapest, a major step forward toward integration was taken with the approval of a joint, coordinated plan outside the separate national plans. The highlight of the plan was the agreement to construct ten joint enterprises.

The push for greater economic coordination was complemented by greater military integration within the Warsaw Pact. At the Budapest meeting of the Political Consultative Council (PCC) in March 1969, several new bodies were established: (1) the Committee of Defense Ministers (CDM), which acts as the supreme military consultative organ; (2) the Military Council, which is subordinate to the Pact's Joint Command and which appears to have responsibility for planning and quality-control functions; and (3) the Technical Council, which apparently has responsibility for the development and modernization of weapons and technology. In addition, a permanent Joint Staff was set up.[15]

The impetus toward closer integration in Comecon and the Warsaw Pact was buttressed by the proliferation of consultations in a number of other fields, particularly ideology and culture, and a general expansion of bilateral consultations. One of the most important examples of the latter was the institutionalization of Brezhnev's annual August meetings in the Crimea with East European leaders. These regular meetings provided an important forum for the coordination of policy on a wide variety of issues.

In essence, what emerged was a process of "directed consensus," in which Moscow's East European allies were given greater participation in bloc councils, but the Soviet Union clearly set the tone and policy guidelines. This is not to suggest that the process was, or is, genuinely consultative. The Soviet Union is clearly the dominant force, but East Europeans were given greater opportunity to express their views, even if they rarely prevailed.

The return to orthodoxy in Eastern Europe was accompanied by a turn to "consumerism," which was made possible by the expansion of economic and political relations with the West as the rigidities of the Cold War gave way to the new impulses unleashed by superpower détente in the early 1970s. East European countries rushed to take advantage of liberal credits being offered by Western banks—often without much regard for how they were going to use or repay these loans. The new prosperity helped to give the regimes a stronger sense of legitimacy and siphon off political discontent. Indeed, the combined impact of the invasion of Czechoslovakia and the rise in the standard of living in the early 1970s were greatly responsible for the lack of vocal dissent in Eastern Europe during this period. The populations were generally either too intimidated or too concerned with "making it" to try to test the boundaries of the system.

The best example of this was Gierek's Poland, where a new, more tolerant attitude was combined with a major effort to expand economic relations with the West. This initially led to a visible rise in the standard of living and earned Gierek accolades in the West. But it manifested itself in other countries as well, particularly Hungary and the GDR, where both leaderships consciously sought to enhance their legitimacy by increasing the standard of living. Even Husak in Czechoslovakia sought to make his politically repressive policy more palatable by increasing the living standard.

**From Cohesion to Corrosion: 1976–1984**   The stability that characterized East European politics during the first half of the 1970s proved to be deceptive and short-lived, however. Beginning in the mid-1970s, the glue that held the East European system together began to come unstuck. By the end of the decade, cohesion had been replaced by corrosion.

*Economic Decline* Several factors contributed to this corrosion in the latter half of the 1970s. Chief among them was the slowdown in economic growth throughout Eastern Europe.[16] Between 1976 and 1980, the average annual growth of produced national income (net material product) declined to 4%, as compared to 7.3% in 1971–1975.[17] This represented the lowest growth rates experienced by Eastern Europe since World War II.

For a variety of reasons—particularly reluctance to reduce growth rates for fear of the political consequences of any serious decline in living standards—the slowdown did not really make itself felt until after 1978–1979. The downturn coincided, moreover, with a general deterioration of East–West political relations as a result of the Soviet invasion of Afghanistan and the Polish crisis, both of which had a negative impact on East–West economic relations.

By 1980, the impact of the slowdown was clearly visible. It was most acute in Poland, which in 1979 suffered a 2% decline in national income—an unprecedented situation in the postwar period. But it was felt in varying degrees in all East European countries. Next to Poland, Romania was the hardest hit, in large part because the Ceausescu regime had blindly forged ahead with plans to expand its oil-refining capacity despite a decline in domestic production and rising world market prices for crude oil. Even Hungary, which had managed its economy fairly well after introducing a far-reaching economic reform beginning in 1968, felt the pinch.

Rather than introducing reforms, East European planners sought to counter the slowdown by expanding imports of Western technology, financed by cheap Western credits, which they hoped would stimulate greater productivity. This large-scale borrowing resulted in a dramatic rise in Eastern Europe's debt to the West—$21.2 billion in 1975 to nearly $60 billion by the end of 1980. Poland had the highest debt ($23 billion), but others such as the GDR ($13 billion), Romania ($10 billion), and Hungary ($8 billion) also faced serious debt problems. The exceptions were Czechoslovakia, which had avoided the problem by severely limiting its trade with the West, and Bulgaria, which actually has been reducing its debt.

East European countries were also hard hit by the recession in Western Europe, which led to a drop in the level of their exports to the West and a deterioration of their terms of trade with the West. Perhaps the most important factor, however, was the Soviet decision to raise the price of its raw materials in 1975. This led to a dramatic increase in the price East European countries must pay for raw materials, particularly oil, and a significant shift in Eastern Europe's terms of trade with the Soviet Union.

To a large extent, the shift in the terms of trade simply offset an unfavorable terms-of-trade balance that Moscow had suffered in the previous decade, during which it had accorded Eastern Europe preferential trade treatment. This preferential treatment amounted in effect to a large implicit transfer of resources from the Soviet Union to Eastern Europe in the form of hidden trade subsidies.[18] The USSR exported relatively underpriced energy and nonfood materials to Eastern Europe in return for imports of relatively overpriced East European machinery and industrial goods. It has been estimated by some Western economists that between 1973 and 1980 these subsidies may have amounted to as much as $60 billion.[19]

Moscow's willingness to provide these subsidies underscores the importance it attaches to maintaining its hegemony in Eastern Europe. Even today, East European countries pay less than market prices for their raw materials. In short, rather than acting like ruthless profiteers determined to make a killing out of the escalation of oil prices, the Soviet leadership, as Philip Hanson has aptly phrased it, "behaved like the better sort of landlord: raising the rent belatedly and by less than the general rate of inflation, and allowing more time to pay."[20] The reason for Soviet "generosity" was undoubtedly Moscow's concern that too steep a rise in prices might exacerbate Eastern European economic difficulties and have a negative impact on political stability.

Nevertheless, despite the Soviet effort to cushion the blow, and despite the continued provision of hidden subsidies, the increase in the cost of Soviet raw materials and the sharp decline in East European terms of trade vis-à-vis the USSR have exacerbated East European economic difficulties and forced East European planners to reduce growth rates in industrial production and investment. Moreover, the difficulties faced by the East European countries are likely to intensify in the coming decade.

At the Thirty-fourth Comecon session in June, 1980, the Soviet Union informed its allies that it would not be able to supply them with oil above 1980 levels. In 1982, the Soviets introduced cuts in deliveries to Czechoslovakia, the GDR, and Hungary, and since then they have made it clear that delieveries over the next 3 years will not be restored to the 1980–1981 levels.[21] (Poland has apparently been exempted from these cuts due to its desperate economic condition; the situation in Bulgaria is unclear.) Bloc members will thus have to look increasingly to outside sources to meet their energy needs and pay world market prices for their oil, aggravating their already acute balance-of-payments problems. And even if the Soviet Union does increase its deliveries of oil to Eastern Europe, the price it charges will undoubtedly rise, causing a further deterioration of East European terms of trade with the Soviet Union. In short, however East European countries seek to resolve their economic dilemmas, they will face severe constraints on economic growth in the future.

Eastern Europe's growing economic difficulties have exacerbated conflicts within CMEA and led to delays in plan coordination. Approval of the 1981–1985 five-year plan, for instance, was delayed almost a year. The plan should have been approved at the Thirty-fourth CMEA Council meeting in Prague in June 1980 but was not presented until a year later at the Thirty-fifth session in Sofia in July 1981. Even then, many of the problems do not seem to have been fully resolved.

Perhaps the most visible problem area, however, has been that of joint investments. In the 1970s, joint investment projects represented the major vehicle for promoting integration. During 1976–1980, about a dozen such projects were initiated, the largest being the Orenburg pipeline. These projects essentially involved an extension of credits to the Soviet Union by the East European countries, in return for which they were guaranteed a share in the planned output of the project. This assured East European countries a stable supply of raw materials while at the same time compensating Moscow for the infrastructure costs associated with extraction and transportation.

The joint investment projects have been controversial, however, and in many cases do not appear to have lived up to expectations. Some East European economists have argued that economic criteria do not play an important enough role in the selection of the projects,[22] while others have complained about the high hard-currency costs of the projects and the low interest rates on credit advances. These complaints appear to have contributed to a decision to downgrade the role of joint investments in the 1981–1985 plan. Instead, emphasis has shifted from direct and joint participation in production back to the old themes of coordination of plans and specialization agreements.[23]

The economic difficulties within the bloc have led to a growing recognition of the need to reassess the whole question of economic integration and regional planning. However, there has been little consensus on the best means by which this integration and planning can be achieved. The Soviets, backed by the Czechs and the GDR, have emphasized the need for the coordination of broad economic policies and have argued that the main direction of communist integration should be in the area of computers and electronics. The Romanians, on the other hand, have emphasized the need to coordinate plans in the area of energy, fuels, and raw materials and have continued to resist any scheme that smacks of supranational planning. Similarly, the Hungarians have opposed efforts to force them to return to comprehensive economic planning and have argued for indirect methods of economic management and market-based integration.

Another source of conflict within CMEA has been the question of economic assistance to poorer member countries such as Mongolia, Cuba, and Vietnam. A number of the more developed countries have been reluctant to provide these countries with economic assistance at a time when they are facing growing economic difficulties of their own. Economic help for the poorer countries has been a source of particular friction with Romania, which would like to have greater access to Soviet raw materials at concessional rates.

Difficulties have also emerged over price formation and trade financing. In May 1981, for instance, Poland proposed that CMEA pricing procedures be reformed.[24] Poland has expressed particular discontent over the lack of convertibility of the CMEA currencies, which means that trade surpluses cannot easily be used to offset deficits with CMEA members. Hungary has expressed similar concerns.

The economic slowdown in Eastern Europe has also accentuated difficulties within the Warsaw Pact and has led to growing East European opposition to Soviet pressures for increased defense spending. The most notable example of this resistance was Romanian President Ceausescu's refusal to accede to Soviet calls for an across-the-board increase in defense spending at the November 1978 Warsaw Pact meeting in Moscow. At the beginning of 1983, Romania also announced that it would freeze defense spending at 1982 levels. While other countries have been less vocal in their opposition to increased defense outlays, there is reason to believe that some share Romania's concerns.

*The Polish Crisis* The economic crisis had its most dramatic impact on Poland. A detailed analysis of the Polish crisis is beyond the scope of this report; but suffice it to say that the deterioration of the economy after 1975 was the main factor in the eruption of the crisis.[25]

The upheaval in Poland in 1980–1981 represented the most serious challenge to Moscow's rule in Eastern Europe since the end of World War II. The Czechoslovak challenge in 1968 was essentially a "revolution from above," led by the party and disaffected intellectuals. The Polish challenge, on the other hand, was a genuine "revolution from below." It was led by the workers and had widespread support throughout the society, including the lower ranks of the party.

There was another important difference. In Czechoslovakia, the Soviets were faced with a wayward party leadership embarked on a dangerous (from the Soviet point of view) path of reform. Thus to halt the challenge, the Soviets could merely replace the top party leadership, which they eventually did. In Poland, however, the Soviets were faced not with a renegade party, but with a massive rejection of the party by the society as a whole.

The existence of an independent trade union posed a major challenge to the very basis of the communist system: the party's monopoly of power. In essence, it threatened a restructuring of the power relationships within postwar Poland. This was something the Soviets could not tolerate. Had it occurred, it would have had serious implications for the rest of Eastern Europe—and for Soviet security interests in the region. Eventually other communist leaderships might have faced similar pressures. Or so the Soviets undoubtedly feared.

The imposition of martial law on December 13, 1981 cut short Solidarity's challenge. But it by no means ended the Polish crisis. While Solidarity has been disbanded, none of the problems that gave rise to its emergence have been resolved. The economy remains in a shambles; the party is in disarray, too divided and weak to provide effective leadership; and the Jaruzelski regime has been unable to win the trust and support of the population. For the foreseeable future, therefore, the Polish crisis is likely to continue to fester, complicating Soviet efforts to manage relations with Eastern Europe and casting a long shadow over East–West relations.

*The Impact of Détente* Another factor which contributed to the erosion of Soviet hegemony in Eastern Europe in the latter half of the 1970s was the impact of East–West détente. The process of détente did not change the basic nature of the East European political systems, but the proliferation of East–West contacts which accompanied détente made Soviet control of Eastern Europe more difficult. And in some countries, such as Hungary and Poland, it contributed to greater social pluralization and liberalization.

The Helsinki Accord, signed in August 1975, played an important role in this process. The Accord did not end abuses of human rights in Eastern Europe, let alone lead to democratization of the East European systems. However, it did legitimize the West's insistence that détente could not be limited to state-to-state relations but had to bring benefits to Eastern European societies as well. Indeed, it was on the level of *society* that the Helsinki Accord had its most important effect—a fact often overlooked by its critics. The signing of the Final Act encouraged a variety of disparate groups in Eastern Europe to speak out more forcefully about abuses of human rights. The result was an upsurge of dissent throughout Eastern Europe in the latter half of the 1970s, which complicated Moscow's efforts to maintain stability and control in the area.[26]

The pattern of dissent varied from country to country. It was most visible and strongest in Poland, where a coalition of workers and intellectuals emerged in the aftermath of riots in Radom and Ursus.[27] Perhaps most important, this new coalition received indirect support from the Catholic Church. Not only did the Church become more outspoken and critical of government policy, but many Catholic intellectuals began to forge close ties to the workers, which were instrumental in Solidarity's success in 1980–1981.

The worker–intellectual–Church coalition was unique to Poland and was not repeated elsewhere. But it was part of a wider process of social ferment that manifested itself to one degree or another in almost every East European country in the late 1970s. In Czechoslovakia the emergence of Charter 77 in 1977–1978 demonstrated that the flame of reform had not been entirely extinguished despite nearly a decade of "normalization." To be sure, the signatories of the Charter Manifesto represented a small minority, mostly intellectuals, and the movement did not have anywhere near the impact of the protests in Poland. But the fact that the movement emerged at all is noteworthy and underscores the inherent fragility of the process of "normalization" in Czechoslovakia.

Romania also witnessed the first serious flickers of dissent in the aftermath of the signing of the Helsinki Accord. Within the intellectual community, the most noteworthy manifestations were the protests by writer Paul Goma. But the impact of these protests was limited. Far more serious from the regime's point of view was the strike by 30,000 miners in the Jiu valley in August 1977, which was settled only after Ceausescu's personal intervention. The strike was a reflection of growing discontent among the working class, which could become more serious if Romania's economy continues to decline.

Hungary also experienced increasing dissent. In Hungary, however, dissent has been limited largely to intellectuals and aimed more at "consciousness-raising" than at direct confrontation with the regime. Its impact has been blunted, moreover, by the relative prosperity that Hungary enjoys vis-à-vis the rest of the bloc, as well as the greater degree of support (or at least tolerance) enjoyed by the party in Hungary, and particularly by Kadar himself. In keeping with its moderate style and image, the regime has tended to deal with manifestations of dissent relatively leniently—usually through enforced emigration for limited periods, as in the case of writers Gyorgy Konrad and Ivan Szelenyi.

Even in the GDR, normally one of the most orthodox regimes, there was greater social ferment. Applications for emigration rose dramatically in the aftermath of the signing of the Final Act, and ferment among the intellectuals increased visibly. From the regime's point of view, however, the most serious and potentially dangerous dissent has come from the emergence of an independent peace movement. While the peace movement has been weakened by emigration since early 1984, it continues to pose a problem to the East German authorities, particularly because of its links to the Evangelical Church and peace groups in the Federal Republic. Indeed, it is this transnational dimension, as Pierre Hassner has pointed out, that gives the peace movement "both its ultimate originality and its political relevance."[28]

The ferment in Eastern Europe, especially East Germany, was also related to the impact of Bonn's *Ostpolitik* and the decline of the "German threat" in recent years. As long as Bonn refused to accept the territorial boundaries that emerged in the aftermath of World War II, Moscow was able to exploit East European fears of German "revanchism," and East European countries (especially Poland) had little choice but to look to Moscow for their security. However, the ratification of the Eastern Treaties in the early 1970s, which formally signified Bonn's acceptance of the postwar status quo, effectively removed the German problem as the key issue of European politics.

This had three important consequences. First, it reduced East European fears of German revanchism, thus depriving Moscow of one of the prime instruments for maintaining its hegemony in Eastern Europe.

Second, it resulted in an expansion of Bonn's influence—particularly economic influence—in Eastern Europe. Finally, it led to an intensification of relations and a proliferation of ties between the two Germanies.

*The Impact of Eurocommunism* Another factor that had an impact on Soviet authority and control in Eastern Europe was the growth of "Eurocommunism" during the mid-1970s. The emergence of more autonomous communist parties in Western Europe, especially Italy, complicated Moscow's efforts to impose unity within the world communist movement and for a brief time in Eastern Europe. The Conference of European and Western Parties held in East Berlin in June 1976 provided the most important example of Moscow's difficulties. During the preparatory meetings leading up to the conference, many of the independent West European parties, backed by the Romanians and the Yugoslavs, stubbornly resisted Soviet efforts to impose a general ideological line, and Moscow was forced to make important concessions to ensure the attendance of the independent West European parties.[29]

Eurocommunist ideas also had an echo among East European dissidents.[30] The Italian communist party (PCI), for instance, openly supported the struggle for human rights in such dissident groups as Charter 77 in Czechoslovakia and KOR in Poland. Moreover, a number of West European communist parties consistently supported the cause of democratic reform in Poland. Again, the strongest support came from the PCI, which publicly and privately made clear its backing for the course of democratization in Poland and its opposition to the use of force to solve the crisis. The PCI's support for Solidarity resulted in open polemics between the PCI and Moscow in 1981 and led to a serious deterioration of relations between the two parties.[31]

One should of course not overdramatize the influence of Eurocommunism. Its impact on Eastern Europe was clearly limited. In addition, its influence was weakened by the decline of the Spanish communist party and the reorientation of the policy of the French communist party back toward a more orthodox, pro-Moscow course at the end of the 1970s. But for a short time in the late 1970s, it did complicate Moscow's efforts to maintain its hegemony in Eastern Europe, and it provided an important source of support for Yugoslavia's and Romania's efforts to pursue more autonomous policies.

*The Soviet Succession Issue* Finally, Moscow's problems in Eastern Europe were exacerbated by the impact of the impending succession in the Soviet leadership. As Brezhnev's health declined after 1976, he was no longer able to exert the vigorous leadership that had characterized his rule in the earlier part of the decade. During the last 5 years of his tenure, Soviet policy was increasingly characterized by immobilism at home and abroad.

This was reflected in Soviet policy toward Eastern Europe. The vacillation exhibited by Moscow during the Polish crisis was one example of this trend; the slowdown in progress toward integration with Comecon was another. In short, Soviet policy lacked a sense of vigor and direction. East European leaders sensed this and reacted accordingly. The recognition that a leadership change was imminent added to the feeling of uncertainty. What resulted was a condition of hesitancy and drift—a reluctance to take new initiatives—which accentuated the mounting problems throughout the region.

Brezhnev's death unleashed a new sense of expectancy in Eastern Europe. Many East Europeans looked to Andropov to provide the strong leadership lacking in Brezhnev's last years. They hoped he would instill a new sense of direction in Soviet policy and support much-needed reforms both at home and abroad. The new Soviet leader's initial efforts to curtail corruption and introduce some cautious and limited reforms in the USSR strengthened these hopes. Andropov did not live long enough, however, to have much of an impact. As his health deteriorated, the early reform impulse lost momentum. His last 6 months were characterized by renewed drift and immobilism. Little effort was made to address the serious problems that faced the region— a fact well illustrated by the continued postponement of the much-heralded Comecon summit of party and state leaders.

Andropov's death in February 1984 has reinforced the hesitancy and uncertainty visible during Brezhnev's last years. Once again the Soviet leadership has been forced to focus its attention on the internal problems of succession, relegating the problems of Eastern Europe to the back burner. Few East Europeans expect much from Chernenko. They see him essentially as a transitional figure who is likely to continue to follow Brezhnev's policy of "benign neglect" toward Eastern Europe. It remains questionable, however, whether the Soviet Union can afford such a policy over a sustained period of time. Moscow's problems in Eastern Europe are likely to grow, and failure to address them systematically could prove costly.

## Notes

[1] Daniel Yergin, *The Shattered Peace* (Boston: Houghton Mifflin Company, 1977), p. 63.

[2] Malcolm Macintosh, "Military Considerations in Soviet–East European Relations," in *Soviet–East European Dilemmas*, ed. Karen Dawisha (New York: Holmes and Meier, 1981), pp. 136–137.

[3] Based on figures from *The Military Balance 1980–1981* (London: International Institute for Strategic Studies, 1980), p. 110.

[4] For a discussion of this point, see Dale R. Herspring and Ivan Volgyes, "Political Reliability in the Eastern European Warsaw Pact Armies," *Armed Forces and Society* (Winter, 1980), pp. 270–296. Also A. Ross Johnson, Robert W. Dean, and Alexander Alexiev, *East European Military Establishments: The Warsaw Pact Northern Tier* (New York: Crane, Russak, 1982).

[5] See Grey Hodnett and Peter J. Potichnyi, *The Ukraine and the Czechoslovak Crisis* (Canberra: Australian National University, 1970). Also Alexander Alexiev, *Dissent and Nationalism in the Soviet Baltic* (The Rand Corporation, R3061-AF, January 1984).

[6] The case of Marshal Zhukov, who was dropped from the Presidium (Politburo) and Central Committee and relieved of his duties as defense minister in October 1957, is perhaps the most notable example of this sensitivity.

[7]Paul Marer, "Has Eastern Europe Become a Liability to the Soviet Union?" in *The International Politics of Eastern Europe*, ed. Charles Gati (New York: Praeger, 1979), p. 61.

[8]Philip Hanson, "Soviet Trade with Western Europe," in Dawisha, *op. cit.*, p. 93; also Marer, *op. cit.*

[9]See Melvin Croan, "A New Afrika Corps?" *Washington Quarterly* (Winter, 1980).

[10]This is one reason why Moscow favors a "No First-Use Pledge." For a cogent argument against abandoning "first use" from a European perspective, see Karl Kaiser, George Leber, Alois Mertes, and Franz-Josef Schulze, "Nuclear Weapons and the Preservation of Peace," *Foreign Affairs* (Summer 1982), pp. 1157–1180.

[11]For a discussion of the dimensions of this modernization, see John Erickson, "The Warsaw Pact—The Shape of Things to Come," in Dawisha, *op. cit.*, pp. 148–171.

[12]For a detailed discussion of the process of Stalinization in Eastern Europe, see Zbigniew Brzezinski, *The Soviet Bloc* (New York: Praeger, 1965).

[13]For a good discussion of the impact of these reforms, see J. F. Brown, *The New Eastern Europe* (New York: Praeger, 1965).

[14]J. F. Brown, "Détente and Soviet Policy in Eastern Europe," *Survey*, (Spring/Summer 1974), p. 50.

[15]For a detailed discussion of these changes and their significance, see Dale Herspring, "The Warsaw Pact at 25," *Problems of Communism* (September–October 1980), pp. 1–15; and A. Ross Johnson, *Soviet–East European Military Relations: An Overview* (The Rand Corporation, P-5383-1, August 1977). Also Lawrence Caldwell, "The Warsaw Pact: Directions of Change," *Problems of Communism* (September–October 1975), pp. 1–19.

[16]See Jan Vanous, "East European Economic Slowdown," *Problems of Communism* (July–August 1982), pp. 1–19.

[17]*Ibid.*, p. 1.

[18]*Ibid.*, p. 6.

[19]See Michael Marrese and Jan Vanous, *Implicit Subsidies and Non-Market Benefits in Soviet Trade with Eastern Europe* (Berkeley: University of California Press, 1983). These figures, however, are regarded by some economists as too high. For a critique of the Marrese–Vanous approach, see Paul Marer, "Intrabloc Economic Relations and Projects," in *The Warsaw Pact: Alliance in Transition*, eds. Jane Sharp and David Holloway [Ithaca: Cornell University Press (forthcoming)].

[20]Hanson, *op. cit.*

[21]B.A. Rahmer, *The Petroleum Economist* (August 1982).

[22]See, for example, Kalman Pecsi, *The Future of Socialist Integration* (New York: Sharpe, 1981).

[23]Cam Hudson, "Are CMEA Joint Investment Schemes Being Downgraded?" RAD Background Report/258 (Eastern Europe), *Radio Free Europe Research* (December 10, 1982).

[24]Cam Hudson, "Poland Proposes New Commercial Arrangements with CMEA Countries," RAD Background Report/135 (Poland), *Radio Free Europe Research* (May 12, 1981).

[25]For a fuller discussion, see Zbigniew M. Fallenbuchl, "Poland's Economic Crisis," *Problems of Communism* (March–April 1982), pp. 1–21.

[26]See Thomas Heneghan, "Human Rights Protests in Eastern Europe," *The World Today* (March 1977), pp. 90–100; also Walter D. Connor, "Dissent in Eastern Europe: A New Coalition," *Problems of Communism* (January–February 1980), pp. 1–17.

[27]For a detailed discussion of the dissent movement in Poland, see Adam

Bromke, "Opposition in Poland," *Problems of Communism* (September–October 1978), pp. 37–51.

[28]Pierre Hassner, "The Shifting Foundation," *Foreign Policy* (Fall 1982), p. 8.

[29]The document issued at the end of the meeting, for instance, made no reference to "proletarian internationalism"—a code word for Soviet hegemony—but rather spoke solely of voluntary cooperation.

[30]For a detailed discussion, see Jiri Valenta, "Eurocommunism and Eastern Europe," *Problems of Communism* (March–April 1978), pp. 41–45.

[31]See in particular the sharp attack on the PCI in *Pravda*, January 24, 1982.

# 30    DALE R. HERSPRING

## The Soviet Union and the East European Militaries: The Diminishing Asset*

Despite the key importance Moscow has assigned the East European armies in Warsaw Pact strategy and the important role they have been expected to play in helping maintain political order, recent trends suggest that their value to Moscow is diminishing in the first area and limited in the second.

On the external front, the increasing qualitative disparities between East European and Soviet weapons systems, as well as nagging—if not increasing—questions concerning their political reliability, are not only undermining Moscow's strategy of "coalition warfare" vis-à-vis NATO, but may be forcing the Kremlin to make some significant changes in its strategy for fighting a war in Europe.

Internally, despite the actions taken by the Polish military on December 13, 1981 to help maintain communist rule in Poland, a careful analysis of the Polish experience over the past 4 or 5 years as well as the East European historical record in general suggests that the government/party's ability to utilize the armed forces in an interal crisis is much more limited than is generally assumed in the West.

Conceptually, the role/function of East European militaries can be divided into two broad categories: external, or the deployment of the armed forces against foreign enemies, and internal, or the use of the military to maintain or strengthen political stability, especially during periods of systemic crisis.

For purposes of this chapter, the external role of the military refers primarily to Moscow's perception of the utility of the East European militaries in an East–West conflict in Europe, although mention will also be made of their value as a tool for maintaining discipline within the "Socialist Commonwealth." The internal role of the military refers to the

*The views expressed in this chapter are those of the author and do not represent official U.S. Government policy. Copyright 1985 by Dale R. Herspring.

armed forces as an institution which can be relied upon to step in to help maintain systemic order and control by the party in a crisis situation. As the following historical analysis will demonstrate, the role and function of the East European militaries—and their consequent value to the Soviets—has changed over time in both of these areas.

## The Historical Evolution of the East European Armies

*1944–1948: The Seizure of Power* While Soviet and East European military historians have argued that the origins of most of the East European armies can be traced back to the common struggle against the Germans during World War II,[1] in fact, with the exception of the Polish and Czechoslovak armies, most of the others (i.e., Slovaks, Hungarians, and Romanians as well as Germans) fought on the Eastern Front against the USSR.[2] Furthermore, even in the case of the Polish military, the memories of the Katyn Forest massacre,[3] Stalin's partition of the country, and Moscow's relatively harsh treatment of those Poles who fell under its control all contributed to an intensification of historical animosities on the part of Poles. As a consequence, Moscow hesitated to introduce a strong system of political controls in the Polish army when it was first created. For example, large numbers of nonparty members were utilized within the political apparatus. One official source reports that only about 13% of all political–educational officers were members of the party in December 1944.[4] And only 56% of officers assigned to the Main Political Administration (MPA)—the most central and politically sensitive component of the political apparatus—belonged to the Communist Party.[5]

Even after the close of World War II, hostility toward the USSR and communism was strong enough throughout the region that the Soviets hesitated to fully Sovietize the East European militaries. In the Polish case, for example, while the MPA continued to function, its importance as a politicizing agent actually decreased. The political officers' school was closed in 1946, and by 1948 only 50% of all political officer positions were filled in the armed forces.[6] Political indoctrination efforts were aimed at imparting a basic understanding of Marxism–Leninism but were not required, and measures traditionally employed as control devices in communist militaries such as self-criticism were largely ignored.

Despite this go-slow policy toward Sovietizing the militaries, Moscow did begin to take steps which were aimed at neutralizing the militaries while at the same time laying the groundwork for building a sense of loyalty toward the newly evolving socialist systems. Thus, hostile elements were removed from the officer corps and replaced by individuals with the proper class background. As a prominent Polish sociologist put it, "for understandable reasons, socio–political criteria took precedence during the period when the army was created—even at the expense of many purely professional criteria."[7]

Little thought was given during this period to the possible deployment of these forces against an external foe. Their equipment was insufficient and antiquated—often of World War II vintage—training rudimentary, cadres unqualified, and neither the Soviets nor the East European leaderships showed any concern with removing the armed forces from their emasculated condition. From Moscow's point of view, the task was to neutralize the armed forces and if this meant making them militarily irrelevant, so be it.

*1948–1952: Stalinism*  With the imposition of Stalinism in Eastern Europe in 1948, all aspects of the various political systems were expected to imitate the Soviet model. This included the armed forces. As a result, national command positions were immediately filled with communist or procommunist officers—often individuals with little or no military experience. The "neutral" officers appointed to senior positions only a few short years earlier were quickly shunted aside. Furthermore, the process of recruiting new officers from hitherto disadvantaged classes (i.e., the worker or peasant classes) was intensified. Thus by 1950 the percentage of officers with a worker or peasant background was 82% in Bulgaria and 60% in Hungary; by 1952 it was 67.7% in Czechoslovakia, and by the end of 1953 it was 50.3% for Poland.[8]

In addition to personnel policies, other areas of military life were also affected by the Sovietization of the Eastern European militaries. Soviet doctrine, training patterns, and internal organization were also introduced. Even the traditionally unique East European uniforms were modified to the point where they were almost indistinguishable from those worn by the Soviets.

To ensure Eastern European military subordination to Soviet command, a number of direct channels of control were introduced by the Soviets. To wit, thousands of military officers were assigned to the East European militaries as "advisors," although in some cases they were actually incorporated into the national armies as regular officers. The most conspicious example of the latter was in Poland where Soviet Marshal Konstantin Rokossovsky became Warsaw's Defense Minister.[9]

Moscow also moved at this time to intensify politicization within the militaries. In Poland, for example, the political officers' school was reopened, and the number of political officer positions was increased. The post of deputy commander for political affairs was introduced at the company level, thereby bringing the political apparatus down to the main working level. Furthermore, throughout Eastern Europe the MPA was given responsibility for the politicization process, and its actions came under increased scrutiny by the party leadership. In addition, the party organization was revitalized and the basic party organization was introduced at the regimental level. Party meetings and discussions now began to be held on a regular basis.

Concurrent with Sovietization of the East European militaries, the Kremlin also began to devote attention to building-up Eastern Europe's military capabilities. By 1949, for example, military conscription had been introduced throughout the region (except for the GDR), and by 1953 the East European armies had expanded to 1.5 million men, organized into roughly 65 divisons.[10] In addition, Soviet equipment began to replace the East Europeans' largely outdated armament inventory. As a Bulgarian source noted in reference to this period: "The troops gradually received new protective weapons (the selfloading rifle 'Simonov,' 'Kalaschnikov' submachine guns), better developed air defense systems, jet aircraft, modern tanks, etc."[11]

While from the Soviet standpoint there was little reason to trust in the internal or external reliability of the various East European militaries at this time, Moscow could at least take comfort in the fact that the basis for a more dependable military had been laid. Furthermore, insofar as a future East–West conflict is concerned, Stalin "may have intended their build-up as a supplement to that of the Red Army itself, which was designed to alter the military balance in Europe to the advantage of the Soviet Union."[12]

*1953–1959: Post-Stalinism and the Founding of the Pact*  The aftermath of Stalin's death was a period of major transition for the East European armies. To begin with, most of the more extreme forms of Sovietization were eliminated. For example, traditional East European military uniforms and songs were reintroduced. In addition, status of forces agreements were concluded with Poland (1956), Hungary (1957), Romania (1957), and East Germany (1957) thereby regularizing the presence of Soviet troops—and in the case of Poland guaranteeing their "noninterference" in Polish domestic affairs.[13] The Soviets also agreed to a Romanian request and in 1958 withdrew all Soviet forces from that country.

From a military standpoint, the most important form of "renationalization" concerned the recall of large numbers of Soviet "advisors" and military officers from the East European militaries. This was most evident in Poland where Marshal Rokossovsky and almost all of his fellow officers were "thanked" for their services and returned to the Soviet Union. They were replaced by "native" communist officers, many of whom had been purged and imprisoned during the Stalinist period.

In addition to the renationalization of the armed forces, the role of the political apparatus was also deemphasized. In Poland, for example, the post of deputy commander for political affairs at the company level was abolished and the time allocated to ideological indoctrination courses shortened. The communist youth organization was also abolished and the focus of party activity shifted from the political apparatus to the party organization. Since only half the officers and even fewer enlisted personnel were party members, the net result was to weaken party influence within the military.

Although ostensibly created as a loosely organized "socialist military coalition" to counter "possible aggression,"[14] the Warsaw Pact, founded in 1955, was equally important to the Kremlin as an institutionalized substitute for Stalin's personalized system of asserting Soviet hegemony over the East European militaries. From the military standpoint, for example, Article 5 of the Treaty provided for a joint military command, and one was established in Moscow in 1956. Nevertheless, in military terms it remained a paper organization during this period. For example, the primary Soviet history of the Pact lists only one major military exercise during the period—involving naval, air, and ground forces from the USSR and Bulgaria.[15] As Thomas Wolfe put it, "the Soviet Union made no effort to weld the Warsaw Pact into an integrated military alliance" during its early years.[16]

Despite Moscow's neglect of the Pact during its first 5 years, important changes occurred in the East European militaries. To begin with, East European forces were cut back by 464,000 men.[17] Concurrently, vigorous efforts were made to improve the educational qualifications of the remaining officers and noncommissioned officers. For example, in Poland the proportion of officers with academic degrees rose from 12% in 1956 to 20% by 1962, in Czechoslovakia from 4.8% in 1956 to 14.4% in 1963, and in Bulgaria by 1960 between 15 and 20% had academic degrees.[18]

With regard to equipment, the motorization of infantry units was pushed, new armored units established, and tactical forces were modified to permit operations under conditions of nuclear war. T-54s gradually replaced T-34s, MIG-17s were added, and improved communication and transportation systems were introduced.[19]

Despite the modernization of East European forces, and the creation of the Pact, their utility to the Kremlin in a strictly military sense was severely limited at this time. The lack of qualified personnel, training deficiencies (especially in the area of combined operations) and the disparity in equipment held by front-line Soviet forces and East European armies meant that their use in conjunction with Soviet forces in an East–West confrontation would be problematical.

If equipment and training shortcomings presented the Kremlin with problems at this time, they were nothing when compared with the questions raised concerning the overall political reliability of East European forces. To begin with, the uprising in East Berlin in 1953 was put down by Soviet forces, due in large part to Soviet concerns over the reliability of East German paramilitary forces. Likewise, during the Hungarian Revolt in 1956, some units fought against the Soviets "with valor, courage, and heroism reminiscent of the best traditions of Hungarian military history,"[20] while the army as a whole stayed out of the fight. Furthermore, in the aftermath of Moscow's suppression of the revolt, the army was decimated by a purge which left large gaps in the ranks of the officer and NCO corps.

From the Soviet standpoint, the events in Poland in 1956 presented an even more dangerous challenge. Not only do the Poles occupy a strategic piece of real estate and possess the largest non-Soviet Pact force, but most senior ranks in the Polish military were at that time occupied by Soviet officers. When troops in Poznan refused to put down demonstrations in June, Polish authorities were forced to call in security forces from Warsaw. Furthermore, in October shortly after Gomulka assumed power, Polish forces played a critical role in ensuring a "Polish solution" to the leadership question. Khrushchev and his compatriots arrived at Okecie airport unannounced and uninvited, in an effort to oust Gomulka. At the same time, Soviet troops in Poland left their barracks and began to move on Warsaw. Meanwhile, Polish forces took up defensive positions around the city making it clear they were prepared to fight if necessary. The threat of resistance by Polish forces at a critical juncture appears to have played an important role in Khrushchev's decision to back down and accept Gomulka. For Moscow the message was ominous. Not even the presence of Soviet officers in the senior ranks of the Polish military could ensure loyalty on the part of the Polish military. If anything, these three events made it clear to the Kremlin that serious problems would have to be overcome before the East Europeans could be considered reliable.

*1960–1968: The Build-up and Czechoslovakia* The significant increase in attention paid by the Soviets to the Pact as a military organization after 1960 appears to have been primarily associated with Khrushchev's plan for shifting reliance in Soviet defense planning and doctrine away from traditional emphasis on ground forces toward greater importance for strategic nuclear forces. He apparently felt he could justify—at least partially—the cutbacks he planned in Soviet ground forces by getting East European military forces to assume a larger role in Pact strategy.

To implement this new strategy, major steps were undertaken to upgrade East European forces shortly after Marshal Grechko took over as Pact Commander-in-Chief in 1960. To begin with, a new Pact doctrine called "coalition warfare" was developed. This doctrine assigned the East Europeans a key role in an East–West conflict. In such a conflict they would be expected to participate jointly with Soviet forces in rapid offensive military operations against NATO. As a result of this new doctrine, East European forces were assigned increasingly important roles. The Poles, for example, were eventually given their own front commanded by a Polish general (the so-called Northern Front), while East German and Czechoslovak forces were assigned important roles in conjunction with Soviet forces on the Central and Southern fronts, respectively.

To make this new doctrine workable, East European military equipment was further upgraded. The process of replacing the World War II vintage T-34 with the more modern T-54/55 was completed and MIG-21 and SU-7 aircraft as well as antitank missiles and self-propelled guns were introduced into Pact inventories. Some East European forces also began to be supplied with nuclear-capable delivery vehicles (although the weapons themselves were kept in Soviet hands). Standardization of weapons systems was pushed forward, and a nascent East German aircraft industry was dismantled in 1961, and Poland renounced further work on advanced jet aircraft in 1967.[21] Considerable effort was also devoted to improving the qualifications of officers. By the end of this period, for example, the percentage of officers with an academic degree in Poland had risen from 18 to 30 and in the GDR from approximately 6 to 13.[22]

A major change also occurred in the area of multilateral training exercises. Where there had been only one in the Pact's first 5 years, there were 19 between 1960 and 1968. Furthermore, while some of the early exercises could be viewed primarily as propaganda devices, by the mid-1960s they had taken on an increasingly important military meaning.

Finally, increased attention was also given to the Pact's high level military organs. They began to meet on an annual basis and while details on the agenda of their meetings are lacking, information available from Soviet and Polish sources suggests they were chiefly concerned with operational matters such as the coming year's training program.[23] Broader defense-related questions appear to have been dealt with by the Pact's highest political organ, the Political Consultative Committee (PCC). For example, "conditions" in the Warsaw Pact forces were discussed at the 1963 PCC meeting.[24]

The increased attention given to training, equipment, and personnel as well as the greater concern being paid to the Pact's defense organs gave the impression that the Soviet Union was assigning greater weight to the role of the East European militaries. There were two developments, however, which raised serious questions on Moscow's part concerning the Pact's overall military utility.

In late 1964, the Romanians unilaterally reduced their term of service from 24 to 16 months. This led to a cut of 40,000 men from the Romanian armed forces. In addition, the Romanians argued that Pact military expenditures were excessive, succeeded in obtaining a reduction in the size of the Soviet military liaison mission in Bucharest, demanded a consultative voice in matters related to nuclear weapons, refused to permit Pact troop maneuvers on Romanian soil, declined to participate in joint maneuvers with combat troops in other countries, and finally proposed that the position of the Pact's military chief rotate among member states.[25] These actions not only undercut Moscow's efforts at upgrading and improving cooperation among Pact members, they also raised serious questions about the utility of Romanian forces in the Southern Region in the event of a war. These developments, as well as the Northern Tier's more strategic location, may help explain the greater attention paid by the Soviets to forces in the Northern Tier.

Following on the Romanian deviation came an even more unsettling development insofar as the Soviets were concerned. In 1968 with the rise of reformist elements in Czechoslovakia, certain segments of the Czechoslovak military—concentrated to a large degree in the political apparatus—began to express openly dissatisfaction with Moscow's domination of the Pact's leadership councils and side with Dubcek in his efforts to "democratize" Czechoslovakia. For example, insofar as the domestic Czechoslovak front was concerned, it has been argued by one Western analyst that conservative officers, opposed to the liberal internal policies advocated by Dubcek, may have planned to intervene in an effort to save the Novotny regime.[26] In fact, a letter sent to the crucial December 1967 Central Committee meeting apparently contained an implied threat by the army to intervene on Novotny's behalf, and certain units of the army were actually placed on alert, while a number of officers planned to "intervene if the Party's deliberations went against

Novotny."[27] The plot was reportedly neutralized by younger pro-Dubcek elements in the officer corps. Despite its inaction during the Soviet invasion—it was ordered not to resist—shortly after the Husak regime was installed, the Klement Gottwald Political Military Academy was closed and a large-scale purge of pro-Dubcek forces followed. According to one source, as a result of the purge and reorganization of the officer corps, personnel in some branches were 10–30% below normal. In the air force, for example, it was admitted to be 20% below normal, making it impossible in the first years of the 1970s to hold proper training and evaluation exercises.[28]

Despite all of Moscow's efforts to up-grade the East European forces, the Romanian and Czechoslovak events suggest that serious problems remained insofar as the reliability of these two Pact members were concerned. Not only did the Romanian military support Ceausescu in his defiance of Moscow, important elements of the Czechoslovak army criticized Soviet leadership techniques in the Pact and supported liberal elements in the country at a critical juncture.

It could, however, be argued that despite the foregoing, the period was not a total loss to the Kremlin. After all, the Soviets were able to convince five of their six allies (the Romanians opted out) to participate in the invasion of Czechoslovakia in 1968. This could be used as evidence to show that the East Europeans are reliable in an intra-Pact policing role. In this writer's opinion, the importance of this event has tended to be overestimated in the West. Ross Johnson put it best when he noted: "The invasion of Czechoslovakia demonstrated that the Soviet Union could mobilize some of its East European allies to interfere in the internal affairs of one of them; it did not demonstrate, however, that East European forces could contribute effectively to military operations against one of their number."[29] There are rumors, for example, that the East German forces aroused considerable resentment on the part of the local populace and had to be quickly withdrawn; that serious morale problems existed among Polish troops (who were embarrassed at being involved, even against a traditional enemy); and that the Hungarians had little heart for the exercise.[30] With the exception of the Soviets, who had morale problems of their own, only the Bulgarians appear to have supported the action. And this occurred against a largely passive population. Thus even an apparent victory in Moscow's efforts to utilize the Pact for its own ends left unanswered important questions concerning the reliability of East European troops when asked to carry out Soviet orders.

*1969–1979: Reassessment and Reorganization* Despite Soviet concern over Pact reliability in the aftermath of the Czechoslovak events, Moscow still felt the East European contribution important. Consequently, efforts were made to strengthen Pact unity. The most important change in this regard was the introduction of modifications in Pact structure. Although raised within Pact councils as early as 1966, they were not formally announced until the March 1969 PCC meeting in Budapest. First, a Committee of Defense Ministers (CDM) was created as the Pact's supreme military consultative organ. The CDM appears to have taken over some of the broader policy-oriented functions previously dealt with by the PCC. As one Soviet source put it, the CDM "works out joint recommendations and proposals for organizing the defense" of the Warsaw Pact and deals "with other questions requiring joint agreement."[31]

The Budapest meeting also established a Military Council, which appears to be subordinate to the Pact's joint command. This council seems to be responsible for some of the planning and quality control functions formerly assigned to the defense ministers and chiefs of staff. For instance, in discussing the work of the Military Council, Marshal V. G. Kulikov, the current commander-in-chief of Pact forces, has stated that it analyzes "the results of combat and operational activities for the preceding year and determines the tasks of the armies and fleets for the coming year."[32]

The third organ that emerged as a result of the 1969 reforms—the Technical Council—does not appear to have a precursor. Not much is known about this body except that it deals with "the development and modernization of weapons and technology, the coordination of the efforts of the unified armies in the area of scientific research and experimental design work of a defensive nature."[33] Yet the relative frequency with which it is mentioned in Soviet and East European writings on the Pact suggests that it plays an important integrative role: To quote Marshal Kulikov, "its creation speeded up the outfitting of the armies and the Warsaw Pact states with new types of weapons and equipment."[34]

As a consequence of these changes, responsibilities in the military sphere became more differentiated. Very broad political–military issues are discussed within the PCC, whose meetings usually include defense ministers as well as foreign ministers. Specific multilateral military issues are handled within the CDM, and the Joint Command oversees the implementation of "decisions by the Communist and Worker's Parties of the (Member) States."[35] The actual planning and organizing of military activities such as "maneuvers, exercises, and war games" are carried out by the Staff of the Joint Command.[36]

Since it was established, the CDM has met annually. The Military Council convenes twice a year on the average—once during the spring and once toward the end of the year. There is no information on how frequently the Technical Council meets.

While formally at least giving the East Europeans a greater role in Pact decision making—a Deputy Minister of Defense serves as Pact Deputy Commander and relays directives from the Pact chief to the national command—most observers agree that in fact key authority remains in the hands of the Soviets.[37] In a wartime situation, for example, East European forces would not be commanded through the Pact, but directly from a Soviet front or theater headquarters. If anything, the new structural changes improved Moscow's ability to coordinate and integrate Pact efforts in the military sphere.

Another manifestation of the mounting effort at Pact integration in the military sphere was the sudden increase in Pact military maneuvers. During the first 14 years of its existence, the Pact held only 20 military exercises, but there were 21 in the period from 1969 to 1972—11 of them in 1969 alone.[38] This striking increase in military exercises appears to have been designed primarily to give Pact forces extensive training on a multilateral level, a prerequisite for efficient deployment of Pact forces under the doctrine of coalition warfare. Such a conclusion is borne out by the great number of certain types of exercises largely ignored in the past. During 1969–1971, for example, five air defense/air force exercises took place, whereas there had been only one previously. Similarly, four rear-services exercises were held between 1969 and 1972.

Apparently satisfied that the groundwork for multilateral cooperation had been laid, Pact officials let the number of multilateral maneuvers drop off after 1972. But Pact military cooperation of a new type, which has generally been overlooked in the West, began to emerge in the mid-1970s. This consists of bilateral cooperation among East European armies, in which the Soviet Union appears to be only minimally involved. Such cooperation is particularly prevalent among the Northern Tier countries. For example, Polish officers attend the GDR's Friedrich Engels Military Academy, and Polish, Czechoslovak, and East German forces train together—without the presence of Soviet military units—and use each other's facilities.[39] Such training significantly enhances the ability of these forces to operate independently of Soviet troops either in rear areas or on a separate front.

Despite the progress which Moscow made in improving the functioning of the Pact as a military organization, major problems began to surface during the 1970s. First, while some Western commentators have suggested that modernization was proceeding apace in the East European forces,[40] the real situation was quite different. According to figures published by the Arms Control and Disarmament Agency, with the notable exception of the GDR, military expenditures in the region increased only gradually throughout the period; certainly not in sufficient amounts to cover even the minimal costs of expensive contemporary weapons systems.[41] This failure on the part of the East Europeans to allocate sufficient funds to cover the costs of contemporary weapons systems during the 1970s is borne out by an analysis of their actual holdings.

The Air Forces.  Most writers on the Pact point to the acquisition by East Europeans of MIG-23s and advanced Sukhoi aircraft during the 1970s as an example of how these military forces are being updated. However, a careful review of East European holdings as of 1979 (see Table 30.1) suggests that while the Soviets were moving ahead to introduce the latest aircraft into their own forces in the region, with a few notable exceptions little was being done to up-grade the East European air forces with modern aircraft such as the MIG-23 and Sukhoi planes.

The Armies.  At a time when there was talk of new tanks and other equipment being introduced in the East European inventories, the

Table 30.1. *Selected East European Air/Ground Holdings: 1979*

| Country | Air Force | Ground |
|---|---|---|
| Poland | MIG-17, 21; Sukhoi-7; some Sukhoi 20 | T-54/55 |
| The GDR | MIG-17, 21 | T-54/55 |
| Czechoslovakia | MIG-17, 21; some 23s | T-54/55 |
| Hungary | MIG-21 | T-54/55 |
| Bulgaria | MIG-17, 19, 21; some 23s | T-54/55 |
| Romania | MIG-17, 21 | T-54/55 |

SOURCE: International Institute for Strategic Studies, *The Military Balance, 1979–80* (London: Institute for Strategic Studies, 1980), pp. 14–16.

Table 30.2. *Selected East European Air/Ground Holdings: 1984*

| Country | Air Force | Ground |
|---|---|---|
| Poland | MIG-17, 21; a few 23s; SU-7; a few SU-20s being added | T-54/55, 70 T-72s; only 800 BMP-1 (½ of those required to meet Soviet norms), 0T64 and obsolescent 0T62 |
| The GDR | MIG-21; a few 23s | T-54/55, large number of T-72s; 40% of combat infantry vehicles are modern and artillery holdings adequate |
| Czechoslovkia | MIG-15, 21; smattering of 23s; SU-7 | T-54/55, 100 T-72s |
| Hungary | MIG-21; 23s beginning to appear | T-54/55, with a few T-72s |
| Bulgaria | MIG-17, 21; a few 23s | T-54/55, with a few T-72s; combat infantry vehicles outdated and major shortfalls in artillery |
| Romania | MIG-17, 21; a few 23s; IAR-93s | Similar to Bulgaria |

SOURCE: International Institute for Strategic Studies, *The Military Balance, 1984–85* (London: International Institute for Strategic Studies, 1984), pp. 24–28.

record shows (see Table 30.1) that the T-54/55 remained the main battle tank in non-Soviet Pact forces.

The Navies. With the exception of East Berlin, which began a major naval build-up in the early 1970s,[42] little was being done by other Pact leaderships to modernize their fleets. The vast majority of the Polish fleet was constructed in the late 1950s and mid-1960s and little was being done to push new construction in the Bulgarian and Romanian navies.

Most weapons systems require considerable lead time, and it could be argued that the delay between a push by Moscow and actual acquisition by the East Europeans of the weapons is related to this process. While the acquisition of new weapons may be influenced somewhat by this process, this does not appear to be a major problem in Eastern Europe. After all, the equipment was Soviet-designed, and since it was being introduced into front line Soviet units at this time, if a high enough priority had been assigned to its acquisition, it could have been obtained. It was clearly available.

The second major problem area for the Soviets during this period occurred in Poland.[43] First, in 1970 riots occurred in Gdansk and while the circumstances are still unclear, the best available information indicates that the military was involved in the suppression of demonstrations by workers. However, despite their involvement, the Polish military reportedly refused to go along with orders from one of Gomulka's representatives in the Gdansk area to use overwhelming force to put down the demonstrations.

This event had two important consequences for the Polish military. First, it had a devastating and demoralizing impact on the Polish officer corps and was the subject of considerable soul searching and debate within the armed forces. Second, the event showed not only that the military would not unquestionably follow the orders of the political leadership, but convinced the high command that the military should at all costs avoid involvement in internal Polish politics.

The 1976 crisis in Warsaw centered around price increases which led to work stoppages by workers in and around Warsaw. According to Polish sources, the Polish military played a key role in Gierek's decision to back down quickly. Jaruzelski's now famous statement, "Polish soldiers will not fire on Polish workers," convinced Gierek of the need to avoid a confrontation.[44]

Taken together, these two events showed that far from being a reliable tool in the hands of the party leadership, the Polish military's utility in an internal crisis was limited. If it was to be successfully utilized at all, it would have to be carefully orchestrated.

By the end of the 1970s, it must have been clear to Moscow that not only were the East Europeans not ready to expend the necessary funds to modernize their armed forces, but that serious questions existed concerning the reliability of one of the Pact's key members.

*1980–1985: The Problems Increase* From the Soviet perspective, events in Eastern Europe over the past 5 years have expanded the problems Moscow faces in utilizing the East European militaries for its own ends. In fact, the difficulties faced by the Kremlin have reached the point where the Soviets may have to consider some major changes in Pact strategy in the event of an East–West conflict in Europe.

The Polish Experience. The actions of the Polish military over the past 5 years have been far from reassuring to the Soviets. To begin with, during the August 1980 events the Polish military remained neutral and refused to become involved in what was viewed as an internal political struggle. For example, Admiral Janczyszyn, commander of the Polish Navy, is reported to have stated at the time that he would not permit the use of Polish troops to put down strike activity by Polish shipyard workers and instead called on the party's Central Committee to approve the Gdansk accords.[45]

Throughout the 15-month period preceding the declaration of martial law, the Polish military stayed in the background. Some Polish sources claim, for example, that Jaruzelski was offered the position of First Secretary at the time of Gierek's ouster, but turned it down. When he did accept it in February 1981 as the internal political stuggle was heating up in Poland, any possibility for him to find a compromise solution to the strike ended with the Bydgoszcz incident in March of that year. At that time, in an effort to gain official recognition, members of Rural Solidarity had been occupying government buildings. Shortly after Polish labor leader Lech Walesa met with General Jaruzelski and hopes had risen over the possibility of a negotiated settlement to the country's problems, the police attacked those occupying the buildings, seriously injuring a number of them. The result was a further intensification of passions on both sides as Solidarity called for punishment of police officials. Walesa reportedly described the affair "as an obvious provocation against the Government of General Jaruzelski; he plainly did not mean that Solidarity members had acted provocatively. . . ."[46] It is generally believed in Poland that the incident was staged by hardline elements within the security services and Polish leadership—perhaps with Soviet support—to prevent any accommodation between the government/party and Solidarity.

Throughout the remainder of the year Poland fell further into internal disarray. The party steadily lost cohesiveness, and there was increasing talk of a full-scale takeover of the party by liberal elements. Frustrated by its inability to get an increasingly beleaguered government/party apparatus to live up to its promises, Solidarity became increasingly radicalized to the point where Walesa's leadership of the union was in serious question at the September 1981 trade union congress. In fact, he succeeded in maintaining control, but only by the smallest of margins and after making a number of concessions to more radical elements in the union.

While we will probably never know exactly who was behind the declaration of martial law on December 13 (i.e., to what degree it was a Polish decision or the result of intense Soviet pressure), contrary to the general Western perception, military involvement was minimal. Regular military units were often not even aware of the declaration of martial law. Furthermore, this writer is not aware of a single incident in which regular military units were involved in the use of force against civilians. The task of implementing the more onerous aspects fell on the shoulders of the security forces—in particular the dreaded ZOMOs. Military participation in the early days was limited to actions such as: Manning of checkpoints on highways and at main urban intersections; 2–3 man patrols in major cities; the transportation of ZOMOs around the country (by the air force); providing communications support to the media; or an occasional drive past key points in tanks or similar equipment in an effort to intimidate the populace. If the West misjudged events in Poland, it was not because it underestimated the ability of the Warsaw leadership to utilize the military in an internal crisis; it was a failure to recognize the tremendous build-up of security forces which had occurred during the 6 months prior to the declaration of martial law.

When it came to a crisis, Warsaw went out of its way to avoid utilizing regular military units in a confrontational situation. The leadership was too unsure of how the soldiers would react if called upon to use force against other Poles. In short, it went out of its way to avoid testing the validity of Jaruzelski's 1976 statement that "Polish soldiers will not fire on Polish workers."

Since December 1981, the Polish military has been used in a variety of functions. First, in addition to General Jaruzelski and those immediately around him, a number of other senior Polish officers have taken on high-level positions (e.g., General Piotrowski, the Minister of Mines and Energy). Second, they have acted as trouble shooters. For example, officers at the level of colonel were assigned to provincial governors who used them to help eliminate supply bottlenecks or deal with other logistical problems. Finally, they served on inspection teams which were assigned the task of ensuring that party and government bureaucrats throughout the country were carrying out the general's orders (they frequently were not). While many of these officers returned to their barracks after martial law ended in July 1983, large numbers are still active in the civilian bureaucracy. In fact, the outlook is for prolonged military presence in the civilian sphere. A return to complete civilian rule would put the same individuals who brought about the 1980 crisis back into power, something the general appears determined to avoid.

The Polish experience has a number of implications for the USSR. First, while the situation in Poland is clearly better than it was on December 12, 1981, to date Jaruzelski has not always done things the way the Soviets would have preferred. He has resisted suggestions to return power to the party. Likewise, Poland has the strongest church in any communist country—if not in all of Europe—the general has not cracked down so hard on dissidents as the Kremlin would prefer, agriculture remains predominantly in private hands, the media is relatively open by communist standards, and the universities retain a significant degree of autonomy. The lesson is that East European generals cannot always be counted on to do Moscow's bidding.

Second, while senior military officers and the security organs were able to hold the line this time, the Kremlin must have continuing concerns over stability in Poland in a real crisis situation. After all, the 1981 takeover took place in the face of a largely passive populace. What if there is resistance next time and the internal security organs prove insufficient? What will the regular army do if called upon to use its weapons?

Finally, looking at Poland's key role in the Warsaw Pact (15 divisions with its own front), Moscow must be worried about the large number of officers who have been engaged in nonmilitary activities. Such activities are likely to detract from the Polish military's combat readiness. Furthermore, the bitterness on the part of the average Pole over the events of the past 4 years as well as continuing support of the ideals of Solidarity are certain to have an important impact on morale and combat readiness.

Modernizing the East European Militaries. Despite some efforts to modernize them, East European militaries appear to be falling further behind Soviet forces in the region.

*Air Forces.* At a time when the Soviet forces will soon have MIG-29s and SU-27s,[47] the East Europeans are far behind. As indicated in Table 30.2, the predominant aircraft in the region remain the MIG-21 and SU-7, though MIG-23s and SU-20s are beginning to make their appearance in East European inventories.

*Armies.* After carefully analyzing the state of Northern Tier forces, one writer has concluded that there are major disparities between Soviet and East European forces. Looking at the Polish army, this writer concludes: "At best, the Polish Army would be hard-pressed to keep up with better organized and equipped Soviet forces and could not be expected to do well some of the very important things that Soviet units could do and Soviet doctrine requires."[48] The Czechoslovak army is in somewhat better shape than the Polish, but it too has serious shortcomings. All in all, "the Czechoslovak Peoples Army, like the Polish Peoples Army, seems ill-structured and ill-equipped to perform a first echelon role."[49] Finally, even the East German army, which is the most modern of all East European militaries, is still inferior to Soviet forces in the region, which are "receiving the newest equipment, tanks, self-propelled artillery and air defense missiles at a much faster rate than the NVA."[50]

*Navies.* With the exception of the East German navy, all of the Pact fleets have serious deficiencies. While the largest, the Polish navy is quickly sinking into obsolescence. The Romanian navy is small and outdated, and the Bulgarian navy is also in need of new ships and equipment.

To the Soviets, the situation among the East European militaries must appear bleak indeed. The quality of their equipment, while improving, lags far behind that of Soviet forces. And while figures from the Arms Control and Disarmament Agency suggest that East European military budgets are increasing,[51] this is not reflected in new weapons systems. One option for the Soviets would be to increase pressure on the East Europeans to purchase more modern weapons. Given the region's serious economic problems—Poland is only the most obvious case—such an approach if carried out could have a serious impact on these countries' economies. In view of the close tie between economic and political stability in the area, it could also have significant political ramifications as well. However much the Kremlin may prefer modern militaries in Eastern Europe, it is doubtful they are prepared to push the

East Europeans in that direction if the result is likely to be increased political instability.

There is also some question as to whether the East Europeans—with the exception of the East Germans—will agree to a significant increase in military budgets. By and large they appear to have other priorities—most particularly resolving internal economic difficulties while at the same time preventing a further deterioration in East–West relations. Recent East European assertiveness on issues such as INF counterdeployments (only the East Germans and Czechoslovaks accepted the SS-12s, and there are rumors that the move was opposed by almost all East European Pact members) as well as participation in the 1984 Olympics (the Romanians went and the Hungarians and Poles held out until the last minute) suggest that within limits the East Europeans are becoming increasingly willing to assert their independence on some issues.[52]

If the past 40 years are any indication, the Soviets still have a long way to go before problems of political reliability will be overcome. The Hungarian revolt in 1956, the Czechoslovak crisis of 1968, the Polish events in the 1970s and 1980s all raise questions concerning their reliability both at home and in an East–West conflict. And while the Soviets may attempt to deal with such problems by pushing cooperation among the various political apparatuses as one writer has suggested,[53] it is unlikely that they will overcome the problem in the foreseeable future.

## The Soviet Dilemma

The increasing technical gap between Soviet and East European weapons systems together with continuing questions concerning the latter's political reliability in a NATO–Warsaw Pact confrontation present Soviet military planners with a number of problems.

*Compensating for East European Forces* One of the major consequences of the Czechoslovak invasion in 1968 was the permanent stationing of five Soviet divisions in Czechoslovakia. The presence of these forces together with the modernization of Soviet forces in Eastern Europe has to a degree helped compensate for shortcomings on the part of East European forces. Since 1968, however, the situation within the East European armies has worsened from Moscow's point of view. One way of dealing with this situation would be to station a greater number of Soviet troops in the region. Alternatively, Moscow could also allocate some of its divisions from the Western regions of the Soviet Union for service in Europe in an emergency.

Both of these options have drawbacks. The first is likely to be resisted by the East Europeans and would be a matter of concern to the West Europeans who would be alarmed by the presence of greater numbers of Soviet troops in the area. It would complicate Moscow's efforts to drive a wedge between the U.S. and its Western European allies and undercut the Kremlin's "peace" policy in Western Europe. The second alternative would create problems in a crisis situation. The mobilization and movement of such forces into position prior to the opening of hostilities would provide NATO with increased warning time.

*Greater Reliance on Nuclear Weapons* Moscow could compensate for the reduced utility of the East Europeans by modifying Pact strategy to eliminate or shorten a conventional stage of a European conflict by moving more quickly to the use of theater nuclear weapons. Such a step would not only increase the danger of a central system exchange, it would almost certainly be picked up by the West during peacetime, help legitimize NATO's reliance on nuclear weapons in the minds of many West Europeans, and create difficulties for Moscow's attempt to downplay the existence of a Soviet threat. To date, this writer is not aware of any movement toward greater reliance on nuclear weapons by the Soviets in a NATO–Warsaw Pact conflict.

*Conflicts Must Be Short and Successful* While there is no doubt that the Soviets can mobilize the East Europeans for an East–West conflict and assure their participation, potential problems with reliability place a premium on a short, successful campaign. Should the USSR suffer reverses or become bogged down, problems with East European troops could quickly emerge. As a consequence, assuming the Soviets decide to utilize the East Europeans, Soviet military planners would be under strong pressure to pick exactly the right time and place to ensure the quick success of any operation against NATO. This obviously limits flexibility in the planning of operations.

*Ensuring the Integration of Pact Weapons Systems* The increasingly obsolescent East European weapons systems will make combined arms operations more difficult. The Pact's continued reliance on a high level of exercises helps somewhat, but as one writer put it with reference to the less technical East Europeans, "the national armies are becoming rapidly less capable than their Soviet counterparts and less able to execute Soviet combined arms operations."[54]

Moscow could, of course, eliminate the discrepancy between its forces and those of its allies by supplying them with modern weapons free of charge. To date, however, the Soviets have not done so. As one East European specialist on national security questions put it in a conversation with the author, "We won't be supplied with the latest equipment for three reasons: first, the Soviets want to make money off of the sale of weapons and we don't have the hard currency. Second, they don't think we will do our part in an East–West conflict and don't want to waste the weapons. Third, they don't trust us and are afraid some of our pilots, for example, will defect to the West with the latest equipment." Assuming the trends outlined in this chapter continue, the Pact's difficulties in carrying out combined arms operations will grow.

*Maintaining Supply Lines* Given the strong anti-Soviet sentiments throughout Eastern Europe, Moscow must also contend with potential problems in ensuring the security of its rear echelons in an East–West conflict. This is particularly true of Poland, where anti-Soviet feelings

are especially strong and through which Soviet forces in East Germany
are normally resupplied. In a European conflict the Soviets could try to
send supplies by sea as they did during the height of the Solidarity
period, but in view of West German naval air and undersea capabilities,
such an approach is fraught with dangers and uncertainties.

*Keeping the Peace in Eastern Europe* The recent Polish experience
shows that while the military can be useful in helping maintain order,
serious questions remain not only about its readiness to carry out
Moscow's will, but concerning its ability to keep the situation under
control if serious bloodshed erupts as well. This means, first, that
Moscow must continue to be prepared to use its own forces in a policing
role in peacetime, and second, that disturbances in rear areas could
cause not only serious logistical problems but instability as well at a time
when Soviet forces were engaged elsewhere.

Observers in the West have traditionally devoted a considerable
amount of attention to NATO's deficiences, both political and technical.
While such attention is appropriate and needed, there has been a
tendency on the part of most Western analysts either to ignore the Pact's
problems or at a minimum to downplay them. As this chapter has
shown, the problems for the Soviets are real and getting worse. It is
doubtful, despite all its problems, that many NATO generals would be
prepared to trade their own forces for those of the other side.

It has often been observed that the Soviet soldier is not 10 feet tall.
This analysis indicates, however, that despite all of the attention and
effort the Soviets have put into the Pact and its East European components, the Pact is also not 10 feet tall. In fact, recent trends suggest
that relative to Soviet forces, its figurative height is decreasing. The
problems for the Kremlin will continue and require actions on the part of
the Soviets to deal with them. While it is not clear at this point how the
Soviets will react, the situation is important enough to warrant more
careful attention on the part of Western analysts than has hitherto been
the case.

## Notes

[1]For a discussion of their origin from the Soviet point of view, see A. V.
Antosyak *et al.*, *Zarozhdenie narodnykh armiy stran-uchasnits varshavskogo dogovora*
(Moskva: Izdatel'stvo nauka, 1975).

[2]See, for example, Peter Gosztony, *Hitlers Fremde Heere* (Dusseldorf: Econ
Verlag, 1976).

[3]For an analysis of the Katyn Forest massacre see J. K. Zawodny, *Death in the
Forest* (Notre Dame: Notre Dame University Press, 1962).

[4]Ignacy Blum, *Z dziejòw Wojska Polskiego w latach 1944–1948* (Warszawa:
Ministerstwo Obrony Narodowej, 1968), p. 180.

[5]*Ibid.*

[6]Lt. Col. Tadeusz Konecki, "Zawodowe Szkolnictwo Ludowego Wojska
Polskiego w Fierwszym Powojennym Dziesiecioleciu," *Wojskowy Przeglad His-
toryczny* no. 2 (1974), p. 341.

[7]Jerzy Wiatr, "Sozio–politische Besonderheiten und Funktionen von Streit-

kraften in sozialistischen Landern," in *Beitrage zur Militarsoziologie*, ed. Rene Konig (Koln and Opladen: Westdeutscher Verlag, 1968), p. 104.

[8]For Bulgaria, see Marian Jurek and Edward Skrzypowski, *Tarcza Pokoju* (Warszawa: Ministerstwo Obrony Narodowej, 1975), p. 240; for Hungary, Sandor Mucs and Erno Zagoni, *Geschichte der Ungarischen Volksarmee* (Berlin: Militarverlag der Deutschen Demokratischen Republik, 1982), p. 170; for Czechoslovakia, Jan Liptak and Milan Spicak, "Die Tschechoslowakische Volks-armee in der Periode des beschleunigten Aufbaus einer Armee sozialistischen Typus," *Militargeschichte*, no. 2 (1975), p. 189; and for Poland, Major Marian Jurek, "Dorobek XX-Lecia ludowego korpusu oficerskiego," *Wojsko Ludowe*, no. 7 (1964), p. 44.

[9]In addition in Poland, the Chief of the General Staff, the Commander of Ground Forces, and the heads of all the service commanders of all four military districts were likewise former Soviet officers.

[10]Thomas W. Wolfe, *Soviet Power and Europe, 1945–1970* (Baltimore: Johns Hopkins Press, 1970), p. 43.

[11]A. Semerdshiew, F. Christow, and S. Penkow, *Geschichte der Bulgarischen Volksarmee* (Berlin: Militarverlag der Deutschen Demokratischen Republik, 1977), pp. 193–194.

[12]A. Ross Johnson, "Has Eastern Europe Become a Liability to the Soviet Union? (II)—The Military Aspect," in *The International Politics of Eastern Europe*, ed. Charles Gati (New York: Praeger, 1976), p. 40.

[13]A. Ross Johnson, Robert Dean, and Alexander Alexiev, *East European Military Establishments: The Warsaw Pact Northern Tier* (New York: Crane Russak, 1982), p. 22.

[14]I. I. Yakubovskiy, ed., *Boyevoyoe sodruzhestvo bratskikh narodov i armiy* (Moskva: Voyenizdat, 1975), pp. 86, 90.

[15]*Ibid.*, p. 273.

[16]Wolfe, *Soviet Power and Europe, 1945–1970*, p. 148.

[17]These figures were arrived at on the basis of data in Stephan Tiedtke, *Die Warschauer Vertragsorganization* (Munich: Oldenbourg, 1978), pp. 23–24.

[18]For Poland see Dale R. Herspring, "Technology and the Political Officer in the Polish and East German Armed Forces," *Studies in Comparative Communism* (Winter 1977), p. 393; for Czechoslovakia, Col. Jan Liptak *et al.*, *Die Tschecho-slowakische Volksarmee* (Berlin: Militarverlag der Deutschen Demokratischen Re-publik, 1979), p. 180; and for Bulgaria, Semerdshiew, Christow, and Penkow, *Geschichte der Bulgarischen Volksarmee*, p. 219.

[19]Liptak *et al.*, pp. 164–165 and Autorenkollektiv des Deutschen Instituts fur Militargeschichte, *Zeittafel zur Militargeschichte der Deutschen Demokratischen Re-publik 1949 bis 1968* (Berlin: Deutscher Militarverlag, 1969), p. 87.

[20]Ivan Volgyes, "The Military as an Agent of Political Socialization: The Case of Hungary," in *Civil–Military Relations in Communist Systems*, ed. Dale R. Herspring and Ivan Volgyes (Boulder: Westview, 1978), p. 152.

[21]A. Ross Johnson, "The Warsaw Pact: Soviet Military Policy in Eastern Europe," in *Soviet Policy in Eastern Europe*, ed. Sarah Meiklejohn Terry (New Haven: Yale University Press, 1984), p. 262. Despite the abandonment of work in these areas, some of the East European states have continued to produce Soviet-design weapons under license (e.g., the Poles are building tanks and ships, the Hungarians and Czechoslovaks infantry equipment and artillery pieces).

[22]Herspring, "Technology and the Political Officer in the Polish and East German Armed Forces," p. 393. The lower educational level on the part of East German officers can be partially explained by the fact that the East German military was not formally established until 1956.

[23]V.G. Kulikov, ed., *Varshavskiy Dogovor—soyuz vo imya mira i sotsializma* (Moskva: Voyennoye Izdatel'stvo, 1980), pp. 274–279 and Jurek and Skrzypowski, *Tarcza Pokoju*, pp. 338–348.

[24]N.N. Rodinov *et al.*, *Organizatsiya Varshavskogo Dogovora, 1955–1976* (Moskva: Izdatel'stvo Politicheskoy Literatury, 1975), p. 75.

[25]Johnson in Gati, *The International Politics of Eastern Europe*, p. 44.

[26]Robert W. Dean, "The Political Consolidation of the Czechoslovak Army," Radio Free Europe Research, Czechoslovakia/14, April 29, 1971, p. 15.

[27]Galia Golan, *Reform Rule in Czechoslovakia* (Cambridge: Cambridge University Press, 1973), p. 183.

[28]Condoleezza Rice, "Warsaw Pact Reliability: The Czechoslovak People's Army (CLA)," in *Soviet Allies: The Warsaw Pact and the Issue of Reliability*, ed. Daniel N. Nelson (Boulder: Westview, 1984), p. 135.

[29]A. Ross Johnson, "The Military in Eastern Europe—Loyalty to Whom?" paper prepared for a conference entitled, "Eastern Europe—Stability or Recurrent Crisis?" by the Department of State at Airlie House, Virginia, November 13–15, 1976.

[30]Even in the primarily Hungarian areas, the Hungarian army was viewed as an occupying army by a hostile population, and the army responded by trying to return to Hungary as soon as possible.

[31]K. Savinov, *Moguchiy faktor mira i stabil'nosti v mezhdunarodnykh otnosheniyakh* (Moskva: Mezhdunarodnyye Otnosheniya, 1980), p. 17.

[32]Kulikov, *Varshavskiy Dogovor*, p. 167.

[33]Savinov, *Moguchiy faktor mira i stabil'nosti*, p. 19.

[34]V. Kulikov, "Chetvert' veka po strazhe zavoevanniy sotsializma i mira," *Voyenno-istoricheskiy Zhurnal*, no. 5 (1980), p. 26.

[35]*Ibid.*, p. 26.

[36]*Ibid.*, p. 26.

[37]See, for example, Johnson in Gati, *The International Politics of Eastern Europe*, p. 51 and Malcolm Mackintosh, "The Warsaw Pact Today," *Survival* (May–June 1974), pp. 122–126.

[38]Material on Pact exercises is taken from Kulikov, *Varshavskiy Dogovor*, pp. 272–293.

[39] See, for example, the reference to GDR–Polish cooperation in a 1975 speech by General Heinz Hoffmann, the GDR Minister of National Defense, during the visit to East Germany by the then Polish Defense Minister Wojciech Jaruzelski in *Zolnierz Wolnosci*, March 14, 1975. See also the Polish report of the result of the visit in *Ibid.*, March 15–16, 1975. There have been numerous other references to widespread Polish–GDR military cooperation in *Zolnierz Wolnosci* and *Volksarmee*. Such cooperation, at least in the form of Polish officers attending the East German military academy, does not appear to have been affected by events in Poland during the past 5 years.

[40]For example, John Erickson, "The Warsaw Pact—The Shape of Things to Come?" in *Soviet–East European Dilemmas*, ed. Karen Dawisha and Philip Hanson (London: Holmes and Meier, 1981), p. 164, and Johnson in Terry, *Soviet Policy in Eastern Europe*, p. 265.

[41]Arms Control and Disarmament Agency, *World Military Expenditures and Transfers, 1972–1982* (Washington, D.C., U.S. Arms Control and Disarmament Agency, 1984).

[42]For a detailed discussion of the East German naval buildup and a comparison of the Volksmarine with the Polish Navy, see Dale R. Herspring, "GDR Naval Build-up," *Problems of Communism* (January–February 1984), pp. 54–62.

[43]The following description of the 1970 and 1976 events in Poland is taken from Johnson, Dean, and Alexiev, *East European Military Establishments*, pp. 51–53.

[44]Dale R. Herspring and Ivan Volgyes, "Political Reliability in East European Warsaw Pact Armies," *Armed Forces and Society* 6, no.2 (Winter 1980), p. 279.

[45]As recounted to the author by a number of Polish sources.

[46]Kevin Ruane, *The Polish Challenge* (London: British Broadcasting Corporation, 1982), pp. 137–138.

[47]James H. Hansen, "Countering NATO's New Weapons: Soviet Concepts for War in Europe," *International Defense Review* 17, no. 11 (1984), p. 1619.

[48]Col. Richard C. Martin, "Disparities in Modernization between Warsaw Pact Armies Opposite NATO's Central Region," paper delivered at the Conference on "Security Implications of Nationalism in Eastern Europe," U.S. Army War College, Carlisle Barracks, Pennsylvania, October 23–24, 1984, p. 10.

[49]*Ibid.*, p. 17.

[50]*Ibid.*, p. 19.

[51]Arms Control and Disarmament Agency, *World Military Expenditures*, pp. 19–42.

[52]Ten years ago the idea of East European leaderships raising questions about, let alone opposing the Soviets on, a key security question such as INF counterdeployments would have been unthinkable.

[53]Christopher Jones, "The Political Administrations of the Warsaw Pact and the Reliability of the East-Bloc Armed Forces," in Nelson, *Soviet Allies*, pp. 67–97.

[54]Martin, *Disparities in Modernization between Warsaw Pact Armies*, p. 4.

# 31

## PAUL MARER

# The Political Economy of Soviet Relations with Eastern Europe*

The most significant general factor in the relations between the Soviet Union and the countries of Eastern Europe,[1] whether individually or collectively, is the large disparity between their populations, territories, resource endowments, and military power. Given these differences, and given the objectives of Soviet policy, intrabloc relations are inevitably asymmetrical, marked by the dominance of a superpower and the dependence of six relatively small client states, and like any relationship of asymmetrical interdependence offering opportunities for the strong to take advantage of the weak.

My focus in this chapter is the evolution of the Soviet Union's economic relations with Eastern Europe since 1945 and the prospects for those relations in the 1980s. The basic question it will attempt to answer is how Soviet–East European relations should be characterized: Has the USSR used its power to dominate the East European countries economically, or has it subsidized them heavily, as some claim? Or is the relationship one of mutual costs and benefits?

First, I trace the Soviet Union's postwar economic objectives and policies under Stalin, relevant because Eastern Europe's economic institutions and structures were established then; their legacies continue to be important even in the 1980s. Next, I describe post-Stalin changes in Soviet economic policies and the main institutions and mechanisms of the Council for Mutual Economic Assistance (CMEA), as essential background for understanding the nature of Soviet economic relations

*Reprinted by permission of the author and publisher from Sarah Terry, ed., *Soviet Policy in Eastern Europe* (New Haven: Yale University Press, 1984), pp. 155–188. The author would like to thank Morris Bornstein, Robert W. Campbell, Ed. A. Hewett, Marie Lavigne, Sarah Terry, and Thomas Wolf for their helpful comments and Michael Marrese and Jan Vanous for making available a pre-publication copy of their book and for clarifying discussions. This acknowledgment should not imply their agreement with any statements or interpretations. Copyright 1984 by Council on Foreign Relations, Inc.

with Eastern Europe. Then, I discuss a most controversial issue: Can it be established statistically and unambiguously that the Soviet Union provides large subsidies to Eastern Europe and, if so, how can that be reconciled with Soviet power and domination of the region? Finally, I describe how Soviet and East European economic performance and prospects are expected to influence Soviet economic policy during the rest of the 1980s, and conclude with a discussion of the USSR's political goals and economic policy options.

## Historical Background (1945–1955)

During World War II, much of the industry of what subsequently became the German Democratic Republic (GDR) was destroyed or severely damaged, and a good part of what remained was dismantled and taken by the Soviets. The economies of Poland and Yugoslavia were also largely destroyed, while Hungary's suffered very serious damage.

Postwar economic recovery was slowed by Soviet exploitation, mainly via conventional types of economic extraction: carting away machinery from the former enemy countries; so-called joint stock companies, through which the Soviet Union took a significant share of Eastern Europe's current output; and by paying less than world market prices for Eastern Europe's commercial exports (particularly well documented in the case of Poland). Reparations represented further unrequited transfers (principally from East Germany but also from Hungary and Romania). The GDR carried the largest combined burden by far, but substantial resources were extracted from the other countries as well. I have estimated the value of the unrequited flow of resources from Eastern Europe to the Soviet Union during the first postwar decade to be roughly $14 billion, or of the same order of magnitude as the aid the United States gave to Western Europe under the Marshall Plan.[2]

With the completion of basic postwar reconstruction by 1948–1949 (later in East Germany), the development strategies of all East European countries followed the Soviet model: increasing the share of investment in national income to very high levels at the expense of consumption and concentrating investment in mining, metallurgy, and machine building. The policies pursued during 1948–1953 and the reorientation of trade from Western Europe to the USSR laid the foundations of an industrial structure that largely determined the course of postwar economic developments in Eastern Europe as well as the subsequent pattern of Eastern Europe's commerical relations with the USSR and with the rest of the world. Therefore, it is of interest whether the adoption of the Soviet model by national communist leaders during the 1948–1953 period was voluntary or imposed.

Long aware of their relative economic backwardness, the East European countries had periodically attempted to overcome it by spurts of import-substitution industrialization, not only in the newly separate Eastern Zone of Germany and in the already highly industrialized parts of Czechoslovakia but in all the other East European countries as well. However, the breakneck speed of industrialization and its extremely skewed pattern were externally imposed. Countless eyewitness accounts testify to the decisive role played by Soviet advisers and shopping lists in the industrialization and trade patterns of Eastern Europe during this early period; many argue that Soviet shopping lists have remained important in determining the composition of the region's industrial output.

Czechoslovakia after the war was already a relatively highly developed country whose industrial base had not been destroyed. The double coup d'état of 1948–1949—of the Communist party over parliamentary democracy and of the Muscovite faction over the rest of the party—was immediately followed by two successive, very large, revisions in the original draft of the First Five-Year Plan (1950–1955). According to an economics text published in Prague in 1969, the first revision arose out of long-term trade contracts with CMEA, especially the 1950–1955 agreement with the USSR, which "raised demands upon Czechoslovak heavy industry, in particular upon the production of heavy machinery and equipment. . . . These articles were highly material-intensive and required the construction of new capacities, or the reconstruction of existing ones." Concerning the second revision in 1951, the same text contended that demands from the military sector were "considerable, and [that] the entire economy was subordinated to them"—indeed, that "these tasks were no longer integrated into a modified plan but represented a plan of their own." As a result, planned growth of industrial output was increased from 10 to 20–25% per annum, while armaments production increased sevenfold from 1948 to 1953.[3]

The situation was quite similar in East Germany. War destruction and dismantling by the Soviets in metallurgy and in the chemical and engineering industries had left the GDR's manufacturing capacity predominantly in light and food industries and light machine building. Yet, while these latter industries often operated below capacity because of supply shortages, and in 1958 were still producing far below 1939 levels, branches founded or expanded to produce for Soviet export (shipyards, railroad equipment plant, precision machinery, electrical machinery, and heavy industrial equipment) were operating above 1939 levels.[4]

The situation appears to have been similar also in Poland and Hungary. As postwar reconstruction was nearing completion, both governments opted for an industrialization drive spearheaded by heavy industry. But it was the subsequent Soviet-inspired upward revisions that became decisive and created extreme hardships. As Poland's onetime economic czar, Hilary Minc, later admitted, the buildup of defense industries at Soviet behest "skimmed the cream of output . . . [and] led to the creation of a half-war economy in 1951–1953."[5]

Romania, Bulgaria, and for a short time Yugoslavia also copied the Soviet model, although trade data do not show that their priorities for heavy industry were imposed on them by Soviet import demands, since much of their exports to the USSR during the 1950s (Yugoslavia until the Stalin–Tito break in 1948) consisted of raw materials, semifabricates, and foodstuffs. But even in Romania there were efforts in its newly created machine-building sector to produce goods such as drilling equipment and ships for export to the USSR.[6]

The primary mechanism through which the USSR imposed its preferences on Eastern Europe during this period has been called the "Soviet embassy system" of plan coordination. The Soviets decided which countries should produce which articles, were involved in the drawing up of long-range plans, and operated certain enterprises in every country except Poland. In the GDR, "all high economic functionaries had their 'partner' in the Soviet embassy whom they consulted for every important move."[7]

A second important instrument of control was the Council for Mutual Economic Assistance, which was formed in 1949 ostensibly to promote multilateral economic integration among its members. CMEA's real purposes were political: as Stalin's reply to the Marshall Plan and to the economic integration of the West European countries that the plan was intended to promote; as an instrument of the Soviet bloc's stand, including initially a trade embargo, against Yugoslavia; and as a means of pre-empting and aborting the several proposals for subregional integration that were being promoted by nearly all the East European regimes in the late 1940s.[8] Far from fostering multilateral links, CMEA served in its first years to enhance Soviet control over each of its individual members; indeed, up to 1955, its activities were confined to the registration of bilateral commercial agreements.

The foregoing evidence leads to the conclusion that during the first postwar decade the USSR was chiefly responsible for turning the East European countries' industrialization strategies, which were probably voluntary and largely balanced to begin with, into an imposed, uneconomical, and excessively paced parallel development of high-cost industrial branches throughout the region. There were probably several interrelated reasons. First, the Soviets apparently did believe that their own pattern of industrialization was ideologically correct and had universal applicability for the new socialist states. This belief was not challenged by the Communist leaders in Eastern Europe, many of whom were trained in the USSR and had witnessed the example of impressive Soviet economic progress during the 1930s and military success during the 1940s. Second, this model also had the beneficial political ramification of placing limits on the East European states' interaction with one another, at least more so than regional specialization would have, and thereby prevented the building up of a politically stronger Eastern Europe. Third, the Soviet policy of encouraging Eastern Europe to specialize in heavy industrial products regardless of their raw material base may have been designed to reorient trade to the USSR and to heighten each state's dependence on Soviet raw materials (which at the time could not readily be sold on world markets) and the Soviet market (at a time when the Western embargo limited Soviet access to Western goods).

The outcome was a grossly inefficient allocation of resources. Its chief manifestations were the building up of parallel industrial capacities in the East European countries and a rapid movement toward all-East

European deficits in raw materials. The forced pace of industrialization led to declining living standards after 1950 and to terrorized and resentful populations, thereby contributing to the political upheavals in the region in the 1950s.

Soviet Policies and the Mechanisms of CMEA Integration (1956–1983)

*Policy Changes after Stalin* There was a sharp break in Soviet economic policy toward Eastern Europe after 1956 as the high political cost of economic extraction and pervasive direct interference was brought home to Moscow by the turmoil of the first post-Stalin years. The essence of the post-1956 policy was to place trade with Eastern Europe on a reasonably equitable commercial basis—a process that began earlier with the dismantling of the joint stock companies—and to activate the CMEA.

After 1956 CMEA became useful as a mechanism through which to maintain and expand Eastern Europe's economic ties with the USSR, while allowing for the formal economic and political independence of the region. Formal, and to some extent real, independence for the East European countries is useful to the Kremlin both for its global foreign policy (because it can be charged less evidently with outright domination and because its allies can support the USSR's global objectives more effectively as nominally independent than as captive states) and for its regional policy (because giving up direct control should help to allay the resentment of the East European populations, which in turn should contribute to the domestic political stability and thus also to the economic viability of these regimes). To be sure, the Soviet Union continued to view its trade with the region as yielding important economic and security, as well as political, benefits.

Although CMEA has not proved to be a strong integrative mechanism, it has played and continues to play a significant role in Soviet–East European economic relations. It is through CMEA that many of the rules of intrabloc commerce are codified. CMEA also serves as the main forum for debating proposals to improve the intrabloc divisions of labor, debates that yield insight into the economic objectives and policies of member countries.

Economic integration among a group of centrally planned economies (CPEs) is fundamentally different from integration among market-type economies. In Western economies much of international commerce is conducted by private enterprise seeking profit opportunities wherever it can find them. Hence, a reduction in or elimination of barriers to the movement of goods, factors of production, and money across national borders goes a long way toward integration. By contrast, under central planning all movement of goods and factors across national borders requires an explicit action by the governments involved. For CPEs, with no mechanism for determining comparative advantage in manufactures, it is difficult to reach agreement about specialization or to implement agreed policies effectively in each country.

*Proposals for Integration* During the first postwar decade the Soviet concept of integration was for each country to carry out Soviet instructions. During the second half of the 1950s the USSR probably had no clear-cut policy on integration. To be sure, large and useful blocwide projects had been completed, such as an electricity grid and other infrastructure projects, which in the CMEA literature of this period were equated with movement toward regional integration. There was much discussion of the need for improved blocwide specialization and integration, but without specifying clearly the economic content of these broad objectives. It is conceivable that during this period the USSR had no definite idea or policy on what type of specialization would provide the Kremlin maximum long-run benefits from intrabloc trade.

By the early 1960s the wastefulness of the parallel industrial development strategies of the 1940s and 1950s became apparent. To remedy the problem, Khrushchev proposed to transform CMEA into a supranational organ: that is, CMEA rather than the national planning authorities would make key new investment decisions ex ante rather than try to coordinate ex post the decisions independently made. This proposal brought to the surface the fear of the East European countries that bloc integration under a supranational authority would mean even more domination by the USSR. The most uncompromising stand against supranationalism was taken by Romania, whose famous 1964 statement brought the conflict to world attention.[9] In the face of Romania's firm stand—and perhaps recalling that earlier pressures on Yugoslavia and Albania had contributed to those countries' defections from the bloc—the USSR decided not to press its proposals.

The 1964–1970 period was one of much debate and experimentation about economic reforms. Domestic reform proposals usually contained suggestions for CMEA reforms also. One proposal, most clearly articulated by the Hungarians, favored greater reliance on market mechanisms for socialist integration. Its advocates predicted better prospects for gains from regional specialization and for the maintenance of greater national autonomy. Other proposals favored planned integration, relying on the traditional concepts and institutions of central planning.

The outcome of the debate was the 1971 Comprehensive Program for socialist integration. Although the document appears to be a compromise between those advocating market mechanisms and those favoring joint planning, the emphasis since 1971 has definitely been on the second approach and on the initiation of joint investment projects in priority sectors. Aspects of the Comprehensive Program stressing the market approach to socialist integration, such as eventual currency convertibility or the establishment of direct and autonomous trade links among enterprises in the different countries, appear in retrospect to have been more a recognition of need rather than a statement of intent.[10] To reduce the fears of the East European countries about supranationalism, an important compromise recognized by the Comprehensive Program that appears to have become a permanent feature of CMEA is the "interested party principle." This permits member countries to confine their participation to those CMEA projects or programs in which they have an interest.

The Comprehensive Program stresses improved plan coordination, joint CMEA investment projects, and cooperation in "long-term target programs." Under the old system, plan coordination meant little more than exchanging background information preparatory to bilateral trade negotiations, after national plans had been completed and the pattern of investment (formally not subject to coordination) had been decided. Improved plan coordination today means that the procedure begins earlier (3 years before the end of the current quinquennium), so that there is at least the possibility that as a result of discussions, a member country's investment plans could be altered.[11] Each country must include a special section in its national plan document elaborating the specific details of its integration measures. In practice, plan coordination appears to involve a standardization of economic information concerning projects that involve a long-term linking of two or more CMEA economies. This should facilitate a better assessment of what is really going on in CMEA and checking of the bilateral and multilateral consistency of national plans, but it does not appear to have brought about fundamentally new modes of CMEA integration.[12]

*CMEA Joint Projects* The joint investment program represented the major new form of CMEA activity during the 1970s. For some time, the Soviet Union had been pressing the East European countries to participate in joint investments in the USSR, pointing out that it alone had the exploitable natural resources and that such investments would represent partial compensation for supplying its CMEA partners with energy and raw materials.

The total value of joint investment projects agreed upon for the 1976–1980 period was approximately $12 billion (at the 1975 official ruble–dollar exchange rate of $1.30). The largest undertaking involving all six East European countries was the Orenburg project, consisting of a natural gas complex at Orenburg in Western Siberia and a 2,677-kilometer natural gas pipeline connecting Orenburg with the Soviet Union's western border. The total estimated cost of the project was between $5 and $6 billion, accounting for about 50% of the value of all CMEA joint investment projects in the 1976–1980 plan period.[13] The second largest joint undertaking was a giant pulp mill at Ust Ilim in Central Siberia.

The two features that distinguished the Orenburg and Ust Ilim projects from all other joint CMEA investment projects were the joint participation of the investing countries in construction on the territory of the host country (other projects were jointly planned but not jointly built, each country being responsbile for construction on its own territory) and the extensive degree of Western participation with technology, machinery and equipment, and financing. The ownership benefits accrue to the USSR, which is repaying the East European countries' investment with a 2% simple interest rate, by delivering to them agreed quantities of gas and pulp, respectively.

In the absence of accurate information about future prices for the commodities used to repay the investment and accurate information about the opportunity cost of investment participation, it is difficult to undertake a meaningful cost/benefit calculation. Some of the East European literature suggests that investing in CMEA joint projects—which take the form of delivery of labor, capital, consumer goods, technical know-how, and hard currency—is not economical. Among the factors cited are: the high manpower costs of these projects (employing East European workers in the USSR costs about three times more than employing them at home, while their contribution is valued by the USSR at Soviet wage rates and overhead schedules); the low interest rate received; the burden of large hard-currency contributions; and the disadvantageous terms of repayment (since the prices of the goods received in payment are tied to world market prices). In short, the East European countries do not obtain ownership benefits for their contribution; however, they do gain assured supplies and will enjoy price concessions as long as CMEA prices are set on the basis of historical world market prices *and* world market prices of energy and raw materials continue to rise steeply.

The joint investment formula à la Orenburg does not appear to have been continued into the 1980s, certainly not on the scale implemented during 1976–1980. No new major multilateral projects have been announced for the 1981–1985 period. East European contributions to Soviet resource development are primarily through deliveries of specialized machinery and equipment as agreed on bilaterally. The reason for this, in addition to those already mentioned, is that such large-scale projects as the pipeline, which lend themselves more readily to joint construction and financing than projects in the manufacturing sector, have been exhausted.

Instead, there appears to be a new emphasis on bilaterally determined investment specialization, with the East European economies providing machinery and other inputs for multilateral resource development projects in the USSR, and on implementing the so-called long-term target programs. The latter involve selected sectors and projects of major importance, where coordination is supposed to take a more binding and all-embracing form: joint forecasting for 15 to 20 years of production, consumption, and trade trends to identify prospective shortages and surpluses; coordination of medium- and long-term plans for the sector's main branches of production and key commodities; and joint research and development programs. Such long-term target programs have been mentioned for five sectors: fuels, energy, and raw materials; machine building; industrial consumer goods; agriculture, especially foodstuffs; and transportation.

It is unclear whether much progress has been or can be made in increasing CMEA specialization under these programs. One problem is that too many priorities means no real priority for any sector. The more general problem, however, is that which hinders CMEA specialization in all sectors: how to determine an economically sound pattern of specialization in production and trade. Calculations of static or dynamic comparative advantage involve comparisons of relative costs in the member countries; but the internal price systems of the CMEA countries cannot provide the necessary information on domestic costs because administratively set prices and exchange rates neither incorporate all relevant costs nor measure relative scarcities of inputs and outputs. This is the reason why intra-CMEA trade is valued at world market prices, an approach that gives rise to a new set of complex problems.

Prompted by unresolved problems relating to the fundamentally unsatisfactory mechanism of economic integration in the CMEA and the immediate economic and trading difficulties experienced by the East European countries in recent years, there have been repeated calls since 1980 for a summit meeting of the first party secretaries and heads of governments of the CMEA countries to deal with the problems. The first publicized summit proposal was made by Romania in June 1980, another by Leonid Brezhnev in February 1981; the latter's formulation of the purpose of the summit was endorsed by Gustáv Husák of Czechoslovakia in April 1981. Yet the disagreements about which problems are the most important and how to solve them are so fundamental that at the time of writing (November 1983) no summit had been convened even though plans have been announced repeatedly to hold one. While Moscow, complaining that ordinary plan coordination as hitherto practiced no longer suffices to support production integration, wants to harmonize the economic systems and policies of the countries and to set up joint production units,[14] the East European countries wish to discuss how the CMEA in general and the USSR in particular can assist them in alleviating the economic crisis they face as a result of their rapidly deteriorating terms of trade with the USSR, hard-currency balance-of-payments problems, and deteriorating East–West political, economic, and financial relations. Romania seeks especially increased supplies of Soviet energy at CMEA prices. Waiting for a clarification of Yuri Andropov's economic policies and prospective reform proposals has been another reason for repeatedly postponing the summit.

*CMEA Price System and Commodity Composition* CMEA countries employ different pricing mechanisms in East–West and intra-CMEA trade. With partners outside the bloc, they try to trade at current world market prices (generally succeeding when they import but obtaining lower prices when they export), while prices in intrabloc trade are linked to world market prices of an earlier period according to successive formulas agreed upon since 1958. Because each CMEA country sets its domestic prices differently and essentially arbitrarily, no country is willing to accept the prices of the others for valuing exports and imports. Therefore, as a practical matter, they formally rely upon an agreed variant of the world market price even though cost ratios and scarcities are different in CMEA from those in the West.

Under the Bucharest formula of 1958, average 1957–1958 world market prices remained in effect until about 1965. For 1965–1970, average world prices of 1960–1064 were used; for the 1971–1975 period, intra-CMEA prices were based on average world prices of 1965–1969. However, in early 1975, prices were revised at Soviet insistence 1 year ahead of schedule, and today are changed annually on a basis of world prices of the preceding 5 years. This procedure will remain in effect at least through the 1981–1985 plan period.[15]

This price-setting mechanism has several problems and consequences. For one, the mechanism prompts bargaining because it is difficult to establish "the" world market price.[16] Bargaining power may be exerted through prices (obtaining high prices for exports and paying low prices for imports) and through quantities (supplying certain goods in specified amounts). Thus, if we find the price of a commodity high or low relative to current world prices, this may be due to (1) the price that is "out of line" being compensated by offsetting deviations in the prices or quantities of other export and import items; (2) one country purposefully exploiting or subsidizing another; or (3) current world market prices having moved much higher or lower than the historical Western prices on which the CMEA price is based.

For energy, raw materials, and other primary products, CMEA prices can be determined relatively easily because these are mostly standardized commodities traded on the world markets at published prices. Since 1973–1974, world prices of energy and many raw materials have risen sharply; CMEA prices, because of the price rule, more slowly. Thus, if the CMEA price rule is observed, the USSR as a net exporter of energy and raw materials will obtain for those goods prices lower than current world prices. One may call this difference an implicit Soviet subsidy to Eastern Europe, though it is important to stress that, to the extent the price rule is followed, the subsidy results automatically from the mechanisms of intra-CMEA price determination, which, for institutional and political as well as economic reasons, it would be difficult for the Soviet Union to change.

For most manufactured goods, there is a range of world market prices for similar but in most cases not identical products. In bilateral bargaining between countries with nonconvertible currencies, prices typically tend to gravitate toward the upper end of the world market price range. One reason for this is that the shortage of convertible currencies causes each side to prefer to import the commodities needed from other soft-currency countries, which places the seller in a position to charge the highest possible price. Indeed, during 1958–1964, when world market prices were comparatively stable, East European computations showed that the intra-CMEA price levels of manufactures were slightly above world market prices, though after 1965 the price level gap apparently narrowed.[17] What has happened to CMEA/world market price ratios for manufactures since then is difficult to say because world market prices of industrial products have also risen rapidly during the 1970s, and there is insufficient reliable information on whether CMEA prices of machinery and industrial consumer goods have kept pace or lagged behind changes in world market prices.

Be that as it may, it is our impression that in the battle of documentation to set prices for manufactured goods in intra-CMEA trade, the USSR has not leaned heavily on its economic and political leverage to obtain favorable prices. In fact, during the 1960s and early 1970s East European negotiators may well have been better equipped with price documentation and thus more skillful price bargainers than those of the USSR, perhaps because of greater initial experience in these matters and because each East European country has relatively more at stake in its trade with the USSR than vice versa. If so, the Soviet Union, as a net importer of manufactures from Eastern Europe, may have granted implicit net price subsidies on this segment of trade also. It must be stressed, however, that the evidence on this point is "soft" and that other considerations must also be taken into account in assessing who is subsidizing whom and by how much in intrabloc trade.

A further important point is that the real value of a commodity is judged by each country's planners not only by its price but also by how strongly it is in demand, either because (1) the exporter is able to meet the technical and marketing specifications of the importer, (2) the import alleviates shortages and bottlenecks in the domestic economy, or (3) the commodity can be sold in the West for convertible currency. Goods in greatest demand are called "hard goods," commodities in surplus "soft goods." Commodities have different degrees of hardness or softness that can change as production patterns and priorities change. Energy, raw materials, and basic food items such as grain that can be sold readily on the world market are the hardest; standard machinery, for which there is not a great deal of demand by the importing country, softest.[18]

CMEA countries try to balance with each trading partner not only total exports and imports but also trade within each category of hardness and softness. This partly compensates for the fact that prices and money balances in CMEA do not play the allocative role they do on the world market. Approximate bilateral balancing of hard goods and soft goods is the practice in all CMEA links except between the USSR and Eastern Europe. This is evident from the commodity composition of Soviet trade with the East European Six combined (Table 31.1) and the corresponding trade balance by main commodity categories (Table 31.2). A brief discussion of the CMEA currency system and exchange rate practices is a useful background for interpreting the data in Tables 31.1 and 31.2. One reason why it is difficult to obtain a firm handle on price subsidization is CMEA's elusive exchange rate system; another is that actual price adjustments do not always follow the formal price rule.

*Currency and Exchange Rates* Intra-CMEA trade transactions valued according to the agreed set of historical world market prices (usually expressed in dollars) are translated into and settled in "transferable rubles" (TRs), an artificial currency whose only function is to serve as an accounting unit. The exchange rate of the TR vis-à-vis the dollar is for all practical purposes the same as that of the Soviet domestic ruble, which remained unchanged at 1.00 Rb = 1.00 TR = \$1.11 until 1972, when both the ruble and the TR began to fluctuate, initially with an appreciating trend, to reflect the depreciation of the dollar in terms of other currencies. Thus, by 1980, 1 TR = \$1.50, which the subsequent appreciation of the dollar changed to 1 TR = \$1.30 by mid-1983.

The significance of a changed valuation of the TR is that, ceteris paribus, it changes the prices of *some* of the commodities traded in

CMEA. If the prices of *all* goods traded were determined each year from a dollar base, a change in the dollar/TR rate would not matter because all prices would change proportionately. But it appears that only the prices of crude oil, of other important primary products, and of newly traded items are derived each year from dollar prices, probably by averaging the dollar prices of the years to be included in the formula and then applying the current dollar/TR rate. The prices of most manufactured goods tend to remain unchanged in CMEA over a longer period and, when changed, the usual method is to adjust the TR price by an agreed percentage. The net result is the existence of de facto multiple exchange rates and the continued separation of domestic, East–West, and intra-CMEA price levels and ratios. These represent significant obstacles to intra-CMEA specialization, especially in the manufactures sectors.

Owing to these difficulties, a significant development during the 1970s was that a growing share of intrabloc trade began to be priced at current world market prices and paid for in convertible currency. These transactions involve mainly hard goods exported to a CMEA partner over and above the quantities agreed upon in the 5-year trade agreements. Thus, a certain portion of Soviet oil and raw materials is sold to the East European countries at current world prices and paid for in dollars, and a portion of Soviet imports from Eastern Europe is also priced and settled in the same way. No systematic information is available on the size and balance of this trade except for Hungary, for which is represents between 8 and 15% of its total "socialist" trade (i.e., with CPEs).

In addition to "direct" there is also "indirect" convertible-currency trade. This refers to the Western import content of East European exports to the USSR that have been paid for in convertible currencies. These have increased very rapidly in recent years, as a growing proportion of imported inputs have had to be obtained from world market rather than CMEA sources. Of course, the Soviet Union can be said to compensate, in part, its East European trade partners for such "embodied" Western imports by providing a certain "ruble content" for Eastern Europe's hard-currency exports to the West. Although calculations of this type are fraught with statistical difficulties, it is interesting to note that during the mid-1970s, the dollar content of Hungary's ruble exports was roughly 20% and rising rapidly, whereas the ruble content of its dollar exports was only about 7%.[19] The point, of course, is that East European "transshipping" of Western goods to the Soviet Union is a benefit the USSR obtains from its CMEA partners, just as Eastern Europe obviously benefits from "transshipping" imported Soviet energy and raw materials in the other direction. The benefits to each side will be determined by the use value as well as by the price (relative to opportunity cost) of the items involved.

*Invisible Transactions and Credits*  Even less is known in the West about so-called invisible transactions in CMEA. Prices of invisibles reportedly are not covered by the CMEA price rules noted above and therefore change infrequently. Poland, for example, is known to be a

Table 31.1. *Soviet Trade with the Six East European Countries Combined, by Main Commodity Categories, 1960–1980 (in Millions of Transferable Rubles)*

| Year | Fuels | Nonfood raw materials and semimanufactures | Agricultural and food products | Machinery | Industrial consumer goods | Total |
|------|-------|-----------|-----------|-----------|-----------|--------|
| *Exports* | | | | | | |
| 1960 | 372 | 1,205 | 476 | 637 | 77 | 2,767 |
| 1961 | 438 | 1,335 | 424 | 784 | 80 | 3,060 |
| 1962 | 527 | 1,438 | 544 | 976 | 89 | 3,574 |
| 1963 | 598 | 1,482 | 504 | 1,081 | 83 | 3,747 |
| 1964 | 668 | 1,717 | 322 | 1,274 | 68 | 4,049 |
| 1965 | 679 | 1,758 | 340 | 1,241 | 79 | 4,097 |
| 1966 | 660 | 1,777 | 380 | 1,327 | 79 | 4,223 |
| 1967 | 682 | 1,836 | 485 | 1,442 | 91 | 4,535 |
| 1968 | 742 | 2,048 | 493 | 1,671 | 118 | 5,073 |
| 1969 | 846 | 2,228 | 559 | 1,826 | 119 | 5,578 |
| 1970 | 914 | 2,600 | 487 | 1,944 | 138 | 6,083 |
| 1971 | 1,051 | 2,653 | 576 | 2,090 | 147 | 6,517 |
| 1972 | 1,174 | 2,740 | 351 | 2,301 | 161 | 6,727 |
| 1973 | 1,324 | 2,849 | 347 | 2,682 | 179 | 7,381 |
| 1974 | 1,577 | 3,185 | 496 | 3,185 | 263 | 8,705 |
| 1975 | 3,138 | 4,344 | 455 | 3,581 | 347 | 11,866 |
| 1976 | 3,717 | 4,610 | 177 | 4,216 | 387 | 13,107 |
| 1977 | 4,692 | 4,878 | 326 | 4,982 | 388 | 15,266 |
| 1978 | 5,670 | 5,115 | 109 | 5,605 | 448 | 16,946 |
| 1979 | 6,977 | 4,968 | 260 | 5,908 | 436 | 18,549 |
| 1980 | 8,582 | 5,478 | 152 | 6,219 | 488 | 20,919 |
| *Imports* | | | | | | |
| 1960 | 187 | 535 | 171 | 1,153 | 470 | 2,516 |
| 1961 | 173 | 586 | 247 | 1,198 | 536 | 2,740 |
| 1962 | 164 | 627 | 229 | 1,551 | 660 | 3,231 |
| 1963 | 164 | 680 | 267 | 1,806 | 816 | 3,732 |
| 1964 | 158 | 757 | 289 | 2,001 | 801 | 4,005 |
| 1965 | 171 | 741 | 366 | 2,113 | 815 | 4,205 |
| 1966 | 158 | 662 | 349 | 1,926 | 922 | 4,016 |
| 1967 | 159 | 733 | 400 | 2,175 | 1,117 | 4,583 |
| 1968 | 145 | 802 | 417 | 2,471 | 1,245 | 5,079 |
| 1969 | 148 | 865 | 475 | 2,645 | 1,278 | 5,410 |
| 1970 | 144 | 962 | 555 | 2,899 | 1,411 | 5,970 |
| 1971 | 174 | 1,001 | 639 | 3,048 | 1,671 | 6,533 |
| 1972 | 205 | 1,202 | 759 | 3,720 | 1,801 | 7,687 |
| 1973 | 211 | 1,152 | 728 | 4,214 | 1,788 | 8,093 |
| 1974 | 196 | 1,208 | 889 | 4,450 | 1,857 | 8,600 |

Table 31.1. *Continued*

| Year | Fuels | Nonfood raw materials and semimanufactures | Agricultural and food products | Machinery | Industrial consumer goods | Total |
|------|-------|--------------------------------------------|--------------------------------|-----------|---------------------------|-------|
| 1975 | 418 | 1,630 | 1,317 | 5,616 | 2,330 | 11,312 |
| 1976 | 407 | 1,798 | 1,226 | 6,321 | 2,474 | 12,226 |
| 1977 | 411 | 1,981 | 1,358 | 7,331 | 2,771 | 13,852 |
| 1978 | 497 | 1,941 | 1,220 | 10,065 | 3,049 | 16,776 |
| 1979 | 471 | 2,155 | 1,506 | 10,196 | 3,163 | 17,491 |
| 1980 | 401 | 2,777 | 1,864 | 10,585 | 3,468 | 19,095 |

SOURCE: Official Soviet foreign trade statistics as compiled, reconstructed, or estimated in *Wharton Centrally Planned Economies Foreign Trade Data Bank*, vol. 1 (Washington, D.C.: Wharton Econometrics, January 1982).

Table 31.2. *Soviet Trade with the Six East European Countries Combined, Total and by Main Commodity Categories, 1960–1980 (in Millions of Transferable Rubles)*

| Year | Fuels | Nonfood raw materials and semimanufactures | Agricultural and food products | Machinery | Industrial consumer goods | Total |
|------|-------|--------------------------------------------|--------------------------------|-----------|---------------------------|-------|
| 1960 | 185 | 670 | 305 | –516 | –393 | 252 |
| 1961 | 265 | 749 | 177 | –414 | –456 | 320 |
| 1962 | 363 | 811 | 315 | –575 | –571 | 343 |
| 1963 | 434 | 802 | 237 | –725 | –733 | 15 |
| 1964 | 510 | 960 | 33 | –727 | –733 | 44 |
| 1965 | 508 | 1,017 | –26 | –872 | –736 | –108 |
| 1966 | 502 | 1,115 | 31 | –599 | –843 | 207 |
| 1967 | 523 | 1,103 | 85 | –733 | –1,026 | –48 |
| 1968 | 597 | 1,246 | 76 | –800 | –1,127 | –6 |
| 1969 | 698 | 1,363 | 84 | –819 | –1,159 | 168 |
| 1970 | 770 | 1,638 | –68 | –955 | –1,273 | 113 |
| 1971 | 877 | 1,652 | –63 | –958 | –1,524 | –16 |
| 1972 | 969 | 1,539 | –408 | –1,419 | –1,640 | –960 |
| 1973 | 1,114 | 1,697 | –381 | –1,532 | –1,609 | –712 |
| 1974 | 1,382 | 1,977 | –393 | –1,265 | –1,594 | 105 |
| 1975 | 2,720 | 2,714 | –862 | –2,035 | –1,982 | 554 |
| 1976 | 3,310 | 2,812 | –1,049 | –2,105 | –2,087 | 881 |
| 1977 | 4,281 | 2,897 | –1,032 | –2,349 | –2,383 | 1,414 |
| 1978 | 5,173 | 3,170 | –1,112 | –4,460 | –2,601 | 170 |
| 1979 | 6,506 | 2,813 | –1,247 | –4,288 | –2,727 | 1,058 |
| 1980 | 8,181 | 2,700 | –1,712 | –4,365 | –2,980 | 1,824 |

SOURCE: Calculated from Table 31.1.

large exporter of transit services, primarily to the USSR, mostly on rails. Uniform CMEA freight rates remained unchanged from 1973 through 1980—a fact that Poland protested strongly—at a time when freight costs rose steeply due to rising energy prices.

Intrabloc tourism is another significant item. Apart from the question of how realistic tourist exchange rates are, net exporters of tourist services—especially Hungary and Bulgaria but also Poland and Romania—provide a high-value service to the net importers because tourists have open access to most of the consumer goods available in the host countries and can thus take advantage of large differences in the availability and relative prices of consumer goods in the CMEA countries.

Another aspect is the settlement of invisible transactions in the balance of payments. Net balances are converted into TRs by an agreed coefficient and settled by shipping goods from the deficit to the surplus country. Depending on the coefficients and the kinds of goods that the deficit country is willing to export to the surplus country, substantial hidden gains or losses may derive from such transactions. It is my strong impression that the USSR and the GDR obtain substantial net benefits on invisibles from the rest of Eastern Europe, but further research would be required to validate and to try to quantify this. That the issue is important was suggested by the headline news when, on August 1, 1979, Romania decreed that all foreign tourists must immediately pay in convertible currency for gasoline and oil purchases. This order, at the height of the summer tourist season, stranded thousands of Soviet and East European tourists in Romania, a country that in effect repudiated the CMEA clearing system for invisible transactions. The decree provided that tourists from the other CMEA countries would be able to pay in their own currencies only after an interstate agreement had been negotiated providing reimbursement to Romania in specified commodities—presumably goods more acceptable than the deficit countries had been willing to ship to Romania up to then.

Credits are among the most important and complex issues in Soviet–East European economic relations. The size of credits, the type of goods or currency in which the loans are supplied, settlement provisions, and the "grant equivalent" of credits jointly determine the distribution of costs and benefits in a loan transaction. In recent years credit transactions between the USSR and the East European countries have been significant, but no comprehensive balance-of-payments-type accounting is available on them. However, since most credit transactions involve the delivery of goods, bilateral trade balances do offer clues.

During 1971–1973 the East European countries combined had a positive trade balance with the USSR of TR 1.7 billion. During 1974–1980, however, Eastern Europe had an import surplus every year, the cumulative total reaching TR 6 billion (Table 31.2). A portion of this surplus represents 10-year Soviet terms of trade credits.

A great deal of uncertainty, however, surrounds the interpretation of observed trade balances because they typically reflect some combination of: delays in planned deliveries by one partner, settlement of balances on invisible transactions, extensions of new credits, and repayment of earlier loans. Matters are further complicated by the involvement of CMEA's International Bank for Economic Cooperation (IBEC) and the International Investment Bank (IIB) in convertible-currency credit transactions because one side of such a transaction will not be reported in intra-CMEA trade statistics. To be specific, in recent years IBEC and IIB have borrowed, jointly on behalf of the USSR and the East European countries, billions of dollars on the Eurocurrency markets, primarily to finance imports from the West for CMEA projects located in the USSR, such as the Orenburg gas pipeline. The East European countries are responsible for servicing their share of these loans, which in the case of IIB amounted to 95% of the total between 1971 and 1978.[20] The USSR repays the East European countries with additional gas shipments that may show up as a Soviet trade surplus with Eastern Europe, while the hard-currency portion of the credits the East European countries grant to the USSR remains invisible. A further important aspect of such credits is that, while the East European countries pay the Euromarket rate of interest on their hard-currency loans (which in recent years has fluctuated between 8 and 20% per annum), they receive interest from the USSR that ranges between 2 and 5% per annum.

Is Eastern Europe an Economic Asset or a Liability for the USSR?

The aggregate growth and structure of Soviet trade with the six East European CMEA countries between 1960 and 1980 are presented in Table 31.1; the trade balance by main commodity categories is shown in Table 31.2. The data presented reveal that the USSR has had a large export surplus in two of the "hardest" commodity groups—fuels as well as nonfood raw materials and semimanufactures—and a large deficit in machinery and industrial consumer goods, which on balance are "softer" commodities.

This pattern of trade is in part a consequence of the energy- and raw-material-intensive development strategy of the East Europeans during the later 1940s and early 1950s, which has in many ways constrained their subsequent pattern of industrial development and trade. It is a consequence also of the relatively poor energy and mineral resource endowment of most of these countries, of the wasteful consumption of inputs that characterizes all CPEs, and of the fact that the East Europeans have redirected some of their domestic output of hard goods to the West to pay for needed imports. As a result, the region's import requirements for energy, raw materials, and semimanufactures, a large part of which were met by the USSR, have grown rapidly over the last three decades. By 1980 the Soviet Union's export surplus in these commodity categories exceeded $16 billion at intra-CMEA prices (TR 10.9 billion at the official exchange rate of approximately $1.5); at prevailing world market prices the surplus would have been significantly higher.

This surplus in Soviet exports of primary products to its CMEA partners, together with the sharp differences between world market and intra-CMEA prices for these products, is an important component of what has been called the USSR's "implicit subsidies" to Eastern Europe. According to the subsidy argument, as presented in its most dramatic form by economists Michael Marrese and Jan Vanous, "the Soviet Union has transferred resources equivalent to almost $80 billion in 1980 dollars during the decade 1971–1980."[21] Their calculations are based on two assumptions: the first concerning the disadvantageous commodity structure of Soviet–East European trade for the USSR; the second concerning the disadvantageous pricing of Soviet trade with Eastern Europe, compared with the hypothetical situation of the same goods being traded by the Soviets with Western countries. An examination of these two assumptions will show that the subsidy argument is open to serious qualification in principle and that the Marrese–Vanous estimate of the burden that Eastern Europe imposes on the USSR is greatly overstated. Let us look first at the commodity structure of trade and then at the question of valuation.

In the 1950s the exchange of Soviet primary products for East European manufactured goods was advantageous for the USSR because its partners were able to supply machinery and other manufactures denied by the Western embargo, and because there was no world shortage of energy and raw materials and therefore no strong demand for Soviet supplies. By the 1960s this pattern had become to some extent ossified: Soviet planners had become used to the routinized supply relationship with East European producers, just as East European planners had come to count on routine acquisition of Soviet primary products and semi-manufactures. Moreover, there was no great economic pressure on the USSR to alter the pattern; on the contrary, it was able to expand energy and raw material production quickly and at reasonable cost.

During the 1970s circumstances began to change. The rapid expansion of Soviet trade with the West increased the opportunity cost of being a large net supplier of hard goods to Eastern Europe, as did the rising cost of extracting and transporting these goods from increasingly remote Siberian regions. Moscow began to complain more persistently that its pattern of trade with Eastern Europe was disadvantageous, but mitigating circumstances still limited the trade patterns' disadvantage. Most important were the substantial windfall gains the USSR enjoyed in the form of improved terms of trade with the West, and to a lesser extent with Eastern Europe, as it benefited from OPEC price increases, the rising price of gold, and its ability to tap into the surplus by selling military hardware for dollars to several newly rich oil-exporting countries.[22]

These windfall gains—which may have yielded as much as $50 billion between 1973 and 1980—enabled Moscow to increase its hard-currency export revenues almost as rapidly as it expanded its hard-currency imports, that is, without incurring excessively large foreign debts. Moreover, in view of systemic limitations on the capacity of the Soviet economy to absorb a greater volume of Western technology than it purchased during the 1970s (indeed it could not utilize fully even what it did import), in view also of supply and transport limitations on the import of larger amounts of grain, the opportunity cost of supplying increased amounts of energy and raw materials to Eastern Europe probably did not appear to be a crushing burden. In addition it should be remembered that Moscow's improved terms of trade with Eastern Europe meant that the growth rate of the volume of Soviet hard-goods exports to its CMEA partners declined steeply during the 1970s, while the volume of Soviet purchases from them accelerated, thus delivering a double-barreled blow to the region's hard-currency balances. On the one hand, the East Europeans were forced to turn to the world market for a growing share of their hard-goods imports; on the other hand, they had fewer exports to pay for them.

Let us now turn to the question of prices in Soviet–East European trade. This is an important issue on which firm, empirically based conclusions are exceedingly difficult to reach. The first problem is the selection of the appropriate standard against which to assess intra-CMEA prices. Although relative scarcities in CMEA are different from those on the world market, in the absence both of meaningful prices within CMEA and of an effectively functioning regional market, most specialists (Western and Eastern) have concluded that current world market prices are the appropriate standard. Next, one must select the appropriate world market price concept: Is it to be the set of prices at which Western countries trade with one another or prices in East–West trade? This is a vital distinction because, although as a rule CPEs are able to import from the West at West–East prices, they are often able to export to the West only at substantially lower prices, especially on finished manufactures.

A further difficulty is how one should interpret the fact that a commodity is traded in CMEA at a higher or lower price than the current world market level. As noted earlier, this may be due to: (1) offsetting deviations in the prices or quantities of other export or import items, (2) changes in world market prices that have not yet been factored into the CMEA formula, or (3) outright exploitation or subsidization. In short, proper interpretation of price anomalies in intra-CMEA trade depends on an evaluation of all aspects of economic (and political) relations among the countries concerned—an evaluation that is made difficult, if not impossible, by the fragmentary nature of available data. It is here, in the interpretation of intra-CMEA prices, that the subsidy argument is most vulnerable to statistical inaccuracies.

Assuming that the USSR could have substituted trade with the industrial West (settled in dollars) for the transactions it entered into with the East European Six countries (settled mainly in TRs), Marrese and Vanous argue that the prices paid to or received from the West represent the Soviets' opportunity cost; hence, trade with Eastern Europe should be revalued in those hypothetical dollar prices. That is, if trade reported by the Soviet Union as balanced in TRs yields a Soviet export surplus in dollars, the surplus is the amount of Soviet subsidy to Eastern Europe; if a deficit, an East European subsidy to the USSR. If trade in TRs is not in balance, an adjustment is made in dollar values. For purposes of their calculations, Marrese and Vanous further divide Soviet–East European trade into two categories: (1) energy, raw materi-

als, semimanufactured products, and agricultural and food products
(primary products); and (2) machinery, equipment, and industrial consumer goods (manufactures).

In the case of primary products, Marrese and Vanous first compute
TR "unit values" for a sample of commodities and then try to find
matching unit values in dollars. For Soviet exports to Eastern Europe,
the dollar values are Soviet-to-West prices for the same commodity; for
Soviet imports from Eastern Europe, they use West-to-Soviet prices. The
ratio of dollar-to-TR unit values are called derived dollar/ruble exchange
rates. The authors compute as many sample derived $/TR ratios as
published trade statistics allow and estimate the hypothetical dollar
value of each commodity category by multiplying the published or
reconstructed TR value by the weighted-average-derived $/TR exchange
rate obtained from unit value samples in that commodity category.
Although gaps in the data force them to make a series of assumptions
that create potentially large margins of error, the dollar values and
corresponding subsidies they compute for trade in primary products
may be accepted as reasonable approximations.

Far more difficult is the establishment of "true" dollar values for
intrabloc trade in manufactures. On the basis of a study done nearly 20
years ago by CMEA experts, Marrese and Vanous estimate that in 1960
intra-CMEA prices of manufactures were 25% higher than West–West
prices for comparable goods. Next, they note that the Soviet Union and
the East European countries could sell to the West the manufactures
they trade with each other only at large discounts from world market
prices—discounts ranging up to 50% and assigned arbitrarily by
country—due to the poor quality and service features of these products.
Each of these assumptions gives a major upward bias to their estimates
of the amount of the Soviet subsidy to each East European country.

Three sets of factors account for the large discounts on East-bloc
exports of manufactures to the West. One is the poor quality of the
East's products. A second is the systemic shortcomings of Eastern
export pricing: exporting on the basis of plan directives, which reduces
the flexibility required to obtain the best price; preference for barter and
compensation deals inconvenient for the Western partner, who therefore pays a low price for such products; and hard-currency balance-of-
payments pressures, which often force Eastern countries to make drastic
price concessions. The third set of reasons for Eastern export price
discounts is Western discrimination—whether in the form of high-tariff
or nontariff barriers to CMEA goods.

Since Marrese and Vanous argue that a portion of Soviet subsidy
arises because the Soviet Union pays more for imports from Eastern
Europe than it would have to pay if the same goods were purchased
from the West, the correct dollar opportunity cost is not East-to-West
export but East-from-West import prices. If the Soviet Union imported
the same manufactured goods from the West, it would not be able to
obtain as large discounts as when the East exports to the West because
the second and third sets of discount factors would be absent. In missing
this point and assuming that they can substitute East European export

prices for Soviet import prices to value Soviet purchases from Eastern Europe, Marrese and Vanous introduce a significant upward bias into their calculations.

There is an even more fundamental criticism of their subsidy computations. Just because an East European machine or consumer product is not of the latest Western design—that it is not equipped with the ultimate series of gadgets, does not have all the assortment, packaging, and other convenience features that characterize the most modern Western products—does not mean that the Soviet importer of these goods provides a subsidy to Eastern Europe equivalent to the western quality discount. There must be many instances where the East European products are as, or even more, suitable to Soviet conditions than the most modern Western counterparts. Thus, while Marrese and Vanous are probably correct that as a net importer of manufactures the USSR provides some subsidy to the exporters, there is simply not enough statistically meaningful information to attach a dollar price tag to the amounts that might be involved.[23]

By breaking the Marrese–Vanous subsidy estimates down into two basic categories—first, those that rise from net Soviet exports of primary products to Eastern Europe (which are acceptable estimates); and second, those that arise from net Soviet imports of East European manufactures (which are unacceptable due to the statistical uncertainties, upward biases, and omitted compensatory gains to Moscow noted above)—we can readily see that 60% of the cumulative subsidy is accounted for by the second, less reliable category (Table 31.3). In addition, more than half the cumulative 1960–1980 total fuel subsidy arose in 1980 due to the explosion of the world market price for crude oil in 1979–1980, which the CMEA price formula and other considerations did not allow the Soviet Union to pass on to Eastern Europe immediately.

Detailed computations covering the period 1971 to 1978, the latest year for which these calculations could be made, show that on trade in fuels, nonfood raw materials, semimanufactured goods, and agricultural products combined, the USSR implicitly provided a net cumulative subsidy of about $14 billion to the six East European CMEA countries. This amount was somewhat greater than 10% of cumulative total Soviet exports to these countries during the period. The distribution of this subsidy total by country was tabulated as follows:

| Country | Total (billion $) | Per capita ($) |
|---|---|---|
| Bulgaria | 3.5 | 390 |
| Czechoslovakia | 2.6 | 170 |
| GDR | 4.8 | 290 |
| Hungary | 1.0 | 100 |
| Poland | 2.1 | 60 |
| Romania | –0.1 | –0.5 |

Table 31.3. *Net Soviet Subsidies (+) and Taxes (−) on Trade with the Six East European Countries Combined, by Major Commodity Categories, 1960–1980 (Millions of Current Dollars)*

| Year | Total (1) | Fuel (2) | Nonfood raw materials and semimanu- factures (3) | Agricultural and food products (4) | Primary products (2) + (3) + (4) (5) | Machinery (6) | Industrial consumer goods (7) | Manufactures (6) + (7) (8) |
|---|---|---|---|---|---|---|---|---|
| 1960–1970 | 3,862 | -2,099 | -3,502 | -594 | -6,195 (-160%) | 4,953 | 5,104 | 10,057 (260%) |
| 1971 | 900 | -31 | -311 | -38 | -380 (-42%) | 472 | 808 | 1,280 (142%) |
| 1972 | 1,134 | -114 | -411 | 22 | -503 (-44%) | 736 | 901 | 1,637 (144%) |
| 1973 | 2,001 | 293 | -132 | 2 | 163 (8%) | 934 | 904 | 1,838 (92%) |
| 1974 | 6,227 | 3,525 | 1,450 | 215 | 5,190 (83%) | 449 | 588 | 1,037 (17%) |
| 1975 | 5,030 | 2,028 | 31 | 496 | 2,555 (51%) | 1,304 | 1,171 | 2,475 (49%) |
| 1976 | 5,144 | 2,547 | 43 | 298 | 2,888 (56%) | 1,155 | 1,101 | 2,256 (44%) |
| 1977 | 5,209 | 2,333 | 106 | 288 | 2,727 (52%) | 1,165 | 1,317 | 2,482 (48%) |
| 1978 | 5,637 | 959 | -145 | 345 | 1,159 (21%) | 2,856 | 1,622 | 4,478 (79%) |
| 1979 | 9,653 | 4,041 | -376 | 481 | 4,146 (43%) | 3,527 | 1,981 | 5,508 (47%) |
| 1980 | 20,482 | 14,294 | -341 | 477 | 14,430 (70%) | 3,933 | 2,120 | 6,053 (30%) |
| 1960–1980 | 65,280 | 27,776 | -3,588 | 1,992 | 26,180 (40%) | 21,484 | 17,617 | 39,101 (60%) |
| 1960–1980 as percentage of total | | | | | | | | |
| 1960–1980 | 100% | 43% | -5% | 3% | (40%) | 33% | 27% | (60%) |
| 1960–1979 | 100% | 30% | -7% | 3% | (26%) | 39% | 35% | (74%) |

SOURCE: M. Marrese and J. Vanous, *Implicit Subsidies and Non-Market Benefits in Soviet Trade with Eastern Europe* (Berkeley: University of California Press, 1983).

The amount of the implicit subsidy is determined largely by the bilateral commodity structure of trade, which has evolved gradually during the postwar period, and by the extent to which an East European country depends on trade with the USSR; but it may also be influenced by the politically determined preferences of Moscow. It seems that for all these reasons Bulgaria has been favored because the amount of the subsidy received by that country, especially in per capita terms, is substantial. Particularly notable is the contrast with Romania, which has been much more oriented toward the West and was self-sufficient in energy until the late 1970s, although political considerations by the Kremlin may also have played a role.

In 1982 crude oil and other fuel prices began to decline sharply whereas intra-CMEA prices continued to rise. If fuel prices were to stabilize at their early 1983 levels or decline further, intra-CMEA prices will equal and then exceed world market prices sometime in 1984 or 1985, so that subsidies in this important commodity category would begin to flow from Eastern Europe to the USSR.

Making similar calculations for manufactured goods is much more difficult for the reasons indicated. Trade in manufactures leads to the question of dynamic gains from trade. Significant trade benefits are foregone by the exporter if the preferential, sheltered CMEA market absorbs over a long time poor-quality goods and obsolete equipment, thereby reducing the incentive to innovate and produce "for the market," causing the exporter to fall more and more behind its competitors on the world market. This cost appears to fall disproportionately heavily on the smaller and relatively advanced CMEA countries like the GDR, Czechoslovakia, Hungary, and Poland; the bill is presented when they must expand their manufactures exports outside the sheltered CMEA market. The importer of shoddy goods loses potential productivity gains, too; yet it may not be able to resist buying such goods if its own producers have become dependent on the same CMEA suppliers for exports and imports.

## Economic Performance of the CMEA Countries and Soviet Policy Options

During the second half of the 1970s two factors that became increasingly important in Soviet calculations were the USSR's own deteriorating economic performance and prospects and the growing economic weakness of the East European countries, with obvious implications for political instability, actual or potential. Since economic performance in the USSR and Eastern Europe represents constraints on Soviet foreign policy during the 1980s, this section will highlight the main trends.

*Economic Performance of the USSR and Eastern Europe* The rate of growth of the Soviet economy declined considerably during the 1970s. The consensus of Western experts is that the slowdown will continue so that, during the 1980s, growth rates are unlikely to exceed the 1 to 2.5% range per annum. Given the Soviet Union's low labor-force growth, growing global commitments, the heating up of the arms race, and the great need for additional investment to respond to bottlenecks in infrastructure, energy, and other sectors, this projected slowing of the growth rate suggests the possiblity of stagnation in the level of per capita consumption, with attendant political difficulties for the Soviet leadership. Thus, from the perspective both of prospects for the Soviet energy sector and of overall economic performance since the late 1970s, the opportunity cost of supplying subsidized energy and other raw materials to Eastern Europe has risen significantly, as have pressures to obtain additional resources from the region.

At the same time, the rapidly deteriorating economic performance of the East European countries caused the Soviet leaders to proceed cautiously about raising export prices too sharply or curtailing energy and raw material shipments too precipitously. Since the late 1970s Eastern Europe, too, has been in a fundamentally new situation that in many ways is more precarious than that of the USSR, and that can best be explained by providing a brief historical perspective.

From the late 1940s until the late 1970s, the East European countries appear to have performed well, some exceptionally well, by international comparisons. One reason for using the word *appear* is that Western experts consider the exceptionally high growth rates reported by some East European countries—Romania, Bulgaria, and the GDR especially—to be exaggerated because of unconventional statistical methods of index number construction, although even after a downward adjustment the rates remain impressive. More important is the fact that the growth rate of output should not be the only performance indicator. The performance of an economy should be judged by multiple indicators, such as efficiency, consumer satisfaction, and its external trade and financial balance. An economy may be able to achieve spectacular growth rates by borrowing large sums abroad. But if the borrowed resources are not put to good use, the high growth rates of one period may be achieved at the expense of stagnation or decline in a subsequent period, as is best shown by the case of Poland.

One reason the East European countries were able to achieve impressive growth rates over the past 30 years was that, until the 1980s, these countries were able to rely on three consecutive sets of temporary support mechanisms. During the early 1950s the regimes used extreme methods to mobilize underemployed resources and to squeeze agriculture and the consumer to finance a rapid growth in investments. These strong-arm methods, however, proved to be economically and politically counterproductive. Political excesses and the absence of material incentives undermined political stability and the economic efficiency of resource use.

During the 1960s the East European economies were boosted by increased trade with the USSR (in the case of Yugoslavia increased trade with, and some assistance from, the West were more important), involving a rapidly growing exchange of inexpensive Soviet energy and raw materials for East European machinery and other manufactured products. However, during the 1970s the annual increments in the volume of Soviet exports to Eastern Europe slowed and became more expensive; by the early 1980s their absolute level began to stagnate and, in the case of some key commodities like oil, actually declined, wherein energy conservation and the recession in Eastern Europe played some role also.

During the 1970s growth rates were helped by official Western credits and private bank loans that became newly available to CPEs. The banks had large surpluses of loanable funds, and lending to Eastern Europe was considered safe because central planning was viewed as synonymous with effective control over the balance of payments (since planners, supposedly, could always cut imports and push exports) and because a Soviet umbrella was believed to exist. Yet in 1981 Poland was forced to reschedule; in 1982 Romania joined Poland, and net lending to Eastern Europe stopped. Most of the other East European countries also experienced debt-servicing difficulties, owing partly to economic and political factors outside their control—such as the Western recession, high interest rates, and the increased level of East–West tensions in the wake of Afghanistan and Poland, which also had an adverse impact on Western trade and the extension of credits.

By the late 1970s all the East European countries were experiencing increased economic pressures: from their own consumers who expected that living standards would continue to improve or at least not deteriorate; from their trade situation with the USSR, whose energy and raw materials had become less readily available and much more expensive; and from Western creditors, who were no longer willing to make large *new* loans to Eastern Europe but expected the countries to service their large debts, which meant a new outflow of resources from Eastern Europe to the West. Depressed economic conditions in the West since the mid-1970s contributed further to Eastern Europe's problems as demand for their products declined, competition (especially from the less developed countries) increased, and protectionist forces in the West grew. The most immediate observable outcome of this new situation has been drastic reductions in growth rates or levels of production, and even more drastic cuts in domestic utilization, as shown in Table 31.4.

Net foreign borrowing makes it possible for domestic utilization— private and public consumption plus investment—to increase more rapidly than production, which it did during the first half of the 1970s in most East European countries. A net outflow of resources—which occurs if the sum of debt service payments and the deterioration in the terms of trade exceeds the sum of new loans obtained from abroad— means that domestic utilization must remain below production, as it has in all these countries except Bulgaria since the late 1970s. This in fact is the adjustment—the price—the borrowing countries have had to pay as debt levels rose too high and as new credits became unavailable.

Although similar pressures are felt by all the East European countries, there are very important differences among them in terms of policies, performance, and prospects, as suggested by the data presented in Table 31.4. Most striking is the case of Poland, where economic mis-

Table 31.4. *Average Annual Growth Rates of National Income Produced and Utilized by the East European Countries, 1971–1982 (in Percentage)*

| Country | 1971–1975 | 1976–1980 | 1981 | 1982[a] |
|---|---|---|---|---|
| *National income produced* | | | | |
| Bulgaria | 7.8 | 6.1 | 5.0 | 4.0 |
| Czechoslovakia | 5.7 | 3.7 | −0.4 | 0.5 |
| GDR | 5.4 | 4.1 | 4.8 | 3.0 |
| Hungary | 6.2 | 3.2 | 2.0 | 1.5 |
| Poland | 9.8 | 1.2 | −12.1 | −8.0 |
| Romania | 11.2 | 7.3 | 2.2 | 2.6 |
| Yugoslavia[b] | 6.6 | 5.6 | 2.0 | n.a.[c] |
| *National income utilized* | | | | |
| Bulgaria | 8.6 | 2.8 | 7.7 | 4.0 |
| Czechoslovakia | 6.1 | 2.2 | − 4.5 | −3.0 |
| GDR | 4.7 | 3.6 | 1.7 | 0.5 |
| Hungary | 5.6 | 1.9 | 0.1 | −2.0 |
| Poland | 11.6 | −0.2 | −12.3 | −12.0 |
| Romania | n.a. | 6.9 | −4.9 | −1.5 |
| Yugoslavia[b] | n.a. | 4.5 | −4.9 | n.a.[c] |

SOURCE: Compiled from official East European reports.
[a]Preliminary.
[b]Social product.
[c]Not available.

management and overly ambitious expansion plans led to costly mistakes, with outcomes that are examined elsewhere in this volume. What economic role is played by the USSR and other members of CMEA in Poland? Although we do not have the full picture, evidence suggests that in 1980 and 1981 the USSR provided economic assistance in the form of additional deliveries to and reduced imports from Poland, as well as substantial hard-currency loans, but that since 1982 only relatively small trade credits have been granted. The East European countries, on the other hand, while clearly being hurt economically by disruptions in Poland's export delivery obligations and the deteriorating creditworthiness of the entire region induced by the Polish and Romanian debt rescheduling, do not appear to have provided large-scale assistance. After the imposition of martial law, the Soviet Union seems to have reduced sharply its economic aid to Poland. This may well be a move motivated not only by economic but also by political considerations: to place the blame for that country's economic hardships on Western sanctions and lack of credits, which Poland's leaders have been doing publically since introducing martial law.

Highly significant also is the dramatic slowdown in Romania's growth. Though due in part to special circumstances, there are similarities with Poland: overly ambitious growth targets in earlier years, serious shortages of consumer goods, economic mismanagement, and a balance-of-payments crisis compounded by external circumstances, such as a disruption of oil imports due to the Iranian revolution and the war between Iran and Iraq.

The growth of the absolute level of the net hard-currency debt of Eastern Europe and the USSR between 1970 and 1982 is shown in Table 31.5. Although since 1981 the debt levels have stabilized, in most cases because of the absolute unavailability of new credits, the debt service ratios (percentage of exports that must be devoted to service the debt) are still very high and will remain high for several years, except in Bulgaria and Czechoslovakia (and the USSR), whose debt burdens are relatively modest.[24] The unavailability of substantial new credits to the East European countries since about 1979 has forced them to adjust quickly, which has meant not only the slowing, leveling, or decline of production growth rates (depending on country) but also the reduction of consumption and especially investment rates or levels.

The basic conclusion concerning Eastern Europe's economic performance is that these countries will continue to face serious difficulties. Although by 1983 the worst of the economic crisis may be over (with the likely exception of Poland), these countries can no longer count on the

Table 31.5. *Net Hard-Currency Debt of Eastern Europe and the USSR to the West, 1970–1982 (in Current Billion U.S. Dollars)*

| Country | 1970 | 1975 | 1980 | 1981 | 1982[a] |
|---|---|---|---|---|---|
| Bulgaria | 0.7 | 2.1 | 2.5 | 2.1 | 1.8 |
| Czechoslovakia | 0.6 | 1.2 | 3.4 | 3.4 | 3.2 |
| GDR | 1.4 | 4.8 | 11.2 | 11.0 | 9.2 |
| Hungary | 0.6 | 2.3 | 5.8 | 6.2 | 6.2 |
| Poland | 1.1 | 7.7 | 22.0 | 23.2 | 24.1 |
| Romania | 1.6 | 3.1 | 9.3 | 9.7 | 8.8 |
| CMEA-Six | 6.0 | 21.2 | 54.2 | 55.6 | 53.3 |
| USSR | 1.0 | 7.8 | 8.7 | 10.8 | 8.0 |
| CMEA banks | 0.3 | 2.2 | 4.1 | 3.9 | 3.6 |
| CMEA-Seven[b] | 7.3 | 31.2 | 67.0 | 70.3 | 64.9 |
| Yugoslavia | 1.9 | 5.7 | 16.8 | 18.0 | 18.3 |
| Eastern Europe and USSR total | 9.2 | 36.9 | 83.6 | 88.3 | 83.2 |

SOURCE: Wharton Econometrics, *Centrally Planned Economies Outlook* (Washington, D.C.: Wharton Econometrics Forecasting Associates, March 1983).

NOTES: Net hard-currency debt to the West is defined as gross hard-currency debt to Western banks, Western governments, and international financial organizations (IMF and the World Bank, in the case of Romania and Yugoslavia), minus deposits in Western banks. Categories of debt included as long-, medium-, and most short-term debts, evaluated at year-end foreign currency/dollar exchange rates.

[a]Estimated
[b]CMEA-Six plus the USSR.

temporary support mechanisms mentioned earlier. Moreover, their continued high debt service obligations, the trade difficulties faced within CMEA, and the related stagnation in consumption but especially the decline in investment levels, indicate that East European growth rates will not soon return to levels achieved to the mid-1970s. The greatest difficulties, of course, will be faced in Poland.[25]

*Soviet Economic Options in Eastern Europe* J. F. Brown has identified succinctly the Soviet Union's policy dilemma in Eastern Europe: conflict between its desire for alliance cohesion and for political viability in the region. Cohesion requires conformity of ideology, of domestic and foreign policies, and of implementing institutions. Viability demands credible and efficient economic performance in Eastern Europe that will increasingly legitimize Communist rule. The two objectives are difficult to reconcile because a uniform set of institutions and policies is at odds with the need for flexible responses to country-specific problems.[26] Stalin opted for cohesion; the post-Stalin leaderships have more and more emphasized viability, as long as East European policies remained within "limits" that were uncertain and constantly changing.

Moscow does not appear to have a great deal of room for maneuver in Eastern Europe. Since it is quite certain that no Soviet leadership will want to give up the ideological, military, political, and economic alliance system it dominates in the region, it cannot contemplate telling the East Europeans that it will change quickly, drastically, or unilaterally the existing institutional arrangements, such as the CMEA pricing mechanism or basic trade patterns. Therefore, the realistic question in assessing Soviet options is this: To what extent and through what mechanisms can the Soviet Union reduce, gradually, the economic cost of its East European empire while increasing the economic and political viability of the regimes in the region?

For the USSR the economic cost of trade with Eastern Europe declines rapidly as the gap between intra-CMEA and world market prices of raw materials and energy products narrows or disappears. A substantial movement in this direction has been taking place since 1980 for most raw materials and since 1982 for energy, owing to the continuing rise in intra-CMEA prices of these products under the CMEA pricing formula, while world market prices have declined. The Soviet Union has also been insisting that the East European countries improve the quality of their manufactured exports.

For the future, one may also envision a gradual change in the pattern of the Soviet–East European division of labor. Given relative factor endowments, including historical traditions and skills, and the Soviet Union's great excess demand for agricultural and food products and industrial manufactures, it would make economic sense to encourage the East European countries to move toward increased specialization in those products for the Soviet market.

Over the next few years much will depend on how the situation evolves. One can envision a scenario in which Poland's economic contacts with the West will continue to decline, and the regime will remain afloat only through substantial Soviet and some East European economic assistance. Such an option would be costly for the USSR. The previously cited evidence for 1981 and 1982 does not suggest that Moscow is prepared to carry a continuous and large economic burden in Poland. For this reason, eventually the Soviet Union will probably support—or at least permit—moves toward political accommodation and economic liberalization, provided that its fundamental security, ideological, and political interests will not thereby be threatened.

Eastern Europe's long-run economic viability can be improved significantly only by undertaking fundamental economic reforms. Economic logic and the evidence cited suggest that reform pressures are gaining strength throughout the region because of the need both for greater efficiency in the use of limited inputs and for expanded production of hard goods, especially manufactures salable for hard currency. Further pressures for reforms come from consumers, neglect of whom has an adverse impact on productivity and political stability.

Given its own economic performance and constraints, the Soviet Union may well become more tolerant of basic economic reforms in Eastern Europe. Yet domestic opposition will remain a major obstacle. Problems in the domestic and international economic environments paradoxically contribute to pressures both for and against reforms. Balance-of-payment pressures add to the tautness of the economy, whereas reforms require some slack—that is, reserves of materials, machinery, labor, consumer goods, and foreign exchange—to cushion predictable and unforeseen difficulties during the transition period. Tautness also means operating under conditions of repressed inflation; thus reforms that give a greater role to market forces are especially feared because of the increased likelihood of rapid, open inflation and possibly significant unemployment. The crisis in Poland warns other East European countries to undertake reforms in time to prevent a crisis, yet the current tense economic and political situation is not conducive to reform initiatives in every country.

What about Soviet attitudes toward economic reforms in Eastern Europe? My view is that, since Khrushchev, the Soviet leadership has become first more ambivalent, then more tolerant, toward a system evolution along the lines of the Hungarian New Economic Mechanism (NEM). There is no question that past and present Soviet leaders have felt and feel more comfortable dealing with Soviet-type centrally planned economies in Eastern Europe than with decentralized ones; the former are easier for them to understand and to manipulate. At the same time, they are aware of the shortcomings of traditional central planning and probably realize also that for historical, cultural, geopolitical, and economic reasons carbon copies of the Soviet model would not be appropriate for all of Eastern Europe. Some surely must also consider that an East European country's reforms may serve as a laboratory to find out what works and what does not and with what consequences.

The East European countries' room for maneuver regarding economic reforms is likely to increase regardless of what happens in Poland. One reason for this is the example of Poland. From the point of view of the

Soviet leadership, the contrast between Hungary's reasonably success-ful economic decentralization[27] versus Poland's economic crisis, which has contributed greatly to an almost complete loss of political control, must be so clear-cut that the Soviets must now realize even more strongly that their own long-term political interests require a much greater stress on economic viability than on political conformity and control over economic decisions. But the manner in which the strong pressures for and against basic economic reforms are to be resolved will be determined by factors that are country specific.[28]

## Notes

[1]For the purposes of this chapter, Eastern Europe is composed of Bulgaria, Czechoslovakia, the GDR, Hungary, Poland, and Romania. Yugoslavia is in-cluded in this chapter only if specifically mentioned.

[2]Paul Marer, "Soviet Economic Policy in Eastern Europe," in *Reorientation and Commercial Relations of the Economies of Eastern Europe*, ed. John P. Hardt, compendium of papers submitted to the Joint Economic Committee, Congress of the United States (Washington, D.C.: U.S. Government Printing Office [hereaf-ter GPO], 1974).

[3]R. Olšovský and V. Průcha, eds., *Stručný hospodářský vývoj Československa do roku 1955* (Prague: Svoboda, 1969), p. 397: cited in V. Holešovský, "The Czecho-slovak Economy in Transition" (unpublished manuscript, 1972).

[4]E. M. Snell and M. Harper, "Postwar Economic Growth in East Germany," in *Economic Developments in Countries of Eastern Europe*, ed. John P. Hardt, compendium of papers submitted to the Joint Economic Committee, Congress of the United States (Washington, D.C.: GPO, 1970).

[5]See, for instance, Minc's speech at the Eighth Plenum of the Polish Central Committee in 1956, cited in J. M. Montias, *Central Planning in Poland* (New Haven: Yale University Press, 1962), p. 123, and S. Ausch, *Theory and Practice of CMEA Cooperation* (Budapest: Akadémia Kiadó, 1972), p. 43.

[6]J. M. Montias, *Economic Development in Communist Rumania* (Cambridge, Mass.: MIT Press, 1967).

[7]F. I. Pryor, *The Communist Foreign Trade System* (Canbridge, Mass.: MIT Press, 1963), pp. 200–201.

[8]Proposals for various kinds of subregional integration schemes, all well documented, included those made by Czechoslovakia with Poland, Hungary with Yugoslavia and Czechoslovakia, Yugoslavia with Bulgaria, and Bulgaria with Romania. See I. Berend, "The Problem of Eastern European Economic Integration in a Historical Perspective," in *Foreign Trade in a Planned Economy*, ed. I. Vajda and M. Simai (Cambridge, England: Cambridge University Press, 1971).

[9]Montias, *Economic Development*, chap. 4.

[10]C. H. McMillan, "Some Thoughts on the Relationship between Regional Integration in Eastern Europe and East–West Economic Relations," in *International Economics: Comparisons and Interdependencies*, ed. F. Levcik (Vienna: Springer Verlag, 1978).

[11]W. Brus, "Economic Reform and Comecon Integration," in *Wirtschaft und Gesellschaft* (Berlin: Duncker und Humblatt, 1979).

[12]For a more detailed discussion of the theory and practice of integration among CPEs, see Paul Marer and J. M. Montias, eds., *East European Integration and East-West Trade* (Bloomington: Indiana University Press, 1980).

[13]See also John P. Hardt, "Soviet Energy Policy in Eastern Europe," in *Soviet Policy in Eastern Europe*, ed. Sarah Terry (New Haven: Yale University Press, 1984), chap. 7.

[14]*Pravda*, October 15, 1982. This article and the material contained in this paragraph of my text were called to my attention by Jozef van Brabant.

[15]Kálmán Pécsi, *The Future of Socialist Economic Integration* (Armonk, N.Y.: M. E. Sharpe, 1981), p. 101.

[16]That there is considerable price bargaining is readily acknowledged even by Soviet experts: "In [intra-CMEA trade] negotiations, both sides cite prices that satisfy their notions of effectiveness of exchange and subsequently arrive at some variant as a result of 'bargaining.'" See N. M. Mitrofanova, "The Economic Nature of Contract Prices in the Mutual Collaboration of CMEA Countries," *Izvestiya Akademii Nauk SSSR (Seriya ekonomicheskaya)*, no. 5 (1977), translated in *Soviet and East European Foreign Trade*, 15 (Spring 1979), p. 9.

[17]Paul Marer, *Postwar Pricing and Price Patterns in Socialist Foreign Trade (1946–1971)* (Bloomington: International Development Research Center of Indiana University, report 1, 1972).

[18]Pécsi, *Future of Socialist Economic Integration*, p. 131.

[19]*Ibid.*, p. 131.

[20]M. Lavigne, "The Soviet Union Inside Comecon," *Soviet Studies* 35 (April 1983), p. 146.

[21]M. Marrese and J. Vanous, *Implicit Subsidies and Non-Market Benefits in Soviet Trade with Eastern Europe* (Berkeley: University of California Press, 1983). These estimates have been prominently reported in influential publications such as the *Wall Street Journal*, January 15, 1982, *Time*, January 18, 1982, and *Fortune*, July 13, 1981.

[22]Ed. A. Hewett, "Foreign Economic Relations," in *The Soviet Economy: Toward the Year 2000*, ed. Abram Bergson and Herbert S. Levine (London: Allen & Unwin, 1983).

[23]Marrese and Vanous have responded to some of the criticisms here and those made by others at the various debates we have had on these issues by including in the appendix to their book (n. 21) a sensitivity analysis, varying the assumed quality discount on intra-CMEA trade in manufactures. However, in their text, summary statements, and press releases they continue to cite only the original high numbers, without qualifications. They also claim that these statistical issues make little difference in any event because much of the subsidy arises on Soviet primary exports to, rather than manufactures imports from, Eastern Europe. I do not agree with their claim; our disagreement on this issue arises from differences concerning the correct statistical formula to use to decompose the total subsidy.

[24]Bulgaria, which had a very high debt burden during the early 1970s, carried out a successful adjustment policy between 1977 and 1982.

[25]A more detailed assessment by country can be found in Paul Marer, "East European Economies: Achievements, Problems, Prospects," in *Communism in Eastern Europe*, 2d rev. ed., ed. Teresa Rakowska-Harmstone (Bloomington: Indiana University Press, 1984).

[26]J. F. Brown, *Relations between the Soviet Union and Its East European Allies: A Survey*, Report R-1742-PR (Santa Monica: The Rand Corporation, 1975).

[27]A comprehensive discussion of Hungary's economic reforms can be found in Paul Marer, "Hungary's New Economic System: Evaluation, Assessment, Prospects," paper read at the conference on Hungary in the 1980s, Columbia University, New York City, October 28, 1983.

[28]The basic features of a traditional centrally planned economic system, the pressures for and against reforms, and the type of reforms that so far have been

introduced in Eastern Europe are discussed in Paul Marer, "Management and Reform in Centrally Planned Economies," in *Readings in International Business*, 3d ed., ed. Richard N. Farmer and John V. Lombardi (Bloomington: Cedarwood Press, 1984).

# 32

# CHARLES GATI

## Soviet Empire: Alive but Not Well*

Give or take a few months, four decades have passed since the Soviet bloc that Stalin conceived began to take shape. During these 40 turbulent years, two types of challenges have confronted Soviet authority over Eastern Europe. First, Moscow has had to cope with popular movements, riots, uprisings, and revolutions such as those that erupted in East Berlin (1953), Poznan (1956), Budapest (1956), Warsaw (1968), Prague (1968), several Polish cities (1970 and 1976), and most recently—and most dramatically—throughout Poland under the banner of the Solidarity movement (1980–1981). When facing more or less spontaneous challenges of this type—popular movements seeking freedom, economic well-being, as well as independence—Moscow, acting directly or indirectly, invariably managed to reestablish most or all of its authority. Second, the Soviet Union has had to cope with regime claims such as those that were advanced by Yugoslavia (1948), Albania (1961), and Romania (1964). When facing more or less controlled challenges of this type—demands by a single communist party leadership for autonomy—Moscow invariably failed to reestablish its authority.

Although both popular outbursts and individual regime claims for autonomy are bound to occur again, Moscow must also find a way to cope with a third and different challenge: the growing dissatisfaction and assertiveness of its essentially loyal allies in the Warsaw Pact. In the mid-1980s—for the first time acting concurrently, though not conspiratorially—several like-minded regimes have come to see the need to make a renewed effort to trim excessive Soviet influence over their policies. Lacking in the dramatic quality of past confrontations and rooted in a common desire for more "elbow room" rather than real independence, the primary challenge today in Eastern Europe is a subtle attempt by several regimes to reach out to Europe without offending or provoking the Soviet Union; indeed, it is an attempt to move toward the

*Reprinted by permission of the author and publisher from *Problems of Communism* 34, no. 2 (March–April, 1985), pp. 73–86. No copyright claimed.

West without appearing to move away from the East. By so trying to square the circle, the East European regimes hope to reap Western economic benefits and gain a measure of respectability at home—and keep Moscow satisfied as well. At a deeper level, they are responding to a sense of European identity and consciousness that has been growing on the continent, east and west. But by proceeding cautiously and by affirming their commitment to the Soviet bloc, that is, to "socialist internationalism," the East European regimes are also responding to the most fundamental political fact of life in the region: their continued dependence on Soviet power for survival.

What are the recent causes and manifestations of this maneuver by East Europe's leaderships? At a time of Soviet leadership changes, is Moscow likely to tolerate a further erosion of its authority in the region? If so, are we witnessing the gradual "decline" of the Soviet empire or merely a new phase in its evolution?

## Causes of Regime Discontent

The current East European maneuver, which is spearheaded by Hungary, Romania, and the German Democratic Republic (GDR), reflects East European apprehensions about the direction of Soviet economic policy toward Eastern Europe since the early 1980s and about the direction of Soviet foreign policy generally.

As for the direction of Soviet conduct abroad, a large segment of the East European communist elites appears to have grown critical of Moscow's lack of diplomatic skill and mistaken priorities. Without disagreeing with broad Soviet foreign policy objectives, they are particularly disturbed by the Soviet Union's heavy-handed treatment of Afghanistan; its inability to improve not only party-to-party but also state-to-state relations with China; and, above all, its clumsy and counterproductive handling of, and subsequent withdrawal from, the intermediate-range nuclear forces (INF) talks in Geneva in late 1983. Although only the Romanian government has addressed these issues directly in public, extensive contacts with Hungarian, East German, and Polish functionaries indicate that, from their perspective too, Soviet conduct appears plagued by miscalculations and missteps.

While granting that the Soviet Union had to do "something" about Afghanistan in 1979, these functionaries wonder if the Kremlin accurately estimated the difficulties the Soviet armed forces would encounter. They wonder if the political and economic costs of the operation will not ultimately exceed the presumed benefits of military victory. Like many a Western observer, they wonder if Afghanistan will turn out to have been "Moscow's Vietnam." Without having specific measures in mind, they speculate whether the Soviet Union should not adopt an "alternative" to the policy it is presently pursuing there. In their view, then, Moscow has allowed itself to be bogged down in a war that it cannot easily win and from which it now cannot extricate itself—but for which Eastern Europe has also had to pay in terms of Western diplomatic complaints and economic penalties.

East European political elites seem to be equally nonplussed over Soviet policy toward China. They applaud the recent improvement in state-to-state relations between China and the Soviet Union and Eastern Europe as well,[1] but they are dissatisfied with the slow pace of the normalization process. Although they share Moscow's suspicions over China's rapprochement with the United States and Western Europe, and believe that Chinese attacks on Soviet "hegemonism" have been unnecessarily harsh, they find the Soviet position altogether inconsistent. If the issue is ideology, they ask, then why does Moscow respond in the same way to present-day Chinese statements and policies as it once did to Mao's statements and policies? If, on the other hand, the primary issue is power rather than ideology, then why cannot Moscow find a diplomatic formula to ease tensions between the two countries? In the East Europeans' view, then, it is primarily though not exclusively the Kremlin's inflexibility that stands in the way of at least partial reconciliation. In the meantime, all of the East European regimes, with the exception of Romania, feel compelled to emulate publicly the Soviet posture toward China which they regard as deeply flawed and believe to be rooted in the Soviet leaderships' grudge against a former—more tractable—ally.

Closer to home, the East European political elites appear especially critical of Soviet policies toward Western Europe in general and of Soviet handling of the INF talks in particular. Rightly or wrongly, it is widely believed among these elites that the Soviet Union could have prevented the deployment of Pershing II ballistic and Tomahawk cruise missiles in Western Europe.[2] They maintain that a more subtle Soviet diplomatic effort—to encourage West European hopes about substantial Soviet concessions—would have so altered the political balance in the Netherlands, Belgium, and even the Federal Republic of Germany (FRG) that the installation of U.S. missiles would have had to be canceled or at least postponed. By first threatening to withdraw from the Geneva INF talks (if the missiles were deployed) and then actually withdrawing (when the missiles were deployed), the Kremlin made it easier for the United States to accomplish that which the Soviet leaders so vigorously and indeed vehemently sought to circumvent. In other words, in the East Europeans' view, Moscow should have temporized, not so much in order to conclude an agreement but in order to keep the Atlantic alliance guessing—and divided.

The common element in the East European elites' critique of Soviet conduct toward Afghanistan, China, and the INF talks is an increasing concern, mixed with condescension, about the recent lack of subtlety in the Kremlin's approach to the outside world. In a critique reminiscent of West European reservations about U.S. foreign policy, East European functionaries think of their Soviet ally as being unduly heavy-handed, inflexible, much too self-righteous and clumsy, and insufficiently appreciative of the merits of quiet diplomacy. They are concerned, clearly, because an intransigent Soviet policy creates an unfavorable atmosphere for the expansion of their own economic, cultural, and political relations with the West, particularly with Western Europe.

The expansion of economic relations with the West is an especially urgent priority for Eastern Europe now, and it is so perceived by all of the regimes in the Soviet bloc (with the possible exception of Czechoslovakia). The main reason for the urgency—and the second general cause of unease with Soviet conduct—is that since the early 1980s, Soviet subsidies to Eastern Europe have steadily declined and there has been a concurrent—and steep—deterioration in Eastern Europe's terms of trade with the Soviet Union. While acknowledging that the Soviet Union has its own economic problems, the East European regimes nevertheless resent getting less in the 1980s than they did in the middle and late 1970s. With a feeling of indignation, they wonder whether the Soviet Union could not afford to do more for them if it did not waste its resources fighting an elusive enemy in Afghanistan, keeping a vast army along its Chinese border, and installing modern and expensive intermediate-range missiles in the GDR and Czechoslovakia.

The essential facts are quite simple and well-known. To alleviate the impact on its East European allies of the sudden rise in the world market price of energy in the early 1970s, Moscow agreed to provide oil and gas to the East European countries at a price that would only gradually catch up with the prices other countries were paying on the world market. Because of cheap energy as well as the overpricing of East European manufactures, Eastern Europe is estimated to have received an implicit Soviet subsidy amounting to U.S. $5.8 billion a year in the 1974–1978 period, about $11.6 billion in 1979, about $17.8 billion in 1980, and about $18.7 billion in 1981. The average subsidy for 1982–1984 is thought to have dropped to $12.1 billion per year, reaching about $10 to $11 billion in 1984.[3] Although some Western economists consider these staggering estimates excessive, there is no disagreement about either the existence of Soviet subsidies in the 1970s or their decline since 1981.[4] Due to the decline and then seeming disappearance of Soviet energy subsidies in 1984, the overall amount has sharply decreased. Concurrently, the steady deterioration in the terms of Soviet–East European trade—by approximately 20% since 1980—means that the East European regimes must sell more of their products in exchange for the same amount of goods received from the Soviet Union. A simple (although admittedly extreme) example illustrates the extraordinary change that has taken place. In 1974, Hungary sold 800 "Ikarus" buses to the Soviet Union in order to purchase 1 million tons of Soviet oil. In 1981, it had to sell 2300 "Ikarus" buses for 1 million tons of Soviet oil. By 1984, the "price" of the same amount of Soviet oil may have reached 4000 "Ikarus" buses.[5]

From a purely economic point of view as well as from the Soviet perspective, changes in Soviet–East European trade relations are fully warranted. The Soviet Union has to cope with its own serious economic stringencies. Keeping up with the United States in the military competition is expensive. The availability of cheap Soviet energy has substantially declined in recent years, while the costs of producing new oil have significantly risen.[6] Why should Moscow not receive the world-market price at long last for the energy its allies so desperately need? The answer from the East Europeans is that they made an implicit contract with the Soviet Union in the 1970s. That contract, or understanding, called for Moscow to protect the East European states from the worst effects of international economic turbulence in exchange for which the East European regimes would maintain domestic stability and support Soviet foreign policy objectives. To the extent that, with the notable exception of Poland, there has been relative peace and quiet in Eastern Europe, the Soviet Union is blamed for reneging on this tacit understanding with the East European leaderships.[7]

Given the decreasing advantage that the East Europeans derive from the Soviet economic connection and their assumption that the Kremlin is assigning decreasing priority to their problems, combined with misgivings about heavy-handed Soviet behavior elsewhere, the East European regimes have ample reason in the mid-1980s to ponder how they will be able to maintain domestic peace as well as support Soviet foreign policy objectives. Thus they have reason to reconsider their relations both with the Soviet Union and the West.

## Manifestations of Concern

Precisely because the current maneuver by several East European governments—the process of inching toward the West—is so incremental, its public manifestations are only occasional and frequently subtle. In fact, one indicator of this trend—the relative share of East European trade with noncommunist countries (see Table 32.1)—shows a decline since 1981, though this is hardly due to political intent in Eastern Europe or even Western Europe. Indeed, it is a function of the region's still-growing hard-currency debt (see Table 32.2), which has made Western credit available to Eastern Europe only on a selective basis since the Polish crisis of 1980–1981. Every country in the area, but especially Romania and Hungary, has made it a top priority to reduce Western imports in order to save hard currency, and Poland has been all but unable to renew its once-extensive commercial ties with the West.

Notwithstanding the temporary setback in East European trade with the West, other trends point to rising political dissonance in the bloc, especially in the GDR, Hungary, and Romania.

Most surprising, and potentially significant, has been the apparent breakdown of synchronization between Soviet and East German approaches toward the Federal Republic.[8] Beginning in November 1983 and continuing after the INF talks had collapsed, the GDR turned out to be only a reluctant supporter of a vehement and vociferous Soviet-led Warsaw Pact campaign against NATO aggressiveness and, later, West German "revanchism."[9] Although all East European leaders, except Nicolae Ceauşescu of Romania, added their denunciations and innuendoes, the GDR's Erich Honecker (as well as Hungary's János Kádár) made a point of pleading for restraint. Honecker asked for a "coalition of reason" in both German states, adding that such a coalition would serve the interests of "the German people"—a formulation contrary to the GDR claim positing the existence of two German nations since the formation of the GDR in 1949.[10] Echoing Kádár's favorite

Table 32.1. *East European Foreign Trade with Noncommunist Countries (Percent of Total Foreign Trade)*

| Year | Exports | Imports |
|------|---------|---------|
| 1960 | 27.6 | 28.5 |
| 1970 | 30.9 | 32.5 |
| 1980 | 36.3 | 38.5 |
| 1981 | 36.0 | 34.5 |
| 1982 | 33.8 | 29.6 |
| 1983 | 31.5 | 27.2 |

SOURCE: Adapted by the author from the U.S. Central Intelligence Agency, *Handbook of Economic Statistics, 1984*, CPAS 84-10002 (Washington, D.C., September 1984), p. 102. Data for 1983 is preliminary.

Table 32.2. *Hard-Currency Debt to the West (in Current U.S. Dollars, Billions)*

| Country | 1970 | 1975 | 1980 | 1981 | 1984 |
|---------|------|------|------|------|------|
| Bulgaria | 0.7 | 2.1 | 2.5 | 2.1 | 2.5 |
| Czechoslovakia | 0.6 | 1.2 | 3.4 | 3.4 | 4.1 |
| GDR | 1.4 | 4.8 | 11.2 | 11.0 | 12.3 |
| Hungary | 0.6 | 2.3 | 5.8 | 6.2 | 8.2 |
| Poland | 1.1 | 7.7 | 22.0 | 23.2 | 27.0 |
| Romania | 1.6 | 3.1 | 9.3 | 9.7 | 8.4 |
| Total | 6.0 | 21.2 | 54.2 | 55.6 | 62.5 |

SOURCE: Jan Vanous, Centrally Planned Economies Service, Wharton Econometric Forecasting Associates, Washington, D.C.

phrase, Honecker also appealed to the "small- and medium-sized states" of Europe to do what they can to "limit the damage" to intra-European cooperation caused by Soviet–American tensions.[11]

Some actions by the GDR were also out of phase with the Soviet campaign against the FRG. In the first half of 1984, the GDR allowed an estimated 25,000 people to leave for West Germany. In July 1984, at the height of the virulent Soviet campaign against the Federal Republic, the two German states reached an agreement that provided for new West German bank credits in exchange for East German concessions concerning emigration, family reunification cases, and the like.[12] Although the GDR's "concessions" were rather minor, the fact that a deal was struck at this time signaled Honecker's desire to distance himself from the latest Soviet position.

True, it is quite possible that, *before* November 1983, the GDR might have been encouraged by Moscow to feign tolerance toward the unofficial East German peace movement and present itself to the West in other ways too as a state dedicated to peace and harmony in Europe. There might well have been collusion between Moscow and East Berlin in an effort to make the West German peace activists believe that both Washington and Moscow were under pressure from their respective allies.[13] Granted the utility of such "fraternal cooperation" prior to the collapse of the INF talks, it is still all but impossible to find similar reasons or, indeed, any rationale from the Soviet perspective for continued dissonance in 1984. Hence, the likely explanation for what happened last year and continues in 1985 is that Honecker, having earlier received either mixed or confusing signals from Moscow and eager to take advantage of leadership disarray in the Kremlin, decided to pursue the inter-German dialogue on his own.

Soviet attacks on the "limited détente" between East and West Germany, and East Germany's spirited defense of it, lend credence to this interpretation.[14] Although Soviet newspapers focused on Bonn's aggressive intentions, the real target was East Berlin. An article in *Pravda* stressed that the relationship between the two German states must be evaluated in the context of general East–West relations and cannot be isolated from them. It reminded East Berlin of NATO's present "crusade against socialism" and of Bonn's desire to "solicit concessions on matters of principle that affect the GDR's sovereignty." Another *Pravda* piece, which repeated some of the same accusations, was meant to underline Moscow's anxiety. It was an unsigned editorial (and hence fully authoritative and official), and it made mention of the Deutsche Mark 950-million credit deal that the two Germanies had just concluded. The editorial expressed specific reservations about travel concessions which, it claimed, would only serve to allow Bonn to have "new channels for political and ideological influence."

At first, the GDR rather vigorously defended its position. Obviously responding to the July 27 *Pravda* article in its August 1 issue, *Neues Deutschland* maintained that Bonn was being pressured both by "revanchist" forces and by "realistic" elements and that it was not self-evident which side would turn out to be more influential. Of course, this was precisely the argument on which Moscow had based its own policies toward the FRG a year or so earlier—but now the situation was said to be different and the old policy was considered untimely and inoperative. In its article, *Neues Deutschland* also asserted that both German states were "independent in their internal and external affairs."

When, under growing Soviet pressure, Honecker ultimately postponed his visit scheduled for September 1984 to the Federal Republic, it was not clear for how long and to what extent the East Germans would place their "internationalist obligations" ahead of their self-interest.[15] Down but not out, Honecker showed up in maverick Romania on the fortieth anniversary of that country's liberation—the only top communist leader from the Soviet bloc to do so.[16] This not-so-subtle expression of displeasure with Moscow notwithstanding, East Berlin shied away from engaging Moscow any further in public disagreements. The compromise they appear to have reached allowed the GDR to improve ties with the Federal Republic and thus continue the dialogue in the spirit of the Helsinki process, on condition that East Berlin proceed slowly, without publicity and summitry, and calibrate each step along the way so as not to embarrass the Soviet Union or counter its policies toward the West.

Ironically but not surprisingly, Hungary—once the object of East Germany's ire for Kádár's reformist experiments—became the primary defender and promoter of Honecker's course. Indeed, it was an authoritative Hungarian statement issued at the beginning of 1984 that gave a much-needed ideological rationale for the GDR's (and Hungary's) approach to European cooperation.[17] Written by Mátyás Szürös, a Hungarian Politburo member and Central Committee secretary in charge of foreign policy, and published in the official party monthly, *Társadalmi Szemle*, the article rejected the traditional (read Soviet) view according to which the "national interests [of the East European states] necessarily had to play a secondary role and generally had to be subordinated to interests and objectives that were seen as common ones." Szürös added: "There is no question of this kind of subordination today." He also argued against "uniform solutions," calling instead for "methods that make optimum allowance for [national] characteristics." Turning directly to the realm of foreign policy, Szürös maintained that, in the absence of a world communist movement with a recognized center, each East European country had the right to take advantage of "specific possibilities." Alluding to one of the "specific possibilities," Szürös wrote: "Historical traditions and contemporary characteristics do make it possible for relations between a particular socialist and capitalist country to flourish [even] when the general trend is one of deterioration of East–West relations and of a narrowing of contacts."

So much for a common front against imperialist machinations! Whether or not Szürös—formerly Hungarian ambassador to Moscow as well as to East Berlin—sent a copy of his article to Honecker will probably never be known, but the East Germans certainly found his arguments useful and convincing. Indeed, when—in the aftermath of a predictable rebuttal by two Prague diehards published in the Czechoslovak party daily *Rudé Právo* and the Soviet foreign affairs weekly *Novoye Vremya*[18]—Szürös reiterated his views in the form of an interview,[19] *Neues Deutschland* promptly reprinted it in full[20] In subsequent articles, too, the Hungarians sought to encourage the GDR's *Westpolitik*, praising Honecker's meetings with the leaders of Sweden, Greece, and Italy, and enthusiastically endorsing his proclaimed preference for diplomatic solutions.[21]

That the normally so very circumspect Kádár regime allowed itself to be embroiled in a debate over the relative merits of international and national obligations was the result of a conscious decision. The original Szürös article was intended to serve four major objectives. First, it was to signal to the Hungarian party apparatus and to the country's attentive public the regime's recognition of the need to back up the economic reform movement at home with an activist foreign policy based to a greater extent than before on the country's national interest.[22] Second, it was to signal to the Soviet Union that while Hungary would remain a loyal ally and fulfill its bloc obligations, it must also look West both for economic reasons and for the purpose of satisfying the public's urge to belong to "Europe." Third, it was to signal to West European governments—to the Federal Republic and Austria in particular—the Kádár regime's commitment to the Western connection even at a time of high tension between the Soviet Union and the United States. Fourth, it was to signal to some of the more orthodox Warsaw Pact states, especially neighboring Czechoslovakia, Hungary's pride in its achievements and its growing impatience with innuendoes questioning the validity of its socialist path.

As for Romania, it has continued to live up to its reputation as the Soviet bloc's leading maverick. It continues to irritate Moscow by maintaining fraternal ties with China regardless of the state of Sino–Soviet relations; by differing from Soviet positions on a multitude of issues, including Afghanistan, Kampuchea, and the Middle East; and by refusing to join the Soviet-ordained boycott of the 1984 Los Angeles Olympic Games. Also, unlike Honecker and Bulgarian leader Todor Zhivkov, Ceauşescu did visit the Federal Republic in October 1984.[23] In addition, Romania remains the only Warsaw Pact state to have officially and publicly opposed both NATO INF deployments and Soviet counter-deployments. Thus, it is a fair guess that the Romanian regime is pleased with the emerging East Berlin–Budapest maneuver. One leading member of the Romanian Communist Party's Political Executive Committee (Politburo) is known to have approached a Hungarian official and informally inquired about the possibility of coordinated political activity.

However intriguing such a constellation might be, Ceauşescu's leadership style precludes consistent cooperation with the other East European states in the Warsaw Pact. Romania suffers not only from a deep economic crisis but also from the consequences of Ceauşescu's apparent megalomania. It has come to be that the President's closest associates, including Politburo members, feel obliged to make recommendations or advance fresh initiatives as if they had been devised by Ceauşescu, for only then do these proposals have a chance of being seriously considered. The resulting alienation of the political elite has led to a paralysis of the decision-making process that no amount of posturing can hide or overcome.[24] The problem is further exacerbated by the President's unwillingness or inability to offer any rationale for his frequent tactical shifts in policy, which seem unrelated to his own professed strategic direction, and by his excessive preoccupation with prestige and protocol at the expense of substance. The upshot of these developments is that Romania's long-standing and potentially still significant position as the semi-independent member of the Warsaw Pact has lost much of the attraction it might have once had for the other East European leaderships. Moreover, as long as the harsh Romanian treatment of the large Hungarian minority in Transylvania continues, Kádár will find it impossible to make common cause consistently with Ceauşescu—and he is unlikely to do so under any circumstances.

Among the other Warsaw Pact members, the Polish regime—overwhelmed by seemingly insoluble economic problems, facing popular hostility, and mired in factional infighting—remains on the sidelines. Czechoslovakia and, to a lesser extent, Bulgaria continue to back Soviet orthodoxy.[25] Thus, the most that can be expected is East European mini-coalitions countering Moscow on some specific issues.

Judging by the admittedly sketchy evidence available about the proceedings of the Council for Economic Mutual Assistance (CEMA), including the 1984 summit meeting in Moscow, such a mini-coalition appears to have come into being, with Romania, Hungary, and the GDR together pressing Moscow for concessions on the present CEMA price structure and on a variety of energy-related issues.[26] If they can further harmonize their views, act concurrently and yet unobtrusively, and place political topics on the agenda of the bloc's multilateral institutions, they could also press Moscow for sufficient "elbow room" in order to protect their Western connections from the vicissitudes of Soviet–American relations. Of course, the central question is how the Soviet Union is likely to treat such a maneuver, however unobtrusive, by a coadjutant East European mini-coalition.

Soviet Dilemmas
There is every reason to assume that Moscow is deeply concerned about the "Europeanization" of East European communism.[27] At the same time, it is not self-evident that this is a process which Moscow can readily arrest or contain. For as James F. Brown once astutely observed,[28] the Soviet Union pursues two competing, if not altogether contradictory, objectives in Eastern Europe. On the one hand, it seeks *bloc cohesion*—strict conformity with its own values, patterns, and policies. This goal, if realized, would help legitimize the Soviet experience at home and enhance the power of the Soviet Union abroad; its implementation, however, would almost certainly entail the use of coercive measures, including Soviet military intervention. To avoid that eventuality, and for other reasons as well, Moscow has as its other goal the *viability* of the East European regimes and indeed the *stability* of the region as a whole. A viable and stable Eastern Europe would, among other benefits, enhance the appeal of Soviet foreign policy to the West, the Third World, and the more independent-minded and presently anti-Soviet communist parties throughout the world.

But the elusive goal of East European stability also demands a high price from the Soviet Union. Short of granting the region independence, an option Moscow is not considering, there are only two noncoercive ways to obtain a measure of stability. One is to allow the East European regimes to attempt economic policies of a kind that produce consumer satisfaction by transforming "gulag communism" into "goulash communism." The other way is for the regimes to adopt political approaches of a kind that satisfy national or even nationalist aspirations by being informed less by Soviet values and interests than by each country's own customs and traditions. In short, the alternatives are bloc cohesion enforced by Soviet military power and economic subsidies or a modicum of East European stability made possible by Soviet tolerance of "goulash communism," "national communism," or some combination of the two.

In the abstract, Moscow does not object to "goulash communism." True, there are Soviet—and East European—diehards who regard excessive reliance on consumer satisfaction as a "petty-bourgeois" deviation. Such stale complaints aside, all communist regimes would like nothing better than economic well-being, partly to demonstrate the superiority of centrally planned economic systems and mainly to take the edge off popular economic and political discontent. The problem is not only that Soviet-type economies have not done well in Eastern Europe; it is also that they are seen not to have done well because the populations in Eastern Europe tend to assess their prevailing living standards less by comparing them with their own past than by comparing them to present living standards in such countries as the Federal Republic, Austria, or Finland. To achieve anything approaching that kind of consumer satisfaction, however, would presumably require larger Soviet subsidies, a reformist course on the Hungarian (or Chinese) pattern, and a political opening to the West to encourage credit, investments, and transfer of advanced technology—measures that entail considerable economic restructuring and political risk. Therefore, despite official endorsements of "goulash communism," the policies that might lead to consumer satisfaction and hence to political stability are, in fact, abhorrent to most Soviet and many East European leaders.

The Soviet Union is also concerned about stability obtained by paying more than lip service to the East Europeans' national or nationalist aspirations. While Moscow does encourage nationalism in the Third World or Western Europe—wherever it might spark anti-American or anti-Western sentiments—it is certainly less favorably disposed toward East European expressions of nationalism. When the GDR celebrates the five-hundredth anniversary of Martin Luther's birth, or Czechoslovakia takes pride in its national hockey team's victories, that's fine. When successive Polish regimes feel compelled to accommodate themselves to the traditional influence of the Catholic Church, that's fine, too, provided that the regime retains its capacity to inhibit and, if necessary, to control the Church's activities. But, in the Soviet view, respect for national values must not entail any policy aimed at fulfilling the region's traditional longing to be accepted by, and indeed to rejoin, the European community. For, as long as the Soviet Union itself is not perceived as belonging to the European community, East European desire to belong is suggestive of anti-Soviet tendencies.

Herein lies the essential reason for the current tug of war between the proprietors of power in the Soviet Union and Eastern Europe. As several East European regimes now see it, they must, for the sake of domestic political stability, actively, if cautiously, inch toward the West. They certainly do not want Soviet interventions; they cannot, as Poland found out, count on sufficient Soviet economic help; and most of them worry about the unforeseeable consequences of market-oriented reforms. The only alternative they see in the mid-1980s, then, is a gradual opening to the West, which, despite obvious risks, offers the promise of public approval. From a Soviet perspective, however, the reasons for such an opening are less compelling. Unlike their junior allies—even the Poles, the Czechs, or the East Germans—many Russians remain genuinely afraid of Western influences. The Soviet leaders also appear to be less apprehensive about, and possibly even to underestimate, the region's persistent instability and the major sources of that instability—nationalist and economic pressures. The Soviet leaders' attitude is also shared by the typical Soviet tourist visiting Warsaw, let alone Budapest, when he asks: "Why are these people complaining when they live better than we do?" It seems that even after 40 years of experience, Moscow cannot accept the fact that East Europeans judge the performance of their political and economic order by European and not by Soviet standards.

Of course, the Soviet Union has gone to considerable lengths to have peace and quiet, if not genuine stability, in Eastern Europe. It has long tried to steer a middle course between the objectives of cohesion and stability, bending now in one direction and then in another and hoping all along that the problem or problems will someday, somehow, disappear.

## "When the Cat's Away. . . ."

Whether Moscow can continue to muddle through in this way in the years ahead depends as much or more on its capacity to shape a *properly calibrated* policy toward the region than on economic conditions. The evidence of the post-Stalin era (see Table 32.3) indicates a significant correlation between the unity or lack of unity of the Soviet leadership, on the one hand, and East European popular movements and regime assertiveness, on the other. Specifically, it has been all but impossible for the Soviet Union to pursue its two competing goals of bloc cohesion and East European stability in a judicious and calibrated fashion at times of unsettled leadership in the Kremlin. Under such circumstances, the Soviet leaders, preoccupied with the struggle for power, have tended to send mixed signals to their East European clients. Sensing confusion in the Kremlin, East Europeans—leaders and people alike—have then tried to use the opportunity to shift the balance of decision-making authority to their side. "When the cat's away, the mice will play."

Of the three periods of Soviet leadership turbulence that have occurred so far, the volatile and highly personalized struggle for power in 1953–1957 resulted in several popular upheavals and considerable elite disorientation in Eastern Europe.[29] To recall briefly, this was the time when Lavrentiy Beria was reportedly rethinking the "German question"; when at first Georgiy Malenkov and then Nikita Khrushchev advocated a "new course" for Eastern Europe; when Khrushchev and Anastas Mikoyan urged, while Vyacheslav Molotov and others opposed, reconciliation with "national communist" Yugoslavia; when a divided Soviet leadership felt it needed Tito's blessing to invade Hun-

Table 32.3. *Kremlin Politics and Eastern Europe*

| State of Soviet leadership | | East European assertiveness | |
| --- | --- | --- | --- |
| Periods of relative turbulence | Periods of relative tranquility | Popular movements | Regime demands for autonomy |
| 1953–1957 | | East Berlin, 1953 Poznan, 1956 Warsaw, 1956 Budapest, 1956 | Poland, 1956 Hungary, 1956 |
| | 1957–1964 | | Albania, 1961 to present |
| 1964–1969 | | Warsaw, 1968 Prague, 1968 | Romania, 1964 to present Hungary, 1968 to present Czechoslovakia, 1968 |
| | 1969–1979 | Polish cities, 1970 and 1976 | |
| 1979 to present | | Polish Solidarity, 1980–1981 | Mini-coalitions, 1983 to present |

gary; and when a visibly shaken Kremlin first tried to obstruct and then grudgingly accepted Wladyslaw Gomulka's appointment as Poland's new leader.

Apparent confusion in Moscow led to unparalleled factional infighting in the East European communist parties, especially in Poland and Hungary. Sensing divisions at the top in Eastern Europe, no wonder that large segments of the attentive public, led by intellectuals, and subsequently the people as well gained courage and expressed their long-suppressed convictions.[30] Of course, in the end they did not get their way, for the Soviet leaders, facing the prospective disintegration of their empire, managed to pull themselves together and reestablish their authority. For about 7 years after the defeat of the "anti-party" group in 1957, they appear to have united behind Khrushchev and followed a rather calibrated policy toward Eastern Europe, one that stressed the goal of cohesion without necessarily stifling every national experiment.[31]

The second—certainly far less volatile—period of Kremlin turbulence began in 1964 as a palace conspiracy against Khrushchev and continued until 1969 or so with intense jockeying for position after his ouster (primarily between Leonid Brezhnev and Aleksey Kosygin).[32] As long as his colleagues refused to give him the kind of extensive authority that Khrushchev had had between 1957 and 1964, Brezhnev was only *primus inter pares*. During the early Brezhnev years, then, Soviet policy in

Eastern Europe once again lacked a sure hand. While Khrushchev's confusing on-again, off-again campaign for CEMA integration was an important factor in Romania's 1964 declaration of semi-independence, the Kremlin preoccupation with Khrushchev's ouster in that year allowed Romania to make stick its claim for a measure of autonomy in the Warsaw Pact.

The Hungarian and Czechoslovak reform movements, which also started in the mid-1960s, received considerable stimulation from the ongoing Soviet debate about economic reform.[33] It is highly instructive that most Czechoslovak leaders were under the strong impression that what they were doing met with Soviet approval. Even after their economic reform movement became the political "Prague Spring" in 1968, many of them continued to believe—and they had reason to believe—that the "Soviet comrades" at least understood and probably supported their efforts for "socialism with a human face." In point of fact, according to Zdeněk Mlynář's vivid testimony and other evidence,[34] *some* of the Soviet leaders did. Even if one accepts the premise that the Czechoslovak reformists around Alexander Dubček were somewhat naive about Soviet intentions, they operated on the basis of frequent consultations with Kremlin leaders at the highest level—and received contradictory signals.

The third, current period of Kremlin leadership turbulence can be traced to about 1979, when Brezhnev's illnesses and absences became chronic. Eventually an intense struggle to succeed him developed between Yuriy Andropov and Konstantin Chernenko. Andropov's rule was short-lived, and Chernenko's rule as *primus inter pares* in the Politburo (as his mentor Brezhnev once was) turned out to be of even shorter duration. This power struggle had been taking place at a time of economic stagnation affecting the entire bloc. For the first time, concerned about a recurrence of a "time of troubles" in the Kremlin, several East European leaders had allowed their preference for or against a specific contender to succeed Brezhnev to come out, with Ceauşescu reportedly opting for Chernenko, and Andropov receiving the endorsements of Kádár and Czechoslovakia's Gustav Husák.[35] As Moscow may see it, the East European regimes, once compelled to accept taxation without representation, have come around to seeking representation without taxation.

In addition to fostering the incipient mini-coalition described earlier in this chapter, the absence of a firm leadership in the Kremlin had affected adversely the management of the crisis of 1980–1981 by the Polish regime. What must be regarded as the paralysis of power in the Kremlin had a profoundly unsettling influence on the Polish leadership, which for almost 18 long months could not decide what it should or should not do.[36] It goes without saying that the rise of Solidarity was primarily a function of internal developments, both economic and political. It is also true that the Polish party has always tended to be deeply divided, probably more so than any other ruling communist party in the world. One can further assume that Moscow, anxious to avoid fighting two wars at the same time (in Afghanistan and Poland)

and concerned about Western sanctions, preferred not to intervene militarily if at all possible. Finally, it is quite likely that the Kremlin kept postponing the decision to act in the hope of further exacerbating the Polish crisis—that it waited for the political order to become chaotic and economic conditions to become unbearable so that the likes of General Wojciech Jaruzelski—surely a "moderate" by Soviet standards—would at last see no alternative to a comprehensive and brutal crackdown.

Yet, the question still remains: Why did the Kremlin tolerate such an extraordinary display of pluralism for a year and a half? What kind of Leninist leadership would hesitate for so long to protect the Soviet empire from such a fundamental challenge to its existence? Indeed, did Moscow seek only to intimidate Poland by completing all preparations for intervention in December 1980 and again in March 1981, or did the preparations for, and subsequent cancellations of, military action indicate vacillation and drift, an inability to take a decisive step?

In my opinion, there is no question but that all Soviet leaders knew what they wanted. In one way or another, they were determined that Poland must remain in the fold. But for well over a year they could not decide how to achieve that goal, primarily because no Soviet leader wanted to be held responsible for the failure of either policy option: accepting the process of "socialist renewal" or ordering an end to it. Responsibility for a failed option would have spelled political defeat for its proponent, and hence no Soviet leader—and certainly none of the contenders for the top position—was willing to press for the adoption of a high-risk alternative. Put another way, an in-between policy of muddling through was a political imperative dictated by political ambitions permeating the intrigue-filled atmosphere of the Kremlin at that time.

Therefore, it is as misleading to assign "prudence" to the Soviet leaders for having waited as long as they did as it is to shout "deception" every time they appear to have emitted confusing signals. Given Brezhnev's incapacitating illnesses, the by then irregular participation of Mikhail Suslov (de facto "second" secretary of the CPSU Central Committee and East European troubleshooter), in the decision-making process, and the intense struggle for succession under way, any but the most cautious or circumspect policy in Eastern Europe was politically unpalatable. Indeed, the ultimate decision to instigate an internal coup that would reestablish communist authority was adopted precisely because it entailed fewer risks than the alternative of direct Soviet military intervention. More important, the fact that such an internal coup was not attempted earlier must be understood as a symptom of Soviet immobility, which, in turn, exacerbated divisions within the Polish party and generated false hopes among the Polish people as well.

## Conclusions

As far as the Soviet Union and its reluctant East European allies are concerned, there is something to be said for the old aphorism that "the foreign policy of large countries is a function of domestic political conditions, and the foreign policy of small countries is a function of external conditions." To the extent that this is a valid observation, it should be stressed that neither regime nor popular defiance and assertiveness in Eastern Europe vis-à-vis the Soviet Union has ever been *caused* by immobility in the Kremlin. Rather, they are due to repression, the gap between economic promise and performance, and the absence of autonomy. These deep-rooted, substantive, and systemic causes of pervasive discontent and defiance generate *crises* mainly when East Europeans sense division and drift in Moscow; when they believe that they can get away with "more"—usually more independence—than they might be able to do when the Soviet leadership appears less preoccupied with the struggle for power. In short, Kremlin turbulence does not create crises in Eastern Europe, it turns inherent tension into explicit regime demands or popular explosions.

Even with Mikhail Gorbachëv at the helm, it is quite likely that the GDR, Hungary, Romania, and possibly Poland, acting alone or together, may succeed in obtaining more "elbow room" from the Kremlin and move inch by inch toward the West. That expectation is based on two assumptions. One is that Gorbachëv *will not* be an unchallengeable leader in the near future—with authority comparable to Khrushchev's between 1957 and 1964 or to Brezhnev's between 1969 and 1979—who could properly calibrate the Kremlin's East European policy. The other assumption is that at least some of the East European leaders seeking more "elbow room" *will* have sufficient authority, experience, and finesse to calibrate the processes of change in their own countries; and that they will not allow popular sentiments to push them beyond the limits of Soviet tolerance. Even if these assumptions, and the forecast of gradual "Europeanization" based on them, turn out to be accurate, it remains wishful thinking to anticipate the "collapse" of the Soviet empire in Eastern Europe. Diversity is not independence; tolerance is not liberty. While Soviet–East European relations are almost certainly entering a new phase, and one or more mini-coalitions are posing a very serious challenge to Moscow's concept of bloc cohesion, the empire, though rather unwell, is still alive.

## Notes

[1]For the improvement in Sino–Soviet relations, see *The New York Times*, December 30, 1984. On January 20, 1985, Xinhua reported the departure of a high-level Chinese trade delegation to Czechoslovakia, Hungary, and Poland to sign economic agreements with those states (see Foreign Broadcast Information Service, *Daily Report: China* [Washington, D.C.], January 23, 1985, p. H/2).

[2]Even that most loyal ally of the USSR, the Czechoslovak government, appeared less than eager to receive Soviet missiles in retaliation for the INF deployments [see RFE–RL, *Radio Free Europe Research* (Munich—hereafter *RFE Research*), December 23, 1983, Czechoslovak Situation Report 21/83].

[3]See Michael Marrese and Jan Vanous, *Implicit Subsidies and Non-Market Benefits in Soviet Trade with Eastern Europe* (Berkeley: University of California Press, 1982). More recent information is derived from periodic reports by Wharton Econometrics, Washington, D.C. See also Charles Wolf, Jr., *et al.*, *The Costs of the Soviet Empire* (R3073-1-NA, Santa Monica, Calif.: The Rand Corporation, 1983).

[4]For an excellent analysis of Soviet–East European economic relations, see Paul Marer, "The Political Economy of Soviet Relations with Eastern Europe," in *Soviet Policy in Eastern Europe*, ed. Sarah M. Terry (New Haven and London: Yale University Press, 1984), pp. 155–188; Marer (p. 179) speaks of a "net cumulative subsidy of about $14 billion" in 1971–1978.

[5]*Magyarország* (Budapest), July 31, 1983. The figure for 1984 is the author's rough estimate.

[6]John P. Hardt, "Soviet Energy Policy in Eastern Europe," in Terry, *op. cit.*, pp. 210–212.

[7]For an up-to-date discussion of East European expectations vis-à-vis the Soviet Union, see F. Stephen Larrabee, *Challenge to Soviet Interests in Eastern Europe: Romania, Hungary, and East Germany* (RAND, forthcoming).

[8]Charles Gati, "East Europe's Communists Are Tugging at Russia's Leash," *The Washington Post*, Outlook Section, July 8, 1984. Ronald D. Asmus has written several perceptive reports on the subject, including "Moscow's Campaign against East-West German Relations," *RFE Research*, August 29, 1984, RAD Background Report no. 160.

[9]Moscow initiated the campaign in late spring 1984, accusing the Bonn government of seeking to revise Europe's postwar borders and of trying to "erode the socialist system in the GDR." For particularly salient examples, see *Pravda* (Moscow), July 27 and August 2, 1984, and *Izvestiya* (Moscow), August 11, 1984.

[10]*RFE Research*, April 30, 1984, RAD Background Report no. 68.

[11]For a survey of the dispute between East Berlin and Moscow over relations with Bonn, see *RFE Research*, August 31, 1984, RAD Background Report no. 158.

[12]On July 26, 1984, the GDR reached a US$330 million (950,000,000 Deutsche Mark) credit agreement with the FRG (see Foreign Broadcast Information Service, *Daily Report: Eastern Europe* [Washington, D.C.—hereafter *FBIS-EEU*), July 26, 1984, p. E/1).

[13]Pedro Ramet, "Church and Peace in the GDR," *Problems of Communism* (Washington, D.C.) (July–August 1984), pp. 44–57; also Ronald D. Asmus, "Is There a Peace Movement in the GDR?" *Orbis* (Philadelphia) (Summer 1983), pp. 301–341.

[14]Lev Bezymenskiy, "In the Shadow of American Missiles," *Pravda*, July 27, 1983; and "On the Wrong Track," *ibid.*, August 2, 1984.

[15]See Ronald D. Asmus, "A Postmortem on Honecker's Visit," *RFE Research*, October 17, 1984, RAD Background Report no. 191.

[16]*FBIS-EEU*, August 24, 1984, pp. H/3–6. En route to Romania, Honecker sent a telegram of greetings to Gustav Husák while flying over Czechoslovak territory (*ibid.*, August 22, 1984, p. D/6).

[17]Mátyás Szürös, "The Reciprocal Effect of the National and the International in the Development of Socialism in Hungary," *Társadalmi Szemle* (Budapest) (January 1984), pp. 13–21.

[18]Michael Stefanak and Ivan Hlivka, "The National and the International in the Policy of the KSC," *Rudé Právo* (Prague), March 30, 1984; "On the National and the International," *Novoye Vremya* (Moscow), no. 16, April 1984.

[19]*Magyar Hirlap* (Budapest), April 4, 1984.

[20]*Neues Deutschland*, April 12, 1984.

[21]See Tibor Thurzó, "GDR Diplomacy: A Sense of Responsibility and Activity," *Népszava* (Budapest), July 26, 1984; and Jenö Bocskor, "East German Foreign Relations: a Multilateral Dialogue," *Magyarország*, August 5, 1984.

[22]On the relationship between Hungarian domestic policies and pressures for increased contacts with the West, see Rudolf L. Tökés, "Hungarian Reform Imperatives," *Problems of Communism* (September–October 1984), pp. 1–23.

[23]For an analysis of the cancellation of the Honecker and Zhivkov visits, see *RFE Research*, October 19, 1984, RAD Background Report no. 189.

[24]For an evaluation of Ceauşescu's recent leadership, see Trond Gilberg, "Romania's Growing Difficulties," *Current History* (Philadelphia) (November 1984), pp. 375–389.

[25]While Czechoslovak official statements echo the Soviet position, Bulgarian statements are more circumspect. For example, during the Sofia celebrations marking the fortieth anniversary of socialist Bulgaria's founding, Mikhail Gorbachëv, the leader of the Soviet delegation spoke of West German "revanchism"; Zhivkov avoided any such references and repeated his suggestion to turn the "Balkan Peninsula into a zone free from nuclear weapons." *RFE Research*, October 5, 1985, Bulgarian Situation Report 12/84.

[26]See *RFE Research*, June 15, 1984, August 31, 1984. October 19, 1984, RAD Background Report nos. 94, 95, 155, and 189. More recently, these countries appeared to differ with Moscow over the terms for renewing the Warsaw pact treaty (see *The New York Times*, March 7, 1985).

[27]See Charles Gati, "The 'Europeanization' of Communism?" *Foreign Affairs* (New York) (April 1977), pp. 539–553.

[28]J. F. Brown, *Relations between the Soviet Union and Its East European Allies: A Survey* (Santa Monica, Calif.: The Rand Corporation, 1975).

[29]Of the vast literature on Soviet politics in the mid-1950s, the East European connection is explored most usefully in Veljko Mičunovič, *Moscow Diary* (Garden City, N.Y.: Doubleday, 1980), and in Strobe Talbot, trans. and ed., *Khrushchev Remembers* (Boston: Little, Brown & Co., 1970).

[30]For two excellent books on Poland and Hungary in 1956, see Flora Lewis, *A Case History of Hope* (Garden City, N.Y.: Doubleday, 1958); and Ferenc A. Vali, *Rift and Revolt in Hungary* (Cambridge, Mass.: Harvard University Press, 1961).

[31]Zbigniew Brzezinski, *The Soviet Bloc: Unity and Conflict* (Cambridge, Mass.: Harvard University Press, 1967).

[32]See, for example, Michel Tatu, *Power in the Kremlin: From Khrushchev to Kosygin* (New York: Viking, 1969).

[33]On the mid-1960s Soviet economic reform debates, see Fyodor I. Kushnirsky, "The Limits of Soviet Economic Reform," *Problems of Communism* (July–August 1984), pp. 33–43.

[34]See Zdeněk Mlynář's, *Nightfrost in Prague* (New York: Karz Publishers, 1980); and for a systematic treatment of differing Soviet positions concerning Czechoslovakia, see Jiri Valenta, *Soviet Intervention in Czechoslovakia, 1968: Anatomy of a Decision* (Baltimore and London: Johns Hopkins University Press, 1979).

[35]See, for example, "Hungary's Hope for Continuity," *Neue Zürcher Zeitung*, February 29, 1984; and *RFE Research*, December 8, 1982, Romanian Situation Report 21/82.

[36]Both before and after the December 1981 "crackdown," Soviet treatment of Poland was marked by a good deal of vacillation and apparently confusing signals. For an early analysis of Soviet options and immobilism, see Charles Gati, "Polish Futures, Western Options," *Foreign Affairs* (Winter 1982/83), pp. 292–308. The release of Lech Wałęsa from house arrest in November 1982, less than 24 hours after Brezhnev's death, prompted Warsaw wits to make up the following story: Andropov, the new Kremlin chief, calls Jaruzelski: "On whose authority did you release Wałęsa?" Jaruzelski: "I'd discussed the matter with Comrade Brezhnev." Andropov: "And what did our beloved Leonid Il'ich tell you?" Jaruzelski: "He said and I quote: 'You may release that no good Pole only over my dead body.'" More recently, the public trial of four security police officers charged with the Rev. Jerzy Popieluszko's murder was also seen in

Poland as a function of General Jaruzelski's ability "to take advantage of what many believe to be disarray in the Kremlin as a result of a struggle to succeed Konstantin U. Chernenko as the Soviet leader" (*The New York Times*, February 9, 1985). That at least *some* Soviet leaders disapproved of such a public trial was indicated by a TASS report, which identified the four security police officers only as "four citizens" who "attributed their act" to their desire to prevent Father Popieluszko from pursuing "activities harmful to the state" (*ibid*).

# VII
## The Far East

# 33 JOHN J. STEPHAN

## *Asia in the Soviet Conception**

As an approach to understanding Soviet perspectives on Asia, this chapter proposes to: (1) identify the salient geographic and historic factors shaping Russian and Soviet attitudes toward Asia, (2) assess the changing role of Asia in Moscow's global priorities, (3) examine Soviet perceptions of current trends, and (4) suggest some of the opportunities that might attract Soviet initiatives in the region.

The escalation of Soviet activities in Asia in general and in Afghanistan in particular has prompted widespread commentary. A good deal of this commentary is oversimplified, creating a misleading impression of certitude that such a complex and elusive subject does not possess. A few cautionary remarks are therefore in order.

Ascertaining Soviet perceptions of Asia is a chastening exercise for anyone seeking to go beyond superficial generalizations. Any expectations of uncovering a coherent conception, let alone a blueprint for action, quickly founder on the shoals of inaccessible data and contradictory evidence. To be sure, one can impose a spurious logic on the subject by taking Moscow's public pronouncements at face value. This approach has the disadvantage of overlooking what a prominent Soviet commentator candidly acknowledged: that expressions of policy can conceal as well as reflect real interests and intentions.[1] Moreover, recent studies have suggested that international affairs and area specialists in the USSR since the early 1960s relied less on ideology as a guide to analysis.[2] Conversely, one can discount Marxism–Leninism as rhetoric and instead explain Soviet perceptions under the rubric of Russian nationalism, geopolitics, group psychology, or some combination thereof. Yet as Alexander Dallin warns, ignoring the role of Marxism–Leninism in shaping Soviet views is as dangerous as overemphasizing its importance.[3]

*Reprinted by permission of the author and publisher from Donald S. Zagoria, ed., *Soviet Policy in Asia* (New Haven: Yale University Press, 1982), pp. 29–56. Copyright 1982 by Council on Foreign Relations, Inc.

At a minimum, Marxism–Leninism molds Soviet perceptions of Asia by providing the conceptual categories and vocabulary with which these perceptions are expressed. To be sure, Marxism–Leninism is consciously wielded as a supple forensic instrument to legitimize Soviet interests in Asia, justify the behavior of allies, appeal to Third World nations, identify "reactionary" and "progressive" elements within capitalist countries, discredit the policies of rivals, and project an image of the USSR being in the vanguard of irresistible historical forces. At the same time, Marxism–Leninism deeply influences patterns of conceptualization and analysis, as can be seen in a widespread tendency of Soviet commentators (privately as well as publicly) to adopt holistic approaches to problems and to explain trends in terms of dialectical processes. The interaction of ideology as a conscious tool and ideology as an unconscious prism is a subtle one that invests Soviet views with an irreducible kernel of ambiguity. This ambiguity is compounded by deceptive appearances. Although wrapped in Marxist–Leninist trappings, some views of Asia in fact antedate the October Revolution. Other views are of recent origin, despite their being depicted as having deep roots in Russia's past.

Another obstacle to generalization is the heterogeneity inherent in the terms *Asia* and *Soviet*. Asia encompasses a kaleidoscopic range of nations and cultures, a range only marginally reduced in this chapter by focusing the inquiry on East and Southeast Asia. Sophisticated Soviet observers know that Asia has no cultural, economic, political, or ideological coherence. Consequently, there is no Soviet view of "Asia" except at the level of rudimentary slogans and stereotypes. Rather, there is a multiplicity of views on individual Asian countries or on subregions within Asia.

Asia's diversity is matched by that of the USSR. It would be misleading to assume that Soviet views are unified or even consistent. Displays of monolithic solidarity at party congresses and habitual use of the first person plural by Soviet spokesmen should not lead one to conclude that there are identical views on Asia within the party or government. If a wider sampling of Soviet society is considered, regional, ethnic, educational, and occupational factors enhance the variety of concepts of Asia.

Finally, the manner in which Soviet perspectives on Asia bear upon foreign policy can only be impressionistically inferred from fragmentary evidence. A considerable number of professional specialists on East and Southeast Asia conduct research at institutes in Moscow and on a smaller scale in Leningrad, Novosibirsk, and Vladivostok. Some of these institutes are heavily engaged in providing background studies for party and government organs. The Institute of World Economy and International Relations is said to maintain especially close ties with the party *apparat*. The Institute of the Far East reportedly has a similar relationship with the Foreign Ministry. The Foreign Ministry, in turn, has its own research and training programs on Asia in the Institute of International Relations. Asian specialists attached to the Institute of the USA and Canada are tapped by party and government alike for their expertise. The formal administrative structure of these institutions is often transcended by personal friendships and unofficial bureaucratic alliances.

The direct influence of Asian experts on policy formulation is probably marginal although one senior Soviet analyst privately opined that it was growing. Sinologist Mikhail Kapitsa is said to have made significant inputs within the Foreign Ministry at certain junctures. Ivan Kovalenko, a section chief in the party's International Department, has been identified as the "commander-in-chief" of the USSR's Japan policy.[4] Kovalenko does publish articles on Japan and China in *Pravda* and in professional journals under the penname I. I. Ivkov. "Ivkov's" pronouncements are said to carry weight because they allegedly represent the views of the Politburo. But it remains an open question to what extent Kovalenko influences, as opposed to reflects, leadership thinking on Asia.

Geographic and Historic Influences

Geography has exerted a pervasive influence on Russian and Soviet perceptions of Asia. Russia and Asia are not contiguous, as the term *Sino–Russian frontier* implies, but overlap spatially and ethnically. Three-quarters of the Soviet Union lies in Asia. One-third of Asia lies within the USSR. Eighty million people (approximately 30% of the Soviet population) live in Asiatic regions of the USSR. Fifty million Soviet citizens (about 20% of the population) are of Asian nationalities.

Asia's spatial interpenetration with the Soviet Union is symbolized by the vast Eurasian plain, which stretches from the Urals to Mongolia. In the absence of major barriers, waves of migrations have moved across the plain for centuries, displacing or absorbing earlier inhabitants. The Russians are but the most recent wave. An awareness of the plain's historic permeability and ethnic evanescence leaves many Russians with a half-formed sense of territorial insecurity that manifests itself not only in the predilection for strong central authority but in what amounts to a national fixation on frontier defense.[5]

The search for natural frontiers, for security, helped propel Russians across Siberia and Central Asia.[6] A similar admixture of anxiety and will to power underlie what Chinese, Japanese, and American observers perceive as Soviet expansionist pressures in Asia and the Pacific today. A metaphorical Eurasian plain with attendant insecurities and outward impulses is still very much alive. Moreover, with the maritime deployment of strategic weapons, the "plain" now extends well into the Indian and Pacific oceans.[7]

History has also left a deep imprint upon Russian views of Asia, particularly selected historical episodes that the regime uses to mobilize and channel public consciousness. Images of the Mongol conquest ("the most traumatic historical experience of the Russian people")[8] are triggered by shrewdly worded propaganda about the territorial appetites of "Great Han chauvinism." Japanese claims in the Kurile Islands are portrayed as following a tradition of predatory designs on the Russian Far East from the Siberian Intervention (1918–1922) to the miniwars around the Manchurian perimeter in 1937–1939. Ominous motives are ascribed to nineteenth-century American commercial interests in the Amur region, to American involvement in the Siberian Intervention, and to Washington's wartime plans to occupy the Kurile Islands. Ubiquitously present in school curricula, books, and museums, these tinted images of the past pervade the Soviet environment and shape the collective historical consciousness.

The cumulative weight of geography and history manifests itself both implicitly and explicitly in Soviet articulations about Asia. First, there is an acute sense of geopolitical vulnerability. It is not uncommon to hear the opinion voiced that the USSR must cope with NATO in the west, China in the south, Japan in the east, and American strategic forces all around. Moreover, there is concern about the tenuous logistical position of the Soviet Far East, connected to European Russia only by the Trans-Siberian Railroad (to be supplemented on its eastern portion by the Baikal–Amur Mainline Railroad [BAM]), air, and circuitous sea routes via the Indian and Arctic oceans. Conversely, it is felt that the United States enjoys the twin advantages of comparatively friendly neighbors along its land frontiers and unimpeded access to the world's oceans.

That spokesmen of the world's largest state profess to feel hemmed in may sound implausible to outside observers. To be sure, Soviet negotiators do wield the notion of geopolitical vulnerability when bargaining with Washington for a margin of strategic advantage vis-à-vis the United States. Nevertheless, there is a real if unstable nexus of anxieties (vestigial fears of "captialist encirclement," insecurity about the USSR's great power status) that tempt Soviet leaders to place emphasis on military power to achieve political goals. The incursion into Afghanistan, which from a Western perspective was an act of unprovoked aggression forming part of a geopolitical strategy aimed at the middle East and Southwest Asia, through Soviet eyes was a response to dangers as well as a probing for opportunities. In Moscow's view, developments in Afghanistan did offer a chance to improve the Soviet position along a portion of its perimeter near the Persian Gulf. But it was also felt that events in Afghanistan in 1979 threatened Soviet credibility globally by jeopardizing the "irreversible" gains of Kabul's 1978 Marxist "revolution."

Second, Soviet views of Asia frequently reflect what a Moscow academic called a "1941 complex": a tendency to see collusion among the USSR's neighbors. The 1941 complex is rooted in events of the 1930s that culminated in Hitler's invasion of the USSR in 1941. Accordingly, Washington is suspected of trying (at its own peril) to use China against the USSR much as Britain and France tried (to their peril) in the 1930s to maneuver Hitler eastward. In the words of Vladivostok analyst Boris N. Slavinsky:

How much our situation today is like that of the 1930's when the western powers armed fascist Germany, trying to push her against the USSR. But, as is well known, Hitler first attacked them! A similar situation could well arise—this time in the Far East—given Peking's geopolitical concepts and expansionist aspirations.[9]

Soviet propagandists exploit the 1941 complex to mobilize popular feelings within the USSR. For example, use of the term *axis* to describe the new relationship among Washington, Beijing, and Tokyo is calculated to evoke images of World War II, which remain very vivid in the general populace. One commentator, in a tactic redolent of the late Senator Joseph McCarthy, portrayed recent contacts between Bonn and Beijing as the work of Nazis among the China specialists within the German Foreign Office.[10]

Third, Soviet attitudes toward Asia betray a craving for status that can be traced to a traditional Russian attachment to rank. Although the original Latin and Manchu documents of the Treaty of Nerchinsk (1689) listed the Chinese (Manchu) emperor before the czar, Peter the Great subsequently reversed the order.[11] A desire to maintain rank among Asian states such as Persia and China is said to have been a stimulus to Russia's late-nineteenth-century reforms.[12] Today, the USSR wants to be treated with the respect it feels it deserves not only as a superpower but as a country with a historically great position in Asia, a position that civil war and revolution eroded but that is now being reclaimed. As an official privately remarked at a recent conference in Khabarovsk: "We are only trying to reestablish our rightful historical interests in Asia and the Pacific." "Rightful historical interests" tend to be equated with the maximum scope of Imperial Russia's interest in any given region—except perhaps Alaska.

The United States plays a special role in the Soviet Union's quest for status in Asia. The United States is expected to deal with the Soviet Union as an equal, to accept the Soviet Union as a major presence with legitimate interests throughout Asia and the Pacific, to include the Soviet Union in regional organizations, and to give priority to relations with Moscow over those with Beijing. Sino–American normalization disturbed Moscow not only because of its geopolitical implications but because by occurring without a corresponding improvement in Soviet–American ties, it suggested that Washington does not give highest priority to relations with the USSR. As Soviet leaders and commentators sense that the USSR is ever closer to realizing its status aspirations in Asia and the Pacific, they increasingly resent any open demonstrations of American superiority. The U.S. mining of Haiphong and bombing of Soviet ships in the harbor still rankle, not so much because of the physical damage sustained but because Moscow suffered a humiliating reminder that the Soviet Union, with all its claims to superpower status, was helpless to deter this naked display of American force. As one Soviet official told the author in 1980: "You'll never be able to do that to us again!" In a broader context a young Soviet diplomat distilled this sense of status restiveness in a remark dropped during a lecture to an American audience on Soviet policy in Asia and the Pacific: "You like being number one, but we are tired of being number two."

Fourth, Soviet views on Asia often exude a half-articulated but one suspects deeply felt expectation of gratitude. To some extent this expectation derives from an unquestioned conviction that the Soviet Union, as heir to the world's first socialist revolution, has borne a major responsibility for the growth and defense of a "socialist community." Analogous feelings can be found among prerevolutionary authors who claimed that Russia deserved Europe's gratitude for having held back the destructive forces of Asia before 1600, thereby ensuring Europe's eventual rise to global preeminence.[13] At present the roles of Europe and Asia are blurred and the ideological content has changed, but a consciousness of selflessness and sacrifice persists. Moscow regularly extols itself for contributions to the struggles of Asian peoples against European and American "imperialism" and "colonialism," Japanese "militarism," and Chinese "expansionism." The achievement of Mongolian "independence" in 1921, the defeat of Japan in 1945, the triumph of the Chinese communists in 1949, the survival of North Korea in 1950–1953, and the unification of Vietnam in 1975 were all supposedly made possible by Soviet power. Yet one can hear only in Ulan Bator and Hanoi expressions of that gratitude that Moscow seeks to sustain its self-image. Beijing has, in Soviet eyes, added insult to injury by not only showing ingratitude for years of assistance but by "slandering" its benefactor. To make up for the shortage of genuine appreciation of perceived Soviet services to Asia, propagandists have assiduously collected and disseminated pro-Soviet testimonials from prominent Asians, including Mao Zedong.[14]

Finally, history and geography have left Russians with ambivalent feelings about their identity vis-à-vis Europe and Asia. Until 1917 Asia to Russians represented variously a source of terror, an exotic subject of romantic speculations, and an object of imperialist idealism. Throughout 1000 years of vicissitudinous relations, there ran a sense of apartness from Asia, notwithstanding the geographic "Asianness" of much of Russia's territory after 1600. But if Russians did not identify themselves with Asians, they also did not fully assimilate European culture. The result was an uneasy suspension between East and West that led Russians, as Dostoyevsky noted, to be regarded as Europeans in Asia and as Asiatics in Europe.[15]

Following the October Revolution, Russian self-images with respect to Asia underwent a significant change. Lenin set about linking the Bolshevik revolutionary mission with anti-imperialist struggles in Asia and wooing Asian nationalities within the fledgling Soviet state. Russians were subsumed with Slavic and non-Slavic minorities into the "Soviet people," who were supposed to possess special qualifications for assisting in the liberation of all Asians.

Moscow has tried in various ways to capitalize on the USSR's self-image as a "Eurasian state."[16] Judicious use has been made of Soviet Asians in dealing with Asian countries.[17] Toasting a visiting Japanese foreign minister in 1941, Stalin proclaimed: "You are an Asiatic, so am I."[18] At international conferences throughout Asia, Soviet delegates of unmistakably Russian ethnicity have been overheard stressing that the USSR is an Asian country. Such expressions of solidarity notwithstanding, it is doubtful that the Russian people as a whole (particularly those subject to the current pull of Russian nationalism) feel ethnically or ideologically close to Asia.

Considerable commentary exists about Russian "gut" feelings toward Asians in general and toward the Chinese in particular. This commentary should be treated with caution, based as it is upon limited and not always reliable evidence. Even knowledgeable observers have fallen into the habit of overgeneralizing, asserting variously that Russian racial feeling against Asians is "strong and widespread"[19] or that Russians are virtually immune from racial prejudice.[20]

Some of the ambiguity inherent in Russian attitudes toward Asia is evident in Russian attitudes toward the USSR's own Asian nationalities, especially those in the Central Asian union republics. On one hand, there is pride in the material advances of these nationalities under socialism. On the other hand, these advances have promoted above-average population growth that portends to alter the ethnic composition of the Red Army and the industrial labor force. Although Russians can take satisfaction in the hostility with which Central Asian Muslims view China (a hostility with deep historical roots), the Islamic revival sweeping the Middle East and Soviet military intervention in Afghanistan raise the specter of an intensification of ethnic consciousness among Muslim intellectuals whose resistance to Russian influence has been greater than any other part of the native population of Central Asia.[21]

Russians, in sum, have complex, ambivalent feelings about Asia and Asians, feelings that are expressed variously under different conditions. Essentially, Soviet images of Asia are inextricably bound up with self-images. Asia is simultaneously part of the USSR and an alien entity. Feelings of propinquity and distance, familiarity and exoticism, affinity and repulsion all appear to be widespread, and may even coexist within the same individual.

Asia in Soviet Priorities   Today, Asia occupies a more important position among Moscow's global priorities than it has at any time in the past. This has occurred in part as a result of the development of Siberia, the Soviet Far East, and Soviet Central Asia. In part, Asia's new significance is a consequence of proliferating strategic, political, and economic linkages within and outside the region, linkages that complicate the USSR's task of defending its national security and that challenge the USSR's self-image as the leader of the "socialist community."

Asia traditionally ranked low in the hierarchy of Russian foreign policy priorities. True, the Mongols preempted attention in medieval Kiev and Muscovy but from the sixteenth century the Asian threat receded behind successive waves of Russian eastward and southward expansion. Europe has consistently been accorded the highest military, political, and economic priority in Russian policies, a priority reinforced repeatedly over the last four centuries by challenges from Poland, Sweden, France, and Germany.

To say that Asia occupied an ancillary position in St. Petersburg's priorities should not obscure the integration of Asian with global policies during the last half of the nineteenth century. The stirrings of this integration occurred during the Crimean War, which opened Russian eyes to the vulnerability of Siberia's Pacific littoral to British and French naval forays. Acquisition of the Amur and Maritime regions from China in the treaties of Aigun (1858) and Beijing (1860), followed by conquests in Central Asia in the 1860s and 1870s, dramatically enhanced Russia's presence in Asia and led to a global rivalry with Great Britain in which Asian issues played a conspicuous role.

Since 1917, Soviet leaders have consistently fit Asia into their conceptions of global objectives. The priority assigned to Asia has varied in accordance with policy adjustments designed to promote national interests within a changing international environment. Lenin saw Asia as the "weakest link" of imperialism and sought to utilize the revolutionary struggle of Asian anticolonial and anti-imperialist movements to promote the international goals of Soviet communism. Security considerations, notably Japan's continental expansion and the rise of Hitler, led Stalin to approach Asia within the context of power politics. Stalin's detachment from most of the Chinese communist leaders, his military aid to Jiang Jieshi (Chiang Kai-shek), and his accommodation with Japan in 1941 bespoke a *Realpolitik* in which survival was the highest priority. In the short term Germany's invasion of the USSR and Japan's advance into Southeast Asia in 1941 reduced the perceived importance of Asia to Soviet security. But in the longer run World War II enhanced Asia's significance in Moscow's eyes. The wartime relocation of industries to Siberia, the invasion and occupation of Manchuria and northern Korea, and the acquisition of southern Sakhalin and the Kurile Islands all gave the Soviet Union a significantly greater stake in Northeast Asia by 1945. Subsequent developments (Soviet–American estrangement, the Chinese communist triumph, the Korean War) reinforced Asia's strategic importance for the USSR. By the time of Stalin's death in 1953, his heirs faced a more formidable challenge in Northeast Asia than ever posed by Imperial Japan. The American forces based along an arc from Hokkaido to Taiwan formed part of a Eurasian network that nearly girdled the USSR. Asia consequently became more closely linked to Europe as a security problem; nevertheless, it still did not rank with Europe as a security priority.

Although Stalin appreciated Asia's strategic significance, he showed less interest in Asian nationalist movements. The triumph of the Chinese communists in 1949 failed to trigger a recrudescence of Leninist support for Asian anticolonial movements. On the contrary a rigid "two camps" doctrine announced in 1947 by Andrei Zhdanov inhibited Moscow from exploiting some of the most powerful political currents gathering momentum in South and Southeast Asia in the decade after World War II.

By revising the two-camps doctrine at the Twentieth Party Congress in 1956, Nikita Khrushchev prepared the theoretical groundwork for courting Third World countries that had bourgeois–nationalist regimes.

Designed to tilt the global balance of forces in favor of "socialism" by allying the Third World to the "socialist camp," Khrushchev's initiative had the effect of promoting Asia among Soviet global priorities in two ways, one of them unintended. First, Moscow began paying more attention to South and Southeast Asia, with gratifying results in India and (for a while) in Indonesia. Second, this doctrinal departure accelerated China's evolution from a regional ally into a global adversary.

Asia's new importance derives, in the words of one Soviet analyst, from its postwar emergence as an "active participant in a new international–political system" whereas Asia had previously been "an object of imperialist policies."[22] Asia has also become more important in Moscow's eyes as a result of a geographical extension of Soviet power and stakes. Moscow is now deeply interested in the whole region, not merely in those areas adjacent to the USSR's frontiers. Moreover, Soviet analysts see Asia as an area fraught with tension. In the words of E. M. Primakov, director of the Institute of Oriental Studies, Asia has become "the most dangerous zone of the development of global contradictions."[23] Dmitrii V. Petrov, a leading Japan specialist, identified those "contradictions" that arouse particular concern:

> In Asia are interwoven the most important contradictions of our time: between the two main social systems, between imperialist states, between industrialized and developing countries. Asia is a region of incessant territorial disputes and border collisions. National discord and social conflict are especially intense here.[24]

Also compelling in raising Asia's weight in the Kremlin's priorities has been the proliferation of what are seen as linkages within and outside Asia. The most disturbing of these new linkages has been Sino–American and Sino–Japanese normalization, which to many Soviet observers is a step toward a Sino–Japanese–American entente held together by common designs against the USSR.[25] Ties between Japan and Europe, and between China and Europe, add more strands to a worrisome network. At the same time, Moscow perceives linkages that could offer the USSR opportunities to exploit friction among its adversaries. Soviet observers have been quick to catch the potential strains that the Iranian and Afghan crises could put on U.S.–Japanese and U.S.–NATO relations.

The manner in which the USSR ascribes new significance to Asia can be inferred by identifying the Asian component at each level of a hypothetical hierarchy of Soviet global priorities.

Dealing with perceived threats to national security posed by strategic nuclear weapons ranks as the highest Soviet military and diplomatic priority. At present only the United States has the capacity to mount an immediate strategic challenge. Despite its nuclear arsenal China is not commonly regarded as an immediate strategic threat, but some Soviet observers concede that it could eventually become one with technical assistance from the United States, Japan, and Western Europe. Japan, by virtue of its industrial base and high level of technology, also is seen as possessing the potential to produce and launch nuclear warheads deep into the USSR.

Real and anticipated American deployment of strategic ballistic weapons in the Pacific and Indian oceans promotes Asia's significance at this highest level of national priorities. Trident II is seen as threatening not only the Far East and Central Asia but all of Siberia and portions of European Russia. Conversely, the Soviet deployment of 30% of the country's ICBMs along the Trans-Siberian Railroad and one-third of the navy in the Pacific, together with the reported use of the Sea of Okhotsk as an enclave for SS-N-18 missiles capable of reaching most of the continental United States, suggests that greater strategic importance is being attached to Asia and its adjacent oceans.[26]

At a second level of priorities Moscow seeks to project its power and influence abroad by a combination of political, military, and economic means, exercised directly or through satellites and allies. In this context Asia also commands demonstratively more importance today than at any time in the past, thanks largely to the People's Republic of China.

China is the first Asian country to challenge the USSR politically on a global level. Soviet media depict Beijing's Maoist leaders as relentless disrupters of international peace, craving hegemony in Southeast Asia, pushing the United States into nuclear war with the USSR, attempting to poison relations between the USSR and its allies, and systematically undercutting Soviet policies throughout the world in league with imperialists, revanchists, fascists, racists, and Zionists. The intensity of Soviet rhetoric about China to some extent derives from ideological considerations, but within the cloud of hyperbole are suspended particles of genuine anxiety about Beijing's new relationships with the Soviet Union's major rivals. Moscow suspects that China's "reckless" anti-Sovietism could be given teeth by economic, technical, and military assistance from the United States, Japan, and Western Europe. In addition Beijing's strident warnings about Soviet "hegemonistic" aspirations are perceived in Moscow as providing ammunition in Washington, Tokyo, and European capitals that seek to undermine détente, rearm Japan, and strengthen NATO.[27]

From published sources alone it is easy to get the impression that Beijing so preoccupies Soviet leaders that Moscow's highest political priority in Asia must be to contain China. Yet in private, Soviet analysts assert that China is too weak to pose, alone, a credible threat to the USSR's vital interests. These analysts concede that China is a global irritant but they maintain that Beijing can confront the USSR with a serious challenge only if modernized and armed by the West. That Washington can to a great extent determine Beijing's ability to threaten Soviet interests reinforces on a regional basis what every Russian observer already knows in a global context: that the United States ultimately commands the highest political as well as strategic priority. One specialist went so far as to assert (in private) that if the two superpowers could only resolve their outstanding differences, all would be well—a polite way of signaling that the United States still remains the USSR's main competitor in Asia.

Asia probably plays a bigger rather than a smaller role in Soviet–American competition since the United States withdrew from Indochina. In Moscow's view the United States is trying to compensate for its setbacks in Vietnam and Iran by making a dangerous commitment to counterrevolution in Southwest Asia, a commitment that conflicts directly with a growing Soviet conviction that the USSR has become the protector of "socialist" Afghanistan and "revolutionary" Iran. Moscow also sees a growing American presence in Southeast Asia in the form of more active overtures to ASEAN nations and a closer association with China's ambitions in the region. Washington's strengthened military alliance with Tokyo, its developing strategic partnership with Beijing, and its reaffirmed military presence in South Korea all impress Soviet observers as disturbing evidence of growing tension in Northeast Asia, where the USSR has vital stakes.

Greater Soviet–American tension from Afghanistan to Japan has enhanced Asia's priority relative to other parts of the world. The USSR has higher stakes in Europe but Soviet–American competition there has occurred within a less volatile environment, although recent events in Poland portend otherwise. Africa and Latin America may offer Moscow more opportunities to extend its influence at American expense but Soviet stakes are relatively lower in those regions than in Asia. Perhaps only the Middle East possesses an equivalent combination of tension, opportunities, and stakes.

Asia's higher position in Soviet priorities does not mean that Asia is perceived as a set of problems separate from other parts of the world. Soviet observers explain President Carter's reaction to events in Afghanistan, for example, as but one of a series of deliberate moves (deployment of Pershing missiles in NATO countries, connivance with congressional opponents of SALT II, flurry about the Soviet combat brigade in Cuba) all designed to gather political support from the "military–industrial complex" and its allies.

Japan's growing regional and global profile has also promoted the Asian component in Moscow's priorities. Soviet analysts appreciate the complex international implications of Japan's new economic stature, even as they tend to overdramatize the significance of Japan's increased defense expenditures. Japan's economic penetration of South Korea, Southeast Asia, and the United States, together with its reliance on Middle East oil, has evoked scenarios of Sino–Japanese and Japanese–American rivalry in which some Soviet commentators speculate (in private) on playing a "Japan card" vis-à-vis Washington and Beijing. On the other hand, there is a growing recognition that Moscow's own problems with Tokyo have acquired more than a bilateral significance. Official denials notwithstanding, Moscow knows that there *is* a territorial problem in Japan's claim to the southern Kurile Islands; moreover, Moscow knows that the impasse on this issue serves Chinese and American objectives insofar as it inhibits a Soviet–Japanese rapprochement.

Just as economic stature raises Tokyo in Soviet priorities, so do an ability and willingness to pursue a regional power role raise Vietnam's importance in the eyes of Soviet policymakers. Moscow now has a powerful ally in Southeast Asia that fulfills a double function of containing China and providing a base for projecting Soviet influence throughout the region. By expelling the United States from Indochina, replacing a pro-Beijing with a pro-Moscow regime in Cambodia, handling China's retaliatory incursion without invoking the recently signed defense treaty with the USSR, guiding Laos into the "socialist community," and offering Danang and Cam Ranh Bay facilities for Soviet air and naval forces, Hanoi has earned a key place in Soviet regional policy considerations. Moscow, to be sure, pays a price for Hanoi's services in terms of military and economic aid, diminished diplomatic maneuverability toward ASEAN nations, and—for a while—eroded influence in Pyongyang (which condemned Vietnam's invasion of Cambodia but remained silent on China's attack on Vietnam).

Moscow's policies toward Japan and Vietnam suggest, in different ways, that economic factors are growing but still remain subsidiary to political objectives. The USSR has a potentially major economic stake in Asia and the Pacific. There are Soviet officials, especially in Siberia and the Far East, who would like to see their country establish strong economic relationships with Asian and Pacific countries, including the United States. But Moscow planners have not yet seen fit to allow the Soviet Far East to assume more than a modest economic profile in the region. Despite impressive increases in percentage terms during the past 20 years, economic ties with Japan remain limited in terms of what one would expect from two major industrial neighbors with many complementary needs. Trade with other Asian countries collectively constitutes less than that between the USSR and Japan. Sino–Soviet commerce has turned upward after years of stagnation but in 1977 it still had not reached one-quarter of the 1960 volume. Political motivations play a key role in economic relations with Mongolia (a strategically located satellite), North Korea (a self-willed object of Beijing's competitive attentions), Vietnam (an important ally), and the ASEAN nations (where the USSR seeks to increase its own influence and reduce that of the United States, China, and Japan).

Moscow's revolutionary expectations for Asia do not loom so prominently as they did in the early 1920s but they have not been discarded. In general the USSR places a higher priority on maximizing Soviet influence with existing regimes and minimizing that of the United States and China. This does not prevent the Kremlin from assisting Hanoi to export a "revolution" to Cambodia or from "protecting a revolution" in Afghanistan when the risks are deemed affordable. It is even conceivable that under certain circumstances some Soviet strategists might be tempted to take a more direct part in promoting certain elements of the revolutionary situation in Iran, but the risks in provoking a strong Muslim, not to mention American, reaction would seem too formidable for this tactic for the time being. In Southeast Asia, Moscow knows that there is a direct relationship between Hanoi's behavior and ASEAN attitudes toward the USSR. Besides, the revolutionary movements in Thailand, Malaysia, and the Philippines have tended to look to Beijing for aid. Making a virtue out of necessity, Moscow portrays China as a subversive intruder nourishing insurrectionary elements in the region.

It does not appear that the USSR has immediate revolutionary expectations in Northeast Asia. Whatever Soviet publications might say about the late President Park's regime and whatever opportunities some strategists might perceive in recent political unrest in South Korea, Moscow has little desire for an upheaval on the Korean peninsula that could trigger a confrontation with the United States and catalyze Japanese rearmament. However, one specialist did hint privately in the wake of Afghanistan's military investment that any closer coordination of Sino–American strategic policies might oblige the USSR to "re-examine" its attitude toward Kim Il Sung, a euphemism for giving Kim more material and political support to implement his revolutionary mission in the south.

If revolutionary expectations do not figure prominently in Moscow's Asian priorities, a truly revolutionary development unforeseen by Lenin is obliging Soviet leaders to accord new weight to Asia: conflict among communist nations. The Sino–Soviet rift, together with recent hostilities between communist states in Southeast Asia (China and Vietnam, Vietnam and Cambodia) pose knotty political and ideological problems to the party. Ideologues have yet to find a solution to what in Marxist–Leninist theory is impossible. The Politburo's late spokesman on ideological matters, Mikhail Suslov, advanced a semantic solution to this paradox by asserting in 1979 that China is not a socialist state. Yet Leonid Brezhnev discussed China under the category "world socialist system" in the secretary general's report to the Twenty-Sixth Party Congress in February 1981.[28] Analysts privately venture that China is socialist insofar as the state owns and controls the means of production and distribution but that China's foreign policy is "antisocialist." Debates on this question are veiled from public view but they will probably continue for the foreseeable future.

## Asian Trends in the Soviet Perspective

As self-professed Marxists, Soviet spokesmen have little choice but to assert that the course of history is ineluctably moving their way even if it needs a Leninist nudge now and then. Pronouncements about the ascendancy of socialism and the crises of capitalism routinely crop up at party congresses and are ubiquitous features of Soviet publications. This global optimism is applied to Asia, producing regular enumerations of "socialist" gains and "imperialist" reverses in the region.[29]

Soviet observers publicly express satisfaction about recent trends in Asia, citing the following in particular. The United States has been expelled from Indochina, leaving a united Vietnam closely allied with Moscow. Pro-Soviet regimes have been installed in Laos and Cambodia. Political and economic ties with ASEAN nations have been established over the corpse of SEATO. A growing economic relationship with Japan can be seen in both trade and investment statistics. Expansion of the

Pacific Fleet and its support bases in the Soviet Far East and Vietnam permits the USSR to enjoy an unprecedented military presence around the Asian littoral. The fall of the Shah in Iran signified a major defeat for American hopes of containing the USSR in Southwest Asia. The ongoing Iranian revolution could eventually move in a direction that would bring "progressive" elements to the fore. The situation in Afghanistan should be "normalized" in the foreseeable future. Indira Gandhi's electoral victory has reinforced Soviet–Indian ties and complicated the American task of arming Pakistan.

On the other hand Soviet expectations in Asia have suffered setbacks, setbacks that the USSR does not always acknowledge publicly but that impinge no less upon perceptions of current trends. No amount of rhetoric can conceal the cost to the USSR of China's metamorphosis from a subordinate ally into a vociferously hostile antagonist cultivating political, economic, and military ties with Japan, the United States, and Western Europe. Moscow has had no success in heading off either a Sino–Japanese or a Sino–American rapprochement, both of which in the Kremlin's view are fraught with dangerous implications. Also, Moscow has not been able to weaken the Japanese–American alliance. North Korea's position in the Sino–Soviet dispute is not satisfactory from Moscow's perspective. Moreover, Pyongyang, for reasons that are not yet clear (but no less disturbing), was the scene of declarations by Cambodian exiles with Chinese connections. South Korea not only has survived but is growing economically. Indonesia has rebuffed Soviet tutelage. Professions of friendship notwithstanding, India is no closer to joining the "socialist community." The situation in Iran is unpredictable and potentially dangerous for the USSR. Reaction to the Soviet move into Afghanistan was unexpectedly strong, not only from the United States but from the Third World as well. The intensity of Muslim nationalism in both Iran and Afghanistan is unsettling in its potential infectiousness. Finally, Brezhnev's collective security proposal for Asia, echoed periodically by Soviet spokesmen since its first enunciation in 1969, seems less and less likely to elicit an appeal outside a handful of client states and Vietnam.

The gap between expectation and reality can be illustrated by reference to an article published in 1961 in the party's theoretical journal predicting the growth of the "socialist camp" during the next 20 years.[30] By 1980, the article proclaimed, the "socialist camp" would be composed of a majority of the world's population and 60% of its industrial production. In fact, the 1 billion members of the "socialist camp" of 1960 has dwindled to 562 million in the "socialist community" of 1980. What was projected to be 54% of the world population is barely 14%. What was anticipated to be 60% of global industrial production is about 30%.[31] Much of this discrepancy can be accounted for by developments in Asia. India and Indonesia have not joined, and China has departed from, the "socialist camp."

One of the more delicate assignments undertaken by Soviet commentators is to explain negative trends within an axiomatically optimistic ideological framework. Under guidelines established by the party, this task is executed in a variety of ways that differ somewhat according to the sophistication of the commentator and of the intended audience.

At a popular level, commentators are wont to portray Asian trends as products of interactions among stereotyped actors: "imperialists" (also "revanchists," "chauvinists"); "socialists" (peace-loving, ever stronger, and led by the Soviet Union); and the Third World (moving ever closer to the socialist countries as the struggle with imperialism deepens). At this level the Sino–American and Sino–Japanese normalizations are treated as a multilevel conspiracy. The Red Army paper *Krasnaya zvezda*, for example, pointed to an emerging alliance of "American imperialists, Japanese revanchists, and Chinese great-power chauvinists."[32] It went on to ascribe grandiose ambitions to all three countries, each of which was said to be temporarily camouflaging its rivalry with the other two in order first to deal with the Soviet Union, which was blocking their "dream of wiping out the peoples' revolutionary gains, redrawing borders, and establishing their own domination in Asia." American imperialists, represented by Zbigniew Brzezinski, are playing the "China card" to create a triangular military alliance while secretly maneuvering Beijing and Moscow into hostilities. Chinese chauvinists are fomenting a Soviet–American nuclear showdown that would "clear the way to world hegemony" for Beijing. Japanese revanchists, restless with postwar subordination to Washington, are nursing expansionist ambitions in Southeast Asia.

At another level of commentary, found mainly in specialized books and journals, one encounters subtler interpretations that share three basic characteristics. First, these analyses do not treat a trend as an isolated phenomenon but relate it to a global "correlation of forces." The correlation of forces embraces a complex interaction between regional and global, political and military, economic and social, and international and domestic issues. Second, close attention is paid to identifying "contradictions" in both bilateral (e.g., Sino–American) and multilateral (Japan–United States–Western Europe) relationships. These contradictions may be temporarily submerged but they are said to resurface inevitably according to "their own logic and law of development" and eventually shift the correlation of forces in favor of the USSR. Third, Soviet analysts distinguish between "subjective" and "objective" trends. The former are supposedly products of political decisions (e.g., Sino–Japanese normalization). The latter (e.g., détente) are said to possess an independent momentum, being part of a historical dialectic.

The single most worrisome subjective trend in Asia today from a Soviet perspective is the network of new relationships attending diplomatic initiatives in Beijing, Washington, and Tokyo. Neither Sino–Japanese nor Sino–American normalization came as a surprise to Soviet analysts. In a 1965 dissertation V. N. Barishnykov speculated that Washington would move toward a rapprochement with Beijing when Taiwan had lost its military significance.[33] Six years later M. I. Sladkovsky (director of the Institute of the Far East) asserted that Japan's "ruling circles," perceiving a weakening of the U.S. position in Asia, were quietly preparing for an alliance with China.[34] Sladkovsky believed that this alliance would have a racial complexion and as such would not be concluded as long as the U.S.–Japan Mutual Security Treaty remained in effect. What neither Barishnykov nor Sladkovsky envisioned was a simultaneous Sino–Japanese and Sino–American rapprochement without any corresponding attenuation of Japanese–American ties.

Analyses of China's new policies toward Japan and the United States stress the interaction of domestic problems with diplomacy. China's masses are portrayed as tired of Maoist socioeconomic upheavals. Mounting popular dissatisfaction has aggravated power struggles between "ideologues" and "pragmatists" within the ruling elite. These two groups are divided not by foreign policy (all current Chinese leaders are portrayed as chauvinists) but by economic, ideological, and personnel questions. The Gang of Four and Four Modernizations campaigns are but tactics to build up China's military power. By emphasizing material development at the expense of social justice, these campaigns have provoked opposition from officials who came to prominence during the Cultural Revolution. To defuse internal tension, the leadership is whipping up chauvinist sentiment, psychologically preparing the country for war, and launching aggressive ventures in Southeast Asia.[35]

What China seeks in a new relationship with Japan and the United States, according to many analysts, is economic modernization at home and a fulfillment of hegemonistic ambitions overseas. Beijing uses anti-Sovietism as "political dollars" to buy American technical and economic assistance. In fact the arms sought by Beijing in the West are for use not against the USSR but against Vietnam, which Chinese leaders see as blocking their expansive designs in Southeast Asia. Similarly, the Sino–Japanese Peace Treaty (1978) is but a tool for exerting leverage on Tokyo. Any Japanese action that incurs Beijing's disfavor can be denounced as a violation of the treaty, making it an instrument to manipulate feelings of cultural affinity and historical guilt that animate segments of Japan's ruling circles and intelligentsia. The U.S.–Japan Mutual Security Treaty is also said to be used by Beijing for its own aims. Beijing in the long run will try to destroy the Japanese–American alliance but for the time being is tolerating it as a device to contain the USSR.

Japan's motives appear to be seen as more complex than those of China because the tactical unity on foreign policy among Beijing's leaders has no counterpart in Tokyo, where different interest groups influence alignments among factions of the ruling Liberal Democratic party and various opposition parties. Moreover, Soviet analysts face phenomena in Japan that do not easily fit into Marxist–Leninist categories. The Japanese communist party, for example, not only has refused to take Moscow's side against Beijing but claims more territory from the Soviet Union than does the conservative Liberal Democratic party.[36]

Published Soviet analyses of Japan's motives for normalizing relations with Beijing stress that elements within the "ruling circles" are seeking to reinforce Beijing's anti-Soviet orientation, increase Tokyo's bargaining leverage vis-à-vis Moscow, secure economic benefits from

China, and gain a margin of independence from the United States.[37] For a while these elements were restrained by "thoughtful and realistic" Japanese who are sensitive to the USSR's "growing international authority," anxious about Japan's international image, aware that China cannot be used to extract territorial concessions in the Kurile Islands, and fearful of complicating relations with the United States. Left to themselves, Japan's ruling circles would probably have opted for caution and have preserved diplomatic equidistance between Moscow and Beijing, but this caution was put aside in May of 1978, when Brzezinski told Tokyo to go ahead and sign a peace treaty with China even if that treaty contained an "antihegemony" clause aimed at the USSR.

Complexities and anomalies have led to disagreements among Soviet analysts of China and Japan. There is no consensus about the existence of "demaofication." Some specialists are prepared to see a degree of demaofication in the pragmatic, technical-oriented aspects of the Four Modernizations campaigns. Others, however, label the new domestic policies as quintessentially Maoist tactics designed to further the Maoist aim of great Han chauvinism. Similarly, there are disagreements on the matter of Japanese "militarism." Some authors play down the subject in their works and privately discount any immediate prospect of militarization, citing the low percentage of armaments expenditures in major corporations and dismissing the far right as an annoyance rather than a powerful threat. Others perceive nationalist tendencies in the irredentist movement for the southern Kurile Islands, in textbook revision, and in the rise of Yasukuni and Ise shrine visitations but they stop short of equating these trends with an upsurge of militarism.[38] Still others, including the authoritative party official Ivan Kovalenko ("Ivkov"), depict an ominous scenario of "militarist trends, a buildup of the armed forces, growing production of modern military hardware, wide-scale ideological indoctrination of the masses and the armed forces in the spirit of revanchism, and the propagation of the cult of violence."[39] There are also divergent appraisals of the Japanese–American alliance, which some commentators assert injures Japan's "national dignity and prestige"[40] but which others concede allows Japan to play a larger role in Asia without arousing the fears of Asian countries. The above differences are alluded to in private conversations but are not articulated in print. Their significance should not be overestimated, for in a larger context Soviet analyses of China and Japan share basic assumptions: internally both countries are beset with economic and social crises, and externally their power aspirations will eventually generate friction with each other and with Washington.

Assessing American policy in Asia presents Soviet analysts with formidable difficulties. A growing awareness of the pluralistic nature of American politics has only complicated the task of determining what Washington seeks in its new relationship with Beijing or how firm Washington's commitment is to South Korea, Thailand, and the Philippines. The enormous volume of raw data is as much a hindrance as an aid to analysis. Pronouncements by administration officials, congressmen, journalists, businessmen, and academics are riddled with inconsistencies that the Soviet observer is unaccustomed to in his own political environment. One specialist wryly confided that it took him some time to realize that the views expressed to him by Asianists at various research institutes and universities were not necessarily those of Washington policymakers.

Soviet publications treat American policy in Asia as an integral part of the global objectives of the country's "ruling classes": to achieve and preserve political and economic domination, to undermine the "socialist community," to keep the Third World in economic bondage, and to crush anti-imperialist movements wherever they may appear. Without changing these ultimate aims, the United States has shifted its tactics in an effort to compensate for recent setbacks and to exploit opportunities presented by Beijing's current anti-Soviet posture.

According to some observers an important shift occurred in the early 1970s, when the United States recognized its inability to impose its will in Southeast Asia. Searching for an alternative means to contain the USSR and to suppress "national liberation movements," Nixon and Kissinger discarded the "politics of strength" approach to Asia in favor of "balancing centers of power," a tactic that involved taking advantage of the Sino–Soviet rift, inhibiting Soviet–Japanese normalization, and strengthening the military alliance with Japan.[41] The Nixon–Kissinger "Beijing connection," which surfaced in 1971, was cultivated within the framework of détente with the USSR. Under Nixon the United States at least formally remained on the sidelines of Sino–Soviet rivalry. However, the Ford and Carter administrations dropped the "realistic" aspect of the Nixon–Kissinger Asia policy by integrating Beijing's anti-Sovietism into American strategic calculations. Soviet analysts attribute this shift to pressure from "conservative" and "military" circles on Carter to take a tougher stance toward Moscow in the wake of "socialist victories" in Indochina, Angola, Ethiopia, and Afghanistan; American reverses in Iran and Guatamala; and escalating tension between the United States and the Third World.

Washington's new political offensive, according to Soviet analysts, became clear with Brzezinski's visit to Beijing in May 1978, when he remarked that the United States and China shared strategic interests. The new American tactic of "using Chinese expansion for the purposes of fighting socialism and progressive forces in general throughout the world" was again demonstrated in January and February of 1979 by the Carter administration's "factual encouragement of Beijing's aggression against the Democratic Republic of Vietnam."[42]

In Moscow's eyes, closer ties between Washington and Beijing have manifold repercussions on other trends within and outside Asia. One of these is that Japanese trade and investment are growing with China but lagging with the USSR. Although Soviet–Japanese trade has made impressive increases in percentage terms since 1960, the USSR occupied a smaller proportion of Japan's total foreign trade in 1977 than in 1967. Moreover, the pace of Japanese participation in Siberian development has shown definite signs of losing momentum, particularly in the wake of the Afghanistan crisis. Among the many obstacles to Soviet–Japanese cooperation, Moscow ascribes a significant role to the machinations of Beijing and Washington.

Moscow also is disappointed with the low level of Soviet–American trade and of American investment in Siberia. Although one writer recently saw "vast possibilities" involving "fantastic projects" in the Soviet Far East and Pacific,[43] expectations raised by the 1972 Soviet–American Trade Agreement have remained unfulfilled, largely because of the Jackson–Vanik and Stevenson amendments. The granting in January 1980 of most-favored-nation status to China will probably intensify Soviet suspicions about Sino–American collusion.

Trends in Southeast Asia have both pleased and dissatisfied Soviet observers. Moscow is generally pleased with Hanoi's invasion of Cambodia, which Ivan Kovalenko asserted "had a salutary effect on the situation in the region."[44] Kovalenko's "salutary effect" referred not only to the demise of the genocidal regime but to the elimination of Beijing's sole client in southeast Asia and the gain of a client for Moscow's ally. China's punitive attack on Vietnam probably caused some moments of concern in the Kremlin but eventually brought gratifying results. Vietnam proved itself capable of handling a Chinese challenge without putting the recently concluded defense pact between Moscow and Hanoi to a serious test. Soviet credibility was upheld at a relatively small risk and Moscow acquired a military dividend: the use of facilities at Danang and Cam Ranh Bay.

Yet Moscow is learning that military power does not necessarily translate into political influence in Southeast Asia. ASEAN nations have diplomatic relations and some trade with the USSR but remain cool to closer political ties. The new regime in Phnom Penh has not achieved international legitimacy despite Moscow's efforts at the conference of nonaligned nations in Havana and in the United Nations. However useful as a military ally, Vietnam may prove to be a political liability in a region where distrust of Hanoi runs deep. The expectation of one Soviet commentator that Hanoi will help ASEAN countries move along a "more balanced course" toward "political and economic independence"[45] has no immediate prospect of fulfillment. Even the utility of Hanoi is subject to the unpredictable and ungovernable impulses of Vietnamese nationalism.

If some current trends in Asia have disappointed Soviet observers, the long-term outlook in Moscow is rather optimistic. For one thing, Soviet analysts are skeptical about China's ability to sustain an economic relationship with either Japan or the United States. They feel that the West has overestimated China's economic stature. One specialist remarked privately that China is "objectively" weaker than Italy and will be further behind the USSR in the year 2000 than it is today. Another asserted that China will sooner or later encounter difficulties in repaying Japan with paraffin-rich oil, which the Japanese cannot refine, and the United States with cheap textiles, which will put Americans out of work.[46] These observers are confident that the limits of Sino–American rapprochement will become apparent as Americans recognize China's low trade and investment potential and realize that Beijing, far from being a Far Eastern NATO, is an expansionist power seeking to drive the United States from the western Pacific.

Second, optimism is also evident in long-term prognoses of Soviet–Japanese relations. Japan, it is felt, will become increasingly interested in Siberian resources as OPEC price hikes and Middle East political instability oblige Tokyo to look for alternate sources of petroleum. Moreover, irredentist sentiment about the Kurile Islands is seen as fading with time, thereby removing an obstacle to closer political relations. An anticipated strengthening of "progressive" forces within Japan is also adduced as a factor supporting long-term optimism.

Third, some (but not all) specialists are prepared to entertain the prospect of a limited Sino–Soviet reconciliation in the foreseeable future. This is envisioned as occurring when Beijing, unable to play off Washington against Moscow and denied additional Western credits, turns to the USSR once again for economic assistance. This shift in Beijing will be brought about by the emergence of a more "sober" and "realistic" leadership that recognizes that "reckless anti-Sovietism" works against China's own interests.

Fourth, basic to Soviet confidence about the long-term future is an awareness that the USSR possesses vast untapped natural resources whereas China is economically weak, Japan depends upon imported raw materials, and the United States is becoming increasingly dependent upon imported sources of energy. The USSR may lag behind the United States in technological matters but Soviet observers feel that their country can always "go it alone" in Siberian development. One analyst went so far as to assert that it is the capitalist countries who will need the USSR in order to survive.[47]

Finally, optimism is generated and sustained by what appears to be a genuine belief in "contradictions" that will eventually disrupt the network of linkages that confront the USSR in Asia. The Taiwan problem and rivalry in the Pacific are seen as inevitably pushing China and the United States apart.[48] Economic competition in Southeast Asia will someday reactivate "deep-rooted Sino–Japanese antagonisms."[49] Even the Japanese–American relationship, held together for more than 30 years by military, political, economic, and social ties, will be "irreversibly" weakened by a combination of "basic contradictions unresolved by the Pacific War," rivalry over access to raw materials and markets, Tokyo's regional political ambitions, and growing Soviet–Japanese ties.[50] Similar contradictions are said to be at work among the three centers of capitalism (the United States, the European Common Market countries, and Japan) and between these centers, on the one hand, and the developing nations, on the other.[51]

It would be an oversimplification to conclude that Soviet optimism about the long-term future is unclouded by doubts. In private, one analyst confided that there were also unfavorable signs within the present "correlation of forces." At home the USSR is confronted with falling industrial growth rates, endemic labor shortages, transportation bottlenecks, and uncertainties about oil supplies. Abroad, the "progressive forces" are in disarray as a result of unresolved contradictions

between the USSR and China, centrifugal tendencies within the "socialist community," and the reformist nature of communist movements in
Western Europe. If Beijing were ever successful in securing significant
military assistance from the West, he continued, China could mount a
serious long-term threat to the USSR. Since these remarks were made (in
1978) the situation in Poland has given grounds for yet more long-
term doubts about the correlation of forces, for events there are being
watched throughout Asia.

The blend of current disappointments with long-term optimism qualified by residual doubts underlies Moscow's readiness to pursue or pass
up opportunities to expand its influence in Asia.

Opportunities and Constraints    Moscow's initiatives in Asia are subject to two contradictory impulses. On the one hand, a deep com-
mitment to struggle propels Soviet leaders to exploit
every opportunity to enlarge the socialist communi-
ty in general and to promote Soviet power in particular. On the other
hand, an unwillingness to take serious risks compels policymakers to
exercise caution.

The term *struggle* reverberates through the lexicon of Soviet discourse: struggle against capitalism, imperialism, colonialism, revanchism, chauvinism, militarism, fascism, and bourgeois ideology; struggle
for socialism, national liberation, and peace. The currently favored
slogan, détente (the literal Russian term is "relaxation of tension"), does
not signify an abdication of a commitment to struggle. On the contrary,
détente is regarded as an "objective" stage in the struggle between
socialist and capitalist systems, a decisive stage in which socialism, led
by the Soviet Union, is to achieve preeminence without nuclear war.
Marxism–Leninism has in this case reinforced a geographical and
historical legacy that long ago made struggle a Russian way of life.

At the same time, the current Soviet leadership has shown little
propensity to push struggle to the point of taking serious risks. Sur-
vivors of a generation baptized by Stalin's purges and World War II, the
aging members of the Politburo have developed the habits of patience,
persistence, and flexibility. Only when the chances of success seem
assured do they act—as in Afghanistan.

Committed to exploiting opportunities yet conditioned to exercise
caution, Soviet policymakers have been frustrated by their lack of
diplomatic maneuverability in Northeast Asia, where four major powers
physically converge, where American strategic weapons are deployed,
where Soviet frontiers with China and Japan are unsettled, where a
volatile situation exists on the Korean peninsula, and where Moscow
hopes to develop some of its richest but most inaccessible resources.
During the 1970s Soviet observers witnessed dramatic realignments
among China, Japan, and the United States, realignments for which the
Kremlin has thus far been unable to devise an antidote. Indeed, recent
Soviet behavior has if anything accelerated the very trend that Moscow
fears: the formation of a Sino–Japanese–American entente.

Curiously, most Russians, including sophisticated Asian specialists, seem unwilling to entertain the notion that the behavior of the USSR itself might be responsible for the emergence of what Moscow terms "anti-Soviet" coalitions in Europe and Asia. Instead, emphasis is placed on the essential fragility of these coalitions and on how the USSR might utilize their internal contradictions. For example, one analyst has written that the USSR can exploit the divergent national interests of the United States, Japan, and the European Common Market.[52] Indeed, strong American reactions to events in Iran and Afghanistan have given Moscow opportunities vis-à-vis Japan and Western Europe. One analyst adumbrated a strategy that Moscow might adopt if the Reagan administration and Congress took "tough" positions on SALT II, defense expenditures, and arms sales to China: "If you want another Cold War, we're ready. Only this time, it will be a Cold War with just you, not with your allies. This time, you're going to be isolated."

This strategy might prove succesful in Asia if the USSR were able to improve its relations with Japan. In the eyes of Soviet analysts, even a limited Soviet–Japanese rapprochement would curtail Beijing's ability to maneuver against Moscow, would weaken the Japanese–American alliance, and would promote greater Japanese participation in Siberian development.

Improving relations with Japan has not been an easy assignment for Soviet diplomats. Some Japan specialists in the Academy of Sciences and the Foreign Ministry have quietly striven to show greater appreciation for Japanese sensibilities in talks, publications, and broadcasts. Refinements in style alone, however, cannot bridge the distance between Moscow and Tokyo. Soviet bids to improve political relations have repeatedly foundered on the territorial issue, which Tokyo insists must be solved before a peace treaty can be signed. Insofar as Moscow has little room or desire to maneuver on this issue, prospects for a political breakthrough with Tokyo are remote.

The political impasse with Tokyo has deprived Moscow of a "Japan card" to play against Washington. Despite the "Nixon shock," chronic friction over trade, and varying views on security responsibilities, Japan and the United States have managed to preserve close political and economic ties for more than 30 years. The resilience of this relationship puzzles at least one analyst, who asked the author:

> How can it be that Japan, which bitterly fought you in World War II, on whom you dropped two atomic bombs, and on whom you imposed a military occupation, should like you and not us, even though we were neutral during most of the Pacific War, did not bomb any Japanese city, and have no troops on Japanese soil?

Opportunities to normalize relations with Beijing have also been limited, in Brezhnev's words, because "the sole criterion which now determines the Chinese leaders' approach to any major international issue is their urge to inflict as much damage on the USSR as possible."[53] That the Soviet leadership has not given up trying, however, is evident from the restraint with which the general secretary spoke about China at the Twenty-Sixth Party Congress early in 1981.

One can assume that Soviet policymakers are quietly seeking out "realistic" elements in Beijing that may come to the fore after the present top leadership passes from the scene. When that time comes, a discreet overture, backed by economic inducements, might elicit a favorable response. Any approach Moscow eventually takes toward China will be conditioned by the prevailing state of Soviet–American relations.

As the USSR's principal global rival, the United States is the ultimate object of any major Soviet initiative in Asia. In the wake of events in Iran and Afghanistan, Moscow can no longer count heavily upon America's post-Vietnam reluctance to become involved in overseas military actions. In the areas where current or potential instabilities offer the USSR opportunities for testing American willpower—Korea, Thailand, the Persian Gulf—Soviet strategists will have to take into consideration the heightened risks of incurring direct American involvement.

Moscow is unlikely to launch any sudden military venture in Asia unless Soviet leaders are confronted with what they perceive as a serious challenge to the USSR's vital interests. Moscow will continue to carry out incremental increases in its military capabilities while probing for soft spots such as Afghanistan, where gains can be had at acceptable risks. There may be more occasions for use of proxies but Moscow will have to take into consideration that Vietnam has its own political and strategic aims, which may not always coincide with those of the USSR, particularly in the event of improved Sino–Soviet relations.

What about the next generation of Soviet leaders? It can be argued that their lack of exposure to the destruction that has made their elders cautious, that their restiveness for more status, emboldened by a perception of American vacillation and a confidence in growing Soviet power, may tempt them to take greater risks. Yet it also can be argued that these same leaders, by shedding some of the insecurity that has gripped their predecessors, may see the logic of giving substance to Brezhnev's 1969 Collective Security proposal and in addition allot higher priority to the problems of food, population, resources, and the environment faced by all Asian nations, including the USSR.

The proportion of challenge, competition, and cooperation in Soviet Asia policy will shift from time to time but the quest for power and prestige is likely to remain a permanent objective. As Asia figures with increasing prominence in the Soviet world view, so should Soviet policies in Asia command more of the world's attention.

## Notes

[1] Aleksandr Bovin, quoted in Morton Schwartz, *Soviet Perceptions of the United States* (Berkeley: University of California Press, 1978), p. 6.

[2] William Zimmerman, *Soviet Perspectives on International Relations* (Princeton: Princeton University Press, 1969), pp. 282–290.

[3]Alexander Dallin, "Introduction," in *Soviet and Chinese Communism*, ed. Donald Treadgold (Seattle: University of Washington Press, 1967), p. 368.

[4]Matsui Shigeru, *Soren no tai-Nichi senryaku* (Soviet Strategy toward Japan) (Tokyo: PHP, 1979), p. 10.

[5]Books and articles about frontier defense form a minor literary genre whose current state was manifested at a 1978 conference on "Literature, Art, and the Defense of Sacred Boundaries of the Motherland." S. Tsvigun, "Khudozhnik i granitsa," *Literaturnaya Gazeta*, January 17, 1979.

[6]Otto Hoetzsch, *Russland in Asien* (Stuttgart: Deutsche Verlags-Anstalt, 1966), p. 124; Andrei Lobanov-Rostovsky, *Russia and Asia* (New York: Macmillan, 1933), p. 36.

[7]On August 21, 1979, *Pravda* carried an article defining Soviet security interests in terms of the range of modern strategic weapons (*Soviet World Outlook*, vol. 5, no. 1 [January 15, 1980], p. 2).

[8]Nicholas V. Riasanovsky, "Asia through Russian Eyes," in *Russia and Asia*, ed. Wayne S. Vucinich (Stanford: Hoover Institution Press, 1972), p. 5.

[9]S. L. Tikhvinsky, ed., *Istoriya mezhdunarodnykh otnoshenii na Dal'nem Vostoke, 1945–1977* (Khabarovsk: Khabarovskoe knizhnoe izdatel'stvo, 1978), p. 550.

[10]Ernst Genri, "Nemetskie revanshisty i Pekin," *Problemy Dal'nego Vostoka* (hereafter cited as *PDV*), no. 4 (1974), pp. 146–158.

[11]Gregor Alexinsky, *Russia and Europe* (London: T. Fisher Unwin, 1917), p. 110.

[12]*Ibid.*, p. 110.

[13]Lobanov-Rostovsky, *Russia and Asia*, p. 24.

[14]*What Peking Keeps Silent About* (Moscow: Novosty Press Agency, 1972).

[15]Feodor Dostoyevsky, *The Diary of a Writer*, vol. 2 (New York: Scribner's, 1949), p. 1048.

[16]M. S. Kapitsa, "Bor'ba SSSR za mir i sotrudnichestvo v Azii," *PDV*, no. 1 (1979), p. 31.

[17]Geoffrey Jukes, *The Soviet Union in Asia* (Berkeley: University of California Press, 1973), p. 64.

[18]*Asahi shimbun*, April 28, 1941.

[19]Sidney Monas, "Amalrik's Vision of the End," in *Will the Soviet Union Survive until 1984?* ed. Andrei Amalrik (New York: Harper & Row, 1970), p. 84.

[20]George Vernadsky, "The Expansion of Russia," *Transactions of the Connecticut Academy of Arts and Sciences*, vol. 31 (July 1933), p. 396; Klaus Mehnert, *Soviet Man and His World* (New York: Praeger, 1962), pp. 282–283.

[21]Alexandre Benningsen and Chantal Lemercier-Quelquejay, *Islam in the Soviet Union* (New York: Praeger, 1967), p. 223.

[22]D. V. Petrov, ed., *Mezhdunarodnye otnosheniya v Aziatsko-tikhookeanskom regione* (Moscow: Nauka, 1979), p. 4.

[23]E. M. Primakov, *International Situation in the Asian Pacific Region: Basic Trends and Developments*, Fourteenth Pacific Science Congress, Khabarovsk, August 1979 (Moscow: Nauka, 1979), p. 2.

[24]Petrov, *Mezhdunarodnye otnosheniya*, p. 262.

[25]Viktor Tsoppi, "Igra s ognem," *Literaturnaya Gazeta*, January 24, 1979; *Krasnaya zvezda*, December 17, 1978.

[26]Japan, Defense Agency, Public Information Division, *Defense Bulletin 2*, no. 2 (October 1978), p. 7; *Hokkaido shimbun*, March 15, 1977.

[27]V. A. Semenov, "Evropeiskaya besopasnost' i pozitsiya KNR," *PDV*, no. 1 (1973), pp. 188–191; V. I. Petukhov, "Problemy Evropy i politika Pekina," *PDV*, no. 2 (1973), pp. 161–166; Yu. I. Mikhailov, "Kitai i zapadnoevropeiskaya integratsiya," *PDV*, no. 4 (1973), pp. 152–159.

[28]Suslov: *Pravda*, September 19, 1979; Brezhnev: *Literaturnaya Gazeta*, February 25, 1981.

[29]Kapitsa, *Bor'ba SSSR.*

[30]S. Strumilin, "The World 20 Years from Now," *Kommunist,* no. 13 (September 1961), pp. 25–36, in *Current Digest of the Soviet Press* (hereafter cited as *CDSP*) 13, no. 38 (October 18, 1961), pp. 3–7.

[31]The official current Soviet statistic is that socialist states account for "more than 40%" of global industrial production. In addition to being a generous estimate, the figure includes China [see *Narodnoe khozyaistvo SSSR v 1978 g.* (Moscow: Statistika, 1979), p. 47].

[32]*Krasnaya zvezda,* December 17, 1978.

[33]Cited in Zimmerman, *Soviet Perspectives,* pp. 240–241.

[34]M. I. Sladkovsky, *Kitai i Yaponiya* (Moscow: Nauka, 1971), pp. 332–333.

[35]M. Yakovlev, "Instability Persists," *Pravda,* October 29, 1978, in *CDSP* 30, no. 41 (November 22, 1978), p. 8; A. Petrov, "Same Goals, Contradictory Course," *Pravda,* December 28, 1978, in *CDSP* 30, no. 51 (January 17, 1979), p. 13; "Reshayushchii faktor mirovogo razvitiya," *PDV,* no. 4 (1978), p. 9; "Itogi 'poteryannogo desyatiletiya' i sovremennoe polozhenie KNR," *PDV,* no. 1 (1979), pp. 56–75.

[36]However, the territorial issue was not mentioned in public communiqués issued after a meeting of Soviet and Japanese communist party representatives in December 1979 [*Soviet World Outlook* 5, no. (January 15, 1980), p. 6].

[37]M. G. Nosov, *Yapono-kitaiskie otnosheniya* (Moscow: Nauka, 1978), pp. 4–7, 169; V. N. Berezin, *Kurs na dobrososedstvo i sotrudnichestvo i ego protivniki* (Moscow: Mezhdunarodnye otnosheniya, 1977), p. 118.

[38]For example, Igor Latyshev, "Natsionalisticheskie tendentsii v politike pravyashchikh krugov Yaponii," *Narody Azii i Afriki,* no. 3 (1971), pp. 45–50.

[39]I. Ivkov, "Japanese Militarism Rears its Head," *Far Eastern Affairs,* no. 4 (1978), p. 43.

[40]A. P. Markov, *Poslevoennaya politika Yaponii v Azii i Kitai, 1945–1977* (Moscow: Nauka, 1979), p. 234.

[41]B. N. Zanegin, "Demokraticheskaya administratsiya i diplomaticheskoe priznanie KNR," *SShA: Ekonomika, Politika, Ideologiya,* no. 3 (March 1979), p. 53; Petrov, *Mezhdunarodnye otnosheniya,* p. 52.

[42]B. N. Zanegin, "Vashington i pekinskaya agressiya protiv SRV," *SShA: Ekonomika, Politika, Ideologiya,* no. 5 (May 1979), p. 80.

[43]Boris N. Slavinsky, "Siberia and the Soviet Far East within the Framework of International Trade and Economic Relations," *Asian Survey* 17, no. 4 (April 1977), pp. 324–325.

[44]Ivan Ivkov, "Victory of Immense Significance," *New Times,* no. 5 (January 1979), p. 4.

[45]B. Ilyichev, "Southeast Asia: Positive Tendencies," *Pravda,* October 29, 1978, in *CDSP* 30, no. 43 (November 22, 1978), p. 164.

[46]Vladimir B. Yakubovsky, "Soviet Policy in Asia," Lecture at East–West Center, Honolulu, April 20, 1979.

[47]Petrov, *Mezhdunarodnye otnosheniya,* p. 6.

[48]*Ibid.,* p. 38.

[49]Primakov, "International Situation," p. 6.

[50]Petrov, *Mezhdunarodnye otnosheniya,* pp. 4, 56, 99; Markov, *Poslevoennaya politika Yaponii,* p. 236.

[51]Petrov, *Mezhdunarodnye otnosheniya,* pp. 6, 12, 38.

[52]*Ibid.,* p. 6.

[53]Quoted in *Far Eastern Affairs,* no. 1 (1979), p. 151.

# 34    ALLEN S. WHITING

## Siberian Development: The Strategic Implications*

**Introduction**   In conventional usage the term "strategic" usually refers to the potential military capability available for combat. When applied to one's own country, this capability is presumed to be for defense against attack. The strategic capability of other countries, however, is usually assumed to have an offensive role.

The tendency toward unilateral justification of military strength is a natural concomitant of nationalism. It also derives from the difficulty—indeed, the near impossibility—of distinguishing defensive from offensive intent by analyzing the nature of particular weapons. Most weapons can be employed in both capacities, although not necessarily with the same effectiveness. Therefore, prudence as well as politics argues for assuming a potential opponent to be arming for attack. It safeguards against unpleasant surprises while justifying one's own military expenditures.

Unfortunately, this practice can lead to misperceptions and arms competition when the strengthening of defensive forces in one country is seen abroad as posing an offensive threat that necessitates a strengthened defense in response. The response may in turn be viewed with alarm, prompting further military expenditures that set off another mirrorlike reaction. The result is the familiar mutual escalation of armaments.

This phenomenon complicates our inquiry. From Moscow's vantage point East Asian Siberia (EAS) requires protection against a possible attack by a numerically superior China, now armed with a growing nuclear missile capability. This perceived threat is rooted in the extremely thin and dispersed population of the area compared with that of its immediate neighbor. It is heightened by heavy dependence, of the

*Reprinted by permission of the author and publisher from *Siberian Development and East Asia: Threat or Promise?* (Stanford, Calif.: Stanford University Press, 1981), pp. 85–111, 247–251. Copyright 1981 by The Board of Trustees of the Leland Stanford Junior University.

region in general and the naval base at Vladivostok in particular, on the Trans-Siberian Railroad, which runs within easy reach of the Chinese border. As a final concern, Soviet access to the Pacific Ocean via the Sea of Japan is by way of straits that can be readily blocked by Japanese and American power, joined in alliance since 1951.

Conversely, Soviet military deployments in East Asian Siberia and the northwestern Pacific Ocean tend to be viewed in China and Japan as posing a threat, albeit in somewhat varying degree depending upon the composition of the forces and their location. In this regard, the United States has relatively little interest in Soviet land-based strength except for intercontinental missiles (ICBM), but it must monitor the Soviet Pacific Fleet both as a regional threat to Japan's sea routes as an economic lifeline and for its contribution to the global strategic threat directed at the United States.

An historical review reveals how a triangle of tension has dominated relations in northeastern Asia over most of the past 100 years. This heritage of mutual suspicion, and at times hatred, prompted each nation to strengthen its defensive capacity against the others while viewing their military efforts as offensively motivated, regardless of the role defensive impulses may have played. Sometimes subjective perceptions accorded with objective reality, as when the Soviets and Chinese feared Japanese militaristic expansion in the 1930s. But sometimes misperception prompted moves that triggered conflicts that might otherwise have been avoided, as when the Chinese and American interaction in 1950 led them into battle on the Korean peninsula.[1]

A full analysis of strategic implications must embrace both reality and perception to the extent possible. We will begin by surveying the present disposition of Soviet military forces in the EAS region. This will provide a base against which we can assess the probable impact of Siberian development on future military capability. Finally, we will touch on how this may be seen from various capitals.

The two central questions at issue are, first, what differences will Siberian development make in Moscow's precombat preparations and posture? Second, once hostilities have begun, what differences are discernible in the Soviet capacity for fighting, and how do these vary according to whether the war is short or long, nuclear or conventional, and local or global? Alternative warfighting scenarios and their various mixtures offer a multiplicity of possible developments that cannot be examined in detail here, but some of the more salient aspects of the most important of them deserve at least cursory review within our framework of inquiry.

In addition to military capability, economic factors can also have strategic implications. Where Siberian development requires foreign capital and technology for which repayment is in local resources, either party in the relationship may enjoy a strategic advantage, depending on the circumstances. At the outset, the Soviet ability to exploit such resources will require continuous access to foreign technology until production is under way, and in some instances afterward. During this time such leverage as may exist will lie with the foreign source of aid.

However, once production begins and payback provides a needed resource in the form of export, the foreign consumer may be at the mercy of Moscow, at least in the narrow, immediate sense. Alternatively, Moscow may need foreign markets to recoup its investment in the specific resources, thereby providing leverage to the consumer.

As an example, gas and oil development in East Asian Siberia is likely to remain dependent on foreign cooperation for the remainder of this century, yet delivery of these energy resources to Japan could be of considerable importance to one or both parties. In this chapter, Soviet–Japanese economic interchange will receive brief analysis for its strategic implications.

Soviet Land-Based Military Capabilities
It is impossible to pinpoint with precision the exact time and size of Soviet military deployments on the basis of foreign intelligence estimates, which are released selectively through various sources. Nevertheless, such figures provide a guide to the rough order of magnitude and period of changes in Soviet force levels, one that must remain general but that is sufficient for our purpose.

According to CIA estimates, 675,000 to 725,000 military personnel were assigned in 1978 to missions directed against China.[2] This number included army, air force, and missile units. On the ground, 43 divisions, nearly one-fourth of the Red Army, faced the People's Republic.[3] Twenty were deployed near the Sea of Okhotsk, mostly in Maritime Krai; 8 stood along the Trans-Siberian between the Amur's eastern bend and Lake Baikal, for a total of 28 divisions in EAS.[4] Another 3 were in Mongolia, east of Ulan Bator, with the remainder in the Central Asian republics. Together with 10,000 medium tanks and 75,000 border guards, they offered an impressive array of power, which was compounded by a crescent of nuclear missiles targeted on China. However, the defensive utility of the force far outweighed its offensive potential if one compares it with China's 3.6 million troops.[5]

This massive military confrontation stood in sharp contrast to the "monolithic unity" of the heyday of the Sino–Soviet alliance, a ritualistic formula intoned by both countries during the 1950s. At that time Moscow provided Beijing with a jet air force of thousands of planes, laid the foundations for a coastal navy and submarine fleet, and modernized its army with tanks and artillery.[6] The industrial base for future production also came through Soviet aid. Least publicized but most far-reaching in importance was a brief but relatively generous nuclear assistance program that equipped China's scientists with the essential training and technology to produce atomic weapons.[7]

This cooperation ended in 1960 when Sino–Soviet differences prompted Nikita Khrushchev to withdraw all economic and technical aid. But despite the ensuing polemics, the relationship did not appear threatening to Moscow until 1964, judging from the fact that only 15 divisions, or 12% of the Red Army, stood opposite China.[8] That year, however, two events occurred to arouse Soviet anxiety. In July Mao remarked to a visiting Japanese Socialist Party (JSP) delegation, "A hundred years ago they [the Russians] incorporated the territory to the east of Lake Baikal, including Khabarovsk, Vladivostok, and the Kamchatka Peninsula. Those accounts are difficult to settle, and we have not settled these accounts with them."[9] Mao supported the demand that Moscow return the Kuril Islands, and his statement suggested that he would lay claim to 1.5 million square kilometers (585,000 square miles) of Siberia and Central Asia that the Qing (Manchu) rulers had ceded to Tsarist Russia. Coming after an upsurge in incidents along the 7500-kilometer (4650-mile) border—more than 4000 allegedly occurred in 1963—his words carried ominous implications.[10]

After nearly 2 months, *Pravda* replied with its editorial "In Connection with Mao Zedong's Talk with a Group of Japanese Socialists":

> It could be expected that Beijing would refute this report, but no denial was forthcoming. . . . The Soviet representative in Beijing asked the P.R.C. Deputy Minister of Foreign Affairs Wang Pingnan for an explanation and the latter declared, "If Mao Zedong said that, I agree with him." On August 1, the Japanese newspaper *Asahi* published a statement by Zhou Enlai [which] actually contained the same ideas as Mao's interview. Consequently no doubt was left that the Japanese press was reporting a true statement of the CCP Chairman. . . . He is not only claiming this or that part of Soviet territory, but is portraying his claims as part of some "general territorial question." We are faced with an openly expansionist program with far-reaching pretensions.[11]

The editorial recapitulated various maps published in China after 1949 that purported to show "lost territories" taken by Tsarist Russia, and charged that "Chinese representatives recently began mentioning with increasing frequency hundreds of thousands of square kilometers of Soviet territory which allegedly belong 'by right' to China." It also noted that "the recent issue of the Beijing magazine Lishih Yanjiu (Historical Studies), No. 4, 1964, contends that Russia actually 'captured vast lands to the north of the Amur River and to the east of the Ussuri River and annexed at various times vast territories in Xinjiang and the northwest area.'" Following a full quotation of Mao's remarks, *Pravda* conceded that "the Czarist government carried out a predatory policy, just as the Chinese Emperors carried one out themselves to the extent of their abilities." But after citing various Soviet gestures at reversing Tsarist practices, such as extraterritoriality, the editorial pointedly quoted Lenin: "Vladivostok is far away but this town is ours."

On October 16, 1964, China detonated its first atomic bomb. Shortly thereafter Premier Zhou Enlai flew to Moscow for discussions following Khrushchev's ouster, but no reconciliation resulted. In February 1965 Premier Kosygin visited Beijing for an equally fruitless meeting with Mao. The Chairman remained implacable on all aspects of the dispute.

These developments apparently prompted the decision to bolster Soviet military defenses against China. Between 1965 and 1969 ground forces in Siberia and Central Asia more than doubled, from 15 to nearly

35 divisions.[12] New airfields, including several in Mongolia, and medium-range missiles encircling northeastern China extended Soviet striking power against key populations and industrial centers.[13]

Speaking on the fiftieth anniversary of the October Revolution in November 1967, Soviet Communist Party General Secretary Leonid Brezhnev warned that any attempt at a surprise attack against the USSR, "wherever it may come from—the north or the south, the west or the east—will encounter the all-conquering might of our glorious Armed Forces."[14] His blunt words placed Beijing in a more hostile role than had previously been depicted at an authoritative level.

The paroxysm of xenophobic violence unleashed by the Red Guards at the height of Mao's Cultural Revolution in 1967 gave cause for heightened Soviet concern. Dissension at the highest policy levels and disruption throughout China's urban centers coincided with violent demonstrations in foreign capitals.[15] The British embassy in Beijing was sacked, and bombings in Hong Kong and violence at the nearby border put the colony's fate in serious doubt. With anarchy seeming to threaten China, the possible spillover effects on the Sino–Soviet frontier could not be ignored in Moscow.

Finally, in March 1969 the first major armed clash between Soviet and Chinese troops occurred at the island of Damansky (Zhenbao) in the Ussuri River. The preponderance of indirect evidence suggests to most observers that the Chinese side initiated the incident.[16] By Beijing's own account Moscow had previously warned that further encroachments on the disputed island would be met with force. The People's Liberation Army (PLA) prepared for this contingency with concealed deployments that inflicted heavy casualties on the Soviet border troops.[17] Tension increased that spring and summer with a Soviet retaliatory blow at Damansky and further fighting elsewhere, especially on the Xinjiang border. Statements in Moscow focused on China as a direct threat to the USSR.[18]

Beyond the sequence of events that prompted Soviet defensive concerns, additional offensive motivations may have entered into Moscow's calculus by mid-1969. That June Soviet bomber units deployed from East Europe to Central Asian bases and flew mock exercises against targets in northwestern China.[19] Soviet diplomats made low-level probes through their foreign counterparts concerning possible reaction to a "surgical strike" against China's nascent nuclear production facilities.[20] At a minimum, the show of force and threat of war could have been aimed at forcing a border settlement on Soviet terms. At a maximum, Moscow may have seriously contemplated an attack on Beijing's nuclear weapons facilities.

But regardless of whatever offensive goals may have been weighed in 1969, the timing, context, and nature of the previous military buildup seems to have been basically prompted by defensive preoccupations. Moscow's concentration of ground and missile units opposite northeastern China is readily understandable. The Trans-Siberian Railroad provides the only lateral land route around this 2400-kilometer (1500-mile) frontier and terminates at the major naval base of Vladivostok. In its final north-south run the line comes within 2.5 kilometers (1.5 miles) of the border at Ebergard, near the Ussuri. Further north, from Dormidontovka to Lesozavodsk, a distance of 280 kilometers (174 miles), much of the track lies fewer than 16 kilometers (10 miles) from Chinese territory.[21] Moreover, the intervening terrain is largely flatland with no natural defense points other than the river itself. By comparison, the much longer east–west run that parallels the border from Khabarovsk to Mogocha is less accessible to ground attack. Its nearest approaches to China, approximately 15 kilometers (9.3 miles), occur at only two points.[22] The remainder is generally twice this distance or further, with the broad Amur River providing a natural barrier.

Interdiction of the Trans-Siberian would cut the one overland supply route to Vladivostok and interrupt the main source of petroleum from West Siberia. The next alternative freight link with the European sector of the USSR is the long sea line to Leningrad and ports on the Black Sea. But this 10,000-mile route transits the Suez Canal and is not reliable in wartime, a factor that compels recourse to the even longer run around the Cape of Good Hope. Under the circumstances, the strengthening of Soviet military defenses in the area, given the events of 1966–1968, reflected prudence more than paranoia.

By 1990 East Asian Siberia will be served increasingly by a new sea route through the Arctic Ocean. In 1978 a nuclear-powered icebreaker accompanied a Soviet merchant ship from Murmansk to the Bering Strait extension of the North Pacific in only 18 days. Soviet sources claim that new nuclear merchant ships will make the Arctic run in 1985, with year-round traffic anticipated later. Until that time, however, overland transport will remain the lifeline for supplies to EAS.

Viewed objectively, the military situation does not pose the nightmare sometimes conjured up by journalistic visions of massive Chinese armies overrunning empty Siberian territory. In contrast to the Soviet side of the border, no lateral railroad traverses northeastern China's frontier region. Instead, eight spur lines terminate at widely separated intervals across this extensive area, in most cases stopping 65 kilometers (40 miles) short of the actual border.[23] The thin road network encounters heavily forested mountains in the northwest and swampy lowlands in the northeast. This inhospitable terrain also inhibits settlement. Although Heilongjiang province has a total population of more than 31 million, the density in most of the frontier area is less than one person per square kilometer (0.39 square mile).[24] By comparison, Soviet territory adjacent to the Amur is much more settled and developed in the lowlands and foothills because of the presence of the Trans-Siberian Railroad.

Yet this objective view is not shared by some sectors of Soviet society, where the crude image of one billion Chinese confronting thinly populated Siberia arouses widespread apprehension. This sinophobia is rooted in historical accounts of the Mongol invasion, which has come to be blended with the perceived Chinese threat into a seamless "yellow peril." Thus, in March 1969, following the clash at Damansky Island, the celebrated poet Yevgenii Yevtushenko exploited this linkage in lurid imagery, referring to "the Chinese God-khan" and more specifically to "Vladimir and Kiev," who "see in the smoking twilight the new Batu khans, bombs rattling in their quivers."[25] His allusion to these classic cases of Mongol pillage struck home. Conversations with Soviet academicians other than China specialists echo the sinophobia encountered more casually in hotel and taxi.[26] A curious exception occurs among residents of Khabarovsk and Vladivostok, which suggests that this fear may increase with distance from China; it is most evident in Moscow.[27]

Whatever the shadings of public opinion, Soviet military planners apparently hold a more rational and relaxed view of the Chinese threat. After the initial bolstering of their capability to defend East Asian Siberia in 1965–1969, the pace of deployment slowed. Many divisions are combat ready, but nearly half are at one-third strength or less.[28] More advanced weaponry comes to the area only after its delivery to Warsaw Pact armies. A qualitative upgrading of weapons has improved firepower without significantly expanding the size of local forces, but the overall disposition of strength is more suggestive of precautionary moves than of preparation for actual combat.

Because the military high command in Moscow has long been sensitive to the logistical weaknesses of the Trans-Siberian Railroad, it undoubtedly supported the decision to build BAM as a second route further removed from the Chinese border. Aside from the danger of hostile interdiction, the Trans-Siberian poses problems of a more mundane nature. It is vulnerable to flooding, on one occasion requiring a prolonged airlift in order to carry supplies to cut-off areas.[29] In addition, it has had to struggle under the burden of steadily growing freight resulting from an expanding civilian economy, heightened military traffic, and increased use of overland transshipment from the Pacific coast to Europe. This has resulted in a 50% expansion in the freight load every 5 years, making bottlenecks and breakdowns more frequent and more difficult to cope with.[30] We will examine BAM's prospects in the next section, but it deserves mention at this point because its emergence as a major project resulted in part from the Sino–Soviet difficulties of the late 1960s.

## Soviet Sea-Based Military Capabilities

By comparison with deployments on land, Soviet naval activity in the Pacific is less susceptible to analysis of its implications for northeastern Asia. Because of their mobility, large naval units offer a greater flexibility of mission and deployment than do land-based armies. The same ships can serve various functions as well as move in and out of the area. The analytical problem is exemplified by the fact that the Soviet Pacific Fleet is also responsible for the Indian Ocean. Thus, in 1977 it registered 5800 ship-days in the Pacific and 6200 in the Indian Ocean.[31] Multiple missions preclude an accurate calculation of the number of ships of different types that would be available in the West Pacific at any future time.

Vietnam became another responsibility during the American mining and bombing of Hanoi and Haiphong in 1972, when the first major Soviet naval contingent positioned itself in the South China Sea.[32] This activity expanded significantly in 1979 when China invaded Vietnam, and it has continued since. Yet as long as Hanoi does not grant the full use of Cam Ranh Bay as a permanent base, Vladivostok must serve this function.

Finally, and most important, the strategic mission of the Soviet Pacific Fleet is part of the global confrontation with the United States. Defensively, it must protect the homeland against attack from aircraft carriers and nuclear submarines with ballistic missiles. Offensively, its ballistic missile submarines are targeted against the United States. These strategic units are based in the main ports of Vladivostok, Sovetskaia Gavan, and Petropavlovsk, with ancillary facilities at Nakhodka and Magadan.[33] However, forces earmarked for defensive or offensive strategic engagement with the United States lie outside our focus on East Asia.

It is worth noting the relationship of the Soviet Pacific Fleet to global considerations as viewed from Moscow. This is apparent in the degree to which the general expansion of the Soviet navy is proportionately reflected in an increased Pacific presence. Table 34.1 illustrates this phenomenon, the percentages indicating the Pacific share of the overall navy. This breakdown shows the relative consistency of smaller allocations to the Pacific Fleet, except for the steady increase in submarines, which strengthens the Soviet strategic capability against targets in the United States. As another indication of its lesser status, the Pacific Fleet

Table 34.1. *Soviet Pacific Fleet Combat Force Levels (Percentages Are % of Total Soviet Fleet Strength)*

| Type of vessel | 1968 | | 1973 | | 1978 | | 1979 |
|---|---|---|---|---|---|---|---|
| | No. | % | No. | % | No. | % | |
| Submarines[a] | 100 | 27 | 101 | 30 | 113 | 32 | 105 |
| Major surface combatants[b] | 58 | 29 | 58 | 27 | 67 | 29 | 78 |
| Minor surface combatants | NA[d] | | 135 | 22 | 113 | 22 | 131 |
| Amphibious ships[c] | NA | | 18 | 25 | 18 | 22 | 17 |
| Mine warfare craft | NA | | NA | | 110 | 25 | 70 |

SOURCES: The figures for 1968, 1973, and 1978 are from Donald C. Daniel, "The Soviet Navy and the Pacific," *Asia Pacific Commentary* (Summer 1979), p. 69; they reflect a reconciling of data from a wide variety of unclassified American, British, German, and Japanese sources, although the totals for 1978 are almost exclusively from the United States Defense Intelligence Agency, *Unclassified Communist Naval Orders of Battle* (DDB-1200–124–78; Washington, D.C., 1978), pp. 1–4. I have added figures for 1979 as compiled in Research Institute for Peace and Security, *Asian Security 1979* (Tokyo, 1979), p. 52.

[a]Includes ballistic missile, cruise missile, and attack boats.
[b]Includes cruisers, destroyers, and frigates.
[c]Includes medium and tank landing ships only.
[d]Not available.

is the last to receive more modern equipment. For example it did not receive its first *Kara*-class cruiser until 1979, although these ships had appeared in other fleets in 1972.[34]

The dual mission, global and regional, of the Soviet Pacific Fleet was amply demonstrated in April 1975 during the world-wide Soviet naval exercise Vesna (Okean II). Four task forces ranged widely in the Pacific Ocean. One grouped 400 kilometers (250 miles) east of Shanghai and moved on station south of Taiwan. Another covered the North Pacific. A third was positioned 480 kilometers (300 miles) east of Japan. The fourth remained near the Tsushima Strait.[35] Their varied activities included antisubmarine warfare, amphibious ship exercises, convoying in the Philippine Sea, and sea-lane interdiction east of Japan. This was an impressive display of power compared with what would have been possible a decade previous. It attracted understandable attention and comment, all adverse, in both Beijing and Tokyo, coming as the final collapse of South Vietnam appeared to symbolize the decline of American power in the West Pacific. Yet it was largely geared to missions outside the immediate area under review.

Narrowing the focus to northeastern Asia, an authoritative naval analyst concludes, "As it has always been for the Soviet Pacific Fleet, the primary mission must be to secure the regional waters that wash Soviet Siberia, particularly the Sea of Japan. The numerous small combatants assigned to the Pacific fleet would be good for little else."[36] This cautions against simply juxtaposing ship totals in the Soviet and American fleets to measure their relative combat effectiveness.

One major problem is securing access to the Pacific Ocean. Three potential choke points confront Soviet naval commanders. The southern route via the East China Sea transits the Tsushima Strait between Korea and Japan. The most direct passage to the Pacific passes through the Tsugaru Strait between the Japanese islands of Honshu and Hokkaido. Further north the Soya (La Perouse) Strait between Sakhalin and Hokkaido links the Sea of Japan with the Sea of Okhotsk, from which the Pacific can be reached through the Kuril Islands. The only alternative to these vulnerable points of passage is the very narrow and shallow Strait of Nevelskoi between Sakhalin and the Siberian mainland. From here ships must cross the Sea of Okhotsk, a distance of 1280 kilometers (800 miles), which is blocked with ice for up to 6 months a year.[37] Considerable time and fuel are additionally required for this route.

Except for the Tsushima Strait, where swift currents impede their use, mines can block movement from the Sea of Japan. Soviet ships could deploy to blue water before a pending crisis erupted into conflict, but they would still need to return to mainland bases for fueling, resupply, and repair. This explains why one-fifth of the fleet consists of minesweepers. Should the choke points be closed, the long route to Vladivostok via the Strait of Nevelskoi could be bypassed in favor of Petropavlovsk, which lies on the Pacific. However, it lacks the facilities of mainland ports, its access is ice-covered from November to April, and it has no rail supply line.[38]

Moscow faces further complications in the need for merchant shipping to supply the Soviet Far East. Enemy submarines could exact a heavy toll along the lengthy route across the Indian Ocean, the East China Sea, and the West Pacific. A revealing statement by Admiral Sergei Gorshkov stressed the limited effectiveness of Allied anti-submarine warfare (ASW) efforts in World War II, warning, "If ASW forces which were so numerous and technically up to date (for that time), possessing a vast superiority, turned out to be capable of only partially limiting the operations of diesel submarines, then what must this superiority be today to counter nuclear-power submarines?"[39]

Any assessment of the actual power of the Soviet Pacific Fleet requires examination of varied combat scenarios, depending on whether the war is limited to East Asia or global in extent and whether it is of short or long duration. This is essential in order to evaluate the American navy's potential role, alternate missions elsewhere, and possible redeployment to the West Pacific. But our brief survey highlights the defensive tasks in northeastern Asia that are an important factor in determining the strength and composition of the Soviet ships in that area.

As for the fleet's ability to support offensive activity, such as an invasion of Japan, the sea power in hand consists of 18 amphibious ships and two naval regiments totaling 4000 troops.[40] Shore bombardment would depend largely on air attack, since the growth of missile-equipped ships has reduced the number of gun-carrying ships available for this purpose. However, any action beyond the range of land-based aircraft must come from the single carrier *Minsk* that is presently in the Soviet Pacific Fleet. Its 12 aircraft and 20 helicopters are basically for antisubmarine warfare.[41] All things considered, Hokkaido faces a far less serious threat than one might judge from its relative proximity to Sakhalin.

In the absence of actual hostilities, the Soviet fleet plays an important political role in projecting an image of power that is heightened in Japan by media attention. This traditional use of a navy to "show the flag" is manifest in the recurrent passage of Soviet ships near Tokyo's territorial waters. More than 300 Soviet naval ships traverse the three major straits of Tsushima, Tsugaru, and Soya each year, and an intelligence ship is stationed in the Tsushima Strait most of the time.[42] In June 1978 a Soviet task force of *Kresta-II*-class missile cruisers and destroyers moved from exercises between Okinawa and Guam to take part in an airlift and amphibious ship operation in the southernmost Kurils that involved the disputed islands of Etorofu and Kunashiri. Again in 1980 small flotillas of Soviet ships transited the Tsugaru Strait between Hokkaido and Honshu as part of the buildup of forces in Shikotan and the Habomais.[43]

The heightened visibility of Moscow's fleet contrasts with the reduced profile of Washington's naval presence in the area. The number of ships assigned to the U.S. Seventh Fleet declined precipitously during the decade 1969–1979, as the gradual winding down of the Vietnam war led to mothballing or reassignment of vessels elsewhere; in 1969 it had 225 ships; in 1970, 145; in 1971, 95; and in 1978, 50.[44] In simple aggregate numbers, as of 1978 the Soviet Pacific Fleet totaled 550 ships to the U.S.

fleet's 50, displaced 762,000 tons to 503,000, and had an average ship-age of 9 years as compared with 15.[45]

The key comparisons depend on whether a war is global or regional. In peacetime, however, public perceptions do not turn on a sophisticated analysis of combat capabilities, missions, and technology. Instead, they tend to rest on a simplistic juxtaposition of aggregate numbers and hypothetical "worst-case" scenarios. This tendency is reinforced by the parochial interest of military bureaucracies in enlarging their budgetary allocation by emphasizing another country's apparent strength. Thus, the Japan Defense Agency's White Paper of 1977 declared that the "buildup of the Soviet Navy cannot be simply ignored since it has ramifications for the region. In particular the advance of the Soviet Navy into the open sea has further heightened the relevant countries' concerns for their security, especially Japan which is positioned close to the straits through which the Soviet Navy passes for its access into the oceans."[46] This overstates the case somewhat. However, it is worth noting as an illustration of some of the strategic implications of Soviet naval activity in peacetime.

Siberian Development: What Difference?

At the outset of this chapter we defined our problem in terms of the difference in military capability that is likely to ensue from Siberian development. In this regard, the best point of departure is BAM, since it is the most strategically important project currently under way.

Russian military performance in the Far East reflects credibly on the capacity of the Trans-Siberian Railroad to meet military needs, at least up to the present. In the 1904–1905 war with Japan, although the Tsarist navy met defeat, an army of approximately 250,000 troops fought fiercely enough to force Tokyo into seeking American mediation.[47] At the time this was an impressive logistical achievement since it was accomplished far from European Russia against an enemy so proximately located. Three decades later—in 1938 at Changkufeng (Lake Khasan) on the Manchurian–Soviet border and in 1939 at Nomonhan (Khalkin-Gol) on the Manchurian–Mongolian border—the Red Army inflicted heavy casualties in division-size engagements with local Japanese units.[48] Japanese intelligence claimed that Soviet strength grew from 20 divisions in 1947 to 30 divisions by 1939, or from 370,000 to 570,000 troops.[49] Although the celebrated commander of the Soviet forces, Marshal G. K. Zhukov, acknowledged transportation problems in his memoir, he singled out the Trans-Baikal military district for special commendation.[50]

Perhaps the most remarkable logistical feat was the massive movement of men and material from the European front to East Asian Siberia in order to attack Japan within the 3 months of the defeat of Nazi Germany, as agreed upon at the Yalta Conference. According to an authoritative Soviet history, in May 1945 a bare 40 divisions equipped with obsolete tanks defended the whole Far East region.[51] By August this force had grown to "eleven field, one tank, three air, and three air-defense armies . . . with over 1,500,000 officers and men, more than 26,000 guns and mortars, and more than 5500 tanks and self-propelled guns."[52] The feat entailed redeployment over distances ranging from 9000 to 12,000 kilometers (5580 to 7440 miles), as well as interfront and innerfront regroupings of up to 1500 kilometers (930 miles) between Blagoveschensk and Maritime Krai. The main body of troops actually came from beyond the Soviet frontier in Europe. Altogether some 136,000 railroad cars were involved; during June and July, between 22 and 30 trains per day ran east of Lake Baikal.

The more recent military expansion opposite China pales by comparison in terms of both the much smaller deployment and the longer time involved. Nonetheless, the doubling of armed strength in Central Asia and Siberia from 15 to nearly 35 divisions between 1965 and 1969 proved the system's ability to meet a sudden military demand, although the movement may well have entailed considerable disruption of normal civilian traffic.

This impressive record notwithstanding, Soviet defense officials undoubtedly were acutely aware of the Trans-Siberian's vulnerability to disruption by human and natural causes. According to an authoritative Soviet source, "The idea of building BAM first arose in 1932" after the Japanese seizure of Manchuria.[53] The result was a spur line running north to Komsomolsk from Volochayevka, west of Khabarovsk. When Japanese pressure erupted in full-scale battles along the border in 1938–1939, further work progressed on "the alignment . . . between Tynda and Sovetskaia Gavan, [which was] determined in 1938–1942." By extending the line east from Komsomolsk to Sovetskaia Gavan and Vanino during World War II, the Soviets provided themselves with an alternate route to Vladivostok via the Sea of Japan in case the Trans-Siberian was disrupted below Khabarovsk, where it paralleled the Manchurian border.[54]

After the war, construction on BAM stopped because of the greater priority given to rebuilding the devastated portions of the Soviet Union, but in the 1960s a coincidence of factors revived Moscow's interest in BAM. We have already noted how Chinese statements and behavior heightened the sense of perceived threat, particularly during the Cultural Revolution. In this regard, a Soviet statement to the effect that it was "possible in 1967 to resume design work on the BAM project in light of improved engineering conditions and devices" is highly suggestive.[55] Of course, the completion of reconstruction in the war-torn areas did gradually free more funds for less developed regions, among which Siberia had long held a special attraction for economic planners.

This attraction was strengthened by postwar surveys and studies that had revealed a wide range of natural resources to be available for exploitation if access and technology could become available. The latter factor, in turn, prompted the decision to involve foreign governments and companies in Siberian development as a means of acquiring the capital and the technology necessary for such a costly and difficult venture.

BAM promised to serve both economic and military needs. In 1974 the massive project was officially launched amid nation-wide fanfare. In strategic terms BAM offers more than adequate assurance against interdiction by ground attack. Its closest approach to the Chinese border leaves it almost 200 kilometers (125 miles) away. Much of it lies between 250 and 270 kilometers (155 and 170 miles) away, and the remainder is even more distant.[56] Moreover, although the Trans-Siberian frequently parallels the Amur and Ussuri rivers on fairly flat ground, BAM is separated from China by mountainous terrain. Should the Trans-Siberian's north–south line to Vladivostok be cut, BAM could still supply the main naval base through Vanino and Sovetskaia Gavan.

The more likely threat of attack by aircraft or missiles is not so drastically reduced. Allowing for the necessity to site Chinese bases well behind the border, the consequent distance of 500 kilometers (310 miles) to BAM offers no decisive advantage for its defense. In addition, the 3145 kilometers (1965 miles) of single track between Ust-Kut and Komsomolsk offers numerous potential choke points. Approximately 3700 bridges and culverts will span bogs and rivers, many of which swell with water from thawing snow and summer rains.[57] More than 140 of the bridges exceed 90 meters (300 feet) in length, and three are 1365 meters (4500 feet), 490 meters (1260 feet), and 412 meters (1375 feet) long.[58] These offer attractive targets for air attack. Less vulnerable, but more disabling if damaged, are the BAM tunnels, which total 24 kilometers (15 miles), including one of 14.4 kilometers (9 miles) and another of 6.4 kilometers (4 miles).[59]

Most of the line passes over permafrost that is unevenly distributed in location and thickness.[60] Here the track must be elevated on a berm of wood or gravel to a height of 2 meters or more (6 plus feet) to guard against the effects of heat and thaw on surface ground.[61] Bridge pilings frequently must be individually designed for depth and stress to allow for the varied subsoil conditions.[62] These factors complicate the maintenance of BAM in wartime. The situation is worsened by the weak infrastructure of service roads, warehouses, and repair stations that would be needed to speed the restoration of traffic following an attack.

An additional vulnerability lies in the plan to electrify the western portion of BAM so as to exploit the large surplus of cheap hydro power available throughout the region and to minimize pollution. Because of the permafrost, lines and installations will be above ground, which increases both their exposure to attack and the cost of protective shelters. The destruction of power lines and stations would paralyze movement until diesel equipment could arrive or the damage be repaired.

Beyond these specific wartime hazards, a host of natural phenomena make BAM a high risk railroad with uncertain reliability.[63] East of Lake Baikal it traverses one of the most active seismic areas in the USSR. Nearly 30 earthquakes of 6 points or greater on the Richter scale have been recorded in the BAM service area with a periodicity of one every 15–20 years. The effects are worsened by permafrost, which heightens the acceleration of transverse waves by a factor of two or more, resulting in greater ground flow, rock debris movements, liquefaction, and mudflows. The concentration of tunnels in the seismic area poses special problems in their alignment and reinforcement.

Landslides and mudflows occur with particular frequency in the central BAM area. Avalanches pose an additional hazard. Icing is a major problem in hundreds of places along the route, with active zones ranging from 1000 to over 1 million cubic meters. Cumulatively, these phenomena pose a threat of interrupted service that could cut freight shipments for weeks at a time, depending upon the origin, severity, location, and timing of the event.

North–south links between BAM and the Trans-Siberian provide alternate routes to bypass afflicted portions, but these are few in number and widely separated. As already noted, service roads and storage points for emergency equipment will be inadequate for many years because of the slowness in developing ancillary facilities, especially in the most hazard-prone sections. Soviet engineers and planners are fully apprised of these problems and have made every effort to anticipate them. Nevertheless, the supply of human, fiscal, and technological resources is extremely limited by comparison with the magnitude of the task.

Taking these various factors into consideration, BAM would appear to have more military value in a precombat situation than in an actual war. It provides a major logistical supplement to the Trans-Siberian for strengthening Soviet forces throughout the area, and facilitates the stockpiling of supplies, including ammunition and petroleum, to sustain prolonged fighting on land and sea. It also provides access to additional territory for the stationing and dispersal of military personnel and installations.

These advantages enhance Moscow's ability to prepare for war in East Asia. Once war begins, however, BAM's liabilities may outweigh its assets. Much depends on the specific circumstances, of course. It can make a considerable difference whether the war is of short or long duration, whether it is fought with conventional or nuclear weapons, and whether the enemy can target with sufficient accuracy and damage to keep BAM inoperative. Regardless of the scenario, the reliability and vulnerability of BAM under conditions of modern warfare remain open to question.

It may be this uncertain prospect that prompted a high Soviet official to remark privately, "Don't overstate BAM's military importance. In the next war, it won't be a question of moving lots of troops over long distances. In the first hours, missiles will be flying and many people will be killed—on both sides."[64] It is impossible to know the degree to which this view is shared by military strategists. A major portion of the labor for BAM's construction was provided by railroad engineering divisions from the Soviet army.[65] It is doubtful that so costly a project, consuming nearly 1% of the annual USSR investment budget, could be undertaken against military opposition.[66]

Yet BAM does not receive the priority in funding of a project that is primarily seen as having strategic importance. Four years after its start, the State Planning Committee had cut the 1978 financing 30.6 million rubles below the previous annual expenditure, and 1979 was still lower.[67] Reporting this, *Pravda* remarked, "Evidently the Ministry of Railroads and Ministry of Transport Construction have still not argued for an intensive work program." The goal of completion by 1983 seems unlikely to be achieved. Soviet officials informally suggest 1985 as the earliest year to begin test runs over the entire line, and perhaps another 2 years will be needed before BAM can be fully operational.[68] This stretched-out schedule implies more than a decade of investment before the returns can begin to be realized. It also implies that Soviet strategists have realistically assessed BAM's limitations, and that they do not envisage the line as improving their Far East capability sufficiently to justify a more accelerated effort.

Whether a similar perception will prevail in Beijing once BAM is completed remains to be seen. Beijing's propaganda, always ready to exploit evidence of a Soviet threat to Japan as well as China, has paid relatively little attention to BAM. A rare reference in early 1978 reviewed the overall effort to develop Siberia east of the Urals, including "construction of the Baikal-Amur Railway," but placed major emphasis on the line's strategic implications for NATO. The commentary claimed the Kremlin's design is to "make the east the rear of its western front" and "to support its major contention in Europe."[69] Japanese firms engaged in engineering projects on BAM experienced no Chinese pressures to desist, and one of the largest companies subsequently won a major contract in the PRC.[70]

For its part, Tokyo shows no sign of giving BAM the strategic significance that was attributed to the Trans-Siberian Railroad at the end of the last century. Although the competition between Russia and Japan for spheres of influence in Korea and Manchuria was the basic cause of conflict in 1904–1905, the war's timing was in large part determined by apprehension that completion of the transcontinental line would permit St. Petersburg to strengthen its military power in the Far East.

No such worries appear to concern officials today.[71] On the contrary, BAM is viewed as advantageous for the exploitation of Siberian resources, particularly timber and coal, to meet Japan's needs. Japanese Export–Import Bank loans are not involved, but the close consultation that takes place in Japan between business and government on such matters makes it likely that official approval underlies the involvement of Japanese firms in BAM's construction. This would not be the case were the railroad seen as significantly increasing the Soviet threat.

In sum, the strategic implications of BAM vary considerably, depending upon whether it is assessed in a precombat or combat context and whether the point of assessment is Moscow, Beijing, or Tokyo. BAM clearly enhances the Soviet ability to strengthen and supply forces in East Asian Siberia and the West Pacific. It also offers defense in depth against a ground invasion that might interdict the Trans-Siberian Railroad. But to what extent these attributes heighten or lessen the likelihood of tension and conflict will depend on specific situations.

For example, if Soviet military planners are more relaxed about the consequences of incidents, escalation, or surprise attack cutting the Trans-Siberian because of BAM's fallback capacity, they might be less likely to unleash a preemptive attack in a Sino–Soviet crisis. If, on the other hand, Chinese military planners anticipate another major expansion of Soviet forces as a consequence of BAM's completion, they might press more vigorously for countervailing measures that would accelerate a local arms race.

On balance, BAM's strategic implications for East Asia are worth noting, but without exaggeration or undue emphasis. By comparison, of much greater interest to Japan and the United States is the effect of Siberian development on Moscow's maritime presence in the Pacific. The most relevant project is the new port of Wrangel. Located across the bay from Nakhodka, by 1990 Wrangel will be able to handle 40 million tons of cargo a year.[72] This will make it possible for many more Soviet merchant vessels to serve the area. Together with BAM, the ships can appreciably augment the logistical flow to meet military needs.

In addition, these ships can perform multiple tasks of intelligence collection and can accomplish the clandestine transport of weaponry.[73] During a conflict, their preplanned conversion to military support roles will offer a valuable auxiliary fleet for the Soviet navy. Wrangel can also relieve congestion at military bases for refueling and repair, depending on the nature of hostilities in the area.

Beyond the direct contributions to military capability offered by BAM and Wrangel, indirect contributions can emerge through the expanding economic infrastructure that will be a consequence of Siberian development. This could result in an enlarged population base and skilled labor force, an improved transportation network, a modern metallurgical industry, and the general upgrading of locally manufactured products. None of these factors is of significance in themselves, but taken together they contribute to the efficiency and effectiveness of a fighting force that is held in place against a distant future contingency. Besides reducing dependence on remote sources for supplies and spare parts, the general development of the region can eventually change the human environment within which the armed services, particularly the army, function.

But this will be slow in coming. The constraints on growth are severe and will remain so. The BAM zone produces only one-third of its present food requirement.[74] The severity and vagaries of local climatic conditions, the effects of permafrost, and the scarcity of arable land combine to prevent the region from becoming self-sufficient in agriculture. As a result, long-distance hauling from more fruitful areas of the USSR raises prices and reduces variety. The cost of living is further increased by the greater expenditure for construction, maintenance, heating, and clothing necessitated by the harsh environment.

These circumstances inhibit migration into the BAM zone. They also induce planners to cluster support services such as hospitals, schools, cultural activity, and entertainment in existing population centers. Yet the continued growth of a few very large cities could pose a risk in wartime. Enemy missiles need only hit Vladivostok, Khabarovsk, and Irkutsk to endanger roughly 15% of the population and a much larger proportion of the industry of East Asian Siberia. All three targets lie within easy range of possible launching sites in northeastern China.

The effect on Soviet strategic thinking is problematic. The vulnerability of these nodal points in the region's economy places a premium on preempting a perceived threat of attack. However, in time defensive concerns should be alleviated to the extent that population and industry can be more widely distributed, as is envisaged for the next decade. Soviet economic analysis suggests that cities of approximately 100,000 persons are optimal for this region, being large enough to justify the necessary services without requiring an excessive network of transportation, supply lines, and sewage disposal facilities.[75] In addition to reducing the problem of defense, the proliferation of new cities would improve the support environment for military units scattered throughout the area.

Economic development will also improve the transportation system throughout the region. This should enhance military logistics in terms of mobility and reliability. In addition to BAM's lateral route, its possible northward extension to Yakutsk will open up previously inaccessible areas for the exploitation of local resources. Maintenance will improve as the necessary manpower and equipment become available. River use may increase with more icebreakers and dredging.

A modern metallurgical industry would also be helpful from a military point of view. The only existing steel works, at Komsomolsk, are inadequate for more than local requirements of low alloy steel.[76] Large deposits of iron ore located near good coking coal offer an attractive base for further development in southern Yakutia, and it seems likely that a major metallurgical base will eventually be built in the region to meet the growing local need and to exploit local resources. This will enhance self-sufficiency, but it may not make it complete. Moreover, all of the prospective sites lie within range of potential Chinese missiles. Reliance on a single point of production could invite a crippling attack. As in other areas, a precombat increase in capability may be offset by wartime vulnerability.

Viewed overall, Siberian development offers only a limited increase in Soviet strategic military capability beyond that already in existence in the area. Its greatest contribution is in its strengthening of the region's logistical and support capacity before hostilities begin. Once a war starts, however, the defensive liabilities appear to outweigh the offensive advantages.

Economic Leverage and Strategic Implications
The exercise of economic leverage on an importing country is a familiar phenomenon in East Asia. Prior to World War II, the United States embargoed the export of strategic goods to Japan—first scrap iron and then oil—to dissuade Tokyo from further aggression. Beginning in 1950 Washington imposed a total embargo on American trade with the People's Republic of China and a strategic embargo on selected items traded by its allies with Beijing. Although the total embargo was lifted at the time of President Nixon's trip to China in 1972, the strategic embargo persisted well after the

"normalization" of relations in 1979 in the form of controls exercised by NATO and Japan.

Siberian development offers Japanese access to energy resources—coal, gas, and oil—as well as such less essential items as timber, asbestos, and copper, which play an important role in the economy. To what extent might Japanese dependency on the Soviet Union for such commodities present a risk in terms of Moscow's ability to manipulate supply for political purposes in peacetime or for military ends in war? As a rule of thumb, Japanese officials indicate a willingness to rely on Soviet supplies for up to a fifth or so of their import total of particular items, but not to go much beyond this limit.[77] Thus, in 1977 the Soviet Union supplied 23.9% of Japan's imported asbestos and roughly 20% of its imported nickel.[78]

According to one official estimate, if the Yakutia natural gas project comes to fruition, the USSR could supply nearly 20% of Japan's total LNG consumption by 1990.[79] However, it is calculated that LNG will contribute less than 10% of the overall energy need.[80] Therefore, the potential Soviet leverage, although it may be pinpointed on certain sectors of the economy, will be minimal for the country as a whole.

South Yakutian coking coal is anticipated to meet from 7 to 10% of Japanese consumption by 1985–1990. With 40% coming from Australia, 25% from the United States, and 15% from Canada, the Soviet potential for leverage will be relatively small. Steam coal will account for only 4% of the total energy requirement in 1990, thereby permitting a somewhat greater increase of such imports from the Soviet Union. Sakhalin oil will amount to only 1% of total petroleum imports, a wholly expendable amount that can be supplied elsewhere.

The combined impact of all four commodities being cut off by Moscow would cause short-term dislocation in selected areas and industries. However, there would be no long-term impact, assuming that other suppliers could increase their deliveries. Japan's various trading partners in the Pacific Basin appear more than capable of filling gaps that might arise from a Soviet embargo on energy exports, although a brief interval might be necessary to increase production and reorient transportation. This fact is so obvious that it presumably would deter Moscow from any such threat, much less action.

Timber is a less critical item, but it looms somewhat larger statistically, 28.4% of Japan's 1977 imports coming from the USSR compared with 63.7% from the United States.[81] Moreover, the higher grade softwoods are North American while their hardwood counterparts originate in Southeast Asia. As with other items, the Soviet supply is useful, but not essential to the economy.

Conversely, the degree to which any such embargo or attempted leverage would hurt the Soviet economy varies from one commodity to another and from one point in time to another. Where the export is in repayment for already acquired capital and technology, Moscow has the advantage, but where it earns foreign exchange needed to pay other bills, for instance, for grain imports, the embargo would inflict a cost on the Soviet economy. In the case of natural gas, Japan will provide the only foreign market other than the United States. There is not likely to be sufficient domestic demand to take up the slack in distribution of output. This in turn would reduce the return on Moscow's original investment. These calculations reveal the symbiosis that characterizes the relationship of the two countries to Siberia's development.

Soviet involvement in the world economy would raise risks on other fronts if Moscow were to apply economic pressure against Tokyo. Reneging on energy exports as payment for acquired technology in Sakhalin and Yakutia would jeopardize the Soviet ability to acquire oil and gas equipment elsewhere. This could paralyze its effort to exploit offshore oil, a vital need in the 1990s.[82] In addition, Washington could support Tokyo with a retaliatory embargo against grain sales to Moscow. Depending upon the availability of alternative supplies, this could hurt, given the chronic vulnerability of Soviet agriculture to bad climate and its continuing inability to raise output.[83] In short, the backlash from singling out Japan for economic leverage could be severely damaging.

Economics aside, it is difficult to define a plausible situation in which Moscow might be tempted to apply such pressure. It would be wholly inadequate for a major goal such as forcing Tokyo to renounce the American alliance or to exclude American bases. It would probably boomerang as an effort to reduce Japanese defense expenditures or to brake a growing Beijing–Tokyo entente. It certainly would not silence public opinion on such issues as the northern territories and fishing incidents, and once such leverage was attempted, no further Japanese cooperation in Siberian development would be likely. This would leave much of the program without hope of realization in this century.

This does not exhaust the examination of the strategic implications for East Asia that may flow from EAS development. In this chapter we have focused primarily on likely military and economic consequences, not on Soviet behavior and the factors that may affect it. To gain a fuller appreciation of alternative future prospects, we must examine in more detail the specific national relationships and perspectives that both affect and are affected by Soviet strategy in the region (i.e., those involving Japan and China). Decision making in Moscow must be forecast in terms of alternative assumptions that posit, on the one hand, future foreign participation in the development of East Asian Siberia and, on the other, a basically unilateral Soviet program. The availability or lack of EAS resources must be weighed in the context of the larger Soviet economy and of global resources in order to evaluate their full strategic significance.

In general terms, East Asian Siberia is likely to be more of a defensive liability than an offensive asset for Moscow during the balance of the twentieth century. It will remain remote from the center of Soviet power. Its logistical vulnerability and environmental constraints will combine to leave the area relatively weak and undeveloped compared with China, a hostile and unpredictable neighbor. Nothing in the anticipated development of EAS will overcome these deficiencies, although some problems may be ameliorated.

# Notes

[1]Allen S. Whiting, *China Crosses the Yalu* (New York, 1960).

[2]*Allocation of Resources in the Soviet Union and China—1978*, hearings before the Subcommittee on Priorities and Economy in Government of the Joint Economic Committee, Congress of the United States (Washington, D.C., 1978), part 4, p. 88.

[3]*Ibid.*, p. 239. According to an unofficial but well-informed source, by late 1979 this had increased to 46 divisions. See International Institute for Strategic Studies, *The Military Balance, 1979–1980* (London, 1979), p. 10.

[4]John M. Collins, *Balance between U.S. and Soviet Armed Forces* (Washington, D.C., 1980), pp. 28ff.

[5]*Military Balance*, p. 60.

[6]Raymond Garthoff, "Sino–Soviet Military Relations, 1945–66," in *Sino-Soviet Military Relations*, ed. Raymond Garthoff (New York, 1966), pp. 84–88.

[7]Morton H. Halperin, *China and the Bomb* (New York, 1965).

[8]*Allocation of Resources*, p. 240.

[9]Mao Zedong, Speech to Japanese visitors, July 10, 1964, in *Mao Zedong sixiang wan sui* (Long live Mao Zedong thought; 1969 ed., Taibei, 1974), pp. 540–541. For a similar version, see Dennis J. Doolin, *Territorial Claims in the Sino–Soviet Conflict: Documents and Analysis* (Stanford, Calif., 1965), p. 44. The English version was translated from *Sekai shuho*, August 11, 1964, which in turn was based on the original Chinese. No authorized transcript was issued by Peking.

[10]Morris Rothenberg, *Whither China: The View from the Kremlin* (Miami, Fla., 1977), pp. 89–90.

[11]*Pravda*, September 2, 1964, in Doolin, pp. 47–52.

[12]Based on the author's access to official U.S. data at the time. For a lower but incorrect estimate, see *Strategic Survey, 1969* (London, 1970); much higher figures were reported by Harrison Salisbury in the *New York Times*, May 24, 1969, and August 31, 1969.

[13]See n. 12 above.

[14]Rothenberg, p. 91.

[15]Edward E. Rice, *Mao's Way* (Berkeley, Calif., 1972), chap. 22, pp. 358–381.

[16]The most careful reconstruction of the incident and examination of alternative hypotheses is Thomas W. Robinson, "The Sino–Soviet Border Dispute: Background, Development, and the March 1969 Clashes," *American Political Science Review* 4 (December 1972), pp. 1175–1202.

[17]Neville Maxwell, "The Chinese Account of the 1969 Fighting at Chenpao," *China Quarterly* 56 (October–December 1973), pp. 730–739.

[18]Rothenberg, *Whither China*, pp. 91–92.

[19]Information available to the author at the time. See also Lu Yung-shu, "Preparation for War in Mainland China," in *Collected Documents of the First Sino–American Conference on Mainland China* (Taibei, 1971), p. 907.

[20]Henry Kissinger, *The White House Years* (Boston, 1979), p. 183.

[21]Data from U.S. Army Map Service, 1:250,000, L-542, Sheet NL 53–7, *Hu-lin, China* (Washington, D.C., 1955). The particular point of proximity to China is above Lazlo. At Lazlo the distance is 5 km (3.1 mi.); see L-542, Sheet NL 53–4, *Pao-ch'ing, China*.

[22]*The World Atlas* (Moscow, 1967), p. 44, shows the Trans-Siberian east–west route on this alignment; a slightly greater distance from China is depicted on another Soviet map, *Baikalo-Amurskaia zheleznodorozhnaia magistral* (The Baikal-

Amur railroad mainline; Moscow, 1977), 1 cm:25 km, published by the Main Administration of Geodesy and Cartography, Council of Ministers, USSR. Both maps agree with the Army Map Service measurements for the north-south line to Vladivostok.

[23]*The Times Atlas of China* (New York, 1973), p. xxix.

[24]*Ibid.*, pp. xvii, 22.

[25]Yevgenii Yevtushenko, "On the Red Russian Snow," *Literaturnaia gazeta* 12 (March 19, 1969), in *Current Digest of the Soviet Press* (hereinafter *CDSP*) 21 (April 30, 1969).

[26]The author visited the USSR in 1972, 1975, and 1978 to consult academic specialists in Moscow and other centers; in 1975 and 1978 he traversed Siberia between Novosibirsk and Khabarovsk.

[27]In addition to those I encountered in private conversations, I have found a similar observation in Victor Louis, *The Coming Decline of the Chinese Empire* (New York, 1979), pp. 175–176.

[28]*Military Balance*, p. 10. John M. Collins, *Imbalance of Power* (San Rafael, Calif., 1978), p. 130, notes that "about half of all Soviet divisions on the Chinese border are Category III. The Kremlin apparently anticipates no early aggression by either side in that area."

[29]Interview with informed Soviet official, September 1978.

[30]Interview with Academician A. G. Aganbegyan, September 27, 1978.

[31]A "ship-day" registers the presence of a single naval vessel, regardless of size of function in a designated area. Thus, Soviet Far East naval movement to and from the Indian Ocean is counted in the Pacific Ocean en route and then in its destination on arrival. Data supplied from Barry M. Blechman and Robert P. Berman, eds., *Guide to Far Eastern Navies* (Annapolis, Md., 1978).

[32]*Ibid.*, pp. 44–45.

[33]*Ibid.*, p. 40.

[34]Research Institute for Peace and Security, *Asian Security 1979* (Tokyo, 1979), pp. 45–49.

[35]Blechman, p. 45.

[36]*Ibid.*, pp. 46–47.

[37]Paul E. Lydolph, *Geography of the USSR* (3rd ed.; New York, 1977), p. 439.

[38]*Asian Security*, p. 55.

[39]Sergei Gorshkov, "Navies in War and Peace," *Morskoi sbornik* 11 (1972), p. 26; my translation was supplied by Donald C. Daniel.

[40]*Asian Security*, p. 49. Of course, these regiments could be supplemented with additional forces from the southern Kurils and Sakhalin.

[41]Stephen S. Kaplan, "Soviet Risk-taking in Asian Countries," in *Soviet Policy in Asia*, ed. Donald S. Zagoria (New Haven, Conn: Yale University Press, 1982).

[42]*Ibid.* Unless otherwise noted, the entire paragraph is based on Kaplan.

[43]*New York Times*, April 1, 1980.

[44]Blechman, *Far Eastern Navies*, pp. 16–17.

[45]*Ibid.*, p. 52.

[46]Japan Defense Agency, *Defense of Japan, 1977 (White Paper)* (Tokyo, 1977), pp. 24–25.

[47]David Walder, *The Short Victorious War* (New York, 1977), p. 80.

[48]Alvin D. Coox, *The Anatomy of a Small War: The Soviet–Japanese Struggle for Changkufeng-Khasan, 1938* (Westport, Conn., 1977), p. 285; Hata Ikuhiko, "The Japanese–Soviet Confrontation, 1935–1939," in *Deterrent Diplomacy: Japan, Germany, and the USSR, 1935–40*, ed. James W. Morley (New York, 1976).

[49]Hata, p. 131.

[50]G. K. Zhukov, *The Memoirs of Marshal Zhukov* (New York, 1971), chap. 7.

[51]M. V. Zakharov, ed., *Finale: A Retrospective Review of Imperialist Japan's Defeat in 1945*, tr. David Skvirsky (Moscow, 1972), p. 69.

[52]*Ibid.*, p. 74.

[53]N. P. Belen'kiy and V. S. Maslennikov, "The Baikal-Amur Railroad: Its Area of Influence and Its Projected Freight Loads," *Zheleznodorozhnii transport* 10 (1974), pp. 39–46, in *Soviet Geography*, October 1975, pp. 507–513. It is also included in Theodore Shabad and Victor L. Mote, *Gateway to Siberian Resources (The BAM)* (Washington, D.C., 1977), pp. 123–133.

[54]Shabad and Mote, p. 72.

[55]*Ibid.*, p. 126.

[56]*Baikalo-Amurskaia zheleznodorozhnaia magistral.*

[57]Shabad and Mote, p. 79.

[58]*Ibid.*, pp. 74–76.

[59]*Ibid.*, p. 74.

[60]E. V. Pinneker and B. I. Pikarski, *Podzemnie vody zony Baikalo-Amurskoi magistrali* (Underground water zone of the Baikal-Amur Mainline; Novosibirsk, 1977). Longitudinal graphs chart the subsoil conditions throughout the BAM zone.

[61]Shabad and Mote, *Gateway*, p. 103.

[62]Interviews, Permafrost Institute, AS-USSR, Yakutsk, October 1978.

[63]Victor L. Mote, "Environmental Constraints to the Economic Development of Siberia," Discussion Paper 6 (December 1978), in AAG. This and the following paragraph draw heavily on Mote's excellent synthesis of Soviet and western literature illuminating the complex interaction of human and natural hazards that confront BAM.

[64]Interview with Soviet official, September 17, 1978.

[65]Mote, pp. 64–69; in subsequent correspondence with the author, he expanded the documentation cited here.

[66]The estimate of BAM's cost as a proportion of total investment was offered by A. G. Aganbegyan in an interview, September 27, 1978.

[67]*Pravda*, May 5, 1979 in *CDSP* 31 (May 30, 1979).

[68]Interviews, September–October 1978.

[69]"What Is the Soviet Union's Intention in Emphasizing Development of the East?" Beijing domestic service in Mandarin, January 12, 1978, in Foreign Broadcast Information Service (hereafter FBIS), PRC, January 13, 1978.

[70]Interviews, Tokyo, July and October 1978. In the fall of 1979, press reports claimed that Komatsu, a major engineering firm involved with BAM, was negotiating the first Japanese joint-venture project in China; FBIS, PRC, October 16, 1979.

[71]Interviews with Japanese officials, Tokyo and Washington, 1978–1980.

[72]For an eyewitness account of Wrangel, see Stephen Uhalley, Jr., *The Soviet Far East: Growing Participation in the Pacific*, Field Staff Report, 21.1 (New York, September 1977).

[73]For specific examples in the Angolan and Ethiopian campaigns, see Robert F. Ellsworth, "Trends in International Maritime Transport," International Symposium on the Sea (Tokyo, 1978), p. 11, mimeographed.

[74]Interview with A. G. Aganbegyan, September 28, 1978.

[75]*Ibid.*

[76]Violet Conolly, *Siberia Today and Tomorrow* (New York, 1976), p. 97.

[77]Interviews, July and October 1978, March 1979.

[78]Richard L. Edmonds, "Siberian Resource Development and the Japanese Economy: The Japanese Perspective," Discussion Paper 12 (August 1979), in AAG.

[79]Unpublished official report of the Japanese Ministry of Foreign Affairs, Tokyo, dated June 1978.

[80]*Asian Wall Street Journal,* September 7, 1979, reporting an official 16-year energy program.

[81]Edmonds, p. 13.

[82]John P. Hardt, Ronda A. Bresnick, and David Levine, "Soviet Oil and Gas in the Global Perspective," in *Project Interdependence: U.S. and World Energy Outlook Through 1990,* a Report by the Congressional Research Service, Library of Congress (Washington, D.C., 1977), pp. 798–801.

[83]Central Intelligence Agency, *USSR: Long-Term Outlook for Grain Imports* (ER 79-10057; Washington, D.C., January 1979).

# 35

## HARRY GELMAN

## *Soviet Policy toward China\**

Today, seven years since Mao Zedong left the scene, two tendencies are visibly contending for predominance in Soviet policy toward China. One current of opinion, which I consider much the weaker of the two, favors more active Soviet steps to conciliate the PRC in order to try to expand the modest areas of improvement in Sino–Soviet relations that have emerged since 1981, and, if possible, permanently to redirect Chinese fears and hostility away from the Soviet Union and toward the United States. The other current, which at present seems to me to have considerably greater strength in Moscow, also would like to see a meaningful Sino–Soviet rapprochement but is highly sceptical that this can be achieved and most reluctant to make significant concessions to Beijing without far-fetching prior Chinese concessions. Above all, those who support this latter tendency appear to be unwilling to sacrifice the concrete geopolitical advantages around China's periphery which Soviet military power achieved in the 1970s at China's expense.

As a result, Sino–Soviet relations now exist simultaneously on two widely divergent tracks. On secondary matters, there continues to be gradual progress; on major matters, there remains a total impasse.

On the one hand, the Soviets and the Chinese both see it as in their interests to continue to pursue a series of slow, step-by-step improvements in certain aspects of their state-to-state relations, particularly in the spheres of economics, sports, and culture. The Soviets sought such improvements immediately after Mao's death, and the Chinese allowed them to begin in 1979 and to acquire new impetus since 1981. This process has reduced tension between the two powers and has cumulatively imparted a certain civility and normality to the relation-

*Reprinted by permission of the author and publisher from *Survey* 27, no. 118/119 (Autumn–Winter, 1983), pp. 164–174. This text is a prepared statement presented in testimony before the Subcommittee on Asian and Pacific Affairs of the Committee on Foreign Affairs of the U.S. House of Representatives on August 2, 1983. Copyright 1983 by *Survey*.

ship. But Chinese intercourse with the Soviet Union, in the economic and every other sphere, is still much more restricted in scope than even American dealings with the USSR.

Meanwhile, side by side with this, on the second track an intense conflict of national interest persists between Beijing and Moscow. The Andropov leadership has thus far preserved intact those Brezhnev policies in Asia—regarding the Soviet military build-up along the Sino–Soviet border, Soviet troops dispositions in Mongolia, Soviet strategic deployments of the Backfire bomber and the SS-20, Soviet support for the Vietnamese conquest of Cambodia, Soviet naval presence at Cam Ranh Bay, and Soviet military efforts to enforce their domination of Afghanistan—which the Chinese regard as grave attacks on their interests or threats to their security. On the whole, the momentum behind this general pattern of Soviet behavior seems quite impressive, and I believe the Chinese are quite pessimistic that it will change.

The Dual Nature of Soviet Policy    This duality in Soviet policy toward China—the desire, on the one hand, to improve relations with Beijing, and the determination, on the other hand, to press Soviet interests that conflict with Beijing's—has been characteristic of Soviet behavior for many years. Throughout the evolution of the Sino–Soviet dispute, a clash of underlying national interests has been a vital factor in the growth of the conflict, changing and broadening and becoming more visible as the years went on.

To be sure, in the early years of the dispute this factor was interwoven with others, notably the personal struggle between Mao and Khrushchev and the ideological clash between Khrushchev's reformism and Mao's fanaticism. But even in the 1950s and early 1960s, when the Sino–Soviet arguments seemed esoteric and the main arena of the dispute was the international communist movement, the focus of the struggle was over the authority to determine whose national interests—Moscow's or Beijing's—should be accorded greater weight in the formulation of communist policy.

It should be remembered that the willingness of Stalin's heirs to sacrifice concrete Soviet interests to propitiate the Chinese rapidly dwindled when it became apparent that China could not be harnessed to Soviet purposes. The early Soviet return of Port Arthur and Dairen to China, and the assistance originally given to the Chinese economy and to Chinese military capabilities, were thus eventually followed by the Soviet effort to control Chinese behavior by demanding establishment of a "joint fleet" dominated by Moscow, by the Soviet refusals to give the atomic weapon to China, and by the punitive withdrawal of Soviet experts from the PRC.

All this is worth recalling now because to some extent the memory of these events a quarter of a century ago still conditions the attitudes of both sides today. On the Soviet side, it reinforces the attitude of those—notably in the military—who tend to be most reluctant to give up existing Soviet geopolitical advantages in Asia for the sake of a conjectural future pay-off in Chinese goodwill. On the Chinese side, the memory of the past remains a continuing lesson in Soviet perfidy toward China, and a warning against over-optimism in dealing with the present Soviet leaders.

**Soviet Motives for the Far East Build-Up**  It is primarily since 1965 that the Sino–Soviet rivalry has been militarized.[1] One of the major legacies of the Brezhnev regime has been the long-term build-up of Soviet forces confronting China, a process which began early in the Brezhnev era and has continued methodically to the present day, in tandem with the growth of Soviet strategic forces deployed against the United States. Khrushchev's successors began this Asian build-up when they decided that Khrushchev's removal had not altered Mao's hostility toward the Soviet Union and that they faced a serious Chinese challenge to the legitimacy of Soviet borders with the PRC. They resolved to undertake a permanent strengthening of their position in the Far East, both to ensure their hold on the frontiers they claimed and, more broadly, to create the means to exert pressure on China. They have come to regard the tank forces they have stationed in Mongolia, threatening the north China plain, as a key element in this pressure. In sum, they have been determined to create and maintain a continuously updated decisive advantage in firepower facing China at every step up the potential ladder of escalation, with the criterion for sufficiency heavily influenced by the need to compensate for dependence on a long and vulnerable railway for reinforcement. All these considerations were strengthened by the Soviet experience in 1969, when the USSR had a long series of border clashes with China, and then further strengthened by the adamant position unheld by Beijing in the border negotiations conducted between 1969 and 1978.

While this initial Soviet motive for the build-up—to deter and overawe China—endures, over the past decade it has been supplemented by additional motives.

First, the Soviets have also come increasingly to rely on their armed forces' dispositions to China's *north* to inhibit China's response to the military initiatives of the Soviets or their clients to China's *south*. The Soviets first discovered this collateral benefit of their Far East build-up during the India–Pakistan war of 1971, when the U.S. feared that the PRC would come to Pakistan's aid despite Soviet support for India, precipitating a Sino–Soviet conflict. This did not happen, and the Soviet leaders are likely to have concluded that Beijing was effectively deterred by the threat of the north.

This conclusion was reinforced in late 1978 and early 1979, when Vietnam launched its *blitzkrieg* into Cambodia after signing a treaty with the USSR that was obviously intended to deter China. Although the PRC responded in February–March 1979 with a punitive temporary and shallow incursion into Vietnam, the Chinese in effect conceded that they believe a more meaningful, far-reaching, and long-lived threat to

Hanoi—an attack which seriously attempted to force Vietnam to withdraw from Cambodia—would entail unacceptable risks of a Soviet military response to the north. The Soviets extracted concrete geopolitical benefits in return for providing this deterrent and other services to Hanoi.

Second, since 1978 the Soviets have been concerned to ensure that their strength in the Far East sufficed to insure a continued Soviet advantage in this arena in the event of the evolution of military cooperation between the United States, China, and Japan. Partly for this reason, over the past 5 years the Soviet Far East build-up has been revitalized. A high command has been established for Soviet forces in the three eastern military districts and Mongolia, in effect formalizing Soviet acceptance of the need for a permanent, self-sufficient, and very large military presence in the area. There has been some tendency toward more forward deployment of forces facing the Soviet Union's neighbors—deployments in Mongolia, in the case of China, and in the Japanese "Northern Territories" (the southernmost Kuriles) in the case of Japan. Over the same period, the Soviet Union has made more visible to China and Japan, through the increasing deployment of the Backfire bomber and the SS-20 missile, the threat of strategic weapons of mass destruction. These trends in Soviet military policy in the Far East are clearly intended to intimidate, and have not been halted despite the dwindling of the ephemeral prospect of Sino–Japanese–U.S. joint military collaboration against the Soviet Union. As in Europe, the Soviet Union continues to count on the pressure created by its growing strength to inhibit the response of its adversaries.

Finally, by the time of Andropov's advent to power in November 1982, Soviet policy toward China had also become intertwined with Soviet efforts to consolidate a series of advanced positions staked out through the use of Soviet military power in Asia during the 1970s. In the 9 months since Andropov took office, the Chinese have seen little change in the thrust of these Soviet efforts.

In Afghanistan, the PRC perceives continuing Soviet punitive war aimed at perpetuating Soviet military control of a country on China's western frontier. The Chinese are scornful of the motives underlying Soviet conversations with Pakistan on the Afghan issue, regarding this as an attempt to separate Pakistan from support of the Afghan rebellion without sacrificing the essence of Soviet domination of Afghanistan.

More important to China than relatively distant Afghanistan is Indochina, where Soviet policy supports Vietnam's military efforts to consolidate its domination over the peninsula and to exclude Chinese influence from a region Beijing has long regarded as essential to its interests. Vietnam is determined to maintain its control over Cambodia, and China is determined to break it; despite some political posturing by both sides, neither really believes that there can be a compromise over these conflicting goals. Meanwhile, in return for Soviet services to Vietnam, Soviet political influence has followed in the wake of Vietnam into Cambodia and Laos and the Soviet Union has secured use of Cam Ranh Bay to support growing naval operations on China's southeastern flank. Soviet authorities must value these military privileges highly, and would be extremely loath to give them up.

Since Andropov came to power, despite some persistent Soviet friction with Hanoi, and despite evident Vietnamese initial fears that the Soviets might betray them for the sake of improving relations with China, this has not happened. The Soviets probably believe that only truly drastic Soviet pressures on Hanoi might possibly bring sufficient Vietnamese concessions to satisfy Beijing, and that the attempted use of such pressures would in the meantime gravely endanger the Soviet relationship with Vietnam and the Soviet presence in Cam Ranh Bay. To run political risks of this magnitude, the Soviets apparently want commensurate payment in advance from Beijing. Thus far, the Soviets have been unwilling to risk losing the bird in the hand—their present advantages in Indochina—for the uncertainties of the bird in the bush— hypothetical Chinese gratitude. The inertia created by existing Soviet geopolitical advantages thus continues to dominate Soviet policy in Indochina, and to perpetuate Chinese resentment.

The Question of Soviet Troop Dispositions
Most important of all is Soviet policy in the north, where the new Andropov regime has thus far been unwilling to make any concessions regarding the disposition of Soviet troops facing China. In the autumn of 1982, the Soviets had dropped a number of public and private hints that they might eventually do so, and Brezhnev shortly before his death had made an allusion to China in an address to military leaders which was also interpreted by many observers as implying the possibility of eventual Soviet conciliatory steps. Since then, however, the Chinese have apparently found, in the two sessions of bilateral talks they have held with the Soviets, that the Soviet leadership has not been prepared to follow through on these hints. The Chinese are evidently particularly disturbed at the Soviet refusal thus far to discuss Soviet forces in Mongolia, which the Chinese see as the most threatening aspect of the Soviet military posture. From the Soviet perspective, as already suggested, these force dispositions in the north are intimately connected with Soviet ambitions in the south. The Soviet forces in Mongolia are, among other things, an instrument of pressure to ensure that China is permanently deterred from intervening in force in response to Vietnam's operations in Indochina. In addition to all other considerations, it is thus quite difficult for the Soviet leaders to be seen making concessions to China regarding forces in the north while fighting continues in Indochina and tension prevails between Vietnam and the PRC.

The Soviets have replied to Chinese demands regarding their forces in Mongolia by asserting that this issue concerns a "third country," and that Beijing can only discuss this with Ulan Bator. From the Chinese perspective, this reply is just hypocritical, since the Mongolian regime, unlike Hanoi, is in fact a Soviet satellite obedient to Soviet wishes. In this context, the Chinese probably regard as ominous the recent Mongolian expulsion of some Chinese nationals. While good evidence is lacking, an explanation for Mongolian conduct which the Chinese may favor is that the Soviet Union has instructed Tsedenbal to create new bilateral friction between Mongolia and the PRC as a pretext to justify continued Soviet intrasigence regarding Soviet forces in the country.

## The Intractable Border Issue

The present Soviet posture, in short, is one of waiting for major Chinese concessions before agreeing to reciprocal Soviet concessions. While one can only speculate as to what the Soviets require from the Chinese, one possibility is a further reduction of existing Chinese security cooperation with the United States. Another is a firm indication of Chinese willingness to settle existing border claims against the Soviet Union.

Although the Chinese have not highlighted these claims in recent years, they have apparently maintained them intact. As spelled out in the years of border negotiations in the 1970s, these involve territories which the PRC claims Russia and the Soviet Union have seized *in addition* to territory given Moscow in a series of "unequal treaties" signed in the nineteenth century. For the most part, this consists of islands in the border rivers in the east, and a large tract in the Pamir mountains in the west. The Chinese for years have demanded that the USSR evacuate every inch of the territory the Chinese define as being in dispute, prior to demarcation of an agreed frontier. It is this demand, in particular, which Moscow wishes Beijing to abandon. While rejecting it, the Soviets have over the years frequently offered China, instead, palliatives such as a nonaggression pact, which Beijing has invariably spurned. The recent Soviet reiteration of the offer of such a pact is thus not regarded by China as a Soviet concession.

On the whole, the border issue has been intractable to date because the Chinese negotiating position has been interwoven with the much broader Chinese geopolitical struggle against the Soviet Union. The Soviets may hope that given enough time, and a relaxation of Chinese attitudes toward the USSR, Beijing may finally change its position and accommodate itself with Soviet wishes.

## The Soviet View of the Internal Chinese Scene

The Soviets today, as often in the past, are making vigorous efforts to appeal to elements in the Chinese elite that they think are the most likely to wish to conciliate the Soviet Union. Although Soviet hopes in this regard were frequently frustrated in Mao's lifetime, since Mao's death in 1976 many Soviet specialists on China have drawn renewed encouragement from the increased Chinese civility in state-to-state relations, from the disappearance of Chinese ideological attacks against the Soviet Union, from the rehabilitation of some older Chinese cadres who in the past had favored a more moderate Chinese attitude toward the USSR, and from the evident divisions within the Chinese elite. They set grounds for hope in the similarities between the Chinese and Soviet social systems and state structures and in the resentment shown by some Chinese leaders over what they regard as the subversive effect of Western influence upon their control over the Chinese population.

Finally, the Soviets have for many years believed that there are hidden elements in the Chinese armed forces with attitudes that may be exploitable for Soviet interests, and they continue today to strive to tap such sentiment in the PLA. They maintain for this purpose a clandestine radio—Radio Ba Yi ("August the First," founding date of the PLA) broadcasting from the Soviet Far East but purporting to emanate from China and to represent a Chinese faction. This radio has in the past violently attacked Deng Xiaoping and other Chinese leaders; although these personal attacks have now been softened for the time being, the Chinese leadership certainly regards Radio Ba Yi as another in a long series of Soviet attempts to interfere in Chinese internal affairs. This perception is not likely to predispose Deng to wish to make further concessions to Moscow.

In general, the societal factors in China that give Soviet specialists hope, while real enough, are thus far more than counterbalanced by the fact that most Chinese continue to believe, as the Chinese Premier recently reiterated, that the Soviet Union continues to pose a grave threat to Chinese security interests around the Chinese periphery.

Soviet Hopes for the Economic Relationship
The Soviets have also for many years sought to get the Chinese to agree to a major expansion of the economic relationship—drastically cut back by the PRC since the 1960s—in the belief that this would help promote the gradual restoration of some Soviet influence in China. To this end, on a number of occasions in the past they have also made specific offers of technological assistance to China, notably in the fields of coal mining, nonferrous metallurgy, and oil development. The last such identifiable Soviet proposal was made many years ago; it is not known whether the Soviets have privately revived any such concrete offer in recent years. Nor is it clear whether the Chinese would accept, in view of their memory of the abrupt withdrawal of the Soviet experts in 1960 and Beijing's traditional resistance to the large-scale return of such agents of Soviet influence or to renewed dependence on the USSR. It is likely that the Chinese response, should the Soviets ever reiterate such an offer, would be conditioned by the nature, scope, and economic relevance of the proposal. It is noteworthy that in one area in which the Soviets have offered technological help in the past—oil exploitation—the USSR no longer has a significant technological advantage over China.

On the purely trading side of the relationship, the Soviets undoubtedly consider that they have made a major advance with the recent Chinese consent to more than double total turnover in 1983 to some $800 million. From the Soviet perspective, this is the most important result yet to emerge from the otherwise marginal recent advances in state-to-state dealings. The Soviets for many years have hoped that the Chinese would eventually be enticed by a desire to secure spare parts and machinery for the large segment of the Chinese industrial base originally built with Soviet help in the 1950s. More recently, the Soviets have counted on a Chinese desire to secure some middle-level Soviet technology more easily assimilated by the Chinese economy than the advanced technology Beijing has bought from the West and Japan. These considerations, along with a PRC desire to conserve hard currency and to diversify its sources of supply, may well contribute to a continued growth of Sino–Soviet trade over the next few years, particularly if total Chinese foreign trade continues to expand. But the growth of Soviet exports to China will continue to be conditioned by Soviet readiness to accept an equal value of Chinese exports every year, since for political reasons the Chinese will accept no imbalances in each year's trading account with the Soviet Union.

Considered more broadly, Sino–Soviet trade today remains only a fairly small fraction of Sino–U.S., let alone Sino–Japanese trade, and this central fact is not likely to change. The PRC is unlikely to abandon its primary reliance upon the capitalist industrialized world for inputs to China's modernization, and the Soviet Union will almost certainly remain a secondary factor in this process. The political advantages that the Soviets can extract from the growth of their economic relationship with Beijing will therefore probably remain rather limited.

**The Sino–American Factor** Soviet conduct strongly implies a belief that Soviet chances of securing further significant concessions from China will be heavily influenced by the future course of Sino–American relations, and that the USSR has a vested interest in the deterioration of those relations. The Soviet leaders thus obviously believe that the growth of Sino–U.S. friction over the Taiwan issue under the Reagan Administration was one important factor that impelled Beijing since 1981 to allow some improvements in Sino–Soviet state-to-state dealings even though the Soviet Union has not yet made any of the geopolitical concessions to China which the PRC had previously posed as prerequisites to any such improvements. Soviet propaganda statements, from those of Brezhnev down, have transparently sought to appeal to Chinese grievances over Taiwan. They have attempted to convince Beijing that those grievances are more important for Chinese interests than the Soviet forces on the Sino–Soviet border or Soviet behavior in Indochina and Afghanistan. They seek to play upon Chinese resentment of the assertions of some Americans that China is dependent on the United States.

At the same time, the dominant forces in the Soviet elite also appear to believe that Soviet intimidation has played a significant role in securing a modification in Beijing's posture toward Moscow since 1981. As they do in Europe, the Soviets seek both to deny the existence of a

Soviet threat to China and paradoxically to encourage a tendency to propitiate Moscow to mitigate the danger created by the threat. The Soviets are well aware of the concerns created in Beijing by the emergence of a two-front confrontation with the USSR and its Vietnamese ally since 1979. They are equally aware of the PRC's grave weakness in military technology and of the desire of the Chinese leadership to limit the diversion to military spending of resources desperately needed for China's economic development. They therefore probably believe that the Chinese decision to permit some improvement in state-to-state relations with Moscow was in large part a move to ease the tensions and reduce the danger created by China's relative weakness and by the Soviet Union's geopolitical hold over China. From the perspective of many in Moscow, however, this Chinese motive is, itself, one good reason to maintain the existing pressure on Beijing, and to make no unilateral concessions.

The dominant forces in the Soviet elite are intensely suspicious of Chinese intentions and, in particular, of Deng Xiaoping, whom they have known, disliked, and fought against for a long time. They are likely to believe that one of the factors underlying Chinese behavior toward the USSR over the past 2 years has been a tactical Chinese desire to use Chinese dealings with Moscow to exert tacit pressure on the United States for bilateral concessions within an overall framework of continued resistance to Soviet policy by both powers. Although they note—and welcome—Chinese criticisms of the United States and the cessation of Chinese calls for a "world united front" against the Soviet Union, they remain highly skeptical of Chinese assertions intended to imply equidistance between the Soviet Union and the United States. They are vividly aware of the extent to which their broad interests and ambitions clash permanently with China's in Asia, of the fact that the United States and the PRC continue to work in parallel to oppose Soviet policy in Indochina and Afghanistan, of the fact that more concrete forms of U.S.–PRC security cooperation evidently continue to exist, of the fact that the PRC continues to seek broader access to U.S. technology with military applications for defense against the Soviet Union, and of the U.S. Secretary of Defense's visit to China. It will therefore seem obvious to the Soviet leadership that despite the many areas of bilateral Sino–U.S. friction, China thus far is still not equidistant; on the contrary, it continues to lean to one side, in fact if not in name. This perception is also likely to reinforce the arguments of those in Moscow who are particularly inclined to maintain an adamant position on the central issues raised in the Sino–Soviet talks.

In sum, for the time being the consensus in Moscow appears to be an inclination to stand firm, and to hope that time will work in the USSR's favor. Although some new symbolic Soviet gesture toward the Chinese is conceivable, the trend of thought in Moscow that favors important unilateral concessions appears to be outweighed by the tendency that does not. The first viewpoint may be influential among some academic China specialists; the second seems likely to be particularly strong among the ideologues of the Central Committee apparatus and within the Soviet military. Meanwhile, Soviets of all persuasions are hoping that the process of slow state-to-state improvements, and the growth of economic and cultural intercourse, will gradually change Chinese international priorities. They hope also that heightened Sino–American frictions over Taiwan may in time incline Beijing to take further steps to conciliate the Soviet Union. Finally, they probably have now begun to await the death of Deng as they once awaited the death of Mao, counting on favorable changes to emerge from the maelstrom of Chinese politics once the man they consider their key opponent has departed the scene.

Implications for the United States

Given the incendiary potential of the present constellation of forces in the Far East and the extent of overall Soviet–American tension world-wide, the modest improvements in Sino–Soviet relations that have taken place in the past 2 years, by reducing the likelihood of Sino–Soviet conflict that might spread to involve the United States, have somewhat improved the prospects for stability in the region, a fact which itself can be welcome to the United States. At the same time, despite some protestations to the contrary, the Soviets clearly tie their hopes for more meaningful improvements with China to hopes for a radical degeneration of Sino–American relations, and thus seek a significant improvement in their position in the Sino–Soviet–U.S. triangle at the expense of the United States. Such a change would be quite harmful to U.S. interests.

A shift of this kind still seems unlikely, primarily because of the assertive dynamism of Soviet foreign policy, which continues to press against Chinese interests around the Chinese periphery in much the same way that it presses against the positions of Japan, the United States, and a variety of other U.S. allies in Asia and other parts of the world. The Soviets are now seeking to consolidate military advances made at the expense of their rivals in the 1970s in Afghanistan and Indochina, and simultaneously to overcome the adverse political reaction—in China and many other states—without abandoning those gains. At the same time, they steadily augment the military power with which they seek to intimidate their opponents on all sides, including China. Given these circumstances, it is in the United States' interest to so conduct its policy toward the PRC as to encourage the Chinese propensity to resist, rather than accommodate, Soviet pressure.

## Note

[1]See Harry Gelman, *The Soviet Far East Build-up and Soviet Risk-Taking against China*, R-2943-AF, August 1982 (The Rand Corporation, Santa Monica).

# 36 DONALD S. ZAGORIA

## The Moscow–Beijing Détente*

I Since the end of World War II, there have been three watersheds in Sino–Soviet relations. In February 1950, the Soviet Union and the People's Republic of China formed an alliance against the West. In the late 1950s, there was the beginning of the historic split between them that transformed international politics. Then, in the early 1970s, there began the Sino–American rapprochement that, by the end of the decade, completely altered the strategic landscape and led to an incipient Chinese–American alliance against the Soviet Union.

A fourth stage in the evolution of the strategic triangle is now underway and will probably continue during the 1980s. Through a variety of winks and nudges, China has responded positively—if still somewhat skeptically and ambiguously—to Soviet overtures for détente. The process of achieving such a détente, if it is successful, will almost certainly be long and difficult. The Soviets, although they have temporarily halted most of their polemics against China, continue to fear that a China modernized with the help of the West will one day be in a position to pursue the "Great Han, chauvinistic and expansionistic" aims which Soviet propagandists have frequently attributed to China during the past two decades. The Chinese, although they have largely dropped the Maoist ideological indictment of the Soviet Union as a "revisionist" country and a "betrayer of Marxism–Leninism," still continue to portray Moscow as a compulsive "hegemonic" power out to dominate the world.[1]

Still, détente is viewed by both adversaries as a means of managing their rivalry, not of eliminating it, and so the trend toward détente is likely to continue. Both the Russians and the Chinese have powerful reasons for desiring an end to the confrontation that has marked their relationship during most of the Maoist era. The big question remains:

*Reprinted by permission of the author and publisher from *Foreign Affairs* 61, no. 4 (Spring, 1983), pp. 853–873. Copyright 1983 by Council on Foreign Relations, Inc.

how far is a Sino–Soviet détente likely to go and what are its implications for the West?

This chapter examines some of the recent developments in Sino–Soviet relations; explores the reasons why both Russia and China are now interested in a détente; identifies some of the substantial limits on that détente; and, finally, analyzes the implications of the new trends for the United States.

II Prior to the death of Mao Zedong in 1976, there were—in addition to Mao's obsessive anti-Sovietism—two basic reasons why the Chinese opposed a détente with Moscow. One was ideological, the other strategic. The ideological concern of Mao and the "radicals" was that too close a relationship with the "revisionist" Soviets could contaminate the Chinese revolution. But once Mao died, the post-Mao leaders quickly purged the radical "Gang of Four," and have since adopted a markedly pragmatic approach to the country's development. They have invited foreign capital into China; they have expanded free markets; they have increased material incentives; and they have even engaged in a virtual de facto decollectivization of agriculture under the rubric of the "household responsibility system." Having replaced revolutionary zeal with a determined emphasis on economic development, the new Chinese leaders now have much less to fear from Soviet "revisionism." In this new context, it would be patently hypocritical for them to continue their ideological critique of the Russians; they can hardly accuse the Russians of "heresies" that they themselves are practicing. So, for several years now, the Chinese have stopped referring to the Soviets as "restoring capitalism" and "betraying Marxism." In sum, Mao's death has worked to remove the ideological barrier to détente.

The second barrier to détente prior to Mao's death was strategic. China's concern about possible military action by Moscow was at its height in the late 1960s and early 1970s. In this period, the Soviets greatly increased the quantity and quality of their military forces on the Chinese border; they invaded Czechoslovakia and proclaimed the "Brezhnev Doctrine," which arrogated to Moscow the right to intervene in the affairs of any "socialist" country; they began to threaten a preemptive strike against the Chinese nuclear missiles; and there were two bloody battles between Soviet and Chinese forces over disputed islands in the Amur River. It was these developments that propelled the Chinese into the arms of the United States in the early 1970s.

Since the death of Mao, however, both the Soviets and the Chinese have been proceeding with much greater caution. The Russians made only verbal threats when the Chinese launched their incursion into Vietnam in February 1979; the Chinese have been behaving more cautiously on the border and there have been no major incidents in recent years. Moreover, the normalization of relations with the United States in 1979 and the stabilization of the Chinese leadership after 1978, when Deng Xiaoping established rather firm control, added to Chinese self-confidence. Thus, by 1979, within 3 years of Mao's death, the ideological barriers to détente were gone and, on a strategic level, some of China's worst fears about the Russians were receding.

In the fall of 1979, the Chinese agreed to participate without preconditions in "normalization" talks with the Russians. These talks took place in Moscow between September and November 1979. According to one authoritative Soviet account, the Chinese raised four points in these talks as preconditions for, or "obstacles" to, the reestablishment of "normal" relations.[2] Beijing called for: (1) a unilateral reduction of the Soviet armed forces in the area bordering on China; (2) a withdrawal of Soviet forces from the Mongolian People's Republic; (3) a discontinuation of Soviet support "in any form" of the Socialist Republic of Vietnam; and (4) a settlement of the longstanding border dispute, talks on which had been going on without result since 1969.

According to this same source, the Soviet response to these demands was rather unyielding. With regard to the first point, the Soviets replied that they took "only necessary defensive measures on the border" and, moreover, that "there were more troops on the Chinese side of the border than on the Soviet side." With regard to Mongolia and Vietnam, the Soviets said that Soviet cooperation with other sovereign states "cannot be a subject of Soviet–Chinese negotiations." And so far as the border dispute was concerned, if the Chinese "were really serious about specifying the border line," all that was necessary was to make sure that the border conformed with the Russo–Chinese treaties of the nineteenth century.

Perhaps the most significant development that took place at the 1979 meeting was that the Soviets tabled what might loosely be called a nonaggression pact. It was a draft declaration of the principles of mutual relations between the USSR and the PRC. According to one Soviet source, this declaration called for mutual recognition of the principles of peaceful coexistence—full equality, mutual respect for state sovereignty, respect of territorial integrity, noninterference in each others' internal affairs, and nonuse of force or the threat of force. In pursuance of these principles, the Soviet side said it would specify and record the commitments of both sides concerning the renunciation of the use or threat of force.

At these 1979 meetings, the Soviets also proposed a discontinuation of "unfriendly propaganda" and an expansion of trade, as well as economic, scientific, technological, cultural, and other peaceful exchanges. Finally, Moscow proposed a variety of meetings, "including summit talks," to speed normalization.

It is not clear how the Chinese responded to these Soviet overtures. According to one account from high-ranking Chinese officials, the Chinese delegation had been instructed to listen to what the Soviets had to say but not to enter into any agreement. Following the conclusion of the talks, the two sides agreed to hold a second round of meetings in Beijing early in 1980. But the Chinese postponed these talks indefinitely after the Soviet invasion of Afghanistan in December 1979. Subsequently, Beijing added a fifth "precondition" for normalization, namely the removal of Soviet troops from Afghanistan.

Throughout 1980, Sino–Soviet relations remained frozen. In 1981, however, the two sides once again began to explore the resumption of normalization talks. On March 7, 1981, Moscow proposed implementing "confidence-building measures" along the border, including advance notification of military exercises, exchange of observers at those exercises, and similar steps.[3] The Chinese gave no official answer. Then, in October 1981, a spokesman for the Chinese Foreign Ministry revealed that a Soviet note of September 25, 1981 had called for a resumption of negotiations. The Chinese made no direct response to this note but, in November 1981, Chinese officials told West Germany's Franz Josef Strauss that a resumption of talks with the Russians was indeed possible and that the West should not "misunderstand." In the same period, China signed a railroad transport agreement with the Soviets and proposed a doubling of bilateral trade. It thus appears as if sometime in the fall of 1981 the Chinese leadership made the decision to respond positively to Soviet overtures. This was a period, it will be recalled, when Sino–American relations were beginning to deteriorate because of Chinese concerns that the Reagan Administration was moving back toward a "two Chinas" policy. Although Chinese dissatisfaction with Reagan's policy toward Taiwan was not the sole, or even the major, factor which brought about a shift in Chinese foreign policy, it was probably one of a number of factors.

On January 8, 1982, Beijing took another step toward negotiations with Moscow when Li Xinnian, a vice-chairman of the Chinese Communist Party (CCP), told an Italian Communist paper: "Why should we be against Sino–Soviet negotiations as long as they can lead to concrete results?" A week later, S. L. Tikhvinsky, rector of the Diplomatic Academy under the Ministry of Foreign Affairs and a prominent China specialist, arrived in Beijing for a 2-week visit. Two years before, Tikhvinsky had been the deputy head of the Soviet team holding normalization talks with the Chinese. During this return visit, Tikhvinsky presumably entered into discussions with Chinese officials on how and when to resume negotiations.

Shortly thereafter, the Soviets sent out an ambiguous signal. On February 18, 1982, Soviet Premier Nikolai A. Tikhonov said in an interview that the Soviet Union is "not going to keep from concrete steps" toward improving relations with China, but that the process "must not be one-sided." This was obviously a reflection of what was being said in private. The Chinese were insisting on some concrete Soviet "deeds" relating to their various "demands." And the Soviets, while not rejecting the need for such action, were calling on the Chinese to reciprocate—presumably by ending "unfriendly propaganda," etc.

A month later, Brezhnev, speaking in Tashkent, signaled a willingness to resume border talks with the Chinese and held out "possible measures to strengthen mutual trust in the area of the Chinese–Soviet frontier." Brezhnev was presumably referring to the "confidence-building measures" that the Soviets had offered earlier in the year. Brezhnev went on to say that Moscow was prepared to come to terms with China but "certainly not to the detriment of third countries."

In September 1982, this time in Baku, Brezhnev again underscored the importance he attached to improving relations with China and, about the same time, the Soviet media began to halt all anti-Chinese propaganda, the fourth such moratorium since the death of Mao. This was a tangible indication that the Russians were now looking forward to some progress in their efforts to improve relations.

In early October 1982, Soviet Deputy Foreign Minister Leonid Ilyichev, Moscow's ranking negotiator with the Chinese, quietly arrived in Beijing for the first round of post-Afghanistan talks with his Chinese counterpart, Deputy Foreign Minister Qian Qichen. The Chinese described these talks merely as "consultations," clearly seeking to retain the option not to go ahead with formal negotiations. According to subsequent Chinese accounts, the Chinese raised three issues with Ilyichev: Afghanistan, the Soviet troops along the border and in Mongolia, and, "above all," the problem of Kampuchea. At this meeting, Qian reportedly proposed a plan for a phased settlement of the Kampuchean conflict. The plan called for a complete withdrawal of Vietnamese troops from Kampuchea over an unspecified but "reasonable period of time" in return for a gradual improvement in Chinese–Vietnamese relations.[4]

In November 1982, the Chinese sent then Foreign Minister Huang Hua to Moscow to attend Brezhnev's funeral and, following a lengthy meeting with Soviet Foreign Minister Andrei Gromyko, Huang announced that he was "quite optimistic" about the prospects for improving Sino–Soviet relations. This visit attracted world-wide publicity. It is not clear whether Huang Hua's immediate dismissal as Foreign Minister upon his arrival back in Peking had anything to do with his expression of optimism in Moscow. But it is likely that the Chinese leaders are divided about how fast to proceed with the Russians.[5]

Soon after Huang's remarks, *Pravda* editor-in-chief Viktor G. Afanasyev, a member of the Soviet Central Committee, told Japanese journalists that the Sino–Soviet discussions could lead to an agreement on troop reductions along the border. The Chinese immediately hailed these remarks as "important" and they now seemed to relax their "preconditions" for normalization. Deputy Foreign Minister Qian told some Austrian journalists in early December 1982 that even "little steps" could improve relations.

At the same time, Qian voiced considerable skepticism about the outcome of the forthcoming dialogue with Moscow. "A complete normalization of relations is only possible," he stated, "if the threat to China's northeastern border is eliminated," if Soviet troops are withdrawn from Afghanistan, and if the Soviet Union agrees to a solution of the Kampuchean problem along Chinese lines. Throughout the coversation, Qian underscored the fact that China continued to look with alarm at Soviet aspirations to world domination. And, he concluded, "the talks will last a long time. They will be marathon talks."[6]

An abrupt revival of polemics between Beijing and Moscow early in 1983 suggested that Qian's caution was not misplaced. In late December, a prominent editorial in *People's Daily* stressed the need to give more moral and material assistance to the guerrillas in Afghanistan, and accused the Soviets of posing a "grave threat" to China's security by massing troops along China's narrow border with Afghanistan. It concluded that the Soviets wanted to turn Afghanistan "into a springboard for its southward drive," and that the "Soviet aggression against Afghanistan is a major step in the Soviet global strategy for world domination."

The Soviets lost little time in firing back. Early in January, a Soviet journal said that Beijing was undermining the fragile movement toward détente by keeping longtime territorial claims and disputes alive and infusing its people with anti-Soviet sentiment. The Soviet journal chronicled in great detail the dissemination in China of claims to territories allegedly seized by the Russian tsars. It concluded that the Soviet impression was that "the Chinese side is keeping the border issue" as an "expedient for retarding the process of normalization."

In February, U.S. Secretary of State George P. Shultz visited China, and this visit was followed in early March by the opening of the second round of Sino–Soviet talks in Moscow.

In sum, more than a year and a half after the Chinese decided to reconsider opening "normalization" talks with Moscow, there have been few concrete results. From this record, it seems reasonable to conclude that the pace of normalization is likely to be rather slow.

III Viewed objectively, both the Chinese and the Russians have a great deal to gain from reducing tensions. For Beijing, the Maoist policy of confrontation was both risky and costly. It was risky because it might have led to an unwanted military conflict for which China was ill prepared. It was costly because it meant increasing military spending at a time when China's resources were spread painfully thin. The post-Mao leaders have evidently decided to reduce both the risks and the costs of confrontation. They believe that their most urgent priority for the next decade or two is to modernize China's economy; to do this, they require a peaceful international climate, increased trade with Russia, and the avoidance of any big increase in defense spending. In a word, the Chinese leaders want a breathing space with Moscow in order to concentrate on economic development.

In this context, the Soviet Union will be a particularly attractive trade partner for China, because, although not so affluent as the West, it will bring with it few ideological or cultural problems and it will trade with China on a barter basis, thus eliminating the kinds of balance-of-payment frictions that have developed with the United States. Moreover, for reasons of proximity, border trade with Russia will be particularly attractive to the Chinese.

By normalizing relations with the Russians, China could also hope to achieve much greater maneuverability and flexibility in the great-power triangle and thus put itself in a position where it could extract concessions from both superpowers. In the earlier situation of frozen relations with Moscow, Beijing could not exert much leverage on either

Moscow or Washington. The Russians saw no advantage in making concessions to China, and the Americans had no need for such concessions.

The Chinese may also hope to manage their adversarial relations with Moscow more effectively through détente. This was, after all, the philosophy behind American thinking on détente with the Russians in the early 1970s. Distancing itself somewhat from Washington also helps China to enhance its image of independence, particularly in the Third World, which China seeks to lead. Also, now that Moscow has a new leader, the Chinese have strong incentives for testing just how far Yuri Andropov is really prepared to go in an effort to improve relations. Finally, China may now see a reduced Soviet capacity for adventurism as an opportunity to test the Kremlin's willingness to compromise. The Russians are bogged down in Afghanistan and Poland, and the tough line of the Reagan Administration toward Moscow is probably one of several reasons why the Russians have been unusually moderate throughout 1982 in the Lebanese war, in Africa, in the Middle East, and even in Central America.

The effort to conclude a détente with Moscow, however, should be seen as only one part of a larger shift in Chinese foreign policy that has been taking place since 1981. That shift involves some distancing from the United States as well as attempts to normalize relations with Moscow, and renewed stress on China's relations with both the "Third" and "Second" worlds. This shift in Chinese foreign policy was doubtless motivated by a variety of factors, but the Chinese must have been somewhat uncomfortable placing themselves in a position where they had become too dependent on the United States. The proud, highly nationalistic Chinese were not suited to be the junior partner of the Americans any more than they were suited to be Moscow's junior partner in the 1950s. Their present stress on "independence" reflects a desire both to gain greater future maneuverability and to carve out a fully independent place in world politics.

The Russians have equally powerful incentives for wanting détente with China. At a time when Soviet relations with the United States are at a low ebb, the Soviets have a strong incentive to try to play their "China card" against the United States. Moscow could hope to put some pressure on the Reagan Administration to be more flexible in strategic arms negotiations. Improving relations with China will also help ease the Soviet Union's two-front problem by undercutting any strategic cooperation between Washington and Beijing. In the long run, of course, Moscow hopes to break up the Washington–Beijing rapprochement. Writing in *Izvestia* on January 31, 1982, the influential Soviet journalist, Aleksandr Bovin, concluded that the Sino–American relationship was no more than a marriage of convenience marked by mutual suspicion and the desire of each partner to outmaneuver the other. He predicted that the relationship would finally come apart as a result of fundamental differences in ideology and global interests.

The wretched state of the Soviet economy is also a factor. Brezhnev's speech to Soviet military leaders just before he died clearly indicated that the Kremlin sees a connection between easing its military and economic burdens, on one hand, and reducing tensions with China, on the other. Calm on the Siberian border could also alleviate the Soviet Union's present crisis of overextension. With 105,000 troops in Afghanistan, a simmering crisis in Poland, and an East European empire that has accumulated a substantial debt to Western banks, Moscow might well welcome a breather with China. Finally, it should be noted that every new Soviet leader since Stalin's death has attached a high priority to trying to improve relations with China. It would be a great coup for Andropov if he could succeed where his predecessors failed.

**IV**  Although there are strong pressures on each side to ease tensions with the other, there are deep-seated suspicions and fears as well as conflicts of geopolitical interest that will make any détente process difficult.

On the Soviet side, there is what Henry Kissinger once called a deep "neuralgic" fear of China, a fear that extends from the leadership down through the entire society, including the dissidents. Even Solzhenitsyn considers the Chinese a long-range enemy of Russia. Soviet political prisoners in prison camps with Andrei Sinyavsky in the 1960s told him they would side with the West in any future war with Russia, but they would fight with Russia against China. In the small towns of Siberia, according to Sinyavsky, most people believe that war with China is inevitable. For some indication of this visceral fear of China at the highest level of the Soviet leadership, one need only consult Nikita Khrushchev's memoirs. His meeting with Mao, said the former Soviet Premier, sent shivers down his spine.

This visceral fear of China is reinforced by the geopolitical vulnerability of Siberia and the Soviet Far East. That portion of the Soviet Union is sparsely populated, it is a long distance from European Russia, it is very difficult to reinforce, and it is very difficult to develop. These problems will only partly be overcome when the new Baikal-Amur Railroad is finished sometime in the next few years. It was for this reason that the Soviets carried out a major military buildup on the Chinese border during the late 1960s and early 1970s—a buildup that has permanently altered the military geography of the frontier with the establishment of underground silos, airfields, missile bases, and new highways. This permanent military transformation of the border is the decisive strategic change that has taken place in the Far East during the past two decades; it will not be altered by symbolic Soviet drawdowns along the border.

Then, too, Soviet fears of China are reenforced by continual Chinese harping on China's "lost territories," which, according to Beijing, were forcibly taken from China by the Russian tsars in a series of "unequal treaties" signed in the nineteenth century. Although the Chinese do not now demand the return of those territories, ever since Mao told some Japanese socialists in 1964 that the Chinese had not yet presented their "bill" to Russia for those territories, the Soviets have had to think about China as a potentially revanchist power once it becomes strong.

Some indication of the deep suspicions of China that exist within the Soviet Central Committee and Foreign Ministry can be gleaned from two articles that appeared in the Soviet journal *Far Eastern Affairs* after Brezhnev's Tashkent speech of March 24, 1982.[7] One was written by "O. Borisov," the pseudonym for Oleg B. Rakhmanin, first deputy head of the Central Committee's Department for Relations with Socialist and Workers' Parties, and one of the most powerful of the China specialists in the Soviet elite. The second article was written by "M. Ukraintsev," the pseudonym for M. S. Kapitsa, recently promoted to Deputy Foreign Minister, and probably the most experienced Soviet diplomat in dealing with China over the past two or three decades.

Rakhmanin's assault on the Chinese was hard-hitting and comprehensive. It included the following accusations:

- The Chinese leaders have adopted practices and doctrines that run "counter to the principles of socialism."

- Beijing's heretical stance has implications that transcend bilateral Sino–Soviet relations and threaten the ideological orientation of the entire international revolutionary movement.

- The struggle against "distortions of scientific socialism" is particularly important at a time when an alliance is shaping up between anti-communism of the Reagan brand, Beijing's social chauvinism, and various brands of opportunists and right-wing nationalists.

- The post-Mao Chinese leaders continue to throw mud at the Communist Party of the Soviet Union.

- Beijing's recent "tactical maneuvers" to improve relations with the Soviet Union are designed to "blackmail the West with threats of improving relations with the Soviet Union."

- The ideological reorientation now under way in China is simply designed to make Maoism more flexible, while retaining its essence of Sinified Marxism plus a hegemonistic foreign policy and anti-Sovietism.

- The changes in China's domestic policy are not significant and they are aimed at providing a more dependable basis for Beijing's anti-Sovietism.

- Under the PRC's constitution and the rules of the CCP, struggle against the Soviet Union is a constitutional and a statutory duty of each citizen and each Party member, reflecting repeated Chinese statements that struggle against the Soviet Union is a long-term task.

- It is up to China to take initiatives to improve relations; the Soviet Union has done all it can.

It seems fair to conclude from this analysis, coming as it did right on the heels of the Brezhnev Tashkent speech, with its overtures to China, that powerful figures in the Soviet Central Committee have deep reservations about the wisdom of making any concessions to China in the interests of détente.

Kapitsa's reservations about détente with China were expressed in more measured terms but were equally apparent. Reviewing the origins of the Sino–Soviet conflict, Kapitsa concluded that it was all the fault of China.

●  After Stalin's death, Mao began claiming to be the leader of the world communist movement.

●  Mao was eager to launch an immense nuclear-missile program whereas the Soviet Union maintained that such a step was unreasonable and would complicate the struggle for disarmament and peace; the Soviet Union had sufficient military strength to protect all the socialist countries.

●  Mao and other Chinese leaders wanted to incorporate Mongolia into China.

●  Finally, in the late 1950s, Mao insisted that the Soviet Union should deliver a nuclear strike at the United States and its allies and that the task of eliminating U.S. imperialism was worth the sacrifice.

Against this background, Kapitsa continued, China split with Moscow and "joined hands" with U.S. imperialism. The Soviet Union then proposed a variety of measures to halt the deterioration of relations, but Mao and his group did all they could to aggravate relations. They staged armed provocations at the border in 1969 both in order to poison the minds of the Chinese people against the USSR, and to make it clear to the United States that China wanted a rapprochement on an anti-Soviet basis.

How did it happen, Kapitsa inquires, that China, initially an ally of the socialist states, could become a junior partner of U.S. imperialism? His answer is that during and after the revolution in China there was a fierce struggle within the CCP between "internationalists" and "national chauvinists" and that, by the end of the 1950s, the "internationalists" had been exterminated or ousted. During the Cultural Revolution, those who survived were sent to reeducation camps or massacred.

This Maoist chauvinism, Kapitsa concluded, was reinforced by several thousand years of Chinese history which dictate that barbarians should be subjugated by other barbarians and that any means from simple deceit to war can be used in the struggle against barbarians.

As to China's reasons for wanting some relaxation of tension with Moscow, Kapitsa sees essentially two motives. First, China wants greater freedom for maneuvering in the international arena; second, China wants to increase trade and scientific and technological exchanges with the USSR.

In sum, although not quite so hostile to China as Rakhmanin, Kapitsa is far from enthusiastic about the prospects for Sino–Soviet détente and rather skeptical about China's motives.

Suspicion of, and skepticism about, the Soviet Union on the Chinese side is equally deep rooted. The Chinese see a long history of Soviet efforts to dominate China and the CCP. They see the Soviet Union as the heir to tsarist Russian imperialism. They are well aware that they cannot hope to deal with the Russians from a position of weakness and, for this reason alone, they will undoubtedly want a continuation of their American connection, both as insurance against, and stimulus to, Moscow. Finally, there can be little doubt that over the next decade or more, the Chinese see Russia as their main threat. After all, it is the Russians who are in Afghanistan, Mongolia, and Indochina; and it is the Russians who maintain such large forces on the Chinese border.

Some indication of the kinds of suspicions and grievances that the Chinese hold about the Russians can be found in an article written in 1979 on Sino–Soviet relations by one of China's leading specialists on the Soviet Union, Liu Keming, Director of the Institute of Soviet Studies in the Beijing Academy of Sciences.[8] At the very moment that the first round of normalization talks was proceeding, Liu ticked off ten basic complaints about the Soviet "hegemonists":

1. They have consistently tried to control China. In 1958, they proposed the establishment of a joint fleet which actually had as its purpose an effort to control the Chinese coastline. After 1959, the Soviets tried to prevent China from acquiring its own nuclear weapons. They wanted to turn China into a "nuclear protectorate" of the USSR.
2. The Russians have repeatedly carried out divisive activities in China's border regions. In particular, they have had an eye on incorporating Inner Mongolia into the U.S.S.R.
3. The Russians have repeatedly carried out subversive activities against China with the aim of establishing a pro-Soviet regime in China.
4. The Soviets have obstructed the solution of the border problem by refusing to acknowledge the existence of disputed areas.
5. The Soviets have greatly increased their troops along the border to strengthen their whole strategic position in Asia and to intimidate China.
6. The Soviets have turned Mongolia into a forward base from which to make military threats against China.
7. With Soviet support, Vietnam has invaded Kampuchea and made territorial claims against China.
8. To obstruct China's four modernizations, the Soviets have tried to interfere in China's trade with the West.
9. The Soviets have sought to isolate China from Japan, the United States, and India.
10. The Soviets have spread lies and distortions about China's positions, seeking to slander China as an aggressive power out to provoke a world war.

In sum, Liu's article contends, the Soviets want to turn China into a client state; they have developed the traditions of Russian imperialism; they cannot allow a strong and powerful China at their side any more than they could allow the emergence of a powerful Europe in the West. To cope with Russia, Liu argues, China must deal from a position of strength. Even if relations were to be normalized on the basis of the five principles of coexistence, he writes, the normalization process would be "protracted, difficult, and complex."

In addition to mutual suspicions and fears, the geopolitical conflicts of interest between the two sides will greatly increase the difficulties of reaching any kind of détente. The Soviet Union is unlikely to withdraw from Afghanistan because such a withdrawal would, under present conditions, ensure the collapse of its client government under Babrak Karmal and lead to an anticommunist and anti-Soviet government. The Soviets are not in a position to force Vietnam to withdraw from Kampuchea and, under present circumstances, it is not in Vietnam's interests to do so. A Vietnamese withdrawal from Kampuchea might well lead to the return to power of the Khmer Rouge, the strongest of the guerrilla resistance forces now fighting against the Vietnamese in that country. Nor are the Chinese likely to withdraw their support from the Khmer Rouge and its partners, Prince Sihanouk and Son Sann, in the tripartite coalition that is actively resisting the Vietnamese occupation. Finally, the Soviets almost certainly will not withdraw their forces from Outer Mongolia, a country that has been a Soviet protectorate since the 1920s. Thus, the prospects do not seem very bright for any substantial compromises on the geopolitical obstacles to normalization raised by Beijing.

# V

Although there are many roadblocks standing in the way of "normalization" of Sino–Soviet relations, the process will still go forward. There will be an increase in trade, particularly in border trade. There will also be increases in cultural, economic, and technological exchanges, and in diplomatic contacts; tensions on the border will continue to diminish; and there will be some reduction in mutual polemics.[9]

Of the various "demands" made by the Chinese for lessening tension, the one issue on which there is some prospect for Soviet concessions is the matter of Soviet troop dispositions on the Chinese border. The Soviets may make a modest and symbolic drawdown of Soviet forces as a gesture of goodwill to the Chinese.

There are, however, thorny problems involved in such a move. First, a symbolic gesture may not go far enough to merit much of a Chinese response. Second, the Soviet troops are deployed quite far forward due to the particular configuration of the border: the trans-Siberian railroad which those Soviet troops guard is located very close to the Chinese border. The Chinese troops, on the other hand, are deployed much further back from the border. Thus, any concessions on the deployment of troops will have to be unilateral Soviet concessions, at least initially. Also, if the Soviets pull back some troops from the border, this might lead the Chinese to argue that the Soviets are now in principle agreeing with them that there are "disputed areas" along the border, something the Soviets have refused to do in the past. Finally, the Chinese are specifically insisting on a pullback of some Soviet forces from Outer Mongolia.[10] This is bound to be a delicate issue for the Russians because it involves their commitment to a country on which the Chinese may well have designs. (According to Kapitsa, Mao wanted to incorporate Outer Mongolia into the People's Republic.)

On the whole, then, progress in détente between Russia and China is likely to be painfully slow. There are two basic reasons: on the Soviet side—inflexibility; on the Chinese side—a tactical interest in going slow.

Soviet policy in the Far East during the past two decades has been described by many Western analysts as "inflexible."[11] There are many reasons for this Soviet rigidity: the geopolitical vulnerability of Siberia; Moscow's classical "two-front" problem; the historical experience of four wars with Japan in the past 100 years or so; the open hostility of China under Mao; the territorial disputes with both China and Japan; the emerging entente between China and Japan, and between China, Japan, and the United States; the slow but steady growth of Japan's defense capabilities; the relative political isolation of the Soviet Union in Northeast Asia and in noncommunist Southeast Asia; and the ultraconservative "political culture" in the Soviet Union. Given this set of factors, it is quite unlikely that the Soviets, even under a new leader, will make any bold concessions toward China or Japan on any of the key issues in dispute. The recent Soviet blast at China for keeping alive the territorial dispute and the attempt to intimidate Japan by threatening nuclear retaliation in response to Prime Minister Nakasone's promise in Washington to turn Japan into an "unsinkable aircraft carrier" are two recent indications that there is not going to be any sweeping change in the Soviet Union's attitudes toward its two major adversaries in the Far East.

On the Chinese side, progress in détente with Russia will be slow because it is not in China's interests to go very fast. The PRC can hope to extract the largest number of concessions from Washington by moving deliberately but slowly toward a new relationship with Moscow. Too rapid progress carries the danger of so alarming the United States as to jeopardize the American connection altogether. China's interest is in worrying the United States about the "threat" of a Chinese détente with Moscow, not in going too far toward achieving such a détente.

Thus, in the coming year or so, while there is likely to be an improvement in "atmospherics" between Russia and China, there will not be any change in the fundamental strategic situation and even the pace of "normalization" will be very deliberate on both sides. In short, the Sino–Soviet détente will remain a "tactical" détente. Both sides will have very limited and very modest objectives. The détente will not constitute a far-reaching strategic change in the international balance of power, as did the U.S.–PRC rapprochement in the 1970s.

VI    A Sino–Soviet détente has both potential dangers and potential advantages for the West. Of course, a great deal depends on how far such a détente goes. But, for reasons that have been advanced, a far-reaching accommodation between the two adversaries is hardly conceivable. More likely is a limited détente which would include an increase in trade and exchanges of all kinds, some limited withdrawals from the border, and some efforts to reduce tensions on a variety of levels.

The dangers can be briefly described. If tensions on the border with China were drastically reduced, the Soviets could contemplate moving some of their troops in the Far East to Europe or the Middle East, thus increasing pressure on the West on other fronts. Such a development, while conceivable, is highly unlikely. The Soviets will not dismantle their Siberian base structure just on the basis of a tactical détente with China. The Soviet military establishment, which is an important constituency for Andropov, will almost certainly veto any such plan. Moreover, the Soviets will want to maintain an overwhelming conventional military superiority over all their adversaries in the Far East— not just China, but Japan and the United States as well. And while the threat of a China–Japan–U.S. alliance against the USSR has temporarily receded, the Soviets cannot be sure that it will not one day be resurrected.

Short of moving troops from one front to another, it is possible that a Soviet Union freed from concern about its Siberian front might become more adventurous on other fronts. But there is no clear relationship between Sino–Soviet relations and Soviet adventurism. The Soviets were on the offensive in the Third World from Angola to Afghanistan in the period from 1975 to 1979 at a time when their relations with China were still relatively frozen. They have been somewhat more passive in the past year or two at a time when their relations with China were improving. This is not to discount the possibility that there *may* be a connection between an easing of Sino–Soviet tensions and Soviet adventurism; it is simply to suggest that many factors influence Soviet foreign policy—internal factors, relations with the United States, estimates of risk, etc. Sino–Soviet relations are only one such variable.

Moreover, if the Soviets, as a result of reducing tensions with China, were to embark on a more adventurous policy on other fronts, it is doubtful that the Sino–Soviet détente would survive. It is not in China's interests to encourage Soviet adventurism. Also, under such circumstances, China's ties with the West would come under enormous strain and the Chinese would probably be forced to choose between the advantages of a tactical détente with Moscow and the much greater economic and strategic advantages of their Western connection.

A Sino–Soviet détente, even of a limited kind, will increase both Chinese and Soviet leverage on Washington, but the advantages of such leverage are not likely to be substantial. As long as Washington is convinced that there are serious limits to any Sino–Soviet détente, it will not pay a high price to avert it.

A more sobering consideration is that a more independent China, particularly a China which continues to adhere to a communist ideology, is likely to support a variety of anti-American movements and sentiments in the Third World. Particularly in the Middle East, Africa, and Central America, China will probably increase its support for countries and movements opposed to American policy.

A more worrisome scenario for Washington would materialize if the Sino–Soviet détente were to be accomplished by a radical deterioration in Sino–American relations. Under such circumstances, the Soviets might be emboldened to increase their concessions to China and the Chinese might become more receptive. And if such developments were accomplished by a further fragmentation of the Western alliance over such issues as the deployment of nuclear missiles in Europe, the overall perception would be one of a Western alliance in disarray. In time, this could lead to a major shift in the balance of power against the West. Thus, it would be unwise to regard the present trends in the great power triangle with complacency.

Viewed in this light, a good deal depends on the stability of American–Chinese relations. The recent visit to China by Secretary Shultz seems for the moment at least to have arrested the process of deterioration. Prime Minister Zhao Ziyang told Shultz he would visit America, and he invited President Reagan to come to China. Significantly, however, Zhao was unwilling to set a date for his trip. The United States and China did not agree during the Shultz visit on preliminary steps to revive high-level military contacts that were largely suspended after the Reagan Administration took office 2 years ago. The Taiwan problem remains a substantial irritant, along with frictions over trade and technology transfers, and these issues will have to be very skillfully managed in the years ahead.

In general, one can be cautiously optimistic about the future of Sino–American relations. The Chinese, skilled in the art of realpolitik, know very well that their long-range interests depend on containing the advance of Soviet power and that an American connection is indispensable in order to achieve this goal. And although the Reagan Administration was initially rather cool toward China, it has in the past year or so demonstrated an increasing awareness of the importance of stable Sino–American relations for the maintenance of a favorable global balance of power.

Barring a radical deterioration in U.S.–Chinese relations, it is difficult to conceive of any great catastrophe for the West as a result of a modest improvement in Sino–Soviet relations. The West, after all, does not have a stake in a very high level of Sino–Soviet tension. Its stake lies in an autonomous, independent China with stable, friendly ties to the West.

Almost all of the benefits that the West has derived from the Sino–Soviet split will continue even under conditions of a modest détente. China, for its own reasons, will continue to serve as a counterweight to Soviet expansion, particularly in such Asian areas as Indochina, Korea, and Pakistan. China will still want American power and influence in Asia, particularly in Japan, in order to counter the Soviets; this is why China continues to oppose any North Korean adventurism against South Korea, and why it does not want to get involved in a war with the United States at a time when it is most concerned about Soviet expansion. China will continue, too, to reduce its support to Southeast Asian insurgencies, because it wants to cultivate relations with the governments of Southeast Asia in order to oppose Vietnam and the Soviet

Union. In sum, for a variety of reasons, the American military burden in Asia will continue to be eased as a result of the adversarial relationship between China and Russia.

Are there any advantages to a limited Sino–Soviet détente? First, war between Russia and China is surely not in anyone's interest. Also, if the two adversaries were eventually to agree on Soviet withdrawals from Afghanistan or Vietnamese withdrawals from Kampuchea, this would benefit and not harm Western interests. Then, too, a Soviet Union that was somewhat less "neuralgic" about China might be more flexible on arms control negotiations with the West.

# VII But the larger point is that Americans need not fear a Sino–Soviet détente because the United States will continue to occupy the pivotal position in the strategic triangle and because there may now be an opportunity to make that triangle more stable.

Both Russia and China want something from the United States that they cannot get from each other. Both want trade and technology. China, in particular, knows that the Russians cannot possibly supply the quantity and quality of technology it desperately needs to modernize its economy.

Moreover, both Russia and China need the United States as a partner. Russia knows that the most crucial relationship for it in the coming decades will remain its relationship with the United States. While it will seek to influence American behavior by applying pressure on, and courting, third parties from Europe to China, the Soviets know that they must come to terms with America, at least to avoid an escalation of the arms race which they can ill afford. The Chinese, for their part, know that the Russians will remain their main adversary over the coming decades, and they will have a common interest with the United States in containing Soviet expansion. Thus, while both Russia and China will seek to maneuver within the triangle in order to improve their bargaining positions vis-à-vis America, both need better relations with the United States.

A limited Sino–Soviet détente could in fact have the long-range effect of producing a more stable and less dangerous great-power triangle. In the 1970s, the Soviets had to worry about a U.S.–Chinese alliance directed against them. There was always the risk that the Soviets might be provoked into some kind of adventurist action to break up the incipient alliance. A gradual buildup of the Chinese armed forces and a developing relationship between the United States and China, even if it contains some military aspects, will look much less threatening to the Russians if there is a Sino–Soviet détente rather than a Sino–Soviet confrontation.

A modest détente between Moscow and Beijing might even improve the chances for a more restrained and cautious Soviet foreign policy. The Chinese will presumably tell the Russians that further adventurism in Asia or Africa comparable to what the Russians did in Angola, Afghanistan, Ethiopia, and Indochina will arrest the prospects for normalization. This will reinforce the similar messages of the Reagan Administration about the conditions for a revival of détente with the United States. Thus, the Russians will have increased incentives for pursuing a more cautious policy in the Third World if they want to improve their relations with both Beijing and Washington.

Also, a modest improvement in Sino–Soviet relations and a slight loosening of ties between Beijing and Washington could lead to greater realism on all sides of the triangle. The Carter Administration oversold the "strategic consensus" with China, and alarmed a number of our Asian friends and allies who see China as a potential long-range threat to their own security. To the extent that the Reagan Administration lowers expectations about what advantages we can derive from China, and they from us, it will lay the basis for a healthier long-term relationship. It was an illusion to believe that the United States and China could become close friends. There are too many differences of ideology, values, and interests. What is possible and desirable is a stable and cooperative long-term relationship based on a common opposition to Soviet aggrandizement and a Western willingness to help China modernize. But neither the United States nor China can be expected to sacrifice any of its basic principles in the process.

The profound ideological differences between China and the West mean that, on the Chinese side, there will always be a fear of Western cultural infiltration and liberal pollution of intellectual life. On our side, we will continue to differ with China not only over the future of Taiwan but over the future shape of much of the Third World and much of the communist world as well. Continued Chinese support for Pol Pot in Kampuchea is one indication of that. China's indifference to the fate of the Polish worker's movement is another. In sum, we ought not to forget that China remains a highly authoritarian communist state with an outlook on the world profoundly different from our own. We can and we should find common ground with such a country, particularly when it comes to opposing Soviet aggrandizement, but we should have no illusions about the strength of those bonds. That is why the Reagan Administration is right to attach a higher priority to Japan than to China. Over the long run, a firm U.S. alliance with a democratic Japan is one of the best guarantees we have of maintaining a favorable balance of power in Asia.

In historical terms, what we are now witnessing is the reassertion of China, after more than a century of weakness, as an independent great power. Such a China cannot be manipulated by either of the superpowers. Just as the Soviet Union found in the 1950s that it could not "use" China against the United States, so the United States has now discovered in the 1980s that it cannot "use" China against the Soviet Union. China is not a "card" to be manipulated in great power politics. It is a great power whose full weight has yet to be registered in international politics. Within several decades, and certainly by the twenty-first century, China will be a superpower in its own right.

What is certain is that an independent, highly nationalistic, and communist China will pursue its own fundamental interests on the world scene. In the 1980s, those interests will include the "normalization" of relations with the Soviet Union to some degree, greater independence from the United States, and a greater role in the Third World. But so long as China is encircled and threatened by Soviet power, and so long as the Soviet Union remains determined to alter the global balance of power in its favor, China will not be able to afford a policy of "equidistance" between the two superpowers. On the key issues affecting the central balance, China will continue to lean to the West.

## Notes

[1] As recently as October 1982, a Chinese journal called Moscow's "détente" policy a tactic to seize global hegemony from the United States. See Zhang Zhen and Rong Zhi, "Brief Discourse on the Soviet 'Détente' Policy," *Guoji Wenti Yanjiu*, no. 4, (1982), in Foreign Broadcast Information Service (FBIS), *Daily Report: China*, February 9, 1983, pp. C1-C9.

[2] M. Ukraintsev (pseudonym for M. S. Kapitsa), "Soviet–Chinese Relations: Problems and Prospects," *Far Eastern Affairs*, no. 3 (1982) (Moscow).

[3] *Ibid.*

[4] Don Oberdorfer, "China Reported to Offer Soviets a Plan to Ease Cambodian Conflict," *The Washington Post*, January 17, 1983.

[5] Ba Yi radio, evidently a clandestine Soviet radio station broadcasting in Mandarin to China, contends that some Chinese leaders are against normalization with Moscow (see FBIS, *Daily Report: China*, January 17, 1983, p. K23).

[6] Quoted in *Die Presse*, Vienna, December 7, 1982.

[7] O. Borisov, "The Situation in the P.R.C. and Some Tasks of Soviet Sinology," *Far Eastern Affairs*, no. 3 (1982) (Moscow); and M. Ukraintsev, *op. cit.* On Soviet pseudonyms, see the forthcoming article in *China Quarterly* by Gilbert Rozman and the doctoral dissertation in progress at Columbia University by Chi Su.

[8] Liu Keming, "Soviet Foreign Policy: On Sino-Soviet Relations," a paper prepared for the Sino–American Conference on International Relations and the Soviet Union, organized by the Research Institute on International Change, Columbia University, November 8–11, 1979, Washington, D.C.

[9] According to Deng Liqum, director of the Chinese Central Committee's Propaganda Department, the situation on the border, both in the eastern sector, in Heilongjiang, and on the western sector, in Xinjiang, has "improved greatly." See Deng's interview with Guiseppe Boffa, *L'Unita*, Venice, January 30, 1983 (reprinted in FBIS, *Daily Report: China*, February 2, 1983, pp. A1-A5).

[10] *Ibid.*

[11] For a recent survey by Western analysts of Soviet policy in the Far East, see Donald S. Zagoria, ed., *Soviet Policy in East Asia* (New Haven: Yale University Press, 1983).

# VIII

## The Third World

# 37

# CENTER FOR
# DEFENSE INFORMATION

## *Soviet Geopolitical Momentum: Myth or Menace?* *

Introduction    Since World War II America has engaged in a struggle with the Soviet Union fierce enough to justify a
large part of our military expenditures, totaling so far over two trillion
dollars, or $10,000 for every American.

We have had no military combat with the Soviets. The struggle has
largely been waged over third countries through diplomacy, aid, trade,
and occasionally military intervention. Since the Soviets brutally occupied Eastern Europe in the 1940s, many Americans have feared that
subversion and conquest would continue until pro-Soviet governments
were installed throughout the world or were thwarted by our efforts.

In the intervening 35 years, there have been hundreds of headlines
that seemed to justify that fear. Recent Soviet advances in Afghanistan,
Angola, Ethiopia, and South Yemen have led *The Wall Street Journal* to
editorialize that "The Soviet Union is engaged in a world-wide geopolitical offensive under the umbrella of its massive military buildup."
Former Secretary of State Henry Kissinger has taken the lead in pop-
ularizing fears of Soviet "geopolitical momentum."

Yet many news stories today and in the past have told of Soviet
reversals. The countries of China, Egypt, and Somalia come to mind. To
make matters more confusing, many new countries have been created,
old ones have changed names, and everywhere hundreds of factions
and governments have risen and fallen. Even experts have trouble
keeping the extent of the Soviet world-wide thrust in perspective.

Looking at the whole world over the past 35 years, we have asked:
Have the Soviets made lasting gains? Where, when, and how have they

*Reprinted by permission of the author and publisher from *The Defense
Monitor* 9, no. 1 (1980), pp. 1–7, 24. Copyright 1980 by Center for Defense
Information.

succeeded? What have been the sources of their failures? What role has the United States played? It is essential that the debate over the complex subject of trends of Soviet influence be more informed and factual than it has been. We hope our analysis will contribute to informed discussion and provide better perspectives from which to view present and future Soviet influence in the world.

The Study    The Center for Defense Information's study of trends of
of Soviet    Soviet world influence covers the period from 1945 to
             mid-1980. Soviet relations with every country in the
Influence    world were examined. In making appraisals for each
country a wide variety of indicators of Soviet involvement, contact, and influence were taken into account. Pertinent data included: treaty relationships; access to military facilities; stationing of troops; military advisors; arms transfers; economic aid; technicians; trade; United Nations voting patterns; high-level state visits; official statements; and opinions of experts.

While some have argued that the only vehicle the Soviets have for obtaining influence is arms, this study has looked at more than the purely military dimension of involvement and influence. An attempt was made to be sensitive to the particular circumstances of different countries. Inputs of aid and military support which might plausibly lead to significant influence in one case might not in another. In identifying periods of Soviet influence special attention was paid to the following factors: the existence of a treaty relationship; Soviet military involvement; Soviet dominance as an arms supplier; the relative role of the Soviet Union versus other major foreign partners of a country; and the views of regional experts.

In attempting such an ambitious and difficult study there are two major problems: danger of oversimplification, and how to measure influence. There are no ready solutions to either of these problems. The richness of detail in the conditions of each country and its complex involvements with other countries is inevitably obscured in a study which seeks to identify patterns and trends over a long time period and involving many countries. There are important gaps in information. This study presents tentative conclusions.

No commonly accepted definition of influence among nations exists, nor is there consensus on determining when it is present. A strict definition of influence would define it as the ability to get another country to do something that it would otherwise not do. By this definition, it would be very difficult to find any country outside Eastern Europe over which the Soviet Union has exercised such influence which approaches control. In order to avoid restricting the study to a handful of obvious cases, a broader, looser, and more subjective concept of Soviet influence was used. Periods in the history of a country when a high level of Soviet involvement and presence are accompanied by a close and cooperative relationship with the Soviet Union have been identified.

However, the existence of a Soviet-influence relationship can only be hypothesized. One can only identify degrees of involvement and closeness which suggest the *potential* for Soviet influence. In the absence of extremely detailed information on decision making (that is generally not available to any outsiders), the presence of significant Soviet influence is a matter of informed estimates. There is no way to measure influence directly. Often what appears to be influence is simply coincidence of interest, the convergence of independent interests on the part of the Soviet Union and another country. It is clear that inputs such as military aid often do *not* lead to real influence. Americans should recognize from their own experience in numerous instances such as Israel and Vietnam the difficulty of converting massive aid inputs into leverage over other countries. In the Soviet case, the easy assumption that various inputs of aid and support and a large Soviet presence automatically lead to Soviet influence has led many observers to exaggerate Soviet influence. Presence does not equal influence. Egypt is a prime example of this.

This analysis has focused on the nature and closeness of the relationship of countries with the Soviet Union. Whether a country has good or bad relations with United States was of secondary importance. The objective was identification of "pro-Soviet" attitudes and behavior, not "anti-American" ones. The two phenomena are not the same thing. There are many countries which are critical of both superpowers.

During the study a number of American government and academic specialists on Soviet foreign policy and regions of the world were consulted. They helped to refine the assessments. Experts differ among themselves on the existence and extent of Soviet influence in particular countries, reinforcing the judgment that assessing influence is more an art than a science. The CDI study does, however, reflect some consensus of expert opinion.

Trends of Soviet Influence  After the 1917 revolution the Soviet Union was generally isolated and ostracized, particularly by Western powers. Despite this isolation, the Soviet Union prior to World War II did have extensive programs of military aid and training for some countries, including Turkey, China, and Germany. But the only country that came under significant Soviet influence was Mongolia.

As a result of Soviet military victory over Germany in Eastern Europe in World War II, the Soviet Union established a number of satellite states which remain today the basic group of Soviet-influenced states. The short-lived Sino–Soviet bloc came into existence with the communist victory in China in 1949. After the death of Stalin in 1953 the Soviet Union substantially expanded its diplomatic and aid activities in other parts of the world and gradually expanded its presence and influence outside the Eastern European sphere of dominance.

A total of 35 countries have had some period of significant Soviet influence in the post-World War II period. There has been frequent shifting in the orientation of countries. It should be noted that the degree of Soviet influence is not the same for each instance of Soviet influence. The period of Soviet influence for each country has its own characteristics.

Since 1945 the number of countries where the Soviet Union has had a degree of involvement that suggests the potential for significant influence has increased, rising from 7 countries in 1945 to 19 in 1980. This category includes some countries where the Soviets exercise clear influence, primarily Eastern Europe, and other countries where Soviet influence is important but substantially less.

While this increase in the number of what one might loosely call "pro-Soviet" countries may superficially correspond to some impressions of Soviet geopolitical momentum, there are several important observations that must be considered.

First, there has been a large expansion of the number of countries in the world since 1945, from about 74 in 1945 to about 155 today. The percentage of Soviet-influenced countries in the world started at 9% in 1945, rose to about 14% in the late 1950s, then declined in the 1960s and finally rose back to about 12% in the late 1960s. It has remained at this level for the past 10 years. According to this indicator, *Soviet world influence was at its height in the 1950s and there has been no significant Soviet geopolitical momentum in recent years.* Considering that nearly all the new countries in the past 35 years have been former colonies of Western powers, the degree of Soviet success in cultivating close friends among these very numerous anticolonial countries is less than one might have expected.

*Importance of Countries* A second important observation is that not all countries are equally important or offer the same benefits to patrons. Whether it is differences in population, size, economic development, natural resources, military strength, or regional importance, some countries are much more significant than others. One of the important features of Soviet world influence is the extent to which it has been most successful among the poorest and least important countries. Nearly half of the 19 countries (most of those outside Eastern Europe) where the Soviet Union has significant influence today (Table 37.1) are poverty-stricken countries at the bottom of the development ladder and in dire need of foreign assistance. Their governments are usually weak. These countries for the most part have little to offer major powers other than the satisfaction of supplying urgently needed assistance for the future prospect of some benefit.

In general, the world's major military powers and industrialized nations are either allied with the U.S. or expect U.S. aid or protection. If impoverished countries are discounted from the aggregation of Soviet-influenced countries, the lack of Soviet geopolitical momentum is even more evident. The Soviet Union has acquired needy friends which place substantial demands on the Soviet Union in return for what are often small or intangible gains. Sometimes the disadvantages of influence may exceed the advantages.

When Daniel Patrick Moynihan was U.S. ambassador to the United

Table 37.1. *Countries with Significant Soviet Influence*

| In 1980 | In the past |
|---|---|
| Afghanistan | Albania |
| Angola | Algeria |
| Bulgaria | Bangladesh |
| Cambodia | China |
| Congo | Egypt |
| Cuba | Ghana |
| Czechoslovakia | Guinea |
| Ethiopia | India |
| East Germany | Indonesia |
| Hungary | Iraq |
| Laos | North Korea |
| Libya | Mali |
| Mongolia | Somalia |
| Mozambique | Sudan |
| Poland | Yemen (Sana) |
| Romania | Yugoslavia |
| Syria | |
| Yemen (Aden) | |
| Vietnam | |

Nations in the mid-1970s, he and his staff made an analysis of which countries were important to the United States. They took into account imports of oil and other critical materials, amount of trade, and size of U.S. investments. Sixty-four countries by these criteria had no bilateral significance for the U.S. According to Moynihan's list, nearly all the pro-Soviet countries outside Eastern Europe are not economically important to the U.S.

Former CIA official Ray Cline in his most recent book on *World Power Trends* provides no power rating for 7 of the 19 countries where the Soviets have significant influence today (Afghanistan, Angola, Cambodia, Congo, Laos, Mozambique, and South Yemen).

*Expanding Influence?* Trends of Soviet influence over the past 35 years have been analyzed by the Center for Defense Information by aggregating Soviet-influenced countries over this period according to their population and Gross National Product (GNP). Indexes of power developed by Ray Cline in his three books on *World Power Assessment* were also examined to make overall appraisals for trends in the 1970s. Because countries are not equally important, these methods of aggregating them may give a better picture of trends of Soviet influence than simply counting the number of countries.

Population and GNP charts show the percentage of the world's total population and GNP for each year from 1945 through 1979 in countries under Soviet influence. With minor differences the population and GNP curves show similar patterns, rising and falling as Soviet influence in the world waxed and waned. Soviet influence rose sharply in the late 1940s with the addition of China and again less dramatically in the late 1950s with the addition of Indonesia and Iraq. Soviet influence plummeted through the first half of the 1960s with the loss of China and Indonesia but then rose in the late 1960s and early 1970s with the addition of Egypt and India. The loss of Egypt and India in the 1970s has been only partially offset by successes in the former Portugese colonies and elsewhere. In the late 1970s with the departure of India from the Soviet orbit there was a dramatic decline in the percentage of the world's population under Soviet influence.

According to Center for Defense Information analyses based on UN, World Bank, State Department, ACDA, and CIA data, 1958 was the high point of Soviet influence in the world. At that time Soviet-influenced countries had 31% of the world's population and 9% of the world's GNP, not including the Soviet Union. In 1979 the Soviets were influencing only 6% of the world's population and 5% of the world's GNP, exclusive of the Soviet Union.

If China and India are excluded, the Soviet Union has been effective in steadily influencing countries outside the USSR with a total of 4–6% of the world's GNP from 1945 to the present. If the contribution of four countries—China, India, Indonesia, and Bangladesh—are excluded, the Soviet Union has been steadily influential in countries with 4–6% of the world's population since 1945.

Ray Cline's indexes of power are based on the combination of a variety of demographic, geographical, economic, and military factors. Dr. Cline has provided power ratings for the world's countries for three different years, 1974, 1976, and 1979. Using his ratings for each year and dividing all countries in the world, including the U.S. and the Soviet Union, into three groups (pro-Soviet, pro-West and China, other), we get a rough impression of the relative share of the world's power possessed by the Soviet Union and its clients. It is also one measure of the trends of Soviet influence in the past 6 years. The results indicate an extremely steady division of the world's power into 20% for the pro-Soviet camp (including the Soviet Union), 70% for the pro-West and China camp (including the U.S.), and 10% other. There was almost no change in these percentages from 1974 to 1979.

*No Soviet Geopolitical Momentum* These comparisons can give only approximate measures of the relative growth or decline of Soviet influence. But they do seem to demonstrate that there is no evidence of inexorable Soviet geopolitical momentum. If these data demonstrate anything, it is the decline of Soviet world influence since the 1950s.

What emerges from the data is that, with the ups and downs over the years, the Soviet Union's bloc of friendly nations has less aggregate importance today than it did in the late 1950s, prior to the loss of China. Soviet efforts at influence-building since 1960 have not brought it back to the plateau it reached before China's defection. *Nothing that has happened since has really made up for the decline in the power of the Soviet bloc relative to the rest of the world that occurred when the Soviets lost China.*

Another major conclusion that may be drawn from these analyses is that a handful of important countries account for nearly all of the significant fluctuation in Soviet world influence: China, India, Egypt, Indonesia, and, to a lesser extent, Iraq. It has been Soviet success or failure with these countries that has been the real story of the rise and fall of Soviet influence. *Soviet inability to hold the allegiance and support of important Third World countries over the long term has been the major weakness of the Soviet Union in attempting to expand its influence.* While smaller countries such as Somalia and Guinea have been at least as forceful in exerting their independence as the larger developing countries, the more important countries have had more resources and options at their disposal to pursue their own road and acquire other patrons.

A final conclusion that may be drawn from this study of trends of Soviet influence is that a closer look at developments in the 1970s reveals a clear absence of expanding Soviet influence. During this period when there have been so many headlines about the American loss in Vietnam and alleged Soviet successes in Africa and the Middle East, the Soviet Union has not in fact expanded its influence. Soviet losses in the 1970s have just about equaled gains (Table 37.2).

**Superpowers and the Third World**   Over the years since the 1940s the Soviets have broadened their influence in the Third World, but they have not been successful in turning any part of it into a zone of their exclusive or even predominant influence. *Third World governments, including those associated with the Soviet Union, jealously safeguard their sovereignty, with or without an American presence or the threat of U.S. intervention.* Even those states which have had a substantial Soviet military presence have sought to maintain their essential independence.

CIA research analysts Orah Cooper and Carol Fogarty conclude:

> Reduced Western influence in Third World countries has not necessarily led to a corresponding rise in Soviet influence. New governments often have translated anticolonialist positions into strong nationalist policies jealous of any foreign influence. Despite the commitment of some LDC (less developed countries) governments to a "Socialist" system, they usually have wanted their own brand of socialism, and have not been attracted to Soviet Communist ideology, either by economic or military aid.

Rather than being mesmerized by the myth of Soviet geopolitical momentum, Americans should have greater confidence in the independence of other countries. For example, it is too simple to maintain, as Zbigniew Brzezinski has, that "Castro is a puppet of the USSR." This is as mistaken an observation as earlier American misconceptions about the monolithic Sino–Soviet bloc and Soviet control of China.

Soviet policies have made adjustments to the needs of Third World countries more often than the latters' decisions have yielded to the

Table 37.2. *Gains and Losses for the Soviet Union, 1945–1979.*

| | 1945 | 1946 | 1947 | 1948 | 1949 | 1950 | 1951 |
|---|---|---|---|---|---|---|---|
| **Gains** | Albania Bulgaria East Germany Poland Romania Yugoslavia | North Korea | Hungary | Czechoslovakia | China | | |
| **Losses** | | | | Yugoslavia | | | |

| | 1952 | 1953 | 1954 | 1955 | 1956 | 1957 | 1958 | 1959 |
|---|---|---|---|---|---|---|---|---|
| **Gains** | Mongolia | | | | Syria | | Indonesia Iraq | Guinea |
| **Losses** | | | | | | Syria | | |

| | 1960 | 1961 | 1962 | 1963 | 1964 | 1965 | 1966 | 1967 |
|---|---|---|---|---|---|---|---|---|
| **Gains** | Ghana Mali | | Yemen (Sana) | Algeria | | Vietnam | Syria | Egypt |

708

Soviet gains and losses in the Third World, 1968–1975:

| | 1968 | 1969 | 1970 | 1971 | 1972 | 1973 | 1974 | 1975 |
|---|---|---|---|---|---|---|---|---|
| **Losses** | China | Albania, Guinea | Indonesia | Iraq, Sudan | Egypt | Algeria | Ghana | Bangladesh |
| **Gains** | Congo, Iraq | Cuba, Somalia, Sudan | | Guinea, India | Bangladesh | | Libya | Angola, Laos, Mozambique |

Soviet gains and losses in the Third World, 1976–1980:

| | 1976 | 1977 | 1978 | 1979 | 1980 |
|---|---|---|---|---|---|
| **Losses** | Mali, Guinea, India, Somalia | North Korea, Yemen (Sana), Iraq | | | |
| **Gains** | | Ethiopia | Afghanistan, Yemen (Aden) | Cambodia | |

preferences of the Soviet Union. As Stephen Kaplan of the Brookings Institution observed in his major study of Soviet political uses of military power, *Mailed Fist, Velvet Glove*, in the Third World "the status of the Soviet Union typically was not that of imperial overlord but that of guest worker." The major impact of Soviet efforts has been to enable other countries to pursue more effectively policies they wanted to follow anyway. In the face of past U.S. rejection of nonalignment, for example, Soviet support enabled governments to more easily implement this policy. India and Iraq are prominent examples. Among other things, Soviet support has made it more difficult for the U.S. to get rid of regimes it does not like.

*American Policy* It is important to note that Soviet reverses, for the most part, have occurred for reasons that have little to do with specific American actions. While the United States has sometimes through diplomacy and other means sought to "expel" the Soviet Union, as in the Middle East, or to constrain it, American actions have usually played no important role in the emergence of conflict between the Soviet Union and its clients. On the contrary, threatening American behavior has often helped solidify Soviet relations with affected countries. This has certainly been the case in Angola, Cuba, and Vietnam, for example.

There may be instances when it is in American interests strongly to oppose Soviet involvements in the Third World. Such action must be based on deep understanding of local circumstances and our own national interests and respect for local capabilities. But in general the Soviet "threat" in the Third World is not the real issue. Both the United States and the Soviet Union have faced enormous and growing obstacles to controlling events around the world. The *inadequacy* of Soviet leverage over possibly disruptive clients may be more a problem than Soviet domination. Vitenam is an example of this today. There has been a dangerous increase in recent years in local international conflict. Neither superpower is able through military or other means to maintain a condition of global stability tilted in its favor. Neither is very successful in controlling a sphere of influence.

*Opportunities for the Soviet Union to gain influence in the Third World have often been the result of questionable policies that the U.S. has pursued.* U.S. policies on such issues as Vietnam, the Middle East, Panama, minority rule in Southern Africa, and various economic matters have tended to isolate the U.S. from the Third World. We should be realistic that certain policy choices are going to have certain consequences we may not like. We cannot have our cake and eat it too. Neither can the Soviet Union. It too faces the problem of reconciling conflicting policies and priorities. For example, the Soviets were unable to maintain good relations simultaneously with Ethiopia and Somalia.

The real problem for the U.S. is how to relate to change in the world and our approach to the Third World. It has been argued by Henry Kissinger and others that there is a deep and natural antagonism between much of the Third World and the U.S. Recent events in Iran have seemed to confirm this for many Americans. For example, a recent

*Washington Post* editorial argued that "the common ground is regrettably narrow" between the U.S. and the Third World. Such attitudes have encouraged support for confrontationist policies which, fortunately, the Carter Administration has tended to avoid.

It is an open question to what extent the U.S. can harmonize its own interests with those of other parts of the world. It should be recognized that the anti-imperialist and anticolonial views of radicals often stem from their nationalist sentiments more than from rigid Marxism and a blind anti-Americanism. Pretending that other countries who are at odds with the U.S. are puppets of the Soviet Union and refusing to deal constructively with them stimulates their alienation.

*Code of Conduct?* While the past record of the Soviet Union in influence-building is very mixed, it may be argued that the past may be no guide to the future. Will the Soviet Union be more adventuristic and successful in the future? Assorted speculations are possible, but the record shows that apocalyptic predictions have been made repeatedly over the past 30 years. Brookings' *Mailed Fist, Velvet Glove* found no clear association between the state of the strategic military balance (and other military measures) and the amount of Soviet political use of military force. Changes "did not seem to lead to more frequent Soviet political–military activity."

Of course, it is obvious that the Soviets are more involved around the world today than 20 or 30 years ago. All countries must take account of the Soviet Union as a force in world affairs. U.S. involvement has also increased. The danger of armed combat between the U.S. and the USSR in the Third World is real. But the situation is not so anarchic and disordered as it may seem. Restraint and caution have sometimes been shown by both the U.S. and the Soviet Union. The Soviet Union has used armed forces to support friends in the Third World occasionally, in circumstances when a vacuum of legitimate rule has been created by the rapid withdrawal of a colonial power (Angola) or when the USSR could assume the position of acting to defend the sovereignty or territorial integrity of a Third World nation (Ethiopia) or to maintain an existing Marxist regime in power (Afghanistan). The long-term gains for the Soviets appear doubtful and marginal.

A very important element of the informal "code of conduct" for superpower behavior in the Third World is the willingness to live with failure. The Soviets in Egypt in 1972 and the Americans in Iran in 1979 could have used force to resist expulsion and did not. *Acceptance of loss of influence without overreaction is necessary for both superpowers in the face of frequent setbacks.* Recognition of the inevitability of ups and downs of influence and the frequently temporary nature of losses should encourage a certain equanimity when confronted by change and instability. The massive Soviet military move into neighboring Afghanistan would appear to be an ill-advised violation of this code.

Another ingredient of the amorphous code of conduct should be a willingness to downplay overblown geopolitical approaches to world affairs, that is, not seeing everything that occurs in the world in terms of superpower competition. Such "strategic" thinking inevitably leads to ignoring local situations and exaggerating the component of superpower conflict and involvement. Both the Carter Administration and the Soviet Union under Brezhnev, with important exceptions, wanted to avoid the kind of linkage of world events which complicates the solution of local problems and entangles the superpowers in conflicts they would rather avoid.

It would benefit both the U.S. and the Soviet Union if they concentrated more on the solution of their own domestic problems and less on trying to influence foreign governments. After Brezhnev and Kosygin replaced Khrushchev in the mid-1960s, they declared that domestic development was the primary internationalist duty of the USSR. In view of the difficult economic problems facing the Soviet Union today this domestic orientation would be even more desirable than in the 1960s. The same is true for the United States.

Conclusions   • American fears of Soviet geopolitical momentum strongly affect U.S. foreign and military policy.

• A comprehensive study of trends of Soviet world influence in 155 countries since World War II does not support perceptions of consistent Soviet advances and devastating U.S. setbacks.

• Outside Eastern Europe, Soviet influence has lacked staying power. Inability to accumulate influence in foreign countries over long periods is a dominant feature of Soviet world involvement.

• Starting from a very low base of political, economic, and military involvement, the Soviets have increased their influence around the world. Starting with influence in 9% of the world's nations in 1945, they peaked at 14% in the late 1950s, and in 1980 had influence in 12% of the world's nations. Of the 155 countries in the world in 1980, the Soviets had significant influence in 19.

• The Soviets have been successful in gaining influence primarily among the world's poorest and most desperate countries.

• Soviet foreign involvement has to a large extent been shaped by indigenous conditions, and the Soviets have been unable to command loyalty or obedience.

• Soviet setbacks in China, Indonesia, Egypt, India, and Iraq dwarf marginal Soviet advances in lesser countries.

• Temporary Soviet successes in backward countries have proved costly to the Soviet Union. They provide no justification for American alarmism or military intervention. U.S. policies should emphasize our nonmilitary advantages in the competition for world influence.

# 38 ROBBIN F. LAIRD

## Soviet Arms Trade with the Noncommunist Third World*

The Soviet Union exports more arms than any other country. In 1980 the Soviets were responsible for 34% of the world's total arms exports, and their significance as an arms exporter to the Third World is even greater than such an aggregate figure indicates, especially with regard to the Arab Middle East. At least 70% of all Soviet arms sales to the noncommunist developing countries in the 1970s went to the Arab Middle East. In 1980 the Soviet Union was the primary supplier for five of the seven major arms-importing states in the Third World (Syria, Libya, Iraq, India, and Vietnam).[1]

The degree to which the Soviet Union dominates the Third World arms sales is best indicated by analyzing the major military equipment end-items shipped to the Third World. In the period from 1979 to 1982, the Soviets were the major supplier of tanks, self-propelled guns, artillery, supersonic combat aircraft, surface-to-air missiles, guided-missile boats, subsonic aircraft, and helicopters. The Western Europeans were the prime suppliers of noncombat aircraft, major- and minor-surface combatants, and submarines. The United States was the prime supplier only of armored personnel carriers and armored cars.[2] In other words, the only significant competitors with the Soviet Union in arms sales to the Third World have been the Western Europeans, especially the French.

Soviet arms sales are motivated by three key factors. First, the Soviet Union believes that the achievement of United States–Soviet strategic

*Reprinted by permission of the author and publisher from Erik P. Hoffmann, ed., *The Soviet Union in the 1980s* (New York: The Academy of Political Science, 1984), pp. 196–213. Adapted with permission of the publisher from Robbin F. Laird, *Soviet Arms Trade with the Non-Communist Third World in the 1970s and 1980s* (Washington, D. C.: Wharton Econometric Forecasting Associates, 1983). The views expressed in this chapter are the author's and do not necessarily represent those of the Institute for Defense Analyses. Copyright 1983 by Wharton Econometric Forecasting Associates.

parity has resulted in an increase in the significance of conventional military power. In the 1970s, the Soviets emphasized conventional arms modernization, and arms sales are a critical component of this program.

Second, the Soviet Union has developed a version of Henry Kissinger's "regional influentials" policy. It uses arms sales to develop ties with key powers in the Third World, regardless of a given country's social structure or its prospects for Soviet-style "socialist" revolution. Western economic power in the Third World is apparently too great for the Soviet Union to compete successfully on that basis. In contrast, the Soviet Union is in a much more favorable position to compete militarily. The economic aid and arms-sale data support such a conclusion. From 1976 through 1980, the value of Soviet arms sales was four times that of economic aid to developing countries.

Third, Soviet arms exports to developing countries are an increasingly important source of the hard currency needed to pay for Soviet imports from the West. In the 1970s, the Soviet Union shifted away from a policy of using arms primarily for geopolitical influence toward a policy that also provided economic benefits by requiring hard-currency payments for arms from virtually all of its customers. This policy evidently applied even to customers valued for political reasons, such as Ethiopia. Approximately 65% of Soviet arms sales to developing countries in the 1971–1980 period were for hard currency. Indeed, arms sales represented 22% of the total export earnings from trade with nonsocialist countries, second only to fuel exports, which reached 56%.

Another economic contribution of Soviet arms sales has been to lower the cost of the Soviet conventional arms-modernization program. By exporting, an economy of scale is created with a lower cost for end-unit items. Current frontline aircraft—Mig-23s and Mig-25s—are sold widely abroad. The new generation aircraft expected to be deployed in the late 1980s—Su-27s and Mig-29s—will probably be available for the export market as soon as they are deployed in the Warsaw Pact countries. In many ways, the only industrial export for the Soviet Union that is competitive with the West is military equipment.

But all is not auspicious for Soviet arms exports. A number of Soviet arms clients in the 1970s began to diversify their sources of supply, particularly for aircraft. For example, Iraq and India have purchased French aircraft because they want a weapons system with the advantages of Soviet equipment (e.g., simplicity of design) but with the superior Western performance characteristics. Many Soviet arms clients are dissatisfied with the service they receive from the Soviets as well.

In the end, the issue is the quality of Soviet military equipment, especially aerospace products. The Syrian debacle in 1982 did not help and has already had an impact on Soviet arms sales. India, for example, is rethinking the wisdom of purchasing the T-72 tank from the Soviets. In short, the Soviet Union now confronts a very tight and competitive arms market. It faces direct competition from Western European and Third World arms producers, while economic pressures impel it to increase either its market share or its profits. Nonetheless, it will be difficult for the Soviets to do so.

Strategic
Deterrence
and Soviet
Arms Sales

The Soviet Union's attainment of strategic-nuclear parity with the United States in the 1970s had an important political impact for the Soviets, because it increased the significance of conventional power as an instrument of foreign policy.[3] Strategic-nuclear deterrence provides a more stable foundation for the Soviet Union's use of conventional power to further its interests than would be the case in conditions of strategic uncertainty. As Roman Kolkowicz observed:

> The Soviets clearly understand that in the nuclear era major powers need the security of a credible strategic-nuclear deterrent force before they can safely adopt limited-war doctrines and policies. The reason for this lies in the logic of deterrence and limited war. To remain limited, wars involving the major powers, whether directly or indirectly, need credible fallback reserves: a strategic (assured destruction) retaliatory threat that will both act to reduce escalatory pressures and provide boundaries. Espousal of limited war without such a credible retaliatory threat would leave the state open to manipulation and blackmail.[4]

From the Soviet point of view, "imperialism" has been "forced" by strategic-nuclear deterrence to exercise its military power in various forms of conventional "armed violence." The most frequent target has been the Third World, where "imperialism" recognizes the existence of the most vigorous and open conflict between capitalism and socialism as world historical forces. As the authors of an authoritative Soviet study of armed conflict in the Third World put it:

> Adapting to changes in the world balance of power and encountering such a factor as the unified military might of the socialist nations, the aggressive forces of imperialism are directing their "local" attacks against individual socialist countries, the revolutionary movement of the proletariat, the national liberation movement, and against developing countries in which progressive regimes have been established. They understand full well that the outcome of the struggle between socialism and capitalism depends in large measure on how the world revolutionary process develops, what path will be taken by peoples which become liberated from the colonial yoke.[5]

The Soviet Union has vigorously countered "imperialist" aggression, precisely to make clear that it will use military power to achieve its political goals. As Colonel D. Volkogonov commented on Soviet aid to Vietnam in its "struggle" against the United States, "the activities of the Soviet Union and other socialist countries in furnishing assistance to the Vietnamese people in their just struggle and the promoting of successful peace negotiations have revealed to the entire world both our firmness and our sincere desire to solve vexing problems through political means."[6]

The Soviet use of its power-projection forces has reflected an acute sense of the political dimensions of the use of military power in the Third World. Above all, the use of Cuban surrogates in a number of

Soviet military interventions reflects a distinct Soviet preference to avoid direct conflict with the United States. By avoiding direct conflict with the United States, the Soviet Union clearly hopes to isolate Third World military action from questions of general United States–Soviet military confrontation.

Stephen Kaplan, in his work on Soviet armed forces as a political instrument, has emphasized the centrality of political considerations in the framing of Soviet military policy toward the Third World:

> In general, Soviet leaders were adept in legitimizing their use of force, timed their introduction of military means well, showed good sense in the types of forces called on, and did not gloat over successes. The Kremlin preferred a naval presence, covert tactical air assistance, logistical support, and the use of Cuban combat formations over the open deployment of Soviet military units in Third World nations. Moscow knew that it was better to create new political facts rather than risk issuing ultimatums.[7]

The centrality of conventional arms in the violence of Third World political development means that military assistance has become a critical tool in the exercise of Soviet influence. Colonel E. Rybkin has underscored this development as follows: "Oppressed and dependent nations waging wars of liberation were no longer alone in the struggle against colonizers. They receive moral, political, economic, and where possible and necessary, military assistance from countries of socialism."[8]

Soviet analysts have increasingly concluded that the military forces in the Third World are the critical elites shaping the development of those countries. Thus, Soviet military assistance is designed to exercise influence over the political orientations of Third World development by shaping the commitments of Third World military elites. As Charles Peterson has noted, "it is certain from the evidence of Soviet writings that the relative importance of military cooperation as an instrument of policy has grown in the measure that Third World military elites have become a leading focus of Soviet attention."[9]

The growing significance that the Soviets have attached to military assistance as an instrument of influence reinforces the importance of further developing Soviet power projection forces. Andrew J. Pierre in his study of the politics of arms sales has described the interrelationship between Soviet military assistance and power projection forces in the following manner:

> During the 1970s the Soviet Union greatly improved its capacity to transport arms over long distances by developing long-range cargo aircraft and by expanding its maritime capabilities. In the previous decade Moscow's ability to aid Lumumba in the Congolese civil war was limited. No such logistical problems hampered the impressive capability of the Soviet Union to bring Cubans to Angola and Ethiopia or to support them with sea and airlift operations, ferrying thousands of tons of arms and military supplies.[10]

In short, a condition of strategic-nuclear parity between the superpowers has not reduced the significance of military power to the Soviet Union. Rather, strategic-nuclear deterrence has increased the significance of the effort to create usable military power—nonnuclear military power. Arms sales have played a key part in strengthening Soviet conventional military power. As Anthony Cordsman noted, "while the linkages involved are often politically complex, there is a clear relation between the expansion of Soviet forces and the expansion of Soviet arms sales."[11] Soviet arms sales to the Third World have been a key dimension of the Soviet conventional arms-modernization process in the 1970s and 1980s.

## The Role of Arms Sales in Soviet Third World Policy

Increasingly throughout Brezhnev's rule, the Soviets came to view noncommunist Third World states as significant global actors in their own right. Whereas in the 1950s and 1960s Soviet interest in the noncommunist Third World was generated primarily by competition with the United States, increasingly the Soviet Union began to perceive the advantages in improving ties for economic and military reasons outside of the superpower framework. Ideologically, the Soviets placed greater emphasis on the legitimacy of developing relationships with Third World states, regardless of their social structure, as long as those relationships provided political, economic, or military benefits to the Soviet Union. It became not only possible but also desirable to expand the network of "mutually beneficial" economic and military ties with noncommunist Third World states.

Nonetheless, the Soviet Union has not always accepted the wisdom or the legitimacy of developing a congruence of interests with the noncommunist Third World. Rather, the Soviet goal historically has been to transform the Third World in the Soviet image. It was only in response to the very mixed results of Soviet Third World involvement in the early post-Stalin period that the Soviets began to lower their expectations or, alternatively, to develop more realistic expectations of the prospects for social transformation in the Third World.[12] The evolution of those expectations went through the following phases:

*Phase One, 1946–1953: The Late Stalin Period* The "National Liberation Movements" in this period were characterized by an effort to remove the formal vestiges of colonialism. While championing the decolonization effort in forums such as the United Nations, the Soviets devoted virtually no economic or military resources to the development of its relations with the Third World. In particular, Soviet military-aid programs in the postwar Stalinist period were mainly limited to China and to North Korea. No military aid was given to any noncommunist Third World state.

*Phase Two, 1954–1957: The Early Post-Stalin Period* In the

immediate post-Stalin period, Soviet leaders expressed interest in the revolutionary potential of the Third World. Khrushchev was an especially visible advocate in this period of extending support to the new regimes in the Third World in order to promote the global process of transformation to "communism." For example, he viewed the 1955 Bandung Conference as an indication of the trend toward Soviet-style socialism in Africa and Asia. This conference was followed by a much publicized trip by Khrushchev and Bulganin to the Near East in late 1955. Concurrently, Soviet arms began appearing in the Middle East (primarily through Eastern European channels, especially Czechoslovakia). It was in this period that Khrushchev developed his "zone of peace" concept. In contrast to the Stalinist concept of the "two camps," Khrushchev put forth an image of the Soviet Union as the ally of all "nonaligned" states. It was argued that there was a virtually automatic commonality of interests between the Soviet Union and the Third World in advancing the cause of "socialism."

This phase included the real beginning of the development of economic and military ties with noncommunist Third World states. Egypt was the first major arms recipient. The initial shipment of arms to Egypt included several Mig-15 fighters, IL-28 jet bombers, T-34 tanks, and several naval vessels. This sale was followed by others in early 1956 to Syria and Afghanistan.

Soviet arms sales were made possible by Western—especially American—unwillingness to supply arms on a favorable basis to key "nonaligned" states in the Third World. For example, Indonesia sought arms in the mid-1950s to strengthen its ability to crush domestic rebellion and to seize control of Western Guinea from the Dutch. When the United States refused to sell arms to them, the Indonesians turned to the Soviets.

A key dimension of the Soviet ability to enter new arms markets in this period was the speed with which the Soviets could deliver equipment. The speed of delivery was facilitated by the stockpiles of surplus equipment made available by the Soviet arms-modernization program of the late 1950s.

*Phase Three, 1958–1964: The Khrushchev Period* During this period, the Soviet Union assumed that socialism would spread throughout the Third World. This would be accomplished by the efforts of "progressive" forces within the Third World itself, which would supposedly seek to ally themselves with the Soviet Union against the common "imperialist" enemy. The Soviets would only have to provide limited economic support that would include the transfer of arms.

In the first part of the period (1958–1960), the Soviet Union was able to enter the Iraqi and Indian markets, Iraq turned to the Soviet Union for arms following the overthrow of the pro-Western monarchy in 1958 by General Kassem. The Soviets entered the Indian market primarily because they were able to meet Indian requirements at a lower cost than the United States and were more flexible in allowing barter terms as well. Initial sales were small, however, being limited to the transfer of transport aircraft and helicopters. Other arms sales in this period were made to Algeria, Guinea, Ghana, and Mali.

The largest recipients of arms in the period from the mid-1950s to 1960 were Egypt and Indonesia. Each received more than $500 million in arms, and together they accounted for more than half of Soviet arms sales. Roughly a third of the sales went to Syria, Iraq, and Afghanistan, each of which received more than $200 million in arms.

Soviet arms sales intensified in the early 1960s. During the period 1961–1964, Soviet arms sales rose in value about 20% over the preceding 6 years. Military sales to India increased significantly in 1962, largely by making good the losses created in fighting with China. Among the most significant Soviet arms agreements with India was the creation for the first time of a coproduction arrangement outside of the Warsaw Pact. The Soviets agreed to build two aircraft plants in India to produce the airframes and engines for the Mig-21 fighters. Arms sales were also dominated by an upsurge of shipments to Egypt and Indonesia in the 1961–1964 period. Egypt, Indonesia, and India accounted for more than 70% of the total. Egypt was the largest recipient of arms with more than $700 million in arms sales. Indonesia and India received more than $500 million each in arms from the Soviet Union in this period.

Sales in this period brought relatively low profits. The Soviet Union provided arms to Indonesia and Egypt on exceptionally favorable terms. The sales to India were more profitable but were still priced below the general arms-transfer market. One must remember, however, that the Soviets were selling older equipment from preexisting stockpiles, and the actual terms of Soviet "military assistance" were often much less generous than appeared to be the case. Rarely did the Soviet Union offer military grants rather than commercial sales. This was in contrast to the American practice at the time of extending large military grants-in-aid to Third World states. Soviet credits for arms purchases usually carried 2–3% interest, repayable over 5, 7, 10, or 12 years. In addition, the provision of arms in exchange for commodities was much less generous than it appeared. Even though Soviet prices were reasonable, massive arms deals could require a significant mortgaging of the commodities production of a given Third World state to the Soviet Union. Clearly, however, economic motivations were secondary to political goals in this period.

*Phase Four, 1965–1969: The Early Brezhnev Years*  In this period the Soviet Union experienced a number of setbacks in the Third World as radical governments allied to the Soviet Union were overthrown by military coups, notably in Algeria and Indonesia. In part, because of such setbacks, the Soviets began to recognize the existence of serious obstacles to the growth of "socialism" in the Third World. Earlier hope of telescoping the Third World's transition to socialism into a relatively brief period was replaced by a more pessimistic assessment. It was now thought that the revolutionary process in the Third World would require "an entire historical epoch." The role of the military in shaping the indigeneous processes of change was given greater significance, although its role was not necessarily considered to be a progressive one. But the military elites seemed a natural target for the exercise of Soviet influence by means of the conduct of Soviet arms trade.

Recognizing the need to influence military elites, the Soviet Union was nonetheless more pessimistic about the prospects for development in the Third World. As one Soviet analyst noted, "the lesson of military upheavals in several states of Asia and Africa is that the army can play a progressive role in the national-liberation movement, but it can also easily turn into a tool of reactionary forces."[13] The experience with Egypt in the early 1970s would cause the Soviet Union further to examine the interests served by its arms trade.

In the early Brezhnev period, India became the largest recipient of Soviet arms, with sales of more than $400 million. Egypt was second, with sales of more than $300 million, while Iraq and Syria each accounted for more than $200 million in sales. Together, Egypt, Syria, and Iraq constituted more than one-half of all Soviet arms sales in the period.

A major Soviet effort in this period was to resupply Egyptian and Syrian forces after the 1967 war. More than 80% of Egypt's losses of military equipment were replaced. In addition, the number of Soviet advisers and technicians increased from 500 to 3000 by the end of 1967. But the support given to Egypt and Syria clearly represented an exercise in the use of arms to achieve direct military and political advantage rather than the use of Soviet arms for economic profit.

*Phase Five, 1969–1975: The Middle Brezhnev Years* Soviet perspectives in this period underscored that "serious obstacles of an objective and sometimes subjective nature" stood in the way of the transition to socialism even in "countries of socialist orientation" and that some of these countries were regressing either by "turning aside from a progressive course or by slowing their advance."[14] The more realistic assessment of Third World developments was conjoined with the increased salience of the military dimension, including a more economically advantageous arms-transfer policy, to the successful exercise of Soviet influence in the Third World.

The debacle in Egypt was a major stimulus to the development of Soviet Third World policy in this period. The expulsion of Soviet military personnel in mid-1972 serves as a traumatic reminder of the reversibility of military ties, because the Soviet expulsion by Sadat came despite massive arms transfers and unprecedented Soviet participation in the active defense of Egyptian air space in 1970.

The period was also characterized by the increased significance of arms sales to petrodollar countries in the Middle East. Iraq and Libya became increasingly significant recipients of Soviet arms, each receiving more than $2 billion in arms. Syria became the leading recipient of Soviet arms, with Egypt close behind. Both received more than $2.5 billion in arms, stimulated largely by the resupply efforts associated with the 1973 war.

*Phase Six, 1975–1982: The Late Brezhnev Period* In this period, the Soviet Union became increasingly pessimistic—or, alternatively, more realistic—in regarding the need to place relations with the noncommunist Third World on a sounder economic and military basis. The Soviets began to recognize that their opponent in the Third World was not only the United States but also the process of indigenous change in the Third World. Opposition by indigenous Third World forces to the exercise of Soviet influence has been a disappointment to the Soviet Union. Historically, it has regarded Third World hostility to Western influence as an acceptance of the Soviet Union and a rejection of the Western powers. The Soviets began to realize that most indigenous Third World forces want independence from both East and West. Specifically, the purchase of Soviet arms has frequently reflected the desire to become independent from the West but not a desire to be under Soviet military tutelage. In the mid-1970s the Soviet Union found itself under increasing market pressure by petrodollar countries able to choose alternative suppliers, such as Iraq and Algeria. These countries favored a mixed arms procurement policy as a means of seeking greater national independence.

In this period several Soviet analysts emphatically contended that there is no automatic commonality of interests binding the Third World to Soviet foreign policy interests. Consequently, the Soviets needed to follow a flexible approach that would take into account such factors as the degree of independence a given country had from the world capitalist system. Some Soviet analysts began to emphasize that the critical line of demarcation in the noncommunist Third World was between dependent capitalist regimes and independent capitalist regimes. It was in the Soviet interest to develop ties with independent capitalist regimes, including the sale of arms, even if such ties would not lead to the ultimate triumph of "socialism."[15]

Table 38.1 indicates that for the period 1975–1979 new arms-sales commitments totaled more than $30 billion, more than double that of the previous 5-year period (these figures include not just Soviet arms sales but arms sales by Eastern Europe as well).

During the late 1970s hard-currency sales of arms to petrodollar countries in Africa and the Middle East began to replace the earlier Soviet practice of providing arms at attractive discounts or terms of payment. With the end of the Soviet–Egyptian arms relationship in 1975, the Soviets focused their arms shipments on Iraq, Libya, and Algeria. Iraq became the largest Third World recipient of Soviet arms. Syria also received large quantities of arms, but, in contrast with Iraq, Libya, and Algeria, Syria made no substantial hard-currency payments for Soviet arms.

Arms sales played a much greater role in overall Soviet hard-currency earnings in the mid-to-late 1970s. Given the importance of hard-currency purchases in Soviet industrial trade with the West, arms sales to the Third World became in effect a major industrial export supporting East–West technology transfer. In terms of manufacturing exports, arms sales became a major end-item for trade in this period.

*Phase Seven, 1982–Present* It is difficult to identify the content of
the Andropov and Chernenko policies toward arms sales with the
noncommunist developing countries. There are, however, a number of
clearly identifiable factors that will affect the formation of policy. First,
the decline in world oil prices will have an immediate impact on the
ability of the Soviet arms clients to pay in hard currency. Second, the
economic stringencies of the 1980s will increasingly pressure the Soviets
to place arms trade on an economically sound footing. Third, the rising
cost of the new generation of Soviet military equipment, especially
aircraft, creates an additional incentive to export in order to reduce the
unit cost of key end-items, such as the new Su-27 and Mig-29 fighters.
Fourth, the defeat of Syria by Israel in the June 1982 war is having
continuing repercussions on the Soviet arms sales markets. The Soviets
have clearly tried to blame Syria for the Syrian defeat at the hands of
Israeli forces. But a number of Soviet arms clients have expressed
concern over the performance of Soviet equipment, and, at a minimum,
Soviet arms clients will increasingly wish to receive the top-of-the-line
Soviet military equipment when at all possible.

In short, the Soviets face a challenging arms-sales market in the
1980s. At the same time, they hope to place their arms sales on an
increasingly sound economic basis in order to support their own military
modernization efforts as well as to support their more general foreign
policy efforts.

## The Basic Structure of Soviet Arms Trade with Noncommunist Developing Countries

More than 70% of Soviet arms sales to the noncommunist developing countries in the 1970s and 1980s have been made with the Arab Middle East. When arms transfers to India are added to the total, more than 80% of Soviet arms sales are accounted for. A major change in the 1970s involved a shift to Syria as the major recipient of Soviet arms in the Arab world. In the decade from 1965 to 1975, Egypt was the single most significant recipient of Soviet arms in the Middle East. With the breakdown of Soviet–Egypt relations in the mid-1970s, Syria became the primary geopolitical actor in the region for whom the Soviets were willing to provide a significant arms transfer that was partially subsidized.

Arab orders for Soviet arms increased dramatically in the 1970s.
Soviet arms sales to the region were five times as great in 1974–1979 as in
the period 1967–1973. In the 1970s, Iraq, Libya, and Algeria became the
key hard-currency customers of Soviet arms. The value of exports
increased in part due to the sale of more expensive late-model equipment, which sometimes predated exports to Soviet Warsaw Pact allies.

The Soviets have sold a broad array of weaponry to the Third World
in the past few years. Some sense of the scope of Soviet arms exports can
be provided by figures contained in Table 38.2, from the Pentagon's
most recent version of its report, *Soviet Military Power*. The table does not
differentiate between communist and noncommunist developing

Table 38.1. *Soviet-Bloc Military-Aid Commitments, 1975–1979 (U.S. Billions)*

| Year | USSR | Eastern Europe | Total |
|------|------|----------------|-------|
| 1975 | 3.3  | 0.64 | 3.94 |
| 1976 | 5.5  | 0.34 | 5.84 |
| 1977 | 8.7  | 0.47 | 9.17 |
| 1978 | 2.5  | 0.55 | 3.05 |
| 1979 | 8.4  | 0.25 | 8.65 |
| Total | 28.4 | 2.25 | 30.65 |

Source: Central Intelligence Agency, *Communist Aid Activities in Non-communist Less Developed Countries, 1979 and 1954–1979* (October 1980).

countries receiving Soviet equipment, but it does provide an understanding of the geographical focus as well as of the major categories of equipment shipped. Overwhelmingly, Soviet arms exports in the 1977–1982 period went to the Middle East, North Africa, and South Asia. This same Pentagon report estimated the value of Soviet military sales agreements to all Third World states at $47.5 billion, of which $29.1 billion went to the Middle East, North Africa, and South Asia. Again, these figures do not isolate sales to noncommunist developing countries.

In the period 1975–1982, the Soviet Union was the major supplier to the Third World of tanks and self-propelled guns, artillery, supersonic combat aircraft, surface-to-air missiles, and guided-missile boats. The major Western European suppliers led in deliveries of major and minor naval surface combatants, submarines, and helicopters. In contrast, the United States led only in deliveries of light armored vehicles and subsonic combat and other aircraft.

The single most successful export has been of Soviet tanks. The Soviet Union has shipped three generations of tanks to the Third World since the 1960s—the T-54/55 MBT in the 1960s and T-62 and T-72 MBTs throughout the 1970s and into the 1980s. In the opinion of many Western experts, the Soviet tank force may be the finest in the world. The evolution of Soviet tank designs has given the Soviet tanks much compatibility among components of the various generations. This provides a significant pool of war reserves.

The large pool of Soviet tanks (more than 50,000 in the Soviet Union alone) and of Soviet client states purchasing tanks provides the opportunity for the Soviets to have large production runs of tanks, thereby significantly reducing the unit cost. In addition, the purchase of significant numbers of Soviet tanks creates a sunk cost for the client state, which in turn creates a key incentive to continue purchasing the evolutionary Soviet tank that is designed for compatibility over time. No Western competitor can compete with the Soviets in the sale of tanks, neither in the length of production runs nor in compatibility of genera-

Table 38.2. *Major Soviet Equipment Delivered to the Third World, 1977–1982*

| | Total | Near East and South Asia | Sub-Saharan Africa | Latin America | East Asia and Pacific |
|---|---|---|---|---|---|
| Tanks/self-propelled guns | 7065 | 5205 | 1140 | 80 | 640 |
| Light armor | 8660 | 6500 | 1590 | 175 | 395 |
| Artillery (100-mm and over) | 9590 | 5115 | 3510 | 420 | 545 |
| Major surface combatants | 32 | 19 | 5 | 1 | 7 |
| Minor surface combatants | 126 | 10 | 45 | 27 | 44 |
| Missile patrol boats | 53 | 33 | 4 | 11 | 8 |
| Submarines | 6 | 3 | — | 3 | — |
| Supersonic combat aircraft | 2235 | 1635 | 220 | 130 | 250 |
| Subsonic combat aircraft | 290 | 150 | 80 | 5 | 55 |
| Helicopters | 910 | 620 | 125 | 35 | 130 |
| Other military aircraft | 345 | 100 | 70 | 65 | 110 |
| Surface-to-air missiles | 11680 | 9495 | 1575 | 435 | 175 |

tions (with the exception of the compatibility of German tanks over time).

A second major category of military equipment widely sold by the Soviets in the 1970s and 1980s has been ground-air defense systems, notably surface-to-air missile (SAM) systems. The cutting edge of Soviet sales in this category has been to politically valued clients under attack from adversaries. In 1970–1971 Egypt was the first noncommunist state to receive the SA-3 low-level SAM system and the mobile ZSU-23-4 radar-controlled antiaircraft gun. In the early 1980s, Syria was the first state outside of the Soviet Union to receive the SA-5s and the first noncommunist state to receive the SA-8s.

The most significant category of sales from the standpoint of hard currency earnings, however, has been military aircraft. Since the 1960s, the Soviet Union has exported three generations of aircraft to the noncommunist Third World. In the 1960s, it exported the first generation Mig-17s and Mig-19s. In the early-to-mid 1970s, it sold second-generation aircraft, most notably the Mig-21. In the mid-to-late 1970s and early 1980s the Soviet Union exported Mig-23s, Mig-25s, and SU-20s.

Soviet aircraft development has been nearly a generation behind American aircraft, and Soviet exports reflect this gap. For example, the Israelis recently destroyed Syrian aircraft with a fourth-generation aircraft that the Soviets only hope to deploy in significant numbers in the late 1980s. The Soviets lag in the development of aircraft generations with respect to Western European producers as well. As a result of the lag in Soviet aircraft development, Western producers are in a much more favorable position to compete with the Soviets than in the case of armored equipment, especially with regard to tanks.

## Major Trends in Soviet Arms Sales

A number of key trends in the practice and structure of Soviet arms sales characterized the 1970s and 1980s.[16] One of the most significant trends has been the shifting of Soviet arms sales from a strictly or mainly political basis to an economic basis as well. Many Soviet arms sales are politically motivated, especially with regard to the communist Third World, notably Cuba and Vietnam. But Soviet arms sales with the noncommunist Third World have increasingly been made to states more capable of paying for Soviet arms.

Even in the case of Syria, for example, there is an economic basis to Soviet policy. With their expulsion from Egypt, the Soviets placed greater reliance on their ties with Syria to maintain their hand in the military confrontation with Israel. But the Soviets have not done so in the absence of an economic motivation. A large portion of Syrian arms imports from the Soviet Union in 1982 was paid for in hard-currency cash. Since Syria is a relatively poor country with no significant oil income, its arms imports were apparently paid for by its Arab neighbors, with Saudi Arabia and Kuwait contributing most of the funds.

Thus, at least indirectly, Saudi Arabia and Kuwait probably became the largest buyers of Soviet military hardware in 1982.

The importance of Soviet arms exports to developing countries in the overall Soviet hard-currency balance of trade and payments has risen dramatically over the last decade. During 1971–1973, when arms sales to Egypt accounted for a major portion of total Soviet arms sales to developing countries, the percentage of arms sold for hard currency was probably below 40%. But after 1973, when Libya and Iraq became increasingly important buyers, the share of hard-currency sales probably exceeded 75%. Estimates prepared by Wharton Econometric Forecasting Associates (WEFA) indicate that during 1971–1980 approximately two-thirds of Soviet arms sales to developing countries—or $21.1 billion—were for hard currency.

According to estimates prepared by WEFA, of all commodities of significant importance in Soviet exports to nonsocialist countries, arms were the most dynamic item. Their share of the Soviet export earnings in developing countries increased from 55% in 1981 to almost 62% in 1982. As for their contribution to total Soviet export earnings in nonsocialist countries (excluding gold), the share of arms increased from 19% to almost 22%, second only to the share of fuels, which reached 56%. Soviet exports of arms to developing countries cannot be viewed only as an instrument of Soviet foreign policy and global military strategy, but are of increasing importance as a source of hard currency and as a means of paying for Soviet imports.

Although outright grants of arms have become much rarer, generous terms still prevail when the Soviet Union wants to keep its hand in the East–West trade competition. For example, the terms of the $1.6 billion sale to India are extremely generous. Repayment is spread over 17 years at an annual interest charge of 2.5%.

The Soviet Union has been able to deliver weapons systems much more quickly than its competitors for arms sales. Soviet arms are extremely attractive to countries in quick need of weapons, because they can be delivered rapidly from stock, something which Western arms suppliers have found difficult or even impossible to match. In addition, the arms offered for sale have been increasingly sophisticated. Recently, the Soviet Union has sold much of its frontline equipment to the Third World states. Especially important in this regard has been the sale of heavy tanks, aircrafts, and multitube artillery.

The increased cost of each successive generation of Soviet aircraft, in particular, has placed pressure on the Soviets to lower costs through the use of exports. By exporting, an economy of scale is created with a lower cost of end-unit items. Current front-line aircraft—Mig-23s and Mig-25s—are sold widely abroad. The new generation of look-down, shoot-down aircraft that is expected to be deployed in the late 1980s—Su-27 and Mig-29s—will probably be available for the export market at the same time as they are deployed within the Warsaw Pact countries.

In addition to the economies of scale advantages, the Soviet Union has been pressured to sell its front-line aircraft to key client states if they wish to remain in the market. The Soviets are in keen competition with the French Mirage 2000 in many of their chief target areas in the noncommunist Third World. Also, the United States sells to many of the states that rival Soviet client states. Soviet clients will pressure the Soviet Union to provide a counter to the United States F-16, which the Soviets apparently believe to be the Mig-29.

There has also been increasing pressure from Soviet client states regarding the quality of service provided by the Soviet Union in maintaining equipment, especially in the case of aircraft maintenance, including engine overhauls. A number of Soviet arms clients have pressured the Soviet Union to build aircraft or at least engine-overhaul facilities in their countries to provide for timely and efficient servicing of their weapons system. Both Peru and Iraq wish to follow the Indian example of having engine-repair facilities on their own soil, rather than having to send aircraft engines to the Soviet Union for repair.

The problem of service has especially intensified with the growing sophistication of military hardware. The more sophisticated the equipment sold, the more pronounced the importance of the continuing relationship between arms supplier and arms user. The value of an average contract between the Soviet Union and one of its arms clients is usually 60% for the cost of the weapon, 33% for support, and 7% for infrastructure. By contrast, the value of an average contract with the United States is 35% for weapons, 35% for support, and 30% for infrastructure. A Soviet arms client therefore relies on its supplier more than United States customers for such things as training support, construction, and technical assistance, which come under the infrastructure category.

As the sophistication of military equipment increases, so do the demands to provide technical training and support to the indigenous personnel using the more advanced equipment. The influx of large quantities of modern, complex military equipment into less-developed countries has demanded a level of military skills that are lacking in the recipient states. This lack of skilled military manpower is exacerbated especially by the speed with which military equipment has been delivered and by the necessity for rapid assimilation. The manpower base in the recipient countries has been unable, in most cases, to supply enough men capable of being trained to command, operate, and maintain much of the more sophisticated Soviet equipment within the necessary time. Hence an important dimension of the Soviet arms sales effort has been to provide training at Soviet military installations for Third World military personnel or to dispatch large numbers of Soviet military technicians to the Third World.

The training dimension of arms transfer may affect the future of Soviet arms sales. On the one hand, the sale of military equipment requiring the creation of increased ties with Third World military elites poses the possibility for expanding Soviet influence with these elites. The Soviets obviously favor such a development. But, on the other hand, the use of military advisers to expand Soviet influence inhibits many Third World states from buying Soviet arms. The expansion of Soviet global military presence poses a threat to many Third World states, and these states do not want to import Soviet influence with Soviet arms.

An additional pressure being placed by Soviet Third World arms clients is to establish coproduction facilities in the recipient country. Coproduction facilities reduce the end-item cost to the recipient country and allow the indigenous manpower base to attain higher skill levels. Coproduction provides the potential for greater independence of the Third World state with the creation of a learning curve for the skilled domestic base.

The only case to date of coproduction arrangements has been India, which has been producing Mig-21s since the 1960s. The Soviet Union offered to coproduce Mig-23s as part of the unsuccessful effort to block the 1978 sale of the Anglo–French Jaguar to India. Evidently as part of the 1980 arms agreement, the Soviet Union and India will coproduce Mig-25s. India was also authorized to produce T-72 tanks as part of the 1980 agreement. Reportedly, Iraq has been especially adamant about establishing coproduction arrangements with the Soviet Union in order to supplement the practice of direct arms-transfer.

Since the early 1970s, the Soviet Union has made a sustained effort to enter new arms markets. A major element of its effort to expand sales to the noncommunist Third World has been an attempt to use the extensive Soviet experience in barter or compensation trade to advantage. Particularly with the capital shortages in the Third World and with the decline in hard-currency available to Third World oil producers in the 1980s, the Soviets hope to play on the desire of Third World states to provide more stable "nonmonetary" exchanges to expand Soviet sales. For example, the Argentinian–Soviet grain arrangements reportedly include an agreement to spend a significant amount of Argentinian earnings in the Soviet market, a provision clearly pointing to the Soviet hope that Argentina will use its Soviet account to purchase Soviet arms. However, the anticommunist Argentinian military has thus far resisted such a purchase.

The Soviets have also faced increasing competition from the suppliers of Soviet-produced or Soviet-copied equipment in the communist countries and the Third World. Such competition simply limits the potential political leverage that the Soviets can obtain from arms sales. It is possible that increased competition from non-Soviet producers or suppliers of Soviet equipment could paradoxically increase the scope of Soviet sales if Third World states could be certain of blocking the Soviets from exercising undue influence from the sale of their arms.

Competition is provided by non-Soviet producers or suppliers of Soviet equipment. Egyptian arms exports consist almost entirely of Soviet equipment. China has continued to produce copies of Soviet equipment and is entering traditional Soviet markets by providing an alternative source of supply, as in Iraq. In 1980, the Soviets embargoed arms shipments to Iraq because of the Iran–Iraq war, but Iraq obtained spare parts and replacement equipment from Yugoslavia, Romania, and Poland.

The Soviets are also facing increasing competition from Western

European arms producers in their traditional arms markets. France especially has aggressively sought to displace the Soviets from key countries in the Middle East, especially in aerospace products, by marketing the Mirage 2000 to Soviet disadvantage in several Third World states. Similarly, Britain has been offering armored products and naval systems in markets that the Soviets have been attempting to enter. West Germany has been selling naval systems and other equipment to several Third World states that do not wish to place themselves under United States domination but also do not wish to purchase Soviet arms.

In the Soviet–Western European competition for arms markets in the Third World, the Western Europeans have a number of advantages over the Soviets. The Western Europeans provide far better service and, in general, a better quality product. And they possess a limited global projection capability, which in turn limits the military influence that can be obtained from arms sales.

The Soviet Union also faces competition from Third World arms producers. The Brazilian armaments and aerospace industries provide a limited supply of armored vehicles and artillery rockets to other Third World states, such as Iraq, which in the past would have purchased them from the Soviet Union.

An additional source of competition has come from arms producers willing to upgrade Soviet equipment. For example, Britain has offered to reengine Soviet tanks for Egypt. Israel is offering an upgrading package for Soviet tanks as well. Several Western European producers have expressed a willingness to provide enhanced avionics packages to countries possessing Soviet aircraft.

In short, the Soviet Union will confront a very tight and competitive arms market in the late 1980s. It faces direct competition from Western European and Third World arms producers, competition that both complements and contests Soviet dominance over the international arms market. The Soviet Union is also indirectly pressured by American arms sales. As the United States exports products like the F-16, the Soviet Union must provide its highest quality weapons at favorable prices. Moreover, there is pressure on the Soviet Union to use counter-trade or barter trade effectively in maintaining its market share. These competitive market conditions come precisely as economic pressure on the Soviet Union compels it to increase either its market share or its profits. It will, nonetheless, be difficult to do so. Furthermore, the Soviet Union has little hope of sustaining the level of hard-currency imports from the West unless it maintains or increases its arms sales. With the net decline in oil prices, the role of arms sales in providing the hard currency for the Soviet Union's balance of payments with noncommunist countries is being enhanced. The Soviet Union will thus seek to sell as many arms to the developing world with as much profit as possible.

The Soviet Union, however, does have several advantages in the competition with Western European arms producers. It can produce and deliver armaments faster, and it can undersell the Western Europeans. The size of the Soviet stockpile provides the option of massive arms transfers when a given client-state is embroiled in military conflict. Also, the size of the Soviet economy allows more flexibility in conducting the sort of barter trade that many Third World countries might well be impelled to engage in throughout the decade ahead.

## Notes

[1]*World Military Expenditures and Arms Transfers, 1971–1980* (Washington, D. C.: Arms Control and Disarmament Agency, 1983).

[2]Richard Grimmett, *Trends in Conventional Arms Transfers to the Third World by Major Supplier, 1975–1982* (Washington, D.C.: Congressional Research Service, 1983).

[3]See Robbin F. Laird and Dale R. Herspring, *The Soviet Union and Strategic Arms* (Boulder, Colo.: Westview Press, 1984), chap. 1.

[4]Roman Kolkowicz, "United States and Soviet Approaches to Military Strategy," *Orbis* 2 (Summer 1981), pp. 322–323.

[5]I. E. Sharova, ed., *Lokal'nye voiny: Istoriia i sovremennost'* (Moscow: Voenizdat, 1981), pp. 5–6.

[6]D. Volkogonov, "Peaceful Coexistence—An Alternative for War." *Kommunist* 19 (October 1973) (translated in Joint Publications Research Service [JPRS], 60454, November 5, 1973) p. 38.

[7]Stephen S. Kaplan, *Diplomacy of Power* (Washington, D.C.: Brookings Institution, 1982), p. 668.

[8]E. Rybkin, "The 25th CPSU Congress and Wars of Liberation of the Contemporary Era," *Voenno-istoricheskii zhurnal* 11 (November 1983) (trans. in JPRS, 072543, January 2, 1979), p. 42.

[9]Charles C. Peterson, *Third World Military Elites in Soviet Perspective* (Alexandria, Va.: Center for Naval Analyses, 1979), p. 37.

[10]Andrew J. Pierre, *The Global Politics of Arms Sales* (Princeton: Princeton University Press, 1982). p. 77.

[11]Anthony H. Cordesman, "The Soviet Arms Trade: Patterns for the 1980s," *Armed Forces Journal International* (June 1983), p. 97.

[12]This section draws on material presented in Steven T. Hosmer and Thomas W. Wolfe, *Soviet Policy and Practice toward Third World Conflicts* (Lexington, Mass.: Lexington Books, 1983).

[13]A. Iskenderov, "Armiia, politika i narod," *Izvestiia*, January 17, 1967.

[14]O. Orestov, "Independent Africa in the Making," *International Affairs*, no. 11 (November 1975), p. 75.

[15]See especially K. N. Brutents, *Osvobodivshiesia strany v 70-e gody* (Moscow: Politizdat, 1979).

[16]This section draws on material presented in various issues of *Aviation Week and Space Technology* as well as in the annual reports on arms sales of the Stockholm International Peace Research Institute.

# 39 ELIZABETH KRIDL VALKENIER

## The USSR and the Third World: Economic Dilemmas*

This study examines four aspects of Soviet economic relations with the Third World in the post-Stalin era: (1) aid and trade policies; (2) views on the operations of the world economy; (3) development theory; and (4) the response to debates about the New International Economic Order.

In every area there has been a marked change. The confident systemic challenge that typified the Soviet entry into the Third World after Stalin's death has given way to far less aggressive and exclusive policies that were induced by various failures and disappointments. Shifts in these four areas indicate significant departures from Moscow's former belief in a common front with the Third World against imperialism and in its ability decisively to challenge Western economic predominance.

Tracing the evolution in practice and ideology enables one to go beyond the simple static assertion that Moscow seeks to expand its influence in the Third World and to add a more dynamic element, that is, how Moscow sees its ability to pursue this goal. The means the Soviet Union has at its disposal and the conception it has of their efficacy qualify the way the USSR promotes its interests. Over the years it has become evident that Soviet economic capabilities do not match Soviet political aspirations. Hence the study's subtitle, "economic dilemmas." It is another way of saying that the USSR's economic capacity and performance are the Achilles' heel of the Soviet presence in the Third World.

My thesis is that the modifications in Soviet theory and practice over the past 25 years have resulted from various disappointments with the initial expectations of easy success for Soviet-type "socialist" policies and institutions in the former colonies. The USSR has had difficulties generating a satisfactory pattern of trade exchanges with these coun-

*This chapter is the English version of a German text written for Stiftung Wissenschaft und Politik, Ebenhausen, Federal Republic of Germany; for elaboration of its central themes, see Elizabeth Kridl Valkenier, *The Soviet Union and the Third World: An Economic Bind* (New York: Praeger Publishers, 1983).

tries; it can no longer afford the aid they still require; Moscow has become disenchanted with the feasibility of speedy "socialist" remedies for the problems of backwardness; and it has come to face the lack of congruence between the Soviet and the Third World programs for restructuring international economic relations.

This thesis—which rests on the perception that increasingly more Soviets have a sense of the limitations on power—runs counter to prevalent interpretations in some Western quarters. Numerous commentators and analysts assume that: (1) the optimistic and competitive goals formulated by Khrushchev remain unchanged and are still the operational code in the Kremlin; (2) the USSR still intends to and is capable of gaining control over the vast raw material supplies of Asia and Africa; (3) the Soviets possess a magic systemic formula guaranteeing success for socialist revolutions in the developing countries; and (4) they command unlimited resources to buy goodwill or to prop up client regimes.

In offering a description of how economic realities have placed the Soviet Union's original politically based aspirations in a bind, I am not chalking up points on some cold war scoreboard. Instead, this chapter hopes to acquaint readers with the evolution in Soviet perceptions of the outside world, which in turn should make it possible to better understand Soviet policies.

## Aid and Trade Policies

The evolution of Soviet economic policies falls rather neatly into three phases: 1954–1964, 1965–1976, and 1977 to the present. The initial, politically aggressive entry was followed by a period of pragmatic consolidation that tried to integrate aid and trade with the needs of the Soviet Bloc. Since about 1976 there are signs that Moscow increasingly realizes it cannot initiate and maintain viable policies on a bilateral basis alone. Hence it is searching for ways to integrate its economic operations into a more multilateral pattern that would give the Bloc more latitude, as well as better returns.

The aid and trade program was initiated without much fanfare in August 1954, when the USSR contributed for the first time to the UN Technical Assistance Program. In the next 2 years, six aid and trade agreements solidified the cordial relations that the post-Stalin leadership sought to establish with the newly independent, less developed countries (LDCs).[1] By 1960, "Soviet economic loans were being presented at a rate of approximately one billion dollars per year." As a percentage of GNP, Soviet efforts nearly equalled American aid commitments. Moreover, in several countries the actual dollar volume of Russian aid exceeded that of the U.S.[2]

What is significant in retrospect is not the volume of Soviet aid during the first decade but its intent and the political impression it produced both in the LDCs and in the West (more lasting in the latter case than in the former, as we shall see). Under Khrushchev the aid–trade policies had three overarching political objectives. First, assistance cemented close relations with radical anti-Western regimes and firmed up the neutralism of others. Thus, Egypt, Indonesia, and India received the bulk (about 80%) of Soviet credits. Second, aid grants were part of a strategy to promote tensions between the LDCs and the West. For example, the lavish loans to Indonesia went hand in hand with Soviet support for Sukarno's irredentist policies against the Dutch in West Irian. Finally, Soviet aid was meant to support neo-Marxist ideology, which was designed to forge an alliance between the Socialist Bloc and the former colonies. By October 1961, at the Twenty-second Communist Party (CPSU) Congress, Khrushchev recognized the middle-class radical leaders of the newly independent countries as "revolutionary democrats" who could transcend the limits of bourgeois revolutions. The economic programs of these leaders received approbation as protosocialist policies. Soviet credits were earmarked to support import–substitution industrialization and the expansion of the state sector, as well as to facilitate the nationalization of Western investment and private business. The goal of the domestic reforms supported by Soviet economic policies was presented chiefly in political terms (i.e., as "economic liberation").

The Soviet entry into the former colonial areas produced a shock in the West. Typical of the alarmist response, shared by political leaders and many scholars, was the comment by the U.S. Undersecretary of State, Douglas Dillon: "The Soviet economic offensive is a means of carrying the struggle against us in its economic aspects to the most vulnerable sector of the free world. The ultimate objective of Soviet leaders continues to be the downfall of the West."[3]

No matter how excessive Western fears proved to be in the long run, it has to be conceded that the first phase of Soviet economic operations in the Third World achieved its political objectives. The Soviet entry broke the monopoly of Western influence and control in the Third World; it contributed to the quickening of self-assertiveness among the LDCs; and it identified the USSR with the liberationist aspirations of these states, providing the Soviet example of rapid industrialization as a model.

Khrushchev's ouster was followed by a retreat from the pursuit of political change through generous aid handouts without much regard for the cost involved. There was a stringent review of the assistance programs, and economic rationality became the guiding criterion.[4] Of course, a sharp eye was kept open for possible political and strategic opportunities, but in cases where radicalism had become an excessive burden—Mali, Ghana, Indonesia, and Burma—the USSR declined to shore up the ailing economies. For roughly 5 years the Soviets concentrated on putting their aid program in order. They started conducting feasibility studies before granting loans; they would often propose to finance the expansion or modernization of existing facilities rather than agree to support a new venture; they would turn down requests; and they began to insist on repayments. As a result, during 1965–1970 the volume of aid disbursement fell for the first time since 1954.

The ideological justification for the practical turn was provided by the new leadership already at the Twenty-third CPSU Congress in 1966. Dispensing with the Khrushchev-era claims about the Soviet ability and obligation to help others, Leonid Brezhnev stressed that the successful build-up of the Soviet economy was the "chief international duty of the USSR."[5]

In due course, specialized Soviet analyses elaborated on the new thrust of the assistance programs. They viewed aid-giving as an alternative to domestic investment and argued that it would be cheaper for the USSR and its East European allies to import certain items than to produce them at home. Rendering aid on such principles would commit the USSR to planning with the LDCs the joint extraction and processing of various natural resources (such as iron ore, lead, zinc, copper, aluminum, and petroleum) and the joint production of some goods (such as textiles).

By the early 1970s, a new pattern of economic relations, based on comparative advantage, had emerged. It was characterized by the following features:

1. The establishment of permanent bilateral commissions with major aid recipients and trade partners for regular consultations, long-range delivery contracts, and the coordination of planning.
2. The expansion of joint-production schemes for the extraction and processing of raw materials (especially oil and natural gas) or the manufacture of finished products, with credits to be reimbursed by a share in the output of these projects.
3. The formation of joint-equity firms with governments or with private companies to promote the sale of Soviet goods, expand shipping, or facilitate banking.
4. The financing of sales of Soviet equipment through outright commercial loans or aid loans at higher interest rates (i.e., at 4% instead of the former 2.5%).

Although the new program was eminently practical and commerically oriented (and most likely because it was precisely that), its theoretical underpinning glossed over this fact. Soviet commentators held that coordination, long-range planning, and "mutual profitability" constituted an alternate system, a *socialist* international division of labor (IDL) far superior to the one offered by the West. In other words, the Soviets still interpreted their economic relations with the LDCs in terms of a political rivalry with the West for the allegiance and resources of the less developed countries. The Third World was being urged to make a choice, with the new forms of cooperation offered by the USSR representing a novel type of integration that would eventually supplant the existing system dominated by the rapacious West.

Some Western specialists have interpreted this third phase of Soviet economic relations with the LDCs as a new anti-Western strategy, whereby the expanding stable division of labor between the Socialist Bloc and the developing countries would bring vast areas of the Third World, especially regions contiguous to Russia's southern borders, into the Soviet economic sphere of influence.[6]

Certain economic indicators lent credence to such prognostications. The LDCs' share in the total Soviet turnover rose from 10.3% in 1964 to 14.6% in 1974. However, the entire European Soviet Bloc did not make a significant breakthrough into Third World markets. By 1975, the LDCs conducted only 6% of their trade with the Socialist countries—a rise of about 1% since 1964.

The dynamism engendered during phase two began to dissipate in the mid-1970s. For example, there was a downturn in Soviet–Third World trade. By 1980, it comprised 12.7% of the USSR's total turn-over, and its annual rate of growth declined from 23.8% in 1974 to 3.8% in 1977. (In contrast, East–West trade began to flourish. From 21.3% of the total in 1970, it climbed to 31.3% in 1974 and inched up to 32.1% in 1979.) Although Soviet aid increased in absolute figures, it declined in relative terms. Thus, the share of the Council for Mutual Economic Assistance (CMEA) in the total aid receipts of the LDCs fell from 8% in the early 1970s to only 2% in 1977.

Several factors undermined the post-Khrushchev plans and expectations. The steep rise in fuel prices enabled some partners to increase imports from the West and, more important, made unprofitable the once advantageous long-term barter arrangements with Moscow. Other partners registered general economic advances that diminished their need for the type of assistance and technological level of equipment that the USSR could supply.[7] Also, the worsening terms of trade made the poorer clients more dependent on larger amounts of aid; and that occurred at a time when the Soviet Union, because of the slowing tempo of domestic growth and the growing demands of the Socialist community, had fewer resources available for foreign assistance.

Yet, despite these setbacks and difficulties the Soviet Bloc planners project increased trade with the Third World for the 1980s and beyond. The draft guidelines for the Eleventh Five-Year Plan (1981–1985), published in December 1980, specified the need to utilize foreign trade to supply the nation with raw materials and other goods, as well as the intention to expand trade with the LDCs. Similar intentions were expressed in the final communiqués of recent CMEA sessions. Statements by the top Soviet leaders and by lesser officials and specialists, both under Brezhnev and since, indicate a persisting and ever-growing interest in seizing the advantage to be gained from foreign trade.

The failure to engender a well-functioning socialist IDL and the persisting need to participate in international exchanges have forced the Soviets to yet another reexamination of economic operations in the Third World. At the heart of the current discussions lies the realization that the USSR and its Bloc cannot manage it alone. What has been emerging since 1975 is an increasingly explicit admission in party-government and academic circles that an alternate international economic order, patterned on the operations of CMEA, is both impossible and impractical. An unresolved but intense discussion is afoot on how to face up to the reality of economic interdependence which dictates East–West–South economic cooperation. It remains unresolved, since— if carried to its logical conclusion—the artificial systemic approach to the

East–West and East–South economic exchanges would have to be scrapped, something that would conflict with the tenets of Soviet diplomacy. Though an open disavowal of traditional ideology has not occurred, both the theoretical discussions and practical policies have taken significant new directions.

A portentous aspect of these discussions is the fact that the same specialists who furnished the economic rationale for the second phase are the ones who now write most openly about the way out of the current impasse. They point out that the assumptions which justified the goal of a socialist IDL were mistaken because they underestimated the strength of the Western position, overestimated the demand for Soviet machinery, and discounted the rise of competition from the LDCs.

These specialized writings offer various proposals to revitalize the lagging Soviet–Third World economic exchanges. Noting the appearance of oil-rich states, they propose that efforts to improve terms of trade center on expanding contracts with the oil producers.[8] They also propose new procedures which would introduce better business practices in cooperation with the LDC partners. For example, they suggest that production cooperation should be improved through equity participation. If the USSR were to invest in the production of raw materials or semifinished industrial goods, it would be better assured of a return flow by virtue of ownership and a voice in the management.[9] Finally, they openly address the question of profit. It is no longer treated as synonymous with capitalist exploitation but as a universal norm of accounting that ensures efficient operations. "Without profitability, i.e., gain, no economy can exist and develop effectively."[10] As a matter of fact, some specialists are so taken with economic efficiency that they even represent the multinationals not as an emanation of the most recent and most exploitative stage of imperialism but as companies that have successfully adapted to the internationalization of production and have devised new management methods to maximize effective operations and profit.[11]

Some departures in Soviet overseas operations coincide with the recommendations scattered in the neorealist economic writings. Thus, the distribution of Soviet aid in Africa after the second wave of decolonization (i.e., following the dissolution of the Portuguese empire) showed that minimal amounts went to the radical states like Angola and Mozambique. Of the $2.7 billion in aid granted to Africa during 1975–1979, $2 billion went for the development of phosphate deposits in the conservative kingdom of Morocco and on a pay-back basis to help relieve the critical fertilizer situation in the USSR.

Soviet competition with capitalist methods has diminished to the point where the USSR is now willing to enter tripartite economic agreements, wherein the West provides the advanced know-how, the Soviet Bloc the intermediate technology, and the LDCs the raw materials plus labor. (By 1980, 226 such agreements had been signed by the Soviet Bloc trade organizations with Western firms and Third World partners.)[12] The recent, largest Soviet tripartite venture, reputed to be worth some $2 billion and signed in 1982, is for the development of the hydroelectric resources of the Cuanza River in the People's Republic of Angola together with Portuguese capital and the Brazil-based engineering firm of Odebrecht. That fact, even better than the phosphate deal with Morocco, testifies to how Soviet economic relations with the LDCs have departed from the ideological, systemic approach that obtained at the outset of the Soviet economic offensive.

The World
Economy
Soviet aid and trade have functioned within the context of explicit doctrinal assumptions about the nature of the international economy and its effects on the LDCs. For some 20 years after Stalin's death the theory of two world economies assured a congruence of Soviet political and economic aims. It posited a shared interest between the USSR and the LDCs and fed hopes for detaching the Third World with its resources from the capitalist camp.

Since the mid-1970s, various failures abroad and difficulties at home have spawned recognition of interdependence and a global outlook which invalidate the former Manichean outlook. But an outright acceptance of a depoliticized interpretation of international economics would undermine the USSR's diplomatic aspirations to guide the Third World against imperialism. Hence a bind prevents clearer formulations.

The doctrine of the disintegration of the "single all-embracing world market" into separate and independent socialist and capitalist markets, promulgated by Stalin in 1951, was not discarded by Khrushchev when he set out to devise neo-Marxist categories to expand Soviet influence into the postcolonial areas.[13] Although Stalin's two world markets theory did not deal specifically with the colonial and dependent countries, it offered three components which guided and justified Soviet actions until the early 1970s. First, it interpreted the expanding industrial production of the Socialist Bloc as a destabilizing challenge to the West. Second, it posited that the socialist and the capitalist systems follow diametrically opposite foreign economic policies. Third, it placed the operations of the two markets in the general scheme of global competition between the two systems.

Following the Twentieth CPSU Congress in 1956—at which Khrushchev stated that the newly independent countries could play a positive role in international relations—Soviet academic research on the LDCs was refurbished and expanded to help furnish appropriate information. However, substantive works on economics were not published for general circulation. To the extent that the economic situation in the newly independent countries was discussed, it was dealt with in the light of the competition between the two camps. The economic writings of those times followed closely the line of 1961 CPSU Program which stated:

The young sovereign states . . . constitute that part of the world that is still being exploited by the capitalist monopolies. As long as they do not put an end to their economic dependence on imperialism, they will play the role of the "world countryside" and will remain objects of semi-colonial exploitation.[14]

Given that context, Soviet economists interpreted the USSR's aid and trade not only as a catalyst for economic liberation but also as a factor that would transform the nature of international economic relations. According to one prominent specialist:

> Within the framework of the world socialist system the basis for a new world system is being created in which the capitalist relations of oppression and exploitation of the weak nations by the strong will be finally liquidated. Relations of genuine equality and mutual aid will be established. An important role in the struggle for the creation of such a world-wide [vsemirnoe] economy is bestowed on the constantly expanding aid of the socialist states to the underdeveloped countries.[15]

Until about 1976, the appearance of politically neutral, universalistic thinking about international economics did not affect Soviet analysis of the Third World's position and prospects. Thereafter we begin to notice a loss of confidence that one part of the world can remain isolated from general laws and the rise of a discussion of how to extend the global thinking to the LDCs.

The recognition of a single world economy made its appearance during the first decade of Brezhnev's rule. There was no formal renunciation of Stalin's doctrine of the two world markets. Nevertheless, an entry on the single world market (defined as "the aggregate of all national markets, seen as linked through mutual economic and trade relations") appeared in the 1974 edition of the *Great Soviet Encyclopedia*.[16] The same year, the first article on the world economy was also published. It explained that the present-day extent and speed of scientific–technological change made it imperative for all countries to participate in the IDL.[17]

Both innovative formulations refrained from placing the LDCs on the new grid of international economic relations. The novel understanding of world economics was directly related to the rise of East–West trade and the Soviet decision to modernize with the aid of Western credits and know-how. But this acknowledgment of interdependence and comparative advantage was kept carefully segregated. Soviet economic relations with the LDCs remained in a separate category wherein the unchanged normative values and political explanations persisted.

Although in actual practice Soviet–LDC exchanges were being reorganized along similar pragmatic lines, the public explanations carefully passed over this fact. Typical was Premier Kosygin's statement at the Twenty-fourth CPSU Congress in 1971: "Our cooperation [is] based on principles of equality and respect for mutual interests [and] is acquiring the nature of a stable division of labor, counterposed in the sphere of international economic relations to the system of imperialist exploitation."[18]

Authorities seemed to be intent on keeping Soviet economic dealings with the West and the South apart in order not to compromise the doctrine of the special relationship between the USSR and the former colonies. One theory that helped to maintain that fiction was that all the LDCs formed a single economic unit with common problems resulting from imperialist exploitation.

However, since the quality of Soviet specialized writings on the Third World was steadily advancing under Brezhnev and the profession was constantly being urged to provide practical advice, the LDCs were less and less viewed as a single entity. Already in late 1970, the preliminary findings on the economic indicators of the development levels of all the nonsocialist countries (i.e., both the advanced and the developing) were published.[19] Elementary as the procedure may seem, it heralded a basic shift in Soviet scholarship. Henceforth, the best minds in the profession conducted research on the LDCs less in terms of socioeconomic categories or systemic competition and more in terms of their actual position in the world economy as well as their domestic potential.

By 1976, the apparent equilibrium between the old theory and the new practice that prevailed during the first decade of Brezhnev's rule began to erode in the wake of the oil crisis, the appearance of petrodollars, the mounting difficulties with the domestic economy, and the failure to institute a viable socialist IDL with the developing countries. As a result, the Party authorities began to urge the specialists in an increasingly open-ended manner to find adequate ideological formulations and to devise appropriate economic policies in keeping with the fact that the USSR has to operate on the capitalist-dominated world market, over which it can exercise no decisive influence and in which the LDCs no longer occupy that "special place" that would tilt them toward the Soviet Bloc.

One cannot as yet speak of a well-formulated or fully articulated new theory. But three interest groupings are discernible in the ongoing discussion on how to acknowledge that global interdependence transcends systemic solutions and how to extend the notion of a single world market to cover the LDCs. First comes the Party apparatus, particularly people in charge of maintaining political power and ideological orthodoxy. They would like to have more effective economic relations without introducing sharp discontinuities in doctrine, the administrative structures, or foreign policy. They recognize the growing necessity to internationalize the Soviet economy but are reluctant to admit an unqualified global interdependence since that would undercut ideological and diplomatic competition.

The economic ministries constitute the second interest grouping. Here, officials and staff are concerned not so much with reconciling their activities with ideology as with achieving practical results. Foreign Trade Minister Nikolai Patolichev is frank about the need to integrate with the world market:

> Today it would perhaps be difficult to find an economic sector in the USSR that is not connected with foreign trade to some extent, or does not receive

effective practical aid in its further development. To put it figuratively, foreign trade has become an important artery in the blood circulation of the Soviet Union's economic organism.[20]

There are two divergent tendencies among the third interest grouping—the academic specialists. The conservatives follow a cautious course that combines a hard ideological line with the search for economic rationality. The modern-minded innovators press for changes in ideological formulations as well as for reforms in institutions and practice. These modernizers see the world economy as an objective phenomenon. It is

> the sum total of not only the national economies of various states but also of the two world systems, socialist and capitalist, each of which develops according to its laws. . . . Despite all the differences and contradictions of the . . . two world markets, they find themselves in a definite mutual interaction. . . . It is possible to take into account not only what divides them, but also a number of common regularities, common tendencies that operate in the world economy as a whole.[21]

Despite the lack of a definite outcome in the debate (it did not die down after Brezhnev's death), three developments offer good prospects for further evolution in Soviet theory and policies: the persistence on the part of the leadership in instituting pertinent changes in the CPSU program; the increasing tolerance toward East European and Western writings on economic issues connected with the Third World; and the advances scored by the evolving discussion thus far.

When Brezhnev first started to mention global problems—ranging from the environment to raw materials—and the need for "constructive cooperation of all countries" to solve them, he did not propose any theory to justify this new view on international economic issues. But, by the Twenty-sixth Party Congress in 1981, he held that the Party's 1961 Program needed revision to account, among other things, for such "new phenomena in international life" as the changed position and role of the LDCs.[22] His successors have not abandoned the quest. In April 1984, Konstantin Chernenko, in his address to the redrafting Commission, referred to "the realities of the world process." The LDCs were not singled out among them, but Chernenko stressed in this context that it was "impossible and inappropriate" to predict the particulars in the struggle between socialism and capitalism. Moreover, he acknowledged that capitalism "still possesses considerable and by no means exhausted reserves of development."[23] The pragmatic intent of these remarks indicates that this approach should help depoliticize many, or at least some, Third World-related economic issues.

The second trend favoring further growth of fresh ideas is the increasing use of East European economic thought and the positive response to Western writings on development. The East European economists, especially the Hungarians and the Poles, analyze conditions of countries that depend on trade, where further development is associated with a greater opening up to nonsocialist markets, and where ideological controls are not very rigid. It seems significant that whereas inter-Bloc academic contacts were quite limited until the 1970s, they have since expanded greatly. I shall cite three telling examples. The translation of Jerzy Kleer's free-wheeling study of world economics was undertaken to introduce Soviet readers—according to the preface—to such "unfamiliar terms" as "open and closed economy," "demonstration effect," and "interdependence."[24] Of more weight is the creation of a joint study group on the economics and politics of the LDCs within the system of the CMEA Academies of Science at which some unorthodox new formulations are being launched.[25] Finally, the Soviet Institute of the Economy of the World Socialist System, which has been initiating the most innovative proposals for improving the terms of Soviet–LDC economic exchanges, has visibly increased its cooperation with the East Europeans.[26]

Recent favorable comments on a major Western work on the economic position of the Third World also indicate greater tolerance for plurality of views. In the early 1970s, Scandinavian publications were thus honored. By the end of the decade, the Brandt Commission report, unlike the earlier Pearson Report, was given a thoughtful review. The Brandt report was commended on three counts: for its global approach stressing the interdependence of all issues as well as of all countries; for suggesting solutions in terms of a constructive dialogue, not of diktats or confrontations; and for including the Soviet Bloc in its analysis and recommendations.[27]

The advances scored in the ongoing debates are the final indication of the direction of change. It is now conceded that some LDCs have attained considerable economic growth and that all have become more closely integrated with the capitalist markets. In early 1978, *Pravda* printed an article by Karen Brutents, an academic specialist on the Third World who also works in the Central Committee's International Department. It offered at least three corrections to the established Soviet view on the economic position of the LDCs: (1) exploitation and ever-deepening dependence were not necessarily the only result of Western activities in the LDCs; (2) capitalist relations had taken large strides in these countries; (3) no immediate likelihood existed that the USSR could offer these countries a better alternative.[28] The same year, Evgenii Primakov, director of the Oriental Institute, wrote in *Kommunist* that the "objective" economic processes were tightly integrating more and more LDCs with the industrialized capitalist countries.[29] Whereas at first such arguments were made as though this situation applied only to the capitalist-oriented states, by 1981 it was admitted that even states of socialist orientation were part and parcel of the capitalist world market.[30] In other world, the Soviets have accepted that the LDCs have not been and cannot be lured into the socialist market.

The second change parallels or follows from the first. There is now frank discussion of the sluggish East–South trade. This trend is attributed to the eroding complementarity in the economic potentials and needs of the two sides.[31] In this context, it seems significant that among the various proposals for revitalizing economic exchanges, those advocating multilateralization are very prominent. Thus, increasingly more is written about East–West–South cooperation or Soviet undertakings with the more advanced LDCs. The first type of venture figures in all the recently concluded long-term cooperation agreements between the USSR and West European states, while the second is now incorporated in the long-term plans the USSR has signed with India.

The third change involves increasingly frank discussion of the need to put an end to concessional agreements with the LDCs. To quote Oleg Bogomolov, director of the Institute of the Economy of the World Socialist System: "It would be erroneous to assert that relations between the socialist world and the developing countries are based on the principle of socialist solidarity."[32] While there is still much circumlocution about the politically embarrassing issue of profit (mainly by way of euphemistic references to "mutual advantage"), it is nonetheless discussed in current writings. Books based on source materials from the State Committee on Foreign Economic Relations—the Soviet Union's foreign aid and economic cooperation agency—proceed from the assumption that profit is a basic consideration in the drive to improve the forms of collaboration and terms of exchange with the LDCs.[33]

A final important breakthrough facilitating discussion of Third World issues in a nonsystemic framework is the inclusion of backwardness among global problems. When global problems were first mentioned, backwardness was not among them. Moreover, *Kommunist* specifically warned that the recognition of global issues in no way signified rapprochement with "bourgeois reformist concepts of globalism [that] . . . give global problems supra-class, supra-social, and supra-national character."[34] These ideological strictures have since evaporated, and before Brezhnev's death economic problems of underdevelopment were interpreted by many experts in a rather depoliticized manner. Acknowledging backwardness as a global problem permitted discussion of this issue without reference to imperialism or neocolonial exploitation and concentration on its consequences but not its causes.

Two important and novel concerns are evident in the writings of the Soviet globalists. For one, their analysis of world raw material resources departs from the hackneyed denunciations of the multinational coporations. Instead, they argue that the growing dependence of all states on these commodities has created a world market which in turn necessitates global regulations to assure the legitimate interests of the producing–developing and the consuming–industrial countries (among which the USSR is included).

On a more important level, the Soviet globalists consider that the deteriorating socioeconomic conditions in the LDCs create situations that threaten world peace and hence demand a cooperative approach of all nations. Those experts who see the nonsystemic, worldwide, and catastrophic aspects of Third World backwardness are the ones who argue that "those powerful objective tendencies, which have given birth to détente and to the growth of international cooperation in many fields, permit one to expect the possibility of attaining an agreed-upon, wise approach to the solution of the problems connected with overcoming backwardness of the developing countries."[35]

Development Theory

Soviet development economics encompass more than theory. The models elaborated by specialists show a close parallelism in time and emphasis with the actual policies Moscow pursues and the official line on the international economy. In tracing development theory through the stages roughly corresponding to changes in Soviet aid and trade policies and views on the world economy, a fundamental shift in perceptions and concerns becomes manifest in three main areas.

Foremost has been the shift from political to economic solutions; the original systemic formulas have been replaced by economic rationality. Closely related is a parallel change in the perceptions of capitalist institutions and of industrialization. Soviet specialists have acquired a sober respect for the sequential nature of development in which capitalist relations and work habits fulfill an economically valid function. Similarly, the Soviets no longer advocate import-substitution industrialization. Acknowledging global interdependence of economic needs, roles, and mechanisms, they now believe that the LDCs should take advantage of their traditional role as raw material producers.

The emergence of a new outlook creates a bind in this area as well. For the Third World continues to believe in the "exploitative" nature of international economic exchanges and to press for an end to dependency rather than to think in terms of interdependence.

During the Khrushchev era, specialists viewed the creation of viable national economies in the LDCs almost exclusively through a political prism. Backwardness was ascribed to colonial rule and its persistence to the survival of capitalist institutions, as well as to the "unequal" ties with the former metropoles. Therefore, curtailing market forces and relations with the West through the build-up of the state sector (i.e., nationalization, planning, industrialization, and extensive dealings with the Soviet Bloc) would produce rapid growth. The almost blind faith in political solutions, grounded on the belief in the efficacy of "economic liberation," was pointed up by the initial Soviet willingness to grant aid for just about any project proposed by the developing country and rejected by the West, without prior investigation of its economic feasibility.

The shift to more pragmatic aid and trade policies after 1964 encouraged a less politically oriented approach to development. It became a widely accepted premise that economic growth entailed prerequisites, stages, diversification, and interrelations among various segments of the economy. Specialists started paying attention to internal retarding factors and not just to the adverse effects of Western domination. In the opinion of one expert, the more backward an economy, the wider the circle of concrete problems that have nothing to do with either capitalism or socialism but will have to be solved through certain basic practical steps.[36]

As a result, policies that used to be favored or condoned were by the late 1960s criticized as harmful "ultra-revolutionary haste" or as "voluntaristic" measures that ignored actual costs and other realities. Such objections covered almost any reform that extended public management and control beyond the state's capacity for efficient administration.[37]

Thus, less rigid planning and a slower rate of industrialization became the most frequently proposed remedies for the malfunctioning of the state sector.[38] There was also a reassessment of the role of foreign investment and of private business. In principle, Soviet hostility to the role of "monopoly capital" remained unchanged. But, in discussing specific situations and needs, the positive contribution of Western capital was often acknowledged. The new consensus was that instead of seeking economic liberation, the new states should seek arrangements that recognized each LDC's sovereignty over its natural resources and industry, and allowed it to retain as large a share of profit at home as possible.[39] As for the private sector, appropriate quotations from Lenin were found to buttress arguments that even during the transition to socialism, capitalist relations could and should contribute to an increased output.[40] Concerning sectoral development, it was now agreed that a simultaneous and balanced growth of industry and agriculture had to be maintained.[41]

It should be noted that no matter how pragmatic or "liberal" the post-1964 views became, they did not affect the overall political analysis. What changed was the understanding of specific domestic policies in the LDCs, not the interpretation of international economics and how they perpetuated backwardness. No one openly questioned the overarching theories of the bifurcated world economy or the unity of the developing countries, which were defined by their uniform dependence. The changed prescriptions were prompted and justified on the grounds of creating conditions for the advent of socialism. The goal of development was still liberation from Western domination and exploitation, as well as the elimination of capitalist relations.

In the period since 1974 Soviet development theory has changed and diversified more than in the preceding decade. Moderate, economically workable policies remain the objective, but they are increasingly being placed in a different conceptual framework. A single world market and pressing global problems have brought a reinterpretation of development, wherein elements of interdependence or universalism often predominate over those of competition and exclusiveness.

Soviet analysts do not agree on how to adapt what Lenin had to say about the conditions of the colonial and semicolonial countries to the vastly different current situation. But the binds and tensions between the traditional political theory and the emerging new understanding of development economics have not stopped the discussion. Moreover, the appearance of three new concepts assures that the evolution will continue.

First, the recognition of the wide economic differentiation among the LDCs calls into question the former theory of unrelieved imperialist exploitation. The application of a purely economic typology to the LDCs appeared in book form in 1976. Since then, classification of the developing countries according to their economic capabilities has gained acceptance on par with the former exclusively political categorization. By 1980, experts were pointing out that some LDCs had attained middle levels of industrial development (analogous to those of Portugal or Greece) while others had become net exporters of capital, acting like "sub-imperialist centers" expanding into the less developed regions. These arguments are opposed by the traditionalists who insist that despite tremendous differentiation the Third World remains a definable political–economic category and that, no matter how much some LDCs manage to advance, they can never transcend the limits of dependence.[42]

The recognition that participation in a global division of labor is essential for overcoming backwardness is another reversal of former tenets. The first cogent exposition of this view appeared in 1976 and was written by Viktor Tiagunenko, the doyen of postwar experts on the Third World. He held that it was impossible to study the "preconditions, nature, and consequences . . . of concrete social and economic changes" without taking into account "worldwide forces with which these processes are closely connected and intertwined."[43] There is still a controversy about where the benefits of interdependence stop and the costs of dependence begin. The conservatives regard the interaction of the LDCs with the West as a necessary evil. But the outspoken proponents of IDL argue that "foreign capitalist enterprise . . . is also one of the forms of 'penetration' of modern production methods into backward countries."[44]

Finally, the recently devised concept of *mnogoukladnost'* explains the multisectoral nature of Third World societies and economies and permits moving outside the predetermined framework of Marxist formulations that imposes the inevitable movement toward socialist institutions and solutions on the LDCs. Aleksei Levkovsky, of the Oriental Institute, is the leading exponent of the more flexible interpretation of *mnogoukladnost'*. He argues that at present most LDCs are going through an "interformation" period of extremely long duration and that it is counterproductive to try to figure out which of the Marxist stages these countries are moving toward. The conservatives object that Levkovsky's theories deviate from historical materialism. But there are scholars who welcome this new analytical tool for having rescued the field from "oversimplifications which tried to fit the whole historical development of the Afro–Asia world into deterministic cells of a linear construction obligatory for all."[45]

Recent Soviet writings on states of socialist orientation (SO) illustrate better than other arguments the degree to which the new terms of reference have permitted the depoliticization of economic views. The policies of the SO states are a highly sensitive issue since the Soviets often note that about a dozen LDCs have chosen to skip the capitalist stage and cite this fact as evidence that the correlation of forces on the world scale is moving toward socialism.

These claims, moreover, are taken seriously by some Western specialists who argue that states like Angola, Mozambique, and Ethiopia have gone through the "final, Soviet-type revolution" and are about to be incorporated into CMEA or an enlarged Socialist Bloc.[46]

When the term SO was first used in the late 1960s, it was synonymous with the concept of bypassing capitalism. As a matter of fact, SO superseded the term "non-capitalist development," devised by Lenin in 1920 to offer the colonial areas the chance to skip the capitalist stage of development. At first the Soviets wrote as though SO was mainly a matter of political resolve. Accordingly, it was stated that the characteristic feature of the states with SO was that "socialist transition starts with the superstructure. . . . The political superstructure creates conditions for reconstructing the socio-economic base." But by 1979, Anatolii Gromyko, director of the Africa Institute, wrote that "the overriding objectively inhibiting factor is backwardness, which has persisted for centuries and cannot, of course, provide foundations for building socialist society, which requires the creation of certain essential material prerequisites."[47]

Current Soviet writings show that these prerequisites involve coming to terms with various aspects of capitalist relations and institutions. First, it is now recognized that SO states remain tied to the capitalist markets. On the ideological level, this admission might diminish Soviet claims to power and leadership. But it makes sense on the economic level. Not only does the admission correspond to fact, but it also eases the USSR's economic burden of having to live up to "socialist solidarity." A recent Soviet commentary on SO asserts that what differentiates the pioneers of this trend (e.g., Mongolia) from the recently formed SO states is that the latter are not dependent on the Socialist Bloc for their economic survival.[48]

Similar changes have taken place in Soviet views on the domestic policies of the SO states. It is clearly articulated that just as on the international level they remain in the capitalist world market, so on the domestic level they are not ready to jettison capitalist relations. To begin with, it is now recognized that the SO states should come to terms with foreign investment. A recent book on SO maintains that it is necessary to attract foreign capital to stimulate economic development, to increase employment, and to satisfy the needs of the consumers.[49]

Similar tolerance toward private domestic capital has also emerged. At first, petty traders and other small-scale private enterprise were accepted as consistent with SO, largely because of the persisting traditions and the needs of the service sector. Now large, modern capitalist enterprise is also acceptable to some authors on the grounds that it is essential for genuine economic development.[50]

What about the role of the state sector? Soviet specialists write at present that it is only the more advanced states like Egypt (before 1973) and Algeria that can afford having a large public sector (i.e., to operate it efficiently). The more numerous and more backward states of Tropical Africa cannot sustain that political luxury. There a large state sector conducts deficit operations that eat up the accumulation created by the private sector. Similar strictures are now extended to other government controls, such as planning. The less developed a country, the less rigorous direct state interference it can afford.[51]

It is interesting to note a change in Soviet attitude toward private ownership. In the past, much was written about the need of progressive states to pass to the more advanced forms of cooperative farming prior to full collectivization. Recent writings admit that this is not the optimal solution, and that for a long time to come a highly differentiated structure of ownership will have to remain. This involves accepting not only small- but also large-scale private farming before conditions are ready for the cooperativization of the peasantry. For the present, and for the immediate future, it has to be recognized that cooperative labor cannot be productive. According to one specialist: "Neither concerted labor nor the use of technology—unavoidably weak due to limited capacities—can compensate for a loss of interest in working on the part of most producers."[52]

The evolution of Soviet development theory in favor of economic coexistence with world capitalism and capitalist relations does not accord with the convictions of the SO states. Their views resemble the one-sided arguments about economic liberation Moscow propounded in the past. Moreover, they expect the USSR to support their radical economics. To quote the General Secretary of the Yemeni Socialist Party:

> Of tremendous importance in class and ideological terms is the fact that our efforts to build up the material and technical basis of the revolutionary transition period have gone hand in hand with the struggle to be completely rid of the control by international capitalism of our national market, and with the further development of our economic cooperation with the socialist world system. . . . After the victory of the Great October Socialist Revolution, Lenin repeatedly emphasized that the stage of capitalist development is not at all inevitable for all countries dominated by feudal and semi-feudal relations. Fraternal assistance from states in which the working class has taken over would help these countries to move faster to socialism. Now, more than 60 years after the October Revolution, with the Soviet state a mighty and steadily growing power . . . the transition to socialism, bypassing the stage of capitalist development, has undoubtedly become easier and has broader prospects before it.[53]

There have been no open Soviet disputes about these issues on the bilateral or interstate level. The fact that CMEA did not accept Mozambique's application for membership—which would have presumably entitled that state to a greater share of the Bloc's assistance—was reported only in Western sources. But the divergence is deep and unmistakable, creating another bind or difficulty in the Soviet Union's bilateral relations with its political allies and protégés.

## The New International Economic Order

The discrepancies in Soviet and Third World thinking about economic issues are evident on the international level. For more than 20 years, Soviet diplomatic cooperation with the LDCs was facilitated by the widely held assumption that the international economic interests of the USSR and these countries coincided. But the appearance of the LDCs' own program of demands

vis-à-vis the industrialized North, coming as it did in the mid-1970s
when the Soviet Union became engrossed in internationalizing its own
economy, has undercut the former harmony. The pursuit of anti-
imperialist diplomacy no longer squares with the Soviet Bloc's growing
involvement in Western markets, where the interests of the USSR and
the LDCs do not necessarily coincide.

A parting of the ways between the Soviet Bloc and the Third World
on international economic issues is taking place. Conflicting aims, even
serious fissures, can be detected from several sources. First, there is the
evolution in the Soviet response to the New International Economic
Order (NIEO). Moscow is now, in effect, presenting a separate program
to the United Nations (UN), one that tries to incorporate elements of
global economic coexistence alongside the old verbiage about imperialism. Second, there is the fact that both Soviet and Third World specialists are increasingly voicing criticism of each other's views and policies.

At first Moscow welcomed and supported the concerted economic
claims the Group of 77 nations began to press against the West in the
early 1970s. It was assumed that the nature of Soviet Bloc–LDC exchanges (i.e., their "equivalent" and "just" character) served as a model
and that any concessions wrested from the West would automatically
bring political and economic gains to the USSR. Accordingly, Andrei
Gromyko welcomed the Declaration on the New International Economic
Order, adopted at the UN in 1974, as "a progressive code of rules by
which states should be guided in their economic relations."[54]

Optimism about the thrust of the LDCs' demands for the reconstruction of global economic relations, the leverage these countries could
exert, and the ability of the USSR to shape the new forces suffused the
joint statement presented by the Soviet Bloc to the IV United Nations
Conference on Trade and Development (UNCTAD) in 1976. In effect, it
was an attempt to weave the demands of the socialist and the developing countries into an alternative to the existing world order dominated
by the capitalist powers.

The statement offered the practices that had evolved in Soviet Bloc–
Third World relations as a model for a "new kind of economic relations"
that would replace the "outmoded system." In general the principles of
planning, long-term intergovernmental agreements, production
cooperation, and compensation agreements were presented as an
appropriate method to establish fair prices and to limit the effects of
market forces, as well as the power of multinationalism.[55]

These assumptions and expectations were not confirmed by the
meeting. Hence, in October 1976, the USSR submitted to the UN
General Assembly a Declaration on NIEO that articulated reservations to
the LDCs' program for the first time. The Soviets objected that it held
the socialist and the capitalist states equally responsible for alleviating
the plight of the LDCs; it ignored the connection between disarmament
and increased aid; and it failed to address the entire gamut of discriminatory practices in international trade.[56]

Given the fact that IV UNCTAD had punctured the fiction about the
common front and interests, it is not surprising that the USSR presented

a very different proposal to the V UNCTAD in 1979. It conceded that the LDCs were being "bound" more closely "to capitalism's main industrial centers." It acknowledged that the closer South–West association made it difficult for the centrally planned economies (CPEs) to "increase their participation in the worldwide division of labor." It stated that what was required was a "comprehensive restructuring of all areas of world trade." And it conceded that it was possible to "democratize" international economic relations even before the "inherent defects of capitalism" had been eliminated from the operations of the world economy.[57] The proposal was interspersed with the old systemic arguments and charges. Yet, it did reflect a fundamental departure, for it offered the principle of nondiscrimination (economically a more neutral term) instead of the elimination of exploitation (a normative political notion) as the basis for restructuring the world economic order.

The new, depoliticized approach to NIEO is much more explicit in Soviet specialized writings. Some economists object to the LDCs' proposals on the grounds that they depart from universal principles. And they posit that given the internationalization and interdependence of the world economy, as well as the intensification of global problems, genuine solutions must be based on the needs and capacities of the entire international economic community.[58] In other words, the formal structure of the NIEO has to be such as to permit the reintegration of the Socialist Bloc. Clearly, the USSR no longer seeks to restructure the world economy in its own image with aid to the LDCs. Lacking the Third World's support, and in a much more vulnerable position, it seeks ways and means to join the world market.

The current Soviet understanding of an ideally functioning world economy is very far from the original premises that permitted an identification with Soviet–Third World interests. Moscow now favors the expansion of international trade based on appropriate specialization by all countries. In that system the LDCs, being the world producers of food, fuels, and raw materials, should specialize in their production since it takes advantage of the natural complementarity between their resources and the needs of the industrial countries. The Soviets tout this plan as an improvement over the "utopian," distribution-oriented program proposed by the LDCs.[59]

Given the USSR's current concern with the supply of raw materials for its own economy and for that of Eastern Europe, these proposals for an optimal IDL (which for the time being relegates the LDCs to a commodity-production-based development) look like a panacea for the Bloc's problems. It is not a program that boldly seeks to restructure the existing situation.

The ideal scenario of global cooperation, where some sort of "invisible hand" would guide the multilevel flow of goods and services among the three groups, would look something like this: While the most advanced countries would find it profitable to invest in the development of Soviet raw materials and industry, the Socialist Bloc with its less advanced technology would in turn find it advantageous to deal with the LDCs. The role of the Third World would be to produce the natural resources to fuel the economies of all the industrialized states, benefiting in turn from their assistance and accumulating funds and know-how for building up processing industries.[60]

The rise of pragmatism concerning international economics creates difficulties and dissension between the USSR and the LDC radicals as well as the Third World establishment.

To placate or bring into line the radicals, Moscow convened an international conference in Berlin in October 1980. Central Committee Secretary Boris Ponomarev delivered a blistering political speech denouncing the multinationals and offering Soviet support for a radical restructuring of international economic relations through the elimination of all discrimination, diktats, and exploitation. But speakers from other Bloc countries were more circumspect, talking about improving the international climate and institutions as well as about coming to terms with the multinationals. Whereas Ponomarev extolled the existing Soviet Bloc–Third World exchanges as paradigmatic, they cited East–West economic cooperation as a good example of effective economic relations.[61]

By contrast, there was no divergence between radical posturing and economic moderation among the Third World delegates. Their speeches were an unrelieved denunciation of capitalist relations on the domestic and international levels. The eradication of these relations was essential for the creation of a new, equitable order. Moreover, the equivocations evident in the pronouncements of the Socialist Bloc were not missed. The delegate from the Communist Party of Réunion made a pointed appeal for the need to "transcend . . . Eurocentrism or any other narrow vision."[62] Despite such comments, Soviet sources claimed after the conclusion of the conference that it had successfully dealt with attempts "to besmirch [the policy of] the socialist states . . . in the struggle surrounding the problems of a new international economic order."[63]

Nor is there greater correspondence between current Soviet views and those of the radical Third World economists who set the tone of the formal demands of the Group of 77. In order to maintain the facade of a common, progressive Socialist–Third World front, extensive criticism of LDC economists is infrequent. What is written tends to center on Samir Amin, director of the Economic Commission of the Institute of Economic Development and Planning in Dakar. To the Soviets he personifies the theoretical extremism of the Third World establishment. He is criticized for flouting the very principles of economics when he argues that the upward revision of raw material prices is a simple matter of political will. Price formation, Soviet experts retort, is part of the international economic mechanism and subject to its objective laws.

Amin's contention that it is impossible to realize the aims of NIEO within the framework of the existing order is rejected. The Soviets maintain that the "reconstruction of economic relations should proceed . . . not by way of abolition" but through gradual reforms.[64] Though the nature of gradualism is not really spelled out, the Soviet statement to the V UNCTAD said that it was possible to democratize international economic relations before the "inherent defects of capitalism had been eliminated," making it clear that the USSR is willing to work with the existing system.

The third set of Soviet objections to the Third World's economic thought concerns self-reliance. While careful to acknowledge the need for economic and political cooperation among the LDCs to weaken dependence on imperialist powers and to speed up development, Soviet experts argue that, pushed to an extreme, the collective approach leads to a "utopian" faith in the viability of autarky. Fears of Third World isolationism are so intense that Soviet economists do not hesitate to lecture Third World audiences that "any attempt on the part of the LDCs to shut themselves up within the framework of [collective self-reliance] would actually mean their deliberate renouncement to share in the world scientific and technological progress."[65]

The Soviets face not only ideological–theoretical difficulties in promoting their version of NIEO but practical binds as well. The structural changes in the world economy have eroded the complementarity between Soviet capacities and the needs of many LDCs. Some countries have petrodollars whereas others produce a wide assortment of capital goods and plan even more sophisticated levels of industrialization. Both groups know that there is practically nothing the East can do that the West does not do better. Soviet hopes to turn exchanges with the Third World into a profitable operation at a time when the USSR has shown its own technological lag by turning to the West for assistance in modernization cannot but face a dim future.

Recent developments in Indian–Soviet relations demonstrate how the improved financial position and advancing development level of a Third World partner introduce elements of competition and expose Soviet inadequacy. In 1970, machinery constituted 64.9% of Soviet exports to India; by 1977, it made up only 15.5%. The decline is due to two factors. Over the years India has become increasingly self-sufficient in basic industrial hardware, and to keep competitive on the world market, New Delhi found it best to have recourse to advanced Western know-how. The deficit operations of many public sector enterprises built with Soviet aid were in part blamed on their simple and outdated technology. When time came for their expansion, India turned to Western sources.[66]

Soviet–Indian trade negotiations in the late 1970s centered on how to restore the "original dynamism." The agreements concluded in 1979/1980 provide both commercial credits and concessional aid for imports of Soviet machinery to help develop India's natural resources. These agreements answered the need of the moment. But they do not bode well for Moscow's pet new project to increase machinery exports—joint ventures in Third World countries. Provision for this cooperation has been part of the formal intergovernment agreements for the past several years, but actual implementation has not gotten off the ground. The Indians do not fancy inviting the USSR into areas where they stand a good chance of getting a large share of the market anyway. As for the traditional method of promoting machinery exports—production cooperation on a compensation basis—the Indians fear that building plants to Soviet specifications would create "captive units" whose production could not be exported anywhere else but to the Soviet Bloc and could give the USSR the possibility of dictating terms.[67]

The Socialist Bloc's version of the IDL, based on a planned and specialized cooperation in production and trade, hardly conforms with reality or with the Third World vision of the new order. This is made amply clear by Deepak Nayyar, an Indian economist who in the past wrote approvingly about the pattern of Soviet–Third World economic relations. He now points out that experts from the Socialist countries mistakenly equate the help rendered by the CPEs in setting up planning machinery in the LDCs with the process of planning itself and thus overestimate the prospects for planned joint action. Second, they assume, also without foundation, that during the 1980s the CMEA countries will increase their trade with the developing countries faster than their total trade. Finally, the composition of that trade is unacceptable, for manufactured and capital goods are supposed to account for an even larger proportion of the Bloc's exports (about 80%), while diversification of Third World exports to the Bloc would basically amount to substituting minerals and fuels for agricultural commodities. In addition to being unrealistic, according to Nayyar, Bloc proposals of this nature are "clearly not the basis for a new international division of labor."[68]


Conclusion   What can one make of the evolution of Soviet views and of the continuing debates? I do not mean to suggest that because the global-minded viewpoint has emerged last, it is bound to prevail and guide Soviet policies in the future. Obviously, any combination of political and economic factors, both domestic and international, can dictate either a more aggressive or even a more isolationist policy. There is nothing inevitable about the USSR's coming to adopt policies that would dilute or moderate competition in the Third World with some degree of cooperation, based on the awareness of interdependence.

Nevertheless, the appearance of new currents of analysis in the USSR should not be either overlooked or discounted. The fact that new interpretations appear most prominently in academic publications does not mean that these opinions do not inform or reflect the policymaking process. Key academic experts supply information and recommendations to people directly responsible for the formulation and implementation of foreign policy. As this study shows, the evolution of Soviet aid and trade practices, as well as Moscow's changing response to the NIEO issues, have followed the course recommended by the academic specialists.

What is more significant is that the discussion, now so clearly articulated, gives evidence of flexibility and adaptation to the changing world. The debates and disagreements outlined in this study belie the contention that the Soviets, because of the straightjacket of Marxism–Leninism, are incapable of adaptation, change, or moderation.

Finally, the two themes of my study have policy implications for the American side. We should be aware that some circles in the USSR are coming to grips with the demonstrable fact that there are limits to Soviet power in the Third World, as well as to the advantages to be derived from close identification with the postcolonial grievances. Some even hold that support of Third World causes is disruptive to Soviet–American relations and threatens world peace. Should this "globalist" view come to shape concrete Soviet proposals, Washington should be ready to respond and not miss the chance to seek mutual restraint or a cooperative relationship.

## Notes

[1]Both at that time and later, it was not possible to draw a clear distinction between aid and trade, since the USSR almost never offered outright grants but only low interest loans to cover the purchase of Soviet machinery and services for the projects to be built with Soviet assistance. Similarly, much of the debt repayment could be made through the shipment of traditional exports. Thus there has always been an automatic conversion of what has been loosely termed "aid" (both by the Soviets and Westerners) into trade flows.

[2]Marshall I. Goldman, "Soviet Foreign Aid since the Death of Stalin," in *Soviet Policy in Developing Countries*, ed. W. Raymond Duncan (Waltham, Mass: Ginn-Blaisdell, 1970), pp. 30–31.

[3]U.S. Department of State, *Communist Economic Policy in the Less Developed Areas* (Washington, D.C.: U.S. Government Printing Office, 1960), Foreword.

[4]Studies on the economic effectiveness of aid and trade were conducted at the Institute of the Economy of the World Socialist System in the early 1960s. But results of this research appeared in print only after 1964 (L. Zevin, "Vzaimnaya vygoda ekonomicheskogo sotrudnichestva sotsialisticheskikh i razvivayush-chikhsia stran," *Voprosy ekonomiki*, February 1965, pp. 72–83), since Khrushchev liked to boast that the USSR followed policies that were "disadvantageous to us economically." *Pravda*, July 13, 1958, p. 4.

[5]*Pravda*, March 30, 1966, p. 3.

[6]R. Lowenthal, "Soviet 'Counterimperialism,'" *Problems of Communism* (November–December 1976), p. 52.

[7]The outcome of Soviet Bloc–Iraqi compensation agreements shows how unexpected changes in the world economy have undone long-range barter plans. In order to increase and diversify their sources of oil supply, the CPEs became readily and extensively involved in assisting Iraq first to exploit the North Rumelia area for the nascent national petroleum company and later to dispose of the nationalized product. Under the terms of the $248 million credit the USSR and its European allies granted Iraq in 1969, the equipment and services for surveying, drilling, pumping, and refining oil, as well as for some other industrial installations, were to be repaid by oil shipments during the following 5 to 6 years. But when the initial barter agreements ran out in 1974, Iraq took advantage of the high prices it could get on the world market and shifted to importing mainly from the West. Consequently, the CMEA's share in Iraqi imports fell from 28% of the total in 1972 to 7.9% in 1975. For the changes resulting from India's technological development, see the penultimate section of this chapter.

[8]R. Andreasian, "Sotsialisticheskoe sodruzhestvo i razvivayushchiesia strany: ekonomicheskoe sotrudnichestvo," *Narody Azii i Afriki* (March–April 1981), pp. 3–13.

[9]G. M. Prokhorov, *Vneshneekonomicheskaya deyatel'nost' sovetskogo gosudarstva: tendentsii i problemy* (Moscow: Mezhdunarodnye otnosheniya, 1983); M. Khaldin, "Sovremennye formy torgovo-ekonomicheskogo sotrudnichestva SSR s razvivayushchimisia stranami," *Vneshniaya torgovlia* (March 1983), pp. 24–29.

[10]R. Andreasian, "Sotsialisticheskoe sodruzhestvo," p. 11.

[11]M. Maksimova, *SSSR i mezhdunarodnoe ekonomicheskoe sotrudnichestvo* (Moscow: Mysl', 1977), pp. 35 ff.

[12]Patrick Gutman, "Tripartite Industrial Cooperation and Third Countries," in *East–West–South. Economic Interaction between Three Worlds*, ed. Christopher T. Saunders (New York: St. Martin's Press, 1981), p. 337.

Even more indicative than the conclusion of tripartite agreements is the evolution of the tripartite cooperation itself. At the start, in the early 1970s, East–West–South cooperation amounted to fortuitous ad hoc arrangements, the result of bidding, and were hardly more than subcontracting procedures. By the decade's end, this cooperation had not only acquired more permanence through interstate agreements for joint activities in third countries, it had also been institutionalized as a regular business practice through the formation of joint East–West companies. In 1977 Moscow for the first time contracted to participate in two such firms. Technicon Spa, established in Genoa as a joint Soviet–Italian company for the construction of steel and tinplate plants in third countries, is a 50–50 partnership between Italpiamti, a subsidiary of an Italian state engineering group, and Litsensintorg, a Soviet foreign trade organization. Another foreign trade association, Energomasheksport, formed a consortium with the Japanese giant in heavy electrical engineering, Hitachi, to supply large-scale electric power plants to developing countries (*ibid.*, pp. 340–341, 362–364).

[13]J. V. Stalin, *Economic Problems of Socialism* (New York: International Publishers, 1952), pp. 26–27.

[14]*XXII S'ezd Kommunisticheskoi Partii Sovetskogo Soyuza. Stenograficheskii otchet 3* (Moscow: Gospolitizdat, 1962), pp. 260–261.

[15]V. Rymalov, "Ekonomicheskoe sorevnovanie dvukh sistem i problema pomoshchi slaborazvitym stranam," *Mirovaya ekonomika i mezhdunarodnye otnosheniya* (February 1960), p. 42 (hereafter cited as *MEMO*).

[16]*Bol'shaya sovetskaya entsiklopediya*, 16 (Moscow: Sovetskaya entsiklopediya, 1974), pp. 322–323; English translation: *Great Soviet Encyclopedia*, 16 (New York: Macmillan, 1977), p. 676.

[17]M. Maksimova, "Vsemirnoe khoziaistvo i mezhdunarodnoe ekonomicheskoe sotrudnichestvo," *MEMO* (April 1974), p. 3–16.

[18]*Pravda*, April 7, 1971, p. 6. For a similar argument by an economist, see L. Zevin's book which argued that joint industrial ventures or mixed companies, when set up by a socialist country, were qualitatively different from similar arrangements by Western companies since neither political advantage nor profit was the primary aim (*Economic Cooperation of Socialist and Developing Countries: New Trends* [Moscow: Nauka, 1975], pp. 198 ff.).

[19]*MEMO* (November 1970), pp. 151–157 and (December 1970), pp. 142–149.

[20]*Vneshniaya torgovlia* (June 1978), p. 3.

[21]M. Maksimova, as reported in *MEMO* (January 1982), p. 138.

[22]Brezhnev first referred to global problems in his report to the Twenty-fifth Party Congress, *Pravda*, February 15, 1976, p. 5. For expanded comments see his speech on the sixtieth anniversary of the October Revolution (*ibid.*, November 3, 1977, p. 3). See also his report to the Twenty-sixth Party Congress (*ibid.*, February 24, 1981, p. 9).

[23]*Pravda*, April 25, 1984.

[24]J. Kleer, *Vsemirnoe khoziaistvo. Zakonomernosti razvitiya* (Moscow: Mysl', 1979).

[25]For example, a report prepared by the Hungarian Academy of Sciences for

the fourth session in 1977 provoked a lively discussion on whether or not the increased economic and political differentiation of the Third World, delineated in the report, invalidated the theoretical notion of the unity of the developing countries [*MEMO* (October 1977), pp. 126–136]. The same idea was broached in the Soviet Union only a year later at a special meeting convened to discuss that topic ["Natsional'no-osvoboditel'noe dvizhenie: nekotorye voprosy differentsiatsii," *Aziya i Afrika segodnia* (June 1978), pp. 28–35].

[26]For one, it publishes books in collaboration with East European scholars, such as *Sotrudnichestvo sotsialisticheskikh i razvivayushchikhsia stran: novyi tip mezhdunarodnykh otnoshenii* (Moscow: Nauka, 1980).

[27]P. Khvoinik, "Mirovoi kapitalizm i razvivayushchiesia strany," *MEMO* (October 1980), pp. 44–57.

[28]"Imperializm i osvobodivshiesia strany," *Pravda*, February 10, 1978, pp. 3–4.

[29]"Nekotorye problemy razvivayushchikhsia stran," *Kommunist*, no. 11 (July 1978), pp. 81–91. See also his "Zakon neravnomernosti razvitiya i istoricheskie sud'by osvobodivshikhsia stran," *MEMO* (December 1980), pp. 24–47.

[30]E. Primakov, "Strany sotsialisticheskoi orientatsii: trudnyi no real'nyi put' prekhoda k sotsializmu," *MEMO* (July 1981), pp. 3–16.

[31]*Sotrudnichestvo sotsialisticheskikh i razvivayushchikhsia stran*, pp. 5–27.

[32]*Strany sotsializma v mezhdunarodnom razdelenii truda* (Moscow: Nauka, 1980), p. 258.

[33]See T. V. Teodorovich and V.V. Efanov, *Sotrudnichestvo pri sooruzhenii ob'ektov za rubezhom. Iz opyta sovetskikh organizatsii* (Moscow: Mezhdunarodnye otnosheniya, 1979).

[34]V. V. Zagladin and I. T. Frolov, "Global'nye problemy sovremennosti," *Kommunist*, no. 16 (November 1976), pp. 94–95.

[35]N. N. Inozemtsev, ed., *Global'nye problemy sovremennosti* (Moscow: Mysl', 1981), p. 98. For a discussion of raw materials, see *ibid.*, pp. 138–159, and S. Glebov, "Problema obespecheniya chelovechestva syr'em i energiei," *MEMO* (October 1980), pp. 30–41.

[36]V. M. Kollontai, *Puti preodoleniya ekonomicheskoi otstalosti* (Moscow: Mezhdunarodnye otnosheniya, 1967), p. 206.

[37]Compare E. A. Utkin, *Problemy planirovaniya v razvivayushchikhsia stranakh* (Moscow: Ekonomika, 1965) with V. Kollontai, "Voprosy planirovaniya v tret'em mire," *MEMO* (July 1969), pp. 91–100, and the discussion in the journal's following three issues of the problems Kollontai raised.

[38]N. P. Shmelev, "Razvivayushchiesia strany: formirovanie khoziaistvennogo mekhanizma," *MEMO* (August 1968), pp. 52–62; R. Andreasian and A. Elianov, "Razvivayushchiesia strany: ekonomicheskaya diversifikatsiya strategiya industrial'nogo razvitiya," *ibid.* (January 1968), pp. 29–40.

[39]See, for example, comments on the 1967 settlement between the Belgian Congo and Union Minière in *New Times*, no. 29 (July 1967), pp. 13–14.

[40]Kollontai, *Puti preodoleniya*, pp. 184–195.

[41]*MEMO* (April 1967), pp. 106–127, and (May 1967), pp. 93–108.

[42]The concept of semi-developed capitalism was outlined by V. Sheinis, "Strany srednego kapitalizma," *MEMO* (September 1977), pp. 105–124. It was subject to public discussion and criticism at an academic conference reported in *Latinskaya Amerika* (January–February 1979), pp. 53–100. For "subimperialist centers," see E. Primakov, "Zakon neravnomernosti razvitiya i istoricheskie sud'by osvobodivshikhsia stran," *MEMO* (December 1980), pp. 28–47; *idem*, *Vostok posle krakha kolonial'noi sistemy* (Moscow: Nauka, 1982).

[43]*Mezhdunorodnoe razdeleni truda i razvivayushchiesia strany* (Moscow: Nauka, 1976), pp. 9–10.

[44]A. Levkovsky, ed., *Inostrannyi kapital i inostrannoe predprinimatel'stvo v*

*stranakh Azii i Severnoi Afriki* (Moscow: Nauka, 1977), p. 17. Tiagunenko's 1976 work observes the more cautious line, as does V. Rymalov's *Strukturnye izmeneniya v mirovom kapitalisticheskom khoziaistve* (Moscow: Mysl', 1978).

[45]See V. Maksimenko's untitled review of A. Levkovsky's *Sotsial'naya struktura razvivayushchikhsia stran* (Moscow: Mysl', 1978) in *Narody Azii i Afriki* (January–February 1979), pp. 208–214. A. U. Roslavlev's "Eshche raz o teorii 'mnogoukladnosti' v strankakh 'tret'ego mira,'" *Rabochii klass i sovremennyi mir* (January–February 1977), pp. 136–145 is an excellent expression of conservative opinions.

[46]Peter Wiles, ed., *The New Communist Third World* (New York: St. Martin's Press, 1982).

[47]"The Theory and Practice of the Non-Capitalist Way of Development," *International Affairs* (November 1970), p. 13. For a later work with a similar bent, see *Afrika: problemy sotsialisticheskoi orientatsii* (Moscow: Nauka, 1976). Also A. Gromyko, "Socialist Orientation in Africa," *International Affairs* (September 1979), p. 103.

[48]K. Brutents *et al.*, *Sotsialisticheskaya orientatsiya osvobodivshikhsia stran. Nekotorye voprosy teorii i praktiki* (Moscow: Mysl', 1982), pp. 35–36.

[49]E. Primakov *et al.*, *Vostok: rubezh 80-kh godov* (Moscow: Nauka, 1983), p. 195.

[50]E. Primakov, "Strany sotsialisticheskoi orientatsii," pp. 8, 16.

[51]K. Brutents *et al.*, *Sotsialisticheskaya orientatsiya*, p. 160 ff.

[52]A. Butenko, "Nekotorye teoreticheskie problemy perekhoda k sotsializmu stran s nerazvitoi ekonomikoi," *Narody Azii i Afriki* (May 1982), p. 77.

[53]Abdel Fattah Ismail, "A New Vanguard Party, *World Marxist Review* 22 (January 1979), pp. 24, 28.

[54]*Pravda*, April 12, 1974, p. 4.

[55]"Joint Statement by the Socialist Countries . . . at the fourth session of the United Nations Conference on Trade and Development," *Foreign Trade* (September 1976), pp. 1–24 (Supplement).

[56]*Foreign Trade* (December 1976) pp. 2–5.

[57]"Evaluation of the world trade and economic situation and consideration of issues, policies, and appropriate measures to facilitate structural changes in the international economy," UNCTAD, TD/249 (April 19, 1979).

[58]A. Chekhutov, "Perestroika mezhdunarodnykh ekonomicheskikh otnoshenii—trebovanie zhizni," *Kommunist*, no. 16 (November 1981), p. 88.

[59]L. Zevin, "The New International Economic Order and Reorientation of the Economic Development Policy of the Developing Countries," *International Social Science Journal* 32 (1980), pp. 776–777.

[60]For one of the earliest descriptions of such a world, see N. P. Shmelev, "Sotsializm i vsemirnoe khoziaistvo," *MEMO* (October 1976), pp. 3–18.

[61]*Working-Class and National-Liberation Movements: Joint Struggle against Imperialism, for Social Progress* (Moscow: Novosti, 1981), p. 43; *World Marxist Review* 24 (March 1981), pp. 36–40.

[62]*World Marxist Review* 24 (March 1981), p. 40.

[63]Karen Brutents, "A Great Force of Modern Times," *International Affairs* (March 1981), p. 84.

[64]*Zarubezhnye kontseptsii ekonomicheskogo razvitiya stran Afriki* (Moscow: Nauka, 1980), p. 153.

[65]V. Yashkin, "Prospects for the Establishment of the New International Economic Order," pp. 17–18 and E. Pletnev, "Major Problems in International Economic Relations," p. 26 in *Joint UNITAR/Foreign Trade Academy Seminar* (Moscow, April 1980), mimeographed.

[66]Kustari Rangan, "Indian is Showered with Soviet Largesse," *New York Times*, December 14, 1980.

[67]K.V. Subrahmanyan, "The Soviet Technology. The Cost of Collaboration," *Economic Times*, April 9, 1979; Jaya Shekar, "Economic Links," *Seminar* (September 1981), pp. 21–26.

[68]See Deepak Nayyar's comments on a paper by I. Dobozi and A. Inotai, "Prospects of Economic Cooperation between CMEA Countries and Developing Countries," presented at the Vienna Institute for Comparative Economic Studies workshop on economic interaction between three worlds, in Christopher T. Saunders, ed., *East–West–South. Interaction between Three Worlds* (New York: St. Martin's Press, 1981), pp. 80–84.

# 40      KAREN DAWISHA

## The Correlation of Forces and Soviet Policy in the Middle East*

For a country whose foreign policy is proclaimed by its leaders to be based on the scientific principles of Marxism–Leninism, the Soviet Union has had its fair share of setbacks in the Near and Middle East. Kicked out of Egypt in 1972, largely excluded from the Arab–Israeli peace process after 1973, astride the wrong horse in the Horn of Africa until 1977, and bewitched and bewildered by the Iranian revolution, the Kremlin cornucopia is hardly overflowing with the fruits of victory. Of all the glittering prizes the area offers any greedy power, prizes of oil, power, wealth, and prime-site real estate for the erection of a strategic colossus, the Soviet Union, at the beginning of the fourth decade of postwar interest and involvement in the area, has only Ethiopia and South Yemen (the PDRY) to show as firm and voluntary adherents to an avowedly Marxist–Leninist course. Afghanistan is being shepherded in the same direction by Soviet troops, but their presence, while marking the victory of Soviet power, also surely demonstrates the frailty, if not the failure, of Soviet influence. Even in Iraq and Syria, both signatories of friendship treaties with the Soviet Union, a quarter-century of dealing with Moscow has enhanced neither the pull of communist ideas nor the position of local communist parties in the two countries. Nor has the Soviet Union found the navigational tools supposedly provided by its ideology sufficient to prevent its goal of building an impregnable phalanx of progressive states from floundering in a sea of regional disputes, conflicts, and coups.

None of these caveats is meant to deny that had the USSR not been prepared to "reap the whirlwind" of Western decline, the West might have been able to contain, if not prevent, the damage wreaked by the postcolonial storm. Equally, cognizance must be taken of the almost

*Reprinted by permission of the author and publisher from Adeed Dawisha and Karen Dawisha, eds., *The Soviet Union in the Middle East: Policies and Perspectives* (New York: Holmes and Meier, 1983), pp. 147–165. Copyright 1983 by The Royal Institute of International Affairs.

inexorable rise of Soviet military power and the global and regional manifestations and repercussions of that power. Yet it is remarkable that a state such as the Soviet Union, contiguous to the Middle East, with long-standing interests there even in prerevolutionary days, should be described by so many analysts as a state without a clear policy, reacting to situations, taking advantage of opportunities, veiling accident as strategy.

While to Western analysts Soviet policy may appear to be inconsistent or even haphazard, this is not how it is portrayed in the Soviet Union. Similar inconsistencies in Western policy are accounted for, or at least disguised by, the disruptive effects of elections and interalliance differences. The Soviet leadership has no similar excuses to hide behind, and its policy must be presented to the public as a cogent and coherent application and development of Marxist principles.

This chapter will examine, therefore, Soviet policy as it is seen in Moscow. In particular it will look at the concept of correlation of forces and the various components of that concept as applied to the Middle East. Any great power wishing to exercise influence in an area such as the Middle East will have to overcome diverse and conflicting religious, tribal, national, and ideological cross-currents. But is Moscow any better equipped than the West to understand these problems? With the constant growth of Soviet power, particularly in the military field, Moscow need no longer be constrained by incapability. Are there any other constraints built into Soviet policy, therefore, and if so how can the West exploit them to its advantage? In particular, at a time when the Middle East has been elevated to an area of vital strategic importance to the West, what risks is Moscow likely to take in order to expand its own presence in that area?

## Correlation of Forces

In the USSR, the application of Marxian ideology to current operative policy issues is determined through the calculus of the correlation of forces (*sootnoshenie sil*). Lenin once called it "the main point in Marxism and Marxian tactics," further stating that "we, Marxists, have always been proud of the fact that by a strict calculation of the mass forces and mutual class relations we have determined the expediency of this or that form of struggle."[1] In the West, while the systematic comparison of one's own capabilities relative to those of one's enemies is usual in military affairs, it is only the Soviets and other socialist countries who carry this concept over into policymaking in the sphere of international relations. The calculation includes both actual and potential shifts in the alignment of forces, thus allowing incredible flexibility of interpretation. The Soviet leaders are accorded, and they claim for themselves, the right to be the ultimate, if not the sole, diviners of policy at any given time, on the basis that it is they who are the most steeped in historical insight and Marxist teachings.

At the center of the concept, distinguishing it from Western notions of balance of power, is its dynamic and manipulative character. It is as much a definition of power as it is a calculus for the application of power. It is, above all, a concept based on the notion not of maintaining the *status quo* but of transforming it, and the leadership is under the compulsion not only to consider the correlation of forces but also to act upon it as the basis both of grand strategy and day-to-day policy.

In the Middle East, it is possible to observe four major elements of the Soviet view of the correlation of forces at work:

1. Soviet policy must take into account, and seek to manipulate, the total correlation between class forces, and not just the balance of power between states.
2. Short-term policy must serve long-term goals.
3. Regional policy should be determined with reference to global strategy.
4. The interests of Soviet socialism must take precedence over the interests of national liberation movements, and similarly the maintenance of the security of the borders of socialism must take precedence over national liberation movements, and in itself forms a basic principle of Soviet strategy.

## Correlation of Class Forces

The first aspect in the "classical" Soviet conception of the correlation of forces is that international relations is concerned with the interaction not primarily between states and governments, as in the Western conception, but between class forces—socialism, capitalism, feudalism, etc. It goes without saying that interaction between these forces is often expressed in the form of state-to-state relations. But the important point here is that because the focus of the Soviet perspective is on the dialectical relationship between class forces, the USSR has absolutely no qualms about openly supporting any communist party, national liberation movement, or separatist group which helps to "tilt the balance in favor of socialism." Looking at the Middle East, one has the example of Soviet support at different times for the Kurds, the Palestinians, the Dhofari rebels in the Sultanate of Muscat and Oman, the Eritreans (while Haile Selassie was in power), and of course all the various communist parties and progressive groupings which fought against British and French rule in Aden, Algeria, and other countries during colonial wars. The point that needs to be made is not that the USSR has always been a selfless and tireless supporter of these groups, because it has not, or that it conducts all its relations "in the open" without needing to resort to clandestine methods, since this also is clearly not the case. Rather, the fact of the matter seems to be that its view of international relations allows it to lend support freely and openly if the cause is deemed deserving.

The West, with a different view of international relations, is considerably more constrained, since support for "nonstate actors," however just the cause, goes against the dominant conception that state-to-state relations reflect and support the *status quo* and are thus the only truly legitimate form of international politics. The West has not lent open, direct, and nonclandestine military support to a single nonstate actor in the Middle East, which is presumably why the picture of former National Security Advisor Zbigniew Brzezinski holding a gun in an Afghan refugee camp in Pakistan in 1980 created such a furor at the time. The West's support tends to be clandestine or through third parties, such as in the case of arms to the Kurds via Iran in the early 1970s (after they no longer received Soviet support) and to the Afghan rebels via Pakistan. Even in the case of aid to a state, the West has often felt constrained to go through third parties or find a means by which its aid can be disguised, as when British aid to the Sultanate of Muscat and Oman to put down the Dhofari rebellion, again in the early 1970s, was either channelled through Iran or took the form of sending contract or loan service personnel from British forces to fight there. The low level of publicity given in the West to the large number of its own personnel stationed throughout the Middle East is in marked contrast to the Eastern bloc, including Cuba, where the press hails the stationing of military personnel and advisers overseas as proof that these countries are fulfilling their international duties.

Short-Term Policy Serves Long-Term Goals

As for the second maxim, that short-term policy must always be made within the framework of long-term goals, application of this principle, if successful, would give Soviet policy an overall coherence often lacking in Western strategy. The provision of massive quantities of economic and military assistance, either gratis or at favorable rates, also could be justified in terms of long-term benefits. Equally, setbacks could be accepted as temporary or tactical retreats on the way to the achievement of more fundamental goals.

In the Middle East, as elsewhere, Moscow's long-term goal is the establishment of Marxist–Leninist regimes integrated into the Soviet-led world communist system; and it has been a feature of Soviet policy since the mid-1970s, perhaps as a result of the reverses suffered in Egypt, that Moscow has devoted much more time to the elaboration of the means by which this long-term goal is to be achieved. There are first of all, certain obligatory steps which a regime must follow before it can embark on "the road of socialist orientation." Articles published in the Soviet press to mark the Twenty-sixth CPSU Congress have outlined the steps as follows:[2] left-wing elements (by no means necessarily communist) within the leadership must strive to eliminate their opponents' control over "the levers of political power" (the police, army, bureaucracy) and put into effect economic measures (confiscation, nationalization, and regulation) designed to eliminate the influence of the bourgeoisie and Western capital. These are measures which have become almost commonplace in the Middle East, but the Soviet Union no longer recognizes them as sufficient guarantees of the continued left-wing orientation of a regime. To this end, the leadership must embark upon a second stage of reforms in which it enacts a wide range of progressive socioeconomic measures, dissociates itself from Maoist-style leftism, and sets about forming a vanguard party in collaboration with local communists using a Soviet-type organizational structure. The establishment of a vanguard party has become a *sine qua non* of Soviet policy, with it now openly being stated that "no group of revolutionaries . . . can ensure the socialist orientation of the bulk of the population and the work of the entire state apparatus without the existence of a vanguard revolutionary party of fellow-thinkers."[3]

Yet Moscow has long realized that it is faced with many problems in trying to achieve its long-term goals in areas such as the Middle East. One Soviet analyst noted some time ago that "here nothing is automatically certain in advance, every step forward has to be won in battle, and progress is often attained at the price of bitter disappointments, mistakes, and searches."[4]

One of Moscow's most intractible problems is that while many Middle Eastern leaders might agree that there is a basis for short-term cooperation, they would totally reject any correlation between short- and long-term objectives. Thus, Soviet willingness to invest large sums of money in the Middle East was based on the assumption that short-term investment would reap long-term benefits. Yet when Egypt's President Sadat abrogated the Soviet–Egyptian Treaty of Friendship, leaving an unpaid debt of $11 billion, this was shown to be a fallacious assumption. The result has been that Moscow has reappraised the notion of the "irreversibility" of socialist gains. In the economic field this shift has manifested itself in a greater emphasis on the principle of "mutual economic advantage" and, as a result, the Soviet Union has become less and less willing to sink large sums of money into states where it enjoys little political control.

Moscow's difficulties become most apparent at the moment when it tries to encourage a regime to make the transition from the first "progressive" and "anti-imperialist" stage of development to the second "socialist" and "pro-Soviet" stage, involving, as mentioned earlier, dissociation from both "rightist" and "leftist" excesses, cooperation with local communists, and the establishment of a vanguard party. The vast majority of the countries of the Middle East have passed through the first stage of development at some time or other since World War II, but very few have made the crucial transition to socialism.

Moscow has suggested that there are four main reasons why states of the Middle East have failed to make this crucial transition. The first, but not necessarily the chief, problem is that elements within the leadership are influenced by "adventurist" and pro-Chinese notions of going "too far, too fast." A basic Soviet work on the Third World quite explicitly stated that "the concept of violent revolution, which the ultra-left opportunists seek to impose upon the national-liberation movement, has nothing in common with Marxism–Leninism. . . . Such revolutionary postures can merely produce a schism in the united anti-imperialist front . . . and hold up its further development."[5] In the Middle East, during the 1970 civil war between the Jordanians and the Palestinians,

*Pravda* explicitly condemned "crazy extremists amongst the fedayeen, governed by the slogan 'the worse it is, the better it is.'"[6] Soviet accounts of the situation in Afghanistan prior to the Soviet intervention similarly make it clear that Amin's major failing had been in pursuing a leftist policy. The following analysis deserves to be quoted in some length:

> The damage that can be inflicted on society if such elements grasp the political initiative is illustrated best by the example of the "great leaps" and "cultural revolution" in China. Still manifestations of leftism and adventurism did take place in some countries of socialist orientation even in the recent past. In Afghanistan, for example, a part of the former leadership tried without justification to accelerate social transformations and to raise them immediately to the level of the people's democratic revolution. This brought about a serious aggravation of the situation which not only internal but also external counter-revolutionary forces were quick to use to their advantage. The country's present leadership made vigorous efforts to rectify the situation, to form a broad front of national-patriotic forces for a consistent solution of the tasks of the national-democratic revolution.[7]

A second problem in achieving the correlation between short- and long-term policy lies in the attitude toward a regime's collaboration with local communists. In order to maintain its influence in the short term, Moscow has shown itself more than willing to gloss over the regime's suppression of its communists. The most graphic example, as discussed in Robert Patman's writings, occurred in Ethiopia during May 1977, when 500 communists were slaughtered on the very weekend that then-President Podgorny arrived in Addis Ababa to consolidate Moscow's shift from Somalia to Ethiopia. In Iraq, the Soviets also initially remained mute to the suppression of local communists by the ruling Baath regime after 1978, although evidence of a shift in Moscow's attitude was evoked by the decision to allow Aziz Muhammad, exiled leader of the Iraqi Communist Party, to use the platform of the Twenty-sixth CPSU Congress to condemn the "cruel repression and persecution" unleashed on the ICP by Saddam Hussein's "reactionary and dictatorial" regime.[8]

A third and major problem arises out of differences over regional rivalries and conflicts which Moscow feels unable to support because they are not directed against Western interests. Thus, for example, having established some considerable influence in both Iraq and Somalia largely through the supply of weaponry, when those weapons were used not against Western interests but against regimes which the USSR sought to nurture (Iran and Ethiopia, respectively), the Soviet Union made its objections clear. But, in doing so, its chances of achieving its long-term goals were considerably reduced. In the case of the Somali–Ethiopian conflict, Soviet losses were minimized by the fact that the shift to Ethiopia represented a net gain in Moscow's eyes. In the case of the Iran–Iraq war, however, failure to support Iraq did not eliminate Iran's suspicions of Soviet motives, and, as I have argued elsewhere, Moscow felt itself to be in a "no-win" situation.[9] Despite the Soviet leaders' determination to prevent any further deterioriation which might lead to the abrogation of the Iraqi–Soviet Friendship Treaty, and their claims that it should be preserved because it served "the fundamental *long-term* interests" of the two countries,[10] the Iraqis made it clear that Soviet refusal to supply arms during the war with Iran would not quickly or easily be forgotten.[11]

Regional conflicts also impede the achievement of another of the Soviet Union's aims, namely the establishment of a united front among all of its allies in the region. Article 10 of its 1979 treaty with the USSR specifically commits the PDRY to help establish a bloc of progressive states in the region, and to this end a friendship treaty between Ethiopia and the PDRY was indeed signed on December 3, 1979. All of Moscow's other efforts in this direction have ended in failure, however. Attempts before 1977 to encourage the formation of a Marxist–Leninist confederation taking in the PDRY, Ethiopia, Somalia, and Djibouti were doomed from the outset, and only displayed the Soviet leadership's own ignorance of national and ethnic rivalries in the Horn. Elsewhere, as of the autumn 1981, Syria and Iraq are arch-rivals; Iraq is publicly committed to the overthrow of the PDRY on account of the latter's support of communist subversion in Iraq; Syria is unlikely to sign a treaty with the PDRY for fear of alienating her Saudi backers; and all of these regimes, anxious to protect their Islamic credentials, will provide the minimum support possible to the Soviet Union's other treaty ally in the area— Afghanistan.

As for Libya's President Gaddafi, even Moscow has kept some distance between itself and this quixotic leader, as manifested by the absence of a friendship treaty between the two states. Indeed, on the occasion of Colonel Gaddafi's visit to Moscow in April 1981 (his first since 1976), President Brezhnev took the opportunity to stress not growing friendship but continuing, if accepted, differences: "Between us there is a defined difference and ideological order. But that does not interfere with our being good comrades. . . ."[12] Equally, Moscow has not been an outspoken supporter of Libya's intervention in Chad, and interestingly, on the occasion of the shooting-down of two Libyan-piloted SU-22s by U.S. F-14s in August 1981, Tass presented both the Libyan and the Pentagon versions of the events.[13] While it appeared for some time that a radical coalition of Iran, Syria, Libya, Algeria, and the PLO might be emerging, particularly in opposition to the nascent Baghdad–Riyadh axis, Israel's actions in bombing the Iraqi nuclear reactor in summer 1981 and supplying arms to Iran diminished the support which radical Arab states could openly show for Iran's war effort against Iraq. However, the announcement of a unified defense pact between Libya, the PDRY, and Ethiopia in August 1981, clearly designed to isolate and encircle Egypt, did represent a step forward for Moscow; and it was hailed by *Pravda* as ushering in a "relatively new stage" in relations between the three signatories.[14]

It is clearly in the Soviet Union's financial interests to promote closer relations with any country, such as Libya, which can pay in hard currency both for its own weaponry and for the Soviet equipment supplied to other Arab states (e.g., with $1 billion reportedly transferred by Gaddafi to Moscow in September 1980 to pay for Syrian arms). It is rather surprising, therefore, that Moscow continued to distance itself from some of Gaddafi's more excessive policies. Ethiopia too has been rather skeptical of Libya's regional intentions, and has been keen both to guard its own preeminent position in the OAU hierarchy against Libyan challenge and to thwart Gaddafi's hegemonistic regional plans by maintaining its own links with both Egypt and the Sudan.[15] Libya's support for Islamic radicals in Eritrea, as elsewhere, also naturally has impaired the friendship between Ethiopia and Libya. These latent conflicts of interest between Moscow's regional allies continue to represent formidable obstacles to the achievement of Moscow's long-term goals. In the case of Libya at least, it seemed that excessive Western pressure on the regime might actually serve Moscow's interests by limiting Gaddafi's options and making him more amenable to Soviet control. Thus, in the wake of the downing of the two Libyan SU-22s, Libyan officials stated that while the USSR had no bases in Libya at the moment and while "Libya will try everything to keep from accepting foreign bases, . . . they could be accepted to defend our freedom."[16]

The fourth and final problem seen in Moscow as jeopardizing the chances of a revolutionary regime fully establishing itself is Western interference. The current Soviet formulation would appear to allow for all forms of Soviet assistance, including direct military intervention, if a regime which is already "oriented" toward socialism is threatened by "external or internal reaction." In his Twenty-sixth Congress speech, Brezhnev made it clear that the USSR reserved the option to lend direct military aid if the situation required it. At the same time, however, he did not give an unequivocal guarantee that the Soviet Union would intervene if socialism were in fact threatened in a client state. He gave only the following assurance:

> We are also helping . . . in strengthening the defense capability of the liberated states . . . for example, in Angola and Ethiopia. Attempts were being made to deal with the popular revolutions in these countries by encouraging internal counter-revolution or aggression from outside. We are against the export of revolution but we cannot agree either with the export of counter-revolution. Imperialism unleashed a real undeclared war against the Afghan revolution. This also created a direct threat to the security of our southern border. This situation forced us to render the military assistance asked for by that friendly country.[17]

By drawing a distinction between Ethiopia and Angola, on the one hand, and Afghanistan, on the other, Brezhnev failed to make an unequivocal statement that established Marxist–Leninist regimes in the Middle East and the Horn of Africa would be protected with the force of Soviet arms and soldiers if necessary. Thus Moscow showed itself unwilling firmly to commit its resources to the forcible achievement of the transition between short-term and long-term objectives. Clearly other factors in the correlation of forces would have to be taken into account.

## Regional Ambitions and Global Strategy

Two extremely important factors in determining Soviet policy in the Middle East at any given time are Soviet strategy and Soviet priorities at the global level. It is interesting that while Moscow resolutely denounces U.S. efforts to establish any linkage between East–West relations and Soviet conduct in the Third World, nevertheless Moscow carefully assesses the relationship between these two policy sets and considers them in their entirety. As outlined at the beginning of the chapter, there are three basic principles that follow on from the Soviet view of the correlation of forces: regional policy should serve global strategy; the interests of Soviet socialism should take precedence over the interests of national liberation movements; and similarly the security of the borders of socialism takes precedence over national liberation movements and itself forms a basic principle of Soviet global strategy. These three principles are seen in Moscow as forming a single unit, and while open to wide and various interpretation are central to the determination of Soviet policy in the Middle East.

Let us look first at the correlation between the USSR's regional and global policy. Many commentators have concluded that with the clear establishment of détente in the early 1970s, the Soviet Union would not take any action at the regional level in the Middle East which would jeopardize the steady improvement of relations with the United States. This was the firm policy adopted at both the Twenty-fourth and the Twenty-fifth Party Congresses, and despite anticipation that détente would be scrapped in favor of proletarian internationalism as the basis of Soviet global strategy, Brezhnev announced at the Twenty-sixth Congress that the USSR remains firmly committed to détente as the overarching principle governing East–West relations, despite recent setbacks.

At the same time, however, Brezhnev emphasized that while the USSR was not in favor of the export of revolution, neither could Moscow any longer "agree" with the export of counterrevolution. In clear terms, the Soviet Union would not invade a country in order to put a socialist government in power, but it reserved the right to provide "fraternal assistance" if an established socialist regime were threatened by counterrevolution. With the extension and development of Soviet military power, the USSR clearly does have the capability to defend the "gains of socialism" in Afghanistan, Ethiopia, the PDRY, and elsewhere in the Middle East if it chooses to do so. Thus it can be seen that both détente and proletarian internationalism are juxtaposed uncomfortably in current Soviet global strategy.

There are two further aspects of that strategy which influence Soviet policy in the Middle East. One is the protection of Soviet borders and the other is the strengthening of Soviet military capability. The enhancement of Soviet military power not only provides the means to pursue a more active policy of proletarian internationalism, but also becomes an end in itself, generating its own dynamics and requirements independent of, or even in contradiction to, other aspects of Soviet global strategy, including both détente and proletarian internationalism. Thus, for example, the continued interest of the Soviet navy in obtaining deep-sea ports has to be seen as a prime motivator of Soviet policy in the Middle East, as shown in the case of Soviet offshore bombardments of positions held by the Marxist-oriented Eritrean liberation movements. This Soviet action illustrated more clearly than most the Soviet adherence to the view that the interests of socialism, defined in this case in terms of military interests, must take precedence over the interests of national liberation movements.

Up to the mid-1970s, Soviet adherence to détente dominated other aspects of Soviet global strategy, and produced a policy in the Middle East that was roundly criticized by progressive leaders in the area for being overcautious. Thus, in the case of the Arab–Israeli conflict, many Arab leaders complained that the Soviet interest in détente took precedence over Soviet support for the Arab cause against Israel. In particular, Soviet reluctance to supply the Arab states with sufficient quantities of the most sophisticated offensive weapons so as to ensure victory against Israel, either prior to the outbreak of hostilities or during a war, was a major cause of disputes between the Arab states and the USSR, and was the chief factor in the expulsion of Soviet advisers from Egypt in 1972 and the gradual exclusion of all other forms of Soviet influence from that country after 1973. Despite continued and long-standing criticisms both from Middle Eastern leaders and from radical elements within the world communist movement itself, notably the Chinese, that the Soviet leaders "are sorely afraid of the revolutionary storm,"[18] Moscow continued to insist that détente, by decreasing imperialist aggression, actually increased the chances of success for national liberation movements.

What creates particular difficulties for Moscow is the Soviet precept that in the event of a clash between what is good for a national liberation movement and what benefits the USSR, the latter must always take precedence. Soviet adherence to this view was most forcefully stated in response to the Maoist doctrine, developed in the mid-1960s, that the revolutionary forces had shifted to the Third World (of which China then considered itself a member). The Soviet response was unequivocal:

> The contentions are designed to refute the Marxist characterization of the current epoch and to substitute for the basic contradiction of our day, which is that between socialism and capitalism, the contradiction between . . . "rich" and "poor" nations. . . . These conceptions in reality seek to push into the background and play down the significance of the revolutionary struggle waged by the peoples of the socialist community of nations. . . . They are completely alien to a class interpretation of the nature of the present epoch.[19]

Yet it is not only the Chinese who have objected to the USSR putting the "interests of socialism" above that of the national liberation movement. Moscow itself concedes that criticism has also come from the Third World, where "leaders of nationalist leanings . . . are fanning a useless argument over which of the two trends are of greater importance."[20] It is a useless argument only in the sense that there is no chance of Moscow changing its view, although it is willing to concede that "the objective fact that the socialist system is a leading factor in the world revolutionary process must in no way be taken to belittle the importance of the . . . fight the oppressed people are waging."[21]

Clearly, until the mid-1970s, Moscow considered the "interests of socialism" to be served by the policy of détente. The strategic and cooperative relationship between Washington and Moscow brought the Soviet Union numerous benefits in terms of technology, trade, disarmament negotiations, and the containment of Chinese efforts to transform the international system from bipolarity to tripolarity.

By the beginning of the 1980s, it certainly was no longer apparent that the "interests of socialism" could be furthered by such a single-minded adherence to détente. In particular, the collapse of the SALT negotiations, the intensification of the arms race, and the diminution of East–West trade and technology transfer, all led Moscow to believe that the benefits on the global level of restraint at the regional level had been minimized. Further, Moscow viewed with great alarm the enthusiasm with which Washington set about constructing a special relationship with the Chinese designed, in the Soviet view, to resurrect the policy of containment and to challenge the Soviet Union not just at the global and strategic level but also at the regional and conventional level.

The enunciation by Zbigniew Brzezinski of the "arc of crisis" theory was considered by Soviet analysts to be a turning-point in U.S. policy. This theory, according to Moscow, became a "factor in the intensification of the military element in U.S. policy toward the region *adjacent to the Soviet Union's frontiers.*" It also "formed the pretext for stepping up U.S. military activity, primarily in the region of the Red Sea, the Persian Gulf, and the entire Middle East."[22] As a result of the growing military involvement of the United States (along with that of the Chinese) in the "arc of crisis" and the U.S. policy of linkage, Moscow was no longer able to pursue a policy of cooperation at the global level and activism at the regional level. Not only had the two levels become linked but, contrary to Soviet interests, the regional level had itself become "globalized." The Middle East had once again become a central arena for East–West rivalry and confrontation in a way which had never seemed possible during the days of détente.

The globalization of the area became most apparent following the Soviet invasion of Afghanistan. Of course, détente already had been seriously damaged before December 1979, and Moscow had already become sensitive to the implications for its posture in the Middle East and South and South–East Asia of the normalization of relations between Peking and Washington. Whereas in the previous 20 years the principle that the security of the borders of socialism was an inalienable part of overall Soviet global strategy had been tested only in Czechoslovakia in 1968, the Soviet Union found that first with the Iranian revolution, and then with the growing turmoil in Afghanistan, the security of its own southern borders was being jeopardized.

Anyone familiar with the Soviet attitude toward conflict on or near its southern borders knows that, in the event of conflict breaking out, almost inevitably Moscow is sooner or later going to issue its time-honored statement about the USSR being "unable to remain indifferent to acts of unprovoked aggesssion in an area adjacent to its borders, and it reserves the right to take the necessary measures dictated by the security interests of the Soviet Union." The Soviet interest in maintaining border security arguably has played a part in the formulation of two rather contradictory policies, including, on the one hand, the Soviet intervention in Afghanistan, of which more will be said below, and, on the other hand, the long (if not entirely unbroken) tradition of "good neighborly relations" with Turkey and Iran. In the case of Iran, relations date back to the early 1920s, when Moscow unceremoniously allowed the collapse of the newly founded independent Soviet Republic of Gilan in northern Iran in return for the 1921 Treaty of Friendship between Moscow and Iran's Reza Shah, the founder of the Pahlevi Dynasty. In the late 1970s, even as opposition to the Shah was growing, the USSR initially refrained from openly supporting his overthrow. Indeed, when on November 19, 1978 Brezhnev delivered the first major statement of Soviet concern over Iran, he made no mention, as one might have expected, of supporting the "democratic aspirations of the peoples struggling to free themselves from imperialist oppression." Rather, his sole concern was that any U.S. attempt to interfere militarily in Iran would constitute a threat to Soviet security interests.[23]

Of course the Soviets were impeded in developing a clear view of the Iranian revolution by virtue of its Islamic character. Prior to the overthrow of the Shah, Moscow considered that Islam had almost always been used in the service of reactionary movements and leaders. The emergence of virulent anti-Western Islamic radicalism made it apparent that this view would have to be altered. The end-process of that review was signalled by Brezhnev at the Twenty-sixth Party Congress when he described the Iranian revolution as "a major international event" and stated that "for all its complications and contradictions, it is fundamentally an anti-imperialist revolution." The broader lessons to be learned from Iran were that "the liberation struggle can develop under the banner of Islam"[24] and that therefore it should no longer be condemned. Indeed, one of the crimes committed by Afghanistan's Hafizullah Amin was that he put into effect reforms which "impinged upon the interests of . . . patriotic elements of the clergy."[25] On the other hand, Brezhnev cautioned that "history shows that reaction also operates with Islamic slogans. . . . Consequently, what really matters is the actual content of a particular movement."[26] As long as the Islamic content of the Iranian revolution works against American interests and does not produce a threat to the security of Soviet borders, Moscow can be expected to support Khomeini, even though the Soviet Union has little opportunity of transforming that revolution along Marxist–Leninist lines. Soviet policy toward Iran is therefore also an illustration of the difficulty faced by the Soviet Union in directing its short-term policy to accord with its long-term goals.

To turn to the case of Afghanistan, the Soviet intervention there certainly was prompted by several of the principles underlying Soviet global strategy, including both proletarian internationalism and Soviet concern for border security. It certainly was not constrained by what remained of détente, although almost all Soviet accounts of that period emphasize that "U.S. attacks on the policy of détente began long before the events in Afghanistan."[27] Nevertheless, the Soviet leaders are willing to concede both that their actions in Afghanistan certainly had a whole series of negative repercussions and that they were "surprised" by the vehemence of Western reaction. The previous constraints on Soviet activism in the Middle East presented by Moscow's adherence to détente were considered to have been removed before the invasion. But what Soviet leaders did not expect, and what they had to deal with after December 1979, was the globalization of Soviet policy toward not only Afghanistan but the whole of the Middle East. The area had become a front line of East–West competition, with Soviet behavior affecting, if not entirely determining, American attitudes to the Soviet Union in other spheres. Thus Soviet efforts to compartmentalize their regional policy and use it in the service of their global strategy had all but failed.

While the globalization of Soviet behavior in the Middle East has been resisted by Moscow, the Soviet Union has itself been responsible for the occurrence of this phenomenon in three ways. First, the increased emphasis on conventional military competition between the superpowers had led to the elevation in importance of areas such as the Middle East and Indian Ocean. Second, the increased emphasis in Soviet policy on military involvement in countries of the Middle East has further alarmed the United States at a time when Middle East oil has become a major strategic commodity. And, finally, Soviet actions in Afghanistan demonstrated to the West the risks Moscow was willing to take in the pursuit and protection of its interests. Thus while Brezhnev may have been genuine in his attempts to reassure the West, in his Twenty-sixth Congress speech, that the Soviet Union has "no intention" of encroaching on "the oil riches of the Near and Middle East or on the oil transport routes," yet the increased emphasis on both the military instrument and military aspect of Soviet policy hardly provides visible proof of pacific intentions.

## Military Aims and Instruments

The preceding discussion has suggested that in several respects the correlation of forces calculus has fallen far short of providing Moscow with a foolproof, scientific framework for the formulation of policy. In particular, Soviet leaders continue to find it extremely difficult to translate short-term policy into long-term gains, often as a direct result of pursuing policies which meet immediate requirements but which at the same time are deleterious to long-term interests. Equally, the USSR has failed to use its regional policy in the service of its global strategy, with its behavior in the region being used by the West as a litmus test of its intentions at the global level. And given the direction of Soviet policy, with its emphasis on the use of the military instrument and the salience of military and security considerations in its strategy, this situation is unlikely to improve.

If one looks first at the use of the military instrument, this can be divided into arms supplies and direct Soviet involvement. The USSR uses arms supplies both to establish and maintain influence and, increasingly, to earn either petrol or petrodollars. Yet the economic imperatives to supply arms may confer on the recipient some considerable reverse influence on the supplier, in addition to the fact that the Soviet Union has found it extremely difficult to turn arms supplies into political influence. Thus, a massive influx of Soviet arms into one client state will almost inevitably generate similar demands among Moscow's other client states in the region, with failure to meet these demands becoming a major issue in bilateral relations and leading to a diminution of Soviet influence. Second, having supplied the weapons, Moscow has often had no control over the end-use of the weapons. As with the cases of the Somali offensive in the Ogaden and Iraq's war with Iran, Moscow was faced with the stark choice of either supporting actions which it did not condone, and which ironically would not have been possible without initial Soviet supplies, or losing influence altogether. And as both of these examples illustrate, although Soviet refusal to continue supplying weapons did prevent the crises from escalating, it did not lead either to the cessation of hostilities or to the reaffirmation of Soviet control. Rather, influence disappeared almost immediately once supplies ceased. A similar problem relating to the lack of control over end-use is that arms are also often supplied to bolster the internal security of a regime against rightist, separatist, or Islamic fundamentalist groups. Yet Moscow on numerous occasions in the past appeared powerless if the regime turned the army or the security apparatus against the communists and other pro-Soviet groups.

Moscow has attempted to resolve some of these problems by increasing its direct military presence in countries of the Middle East, both in pursuit of greater political control and in the protection of its own distinct military interests in the area. East German and Cuban assistance in the organization and running of the military and the internal security services in countries such as the PDRY, Ethiopia, and Afghanistan has done much to bolster Moscow's political control in countries of the so-called "Communist Third World."

The growth of the Soviet Union's military capabilities undoubtedly has produced a greater confidence among its allies in the Middle East that it will come to their assistance in the case of need. Thus, for example, while previous treaties between the USSR and states of the Middle East make only general reference to mutual consultation in situations which threaten peace, Article 6 of the October 1980 treaty with Syria does take the formulation one important step further by declaring that in the event of a crisis the two parties "shall immediately enter into contact with each other with a view to coordinating their positions *and cooperating in order to remove the threat which has arisen and to restore peace."*[28] And the Syrian Minister of Information has made it clear that Damascus welcomes the treaty as a guarantee of Syrian security providing for the dispatch of Soviet troops to Syria in case of need.[29]

While increased Soviet military capability multiplies Moscow's options for the support of local clients and the promotion of its interests, in any sense, the very growth of that influence presents almost equally severe problems for the future of Soviet policy in the area. First, the enhancement of Soviet capabilities means that Moscow will no longer be able to beg lack of capability as the reason for its nonsupport of local clients if they get involved "above their heads" in regional conflicts which Moscow really does not want to support. As a result, tension between Moscow and its clients certainly need not disappear with the growth of Soviet military power and may indeed even increase. Second, the physical presence of Soviet troops in the various states of the Middle East almost without exception has produced not only widespread anti-Soviet (specifically anti-Russian) sentiments, but also the feeling that local independence is being infringed. These feelings manifest themselves both at the popular level and, more important, in the army, thus often producing a subsequent anti-Soviet backlash, the most notable example being the transition from Nasser to Sadat. Third, the growth of Soviet naval power, while used successfully in the support of local clients in Ethiopia and Syria (when joint maneuvers in the summer of 1981 were part of the minatory diplomacy employed by Moscow to remind the Israelis of the dangers of escalating the Lebanese crisis), also increasingly creates its own demands in terms of requirements for ports and onshore facilities, a subject of considerable tension in negotiations between Moscow and its Middle Eastern clients, whose determination to protect their hard-won sovereignty persists. And, of course, sensitivities of this type were not allayed by the Soviet invasion of Afghanistan, which did more than anything to signal to the Middle Eastern states the length to which Moscow was willing to go to protect its own interests.

Military aims and instruments have thus come to the forefront of Soviet policy in the Middle East. While undeniably establishing the USSR as a superpower in the area, the promotion of Soviet military power has emphasized the failings of Moscow's political and ideological offensive, and itself has brought with it problems which the Soviet leaders have yet to resolve. Unless they are resolved, Moscow's optimism that the correlation of forces is shifting in its favor may be misplaced.

## Notes

[1]V. I. Lenin, *Sochineniya*, vol. 22 (2d ed. Moscow, 1929), p. 265.

[2]See in particular E. Primakov, "Zakon neravnomernosti razvitiya i istoricheskiye sud'by osvobodivshikhsya stranam," *Mirovaya ekonomika i mezhdunarodnyye otnosheniya* 12 (1980), pp. 28–48; Yu. N. Gavrilov, "Problemy formirovaniya avangardnoy partii v strankh sotsialisticheskoy orientatsii," *Narody Azii i*

*Afriki* 6 (1980), pp. 10–24; and the articles by N. Simoniya, A. Iskenderov, and Anatoly Gromyko on the Twenty-sixth CPSU Congress and the International Liberation Movement in *Asia and Africa Today* 3 (1981), pp. 2–11.

[3]N. Simoniya, "The Present Stage of the Liberation Struggle," *Asia and Africa Today* 3 (1981), p. 4.

[4]K. Ivanov, "The National-Liberation Movement and the Non-Capitalist Path of Development," *International Affairs* (Moscow), 2 (1966), p. 12.

[5]Yu. Zhukov, L. Delynsin, A. Iskenderov, and L. Stepanov, *The Third World* (Moscow: Progress Publishers, 1970), pp. 23–24.

[6]*Pravda*, October 17, 1970.

[7]Simoniya, "The Present Stage," p. 4. This view was also expressed by Evgeni M. Primakov, "The USSR and the Developing Countries," *Journal of International Affairs* 34 (1980/81), p. 276.

[8]*Pravda*, March 2, 1981.

[9]Karen Dawisha, "Moscow's Moves in the Direction of the Gulf—So Near and Yet So Far," *Journal of International Affairs* 34 (1980/81), pp. 219–235; Karen Dawisha, "Moscow and the Gulf War," *The World Today* (January 1981), pp. 8–15.

[10]Message of congratulations to Saddam Hussain from Brezhnev and Tikhonov on the ninth anniversary of the signature of the Soviet–Iraqi Friendship Treaty, *Pravda*, April 11, 1981 (italics mine).

[11]Press conference of Saadoon Hammadi, Iraqi Foreign Minister, in London, March 11, l981, Arabic transcript issued by the Iraqi embassy, pp. 7–8.

[12]*Pravda*, April 27, 1981.

[13]*The Times*, August 20, 1981.

[14]*Pravda*, August 24, 1981.

[15]The links between Ethiopia and Sudan were recently cited by Moscow as an example of how "the coming to power of progressive regimes contributes to lower tension on a regional level and has a stabilizing effect on international relations as a whole" (Evgeni M. Primakov, "The USSR and the Developing Countries," p. 272).

[16]*The Guardian*, August 26, 1981.

[17]Brezhnev's Twenty-sixth Congress speech, February 23, 1981, BBC, *Summary of World Broadcasts* (*SWB*), part I, SU/6657/C/8.

[18]*Jen-min Jih-pao*, October 22, 1963, quoted in Raymond Garthoff, *Soviet Military Policy* (London: Faber, 1966), p. 212.

[19]A. Iskenderov, "The National Liberation Movement in Our Time," *The Third World* (Moscow: Progress Publishers, 1970), p. 30.

[20]L. Delynsin, "Socialism and the National-Liberation Struggle," *ibid.*, p. 247.

[21]A. Iskenderov, "The National Liberation Movement," p. 31.

[22]Primakov, "The USSR and the Developing Countries," p. 274 (italics in original).

[23]*Pravda*, November 19, 1978.

[24]Brezhnev's Twenty-sixth Congress speech, February 23, 1981, *SWB*, SU/6657/C/8.

[25]Primakov, "The USSR and the Developing Countries," p. 276.

[26]Brezhnev's Twenty-sixth Congress speech, February 23, 1981, *SWB*, SU/6657/C/8.

[27]Primakov, "The USSR and the Developing Countries," p. 275.

[28]*Pravda*, October 9, 1980 (italics mine).

[29]Interview with Syrian Minister of Information, Ahmed Iskandar, in *al-Moustaqbal* (Paris), September 26, 1980.

# 41 ALVIN Z. RUBINSTEIN

## The Soviet Union and the Peace Process since Camp David*

The Soviet Union's opposition to the Camp David accords of September 1978 is a logical outgrowth of its Arab–Israeli policy, which took form after the June 1967 War and was colored by events of the post-October 1973 War period. The cease-fire hardly had taken effect in late October 1973 when Sadat dashed the Kremlin's expectations of a key role in the negotiations by resuming diplomatic relations with the United States and plumping his eggs in Washington's basket, leaving the USSR empty-handed, angry, and odd-man-out in the peace process whose deliberations under a U.S.-imprimatur were profoundly to alter the political environment of the Arab–Israeli sector of the Arab East. Moscow sought a role and a constituency for itself by supporting Syria—the arch opponent of Sadat's U.S. strategy—arming Iraq and Libya, and espousing the Palestinian cause, which gained adherents and international prestige in the mid-1970s.

In my view, there have been no surprises in the USSR's record. Since Camp David, its approach continues to be characterized by the mixture of opposition, opportunism, and commitment to keeping key clients in power that has been very much at the heart of Soviet diplomacy since the June War. I propose to examine this record by focusing on four questions.

- What have been the Soviet perceptions of, and attitudes toward, the peace process since Camp David?

- What have been the Soviet policies, that is, what did Moscow do or try to do to frustrate the peace process?

- What has been the impact of Soviet policies on the peace process and on the key actors?

*Reprinted by permission of the author and publisher from *The Washington Quarterly* 8, no. 1 (Winter, 1985), pp. 41–55. Copyright 1985 by The Center for Strategic and International Studies, Georgetown University.

• What are the options open to Moscow and, in light of the record, what is likely to be Moscow's probable behavior in the foreseeable future?

Perceptions   After Camp David, most Soviet analysts expected the adoption of some form of the accords—the first, dealing with Egyptian–Israeli relations, the second, with the West Bank and Gaza. Over the years, the focus of their attention shifts but certain themes recur, their timing and emphasis being very much a function of developments in the region. Taken together and systematically traced, these themes constitute a composite of what might be called the official Soviet perception of the peace process. To best evaluate this basic, rather unvarying, perception and relate it to ongoing policy, a thematic approach, rather than a chronological one, will be used on the assumption that the latter would involve a repetitiveness that can safely be dispensed without any risk of overlooking some sudden or subtle change in Soviet attitude.

A few days after the Camp David accords were announced, Leonid Brezhnev, speaking in Baku, conveyed the essence of the Kremlin's attitude toward the peace process. He criticized the exclusion of "lawful participants" and the sacrificing of their interests; deplored the attempt of the United States to fashion a settlement that would split Arab ranks and enable Israel to retain "the fruits of aggression"; and stipulated—repeating what was and has remained the official Soviet position since 1967—that the only basis for a real solution of the Arab–Israeli conflict required "the complete liberation of all the Arab lands occupied by Israel in 1967; full and unequivocal respect for the lawful rights of the Arab people of Palestine, including the right to set up their own independent state; and ensuring reliably guaranteed security for all the countries in the region, including of course Israel also."[1] All subsequent Soviet commentaries and formulations stem from these fundamental statements and the perceptions that underlie them, as is evident from a careful examination of Soviet writings.[2]

For analytical purposes, Soviet perceptions of the peace process since Camp David may be divided into two periods: from Camp David in September 1978 to Israel's invasion of Lebanon in June 1982, and from then to the present. Some commentary on the key themes comprising the Soviet perception may be useful. From September 1978 to June 1982, the following themes predominated:

• Sadat's "betrayal" of Arab cause;
• Disregard of the rights of the Palestinian people;
• U.S. ambitions and manipulation of the peace process;
• anti-Sovietism;
• Soviet participation as a prerequisite for any lasting solution.

*Sadat's "Betrayal"*   The day after Camp David, Tass decried Sadat's "betrayal" and "surrender" to the diktat of Washington and Tel Aviv.

Until his assassination 3 years later, Sadat remained the butt of Soviet fulminations. In the main, he was portrayed as a pawn in U.S. policy, manipulated by a combination of military pressure and economic assistance. However, the alacrity with which he fostered military and strategic cooperation between Egypt and the United States clearly discomfited Moscow and undercut its basic argument, for he often seemed ally, not victim.

Moscow reiterated that Sadat's "capitulation" institutionalized Israel's absorption of East Jerusalem and occupation of the West Bank and Gaza, as well as its stranglehold on most of the Golan Heights. It berated him for ignoring the interests of other Arab countries and the plight of the Palestinian people. By making peace with Israel, he was playing Israel's game, allowing it to neutralize Egypt and giving it a free hand to attack its Arab neighbors (this point received particular attention after June 1982). The Soviet establishment contends that Tel Aviv's aim is to keep the Egyptian front quiet in order to deal with the other Arab parties on its borders, and that as long as the Egyptian–Israeli treaty is operative, the Arab countries are deprived of a military option against Israel, for without Egypt, their strongest component, they lack military credibility. (What Moscow leaves unsaid is its consequent need to play an even greater role in Syria's defense.)

Up until the final Israeli withdrawal from Sinai in April 1982, a number of Soviet commentators suggested that Israel might not withdraw and that the Camp David settlement would unravel. But what the Soviet media consistently stressed was that even if Israel did pull out, control of Sinai would still be in foreign hands, and this time the "change of occupation forces" would bring in U.S. troops as part of a multinational force and limit Egypt's exercise of sovereignty. After Sadat's assassination, Soviet criticisms of Egypt's policy eased somewhat, as Moscow watched to determine Mubarak's course. Gradually, in the wake of the coolness that has affected Egyptian–Israeli relations since Israel's involvement in Lebanon, Moscow has tempered its attacks on Egypt, responded to Mubarak's interest in diplomatic normalization, and looked for new breaches to exploit in Egyptian–Israeli relations.

*Disregard of the Rights of the Palestinian People*  In keeping with previous Soviet statements of support for the creation of a Palestinian state, Moscow dwelt on the failure of the Camp David agreements to deal with the Palestinian question or even to mention the Palestine Liberation Organization, which it avers is "the only legal respresentative of the Palestinians." In a slashing article, V. Kudriavtsev, a leading hardline Soviet commentator on the Middle East, said that even though Camp David rubber-stamped Israel's policy in the occupied territories, "it is impossible to eliminate an entire people at the stroke of a pen"; he accused Israel of seeking "the physical annihilation, if not of the [Palestinian] people as a whole which is simply beyond its strength, then at least of that segment which is struggling actively for the Palestinians' legitimate rights"; and he accused Washington and Tel Aviv of conniving at Camp David to liquidate the radical Palestinians in what is "a deal on active genocide.''[3] With more restraint, Evgenii Primakov, a Middle East scholar and director of the Institute of Oriental Studies of the USSR Academy of Sciences, called the Camp David agreement on the Palestinian issue "nothing but an attempt to artificially eliminate the Palestinian problem and create conditions for Israel's annexation of the territories where the Palestinian people live."[4]

The Soviets insist that the plight of the Palestinians is the crux of the Arab–Israeli conflict and that Camp David does nothing but complicate the problem, making a solution even more remote. Moreover, Camp David gave the Israelis a green light to attack the PLO in Lebanon and expand the Jewish settlements on the West Bank, and it encouraged those elements in Israel that are opposed to any concessions whatsoever.

Moscow denounces Camp David's provision of autonomy talks to decide the fate of the Palestinians living under Israel's occupation and calls for "the Arab people of Palestine" to be permitted to create their own independent state. In aligning itself since the October War with the Arab position espousing statehood for the Palestinians, it has, however, carefully refrained from specifying the precise boundaries of such a state, preferring not to alienate any Palestinian or Arab client and also to retain a bargaining chip in future negotiations with Israel. When the Soviets talk of the need for "a just peace," what they have in mind varies with audience and circumstance. For example, in line with UN Security Council Resolution 242 of November 22, 1967, Moscow stands for a return of "territories" seized in the June War, leaving open the possibility of border adjustments. However, since the October War, it has emphasized the return of "all lands" seized in 1967, implying that it believes a Palestinian state should be established on, and confined to, the borders existing on June 4, 1967. Indeed, in the chilled atmosphere since 1982, some Soviet writers have even hinted at possible support for a rollback to the boundaries laid out in the 1947 partition plan.[5] The issue is very much a part of the disparate signalling in the wings of offstage diplomacy.

*U.S. Ambitions and Manipulation of the Peace Process* Soviet writers maintain that the aim of Camp David was to improve the U.S. strategic position in the Middle East, with a view toward securing U.S. oil interests and excluding the Soviet Union from the region. Luring Egypt to accept a major supporting role, strengthening Israel, and obtaining a military foothold in Sinai were steps to this goal. They point out that with Israel serving as a "strike force" against "progressive" and anti-U.S. Arab regimes, and Egypt providing valuable facilities and access, the United States has greatly augmented its diplomatic assets in the area.

In its efforts to limit the extent of direct U.S. involvement, Moscow opposes the introduction of U.S. troops into the Middle East. It regards the contingent assigned to the non-UN multinational peacekeeping force in Sinai as an extension of the Rapid Deployment Force and, as such, an aggravation to regional tensions and a threat to friendly Arab regimes. The Soviet military press, in particular, reflected this concern, Thus, *Krasnaya zvezda* devoted considerable attention to the different ways that the U.S. military presence was being strengthened—from U.S. involvement in Sinai to the construction of new air bases for Israel in the Negev.

Throughout the post-Camp David period, Soviet commentators have warned that the accords fashioned by U.S. pressure were ephemeral and could not permanently or significantly change the Arab–Israeli conflict. Alexander Bovin, one of *Izvestiia's* top correspondents, called Camp David "an unstable diplomatic mirage."[6] Without the creation of a Palestinian state and the withdrawal of Israel from all Arab lands, no lasting settlement was possible. On the eve of the signing of the Egyptian–Israeli treaty, *Pravda* expressed the Kremlin's innate skepticism.[7] Also, Soviet scholars probed what they called the "contradictions" inherent in Camp David.[8]

*Anti-Sovietism* Soviet analysts criticize Camp David and the peace process for their inherent anti-Soviet bias and animus. Demchenko made this point, noting that *The Washington Post* acknowledged that "anti-Sovietism was the fourth participant in the Camp David talks. It was anti-Sovietism which largely helped the sides to reach agreement."[9] As Moscow sees the situation, it makes no difference whether it is the U.S.–Israeli strategic relationship, U.S.–Egyptian military cooperation, or the (abortive) U.S. involvement in Lebanon, the cutting edge of the U.S. thrust is intended to weaken the Soviet Union.

*Soviet Participation as a Prerequisite for Any Lasting Solution* Time and again, Soviet officials have insisted that a conflict on the scale of the Arab–Israeli conflict cannot be settled without the cooperation of the Soviet Union. They say "it is not a question of national pride or prestige," but a matter of vital national interest.[10] Moscow believes that any agreement on the Middle East made without its participation is not only anti-Soviet in purpose but also seriously lacking in political realism. The question of what kind of settlement Moscow favors or would support—and Western analysts are sharply divided on this matter—is not our concern here. What is pertinent is that Moscow calls for an international conference on the Middle East that would include the PLO and be cochaired by the United States and the Soviet Union. These have been the staples of official Soviet statements not only since Camp David but ever since the briefly convened and quickly adjourned Geneva Conference of December 1973. In the Soviet view, a return to Geneva is a prerequisite for progress toward a permanent Middle East settlement.

These Soviet perceptions were strongly reinforced by Israel's June 1982 invasion of Lebanon. Soviet commentaries hammered away at the connection between the neutralization of Egypt and Israeli "aggression." Moscow minced no words in blaming Camp David for Lebanon. On October 1, 1982, in his speech to the UN General Assembly, Soviet Foreign Minister Gromyko asserted that "the root cause of the Lebanese tragedy lies in Camp David"; because of it, Israel acted with impunity to "commit aggression and perpetuate genocide against the Palestinians.[11] When, on May 17, 1983, the (short-lived) Israeli–Lebanese treaty was signed, Moscow castigated the United States for foisting this "version of the Camp David separate deal" on hapless Lebanon, caustically describing Washington's peacemaking as a mixture of intimidation, force, disregard of Palestinian rights, partition, and loss of sovereignty.[12]

The U.S. armed intervention in Lebanon heightened the concern of Soviet officials, who dismissed the Reagan plan of September 1, 1982 as "anti-Arab," an obvious play to ensure Israeli dominance over the West Bank, while enticing Jordan into the "peace process."

> The policies of the Reagan administration are creating a dangerous level of tension within the regions of the Near and Middle East.
> Under the influence of U.S. policies, the region as a whole is turning into a powder keg. The goal of these policies consists of the following: the establishment of U.S. military control over the resources of the Near and Middle East; the creation of a hotbed of tension close to the Soviet border; the imposition of constant pressure on the USSR from the south; the neutralization of the forces of peace which are struggling to create a zone of peace in the Indian Ocean and to mediate the conflict to the Middle East.[13]

When U.S. troops were withdrawn from Lebanon in February 1984, Moscow hailed the move as evidence of the failure of Reagan's policy and of the dead end to which the Camp David peace process had come.

The overall Soviet perception provided a coherent and consistent explanation for the limits of the Camp David peace process and proved capable of accommodating policy to the possibilities that existed for frustrating U.S. aims and affecting regional developments.

**Policy**   After Camp David the Soviet government found its options severely limited, but Middle East policies have long shown that a superpower intent on staying in the region's great game has opportunities for tactical maneuvering that can have long-term consequences. Patient and wedded to an imperial-minded outlook that emphasizes the need to nurture a strategic environment congenial to the promotion of its diplomatic objectives, Moscow supported regional clients in their efforts to pursue their own bent.

First, Moscow encouraged the Steadfastness Front—the Arab actors (Algeria, Syria, Libya, the People's Democratic Republic of Yemen, and the PLO) committed to war against Israel and opposition to Sadat's policy of reconciliation with Israel—and lent international respectability to the criticisms of a U.S.-engineered peace process. Syrian, Algerian, and Palestinian leaders visiting Moscow received assurances of assistance for improving their "defense potential." In the flush of the initial anti-Camp David mobilization effort, the rival Baathist leaderships of Syria and Iraq signed a unity agreement in October 1978. This, however, ended the following June, when Iraqi President Bakr resigned in favor of Saddam Hussein, who was not interested in any merger with the Syrian

Baathist Party of Hafez Assad and whose ambitions lay in the Gulf rather than the Eastern Mediterranean.

It was Moscow's hope that enhancing the importance of the Steadfastness Front would force the moderate Arab states, especially Jordan and Saudi Arabia, to distance themselves from the United States and to improve relations with the USSR. To Jordan, the Kremlin extended an offer of arms and intercession with Syria to meliorate their tensions. It sent a military delegation in October 1980, and King Hussein went to the Soviet Union in May 1981, but these and related talks accomplished little. Hussein's suspicions of Assad's ambitions in Lebanon, intrigues to fashion a Palestinian leadership dependent on Syria, past hostile actions against the Hashemite monarchy, and assistance to Iran in the Gulf War all militated for a continued basic orientation toward the United States. Nor was Moscow any more successful with Saudi Arabia. Several overtures, manifested in highly favorable articles written in early 1979 in *Literaturnaya gazeta* by Igor Belyaev who is a leading Middle East specialist, and in statements by Soviet officials visiting Kuwait after the fall of the shah of Iran, fell flat once Soviet forces invaded Afghanistan. In the absence of a united Arab approach to countering the consequences of Camp David, there was little Moscow could do but tailor its diplomacy to each Arab leadership, which was often as wary of its ostensible Arab allies as it was of the Soviet Union. Nonetheless, there was benefit of sorts, because the members of the Steadfastness Front each saw utility in strengthening ties with the USSR. From Moscow's perspective, the repolarization of the Arab world held long-term value in the ongoing rivalry between the USSR and the United States.

Second, by brandishing the prospect of a veto in the UN Security Council, the Soviet Union forced disbandment of the UN supervisory force in Sinai, established after the October War for purposes of overseeing Israel's pullback from the Suez Canal and preventing violation of the 1973–1974 limited disengagement agreements. To have acted otherwise would have implied approval of the Egyptian–Israeli treaty and angered the Arabs it was courting.[14] Left to its own devices, Moscow might have opted for some variant of a UN presence rather than to see the creation of the non-UN multinational peacekeeping unit in which U.S. troops participated as the principal component, once the UN mandated force had been terminated. But in UN forums the Soviet Union is the follower, not the fashioner, of hard-line Arab positions on Arab–Israeli issues; and for Arab governments, militant and moderate alike, the primary objective was to deprive the treaty of any UN imprimatur: in their eyes, the attendant low-level U.S. troop deployment was relatively insignificant.

Third, Moscow accommodated the Arab states' efforts to enhance the PLO's international position, though in measured fashion. Originally, this meant nothing new operationally. Moscow continued to supply the PLO with arms and military training, issue statements calling for the establishment of an independent Palestinian state, and support pro-Palestinian resolutions in international forums. Not until October 1981, 3 years after Camp David—and 2 weeks after Sadat's assassination, a timing more coincidental than causal—did the Soviet Union take the ultimate diplomatic step and grant full accreditation to the PLO mission in Moscow. Prior to that, from 1976 to 1981, the PLO had been accredited to the Afro–Asian Solidarity Committee, a nongovernmental Soviet front organization that lacks diplomatic symbolism. When, in December 1983, a Syrian-backed faction challenged Yasir Arafat's leadership in the wake of PLO setbacks in Lebanon at the hands of Israel, Moscow was noticeably upset by the split in the PLO and urged reconciliation, but it was not prepared to jeopardize its special ties to Syria by taking sides in an internecine conflict.

Fourth, the centerpiece of Soviet policy was support for Syria, the key to effective Arab opposition to the Camp David peace process. At Assad's importuning, a friendship treaty was signed in October 1980. Previously Moscow had been the one that coveted a close and more formal connection, but in the fall of 1980 it could not have been eager for additional commitments, given the serious challenges it faced in Poland, in Afghanistan, in relations with Iran, and in trying to find a suitable policy toward the Iran–Iraq War—not to mention its deteriorating relations with the United States. The Kremlin must have approached the prospect of deeper involvement with Syria, whose ambitions in Lebanon had occasioned Soviet criticism as far back as 1976, with strong feelings of characteristic caution and some trepidation. The military stakes rose in the spring of 1981, when Syria moved surface-to-air missiles into the Bekaa Valley of Lebanon and Israel bombed Iraq's nuclear reactor. These events led to the first Soviet–Syrian joint naval exercises in July and to continued Soviet strenthening of Syria's armed forces.

After the 1982 Lebanese crisis erupted, in addition to these four components of Soviet policy, two other perennial components assumed particular prominence, namely, arms transfers and anti-Semitism. Moscow's initial reaction to Israel's invasion and stunning military victories over the PLO in southern Lebanon and the Syrian air force in the Bekaa Valley was uncharacteristic silence. Three days later, on June 9, Brezhnev sent President Reagan a hotline message warning of the dangers of a spreading conflict,[15] but there were no military movements, no major resupply effort, no threats. On June 14, Tass issued a statement denouncing "Israel's blatant brigandage" and demanding a stop to the fighting—a tame arraignment by Soviet standards. All of this, coupled with the absence of authoritative Soviet commentaries, led to the ascendancy in U.S. official circles of the assessment that the Kremlin was experiencing a crisis over what to do or, indeed, whether to do anything. Some even contended that Lebanon was Moscow's worst defeat in the Arab world since 1956 (though this writer has difficulty understanding on what ground such views were based). As so often in the past, Washington misjudged the depth of Moscow's determination to stay in the Middle East game.

If there was uncertainty in the Kremlin over how best to proceed, Reagan's announcement on July 6 of a U.S. agreement to provide troops for a peacekeeping force in Lebanon may well have hastened and sharpened the USSR's response. Brezhnev promptly warned that if U.S. troops were sent to Lebanon "the Soviet Union would build its policy with due consideration of this fact."[16] At about the same time, Tass noted that the USSR was helping Syria "to bolster its defense capability," thereby publicly acknowledging what U.S. intelligence had been reporting for 2 weeks—the transfer of Soviet weapons to Syria by ship.[17] As always, arms were the strong suit in Moscow's hand.

Credit the Kremlin with keeping its perspective and priorities clear. For almost 4 years after Camp David, it had persisted, doing its best to strengthen clients and disrupt the peace process, in the meantime waiting upon new developments to bring new opportunities. Israel's invasion set in motion a set of dynamic, and unpredictable, forces. As Syria was in no immediate danger, Moscow took time to decide on its response. Its delayed and low-key reaction to the Israeli attack did not connote any wavering in its commitment to the Assad regime or basic reappraisal of the centrality of the Syrian connection in its Arab world policy. Nor, given the steady arms flow that started soon after the fighting began—first, replenishment, then, a vastly expanded buildup—it is easy to decipher why Western analysts were ascribing passivity—or crisis, for that matter—to Soviet policy. Even such a consistently perceptive observer of Soviet foreign policy as William Hyland thought Brezhnev's "passivity" remarkable and as possibly portending a "fundamental change" in policy.[18] But there was no change, only consistency; and certainly, no "passivity":

[Within a little more than a year] Moscow provided some $2.5 billion worth of equipment, roughly double what had been lost during the 1982 war, and including advanced fighter aircraft and tanks in numbers exceeding what had been destroyed by the Israelis. It also provided Syria with sophisticated surface-to-air missiles [SA-5s]; 8,000 Soviet personnel—most of them to man these air defense installations and related communications centers, the rest to train Assad's army—and a number of surface-to-surface missiles possessing greater accuracy—though not longer range—than any previously in the Syrian inventory.[19]

The decision to send SA-5s and air defense crews to Syria in late 1982 showed that the Kremlin was not disinclined to enmesh itself still further in the Middle East—that, on the contrary, it had every intention of defending Syria against attack and of striving to reverse U.S. gains from the Lebanese crisis.[20] Although the actual deployment of the SA-5s began in December 1982–January 1983—after Brezhnev's death in November 1982—it was most probably the result of a decision taken before Yuri Andropov succeeded to the leadership (November 1982 to February 1984). If this is so, it buttresses the contention that the Soviet succession problem did not materially constrain Soviet moves in the area: the stewardship of Foreign Minister Gromyko ensured continuity in implementing the essential consensus on Arab–Israeli issues that had existed in the Kremlin since the June War.

The final facet of the Soviet response to Camp David is none other than recourse to the hoary demon—anti-Semitism. On the eve of Camp David, Tass analyst Yuri Tissovskii, and experienced Middle East hand, inserted an anti-Semitic jibe in his commentary: "The name Camp David is also symbolic, as the Israeli flag with the 'Star of David' has always been given preference in Washington to national colors of any Arab country. This is going to happen again."[21] Tissovskii of course did not tell his Soviet readers that the Maryland retreat, originally built for Franklin D. Roosevelt during World War II, was named by President Eisenhower after his grandson David.

Under the best of circumstances, Soviet attacks on Israel and Zionism, those staples of Soviet propaganda, approach the threshold of openly anti-Semitic calumnies, as when the Soviet media denounce "Zionism," whose condemnation by the UN General Assembly in 1975 as "a form of racism was," they proclaim, "no accident."[22] When they cross that threshold, as during the most dangerous period of Nasser's so-called war of attrition in the spring of 1970 and after Israel's invasion of Lebanon in June 1982, they can only be described as obscene. Reeking of hate and catering to base racist emotions, Soviet media denounce "the evils of Zionism," accuse Israel of using Nazi techniques, and allege that there is "much in common between Nazism and Zionism."[23] The caricatures appearing in leading Soviet newspapers would have done Hitler proud. Anti-Israeli, anti-Zionist, and anti-Jewish diatribes are all lumped together; there is no differentiation among them—and none is intended.

There are various explanations for this persistent motif in the USSR's Middle East policy, but in general few analysts consider it an important determinant of Soviet policy, seeing it rather as convenient grist for the Soviet propaganda mill, which can be stepped up or slowed down, depending on the circumstances in the region. Nonetheless, a few comments may be in order concerning the motivations underlying the Soviet Union's current anti-Israel/anti-Jewish campaign. To understand the Kremlin's recourse to it one must never overlook Soviet domestic politics. From Stalin's time, anti-Semitic campaigns have been a corollary of internal crackdowns on larger groups of supposed enemies. The most recent one acquired special intensity under the short-lived tenure of Yuri Andropov. By creating the Anti-Zionist Committee of the Soviet Public in April 1983, the former head of the KGB sought not only to discredit and isolate refuseniks and other dissidents but also to give bite to his campaign for tightened controls and discipline in Soviet society. Konstantin Chernenko has broadened and intensified the stress on ideological orthodoxy.[24]

Kremlin rage triggered the current campaign. Unable to deter an Israeli attack it had repeatedly predicted or to protect its most important Arab client from a severe drubbing—prompting the old canard about the inferiority of Soviet weapons—Moscow struck back with weapons of unquestionable potency—words if not guns. The aim was to wound Israel, and the comparisons with both Nazi policy and Hitler accomplished it. This language, it knew, was not only profoundly offensive to

Israel but was an immediately useful contribution to the Arab effort to brand Israel an outlaw state and foster its international isolation.

Another consideration was undoubtedly the extremely poor relationship with the United States. Given the tattered condition of détente, Moscow felt it had little more to lose from an internal crackdown that would bring U.S. criticism.

Moscow tried to deflect attention away from its own failure to render any effective help to the PLO by fulminations linking the United States to a Jewish–Zionist–Israeli cabal conspiring against the Arabs. It knows that it has no obligation, moral or legal, to defend the PLO, that its support has been consistently tactical, a function of its perceived need to align itself with hardline positions, but not all Arabs appreciated the cynicism underlying Soviet policy toward the PLO—hence the usefulness, from Moscow's perspective, of its anti-Semitic campaign.

Impact    The Lebanese crisis perfectly exemplifies the importance of persistence and patience in foreign policy. That the Soviet Union intends to remain an active participant in the Arab–Israeli sector of the Middle East has been clear since 1967; its opposition to Camp David is but one of a continuing series of cautious but unequivocal steps along an indeterminate political path. Though in the short term thwarted by its inability to prevent the Egyptian–Israeli reconciliation, in the longer term Moscow has not been without influence in adversely affecting the erratic peace process and frustrating further progress toward a comprehensive settlement under the aegis of the United States. Like a seasoned gambler playing in a high-stake game of diplomatic roulette, it backs several numbers at the same time, hoping to parlay a small investment into a big payoff and prevent the United States from coming out ahead. Opportunism underlies Moscow's placing of bets, and specific moves have evolved out of specific circumstances.

The USSR's impact on the peace process has been profound. First, and most important, Soviet military commitments enable Syria to stay in the political game after being trounced by Israel in Lebanon in the summer of 1982, and to emerge 2 years later as once again the predominant force in Lebanon. Soviet arms and military personnel signaled Moscow's intention to protect Syria from attack. Secure under this military umbrella, Hafez Assad fashioned a remarkable political comeback in Lebanon in 1983 and 1984, in the process showing himself to be a consummate strategist. He outintrigued Israel, outmaneuvered the United States, and isolated the Christian Phalange in the Lebanese labyrinth after the assassination of Beshir Gemayel and the massacre at Sabra and Shatila in September 1982 had set in motion powerful and unexpected currents, whose effect was to transform Israel's triumph into a quagmire. Assad's political fortunes—indeed, his very survival—would have been placed in serious jeopardy were it not for regime-sustaining Soviet military support.

Second, by backing Syria, Moscow frustrated U.S. objectives. Indeed, it was instrumental in undermining Washington's involvement in Lebanon: the peacekeeping force dispatched in September 1982 to protect the fledgling government of Amin Gemayel and nudge him toward a formal reconciliation with Israel could not withstand the bitter communal violence unleashed by Syria and had to be withdrawn in February 1984; the U.S.-engineered Israeli–Lebanese agreement of May 17, 1983 had to be scrapped by the Lebanese government a year later, and the effort to extend the Camp David process to include Lebanon and possibly Jordan was shelved indefinitely. Never was the ability of Soviet power to undercut a U.S. initiative in the Middle East through a strengthening of an anti-U.S. client more dramatically revealed. One Soviet analyst, Yuri Glukhov, summed up the Soviet sense of having countered Washington's aims this way:

> We are witnessing the collapse of Washington's Near East strategy elaborated at Camp David and later updated as the "Reagan Plan."
> The mirror of Lebanon's tragedy reflects particularly clearly the grave consequences which resulted from Washington's so-called "peace initiatives," the course of dealing with the Arab countries "separately," in isolation. As a result, the complex problems, far from being unraveled, were drawn still tighter.[25]

By its policy during the Lebanese crisis, when the situation had seemed conducive to the entrenchment of a U.S. military presence, the Soviet Union allayed its clients' anxiety by exposing the limits of the U.S.–Israeli "strategic cooperation."

Third, Soviet arms transfers and willingness to assume extensive military commitments seek to foster regional conflicts and exploit existing tensions and instability. As long as there are key Arab actors who are unwilling to participate in U.S.-sponsored negotiations, Moscow, by supplying them with the military wherewithal to pursue other options, enables their opposition and reaffirms its own determination to prevent a *Pax America* in the Middle East. Moscow's message is that there can be no comprehensive settlement without its cooperation. Notwithstanding setbacks and losses, the Soviet arms-tap remains wide open, and thousands of tanks and hundreds of planes flow into anti-Camp David Arab arsenals. The war in Lebanon shows once again that Soviet arms can keep a client in the regional power game and deprive U.S. clients of permanent gains.

Fourth, Soviet policy also has indirect consequences for the peace process. By its tenacity, the Soviet Union has shown that it cannot long be ignored, that friendship brings benefits and hostility costs, and that improved relations with Moscow can provide a leadership with useful bargaining chips in dealing with the United States and in intra-Arab politics. For example, it is reasonable to assume that the Soviet–Syrian recovery in Lebanon was one of the considerations that influenced King Hussein's refusal to go along with the Reagan plan and become part of the peace process and that it contributed to Hosni Mubarak's decision to normalize Soviet–Egyptian relations as epitomized by the exchange of

ambassadors in September 1984. In both situations, Moscow's resolve to
play an often poor hand, its willingness to increase the ante required to
counter U.S. and Israeli moves, its skill in exploiting unanticipated
developments, and its potential for significant intrusiveness were all
responsible for its remaining very much an integral member of the
ongoing political–strategic game in the Arab–Israeli sector.

Options    As Moscow looks ahead, it sees five basic possibilities, each
             of which has very different policy implications.

First, the Soviet Union can continue its present policy of placing
particular emphasis on strengthening ties with Syria, aiding other
opponents of Camp David, and awaiting regional developments for new
opportunities. Essentially, this means that Moscow does not expect any
major changes to take place in existing bilateral or regional alignments;
that it is content to wait for contradictions to develop between, for
instance, the United States and Egypt, the United States and Israel, and
Egypt and Israel; and that it does not expect any U.S.-generated breakthrough to carry Camp David forward. Time, Moscow may well believe,
is more likely to bring the Arabs closer to the Soviet Union than to the
United States—whether out of their frustration with the U.S. reluctance
to pressure Israel or whether out of internal pressures that place a
premium on pursuing a policy of equidistance. Looking back on its
disappointments after the October War and the Camp David initiative,
Moscow may conclude that the United States had made as many gains
as it is apt to, and that for the foreseeable future regional trends seem
likely to bring an enhanced position and role for the USSR.

A second possibility is that the Soviet Union could find itself faced
with another dramatic Sadat-type initiative by one of the Arab confrontation parties. However unlikely, this has the potential to place the
entire Soviet position in the area in jeopardy, and as such it merits
careful monitoring. Thus, should the PLO recognize the existence of the
state of Israel and agree to negotiate in accordance with the principles
set forth in UN Security Council Resolutions 242 and 338, or should
Assad suddenly emulate Sadat and offer Israel a peace treaty in return
for the Golan Heights and justice for the Palestinians along the lines
noted above or as contained in the Reagan plan, the United States would
again become the diplomatic hub of all activity, and the Soviet Union
might again find itself outside the peace process. Of course, it is possible
that a PLO or Syrian turnabout might be predicated on providing a key
role for the Soviet Union. But the unpredictabilities inherent in such a
contingency are too great, so that Moscow, which dislikes surprises, is
quite satisfied to give Assad the means and the backing to sustain his
preferred line of policy.

A third possibility is that the Soviet Union would have to reconsider
its client relationships in the event that the United States decided to
pressure Israel to make major concessions in order to invest the Camp
David process with new life. This assumes that the U.S. president
would be prepared to make a Middle East settlement the centerpiece of

his foreign policy and to wage an intense domestic campaign to obtain support for such a policy. Though unlikely for many reasons, including the centrality of U.S.–Soviet tensions in the foreign policy pre-occupations of official Washington, such an initiative would bring the United States great prestige in the Arab world and force Moscow to decide how far it would be prepared to go to make itself an indispensable part of the process. For example, would it be prepared to resume diplomatic relations with Israel? Encourage concessions by its clients? Stay aloof in the early stages and wait before acting? Any of these questions has enormous implications for Soviet relations with hardline Arab parties; none has any obvious answers.

Fourth, the Soviet leadership has to consider what its position would be if there is a return to the Geneva Conference. This possibility implies Washington's recognition that no further movement on a comprehensive settlement is possible without Soviet participation (and this could grow out of a U.S. president's frustration with Israel's footdragging), and that only the USSR could persuade Syria to participate. A revival of U.S. interest in a joint U.S.–Soviet effort to find a solution to the Arab–Israeli conflict might take hold if a U.S. president: wanted to improve relations with the Soviet Union and tested the waters, so to speak, by calling for cooperation in the Middle East (an approach Jimmy Carter ineffectually tried in October 1977); did not see the USSR as a major source of tension in the Middle East and did not consider the U.S.–Soviet rivalry there as a zero-sum situation; sought to lessen the possibilities of inadvertent confrontation in the future; and was prepared to risk negotiations that could prove counterproductive to U.S. interests.

For Moscow, a return to Geneva would represent a triumph and vindication of its basic approach to the region. However, it does not see such a possibility crystallizing in the foreseeable future.

A final, and even less likely, option would be for the Soviet Union to exercise pressure on its clients to make concessions and agree to a negotiated settlement. Such a position presupposes that the Kremlin, assessing the costs and benefits that almost two decades of intense engagement in the Arab–Israeli conflict have brought, would have concluded that: the advantages had been modest compared to the disadvantages; this sector of the Middle East was really not worth the risks of further worsening the already poor relations with the United States or of inadvertently becoming involved in a highly explosive regional conflict, the outcome of which was not vital to the promotion of its national interest; and the time had come to put a brake on clients determining the level and intensity of Soviet involvement in Third World conflicts. In a word, Moscow would have to decide that the Arab–Israeli game had not been worth the effort and that the the time had come to put Soviet involvement in the region into a broader political-strategic perspective.

Of these options, continuity is the most likely. Not only is the momentum of a policy-in-motion a force of considerable significance for Kremlin decision makers, but they also have reason to find in the present configuration of players and underlying pressures sufficient basis for optimism about their prospects and about U.S. difficulties to warrant adherence to the essential consensus that has been in place since 1967. As long as Israel is mired in southern Lebanon and the United States is uncertain as to what to do next, the Camp David peace process is no threat to Soviet interests or to a continued Soviet presence in the region.

# Notes

[1]*Pravda*, September 23, 1978.

[2]V. Kudriavtsev, *Pravda*, October 11, 1978.

[3]*Izvestiia*, October 28, 1978.

[4]FBIS/USSR International Affairs, December 19, 1978, F 1.

[5]Sergei Losev, "Ugroza miru na blizhnem vostoke," *SShA* (February 1984), p. 5.

[6]*Izvestiia*, September 20, 1978.

[7]*Pravda*, April 2, 1979.

[8]E.g., A. K. Kislov, "Blizhnii vostok i Kemp-Devidskii Turik," *SShA* (March 1982), p. 37.

[9]*Pravda*, October 13, 1978.

[10]FBIS/USSR International Affairs, December 12, 1983, F 2.

[11]*The New York Times*, October 2, 1982.

[12]FBIS/USSR International Affairs, December 12, 1983, H 2.

[13]See, e.g., Viktor Kremenyuk, *SShA: Bor'ba protiv natsional'no-osvoboditel'nogo dvizheniya* (Moscow: Mysl, 1983), p. 195.

[14]A recent Soviet monograph on the role of the United Nations in the Arab–Israeli conflict, notable for its fairly straightforward and unpolemical presentation, does not mention the UN supervisory force or the policy of the Soviet government on the issue. Soviet writings on the Middle East seldom include much about Soviet policy. [M.E. Khazanov, *OON i Blizhne-vostochnyi krizis* (Moscow: International Relations, 1983)].

[15]Alexander Haig, Jr., *Caveat: Realism, Reagan, and Foreign Policy* (New York: Macmillan, 1984), p. 339.

[16]Excerpt from a letter that Brezhnev sent to Reagan, which Tass issued, as quoted in *The New York Times*, July 9, 1982.

[17]*Baltimore Sun*, July 9, 1982, p. 5.

[18]William G. Hyland, "What's the Soviets' Role in the Mideast?" *Washington Post*, October 3, 1982. See also Dimitri Simes, "Moscow's Middle East," *The New York Times*, November 10, 1982.

[19]Larry L. Fabian, "The Middle East: War Dangers and Receding Peace Prospects," *Foreign Affairs: America and the World 1983*, pp. 634–635.

[20]For a different line of argument see, for example, Karen Dawisha, "The U.S.S.R. in the Middle East: Superpower in Eclipse?" *Foreign Affairs* 61, no. 2 (Winter 1982/83), p. 449.

[21]FBIS/USSR International Affairs, September 7, 1978, F 4.

[22]*Izvestiia*, October 9, 1982.

[23]For example, see FBIS/USSR International Affairs, July 14, 1982, H 1-2; FBIS/USSR International Affairs, January 20, 1984, CC 17: and *Pravda*, January 17, 1984.

[24]*The New York Times*, September 26, 1984.

[25]FBIS/USSR International Affairs, February 23, 1984, H 1.

# 42

## MARIAN LEIGHTON

## Soviet Options and Opportunities in Southern Asia

As the fifth anniversary of Moscow's invasion of Afghanistan passed, it became clear to all but the most inveterate optimists that the Soviets intended to occupy the country permanently and to fight to the last Afghan if necessary. Already, the Soviet military presence and infrastructure in Afghanistan have wrought a profound change in the strategic balance of power throughout the region. Pakistan is now a "frontline" state in the Western effort to ward off Soviet military expansion into the subcontinent, and India, which aspires to regional hegemony in South Asia, hovers in the lengthening shadow of Soviet military might.

Historically, Afghanistan served as a buffer between the British and Russian empires. If Tsarist Russia had taken over Afghanistan in the nineteenth century, maintenance of British control of India—the "crown jewel" of the empire—would have been jeopardized. Neither Great Britain nor Russia was able to subdue the fierce Afghan tribes, however.

During the 1920s the young Communist revolutionary regime in Russia launched a counterinsurgency campaign against the "Basmachi"[1] in Central Asia. The rebels, representing various Muslim tribes that resisted impending Sovietization, used Afghanistan as a sanctuary. Russian diplomatic pressure finally forced the Afghan government to move the insurgents' encampments away from the banks of the Oxus (Amu Darya) River along the Soviet–Afghan border and further into the hinterland. This move, which stretched out the rebels' supply lines and hampered their communications and logistics, was regarded as a turning point in the conflict. Moscow currently is applying the same type of pressure against Pakistan, which has permitted the Afghan mujahideen (variously translated as "freedom fighters" or "holy warriors") to operate along its 1500-mile border with Afghanistan.

Having conquered most of what is now Soviet Central Asia by the 1930s, the Kremlin paid relatively little attention to Afghanistan and the Indian subcontinent until after World War II. India's independence from Great Britain in 1947 and the ensuing establishment of Pakistan created a new configuration of power in the region, but Moscow still tended to regard these states as part of the Western sphere of influence or, at best, as unfriendly neutrals. Only after Stalin's death in 1953 did the Soviet Union begin to court some of the countries of southern Asia. Nikita Khrushchev and Nikolai Bulganin, his prime minister, toured India and Afghanistan (as well as Burma) in 1956. Pakistan at that time was a member of the Baghdad Pact, composed of Iran, Iraq, Turkey, and Britain (the name was changed to Central Treaty Organization, or CENTO, after Iraq dropped out). This was a pro-Western alliance system that encompassed the northern tier of the Middle East and effectively blocked Soviet expansion into the Arab world (despite the famous Soviet arms deal with Egypt in 1955). The United States and Pakistan signed a bilateral defense treaty in 1959 to give the Pakistanis extra assurances about their security.

Afghanistan was officially neutral in the mounting East–West rivalry in the Third World, but it developed close ties with the USSR, which provided economic and military assistance, technical advisers, and road-building teams that constructed the arteries over which Soviet troops and tanks later invaded the country. Afghan requests for American military aid reportedly were rebuffed.

The Soviets developed a keen interest in India, not only for its strategic importance but also because it became a leader of the non-aligned states and, as Sino–Soviet relations broke down in the 1960s, a counterweight to China in Asia (a role also attributed to China by the United States). India and China fought border wars in 1959 and 1962. The USSR refused to support its fellow Communist state and instead supplied arms to India, initiating a military supply relationship that endures to this day. Then, in the mid-1960s, the Soviet Union seized an opportunity to win Pakistan's friendship. An Indo–Pakistani war erupted in 1965. Washington embargoed arms to both belligerents. The Soviets accelerated their military deliveries to New Delhi. In January 1966, after the war ended, Soviet Premier Aleksei Kosygin invited Indian Prime Minister Lal Bahadur Shastri and Pakistani President Mohammed Ayub Khan to Tashkent for what proved to be the first Soviet mediation of a conflict between two non-Communist nations. When war broke out anew in 1971, however, Moscow supported India unequivocally.

An Indo–Soviet Treaty of Peace, Friendship, and Cooperation was signed on August 9, 1971. The salient portion of the accord, Article 9, stipulated that: "In the event of either Party being subjected to an attack or a threat thereof, the High Contracting Parties shall immediately enter into mutual consultations in order to remove such a threat and to take appropriate effective measures to ensure the peace and security of their countries."

Negotiations for the treaty evidently had been underway since about 1968, but events in East Pakistan during 1971 provided new impetus. A secessionist movement there among the majority Bengalis flared into open rebellion against the central government in West Pakistan. Millions of refugees fled to India, severely straining its economy. The period between the signing of the Indo–Soviet treaty and the outbreak of war with Pakistan in December witnessed visits to New Delhi by such top Soviet officials as Foreign Minister Andrei Gromyko (who initialed the treaty), President Nikolai Podgorny, Deputy Foreign Minister Nikolai Firyubin, Air Marshal Pavel Kutakhov, First Deputy Foreign Minister Vasily Kuznetsov, and commander of the air defense forces Gen. Pavel Batitskiy. Moreover, Indian Prime Minister Indira Gandhi made a hastily arranged trip to Moscow in September 1971.

On the eve of the Indian invasion of Pakistan, Moscow airlifted large quantities of sophisticated military hardware to New Delhi. This equipment was viewed generally as proving decisive in the Indian victory. Once all-out war erupted on December 3,[2] the Soviet Union staged a naval demonstration in the Bay of Bengal that evidently aimed to head off U.S. attempts to assist Pakistan. In the international diplomatic sphere, Moscow vetoed a U.N. Security Council resolution demanding a ceasefire and withdrawal of Indian troops from Pakistan. By this action, the Kremlin bought the time that India needed to win a decisive military victory.

The successful outcome of the Indian invasion, which made possible East Pakistan's transformation into the independent nation of Bangladesh, redounded to the benefit of Moscow as well as New Delhi. The USSR emerged as a reliable ally of India, and, by implication, of other Third World nations that might choose to strengthen their ties with Moscow as a means of advancing their regional objectives. The Kremlin's treaty relationship and military assistance to New Delhi also launched it into the role of a key arbiter of South Asian affairs.

While it was generally unrecognized as such at the time, the Soviet-backed Indian attack on Pakistan can be regarded as the opening thrust in Moscow's efforts to construct an Asian collective security system under its aegis. This scheme was first broached publicly by Soviet media in August 1969. A Radio Moscow announcer stated on August 17 that "India, Pakistan and Afghanistan would form the nucleus of the system, which would eventually embrace all countries from the Middle East to Japan." The function and purpose of the scheme were left deliberately vague, but the proposal evidently was directed against the spread of both U.S. and Chinese influence in Asia.

Many Western observers looked upon the USSR's invasion of Afghanistan as a stepping-stone toward eventual Soviet seizure of Iran and the oil fields of the Persian Gulf.[3] Afghanistan, however, is a gateway to the Indian subcontinent rather than to the Gulf. Pouring military manpower and financial resources into Afghanistan arguably detracts from an effort directed against Iran. In any case, there are easier ways to attempt a takeover of Iran, as the Kremlin demonstrated at the end of World War II when it established two Soviet-type "republics" in the northern part of that country under the protection of the Red Army. Considerable Western diplomatic pressure was needed to dislodge the Soviet presence.

Moscow is more likely to seek control of Iran through subversion than overt aggression, but small-scale clashes already have occurred along the Afghan–Iranian frontier, the USSR has denounced Ayatollah Khomeini's regime for aiding the Afghan insurgents, and the deployment of sophisticated Soviet warplanes to Afghanistan has brought Soviet airpower within 2 to 3 hours of the Strait of Hormuz. Moreover, the Soviets perceive a direct strategic link between the Indian subcontinent and the Persian Gulf. Leonid Brezhnev used the occasion of his address to the Indian parliament in December 1980 to propose a five-point plan that essentially called for demilitarization of the Gulf under a Soviet guarantee.[4]

As of this writing, India remains the Kremlin's most dependable ally in South Asia, Pakistan is resisting Soviet blandishments to become more obedient to Moscow's dictates, and active combat continues in Afghanistan. Trends are evolving, however, that may alter the outlook for all three of these South Asian countries.

Indira Gandhi, one of Moscow's most stalwart friends in the Third World, was assassinated in October 1984. Her son and successor, 40-year old Rajiv, is essentially an unknown quantity in the international arena. He pursued a career as a commerical airline pilot while Indira groomed his younger brother, Sanjay, as her heir-apparent. After Sanjay's untimely death in 1980, the prime minister steered a reluctant Rajiv into politics.

Having won an overwhelming majority in the parliamentary elections held in December, Rajiv enjoys a popular mandate that should afford him considerable flexibility in choosing and implementing his policies. Moreover, he has an Italian wife and evidently admires Western technological prowess, managerial expertise, and culture. Rajiv may move toward a more genuine nonalignment without abandoning India's longtime friendship with the USSR (during his mother's rule, Rajiv made four journeys to the Soviet Union). He visited Moscow in May 1985 and Washington in June 1985 and sought closer ties with the United States in the fields of economic and scientific cooperation. The new prime minister also may authorize selective arms purchases in the West without jeopardizing the longstanding Indo–Soviet military supply relationship. In the Third World, Rajiv may be less effective than his mother in providing a diplomatic entree for the Soviets, simply because he lacks Indira's clout. Rajiv has a low-key personality that is devoid of his mother's arrogance. It is too soon to predict, however, whether his policies will provide a change in substance or only in style.

Pakistan, India's neighbor and traditional adversary, also faces a shifting political landscape, but as in the Indian case it is not yet clear whether substantive or merely superficial changes can be expected. General Mohammed Zia ul-Haq, the country's president and chief martial law administrator, has held the reins of power since he deposed Prime Minister Zulfikar Ali Bhutto in a bloodless coup in July 1977 and dissolved the parliament. Bhutto was executed in March 1979 on charges of conspiring to murder a political opponent, but the Pakistan People's Party, which he headed, remains the largest political party in the nation. It is outlawed, as are all political organizations. Bhutto's family is in self-imposed exile but still politically active. A daughter, Benazir, is based in London, where she is seeking international support for an end to the martial-law regime in Islamabad. Bhutto's sons founded an organization, Al-Zulfikar, which has sought to avenge their father's death by terrorist as well as nonviolent means. Al-Zulfikar reportedly has moved its base from Afghanistan to Libya but retains offices in Kabul and New Delhi. It has received varying degrees of support from the Soviet bloc and radical Third World nations.

The major opposition force within Pakistan is the Movement for the Restoration of Democracy (MRD), a coalition of eight banned political groups that ranges across the ideological spectrum but harbors a disproportionate number of leftist (including Marxist) elements. In the autumn of 1983 the MRD launched a nationwide civil disobedience campaign demanding free elections and the restoration of constitutional government. The campaign continued for 3 months but evidently garnered large-scale support only in Sind, Bhutto's home province. A substantial number of politically aware Pakistanis appear to share the contempt of Zia and the military for the country's politicians, who compiled a dismal record of corruption and ineptitude during the period of civilian government in Pakistan.

Having reneged on numerous occasions on his promises to hold elections, Zia finally permitted balloting for local offices at the end of 1984. Then, in January 1985, he announced that voting for the lower chamber of the federal parliament would take place in February, followed by balloting for provincial legislatures, each of which, in turn, would elect members of the upper house of the parliament.[5] However, the election was strictly a nonparty affair, and the continuing existence of Zia's handpicked 350-man advisory council (heavily military in composition) raises doubts as to the authority and prestige that the reconstituted parliament will enjoy.

The new facade of civilian government may give Zia a reprieve from the political discontent simmering in Pakistan and from the pressure of his critics in the West, but it does little to allay the mounting threat to Pakistan's security that stems from the war in neighboring Afghanistan. An unidentified "senior Western diplomat" told a *Wall Street Journal* reporter in late 1984 that:

> Pakistan is in the most difficult foreign-policy predicament it has had for years. Its policy during the . . . Afghanistan conflict has been to avoid angering the Soviets too much by giving the resistance only limited support and by publicly denying any role. But at the same time, it assists anti-Soviet guerrillas by allowing them relatively free movement to and from Afghanistan, by acting as a conduit for arms, and by giving sanctuary to their political parties. Zia has been walking the tightrope very effectively, but the question is whether he can continue doing so if the Soviets continue huffing and puffing.[6]

Faced with the virtual impossibility of trying to seal the Pak–Afghan border, the Soviets have resorted increasingly to "hot pursuit" of the Afghan mujahideen in Pakistan. Soviet and Afghan aircraft almost routinely violate Pakistani airspace. Ground and air attacks have been conducted against Afghan refugee facilities on Pakistani soil, and Pakistani villages nearby have been bombed. This Soviet military activity has been accompanied by dire warnings from Moscow about Islamabad's continuing support for the Afghan resistance.

There are approximately 3 million Afghan refugees in Pakistan; together with some 1.5 million in Iran, they account for one-quarter of the entire population of prewar Afghanistan. Much of the area they occupy in Pakistan is under the writ of tribal leaders rather than the central government. Clashes have occurred between the Afghans (all of whom are armed) and the local Pakistani authorities, as well as among representatives of different refugee groups, which are organized along ethnic and religious lines. This volatile situation is perfectly tailored for the infiltration of Soviet agents-provocateurs into the refugee encampments. The growing dangers to Pakistani security have prompted some officials of the country's outlawed political parties to call for concessions (including Pakistan's diplomatic recognition of the Babrak Karmal regime in Kabul) that would permit the return of the Afghan refugees to their homeland. How steadfastly Zia can resist the internal and external pressures for a halt to Pakistani support of the Afghan freedom fighters will determine the pace of the Soviet Union's efforts to pacify Afghanistan and perhaps direct its expansionist ambitions elsewhere in southern Asia.

Afghanistan seems destined for absorption into the Soviet empire, but the astonishing scope of the resistance offers some assurance that the USSR's timetable will have to be extended and that the military and financial burden of empire building will be considerably greater than the Kremlin's planners had anticipated. Soviet terror tactics—carpet bombing of the mujahideen and innocent civilians alike; burning crops, poisoning wells, and exterminating livestock in order to force Afghans off the land ("migratory genocide"); killing and maiming Afghan children through the use of booby traps fashioned like toys, and press-ganging young men off the streets and out of schools to serve in the puppet army—finally have awakened Western consciousness to the extraordinary brutality of the war. Whether indignation will be matched by more actions in support of the insurgents remains to be seen. The Western media have maintained a remarkable silence about events in Afghanistan—a silence punctuated only on occasion with reports of a Soviet atrocity or the valor of a resistance fighter.

In 1984 the United Nations General Assembly resolution demanding the withdrawal of Soviet troops from Afghanistan drew an even more lopsided majority (119–20 with 14 abstentions) than in previous years.[7] There has been some speculation that sympathetic Western and Islamic countries might be prepared to grant recognition to an Afghan government-in-exile if the political representatives of the various insurgent factions could create a unified organization. In addition, prospects have brightened for the delivery of more and better weapons for the mujahideen. Actions undertaken by the international community on behalf of the Afghan freedom-fighters help to reduce the physical and psychological burden on Pakistan, which up until now has been left virtually alone to bear the wrath of the Soviet Union.

Much has been written about the disunity among the mujahideen, particularly the animosity between the fundamentalist Islamic groups and the more moderate, secular-oriented elements. These differences have precluded efforts to establish an umbrella organization of resistance groups that could coordinate and distribute supplies from abroad and perhaps could create a government-in-exile with broad international support. The internecine political rivalry among mujahideen groups, however, should not obscure the fact that "allegiances and rivalries in Peshawar often have nothing to do with arrangements on the ground inside Afghanistan."[8] There is evidence of tactical collaboration between various mujahideen groups in military operations and intelligence-sharing arrangements directed against the Soviet invaders.

In surveying Moscow's options and opportunities in southern Asia, it is worth keeping in mind that Soviet domestic problems are not severe enough to hamper the conduct of foreign policy. The Kremlin has experienced rapid shifts in the ranks of its top leadership during the past few years after a prolonged period of stability. General Secretary Leonid Brezhnev, who had been in power since 1964, died in November 1982. His successor, former KGB chief Yuri Andropov, held the reins for only 15 months, during which he was physically incapacitated more than one-third of the time. When Andropov died in February 1984, Konstantin Chernenko, a loyal Brezhnevite, became general secretary. By the end of the year, Chernenko, too, was succumbing to illness and old age. In the meantime, Defense Minister Dmitri Ustinov, a fixture in the Kremlin for more than 40 years, died and left another gap in the ruling Communist Party Politburo. Ustinov, like the three top leaders mentioned above, was in his seventies. His successor, Marshal Sergei Sokolov, also is a septuagenerian. Still another important shift in the Soviet leadership occurred with the abrupt removal in September 1984 of Marshal Nikolai Ogarkov, chief of the general staff. Ogarkov was not a Politburo member but evidently was politically ambitious and also voiced ideas about the allocation of national resources that contradicted the prevailing consensus. Mikhail Gorbachev's accession to the top post of the Kremlin, upon the death of Chernenko in March 1985, marked the start of a shift in political power from the gerontocracy to a younger generation. At 54, Gorbachev is the "baby" of the Politburo. Other prominent Politburo members among the new generation include 62-year-old Grigory Romanov, head of the powerful Leningrad party organization, and Geidar Aliyev, 61, a First Deputy Premier and former KGB official from Azerbaijan, who reportedly plays a significant role in Soviet Central Asian affairs. Within weeks of becoming General Secretary, Gorbachev named three new men to the Politburo: Viktor Chebrikov, 62, head of the KGB; Yegor Ligachev, 64, a supervisor of party personnel policy; and Nikolay Ryzhkov, 55, a specialist in the administration of heavy industry.

Those in the West who place their hopes in the upcoming generation of Soviet officials to bring about a mellowing in Moscow's policies have produced no convincing evidence to support their optimism. The younger apparatchiki have witnessed the rise of the USSR from the brink of defeat in World War II to the achievement of superpower status.

By all accounts, they are proud, self-confident, and steeled in the techniques—from disinformation to subversion to coercion and outright aggression—that have advanced Soviet power and influence into every corner of the globe. The new generation of leaders will be no more inclined than were their predecessors to compromise what they regard as vital national interests for the sake of détente abroad or consumerism at home.

It is reasonable to suppose that the war in Afghanistan is more of an embarrassment than an onerous burden for the USSR. Compared with U.S. expenditure of blood and treasure in Vietnam (with which Afghanistan often is erroneously compared), the casualties are minimal and the costs miniscule. Some 5,000–10,000 Soviet soldiers have been killed in the conflict and another 15,000–20,000 wounded.[9] The greatest toll has been taken by disease. The Kremlin has spent $3–$4 billion annually on the war to date; it spends twice that much on a yearly basis to support Cuba. Equipment—notably aircraft—losses in Afghanistan are rising but by no means have reached an intolerable level. The relatively protracted nature of the conflict may have surprised some Soviet military officials who had envisioned a quick victory over ragtag bands of opponents. Politically, however, the Soviets are infinitely patient. Aware of the hopelessness of trying to wean the present generation of Afghans from their socioeconomic customs and religious heritage, they are focusing on converting the next generation to Communism. Thousands of small Afghan children are forcibly separated from their parents and sent to the USSR for education-cum-political indoctrination. This formula worked in Soviet Central Asia and Mongolia; there is no reason to doubt that it can be applied successfully to Afghanistan as well.

Weighed against the disadvantages that the Soviets have encountered in Afghanistan—the elusiveness of the mujahideen, the dramatic and deadly attacks against Soviet personnel and installations, the inability to field a reliable army of Afghans, the failure to reconcile the feuding Khalq and Parcham factions of the Afghan Communist party, the opprobrium generated against Moscow among Third World and Islamic states—are a number of benefits. Afghanistan constitutes a laboratory for testing and refining new Soviet weapons and counterinsurgency techniques (not to mention more odious phenomena such as poison gases). It also offers extensive terrain for the emplacement of infrastructure and arms that can serve Soviet objectives beyond the borders of Afghanistan. The reach of Soviet military power thus has been extended further to the south and west than would have been possible without the invasion. Moscow's enhanced power position in South and Southwest Asia is the foundation and prerequisite for a "correlation of forces" in the region in favor of the Soviet Union. Operating from a favorable "correlation of forces" (of which military power is the primary but by no means the sole component), the Soviets will attempt to persuade India, Pakistan, and other neighboring states that resistance to Soviet predominance in the region would be futile and that accommodation to the Kremlin's power is therefore necessary.

From this perspective, the Soviet Union's military occupation of Afghanistan could intimidate the rest of South Asia to the extent that it would bow to Moscow's dictates. In this sense, moreover, Moscow is utilizing the opportunity afforded by its presence in Afghanistan to circumscribe the foreign policy options of the states in the region and their Western friends.

It is clear from the USSR's disinclination to pursue a negotiated settlement to the Afghan conflict that it is determined to prevail militarily rather than to seek a face-saving solution that would provide a "decent interval" for Afghanistan to revert to its former neutral, buffer status in South Asia. "Proximity talks" in Geneva between Afghan government and Pakistani representatives are taking place on an episodic basis under the sponsorship of Diego Cordovez, the U.N. special envoy to Afghanistan. He shuttles between the rooms where the Pakistani and Afghan negotiators are housed, because Islamabad does not recognize the Soviet puppet regime in Kabul. The question of mujahideen representation at the talks seems never to have been seriously addressed.

If U.N. Secretary General Javier Perez de Cuellar is seeking a formula for a graceful Soviet retreat from Afghanistan, he has not yet understood that the USSR is not interested in retreat—graceful or otherwise. Instead, the Soviets are engaged in a "fight–talk" strategy of the sort that Moscow and Hanoi pursued so brilliantly during the Vietnam War. Applying a mixture of threats and cajolery toward Pakistan, the Soviets are stepping up air and ground raids across the Pak–Afghan frontier while professing to world public opinion their willingness to withdraw from Afghanistan as soon as "interference" in that country by Western "imperialists" ceases. Soviet propaganda portrays Pakistan alternately as a tool of the U.S. "imperialists" and as an instigator in its own right of anti-Soviet activities in Afghanistan.

In essence, the USSR's demarches at the Geneva talks amount to a series of nonnegotiable demands involving an end to all forms of U.S., Pakistani, and Chinese resistance to the Babrak Karmal regime, acceptance of the "irreversibility" of the Afghan revolution, and carte blanche for the Soviets to pacify the country behind the kind of impenetrable curtain they drew down over Eastern Europe 40 years ago. "Indeed," as Soviet specialist William G. Hyland pointed out, "the idea of neutralization and negotiations seems closely linked to several dubious conclusions about the Soviet invasion: that it was the work of the sinister Soviet marshals who overrode the more prudent Kremlin doves (how these doves keep their jobs decade after decade is amazing); that the decision was taken while Brezhnev and Kosygin were on sick leave; that Soviet motives were purely defensive; that they hopelessly miscalculated; that they are stuck in a quagmire. . . ."[10]

Having foreclosed the option of a peaceful settlement in Afghanistan, Moscow must attempt to reconcile India and Pakistan to the extension of its writ into southern Asia. It will be especially wary of moves by those two countries, which have fought three wars since 1948, to sign a nonaggression pact or undertake other measures that will improve their relationship dramatically. The Soviets also will try to prevent any expansion of U.S. or Chinese influence in the Indian subcontinent. Such an expansion could occur if longstanding Sino–Indian border problems and other differences were resolved and India sought Chinese support as a counterweight to growing Soviet military power in the region. It could occur also if the new Indian prime minister pursued an across-the-board improvement in relations with the United States, especially a marked increase in trade that would jeopardize Moscow's virtual monopoly as an arms supplier and purveyor of advanced technology to New Delhi.

As for Pakistan, the current level of its relationship with the United States may be worrisome to the Soviets, but compared with the period when Pakistan belonged to two U.S.-backed military pacts and harbored a then-secret U-2 air base facility on its territory, it would be surprising if Moscow did not perceive a change for the better. Even the extent to which the U.S.–Pakistani bilateral treaty commits Washington to rush to Islamabad's aid in a crisis is uncertain. The Sino–Pakistani link presents more of a symbolic challenge than a military threat to the USSR. In the event of a military confrontation, India probably could handle a Chinese-assisted Pakistani challenge even without direct support by Moscow to New Delhi. In fact, the Kremlin could contribute most meaningfully to an Indian victory by threatening an incident on the Sino–Soviet frontier, thereby obliging China to concentrate its forces there rather than in the area near Pakistan.

During the early part of the Afghan war, Soviet troops annexed the strategically situated Wakhan Corridor in Afghanistan's northeastern panhandle. The 185-mile-wide Corridor, which has formidable terrain and an extremely sparse population, was purposely left in Afghan hands by Great Britain and Russia in order to form a buffer between their empires. The annexation of Wakhan sealed off Afghanistan's only direct border with China and created a Soviet-Pakistani border in Pakistan's northwest corner. Occupation of the Corridor also gave the Soviets control of the western end of a road leading into China. As a result, the Karakorum Highway across the mountains at the "top of the world" is China's only remaining road link to Pakistan. The Wakhan reportedly is administered directly by military authorities in the USSR, rather than by the Soviet military command in Afghanistan.[11] The Wakhan Corridor is an improbable staging area for a Soviet invasion of Pakistan, but the occupation of this finger of territory adds to the psychological, if not physical, isolation and vulnerability of Pakistan.

Moscow's ultimate intentions toward Pakistan are unclear and may be the subject of deliberations at the highest levels of the Soviet political and military leadership. Beyond doubt, however, is the fact that Islamabad's support of the Afghan mujahideen offers Moscow an excellent pretext for destabilizing the country, either through aggression or subversion. The Kremlin's most viable options—to be pursued singly or in combination—appear to be influence-peddling among Pakistani political figures and bureaucrats (notably in the foreign ministry); agitating for the revival of political parties (in the hope that the Communists and their sympathizers could organize freely and work toward creation of a broad coalition of "progressive" forces in the country); stepping up the infiltration of Afghan refugee communities with the goal of exploiting differences among the insurgent organizations and provoking further clashes between Afghans and Pakistanis in the Northwest Frontier Province; and fomenting separatist movements, particularly in Pakistani Baluchistan, which borders on the Indian Ocean. Both the Baluchi and the Pushtun tribes have ethnic kin in Afghanistan; the Pushtun issue inflamed the Pak–Afghan border area and poisoned political relations between Islamabad and Kabul many years prior to the Soviet invasion.[12]

Islamabad, recalling the role that the Soviet Union (in collusion with India) played in the war leading to East Pakistan's transformation into the independent nation of Bangladesh, is concerned that Moscow will abet renewed dismemberment of Pakistan. Ironically, however, the Soviet Union may be inhibited by fear of India's reaction to a further partition of Pakistan. Although New Delhi probably would not object to the fragmentation of Pakistan into a number of small autonomous entities, Soviet attempts to dominate those entities would pose a grave threat to India's military security, as well as destroying India's aspiration to remain the paramount power in South Asia.

In the period immediately preceding Indira Gandhi's assassination, Indo–Pakistani tensions rose to such a fever pitch that many observers predicted war. Is it now possible that these traditional foes will perceive a commonality of interest in preventing the establishment of Soviet hegemony in the subcontinent? It is paradoxical that the Soviet invasion of Afghanistan was the catalyst in revitalizing Pakistan's military relationship with the United States and strengthening its military cooperation with China, thus forcing India into greater dependence on the Soviet Union for modern arms. New Delhi now has an opportunity to break the cycle of military dependence on the USSR by seeking reconciliation with Islamabad. As one scholar observed recently, "Were India to conclude that closer ties to Pakistan lessened its own need for Soviet arms, and that its own power was . . . sufficient to enable it to negotiate on an equal basis with China, it might strike deals with both Islamabad and Beijing and emerge as a powerful regional leader, free from the stigma of the Soviet military connection."[13]

Taking this scenario one step further, however, the USSR might well view Indian moves toward greater independence and regional predominance as a threat to Soviet security interests in South Asia—particularly if Moscow perceives the outlines of an Indo–Pak–Chinese strategic partnership. The Soviet Union then might attempt to foment trouble inside India, either through use of the pro-Soviet Communist Party of India or through manipulation of the multitude of dissident groups that pose a challenge to India's unity.

Although New Delhi may wish to loosen its military ties with Moscow, it is unlikely to undertake any policies that will strain Indo–Soviet friendship beyond tolerable limits. Even the Janata party government that wrested power from Indira Gandhi and her Congress Party in 1977 and held it until January 1980 did not alter the basic parameters of

Soviet–Indian relations. Prime Minister Morarji Desai, head of Janata, repeatedly invoked the virtues of "positive nonalignment," but he made no move toward abrogating the Indo–Soviet friendship treaty or supplanting the USSR as India's principal arms supplier. Rajiv Gandhi probably will follow in Desai's footsteps in these respects—not only to avoid antagonizing Moscow unduly but also because it is almost impossible to envisage an alternative supplier of arms that could match the quantities and generous repayment terms proffered by the Soviets.

Since it signed its first arms agreement with Moscow in November 1960 (covering aircraft and helicopters worth about $300 million), New Delhi has established a pattern of acquiring not only finished equipment but also the technology and the licenses to produce many Soviet military items in Indian arms factories. Non-Communist India receives weapons and equipment of higher quality than do such "fraternal" countries as Vietnam and Cuba. Moreover, India has acquired a number of items that were not yet delivered to the Warsaw Pact countries or even in quantity to the Soviet armed forces themselves. The late Defense Minister Ustinov paid three visits to India—the only non-Communist nation to which he ever traveled. His visit in May 1980 resulted in an arms deal that was valued officially at about $1.6 billion but, in fact, was worth more than double that figure when the nominal interest rates, generous arrangements for amortization, and 17-to-20-year repayment period were taken into account. Ustinov's journey to New Delhi in March 1982 was notable for the large, high-powered delegation that accompanied him—some 80 people in all, including Gen. Pavel Kutakhov, the air force chief of staff; Colonel General Vladimir Yakushin, deputy chief of staff of the army; and Admiral of the Fleet Sergei Gorshkov. Although no new arms deals were announced at the time of the visit, arrangements were discussed during a subsequent trip to Moscow by the Indian defense minister and during other exchanges among defense officials for India to receive such ultramodern systems as the MIG-19 "Fulcrum" fighter aircraft, the T-80 tank, the AN-32 and IL-76 transport planes, sophisticated naval equipment, and the latest generation of air defense missiles.[14]

Ustinov made a week-long visit to India in March 1984, and the Indian defense minister was in the Soviet Union in October when Indira Gandhi's assassination forced him to cut short his trip. Commenting on Ustinov's visit, the *Times of India* wrote:

> Details of the military hardware, the supply of which has been discussed in New Delhi, are not yet known. But from what has been said, it can be deduced that the future supplies might cover MIG-29s and even MIG-31s for the air force, more and newer submarines as well as marine reconnaissance aircraft for the navy, and advanced missiles and artillery for the army. Whether the upgrading of the T-72 tanks to T-80 ones has also figured in the discussions is not known. However, much more important than the range and quality of the arms proposed to be supplied are three other facts which merit attention.
>
> The first and foremost of these is that never before in their dealings with any friendly country, including India, have the Russians ever agreed to

the transfer of equipment still being developed within the Soviet Union itself. In the late sixties they were chary of even discussing the MIG-23 and the Sukhoy-7. Now for the first time, they have freely discussed the MIG-31 which, according to U.S. intelligence, will not be operational for another two or three years. Secondly, as always, the latest Soviet promise is accompanied by Moscow's willingness to transfer the technology for their eventual manufacture in India. And thirdly, it would be entirely wrong to look at the supplies under discussion in the context merely of the massive transfer of highly sophisticated U.S. arms to Pakistan. As Marshal Ustinov has himself hinted in one of his speeches, the wider developments in the Indian Ocean have raised the Soviet Union's stakes in strengthening the defenses of an India determined to uphold its policies of peace, non-alignment and independence.[15]

Indian enterprises produce MIG-23 Flogger aircraft, engines for the T-72 tank, and a wide variety of other up-to-date equipment, and arrangements reportedly have been finalized for the manufacture in India of the advanced versions of Soviet infantry combat vehicles (ICVs).[16] New Delhi has continued to make selective arms purchases in the West, of which the British Jaguar aircraft, French Mirage 2000 fighter planes, West German submarines, and British-made Sea King helicopters and Sea Eagle missiles are the most significant. In addition, India displays interest in buying an airborne early warning control system (AWACS) from the United States. Nevertheless, for the foreseeable future the Soviet Union will continue to supply India with the vast majority of its defense needs.

India's numerical as well as qualitative edge over Pakistan appear so overwhelming that it is difficult to comprehend why the recent arms deal between Pakistan and the United States should cause alarm in New Delhi. The $3.2 billion deal covers both military and economic assistance and carries along with it the provision of 40 F-16 fighter aircraft. Islamabad also seeks to acquire AIM 9L "Sidewinder" missiles and the Grumman E-2 Hawkeye early warning system for the Pakistani air force. Soviet propaganda had a field day exploiting India's concern over Pakistan's forthcoming acquisitions and delighted in contending that Islamabad would not dare use the F-16s against superior Soviet forces in Afghanistan and therefore would deploy them against India.

According to Moscow, the United States is fueling an arms race in the Indian subcontinent, but this contention is far wide of the mark. The real danger in the region is that of nuclear proliferation—a danger that Moscow is virtually helpless to control. India exploded its so-called peaceful nuclear device in 1974. It subsequently has foresworn any intention of becoming a nuclear power but has adamantly refused to sign the nuclear nonproliferation treaty and has studiously ignored suggestions from any quarter concerning the possible transformation of the subcontinent into a nuclear-free zone. On a number of occasions, speculation was rife that India was about to launch a preemptive attack against Pakistan's fledgling nuclear facility before the Paks had an opportunity to test a weapon. Whether or not Pakistan actually has acquired a nuclear device—the "Islamic bomb"—it is generally agreed that a nuclear test would doom further military assistance from the United States. As of this writing, the nuclear fever in South Asia has subsided considerably. Moscow presumably is as reluctant as Western capitals to inject the dangers and uncertainties of the nuclear issue into the volatile politics of the subcontinent.

The most seriously destabilizing element in the balance of power in South Asia is the Soviet military buildup in Afghanistan. Many of the weapons being deployed there (MIG-23 Floggers and IL-38 electronic-control planes, for example) have less relevance for counterinsurgency operations than for power projection and warfighting capability beyond Afghanistan's borders.[17] The introduction of greater numbers of Red Army troops, including elite commando units, into Afghanistan and the upgrading of other forces on the Soviet side of the border with Afghanistan also cannot help but have a sobering effect on the countries of South Asia. The takeover of Afghanistan placed the Soviet army at the Khyber Pass, the historical invasion route into the subcontinent.

The 85,000-man force[18] that carried out the invasion and the initial occupation of Afghanistan was composed of a substantial percentage of draftees from Soviet Central Asia. When it became obvious that these troops were prone to fraternize with their Afghan counterparts (who were ethnically and religiously kindred), they were replaced with Slavic contingents. Nevertheless, the Soviets have faced an uphill struggle in fashioning an Afghan army willing to serve as cannon fodder in their suppression of the insurgency. Approximately 80,000 Afghans were in uniform at the time of the invasion. Defections to the mujahideen and desertions have taken their toll, and fewer than 30,000 Afghans are fighting with the Soviets today. "Afghanization" of the war is not in the cards. Soviet forces in the country have been increased to about 120,000, and the percentage of combat to support forces seems to have risen. The Communist Party Politburo evidently vetoed a proposal by the Soviet military command in Afghanistan to bolster Soviet strength by a heftier margin, but some 40,000 airborne troops committed to the Afghan theater stand poised in Soviet Central Asia to deploy for "specific operations south of the border," according to Western diplomatic sources. Some of these troops have participated in Soviet attacks on the strategically situated Panisher Valley.[19]

Currently, the USSR is in effective control of Afghanistan's major cities and transportation arteries, even though Kabul and other urban centers remain subject to rocket attacks by the mujahideen and ambushes of Soviet convoys occur regularly. More of the war has moved into the air, where the Soviets enjoy an overwhelming superiority through use of their helicopter gunships and high-flying Sukhoi-25 and other aircraft that are virtually immune to attack by the freedom fighters.

Soviet military infrastructure in Afghanistan is impressive and is expanding steadily. It is clearly designed to cope with military contingencies both within the country and further afield. A permanent bridge now spans the Amu Darya river, other bridges and tunnels are under construction, the highway system built in prewar years is being upgraded and extended, and a railroad is planned that will integrate Afghanistan into the grid in the USSR. An overall improvement in transportation and satellite communications facilities is enhancing Soviet logistical and battle-management capabilities within Afghanistan and has obvious implications for neighboring countries that could become future targets of Soviet expansionism. Soviet-built radar sites for early warning and other uses and air defense missiles suggest that Afghanistan is becoming part of the forward defense area for the USSR. In addition, there are unconfirmed reports of underground missile sites in Afghanistan that are heavily guarded and off bounds to Afghans.[20] Moreover, the deployment of SS-20 mobile missiles along the USSR's southern frontier areas in Central Asia has extended the range of Soviet offensive power into areas that previously were beyond reach.

More than a dozen major airfields in Afghanistan have been built or modernized by the Soviets. Many of them are capable of handling the most advanced Soviet aircraft, including Backfire bombers. The construction of an airfield in the Helmand Valley, which began in 1984, is particularly suitable for Soviet reconnaissance flights and tactical operations in the Strait of Hormuz and the Arabian Sea.[21] The Soviets could use their huge airbase at Shindand, in western Afghanistan near Iran, to monitor U.S. naval forces in the Indian Ocean. The air assets assembled at Shindand and other airfields in Afghanistan also could be used to provide air cover for Soviet warships in the Indian Ocean in the event of a conflict.[22] More generally, the buildup of offensive airpower in Afghanistan is a complicating factor in U.S. contingency planning for the Rapid Deployment Force to support American allies in the Middle East or Asia in a crisis. U.S. military planners originally envisaged use of the Force to counteract a Soviet invasion southward from the USSR. The arsenal deployed in Afghanistan during the past few years necessitates coping with the additional threats of a Soviet attack from that country eastward toward Iran and the Persian Gulf or westward toward the Indian subcontinent.[23]

In the words of one South Asian specialist, "The USSR has been willing to pay a stiff price for its Afghan war, not because it sees Afghanistan as a route to the warm waters of the Indian Ocean (or even the Persian Gulf), but because Afghanistan now falls into the category of allied border states that includes Mongolia and Eastern Europe."[24] One can argue about the harshness of the penalty Moscow has paid, but it is clear that Soviet policy toward Afghanistan represents a continuation of the time-honored pattern whereby the Russian Empire successively absorbed the weak states of Central Asia into its domain.

During the past two decades, the wall of containment that the Western powers erected along the Soviet Union's southern periphery has been breached irreparably. Soviet action has demonstrated once again the pertinence of the cliché that nature abhors a vacuum. Although there are many cogent explanations for the Soviet military takeover of Afghanistan, notably the fear of the political and ideological consequences that would flow from the collapse of a Communist regime under insurgent pressure, the concept of the vacuum retains relevance.

The West had largely opted out of South Asia militarily and had even failed to prop up the Shah of Iran, its security pillar in the Persian Gulf, during his time of crisis. It is unlikely that the USSR anticipated the establishment of an Iranian-style fundamentalist Islamic regime in Afghanistan, but a collapse of Afghanistan into civil war and anarchy was a troubling prospect. These circumstances, added to the compelling fear of an unprecedented collapse of a Communist regime, made the invasion appear inevitable in the Kremlin's eyes.[25] To what extent the occupation of Afghanistan expands or contracts Moscow's future options in South Asia depends to a large extent on whether the states of the region develop a modicum of cooperation among themselves or whether renewed conflict erupts that will render them tempting targets of opportunity for Soviet meddling.

## Notes

[1]"Basmachi," translating roughly as "bandits," is a term of derision applied by the Russians to the Central Asian insurgents. The correct term for the insurgency is *Beklar Hareketi*, translated from Turkish as Freemen's Movement. See Martha Brill Olcott, "A Basmachi or Freemen's Revolt in Turkestan," *Soviet Studies* (July 1981), p. 362.

[2]India apparently timed its invasion to ensure that snow blocked the Himalayan passes through which China might have rendered aid to Pakistan.

[3]The Chinese seem to share this view. The 6 June 1983 issue of *Beijing Review* charged that Moscow's strategic goal was "opening a southern passage to the Persian Gulf through Afghanistan."

[4]For Moscow, the virtue of neutralization would be the removal of the Western naval presence from the Gulf region so that the Soviet Union, by virtue of geography, would be the dominant power.

[5]AP, Islamabad, 12 January 1985.

[6]*The Wall Street Journal*, 12 November 1984.

[7]AP, 15 November 1984.

[8]*Washington Post*, 17 October 1983.

[9]See, e.g., *The New York Times*, 19 December 1984.

[10]*Manchester Guardian Weekly*, 23 March 1980.

[11]*Christian Science Monitor*, 4 March 1981.

[12]A "national liberation movement" has been created in Pakistani Baluchistan; its members reportedly receive training and support in Afghanistan. Baluchis also inhabit southeastern Iran.

[13]Stephen P. Cohen, "South Asia after Afghanistan," *Problems of Communism*, January-February 1985, p. 24.

[14]See, e.g., Ahsan Ali Khan, "Military Balance in South Asia," *Asia-Pacific Community*, Summer 1984, pp. 102–105.

[15]*The Times of India*, 12 March 1984.

[16]Ahsan Ali Khan, *op. cit.*, p. 104.

[17]The Floggers are suitable for ground attack support and also could be used to take on any F-16's that Pakistan might send aloft in response to a Soviet air incursion into its territory.

[18]Soviet propaganda labeled this force a "limited contingent."

[19]*Washington Post*, 4 November 1984.

[20]See, e.g., *The Washington Times*, 20 September 1983 and *Business Week*, 4 April 1983, p. 52.

[21]*The New York Times*, 9 April 1984.

[22]*Ibid.*, 6 November 1983.

[23]See, e.g., *The New York Times*, 14 November 1982.

[24]Stephen P. Cohen, *op. cit.*, pp. 24–25.

[25]It is worth speculating whether Soviet troops would have entered the Vietnam War if the Communist regime in Hanoi were in imminent danger of collapse.

# 43      DAVID E. ALBRIGHT

## New Trends in Soviet Policy toward Africa*

The 1980s have witnessed some important changes in Soviet policy toward Africa. These have involved Moscow's broad political strategy with respect to the continent, the means by which it pursues its ends there, and the expectations that it brings to its undertakings.

**Elements of Continuity**    To put the new features in proper focus, it is essential to bear in mind that a number of key aspects of Soviet policy have not altered. The geopolitical priorities that Moscow attaches to Africa have remained essentially the same. In the hierarchy of Soviet global concerns, Africa as a whole continues to rank behind Europe and East Asia, and North Africa retains greater significance than sub-Saharan Africa. Within sub-Saharan Africa, the Horn is still the area of top interest to the USSR.

No state in Africa has emerged as an actual potential rival to the Soviet Union on a global scale, and none has come to pose a security threat to it. Nor has the USSR developed a major dependence on any of the continent's resources. Thus, Africa continues to be an arena in which Moscow's fundamental goals transcend the local setting.

As for these objectives, they too have stayed more or less constant—indeed, they have not changed appreciably since the mid-1960s. In keeping with a more generalized determination to substantiate the USSR's global power status, Soviet leaders have doggedly persevered with efforts to enhance Soviet presence and influence in Africa. They have also persisted in seeking to reduce the roles of the West and China on the continent. Although countering Chinese influence has lost some of the urgency that it had prior to the 1980s, it has retained a high

*Reprinted by permission of the author and publisher from *Africa Notes*, no. 27 (April 29, 1984), pp. 1–10. The views expressed in this chapter are the author's and do not necessarily reflect those of the U.S. Air Force or the U. S. Government. Copyright 1984 by The Center for Strategic and International Studies, Georgetown University.

position on the Soviet agenda. China's attempts—particularly since 1982—to refurbish its image as an alternative Communist source of succor for Africans are not taken lightly.

There has even been carry-over in a key element of Soviet assessments of opportunities in Africa. In the wake of the ousters of radical governments in such countries as Ghana and Mali in the mid-1960s, Soviet analysts concluded that the prospects for fostering a transition to "genuine socialism" anywhere on the continent were dim for the foreseeable future; hence, they greeted the appearance of a number of self-styled Marxist–Leninist governments in the mid-1970s with both caution and skepticism. Their reservations about the near and medium-term outlook for these states was reflected in, among other things, the label that they applied to the ruling parties there—"vanguard parties," as carefully distinguished from Communist parties. Events of the 1980s have done nothing to alter basic Soviet judgments about the chances for "true" revolution in these countries in the years immediately ahead.

The shifts that have taken place in Soviet policy toward Africa in the 1980s, in short, fall primarily into the "how to accomplish" rather than the "what to accomplish" category. The fact that they add up to something less than a complete overhaul of the Soviet approach to the continent does not diminish their consequence. Soviet behavior toward Africa today differs markedly from what it was during the last half of the 1970s.

## Political Strategy in the 1970s

Of the recent modifications in Soviet policy toward the continent, those in the USSR's general political strategy have had the most far-reaching effects.

During the 1970s, and especially from mid-decade on, Moscow believed that ideological affinity offered the most promising openings for pursuing its ends on the continent. This conviction, to be sure, did not blind it to the value of ties with major African states and parties that failed to profess a "socialist orientation." On the contrary, the USSR courted Nigeria vigorously throughout the decade, and in 1976 agreed to help build an iron and steel complex at Ajaokuta which, when completed, will constitute the largest such enterprise in Africa. Morocco also received a great deal of attention. Negotiations that began in 1975 on joint development of phosphate deposits at Meskala eventually resulted in a 1978 agreement whereby the USSR extended $2 billion in assistance to Morocco in return for guaranteed deliveries of phosphate rock for 30 years. This is the largest commitment that Moscow had ever made to a single project in the Third World.

Nonetheless, Soviet leaders clearly felt that elements of ideological similarity afforded them the greatest room for maneuver. A 1976 book on the "socialist-oriented" states of Africa affirmed this viewpoint in the following fashion:

> From the first day of their arising these countries invariably support all basic foreign policy actions of the Soviet Union and of the other socialist

states directed toward the affirmation of the principles of peaceful coexistence in international relations, the repulsing of imperialist aggression, the
struggle against colonialism and neocolonialism and for relaxation of
world tension.[1]

In accordance with such a perspective, the bulk of the USSR's efforts
in Africa went to courting "socialist-oriented" states and parties—
particularly the more radical among them, which Soviet analysts termed
"revolutionary democracies" and "revolutionary democratic parties."
Treaties of friendship and cooperation were concluded with five African
countries during the 1970s—Egypt, Somalia, Angola, Mozambique, and
Ethiopia. All qualified as "revolutionary democracies" in Soviet eyes at
the time of the signing of the treaties, although both Egypt and Somalia
had lost the status by the end of the 1970s and had even renounced their
respective treaties. The most significant aspect of these documents lay in
the provision for consultation between the two signatories in the event
of a security threat to either. Prior to the 1970s, Moscow had maintained
this type of treaty relationship only with Communist states.

Beginning in the mid-1970s, the Communist Party of the Soviet Union
(CPSU) forged strong links with four ruling parties on the continent (in
Angola, Mozambique, Benin, and Congo) and one commission set up to
create such a party (in Ethiopia). These ties encompassed advice on
ideological and organizational matters. All of the countries involved
were "revolutionary democracies."

Soviet economic assistance to African countries during 1975–1979
amounted to $2.7 billion. If the $2 billion to Morocco is excluded from
this total as exceptional, five "revolutionary democracies" (Algeria,
Ethiopia, Angola, Mozambique, and Somalia) accounted for $500 million
of the remaining $700 million. Six other "revolutionary democracies"
(Guinea, Guinea-Bissau, Cape Verde, Madagascar, Congo, and Tanzania) received an additional $71 million.

In 1977, a total of 35,490 Soviet and East European economic technicians were working in Africa, of whom 24,575 were in "revolutionary
democracies." The list of states included Algeria, Angola, Ethiopia,
Guinea, Libya, Mozambique, Somalia, and Tanzania. By 1979, the
figures had become even more striking. Of 49,035 Soviet and East
European technicians on the continent, 41,020 were on assignment in
"revolutionary democracies." They were posted to all of the countries
just mentioned except Somalia, plus Madagascar, Sao Tomé and Prín-
cipe, and Guinea-Bissau.

As for military assistance and sales, $10.5 billion worth of arms went
to African states during 1975–1979. Of that total, $8.88 billion went to
"revolutionary democracies"—Algeria, Angola, Ethiopia, Libya,
Mozambique, and Somalia. Another seven "revolutionary
democracies"—Benin, Cape Verde, Congo, Guinea, Guinea-Bissau,
Madagascar, and Tanzania—accounted for $540 million of the rest.

In 1977, the USSR and its East European allies supplied 5715 military
technicians to African countries, and at least 3075 of them were to be
found helping the militaries of "revolutionary democracies"—Algeria,
Libya, Angola, Ethiopia, Guinea, Guinea-Bissau, and Mozambique. By

1979, the concentration of Soviet and East European technicians in the "revolutionary democracies" of the continent was even higher. Of the 6825 military technicians from the USSR and Eastern Europe in Africa, 6155 were operating in the seven states noted.

## The Afghanistan Watershed

As the 1970s drew to a close, some prominent Soviet analysts were beginning to question the key assumption that underlay the USSR's political strategy with respect to Africa. Specifically, it was argued that the strategy placed too much stress on the ideological outlooks of Africans and ignored other relevant considerations.

Karen Brutents, a deputy director of the International Department of the CPSU, provided perhaps the most detailed critique of the strategy.[2] In somewhat esoteric fashion, he maintained that even countries under "revolutionary democractic" rule normally did not adopt a steadfast posture on political issues of either a domestic or an international nature. He attributed this wavering to class conflict within the ranks of the "revolutionary democrats," and contended that such conflict could result in backsliding and even abandonment of "progressive" attitudes—in part because Western "imperialism" retained strong economic positions in most African states and remained unreconciled to a "socialist orientation."

Departing from the prevailing Soviet assessment, Brutents also argued that only a few ruling groups on the continent had yet to select a path of development, and he pointed out that more had opted for a "capitalist" than for a "socialist" path. Choosing the capitalist option did not eliminate the antagonism between these countries and "imperialism," however, for "imperialism" sought to keep them developing along a "dependent capitalist" instead of a "national capitalist" line. In these circumstances, Brutents reasoned, the "national capitalists" would find it in their interest to cooperate with the USSR and other Communist states to secure a counterweight against "imperialism."

Implicitly, Brutents was proposing that Moscow pay less attention to ideological affinities and pursue a more eclectic policy in advancing its interests in Africa. The Soviet invasion of Afghanistan in December 1979 set in motion a series of events that led to the policy shift proposed by the Brutents school. In the vote on the UN General Assembly resolution calling for the withdrawal of Soviet forces, none of the non-"socialist-oriented" states of the continent backed Moscow on the issue, and the only "revolutionary democratic" countries in Africa that supported the Soviet position were Angola, Ethiopia, and Mozambique. The lesson that Moscow drew from these results was not only that the loyalty of the "revolutionary democratic" countries had limits, but also that more attention should be devoted to developing ties with the non-"socialist-oriented" states.

Since the latter part of 1980, Soviet commentaries on Africa have increasingly reflected the Brutents perspective. Although some analysts continue to be highly laudatory of the continent's "revolutionary democrats," most observers today take care to note their deficiencies as well as their virtues. This new candor is even applied to "revolutionary democrats" in Angola, Mozambique, and Ethiopia. Perhaps more significant, Soviet observers now single out bases for cooperation with political forces not of a "socialist" persuasion. The distinction between "national capitalism" and "dependent capitalism" has become commonplace in Soviet writings and speeches, and even Islamic fundamentalism has received endorsement as a positive factor in certain contexts.

Foreign Minister Andrei Gromyko, a senior member of the CPSU Politburo, placed his personal stamp of approval on the revised strategy in June 1983, when he told a session of the Supreme Soviet: "The Soviet Union's international ties *with states representing a broad political spectrum* testify to recognition of the high prestige of our country, to realization of the fact that practically not a single serious question of world politics can be solved—nor is in fact solved—without its participation. That is as it should be" [italics added].

## Carrying Out the New Strategy

Implementation of this new approach to Africa has taken many forms.

1. An attempt to set some bounds on relations with "revolutionary democrats." Moscow has in no sense forsaken the "revolutionary democrats." Algeria, for example, continues to be the African country with which the USSR maintains the most extensive and diverse economic ties. Libya remains the chief customer for Soviet arms. Since Ethiopia committed itself to establish a vanguard party by September 1984, the CPSU has provided extensive assistance to help it meet this goal. Numerous Ethiopian delegations have visited the USSR to observe the work of the CPSU at all levels: the major groups alone totaled no less than 12 in 1983, and some consisted of 30 or more people. The ruling parties or developing parties of Algeria, Angola, Mozambique, Ethiopia, and Congo received invitations to the Twenty-sixth CPSU Congress in February–March 1981, and high-level representatives from all of them addressed main sessions of the gathering.

The new aspect of the Soviet relationship with the "revolutionary democrats" is that Moscow has sought to make plain its intention to define the terms, and where necessary establish the limits, of the relationship. For instance, despite repeated public statements from Maputo in 1981 that Mozambique would soon become a member of the Soviet-dominated Council for Mutual Economic Assistance (CMEA), membership in that body did not materialize. Nor did the extensive Soviet military aid that was sought in 1981–1982 to cope with the growing threat posed by the antigovernment guerrilla activities of the South African-backed *Resistência Nacional Moçambicana* (MNR).

Libya had a similar experience in 1983. In the wake of another downturn in relations with the United States and Egypt, Mu'ammar al-Qaddafi sent his second in command, 'Adb as-Sallam Jallud, to Moscow in search of a treaty of friendship and cooperation with the USSR, but Jallud came home with just a "preliminary agreement" to "contract a treaty" of this sort. To date, no treaty has been concluded.

2. Courtship of states deemed to have carried out a major ideological retreat in recent years. Egypt affords perhaps the best illustration of this new tack, but Somalia deserves brief mention as well.

During the 1970s, it will be recalled, Egypt fell from the ranks of "socialist-oriented" countries when President Anwar al-Sadat reversed many of the "anticapitalist" policies of the Nasser period, reopened the doors to Western private investment in the Egyptian economy, turned to the United States for military and economic assistance, and signed a peace treaty with Israel. In the process of these undertakings, he tore up the treaty of friendship and cooperation that he had signed with the USSR in 1971 and dismissed the Soviet military advisers who had been working with the Egyptian armed forces. Shortly before his assassination in October 1981, he even accused the Soviet Embassy in Cairo of maintaining contacts with opposition groups plotting his overthrow, and he summarily expelled the offending diplomats as well as all Soviet economic technicians still involved in development projects in Egypt.

Mohammed Hosni Mubarak, Sadat's successor, has done nothing to restore Egypt to "socialist-oriented"status, but he has indicated a desire to improve relations with the USSR. Moscow has labored mightily to capitalize on this opening.

When Egypt in 1982 asked for the return of a number of Soviet technicians for a specific period to complete projects not finished when they had departed in 1981, Moscow rushed to oblige. By the end of the year, more than 60 Soviet technicians had resumed work in Egypt, and the total has grown since. The possibility of cooperation in laying new electrical power lines and in other sorts of economic ventures is being studied.

An Egyptian trade delegation visited Moscow in February 1982, and by the end of the year an agreement had been concluded that provided for Soviet purchase, for the first time since 1978, of Egyptian cotton. On May 26, 1983, Soviet and Egyptian representatives meeting in Moscow signed a number of other trade agreements, including a protocol calling for a "dramatic increase" in trade.

Following up on this breakthrough, Moscow dispatched a 12-man economic team to Cairo in late November 1983 to negotiate a new trade protocol for 1984. The document that emerged from these negotiations on December 1 envisions an increase in the volume of trade turnover from 400 million pounds sterling (about $600 million) in 1983 to 500 million pounds sterling (about $750 million) in 1984.

In April 1983, a Soviet delegation spent 5 days in Cairo discussing the normalization of cultural and scientific relations. Out of these talks came a protocol covering cooperation in culture, science, education, information, and sports for 1983–1984. In September 1983, Oleg Grinevskiy, chief of the Foreign Ministry's Department of Near Eastern Countries, conferred with Egyptian officials in Cairo for 4 days on bilateral relations and the situation in the Middle East. During late August and early September 1983, Soviet trade union leaders played hosts to two groups of Egyptian trade union representatives at a world trade union conference on social and economic effects of disarmament on the power industries. Then in December it was announced that for the first time in a decade a Soviet trade union delegation would visit Egypt in February 1984.

Moscow's recent overtures to Somalia have been more tentative than those to Egypt (in part because of the lower level of receptivity in Mogadiscio); however, they are of particular interest because of the priority accorded the Horn region by both the USSR and the United States.

Somalia lost its classification as a state of "socialist orientation" during the 1970s on two grounds. The government of President Mohammed Siad Barre (1) abandoned a "progressive" course in domestic affairs and (2) invaded the Somali-inhabited Ogaden region of Ethiopia in July 1977 and subsequently renounced its 1974 treaty of friendship and cooperation with the USSR after Moscow refused to back the annexation effort. Particularly galling to Moscow were the cancellation of Soviet military access to facilities at Berbera and elsewhere, and the expulsion of some 1600 Soviet military advisers posted to Somalia.

Siad Barre's actions in the early 1980s reinforced Soviet judgments about Somalia's deviation from the path of "socialist orientation." In the face of rising internal opposition, he paid less and less heed to social and economic matters, concentrated upon repressing his opponents, and sought military aid from the United States to help him stay in power.

Nevertheless, Moscow recently has sharply reduced its statements of support for the opposition Democratic Front for the Salvation of Somalia (DFSS), and in July 1983 the USSR reached agreement with the Siad Barre government on reestablishing Soviet diplomatic representation in Mogadiscio at ambassadorial level.

3. Maneuvering to find nonideological grounds for links with "socialist-oriented" governments wary of the USSR. Although the new governments that came to power in Uganda and Zimbabwe in the early 1980s are clearly "socialist-oriented" by Soviet criteria, both President Milton Obote and Prime Minister Robert Mugabe had good reason to hold the USSR at arm's length. During his earlier tenure as prime minister and then president of Uganda (1962–1971), Obote had developed fairly substantial ties with the USSR, yet when Major-General Idi Amin Dada took power in 1971, Moscow did not hesitate to establish links with the new regime. Indeed, it was Soviet military aid that permitted the despotic Amin to maintain his rule until 1979. In the case of Zimbabwe, Moscow had focused its attention and military assistance exclusively on the Zimbabwe African People's Union (ZAPU) led by Joshua Nkomo throughout the "war of national liberation," and the sweeping victory of Mugabe's Zimbabwe African National Union (ZANU) in the 1980 preindependence elections came as a surprise to Soviet leaders.

The USSR took its initial steps to rebuild relations with Obote in 1981. These included the dispatch to Kampala in October of a delegation of the Soviet Afro–Asian Solidarity Committee. But it was not until 1982 that the basic economic thrust of Moscow's approach to the achievement of its aim became evident. In January of that year, the Soviet Embassy's commercial counselor met with Minister of Commerce J. Aliro-Omara to discuss the expansion of trade between their two states, and the Soviet official indicated that Moscow would increase imports from Uganda and was even willing to extend credits to facilitate purchases from the USSR. The following June, a ministerial-level Ugandan delegation visited Moscow to talk about problems associated with the country's rehabilitation. This visit eventually resulted, in March 1983, in an $11 million Soviet credit, earmarked largely for specialists and equipment for an agricultural college.

In August 1983, Moscow went even further. It agreed to cancel a sizable portion of Uganda's debts to the USSR, to reschedule repayment of the rest to begin in 15 years, and to extend a loan for the rehabilitation of the Lira spinning mill and the expansion of Busitema agricultural college. Both of these projects had originally been launched with Soviet aid in the 1960s. The USSR also undertook to send experts and doctors to Uganda and to train Ugandans at Soviet universities.

To underline its humanitarian concerns, Moscow adopted some additional measures. In November 1983, for instance, the Soviet Red Cross Society donated more than 1.5 tons of children's food to assist in the care of displaced persons in Luwero, Mubende, and Mpigi.

During the long period when Mugabe stalled on the opening of formal diplomatic relations with the USSR (from independence in April 1980 to February 1981), Moscow confined its wooing efforts to positive comments in the Soviet media on the government's accomplishments. Since the establishment of an embassy in Harare in 1981, the primary strategy appears to have been to create a web of diversified functional contacts between the two countries.

There have been several Soviet initiatives in the realm of media cooperation. A television and radio accord signed in July 1982 provides for exchange of television films, programs, and newsreel material on the political, economic, and cultural life of the USSR and Zimbabwe. An agreement signed by the Zimbabwe Inter-African News Agency and TASS in December 1982 envisioned an exchange of information and other forms of cooperation. Perhaps most important, TASS in 1983 reacted quickly to Harare's expressed desire to obtain and disseminate news on the international situation from socialist as well as capitalist sources, and in July of that year a contract for TASS servicing was signed. Since 1981, Moscow has dispatched a number of cultural and friendship groups to Zimbabwe. Those arriving during 1983 included a women's delegation, the Bolshoi Ballet, and a general friendship delegation.

In July 1983, Soviet trade union officials received a group of leaders of the Zimbabwe Congress of Trade Unions. During the course of the visit, an agreement was signed on basic principles for the development of friendly links and cooperation, and the Soviet hosts "gratefully accepted" an invitation to send a trade union delegation to Zimbabwe in 1984.

Late 1983 brought still another addition to the list of functional areas in which the USSR is active. The first Soviet trade group to visit Zimbabwe arrived in December of that year.

Since early 1983, however, Soviet cultivation of the Harare government has assumed a more straightforwardly political dimension as well,
in response to Mugabe's publicly expressed desire to follow a genuinely
nonaligned course. In May 1983, the Soviet media applauded the prime
minister's 11-day tour of Hungary, Czechoslovakia, and East Germany,
and his statement that he would visit the USSR soon. During Mugabe's
official visit to the United States in September, Soviet commentaries took
note of the friction with the Reagan administration over Zimbabwe's
abstention in the UN Security Council vote on the shooting down of
Korean Air Lines Flight 007. In October, Zimbabwe's cosponsorship of a
vetoed Security Council resolution condemning the U.S. intervention in
Grenada was underscored.[3] At the end of the year, the Reagan administration's decision to cut aid to Zimbabwe was deplored, and it was
attributed (not inaccurately) to the Harare government's actions on the
KAL and Grenada issues.[4]

4. Maintenance, on a gradated basis, of party-to-party contacts with a
wide array of ruling African parties. During the 1970s, the CPSU carried
on official contacts with a number of ruling African parties, especially
those of a "vanguard" type, but the 1980s have produced a major
expansion of the targets and the substance of such contacts.

Governing "revolutionary democratic" parties continue to garner the
most attention from the CPSU, and their relations with the Soviet party
remain broader in scope than those of any other ruling African parties.
Yet "socialist-oriented" parties of a non-"revolutionary democratic"
kind have acquired additional status in the eyes of the CPSU in the
1980s. This change was readily apparent from the list of governing
African parties that received invitations to attend the Twenty-sixth
Congress of the CPSU in February–March 1981. Names found on the
1981 list that were not on the list for the Twenty-fifth CPSU Congress in
1976 included Burundi's *Union pour le Progrès National*, Mali's *Union
Démocratique du Peuple Malian*, Sierra Leone's All-People's Congress, and
Zambia's United National Independence Party (UNIP).

As the handling of Zambia's UNIP since the turn of the decade
illustrates, increased Soviet efforts to engage in interaction with
"socialist-oriented" non-"revolutionary democratic" parties have
tended to go along with the upgrading of their standing. In April 1981,
CPSU representatives signed an accord with UNIP officials to establish
interparty dialogue. Under this broad umbrella, a two-man UNIP delegation left Lusaka in August of that year for a 3-week study tour of the
USSR. In March 1982, L. K. Shepetis, secretary of the CPSU's organization in the Lithuanian Republic of the USSR, journeyed to Lusaka for
conversations with key UNIP officials, and 3 months later Humphrey
Mulemba, secretary-general of UNIP, headed a delegation to Moscow.
Another UNIP group was in the USSR in November and December 1982
for the purpose of studying agriculture. In March 1983, a CPSU group
met with UNIP officials in Lusaka to work out proposed party contacts
for 1983–1984. The following August, a UNIP delegation headed by O.
Muskua, minister of state in the Zambian Ministry of Foreign Affairs,
spent about 2 weeks in the USSR.

An even more revealing aspect of the new approach has been CPSU cultivation of contacts with parties not deemed to be "socialist-oriented" at all. In May 1981, for instance, A. H. Mivedor, a member of the Political Bureau of Togo's ruling *Rassemblement du Peuple Togolais*, journeyed to the USSR at Soviet invitation for a stay of nearly 2 weeks. The following July, a delegation from the governing National Party of Nigeria, led by the party chairman, A. M. A. Akimloye, visited the USSR for the first time.

Such contacts, to be sure, are not pursued with the depth and intensity of those with "socialist-oriented" parties and particularly those categorized as "revolutionary democratic," but careful thought clearly goes into each overture and the follow-through. An October 1, 1983 Radio Moscow commentary in honor of Nigeria's national day removed any doubt on this score. The recent Nigerian elections were credited with proving that the country's "internal stability and national unity" were "firm enough," and the "stronger unity and stability" evident were attributed "to the fact that Nigeria's ruling National Party pursued the right course in its economic and social policy."

5. Wooing of important countries with a "capitalist orientation" to which the USSR had paid relatively little heed in the 1970s. The three countries that best demonstrate this new dimension of Soviet policy in the 1980s are Zaire, Tunisia, and Kenya.

The courtship of Zaire evidenced itself in 1981, when the first exchange of parliamentary delegations took place between the two states. Representatives of the Supreme Soviet visited Kinshasa in May, and a parliamentary group from Zaire traveled to Moscow in August. Although Moscow was critical of Mobutu's signature of a 5-year military cooperation agreement with Israel in January 1983,[5] the courtship of Kinshasa has continued. In late January and early February 1983, representatives of the Central Committee of the USSR Union of Workers in the Construction and Building Materials Industry spent 7 days in Kinshasa, and they signed a joint communique with the *Union National des Travailleurs du Zaire* at the conclusion of the visit. Of more significance is an agreement on cultural and scientific cooperation and a protocol on specific forms of cooperation negotiated by Deputy Foreign Minister L. F. Ilichev and Linguema Douliza, secretary of state for international cooperation in Zaire's Ministry of Foreign Affairs, in Moscow in April 1983. In December 1983, the fifth session of the joint Zaire–Soviet Union Cooperation Commission met in Zaire. This gathering produced an agreement for cooperation in the merchant marine field.

In the case of Tunisia, Moscow began to lay the groundwork for a closer relationship in 1982. In August of that year, a major delegation from the Supreme Soviet arrived in Tunis, where they met with President Habib Bourguiba and other top leaders. In mid-May 1983, a delegation headed by the president of the Presidium of the Union of Soviet Societies for Friendship and Cultural Relations with Foreign Countries visited Tunis, and its members also saw President Bourguiba, Prime Minister Mohammed Mzali, and Foreign Minister Beji Caid es-

Sebse. In September, Mahmoud Mestiri, Tunisia's secretary of state for foreign affairs, travelled to Moscow for discussions on both bilateral and general international problems with officials of the Ministry of Foreign Affairs.

In October 1983, Yakov Ryabov, a chairman of the USSR State Committee for External Economic Relations, was in Tunisia to take part in the opening ceremonies for the Jumin River dam, a project conceived by specialists at a Kiev institute. During Ryabov's visit, a new agreement for economic and technical cooperation in the construction of hydrotechnical projects was signed. Under its terms, Moscow promised to provide aid valued at 17 million Tunisian dinars (about $25 million) to build an irrigation complex at Sidi al-Barak and three dams on the Tin, Douimis, and Melah rivers. In addition, the USSR assumed responsibility for study and prospecting work, the supply of necessary equipment and specialists, and training of Tunisian personnel to build and operate the project.

Of comparable significance were the talks that T. B. Guzhenko, minister of the maritime fleet, had with Tunisian officials in December 1983. These yielded a maritime transport agreement whereby the USSR and Tunisia are to work together in establishing a regular line between Tunisian and Soviet ports, in carrying out advanced maritime training, in planning a port workers' training center and a naval repair center in Tunisia, and in bringing about cooperation between the merchant marine administration and Tunisian port authorities.

The Soviet approach to Kenya remained low-key until 1983. In December 1981, the two governments concluded a protocol for scientific and cultural cooperation (which included provisions for the extension of scholarships to Kenyan students and postgraduates to study in the USSR, and for the exchange of teachers, scientists, and artists). When a fairly low-level delegation visited Nairobi in November 1982, a member of the Soviet Embassy staff urged President Daniel arap Moi to present a tangible proposal to Soviet authorities in elaboration of his verbal appeal for more technical cooperation between Kenya and the USSR, especially in the training of graduate students.

But it was only in 1983 that Kenya became a focus of major activity. In March of that year, a delegation from the USSR Chamber of Commerce and Industry visited Nairobi and entered into an agreement with the Kenyan Chamber of Commerce to promote increased trade. In July, a visiting four-man Soviet trade delegation headed by the USSR's deputy minister of foreign trade proposed to Kenyan officials the signature of a formal trade agreement. At about the same juncture, a Kenyan trade group was in Moscow negotiating with Soviet representatives. A trade accord was subsequently signed.

In early December, agreement was reached on a new plan for cultural and scientific cooperation, which included provisions for 60 scholarships for Kenyan students to attend Soviet educational institutions and for eight Soviet doctors to work in Kenyan hospitals. At year's end, a Soviet delegation headed by a deputy chairman of the Presidium of the USSR Supreme Soviet participated in the celebrations of the Twentieth anniversary of Kenya's independence.

6. Cultivation of ties with minor non-"socialist-oriented" states. Distinguishing "less important" from "more important" African countries poses problems, for physical dimensions, sizes of populations, and gross national products do not suffice as criteria. Strategic location or the possession of a critical resource can give significance to a state that fails all other litmus tests. Nevertheless, few observers would quarrel with the judgment that Senegal, Gambia, Togo, Cameroon, and Lesotho belong in the minor category from the Soviet perspective.

In 1983 alone, the USSR made at least one major overture toward each of these countries. During the year, two Soviet delegations of consequence arrived in Senegal: a group from Baku toured Dakar in March, and a parliamentary group visited Senegal in November (and invited the National Assembly to send a delegation to the USSR). The parliamentary group subsequently was the guest of the Gambian legislature for several days.

In the case of Togo, Soviet trade union leaders played hosts to Barnabo Nangbog, secretary-general of the *Confédération Nationale des Travailleurs du Togo*, and several of his associates in May, and the two sides signed an agreement on ties and cooperation between their organizations. Perhaps more important, a delegation from the Soviet Afro–Asian Solidarity Committee met with President Gnassingbe Eyadéma while on a visit to Lomé in August.

New relationships with Cameroon included the signature in late March of an agreement between the Soviet news agency TASS and the *Société de Presse et d'Edition du Cameroun* on exchange of information and Soviet assistance in the training of Cameroonian specialists in communications. In August, a delegation led by S. Tandeng Muna, chairman of Cameroon's National Assembly, met with various officials (including V. P. Ruben, president of the Soviet of Nationalities of the USSR's Supreme Soviet) in the course of a visit to Moscow.

Prime Minister Leabua Jonathan of Lesotho made an official visit to the USSR in May, and the following month the first resident Soviet ambassador arrived in Maseru.

7. Diversification of contacts with opposition political elements in key non-"socialist-oriented" states. Moscow's new emphasis on government-to-government relations across a broader ideological spectrum implies no commitment to refrain from relations with other local political forces. Indeed, Soviet relations with opposition groups today tend to be more diverse than they were in the 1970s, when Soviet interest focused almost exclusively on "socialist-oriented" segments of the opposition (and often just the Marxist–Leninist ones). Morocco and South Africa provide two somewhat different kinds of examples.

In Morocco prior to the 1980s, the USSR lavished nearly all attention not directed toward the government on the *Parti du Progrès et du Socialisme* (PPS), the local Communist party. Beginning in 1982, however, Moscow established links with other political elements. In April of that year, a Soviet delegation attended the Eleventh Congress of the Istiqlal Party. In May, a CPSU group headed by Karen Brutents, which was visiting Morocco at the invitation of the PPS, met with the leaders of both the Istiqlal and Morocco's *Union Socialiste des Forces Populaires*

(USFP). In the discussions with the latter, even the possibility of formal party ties with the CPSU was raised. In April 1983, N. N. Ponomarev, deputy chairman of the USSR People's Control Committee, attended the Fourth Congress of Morocco's *Union Nationale des Forces Populaire*, (UNFB). The following December, Brutents, in Morocco again for the fortieth anniversary of the founding of the PPS, conferred with Abderrahim Bouabid, first secretary of the USFP, on their shared interest in developing party contacts and ties.

Soviet attitudes toward South African opposition forces are more complicated than is generally perceived. For many years, the USSR's attention and support was concentrated in the South African Communist Party (SACP) and the African National Congress (ANC), in which the SACP has some important representation. In the 1980s, however, Moscow has been showing increasing sensitivity to the proliferation of significant political forces. For example, the Soviet media has paid close heed to the recent constitutional changes that will establish elected Coloured and Asian houses in a new tricameral parliament—albeit in commentaries that view this development as another Afrikaner attempt to divide and rule. More striking yet, Soviet diplomats in Washington responded positively to the request of Gatsha Buthelezi, KwaZulu's chief minister, to meet with them during his visit to the United States in October 1982.

## Means

During the 1980s, the weight that the USSR accords military instruments in pursuing its ends in Africa has decreased, and there has been a corresponding rise in the importance that it attaches to other instruments—particularly economic ones. These alterations have been relative in nature, however, and military instruments still play the dominant role in overall Soviet operations.

Some figures will help to clarify the extent of the shifts. During 1975–1979, as noted earlier, the USSR delivered $10.5 billion, or $2.03 billion a year on the average, worth of arms to African states (plus an unknown sum to movements such as the ANC, SWAPO, and ZAPU). Commitments of economic aid during the same period amounted to $2.7 billion, or an annual average of $450 million. If, as suggested earlier, the $2 billion in assistance to Morocco is treated as something out of the ordinary, the figures were $700 million and $140 million, respectively. For the years 1977–1979, the USSR's trade turnover with African countries averaged a little more than 1.4 billion rubles (or roughly $1.8 billion). Of this total, exports to the continent accounted for nearly 630 million rubles (about $820 million); imports from there, almost 780 million rubles (about $1.02 billion).

In contrast, Soviet commitments in 1981–1982 to provide arms to African states—a more sensitive indicator of the change in Moscow's policy than deliveries, because an interval normally passes before arms promised actually arrive—reached only $2.43 billion, or an annual average of $1.215 billion. During 1980–1982, the USSR extended $1.4 billion, or $467 million a year on the average, of economic aid to African countries. Its trade turnover with African states during the same period averaged about 2.4 billion rubles (more than $3 billion) a year—nearly twice the figure for 1977–1979. The annual average for exports exceeded 1.1 billion rubles (almost $1.5 billion), while that for imports fell only a little shy of 1.3 billion rubles (about $1.7 billion).

The increased stress on economic instruments has been particularly evident with respect to specific countries. Four states have received considerably more economic credits since the beginning of the 1980s than they did during the last half of the 1970s:

• Algeria stands at the top of the list. During 1975–1979, Moscow made no new commitments of economic assistance to Algeria; the figure for such commitments thus far in the 1980s has exceeded $600 million. Major projects involved include the construction of a gas pipeline through the Algerian Sahara and the building of a strategic railroad line on the western part of Algeria's high plateau.

• Mozambique and Angola signed 10-year economic agreements with the Soviet Union in 1981 and 1982, respectively, and significant extensions of Soviet economic aid to these countries followed soon thereafter. Whereas the USSR undertook to furnish only $5 million in economic assistance to Mozambique during 1975–1979, the total of its commitments in the 1980s has now mounted to somewhere in the neighborhood of $100 million. One of the major undertakings for which this assistance is earmarked is the establishment of 11 large farming cooperatives intended to be the producers of more than half of Mozambique's cotton. It should also be noted that East Germany has committed itself to provide substantial help for the rehabilitation of Mozambique's railroads.

At the time the 10-year agreement with Angola was signed in early 1982, Soviet officials reportedly spoke in terms of $2 billion of assistance over the period of the accord—a significant jump from the $15 million extended to the Luanda government in 1975–1979. To date, aid valued at more than $400 million has been announced for a number of specific projects. Perhaps the most important of these is a hydropower station to be constructed on the Cuanza River in Malanje District that will double the aggregate capacity of Angola's power-generating facilities; a dam to be built nearby would create a water reservoir sufficient to irrigate more than 400,000 hectares of land. Other major projects include the launching of three cotton enterprises and the setting up of an agricultural experimental laboratory.

• Madagascar, which got $20 million in Soviet economic credits in 1975–1979, has received something approaching $100 million worth of such credits in the 1980s. The construction of a 225-kilometer road through a key agricultural area of the island (from Ambalabe through Mahanoro to Marolambo) is one of the projects to be supported by this assistance.

Three other states have benefited in more modest ways from Moscow's greater willingness to extend economic help to African countries. Uganda and Benin, which obtained no economic aid whatsoever from the USSR in the 1975–1979 period, have received economic aid amounting to perhaps as much as $25 million and to $5 million, respectively, in the 1980s. Ghana, which obtained Soviet aid totaling about $1 million in the 1975–1979 period, has begun to get assistance in a variety of forms since the Rawlings government signed an agreement on economic and technical cooperation in late 1982. Under the terms of this accord, Moscow undertakes to provide technical assistance to help Ghana complete and make operative a factory in Tarkwa for purifying gold, a school in Tema for professional technical training, a ferroconcrete construction plant in Accra, and other projects. Soviet specialists will also conduct the geological survey and planning work for the building of a hydroproject on the Black Volta River, and the USSR will supply the equipment to construct the project.

Figures for Soviet trade with a sampling of African countries are equally revealing. In 1980–1982, the average annual trade turnover with four African states jumped sharply in comparison with that for 1977–1979. With Ethiopia, it rose from 52 million rubles (about $67 million) to 166 million rubles (about $216 million); with Libya, from 231 rubles (about $300 million) to 800 million rubles (about $1.04 billion); with Morocco, from 112 million rubles (about $146 million) to 218 million rubles (about $283 million); and with Nigeria, from 59 million rubles (about $77 million) to 188 million rubles (about $244 million). Soviet sales accounted for the bulk of the upswing in the cases of Ethiopia and Nigeria. Both Soviet sales and Soviet purchases were responsible for the increase in the figure for Morocco. The growth in Soviet–Libyan exchanges is attributable primarily to Soviet purchases.

There has also been significant, if less pronounced, expansion of the USSR's trade with three additional African countries. The average yearly turnover in trade with Algeria went from 139 million rubles (about $181 million) in 1977–1979 to 177 million rubles (about $230 million) in 1980–1982; with Angola, from 67 million rubles (about $87 million) to 88 million rubles (about $114 million); and with Mozambique, from 15 million rubles (about $20 million) to 36 million rubles (about $47 million). A new 3-year trade agreement signed with Mozambique in 1983 envisions a trade turnover of some $300 million during the period of the accord. In all three of these cases, mounting Soviet sales have been the primary factor behind the increase in overall trade.

Soviet
Worries

As the 1980s have progressed, Moscow has recognized that the attainment of its goals in Africa may entail far greater costs than it anticipated earlier. In the economic realm, Soviet commentators have more and more frequently conceded that Africa confronts an "agonizingly difficult" path in "advancing toward prosperity and progress." Writing in *Izvestiya* on June 15, 1983, after the Organization of African Unity summit in Addis Ababa, for example, Aleksandr Bovin held that enormous problems impede the development of African states, and he mentioned specifically the continent's uncontrolled urbanization, its growing inability to supply itself with food, its large number of refugees, and the sharp fall in the world prices of its raw materials in recent years.

These severe conditions, Soviet observers now grant, preoccupy African leaders. Implicit in this open admission is an acknowledgment that a would-be global power cannot blindly cling to the position set forth by Soviet Foreign Minister Gromyko in a memorandum he submitted to the United Nations in October 1976. This maintained that "the Soviet Union cannot fail to be concerned for the well-being of its own people" and declared that the USSR's "potential for rendering economic assistance is not infinite."

Indications of a revised Soviet assessment of the burdens that involvement in Africa may impose can be found in the military sphere too. These have related principally to South Africa.

After South Africa ended its direct intervention in the Angolan civil war in 1976, Moscow assumed that protecting Soviet friends in southern Africa, especially the new governments in Mozambique and Angola, would not require major outlays. The Luanda government requested that Cuban troops remain in Angola at Angolan expense to help stabilize the situation in that key country, and the rest of the southern African region did not appear likely to make heavy demands on the USSR. Thus, Soviet leaders concluded that they could confine their military undertakings in the region to dispatching military advisers to improve the performance of local military forces and to supplying the sort of standard arms and equipment that the USSR produces in great quantity.

But South Africa's behavior in the 1980s has undermined Soviet calculations. From 1981 until the end of 1983, the South African Defense Force repeatedly violated the borders of Mozambique and Angola to strike at local sanctuaries for political elements carrying on opposition activities in Namibia and South Africa proper, and Pretoria rendered substantial assistance to guerrilla movements seeking to unseat the governments in Maputo and Luanda. Moscow's awareness of the implications for the USSR of South Africa's actions was evident in the message conveyed directly to South African officials in New York in November 1983 and underscored in the statement issued by TASS in January 1984. The latter demanded an end to "direct and indirect" South African "aggression" against Angola, called for the withdrawal of South African troops from that country, and warned that "aggression cannot be left unpunished."

Thus far, Soviet leaders have responded ambivalently to their growing realization of the potential costs of their present approach to Africa:

On the one hand, Moscow has shown some willingness to incur higher costs than it had previously expected to pay, in order to try to ensure a major Soviet role on the continent. As noted, it has proved far more forthcoming in economic dealings with African states in the 1980s than it did in the 1970s. It has also poured large amounts of arms and equipment into Angola in recent years—including items of an advanced technological nature, such as MiG-23 aircraft and SA-9 surface-to-air missiles. It did not even flinch at staging a direct show of force when the military pressure from South Africa and the *União Nacional para a Independência Total de Angola* (UNITA) reached its peak in late 1983. A Soviet naval detachment composed of an aircraft carrier and three other major surface ships called at Luanda in November and then rounded the southern tip of the continent for a stop at Maputo. This constituted the most powerful naval detachment from the USSR that had ever sailed past the Cape of Good Hope.

On the other hand, Moscow has evinced uneasiness about the mounting burdens that heavy involvement in Africa is generating. This flows from two distinct considerations:

First, the Soviet leadership has doubts about the USSR's capabilities to meet the costs that may ultimately be involved as it tries to win global-power status on the continent. For instance, Soviet commentators have become increasingly sensitive on the issue of the USSR's aid to African countries. This sensitivity was aptly illustrated in an interview with Anatoliy Gromyko, director of the Africa Institute of the USSR Academy of Sciences, that appeared in *Moscow News* on December 18, 1983. When questioned about the contrast often pointed out by Western observers between Soviet stress on the importance of economic assistance to African countries and the "very insignificant volume" of the USSR's assistance to them, Gromyko countered that Soviet economic aid was not inconsequential, and he went on to depict it as special because it "is sincere and requires no exorbitant dividends either now or in the future."

On some recent occasions, the USSR has also downplayed its ability to deliver militarily for its African clients. The South African and UNITA offensive in Angola in late 1983 affords the best example. To be sure, the new burdens that a more extensive and direct Soviet role in the conflict would have entailed gave Moscow good reason to employ means short of direct military intervention to attempt to stop the drive, but there were hints as well of a Soviet concern that the USSR could not bring adequate military force to bear on the situation quickly enough to keep the existing Angolan government in power. Hence, the initiative to dissuade Pretoria from pushing toward a full-scale confrontation with the USSR.

Second, the Soviet leadership has a mounting anxiety that no matter how extensive its efforts in Africa, the envisaged payoffs may be elusive. Soviet officials, for example, have watched with open consternation the extent of Mozambique's evolution since 1982. Samora Machel's government has turned sharply toward the West for economic succor, established closer relations with the United States, and entered into a remarkably detailed nonaggression pact with South Africa in March 1984.[6] In December 1983, the Soviet ambassador in Maputo even felt compelled to give an interview to the Mozambican news agency to deny that Soviet–Mozambican relations had deteriorated and to highlight the increase in economic ties between the USSR and Mozambique during the year.

Moscow has likewise displayed disappointment that, despite the scope of Soviet overtures toward Egypt described earlier, the Mubarak government has manifested no inclination to look to the USSR as a counterweight to the United States. Indeed, Cairo has even dragged its feet on "normalizing" bilateral relations (i.e., exchanging ambassadors again). Worse yet, the reintegration of Egypt into the Arab mainstream has begun in a manner that minimizes Moscow's opportunities to revive its influence in Cairo. Yasser Arafat's visit to Cairo in late 1983 after his expulsion from Lebanon tended to erase the stigma of betrayal of the Palestinian cause that Sadat's recongition of Israel had generated, and it did so without necessitating Egyptian responses that might have undermined the foundations of the Mubarak government's existing policies toward the United States and Israel.

## Conclusion

Perhaps the crucial question about the new as well as the old elements of Soviet policy is how lasting the current amalgamation will prove to be. In considering this question, three points are worth underscoring:

First, the geopolitical priorities that the USSR assigns to Africa and Moscow's objectives on the continent have not essentially altered since the mid-1960s, and there is little to suggest that they will change significantly in the foreseeable future. The one development that might spark a shift would be a rising tide of radical revolutions across Africa, but such a phenomenon appears most unlikely in this decade.

Second, the shifts that have taken place in the political strategy, means, and expectations of Soviet policy in the 1980s have derived basically from Moscow's judgments of African conditions. It follows that the impetus for any modification of these aspects of policy in the years immediately ahead is likely to come from the same source. The possible exception concerns means. Adversities that currently beset the Soviet economy could compel Moscow to turn its back once again on African needs—especially if the economic situation worsens.

Third, Soviet strategy, means, and expectations with respect to Africa appear better attuned to the continent's realities today than they have been at any time in the past. It is conceivable, of course, that African events might create a disjunction between these elements of policy and African conditions that would induce Moscow to reevaluate its perspectives. Although the continent is highly unstable, no specific developments of this kind loom on the near horizon.

## Notes

[1]N. I. Gavrilov and G. B. Starushenko, *Africa: Problems of Socialist Orientation* (Moscow: Nauka, 1976), p. 419.

[2]Karen Brutents, *The Liberated Countries in the '70s* (Moscow: Izdatelstvo politicheskoi literatury, 1979).

[3]Michael Clough, "Whither Zimbabwe?," *CSIS Africa Notes*, no. 20 (November 15, 1983).

[4]Carol Lancaster, "U.S. Aid to Africa: Who Gets What, When, and How," *CSIS Africa Notes*, no. 25 (March 31, 1984).

[5]J. Coleman Kitchen, Jr., "Zaire and Israel," *CSIS Africa Notes*, no. 10 (March 21, 1983).

[6]John de St. Jorre, "Destabilization and Dialogue: South Africa's Emergence as a Regional Superpower," *CSIS Africa Notes*, no. 26 (April 17, 1984).

# 44

# WILLIAM H. LUERS

## The Soviets and Latin America: A Three Decade U.S. Policy Tangle*

Growing Soviet activity outside of the Atlantic Treaty area has been the major influence in recent years in shaping U.S. public attitudes and official policies toward the Soviet Union. The intensifying Soviet–Cuban military partnership in Africa, the Soviet-sponsored Vietnamese occupation of Kampuchea, and the Soviet invasion of Afghanistan have resulted in the most troubled U.S.–Soviet relationship since 1962. What makes this period more disturbing than the 1960s is the rising scale of Soviet strategic and conventional arms preparedness, the increasing willingness of the Soviets to use force beyond the periphery of the USSR, and the military-security orientation of the new Soviet leadership. The Soviets seem now to be seeking through expanded influence in the Third World to achieve parity with the United States in political power that will match their parity in military power.

Political leaders of all ideological persuasions in the United States have been reexamining the assumptions that led this country through 6 earlier administrations to seek a relaxation of tensions with the other superpower. As U.S. leaders grapple with designing a U.S.–Soviet relationship that can reduce the risks of nuclear war while not implying acquiescence to Soviet military activities in the Third World, increased Soviet interest and involvement in the Latin American region make it more urgent, yet more difficult, to reach a consensus on how to restrain Soviet power:

• More urgent because the risk of a Soviet miscalculation in the Western Hemisphere and the deteriorating situation in Central America hold a greater potential for provoking a crisis between the superpowers

*Reprinted by permission of the author and publisher from *The Washington Quarterly* 7, no. 1 (Winter, 1984), pp. 3–26. The views and opinions expressed in this chapter do not necessarily reflect the views of the U.S. Department of State. Copyright 1984 by The Center for Strategic and International Studies, Georgetown University.

than in any other non-NATO area, with the possible exception of the Middle East.

• More difficult because the mere discussion in the United States of "communism," "Soviet threat," or "Cuban threat" in the Caribbean or Latin American regions confuses, angers, and polarizes the American foreign policy managers and commentators who are often as uninformed on Latin America as they are concentrated on the problems of containing Soviet power.

Soviet policy toward Latin America has become more focused and activist over the past 20 years as Moscow has learned from a series of events, most of which were beyond Soviet ability to initiate or control. In 1983, Soviet policy for the first time is openly directed toward the violent overthrow of the governments of El Salvador and Guatemala. This more aggressive Soviet posture in Central America is the product of Soviet perceptions of conditions in the region, of U.S. capacities and policies, and a more bold, military emphasis to Soviet competition with the United States outside the NATO area. A major factor urging and assisting this Soviet posture is its superclient Cuba which seems to have convinced Moscow after over 20 years of debate that the promotion of violent revolution in Central America is a wise, relatively low-risk policy.

This chapter will discuss the public policy problems involved in designing a coherent policy to deal with Soviet–Cuban involvement in this hemisphere, analyze the evolution of Soviet–Latin American relations, look at the militarization of the Soviet–Cuban superpower, and periodically offer some thoughts on U.S. interests and policies toward the Soviet–Cuban involvement in Latin America. This chapter does not pretend to be a comprehensive survey of Soviet "penetration" of Latin America; rather, it is an analysis of trends in the Soviet and Latin American relationship that have resulted in an increased Soviet commitment to affect the course of events in the Caribbean Basin.

## The Problems of Public Policy

The United States finds it more difficult to sustain coherent, consistent policies toward the Soviet Union and toward Latin America than toward any other regions or nations of the world. In dealing with the Soviet Union, U.S. policies tend to be inconsistent because the American body politic is so deeply divided between its fear and distrust of Soviet communism and its desire to reduce the likelihood of nuclear war. Part of the problem is that the United States finds it difficult to deal with adversaries, and the Soviet Union is a particularly enigmatic adversary. Americans have little or no contact with the Soviet Union, but harbor both vague and very specific anxieties about Russians or communism. Americans are strongly distrustful of dealings or agreements with the Soviets, yet sense that they cannot be ignored or else nuclear war could be a result. U.S. foreign policy since World War II has been shaped by periodic surges of accommodation with this powerful, unknowable adversary followed by periods of revulsion from it.

The lack of consistency in managing our relations with Latin America stems from quite different attitudes. Americans generally have some close contact with or knowledge of one or more aspects of the Latin American world through tourism, migration, trade, or proximity to the growing U.S. Hispanic–American community. Yet, few Americans know much about the issues that form our relationship with the other American states. If U.S. policymakers and opinion makers have tended to be obsessed with the U.S.–Soviet relationship, they have generally been indifferent to or ignorant of Latin America. It has been difficult, therefore, to sustain constructive policies toward Latin America unless the Soviet threat was present or imagined.

Real or imagined Soviet threats to U.S. interests in the Western Hemisphere have evoked forceful and often violent reactions from U.S. governments for three decades. Policymakers, journalists, and academics who normally discuss dispassionately and rationally Middle East problems, China policy, and even U.S.–Soviet relations and nuclear arms issues, find themselves mixing anger with exaggeration when discussing Cuban policy, revolutionary change in Central America, and "communism in our backyard." Often the detailed knowledge and measured judgments of U.S. foreign policy experts on East–West matters are matched only by their ignorance of Latin American issues.

The excesses of the U.S. responses to the perceived Soviet threat in Latin America are part of the heritage of "U.S. interventionism." The U.S. promotion under the Eisenhower administration of the overthrow of the Arbenz government in Guatemala was crude and probably based on incorrect premises. The Kennedy administration, to the surprise of Camelot, became even more anticommunist than John Foster Dulles with regard to Latin America, even though the Kennedys were more creative in formulating and sustaining a U.S. response. The Alliance for Progress was shot from the guns that were silenced in the Bay of Pigs. Johnson's decision to send marines to the Dominican Republic stemmed as much from his administration's distraction and frustration over the Vietnam War as it did from a misreading of events in Santo Domingo. Even though today democratic Dominicans will whisper secretly that the U.S. "intervention" was possibly a constructive event in Dominican history, most Latin Americans condemn ritualistically the U.S. role there. Looking back on Guatemala, the Dominican Republic, and a series of lesser "threats," it is clear that the Soviet threats to which the U.S. thought it was responding were exaggerated. Moreover, Castro's conversion to communism gave an energy and coherency to U.S.–Latin American relations in the 1960s which we had not had before and have not had since. In other words, U.S. concern over "communism" has clearly shaped the nature of our modern relationship with Latin America.

In 1983, therefore, official statements about a potentially dangerous shift in Soviet and Cuban strategy toward the American states are greeted with a sense of *déja vu* and outrage from some, and a resounding "we told you so" from others who have advocated a policy of intervention against communism since World War II. Let us review why a U.S. government in the 1980s finds it difficult to formulate and implement consistent policies designed to constrain the Soviets from seizing opportunities for military involvement in the Caribbean Basin.

First, when U.S. administrations say "communist threat in Latin America," Latin Americans and many U.S. citizens hear "U.S. intervention." U.S. administrations have been justifying activist and interventionist policies toward Latin America for decades by invoking the communist threat. U.S. intervention in the Caribbean Basin has been the major issue of contention between the United States and Latin America throughout the twentieth century. In every case, no matter how concerned Latin Americans become about the Soviet–Cuban threat, they have historically worried first about real or imagined U.S. intervention. We have cried wolf for decades—now the real wolf may be at the door.

Second, there is a divided community of foreign policy specialists in the United States that severely inhibits the formulation of U.S. policy on questions involving the Soviets and Latin Americans. In its most simplistic form the division is between those foreign policy experts, journalists, and academicians who concern themselves with East–West issues and those who concern themselves with North–South issues. The East–West specialists, who have tended to dominate in the State Department, the NSC, Defense, and every other agency of government involved with national security since World War II, focus on arms and arms control, NATO and alliance politics, defense strategies, and Soviet power and policies. When presidents and secretaries of state have begun to think about foreign policy, the East–West issues were central for many historical, cultural, and logical reasons. No president or secretary of state of the United States has come to office with knowledge of or experience in Latin America since World War II.

The North–South group of specialists are relatively new to academia, journalism, and government. The North–South specialists, often younger than their East–West counterparts, think about Africa, Latin America, and South Asia, international financial institutions, bilateral aid, development economics, commodity trade, nonproliferation, military coups, human rights, and social justice. The difference in mind-sets between Sovietologists and Latin Americanists is most striking. One only needed to attend meetings of the American Association for the Advancement of Slavic Studies (AAASS) and its Latin Americanist counterpart, the Latin American Studies Association (LASA), over the past 20 years. The participants' vision of foreign policy and U.S. society are at opposite polls of the American political spectrum. The Latin Americanists are often influenced by the Latin left, severely critical of the U.S. government and the U.S. private sector, sympathetic to and supportive of Latin criticism of the United States, worried about people and development problems. They tend to be idealistic about the U.S. ability and desire to shape events and about Latin American motivation.

The Russian–East European specialists tend to be critical of the Soviet Union, communism, and revolution. They are not given to idealism, are hard nosed about the limits of U.S. policy, and convinced that there are virtually no issues so important as those involved in the U.S.–Soviet relationship. Soviet specialists and Europeanists in general give low priority to North–South issues and tend to be either patronizing toward those who do, or worse, instant experts when they engage the issues. The first and most distinguished East–West historian–diplomat, George Kennan, wrote in 1950 a memorandum in the State Department giving his negative views on Latin America: "It seems unlikely that there could be any other region of the earth in which nature and human behavior could have combined to produce a more unhappy and hopeless background for the conduct of human life than in Latin America."

This low regard for Latin America's role in world affairs by the dean of U.S. Russian experts is matched by the instant wisdom of Seweryn Bialer, the top U.S. Sovietologist whose writings on Soviet foreign and domestic policy are the best available. Bialer, in a *New York Times* article following a recent trip to Central America, an area he has previously known little about, writes: "Clearly then it is unrealistic for the United States to hope to defeat Communist—or potentially Communist—regimes in the region (Central America)."

These two writers are in the first line of U.S. scholarship on the Soviet Union but neither should be expected to offer wisdom on Latin America. The Soviet specialists tend to think of Latin America as a minor side show in U.S. foreign policy. To the Latin Americanists the region is of major interest to the United States for humanitarian and political reasons which are only confused, in their view, by the introduction of "extraneous" East–West issues. Therefore the Soviet and Latin American specialists tend at times to reinforce each others' low tolerance for discussing seriously the Soviet threat in the Caribbean Basin but for completely different reasons.

One example of this North–South–East–West debate is particularly important. During the 1978 Soviet–Cuban military entry into Ethiopia, the debate within the U.S. government and in the public domain became sharply polarized. The Africa North–South group, who dominated thinking in the State Department on this issue, took a firm stance against U.S. action, arguing that the Soviet–Cuban forces were defending Ethiopia against the Somalia invasion. "We should do nothing to back Somalia because they were the offending nation; the way to avoid future Soviet–Cuban interventions is by precluding future African problems with wiser U.S. policies." Moreover, the North–South position argued, the Soviets have yet to establish a satellite or client state in Africa. They will fail eventually in Ethiopia as they did in Ghana and Egypt. The Europe East–West specialists, in the NSC and Defense, argued, on the other hand, that the Soviet–Cuban military move into Ethiopia represented a significantly bolder projection of Soviet power in Africa. "If the U.S. does not take a series of actions to demonstrate to the Soviets the cost to them of this more adventurous thrust, then the Soviets would be encouraged to take bolder steps in the future." Moreover, argued the East–West specialists, the combination of Soviet–Cuban military power, Ethiopian revolutionary needs, and increased

Soviet experience might enable them to get a hammer lock on Ethiopia similar to the relationship they have developed with Cuba. The U.S. government was immobilized by the heat and anger of this debate. Policies and actions were muddled. The Soviets, Africans, and Arabs all were aware of our inability to reach agreement on policy or on action. The U.S. government should have recognized that both groups were correct and developed policies that would communicate forcefully to the Soviets that their actions affected our relations while not involving us in military conflict in Africa, particularly one in which our potential clients were the invaders. We could have been tougher on the Soviets and improved our African strategy at the same time.

Third, there is the debate over Soviet intentions that affects U.S. thinking about Latin America. Do they seek world conquest? To communize the world? Or only secure borders? Are they only desirous of equal status and equal influence as a superpower? Or more ambitiously to change the "correlation of forces?" These are legitimate and difficult questions. One can almost position a foreign policy expert on the political spectrum between conservative and liberal ("A" and "B" team) as to how he or she answers these questions. Conservatives stress Soviet expanionism, world strategy, and conquest. "Realists" and liberals tend toward a somewhat more benign view of Soviet motives—secure borders and equal status as a superpower. One influential group of East–West specialists has found it convenient to avoid the debate entirely by arguing that, since we cannot know Soviet intentions, we should conclude that they are unimportant. Instead we should look only at Soviet actions and capabilities. This latter position is essentially a military view of the "enemy" and can lead to distortions in either extreme. Of course, Soviet intentions are important. They are particularly important when the United States is seeking to evaluate Soviet actions or nonactions where U.S. interests are directly and intimately involved, such as in Central America and the Caribbean. However difficult it is to evaluate Soviet motives we must make the effort, and constantly re-evaluate our estimates. Just how high a priority do the Soviets give to Central America? What type of economic commitment would they take on for one or two more client states? Would they risk damaging state-to-state relations with Mexico, Brazil, even Argentina by a higher military–political profile in the Caribbean Basin?

The split in American society over foreign policy objectives and assumptions has proved profound. The Vietnam War punctuated explosively the gap between generations, reshaped America's vision of itself, and virtually paralyzed the U.S. capacity to use its military power. The tensions between the executive and legislative branches, between media–academia and the government are mounting again, recalling the strains in the American political system of the 1960s. The United States is so deeply divided over policies toward the Soviet Union and Latin America that should we be facing now a step-by-step escalation of a Soviet military presence in this hemisphere over the next 5 years we could find it difficult, if not impossible, to formulate a policy that would balance our important interests in Latin America against our need to define clear limits on the type and scale of Soviet–Cuban activities we can accept in the Caribbean Basin. We, in the United States, must open up the debate over U.S. interests and policies in the Caribbean Basin. U.S. government public policy must include a serious effort to bridge these deep divisions within the American political system.

| The Evolution of Soviet–Latin American Relations | Until the late 1960s the Soviet Union placed Latin America at or near the bottom of its foreign policy agenda and, with the exception of Cuba, had minimal involvement in the region. The reasons were obvious: geography, history, and their limited capacity to project military power at great distances. |

With the temporary cessation of Cuban revolutionary activity in the Hemisphere in 1968, the advent of détente between the superpowers, and the growing self-confidence and global assertiveness of Latin American nations in the 1970s, the Soviets began to expand their state-to-state diplomatic–commercial ties in the Western Hemisphere.

In 1960 the Soviet Union had diplomatic relations with only three countries in Latin America—Cuba, Brazil, and Argentina. By the mid-1970s virtually every major South American and several Caribbean and Central American countries had opened relations with the Soviets. Diplomatic relations were usually accompanied by substantial diplomatic presences and expanded commercial and cultural relations. Trade grew tenfold between 1970 and 1977.

Much has been written about the expanding Soviet presence in Latin America. Most books and articles on the subject fall into the "penetrationist" school of analysis of Soviet policy, the argument being that the more expanded Soviet presence including the trade and cultural ties represented a significant new Soviet threat to the security and independence of Western Hemisphere. The penetrationists fail usually to point out that in most South American countries, the strongly independent governments are sensitive to the problem and often adequately equipped to restrict Soviet intelligence activities. Moreover, the larger Latin countries saw definite advantages from such relations. The balance of trade with the Soviets was overwhelmingly in favor of Latin American exports, even though the total turnover was not much over one billion dollars by the late 1970s. Latin American countries found that a measured low-key relationship with the USSR could be economically and politically profitable in the bipolar world dominated by two superpowers.

This "penetration" enabled the Soviet Union to work more closely with Latin American communist parties and other Marxist–Leninist groups, both legal and illegal, and permitted disruptive subversive activity in smaller, more vulnerable countries. But this traditional type of Soviet activity has not, as yet, resulted in any "successes" for Soviet policy in the region. Moreover, the Soviets still give relatively low priority to Latin American nations which stand far below those of other regions of the world as recipients of Soviet aid or military assistance or as Soviet trading partners. It is not the size of the Soviet presence in this large, diverse, and increasingly assertive region that should concern the United States; it is the location, the purpose, and the quality of that presence to which we must direct our analysis and policies.

In order to analyze how the Soviets are changing their objectives, assumptions, and involvement in the Western Hemisphere, we should look at those experiences that have shaped Soviet policies and thinking about Latin America. It is difficult to discern a unifying coherent strategy that has driven Soviet policies toward the Latin region other than the objective of increasing their influence. Kissinger is correct in saying that the United States and the Soviets tend "to ascribe to the other a consistency, foresight and coherence that its own experience belies." In Latin America the Soviets have stumbled, stepped back, and probed further with limited understanding of the region or vision about how to pursue their own interests. We often make the mistake of believing that the Soviet steps are sure-footed and carefully planned years in advance. The patterns seem to confirm Professor Alexander Dallin's thesis that: "Soviet foreign policy behavior can be seen as the product of an encounter between expectations and values of Soviet decision makers and the reality as they found and perceived it. In practice, it has required (and in turn reflected) a series of adaptations—an imperfect learning process."

The Soviets have shifted tactics and reevaluated assumptions over the past 25 years in their evolving relations with Latin America. Some of their shifts have been affected by factors extraneous to Latin America, but much of their behavior has been in direct response to opportunities that presented themselves in the Western Hemisphere. This imperfect learning process could be leading them into a set of involvements in the Caribbean Basin region or to a miscalculation about U.S. reactions that could result in a major crisis in U.S.–Soviet relations. U.S. policy must be designed to head off such a Soviet miscalculation.

The first and only real "success" of Khrushchev's post-Stalin decade (1954–1964) of efforts to project Soviet influence into the developing world was Cuba. Earlier Soviet efforts, in the Congo, Ghana, and Indonesia, to take advantage of opportunities arising out of the dissolution of colonial empires in Asia and Africa were eminently "Khrushchevian"—personalized, ideologically justified, copied from the United States, poorly executed, and ultimately failures. It was the serendipitous Castro revolution in a part of the world least pursued by and most inaccessible to Soviet power that provided the first new "socialist state" to the Soviet camp.

We will not review here the events which brought Cuba and the Soviet Union together. It is useful, however, to review in some detail the nature of the Soviet–Cuban disagreements over revolution, since the issues that divided Moscow and Havana so deeply in the 1960s are at the center of Soviet–Cuban activities today in Central America. At the core of the debate was Castro's desire to promote revolution in several Latin countries, most particularly in Venezuela, working with trained guerrillas and bypassing communist parties. The Soviets were opposed to Cuba's promotion of armed struggle in Latin America because they did not consider the region ripe for revolution, they wanted to establish state-to-state relations with Latin nations, and they did not want to risk confrontation with the United States. Moreover, the Soviets in the 1960s were trying desperately to hold together the world structure of Moscow-lining communist parties that buttressed Soviet foreign policy. The Chinese and Cubans in their different ways were discrediting and dividing the communist movement. Castro, more a revolutionary than an ideologue, depended first on Che Guevara, then on Regis Debray, to formulate Cuba's position in this international communist debate. Stated simply Castro/Debray held that: The duty of a revolutionary is to make revolution; revolution must be carried out by trained, armed guerrillas who are organized into fighting forces; political organization, parties, and front groups must be secondary and dependent on the fighting force; the fighting must be in rural areas because of the baneful influence of the city on organization, motivation, and support; once in power, the fighting force transforms itself into the governing power and the Marxist–Leninist political organization that mobilizes the masses.

For Castro, guerrilla warfare was the strategy whereas for the Soviets, guerrilla warfare was only one tactic among several toward achieving power and influence. The Soviets placed political organization first— particularly the leading role of the communist party; they gave greater emphasis to urban activities where the proletariat were; and they believed that the fighting force needed to be subordinate to the political vanguard that would take power. The Soviets, in a tactical gesture to achieve Cuban support for the traditional Latin Communist parties and in order to undercut a potential Chinese Communist alliance with Castro, conceded some ground on this "revolution" issue at the November 1964 Havana Conference of 22 Latin American Communist Parties. In exchange for Castro's agreement to work with CPs "the Soviets and their parties conceded the necessity of supporting guerrilla warfare in several areas." This agreement lasted less than a year during which time the Soviets tried to extract from the Cubans three additional concessions in exchange for increasingly large Soviet assistance; rationalization of the Cuban economy to minimize waste of Soviet assistance; strengthening of the Cuban Communist Party to make Cuban communism less dependent on the person of Castro; Cuban support for peaceful coexistence with the United States.

Castro complied, in his way, to these three demands by encouraging the foreign adventures of Che Guevara who had opposed Soviet ideas on Cuban economic development, by creating a communist party but throwing out the Moscow-lining members, and by making gestures to the United States, such as agreeing to permit the exodus of some Cubans. But on the core issue of revolution the Cubans proceeded to press for revolution against the "revisionists" (read Soviet-lining communist parties). Moreover, the Cubans held the January 1966 Tricontinental Conference in Havana which ended in Castro's overturning the 1964 Soviet–Cuban agreement in Castro's commitment to strengthen

Cuba's ties and support for genuine revolutionary movements, as opposed to supporting Moscow's communist parties in Latin America.

The second and closely related experience which shaped Soviet policies toward Latin America was played out in Venezuela.[1] Throughout the 1960s the Cubans sought to overthrow the democratic government of Betancourt in Venezuela which had come to power at about the same time as Castro. Betancourt and Castro had both taken over from dictators in 1959. Betancourt, the reformist democrat, was seen by Castro as a far greater threat to his revolutionary agenda than the other regimes in the region. The Cubans, therefore, centered their debate with the Soviets on support for the guerrilla warfare in Venezuela. The Cubans worked closely with the dissident Venezuelan FALN and other guerrilla groups; the Soviets worked with the Communist Party. Eventually Soviet and Cuban differences were a critical factor in splitting and fatally weakening the guerrilla movement. The Cubans strongly criticized the Soviets for failing to assist materially and politically the guerrilla movement. The Soviets accused the Cubans of pursuing left-wing extremist policies.

The Venezuelan government's victory over the guerrillas was first and foremost the result of nearly a decade of combining wise political and economic policies with forceful military action, supported, by the way, with substantial U.S. military assistance. The failure of the guerrilla movement in Venezuela in the late 1960s persuaded the Soviets that the Cuban vision of revolutionary potential was wrong and was not in line with Soviet interests. The failure in Venezuela helped to persuade the Cubans that they needed to take two steps backward on the revolutionary issue.

The Soviets, in order to pressure Cuba to change its policies, applied economic sanctions (a cutback in vital oil deliveries in 1967). The Cubans were finally brought into line in 1968, as symbolized by Castro's open endorsement of the Soviet invasion of Czechoslovakia. Cuba suspended support for revolutionary movements in Latin America and began to accept Soviet suggestions on economic policies. In the early 1970s Cuban policies began to parallel and be largely subordinate to Moscow. In return Castro received large-scale economic assistance, a modern military establishment unequaled in Latin America, and a substantial implicit Soviet protection of the Cuban revolution flowing out of the U.S.–Soviet unwritten "understandings" of 1962 and 1970 which involved U.S. willingness not to invade Cuba in exchange for Soviet restraint in using Cuba for strategic purposes.

We will return to the Cuba relationship later. It is important to underscore, however, that Castro, who came to power as a result of no Soviet action, and who joined the Soviet camp for his own purposes and to the surprise of the Kremlin, became the crucial wedge for the first significant Soviet involvement in Africa and Latin America, despite the Cuban–Soviet divisions over the way to pursue revolution.

The third formative set of experiences that shaped Soviet attitudes and policies toward Latin America related to the emergence in the late 1960s of "progressive" military regimes, particularly in Peru. The

Soviets traditionally had "regarded the armed forces mainly as a weapon of reactionary coercion and class domination" and as "praetorian guards of the Pentagon." Moscow's attitude toward the 1968 military coups in Peru and Panama were entirely negative. The Peruvian generals were called by the the Soviet press "gorillas who established in the country a regime of ferocious military dictatorship." When the Peruvian regime undertook reforms undercutting the oligarchs, nationalization of U.S. oil companies, and the expulsion of U.S. military advisers, the Soviets were pleasantly surprised. They changed their attitudes and policies quickly. By the 1969 Moscow meeting of communist parties, the Soviets stated that "patriotic and democratic trends are gaining ground in the armed forces of some countries." Moscow believed that a new model might have emerged for Soviet partnership in Latin America. The progressive military junta proceeded to open diplomatic and trade relations with the Soviets and, more significantly, developed a close military relationship including the purchase of sophisticated Soviet military equipment and training of Peruvian military in the USSR.

Over the dozen years of the Soviet–Peruvian relationship, the Peruvians bought, on excellent terms, over one billion dollars in Soviet military equipment including jet fighters, helicopters, missiles, and tanks. Nearly 150 Soviet advisers went to Peru and over 2000 Peruvian military officers passed through Soviet training. The Soviets also offered some economic assistance programs to the Peruvians but economics were not key to their approach. By the late 1960s the Soviets were beginning to realize that in trade and economic assistance they were no competition for Western nations. While not holding that the military could, in any way, substitute for the communist party, the Soviets did begin to believe that the military relationship seemed to be a route to sustain influence in some countries of the Third World.

The Soviets expected, then, that the Peruvian experience would prove to be a fruitful and enduring one that would repeat itself in other Latin countries such as Panama and Bolivia. They were wrong. When, in 1980, the military junta turned rule back to the civilian President Belaunde, the long experiment with the progressive military was set back, but not over. The Soviets continue to maintain a close relationship with their Peruvian military clients even though their clients did not manage to establish a revolutionary model that was compatible with Soviet objectives. While there has by no means been a clear break with the Soviets, Peru turned out to be an isolated case and an ephemeral success for Soviet foreign policy. The Soviets, nonetheless, continue to give the Latin American military a high priority for their favors—with little evident success. The Brazilians, for example, who are agreeable to profitable trade and technology relations with the Soviets, still refuse to accept Soviet military attachés. At the same time, this positive experience with progressive military regimes reinforced the Soviet view of the 1960s and early 1970s that the Soviets should not support the Cuban approach to violent revolution in Latin America.

The fourth important event that shaped Soviet thinking about and policies toward the Western Hemisphere was the 1970 election of Allende in Chile. Allende's peaceful acquisition of power seemed further to confirm the correctness of Soviet tactics in Latin America and the errors of Castro's earlier policies. During the 1960s, for practical reasons, and the early 1970s in an effort to encourage détente with the United States, the Soviets and virtually all of the orthodox (pro-Moscow) communist parties espoused the "peaceful route to power"—elections. Such policies enabled the Soviets to expand state-to-state relations and did not provoke the United States. They seemed the most practical policies to pursue in conservative Catholic societies with large military establishments as well as with growing proletariats and leftist political parties—Latin America began to look to the Soviets like Southern Europe. The Soviets, a decade earlier, had considered the Cuban revolution a fluke. Allende represented for the Soviets the important first phase toward peaceful change to socialism and confirmed policies of promoting united fronts as opposed to the *lucha armada* (armed struggle).

Allende himself, however, was not the answer. The Soviets moved as cautiously with Allende as he did with the Soviets. The Soviets had been surprised by Castro's conversion to communist orthodoxy after the Bay of Pigs and they were not about to take on another costly and unpredictable Latin American. The Soviets did not suggest that the Allende government was "building socialism." They understood that counterrevolution was part of Chilean reality. The Soviets like to preserve their options until they can see that a revolution has become irreversible. The extension of the Brezhnev doctrine beyond Eastern Europe has never been articulated, but the Soviet commitment to the maintenance of the Cuban system is substantial. The Soviets had no intention of making such a commitment to Allende.

Nonetheless, Allende's downfall shook the communist world. The Chile experience led to a debate throughout the communist movement. It demonstrated to Moscow that U.S. policies were still directed toward excluding Marxist governments from power in the Western Hemisphere. The debate did not, however, concern itself primarily with CIA destabilizing activities, but concentrated on the lessons to be learned by communists:

• Communists should prepare more effective methods of taking over a recalcitrant military establishment or, if necessary, opposing it with masses and a popular militia. There is a high price to pay when the focal points of counterrevolution are not destroyed or neutralized at an early stage.

• Communists should analyze Allende's other serious mistakes such as moving too quickly to redistribute resources and not making adequate use of other progressive political forces in the early stages.

• The communist party must play the dominant and innovative role in any revolutionary movement; it must be the vanguard of the revolution.

This debate,[2] which ensued for many months after Allende's fall, was one of the most important, soul-searching, and divisive self-criticisms by communist orthodoxy since the "destalinization" discussion of the 1950s and the Sino–Soviet split in the 1960s. The lessons and the tactics that emerged from the Allende experience moved Latin American communist parties and the Soviets toward a more flexible attitude toward the armed struggle in Latin America. The Allende experience reopened the Soviet–Cuban debate of the 1960s.

The fifth experience that has shaped Soviet policies toward Latin America is the long evolving relationship with Argentina. The Soviets and Argentinians began exploring bilateral relations in the early 1920s. The Soviets established relations with Argentina in 1946 and signed their first bilateral treaty agreement with any Latin country with Argentina in 1953. With the return of Peron to power in 1973 both nations began to take their mutuality of interests seriously. From the Soviet viewpoint Argentina was a logical partner for a long-term state-to-state relationship. Argentina is the second largest nation of South America, strategically positioned, traditionally the maverick of Western Hemisphere nations, and consistently at odds with the United States. Moreover, Argentina was a major supplier of much needed agricultural products, a fact that paid off handsomely in 1980 when Argentine grain exports helped the Soviets withstand the parital U.S. grain embargo.

From the Argentine point of view since 1979, the Soviets have been a major dependable market for Argentine exports. In 1980 the USSR took 33.7 % of Argentine exports for a total of 2.9 billion dollars when Buenos Aires purchased only .3% of its imports from the Soviets. Moreover, the only major Soviet economic cooperation programs in Latin America, except for Cuba and Nicaragua over the past decade, have been with Argentina. Argentina receives Soviet-supplied heavy water, enriched uranium, and technological assistance under a bilateral nuclear energy agreement. This close Soviet relationship with the most advanced nuclear program in Latin America, one probably capable of producing a nuclear explosion in a few years, is a disturbing factor in Latin American and U.S. efforts to limit nuclear proliferation in the Western Hemisphere.

This close relationship survived the 1976 Argentine coup and the past 7 years of repressive military governments. The Soviets emerged in international fora to defend the Argentine military governments who were busy "disappearing" alleged revolutionaries, subversives (probably including communists), and Marxists at home by the thousands. The Argentine Communist Party had not come out strongly against the repressive policies of recent Argentine governments until the recent political campaign. The Soviets have supported Argentina in the dispute over the Falklands and the dispute with Chile over the Beagle Channel. It has become a relationship of mutual convenience that is likely to survive repeated Argentine governmental crises, and may evolve into an even closer relationship should the Soviets achieve their goal of becoming a major arms supplier to the Argentines. Thus far, however, even in the wake of the Falklands–Malvinas War, the Argentines have avoided a military relationship with the Soviets.

The Soviet and Argentine objectives in this increasingly pragmatic, close, but not intimate, relationship are obvious—economic, political, and possibly military. Argentine governments, pathologically anti-communist over the past decade, have believed they can manage the Soviets internally. The Soviets have been restrained in meddling in internal Argentine affairs even though Cuban ties with Argentine insurgents have been close over the years. It is a relationship not unlike that between the USSR and India. But the endemic Argentine political–economic disorder may offer the Soviets a future opportunity to change the current relatively straight-forward relationship with Argentina—a country strategically positioned in the South Atlantic.

Finally, the event that has influenced Soviet thinking and policies toward Latin America more than any other since the Castro conversion was the Sandinista victory in Nicaragua in 1979. Sergio Mikoyan, editor-in-chief of the Soviet publication *Latinskaya Amerika*, in 1980 declared that the Sandinista revolution was of "colossal international importance—one of those events that demand reexamination of established concepts."

The Somoza regime had dominated not only Nicaragua, but much of Central America for decades. Military officers in Honduras, El Salvador, and Guatemala looked to Somoza and to his U.S. political–military contacts for support. These conservative, backward societies had traditionally been held in place by strong, often repressive military institutions, well established small economic elites, and the Catholic Church. The combination of liberalizing church policies in the 1970s, the effects of modernization and economic growth, and the decision of a U.S. administration not to give unquestioning support to repressive governments opened the way for the development of more bold guerrilla and other opposition movements in Central America. The reasons why social–political modernization and guerrilla warfare began to change the shape of these Central American countries in the late 1970s and early 1980s flow from many factors. A common drive was the need for social justice and economic reforms. Certainly, once Somoza departed Nicaragua, the lid was off and the pressures for change rapidly grew, there and elsewhere in the subregion.

The small smoldering Sandinista movement caught fire in Nicaragua in 1977 for a series of reasons peculiar to Nicaragua. Although very much a Nicaraguan anti-Somoza movement, it was made up of many parts. The leaders had for years been trained in Cuba and most of them were Marxist–Leninist. The fact, however, that these *comandantes* received widespread support from inside and outside Nicaragua attests to the hatred in the region against the Somozas. The then-governing Venezuelan Accion Democratica leader Carlos Andres Perez claimed that Venezuelan dictator Perez Jiminez had convinced his pal Somoza to bomb from the air a section in San Jose, Costa Rica in which AD leaders, including Perez, were spending their exile in the 1950s. That Panama,

Venezuela, Costa Rica, and tens of thousands of Nicaraguans joined in support of the growing Sandinista movement was not surprising, therefore, given the fact that throughout the region Somoza stood as the last and most hated of the Caudillo dictators of the Caribbean Basin.

It is instructive to review briefly a few of the key steps by external actors that brought the Sandinistas to power in the summer of 1979:

• In July 1978 the Cubans brought together in Havana the leaders of the three major Sandinista factions and imposed unity on them as a precondition for Cuban military support. From that moment of guerrilla unity—a key objective in Cuban strategy in Central America—the two Sandinista factions in the north of Nicaragua received increased Cuban support. Up to that point the two northern groups had depended heavily on money provided by the wealthy Salvadorian guerrilla/terrorists to buy arms. Salvadoran terrorists in the mid-1970s found lucrative sources in robbing banks and kidnappings, a source which dried up with the departure of the rich families.

• In the fall of 1978, Panama's Torrijos, Venezuelan President Perez, and Costa Rican President Carazo agreed to provide military and logistical support to the Sandinista faction fighting on the southern Nicaraguan border. This group—the Terciario faction—had as one of its leaders Eden Pastora, or "Comandante Cero," who had achieved fame by his temporary seizure in August 1978 of the Palace in Nicaragua. Torrijos, Perez, and Carazo believed Pastora to be a democratic revolutionary, the most charismatic leader of the Sandinistas, and a likely leader of a post-Somoza regime. The three leaders set out, therefore, in late 1978 and early 1979 to provide significant support to Pastora, to tell Castro to stay out of the Sandinista struggle, and to pressure the Carter administration to move Somoza out prior to a complete Sandinista victory, thus permitting a "moderate" coalition including Pastora. Perez believed that the Marxist–Leninist–Cuban involvement and dominant role was cheating the Latin democratic left of the revolutionary banner that had brought democracies to Venezuela and Costa Rica.

• In March 1979, following the departure of Perez from the presidency in Venezuela and the failure of the Carter administration to bring about the departure of Somoza, the Cubans, with support from Costa Rica's Carazo, began a large-scale airlift of arms, volunteers, and supplies to the Sandinistas. A Cuban command center was set up in San Jose, Cuban military aircraft openly landed in Costa Rica to offload arms and equipment for the Sandinistas, and staging camps and air strips were set up in Costa Rica on the Nicaraguan border. Within 2 months the Cubans had turned the two northern Sandinista factions (headed by the Ortega brothers) into effective military fighting units. The Pastora group was now cut off from Venezuelan assistance. It became the weakest of the fighting groups. The Costa Rican Legislative Assembly undertook a special investigation of the Cuban and Costa Rican Government cooperation in this major airlift. The 1981 report of that Commission is an important source of information on this shift in Cuban strategy which brought the Sandinistas to power.

The Sandinistas' victorious entry into Managua in the summer of 1979 would not have taken place without the financial help in the pre-1977 period from Salvadoran guerrillas, rich from kidnapping and bank robberies, and without large-scale help from a few of the region's democratic leaders. But there is little doubt that the major change that took place in the military situation in May–June 1979 came from the large-scale assistance provided from Cuba including trained guerrillas from Cuba's international brigade of Central and South American revolutionary fighters. The dramatic and surprising shift in the Sandinista fighting ability had a devastating psychological and military impact on the already demoralized Nicaraguan National Guard which collapsed in June 1979.

The Sandinista victory was complete in that it resulted in the departure of all of the Somozas and the destruction of the National Guard. It was a complete victory largely because Somoza would have it no other way—if he had to leave, he would assure the deluge would follow. The provisional government, made up of Sandinistas and moderate sympathizers, came to power amidst great hope and support within the region. Within 2 years virtually every moderate had left the government—Robelo, Pastora, Mrs. Chamorro. The Marxist–Leninist *comandantes* had established themselves in full control.[3]

The Nicaraguan Revolution must be seen in the context of the Soviet–Cuban debate over revolution that extends back to the early 1960s. It seems clear that the Sandinista victory confirmed, at least in this case, the Castro–Debray thesis in that: The revolution was won by trained guerrillas who fought almost exclusively from a rural base, who were not dependent on a political organization (read the communist party), and who took over directly as the Marxist–Leninist government after seizing power.

The Sandinista victory also seemed to answer many of the questions raised by the Allende failures, particularly on how to neutralize or eliminate military opposition. Moreover, the Sandinista revolution simply could not have been won without large-scale military assistance from abroad. Finally, since achieving power, the Sandinistas have moved more cautiously than Allende did in the distribution of resources, in dealing with the private sector, and in dealing with western banks and governments on financial matters.

The Soviets' attitude toward this new phase of what Dallin termed their imperfect learning process in expanding their influence in Latin America is therefore important, since the Soviets had not played a key role in bringing about the revolution. They even seemed surprised by its remarkable and rapid success. The Soviets realize that the Cuban position on revolution has been vindicated by the Nicaraguan experience. A reading of the Soviet literature suggests that Moscow recognizes this fact and for the first time, in Central America and the Caribbean region, is now openly supportive of the Cuban position on revolution. In an important article on revolution in the July 1982 issue of *Latinskaya Amerika,* M. F. Gornov says:

The victory of the people's democratic revolution in Nicaragua has been a colossal triumph for the popular movement in Latin America in the 1980s. The present stage of the anti-imperialist struggle in Latin America is obviously the next logical step after events such as the Cuban revolution, the revolutionary wave of the mid-1960s, the foundation of revolutionary democratic governments in Peru, Bolivia and Panama in the late 1960s and early 1970s, the Chilean revolution of 1970–1973 and the revolutionary outbursts of the early 1970s in Uruguay and of the mid-1970s in Argentina. They have culminated in the victory of the Sandinista revolution in Nicaragua, which simultaneously marks the beginning of a new stage in the continent's revolutionary struggle.

Soviet official pronouncements over the past 3 years regarding Nicaragua and other Central American developments demonstrate an important shift in Soviet tactics—support for the *lucha armada* and a remarkable increase in attention to the area. For example, the July 1982 issue of the Soviet publication *Latinskaya Amerika* was devoted entirely to the Central American Revolutionary Process. The lead editorial sets the tone for the entire issue:

> Today this region (Central America), which was considered hopelessly backward not long ago, is marked by an amazingly high degree of mass political awareness, high level of mass revolutionary organization, progressive forms of struggle, the skillful combination of these forms to fit the particular situation and the maturity of the political programs of this struggle. The region is explosive, not only from the standpoint of the internal situation. Suddenly, literally within the last few years, it became apparent that the development of this conflict situation was leading to the increasing involvement of various forces of global dimensions in this situation.

Yet, a certain caution has governed direct Soviet involvement in Nicaragua. Soviet eastern bloc military security personnel in Nicaragua have been kept under 300 while Cuban advisers number in the thousands. Soviet arms have been shipped to Nicaragua, in the past through third parties, such as the Cubans, Algerians, and Libyans. For months the Bulgarians were training Nicaraguans to fly MIG-fighter-bombers, but the MIGs have not appeared, possibly because of the strong criticism from the United States and other Hemisphere governments that Nicaragua was escalating the regional military arms race. The Soviets appear determined not to make a mistake by escalating too rapidly their involvement. Thus far they have not indicated a willingness to take on Nicaragua as a full-fledged economic and military client. The internal Nicaraguan dynamics combined with outside pressures may force events and require a Soviet decision or a higher level of material support.

Now that we have briefly reviewed the formative events of the past 25 years in Soviet–Latin American relations, I would like to draw some conclusions and make some effort to examine Soviet motives.

First, over the period we have discussed, the Soviets have cautiously explored a variety of relationships in the Western Hemisphere with the view to expanding their influence in the region while minimizing the potential for conflict with the United States. The traditional Moscow-lining communist parties have been an important vehicle for Soviet policy but increasingly state-to-state relations in most of the Hemisphere have been the primary focus of Soviet activity.

Second, in South America the Soviets have, by and large, sought to establish long-term stable government relations, with traditional trade, economic, and political objectives with a few exceptions, such as Chile (the Allende heritage has left the Chilean communists advocating violent revolution there), and Colombia (where the communist party for peculiar historical reasons has an active violent wing). Yet, the Soviets try to maintain the picture of legitimate relations with the Colombian government while the Cubans support the most troublesome guerrilla movement—the M-19. The political consequences of the current severe economic-monetary strains in South America and the development of greater regional tensions over border–subregional problems could create opportunities for Soviet meddling and expanded influence. For now, however, neither the South American nations nor the Soviets seem to anticipate a fundamental shift in the pragmatic ties that have evolved there over the past decade. A dramatic shift toward revolutionary changes in Central America could change South American thinking on relations with the Soviets.

Third, in Central America and in the Caribbean the Soviets have clearly shifted toward a more activist set of policies as a result of the Sandinista victory and the subsequent events in Central America that indicate the emergence in the area of unstable, revolutionary societies. That Moscow's orthodox communist parties have openly declared and physically engaged in the tactics of violent revolution is a significant shift in Moscow's policies. This shift places the Soviets in a conflictive posture with the United States in our immediate neighborhood. That the Soviets have been cautious thus far in direct military involvement, and in direct confrontation with the United States, is deceiving since Soviet clients, Cuba, East Germany, Bulgaria, and radical Arab groups have been expanding their physical presence in Nicaragua and their assist-ance to guerrilla movements elsewhere in Central America. The Soviets and Cubans probably wish first to see the Sandinistas consolidate authority, believing that time will lead to greater regional acceptance of change in Nicaragua and to a more powerful government in Managua. A second objective is probably a victory for the guerrillas in El Salvador, but not at the cost of the Sandinista revolution. The Soviets are probably not now seeking a full client state in Nicaragua, but over time the Soviets might take on significantly greater responsibilities there. Above all the Soviets will want more evidence than they have to date that they can exercise control over key Sandinista decisions before they take them as high cost clients.

The Kremlin decided long ago that any area of the world is fair game for the superpower competition for influence. The Soviets would prob-ably say they confirmed their inclination to so compete by watching us play the "China card" and succeed in excluding them from much of the Middle East. Central America now appears to them ripe, if a little risky, for that competition. One key question is to what extent the Soviets are prepared over a long period of time to increase their military presence in Nicaragua. That Soviet decision will depend largely on other regional developments, most particularly on Soviet estimates of the U.S. reaction. A second key question is to what extent this victory of the Cuban view of support for violent revolution in the Western Hemisphere will lead to more bold Soviet action in support of shaping other Marxist–Leninist regimes in Central America and in the Caribbean.

What does this shift to a more focused, action-oriented Soviet policy in Central America imply about Soviet policy, about the relationship with Cuba, and about the superpower competition?

## The Soviet–Cuban Superpower: Marching toward Militarism

As the Soviet Union set out in pursuit of a "global vocation" under Khrushchev in the late 1950s its vision of what superpower status meant was drawn from watching the United States. Khrushchev drove the party to "catch up with and pass the United States" in the production of everything from milk to steel. The party's stated goals were first and foremost to match the United States as an economic power which, combined with growing Soviet influence in the collapsing colonial world, would shift the "correlation of forces" to favor the socialist camp. Military power was to play a role but not the primary role. The Soviet Union as an economic, technological power able to pick up the residue of empires and to give ideological sustenance to a new world of leaders would challenge the United States' predominance in the developing world.

From 1964 when Brezhnev and his colleagues threw out the "harebrained schemer" Khrushchev, until the death of Brezhnev in 1982, emphasis shifted dramatically on how to achieve superpower status. Khrushchev's dream was not realized. On the contrary by 1982 the gap between U.S. and Soviet production was nearly as great as it was when Stalin died. In technology, with the possible exception of some military technology, the Soviets were hopelessly still far behind the United States.

The Brezhnev era brought the Soviet Union to superpower status as a military, not an economic nor an ideological power, thereby turning Khrushchev's dream on its head. During Brezhnev's rule the USSR underwent the largest-scale development of military power the world has ever witnessed. The armed forces grew in size as did their share of resources. Military projects demanded and received the best personnel and materiel. In strategic and conventional weaponry and in their capacity to deliver their power anywhere in the world, the Soviet Union became the equal of the United States.

This creeping militarization of Soviet power and society should not be overdrawn. The communist party is still in charge. On the Central

Committee or other leadership bodies there has not been a significant increase in military representation. But Brezhnev's vision of superpower status succeeded where Khrushchev's failed, and that military emphasis in Soviet development over the past 18 years has affected the party, Soviet society, and Soviet foreign policy.

This military emphasis in Soviet foreign policy has made the Kremlin such a formidable and disturbing competitor in the third world, and particularly in the Western Hemisphere.

First, the Soviets came to learn by the 1970s that in the trade–economic assistance, area of relations with the LDCs, they are severely handicapped in competing with the United States or West Europeans. By the mid-1970s their economic aid programs had become stabilized and been relegated to a relatively minor role except with client states (Vietnam and Cuba). Arms sales and military assistance, on the other hand, had become a major and highly lucrative lever in dealing with foreign countries. Soviet arms sales to noncommunist LDCs reached 8.8 billion dollars in 1980 compared to new economic aid commitments that year of less than 2.6 billion dollars. Although this enormous growth in military assistance, largely to Arab countries, did not always buy influence, it did increase the role of the Soviet military in the management of foreign affairs. Moreover, when the Soviets learned that they were at a disadvantage when the issues were economic, they also learned that in the post-Vietnam era they held the advantage when the issues were military. Therefore, in areas of critical interest to them, the maintenance of regional tensions offered opportunities for deeper or sustained Soviet involvement. Second, the Soviet–Cuban involvement beginning in 1975 in Angola, in Ethiopia, and in a series of smaller countries in Africa and the Middle East was conducted primarily through military channels. The remarkable air and sealift mounted to Ethiopia was preplanned in Moscow between Cuban Defense Minister Raul Castro and Soviet Defense Minister Ustinov, and was executed out of a Soviet military command and control center run by a Soviet general in Addis Ababa. These successes of Soviet–Cuban foreign policy in Africa have been characterized by remarkably effective military coordination between the Soviet and Cuban military high commands. Supported by extensive technical personnel from Soviet and Eastern European countries, the military seem to have had the upper hand in mounting the plunges of Soviet power into Africa. They also retain a firm control over ongoing military-security ties with the client states and leadership, possibly seeking not to repeat past bad experiences the Soviets have had leaving local revolutionary leaders to their own devices. The military–security forces seek to ensure stable, controlled clients where the Soviet party and government had failed in the 1960s. The Soviet military was humiliated by their ouster from Egypt by Sadat and wants to avoid such a repeat performance in Africa and elsewhere in the Third World.

Inevitably one must ask whether this increased use of Soviet military power for political purposes is becoming more effective and more permanent in Africa and in the Third World in general. In the 1981 detailed study by The Brookings Institution, "Diplomacy of Power—

Soviet Armed Forces as a Political Instrument," Stephen Kaplan concludes that the 1970s saw, on balance, greater success for Soviet power: "With the partial exception of the Arab side in the 1973 Middle East war, no Soviet ally involved in the Third World cases examined occurring after the 1967 Middle East war was defeated by a Chinese or Western ally or an actor supported by a Western proxy. Nor was any regime receiving Soviet political–military support overturned."

Yet, Kaplan is wisely cautious. He also concludes that Soviet political–military influence, while increasingly effective, is conditional on the attitudes of the receiving Third World state—such as how palatable are Soviet demands, and how secure is the state. The Soviets have, since their setbacks in Egypt and Indonesia, placed increasing emphasis in the 1970s and 1980s on political control over clients.

One additional point needs to be made about Soviet motives in Angola and Ethiopia. It has often been argued that the Soviets, pushed slightly by the more bold Cubans in August–October 1975, began the Angola intervention because détente was beginning to unravel and they felt less fettered by the close U.S.–Soviet relationship. On the contrary, the Soviets most assuredly believed then, and perhaps even more so today, that the benefits or obligations which flow from equal status as a superpower include the seizure of opportunities to expand influence outside the NATO area. Competition in Africa, Asia, and indeed Latin America was and is, in their view, part of the détente relationship, not alien to it. The Soviets would clearly argue that the successful efforts of the United States to exclude the Soviet Union from the Middle East peace process after the 1973 war, the ouster of the Soviets from Egypt and, even more disturbing, the United States playing the China card, all demonstrated that Washington for its part was determined to seek advantage and not a "condominium of superpowers" in its approach to the Third World.

A third more obvious Soviet military control over the management of foreign affairs came with the Soviet invasion and tormented, prolonged occupation of Afghanistan. The war in Afghanistan, involving 100,000 Soviet troops, has been the largest, longest, sustained military conflict the Soviets have engaged in since World War II. Because of the nature of that mountain war against the tenacious Afghan partisans, the Soviets have not even had much satisfaction that they can test out new military equipment. The war in Afghanistan occupies a large place in Soviet thinking about foreign affairs. Although we can not know for certain, Politburo meetings must devote a great deal of time to sorting out how to manage the "Soviet Vietnam." Although the military invasion was undertaken for political purposes, military prestige and thinking must play a major role in these policy discussions. It is a military conflict, conducted by the military, who are most certainly reluctant to leave Afghanistan without victory, whatever victory could possibly mean to the Soviets in this situation.

Finally, there is the example of Poland where the army has taken over from the Polish Communist Party which had virtually disintegrated. General Jaruzelski is still, first and foremost, a Polish military officer, second, the head of the communist party. The militarization of the Polish Communist Party haunts the Soviet leadership. Moreover, it is not difficult to imagine that Jaruzelski still is more comfortable communicating with Moscow through old military channels than through party channels, thus again placing the Soviet military in the forefront of critical Soviet foreign policy problems.

Andropov became General Secretary of the CPSU at a time, therefore, when the Soviet military had achieved a larger role in the conduct of Soviet foreign policy than at any point in Soviet history. His main allies in the Politburo were, not surprisingly, Minister of Defense Ustinov and Minister of Foreign Affairs Gromyko. This national security triumvirate had been promoted to full membership in the Politburo in the mid-1970s. It is, therefore, not surprising that the new military thrusts to Soviet foreign policy began in this same period with the Soviet–Cuban move into Angola. The military role, long a major factor in Soviet moves in Hungary, Egypt, and Czechoslovakia, now seemed to take on new prominence.

Kaplan's extensive research in "Diplomacy of Power," cited earlier, appears to support the view that even the Soviet military leadership became "more confident about the USSR's ability to use military power to successfully influence events in the Third World" after their airlift of military equipment to Egypt during the 1973 Middle East war. Kaplan cites Marshal Grechko's article in a 1974 issue of the Soviet journal "Questions of CPSU History":

> At the present stage the historic function of the Soviet armed forces is not restricted merely to their function in defending our motherland and other socialist countries. In its foreign policy activity the Soviet state actively and purposefully opposes the export of counterrevolution and the policy of oppression, supports the national liberation struggle, and resolutely resists imperialist aggression in whatever distant region of our planet it may appear. The party and Soviet government rely on the country's economic and defense might in fulfilling these tasks. . . . The development of the external functions of the socialist armies is a natural process. It will continue.

The new Secretary General came to this job after 15 years heading the powerful KGB and as an ally of the Minister of Defense—a job preparation that may have in it the seeds of his own undoing but that also presents a serious challenge to the United States. His first decisions reflected his bias for greater discipline in the economy and in society. His key appointments are largely from the government and intelligence side, reflecting a bias against the traditional party faithfuls and regional party secretaries. His repeated suggestion that "we will not solve our problems with slogans" indicates a more pragmatic approach than his predecessors. This tough pragmatic line may help Andropov see more clearly than his predecessors the need for economic reform. But reform apparently means discipline and tinkering. Andropov's approach to the economy seems to be to adopt the management techniques from Soviet defense industry to the broader industrial base.

The other side of Andropov's problem is that he has had no prior experience in managing the giant Soviet economy, nor within the party apparatus dealing with economic, industrial, or agricultural issues. To the extent that he ignores or plays down the enormous party apparatus that is concerned with these matters, he may risk alienating the Central Committee or even part of the Politburo. Andropov's ascent to power reinforces and confirms the trends described above that have progressively increased the role of the military and security institutions and considerations in the conduct of Soviet foreign policy.

There is another critical factor that must be considered in examining the evolution of the Soviet Union as a military superpower—Cuba. Without the Cuban fighting force and without the Cubans' ready access to and knowledge of Third World countries, the Soviets would be a less adventurous and a less successful competitor with the United States. Cuba is probably the closest, most dependable, and most effective ally the Soviet Union has not excepting even East Germany and Bulgaria. The Soviet package for helping Third World countries, whether Angola, Ethiopia, Nicaragua, or Grenada, involves Cuban military advisers and East German security guards, the latter often expert at training and keeping close watch on the valuable national leaders of the country where they are serving. Cuba in 1982 had 70,000 military troops and advisors as well as civilian advisors in 23 countries worldwide—in most cases enhancing Soviet political influence in those countries.

The militarization of Cuban society has been evident in Cuba over the past decade, as its innovative approach to development has waned and as its economy has become more and more dependent on Soviet economic assistance—over 3 billion dollars in Soviet economic support last year alone. Soviet arms transfers to Cuba in 1981–1982 amounted to about 66,000 tons in each year—a staggering amount clearly designated in part to back up Cuban support for Central American revolution, since shipments for Africa go directly to Angola and Ethiopia. Moreover, Raul Castro as Minister of Defense is principal liaison with Moscow for his brother Fidel, leaving Carlos Rafael Rodriquez to deal with the Soviets on economic issues.

The true relationship between the Soviets and their "privileged ally" Cuba is the subject of continuing debate within the official government and academic communities. Officially and publicly, U.S. leaders since Kissinger have delighted in belittling Castro by calling him a "proxy," "surrogate," "pawn," or "puppet" or any number of even less flattering names. From a policy point of view, as the U.S. government seeks to restrain Cuban behavior, it is perhaps a convenient device to depict Castro as a mindless tool—it annoys Castro and simplifies policy. But such a description is clearly not adequate to evaluate this unique military alliance that has played such a critical role in shaping a more bold Soviet superpower. Castro's willingness to accept dependency has been balanced by the large role he has played in world events. Castro, as the longest surviving world leader today, also most certainly tries to promote the image of a successful Hispanic leader to the millions of Hispanic Americans who have felt themselves second-class citizens in the New World. The Cubans have not so much helped the Soviets take risks—they are still cautious when it comes to potential conflict with the United States—rather, the presence of the Cubans has allowed the Soviets to reduce their estimate of risk for involvement in Africa and in Latin America. The Cubans tend to take the initial and major risks such as in Angola, Nicaragua, and El Salvador. In Ethiopia, where the Soviets presumably had a strategic objective and the risks appeared low, the Soviets were prepared to play a more prominent role. Yet Castro's 1977 visit to Ethiopia must certainly have convinced him that Mengistu was as close to an African version of Castro as would come along.

There are a series of tensions in the relationship that do not lend themselves readily to external, particularly U.S., exploitation—but tensions nonetheless.

The Cubans know that in case of a threat of superpower conflict they would be the target of swift U.S. military action. The defense of Cuba would be a low priority for the Soviet Union in such a situation. Cuba's distance from the Soviet motherland imposes critical limits on a response, even if the Soviets were inclined to make one. This ambiguous Soviet commitment to the defense of Cuba must rankle Castro and the Cuban leadership.

Castro's decision to trade much of his independence of action for his superclient status has brought Cuba mixed benefits. It has enabled Cuba to become part of a superpower projection into the developing world. It has also, at times, set back significantly Cuba's objectives. Cuba's support for the Soviet invasion of Czechoslovakia was costly but eventually forgotten by the developing world. Cuba's emergence as the leader of the nonaligned movement and desire for a United Nations Security Council seat in 1980–1981 were severely set back by Cuban support for the Soviet invasion of Afghanistan. Castro's hubris or other interests may at some point require him to split with the Soviets over foreign policy issues. The Soviets would not look kindly on a dissident Castro.

More threatening than Cuba's military vulnerability and political dependency is its fragile economic status. Should the Soviets and the Eastern European communist states decide, for political or other reasons, to apply sanctions on the Cuban economy, Castro would have limited options. Soviet economic support, particularly the major commitment to supply energy to Cuba, is so crucial (even more so today than in 1968 when the Soviets successfully applied sanctions) that Castro would either have to comply with Soviet demands or turn elsewhere rapidly. Some scenarios [see "Cuba Faces the Economic Realities of the 1980s" (1982 Joint Economic Committee report of Congress)] suggest that the Soviets may even find it necessary over the next 5 years to reduce drastically their energy subsidy to Cuba for economic reasons. Other scenarios suggest the Cubans may not want to pay back their debt that begins coming due to Moscow in 1986. Whatever the circumstances, the Cuban economy is so dependent on outside support that it would probably have to be prepared to pay a high political price to gain economic support from other sources if necessary.

Castro's desire to promote political change and revolution in the Western Hemisphere has been at the center of Soviet–Cuban tensions for over two decades. Castro's failure in the 1970s to establish Cuba as a model in the Western Hemisphere and his failure to establish constructive stable state-to-state relations with the major Latin countries— except for the peculiar relations with Mexico and Argentina—have led him back to his original commitment to revolutionary change in Hispanic America as the best long-term source of security for the Cuban revolution. In the company of several revolutionary regimes in the Western Hemisphere, Cuba would be less vulnerable. This Castro neo-Trotskyite or left-wing extremist view of revolution may not be compatible for long with the more pragmatic tactical Soviet approach to political change. Open Cuban support for the M-19 guerrilla group in Colombia embarrassed the Soviets. Moreover, the bold Cuban support for the successful Sandinista revolution required the Kremlin to revise some of its thinking about guerrilla warfare or risk being left behind a revolutionary tide. There must still be differences of view between Moscow and Havana over the timing and scale of Soviet support for Nicaragua and over the pace at which the revolutionary struggle should be pressed in the Western Hemisphere, even though the Soviets appear to have accepted the Cuban line on the *lucha armada* in a few Central American countries.

An esoteric but important sectarian aspect of Soviet–Cuban differences has always been the proper role for orthodox Moscow-lining communist parties in political and revolutionary change. Moscow's differences with other parties over the many facets of this seemingly theoretical issue have been central to the breakup of international communist unity. The role of the party has been at the center of Soviet disputes with China and Soviet actions against Hungary, Czechoslovakia, and Poland. Even though Andropov may give less prominence to the communist party role than Brezhnev, as official ideology continues to decline as a factor in Soviet behavior, there is evidence in the Soviet exegesis of events in Central America that this issue is a continuing source of difference with Cuba. Castro clearly prefers and has always preferred to deal with guerrilla leaders than with communist party bureaucrats. In an extended discussion of this problem in the special *Latinskaya Amerika* issue discussed above, M. F. Gornov invokes Lenin to support his basic point on the role of the party. "It is not enough simply to call our selves the 'vanguard' or 'advance detachment', we must also act in such a way that all other detachments realize and admit that we are taking the lead. This charge of Lenin must not be forgotten today," adds Gornov, "now that various forces have joined the anti-imperialist movement."

The Soviets were somewhat embarrassed by the failure, at Moscow's insistence, of the "Nicaraguan Socialist Party" (the Soviet-lining communist party in Nicaragua) to play an important role in the Sandinista revolution. T. Ye. Vorozheykino spoke in *Latinskaya Amerika* of "the regrettable experience of the Nicaraguan Socialist Party which clearly demonstrated that a party which does not unite with other leftist forces faces the root danger of being left on the sidelines of the revolutionary struggle." Therefore, even though Moscow has now instructed its toady parties in such places as El Salvador not to be on the sidelines, the Soviet leadership wants to regain some control over the course of events. How will Castro feel about that?

The Soviets have learned to tolerate and to exploit on occasion Castro's international stature and his revolutionary hubris as part of their superpower reality. But the Soviets must also build for the future and work to preserve a close, useful relationship with Cuba after Castro. Soviet efforts to control and influence the Cuban Communist Party and the secret police have created tension in the relationship in the past. Even though brother Raul Castro seeks to preserve Fidel's interests within the military, it is likely that the growing intimacy and greater degree of coordination between the Soviet and Cuban military institutions over the past decade have offered to the Soviets a vital insurance policy for Soviet interests on the departure of Fidel Castro. Cuban awareness of these realities of Soviet interests constitutes still another source of Cuban–Soviet tensions.

Having outlined the growing military thrust of Soviet foreign policy, discussed the military–security bias that Andropov brings to the Kremlin leadership, and mentioned some of the aspects of the relationship that make the Soviet Union and Cuba together a military superpower, I will now review briefly what Soviet behavior suggests—namely, that there is something new since 1980 in their approach. The Soviets have set in motion a series of action-oriented policies toward Central America.

Between 1980–1982 the Soviets significantly modernized and expanded the Cubans' military hardware inventory. During those 2 years the Soviets sent to Cuba the largest supply of military equipment since the year after the Bay of Pigs. These Soviet shipments served two purposes: They partially satisfied Castro's late 1980 appeal for evidence of heightened Soviet commitment in the face of suggestions that the Reagan administration might use force against Cuba; they provided surplus weapons to be available for shipment to Nicaragua and to guerrillas in Central America.

Beginning in 1980 the Soviets began to enlarge their presence in Nicaragua and they supplied through intermediaries T-54 tanks, Ml-8 helicopters, and an ample package of military and security advisors from Cuba, East Germany, and other East European states. The Soviets have not been so ostentatious as they have been in some African and Asian client states, so as not to alarm the United States, the West Europeans, or the South Americans. But Soviet allies, tanks, and helicopters are present in abundance.

The Moscow-backed communist parties of El Salvador and Guatemala declared that they were joining the guerrilla movement and advocating violent revolution in late 1979 and early 1980. This shift was significant not because the parties are major revolutionary organizations, but because they are the best indicator of Moscow's plans and policies. The main revolutionary forces within those countries are led by former Moscow-line communists who left the party earlier precisely because Moscow was opposed—then—to supporting guerrilla warfare.

Once Soviet and Salvadoran communist party commitment to violent revolution in El Salvador was decided in early 1980 the Soviets undertook to provide increased material support to the communist guerrillas agreed upon when Salvadoran communist leader Handel visited Moscow and other East European capitals in 1980. The Soviets later minimized their direct involvement with Salvadoran communist guerrillas, presumably to avoid raising the risk to them of being exposed.

The Soviet and Cuban agreement in early 1980 not to press for an immediate espousal of a Marxist–Leninist revolutionary victory was key to enabling the Salvadoran guerrilla groups and their external supporters to place the Social Democratic leader Guillermo Ungo at the head of the political front organization. Ungo's public and credible espousals of democratic principles have been crucial to the FMLN's strategy of developing broadly based West European and Latin American sympathy for Salvadoran guerrilla objectives and reasonableness.

In Grenada, the Soviets and Cubans are assisting in the construction of a new heavy duty international airport and a deep water seaport. The Soviets agreed to Bishop's request in Moscow in mid-1982 to increase Soviet material and political support to that revolutionary regime.

The discussion of events in Central America in the Soviet press, as indicated earlier, strongly supports the contention that the Soviet bureaucracy sees a significant change in Central America following the Sandinista victory, which offers important new opportunities and challenges to the Soviet Union to support revolutionary change in that region. The Soviet leadership has been cautious in its public references to revolutionary developments in Central America.

Thus far, the Soviets have held back from large-scale Soviet military involvement in these new areas. Their caution may well reflect a belief that the present Washington administration would take forceful action in response, and a desire not to give West Europeans and Latin Americans reason to cease their criticism of the United States and their support for the Sandinistas. There are pressures other than clever public policy objectives that restrain more bold Soviet involvement in the Western Hemisphere. The Soviets may, with Afghanistan, Poland, Southeast Asia, economic troubles at home, and not fully satisfactory developments from their earlier adventures in Africa, believe that they are overextended. The bold policies of the past decade in other parts of the world which have brought them their superpower status may now require some rethinking.

Why then would the Soviets decide to change their traditionally cautious policies toward a part of the Western Hemisphere? Even though the cost of a Soviet miscalculation could be very high, the circumstances that have led the Soviets to take this more action-oriented posture in Central America are precisely those that could lead to miscalculation. What would be their motives? One can only speculate, since we cannot know the answer.

Whether or not the Soviets have a global strategy, they most certainly are determined to increase their political influence in the world. Since they find it difficult or impossible to exercise that influence through international economic, financial, or trading bodies or through regional groups, they seek instead to build military–political clients. The evolution of Soviet involvement in Africa, Southeast Asia, the Middle East, and the Caribbean Basin attest to this Soviet desire for influence through close alliances with willing or threatened nation states. The Soviets in this way seek to establish parity with the United States as a superpower, not only in the military but also in the political sphere.

The largely restrained Soviet foreign policy of the 1960s and early 1970s has been changed by the relationship with Castro. Cuba has given the Soviets the tools and the rationale for extending their power into the developing world at low risk. Now in Central America and the Caribbean, where Castro has again challenged the role of the communist parties and threatened to take charge of a growing revolutionary situation, the Soviets must engage the issues or be left behind. Central America does indeed appear ripe for revolutionary change and the Soviets, therefore, must be involved.

The Soviets have no economic interests in the Caribbean Basin. Economic issues, as we have seen, have played a decreasing role in Soviet policies toward the Third World. The Soviets believe that where their political and military influence expands is where regional strife is high. Central America seems now to be ripe for greatly expanded Soviet influence over the next few years as long as the Soviets can control and establish a military–security presence. The eventual financial cost of expanded influence and involvement in the region is not likely to be high even if it should eventually involve another client state. The current costs are low.

An increasingly important factor in Soviet thinking must also be the competition with the United States as seen through the eyes of the military–security elements in the Soviet Union who have been playing a larger role in Soviet foreign policy in the past decade. The "correlation of forces" in military and political terms would clearly take a surge in favor of Soviet power should Central America enter a period of prolonged regional warfare and should one or more Marxist–Leninist regimes emerge in the region.

The Soviet decision to take a more activist approach to the Caribbean Basin is the result of this extended and imperfect learning process that we have examined—and probably not the result of the current low state of U.S.–Soviet relations. On the contrary, some of the caution in 1984 (not delivering the MIG fighters to Nicaragua and restrained Soviet leadership commentary on Central America) may reflect a Soviet decision not to give Washington justification for an even harder line on Moscow. Soviet behavior in the Third World, in general, and Latin America, in particular, has generally been governed more by perceived opportunities and developments in the region than by the current state of U.S.–Soviet relations. In the case of Central America, part of the Soviet perception relates to the developing revolutionary situation, the inability of the United States for domestic and historic reasons to react coherently and effectively, and the Soviet desire to reinforce growing divisions within the Western alliance over such issues as missile deployments in Europe and U.S. management of developments in Central America.

Whatever the Soviet reasons, the trends are sufficiently disturbing to argue for a more serious and studied discussion of the implications for the United States.

## Notes

[1] Soviet and Cuban differences in the 1960s have been analyzed in several studies. One of the best ones is D. Bruce Jackson, *Castro, The Kremlin, and Communism in Latin America,* The Washington Center for Foreign Policy Research (Baltimore: The Johns Hopkins University Press, 1969).

[2] See, for example, L. Gouré and D. Rothenberg, *Soviet Penetration of Latin America* (Center for International Studies, University of Miami, Florida, 1975), Chapter IV.

[3] See Umberto Ortega's August 25, 1981 speech on the role of Marxism–Leninism as the political doctrine of Sandanism.

# IX
## The Future

# 45

## RICHARD PIPES

## *Can the Soviet Union Reform?* *

I American–Soviet relations can be approached in two ways. One approach avails itself of the techniques of meteorology, in that it concentrates on taking regular readings of the East–West climate as manifested in the level of rhetoric emanating from Washington and Moscow, the prevalence or absence of dialogues and negotiations, and the intensity of their competition in regions outside their immediate control. This approach is favored by journalists because it focuses on concrete events which they can report as news and subject to instant analysis. It also prevails in liberal circles whose adherents believe that there exist no genuine differences of either values or interests among nations and that such conflicts as do occur derive from mutual mis-understanding or lack of conciliatory spirit, mainly on the part of U.S. administrations.

The alternative approach has more in common with the science of geology. It perceives the East–West conflict as rooted in fundamental differences dividing the two societies, differences which are imbedded, as it were, in their respective ideological substances and political struc-tures. Firm diplomacy and military preparedness may prevent these disagreements from erupting into overt hostility, but they cannot alter the reality of an inherent antagonism. This second approach, dominant among Western conservatives, happens also to be shared by the Soviet leadership.

Neither of these approaches is entirely satisfactory. Surely, relations among sovereign states involve more than atmospherics; there un-questionably exist significant differences in the nature and operations of democratic and communist societies that neither enhanced human con-tacts, nor good will, nor proper negotiating techniques can eliminate.

*Reprinted by permission of the author and publisher from *Foreign Affairs* 63, no. 1 (Fall, 1984), pp. 47–61. This chapter is an expanded version of a section in the author's book, *Survival Is Not Enough* (New York: Simon and Schuster, 1984). Copyright 1984 by Richard Pipes.

These differences affect relations of the two societies because of the close and direct relationship that exists between a country's internal condition and its external conduct: Foreign policy, after all, is driven mainly by domestic interests and shaped by a society's political culture. If this is the case, then the decisive factors influencing the course of East–West relations must be sought elsewhere than in the day-to-day decisions of the leaders of the respective blocs, and an understanding of the drift in their relations requires a greater effort than that involved in readings of the political barometer with its fluctuations between the extremes of sunny détente and bleak cold war. These factors reside in the political, social, and economic systems and cultures prevailing in Eastern and Western societies.

This point conceded, it must be said in criticism of the conservative view that nothing in nature is permanent and immutable: After all, even geological formations undergo evolution, slow and imperceptible as it may appear to the human eye. If continents shift, so do man-made institutions. If one postulates, therefore, that foreign policy is a function of domestic politics, then one has some assurance that as internal conditions in the blocs change, so too will their external conduct. The leadership of the Soviet Union is extremely anxious to create the impression that all changes occurring within its realm are the result of its own conscious and deliberate decisions; it is quite obvious, however, that it, too, must respond to the pressure of changing conditions brought about by such independent factors as the emergence of a large, well-educated technical intelligentsia, demographic developments, and the change in mood of the young generation.

II  Western commentators on East–West relations, however, persistently ignore the relationship between internal conditions in the USSR and Soviet foreign policy. The level of analysis in the existing literature on the subject, including many academic monographs, rarely rises above that of journalism in that it concentrates attention on actions and events rather than on structures and processes, treating foreign conduct as if it were an entirely discretionary activity. This practice disregards the insights of the most outstanding dissidents from the USSR and Eastern Europe (e.g., Andrei Sakharov, Aleksandr Solzhenitsyn, Milovan Djilas, and Adam Michnik) who see the root of Soviet aggressiveness and the threat to international peace that it represents in the internal conditions prevailing in the Communist bloc. These writers argue that the manner in which the self-appointed and self-perpetuating elites of these countries treat their own citizens has critical bearing on the way they behave toward other states. From this premise they deduce that the West ought to concern itself with political and economic conditions inside communist societies, not only from philanthropic and idealistic motives but also from those of the most narrow self-interest. In an appeal issued recently to Western "peace" movements, which act on the premise that peace is endangered by the existence of weapons, a group of Polish Solidarity intellectuals sought to make this connection explicit:

> States with totalitarian political systems are a threat to world peace; the necessity for aggressive expansion arises wherever authority is based on force and lies, wherever societies are deprived of the possibility of influencing government policy, wherever governments fear those over whom they rule and against whom they conduct wars. . . . The sole ideology of the adherents of totalitarianism is the maintenance of power by any means. In the present crisis, even war can be considered an acceptable price for this aim.[1]

In response it can be argued that even if this thesis is correct, it is irrelevant since totalitarian regimes are by definition incapable of evolution from within and impervious to change from without; hence Western attempts to attenuate Soviet aggressiveness must limit themselves to modest efforts at removing points of friction through treaties and "dialogues." This rejoinder is unconvincing. A deeper insight into internal conditions of communist societies, the Soviet Union included, indicates that they are in the throes of a serious systemic crisis which sooner or later will require action of a decisive kind—action which, in turn, will exert the most profound influence on Soviet external policy. It is much less clear whether this change of course at home will lead to heightened or to lessened truculence abroad, whether it will express itself in a turning inward toward peaceful reform, or seek outlets abroad in enhanced military aggression as a surrogate for reform.

III The current crisis of the Soviet system has two aspects, a political one and an economic one. Speaking in the broadest terms, both arise from a growing discrepancy between the responsibilities assumed by the communist elites at home and abroad, and the human and material resources with which to carry them out. The political crisis is, first and foremost, the crisis of the Communist Party establishment. The Party was originally designed as an infinitely pliable instrument in the hands of its leadership with which to force a reluctant population toward the vision of a utopian society conceived by a band of radical intellectuals. Over the years, however, it has evolved into a self-serving, privileged class that in its highest echelons, the so-called *nomenklatura*, has turned into a completely parasitic stratum. Corrupted by privilege and peculation, it has lost, since Stalin's death, any sense of service or obligation, whether to the ideal of communism or to the nation: It so dreads any change in the Stalinist system, from which its power and privilege largely derive, that it chooses ever weaker general secretaries as Party leaders. A Party thus self-serving and estranged from the population, and weakened by lack of decisive leadership, is in grave danger of losing control. This was demonstrated in Poland in 1980–1981, where the Communist establishment found itself pushed aside by a discontented populace and forced to hand power over to the military. The political crisis also afflicts the Soviet empire, which is overexpanded and whose inhabitants make political and other demands that Moscow is ever less capable of either satisfying or beating back.

The economic crisis is due to inadequate productivity; this, in turn, is caused by two factors: excessive centralization of economic decision making in the hands of Party organs, and inadequate incentives offered to workers and farmers, who are essentially paid not in proportion to output but according to the time spent working. Declining rates of economic growth adversely affect the ability of Moscow to engage in its ambitious military and imperial ventures. For more than a decade now, Soviet planners have been forced to transfer resources from the capital investments sector into the military sector, which ensures in the long run further declines in industrial growth. The country's productive resources are stifled by an economic system that is designed primarily to ensure the security and power of the nomenklatura. The government theoretically could, but in reality does not dare to, decrease further the impoverished consumer sector for fear of strikes and riots in industrial centers, preferring instead to risk undermining the country's industrial future. One of the by-products of the economic crisis is declining birth rates, caused in good part by fantastic abortion rates (estimated at ten per Russian female): for the first time in recorded history, the Russian population, once with the highest reproduction rate in Europe, is not replacing itself, as each year more Russians die than are born.

## IV

A crisis of such dimensions, camouflaged by massive disinformation and saber-rattling, fits very well the concept of a "revolutionary situation" as defined by Lenin. The term meant to him a condition of stalemate between the ruling elite of a country and its population: The former could no longer rule, and the latter would no longer let themselves be ruled in the old way. Once a society reached this stage it was objectively ready for revolution. But for revolution to break out, another element, subjective in nature, was required as well, and that was the ability and the will of the people to act—"it being a rule," in Lenin's words, that "the old government . . . never, not even in a period of crisis, 'falls,' if it is not toppled over."[2] When this subjective element is missing, as, according to Lenin, it was at certain critical moments in nineteenth-century Germany and Russia, then the "revolutionary situation" dissipates without issue.

Were Lenin alive today, he would very likely conclude that conditions in his country and its empire meet the criteria which he had established for "revolutionary situations." Certainly, the Soviet bloc is currently in the throes of a much graver economic and political crisis than either Russia or Germany had experienced a century ago. What is lacking today, as it was then, however, is the subjective element, the ability and the will of social groups and political parties to transform the "revolutionary situation" into a revolution. The ability to revolt is frustrated by the apparatus of repression which communist regimes have developed to a degree never before known; having come to power by revolution, they are determined to prevent being overthrown in the same way.

But a way could be found around even this obstacle, as events in Hungary, Czechoslovakia, and Poland have shown, if the revolutionary will were there. In Russia, at least, it is missing. Historical experience since 1917 has caused Russians of every political orientation to fear the collapse of authority even more than despotism and to reject violence as an instrument of change. Before 1917, the Russian intelligentsia had unbounded faith in the innate goodness and democratic spirit of its people. It was convinced that as soon as Tsarism fell democracy would emerge and triumph all along the line. These Rousseauean illusions were shattered by the experiences of the revolution. The present generation of the educated in the Soviet Union has been cured of all revolutionary romanticism. It believes that if the Soviet government were to collapse, the result would be a political vacuum that would only give license to the quarter of a billion inhabitants to settle old scores: Village would move against city, nationalist against communist, Russian against Jew, Muslim against Russian, Armenian against Muslim, in a murderous Hobbesian war of all against all. But even the few who might be prepared to pay this price if it would rid the country of communist tyranny no longer believe that it will purchase anything worthwhile. Having experienced revolution in all its fury, Russians have learned not only its terrible costs but also its futility: No matter how many eggs it breaks, it somehow never produces an omelette.

Thus, there is universal disillusionment with political violence in the Soviet Union—at any rate, no prominent dissident of either the democratic or the nationalist opposition is known to advocate it. The two camps are in agreement that if Russia is to emerge from its crisis it must do so by means of gradual and peaceful changes; if this requires the Politburo and the rest of the nomenklatura to stay in power, so be it—at any rate, for the time being. The following passage from a recent *samizdat* tract, strongly anticommunist in content, is typical in this respect:

> In its mass, the population of the USSR is far from ready for direct democracy. And we will assert that a new revolution in the USSR would be a genuine misfortune for the country. Solzhenitsyn believes that the moral level of the people today is even lower than it was in 1917. I do not know. Perhaps. In any event, it is entirely clear that without sufficiently prolonged experience of *consistent democratization of the existing sociopolitical order* one cannot take the risk of involving millions of politically uneducated people in the immensely complex task of sociopolitical transformation of the country. . . . The structural improvement of the country is preferable to its destruction. A reformed system has many advantages over one newly brought into being. The experience of Western democracies is for us a guarantee of this. Where the principle of continuity between the old and the new is strictly observed . . . there the result is a stable system of representative democracy of the English or Swedish type.[3]

Widespread conservatism of this kind among the educated classes provides no assurance, of course, that a revolution will not break out on its own, uncalled for and unwanted, from a collapse of authority. Lenin's insistence that if governments are to fall they must be toppled is too rigid, considering that the Tsarist regime did fall under its own weight when it proved unable to cope with the strains of war. Nevertheless, the likelihood of a revolutionary explosion in the Soviet Union is certainly much reduced by virtue of the fact that the nomenklatura has public opinion on its side on this issue. Essentially, its opponents do not want to overthrow it and take power, but prefer to circumscribe its authority by expanding the private sphere; this desire may be dangerous to a totalitarian regime, but it does not threaten it with uncontrollable violence.

V   If revolution is expanded, the Soviet regime faces three alternatives: reversion to Stalinism, intensified external aggression leading to a world war, and internal reform.

Among the nomenklatura and the less educated public there is much nostalgia for the days of Stalin—not, of course, for his genocidal savagery, but for an idealized regime of order and discipline, when everyone did his duty and corruption was pitilessly punished. Such glorified Stalinism seems to offer a way out of the difficulties that Soviet society faces, without resort to dangerous reforms. But this is an idle fantasy.

Stalinism cannot be restored for any number of reasons, the most weighty of which is the impossibility of running the country's present-day sophisticated industrial plant and military establishment by brute force and in isolation from the rest of the world. Nor can the nomenklatura have forgotten how insecure and hard its life under Stalin was and how many of its people perished in his wholesale massacres. In any event, after 30 years of gradual dismantling and decay of Stalinism, it is senseless to speak of its restoration; it would have to be recreated and reimposed anew. One suspects that those who recall it so wistfully realize this, and Stalinism is the last thing they want or would put up with if it really returned. The current nostalgia for Stalinism is very reminiscent of the longing of Russian bureaucratic and conservative circles during the "revolutionary situation" of the 1870s and 1880s for the "good old days" of Nicholas I (1825–1855), when the peasants had been kept in their place by serfdom and the government suppressed all dissent. Then, as now, this habit of looking backward was symptomatic of the unwillingness of the ruling apparatus to face up to changed realities and to venture on painful but unavoidable reforms.

In some ways the easiest, if most dangerous, way out of a crisis is to keep raising the level of international tension. War scares, one of the major products of the Soviet propaganda industry since the 1920s, divert the masses' attention from their own condition and make it possible to demand extraordinary sacrifices from labor as well as to silence the opposition in the name of patriotism. The constant harping on memories of World War II in the Soviet Union and the linking of "fascism" with American "imperialism" serve this purpose. But war scares are risky, because they have a way of getting out of hand: The logical outcome of war scares is war. The possibility of the nomenklatura taking a chance on war as a way of avoiding internal reforms cannot be precluded; in the opinion of some East European observers it is a risk that the nomenklatura would take if it felt sufficiently endangered internally. The greater the likelihood of quick and cheap victory, the greater the temptation to use this avenue of escape from an intolerable internal predicament. Clearly, the more the West forecloses this option with its own military counterpreparations, the less attractive will it appear.

# VI
If revolution is set aside because it lacks social support, a return to Stalinism because it is unrealistic, and recourse to war because of its uncertain outcome, reform looms as the only viable way out of the "revolutionary situation" which the Soviet Union faces. The vital question for Russia, its subjugated nations, and the rest of the world is whether the nomenklatura will come to see its predicament in this light, whether a dispassionate analysis of the facts will prevail over bluster and the "after us the deluge" mentality. The nomenklatura is not the first ruling elite to face the choice between holding on to all its power and privilege at the risk of losing it all, or surrendering some of both in the hope of holding on to the rest. History knows both outcomes. England has avoided revolution for three centuries because its monarchy, aristocracy, and middle classes have always seen in time the inevitability of change and made the necessary concessions. In Imperial Russia, die-hard sentiment was much stronger, and so it is today in Latin America.

The behavior of the Soviet nomenklatura under these circumstances is a subject on which expert opinion is divided.

A rather pessimistic assessment is provided by Milovan Djilas, the Yugoslav author of a pioneering study of the nomenklatura under the title *The New Class*, and a person who, as a close associate of Tito, has had much opportunity to learn at first hand how the Soviet elite thinks. "In my opinion," he writes,

> changes in the Soviet system are least likely. One reason is that this system is more than the other systems permeated, one might say, with imperialist class privileges. I believe that the Soviet system has no internal potential for change, just as Soviet imperialism cannot stop of its own will. In theory, the only possibility of change in the Soviet Union lies in the creation of some kind of enlightened absolutism which could initiate reforms, but even then bureaucratic repression can strangle the process of democratization. Even for such an enlightened autocrat to emerge, it is imperative that there be some sort of a *national crisis*: a military crisis or a revolutionary crisis, or both at the same time. Such a perspective, it must be noted, is in accord with Russian history.[4]

Djilas's conviction that nothing short of a catastrophe will induce the apparatus to undertake reforms is shared by many dissenters as well as loyal but apprehensive Communists in the Soviet Union.

Others maintain that the nomenklatura will soon have no choice in the matter, that life will push it onto the path of reform whether it likes it or not. An articulate spokesman for the more optimistic school of thought is Valerii Chalidze, a pioneer fighter for human rights in the USSR:

> Russia is filled with the sharpest contradictions. They are so numerous that sometimes it seems as if this were done on purpose, so that one contradiction would eclipse all the others. But should all these contradictions speak up, then the government will not be able to confine itself to promises and repressions, as it is doing now, because the entire people will be pulled into this mass of internal contradictions. The government will have to disentangle these contradictions: it will have to busy itself improving internal conditions and organizing economic as well as social relations. And then, for a time, all the imperial dreams will fade, compared with the importance of internal problems.
>
> One may object that the authorities will not bother to improve social relations, and instead resort to mass repressions. I think this will not happen. The country is ruled by a class of professionals who are interested in the Empire's stability and grandeur. Any outburst of dissatisfaction can be suppressed by force: no need to consider the morality of the rulers. But the growing social tension in the whole country, the sharpening of the many contradictions will cause these professionals to react in a manner that endangers the stability neither of their position nor that of the empire; this will compel them to carry out social reforms, and these reforms will mark a piecemeal, gradual transition to a more democratic system of government. The authorities are ready for such reforms as long as they do not threaten stability: being gradual, they will not do so.[5]

The difference between the two schools of thought, the one more optimistic, the other less so, is really one of degree: Mr. Chalidze believes the conditions for an acute crisis to be much closer at hand than does Mr. Djilas. They agree, however—and this is of essential importance to Western policy—that reforms are conceivable only as a result of major internal and external setbacks, that they will come about only when the nomenklatura concludes that they are the price it must pay for its survival.

The intimate link between crises and reforms to which Mr. Djilas refers is corroborated by the record of Russian history. Russia is an extremely conservative country, so much so that even its socialism has acquired a thoroughly reactionary character. It is so vast and complex and so loosely held together that its leaders have always feared and rarely volunteered changes. They have consented to make changes only under duress caused either by humiliations abroad or upheavals at home. Tsarism finally screwed up its courage to abolish serfdom and introduce both an independent judiciary and local self-government when the defeat in the Crimean War demonstrated Russia's backwardness. Nicholas II was determined to preserve the autocratic system that endowed him with a monopoly on legislative authority until Russia's drubbing at the hands of Japan, and the internal disorders which followed, compelled him to grant the country a constitution and a parliament. Even Lenin had to veer sharply toward more liberal economic practices in 1921, when social unrest and the near collapse of the economy placed his regime in jeopardy.

Russian history thus strongly suggests, and informed Russian opinion corroborates, that such *changes for the better that one can expect in the nature of the Soviet government and in its conduct of foreign relations will come about only from failures, instabilities, and fears of collapse and not from growing confidence and sense of security.* This assessment is antithetical to the one that underpinned détente and that continues to dominate thinking in the foreign services and liberal circles in Europe and the United States— that the more confident and secure the Soviet elite feels, the more restrained its conduct will be. The latter thesis cannot be supported by any evidence from the past and can only derive from ignorance of the mentality of the Soviet elite and the record of Russia's past.

VII  Clearly, it makes a profound difference for U.S. foreign policy which of these two interpretations is correct. Assuming that the crisis– reform thesis is correct and the "revolutionary situation" will ripen to the point where something must be done, what kind of reform can one reasonably expect from the Soviet leadership?

Speaking very generally, the trouble with the Soviet system as presently constituted is that it has the worst of both worlds: It suffers from all the drawbacks of a regime based on the command principle, but it no longer enjoys many of the benefits that this principle has to offer. Man can be motivated either by fear or by hope, either by threats or by inducements. Communists have always preferred to rely on the first of these methods. This practice has not given them the stability and productivity of democratic and free-market societies, but it has enabled them to concentrate the limited resources at their disposal on whatever goals to which they chose to assign high priority. What they lacked in quantity, quality, and diversity of resources, they made up for with the ability to mobilize resources for crash programs.

This ability has been eroding for some time. In a sense, the current crisis of communism is due to its vegetating in a kind of limbo between compulsion and freedom, unable to profit from either. The all-pervasive fear that Stalin's regime had instilled in the people is gone beyond recall, and one can no longer rely on the faint memory it evokes to exact hard work and unthinking obedience: For Communist bloc citizens under 40—that is, the majority of them—Stalinism is ancient history. But fear has not been replaced with hope and inducements. As a result, the creative energies of the people living under regimes of the Soviet type are directed into private and opposition channels that not only bring those regimes no benefit but in many ways do them positive harm. The normal and healthy spirit of economic entrepreneurship, deprived of legitimate channels, seeks outlets in semilegal or illegal activity connected with the "second economy," bribery, and the black market. Citizens concerned with public affairs take to overt or concealed dissent, which the regime is unable to wipe out and can only try to keep within safe bounds. In other words, everything dynamic and creative, whether in economic or intellectual activity, is driven by the system into criminal channels; forces which should strengthen the regime are made to undermine it.

This, in a nutshell, is the problem that post-Stalinist regimes have had to face and with which sooner or later they must come to terms. A way has to be found of reconciling the interests of the state and its ruling elite with the creative energies of its citizens. This cannot be accomplished unless the elite is prepared to sacrifice some of its authority and bring society into partnership, if only of a limited kind.

There is no need to spell out possible reform programs for the Soviet Union and its colonies in any detail. It is more useful to indicate the principles on which reforms must rest if they are to be of any benefit. The basic task is to harness the creative forces of the country in public service, to bridge the gap between the pursuit of private goals—presently the sole objective of the vast majority of citizens in communist countries, their leaders included—and the interests of the whole. To this end, three reforms appear essential.

One is legality. The citizen of communist society need not necessarily participate in the making of laws—this is a right which the nomenklatura would certainly not concede of its own will—but he must be assured that those laws that are on the books are binding on all, representatives of state authority included. For the citizen to know what he can and cannot do is a sine qua non of any properly functioning society. This requirement entails, among other things, strict judiciary control over the Party bureaucracy—that is, an end to the tradition inherited from Tsarism that servants of the government are above the law. Since legality is compatible with authoritarian methods of government, this innovation should not prove unacceptable, once reforms are decided upon.

The other is wider scope for private enterprise. The economy directly controlled by the regime must link up with the second, private sector, and draw on its dynamism. This calls for the decentralization of industrial decision making, the dismantling of collective farms, the adoption in industry and agriculture of the contractual principle as the rule rather than the exception, and the turning over of a good part of the consumer and service sectors to private enterprise.[6] The consequence of such reforms would be a mixed economy, in which the state and the Party establishment would continue to wield immense power but no longer stifle productive forces. That which the nomenklatura would give up in managerial authority it would gain many times over in increased productivity.

The third is administrative decentralization of the USSR. The nomenklatura will have to acknowledge that the days of colonialism are over, that it will never succeed in creating a synthetic "Soviet" nation by having the ethnic minorities dissolve tracelessly among the Russians. There is no likelihood that the Soviet government will voluntarily dissolve the Soviet Union into its constituent republics, but genuine federalism of some sort, with broad self-rule for the minorities, is not inconceivable; it calls only for making constitutional fiction constitutional reality. Such a step would go a long way toward reducing the ethnic tensions that now exist.

Viewed superficially, the fate of reforms in communist societies may appear to hold merely academic interest for citizens of other societies. After all, it is not for them to tell Russians how to manage their affairs; all that matters to them is that the Soviet Union respect international standards of conduct and cease its aggression. But because of the intimate relationship between a country's internal system and its conduct abroad, the issue is exceedingly relevant. Soviet militarism and aggressiveness are not, as widely believed, the product of a mythical paranoia brought about by centuries of foreign aggression: It requires only a slightly deeper acquaintance with the history of Russia to realize that that country has engaged in aggression against its neighbors far more often and more persistently than its neighbors have ever acted against it.[7] Imperialism is endemic to the Soviet system in part because its ruling elite has no other justification for maintaining its power and privilege than to create the phantom of an ever-present external threat to the country's survival, and in part because it seeks to compensate its citizens for deprivations at home by manifestations of its might abroad. The root of the problem—and the principal threat to world peace today—is the political and economic system of Stalinism which the successors of Stalin have retained even as they turned its originator into a virtual nonperson. As long as the nomenklatura remains what it is, as long as the Soviet Union lives in a state of lawlessness, as long as the energies of its peoples are not allowed to express themselves creatively, so long there can be no security for anyone else in the world.

VIII The key to peace, therefore, lies in an internal transformation of the Soviet system in the direction of legality, economic decentralization, greater scope for contractual work and free enterprise, and national self-determination. The obstacles to such reforms are formidable. The nomenklatura will resist changes of this nature as long as it can, and that means, in effect, as long as it is able to compensate for internal failures with triumphs abroad. It will always find the pursuit of an aggressive foreign policy preferable to coping with internal problems, because in the former case it can buy time with tactical maneuvers of all sorts, whereas internal problems call for structural changes which are far more difficult to undo.

The point is that the majority of inhabitants of any country, the USSR included, are not deeply concerned with foreign policy. They may be disgusted with their country's humiliations and elated by its triumphs, but they experience the effects of such events only indirectly. What happens at home, however, is to them of immediate and direct relevance; here, every citizen is an expert. Competing against democracies, which only want to be left in peace to pursue their commercial interests, a government like the Soviet one can always stay on the offensive. At home, by contrast, it is forever waging a defensive campaign against its own people, who are ready to exploit every opportunity, every sign of weakness, to arrogate for themselves more economic and political power. Once they have seized a position, they are difficult to dislodge.

These difficulties conceded, it is nevertheless true that the Stalinist system now prevailing in the Soviet Union has outlived its usefulness and that the forces making for change are becoming well-nigh irresistible.

A Soviet Union that will turn its energies inward will of necessity become less militaristic and expansionist. It is a precondition of all Soviet reforms that the nomenklatura surrender some of its authority to the people over whom it rules, that it restrain the arbitrary powers of its members, that it allow law and contractual relations to replace bureaucratic whim. Anything that occurs in this direction has to act as a brake on the regime's hitherto unbridled appetite for conquests because, much as they may be flattered by the might of Russia, its citizens have other concerns closer to home. The immense task of internal reconstruction that confronts the country cannot be undertaken so long as military expenditures remain at their present levels. Cutbacks in military budgets, however, demand a more pacific foreign policy. In other words, the greater the pressures on the Soviet regime to deal with genuine crises at home instead of artificially created crises abroad, the greater its dependence on its citizens, and the greater, in consequence, the ability of these citizens to deflect their governments from foreign adventures. This point was already made by Friedrich Engels a century ago:

> This entire danger of a world war will vanish on the day when a change of affairs in Russia will permit the Russian people to put an end to its tsars' traditional policy of conquest and attend to its own vital domestic interests—interests which are endangered in the extreme—instead of fantasies of world conquest.[8]

Anyone who doubts this prospect has only to consider the evolution of China since Mao's death. As long as Mao ruled China, that country conducted an exceedingly truculent foreign policy, threatening to set the Third World afire with campaigns of "national liberation" and even making light of nuclear war. Washington took these threats so much to heart that it sent hundreds of thousands of men halfway around the world to prove its ability to cope with them. Mao's successors, however, decided that their first priority had to be economic modernization; once this decision had fallen, aggressive actions and words miraculously ceased. Economic modernization entailed a series of reforms, including decentralization of decision making, the gradual dismantling of the collective-farm system, and greater latitude for the private sector. Concurrently, attempts have been made to introduce greater legality into relations between state and citizenry. The entrenched bureaucracy has been sabotaging these measures in its own quiet way, but even so their effect on foreign policy has been startling. Realizing that better relations with the West were essential to the modernization program, China has cautiously moved to establish with it closer economic, political, and military relations.

Thus, it was not success but failure that caused Communist China to turn from a mortal enemy of the "capitalist" countries into their quasi-partner—not promises of assistance from the West, but the desperate need for such assistance. And even after due allowance is made for the fact that Russia is not China, it is difficult to see why the experience of the one Stalinist state is not of immediate relevance to the other.

The implications which these observations hold for Western policy should not be difficult to draw. The West would be well advised to do all in its power to assist the indigenous forces making for change in the USSR and its client states, forces that are eating away at the Stalinist foundations of communist regimes. This end it can partly promote by staunch resistance to Soviet expansion and military blackmail: Such resistance will have the effect of foreclosing for the nomenklatura the opportunity of compensating for internal failures with triumphs abroad. Second, by denying to the Soviet bloc various forms of economic aid, it can help intensify the formidable pressures which are being exerted on their creaky economies. This will push them in the direction of general liberalization as well as accommodation with the West, since this is the only way of reducing military expenditures and gaining access to Western help in modernization.

Experience has repeatedly shown that attempts to restrain Soviet aggressiveness by a mixture of punishments and rewards fail in their purpose because they address the symptoms of the problem, namely aggression, rather than the cause, which is a political and economic system that induces aggressive behavior. The West, therefore, should in its own interest encourage anti-Stalinist forces and processes active inside the Soviet bloc. Such a policy calls not for subverting communism but for letting communism subvert itself.

## Notes

[1]Cited in *The Wall Street Journal*, October 7, 1983.

[2]V. I. Lenin, "The Collapse of the Second International," *Collected Works*, Vol. XXI (London: Lawrence & Wishart, 1963), p. 214.

[3]Iu.K. Petrov, pseud., "Metamorfozy russkogo liberalizma," pp. 109–110; manuscript in the author's possession.

[4]*Sintaksis*, Paris, no. 6 (1980), pp. 112–113.

[5]"O politicheskom prosveshchenii naseleniia Sovetskogo Soiuza," *Problemy Vostochnoi Evropy* (New York, no. 2, 1981), pp. 133–134.

[6]Under the contractual system of work, which is practiced here and there in

Soviet agriculture and industry, groups of farmers and workers enter into agreements with state enterprises which allow them to be compensated by the product they turn out rather than draw standard wages for the fulfillment of norms.

[7]In 1898 the Russian Imperial General Staff completed a study of Russian warfare through the ages. The editor, in the concluding volume, assured readers that they could be proud of their past and face the uncertain future with confidence: Of the 38 military campaigns that Russia had waged in the preceding 200 years, 36 had been "offensive" and only two defensive (N. N. Sukhotin, *Voina v istorii russkogo mira* [St. Petersburg, 1898], pp. 13–14).

[8]Friedrich Engels, "Die auswaertige Politik des russischen Zarenthums," in *Die Neue Zeit*, Vol. VIII (Stuttgart, 1890), p. 202.

# 46

## TIMOTHY J. COLTON

## *The Changing Soviet Union and the World**

Foreign and
Domestic
Policy in
Interaction

Everywhere in the contemporary world, the interaction between foreign and domestic issues has widened and intensified. The causes are various: breakthroughs in communications and transportation technology, shrinking the distances between peoples and spilling information and controversy across state borders; the calculus of modern warfare and military deterrence, requiring the mobilization of the resources of society as a whole for the sake of defense; mutual vulnerability to global demographic and ecological problems; trends in the world economy, now earmarked by growing competition, technological borrowing, and interpenetration of national industry and finance. For the great powers, there is a supplementary and more expressly political logic: Elected leaders and dictators, in addition to tending to domestic constituencies, are custodians of universalist ideologies that must be upheld abroad, and their performance in office is judged accordingly.

For decades, the Soviet regime denied much of this reality. Stalin's teaching of "socialism in one country" envisioned the USSR as self-sufficient in most essential respects—as a source of revolutionary enlightenment and energy for the world, but not actively engaged with it in many other ways. Since his death, the Soviet attitude has changed greatly. Yuri Andropov put the new consensus starkly while still in the KGB:

> We do not live behind a fence shutting us off from the external world. The internal development of the Soviet Union is closely tied to the state of affairs in the world arena. We must take precise account of what happens there in drawing up our plans and defining the articles of expenditure in our budget. By the same token, the achievements of the Soviet Un-

*Reprinted by permission of the author and publisher from Timothy J. Colton, *The Dilemma of Reform in the Soviet Union* (New York: Council on Foreign Relations, 1984), pp. 80–100, 111–113. Copyright 1984 by Council on Foreign Relations, Inc.

ion . . . now exert a powerful influence on the development of the entire world.[1]

Fuller participation in international life, especially on the economic plane, was arguably one of the major developments in the Brezhnev era. Leonid Brezhnev, it has been said, "brought foreign policy home to the USSR," tying it more closely to domestic concerns and exposing the country to international and transnational currents as never before.[2]

If reciprocal domestic–foreign effects are certain to figure in Soviet politics in the decade ahead, the perplexing question is on what scale and with what significance. How, in concrete terms, will external events impinge on Soviet internal politics, and with what force will they make themselves felt on the prospects for moderate reform? In turn, what practical differences will the internal Soviet situation spell for Soviet foreign activity? And what, finally, are the implications for Western policy?

## General Effects: Political Succession, Regime Goals, Constraints

We can begin by noting the three main ways Soviet domestic and foreign policy interact: by the recruitment of leaders, in the goals and aspirations of the regime, and through the constraining power of internal and external events on regime choices.

*Political Succession and Foreign Relations* A cardinal feature of Soviet politics today is the advent of new top leaders and of a younger elite generation. Political succession could both be affected by external events and exert a perceptible influence on Soviet foreign conduct.

The accession of Andropov and then Chernenko took place in an international climate marked by embittered East–West relations and by concurrent Soviet setbacks within the USSR's own camp (especially in Poland) and in selected parts of the Third World (notably in Afghanistan). Most dramatic was the clash with the United States. In both previous Soviet successions, a new American leader (Dwight Eisenhower in 1953, Lyndon Johnson in 1964) had recently pointed American policy in what Moscow saw as a markedly more combative direction. This time the situation was worse: The new occupant of the White House, Ronald Reagan, was out of deep conviction the most anti-Soviet chief executive since the 1940s, and the edge of American hostility was further honed by the widespread disillusionment over the unravelling of the U.S.–Soviet détente of the 1970s. Brezhnev was not far wide of the mark in observing at one of his final public appearances that the Soviet Union's global adversary had "deployed a political, ideological, and economic offensive" against it.[3]

The charged international atmosphere has had little apparent effect thus far on politics within the inner Soviet leadership. Andropov, it is true, had better foreign policy credentials than any of the other contenders in 1982, or indeed than any incoming General Secretary previously, and this may have served him well in the struggle for power. It is also conceivable, though unprovable, that a desire to present a united front against the Reagan crusade contributed to Andropov's tardiness in disposing of competing or superannuated Politburo colleagues such as Konstantin Chernenko and Nikolai Tikhonov. And yet, it was Chernenko, a man with negligible involvement with foreign policy, who took Andropov's place in 1984. As best we can ascertain, domestic considerations were decisive in the 1982 and 1984 rounds of the succession contest and are apt to be so again. Symptomatic of this is that the two favorites to follow Chernenko as head of the party, Mikhail Gorbachev and Grigori Romanov, have had even less exposure to international affairs than he has.

What has been and will be the reverse effect of leadership succession on Soviet foreign policy? As a general point, the same factors that propel the regime toward moderate internal reform also prod it to consider initiatives to break foreign policy log-jams. Politburo successions shake up coalitions and bring new individuals and teams into high office. They grease the machinery of policy change and often lead to a reaction against the less successful ideas of the previous leader. We see already some limited evidence of reappraisal of foreign policy under Andropov and Chernenko, particularly in the sweetening of Soviet proposals on arms control, in the hastened effort to mend fences with Peking, and in the several attempts to lessen frictions with the West (such as the 5-year U.S–Soviet grain deal, the signing of the Madrid accord on European security, the gestures on human rights, and recently Chernenko's call for a resumption of détente).

On the other hand, one can only be struck by how much more listless the regime's initiatives have been in foreign than in domestic policy. Many central elements of Brezhnev's policy have gone unaltered—witness the continuing quest for victory in Afghanistan (where the Soviets have now fought longer than in World War II), the paucity of progress in negotiations with China, the unyielding line in Poland, and the deterioration of relations with Washington in the fall of 1983, brought to a new nadir by the Korean Air Lines incident and the Soviet suspension of talks over limiting intermediate and strategic nuclear forces. Changes in key personnel have been avoided, and Moscow's chief international spokesman for the last quarter-century—75-year-old Foreign Minister, Andrei Gromyko—has been upgraded in status (he became one of three first deputy chairmen of the Council of Ministers in March 1983).

Interpretations vary as to this relative immobility. One is that the new leaders want to make large changes in foreign policy but are unable to do so because of political opposition from within the Soviet establishment. This theory is not convincing, because Andropov and Chernenko both made brisk headway in consolidating their power, and their political standing has been sufficient for them to make a solid start on domestic innovations. We know that in the mid-1950s a new Soviet leader whose authority was no greater than that of the two new General Secretaries of the 1980s, Nikita Khrushchev, pushed through important foreign policy reforms (the Korean armistice, the Austrian peace treaty, the rapprochement with Tito's Yugoslavia, and overtures to the Third World) and, what is more, used these to help augment his prestige and win adherents within the party.

A more persuasive explanation is that the Soviet elite, and Andropov and Chernenko with it, has been less dissatisfied with recent foreign policy than with domestic policy. Particularly in the Third World, the second half of the 1970s was a time of external Soviet gains, with the acquisition of new clients in Indochina, Angola, Mozambique, Ethiopia, South Yemen, and Afghanistan. Present difficulties notwithstanding, external developments do not represent nearly the threat to the regime's vital interests that the internal economic slowdown and erosion of public morale do. Furthermore, the regime's objective opportunities for reversing setbacks are less in foreign than in domestic affairs. This is an unavoidable result of the difference between international and domestic politics: In the world of states, there is no common law or culture, and each player must live by his wits to an extent unheard of within civil society. The Soviet bosses respond to this contrast more than most leaders, for they are used to an abnormal degree of control in their domestic affairs. Vexing though Soviet society at times may be to them, it does not present them with challenges as maddeningly beyond their reach as those raised by a Ronald Reagan or an Anwar el-Sadat. Because the international environment is so complex and unpredictable, Soviet conservatives have an easier time arguing for constancy in foreign policy. The reformist impulse is weaker here than in domestic policy, the grip of inertia greater, and the difference between reformers and conservatives slighter.

Control over the supreme political positions aside, what of the more pervasive changeover of generations within the policymaking elite? In tandem with the bureaucracies concerned with internal affairs, the foreign policy establishment will, over the next 5 or 10 years, come at all levels under the control of members of the post-Stalin generation. As in domestically oriented institutions, the newcomers are better educated and informed than their elders. They also have traveled far more widely abroad, including in the West, and tend to have fewer preconceptions about the evils of capitalism and the perfection of the Soviet system. In their published writings, at least, experts from the younger age groups subscribe to

> a less theological, increasingly pragmatic and objective world out-
> look . . . endorse a more hopeful view of capitalist foreign policy than did
> their Stalinist predecessors . . . [are] more optimistic about the prospects
> for coexistence and accommodation . . . [and] seem to have developed a
> particularly acute appreciation of the advantages which a relaxed in-
> ternational atmosphere holds for Soviet diplomacy.[4]

Within the limits posed by their acceptance of the fundamentals of Soviet ideology and superpower ambitions, these younger figures are inclined to be more interested than the old guard in good relations with the United States, in greater East–West contact, and (least clearly) in steps to manage the U.S.–Soviet tug-of-war in the nonaligned world.

Leadership and generational change thus hold out some prospect of the Soviets modifying certain of the more confrontational and less effective facets of their foreign behavior. The door to an adjustment in policy and style is more open under the post-Brezhnev Politburo than it has been in some time, although Andropov's cautious opening moves and the appallingly unsophisticated Soviet reaction to the political afterclap of the KAL affair warn us against assuming too much too soon. The influx of younger officials in the late 1980s should, other variables held constant, help moderate Soviet policy, albeit in ways at which we can only guess today. Because the amount of policy distress, however, is at present less in foreign than in domestic affairs, and the possibilities of real change more dependent on forces immune to Kremlin control, the changes stemming from political succession will in all likelihood be less pronounced than in internal policy.

*The Regime's Goals, Foreign and Domestic*   Foreign and domestic agendas can also be linked by the objectives and aspirations of a country's political leadership. For example, politicians may decide that their domestic program has to be set aside because foreign problems are more pressing, or they may seek out adventures in foreign policy to distract public attention from their domestic troubles, or their ideologies or outlooks may prescribe reinforcing programs at home and abroad. Does any of these three examples apply to the Soviet regime over the next decade?

The first example is certainly not relevant. Andropov and Chernenko have taken more vigorous action on the domestic than on the foreign front, not less, indicating a bias toward internal issues that their successors will likely share. The political success of the top leaders will be determined in some measure by performance in foreign policy—but not at the expense of domestic issues. Andropov, for one, said that domestic improvement, vital in its own right, is also a prerequisite for success in foreign policy. "It is not difficult to understand," he told Moscow factory workers in early 1983, "that the greater our successes . . . [and] the better things stand in our national economy, then the sounder will be our international position."[5]

Nor should one suppose that the regime will look for diversions on foreign soil flashy enough to obscure domestic misery. In the past, hazardous ventures abroad have not been timed to ease the mood of the Soviet population. When they have been undertaken, say, the sending of Soviet pilots and air defense crews to Egypt in 1969–1970 or the occupation of Afghanistan in 1979, they have been hushed up rather than played up in the Soviet media.

Can we foresee the third type of linkage, a broad sort of congruence between foreign and domestic goals? At a certain level of abstraction, some such harmony assuredly must be preserved. "It is virtually impossible," one eminent American authority on Soviet foreign policy writes, "to conceive of the Soviet system's survival in its present form were its rulers to abandon explicitly, or even implicitly, the main premises behind their foreign policy."[6] Many integral features of the USSR's domestic authoritarianism derive support from the Soviet doctrine of a divided world, in which American-led "imperialism" pursues nefarious designs against the USSR and its allies. Still, as the same scholar attests, the Soviets enjoy great tactical flexibility in defining the external situation of the moment. They fluctuate between two general perspectives on the world: One, analogous to that of the rentier in business, counsels caution, timely concessions to the United States, and a biding of time as investments pay off and contradictions within the opposing coalition ripen; the other, the mentality of the speculator, is in more of a hurry, more assertive and open to risk, and less skittish about resistance by the capitalist powers.[7]

Each of these orientations is consistent with the maintenance of core Soviet institutions, as each justifies a high degree of domestic control by the party and its agents. Historically, periods of militancy in foreign policy have not been clearly associated with internal repression and conservatism, nor has a more accommodating foreign policy necessarily coincided with domestic reformism.[8] In the decade to come, it is likely true that several of the more drastic (and more improbable) internal outcomes—such as revolutionary collapse or radical reform—would be incompatible with continuation of Soviet foreign policy in either its rentier or its speculator form. But moderate reform, the most plausible domestic path, is caught in no such bind, since it is trained on economic issues and not on the beliefs and myths underlying party rule. It would dovetail with either version of the basic Soviet foreign policy philosophy.

The rentier outlook, however, would make moderate reform somewhat easier, if for no other reason than it involves fewer gambles and obligations and leaves Soviet leaders a freer hand to attend to domestic problems. All things being equal, therefore, moderate reform should predispose the regime toward the less strident of the two broad foreign policy alternatives open to it. While scarcely embracing the international status quo or ceasing their opportunistic exploitation of what they call the shifting "correlation of forces," Soviet leaders are likely to be more concerned with getting their own house in order. Among other things, they will be more open to détente with the West and the United States—on the assumption, in Andropov's phrase, of "the necessity and mutual advantageousness of a lengthy peaceful coexistence of states with diverse social systems"—and more willing than they were in the 1970s to tone down Soviet expansionism in order to make détente possible.[9] This will be rationalized as the best means in the current setting of promoting ideologically sound goals. To quote Andropov in November 1982: "The steady uplift of our economy and the improvement of public welfare are both our duty before the Soviet people and our international duty." The party, Andropov said, using the words of a speech given by Lenin at the end of the Russian Civil War in 1921, has to be "guided by the Leninist dictum that we have our main influence on the world revolutionary process through our [domestic] economic policy."[10] In other words, turning a blind eye to domestic ills today may sacrifice Soviet power tomorrow and lessen the ultimate Soviet contribution to progressive change in the world.

*Domestic and Foreign Problems as Constraints on Soviet Policy* The Soviet preoccupation with problems at home and the arduous task of implementing even moderate reform should discourage a forward, high-cost stance in dealings with the West. The most noticeable change is likely to be fewer new commitments, particularly in the Third World. The Soviets are apt to be rather less primed than in the 1970s to seize opportunities and, because the anticolonial revolution in Asia and Africa has now nearly spent itself, occasions for inexpensive extension of Soviet influence should be fewer in the decade ahead in any case. A Politburo occupied with political succession, fighting corruption, restructuring industry, and the like will have less time and energy for distant adventures. It will also be easier for the Soviet leadership to argue as Andropov did in June 1983 that "the social progress of these [developing] countries can . . . only be the result of the labor of their peoples and the correct policy of their leaderships."[11]

The Soviet attitude on standing commitments such as Afghanistan, the alliance with Syria, and the stormy negotiations over intermediate-range nuclear forces in Europe, however, promises to change less. There are good psychological reasons for this. The same feeling of vulnerability that prompts the Soviets to weigh internal reform and balk at added foreign responsibilities also puts them on guard against concessions on foreign policy giving the appearance (to either external or internal audiences) of lack of strength or will. A prickliness on this point is evident in Soviet statements, today, which remonstrate noisily about "the plans of those who count on 'the weaknesses' of the Soviet Union."[12] It follows that Soviet cave-ins to pressure will be few and that there will be no Soviet pullbacks (in Afghanistan or anywhere else) unless face-saving formulas are found. Under no conditions will the Kremlin feel it need accept humiliation or abandon bedrock objectives.

Do foreign developments in turn constrain the Soviet leaders' ability to pursue their domestic goals? No one—certainly no one in Moscow with whom I have ever discussed the issue—doubts that an easing of international relations, and especially a thaw in relations with the United States, would lighten the political task of moderate Soviet reformers. Antagonism with foreign adversaries reinforces the Stalinist garrison mentality so closely connected with economic overcentralization and vigilance against criticism. In an environment of foreign policy crisis, certain moderate improvements would probably be ruled out entirely (such as cutting the defense budget), some changes would be delayed, others would be watered down for lack of adequate political and material resources, and generally the authoritarian aspects of the changes would be accentuated.

Extreme challenges from without might conceivably drive the regime completely away from moderate reform. One such challenge would be an assault on the established order in Eastern Europe. To achieve the maximum impact, this would have to involve—as it never has in the past—national uprisings culminating in Soviet military intervention in more than one country in the region. Mayhem in the East European empire might play into the hands of Soviet hardliners and superpatriots or, to the same effect, activate the survival instincts of middle-of-the-roaders in the regime. The leadership could then wind up declaring a bloc-wide state of siege, delegating new control powers to the army and KGB, and clamping down for a time on even whispers of reform.

Similar consequences could flow from an emergency in relations with the United States, and particularly one in which the Politburo came to the conclusion that the Americans were preparing to unleash a general war. A Moscow–Washington confrontation would most likely be sparked by a local conflict involving allies or proxies in a tinderbox region like the Persian Gulf, the Caribbean, or the Korean peninsula. No such scenario can be precluded for the 1980s and 1990s. But it would seem that the most likely forms of superpower sparring will not divert the regime from trying limited kinds of internal improvements. Events since Brezhnev's death are instructive. Yuri Andropov obviously saw no inconsistency between acknowledging (and contributing to) an extraordinary level of East–West enmity—an ideological fray that he described as "unprecedented in the entire postwar period for its intensity and sharpness"—and getting a program of moderate domestic reform off the ground.[13] There probably are those in the Soviet hierarchy who see rawer conflict with the West (short of war) as constituting one of the strongest arguments for internal reform, on the premise that only a more efficient Soviet system can prevail in the long-term struggle with the capitalists.

## Specific Effects: Five Hybrid Issues

Beyond the general interaction of foreign and domestic priorities, Soviet decision makers must deal with similar linkages in specific instances. Five of these will be touched on here: ethnic and regional problems; defense spending; foreign economic ties; change in Eastern Europe; and human rights. In each case we want to know how the internal and external aspects of the issue interlock and how they bear on moderate domestic reform.

*Ethnic and Regional Questions* One cluster of internal problems of some significance to foreign policy has to do with relations among the Soviet Union's numerous ethnic groups and geographic units. It is probably true, for example, that the party's ambitious Siberian development projects of the 1960s and 1970s, among them the start in 1974 on construction of a second trans-Siberian railway, were designed in part to fortify Siberia against possible Chinese encroachment and to pave the way for Soviet–Japanese cooperation in extracting the region's mineral and energy riches. Thus, foreign policy considerations apparently favored the budgetary claims of Siberia, populated mainly by Russians, over those of such non-Russian areas as the Ukraine and Central Asia. Similarly, many have thought, the 1979 decision to invade Afghanistan was inspired partly by the Politburo's anxiety over the Islamic revival in Iran and Afghanistan spreading to Soviet republics like Uzbekistan and Tadzhikistan, and the condemnation of the rise of Solidarity by a fear of Polish events contaminating the Baltic republics.

In actuality, the interaction between foreign and domestic concerns of this sort has not been particularly strong in the recent Soviet past. It is not likely to be so in the immediate future, whether or not the Kremlin embarks on moderate internal reform. Concerning regional development, calculations of the domestic economic payoff rather than national security considerations have always been foremost in such Soviet decisions, including decisions about Siberia. While certain areas would profit greatly from massive foreign investment in Soviet resource development schemes—of the sort with which the Japanese declined involvement in the 1970s but which they continue to explore—precedent indicates that the Soviet authorities will approach such plans with an eye to maximizing the total benefits to the USSR, not to any individual region.[14]

The ethnic question also is but weakly connected to Soviet foreign policy appraisals. Soviet hostility to Solidarity was amply fueled by Solidarity itself and owed little to ethnic developments on the Soviet side of the border (which, in any event, have a vigorous life of their own in the Baltic region). The Moslem nationalities of Central Asia, which are of the greatest long-run worry to the Russian rulers, have to date found little if anything to admire in Khomeini-style fundamentalism. Soviet troops entered Afghanistan mostly to prevent a newly established satellite regime from leaving the Soviet orbit, and apprehensions about nearby Moslem areas in the Soviet Union appear to have had scant weight in the decision.[15] All things considered, external threats to the ethnic balance will be minimal in the decade to come, so long as Moscow's control over the non-Russian communities remains as sturdy as it has been. Moderate, economic-centered reform should not have much direct effect on either the Soviet ethnic problem or its relevance for foreign policy.

*Defense Spending* It is clear that defense policy, at once a claimant on national treasure and a means of projecting Soviet power abroad, straddles the demarcation line between domestic and foreign issues. A modern military establishment never comes cheap, but for the USSR, with its traditional nervousness about invasion, its global ambitions, and its resolve to compete militarily with an American colossus which has almost double the Soviet economic capacity, the costs have been unique. Soviet military outlays stood at 13 or 14% of total GNP in the early 1980s. As a proportion of the national economy, they have for five decades exceeded the military spending of all other industrial countries (including the United States, where the ratio to GNP is some 7%).

At first glance, the faltering economy and the pressure of maintaining or improving rates of investment and mass consumption would seem to give the Soviet leaders ample reason to reduce the mammoth military budget. Will this, however, be the case? Will the needs of internal retrenchment and reform necessarily prompt them to slacken their military effort and exercise restraint abroad? There are no simple answers to these questions, and no automatic connection between the internal and external dimensions of the defense-spending issue.

For one thing, the regime has almost always given primacy to national security objectives in deciding on military appropriations. It reduced the rate of growth of military spending to around 2% in 1977, from 4 or 5% in the preceding decade, but this was during a period of still relatively relaxed East–West relations, and it could well be reversed under new circumstances. The leaders have consistently been prepared, even at moments of great domestic strain, to make formidable sacrifices to keep Soviet military readiness at the level dictated by perceived foreign policy needs, however inflated these may look to foreign observers. It can be inferred, therefore, that deep cuts in Soviet defense spending are not in the cards unless the Politburo comes to believe that external conditions, and above all relations with the United States, warrant them.

For another thing, there is no iron link between reductions in the military budget and domestic reform. Redirecting defense rubles to other needs would be only one of several items in a package of moderate reforms, and reform can be launched with or without it. Failure to slash military outlays would make economic reform more difficult but not impossible, and by keeping resource use taut it arguably would simply make some other aspects of economic reform more imperative. Further, a steady-state or even a leaner military establishment, were that to be accomplished, would not necessarily involve a more conciliatory Soviet foreign policy. In the Third World, at least, the Kremlin (like the White House) may find ways to use stable or smaller forces more efficiently and aggressively. The Soviet action that has most incensed the West— the occupation of Afghanistan—occurred at a time of reduced growth in Soviet military spending, and probably could be sustained by a Soviet military machine half its present size. From the point of view of American interests, it is worth noting that one element of defense spending that is among the least onerous in budgetary terms is the development and procurement of strategic nuclear weapons.[16] If the Soviets are to be more forthcoming in negotiations over these weapons—and there is good reason to think that they will be—it will be because they see arms control as a prudent security policy, not because they do not have the wherewithal to stay in the competition. If financial savings were the sole desideratum, the Soviet Union could recoup as much or more by achieving détente with China and demobilizing some of the mainly conventional forces (more than fifty divisions) stationed along the Chinese frontier since the late 1960s.

The Soviet leaders have long referred to defense spending as a burden on their economy, and lately they have repeated the claim that arms reductions would enable "the release of material resources senselessly wasted in the arms race" to other uses.[17] The regime's obsessive secrecy about national security matters makes it difficult to know how large they think the savings might be, but others have made rough estimates.

Most of these studies suggest that the economic benefits of cutbacks in Soviet defense spending would be surprisingly modest and slow to materialize. Consumption standards would be helped more than aggregate growth, but in neither case would the impact be great. A U.S. government report on the effects of zero growth in Soviet military spending over the remainder of the 1980s estimates that long lead times in converting military assembly lines, supply and transport bottlenecks, and other problems would limit the improvement in the annual rate of growth of GNP to somewhere between one-tenth and one-fifth of a percentage point through 1990. Per capita consumption would do a little better, rising by an extra 0.5% a year. Another analysis, by two private economists, looks at the effects of varying the annual increase in defense outlays up or down from the rate of 4 to 5% recorded from the mid-1960s through 1976. With defense spending at the pre-1977 baseline, Soviet GNP would increase in the latter half of the 1980s by 2.2% a year and consumption per capita by 0.1% a year. Defense growth of only 2.5% a year, roughly its post-1976 rate, leaves GNP growth unchanged and boosts consumption growth to a still puny 0.6% a year. The most interesting outcome is of an acceleration of Soviet defense expenditures. If they grew by 7.5% a year, there would still be little impact on GNP (up 2.1% a year), but per capita consumption would *go down* by 1.0% a year. Under this projection, the defense sector would by 1990 comprise 22% of the entire economy, defense production would account for 65% of all new output, and the total stock of new machinery produced by Soviet workers would be delivered to the armed forces.[18]

Two conclusions emerge from these figures, each consistent with my earlier prediction that domestic factors will not soon compel the Soviets to rethink standing policy commitments but may discourage new adventures. First, the economic implications of failing to cut the defense budget are not catastrophic. The burden of either the most recent tempo of increase or the somewhat higher rate sustained before 1977, while heavy for state and society, is probably bearable, and lowering it would be no panacea for Soviet economic problems. Yet, second, the consequences of upping the rate of growth of military expenditures are much more chilling from the Kremlin's perspective. If the regime insists on quickening its military buildup in the 1980s, the result will in all probability be an absolute decline in living standards, a very different situation from slow growth or even stagnation. This is not a prospect that even the most hawkish Politburo could contemplate with equanimity. The Soviet leadership, while perhaps being prepared to persevere in the arms race, is almost certain to be receptive to reasonable accommodation with the West, saving it from running faster than it can safely run.

*Foreign Economic Ties* A steady move away from economic autarchy is one distinctive legacy of the Soviet 1960s and 1970s. The ratio of imports to GNP, which was less than 1% in the isolationist 1930s and about 3% in the mid-1960s, climbed to roughly 5% at the beginning of the 1980s, low by world standards but high by Russian standards. Especially large was the growth posted in trade with the industrialized Western countries. Western imports rose from 20% of the Soviet total in 1965 to approximately 35% in the early 1980s. Procurements were massive of Western grain and of machinery and equipment for the automotive, fertilizer, petroleum, and other industries embodying a higher level of technology than that prevalent in the USSR.[19] Although precise calculation of the effect of increased trade on the Soviet economy is difficult, there is general agreement that it has been of substantial benefit. It has been said, to take one estimate, that the $7 billion the Soviets spent on grain imports in 1982 was $32 billion less than it would have cost them to produce the extra grain themselves. According to a British economist, imports of advanced Western equipment netted the Soviet economy about one-half a percent a year in additional growth in the 1970s, and some Western experts put it higher than that.[20]

One could well imagine a strategy for internal Soviet reform that placed a high value on expanding foreign economic ties and coupled this to modernization of domestic industry. Importing more high-technology goods would be the centerpiece of such a strategy, supplemented perhaps by greater contacts with foreign scientists and industrialists, joint ventures with foreign capital, grooming certain industries for export production at world prices, and maybe even applying for admission to the International Monetary Fund. Such a program, attractive though it may look on paper, seems improbable.

One negative factor is the deterioration of the conditions that assisted the rapid expansion of Soviet imports in the 1960s and 1970s. This trend was taking hold well before Brezhnev's death. Growth in trade with the Western nations, which was 28% a year from 1971 to 1975, slowed to 16% a year from 1976 to 1980 and 9% a year in 1981–1982, and the official plan (which now looks unrealistic) has it averaging a mere 2% in 1981–1985.[21] Worsening relations with the West, and the United States in particular, help account for the drop—a situation apt to improve only slowly, if at all, in the near future—but the most important explanation is the poor performance of Soviet hard currency earnings, the USSR's preferred way of financing imports. These jumped with world oil and gold prices after 1973 (mineral fuels are by far the biggest Soviet export to the West), only to level off at the end of the 1970s when these prices sagged. The prognosis is that the Soviets will do well over the next decade to hold hard-currency earnings at their present level, using exports of natural gas to Western Europe to offset a predicted drop in oil exports.[22]

In theory, the Soviets could achieve a big increase in foreign trade the way many of their East European allies did in the 1970s: by borrowing more heavily from foreign governments and banks. In practice, this path is all but closed. In the post-détente age, most Western governments have little interest in underwriting major new Soviet borrowing, and private lenders are being deterred by the general crisis in international finance and by Poland's wretched performance with its huge debt. The Soviet leaders, who are congenitally cautious about foreign borrowing, seem determined not to see their current obligations to the West—$10.1 billion as of January 1983, as compared to under $600 million in 1971— swell much further. This resolve already seems firmer now than it was under Brezhnev, if one is to judge from Soviet commentary on NATO's plans to use a "credit trap" to increase Soviet indebtedness and susceptibility to Western pressure.[23]

The debt question aside, the regime has given signs since the late 1970s of growing disenchantment with East–West commerce, and in particular with imports of high-technology machinery. Nothing seems likely to reverse that mood in the period ahead. Even proreform advisers long favorable to greater trade now concede that the Soviet Union is today "forced to approach collaboration with the West more selectively."[24] Both conservatives and reformists have been affected by two considerations: first, a backlash against the failure of the United States to deliver on the most-favored-nation status for tariffs and sharply expanded trade promised in the early 1970s, and against the several partial trade embargoes led later by Presidents Carter and Reagan; and second, a more deep-seated recalculation of the economic dividends of technology transfer. Western imports, it is now being stated widely in the Soviet media, are ultimately not a substitute for indigenous Soviet technology, and are often utilized ineffectively themselves because of poor Soviet planning and management. Therefore, the argument goes, the Soviet Union will get better results by improving its own science and industry, and its capacity to assimilate better current levels of imports, than by trying to bypass the problem by bigger purchases abroad.

The prospect of static or perhaps reduced trade with the West does not obstruct the chances of moderate Soviet reform. Soviet–Western trade thrived under a Brezhnev regime that refused to make more than minimal changes at home and seemed often to see imports as a way of avoiding more systematic improvements. Brezhnev's heirs, with less access to the implicit short-term subsidies provided by expanded imports, now have all the more reason to direct their main energies to moderate domestic reform.

For the West, this turn of events can mean only one thing: less and not more opportunity to alter Soviet conduct by economic means. Western economic leverage over the Soviet Union was never great to begin with, on account of Western disunity and the Soviets' low dependence on foreign trade. In 1980 total Soviet imports came to 5.0% of the country's GNP, imports from the West to 1.7%, and imports from the United States to an insignificant 0.1%. If, as can be anticipated, the already low importance of imports to Soviet strategy declines, so will the capacity of Western governments to exercise short-term economic influence over Soviet policy.

*Eastern Europe* Because the six allied states in Eastern Europe are politically, economically, and militarily so closely tied to their Soviet patron, their internal affairs and foreign policies are separated by only a porous boundary from the domestic concerns of the Soviet leadership.

Circumstances in Eastern Europe differ in several ways from those during previous periods of political succession in the Soviet Union. First, the viability of the communist regime of the most important country in the area, Poland, is in doubt after almost 4 years of turmoil. Some kind of pro-Soviet government will remain in power in Warsaw, but rule by an orthodox communist party, such as existed before the hammer blows of the Solidarity rebellion and military takeover, may not be seen again for years to come, if ever. Second, all of the USSR's partners from the Baltic to the Black Sea are mired in severe economic difficulties, ranging from acute crisis in Poland (which may not regain 1978 production levels until 1990) to a growth deceleration of Soviet dimensions in some of the other countries. Total hard-currency indebtedness was $58.3 billion in 1981 (it had been only $6.0 billion in 1970).[25] Third, the East European economies are receiving subsidies from Moscow far surpassing those in earlier Soviet successions, transfers that crimp the Soviet Union's ability to minister to its own economic ills. Soviet aid, mostly in the form of marketings of petroleum at prices below world par, peaked in 1981 at $21.1 billion and is scheduled to fall to $17.5 billion by 1985, still a sizable sum.[26] Fourth, economic difficulties are forcing at least debates over moderate economic reform in almost all the bloc countries. While few leaderships are likely to go as far as the Hungarians have, even regimes as conservative as the Czechoslovak and Romanian are discussing serious changes.

How will the Soviets respond to this welter of problems? Two immediate policies inherited from Brezhnev will definitely be carried through. One is to bring continuing pressure to bear on the Polish regime and nation to refrain from repeating the Solidarity experiment. The enormity of Poland's foreign debt may give Western governments some small means of discouraging Soviet-backed repression, by manipulating negotiations over repayment and supplementary credits. The other urgent Soviet priority is to reduce the East European drag on the Soviet economy. Soviet planners have begun to do so, mainly by cutting oil deliveries, hiking energy prices, and requiring that customers unable to afford the increases enter into explicit credit arrangements to cover the shortfall.

But what of the longer haul? Is a more comprehensive strategy taking shape, and would it be affected by execution of a program of moderate reform within the Soviet Union? There are some signs that, despite Soviet opposition to Solidarity, Moscow has not foreclosed economic and social changes in Eastern Europe. Andropov stressed that "big differences in economics, in culture, and in the ways and methods of developing socialism" are inescapable within the bloc. "This is natural, even if at times it seemed to us that [the development of communism] would be more uniform."[27] Other Soviet spokesmen, one presumes with Politburo clearance, have described East European reforms as essential, spoken approvingly of how "these reforms are taking on a more radical (*radikalnyi*) character," and emphasized that "each country [in the alliance] has its particularities" and that reforms can be expected to "differ in terms of depth, tempo of implementation, complexity, and many concrete features."[28]

If Soviet tolerance of policy innovation in Eastern Europe is increasing, Moscow also has a list of specific Soviet interests to promote. It wants to reduce energy subsidies further after 1985 and is openly twisting its allies' arms to produce more food for Soviet cupboards and to accept greater coordination of industrial and science strategies. It is demanding an end to increases in hard-currency indebtedness. It also is more anxious than ever about monitoring and controlling domestic change in the bloc countries, especially in the political dimension. The limits to acceptable change may be wider in the years to come, but the Soviets also intend them to be more meticulously observed. Soviet conservatives fear, of course, that another Prague Spring or Solidarity may be the surprise result of national experimentation. But it is also proreform officials and specialists in Moscow who advocate greater "exchange of experience," mutual consultation, and Soviet supervision of local developments.[29] Evidently they count on East European reform to demonstrate the practicality of analogous changes to Soviet skeptics, and they dread that botched reforms or loss of political control by any of the client parties will make the work of moderate reformers within the Soviet Union harder. The emerging Soviet design for Eastern Europe is thus not unlike the blueprint for moderate change at home: greater economic diversity and dynamism, but as much if not more political conformity among the populace. It remains to be seen whether Soviet leaders can make such a two-track strategy work.

*Human Rights* No Soviet domestic issue was more internationalized in the Brezhnev years than that of human rights. Two sides of this multifaceted question acquired particular prominence: government treatment of political dissidents, individuals openly discontented with the Soviet system; and emigration of Soviet citizens, something which had been practically impossible for most of Soviet history but in the 1970s was permitted for about 400,000 persons, about two-thirds of them Jews. The human rights issue mattered most in relations with the United States, where initially Congress and private groups took the lead but eventually Presidents Carter and Reagan, too, espoused the cause. American elite and mass attitudes toward the Soviet Union were greatly affected by Soviet behavior, as were the course of U.S.–Soviet economic relations and the timing if not the substance of American arms control proposals. The Soviets, for their part, reluctantly accepted the need to bargain over aspects of human rights as a price of dealing with Washington, and used carefully rationed concessions to secure American favor and repressive measures to convey displeasure with American policy.

The limited East–West dialogue over human rights all but ended after the Soviet invasion of Afghanistan, as Jewish emigration fell sharply, prominent dissidents were jailed and exiled, and new restrictions were slapped on postal, telephone, and radio communication. Under Yuri Andropov, who as KGB chief was responsible for implementation of the post-Afghanistan crackdown, the hard line was continued and even stiffened. There is little chance of it softening soon. Domestic reforms of some genre may be on the horizon, but these are being proposed only in economic and socioeconomic areas and will not involve liberalization, to say nothing of democratization, in the political and cultural fields. Moreover, the regime may well decide that an era of moderate internal reform, with all its attendant divisions and stresses, will require that certain individual freedoms be further curtailed, not enlarged. Wholesale violence of the sort under Stalin is unlikely and maybe even impossible, but the regime doubtless will be quick to stamp out any popular resistance to new economic and socioeconomic policies. At such a time, the authorities may also want to limit cultural contact with the West as much as possible.

This does not mean that foreign governments can have no influence on Soviet human rights policy. Despite its generally rigid line at home, the post-Brezhnev regime has hinted at some flexibility. It withdrew the Soviet Union from the World Psychiatric Association in the spring of 1983, mostly, it seems, to prevent investigation of the use of mental clinics and prisons against political dissidents. Later in 1983, however, it also signalled publicly and privately that Jewish emigration might be resumed and prominent dissidents like Andrei Sakharov allowed to leave, and it granted visas to a family of Siberian Pentacostalists who had lived in the U.S. embassy in Moscow for years awaiting exit permission. It also made concessions at the Madrid review of the Helsinki agreements on European security, giving slightly fuller paper assurances on family reunification and foreign journalists' rights and agreeing to a new round of discussion at experts' meetings on human rights and human contacts to be convened in 1985 and 1986.

Western efforts to sway the Soviets on human rights abuses must continue, but they must also keep in mind three painful realities. First, partial and highly selective improvements are the most to be expected. The regime may be persuaded to bend its rules in particular instances— usually for people fortunate enough to have articulate defenders in the Western democracies—but external influence thus far has had almost no impact on the rules themselves. It is a delusion to imagine that Western leaders can negotiate a liberalization of the Soviet system even in the sunniest East–West climate. Second, Soviet willingness to accommodate Western pleas is likely to be considerably less in the near future than it has been in the past. And third, the best tactic for achieving such limited results as are attainable is one of quiet diplomacy and behind-the-scenes pressure. Attempts to dictate Soviet emigration policy, such as the 1974 Jackson–Vanik amendment to the U.S. Trade Reform Act, will be even less successful in the future than they have been in the past.

## Implications for Western Policy

Coping with the Soviet Union has always been difficult for Western societies, and it will not be less so in the coming decade. While sensitivity to the domestic agenda facing Soviet leaders may not tell us all we need to know in designing U.S. and allied policy, it does help inform policy in important respects. Several insights flow from a hard look at the Soviet system as it is and as it is likely to evolve.

*First, we must be realistic about internal conditions in the Soviet Union.* Western decision makers, especially in Washington, have vacillated in recent years between two contrary and equally misleading images of the Soviet Union. One treats it as a country of almost supernatural strength, a monolith ruled by obdurate ideologists who pay no heed to public wants and are at liberty to proceed with foreign adventures and conquests as they please. In the other image, the USSR is, as President Reagan said of it in his June 1982 address to the British parliament, "inherently unstable," a society riddled with conflicts and tensions and experiencing a "great revolutionary crisis," which before long will climax in the downfall of its institutions.[30]

Neither impression bears much resemblance to Soviet reality and neither forms a reliable foundation for Western policy. The Soviet system today is stable in its fundamentals. The USSR is not Poland—its regime is far older, stronger, wilier, and more generally accepted by the average citizen. There is no revolutionary crisis in the Soviet Union today. Nor is there total mastery over events by the regime or an ability on its part to disregard utterly the demands of the population. The ruling party gives every indication of turning onto a road of moderate internal reform in which economic and socioeconomic policies will be seriously retooled in an effort to revive economic growth and improve popular welfare. The authoritarian Soviet system is responding to problems that have been brewing for some time, reflecting a capacity for change and for averting a collapse in which everything will change.

*Second, internal factors make moderation in Soviet foreign behavior more likely but not necessary.* In a time of political succession, economic woes, and limited domestic reform, the Soviet leaders will be reevaluating unsuccessful and self-defeating policies as well as avoiding additional undertakings abroad. Western statesmen are thus in a better position today to work toward containing and accommodating Soviet power than they were in recent times. It is crucial to realize, however, that there is no absolute necessity for the Soviets to modify their foreign policy for domestic reasons, and no grounds for thinking that they will make important concessions on established points of controversy because of them.

Partial domestic reform can be pursued with or without shifts in foreign policy. The USSR is not strong enough to keep on piling up costly foreign commitments or to step up the arms race, but it is strong enough to persevere with most of its existing commitments. Awareness of Soviet liabilities must not blind us to Soviet assets. The USSR is still the largest country on the globe and ranks first in the size of its army, second in economic strength, and third in population. The Soviet bear may have an ache in its belly and a limp in its gait. This still leaves it a very big bear, with teeth and claws and a tough hide to match. It is far from being crippled, and, if cornered, it will be dangerous.

*Third, we have a limited capacity to influence the Soviet domestic system.* If moderate reform does indeed occur in the Soviet Union, this will be chiefly due to trends and pressures from within. In the short term, the West's leverage over Soviet domestic developments is not great. Loose talk about destabilizing the Soviet system is at best a diversion from the practical business of foreign policy, and at worst a flight from reason inviting a comparably immoderate response from Moscow. Economic boycotts, arms buildups, propaganda offensives, intervention on behalf of specific domestic groups, and the like may or may not deter or punish specific Soviet foreign policy decisions. But they have little potential for influencing in a way congenial to Western interests the domestic environment within which such decisions take place. If anything, they have less promise of doing so today than they did one or two decades ago.

American liberals sometimes propose that a set of more affirmative measures—expanded trade, scientific contacts, and so forth—be used to rehabilitate the Soviet system, lending support to its development in the direction of greater social and political pluralism. Unfortunately, carrots from the West can be used to equal effect by Soviet reformers or counterreformers. We have little control over the result. Moreover, changes of any genuine significance gestate over long periods. Altered attitudes and values take generations; they cannot be reformed from year to year.

The ultimate Western resource for influencing Soviet society is not grain, optical fibers, or gas turbines but the slow-acting magnet of Western culture.[31] The essence of that culture is a belief in the sovereignty of the individual. Russian rulers since the reign of Peter the Great in the early eighteenth century have sought to trade with the West without buying, indeed, guarding against, this core value. Modern communications make the screen more penetrable, yet the pace of change will be glacial at best. It can be speeded up only a bit by external effort, and then only in a climate of improved political relations between East and West. Political détente, if it can be arranged, gives slightly, but only slightly, freer play to those irreverent forces—in literature, modern music, sport, the laboratory, and elsewhere—that celebrate the individual's right to think and act for himself.

*Fourth, we should address Soviet foreign behavior directly, not indirectly by way of Soviet society.* Efforts to affect the internal evolution of the Soviet Union are no proper replacement for a coherent program for curbing Soviet mischief abroad and encouraging a constructive Soviet approach to disputed issues and common interests. If the USSR were a bit player on the world stage, we might afford the luxury of trying to remake its institutions in the image of our own, but it is not. Whatever our admiration for those who oppose it from within, our interests give us no alternative to dealing sensibly with it as it exists. George Kennan, the dean of American Sovietologists, speaks the truth:

American sympathies are, of course, engaged in behalf of people who fall afoul of any great political police system. This neither requires nor deserves any concealment. But, if what we are talking about is the official interrelationship of great governments, a choice must be made between the interests of democratization in Russia and the interests of world peace. In the face of this choice, there can be only one answer. Democracy is a matter of tradition, of custom, of what people are used to, of what they understand and respect. It is not something that can be suddenly grafted onto an unprepared people—particularly not from outside, and particularly not by precept, preaching, and pressure rather than by example. It is not a concept familiar to the mass of the Russian people; and whoever subordinates the interests of world peace to the chimera of an early democratization of the Soviet Union will assuredly sacrifice the first of those values without promoting the second. By the nature of things, democratization not only can but must wait; world peace cannot.[32]

Little faith should be invested in the false notion that we can soon tame Soviet foreign behavior by changing Soviet society. The West's best means for addressing Soviet power are the same as they have always been: economic strength, cohesion around democratic principles, sufficient military power, and intelligent use of the traditional instruments of statecraft and balance of power. As usual, the leading role must be taken by the United States. So long as it seeks safety and not superiority, American policy has it well within its means to succeed. There is room for both superpowers, and their mutual security can be fashioned from a reasonable regard for each side's national security. Even with that accomplished, the rivalry between the two camps, rooted in different ideals and experiences, will continue, finding new forms of expression and levying new costs that the Soviets are not likely to shirk. The United States and the Western democracies need not fear their ability to compete, though everyone has reason to fear a competition that cannot be kept peaceful. Opposing Soviet aggression and balancing Soviet strength are necessary elements of Western strategy. They should be undertaken calmly and honestly, in a spirit that neither trivializes the Soviet challenge nor fantasizes it to be the source of all that ails the world. Equally vital are negotiations over mutually acceptable means of defusing the military component of the East–West contest, ground rules in the Third World, and ways of safeguarding common human values. Provided the United States and the allies retain their self-confidence and sense of proportion, a balanced policy toward a changing Soviet Union promises gratifying, if less than perfect, results.

# Notes

[1]Yu. V. Andropov, *Izbrannyye rechi i statyi* (Selected Speeches and Articles) (Moscow: Politizdat, 1979), p. 180.

[2]Alexander Dallin, "The Domestic Sources of Soviet Foreign Policy," in *The Domestic Context of Soviet Foreign Policy*, ed. Seweryn Bialer (Boulder, Colo.: Westview Press, 1981), p. 350.

[3]*Pravda*, October 28, 1982, p. 1.

[4]Morton Schwartz, *Soviet Perceptions of the United States* (Berkeley: University of California Press, 1978), p. 159. See also Jerry F. Hough, *Soviet Leadership in Transition* (Washington, D.C.: Brookings Institution, 1980), chap. 6.

[5]*Pravda*, February 1, 1983, p. 2.

[6]Adam B. Ulam, "The World Outside," in *After Brezhnev: Sources of Soviet*

*Conduct in the 1980s,* ed. Robert F. Byrnes (Bloomington: Indiana University Press, 1983), p. 348.

[7]*Ibid.,* pp. 355–359.

[8]See Dallin, pp. 344–347; and Charles Gati, "The Stalinist Legacy in Soviet Foreign Policy," in *The Conduct of Soviet Foreign Policy,* eds. Erik P. Hoffmann and Frederic J. Fleron, Jr. (New York: Aldine, 1980), pp. 650–656. See, by way of comparison, the statement that "significant economic reform [in the Soviet Union] is generally dependent on political and military détente, and advocacy of the two tends to go together." Jerry F. Hough, "Soviet Succession: Issues and Personalities," *Problems of Communism* 31 (September–October 1982), p. 27.

[9]*Pravda,* June 16, 1983, p. 2.

[10]*Ibid.,* November 23, 1982, p. 2. Andropov's quotation (for which he did not give a source) can be identified as Lenin's closing address at the Tenth Party Conference in May 1921, which also stated that, out of international considerations, "for us questions of economic development become of absolutely exceptional importance."

[11]*Pravda,* June 16, 1983, p. 2.

[12]M. A. Milshtein, "Uroki Stalingradskoi bitvy" (Lessons of the Battle of Stalingrad), *SShA: Ekonomika, politika, ideologiya,* no. 1 (January 1983), p. 15. This same note was sounded several times by Andropov—for instance in his assertion to the Central Committee following his appointment that the Soviet Union would never "request peace from the imperialists," or in his later warning that Soviet willingness to improve relations with Washington "must not be understood as a sign of weakness" (*Pravda,* November 13, 1982, p. 1, and September 29, 1983, p. 1).

[13]Statement from *Pravda,* June 16, 1983, p. 1.

[14]Discussion in Allen S. Whiting, *Siberian Development and East Asia: Threat or Promise?* (Stanford: Stanford University Press, 1981), especially chap. 4; and Robert W. Campbell, "Prospects for Siberian Economic Development," in *Soviet Policy in East Asia,* ed. Donald S. Zagoria (New Haven: Yale University Press, 1982), pp. 229–254.

[15]See on this point V. Stanley Vardys, "Polish Echoes in the Baltic," *Problems of Communism* 32 (July–August 1983), pp. 21–34; and Martha Brill Olcott, "Soviet Islam and World Revolution," *World Politics* 34 (July 1982), pp. 487–504. A different reading of Soviet concerns in Afghanistan can be found in Alexandre Bennigsen, "Soviet Muslims and the World of Islam," *Problems of Communism* 29 (March–April 1980), pp. 38–51; and Eden Naby, "The Ethnic Factor in Soviet–Afghan Relations," *Asian Survey* 22, no. 3 (1980), pp. 237–256.

[16]In the late 1970s the strategic rocket forces' share of the Soviet defense budget was less than 10%. Abraham Becker, "The Meaning and Measure of Soviet Military Expenditures," in *Soviet Economy in a Time of Change,* Joint Economic Committee, U.S. Congress (Washington, D.C.: U.S. Government Printing Office, 1979), I, p. 361.

[17]*Pravda,* September 29, 1983, p. 1.

[18]Gregory G. Hildebrandt, "The Dynamic Burden of Soviet Defense Spending," in *Soviet Economy in the 1980s: Problems and Prospects,* Joint Economic Committee, U.S. Congress (Washington, D.C.: U.S. Government Printing Office, 1983), I, pp. 331–350; Daniel Bond and Herbert Levine, "The 11th Five-Year Plan, 1981–85," in *Russia at the Crossroads: The 26th Congress of the CPSU,* eds. Seweryn Bialer and Thane Gustafson (London: George Allen & Unwin, 1982), pp. 100–106, using figures for low productivity growth. Both the Hildebrandt and the Bond–Levine projections were done before the post-1977 slowdown in Soviet defense spending was known. Some guidance on this latter

question can be found in Richard F. Kaufman, "Soviet Defense Trends," staff study prepared for Joint Economic Committee, U.S. Congress (Washington, D.C.: Processed, September 1983).

[19]William H. Cooper, "Soviet-Western Trade," in Joint Economic Committee, *Soviet Economy in the 1980s*, I, p. 460.

[20]Jan Vanous in *The Washington Post*, October 10, 1982, p. C5; Philip Hanson, *Trade and Technology in Soviet–Western Relations* (New York: Columbia University Press, 1981), p. 155.

[21]Cooper, p. 461; Central Intelligence Agency, Office of Soviet Analysis, "USSR: Economic Trends and Policy Developments," briefing paper for Joint Economic Committee, U.S. Congress (Washington, D.C.: Processed, September 1983), p. 12.

[22]Joan Parpart Zoeter, "U.S.S.R.: Hard Currency Trade and Payments," in Joint Economic Committee, *Soviet Economy in the 1980s*, II, pp. 479–506.

[23]V. Shemyatenkov, "'Ekonomicheskaya voina' ili ekonomicheskoye sorevnovaniye" ("Economic Warfare" or Economic Competition), *Mirovaya ekonomika i mezhdunarodnyye otnosheniya*, no. 3 (March 1983), p. 32.

[24]O. Bogomolov, "Nauchno-tekhnicheskii progress v SSSR i yego vneshnepoliticheskiye aspekty" (Scientific–Technological Progress in the USSR and its Foreign Policy Aspects), *Planovoye khozyaistvo*, no. 4 (April 1983), p. 113.

[25]Jan Vanous, "East European Economic Slowdown," *Problems of Communism* 30 (July–August 1982), p. 4.

[26]Michael Marrese and Jan Vanous, "Soviet Policy Options in Trade Relations with Eastern Europe," in Joint Economic Committee, *Soviet Economy in the 1980s*, I, p. 115.

[27]*Pravda*, June 16, 1983, p. 2.

[28]O. Bogomolov, "SEV: ekonomicheskaya strategiya 80-kh godov" (CMEA: Economic Strategy of the 1980s), *Kommunist*, no. 7 (May 1983), p. 79.

[29]For example, *ibid.*, p. 80.

[30]U.S. Department of State, *Current Policy*, no. 399 (June 8, 1982), pp. 2–4.

[31]The case for the slow seepage of Western cultural values into Soviet life is brilliantly made in S. Frederick Starr, *Red and Hot: The Fate of Jazz in the Soviet Union*, 1917–1980 (New York: Oxford University Press, 1983).

[32]George Kennan, "Breaking the Spell," *The New Yorker*, October 3, 1983, p. 53.

# 47

# SEWERYN BIALER

## Socialist Stagnation and and Communist Encirclement*

The Soviet Union will encounter formidable obstacles in its efforts to sustain and advance its world power during the 1980s. Much of its success will depend on circumstances beyond Soviet control—not the least of them being the changing international environment and the capacity of the United States to mobilize, expand, and effectively utilize its own vast resources. The growth of Soviet power will also depend on how successfully the new leadership in Moscow responds to the more predictable, well-defined, and immediate problems under its direct authority.

Soviet power cannot grow unless the Soviet leaders arrest the adverse trends in their domestic economic, social, and political environment; unless they manage, despite these trends, to sustain their military buildup; unless they contain and minimize the repercussions of the disaffection within their "internal" and "external" empires; unless they stabilize their periodically explosive relations with China; and unless they evolve a coherent, imaginative, and active foreign policy to replace the failed détente with the United States. Moreover, these sources of instability must be confronted at a highly vulnerable time, when a new leader is attempting to consolidate his authority and the governing hierarchies are replacing the current leading elites.

Socialist Stagnation    The profound economic, social, and political problems that Brezhnev bequeathed to Andropov and Chernenko represent the cumulative effects of the inherent weaknesses in the basic Soviet structures. The most immediate problems facing the Soviet Union are in its economic structure. Without decisive

*Reprinted by permission of the author and publisher from *The Soviet Union in the 1980s*, ed. Erik P. Hoffmann (New York: The Academy of Political Science, 1984), pp. 160–176. Full version in Adelphi Papers, no. 189 (Spring, 1984), pp. 13–30. Copyright 1984 by The International Institute for Strategic Studies.

action by Chernenko, the situation promises to become even more acute as the 1980s progress. If the economic situation is not so catastrophic as some analysts in Washington believe, it is far from being as routine as Soviet leaders say it is. For many decades the political "superstructure" has shaped the socioeconomic "base" in the Soviet Union. Now the time has come for the "base" to take its revenge on the "superstructure."

Soviet economic problems are well known to specialists. Some have their sources in the economy's maturity, some are directly connected to the archaic and cumbersome economic system, some are the consequence of specific policies and their inertial continuation, and some are exogenous. Among the problems facing the Soviet economy is that its planning system is geared to one indicator, the size of output. Prices, costs, and profits provide no true measure of performance, and managerial and incentive systems primarily reward quantity, not quality, of production. The list of economic problems also includes the scarcity of investment capital; the limited ability to pay for technological imports; unfavorable demographic trends that bring fewer newcomers annually to the labor force; the inability of agriculture to keep pace with population growth; the lack of a satisfactory infrastructure; the exhaustion of cheap, abundant raw materials; the slow and uneven growth of energy resources; and the backwardness of the machine-building industry. Given all these problems, in the 1980s the Soviet gross national product will grow at the rate of 2 to 3% annually, according to optimistic estimates. Even more significant is the low quality of both the inputs and the outputs of that growth.

Although there are not more economic problems now than at many other troubled times in the past, the problems are qualitatively different in two important respects. First, the economic problems of today are associated with stagnation; those of the past were associated with growth. Second, the Soviet leaders can no longer use the only means that the system provides to combat problems—crash mobilizations of people, capital, and resources. In place of *extensive* sources of growth, *intensive* sources are needed—high technology, high quality, and high labor productivity. To mobilize these new sources of growth would require major reforms. The alternative is a faltering economic performance.

Until now, the Soviet Union has not experienced economic stagnation. In this sense, the 1980s will be very different from the past, and therefore it is unknown to what extent economic stagnation will encourage social instabilty. Stalin ended the threat from the countryside by crushing the independent peasantry and establishing a coercive agricultural system. After Stalin, the threat to social stability came from the "intelligentsia," the youth, and the open dissenters. But the new "intelligentsia" remains clearly within the system—career-oriented and materialistic. The youth, unlike that of any other industrial country, has not made its "revolution," and the dissenters have been successfully isolated.

In the 1980s social instability may come primarily from a more critical stratum, the industrial workers. The factors that have ensured labor peace in the past will be considerably weakened in this decade. The repressive police state will most probably become even stronger and more active. Yet it is difficult to predict how urban workers will react to the stagnation or decline in their standard of living, which has been steadily rising for two decades. Their plight could be further exacerbated by any serious industrial reform that would bring a combination of economic austerity and state pressure for improved performance. Finally, the intergenerational mobility of workers into the middle and professional classes is declining and will continue to decline as a result of competition from the extensive middle class, stagnation or even a decrease in educational expenditures, and reduced economic growth.

Another potential source of social instability emanates from the non-Russian nations of the federation. The many factors that have ensured social peace in these nations will be considerably weakened in the 1980s as the economic base erodes. The nationality problem, however, is unlikely to constitute a main source of social instability in this decade—even if it remains potentially the most resistant to an enduring resolution and the most destructive to the existing system.

Economic and social problems will most likely exacerbate the political problems generated by the irrefragable legacy of political Stalinism and the complex succession process. The new leadership must contend with age-old (tsarist and Soviet) problems of social discipline and bureaucratic inertia and corruption. Social discipline has recently deteriorated remarkably, even by Soviet standards. One finds surging absenteeism, unacceptably high worker turnover, substandard quality of production, rampant alcoholism, and so much theft that it amounts to a secondary redistribution of national income. Some Soviet sociologists and economists question whether official attempts to stimulate a greater sense of responsibility and improved work habits can impress the present generation of workers at all.

The recent bureaucratic stagnation has no close parallel in past Soviet history, except perhaps that of the last years of Stalin's rule. The already cumbersome process of decision making became even more intractable during Brezhnev's decline. Bureaucratic routine prevailed at every level. At the center, crucial decisions were delayed too long. Costly investment policies were pursued without alteration, even though they yielded few of the expected results. The stability of cadres was higher than at any previous period as the older elite barred advancement to an entire generation of middle-aged officials in middle-level positions. Meanwhile, clientalism, patronage, and corruption pervaded the entire party-state apparatus from Moscow to the smallest district.

Another potential source of political instability lies in the relations among the various elites and bureaucracies. Here, too, the factors that have ensured political peace will be considerably weakened by declining economic growth. Inevitable scarcities and austerity will undermine the enduring equilibrium of the Brezhnev years as competition for growth resources divides spokesmen for the military and civilian sectors, for agriculture and industry, and for the territories of European Russia, Ukraine, Siberia, and Central Asia.

Decisions on economic reform will have to be made in the 1980s. Only when survival is at issue will Soviet leaders accept the high political cost of radical reform. Economic reforms require a withdrawal of subsidies from the basic commodities and would draw strong opposition from middle-rank officials and managers who have learned to take advantage of the existing system. The repercussions of limited reform—not to speak of radical reform—are perhaps the major domestic political problems of the 1980s.

The extent to which Soviet domestic problems will affect the growth of Soviet power in the 1980s remains to be seen. Both economic and military power will probably advance at lower rates than during Brezhnev's first decade. The drop in the annual growth rate to about 2.5% will complicate decisions concerning military appropriations. The choice is not between guns and butter but between an increase in the current direct expenditures on arms and maintenance of the military forces and an increase in the large-scale investment in the military–industrial plant to support future military growth. To maintain both at their 1970s levels is economically and politically impossible.

Major impediments to sustained, high-quality military development will originate either on the demand side, from cuts in military spending, or on the supply side, from the inability of the economy to deliver the necessary resources. The continued separation of the military and civilian sectors also inhibits technologically advanced military growth. The technological base of the Soviet economy is too small and narrow to support large-scale military progress at a reasonable cost. The traditional route to success in the military area—concentration on a very few priorities regardless of cost—is no longer open. The number of priorities is growing, the strength of competing claimants is increasing, and the width of the technological gap between the military and civilian sectors makes the transfer of resources very difficult. Finally, the quality of the Soviet armed forces may be seriously impaired by the combined effects of long-neglected health services, low educational levels, and a shift in the ethnic mix of Soviet recruits toward non-Slavic minorities. Political tensions may result from the association of Slavic officers and non-Slavic draftees, while the armed forces in general may become less reliable as a major socializing agency in the party-state.

This assessment does not imply that Soviet leaders will fail to match American efforts in a continuing or accelerating arms race. It demonstrates, however, that the economic, social, and political costs of the arms race to the Soviet Union will be much higher than in the past. It suggests that the Soviet leaders may prove more responsive to serious proposals on decelerating the pace of arms production. For the immediate future, the Soviet leaders will be preoccupied with major domestic problems. This situation reinforces the basic mode of retrenchment that has been characteristic of Soviet foreign policy in recent years. This retrenchment, however, does not depend on internal sources alone. It also reflects the failure to conceive an alternative to the coherent foreign policy structured around détente with the United States, the need to perpetuate détente with Western Europe, the reluctance to test

Reagan's hard line, and, not least, the consequences of "communist encirclement."

Stalin's successors inherited the concept of the dread *"capitalist* encirclement," which energized Soviet military and foreign policy. To the degree that fears of the consequences of capitalist encirclement have receded with the growth of Soviet power since Stalin's death, another set of problems that may be termed *"communist* encirclement" has become more central in policy formulation.

This second type of encirclement may be seen as four concentric arcs at different spatial and political distances from vital Soviet interests, each of which over time generates problems of varying intensity and danger. The first arc, nearest to the center both physically and politically, encompasses the Soviet "internal empire," the belt of non-Russian nations dominating the periphery of the USSR. The second arc includes the Soviet "external empire," the phalanx of Eastern European nations that owe their existence and survival as communist states to Soviet force, threatened and actual. (Cuba and Vietnam should be regarded as separate cases.) The third arc, farther yet from the center, consists of China, the colossus risen from an authentic revolution and transformed into a long-range threat on the Soviet eastern border. The fourth arc, farthest from the center, collects those remains of a once cohesive international movement dominated by Moscow, the many communist parties that now exhibit a troublesome autonomy. This chapter will focus on the second and third arcs.

**The Second Arc: The Eastern European Empire**   Soviet leaders from Stalin to Chernenko have remained determined to preserve and dominate the "external empire." It is a commitment that differs little from the commitment to protect the integrity of the "internal empire." But security interests alone cannot explain the depth of the Soviet determination to maintain the Eastern European empire regardless of the cost. Soviet leaders, of course, see the retention of this extensive buffer zone between the USSR and Western Europe and the ability to mobilize the miltary and economic potential of Warsaw Pact members as a necessary counterbalance to NATO. These security considerations, however, do not require a high level of Soviet control over the social and political developments in the Eastern European countries. If security interests do not account for the depth of commitment, neither does the utility of Eastern Europe in advancing Soviet global ambitions—for example, the dispatch of Eastern European security and military forces to the Third World.

The explanation goes well beyond pragmatism. Victory in World War II was the key legitimizing experience of Soviet rule at home, and control over Eastern Europe was the major spoil of war. A determination to retain the Eastern European empire creates a fundamental bond between the Soviet government and its Great Russian and other Slavic populations. It also constitutes a key justification for the preeminent role of the political leadership and party elite within the complex elite structure.

Loss of control over Eastern Europe, not to mention the disintegration of the "external empire," would probably strengthen centrifugal tendencies within the "internal empire." Therefore, the key question concerning Soviet policy in this area is not whether the Soviets will relinquish their hold but what means they will choose to preserve their domination and how successful they are likely to be.

Since 1953 the Soviet Union's position has been intransigent with regard to maintaining the Communist parties' monopoly of power, the highly monolithic and orthodox character of these parties, and their organization in accordance with Leninist principles. The Soviet leaders have insisted that the security and armed forces of the satellite nations be subordinated to a dual system of native party supervision and direct control by the Soviet security and military command. They have unswervingly placed the communications media under strict party control and have carefully monitored breaches in censorship and criticism of the Soviet Union. They have not permitted any autonomous political organizations to exist, let alone to challenge the party's monopoly.

Soviet controls, however, have been relaxed in some areas, particularly in economic organization and reform. The Soviet leaders have reluctantly tolerated economic experimentation, leaving initiatives to native party leaders. They have limited their efforts to harness satellite economies to the service of Soviet goals. There has been little economic integration of Eastern European economies with the Soviet economy. The Soviets have also tolerated a relaxation of restraints on private if not political freedoms, again leaving the decisions to local party leaders. And, until the recent events in Poland, direct daily supervision of satellite party activities had been less stringent than under Stalin.

After three decades of Soviet domination, one must conclude that the Soviet "external empire" has peaked; its decline has commenced. However Soviet leaders evaluate the trends, evidence of decline may be found in economic, military, political, and ideological areas.

Economically, the Eastern European countries have become a burden for the Soviet Union. Not only would the Soviet Union receive higher prices in world markets for the raw materials it now sells to its economically dependent satellites, but it would also earn enough to purchase highly essential advanced technology. Instead, in exchange for its raw materials, the Soviet Union routinely accepts Eastern Europe's inferior goods, which are unsuitable for sale in the world markets. Furthermore, Eastern European countries apparently do not bear their proportional share of military expenditures as members of the Warsaw Pact.

Militarily, the potential contribution of Eastern European countries to Soviet conventional war capabilities is severely limited; it is probably even a minus factor. In case of war, the Soviets could rely only on select Eastern European elite units to supplement Soviet forces. In case of protracted war, the Soviet Union would most likely have to provide more troops to ensure Eastern Europe's political reliability than Eastern Europe would provide for the front line. This assessment, however, does not apply to the potential value of deploying select Eastern European military units in Third World countries to enhance Soviet influence and expansion, as has been done with Cuban troops.

Politically, the "external empire" has probably become an embarrassment and a handicap to the Soviet Union in its pursuit of foreign political objectives. Soviet domination of Eastern Europe seriously inhibits a renewal of détente with the United States. It cements the defensive military and political alliance of Western Europeans who daily witness its military–colonial dimension. It stands as the most significant obstacle to a cohesive international communist movement under Soviet direction and accounts for the spread of Eurocommunism. The United States cannot accept détente with a power that intervenes dramatically in Eastern Europe. As Europeans, America's NATO allies are especially sensitive to this blatant expression of Soviet imperial appetites. Furthermore, there is little difference between the European right and left in condemning repressive communist measures that are directed not only against dissidents and intellectuals but also against workers and free trade unions. Indeed, an enduring Soviet détente with Western Europe will lapse only on the day that Soviet troops invade an Eastern European country.

The Eastern European countries are also a prime example of the failure of Soviet ideology and the Soviet model of "socialism." For decades, Soviet leaders and ideologues have accounted for political repression, intellectual intolerance, economic backwardness, and social inequality in their country by referring to tsarist underdevelopment, to the isolation of Russia's revolution, and to capitalist encirclement. Yet these basic features of Soviet power have not essentially altered, despite the added security of westward expansion. And now they characterize some countries that enjoyed more democratic traditions and others that had higher levels of industrialization before the Soviet takeover.

The Eastern European empire will decline because almost all of the component states lack internal legitimacy. Soviet and satellite leaders had expected that the governments imposed on the area in 1944–1948 by Soviet force behind narrow native communist bridgeheads would, over time, erase the popular memory of their violent origins. Almost 40 years later, these governments have failed to do so.

The legitimacy of regimes spawned by revolution, whether "authentic" or "inauthentic," may derive from popular support expressed in traditional or legal forms, from elite support reflecting the cohesion and interlocking strength of key power centers, and from performance. Legitimacy grounded in popular support did not obtain, because patent Soviet controls and interventionism denied a native government its traditional source, nationalism, and its legal source, free elections at all levels. Legitimacy grounded in elite support did obtain under ordinary circumstances, but the cohesiveness of the power structure and the reliability of support from other power centers (the security and armed forces, the communications networks, the official trade unions, and so forth) weakened in times of crisis (1953, 1956, 1968, 1980, and 1981). This form of legitimacy ultimately depends less on internal structures than on external coercion. It is only through performance that East Germany and Hungary gained a limited and grudging acceptance among the population. Yet legitimacy grounded in performance is the most fragile and least dependable form of all.

The real test of a regime's legitimacy occurs during crises when rulers attempt to mobilize reserves of support. The paucity of such reserves in Eastern Europe demonstrates that satellite governments rely on Soviet power and determination to sustain them and on popular fears of the danger from the East. Especially disquieting for the Soviet leaders is the report that the younger generations of Eastern European countries exhibit a level of dissatisfaction with communist regimes equal to or higher than that of the older generations.

The native power elites' dilemma is insoluble. On the one hand, they can gain strong popular support only by advocating the anti-Soviet cause of national independence with the accompanying risks of Soviet military intervention. On the other hand, they can retain power only by ensuring unqualified Soviet support and, if necessary, Soviet military intervention. Communism was victorious in the twentieth century primarily because the regimes that were forged in "authentic" communist revolutions identified themselves with national interests, nationalism, and independence. It is the crucial flaw of communist regimes in Soviet-controlled Eastern Europe that they cannot do so.

Yet other circumstances work to thwart an acceptance of these regimes as legitimate. First, in contrast to the Soviet Union, Eastern Europe has failed to produce professional classes that identify more than superficially with the regime. While persons with a higher education in the Soviet Union do not exhibit the hallmark of an "intelligentsia," that is, a critical political attitude, Eastern Europe boasts a genuine intelligentsia, created under communist rule, that is potentially or actually hostile to communist leadership. Second, Eastern Europe remains immune to Soviet Russian cultural influence. The contempt for Soviet Russian culture, the shallow acceptance of dogmatic Marxism–Leninism even in the party, the deep attachment to religion and church, and the attraction to Western values and traditions—all combine to reduce the communist leadership to an alien and superficial stratum markedly different in stability and effectiveness from its counterpart in the Soviet Union. Third, almost unique among historical empires, the Soviet dominator surpasses the dominated in only one attribute—absolute military power. It lags behind in standard of living, economic development, educational levels, and cultural richness.

Absolute military power, however, has so far sufficed and will most likely continue to forestall defection, not to say disintegration. After all, historically, empires do not disintegrate when the metropolitan power is at the peak of its military strength. But if apocalypse does not threaten the Eastern European empire in the next decade, serious instability surely will.

In the 1980s, legitimacy grounded in performance may wreck on the shoals of economic distress. Because the Eastern European regimes base their legitimacy on economic performance, a pattern has emerged, according to which economic discontent translates into social and political instability. Virtually the same serious economic problems confront Soviet and Eastern European leaders. Much-needed improvements in economic performance for both will depend essentially on a successful shift from extensive to intensive sources of growth. But the difficulties in Eastern Europe are more serious economically, more dangerous politically, and more unpredictable in their likely outcome.

Eight circumstances aggravate the situation for Eastern Europeans and herald an even greater general destablization there in this decade than in the Soviet Union:

1. Eastern European economies have already utilized intensive sources of growth to a much greater extent than the Soviet Union. Fewer reserves exist for correcting the irrational organization of production, incentives, and diffusion of high technology than in the Soviet Union.
2. In the Eastern European economies, the growth of military expenditures is even more burdensome than in the Soviet Union.
3. Economic difficulties will probably force the Soviets to reduce or eliminate their subsidies that take the form of selling energy and other raw materials below world prices and of buying inferior goods that would not find other markets.
4. Eastern Europeans will find it increasingly difficult to compete in Third World markets and to enter Western markets, where near-term recovery will proceed mainly from utilizing existing industrial capacity.
5. All Eastern European countries must service foreign debts that are sizable and, in the case of Poland, catastrophic, while pressing for export production that will further constrict domestic consumption.
6. Poland's insolvency sorely disturbs regional economic development; not only has Poland failed to deliver goods and credit repayments to its eastern neighbors, but these last must also commit substantial resources to alleviate Poland's difficulties.
7. All Eastern European countries have undertaken and will have to sustain well into the 1980s austerity programs that strike the working class and undermine efforts to raise labor productivity.
8. In the 1980s Eastern European leaders will find it difficult to alleviate their economic difficulties by accelerating the implementation of existing reforms or initiating new ones.

The Soviet bloc's economic dilemmas of the 1980s will in all probability have a greater destabilizing impact on Eastern Europe than on the USSR. The expectations of Eastern European populations far exceed those of the Soviet working class, and the gap between what is and what they think should be will certainly increase their dissatisfaction. Moreover, should the austerity programs disproportionately burden the Eastern European working classes, as seems probable, the disparity in living standards among diverse groups will reinforce the sense of injustice that was the single most important impulse in the Polish eruption of 1980. This cause of discontent may erupt more dramatically in Hungary, where the differentiation of personal income and the standard of living is more visible if not much greater than in neighboring eastern states. The Eastern European working classes' dissatisfaction will also feed on the consequences of reduced educational expenditures in a time of budgetary constraints. Education has been the most important avenue of intergenerational mobility and a major guarantor of relative stability.

Only the prolonged Polish crisis indicated to the Soviet political elite and their advisers the systemic nature of the crisis in Eastern Europe, with its threat of imperial decline. The Polish case demonstrates the disruptive potential of these complex underlying problems common to all Eastern Europe and the Soviet determination to secure its dominion at any cost.

The Polish case is unique in several respects. Major groups of the working class initiated, sustained, participated in, and provided leaders for the organized defense of their rights. The workers' movement merged with a majority of the intelligentsia and later with part of the peasantry to express a unified Polish national stance against communism. Security and elite military forces neither disintegrated nor betrayed the formal government in Poland as they did in Russia's revolutionary year of 1917. If in both historic situations the minority emerged victorious over the majority, Poland's fate, unlike Russia's, was decided by an overwhelming external force.

Other examples of uniqueness can be cited. The proposed economic and political socialist alternative to orthodox communism exhibited depth and coherence. The disintegration in the party and state apparatus ceased only with the forced installation of a military-security government. And even after the imposition of martial law and the crushing of Solidarity, the Polish nation's nonviolent active resistance to military rule and Soviet communism persisted. Finally, Poland's military contribution to the Warsaw Pact was eliminated, an alarming turn obliging the Soviets to redesign contingency plans for a war in Europe.

The installation of a military-security government represented an act of desperation for Polish communists and their Soviet mentors—not an act of long-range planning. It avoided the more costly and unpredictable alternative of direct Soviet armed intervention; but from the Soviet perspective, nothing has been solved. The pope's visit in June 1983 exposed the vast gulf between a hybrid government without subjects and a disaffected population without influence. Solidarity was defeated as an organization and the representative of dual power, but the other power, the Catholic church, emerged even stronger in authority and more radical in aspirations. At the same time, the communist establishment has been divided dangerously along two axes—the party versus the military and the moderates versus the hardliners. Since its very inception, military rule with the attendant military infiltration of the weakened party apparatus at all levels has appeared to be the only alternative to greater chaos.

Tsarist and Soviet tradition firmly upholds the principle and practice of civilian and party ascendancy over the military. Today Soviet leaders are paralyzed, on the one hand, by the fear of prolonging a military regime in Poland and the fear of abolishing it in favor of civilian party rule, on the other. To avert a popular explosion, to prevent a resurgence of Solidarity, and to ensure a minimum of political instability in Poland are the immediate Soviet objectives. Only a military-security government would appear capable of achieving them.

Neither Polish citizens, Polish communists, nor Soviet leaders can find comfort in the prospects for the future. A violent outbreak remains possible, with its inevitable armed response from the East. If such developments do not occur, the restoration of an orthodox communist regime will be impossible for the next 3 to 5 years because it could provoke civil war. Also, a competing political organization modeled on Solidarity cannot be restored because it would provoke Soviet invasion.

The sole feasible short-term solution would involve a political compromise mediated by the church that would gradually reorganize the communist regime and return its overall political monopoly and at the same time grant certain demands of the defunct Solidarity to officially sanctioned trade unions. The restored regime would recognize the church's place in Poland's spiritual and, to some extent, secular life. It would redirect its economic planning to satisfy modest goals of the consumer. A number of years will be required to stabilize the economic and political situation, to achieve pre-Solidarity levels of production, and to plan for major changes in the Polish economic system. The level of political, social, and economic stability in Poland will likely remain low through the 1980s, and changes in policies and structures will be introduced gradually and with only partial effect.

The Soviet leaders are now persuaded that they committed a number of mistakes in Poland. Impressed in the early and mid-1970s by the satellite's drive to build a "second industrial Poland," fueled largely by Western credits, the Soviets failed to press for alterations in goals and means. Surprised by the extent of labor unrest in the summer of 1980, the Soviets failed to intervene decisively in internal Polish party matters or in relations between the party and Solidarity. The Polish case illustrates the independence of the native communist leadership in Eastern Europe with regard to domestic and especially economic questions, the USSR's slack monitoring of internal developments, and the unsatisfactory initial Soviet response to the Polish turbulence.

Soviet economic difficulties in the 1980s, which have been exacerbated by the state of the international money and commodity markets, have seriously impaired the Soviet Union's ability to bear the burden of substantial subsidies to Eastern Europe (as well as to Cuba and Vietnam). This burden now absorbs between a quarter and a third of the increments of Soviet investment growth. At the same time the party leadership is becoming increasingly impatient with the modest level of Eastern European participation in Soviet economic development.

Eastern Europe's vulnerability to social unrest significantly complicates Soviet relations with the West and presents irreconcilable con-tradictions to Soviet policymakers. Soviet officials fear Eastern European economic dependence on the West (what the Soviet press calls "the imperialist trap"), while acknowledging that Western European support of Eastern European economic development might ease pressure on Soviet resources. Social peace with a degree of cultural liberalism in Eastern Europe cements the Soviet détente with Western Europe and underpins any hope for restoration of détente with the United States. Improved relations with the West, and especially with the United States, however, encourage liberal forces in Eastern Europe and impede Soviet efforts to contain them.

It has often been stated in the specialized and general Soviet press that the USSR should learn from the experience of Eastern Europe, especially that of Hungary and East Germany. In Eastern Europe, however, the Soviet leaders are not pressing to introduce economic reforms where they do not already exist—in Czechoslovakia, for ex-ample. Nor, on the other hand, are they pressing for a return to orthodoxy in countries where reforms are well advanced. The primacy of political over economic considerations lies at the root of the in-consistency. The Soviets apparently accept established reforms and their economic consequences while fearing the political consequences of new or bolder reforms. Thus the major influence on Soviet attitudes comes from Poland, not Hungary.

Soviet policy in Eastern Europe during the 1980s will stress political stability over economic development. That stability ultimately depends on improved economic performance, which in turn depends on poten-tially destabilizing economic reform. This predicament mirrors the con-tradiction between the two key Soviet goals in Eastern Europe—preserving Soviet dominion and ensuring domestic stability. The first requires orthodoxy. The second requires innovation.

No survey of the Soviet Union's "second arc" would be complete without exploring its significance for the domestic and foreign policies of the imperial power itself. Eastern Europe is a bridge between Western countries and the Soviet Union, at least for technological transfer and economic experimentation. The far greater significance of the Eastern European empire, however, is its very existence and its endemic in-stability. Eastern Europe inhibits political and economic liberalization in the USSR. The Soviet leaders fear the consequences across borders in either direction of any departure from a sterile orthodoxy.

The effect on Soviet foreign policy is even more complex and con-tradictory. First, the commitment to hold the Eastern European empire is far more important to Soviet leaders than the commitment either to secure a durable rapprochement with the West or to expand their power in the Third World. Second, Eastern Europe (especially East Germany and Czechoslovakia) significantly contributes to the extension of Soviet influence in the Third World—through military and security advice and through training, weapons delivery, and economic exchange and aid. Third, given that priorities in Soviet policy are directly correlated with distance from Moscow, difficulties in Eastern Europe tend to reinforce retrenchment in foreign policy, as the Polish case shows. Fourth, the situation in Eastern Europe bears heavily on the policy of détente with Western Europe and the United States.

Because of the importance of the European détente to Soviet interests, Western Europe has the leverage to moderate Soviet policies in Eastern Europe. Less discussed but more important is the leverage that dominion over Eastern Europe affords the Soviet leadership vis-à-vis Western Europe. Twenty-two million East German hostages serve as a powerful restraint on West German policy toward the Soviet Union and on West German willingness to support American postdétente policy toward the Soviet Union. Moreover, the rebirth of strong German nationalism, this time on the left of German politics, has again raised the question of German reunification, not as a long-range historical prospect but as a question to be resolved in this century. Such considerations give the Soviet Union room for manipulation in German politics. As for the United States, the Soviet leaders must decide whether the advantages of a renewed détente—so far the central and seemingly irreplaceable focus of Soviet foreign policy—outweigh the disadvantages in the form of inevitable pressures for liberalization and independence in Eastern Europe.

If successive explosions fail to rock Eastern Europe during the remainder of the 1980s, serious tensions will persist within client states and between them and the imperial center. For years to come Poland will remain the focus of Soviet attention and fear in the area. It remains to be seen whether Western Europe will exercise its virtually unused leverage to affect the Soviet imperial policy and the direction of Eastern European development. (Without some semblance of détente with the Soviet Union, the United States holds practically no such leverage.) The situation in the second arc during the 1980s will act as a restraint on various Soviet policies toward the outside world, but it is futile to hope that Soviet foreign policy will abandon global objectives to concentrate on either imperial or domestic problems.

For 40 years the Soviet Union has had the good luck to confront crises in only one Eastern European country at a time. Even if this luck holds in the 1980s, Eastern Europe will spotlight Soviet weaknesses and failures. Even more important, it may generate the sparks that could ignite a large-scale military conflict. Soviet–Eastern European relations will impede East–West cooperation, especially in the area that affects all mankind—the control and reduction of nuclear weapons.

## The Third Arc: China

Ever since Khrushchev discredited Stalin's legacy in 1956, Soviet leaders have encountered the greatest risks and costs of communist encirclement in its relations with China. Along thousands of miles of eastern and southeastern borders, vast quantities of men and matériel were fixed in varying degrees of readiness against this once-loyal communist ally, while military planners were obliged to make complex preparations for war on two fronts. Since 1979, however, the conflict between the Soviet Union and China has moderated. Both sides have cautiously and slowly moved toward a normalization of state relations. They will probably soon achieve a degree of rapprochement that would have appeared highly unlikely to most informed observers just a few years ago.

Most important, China has gradually modified its position on the three preconditions essential for serious negotiations and improved relations. For some time, China had insisted on Vietnamese withdrawal, from Kampuchea, Soviet withdrawal from Afghanistan, and Soviet reduction of forces on the Chinese border, together with total withdrawal from Mongolia. Following 2 years of cautious modification, China now appears ready to negotiate if the Soviet Union is willing to begin a partial fulfillment of any one of the preconditions.

Why has China shifted its policy to this extent, especially in the last 3 years? The answers lie in its evaluation of the Chinese domestic situation, the balance within the Sino–Soviet–American triangle, and the changing international environment. President Reagan's policy toward China has clearly damaged Sino–American relations and accelerated the process of Sino–Soviet rapprochement. Ironically, the United States's consistent hard line toward the Soviet Union—a posture that China urged in the past—now works to distance China from the United States. Reassured by Reagan's strong stance against the Soviet Union, China can relax its vigilant warnings about Soviet hegemonism. Indeed, one can argue that poor Soviet–American relations draw China toward the Soviet Union while good Soviet–American relations draw China closer to the United States.

The softening Chinese position on the preconditions for normalization with the Soviet Union stems less from specific American policies, however, than from the need for stabilized relations with a less threatening neighbor in order to pursue internal modernization. The Chinese leaders perceive less danger from a Soviet Union beset by domestic and especially economic difficulties, and they expect the phase of retrenchment to persist in Soviet foreign policy. All of these considerations strengthen the position of those in the Chinese elite, especially the Chinese armed forces, which favor more independence in China's position within the strategic triangle and criticize excessive leaning toward the United States.

Difficulties encountered in implementing the ambitious program of reforms in China demand a greater concentration on domestic affairs and a greater need to minimize the danger from the Soviet Union. Of the "four modernizations," China places military modernization last. Abandonment of old slogans, devolution of economic power, reevaluation of the past, and uncertain plans for the future—all heighten the anxiety among the leaders and bureaucracies that control over the population, particularly the youth and the intelligentsia, will be lost. They strenuously seek a new ideological compass by which to guide the population and strengthen authoritarian control. In this regard the West constitutes a greater danger than the Soviet Union, as the leadership acknowledged by terminating the short-lived "democracy" campaign. As a matter of fact, China is becoming more interested in certain phases of Soviet historical development. The process of post-Mao evolution has many elements in common with both the New Economic Policy (NEP) and with the post-Stalin experience.

Several years ago, Western policymakers and analysts tended to exaggerate the unalterability of Sino–Soviet tensions. Now they tend to exaggerate the likely consequences of reconciliation and its susceptibility to Western, especially American, influence. Although it is impossible to predict the detailed progression of the Sino–Soviet rapprochement, it is possible to be quite certain about its limits. Normalization would end the reciprocal vilification in the press; stimulate scientific, educational, cultural, and athletic exchange; increase the communication of unclassified materials and facilitate the visits of journalists and economic experts; reduce the isolation of accredited diplomats; reinstate Chinese relations with pro-Moscow communist parties; and, more important, expand trade, perhaps even substantially. Quite possibly, the Sino–Soviet border dispute will be resolved by compromise. Eventually, a Sino–Soviet agreement could produce mutual troop reductions along the border, and a nonaggression treaty might be signed.

Normalization, however, will bring no Sino–Soviet political or military alliance—not even détente. Nor will it restore friendly relations between the two communist parties. Normalization will reduce tensions, but it will not erase China's suspicions of Soviet hostility to Chinese ambitions. It will not deter Chinese efforts to reach agreement with Japan on issues of defense and trade. Finally, China will perpetuate Sino–Soviet tensions in the Third World by opposing Soviet "hegemonist" expansion there.

Normalization of Sino–Soviet relations will leave certain cardinal facts of the Sino–Soviet–American triangle unaltered. The Soviet Union and China remain potential enemies whose security is measured only in relation to each other's weaknesses. The Soviet Union remains a present and future danger to China, while China will continue to fear little and gain much from the United States while it is hostile to the Soviet Union. Regardless of normalization, the Soviet Union aims to prevent or delay China's attainment of genuine great-power status. Prejudice and fear govern Soviet relations with a country with which it shares a border of 6,000 kilometers, contains the largest population in the world, and possesses the will and resources to reclaim its historic greatness. As long as the Soviet threat persists, the United States has no reason to oppose the growth of Chinese power and international stature, even if it has no enthusiasm for underwriting the Chinese process of modernization.

Normalization will not obviate the need to keep one-third of the Soviet armed forces and one-quarter of the Soviet rocket forces opposite China. Nor will it relieve Soviet military planners of the necessity to plan for a two-front war and economic planners of the necessity to finance it. Nor will normalization facilitate the more central Soviet goals of destroying the Western alliance or restoring a semblance of détente with the United States.

Normalization will strengthen China's position in the strategic triangle, but it will not secure China a place equidistant from both partners.

Given Chinese fears, needs, and interests, its position in the triangle will remain skewed in favor of the United States. Sino–American relations will remain closer than either Sino–Soviet or Soviet–American relations. The United States remains the pivotal country in the strategic triangle and derives more advantage from it than either of the other two powers.

Current Soviet policy exhibits a new urgency and flexibility that is rooted in the disintegration of the Soviet–American détente, the threatening American military buildup, and the potentially greater Japanese military presence. If Soviet fears of encirclement subsided during the early 1970s, they surfaced again by the end of the decade. The Soviet Union not only began to see itself as the object of an unfriendly encirclement, both "capitalist" and "communist," but it also began to exaggerate the growth of both Western and Eastern components of the encirclement.

Conclusion   Since the mid-1970s, the Soviet Union has been expanding externally while declining internally, and now contradictory pressures vastly complicate the policy choices of the Soviet leaders. On the one hand, the magnitude of domestic difficulties demands urgent and concentrated attention. On the other hand, the international environment offers considerable opportunities to expand Soviet power and influence, especially in the Third World. Internal decline will surely continue or even accelerate during the remainder of the 1980s. The desire to translate newly achieved Soviet global military power into international influence will perhaps heighten the risk of active Soviet intervention in the world's most troubled regions. The key question is whether the Soviet leadership will alleviate and resolve problems within the Soviet Union and its empire or pursue external advantages.

As for China, the pursuit of a new direction in foreign policy represents merely another, though significant, expression of how its leaders regard their national interests. The process of normalization has an internal and profound dynamic, which is neither sparked nor guided by the conduct of the United States. If President Reagan's policies toward China have had an impact on the direction of Sino–Soviet rapprochement, they certainly do not explain it. Former officials of the Carter administration accuse Reagan of losing "our China card," thereby perpetuating vain illusions and a shortsighted manipulative approach to relations with China. The United States would be well advised to forget the "China card" and be satisfied with the existence of an independent China. Its geographical location, its historical attitude toward Russia, its military power, and its experience with Soviet leadership provide an important obstacle to the expansionism of the Soviet Union.

The United States and its Western allies have greater opportunities now than they had in the 1970s to influence Soviet international behavior. The combination of circumstances within and outside the Soviet Union encourages prospects for moderating the inevitable conflict between East and West by devising acceptable rules of international conduct on both sides and by achieving agreements on limiting, reducing, and stabilizing the arms race. The Soviet Union will be more amenable to serious negotiations while it is preoccupied with domestic and imperial problems, while it contemplates the escalating costs of a new arms race, while the Kremlin successions have interrupted the inertial drift of Soviet policies, and while Soviet leaders are learning that there is no substitute for better relations with the United States and for a controlled management of the East–West conflict. The principal question of the 1980s is not what Chernenko will do. Rather, it is what the United States and the Western alliance will do, for the policies of Moscow's new leader will largely depend on their actions.

# 48     VERNON V. ASPATURIAN

## Soviet Global Power and the Correlation of Forces*

For some time now, the USSR's behavior in the international arena, and particularly in the Third World, has been debated within the context of whether Moscow is executing a "grand design" or "global strategy" or merely responding to "targets of opportunity." Actually, Soviet policy amounts to something less than a master plan (grand design) or a 5- or 10-year plan (global strategy), yet it is something much more than a sequence of responses to targets of opportunity. The Soviet invasion of Afghanistan at the end of 1979 was clearly in part an initiatory act and not exclusively a reactive one. Even more important, the USSR's recent insistence, in advance of any definition or occasion, that as an equal to the United States it must be consulted in principle on all major issues everywhere, hardly seems like a passive, reactive policy that a targets-of-opportunity hypothesis would convey. The Soviet Union responds to targets of opportunity, it often creates its own opportunities, and it behaves in the absence of opportunities.

In short, the Soviet Union has developed a *global policy* to correspond with its as yet modest global capabilities. This chapter will explore that policy and its complexities and ramifications from Moscow's standpoint.

**Assertion of Global-Power Status**    "Today," declared Foreign Minister Andrey Gromyko at the Twenty-fourth Congress of the Communist Party of the Soviet Union (CPSU) in April 1971, "there is no question of any significance which can be decided without the Soviet Union or in opposition to it."[1] This public, if somewhat premature, self-anointment by Moscow as a global power represented more pretension and anticipation than reality. Although for most of the postwar era, the international system had functioned along bipolar lines, with two powers dominating the international landscape,

*Reprinted by permission of the author and publisher from *Problems of Communism* 29, no. 3 (May–June, 1980), pp. 1–18. No copyright claimed.

the United States at that juncture still constituted the only authentic global power.[2]

To be sure, Nikita Khrushchev had made a bid for global status in the late 1950s and early 1960s, when he thought that Soviet space achievements had set in motion a psychological momentum that could be converted into Soviet power. But this early and highly premature bid had failed, just as had Khrushchev's boast that the Soviet Union would soon overtake the United States in science, technology, and certain sectors of the economy.[3]

Within a year after Gromyko revealed Moscow's self-image as a global power, however, the Soviet Union was formally, if inadvertently, enshrined as a global power when, at the SALT I ceremonies in Moscow, the United States voluntarily recognized the Soviet Union as an equal *strategic power*, as reflected in the principle of strategic parity. One prerequisite "for maintaining and strengthening peaceful relations" between the USSR and the United States, reads the "Basic Principles of Relations between the United States of America and the Union of Soviet Socialist Republics," is "the recognition of the security interests of the Parties based on the principle of equality."[4] Although the Soviet Union in 1972 was not yet a global power, Moscow considered that the SALT I agreements and the principle of strategic parity invested the USSR with the mantle of global status and all of the entitlements and deference such a status presumed and implied.

About 1974, the Soviet Union's global character finally took shape, when the USSR developed a modest but growing global capability to match its global pretensions. Taking advantage of the temporary paralysis induced in the United States by the post-Vietnam malaise and Watergate, the USSR cautiously embarked upon its first global excursion by orchestrating from Moscow an ingeniously conceived and effective military intervention by its Caribbean client state, Cuba, in the remote reaches of Southern Africa. The fact that Moscow could logistically conceive and execute such a military operation was a tangible confirmation of its global reach. To be sure, the USSR still does not possess the resources and capabilities to intervene in all parts of the globe with equal effectiveness, and its capabilities fall short of America's global capabilities. But it does possess sufficient reach to carefully select its targets around the globe, depending upon opportunities, risks, and chances of success.

As befits a global power, the Soviet Union included in the new constitution adopted on October 7, 1977 an entire chapter on foreign policy which elaborated the foreign policy aims and functions of the Soviet state in comprehensive global terms. Article 28 reads:

> The foreign policy of the USSR is aimed at ensuring international conditions favorable for building communism in the USSR, safeguarding the state interests of the Soviet Union, consolidating the positions of world socialism, supporting the struggle of peoples for national liberation and social progress, preventing wars of aggression, achieving universal and complete disarmament, and consistently implementing the principle of the peaceful coexistence of states with different social systems.[5]

After the USSR had functioned as a global power for about 5 years, the Soviet leadership apparently calculated that the combination of the United States' acceptance of the USSR as a military equal—indeed, the general perception that the Soviet Union might even be militarily superior—and the USSR's new global capabilities entitled it to be recognized as an overall equal to the United States. In fact, it often acted as if it were ready to supersede the United States as the paramount power in the interstate system, with its behavior assuming increasingly interventionist and expansionist dimensions. Such behavior culminated in the massive invasion of Afghanistan at the end of 1979.

Although Soviet leaders and Soviet writers often suggest that the USSR is entitled to both global *status* and *equality* with the United States as some sort of divine right ordained by history, they clearly realize that the situation is more complicated than they imply. From an objective analytic standpoint, no state, not even the United States, is *entitled* to be a global power. The position of the United States in the international system was not granted to it by divine right, history, or the consent of the international community. It was self-asserted and must be self-sustained. Similarly, the Soviet Union does not possess any "right" to global status; it must be self-achieved, self-asserted, and self-sustained.

In recognition of this reality, Moscow has developed the independent capabilities to function on a global level. Thus, there is little question that the Soviet Union is a global power, whether the United States recognizes it as such or not.

Likewise, no state is *entitled* to be equal with any other state. Just as there are superpowers and superpowers, there may also be distinctions between global powers, even if the exclusive club is restricted to two members. Moreover, equality—unlike global status, which is independently determined—is a relative term and is measured against others. Of perhaps greatest significance, equality, as even Soviet observers implicitly concede, is *ascriptive* in character and depends upon the recognition and policies of others.

Yet when the United States in 1972 accepted the Soviet Union as a strategic equal—that is, as an equal military power—this did not mean that the United States recognized the USSR as an equal *global* power. To the contrary, Washington perceived the SALT I agreements as instruments designed to domesticate and contain Soviet power, not unleash it. Of this fact, Moscow is exceedingly conscious. To American criticisms of Soviet behavior in Africa and the Third World more generally as incompatible with détente, for instance, Moscow has complained defensively that the United States is refusing to treat the USSR as an equal, is attempting to deny its global credentials in practice while recognizing them symbolically.

Thus, as we shall see in detail later, Soviet leaders are painfully aware that the favorable military equation which they have achieved largely by default, because of the continuing state of the internal situation in the United States in the wake of Vietnam and Watergate, is the critical factor in what they perceive as a favorable "correlation of forces" and may prove temporary, should Washington decide upon new objectives and priorities. What they have to calculate is the degree to which they can take advantage of what observers often call a "window of opportunity" during the next few years, without running the risk of prematurely provoking a renewed arms race with the United States, which, in light of the unrealized military potential of the American economy, they would surely lose.

In addition, Soviet leaders recognize the enormous resources of Washington's allies, most of whose productive energies and outputs have been devoted to the civilian sector of the economy. And, finally, there is China and the notorious "China card," which the United States could seriously exploit as part of its global policies. For example, the Soviet achievement of equality by ascription has posed the question of why only the USSR is entitled to equality with the United States. Moscow itself never raises this issue, and when others raise it, Soviet spokesmen are very evasive. Thus, at a press conference in Bonn on November 23, 1979, Foreign Minister Gromyko responded to a query about equality for other powers within the context of a possible SALT III negotiation in the following fashion: "But one asks . . . after all, other countries also have strategic arms. What types of weapons and what countries should have equality? Why should the Soviet Union always proceed from the premise that the subject under discussion should be equality only between the U.S. and the Soviet Union? . . . None of these matters have been settled."[6]

It is this enormous material and human potential, whose military convertibility has only barely been tapped—while the USSR has strained and stretched its resources to maintain the current balance—that the Soviet leadership must worry about as it contemplates its future actions. But potential is potential, and possibilities are only possibilities. Hence, Soviet leaders must also crank into their calculations the intangible factors of leadership, public support, internal stability, and various other factors operating in these countries and arrive at a judgment as to whether the undoubted potential that the United States could mobilize can indeed be transformed into a "correlation of forces" favorable to Washington.[7]

## Soviet Apprehensions

Obviously, the Soviet Union cherishes its equality with the United States and is reluctant to share it with third powers—most notably, China. But much of the Soviet literature reflects an apprehensiveness on this matter from two directions. The first is that the United States may seek to bestow equality upon other states (e.g., China). Soviet writers *conspicuously avoid* this theme. The second is that the United States may attempt to withdraw its conferral of equality. Three major themes concerning the legitimacy and durability of Moscow's equal and global status can be discerned in Soviet writings, and while they are inconsistent, these inconsistencies mirror anxiety about the permanence and "objective" quality of the Soviet Union's equal and global status. These three themes can be summarized as follows: (1) The United

States, by lecturing the USSR on the unacceptability of its internal and external behavior, is not treating the USSR as an equal; (2) the United States is threatening to seek "military superiority," which is incompatible with the principle of equality; (3) the Soviet Union's equality has been established by the "correlation of forces" and the objective processes of history, and the Soviet Union is fully capable of preventing the United States from attaining military superiority.

U.S. lectures on the acceptability and appropriateness of Soviet internal and external behavior have evoked great Soviet resentment, since they have recently been coupled with threats of rewards and punishment by the United States if Moscow continues to misbehave—hardly the way that one equal would treat another equal. The Carter administration's condemnation of Moscow's violations of "human rights" and restrictions on the emigration of Soviet citizens and contraventions of Basket III of the Helsinki agreement have been viewed as particularly arrogant attempts by the United States to sermonize and impose its own values and norms upon the Soviet Union. These acts, according to Moscow, are incompatible with the elementary norms of international law and sovereignty and would represent bad form even when directed against smaller and vulnerable powers, to say nothing of the fact that they are directed against a power equal to the United States. Thus, on March 21, 1977, no less a personage than Leonid Brezhnev charged: "Washington's assertions that it is entitled to teach others how to live cannot, I believe, be accepted by any sovereign state. . . . Let me repeat: we shall not tolerate interference in our internal affairs by anyone, under any pretext. The normal development of relations on such a basis is, of course, unthinkable."[8]

Moreover, when President Carter, after the invasion of Afghanistan, shifted from lecturing Moscow on proper behavior to "punishing" the Soviet Union for improper deportment and further threatening to withdraw "rewards," Brezhnev's response, while clearly a rebuff, nevertheless betrayed an apprehension that the United States was indeed still capable of "punishing" and "rewarding" its putative equal:

> The sum total of steps taken by the American administration in connection with the events in Afghanistan—the freezing of the Salt II treaty, the refusal to deliver to the USSR a whole series of commodities, the suspension of talks with the Soviet Union on a number of questions . . . indicates that Washington is again, as it did decades ago, attempting to talk to us in the language of the cold war. . . . Of course, we will get along without these ties with the United States—in fact, we never begged for them, believing that they were mutually advantageous. . . . However, Washington's arbitrary arrogation to itself of some kind of "right" to "reward" or "punish" independent sovereign states poses a question of principle. In fact, these actions of the U.S. government strike a major blow at the system of relations among states regulated by international law.[9]

Although from Moscow's standpoint U.S. lecturing and sermonizing are insulting and humiliating to the Soviet Union and debase the image of equality it seeks with the United States, they are not by themselves threatening. But Soviet spokesmen also contend that the United States is threatening to attain military and strategic superiority once again. Such an undertaking would not only automatically strip the Soviet Union of its equal status but require a large-scale, fundamental, and even destabilizing reexamination and restructuring of Soviet internal and external policies and a reordering of priorities. It could undermine the credibility of the economic and military commitments of the USSR to its allies and client states, especially those remote from the Soviet Union, And finally, should the United States attain military superiority at a time when the Soviet Union is confronted with a leadership succession crisis, the Soviet regime could be seriously crippled.

Growing out of this second theme have been uncharacteristically modest disclaimers that the USSR has either attained or is striving for military superiority. These appear to be essentially a prudent gesture designed to undercut those in the United States who charge that the Soviet Union either has or soon will attain military superiority.

No less authoritative a figure than Leonid Brezhnev was the first to enunciate such a disclaimer. In a speech at the Soviet city of Tula in January 1977, he asserted: "Of course, comrades, we are improving our defenses. It cannot be otherwise. We have never neglected the security of our country and the security of our allies, and we shall never neglect it. But the allegations that the Soviet Union is going beyond what is sufficient for defense, that it is striving for superiority in armaments in the aim of delivering a 'first strike,' are absurd and utterly unfounded."[10]

To further indicate to Washington and the West that the disavowal of military superiority was more than a unilateral assurance, and simultaneously to ensure that the United States would be bound by formal commitments not to seek military superiority, the USSR entered into a joint renunciation of the intention to seek military superiority, in the Joint Soviet–American Communiqué executed in Vienna in June 1979 as part of the SALT II arrangements. This read: "Each [side] stated that it is not striving and will not strive for military superiority, since that can only result in dangerous instability, generating higher levels of armaments with no benefit to the security of either side."[11]

In Berlin in October 1979, Brezhnev reiterated his disavowal of any inclination to seek military superiority, in even stronger words than he had used in 1977: "As far as the Soviet Union is concerned, I repeat again and again: We do not seek military superiority. We have never intended and do not now intend to threaten any state or group of states. Our strategic doctrine is a purely defensive one. Allegations that the Soviet Union is building up its military might on the European continent on a scale not called for by its defense requirements have nothing to do with reality. This is a deliberate deception of the public at large."[12] But this time he coupled it with a charge that the United States was seeking to regain military superiority: "The dangerous plan for the deployment of new American nuclear missiles on the territory of Western Europe . . . would substantially change the strategic situation on the continent. Their objective is to upset the existing balance of forces in Europe and to try to ensure military superiority for the NATO bloc."[13] Both the change and the disclaimer obviously were aimed at deterring the United States from what he feared it was capable of doing.

The recurring anxiety that the United States might once again make a bid for military superiority and succeed became even more pronounced after the Soviet invasion of Afghanistan. It appeared to some Soviet commentators that although Soviet leaders had indeed correctly calculated that the risk of American military counteraction in response to such an invasion would be low, they may nevertheless have overplayed their hand to gain a local, if admittedly important, advantage. That is, they had miscalculated the impact the invasion would have upon the fears and attitudes of the U.S. public, particularly during a presidential election in which the principal Republican contender was an undoubted advocate of regaining American military superiority.

Despite the enigma and paradox that the Carter administration constituted for the Kremlin leaders, and despite its annoying messianic sermonizing about human rights, the administration had exhibited a deep aversion to the use of force or had been easily deterred from employing it because of its perception of Soviet power and Moscow's willingness to use it. As Moscow saw things, the Carter administration had refused to react to the continuing Soviet/Cuban intervention in Angola; shunned an opportunity to confront Moscow and Havana on the Horn of Africa by supporting Somalia; huffed, puffed, and retreated on the issue of the Soviet combat brigade in Cuba; and allowed itself to be paralyzed by the seizure of the American embassy in Teheran.[14] Furthermore, in the Soviet view, this administration had shown itself to be particularly susceptible to Soviet pressures and persuasion. In the face of Soviet complaints and mild threats, Jimmy Carter had canceled the B-1 bomber, vetoed construction of another attack carrier, decided not to build the neutron bomb (after pressuring European leaders to publicly accept it even at some cost in terms of their internal political support), and retreated on a whole host of issues connected with the SALT II agreements, including matters connected with the cruise missile, the Backfire bomber, ICBM ceilings, and verification capabilities.

But now, the assessment went, the Kremlin by its move into Afghanistan may have created a real possibility that the "hard-liners" in the American ruling class would succeed in replacing the Carter administration and launch the United States on a course to achieve military supremacy. Some Soviet leaders, as the Soviet literature indicated, were already convinced that the "hard-liners," in the person of the President's national security adviser, Zbigniew Brzezinski, had already taken over from the "moderates," as represented by Paul Warnke, former Director of the Arms Control and Disarmament Agency, and Cyrus Vance (soon to be former), Secretary of State, and that this shift had clearly been in process before the invasion of Afghanistan. Yet, as the initial Soviet comments on presidential candidate Ronald Reagan reveal, the rejoinder to that judgment by some Soviet circles might well be a Russian version of "if you think Brzezinski is a 'hard-liner,' you ain't seen nothin' yet."

The apprehension in much of the Soviet literature and the speeches of

Soviet leaders that the United States is still fully capable of reversing the direction in which the "correlation of forces," particularly in the military sphere, had been moving, is quite evident, even though coupled with these fears are the familiar assertions that the existing alignment of power is irreversible and such that U.S. efforts would be futile. Not only do Soviet spokesmen recognize that a renewed U.S. effort to regain strategic superiority would stretch Soviet resources to their limits, but they also acknowledge that despite the maximum Soviet effort, American potential remains great enough that the United States could reverse the existing "correlation of forces" simply by enhancing its military power—not to speak of doing other things, to be discussed below.

Thus, the Kremlin's leading Americanologist, Georgiy Arbatov, warned the Soviet leaders obliquely of such a possibility:

> Despite a sustained period of détente, the U.S. ruling class has still not completely put behind it its past global pretensions . . . to break with the guidelines, notions, and traditions of a whole period—a period right after World War II, in which America found itself in an exceptional position by virtue of an aggregation of unique and transient historical circumstances (although the Americans, understandably, wanted to see these circumstances as the natural and eternal order of things).

Furthermore, he even singled out closer relations with China as a conceivable means whereby the United States could temporarily remedy the existing unfavorable balance confronting it until it could rectify the situation through its own resources. The Americans, he said, are gripped with "illusions to the effect that a rapprochement with the chauvinistic Chinese leadership . . . can change the balance of forces, strengthen America's position, and enable it to . . . again lord it over the planet to its heart's content." Simultaneously, Arbatov issued a caveat to Washington that the Soviet Union could still muster sufficient resources to maintain parity, at least in the military field: "The Soviet Union today has greater possibilities than ever before to frustrate such plans [the achievement of military superiority] and to maintain parity in the military field."[15]

Widely prevalent in Soviet commentary is the view that the United States is not merely interested in reclaiming military superiority but yearns to restore itself to the apex of the international system as the principal arbiter of the planet's destiny, to renounce its agreement to accept the Soviet Union as an equal partner and behave once again as if it were the world's only authentic global power, with the self-asserted right to set the international agenda, resolve disputes, and in general regulate and manage the international system. These fears masquerading as accusations simultaneously afford retrospective insight into the real image which Moscow had earlier of America's position in the international system and disclose the Soviet nightmare that while the United States may not develop sufficient power to roll back the wheels of history, it may once again be able to seize its helm. Despite all their bravado about the favorable alterations in the "correlation of forces" during the past decade, Soviet leaders continue to have a deep and even awesome respect for the enormous economic, scientific, and technological resources of the United States and the realizable military potential inherent in them—potential which the favorable shift in the "correlation of forces" has obviously left intact. The anxiety that results is implicitly but clearly spelled out in *Pravda*'s editorial denouncing President Carter's State of the Union message of January 23, 1980: "The message and the speech . . . openly state the U.S. claim to a 'leading role' in the world. What 'leading role' means is Washington's intention to dictate its system in any region and to any state, and, when the U.S. administration deems it expedient, to use any means, including weapons, to oppose national liberation, revolutionary, and all progressive movements. Thus, what we see here is a new American claim to world supremacy."[16]

Accompanying the Soviet accusation and fear that the United States refuses to accept the USSR as an equal and is striving for military superiority is the not wholly confident reiteration that Soviet equality has been determined by recent irreversible changes in the "correlation of forces" and that the Soviet Union is capable of thwarting U.S. ambitions to attain military superiority and regain world supremacy. In a book written before the advent of the Carter administration, two Soviet writers had already heralded a historic shift in the "correlation of forces" in favor of socialism:

> In the mid-1960's, far-sighted leaders in the imperialist camp were compelled to recognize that the historical initiative in world affairs was steadily passing into the hands of the Soviet Union and other socialist countries. A change in the balance of power was steadily developing. . . . Experience has demonstrated that the process of change in the relationship of forces between the two systems is an objective process which arises out of the advantages of the new social system. This process can rightly be called irreversible because it has been dictated by the objective laws determining the contest between the two systems.[17]

With specific reference to the actions and responses of the Carter administration to the USSR's invasion of Afghanistan, Soviet Foreign Minister Gromyko warned that a U.S. effort to free itself from parity and seek superiority would fail: "The common objective of all these actions is clear: to break the rough parity that now exists between the military power of East and West, of the Soviet Union and the U.S., and to try to achieve superiority over the socialist commonwealth. . . . We have stated several times—and at the most authoritative level—that we will not allow this. L. I. Brezhnev talked to the American President about this in Vienna."[18] Unlike the "far-sighted leaders of the mid-1960's," President Carter, according to the *Pravda* commentary on his 1980 State of the Union message, refuses to recognize or accept realities and therefore adjust accordingly:

> On the whole, it follows from the President's message that the country's ruling circles, having run up against the realities of today's world and the

objective growth of the forces of peace, progress, and socialism, clearly are reluctant to construct their policy in accordance with the United States' actual weight in today's world. Apparently, they cannot rid themselves of imperial, hegemonistic thinking, do not want to reckon with the existing alignment of forces in the international arena.[19]

In sum, then, Soviet writers implicitly recognize that the equality which they so passionately cherish remains essentially an ascriptive one. Although they express confidence that the impersonal but objective forces of history will render it permanent, and thus free Soviet equality from its dependence upon American recognition, they are aware that for the time being, it is not. Moreover, it is clear that a successful U.S. decertification of the Soviet Union as an equal could have a traumatic impact upon the Soviet leadership. In response to the aftermath of the Soviet invasion of Afghanistan, for example, Leonid Zamyatin moaned: "The difficulties arise . . . from the American leaders' unwillingness or inability to understand that equality in international affairs means just that—equality; that parity in the alignment of international forces means parity; and that equal security means equal security.[20]

Soviet concerns on this matter seem to have had an effect on Soviet discussions of the "correlation of forces." This has been fairly complex. Soviet spokesmen have affirmed that while, as Brezhnev stated to the West Germans in May 1978, "the Soviet Union believes that rough equality and parity are sufficient for defense needs" and does not set itself "the aim of achieving military superiority,"[21] it explicitly welcomes and seeks a favorable shift in the "correlation of forces." These two propositions would, on the face of things, appear to be mutually incompatible. The discrepancy thus requires some extended explanation. In response, Soviet spokesmen have offered a more elaborate exegesis of the concept of the "correlation of forces" and have attempted to distinguish it carefully from the concept of the "balance of power," particularly the *military* balance of power.

Cognitive Deception    Although the resulting Soviet position does not represent outright falsehood, it amounts to a kind of "cognitive deception." Since a critical, if not always decisive, component of the "correlation of forces" is the state of the military balance, the two are obviously interrelated, and whereas it is possible to achieve superiority in the "correlation of forces" without at the same time enjoying military superiority, it is nevertheless true that the military component of the "correlation of forces" is the most precise, measurable, and visible component in the calculation. Furthermore, changes in the military balance affect changes in the overall "correlation of forces" more immediately and reliably than changes in any other component, many of which are intangible and amorphous, thus making their calculation and exact weight elusive and subject to differing intuitive estimates and judgments rather than precise and unambiguous measurement. As even a Soviet commentator has conceded, "the military strength of a state is by all means a decisive element of its position in the world."[22]

To appreciate the character of the new exegesis, it is essential to have a clear understanding of the traditional Soviet approach to the "correlation of forces." Because the Soviet Union has survived and developed its capabilities for decades when it was militarily weak and had to rely upon factors other than the conventional elements of national power to make up for its military deficiencies, the Soviet leadership is experienced and well versed in the manipulation and mobilization of various "exotic" nonmilitary elements that can be factored into the "correlation of forces." One writer recently capsulized these in the following fashion: "The foreign policy potential of a state depends not only upon its own forces and internal resources but, to a considerable extent, on such external factors as the existence of reliable, sociopolitical allies among other states, national contingents of congenial classes, mass international movements and other political forces active in the world scene."[23] As the well-known Soviet Americanologist Genrikh Trofimenko has pointed out, such elements even embrace the internal social and political alignments and forces within the United States:

> Political reality also includes the domestic political situation in the U.S. itself, where the popular masses are demanding increasingly, decisively, and loudly the renunciation of military adventures abroad and the administration's turning to face the internal socio-economic problems. . . . Moments arise when the split between the sentiments and feelings of broad public circles and official policy proves so deep that a bourgeois government, wishing to remain in power, either has to correct official policy or resign from power. . . . The . . . administration must take into account the opinion of the overwhelming majority of voters who support . . . the reduction of U.S. military commitments abroad.[24]

Soviet leaders, in short, have long recognized that social conflicts, tensions, frustrations, and resentments, particularly between classes, conceal tremendous reserves of pent-up social power, which can be detected by dialectical analysis and then tapped, mobilized, and transmuted into concrete political power subject to the manipulation of Soviet policy. These stored-up social energies of a world in ferment and convulsion are released with tremendous force during periods which Lenin described as "revolutionary situations." In calculating the international "correlation of forces," or "the relation of forces in the world arena," these internal social factors, and the direction of their movement—for or against the status quo—constitute important elements in the power equation.

However, Soviet leaders also know that the most direct and quickest way to affect the "correlation of forces" is to increase one's military strength. After all, Nazi Germany's rise to power in the 1930s eloquently demonstrated how the "correlation of forces" could be radically reversed within a short period of time. Instead of "realistically" adjusting to the "realities" and "correlation of forces" as they existed in 1933,

Adolph Hitler set out to willfully and successfully revise both reality and the "correlation of forces." His principal means was to transform Germany's human and material resources into military power.

Similarly, the USSR has actually been devoting an inordinate share of its own resources to military development. But given the imbalance in the productive capabilities of the Soviet Union and the United States, between socialism and capitalism, Moscow has also sought to downgrade the salience and possible decisiveness of the military contribution to the "correlation of forces." It stresses the decisive character of the nonmilitary factors, particularly those intangible and elusive (but nevertheless real) social, revolutionary, and progressive "forces" in the overall equation, which are fortuitously inevitable, irreversible, and favorable to the Soviet side.

Hence, the concept "correlation of forces," while useful as a mode of analysis for Soviet leaders in assessing and building strength, is far less useful and relevant for the U.S. and Western leaders. The West is not so versed as the Soviet side in manipulating or adjusting to the manifold social, political, and revolutionary processes which contribute to the "correlation of forces" equation, and for this reason Western analysts and policymakers are likely to put greater stress upon the "elements of national power" and the "balance of power" in the traditional sense as their basic calculus. Attempts to develop a formula which goes beyond the economic and military factors in the balance equation and incorporates assessments of processes in various parts of the globe, while hypothetically possible for Western decision makers, usually turn out to be dysfunctional and counterproductive, paradoxically because of both the amorphous character of Western ideologies as a guide to Western policies and the rigidity and inflexibility of whatever ideological baggage is employed.

At any rate, the Soviet concept "correlation of forces" differs fundamentally from the concept "balance of power." While the balance of power can be the product of deliberate policy, the "correlation of forces" represents "balance" determined by social and historical processes in which the policy of states is only a component. As developed by Soviet writers, the "correlation of forces" constitutes the basic substructure upon which the interstate system rests. The latter, like any superstructure, is governed by man-made rules and is the product of deliberate policy processes of various states, whereas the "correlation of forces" derives from a myriad of cross-cutting and interacting variables which operate independently of decision makers and state policies. Thus, the "correlation of forces" can be affected only marginally by state policy, but, in general, state policies are shaped by the changing "correlation of forces." Whatever changes take place in the substructure are inevitably reflected in the superstructure of the interstate system.

Soviet writers have been focusing on the changing "correlation of forces" for decades, but only recently have they been discussing the transformational processes at work in the international system. "The Marxist–Leninist approach to the relationship of forces between classes, groups of states, and individual states," contend two Soviet commentators, "differs fundamentally from the approach to these matters taken by bourgeois politicians and ideologists." For Marxist–Leninists,

> international politics is above all an area of struggle and the interaction of diversified class, political, national, and other factors, with class factors always playing the decisive role. These have ultimately shaped the picture of international relations as a whole and in any given period of time.
>
> The changing relationship of forces between the two systems has provided the basis on which new, positive processes in world affairs can now develop. This change means a definite and irresistible tendency toward the increased influence of socialism on the course of world developments. **It is quite obvious that the alteration in the balance of power between socialism and capitalism is mainly a change in the relationship of class forces.**[25]

On the other hand, "some spokesmen for modern bourgeois political sciences, basing themselves on conceptions first formulated in the last century,"

> have made the preservation of peace and all the important processes of international relations contingent on the maintenance of an equilibrium of strength. This equilibrium (or balance of power) is presented as the main and crucial factor in the preservation of peace and the stable development of relations between states and groups of states. From this premise, the maintenance of a definite equilibrium or balance or power between states or groups of states is declared to be the basic factor in the further development of international relations and the key instrument for preserving stability.[26]

Thus, according to this line of analysis, any attempt to function outside the "correlation of forces" ordained by the historical process is bound to fail. Increasingly, the military power of individual states can have only restricted and temporary effects, slowing down the process, speeding it up, or modifying and diverting it in marginal dimensions. Since the changes are in directions unpalatable to the old order, it justifies efforts to arrest or reverse the process by ascribing the movement to the intrigues and machinations of the Soviet Union, as if the processes were the simple product of a contest between states. But while interstate behavior is governed by and dependent upon the underlying "correlation of forces," it does not determine them, and the two spheres are not interchangeable or continuous: "The socialist countries draw a clear line between the spheres of class struggle and interstate relations, and oppose any attempts to erase this line. As for the imperialists, their persistent attempts to interfere in the socialist countries' internal affairs reflect their intention to transfer the class struggle to the sphere of interstate relations, to substitute one for the other."[27] Consequently, while it is both possible and desirable for countries in their interstate relations to make agreements not to seek military superiority, Soviet observers maintain, "no one can 'put a freeze' on the world sociopolitical development on the pretext of détente," and "international agree-

ments cannot alter the laws of class struggle."[28] Simply because the
Soviet Union and socialism happen to be the principal beneficiaries of
these processes, the net consequences of these processes in terms of the
"correlation of forces" are incorrectly translated into a Soviet passion for
military superiority.

At Vienna in 1979, Brezhnev himself responded to President Carter's
complaints about Soviet/Cuban activity in Africa by saying in effect that
the President should direct his grievances not at the Kremlin, but to the
Muse of History:

> The opponents of mutual understanding between the USSR and the U.S.
> make active use of the legend about a so-called "Soviet military
> threat.". . . There are also continuing attempts to depict social processes
> in one country or another and the struggle of peoples for independence
> and social progress as "Moscow's intrigues and machinations.". . . Our
> appraisals of political regimes in various countries sometimes differ
> strongly from the appraisals made by certain circles in the U.S. . . . We
> believe that every people has the right to decide its own destiny. **Why then
> pin on the Soviet Union the responsibility for the objective course of
> history and, moreover, use this as a pretext for worsening our relations?**[29]

As noted earlier, there is more than a little disingenuousness in Soviet
attempts to draw a sharp distinction between their actions and behavior
and what they call the "processes" or "forces" of history. While one can
plausibly explain revolutionary movements and social ferment as the
product of underlying historical forces and trends, one can hardly
burden history with the decision to airlift and support thousands of
Cuban soldiers in Angola and Ethiopia, or to send 85,000 Soviet troops
into Afghanistan. Even in accordance with Soviet definitions and conceptions, these are the acts and results of deliberate state policy, decisions taken within the context of the interstate system and not in the
abstract arena where class struggles occur.

The uncoupling of the concepts "correlation of forces" and "military
superiority," in sum, appears to be designed not so much for method-
ological and cognitive clarity as to send out conflicting signals to two
separate audiences. To its partisans and supporters, Moscow is conveying the message that the balance of power has shifted or is about to shift
in favor of the Soviet Union; to the West, it is saying that the balance has
not and is not about to do so.

Policy               Intellectually dubious though the Soviet distinction
Implications         between not seeking or striving for military superiority
                     and anticipating a favorable "correlation of forces"
may be, it does have certain implications for Soviet policy. These are
fourfold: (1) Soviet leaders will not explicitly claim military superiority or
make its attainment a matter of official policy; (2) they will, however,
accept military superiority and act upon it if they attain it by default (i.e.,
if the United States fails to maintain military parity with the Soviet
Union); (3) Soviet leaders will accept military parity as sufficient for their

defense and security interests, but they will conspicuously avoid saying that they will *strive* for or *seek* parity (i.e., *they will neither strive for nor seek parity or military superiority*); (4) they will, however, strive for and seek a favorable "correlation of forces," since this striving and seeking presumably takes place in the "international arena of class struggles" and not the "international arena of state relations."

These distinctions are important from the USSR's standpoint, for they serve to relocate what Moscow itself mockingly calls the "Soviet threat" or "menace," out of the arena of state relations and into the arena of class struggles. Soviet leaders and writers do not refrain from conceding that "socialism" and the USSR constitute a "menace" or "threat" to capitalism, imperialism, colonialism, reaction, and other assorted evils. Indeed, they exult in the fact, and the new Brezhnev constitution establishes as two of the concrete aims of Soviet policy "consolidating the positions of world socialism [and] supporting the struggle of peoples for national liberation and social progress," which are activities defined even within the Soviet context as belonging to the sphere of "class relations" rather than "state relations."

Yet ever since Leonid Brezhnev resurrected the title of General Secretary of the CPSU, the distinction between "party" and "state" has been losing its relevance insofar as Soviet foreign policy is concerned. For decades, the Soviet leaders found it advantageous and preferable to maintain a scrupulous distance between "party" and "state"—Party Secretary and Premier—in foreign policy, but the practical significance of the distinction diminished under Brezhnev, even before he assumed the post of Chairman of the Presidium of the USSR Supreme Soviet in 1977. Increasingly after 1966, Brezhnev played a more conspicuous and "official" role in diplomacy and even signed bilateral and multilateral treaties in his capacity as General Secretary of the CPSU, a title which appears boldly on both the SALT I Treaty and the Helsinki Final Act. It is true that he received special plenipotentiary authority to officially represent the Soviet state on these occasions; nevertheless, it was highly unusual for him to attach his party title to formal interstate documents, since the party has absolutely no standing under international law.

Moreover, with Brezhnev's assumption of formal state authority as head of the Soviet state and simultaneous retention of his post as General Secretary of the CPSU, the distinction between the two spheres has been virtually obliterated. Never before in Soviet history have the posts of head of the Soviet state and head of the Soviet party been joined in one person. Neither Vladimir Lenin nor Iosif Stalin nor Nikita Khrushchev was ever head of state; they all were head of government, a lesser position under international law.

Thus, the notion that Leonid Brezhnev, in his capacity as General Secretary, is free to threaten and menace capitalism but nevertheless constitutes no threat to states or countries, simply boggles the imagination. In a curious appropriation and imitation of devices employed in the past by those who tried disingenuously to draw a distinction between the Comintern or international communism, on the one hand, and the USSR, on the other—which Moscow never accepted—the Soviet Union expects the world to believe that its hostility toward capitalism and imperialism as abstractions should bear no relevance to Soviet relations with "capitalist" or "imperialist" states. But now that the Soviet state freely crosses over into the sphere of class struggles, where it can openly threaten and menace capitalism and imperialism and support revolutionary and national liberation movements, one can hardly accept that when it returns to the sphere of interstate relations, its menacing and threatening baggage has somehow been conveniently left behind. There is little question that the baggage is inseparably tied to the Soviet state, no matter within what sphere it chooses to operate.

Even Soviet writers seem to be having an increasingly difficult time sustaining the distinction and justifying the Soviet threat in one realm and denying it in another. For example, they assert, on the one hand, that "the Soviet Union has never pledged itself to work for the maintaining of the status quo in other countries" and then insist, on the other, that "social changes occurring in the world . . . serve to strengthen the positions of the democratic and socialistic forces. . . . [and] create a much more favorable international setting for each of the three revolutionary streams of our day—world socialism, the international working class movement, and the national liberation movement—to achieve their goals."[30] The difficulty is compounded by the Soviet constitution's stipulation that the foreign policy of the Soviet state is pledged to support two of these revolutionary streams—world socialism and the national liberation movement—and the fact that the Soviet head of state in his capacity as General Secretary of the CPSU presides over, if does not direct, the third (i.e., the international working-class movement).

Leadership Divisions    The foregoing analysis is not meant to leave the impression that Soviet leaders and their various support constituencies agree about the best course of action to take at a time when opportunities appear to be running high and risks low. Indeed, there is substantial evidence to suggest that Soviet leaders have been divided—certainly confused—about how to respond and react to what they have described as the capricious, arbitrary, unreliable, and inconsistent behavior of the Carter administration. This evidence indicates uncertainty about whether such behavior represents deep cunning, traditionally associated in the Bolshevik mind with the kulak, or whether it represents naiveté, inexperience, or even ineptitude.[31] Soviet commentaries on the Carter administration have reflected the entire spectrum of perceptions mentioned—individually, selectively grouped, or, in some cases, all together.

In particular, Soviet leaders and observers found bewildering the U.S. President's rhetoric in favor of détente, SALT II, and cooperation with the Soviet Union and his conspicuous aversion to the use of force, on the one hand, and his stern moralizing about the USSR's violations of "human rights" and its inappropriate behavior in Cuba and Africa, on the other, for this combination of positions, all often in the same speech or statement, implicitly carried a message that American attitudes and policies toward the Soviet Union would be conditional on good marks for Soviet deportment and behavior. Thus, *Pravda*, in response to President Carter's speech before the U.S. Naval Academy on June 7, 1978, registered what was a then a typical complaint:

> Recent evidence indicates that American policy is undergoing changes. . . . The U.S. government is also undertaking actions whose aim is difficult to understand. . . . Some administration officials . . . have [caused] . . . considerable confusion in the minds of U.S. allies and among their fellow citizens. President J. Carter's recent speech in Annapolis . . . was supposed to dispel this confusion. However, the U.S. President definitely failed to clarify the American policy, particularly policy toward the USSR . . . for the simple reason that the speech was an attempt to reconcile the irreconcilable—to combine reassurances of devotion to the ideas of détente and improved Soviet-American relations with undisguised attacks against the Soviet Union . . . with a prejudiced and distorted description of Soviet reality of the kind that has rarely appeared since the cold war, even in the most malevolent American newspapers.[32]

While Soviet leaders could fall back on the familiar view that the contradictions and resultant confusion almost certainly represented divisions between the moderates and hard-liners in the American ruling class, the inadequacies of this standard litany as an explanation were quite apparent to them. Moreover, the enigmatic image projected by the Carter administration resulted in disorientation and distortion of the general character of the Soviet internal debate, for the various sides in the Soviet leadership found it difficult to bring into focus a clear image of what they were responding to. Under such circumstances, Soviet observers were moved to shift to personality explanations of U.S. behavior. Even Brezhnev himself did so soon after the invasion of Afghanistan:

> As a result of the Carter administration's actions, the world is getting an even clearer picture of the United States as an absolutely unreliable partner in interstate ties, as a state whose leadership, prompted by some whim, caprice, or emotional outburst or by considerations of narrowly understood immediate advantage, is capable at any moment of violating its international commitments and nullifying treaties and agreements it has signed; there is no need to explain what a dangerous destabilizing influence this has on the entire international situation—all the more so because the leadership that is behaving this way is that of a major and influential power, from which the people are entitled to expect a carefully considered and responsible policy.[33]

At the same time, it is by no means clear that the Soviet internal debate can be shaped in a preferred direction by external influences—notably, the United States. That external factors have an impact upon the debate cannot be questioned; at issue is what that impact is likely to be.

The emergence of a limited semipluralistic decision-making process in the Soviet system, somewhat akin to an idiosyncratic combination of Graham Allison's bureaucratic and organizational process models,[34] has created the impression that such decision-making processes will almost automatically produce moderate decisions and policies. While the current Soviet decision-making process does often result in more hesitation, vacillation, and involuntary self-restraint in the formulation and execution of decisions and can seriously affect their timing, its impact on the substance or quality of the decision is likely to be much less. In fact, what the process means is that Soviet decisions are increasingly uncertain and unpredictable, and frequently even ambiguous, ambivalent, and reversible.

One of the hidden shoals of Brezhnev's generally successful consensus style of conflict resolution and decision making—which has resulted in policies commanding the widest possible base of support and, hence, has entailed shared responsibility—has been the definition of his policies, and in particular détente, almost entirely in *utilitarian*, rather than in *normative* or *value*, terms. Détente, for example, is never described as a substantive goal or an objective value in itself; instead, it is discussed in terms of whether it promotes or hinders the achievement of traditional Soviet ideological and other objectives. And it is often referred to as the *best* means or vehicle for achieving substantive ends. Presumably, such references can only mean that if détente hinders the attainment of Soviet goals or can be shown to be less effective than another policy, then détente is likely to be replaced.

The utilitarian and pragmatic dimension of Soviet policies, thus, can lead to the replacement of a policy, no matter how valuable for its own sake or for various vested interests, with one that is more utilitarian and successful in achieving substantive Soviet goals. Precisely such a situation appears to have arisen in the case of the Soviet decision to invade Afghanistan. The self-restraint imposed by détente was increasingly perceived as functionally deleterious to Soviet policy as opportunities increased and risks decreased, and a better utilitarian argument could be made in favor of an invasion than against it, although such a decision would run the risk of rupturing détente. Furthermore, as the course of events in Afghanistan became ominous from the Soviet standpoint, the utility of a policy of not heightening international tensions (i.e., détente) correspondingly diminished. Even though individuals and groups within the Soviet Union may, in varying degrees of intensity, take positions for or against détente because of vested interests of different kinds, they must still debate the policy within the context of the utility of détente for the achievement of the Soviet equivalent of national goals.

Moreover, the appearance of hard- or soft-liners in Washington does not automatically produce counterparts or opposites in Moscow. The symbiotic relationship that exists between various kinds of "-liners" in the two capitals is extremely complicated and depends upon many unknown and unknowable variables. In addition, the state of the military balance—strategic and conventional, global and regional—critically affects the impact that one set of decision makers and decisions has upon the other set. For instance, the flourishing of moderate forces within the Soviet leadership is not encouraged if the United States allows its end of the strategic balance to tip adversely and refuses to sustain and maintain strategic parity, for excessive weakness and lack of resolve on the U.S. part, whether real or perceived, arouse appetites in the USSR which otherwise can be successfully depicted as unattainable as long as the United States continues to be powerful and its willingness to use that power remains credible. Although power corrupts (mainly the holder) and maims (both the holder and the adversary), impotence excites and incites those whom power corrupts. Thus, moderation is more likely to prevail in the Soviet Union if the United States is strong but not threatening, is prudent and generous from "positions of strength."

One important caveat ought to be registered here, however. While it is true that the Soviet internal debate has an indirect and opaque quality for external audiences, the same is probably the case for internal audiences. Soviet advocates of détente or a relaxation of international tensions, whether as a value in its own right or as a means of serving the interests of particular individuals and groups, must still make their arguments and justifications in utilitarian terms. Therefore, it is essential not to take the often extravagant Soviet claims about how successful détente will be in altering the "correlation of forces" or promoting socialism, revolution, and national liberation as evidence that détente must be a bad policy for the West since it is simultaneously expected to perform miracles for Moscow. Such Soviet claims may simply be attempts to win arguments against internal opponents of détente.

## Conclusions and Prospects

As noted at the outset, one does not have to assume that Soviet intervention abroad in the 1970s reflects a Soviet grand design or global strategy to recognize that the Soviet Union has developed a global policy, representing an intersection of Soviet global capabilities and residual universalist ideological goals. The Soviet move in Afghanistan must be linked with earlier and continuing Soviet/Cuban moves in Africa. As Zbigniew Brzezinski, President Carter's national security adviser, has pointed out, there is indeed an "arc of crisis" stretching along the western edge of the Indian Ocean from Mozambique to Pakistan.

To be sure, Soviet initiative in virtually all parts of the arc has been distinguished by its absence. The apparent unwillingness of the United States to support its local clients probably had more to do with the development of the crises there than did the Kremlin's political/diplomatic engineerings. Of equal importance, the revolutions in Mozambique, Ethiopia, South Yemen, and Afghanistan were the result of indigenous activity to which the Soviet Union responded, usually following an invitation either from a new regime or one of the factions in an internal civil struggle. And although the USSR did attempt to inflame passions in the final stages of the upheaval in Iran, there is no evidence that Moscow fomented the revolution or had much impact on its ultimate course.

Nevertheless, the overall consequences of Soviet behavior within a global context may eventually be indistinguishable from the execution of a grand design. What is more, the opportunities that have inadvertently and fortuitously been created may induce the Soviet Union to operate as if it is pursuing a grand design or stimulate it to formulate one to take systematic advantage of the situation. In this context, the threat and danger of Soviet envelopment of the Middle East and Persian Gulf region from the north are real. Since the Middle East is adjacent to Soviet borders, the natural resources of the region are close to the centers of Soviet power and lines of communication. Furthermore, no large bodies of water separate the USSR from these natural resources, and the countries lying between the USSR and the resources are small, internally unstable, and subject to both domestic turmoil and external penetration. That Soviet influence and penetration are more likely to result from internal upheavals and invitations for support extended to Moscow rather than from Soviet military initiatives does not significantly reduce the importance of these considerations.

In the recent past, Moscow has placed its ideological goals in cold storage, largely because it deemed too vocal an expression of them counterproductive and because the USSR did not have the capabilities to implement them in any case. But if Soviet global capabilities continue to grow while the capabilities of the United States wane, there could be a resurgence of ideology as a shaper of Soviet foreign policy. The apparent Soviet decision to give global and universalist application to the so-called Brezhnev doctrine affords an ominous reminder of this possibility.

Since the enunciation of this doctrine in the late 1960s, the Soviet interpretation of it and its application had remained something of a mystery. While it surely applied to the Warsaw Pact states and perhaps the "socialist commonwealth," Moscow never defined the latter unambiguously, thus leaving open to question whether it intended the doctrine to cover China, Yugoslavia, Albania, and other Communist states.[35] However, in a speech in April 1980, the Soviet ambassador to France, S.V. Chervonenko (the same Chervonenko who staged and orchestrated the massive intervention in Czechoslovakia by the Warsaw Pact states in 1968 from his vantage point as Soviet ambassador to Prague), went a long way toward clearing up this matter and explaining the precise mechanics whereby the doctrine is applied. Chervonenko asserted in connection with the Afghanistan invasion that the Soviet Union "would not permit another Chile"—a rather imperious and arrogant pronouncement in itself—and made the extraordinary statement that now any country, in any region, anywhere on the globe, "has the full right to choose its friends and allies, and if it becomes necessary, to repel with them the threat of counter-revolution or a foreign intervention."[36] This expanded Brezhnev doctrine serves not only to justify the invasion of Afghanistan but also retroactively to justify the Cuban/Soviet military interventions in Angola and on the Horn of Africa, and it poses an immediate threat to Iran or any other country where internal chaotic conditions can generate "invitations" to Moscow for support to quell internal counterrevolutions or external intervention. Czechoslovakia 1968 and Afghanistan 1979 provide sufficient cause for concern that Soviet leaders are not overly fastidious in examining their invitations and are fully capable of inviting themselves, should no invitation be forthcoming.

To give a further global dimension to his remarks, Ambassador Chervonenko gratuitously warned that the Soviet Union would not recognize any assertion by the United States that the Persian Gulf or any other region was a special area of vital interest to the United States. Indeed, he indicated that the USSR would contest any such claim. In this connection, the Soviet ambassador emphasized the USSR's claim to equality with the United States not only as a military power but also as a global power, and he contended that the Soviet Union had a right equal to that of the United States to be consulted and involved everywhere in the world on all major issues. This contention contained an implicit threat of intervention to sustain such a right.

Even without such an ideological resurgence, however, there appears to be a Soviet global policy—if not yet a grand design woven out of targets of opportunity—that only transparently conceals a powerful Soviet ambition to supplant the United States as the paramount international power—to become the world's principal manager and regulator. The kind of management and regulation that the USSR promises to deliver can already be faintly discerned in the Soviet scholarly and journalistic literature. In the mid-1970s, it emerged vaguely in discussions of the role of Leninist ideas and the "correlation of forces" in achieving an extensive restructuring of the international system which would be "designed to completely exclude from international relations *imperialist* violence and threats" (i.e., a system in which American and Western power is neutralized or nullified). One Soviet author wrote:

> The change in the balance of forces of the two social systems constitutes a decisive factor in restructuring the system of international relations, because this balance is a key issue determining its very nature. The weight of the socialist community in the economic, moral, political, and military balance of forces in the world today has been constantly growing, just as, on the whole, the role it plays in world politics has also increased. The foreign policies of socialist countries have become far more effective, and the coordination of their joint action in solving major issues of our day has become more close and purposeful. As soon as the balance of forces in the world began to change in favor of socialism, possibilities for establishing international relations on truly just and democratic principles were extended.[37]

Several years later, the same author offered a much more revealing observation: "The new style international relations that have taken shape and are developing among the socialist countries provide a convincing model of relations among nations and represent a major factor influencing the development of the present-day world."[38]

This notion of an international system restructured in accordance with Leninist norms should not be confused with the crude Soviet ideological approach of earlier years that sought to stimulate world revolution to achieve world communism. Revolution and communism will continue to be supported and promoted, but only in areas where they are supportable and promotable. As the paramount global power, the USSR would make appropriate adjustments to both the developed capitalist world and the underdeveloped Third World—and although the Kremlin would coordinate and manage all three worlds, it would pursue separate policies with respect to each.

When overall Soviet behavior in the international arena is viewed within this context, one can begin to understand why Moscow has been eager to expand and diversify its strategic arsenals far beyond its defense and security needs. One can understand, too, why it pursues a flexible ideological policy—with the Eurocommunists in Western Europe, the do-it-yourself Marxist–Leninists in Africa, the various nationalist and revolutionary movements throughout the Third World, and a motley assembly of traditional and conservative regimes sprinkled around the globe.

Whether or not the USSR will realize its ambition will depend in large measure on how resolutely the challenge of Soviet power is met. The Soviet Union is probably in Afghanistan to stay, but it is by no means inevitable that the Middle East and the Persian Gulf region will pass under Moscow's control and influence.

## Notes

[1]*Pravda* (Moscow), April 4, 1971.

[2]Both the USSR and the United States, it is true, had by 1960 achieved recognition as "superpowers." As such, they shared a number of salient common characteristics which set them apart from the other states in the international community. Each had a large, diversified, and highly skilled population; boasted a powerful industrial–technological capacity; occupied a large, strategically located territory; was the leader of an ideological–military alliance; and gathered around itself a retinue of client states from various parts of the world. Most important, each had or was soon to develop a capability sufficient to unilaterally and almost instantaneously incinerate the globe. Perhaps it is this last characteristic, gruesome as it may be, that constitutes the ineffaceable stigmata of a global power—more, perhaps, by adumbration than designation, since the crude capacity to destroy the entire planet does not by itself enable a country to function as a global power.

Although the distinction between the concepts "superpower" and "global power" has not always been recognized and the two concepts have often been used interchangeably, the difference is fundamental, if subtle. The term "superpower" has primary reference to the magnitude of power which a state possesses. While the unilateral capacity to destroy the entire planet constitutes an indispensable prerequisite for global power status, however, it is by no means sufficient for a state to qualify as a global power, for the concept of a "global power" involves not only the magnitude of power that a state possesses but also the range and reach of that power. Thus, countries such as China, France, West Germany, and Japan have superpower potential because of their material and human resources, but it is doubtful that any country aside from the U.S. and the USSR, with the possible exception of China, can assemble the complicated and intricate complex of intersecting and reinforcing economic, scientific, technological, military, demographic, and geographical capabilities necessary to function as a global power.

[3]See Khrushchev's report to the Extraordinary Twenty-first Congress of the CPSU in *Pravda*, January 28, 1959.

[4]The full text of this document, signed on May 29, 1972, appears in *The Department of State Bulletin* (Washington, D.C.), June 26, 1972, pp. 898–899. It is not entirely clear that President Richard M. Nixon and his national security adviser, Henry Kissinger, anticipated, much less intended, that the principle of strategic parity and equal security should or would invest the Soviet Union with global power status. Certainly, the United States strongly contested such an interpretation once the USSR began to behave like a global power.

[5]A full text of the new Soviet constitution can be found in *Konstitutsiya (Osnovnoy Zakon) Soyuza Sovetskikh Sotsialisticheskikh Respublik* (Constitution [Basic Law] of the Union of Soviet Socialist Republics), Moscow, 1978. Article 28 is on p. 21.

In contrast to the 1977 document, the 1936 constitution contained no special section on foreign policy, and it did not even include any extravagant statements on the aims of the Soviet foreign policy. The sweeping ideological tone of the foreign policy section of the 1977 constitution harkens back to the 1924 constitution. The latter's Preamble began with a grandiose description of a "world . . . divided into two camps . . . the camp of capitalism: national hate and inequality, colonial slavery and chauvinism, national oppression and massacres, brutalities and imperialist wars . . . [and] the camp of socialism: reciprocal confidence and peace, national liberty and equality, the peaceful coexistence and fraternal collaboration of peoples." Its final words were that "the Union of Soviet Socialist Republics . . . will serve as a bulwark against world capitalism and mark a new decisive step toward the union of the workers of all countries in one World Socialist Soviet Republic" [*Istoriya Sovetskoy Konstitutsii, 1917–1956* (History of the Soviet Constitution, 1917–1956) (Moscow, 1957), pp. 458–460].

Whereas the words of the 1924 constitution reflect revolutionary bravado, ideological candor, and naiveté, the passages in the 1977 constitution reflect the power and self-confidence of Leonid Brezhnev's Russia. The absence of sweeping ideological verbiage concerning foreign policy in the 1936 constitution mirrored Moscow's prudence when it was developing the capabilities enabling it subsequently to openly reassert its ideological foreign policy goals in a constitutional document.

[6]*Pravda*, November 25, 1979.

[7]That the unrealized military potential of the United States and its allies might become a force for the disruption of the evolving "correlation of forces" that Moscow has deemed favorable to it, is cause for grave concern in the Soviet Union. Even theory is distorted to discount the possibility. One Soviet writer, for example, maintains that "the military potential of the Western powers can no longer serve as the main criterion of their role in the world arena" and goes on to elaborate: "Marxist–Leninist theory proceeds from the fact that the category of correlation of forces in the world cannot and should not be reduced to the correlation of states' military potentials and that in the ultimate end this correlation is nothing but the correlation of class forces in the worldwide system of international politics" [A. Sergiyev, "Leninism as a Factor of International Relations," *International Affairs* (Moscow) (May 1975), p. 101]. For an excellent assessment of Soviet military potential, see Andrew Marshall, *Sources of Soviet*

*Power: The Military Potential in the 1980's,* Adelphi Papers, no. 152 (London, International Institute for Strategic Studies, Summer 1979), pp. 11–18.

[8]*Pravda,* March 22, 1977.

[9]*Ibid.,* January 13, 1980.

[10]*Ibid.,* January 19, 1977.

[11]See *The Department of State Bulletin,* July 1979, p. 55.

[12]*Pravda,* October 7, 1979. In order to give this theme greater force, Defense Minister Dmitriy Ustinov shortly afterward, in an article entitled "Military Détente Is a Command of the Times," cited this passage as evidence that the Soviets did not have and were not seeking military superiority (*ibid.,* October 25, 1979).

[13]*Ibid.,* October 7, 1979. Soviet writers and the Soviet press have devoted an extraordinary amount of space to the theme of the necessity of "military détente," while simultaneously castigating the idea of "ideological détente." The stress on the desirability of military détente betrays the Soviet fear of a resurgence in U.S. military strength. See, for example, the following: A. Voronov, "The Chimera of Military Superiority," *International Affairs* (February 1980), pp. 18–27; A. Svetlov, "The Soviet Union's Struggle for Military Détente," *ibid.* (February 1976), pp. 93–101; D. Proektor, "Military Détente: Primary Task," *ibid.* (June 1976), pp. 35–43; editorial on "European Security and Détente," *ibid.* (February 1980), pp. 3–7; and Y. Zakharov, "International Cooperation and the Battle of Ideas," *ibid.* (January 1976), pp. 85–95.

[14]See Vernon V. Aspaturian, "Moscow's Afghan Gamble," *The New Leader* (New York, N.Y.), January 28, 1980, pp. 7–13, for the author's elaboration of this point. Also see Jiri Valenta, "Afghanistan—The Soviet Invasion," a four-part article in *The Baltimore Sun,* February 19, 20, 21, and 22, 1980; *idem,* "Soviet Invasion of Afghanistan: The Difficulty of Knowing Where to Stop," *Orbis* (Philadelphia, Penn.), Summer 1980.

[15]"On the Threshold of a New Decade," *Pravda,* March 3, 1980.

[16]*Pravda,* January 29, 1980.

[17]Sh.P. Sanakoyev and N. I. Kapchenko, *Socialism: Foreign Policy in Theory and Practice* (Moscow: Progress Publishers, 1976), pp. 126–163.

[18]*Pravda,* February 19, 1980.

[19]*Ibid.,* January 29, 1980.

[20]"Restore a Climate of Détente and Trust," *Literaturnaya gazeta* (Moscow), February 27, 1980, p. 14.

[21]*Pravda,* May 4, 1978.

[22]A. Sergiyev, "Leninism on the Correlation of Forces as a Factor of International Relations," *International Affairs* (May 1975), p. 101.

[23]*Ibid.,* p. 103.

[24]G. Trofimenko, "Political Realism and the 'Realistic Deterrence' Strategy," *SShA* (Moscow), no. 12, 1971.

[25]Sanakoyev and Kapchenko, *op. cit.,* p. 160. Emphasis added.

[26]*Ibid.,* p. 162.

[27]V. Kortunov, "The Leninist Policy of Peaceful Co-existence and Class Struggle," *International Affairs* (May 1979), p. 91.

[28]*Ibid.,* p. 93.

[29]*Pravda,* June 17, 1979. Emphasis added.

[30]Kortunov, *loc. cit.,* p. 94.

[31]See Aspaturian, "Moscow's Afghan Gamble," *loc. cit.,* and Alexander Dallin, *The United States in the Soviet Perspective,* Adelphi Papers, no. 151 (London: International Institute for Strategic Studies, Summer 1979), pp. 13–21.

[32]*Pravda,* June 17, 1978.

[33]*Ibid.*, January 13, 1980.

[34]See his *Essence of Decision* (Boston, Mass.: Little, Brown and Co., 1971).

[35]For various definitions and views of the "socialist commonwealth" within the Communist world, see Vernon V. Aspaturian, "The Metamorphosis of the Socialist Commonwealth," in *Sozialismus in Theorie und Praxis* (Socialism in Theory and Practice), ed. H. Horn *et al.* (Berlin, 1978), pp. 249–320.

[36]As quoted in *The New York Times*, April 22, 1980.

[37]N. Kapchenko, "Socialist Foreign Policy and the Restructuring of International Relations," *International Affairs* (April 1974), p. 5.

[38]N. Kapchenko, "Leninist Foreign Policy: A Transformative Force," *International Affairs* (October 1978), p. 7. See also Philip Windsor, *The Soviet Union in the International System of the 1980's*, Adlephi Papers, no. 152 (London: International Institute for Strategic Studies, Summer 1979), pp. 2–10; and Curt Gasteyger, "Soviet Global Strategy," *Survival* (London) (July–August 1978), pp. 159–162.

# 49 ALEXANDER DALLIN

## KAL 007: Perceptions and Politics*

Of all the incidents between East and West since World War II, the Soviet downing of Korean Airlines flight 007 on September 1, 1983 was the disaster most costly in human lives. The fate of the unfortunate airliner highlights the volatility of the international order. An unforeseen incident or accident, a single plane or a single person—and *a fortiori* a single nuclear device—can create an international crisis of the first order, whatever the intentions of the so-called policymakers. And once an incident occurs, each side sees itself compelled to respond—to speak out or to act—and to do so fast and firmly, as if it knew what it was all about. The dangers that inhere in such a pattern of behavior are only too obvious, yet so are the pressures that bring it about.

The flight of KAL 007 challenged a number of beliefs and illusions. Some of these stem from our general faith in science and technology. Thus, there has been widespread acceptance of the notion that a variety of technological innovations—radar, satellite photography, electronic communications networks, sonar detection—have made deterrence of aggression and intrusion, nuclear as well as conventional, more reliable and therefore stable, and have made unilateral verification of arms-limitation agreements more foolproof and violations less likely because of the greater probability of detection. The opponents of arms-control agreements have likewise invoked the reliability of weapons technology (say, in the ability to "launch on warning") as part of the argument that security is better assured by technical than by political means.

The crisis over KAL 007 does not disprove these arguments. It does underscore not only the limits of technology but in particular the hazards of inadequate technology (such as Soviet radar that could not tell that a Boeing 747 was not an RC-135; or the inability of air traffic ground controllers to check independently on the accuracy of pilots'

*Reprinted by permission of the author and publisher from *Black Box: KAL 007 and the Superpowers* (Berkeley, Calif.: University of California Press, 1985), pp. 100–105, 122. Copyright 1985 by University of California Press.

position reports; and perhaps the malfunctions, if there were any, on board the KAL 007). It bodes ill for the enthusiasts of "star wars" in the uncertain future. More immediately, it illustrates how, regardless of science and technology, it is ultimately human judgments, human choices, human errors, politics, and preconceptions that shape political and military decisions.

To many American military analysts, the unreliability of Soviet early-warning systems is troublesome—especially at a time when Pershing-2s are being deployed in Europe. In the end, it was not the inadequacy of Soviet technology, such as the communications link between Sakhalin and Moscow, that was the problem in the Korean airliner crisis, but the choices which the key actors made, such as the decision to shoot down the jet rather than to let it "escape" scot-free. Whether the failure of the airliner to respond to the signals from Soviet fighters and ground stations was a matter of human choice or technology is, of course, one of the questions to which we lack a definitive answer. In fact, one may speculate that greater human ingenuity might have permitted KAL 007 to "escape" even when the Soviet interceptors were in hot pursuit during its final minutes over Sakhalin, had it acknowledged their signals and feigned compliance while changing altitude and speed to get away over international waters.

Still, the lessons Moscow is apt to have drawn from the incident are likely to have borne in both directions—training as well as technology. In the latter group, while Moscow obviously knew of the extensive American effort to intercept and decode Soviet communications, it is possible that the revelations by the American and Japanese authorities brought home to the Soviet political leadership its vulnerability to foreign "ears" listening in—an unwitting Soviet exposure, a nakedness (as Soviet officials have at times referred to it), ranging apparently from missile test telemetry to perhaps civil and military communications across the country. One prompt response was reportedly a change of codes and radio frequencies on Soviet military aircraft transmissions, within literally a few days of the Japanese and American disclosure of the intercepts.[1] How extensive such changes have been cannot be judged by those outside the area of classified information.

Both sides to a dispute—both sides in a crisis—feel compelled to make decisions under conditions of imperfect information.[2] Under such conditions, each party, in its attempt to interpret such facts as are available, to fit them into some explanatory or conceptual framework, and to move toward some action strategy, inevitably tends to fall back on prior images, assumptions, and suspicions regarding the adversary power and its intentions and capabilities—images and assumptions that must always be close to the surface but come into the open only under such special circumstances. And when—as in this case—the events are such as to permit both sides to impute the worst to, and believe the worst about, the adversary, there is indeed a strong predisposition to go for "worst-case" scenarios, that is, to select from the whole range of possible interpretations the one which assumes the worst about the other side's intentions and capabilities—a tendency which, more often than not, has an inherent propensity toward self-fulfilling prophecy.

Most striking in the case of KAL 007 was the mind-set—the set of assumptions and beliefs dominant from the outset in official circles both in Moscow and in Washington. In their eagerness to make political capital and to impute criminal intent to their adversary, the policymakers in both the United States and the Soviet Union ruled out categories such as accident, confusion, incompetence, or error on the part of the other side as a possible explanation for the events. For Moscow to make such a defense of its behavior would have meant to admit fault and imperfection. For Washington so to brand Soviet behavior would have blunted the ideological edge of its outrage. As a result, each side was programmed to present the whole episode as more calculated by the adversary and more overdetermined by the totality of "objective" and "subjective" forces than was warranted by the facts. Thus, they revealed instead a natural predisposition to impute purpose—hostile intent, subversion, or willful brutality—to the adversary: a dangerous but rather characteristic practice.[3]

In fact, this tendency was not limited to government analysts but included Soviet radar technicians, pilots, and ground controllers: Operating in an atmosphere of perennial "dueling" with the Americans, the question whether what they "saw" was conceivably a commercial plane with civilian passengers, and whether the aircraft might have made an error in navigation, does not seem to have been seriously explored by the Soviet air defense personnel. The built-in bias under such conditions is to avoid alternatives that make one appear weak, soft, or naive. Hence the tendency never to give the adversary the benefit of the doubt: in neither system is one likely to be punished for playing it tough and "going by the book."

This pervasive tendency is further strengthened by a peculiar nuclear anticipation that has developed over the past generation: The Soviet fighter pilots interviewed on television, some 2 weeks later, spoke (quite characteristically) not only of the broader pattern of American mischief into which the intruder-plane's action seemed to fit but also of the belief that, if indeed this plane's flight was in some respects an unprecedented phenomenon, this might be all the more dangerous. After all, who knows whether it might not be carrying a bomb or some nuclear device?

Nor was the American perception much more balanced or cautious. Why and how KAL 007 wound up where it did does not seem to have intrigued those analyzing the events when the news of the disaster first came in. How the Soviet authorities were bound to have seen it was irrelevant. That Soviet air defense personnel might have tried to signal it or get it to land was apparently ruled out as incongruent with the explanatory syndrome of inhumanity and purposive brutality. Instead, purpose, conspiracy, and provocation became the dominant assumptions on both sides. And on the American side, too, that image of evildoing was promptly fitted into a broader canvas that ranged from Afghanistan to forced labor, and soon (as in President Reagan's and Ambassador Kirkpatrick's speeches) the shooting down of the airliner came to be seen as an instance of natural, almost inevitable behavior for a totalitarian regime whose assessment this Administration saw dramatically validated by this crisis.

The crisis over the downing of KAL 007 thus served as a sort of political Rorschach test which made manifest each elite's propensities, and especially its fears and images of the adversary. Alas, the images on both sides were seriously wide of the mark. If the Soviet image of the United States was close to a caricature, the American image of the Soviet Union—both among government spokespersons and in the media—revealed an amazing lack of knowledge, feel, and understanding of the Soviet scene. To point to only one widespread misconception: In a real sense, the episode teaches us nothing about Soviet foreign policy decisions, for shooting down the airliner was not an act implementing a foreign policy decision of the Kremlin's leadership. Contrary to many pundits, it did not mark the beginning of a new policy. Yet one inevitable outcome of the crisis was to heighten mutual suspicion and to insulate even further each side's perceptions and rhetoric from critical testing by interaction with the other side.

In the end, however, the symmetry between the two sides breaks down. Though we have some good surmises, we do not know why KAL 007 went astray. We do know who shot it down. Politically and morally, the whole episode amounted to an international fiasco for the Soviet Union, whose leaders—once the crisis occurred—could not see any ready way out of the difficulties, which they were loath to acknowledge. Still, the United States, too, emerged from the crisis paradoxically confused—seemingly "victorious" though uncertain just what it had won, feeling morally united and superior but also conscious of serious unanswered questions and gnawing doubts.

Political scientists may, of course, argue that what we have dealt with here was not properly a war-threatening international crisis. For one thing, if we take a widely accepted definition, such a crisis requires surprise, a high level of threat, and a short decision time.[4] While the element of surprise was present in this case, there was no high threat; and the short decision time, on the American side, was self-imposed. The circumstance that it was not a war-threatening crisis (such as the Cuban missile crisis had been) but rather what has been called a "politically damaging crisis" (as had been true also, for instance, of the U-2 incident in 1960 and of the discovery of the so-called Soviet brigade in Cuba in 1980) made it easier for the U.S. not to escalate without losing face—especially as it was by no means clear what escalation could have achieved.

For another thing, if we take the standard view that war-threatening crises are essentially bargaining situations[5] or occasions for what has been labeled "coercive diplomacy,"[6] the KAL 007 episode again does not fit the mold. The incident was hardly planned to create a negotiating situation. The Soviet Union was not trying to coerce the United States to admit its responsibility for the flight; nor, in fact, was the U.S. trying to coerce the USSR: Rather it was trying to "expose" and pillory it and perhaps was hoping to punish it. As in other instances, anti-Soviet sanctions were adopted more as tokens of outrage and solidarity (or, others would say, as U.S.-inspired propaganda gestures) than as credible efforts to get Moscow to admit its responsibility, to provide compensation to the families of the victims, and to learn the proper lessons from the events.

Actually, when it comes to learning lessons, in all likelihood the two superpowers agreed only on the most limited, technical lessons (such as the need for better civil–military air traffic communications). Beyond that, rather than bringing them closer together, what each side learned from the incident—over the outrage, both genuine and sham, directed at each other—served to place them even farther apart. In the absence of the real "black box" from KAL 007, each side filled its mental, imaginary black box with opposite and incompatible assumptions about the adversary—assumptions which, each believed, were validated by the so-called facts in the case.

## Notes

[1]"Russians Said to Use New Codes," *Washington Post*, September 9; *TIME*, September 19, p. 14.

[2]For technical discussions of the psychological problems involved, see the papers in Daniel Kahneman, Paul Slovic, and Amos Tversky, eds., *Judgment under Uncertainty: Heuristics and Biases* (Cambridge, England: Cambridge University Press, 1982).

[3]See the excellent discussion in Robert Jervis, *Perception and Misperception in International Politics* (Princeton, N.J.: Princeton University Press, 1976), especially chap. 8.

[4]Ole R. Holsti, "Theories of Crisis Decision Making," in *Diplomacy: New Approaches in History, Theory, and Policy*, ed. Paul Gordon Lauren (New York: Free Press, 1979), p. 101; and Charles Hermann, *Crises in Foreign Policy* (New York: Bobbs-Merrill, 1969).

[5]Thomas C. Schelling, ed., *Arms and Influence* (New Haven: Yale University Press, 1966); Glenn H. Snyder and Paul Diesing, *Conflict among Nations* (Princeton, N.J.: Princeton University Press, 1977); Paul Gorden Lauren, "Theories of Bargaining with Threats of Force: Deterrence and Coercive Diplomacy," in *Diplomacy*, pp. 186 ff.

[6]Cf. Alexander George *et al.*, eds., *The Limits of Coercive Diplomacy* (Boston: Little, Brown, 1971).

# 50 MARSHALL D. SHULMAN

## What the Russians Really Want: A Rational Response to the Soviet Challenge*

Like travelers who come upon an unmarked fork in the road, we find ourselves obliged by the change in leadership in the Soviet Union to stop and think. The transition, with all the uncertainties it presents, compels us to consider where we are going in our fateful relationship with the Russians, and why, and whether we should be going in another direction.

Almost seven decades have passed since the revolution that led to the founding of the Soviet Union. For most of those years, relations between that country and our own have been animated by hostility, relieved only by brief intervals of abatement and passing hopes of some easement.

Each such interval, however, has been followed by an ever stronger expression of the conflict of power, beliefs, and purposes between the two nations. That conflict is now so deeply rooted and so intense that it evokes the destructive energies of both societies, weakening them and the fabric of the international system, threatening the possibility of catastrophe.

That hostility did not grow out of any natural antipathy between the peoples of the two countries, but with the passage of time each has come to be so persuaded of the malign intent of the other that it has become difficult to distinguish what is real and what is fancied in the perceptions each holds of the other.

In the conduct of our foreign relations, Walter Lippmann observed, we operate on the basis of "pictures in our heads." The images of the Soviet Union held most widely in this country are stereotypes, and they warp our thinking in a number of ways. They are simple caricatures of a complex society. They are static and do not take into account the

*Reprinted by permission of the author and publisher from *Harper's Magazine* (April, 1984), pp. 63–71. Copyright 1984 by *Harper's Magazine*.

changes that have taken place, particularly since the death of Stalin. They are based on prevalent assumptions that do not bear critical examination. They misrepresent the ways in which the Soviet people react to our actions and to our words. They do not distinguish between atmosphere and substance. Finally, as oversimple images informing oversimple policy, they make it difficult for us to resolve the dilemma of whether we should try to change the Soviet system or try to improve our relations with it.

After almost four decades spent studying the Soviet Union and after about 30 trips there, what continues to strike me most forcefully is the sharp contrast between the complex reality of that country and the primitive perceptions of it that dominate our discussions, and the contrast between the way the world looks from Moscow and the way it appears from Washington. Even more troubling is the problem we face in bringing our values, our emotions, our apprehensions, and our judgments about the Soviet Union into some kind of reasonable balance with our relations with it.

To many Americans, including many specialists on the subject, it seems contradictory to recognize that the Soviet Union is repressive and expansionist and also to believe that we should seek to manage rationally the fundamentally competitive Soviet–American relationship. What has been absent from our thinking is the maturity to carry such apparently contradictory notions in our heads at the same time.

Good and reasonable people often come to hold fundamentally different views of the Soviet Union. There is much about that secretive society that we do not know. Into this uncertainty people tend to project either their fears or their hopes, according to their temperaments or their political prejudices or, perhaps, their experiences: A businessman who has been royally treated on his visits to the Soviet Union will have a very different picture in his mind than an émigré who may have spent years in a labor camp or years battling bureaucrats for an exit visa; a military game theorist will see the Russians as the enemy, ruthless, omnicompetent, poised to attack.

The problems presented by the Soviet Union are serious. But stereotypes do not provide us with an adequate basis for responding intelligently. My purpose here is to suggest a way of thinking about these problems, beginning with a realistic view of the Soviet Union and its behavior and ending with some guidelines for the conduct of our relations with Moscow. Not everyone, and certainly not all of those who study Soviet behavior, will agree with what I regard as realistic or with my conclusions. But I believe that the time is overdue for us to address head-on some of the questions that underlie our present thinking about that country in order to contribute to a more rational discourse, beyond the level of partisan polemics.

1. *In seeking to expand its power and influence around the world, are the Soviet Union's aspirations unlimited? Does it accept practical limitations on realizing its status as a superpower? Might it even become willing to live according to the norms of the international system?*

Over the last 67 years, we have witnessed the ascendancy of nation-state interests over revolutionary expectations and ideology as the primary motivation of Soviet foreign policy. It became apparent to the Soviet regime in its early years—and even more so after World War II—that the proletariat of the West was showing no signs of the revolutionary potential that Lenin had ascribed to it. In response to this fact, Soviet policy was adapted to address the bourgeoisie of both the Western industrial societies and the developing world for the purpose of influencing governments to act in ways favorable to Soviet interests. Although revolutionary ideology is still part of the official rhetoric and although it is bolstered by a bureaucratic apparatus that has a stake in it, it has been modified in such a way as to put off to the indefinite future the realization of apocalyptic goals. Peaceful coexistence, which to Lenin meant a breathing spell, has become a long-term political strategy of competition by means short of war.

While it is impossible to predict whether Soviet foreign policy will evolve in directions we would wish, it can be said that it has evolved more than is generally appreciated, largely as a result of Soviet efforts to adapt to changes in international politics, including options created by policies of the United States.

Coincident with this development—which has included Soviet policy toward favoring traditional balance-of-power maneuvers—has been a continuous movement away from the autarkic reliance on the Soviet economy promised by Stalin's commitment to "Socialism in One Country." In fact, the Soviet Union has become ever more deeply involved in the world economy, and the proportion of its gross national product derived from foreign trade has risen steadily.

While it does not seem likely that these trends will be reversed, it is clearly too much to say that they will necessarily lead to Soviet acceptance of the international system to the extent of being willing to act as a partner in preserving the system's stability. The Soviet Union has an interest in maintaining the status quo in Eastern Europe, but not elsewhere. A broader commitment would require a much greater departure from its residual faith that capitalist systems contain the seeds of their own destruction than any signs now indicate is likely.

2. *Are Soviet leaders, then, guided by the ideology of Marxism–Leninism?*

If you were to ask them that question, their answer would be "Of course." None of them would say otherwise, and they seek sanction for every action, speech, article, or book by quoting from the storehouse of the writings of Marx, Engels, and, especially, Lenin.

Marxist–Leninist ideology, of course, is based on the prediction that capitalist systems are doomed to decay and collapse, that they will seek to stave off this outcome by imperialist aggression, but that, in the end, "socialism" as the Soviet Union defines it will prove more effective and will emerge as the universal form of social organization. In practice, Soviet theoreticians have had to take into account the fact that these predictions from the nineteenth and early twentieth centuries have not received much confirmation. The lesson has not been lost on Soviet theoreticians, who have reinterpreted some parts of the ideology while clinging to others, seeking legitimacy in hoped-for improvements in performance, or what Khrushchev called "goulash communism." In truth, there is as much variance in the Soviet interpretation of Marxism–Leninism today as there is in American Protestantism.

To say that Soviet political figures and writers claim consistency with Marxism–Leninism is not to say that their actions are derived from ideology. Certainly the historical analysis of capitalism influences the way the older Soviet political elites interpret events, but the sacred texts offer less and less guidance for making the practical decisions demanded by the complex society that the Soviet Union has become. With rare exceptions, even those youths who aspire to become members of the Soviet establishment master their catechism with cynicism (the sound of shuffling feet during lectures on "diamat"—dialectical materialism—is reminiscent of the noise during lectures for GIs on social hygiene), suggesting that when they take the levers of power into their hands, the ideas that will shape their thoughts and guide their actions will bear only the slightest resemblance to the ideas that inspired the Revolution.

3. *Is the Soviet Union nevertheless* inherently *expansionist?*

Some have argued that the answer to this question is yes. Should that be true, it would follow that in order to move Soviet behavior in the direction of greater restraint and responsibility it would be necessary to change the Soviet system in fundamental ways, and that this should be the primary objective of American policy. Those who take this position claim that it is only by external aggrandizement that the Soviet leadership can cement its power, claim legitimacy, and validate its view of history. Some even argue that there is a parallel between the Soviet Union and Nazi Germany, and that just as appeasement served to whet the Nazis' appetite, any accommodation with the Soviet Union can "only lead to disaster."

The study of Soviet behavior, however, suggests that Soviet actions are more consistently explained by reference to the pursuit of nation-state interests than by some inner compulsion related to the structure of the system. The leadership is strengthened by successes and weakened by failures, as is the case in any country, but there is no sign that Soviet adventures abroad have resulted in increased popular support. On the contrary, foreign adventures, whether in Hungary or Afghanistan, are regarded uneasily by Soviet citizens.

There is an expansive tendency in the Soviet Union's behavior but it is impelled not by the nature of the system but by the sense that the country has grown into a great power. Moreover, it has been activated by opportunities that the Soviet Union itself has not created, and it has been guided by a careful calculus of risks and gains as well as by a capacity for prudence. This was illustrated most recently by the absence of an immediate Soviet reaction to the attacks on Syria during the Israeli invasion of Lebanon.

The Nazi parallel is particularly misleading. Unlike the Nazis, Soviet leaders do not seek war. No one doubts that who has seen firsthand how fresh are the memories of the destruction and loss of life in World War II, or how universal is the appreciation of the consequences of nuclear war (much more universal than is the case in the United States).

Soviet leaders have accepted and accommodated themselves to the practical constraints on their expansionist tendencies. They may hope that the future will bring more favorable opportunities, but faith in their historical inevitability has become ritualistic, and is advanced on national holidays with diminishing conviction.

4. *Even if the Soviet Union is not inherently expansionist, is it possible for us to maintain peaceful relations with it so long as it seeks to maximize its power and influence?*

We have to accept the fact that the Soviet–American relationship is fundamentally competitive and is likely to remain so for the foreseeable future. What we must decide is whether it is in our interest to compete at a high level of confrontation or whether it is more sensible to manage the competition at lower levels of tension. If we seek to force the pace of military competition and to maximize pressure on the Soviet Union by cutting back diplomatic contacts, trade, and all forms of cooperation, the effect will be to increase the level of conflict and the risk of war and to push both societies toward greater, and destructive, militarization.

It is sometimes said in this country that the so-called détente of the early 1970s was a failure and a deception, and that it proved that the effort to moderate relations is bound not to work, leaving us at a disadvantage. But the principal reason why détente was not successful was that neither side fulfilled the two main requirements for reducing tensions. Those requirements are the management of the nuclear competition at lower and more stable levels and the codification of the terms of political competition in the Third World. On each side there were impediments to exercising the restraint that is essential to reducing the risk of war.

On the Soviet side, the main impediments to the stabilization of the nuclear competition appeared to stem from the influence of the military bureaucracy in Soviet politics; tendencies toward overinsurance in military matters; an inclination to think in prenuclear terms; a fear of the U.S. advantage in advanced military technology; a fear of appearing weak and therefore vulnerable to American pressure; and a mistaken belief that a strengthened military posture would make the United States more pliant in negotiations. In the Third World, the main impediment to restraint was the Soviet Union's commitment to expand its influence wherever it could do so at acceptable costs and risks, which it rationalized as support for what it chose to call national liberation movements. The increase in Soviet logistical capabilities and conventional weapons and forces made such interventions more tempting.

On the American side, the impediments to the stabilization of the nuclear competition included a lack of rationality in defense policy-making, as a result of which decisions were dictated by parochial economic and service interests; a residual commitment to superiority rather than parity as the basis for national security; a post-Vietnam fear of appearing to be weak; and a mistaken belief that a strengthened military posture would make the Soviet Union more pliant in negotiations. Moreover, a resurgence of nationalism, a universal phenomenon throughout the industrialized world, made any form of accommodation with the Soviet Union politically difficult. The basic impediments to stabilizing the U.S.–Soviet competition in the Third World were America's inexperience in international affairs, its parochialism, and its ignorance of the areas involved. That led the United States to regard countries of the Third World as abstract counters in the East–West competition, driving all radical movements into the Soviet camp, and to rely primarily on military instrumentalities for dealing with them.

In addition, there have been external impediments to a regulation of the competition. This period of international politics has been characterized by an extraordinary turbulence involving dramatic transformations in the industrialized nations, postdecolonization travails in the developing ones, and anarchy in the international system. Under the best of circumstances, it would have been remarkable if Soviet–American relations had not become roiled.

5. *Has Soviet foreign policy, emboldened by what some analysts see as military supremacy, become more aggressive in the years since détente?*

There is a two-part answer to the military question. Certainly the improvements in the Soviet Union's conventional capabilities, the increase in the firepower and mobility of its forces, and its greater logistical capabilities—demonstrated in the impressive airlift of matériel to Ethiopia—have made it possible to intervene where it might not have been able to a decade ago. But despite the expanded Soviet strategic nuclear arsenal, it is wrong to speak of supremacy, and there are no grounds for believing that the strategic balance influenced the Soviet decisions to act as it did in Angola, Ethiopia, or Afghanistan.

The lack of restraint shown by the Soviet Union in exacerbating local conflicts cannot be justified, but its interventions have represented a continuation of its longstanding policy of seeking to exploit opportunities, whatever their cause. The 1975 intervention in Angola, for example, was a response to the collapse of the Portuguese position in Africa. (The Soviet Union was able to respond to that collapse more effectively than was the United States, tied as we were to our Portuguese ally and restrained as we were by the post-Vietnam inhibitions against foreign interventions.) In Ethiopia, it was Chairman Mengistu Haile-Mariam's alienation from the United States and his turning to the Soviet Union for support that created the Soviet opportunity, and there, as in Angola, the messianic mission of Fidel Castro gave the Soviet Union the benefit of Cuban soldiers. (In contrast, the Soviet invasion of Afghanistan was a response not to an opportunity but to a perceived threat; it can best be understood as a gross political and military miscalculation, reflecting Soviet paranoia about the security of its borders.)

Of course, even though these Soviet interventions were responses to opportunities rather than manifestations of a more aggressive policy, they are still a matter for concern. But it lies within our power to reduce such opportunities by understanding better what local factors generate upheavals and conflicts, and by responding to them more appropriately ourselves.

*6. Does the Soviet Union's military buildup indicate that it has accepted the risks of nuclear war?*

The great increase in its conventional forces does raise the possibility that the Soviet Union is prepared to intervene in behalf of its newly acquired global interests. And in its production and deployment of nuclear weapons like the SS-18, an intercontinental missile capable of delivering ten warheads of 500 kilotons each with great accuracy, and the SS-20, an intermediate-range missile targeted on Europe and the Far East, it has not shown reasonable restraint and has aroused concerns in the West that have had the effect of reducing its own security. (In this respect, neither Soviet nor American defense policies have been marked by much rationality or foresight.) But it strains any plausible scenario to see Soviet strategic forces as capable of anything other than preventing a military attack or political intimidation.

Monetary measures of the Soviet Union's military effort have some-times been used to show that its programs are alarmingly larger than ours, but these are not a reliable basis for comparison. The statistics cited in such comparisons are questionable: They depend on estimates of what it would cost us to produce Soviet weapons using American labor costs, and also on calculations of dollar-ruble equivalencies; they do not take into account the actual Soviet production costs; and even if it is argued that the percentage of the Soviet gross national product devoted to military programs is twice that of the United States, it must be borne in mind that the Soviet GNP is half our own. Moreover, the CIA has recently revised downward its estimates of Soviet military expenditures; those estimates now suggest that after annual increases of about 4% a year beginning in the early 1960s, the rate of increase began to level off in the mid-1970s, once the Soviet Union reached parity with the United States.

Judgments about parity are, of course, inexact, seeking as they do to compare quite different force structures (the Soviet Union has three-quarters of its strategic force in land-based intercontinental missiles, compared with only one-third of ours; the rest is in bombers and submarines). The Soviet Union fears that America's superior industrial technology may give us an edge in the future, and it continues to develop new weapons, duplicating our innovations when it can and compensating for others simply by doing more of what it can do. By any measure, however, it is apparent that given the destructiveness of nuclear weapons, neither side has or can hope to have a usable military superiority over the other. But neither country has had the self-confidence to regard a secure retaliatory force as sufficient.

It has been said that Soviet military writings imply that Soviet leaders believe they can fight and win a nuclear war, but that argument reflects a superficial reading of the literature. Soviet military doctrine has evolved considerably since the time of Stalin, when nuclear weapons were discussed in pre-nuclear-age terms, and the authoritative state-ments of Yuri Andropov, Konstantin Chernenko, Minister of Defense Dmitri Ustinov, and Chief of the General Staff Nikolai Ogarkov have shown unequivocal awareness that nuclear war would be a danger to the security of their country.

*7. Does it follow, then, that the Soviet Union is prepared to engage seriously in arms-control negotiations?*

Arms-control negotiations about nuclear weapons seemed a radical idea to the Russians when they were first proposed in the Baruch plan in 1946. In the early years of the Strategic Arms Limitation Treaty negotiations, which began in November 1969, the Russians were obviously reluctant to consider entrusting their security to such arrangements— perhaps because they didn't feel strong enough, or their military was resistant, or they did not trust us any more than we trusted them. Most of the SALT proposals were advanced by the American negotiators, and many of the Soviet proposals (for nonaggression agreements, a ban on first use of nuclear weapons, and international conferences to discuss disarmament) had an agitprop character. Although the Soviet Union accepted the American proposal for strategic arms limitation talks, it did not appear to have accepted the fundamental SALT concepts: parity, mutual deterrence, and strategic stability.

But the situation has changed in two respects. We have changed. Despite our formal acceptance of deterrence as a guiding principle, we have moved toward developing war-fighting capabilities. Our defense plans are now based on the requirement that we be able to prevail in a prolonged nuclear conflict. In this respect, both the declaratory and the actual policies of the two countries have moved closer.

The Soviet Union has also changed: It became more than a passive partner in the negotiations. In the SALT II talks, it offered considerably more major concessions than did the United States; it was also prepared to agree that no new land-based intercontinental missiles be allowed, had we been willing to agree to what had originally been an American proposal. The Russians were stubborn bargainers, but they manifested a serious interest in limiting the nuclear competition.

*8. What does this say about the belief that the United States must develop "positions of strength" in order to make the Soviet Union negotiate in good faith or accept our deterrent as credible?*

To the Soviet Union, it appears that a military balance now exists and that American efforts to secure "positions of strength" mask attempts to achieve superiority. The Soviet reaction will be contrary to what is expected. Instead of feeling pressured to make concessions at the negotiating table, the Soviet Union will match every new American program with one of its own (as it has done in the past, for example when we introduced multiple-warhead systems). It is for this reason that the search for such "positions of strength" will lead to an upward spiral in the nuclear military competition, involving weapons that are less stable (the MX missile and the proposed space-based defense system) and less verifiable (cruise missiles) than those now in existence, with the consequence that it will be increasingly difficult to achieve any agreement.

*9. Is the Soviet system capable of change?*

It is here that we come to a question that is absolutely fundamental to the way we think about the Soviet Union, and it is here that our stereotypes are most strikingly out of date. Since the Revolution, the Soviet Union has evolved from a predominantly peasant society to one that is largely urban and industrializing. Although the process of industrialization has moved forward unevenly, and although large parts of the country do not seem to have changed in the past 100 years, the spread of education and the growth of cadres of specialists have made for a much more complex society, in which controls have been increasingly internalized and "privatization" stubbornly protects pockets of autonomy from intrusion by the central authorities. Leaving the intellectuals aside, for most people the system works, since they compare their living standards not with those of other countries but with their own in the past.

The engine of change is the emergence of new generations, with new expectations and experiences, and a vast generational shift is already in progress. Although it is not yet reflected in the composition of the top party leadership, it is to be seen at lower levels of the party, in the military, and in the various bureaucracies. The younger elite are well educated and competent. Not liberals in a Western sense, their thinking is nevertheless far more sophisticated than that of high-level party members, which has been characterized by parochial fundamentalism. They are free of the formative influences of the Revolution and the Stalinist terror and are relatively knowledgeable about the outside world and prepared to learn from it.

The prevailing Western images of the Soviet elite, based on monolithic totalitarian models, tend to stereotype Soviet officialdom, leading some observers to conclude that the system is brittle and cannot change without risk of collapse. This obscures the spectrum of views to be found even within the party establishment, which encompasses not only those who are careerists and bureaucrats supreme but also those who might be called "within-system critics," those who, within the bounds of loyalty to the system, possess and sometimes express unorthodox views about modernization. Because the changes they favor may provoke resistance, in the short run their activities may reinforce or even increase the authority of the political police. Whether in the long run such changes will moderate the repressiveness of the Soviet system may depend in part on the international climate.

In the end, one must wonder if the system will be able to cope with its enormous problems. That is a question no one can answer, not even the Soviet leadership. The decline in the country's growth rates is symptomatic of the contradiction between the rigidities of its political structure and the requirements of advanced industrialization. No one was more severe in cataloguing the deficiencies of the Soviet system than Yuri Andropov. The new leadership is also aware of the problems it faces. But it must deal with a profoundly conservative society, changing but resistant to change, fearful, above all, of the effects of reform on the party's control.

How these contending forces will resolve their differences is the most intriguing question of all, and the answer, when it becomes clear, will affect our thinking about our future relations with the Soviet Union.

There are, of course, other questions that we might wish to ask, but the issues we have already touched on point toward something that should be taken into account far more than has been the case: the factor of change. If instead of viewing the Soviet Union as a static system we view it as one in the midst of a historical transformation, then the starting point for thinking through our own policies should be to ask ourselves how they are likely to affect the processes of change in the Soviet system, Soviet conduct in the world, and opportunities for peaceful relations between the two countries.

Our capacity to influence the nature of change in the Soviet Union is limited. At the very least, however, we should exercise care lest our actions and words impair the prospects for changes we would like to see. It should be clear from past experience that if we are perceived to be bellicose, or if we declare our intent to undermine the Soviet order, we strengthen the backward elements in the Soviet political system.

It follows that our long-term policy should have an evolutionary purpose: It should be designed to encourage future generations of Soviet leaders to see that acting with restraint and enlarging the area of genuine cooperation between the United States and the Soviet Union serve their own self-interest. The main objective of our policy should therefore be to respond to the Soviet challenge in ways that will protect our security, our interests, and our values, rather than to try to force changes in the Soviet Union or to bring about changes in its foreign policy indirectly by seeking to undermine the Soviet system.

This does not mean that we are not interested in what happens inside the Soviet Union, nor that we should put aside our humanitarian concern about its repressive practices. None of us can remain unmoved by the cruelty with which the Soviet police apparatus deals with dissidents or with those who wish to emigrate. But we should have learned from our recent experience that it is counterproductive for our government to make the human rights issue an instrument in a political offensive against the Soviet Union and to engage the prestige of the Soviet leadership by frontal, public ultimatums, as it did with the Jackson–Vanik amendment and in the tragic cases of Andrei Sakharov and Anatoly Shcharansky. We should also remember that although decreased international tension may in the short run inspire campaigns of ideological vigilance designed to control the spread of bourgeois ideas within the Soviet Union, increased levels of international tension reduce the restraints on the Soviet police apparatus and encourage greater pressures for retrogressive movement toward neo-Stalinism.

Perhaps the best that can be hoped for in our relations with the Soviet Union, in the aftermath of the transition to the Chernenko leadership, is a Cold Truce, an improvement in the climate of confrontation that is now patently leading toward greater military competition and a greater risk of misperception and miscalculation in responses to local crises. Beyond the immediate period, we should recognize that the only sensible alternative to a relationship based on confrontation is one that seeks a *modus vivendi*, in order to manage the competition between us at a less destructive level of tension.

The most important aspect of such a policy is the military competition. Clearly, a military balance is required, but what kind, and at what level? If our political leaders and the public really accept the proposition that our security is better safeguarded by a stable nuclear balance than by unregulated competition, it follows that we should accept stability, parity, and mutual deterrence. We pay lip service to these concepts but have not been guided by them in practice. Their genuine acceptance would make possible serious negotiations that would take into account legitimate Soviet security concerns, as well as our own. Neither in the negotiations on strategic systems nor in those on theater nuclear weapons in Europe are the positions of the two sides so far apart that they cannot be bridged. That is also true of the negotiations on treaties for a comprehensive test ban and on the use of chemical weapons, among others. Meanwhile, it does not make sense for us to introduce systems that are destabilizing, systems that will make us more trigger-sensitive. There also must be a balance in conventional weapons. There, too, our long-term objective should be to seek a balance at a moderate level through negotiations, on the basis of the same kind of mutual deterrence that should guide our nuclear weapons policy.

In the political competition between the United States and the Soviet Union, containment by military force is clearly an inadequate response. There may be occasions when we will need sufficient forces on the ground to prevent Soviet intervention, but this is only a negative capability. More important, we must learn to respond to the causes of the strains and instabilities that create opportunities for exploitation by the Soviet Union. For example, we have allowed our relations with our allies among the industrialized nations to become strained by economic tensions and by their growing lack of confidence in the sobriety and wisdom of our leadership. Yet it ought to be the very heart of our policy to maintain the closest possible ties with them. In the Third World, we must show greater awareness of the sources of instability than we have so far. If we are prepared to deal with the causes of revolutionary change, to address the issues of health, food, literacy, and equity with more understanding, we will be able to respond to these problems before all hope of peaceful resolution is lost and the only solution becomes military arbitration between equally unsavory extremes.

In our relations with the Soviet Union we should rely on incentives as well as on constraints. This means that we must sustain a reasonable level of trade and exchanges and encourage limited measures of cooperation. Holding out the prospect of widening ties as the Soviet Union shows its readiness to act responsibly is a token of our hope that the relationship can move to a less dangerous stage. This, indeed, is the link to our longer term policy. We cannot assume that Soviet behavior will evolve in this way, but we can let future generations of Soviet leaders know that if they do move in this direction we are prepared to accept this more productive relationship.

At the center of our thinking should always be the concern that the protection of our security and our values depends not only on the sensible management of relations with the Soviet Union but on the condition of the international system itself, on those fragile restraints on the behavior of nations that have been created so slowly and painfully over the years. It must be strengthened against the anarchy and chaos that now threaten it. To do this we must seek not to preserve the status quo but to codify processes of nonviolent change. We must work toward placing constraints on the use of force to produce or to prevent change, and we must be willing, ourselves, to live within these constraints.

One more thing needs to be said. Essential to a *modus vivendi* are diplomatic communications with the Soviet Union, firm but not bellicose, conducted with civility and common sense—recently so uncommon in American politics.

# 51  ZBIGNIEW BRZEZINSKI

## *The Future of Yalta**

Yalta is unfinished business. It has a longer past and it may have a more ominous future than is generally recognized. Forty years after the fateful Crimean meeting of February 4–11, 1945, between the Allied Big Three of World War II, much of our current preoccupation with Yalta focuses on its myth rather than on its continuing historical significance.

The myth is that at Yalta the West accepted the division of Europe. The fact is that Eastern Europe had been conceded de facto to Josef Stalin by Franklin D. Roosevelt and Winston Churchill as early as the Teheran Conference (in November–December 1943), and at Yalta the British and American leaders had some half hearted second thoughts about that concession. They then made a last-ditch but ineffective effort to fashion some arrangements to assure at least a modicum of freedom for Eastern Europe, in keeping with Anglo–American hopes for democracy on the European continent as a whole. The Western statesmen failed, however, to face up to the ruthlessness of the emerging postwar Soviet might, and in the ensuing clash between Stalinist power and Western naïveté, power prevailed.

Yalta's continuing significance lies in what it reveals about Russia's enduring ambitions toward Europe as a whole. Yalta was the last gasp of carefully calibrated Soviet diplomacy designed to obtain Anglo–American acquiescence to a preponderant Soviet role in all of Europe. At Yalta, in addition to timidly reopening the issue of Eastern Europe, the West also deflected, but again in a vague and timorous fashion, Soviet aspirations for a dominant position in the western extremity of the Eurasian land mass.

Yalta thus remains of great geopolitical significance because it symbolizes the unfinished struggle for the future of Europe. Forty years after Yalta that struggle still involves America and Russia, but by now it

*Reprinted by permission of the author and publisher from *Foreign Affairs* 63, no. 2 (Winter, 1984–1985), pp. 279–280, 294–302. Copyright 1984 by Zbigniew Brzezinski.

should be clear that the issue is unlikely to be resolved in a historically constructive manner until a more active role is assumed by the very object of the contest, Europe itself.

As President Mitterrand put it some 2 years ago, "*tout ce qui permettera de sortir de Yalta sera bon. . . .*" But how to escape from Yalta? Forty years later, there must be a better option for both Europe and America than either a partitioned and prostrated Europe that perpetuates the American–Soviet collision, or a disunited Europe divorced from America acquiescing piecemeal to Soviet domination over Eurasia. And there is such a third option: the emergence of a politically more vital Europe less dependent militarily on the United States, encouraged in that direction by an America guided by a timely historic vision, and leading eventually to a fundamentally altered relationship with Eastern Europe and with Russia.

This third option requires a long-term strategy of the kind that the West simply has not devised in dealing with the enduring post-Yalta European dilemma. The point of departure for such a long-term strategy has to be joint recognition of the important conclusion which the experience of the last several decades teaches: *The historic balance in Europe will be changed gradually in the West's favor only if Russia comes to be faced west of the Elbe rather less by America and rather more by Europe.*

Thoughtful Europeans realize, moreover, that the future of Europe is intertwined with the future of Germany and of Poland. Without spanning, in some nonthreatening fashion, the division of Germany, there will not be a genuine Europe; but continuing Russian domination of Poland makes Russian control over East Germany geopolitically possible. Thus the relationship between Russia, on the one hand, and Germany and Poland, on the other, must be peacefully transformed if a larger Europe is ever to emerge.

Both Americans and Europeans must also face up to the implications of the fact that the division of Europe is not only the unnatural consequence of the destruction of Europe in the course of two world wars; in the long run it is also an inherently unstable and potentially dangerous situation. It is likely to produce new explosions in Eastern Europe and it could also generate a basic and destabilizing reorientation in Western Europe, especially since for many Europeans the existence of the two alliances across the dividing line in the middle of Europe is seen as an extension of superpower efforts to perpetuate the status quo.

Accordingly, concentration on the purely military dimension of the East–West problem, or trying to get the West Europeans to hew to the U.S. line in the Middle East or in Central America, is not going to preserve Western unity. America has to identify itself with a cause which has deeply felt emotional significance to most Europeans. Undoing the division of Europe, which is so essential to its spiritual and moral recovery, is a goal worthy of the Western democracies and one capable of galvanizing a shared sense of historic purpose.

But that objective, so essential to Europe's restoration, cannot be accomplished as an American victory over Russia. Nor will it be achieved by an explicit Russian acceptance, through a negotiated agreement, of Eastern Europe's emancipation from Russian vassalage. Moscow will not yield voluntarily. A wider Europe can only emerge as a consequence of a deliberately but subtly induced process of change, by historical stealth so to speak, which can neither be quickly detected nor easily resisted.

The West must shape that process and give it historical direction. As the point of departure for seeking the common goal, one can envisage a strategy combining five broad political, economic, and military dimensions. Some involve relatively simple acts and can be summarized succinctly; some require more complicated processes of change, are bound to be more controversial, and thus require a fuller justification.

*First*, on the symbolic plane, it would be appropriate for the heads of the democratic West as a whole, perhaps on February 4, 1985, to clarify jointly, through a solemn declaration, the West's attitude toward the historic legacy of Yalta. In publicly repudiating that bequest—the partition of Europe—the West should underline its commitment to a restored Europe, free of extra-European control. It should stress its belief that there now exists a genuine European political identity, the heir to Europe's civilization, which is entitled to unfettered expression. It should affirm the right of every European nation to choose its sociopolitical system in keeping with its history and tradition. It should explicitly reject and condemn Moscow's imposition on so many Europeans of a system that is culturally and politically so alien to them. Finally, by drawing attention to the positive experience of neutral Austria and Finland, it should pledge that a more authentic Europe would not entail the extension of the American sphere of influence to the European state frontiers of the Soviet Union.

*Second*, and in direct connection with the renunciation of Yalta's burden, the West should simultaneously reconfirm its commitment to the Helsinki Final Act. This is absolutely essential, for otherwise the repudiation of Yalta could give the Soviets the convenient argument that the territorial integrity of Poland and of Czechoslovakia is thereby again endangered. The Helsinki agreements confirmed the durability of the existing frontiers in central and eastern Europe, and the eastern nations must be reassured on this score. At the same time, the Helsinki agreements legalized and institutionalized the notion that the West has a right to comment on the internal practices of East European governments and that respect of human rights is a general international obligation. Accordingly, the repudiation of Yalta's historic legacy should be accompanied by the reaffirmation of the West's commitment to peaceful East–West relations, to the maintenance of the existing territorial status quo, and to the indivisibility of the concepts of freedom and human rights.

Moreover, reaffirmation of the continued Western commitment to the Helsinki Final Act could help to resolve the potentially fatal European ambivalence regarding Germany. The fact is that, while the Europeans resent their historic partition, they fear almost as much a reunited Germany. Therefore, the renunciation of Yalta's legacy—the division of Europe—should be accompanied by an explicit pledge, through the reaffirmation of Helsinki's continued relevance, that the purpose of healing the East–West rift in Europe is not to dismantle any existing state but to give every European people the opportunity to participate fully in wider all-European cooperation. In that context, the division of Germany need not be undone through formal reunification but by the gradual emergence of a much less threatening loose confederation of the existing two states.

*Third*, much in keeping with the spirit of these symbolic acts, Western Europe should strive to create the maximum number of opportunities for East European participation in various all-European bodies. There is today a proliferation of such institutions, both private and public. East Europeans should be encouraged quietly but systematically to increase their participation—even if initially only as observers—in such bodies as the European Parliament, as well as the myriad of more specialized technical agencies. The fostering in Eastern Europe of the European spirit, and of greater East European recognition that there is more to Europe today than meets the eye, is clearly in the interest of all Europe. But a new burst of energy in this regard is much needed.

It would also be appropriate for the major West European nations, as well as for America, to sponsor during the Yalta year of 1985—on either a private or public basis—a series of seminars and conferences on the future of post-Yalta Europe. A special effort should be made to invite East Europeans to participate, on whatever basis is possible, in deliberations designed to forge during that year a wider consensus on how best to undo peacefully Yalta's legacy.

In addition, Western Europe should reactivate efforts previously initiated but lately dormant designed to encourage closer contacts and eventually even some form of collaboration between the Common Market and Eastern Europe. In different ways, both East Germany and Yugoslavia today have practical relationships with that important West European entity. Precisely because the present Soviet leadership has stepped up its efforts to integrate Eastern Europe into COMECON and thus to bind it to the Soviet economy, additional initiative on the part of the Common Market is now badly needed. Even if the East Europeans, under Soviet pressure, were to rebuff such Western efforts at closer contacts, exchange of information, and some cooperative projects, the Western initiative would still have a positive effect. The recent East German willingness to risk Soviet displeasure at growing inter-German ties reflects the widespread desire as well as economic need of Eastern Europe for closer links with the rest of Europe. The continued economic stagnation of the Soviet-type economies makes the timing for greater Western activism in this regard particularly propitious.

*Fourth*, and in no way in conflict with the preceding, Europe should intensify its aid to those East Europeans who are struggling actively for the political emancipation of Eastern Europe. That struggle is the necessary concomitant and at least partially also the cause of evolutionary change in Eastern Europe. Only too often do West European well-wishers of a more independent Eastern Europe look askance at those in the East who undertake more direct forms of struggle. While cultivation of East European officials enjoys a certain fashionable prestige in Western circles, tangible assistance to those resisting totalitarianism is viewed only too frequently as somehow "in the spirit of the cold war."

Yet a division of labor between America and Europe in which the former is seen as alone in supporting dissident "subversion" while the latter engages exclusively in official courtship would be self-defeating. West Europeans should undertake to provide support for some of the activities that America has quite generously, for Europe's sake as well as for its own, sustained for more than three decades. The French recently have done so for the Polish Solidarity movement, and so have some other Europeans. Radio Paris has been gaining more East European listeners. But much more needs to be done. Germany, for example, after Chancellor Helmut Schmidt in effect endorsed Wojciech Jaruzelski's martial law in Poland, confined itself to truly humanitarian private philanthropy; it has not been so active as it could be in sustaining various forms of East European political activity designed to induce the existing regimes to transform themselves.

In subtle but sustained fashion Western Europe could aid the East Europeans in such efforts, because in the age of transistors and mass communications totalitarian control can be pierced, with positive political effect. Western Europe should, after all, be a direct partner in the struggle for Europe's future, and a well-funded Franco–British–German–Italian consortium (a Foundation for a Post-Yalta Europe) to aid East European efforts to emancipate peacefully the eastern portion of Europe would be an appropriate and long overdue contribution.

*Fifth*, the time has come for a more fundamental rethinking of the relationship between Western security and political change in Europe as a whole. The West can make the needed adjustment, and America— since it plays the central military role—should take the lead to that end. America is needed in Europe to deter Russia not only from military aggression but from political intimidation. That is obvious and it justifies NATO and the American military presence on the continent. But an American military presence that reduces the incentive for the Europeans to unite politically, yet simultaneously increases the incentive for the Soviets to stay put militarily in central and eastern Europe, is a military presence not guided by a subtle political–historical calculus. A more sensitive calibration of the political–military equation is needed in order to safeguard Western Europe while promoting change in the East–West relationship.

If Europe is to emerge politically, it must assume a more direct role in its own defense. A Europe that plays a larger defense role will require a lesser, or at least a redefined, American military presence. A Europe that can defend itself more on its own is a Europe that is also politically more vital, while less challenging to the Soviet Union from a purely military point of view, than a Europe with a large American military presence in its very center. Such a Europe would then be better able to satisfy the East European yearning for closer association without such association being tantamount to an American defeat of Russia.

But Europe must be prodded to move in that direction. Left as it is, Europe's cultural hedonism and political complacence will ensure that not much is done. Even the modest 1978 NATO commitment to a 3% per annum increase in defense expenditures was not honored by most European states. America, therefore, should initiate a longer-term process to alter the nature of its military presence in Europe gradually, while making it clear to the Europeans that the change is not an act of anger or a threat (à la the Mansfield resolution) but rather the product of a deliberate strategy designed to promote Europe's unity and its historic restoration.

Ultimately, the United States in NATO should be responsible primarily for offsetting Soviet strategic power, thus deterring both a Soviet attack or nuclear blackmail. But on the ground, the defense of Europe over the next decade should become an even more predominantly European responsibility. The needed process of replacing gradually but not totally (and certainly not in Berlin) the U.S. ground combat forces could perhaps be accelerated if, through the Mutual and Balanced Force Reductions talks or otherwise, the Soviet Union were willing to reciprocate by comparable withdrawals of its own ground forces. But, in any case, it should be accompanied by appropriate European efforts to assume greater responsibility for the defense of Europe not only on a purely national basis but through enhanced European defense coordination.

The United States particularly should encourage efforts at increased Franco–German military cooperation and eventual integration. France has a historic awareness of a European identity, while Germany chafes under Europe's partition. A Franco–German army would have the manpower, the resources, and the fighting potential to pick up the slack created by a gradual decrease in the American combat presence on the ground. The eventual fusion of these two national forces into a joint combat force would represent a giant step toward a politically more vital Europe, yet a Europe which would be less conflictual with the Soviet Union than a Europe hosting a large U.S. army and less threatening to Eastern Europe than a Europe with a powerful separate German army. A gradually reduced U.S. ground presence would in turn create pressure from even the existing East European regimes for a commensurate Soviet redeployment, thereby gradually creating a more flexible political situation.

To move Europe in this direction, the United States will have to take the first steps, even perhaps unilaterally through a 10-year program of annual cuts in the level of the U.S. ground forces in Europe. But these steps should be taken in the context of an articulated strategy that has a constructive political as well as military rationale. Its political purpose should be openly proclaimed: to create the setting for Europe's restoration and, through it, also for a more stable East–West relationship. It would also have to be made clear that some American combat forces would remain in Europe, as they do in Korea, thereby ensuring immediate American engagement in the event of hostilities. Moreover, continued American strategic protection of Europe should not remain confined only to the possible employment of nuclear weaponry. It should over time, with technological advance, be enhanced to include also some strategic defense. As strategic defense for America becomes more viable, it should be a major American goal to extend some of its protection to Europe as well.

A division of labor in NATO along the foregoing lines would make it much easier to consider by Yalta's fiftieth anniversary also those East–West security and political arrangements which at the moment seem premature, unrealistic, or excessively threatening to America or to Russia. These could include demilitarized or nuclear-free zones or extension of the Austrian-type neutrality to other areas, including later even to a loosely confederated Germany. It would encourage a process of change permitting the latent or frustrated West and East European impulses for the restoration of Europe gradually to surface. Eventually, it would permit Europe to emerge, and to play a major role on the Eurasian continent, along with the Soviet Union, India, and China, while helping to ensure through its links with America that no single power dominates that geopolitically vital continent.

The fiftieth anniversary of Yalta is only 10 years away. It should be our shared goal to fashion by then political–military arrangements which, instead of perpetuating the division of Europe and perhaps even prompting Western Europe's political decay, create the preconditions for peacefully undoing Yalta. A Western Europe essentially self-reliant in regional defense, while covered by the U.S. system of nuclear deterrence and also eventually by U.S. strategic defense, would be a Western Europe more capable of pursuing a positive policy toward the East without fear of domination by Moscow. In the final analysis, only Europeans can restore Europe; it cannot be done for them by others.

To be sure, Moscow will resist the aspirations of the Europeans. No empire dissolves itself voluntarily—at least not until it becomes evident that accommodation to gradual dissolution is preferable to the rising costs of preserving the imperial system. So it will be also with the Soviet empire. Moscow will violently protest any Western disavowal of Yalta's legacy and will accuse the West of worsening East–West relations; that is only to be expected. But such public disavowal is the necessary point of departure for more focused efforts by all the Europeans gradually to undo their continent's division. Once that historic commitment has been made, these efforts, as recommended here, need not be either aggressive or initially even very explicit. As time passes, with the organic growth of a larger Europe gathering momentum, it will become more and more difficult for the Kremlin to resist a process that over time may acquire the hallmarks of historical inevitability. At some point, then, even the Soviets may find it useful to codify some new neutrality arrangements in central Europe and to reduce and eventually to remove their occupation forces.

One should not underestimate in this connection Moscow's adaptability. Despite his ruthlessness, even Stalin accommodated himself to the reality of an independent Catholic Church in Poland; Khrushchev to a Polish peasantry free from collectivization and to a separate Romanian foreign policy; Brezhnev to "goulash communism" in Hungary and to army rule in Poland. Why then should not the next generation of Soviet leaders be pressed also to come to terms with the fact that even the interests of the Soviet people would be better served by a less frustrated and oppressed east–central Europe, partaking more directly of the benefits of all-European cooperation?

As divided Europe enters the fifth decade after Yalta, it is important to reiterate that undoing Yalta cannot involve a precise blueprint or a single dramatic initiative. The shape of the future cannot be reduced to a neat plan, with specific phases and detailed agreements. Rather, it requires an explicit commitment and a sense of strategic direction for a process of change that is bound to have also its own dynamic. In any case, for America the emergence of a more vital Europe would be a positive outcome, for ultimately a pluralistic world is in America's true interest. Moreover, such a development would avert the major danger that if Yalta's legacy is not deliberately—though peacefully—undone in the East, it will eventually become the reality in the West. In other words, Yalta must be consigned to Europe's past if it is not to become Europe's future.

# 52

## GEORGE P. SHULTZ

## *Managing the U.S.–Soviet Relationship over the Long Term**

*Following is an address by U.S. Secretary of State Shultz before the Rand/UCLA Center for the Study of Soviet International Behavior, Los Angeles, California, October 18, 1984.*

This distinguished audience knows well that the Soviet Union presents us with a conceptual as well as a strategic challenge. Let me take advantage of this occasion, therefore, to raise what I see as some of these larger conceptual issues that face us in managing U.S.–Soviet relations over the long term.

**Differences between the Systems** The differences between our two countries are profound. You and I know that, yet we need to reiterate it, remind ourselves of it, and reflect upon it. The United States and the Soviet Union have different histories, cultures, economies, governmental systems, force structures, geographical circumstances, and visions of the future. We cannot analyze the Soviet Union as if it were a mirror of ourselves.

We Americans stand by our values and defend our interests, but we also put great store by pragmatism, compromise, and flexibility in international life. Marxist–Leninist ideology subordinates all of these qualities to the so-called objective, scientific, and inevitable laws of history. We can debate how fully Soviet leaders follow this ideology. No doubt, however, it helps shape a political culture that does not accommodate well to compromise or truly positive relations with op-

*Reprinted from *Current Policy*, nos. 624 and 650, U.S. Department of State, Bureau of Public Affairs, Office of Public Communication, Editorial Division, Washington, D.C., October 18, 1984 and January 31, 1985. In the public domain—no copyright claimed. The postscript is reprinted here by permission of the author and publisher from "New Realities and New Ways of Thinking," *Foreign Affairs* 63, no. 4 (Spring, 1985), pp. 705–709. Adapted from Secretary Shultz's statement before the Senate Foreign Relations Committee, Washington, D.C., January 31, 1985.

ponents. Their doctrine of history teaches them that their opponents are doomed to crisis and decline—and that the struggle between the two systems is a mortal struggle.

Most notable, perhaps, is the very different relationship between the government and the people in the Soviet Union and in the United States. Our national policies are the product of open debate, deliberation, and political competition guided by constitutional processes. In the Soviet Union, policy is the exclusive domain of a self-perpetuating ruling elite. Soviet leaders do not ignore public opinion; on the contrary, they vigorously seek to control it. Theirs is a system marked by repression and hostility to free political, intellectual, or religious expression. A nation whose system is the legacy of Marx, Lenin, and Stalin obviously bears scant resemblance to one that draws its inspiration from Washington, Jefferson, and Lincoln.

When we in America conduct foreign policy, we must meet certain requirements that Soviet rulers can disregard. An American president must win and sustain support from the Congress and the American people if he is to lead the nation on any path, if our policy is to follow a steady course and a coherent strategy. Through this process, we gain the sustenance and commitment that come from democratic participation. And in the complex world of the 1980s and 1990s, the effectiveness of our dealings with the Soviets will benefit from a level of national understanding of the Soviet Union beyond what we have required, or had, in the past. That is why what the Rand/UCLA Center seeks to accomplish is so important, and why I look forward to the contribution that you can make.

## The Complexity of Managing the Relationship

Today, despite these profound differences, it is obviously in our interest to maintain as constructive a relationship as possible with the Soviet Union. The Soviet Union is powerful; it occupies a very large part of a shrinking world; and its military strength, including its vast nuclear arsenal, is a reality that we cannot ignore. Its people are a great and talented people, and we can benefit from interchange with them. And we owe it to our own people, and to the future of the planet, to strive for a more constructive pattern of relations between our countries.

A brief review of the postwar period reminds us of how complex a task this is. For the past two decades, Soviet defense spending has grown at a rate of 3–5% a year, even when the United States was cutting back its own defense expenditures. And the Soviets kept up this military expansion even in the face of mounting economic difficulties.

In the postwar period, the United States never sought to expand its territory nor used force to impose its will upon weaker nations, even when we were the world's preeminent power. The Soviets, however, have used force frequently—in East Berlin, Hungary, Czechoslovakia, and Afghanistan. And it was their threat of force that imposed martial law on Poland.

It has been argued that Soviet behavior is partly motivated by a historical insecurity, that they suffer from an endemic paranoia stemming from centuries of war and foreign invasions. But this analysis is clearly inadequate. The problem is that the Soviets seek absolute security in a way that guarantees insecurity for everyone else. Their policies have created antagonism when opportunities existed for better relations; their vast military power—and their demonstrated willingness to use it—go far beyond legitimate self-defense and pose objective problems for the world community. The Soviets' interventionist policies in the Third World, for example, seem the result of ideology combined with new capability, not the product of "insecurity." In the past two decades they have expanded their influence in Asia, Africa, the Middle East, and Central America by purveying arms and backing those who subvert neighbors or block peace.

The record shows that when the Soviets have perceived weakness, when they have seen a vacuum, they have seized the opportunity to gain an advantage. Their code of behavior has not included categories for voluntary restraint or self-denial.

And they have not hesitated to persecute those of their own people—whether intellectuals, religious figures, or average citizens—who dared to speak or write freely, or who sought to emigrate. After signing the Helsinki Final Act, which confirmed that human rights were a vital part of the diplomatic dialogue on peace and security in Europe, the Soviets and their East European allies even suppressed the very citizens' groups that were formed to monitor compliance with the Helsinki accord.

We are left with two inescapable truths: In the nuclear age we need to maintain a relationship with the Soviet Union. Yet we know that they have acted in ways that violate our standards of human conduct and rule by law and that are repugnant to us—and they will likely continue to do so in the future. What kind of relationship can we reasonably expect to have in these circumstances? How can we manage U.S.–Soviet relations in a way that can endure over a long period?

## The Questions of Linkage

The U.S.–Soviet relationship, of course, is a global one. We impinge on each other's interests in many regions of the world and in many fields of endeavor. A sustained and sound relationship, therefore, will confront the fact that the Soviets can be expected periodically to do something abhorrent to us or threaten our interests.

This raises the question of linkage. Should we refuse to conclude agreements with the Soviets in one area when they do something outrageous in some other area? Would such an approach give us greater leverage over Moscow's conduct? Or would it place us on the defensive? Would it confirm our dedication to fundamental principles of international relations? Or would it make our diplomacy seem inconsistent? Clearly, linkage is not merely "a fact of life" but a complex question of policy.

There will be times when we must make progress in one dimension of the relationship contingent on progress in others. We can never let ourselves become so wedded to improving our relations with the Soviets that we turn a blind eye to actions that undermine the very foundation of stable relations. At the same time, linkage as an instrument of policy has limitations; if applied rigidly, it could yield the initiative to the Soviets, letting them set the pace and the character of the relationship.

We do not seek negotiations for their own sake; we negotiate when it is in our interest to do so. Therefore, when the Soviet Union acts in a way we find objectionable, it may not always make sense for us to break off negotiations or suspend agreements. If those negotiations or agreements were undertaken with a realistic view of their benefits for us, then they should be worth maintaining under all but exceptional circumstances. We should not sacrifice long-term interests in order to express immediate outrage. We must not ignore Soviet actions that trouble us. On the contrary, we need to respond forcefully. But in doing so, we are more likely to be successful by direct measures that counter the specific challenge.

When the Soviets invaded Afghanistan, President Carter said his opinion of the Soviet Union and its goals had changed more in 1 week than throughout his entire term of office. He canceled the grain agreement, withdrew his own arms limitation treaty from Senate consideration, refused participation in the Olympics, and stopped the annual meetings with Foreign Minister Gromyko. But did his actions serve our economic interests? Did they further progress toward a better arms agreement? Did they get Soviet troops out of Afghanistan?

When the Soviets shot down the Korean airliner, in contrast, President Reagan was not derailed from his steady, firm, and realistic course. He never had illusions about the Soviet Union. After the KAL (Korean Air Lines) shootdown, he focused attention on the menace to civil aviation posed by such conduct. He made sure the world knew the truth about the incident. But he also sent our arms control negotiators back to Geneva, because he believed that reducing nuclear weapons was a critical priority.

In the final analysis, linkage is a tactical question; the strategic reality of leverage comes from creating facts in support of our overall design. Over the longer term, we must structure the bargaining environment to our advantage by modernizing our defenses, assisting our friends, and showing we are willing to defend our interests. In this way we give the Soviets more of a stake, in their own interest, in better relations with us across the board.

## The Need for a Long-Term Strategy

Sudden shifts in policy, stemming from emotional and perfectly understandable reactions to Soviet behavior, are not the way to pursue our interests. It seems to me that the West, if it is to compete effectively and advance its goals, must develop the capacity for consistency and discipline and must fashion—and stick to—a long-term strategy.

But consistency is difficult for a democracy. Historically, American policy has swung from one extreme to the other. We have gone through periods of implacable opposition—foregoing negotiations, building up our defenses, and confronting Soviet aggression. Then, concerned about confrontation, we have entered periods of seeming détente, during which some were tempted to neglect our defenses and ignore Soviet threats to our interests around the world—only once again to be disillusioned by some Soviet action that sent us swinging back to a more implacable posture.

We have tended all too often to focus either on increasing our strength or on pursuing a course of negotiations. We have found it difficult to pursue both simultaneously. In the long run, the absence of a consistent, coherent American strategy can only play to the advantage of the Soviet Union.

Therefore, we must come to grips with the more complex reality of our situation. A sustainable strategy must include all the elements essential to a more advantageous U.S.–Soviet relationship. We need to be strong, we must be ready to confront Soviet challenges, *and* we should negotiate when there are realistic prospects for success.


## The Purposes of Negotiation

Winston Churchill understood both the limits and the necessity of negotiating with the Soviet Union. In May 1953, he said: "It would, I think, be a mistake to assume that nothing can be settled with the Soviet Union unless or until everything is settled." In the 1980s, as then, the process of U.S.–Soviet negotiation has as its purposes both to avert dangerous confrontations and to reach agreements that are in our mutual interest.

If we are to be effective in negotiations, we need a clear sense of what we want to achieve.

The United States seeks an international environment that enhances the freedom, security, and prosperity of our own people, our allies and friends, and of all mankind. We know that such a promising future depends, above all, on stability and global security. It cannot be achieved in a world where aggression goes unchecked and where adventurous foreign policies succeed. Nor can it be achieved in a world where the two largest powers refuse to engage in constructive relations.

To pursue our goals successfully we must persuade the Soviets of two things: first, that there will be no rewards for aggression. We are strong enough and determined enough to resist attempts by the Soviet Union to expand its control by force; and, second, that we have no aggressive intentions. We mean no threat to the security of the Soviet Union. We are ready and willing, at all times, to discuss and negotiate our differences.

The conditions for successful negotiation exist when both sides stand to gain from an agreement or stand to lose from the absence of an agreement. We have to accept the fact that on many issues, our respective goals may be incompatible, making agreements impossible to reach. When this occurs, we should not despair or panic about the state of our relations. Certainly, we should never accept disadvantageous agreements for the sake of making negotiations seem successful. Occasional disappointments are part of the long-term process, and we should move on to seek negotiations when and where the conditions are ripe for progress.

Some argue that if you cannot trust the Soviets, you should not negotiate with them. But the truth is, successful negotiations are not based on trust. We do not need to trust the Soviets; we need to make *agreements* that are trustworthy because both sides have incentives to keep them. Such incentives operate best when there are clear and working means to verify that obligations undertaken are, in fact, carried out.

Each side will watch the other carefully to ensure that neither can gain a one-sided advantage by violating an agreement. If we spot Soviet violations, we must do what is necessary to protect ourselves and to raise the cost to the Soviets of further violations. We cannot allow them to use negotiations or agreements as a cover for actions that threaten our interests.

Sometimes it is said that plain statements by us about Soviet violations of agreements, whether on arms or human rights, harm our relationship. In our system, it is our obligation to speak out and tell the truth—to the Soviets, to the world, and to the American people. Our own values have claims on us, both to speak out honestly and to use our leverage when we can, and often quietly, for humanitarian goals. Those goals are not a burden on the U.S.–Soviet relationship; they are, for us, a key part of that relationship. If we can help a Shcharansky or Sakharov, or prevent the jailing of a priest in Lithuania, or ease the plight of Soviet Jewry, we have gained something worth negotiating for and worth using our influence to obtain—not to score points against the Soviets but because we are a moral people.

The experience of negotiations shows that the Soviets recognize reality and that tough, sober bargaining, when backed by American strength, can lead to mutually advantageous results. Negotiation without strength cannot bring benefits. Strength alone will never achieve a durable peace.

A Policy of Strength and Negotiation   Throughout this Administration, President Reagan has adhered to this approach. He has based his policies toward the Soviet Union on a solid foundation of realism, strength, and negotiation. This approach has created the objective conditions for a safer, more constructive relationship in the years ahead.

In light of Moscow's history of taking advantage of any weakness, it is not surprising that we suffered setbacks in the 1970s. In light of the recent clear improvement in our relative position, it is not surprising that Moscow is complaining about our policy. The 1970s were a time when our economy was deeply troubled, when our military capabilities were eroding, and when our self-confidence and sense of purpose both at home and overseas were at a low ebb. The Soviets had grounds for believing that what they call "the global correlation of forces" had shifted in their favor. And we, in turn, had grounds for fearing that they might overreach themselves and present us with a challenge that we could neither ignore nor effectively counter.

Since then, the United States, in particular, and the West, in general, have made an impressive turnaround. We have begun to recover lost ground and to move ahead.

• Our own economic recovery is well underway. Sustained growth without inflation is within reach. The American economy has bounced back and is giving welcome impetus to global recovery.

• The much-needed modernization of Western defense capabilities is on track. The gaps in the East–West military balance that were expanding in the 1970s are being narrowed and closed. The Soviets' temptation to preempt or intimidate at any point on the spectrum of deterrence must be diminishing.

• We have restored the relations of confidence and harmony with our key allies in Europe and Asia, which have been the bedrock of American security throughout the postwar era. We have provided leadership in the community of nations joined to us by common values and common interest. Disagreements have, at times, been sharp, and debate vigorous, just as they are in our country. The result, however, just as here, has been increasing consensus on the challenges to the common security and widening agreement on what is required to meet those challenges.

• Most important, we have restored our own confidence in ourselves. We know that we are capable of dealing with our problems and promoting our interests and ideals in a complex and dangerous world. We have renewed our commitment to democratic values and human rights, a commitment that joins us not only to our allies but to other millions across the globe.

These achievements put our relationship with Moscow on a substantially safer, sounder, and more durable basis. Our credibility as a strong and resolute nation has been enhanced. In contrast to the 1970s, Moscow has not only failed to add any new territory to its extended empire in the 1980s but it has been unable to prevent adverse trends in Central America, the Caribbean, Asia, and southern Africa. Some in Moscow must wonder if the "correlation of forces" is not shifting against them.

We hold to the principle that America should not negotiate from a position of weakness, and this Administration has ensured that we need not face such a prospect.

But we reject the view that we should become strong so that we need not negotiate. Our premise is that we should become strong so that we are able to negotiate. Nor do we agree with the view that negotiated outcomes can only sap our strength or lead to an outcome in which we will be the loser. We will stay strong to enforce the peace; we will bargain hard to ensure that any agreement we sign is reliable and verifiable; and we will negotiate seriously to find solutions that endure.

In bargaining with the Soviets, we are prepared for modest advances as well as major breakthroughs. We have made limited proposals designed to stabilize the current state of relations. And we have made ambitious proposals that, if accepted, could put the Soviet–American relationship on a fundamentally new and safer footing.

In conducting negotiations and discussions in the major areas of U.S.–Soviet relations—arms control, regional issues, human rights, and bilateral cooperation—we have been guided by four basic principles.

- First, we must have a strong defense. The United States does not seek military superiority over the Soviet Union. But the Soviets must know that in the absence of equitable and verifiable agreements, we will proceed with defense programs that will deny them superiority. The test of arms control is whether it reduces the danger of war. An arms control agreement that controls the United States but does not control the Soviet Union would only increase the danger of war. We know we will adhere to agreements; based on their conduct, we cannot be sure they will. Therefore, agreements *must* be reliable and verifiable.

- Second, we must be united both at home and with our friends and allies. We must continue to strengthen our alliances and friendships and, above all, reaffirm and reinvigorate our own bipartisan consensus about the need for a foreign policy based on realism, strength, and negotiation.

- Third, we must be patient. We cannot abandon negotiations or change our whole strategy each time the Soviets misbehave. We must not allow ourselves to panic or overreact to every fresh demonstration of incivility or intransigence. Nor can we abandon our defenses or forget the importance of our friends and allies each time there is a period of negotiating success.

- Fourth, we must be purposeful, flexible, and credible. We must negotiate with the Soviet Union on the basis of equality and reciprocity, in ways that demonstrate to the Soviets and to our friends our commitment to reaching agreements that are in the interests of both sides. We stand ready to join the Soviets in equal and verifiable arms reduction agreements, and we are prepared to move rapidly to discuss both offensive and defensive systems, including those that operate in or through space.

## Future Prospects

This was the spirit in which President Reagan and I conducted our recent discussions with Deputy Prime Minister Gromyko. We set out for him our agenda for the years ahead. We presented some new ideas for getting nuclear arms control negotiations on track and for achieving some worthwhile results. We offered a dialogue on regional issues, to avoid crises and aid the search for peaceful solutions. We urged the Soviets to take steps in the human rights area. And we outlined constructive measures to improve bilateral cooperation in a variety of fields.

Our discussions with Mr. Gromyko lead me to conclude that the

Soviets are interested in continuing our dialogue and in exploring ways to enrich that dialogue and turn it into concrete results.

What can we expect? The Soviets may now realize that it is in their interest to engage with us on the larger issues in a constructive way. Their intransigence in walking away from negotiations has brought them nothing.

A patriotic Russian looking back over the history of our relations would find it difficult to construe how the policy of rejection that Moscow has been following has served his country well. And he would surely realize that such a policy will prove even more costly in the future. In weighing his present choices, he would have to ask some very pointed questions.

- If the Soviet Union will not accept equitable arms agreements, then the United States and its allies will continue their modernization programs. Is there any Soviet gain in this result?

- If the Soviet Union pursues aggressive policies in the Third World, and not least in our own hemisphere, that threaten us and our friends, then we will respond equally strongly. Isn't the level of armed conflict in the Third World too high already?

- If improvement in Soviet human rights performance continues, as in the past, to be nothing more than the cynical manipulation of human lives for political purposes, then the Soviets cannot expect that international—and internal—pressures for better performance will stop growing. Doesn't the Soviet Union pay a price for this censure and for the isolation that goes with it? The price is large and steadily increasing.

We pose these questions knowing full well that a state founded on the theory that the global correlation of forces *must* move in its direction does not easily alter its course to suit new and changed circumstances. The temptation, if not the compulsion, is always present to create new facts to confirm an old theory. Therefore, we should not count on, or even expect, immediate and exciting breakthroughs.

But the way is wide open to more sustained progress in U.S.–Soviet relations than we have known in the past. In recent months, there have been at least a few signs of Soviet willingness to meet us halfway on some secondary but contentious issues. We have been able to agree to upgrade the Hot Line, to extend our 10-year economic cooperation agreement, and to open negotiations to expand cultural exchanges. And, of course, Moscow has made it possible for us to resume high-level contacts. These are welcome steps: They just may herald more substantial and productive moves to come. And I can tell you, certainly, that President Reagan welcomes yesterday's statement by Chairman Chernenko that the Soviets are ready to pursue a constructive dialogue with us.

We cannot confidently fathom, much less predict, the direction of Soviet policy. We recognize that much of Soviet behavior stems from problems and pressures within their own system. Our statements and our actions are often far less relevant to their decisions than some might think. During this Administration, President Reagan has had to deal not with one Soviet leader but three, which has not made the negotiating process any easier.

What we have begun to do over the past 4 years, and can continue to do in the future, is to persuade Soviet leaders that continued adventurism and intransigence offer no rewards. We have provided persuasive reasons for the Soviets to choose, instead, a policy of greater restraint and reciprocity. We must be comfortable with the requirements of such a strategy, including its price, its risks, and its predictable periodic setbacks. We must be able to deter Soviet expansionism at the same time as we seek to negotiate areas of cooperation and lower levels of armaments.

These are the essential elements of our long-term policy. If we pursue such a strategy with wisdom and dedication, we have a much better prospect of achieving our goals: countering the Soviet challenge, directing the competition into less dangerous channels, and eventually forging a more constructive relationship.

Postscript      The U.S.–Soviet relationship, for better or worse, remains a crucial determinant of the prospects for world peace, even though the political predominance of the two superpowers is less than it was a few decades ago. How to manage this relationship as conditions change remains a major conceptual challenge for the United States.

So long as the Soviet system is driven by ideology and national ambition to seek to aggrandize its power and undermine the interests of the democracies, true friendship and cooperation will remain out of reach. The West must resist this Soviet power-drive vigorously if there is to be any hope for lasting stability. At the same time, in the thermonuclear age, both sides have a common interest in survival; therefore both sides have an incentive to moderate the rivalry and to seek ways to control nuclear weapons and reduce the risks of war. We cannot know whether such a steady Western policy will, over time, lead to a mellowing of the Soviet system. Perhaps not. But the West has the same responsibility in either case; to resist Soviet encroachments firmly while holding the door open to more constructive possibilities.

Today, with the accession of Mr. Gorbachev, there may be a fresh opportunity to explore these more constructive possibilities. President Reagan is approaching this prospect in a positive spirit, as well as with a realistic appreciation that the difficulties between our countries are grounded in objective problems that we must work hard to resolve.

The democracies, unlike the Soviets, have long had difficulty maintaining consistency, coherence, discipline, and a sense of strategy. Free societies are often impatient. Western attitudes have fluctuated between extremes of gloom and pessimism, on the one hand, and susceptibility to a Soviet smile, on the other. Our ways of thinking have tended too often to focus either on increasing our strength or on pursuing negotiations; we have found it hard to do both simultaneously—which is clearly the most sensible course and probably the only way we can sustain either our defense programs or our ability to negotiate.

In the last 4 years, nevertheless, the underlying conditions that affect U.S.–Soviet relations have changed dramatically. Ten to 15 years ago, when the United States was beset by economic difficulties, neglecting its defenses, and hesitant about its role in the world, the Soviets exploited these conditions. They relentlessly continued to build up militarily; they and their clients moved more boldly in the geopolitical arena, intervening in such places as Angola, Cambodia, Ethiopia, and Afghanistan, believing that the West was incapable of resisting. They had reason for confidence that what they call the global "correlation of forces" was shifting in their favor.

Today, our key alliances are more united than ever before. The United States is restoring its military strength and economic vigor and has regained its self-assurance; we have a President with a fresh mandate from the people for an active role of leadership. The Soviets, in contrast, face profound structural economic difficulties and restless allies; their diplomacy and their clients are on the defensive in many parts of the world. We have reason to be confident that the "correlation of forces" is shifting back in our favor.

Nevertheless, history will not do our work for us. Experience suggests that the Soviets will periodically do something, somewhere, that is abhorrent or inimical to our interests, dampening hopes for an improvement in East–West relations. Witness the examples of Czechoslovakia, Afghanistan, the Korean Air Lines shootdown, and Soviet human rights practices. The question is how the West should respond to such outrages. Clearly our objective should be to act in a way that could help discipline Soviet behavior; at the same time, our posture should not leave our own strategy vulnerable to periodic disruption by such shocks.

We must never let ourselves be so wedded to improving relations with the Soviets that we turn a blind eye to actions that undermine the very foundation of stable relations; symbolic responses to outrageous Soviet actions have their place, and so do penalties and sanctions. Experience also shows, however, that as a practical matter we can best deter or undo Soviet geopolitical encroachments by helping, in one way or another, those who are resisting directly on the ground. And many negotiations and endeavors we undertake with the Soviets serve mutual interests—indeed, they all should.

Thus we are left with tough choices. Whether important negotiations ought to be interrupted after some Soviet outrage will always be a complex calculation. When the Soviets shot down the Korean airliner in 1983, President Reagan made sure the world knew the full unvarnished truth about the atrocity; nevertheless, he also sent our arms control negotiators back to Geneva because he believed that a reduction in nuclear weapons was a critical priority.

In short, our "mode of thinking" must seek a sustainable strategy geared to *American* goals and interests, in the light of Soviet behavior but not just in reaction to it. Such a strategy requires a continuing willingness to solve problems through negotiation where this serves our interests (and presumably mutual interests). Our leverage will come from creating objective realities that give the Soviets a growing stake in better relations with us across the board: by continuing to modernize our defenses, assist our friends, and confront Soviet challenges. We must learn to pursue a strategy geared to long-term thinking and based on both negotiation and strength simultaneously, if we are to build a stable U.S.–Soviet relationship for the next century.

The intellectual challenge of a new era faces us in a related dimension, namely arms control. The continuing revolution in technology means that the strategic balance—and the requirements of deterrence—are never static. Unfortunately, conventional modes of thinking about many of these questions continue to lag behind reality.

Standard strategic doctrine in the West has ultimately relied, for decades, on the balance of terror—the confrontation of offensive arsenals by which the two sides threaten each other with mass extermination. Deterrence has worked under these conditions, and we must not let go of what has worked until we know that something better is genuinely available. Nevertheless, for political, strategic, and even moral reasons, we owe it to our people to explore the possibility that we can do better than the conventional wisdom that our defense strategy *must* rely on offensive threats and *must* leave our people unprotected against attack. The Soviets, for their part, have always attached enormous doctrinal and practical importance to strategic defense, including not only air defense and civil defense but a deployed and modernized antiballistic missile system around Moscow—and intensive research into new defensive technologies.

Adjusting our strategic thinking to the constant advance of technology is never an easy process. The vehemence of some of the criticism of the President's Strategic Defense Initiative (SDI), in my view, comes less from the debate over technical feasibility—which future research will settle one way or another in an objective manner—than from the passionate defense of orthodox doctrine in the face of changing strategic realities. We are proceeding with SDI research because we see a positive, and indeed revolutionary, potential: Defensive measures may become available that could badly disrupt any attack on us or our allies and thereby render obsolete the threat of an offensive first strike. A new strategic equilibrium based on defensive technologies and sharply reduced offensive deployments is likely to be the most stable and secure arrangement of all.

Our concept can be described as follows: During the next 10 years, the U.S. objective is a radical reduction in the power of existing and planned offensive nuclear arms, as well as the stabilization of the relationship between offensive and defensive nuclear arms, whether on earth or in space. We are even now looking forward to a period of transition to a more stable world, with greatly reduced levels of nuclear arms and an enhanced ability to deter war based upon an increasing contribution of nonnuclear defenses against offensive nuclear arms.

This period of transition could lead to the eventual elimination of all nuclear arms, both offensive and defensive. A world free of nuclear arms is an ultimate objective to which we, the Soviet Union, and all other nations can agree.